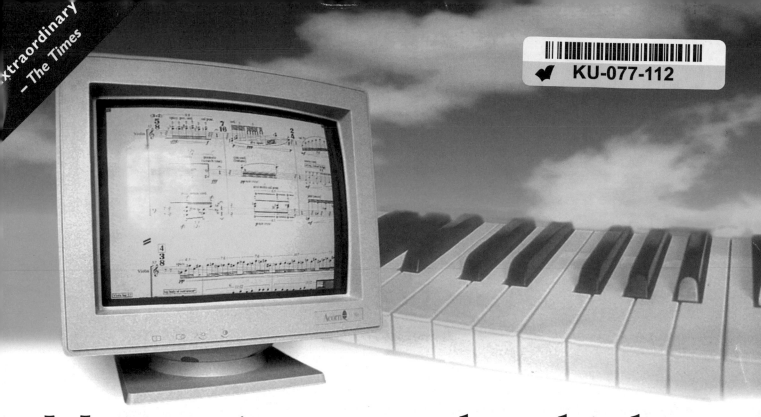

Manuscript paper that thinks.

SIBELIUS is the state-of-the-art computer software for writing, playing and printing music. It's used by composers, arrangers, performers, publishers, teachers and students worldwide.

And because *Sibelius* is **'far more powerful and sophisticated than any other score-writer'** (*Personal Computer World*) and produces **'engraving of quite exceptional quality'** (Piers Hembry, Production Director, Faber Music), in just five years it has become the UK industry standard for music publishing.

But don't just take our word for it.

A list of *Sibelius* users reads like a complete *Who's Who* of music – including top publishers such as **Peters Edition** and **Faber Music**, composers and performers in every field from film to avant garde, the **BBC**, **National Theatre**, and virtually every major conservatoire in Britain, incuding the **Royal Academy of Music** and **Royal College of Music**. (More famous *Sibelius* users are listed below.)

Whether you're a computer expert or a technophobe, you'll find *Sibelius* **'as easy to use as pen and ink'** (*Sunday Times*) – and master it in a matter of just hours, not months.

So phone us on **01223 302765** for a complete information pack, and free tickets to any of our demonstrations around Britain.

"I have found *Sibelius* a powerful and effective tool in preparing my scores"
– **Michael Tilson Thomas** (conductor)

"This extraordinary computer program has changed the music profession forever. It may soon redefine the very nature of composition"
– *The Times*

"In a totally different league from anything else"
– Paul Patterson, **Royal Academy of Music**

"Other systems take months to learn…
Sibelius can be used at once by a novice"
– *Sunday Times*

"*Sibelius* can notate, print and play a musical score at a pace even more rapid than Mozart at his most fecund… Imagine what wonders Bach could have worked with such technology; or Richard Strauss, or Britten. Or the composer of *Finlandia* himself"
– *The Times* leader column

"Dramatically reduces the time it takes to compose a piece of music and produce a score" – *Financial Times*

CLAUDE DEBUSSY
(1862-1918)

heveux de lin
(e flaxen hair)

Cédez   Mouvt.

Composers: James Dillon, Giles Swayne, Steve Martland, Nicholas Maw, Barry Guy, John McCabe, John Rutter, David Fanshaw (*African Sanctus*), Richard Stilgoe (musicals), Mike Townend (commercial music), Peter Graham (brass band), Piet Kee (organ), Peter Sculthorpe, Howard Snell (brass band), Barry Forgie (jazz & big band) • ***Film/TV:*** Lalo Schifrin (*Mission Impossible, Dirty Harry*), Trevor Jones (*Last of the Mohicans, Cliffhanger, Richard III, Brassed Off, G.I. Jane*), Karl Jenkins (best-selling *Adiemus* albums, Delta Airlines and Diamonds Are Forever adverts), John Altman (*Goldeneye, Peak Practice, Hear My Song*), Geoffrey Burgon (*Life of Brian, Tinker Tailor Soldier Spy, Brideshead Revisited*), Ed Welch (*National Lottery Live, Spike Milligan, One Foot in the Grave*), Howard Goodall (*Blackadder, Mr Bean*) • ***Conservatoires:*** Royal Academy of Music, Royal College of Music, Royal Northern College of Music, Royal Scottish Academy of Music & Drama, Trinity College of Music, Juilliard School (New York), Oxford University, Purcell School, King's College Choir School (Cambridge), Yehudi Menuhin School • ***Performers/conductors:*** Michael Tilson Thomas (conductor), Howard Shelley (piano), Denis Wick (trombone), John Miller (trumpet), Chris Kilvington (guitar), James Wood (percussion), Richard Benjafield (percussion), Neil Jenkins (tenor), The King's Consort (early music), The English Concert (director Trevor Pinnock), Andrew Parrott (director of Taverner Choir & Consort) • ***Publishers:*** *Sibelius* has produced scores for Peters Edition, Faber Music, Schott's, Bärenreiter, Music Sales, Boosey & Hawkes, Oxford University Press, Chester Music, Novello • ***Others:*** Royal Opera, Opera North, D'Oyly Carte Opera Company, National Theatre, Salvation Army, Royal Marines Band

Sibelius Software

Sibelius Software Ltd, FREEPOST CB344, Cambridge CB1 1BR
Tel: 01223 302765 • Fax: 01223 351947
email: info@sibelius-software.com • www.sibelius-software.com

Other offices in London and Los Angeles. Software available worldwide
Sibelius is a trademark of Sibelius Software Ltd

Contents

Key and Abbreviations. xi

Preface and Acknowledgements. xvii

The British Music Year by Keith Clarke xiii

Organisations

The Queen's Household. 2

The Foundation for Sports and the Arts 3

Department for Culture, Media and Sport 2

London Boroughs Grants Committee. 3

British Council 2

Music Information Centres. 5

Arts Council of England. 2

Regional Arts Boards 5

Arts Council of Northern Ireland 3

National Music Council 6

Arts Council of Wales 3

Associations 7

Scottish Arts Council 3

Musicians' Union 28

Isle of Man Arts Council 3

Music and Disability. 29

International Arts Bureau 3

Artists and Agents

Symphony and Chamber Orchestras 35

Instrumentalists 129

Opera, Dance and Music Theatre. 53

Singers 159

Choirs and Choruses. 59

Opera Producers 172

Military and Brass Bands 71

Composers. 173

Agents and Managers 75

Librettists and Translators 189

Ensembles. 97

Jazz and Light Music Agencies 191

Solo Performers 123

Regional Jazz Organisations. 191

Conductors 123

Venues and Promoters

Concert Halls and Theatres 197

Music Clubs and Societies 223

Local Authority Promoters. 211

Music in Places of Worship 229

Concert Promoters 221

Music Festivals 237

Early Music

Early Music Fora 246

Early Music Ensembles 257

Early Music Instrument Manufacturers 247

Early Music Instrumentalists 268

40th ANNIVERSARY YEAR

Finchley Children's Music Group

President SIR COLIN DAVIS

Musical Director NICHOLAS WILKS

Past Events
Four premier performances of Piers Hellawell's *Do Not Disturb* at the Barbican with the LSO and Sir Colin Davis (May 97); a recording of Britten's *A Ceremony of Carols* and *Noye's Fludde*; Gala concert at the Royal College of Music; *Carmen* at the Royal Albert Hall (Feb 97) with the BBC Concert Orchestra; TV and radio appearances including *Joy to the World* and *Children in Need* in 1996; *The Nutcracker* (Snowflakes Chorus) with English National Ballet; leading the children's choruses for VE and VJ Day celebrations at Hyde Park/Horse Guards Parade (1995); concerts at Westminster Abbey, Sherborne Abbey, Queen Elizabeth Hall, St. James's Piccadilly, the Royal Festival Hall, and the Royal Albert Hall.

Forthcoming Appearances/Performances
Education project with James MacMillan and the Philharmonia Orchestra at the Royal Festival Hall; Christmas Concert at the Barbican; Spring tour with Ukranian chamber choir *Cantus*; world premier of opera *The Fabulous Adventures of Alexander The Great*; performances with the LSO at the Barbican of Britten's Spring Symphony with Andre Previn, and Mahler's *3rd Symphony* with Myung Whun Chung; a joint commission with the LSO to be performed at the Barbican. Children from FCMG have unparalleled opportunities to perform and receive regular group (and individual) tuition, and to attend a residential Summer School, Workshops and Masterclasses.

New Members Always Welcome!
Rehearsals take place every Sunday in north London. Interested children, parents and visitors are always welcome to observe rehearsals – an appointment is not necessary. Please call the FCMG office to find out more about the group's availability and for auditions.

> **Infant Choir** (from 5 years) trained by Simon Kent, Consultant - Susan Digby.
> **Junior Choir** (from 7 years) trained by David Joyner, Professor of Singing – GSMD.
> **Senior Choir** (by audition) trained by the Musical Director, Nicholas Wilks M.A. (Oxon).
> **SATB** (for boys with broken voices & older girls) trained by Nicholas Wilks.

"A challenge expertly met by the young singers of The Finchley Children's Music Group" – (Daily Telegraph)

"The first section of Do Not Disturb, an LSO commission...was tossed in youthful antiphony between sections of the FCMG ...I loved it" – (Independent)

"...confident singing from the FCMG and Colin Davis's careful conducting got the balance right" – (The Times)

For information contact The Administrator on Telefax 0181-343 3847 or write to 69 Etchingham Park Rd, Finchley, London N3 2ED.

Founded 1958. Patrons: **RAYMOND GUBBAY, NICHOLAS HYTNER, LUCIE SKEAPING.** Registered Charity No. 290334

Recording and Broadcasting

Radio and Television 272

Record Companies 280

Recording Studios 284

Recording and Sound Duplication:

Location Recording Services 289

Record Pressing, Cassette Duplication,

CD Mastering 293

Sound Recovery and Restoration 293

Specialist Record Dealers 294

Competitions and Scholarships

Competitions:

Competitions for Performers and Conductors 301

Competitions for Composers 305

Brass Band Championships 307

Scholarships and Grants 308

Scholarships for Study Abroad:

Organisations 312

Scholarships 312

Education

Choir Schools 317

Specialist Music Schools 321

Independent Schools Offering Music Scholarships . . . 323

Junior Departments at the Conservatoires 342

Colleges of Further Education 343

Music Degrees and Diplomas 347

Colleges of Higher Education 349

Conservatoires 353

Universities 357

External Examining Institutions 365

Alexander Technique Training Courses 369

Arts Administration Courses 369

Instrument Making and Repair Courses 369

Professional Development Courses for

Private Music Teachers 369

Psychology for Musical Performance Courses 369

Recording and Technology Courses 371

Services Schools of Music 371

Colleges of Bagpipe Music 371

Youth Orchestras and Bands 373

Youth Choirs 377

Organisations for Young Performers 380

Festivals for Young Performers 380

Summer Schools and Short Courses 381

Libraries 394

Museums and Other Collections 400

Marketing, Fundraising and Related Services

Marketing and Organisational Management 405

Concert and Personal Management 407

Public and Media Relations 409

Advertising: Agencies; Media Buying

and Media Sales 411

Design and Print 411

Photographers 413

Leaflet Distributors 417

Box Office Services 417

Fundraising and Sponsorship 419

Photo: Coneyl Jay   Medieval Image courtesy of the British Museum

THE DUFAY COLLECTIVE

Management: Magenta Music Int.

Suppliers and Services

Orchestral Contractors 422

Music Publishers 423

Subsidiary Music Publishers 440

Book Publishers 443

Orchestral Hire Libraries 446

Copyright 447

Music Journalism 448

Instrument Manufacturers 453

Retailers 459

Antiquarian and Specialist Music Booksellers 485

Musician Services:

    Accessory Distributors 487

    Accountancy and Taxation Services. 487

    Computer Systems Consultants 487

    Diary and Answering Services 489

    Equipment Hire. 489

    Equipment Manufacturers 491

Freight Forwarding 491

Information Services 491

Instrument Auctioneers 491

Instrument Hire 493

Instrument Technicians 495

Insurance and Financial Services 499

Internet and Website Services. 499

Medical Support Organisations. 499

Music Copyists, Setters, Engravers and Printers . . . 501

Musical Giftware and

    Novelties Manufacturers and Retailers 505

Practice Studios 505

Programme and Sleeve Notes 507

Solicitors 511

Tour and Travel Companies 511

Video Companies 513

Word Processing Services. 513

International Directory

International Directory Contents 517

Preface 517

The International Music Year by Keith Clarke 519

Music Information Centres and Organisations 525

Agents and Promoters 531

Symphony Orchestras 547

Opera Companies 559

Choirs and Choruses. 570

Trade Fairs 573

Music Publishers. 575

Competitions:

    Competitions for Performers and Conductors 583

    Competitions for Composers. 592

Music Festivals 596

Summer Schools and Short Courses. 609

Indexes

Alphabetical Index of Advertisers 616

Alphabetical Index of Subjects 621

Editorial Entry Forms 625

Key and Abbreviations

The geographical scope of the *British Music Yearbook* includes England, Scotland, Wales, Northern Ireland, the Isle of Man and the Channel Islands. In lists arranged in alphabetical order of places, London entries are grouped together at the beginning. The *International Directory* includes information from the rest of the world.

The postal address is followed by the full telephone, fax and email numbers. In the *British Music Yearbook* international telephone numbers are given complete wherever possible, with the UK international access code first, the country code, the local area code, followed by the subscribers number. (If dialling the number from within the relevant country, the international access code and country code are omitted and a zero is added at the front of the area code.) In the *International Directory* the UK international access code is omitted and replaced with a '+' sign.

In addition to conventional abbreviations, the following (referring mainly to voices, instruments and performing groups) are used throughout the book.

Musical Performance

acc	accompanist	f-pno	fortepiano	rcdr	recorder
bar	baritone	gui	guitar	sax	saxophone
br	brass	hn	horn	sop	soprano
bs	bass	hp	harp	str	string
bs-bar	bass-baritone	hpd	harpsichord	tb	tuba
bsn	bassoon	inst	instrument, instrumental	ten	tenor
chmbr	chamber	m-sop	mezzo-soprano	timp	timpani
cl	clarinet	mus	music, musical	tpt	trumpet
clvd	clavichord	ob	oboe	trb	trombone
con	contralto	ob d'am	oboe d'amore	vc	violoncello
cor	cor anglais	orch	orchestra, orchestral	va	viola
c-ten	counter-tenor	org	organ	va d'am	viola d'amore
db	double-bass	perc	percussion	vib	vibraphone
eh	english horn	picc	piccolo	vn	violin
ens	ensemble	pno	piano	w/wind	woodwind
fl	flute				

Organisations, Orchestras and Halls

BBCPO	BBC Philharmonic	LCM	London College of Music	RNCM	Royal Northern College of Music
BBCSO	BBC Symphony Orchestra	LPO	London Philharmonic	ROH	Royal Opera House
BBCSSO	BBC Scottish Symphony Orchestra	LSO	London Symphony Orchestra	RPO	Royal Philharmonic Orchestra
BMIC	British Music Information Centre	PO	Philharmonia Orchestra	RSAMD	Royal Scottish Academy of Music and Drama
CBSO	City of Birmingham Symphony Orchestra	QEH	Queen Elizabeth Hall		
		RAH	Royal Albert Hall	TCL	Trinity College London
		RAM	Royal Academy of Music	WCMD	Welsh College of Music and Drama
ECO	English Chamber Orchestra	RCM	Royal College of Music		
ENO	English National Opera	RFH	Royal Festival Hall	WNO	Welsh National Opera
GSM	Guildhall School of Music and Drama	RLPO	Royal Liverpool Philharmonic Orchestra		

Positions

admin	administrator	co-ord	co-ordinator	mkt	marketing
arr	arranger, arranged by	dir	director	offr	officer
asst	assistant	ed	editor	sec	secretary
chmn	chairman	gen	general	subs	subscription(s)
cond	conductor	mgr	manager, managing		

Other

accs	accessories	ext	extension	snr	senior
coll	collection	jnr	junior	tel	telephone number
educ	education, educational	m/class	masterclass	w/end	weekend
elec	electronic	max	maximum	w/shop	workshop
email	electronic mail				

The first step in a life long passion

Music making can be enjoyed by everyone, throughout their lives.
The Primavera range of violins, cellos and guitars offers that important first step.

The Primavera Violin Range comes in a choice of sizes and prices to suit almost everyone and promises to offer teachers, students and parents tremendous advantages over other entry level instruments. All violins are supplied with a lightweight case and a bow - everything you will need for your first step in a life long passion.

Quality, hand-crafted violins, cellos and guitars for students

For more information and details of your local stockist call 0500 001812

The Sound Post, Unit 1 Heliport Industrial Estate, Lombard Road, London SW11 3SS Telephone 0171 223 3338 Fax 0171 223 7333

The British Music Year

by Keith Clarke

Geoffrey Rush as David Helfgott in the hit movie Shine - *the real Helfgott's concerts drew critical fire*

Soprano Rosalind Plowright, seen here with actor Derek de Lint, took to the small screen as a fiery diva in Jilly Cooper's The man who made husbands jealous

If 1996 had seen much lip service to the need to change the national lottery, 1997 was when something started to be done about it. The lottery guidelines, allowing money to flow only into capital projects, had raised the spectre of spanking new arts centres with no performers, since core funding for performing groups was in its fifth year of standstill. A relaxation of the guidelines led to an Arts for Everyone in-itiative from the Arts Council, catchily abbreviated as A4E, which allowed money to flow into development costs, fees, ma-terials, travel, research, administration, marketing and audience development.

The new scheme came in two parts - the main A4E programme, which offered between £500 and £500,000 to established organisations, both professional and amateur, for new arts activities, and A4E Express, offering between £500 and £5,000 to small groups, who may never have received any kind of funding at all. Despite early teething problems, a pilot scheme was deemed to be a huge success, with the Arts Council declaring itself overwhelmed by the number of applicants. In the first distribution for the two programmes, some 2,138 groups shared £17m.

Later in the year, of course, the country saw a rather bigger change than a bit of tinkering with the lottery, and after 18 years in the wilderness New Labour marched in with fire in its belly. The Department of National Heritage, deemed a stuffy title for the wild and wacky world

of arts, was retitled the Department for Culture, Media and Sport, and promptly announced a comprehensive review of the lottery. This rattled a number of arts organisations, who feared that the new team may want to channel money away from anything it deemed elitist. The fears seemed well founded when the arts made a rare appearance as the front page lead of the *Daily Telegraph*, which reported that the government was to impose a £100m cap on national lottery arts funding - less than half what the Arts Council had been expecting. The Department and the Council swiftly moved in to quash the story, dismissing it as a wildly inaccurate piece in the fine tradition of the silly season.

Whatever fascination the lottery may hold, the arts story that the national papers kept on the front burner was opera, with crisis-ridden this and beleaguered that filling acres of newsprint. Opera insiders took a dim view of this, feeling that the good news stories - like English National Opera offering seats for a fiver - were ignored in the stampede to gloat at opera's troubles. But troubles there certainly were. After years of uncertainty, the Royal Opera House finally closed its doors for the much publicised refurbishment in the summer of 1997, and controversy raged until the very last bolt was shot. In 1996 the house was licking its wounds after the celebrated television documentary on the subject left people with the impression of incompetent management. In an effort not to disappoint

expectations, the house spent the better part of 1997 lurching from one crisis to another.

First there was the little matter of not having anywhere to go to during closure. A proposed development at Tower Hill went well into injury time before falling through, and for a while it looked as though the opera and ballet companies would be setting up tents on Shepherds Bush Green and other cultural centres. In the end, the ROH proudly announced what it had managed to cobble together in the way of alternative venues, an achievement which the new secretary of state declared 'a shambles'.

With venues as far away from Covent Garden as the Prince's Theatre (five minutes' walk) the unions promptly put in for a touring allowance, lighting a blue touch paper which fizzled gaily.

All of which might have taken minds off the other ROH story, had it not been such a whopper. New chief executive Genista McIntosh hit the headlines in May with the announcement that she was leaving after just a few months because of what chairman Lord Chadlington called 'ill-health'. The nature of this 'illness' was debated endlessly, many coming to the conclusion that the symptoms consisted of turning red with frustration when presenting the board with plans for greater accessibility to the house.

Chadlington's solution was to appoint the Arts Council's then secretary-general Mary Allen to the post. This was odd, since

To the relief of many, Barbican Centre managing director John Tusa oversaw the removal of the Nine Muses from the centre's main entrance

The first community opera to take place at Glyndebourne was met with great enthusiasm on both sides of the footlights

she had been on the interviewing panel as an Arts Council observer, and was therefore to all appearances appointed to a job for which she had not applied nor been interviewed. Two days into his new job, culture secretary Chris Smith was faced with Chadlington & Co assuring him that this was the best solution and everything was perfectly above board. In the coming weeks, there was much talk of his having had the wool pulled over his eyes and he was said to be incandescent with rage. His reaction, admirably equitable in the circumstances, was to set up an enquiry into the house and its workings. Meanwhile, Mary Allen was invited to clear her Arts Council desk so that none of the Bow Street mud should besmirch it.

Round the corner in St Martin's Lane, English National Opera started off the year with the release of a consultation paper which suggested that the company should move to a newly-built venue rather than refurbish the London Coliseum. Many of the arguments about the limitations (and comparative financial implications) of developing a land-locked site made a lot of sense, but a mishandled presentation added a few more cats to the pigeons who, like their colleagues in neighbouring Trafalgar Square, have grown to love the place, warts and all.

ENO was in the news again for postponing Gavin Bryars' new work, *Dr Ox's Experiment*, to help it cope with the ongoing cash crisis. The smaller appetite for good-news stories convinced the company that the press was out for blood, come what may. And what came next was Dennis Marks' hasty departure from his job, in a move that was widely thought to be connected to his determination to take the company out of the Coliseum.

Down on the leafy Sussex downs, Glyndebourne also announced the departure of its general director Anthony

Whitworth Jones, though with rather less haste - he leaves at the end of the 1998 festival. (Another 1998 departure is Patrick Deuchar, chief executive of the Royal Albert Hall, who has breathed new life into the hall.) Earlier in 1997, Glyndebourne presented its first community opera. (The outreach department has been active for years, of course, but this was the first such work to be put on in the house itself.) *Misper*, police slang for missing person, put a massive amount of young enthusiasm on stage and it seemed matched by that in the auditorium. Later in the year, the more traditional story of the house was told in a Radio 3 documentary, *The Christies of Glyndebourne*, with generous whole-act chunks of opera along with the chat.

Country house opera on a smaller scale hit the headlines when the neighbours at Garsington turned bucolic, setting out to ruin the first night of the season with a chorus of mowers, strimmers, car alarms and even a light aircraft. The local council's complaints about the noise were dismissed by the courts, but it showed its disdain for the decision by raising the entertainment licence from £460 to a whopping £12,400. The barny was greatly enjoyed by the press, which filled much space telling the tale.

Opera in Scotland and Wales continued to cause concern. Despite the rude artistic health of Scottish Opera and Welsh National Opera, the companies had more than their share of woe, the Scots fielding financial crises and the Welsh watching their hopes for a new performing venue wax and wane.

Having won a bid to run a Year of Opera and Musical Theatre as part of an Arts Council initiative to celebrate Britain's artistic achievements throughout the decade leading up to the millennium, the east of England put on a comprehensive range of productions, including the

KATERINA JEBB/EMI

Nigel Kennedy returned to the classics with a recording of the Elgar violin concerto and a Royal Festival Hall comeback concert

region's first complete *Ring* cycle, courtesy of Norwegian Opera. But the project ran into trouble as a result of a slow start to fund-raising, largely due to three changes of chief executive at the Eastern Arts Board and the late appointment of a chief executive and deputy for the year. In June, chief executive and artistic director Peter Sarah resigned, his departure being seen as part of an administrative restructuring in the face of a shortfall in funding.

Despite the problems, the year was deemed an artistic success, with productions which included the National Youth Music Theatre's new show *Warchild*, a production of *The Mahabharata* given in five episodes in five towns, and an enterprising work by Rose English which involved a Bulgarian women's choir and ten horses.

On the orchestral front, the London Symphony, the London orchestra most favoured by fortune, consolidated its reputation for slick manoeuvres by landing a series of free advertisements in the *Financial Times* worth half a million pounds. In an enterprising piece of sponsorship, the space was paid for by an ad company that was out to consolidate its own position. Earlier in the year, the orchestra had been prevented from carrying out another slick move, offering a series of concerts to Radio 3 at a bargain price. Once the business got wind of something which would have put other

orchestras at an unfair disadvantage, agents moved in to scupper the plan.

But luck was back with the LSO later in the year when it was chosen as one of the orchestras to benefit from another Arts Council pilot project, a stabilisation scheme whereby organisations would put together a business plan with the aid of consultants and then be granted money to put it into action. It was generally felt that the LSO was the last of Britain's orchestras to need any help with stability, but it did indeed win a slice of the cash, with Arts Council chairman Lord Gowrie adamant that the orchestra had put forward a five-star proposal for widening its outreach work.

Other orchestras to benefit from the scheme were the Bournemouth orchestras and the Northern Sinfonia, while other winners included English National Opera and Inner City Music Ltd of Manchester. That city continued to enjoy something of a renaissance. The Royal Northern College of Music gained a new extension, and the Hallé basked in the glory of the new Bridgewater Hall, but faced a number of setbacks. With the resignation of Alan Dean, the orchestra was looking for its third chief executive in as many years, but it had high hopes of retaining its high-profile music director Kent Nagano into the new millennium.

The Royal Liverpool Philharmonic continued to exercise a deft sleight of hand, producing artistically excellent work while

the financial storm clouds lowered ever darker. The orchestra's many supporters talked of great things ahead with the arrival of new principal conductor Petr Altrichter.

While Bridgewater continued to pack in the Manchester audiences, making a significant contribution to the regeneration of the city, Liverpool announced plans for a new hall following a decision by the Millennium Commission to part-fund a new media centre. The £120m National Discovery Park, which was expected to start building before the end of the year, will include a 3,000-seat covered arena which will open up to include 10,000 open-air spaces in surrounding park land. The new venue, due to open in 2000, was seen as a new home for the RLPO Summer Pops along with other classical and pop events and possibly opera and dance.

The South Bank Centre suffered another delay to its proposed redevelopment when the Arts Council deferred a decision. The centre had netted a multi-million-pound donation from the philanthropist Paul Hamlyn and as a result, announced that it would be renamed the Paul Hamlyn Arts Centre on the South Bank if the scheme goes ahead. It is hoped that the £151m scheme, which involves the full restoration of the Royal Festival Hall, will be completed in time for the hall's 50th anniversary in May 2001. At the Barbican Centre, managing director John Tusa oversaw the removal of the Nine Muses from the main entrance - to the relief of many. Behind the scenes, he set about restoring confidence in a venue which had been through a difficult period but in 1997 celebrated its first 15 years in business.

As the millennium approached, Radio 3 announced an ambitious plan to celebrate the music of the 1900s with a three-year festival of 20th-century music, *Sounding the Century*, which involves BBC2 and all the major UK orchestras, opera companies and ensembles. It was another big-is-beautiful project, following hard on the heels of Radio 3's mammoth survey of British music, *Fairest Isle*. Less welcome at Radio 3 was the rumpus caused by rumours that the network was to move further towards Classic FM-style broadcasting. Network controller Nicholas Kenyon moved to allay fears, but insiders remained uneasy.

Wearing his other hat, as director of the Proms, Nicholas Kenyon had fewer battles, despite the traditional complaints that this or that composer was under-represented. The season boasted some 30 world, European, UK and London premieres, including seven BBC commissions. With Radio 3 relaying all the concerts and BBC Television taking a selection, the Proms maintained their reputation as an unrivalled concert and broadcast series.

In the summer, Britain's other classical station, Classic FM, started broadcasting in South Africa. Earlier in the year it lost its founder, programme controller Michael

Before the Last Night festivities the 103rd season of Proms packed in some 30 world, European, UK and London premieres, including seven BBC commissions

Buhkt, who gave up his post due to ill health. He will continue to work for the station in a consultancy role as well as providing recipes under the guise of crafty cook Michael Barry. The issue setting broadcasters' pulses racing was the advent of the digital broadcasting age, although they remained divided over the significance of it. At the Association of British Orchestras annual conference at the beginning of the year, Michael Buhkt had little to say in its favour, but Radio 3 controller Nicholas Kenyon delivered a speech of Messianic zeal, pointing the way to a bright new future in which multi-choice, CD-quality broadcasting will be at everyone's fingertips, if they can afford it.

The big ticket in 1997 was for David Helfgott, the Australian pianist whose battle with mental illness was the subject of the sell-out film, *Shine*. While music critics sat and chewed their pens as Helfgott grunted and waved his meandering way through the music, he clearly had the audiences on his side.

On the small screen, soprano Rosalind Plowright got the chance to play the grand opera diva in an adaptation of Jilly Cooper's *The man who made husbands jealous*, playing a candelabra-throwing scene with so much conviction that her co-star ended up with a very real lump on his head. Later in the year she was back at the London Coliseum, returning in triumph as Tosca in a revival of the production she had to quit a few years ago when she was troubled by vocal cord trouble.

A diva on the truly grand scale hit the London stage when Patti LuPone took on the daunting task of portraying Maria Callas in Terry McNally's Tony Award-winning play, *Master Class*. Critics were divided on the success of this, and

predictably, Callas worshippers were waspish in what many saw as a travesty of their heroine. But LuPone certainly had the chutzpah to bring off the part, and theatregoers got an evening of drama which sent them off wanting to take the real thing off the record shelves, which can be no bad thing.

Classical record sales took something of a nose-dive in 1997, sending record executives from the larger companies into a bit of a flutter. Some entertained dark thoughts about how people were spending all their leisure time on computers instead. Those who did had plenty of music-related material to deal with, since music organisations were setting up world wide web pages quicker than you could say hypertext. Among those joining the throng was the South Bank Centre, whose site came complete with sound effects for a Thames barge but no music, although the South Bank whizz kids soon sorted that.

Musicians were increasingly convinced that the internet was more than an all-bells-and-whistles executive toy, and conductor Stephen Layton put his mouse to good effect, tracking down neglected choral repertoire for a Hyperion CD. Also making the most of high-tech was music publisher Schott, which put out a series of multimedia study aids on CD-Rom which it felt would also serve to counter-attack photocopy pirating of its material. The idea was to offer additional features which the humble printed page could not offer - like the ability to print, listen, play, and so on - so that copying would become less attractive.

Returning to the classical fold in 1997 was *enfant terrible* Nigel Kennedy, who not so long ago had denounced the classics as 'not his fing'. After a brief showing at the Gramophone Awards, he was back in

the recording studios, laying down the Elgar concerto, and a Royal Festival Hall comeback concert was planned for the autumn.

Among those celebrating birthdays and anniversaries in 1997 were Ligeti and Walton's *Façade*, both 75, the ever youthful Vladimir Ashkenazy, who reached 60, and two ensembles who made it to a quarter century - the Chilingirian Quartet and the Pauk, Frankl, Kirshbaum trio.

Checking out from the earthly concert hall were pianist Sviatoslav Richter, harpsichordist Ruth Dyson, violinist and pedagogue Sándor Végh, cellists Antonia Butler and Timothy Mason, viola player Watson Forbes, bassoonist Charles Cracknell, recorder pioneer Carl Dolmetsch, oboist, composer and pianist Mary Chandler, singers Kenneth Neate, Mary Thomas and Karl Riddersbusch, conductors Sir Georg Solti, Albert Rosen and Hans-Hubert Schönzeler, composers Conlon Nancarrow, Paul Reade and Tristan Jeuris, librettist and critic Myfanwy Piper, Delius' amanuensis Eric Fenby, composer and writer David Cox, harpsichord maker and player David Thomas, pianist and teacher David Hartigan, musicologist and critic Arthur Jacobs and author Anthony Baines.

Perhaps it would be appropriate to end with the news that musicians continued to run, jump, cycle, parachute, walk, dance, go-cart, bunjee jump and heaven knows what else in order to raise money for their colleague, trumpet player Clarence Adoo, paralysed in a car accident. Nothing serves better to illustrate that whatever the financial constraints of making a living in music, when it comes to helping out a chum, musicians are the most generous people in the world.

Preface and Acknowledgements

Welcome to the twenty fourth edition of the *British and International Music Yearbook*. This edition aims, as always, to provide accurate information for everyone concerned with the classical music business; for those who have been involved in the industry for years as well as those who have just stepped out of music college and are aiming to carve a career in this difficult but exciting world.

Electronic communication is becoming increasingly important within the music industry. Many more musicians and organisations are realising the necessity of having a 'presence' on the World Wide Web, whether it be their own full-blown website or a mention on another site, and many companies exist to provide these services. The companies that provide specialised sites for musicians, or who have experience in setting up sites for the music business, are listed in the new *Internet and Website Services* section which can be found under **Musician Services**.

The *International Directory* has continued its modest growth with the addition of comprehensive listings of the National Music Committees on the International Music Council into the **Music Information Centres and Organisations** section. The International Music Council aims to develop and strengthen friendly working relations between all the musical cultures of the world, and is therefore concerned with music creation, music education, music performance and dissemination, music research and documentation, social problems of musicians and all other aspects of music life. The IMC membership covers an unparalleled range of expertise in musical matters.

Telephone codes continue to change in the international arena. Numbers for Warsaw now contain an extra digit, and several Australian cities also have had an extra digit added. The Slovak Republic now has the distinction of having an international access code separate from the Czech Republic; it has changed from +420 to +421.

It is not an easy task to keep track of the wealth of changes taking place in the music industry from year to year. I am therefore extremely grateful to the organisations and individuals who take the time and trouble to respond to mailings, phone-calls and faxes and enable the high standards of accuracy demanded by this directory to be met. Many organisations also provide membership lists which are used to contact new groups and individuals to offer them a chance to appear in the *British and International Music Yearbook*. Without this regular flow of information the compilation of this directory would be an impossible task, and my thanks go to the many thousands of people who have helped to make my job easier over the past years.

This is rather a sad article to write, as it will unfortunately be my last. After being involved with this publication for eight years, it is time for me to move on to 'pastures new', but not without regret; for there have been many enjoyable moments that have made producing this book worthwhile. There have been many pleas for duplicate proof forms because the family pet thought it would make a tasty treat; one very pink-tinged form with a note apologising for the wine stain, but with reassurance that the party had been very worthwhile; and the rather dusty proof form returned with a note saying 'Sorry for the mess, the police fingerprinted this form after we were burgled.' It amuses me to think that a discerning burglar thought the form valuable enough to handle, but not valuable enough to steal . . .

My thanks must go to all my colleagues at Rhinegold for the commitment and hard work that has gone into the preparation of this book, especially to Sheena Barbour, the editor of the *British Performing Arts Yearbook,* for the preparation of the listings of concert halls and theatres, local authority promoters and music festivals. My two assistant editors, Laura Dollin and Karen Harman, deserve the highest accolade I can give them for the dedication they have shown in making this book as accurate as possible, and I wish them every success with future editions.

Felicity Rich
London 1997

Editor
Felicity Rich

Assistant Editors
Laura Dollin
Karen Harman

Publishing Manager
Sarah Williams

Advertising Managers
Catharine Pitt
Alison Warder

Advertising Sales
Madeline Ashcroft
Pauline Futeran
Robert Holmes
Matthew Peacock
Hannah Saunders
Dominic Sewell
John Simpson

Advertising Production Manager
Joanna Moore

Advertising Production
Catherine Hall

Art Director
Sarah Davies

Designers
Steve Talkington
Barbara Walker
Phil Wingrove

Book Sales Administrator
Penny Mills

Marketing Manager
Richard Thomas

Marketing Director
Keith Diggle

Managing Director
Tony Gamble

Organisations

2

The Queen's Household

Master of the Queen's Music: Malcolm Williamson CBE AO. c/o Campion Press, Sandon, Buntingford, Herts SG9 0QW *tel:* 01763 247287 *fax:* 01763 249984.
Organist, Choirmaster and Composer, HM Chapels Royal: Richard Popplewell MVO FRCO FRCM. St James Palace, London SW1A 1BG *tel:* 0171 930 3007.
Organist and Choirmaster, HM Chapel Royal: Carl Jackson. Hampton Court Palace, East Molesey, Surrey KT8 9AU *tel:* 0181 781 9598 *fax:* 0181 977 4771 *email:* carl_jackson@ccis.org.uk.

Department for Culture, Media and Sport

2-4 Cockspur St, London SW1Y 5DH *tel:* 0171 211 6000. Rt Hon Chris Smith MP, Secretary of State; Rt Hon Tom Clarke CBE MP, Minister of State; Hayden Phillips, Permanent Secretary; Andrew Marre, Head of Information. The Department for Culture, Media and Sport exercises responsibility for arts, sports, national lottery, libraries, museums, galleries, broadcasting, media, volunteering, heritage and tourism.

British Council

10 Spring Gardens, London SW1A 2BN *tel:* 0171 930 8466 *fax:* 0171 839 6347. Sir John Hanson KCMG CBE, dir gen. The British Council defines its aims as the promotion of a wider knowledge of Britain and the English language abroad, and the development of closer cultural relations with other countries.

The Arts Division of the British Council

11 Portland Pl, London W1N 4EJ *tel:* 0171 930 8466 *fax:* 0171 389 3199. John Tod, dir; Simon Milner, head of mus; Andrea Rose, head of visual arts; Simon Gammell, head of drama and dance. Paul Howson, head of film and television; Alastair Niven, head of literature; Christopher Wade, head of exhibitions, media and design.

Visiting Arts

11 Portland Pl, London W1N 4EJ *tel:* 0171 389 3019 *fax:* 0171 389 3016 *email:* visiting.arts@britcoun.org. Terry Sandell OBE, dir; Camilla Edwards, deputy dir; Richard Lambert, chmn; Nelson Fernandez, Melissa Naylor, asst dirs. Visiting Arts is a joint venture of the Arts Councils of England, Wales and Northern Ireland and the Scottish Arts Council, the Crafts Council, the Foreign and Commonwealth Office and the British Council. Visiting Arts is an advisory, consultancy and information organisation which promotes and facilitates the inward flow of foreign arts into England, Scotland, Wales and Northern Ireland in the context of the contribution they can make to cultural relations, cultural awareness and fostering mutually beneficial international arts contacts and activities at national, regional and institutional levels.

Arts Council of England

14 Great Peter St, London SW1P 3NQ *tel:* 0171 333 0100 *fax:* 0171 973 6590 *email:* http://www.artscouncil.org.uk. Lord Gowrie, chmn; Graham Devlin, acting sec gen; Hilary Carty, dance dir. Music Department Staff: Kathryn McDowell, head of mus dept; Rachel Dominy, opera, music theatre, contemporary music; Andrew Pinnock, music education, early music, amateur and music for youth; Olivia Lowson, orchestras; Rajan Hooper, traditional music, jazz and non-western music, recordings; Graeme Wall, new mus. The Arts Council receives a grant-in-aid from the government, and is incorporated under Royal Charter with the following objects: (a) to develop and improve the knowledge, understanding and practice of the arts; (b) to increase the accessibility of the arts to the public and (c) to advise and co-operate with Government departments, local authorities and other bodies on any matters concerned whether directly or indirectly with the foregoing objects. The members of the Council, who may not exceed 20 in number, are appointed by the Secretary of State for the National Heritage. Funds from the National Lottery for the Arts in England are administered by the Arts Council of England's National Lottery Department, which aims to give the maximum benefit to the public by supporting arts projects which make an important and lasting difference to the quality of life of people throughout England.

Arts Council of Northern Ireland

MacNeice House, 75-77 Malone Rd, Belfast *tel:* 01232 381591 *fax:* 01232 661715. Brian Ferran, chief exec; Philip Hammond, dir of perf arts. The Arts Council of Northern Ireland, funded by the British Government via the Department of Education for Northern Ireland, has functions of subsidy and promotion similar to those of the Arts Council of England.

Arts Council of Wales

9 Museum Pl, Cardiff CF1 3NX *tel:* 01222 394711 *fax:* 01222 221447. Emyr Jenkins, chief exec; Roy Bohana MBE, mus dir.

Arts Council of Wales North Wales Office. 10 Wellfield House, Bangor, Gwynedd LL57 1ER *tel:* 01248 353248 *fax:* 01248 351077. Sandra Wynne, dir. *Conwy, Denbighshire, Flintshire, Gwynedd, Isle of Anglesey, Wrexham, Montgomeryshire area of Powys.* Regional Office at Library, Museum and Arts Centre, Earl Rd, Mold, Clwyd CH7 1AP *tel:* 01352 758403.
Arts Council of Wales South East Wales Office. Victoria St, Cwmbran, Gwent NP44 3YT *tel:* 01633 875075 *fax:* 01633 875389. Nigel Emery, acting regional dir. *Brecknock and Radnor districts of Powys, Blaenau Gwent, Caerphilly, Bridgend, Cardiff, Torfaen, Merthyr Tydfill, Rhondda, Cynon Taff, Vale of Glamorgan, Monmouthshire, Newport.*
Arts Council of Wales West Wales Office. 6 Gardd Llydaw, Jacksons La, Carmarthen SA31 1QD *tel:* 01267 234248 *fax:* 01267 233084. *Carmarthenshire, Ceredigion, Pembrokeshire, Swansea, Neath Port Talbot.*

Scottish Arts Council

12 Manor Pl, Edinburgh EH3 7DD *tel:* 0131 226 6051 *fax:* 0131 225 9833. Seona Reid, dir; Matthew Rooke, mus dir.

Isle of Man Arts Council

10 Villa Marina Arcade, Douglas, Isle of Man IM1 2HN *tel:* 01624 611316 *fax:* 01624 615423. Lynda Cannell, sec; Dawn Lancaster, arts offr.

International Arts Bureau

4 Baden Pl, Crosby Row, London SE1 1YW *tel:* 0171 403 7001 *fax:* 0171 403 2009. Rod Fisher, dir; Anne Cockitt, admin. Established in 1994 to provide for the Arts Council of England, the Regional Arts Boards and the arts constituency and funding system a range of monitoring, research, publication and training services. Free enquiry service on international arts funding, policies, contracts etc. Tue-Thu 10am-1pm and 2pm-5pm on above number. Publishes *International Arts Navigator* and, for the Arts Council of England, a quarterly *International Arts Digest.*

The Foundation for Sports and the Arts

PO Box 20, Liverpool L13 1HB *tel:* 0151 259 5505 *fax:* 0151 230 0664. Grattan Endicott, sec to the Trustees. The FSA was established in 1991 by members of the Pool Promoters' Association who are channelling £30 million into the fund on top of £15 million which the promoters are enabled to add in consequence of a reduction in pools tax. A third of this fund is allocated to the arts.

London Boroughs Grants Committee

5th Floor, Regal House, London Rd, Twickenham, Middx TW1 3QS *tel:* 0181 891 5021 *fax:* 0181 891 5874. Andy Ganf, arts, recreation and environment leader. This organisation supports a wide range of arts projects including theatres, arts centres, touring groups, festivals, one-off events, advice and information groups and museums.

Music Information Centres

There are three centres in mainland Britain and one in the Republic of Ireland set up to increase public awareness of music and to disseminate information. They take particular responsibility for living composers and contemporary music.

British Music Information Centre. 10 Stratford Pl, London W1N 9AE *tel:* 0171 499 8567 *fax:* 0171 499 4795 *email:* bmic@bmic.co.uk; http://www.bmic.co.uk. Matthew Greenall, dir.
Irish Contemporary Music Centre. 95 Lower Baggot St, Dublin 2, Ireland *tel:* 00 353 1 661 2105 *fax:* 00 353 1 676 2639 *email:* info@cmc.ie; http://www.cmc.ie. Eve O'Kelly, dir.

Scottish Music Information Centre. 1 Bowmont Gardens, Glasgow G12 9LR *tel:* 0141 334 6393 *fax:* 0141 337 1161 *email:* smic@glasgow.almac.co.uk; http://www.music.gla.ac.uk/htmlfolder/resources/smic/homepage.html. Kirsteen McCue, gen mgr; Alasdair Pettinger, info offr.
Welsh Music Information Centre. University of Wales, Cardiff CF1 1XL. *Written enquiries only.*

Regional Arts Boards

English Regional Arts Boards. 5 City Rd, Winchester, Hants SO23 8SD *tel:* 01962 851063 *fax:* 01962 842033 *email:* info.erab@artsfb.org.uk; http://www.poptel.org.uk/arts/. Christopher Gordon, chief exec; Carolyn Nixson, asst. The ten Regional Arts Boards in England exist to promote and develop the arts and the audience for the arts in their regions. They provide information, help and guidance to all kinds of arts organisations in their area and in many cases can provide financial assistance. English Regional Arts Boards is the representative body for the ten RABs. Its Winchester secretariat provides project management, services and information for the members and acts on their behalf in appropriate circumstances.

East Midlands Arts Board. Mountfields House, Epinal Way, Loughborough, Leics LE11 0QE *tel:* 01509 218292 *fax:* 01509 262214 *email:* info.ema@artsfb.org.uk. John Buston, chief exec; Penny Hefferan, arts offr, orch mus; Helen Flach, head of perf arts; Karl Chapman, arts offr, contemporary mus. *Derbys (excluding the High Peak District), Leics, Northants and Notts. The Board aims to enrich life in the East Midlands by offering the opportunity for everyone to participate in and enjoy the arts.*
Eastern Arts Board. Cherry Hinton Hall, Cambridge CB1 4DW *tel:* 01223 215355 *fax:* 01223 248075 *email:* info@eastern-arts.co.uk. Lou Stein, chief exec; Kate Tyrell, mus offr. *Beds, Cambs, Essex, Herts (other than London borough overlap), Lincs, Norfolk, Suffolk.*
London Arts Board. 3rd Floor, Elme House, 133 Long Acre, London WC2E 9AF *tel:* 0171 240 1313 *fax:* 0171 240 4580 *email:* ame@lonab.demon.co.uk. Trevor Phillips, chmn; Andrew McKenzie, principal mus offr. *Covers the area of 32 boroughs of London and the Corporation of London.*
North West Arts Board. Manchester House, 22 Bridge St, Manchester M3 3AB *tel:* 0161 834 6644; 0161 834 9131 *fax:* 0161 834 6969 *email:* nwarts-info@mcr1.poptel.org.uk; http://www.poptel.org.uk./arts/. Debra King, perf arts offr (mus). *Cheshire, Greater Manchester, High Peak (Derbys), Lancs, Merseyside.*
Northern Arts Board. 9-10 Osborne Terrace, Jesmond, Newcastle upon Tyne NE2 1NZ *tel:* 0191 281 6334 *fax:* 0191 281 3276 *email:* norab.demon.co.uk. Andrew Dixon, chief exec; Brian Debnam, head of perf arts; Mark Monument, offr for perf arts. *Cleveland, Cumbria, Durham, Northumberland, Tyne and Wear.*

South East Arts. 10 Mount Ephraim, Tunbridge Wells, Kent TN4 8AS *tel:* 01892 515210 *fax:* 01892 549383. Debra Reay, dir perf arts; Jonathan Dabner, mus officer; Felicity Harvest, chief exec. *Kent, Surrey, E and W Sussex.*
South West Arts. Bradninch Pl, Gandy St, Exeter EX4 3LS *tel:* 01392 218188 *fax:* 01392 413554 *email:* swarts@mail.zynet.co.uk. Graham Long, chief exec; Nicholas Capaldi, dir of perf arts; Keith Nimmo, arts development mgr (perf arts); Ouvrielle Holmes, perf arts admin. *Bath, Bristol, Cornwall, Devon, Dorset (excluding Bournemouth, Poole, Christchurch), Glos, N Somerset, N E Somerset, Somerset, South Glos.*
Southern Arts Board. 13 St Clement St, Winchester, Hants SO23 9DQ *tel:* 01962 855099 *fax:* 01962 861186 *email:* sarts-info@geo2.poptel.org.uk. Robert Hutchison, chief exec; Michael Marx, mus offr; Jane Bryant, educ and planning offr. *Berks, Bucks, SE Dorset (Bournemouth, Christchurch and Poole), Hants, IoW, Oxon, Wilts.*
West Midlands Arts. 82 Granville St, Birmingham B1 2LH *tel:* 0121 631 3121; 0121 693 6878 (lottery info) *fax:* 0121 643 7239 *email:* west.midarts@midnet.com; http://www.arts.org.uk/. Sally Luton, chief exec; Anne Gallacher, planning offr, educ; Val Birchall, mus offr. *Hereford and Worcester, Shrops, Staffs, Warwicks, W Midlands.*
Yorkshire and Humberside Arts. 21 Bond St, Dewsbury, W Yorks WF13 1AX *tel:* 01924 455555 *fax:* 01924 466522 *email:* yharts-info@geo2.poptel.org.uk. Roger Lancaster, exec dir; Jim Beirne, dir of perf arts; Glyn Foley, mus offr. *S Yorks, W Yorks, N Yorks, N Lincs, NE Lincs, E Riding and Hull and York cities.*

National Music Council

Francis House, Francis Street, London SW1P 1DE *tel:* 0181 347 8618. Sir Michael Tippett OM CH CBE, hon president; Russell Jones, chairman; Mark Isherwood, deputy chairman; Chris Hodgkins, hon treasurer; Jennifer Goodwin, administrator.

Founded in 1953, the National Music Council is an organisation dedicated to promoting and representing the interests of those working within the field of music in the United Kingdom. It is also the UK representative on the International Music Council (UNESCO) through which it acts as a voice for British music within Europe and throughout the world.

The Council co-ordinates the publication of a regular newsletter and an annual programme of seminars and meetings thus providing a forum through which shared interests and concerns can be voiced, and the means for concerted action agreed. Membership is open to all organisations with an interest in the development of music in the UK; professional, voluntary and amateur, subsidised and commercial, creative and educational.

The Council is also committed to promoting the advancement of music education and provision. Each year, in collaboration with the Association of County Councils, the Association of District Councils and the Association of Metropolitan Authorities acting through the Council of Local Education Authorities, the National Music Council presents awards to those local authorities and local education authorities that have demonstrated an outstanding commitment to music.

Executive Committee Members 1997-98

Association of Professional Composers
Association for Business Sponsorship of the Arts
British Phonographic Industry Ltd
Council of Local Education Authorities
Jazz Services Ltd
Mechanical-Copyright Protection Society Ltd

Music Education Council
Music Industries Association
Musicians' Union
National Federation of Music Societies
Performing Right Society Ltd

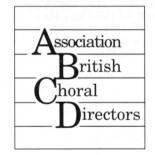

Associations

This list includes musical societies devoted to a named composer or instrument. Organisations for and on behalf of people with disabilities (including organisations for the practice of music therapy) are grouped together in a separate list immediately following this section (*see* **Music and Disability**). The **Musicians' Union** regional offices are listed at the end of this section.

Adult Residential Colleges Association (ARCA). Headlands, Church La, Washbrook, Ipswich, Suffolk IP8 3HF *tel:* 01473 730737 *also fax. Short courses averaging 2 to 7 days. Many member colleges include mus in the range of subjects covered.*

Alkan Society. 21 Heronswood, Salisbury, Wilts SP2 8DH *tel:* 01722 325771 *also fax.* Peter Grove, hon sec. *Founded in 1977. Publishes a bulletin 3 times pa, also discography. 1 all-day meeting pa in London.*

Alwyn (William) Foundation. Lark Rise, Dunwich Rd, Blythburgh, Halesworth, Suffolk IP19 9LT *tel:* 01502 478331 *also fax; email:* http://www.cityscape.co.uk/users/dy25/alwyn/. Mary Alwyn, archivist. *Promotes the study, performance and recording of the mus and writings of William Alwyn.*

The Alwyn (William) Society. 122 Vernon Av, Old Basford, Nottingham NG6 0AL *tel:* 0115 978 0863 *fax:* 0115 913 0860 *email:* http://www. edu.coventry.ac.uk/music/alwyn/. Andrew Palmer, sec; Mary Alwyn, president. *Aims to widen knowledge and encourage the performance of Alwyn's work. Regular newsletters; information on Alwyn's life and work.*

Arnold (Malcolm) Society. 6 Walton St, Barnsley, S Yorkshire S75 2PE *tel:* 01226 284116 *also fax.* Keith Llewellyn, hon sec. *Exists to promote the mus of Sir Malcolm Arnold. Quarterly newsletter, concert details, reviews and details of recorded mus.*

The Arts Foundation. The Countess of Huntingdon's Chapel, The Vineyards, Bath BA1 5NA *tel:* 01225 315775 *fax:* 01225 317597. Prudence Skene, dir. *A private, charitable organisation established to foster innovation and patronage in the arts by awarding Fellowships to individual artists. No open applications accepted; nominations only.*

Arts Marketing Association. Bolton's Warehouse, 23 Tenison Rd, Cambridge CB1 2DG *tel:* 01223 578078 *fax:* 01223 578079. Helen Robbins, mgr; Roger Tomlinson, chmn. *National body for arts marketers providing advice, speaker's tours, mentoring, newsletters, jobwatch and an annual conference.*

Associated Board of the Royal Schools of Music. 14 Bedford Sq, London WC1B 3JG *tel:* 0171 636 5400 *fax:* 0171 436 4520 *email:* chiefexec @abrsm.ac.uk. Richard Morris, chief exec. *Established in 1889 to offer a graded system of mus exams at all levels from preparatory to professional diploma. Over half a million candidates are examined worldwide. Also a mus publisher and offers professional development courses for inst and singing teachers.*

Association for Business Sponsorship of the Arts. Nutmeg House, 60 Gainsford St, Butlers Wharf, London SE1 2NY *tel:* 0171 378 8143 *fax:* 0171 407 7527. Colin Tweedy, dir gen. *National organisation promoting business support for the arts. Manages the Pairing Scheme (formerly Business Sponsorship Incentive Scheme BSIS), and Business in the Arts (BIA), on behalf of Department for Culture, Media and Sport.*

Association for Business Sponsorship of the Arts (Northern Ireland). PO Box 496, 120 Malone Rd, Belfast BT9 5GL *tel:* 01232 664736 *fax:* 01232 664500. Caroline Kieran, dir. *Independent trade association promoting the concept and good practice of arts sponsorship to both arts and business communities in Northern Ireland.*

Association for Business Sponsorship of the Arts (Scotland). 100 Wellington St, Glasgow G2 6PB *tel:* 0141 204 3864 *fax:* 0141 204 3897. Peggy MacLeod, dir. *To provide services and advice to the business and arts communities on business sponsorship; to run the government's Pairing Scheme and Business in the Arts, and promote business support of the arts.*

Association for Business Sponsorship of the Arts (Wales and South West England). 16 Museum Pl, Cardiff CF1 3BH *tel:* 01222 303023 *fax:* 01222 303024. Gavin Backley, dir; Llinos James, mgr.

Association of British Choral Directors (ABCD). 46 Albert St, Tring, Herts HP23 6AU *tel:* 01442 891633 *also fax.* Howard Layfield, chair; Marie-Louise Petit, gen sec. *The association and forum for choral conductors. Promotes educ, training and development for choral conductors and teachers in all sectors of activity.*

Association of British Jazz Musicians. Jazz Services, Africa House, 64-78 Kingsway, London WC2B 6BD *tel:* 0171 405 0737 *fax:* 0171 405 0828 *email:* jazz@dial.pipex.com. Chris Hodgkins. *Represents the interests of jazz musicians in the UK who are members of the Musicians' Union.*

Association of British Orchestras. Francis House, Francis St, London SW1P 1DE *tel:* 0171 828 6913 *fax:* 0171 931 9959 *email:* abo@ orchestranet.co.uk; http://www.orchestranet.co.uk. Libby MacNamara, dir. *Representation of the collective interests of professional UK orchs: conferences, seminars, negotiation, training and general advocacy. Incorporating Opera and Music Theatre Forum.*

Association of Educational Advisers in Scotland. Summerhill Education Centre, Stronsay Dr, Aberdeen AB2 6JA *tel:* 01224 208205. Alistair Horne, president; Elisabeth Sharp, sec.

Association of English Singers and Speakers. 13 Shaftesbury Av, Bedford MK40 3SA *tel:* 01234 355787 *also fax.* Jacob de Vries, chmn. *To encourage the communication of English words in speech and song with clarity, understanding and imagination.*

Association of Heads of Independent Schools. Wispers School, Haslemere, Surrey GU27 1AD *tel:* 01428 643646 *fax:* 01428 641120. L H Beltran, chmn. *Member schools, accredited by ISJC, tend to be small all-ability schools, both boarding, weekly boarding and day.*

Association of Irish Choirs. 4 Drinan St, Cork, Republic of Ireland *tel:* 00 353 21 312296 *fax:* 00 353 21 962457. Barbara Heas, admin. *Established in 1980 to promote choral mus and singing. Organises annual summer school and other courses; publishes choral mus; administers the Irish Youth Choir; issues newsletter In-Choir.*

Association of Medical Advisers to the British Orchestras (AMABO) *see* **British Performing Arts Medicine Trust**.

Association of Professional Composers. The Penthouse, 4 Brook St, London W1Y 1AA *tel:* 0171 629 4828 *fax:* 0171 629 0993 *email:* a.p.c @dial.pipex.com. Rosemary Dixson, admin. *The APC represents professional composers working in most fields of mus and advises them on professional and artistic matters.*

Association of Professional Music Therapists. 38 Pierce La, Fulbourn, Cambs CB1 5DL *tel:* 01223 880377 *fax:* 01223 881679. Diana Asbridge, admin. *Deals with the needs of professional mus therapists in relation to standards of practice, employment career structure, training, etc.*

Association of Professional Recording Services LTD (APRS). 2 Windsor Sq, Silver St, Reading, Berks RG1 2TH *tel:* 0118 975 6218 *fax:* 0118 975 6216 *email:* info@aprs.co.uk. Philip Vaughan, chief exec. *Trade association for businesses and individuals involved in professional sound recording and associated fields; organises annual international APRS Audio Exhibition in London.*

Association of Religious in Education. 53 Cromwell Rd, London SW7 2EH *tel:* 0171 584 6617. Sister Louisa Poole, president; Sister Winefride Fitzgerald, sec. *National association that supports, informs, encourages and represents the religious in education, pastoral and chaplaincy work.*

Association of Teachers and Lecturers (ATL). 7 Northumberland St, London WC2N 5DA *tel:* 0171 930 6441 *fax:* 0171 930 1359 *email:* info @atl.org.uk; http://www.atl.org.uk. Peter Smith, gen sec. *Provides over 150,000 members (4,877 mus teachers) with full trade union services. Also curriculum development.*

Association of Teachers of Singing. 146 Greenstead Rd, Colchester, Essex CO1 2SN *tel:* 01206 867462 *also fax.* Coral Gould, membership sec; Norman Tattersall, conference sec; Colin J Schooling, sec and treasurer. *For qualified teachers of singing; holds annual conference in different venues and spring and winter conference in London.*

Association of University Teachers. United House, 9 Pembridge Rd, London W11 3JY *tel:* 0171 221 4370 *fax:* 0171 727 6547 *email:* hq@ aut.org.uk. David Triesman, gen sec.

Association of University Teachers (Scotland and Northumbria). 6 Castle St, Edinburgh EH2 3AT *tel:* 0131 226 6694 *fax:* 0131 226 2066 *email:* scotland&ne@aut.org.uk. David Bleiman, asst gen sec; Tony Axon, research offr. *Professional association for academic and related staff in universities.*

Association of Woodwind Teachers. 90 Becmead Av, Kenton, Middx HA3 8HB *tel:* 0181 907 8428; 0410 520539. Angela Fussell, chmn; Caroline Barlow, sec. *The aims of the association are to promote and encourage high standards of w/wind teaching and to give support and practical help to teachers who teach insts other than their principal study. Also provides opportunities for w/wind teachers to meet, discuss and exchange ideas and information, as well as mutual support and encouragement through meetings and courses.*

Association of Workers for Children with Emotional and Behavioural Difficulties. 18 Thornton Ct, Girton, Cambridge CB3 0Ns *tel:* 01223 277096 *also fax.* Sue Panter, gen sec. *Serves all disciplines involved with children with emotional and behavioural difficulties.*

Audio Engineering Society Ltd. PO Box 645, Slough SL1 8BJ *tel:* 01628 663725 *fax:* 01628 667002 *email:* aesuk@aol.com. Heather Lane, admin. *International society of 11,000 members in the world of audio. Over 650 members in British section.*

Australian Music Centre. 51b Dartmouth Rd, London NW2 4EP *tel:* 0181 208 1541 *also fax.* Tony Gray, UK rep. *Object is to promote performance and awareness of Australian mus in Britain. Library of scores and recordings.*

The Bagpipe Society. 25 Baden Rd, Evington, Leicester LE5 5PA *tel:* 0116 273 4453. Tim Garland, publicity offr. *For all types of folk, early and art bagpipes. Regular newsletters, journals, diary of bagpipe events and other publications.*

Bantock Society. St Barnabas Vicarage, Daventry Rd, Knowle, Bristol BS4 1DQ. Roger Dubois, hon sec.

Baptist Music Network. 19 Limefields Way, East Hunsbury, Northampton NN4 0SA *tel:* 01604 760928. Paul Lavender, chmn and training offr; Lesley Goulbourne, admin. *Offers practical help and encouragement to those involved with mus in churches.*

Barbirolli Society. 2 Cedar Close, Uttoxeter, Staffs ST14 7NP *tel:* 01889 564562 *also fax.* Pauline Pickering, chmn. *Dedicated to keeping alive the art of Sir John Barbirolli through the re-issue of his recordings.*

BBC Education. White City, Wood La, London W12 7TS *tel:* 0181 746 1111. *Supplies information concerning forthcoming schools radio and TV broadcasts as well as supporting publications, time-tables, etc.*

Beecham (Sir Thomas) Trust. Denton House, Denton, Harleston, Norfolk IP20 0AA *tel:* 01986 788780. Shirley, Lady Beecham, trustee; A M Mackarel Davies, trustee; Christopher R Hopper MVO, chmn. *The provision of scholarships and awards at certain universities and musical institutions throughout the UK.*

Benslow Association. Little Benslow Hills, off Benslow La, Hitchin, Herts SG4 9RB *tel:* 01462 459446 *fax:* 01462 440171. Chris Blackman, chmn. *The Friends of Benslow Music Trust.*

Benslow Music Trust. Little Benslow Hills, off Benslow La, Hitchin, Herts SG4 9RB *tel:* 01462 459446 *fax:* 01462 440171. Keith Stent, mus adviser. *National centre for residential mus courses and meeting place for amateur musicians of all standards. Over 100 short courses each year.*

Berkshire Young Musicians Trust. Mockbeggar, 25 Whiteknights Rd, Reading, Berks RG6 7BY *tel:* 0118 966 5015 *fax:* 0118 935 3419. David Marcou, principal. *Provides a wide range of musical opportunities in schools, mus centres and at county level.*

Black Music Vox. PO Box 7674, London NW10 1AF *tel:* 0181 453 1643 *also fax.* Lydia Batchelor, chair; Vicky Okolo, vice-chair. *Offers services for its members by using the BMVOX counsellors' vast experience of the mus industry. Seminars and newsletter.*

The Bliss Trust. c/o Taylor Joynson Garrett, Carmelite, 50 Victoria Embankment, Blackfriars, London EC4Y 0DX *tel:* 0171 353 1234 *fax:* 0171 936 2666. Sarah Faulder, chmn. *To promote understanding and awareness of the mus of Arthur Bliss through performance, recordings, research, academic writing and publication. Awards, prizes and scholarships are offered mainly through centres of learning and educ.*

Boughton (The Rutland) Music Trust. 526a Hitchin Rd, Stopsley, Luton LU2 7UE *tel:* 01582 400824. Carolyn Boughton, sec; Vernon Handley, president. *Registered charity established in 1978 to promote the works of Rutland Boughton. Mailing list. Publicity leaflet available.*

Brian (Havergal) Society. 5 Eastbury Rd, Watford WD1 4PT *tel:* 01923 224607 *also fax.* Alan Marshall, admin sec. *To further public knowledge of Brian's work by supporting and sponsoring its publication, performance and recording.*

Bridge (Frank) Trust. 14 Barlby Rd, London W10 6AR *tel:* 0181 969 3579. John Bishop, admin. *Acts as a centre of information about all aspects of Bridge's mus; publishing and recording programme.*

British Academy of Songwriters, Composers and Authors (BASCA). The Penthouse, 4 Brook St, Mayfair, London W1Y 1AA *tel:* 0171 629 0992 *fax:* 0171 629 0993 *email:* basca@basca.org.uk. Guy Fletcher, chmn; Amanda McCarthy, membership; Joanne Brown, BASCA News. *Europe's largest composer body. Represented on PRS and MCPS boards. Campaigns on the Continent. Business and songwriting surgeries. Quarterly magazine. Song for Europe. Presents annual Ivor Novello Awards.*

British Actors' Equity Association. Guild House, Upper St Martin's La, London WC2H 9EG *tel:* 0171 379 6000 *fax:* 0171 379 7001 *email:* equity @easynet.co.uk. Ian McGarry, gen sec. *The union representing British actors, singers, dancers, variety artists, stage mgrs, theatre dirs and designers, broadcasters and others in the entertainment business.*

British American Arts Association. Third Floor, 118 Commercial St, London E1 6NF *tel:* 0171 247 5385 *fax:* 0171 247 5256. Jennifer Williams, exec dir. *Arts service organisation providing information and advice to artists and arts administrators working in transatlantic cultural exchange; does not run programmes or give funds.*

The British and International Double Bass Forum. Studio Ten, Farnham Maltings, Farnham, Surrey GU9 7QR *tel:* 01252 319610 *also fax.* David Heyes, admin. *Promotes the db in all aspects of performance and educ. International membership. Quarterly newsletter.*

British Arts Festivals Association. 3rd Floor, Whitechapel Library, 77 Whitechapel High St, London E1 7QX *tel:* 0171 247 4667 *fax:* 0171 247 5010 *email:* bafa@netcomuk.co.uk. Gwyn Rhydderch, co-ord. *Association of more than 50 leading professional arts festivals for promotion of festivals to audiences at home and abroad and as a forum for exchange of expertise. Includes Festivals Education Group for festival personnel organising educ and community programmes. Free annual arts festivals brochure.*

British Association for Early Childhood Education. 111 City View House, 463 Bethnal Green Rd, London E2 9QY *tel:* 0171 739 7594 *fax:* 0171 613 5330. Mrs B Boon, snr admin offr; Mrs J Rabin, project mgr. *BAECE is concerned with all aspects of learning for children aged 0-9. Organises national conferences, seminars and meetings; also publishes a newsletter.*

British Association for Performing Arts Medicine *see* **British Performing Arts Medicine Trust.**

British Association of Barbershop Singers (BABS). 7 Northcote Rd, Clifton, Bristol BS8 3HB *tel:* 0117 973 6591 *also fax.* Gerry Hughes, PR offr. *BABS is an association of male singers and 54 harmony clubs singing a capella 4-part close harmony known as barbershop.*

British Association of Christian Bands. Winyards, Lytton Rd, Woking, Surrey GU22 7BH *tel:* 01483 760904. Norman Gerhold, hon sec; Trevor Austin, hon chmn. *Brings Christian musicians together for fellowship and to learn from experienced conductors. Branches in Andover, Nottingham, Tyne and Wear and Faversham.*

British Association of Symphonic Bands and Wind Ensembles (BASBWE). 7 Dingle Close, Tytherington, Macclesfield SK10 2UT *tel:* 01625 430807 *also fax; email:* basbwe@interbs.demon.co.uk; http:// www.interbs.demon.co.uk/basbwe. Liz Winter, sec; Colin Touchin, chmn; Sir Simon Rattle, president. *Promotes interest nationwide in wind bands and wind ens. Quarterly journal* Winds.

British Choral Institute. 18 The Rotyngs, Rottingdean, Brighton BN2 7DX *tel:* 01273 300894 *fax:* 01273 308394 *email:* britchorinst@fastnet. co.uk. Roy Wales, dir; Christine Wales, admin. *Advisory, promotional, educ and training body for choral singers, conductors, choral administrators and organisers, with a special emphasis on developing international choral projects.*

The British Clavichord Society. 3 East Castle Rd, Edinburgh EH10 5AP *tel:* 0131 229 8018 *email:* 100603.2732@compuserve.com. Sheila Barnes, membership sec. *Encourages understanding and enjoyment of the clavichord, promoting recitals and organising educ activities. Publishes a newsletter 3 times pa, and a comprehensive* Register *which lists performers, makers, tuners and teachers is available free of charge to all members.*

British Copyright Council. 29-33 Berners St, London W1P 4AA *tel:* 0171 306 4069 *fax:* 0181 371 9993 *email:* british.copyright.council@dial. pipex.com. Heather Rosenblatt, sec. *Liaison committee of professional associations, trade unions and collecting societies whose individual members own copyright in original library, dramatic, musical and artistic works, together with publishers' and performers' organisations.*

British Double Reed Society. 9 Hamlyn Gardens, Church Rd, London SE19 2NX *tel:* 0181 653 3625. Sarah Francis, chmn; David Moore, hon sec. *Registered charity established to further the interests of all involved with the ob and bsn.*

British Fasch Society. 55 Ballindean Rd, Dundee DD4 8NS *tel:* 01382 500296 *also fax; email:* brianc@argonet.co.uk. Brian Clark, sec. *Publishes and encourages performances of mus by Johann Friedrich Fasch. Affiliated to Internationale Fasch-Gesellschaft.*

British Federation of Audio. 19 Charing Cross Rd, London WC2H 0ES *tel:* 0171 930 3206 *fax:* 0171 839 4613. C I C Cowan, sec. *Trade association for British manufacturers of hi-fi audio equipment.*

British Federation of Brass Bands. 17 Kiln Way, Badgers Dene, Grays, Essex RM17 5JE *tel:* 01375 375831. Norman Jones, gen sec; Peter Parkes, pres. *The national body representing the interests of br bands throughout the UK.*

British Federation of Festivals. Festivals House, 198 Park Lane, Macclesfield, Cheshire SK11 6UD *tel:* 01625 428297 *fax:* 01625 503229 *email:* festivals@compuserve.com; http://ourworld.compuserve.com/ homepages/festivals. Elizabeth Whitehead, chief exec. *Headquarters of the amateur mus, speech and dance festival movement.*

British Federation of Young Choirs. Devonshire House, Devonshire Sq, Loughborough, Leics LE11 3DW *tel:* 01509 211664. Susan Lansdale, dir; Andrew Fairbairn, hon sec. *Offers events, courses, training and encouragement to people of all ages involved with choral singing. Choral animateurs employed in Scotland, Northern Ireland, the South East, Midlands, East Anglia and London.*

British Flute Society. 61 Queen's Dr, London N4 2BG *tel:* 0181 802 5984 *fax:* 0181 809 7436. Ann Cherry, sec; Nick Wallbridge, membership sec. *Promotes fl playing from beginner to professional standard. Events held throughout the country. Quarterly journal* Pan.

British Horn Society. Freepost WC 4386, Epsom, Surrey KT19 0BR *tel:* 0181 393 6067 *email:* 100530.2575@compuserve.com; http://www.foresight.co.uk/horn/. Margaret Humphries, sec; Shirley Hopkins, chmn. *Promotes the hn and its mus. Student, amateur and professional membership. Organises festivals, w/shops and publishes* The Horn *magazine.*

British Institute of Organ Studies. c/o 17 Wheeleys Rd, Edgbaston, Birmingham B15 2LD *tel:* 0121 440 5491 *also fax.* Jim Berrow, sec; Nicholas Thistlethwaite, chmn. *Dedicated to the study and conservation of historic British organs, their source materials and repertoire. Operates an advisory service and administers the British Organ Archive, the National Pipe Organs Register and the Historic Organs Certificate Scheme. Regular day and residential conferences and publications.*

British Kodály Academy. 13 Midmoor Rd, London SW19 4JD *tel:* 0181 946 6528 *fax:* 0181 946 6561. Celia Cviic, treasurer and courses sec; John Wood, chmn. *Offers teacher training according to the Kodály concept in mus educ through w/shops and INSET courses throughout the UK. Also w/end courses, diploma courses and an annual summer school.*

British Music Information Centre. 10 Stratford Pl, London W1N 9AE *tel:* 0171 499 8567 *fax:* 0171 499 4795 *email:* bmic@bmic.co.uk; http://www.bmic.co.uk. Matthew Greenall, dir; Tom Morgan, information mgr. *Reference library of 20th C British classical mus. Free admission; open Mon-Fri noon-5pm. Concerts, usually Tue and Thu 7.30pm.*

British Music Society. 30 Chester Rd, Watford, Herts WD1 7DQ *tel:* 01923 230111. David Burkett, hon sec. *Concentrates particularly on promoting an interest in neglected British composers through learned publications, professionally produced recordings and live concerts.*

British Performing Arts Medicine Trust. 18 Ogle St, London W1P 7LG *tel:* 0171 636 6860/6960 (helpline) *fax:* 0171 636 6880 *email:* bpamt @dial.pipex.com. Alex Scott, admin. *Specialist charity offering help and advice regarding medical problems to all performers. Administers the British Association for Performing Arts Medicine and the Association of Medical Advisers to British Orchestras.*

The British Phonographic Industry Ltd. 25 Savile Row, London W1X 1AA *tel:* 0171 287 4422 *fax:* 0171 287 2252 *email:* general@bpi.co.uk. John Deacon, dir gen. *Trade association for British record companies.*

British Piano Duo Association. 15 Birchmead Close, St Albans, Herts AL3 6BS *tel:* 01727 858485 *also fax.* Harvey Dagul, president; Isabel Beyer, president. *Encourages the study and performance of the pno duo repertoire on one and two pnos.*

British Radio & Electronic Equipment Manufacturers Association. 19 Charing Cross Rd, London WC2H 0ES *tel:* 0171 930 3206 *fax:* 0171 839 4613. H Peltor CBE, dir. *Trade association for manufacturers in the consumer electronics industry.*

British Society for Music Therapy. 25 Rosslyn Av, E Barnet, Herts EN4 8DH *tel:* 0181 368 8879 *also fax.* Denize Christophers, admin. *The BSMT promotes the use of mus therapy in the treatment, educ and rehabilitation of children and adults suffering from emotional, physical or mental handicap. Holds meetings and conferences, publishes papers and a journal for members. Membership is open to all interested in mus therapy.*

British Suzuki Institute. 39 High St, Wheathampstead, Herts AL4 8BB *tel:* 01582 832424 *fax:* 01582 834488. Birte Kelly, gen sec. *Suzuki teacher training in vn, pno, vc and fl. P/t courses lead to Diploma of European Suzuki Association.*

British Tape Industry Association. Ambassador House, Brigstock Rd, Thornton Heath, Surrey CR7 7JG *tel:* 0181 665 5395 *fax:* 0181 665 6447. A C Skipper, sec. *Representative organisation for manufacturers of blank audio and video tape and computer media.*

British Trombone Society. PO Box 817, London SE21 7BY *tel:* 0181 658 0405 *also fax;* 01763 848208. John Edney, membership sec; Christopher Greening, ed. *Open to all ages and abilities interested in the trb.*

Calouste Gulbenkian Foundation. 98 Portland Pl, London W1N 4ET *tel:* 0171 636 5313 *fax:* 0171 637 3421. Ben Whitaker, dir. *Grant giving foundation which also publishes books within the three policy areas of social welfare, arts and educ.*

Cambridge Society of Musicians. 122 Horton Rd, Manchester M14 7GD *tel:* 01426 241423 (24hr message line). Lee P Longden, dir; Ian Roche, admin dean; Nicholas Groves, academic dean. *A learned society which elects experienced musicians to membership, and formally qualified musicians to the higher grades of Associateship and Fellowship. The Society's College, Phillips College, offers certificate and diploma exams.*

Careers and Occupational Information Centre. PO Box 298a, Thames Ditton, Surrey KT7 0ZS *tel:* 0181 957 5030 *fax:* 0181 957 5019. *Publishes a wide range of careers and occupational books.*

Careers Research and Advisory Centre (CRAC Ltd). Sheraton House, Castle Pk, Cambridge CB3 0AX *tel:* 01223 460277 *fax:* 01223 311708 *email:* enquiries@crac.org.uk; http://www.crac.org.uk/crac. Alison Manners, snr admin, business relations; Donald McGregor, dir. *CRAC is an independent development agency and registered educ charity founded in 1964. It provides information, informs policy, anticipates developments and identifies practical solutions in the careers and guidance field.*

Carreras (José), Friends of. 89 Gordon Rd, Corringham, Essex SS17 7QZ *tel:* 01375 678788 *also fax.* Joan Sheppard, chmn. *Appreciation society; career information. Leukaemia Foundation fundraising. 1000+ members worldwide.*

The Carreras (José) Society. 26 Denbydale Way, Royton, Oldham OL2 5TJ *tel:* 0161 624 5264 *fax:* 0161 287 8234. Patricia Chantler, organiser. *Artistic appreciation society and support group for the José Carreras International Leukaemia Foundation worldwide membership.*

Cathedral Music, Friends of. 26 Dumbrells Ct, North End, Ditchling, W Sussex BN6 8TG. Vincent Waterhouse, hon sec; Alan Thurlow, chmn. *To assist cathedrals financially in maintaining their mus and to increase public awareness of the unique heritage of cathedral mus.*

Cathedral Organists' Association. Royal School of Church Music, Cleveland Lodge, Westhumble, Dorking RH5 6BW *tel:* 01306 877676 *fax:* 01306 887260. Harry Bramma, sec. *Association of present and former cathedral organists.*

Catholic Stage Guild. Corpus Christi, 1 Maiden La, London WC2E 7NP *tel:* 0171 240 1221. Ann Rutherford, hon sec. *For Catholics engaged in the theatre, films, TV, radio and allied arts including actors, directors, writers, performers, musicians and technicians.*

Cello Club. 12 Pierrepoint Rd, London W3 9JH *tel:* 0181 248 9067 *also fax; email:* celloclub@wbruce.demon.co.uk. William Bruce, dir; Christopher Bunting, president. *A non-profit making national club for young cellists. Members receive three magazines and three newsletters each year on everything to do with the vc world, the opportunity to participate in special vc events and discounts on vc supplies.*

Chance for Children Trust. 5 Summerfield Rd, Ealing, London W5 1ND *tel:* 0181 997 5831. Helen Ranger. *Mus w/shops for children and young people who have been through a period of trauma.*

Children's Music Foundation In Scotland. 537 Sauchiehall St, Glasgow G3 7PQ *tel:* 0141 248 1611 *fax:* 0141 248 1989 *email:* childclasscon@compuserve.com; http://www.childclassic.co.uk. Louise Naftalin, Lizanne McKerrell, mgrs. *Organises the 'Children's Classic Concerts' series, and encourages an appreciation of classical mus in children through concerts and educ w/shops.*

Choir Schools' Association. The Minster School, Deangate, York YO1 2JA *tel:* 01904 624900 *fax:* 01904 632418. Mrs W A Jackson, admin. *Membership includes over 40 schools which educate boy and girl choristers for cathedrals, churches and collegiate chapels. Also administers a Bursary Trust Fund, which aims to ensure that no chorister is denied a place at choir school on financial grounds.*

The Chopin Society (London). c/o 39 Emperor's Gate, London SW7 4HJ *tel:* 0171 370 4943 *also fax.* Gives monthly concerts at the Polish Institute, 20 Prince's Gate, London SW7 (opposite Hyde Park).

Christian Copyright Licensing (Europe) Ltd. PO Box 1339, Eastbourne, E Sussex BN21 4YF *tel:* 01323 417711 *fax:* 01323 417722 *email:* info@ccli.co.uk. Geoff Booker, mgr dir. *Issues and administrates the Church Copyright Licence on behalf of over 2000 copyright owners. The licence allows reproduction and recording of the words of copyright worship songs and hymns to churches, schools and Christian organisations for non-commercial use.*

Church Music Society. 8 The Chandlers, The Calls, Leeds LS2 7EZ *tel:* 0113 234 1146 *also fax.* Simon Lindley, hon sec. *Leading publisher of all kinds of church mus in association with OUP mus dept. Annual lecture and other events.*

Clarinet and Saxophone Society of Great Britain. 167 Ellerton Rd, Tolworth, Surbiton, Surrey KT6 7UB *tel:* 0181 390 8307. Susan Moss, membership sec. *Advice and consultancy service; library, discount insurance, quarterly journal (including* Young Reeders *supplement), annual conference, teachers' course, regional events.*

Clarinet Heritage Society. 47 Hambalt Rd, London SW4 9EQ *tel:* 0181 675 3877. Stephen Bennett, hon sec. *Publishes and records new and rare cl mus and promotes the image of the cl.*

Clarinetwise. Pengribyn, Cilrhedyn, Llanfyrnach, Pembs SA35 0AA *tel:* 01239 698602. Jacqueline Browne, events organiser and ed; Michael Collins, president. *W/shops, m/classes, competitions, courses, playing days; quarterly journal.*

The Clarsach Society. 22 Durham Rd South, Edinburgh EH15 3PD *tel:* 0131 669 8972 *fax:* 0131 445 2022 *email:* arco@globalnet.co.uk. Alistair Cockburn, admin. *Promotes the teaching and playing of the celtic harp; organises the Edinburgh Harp Festival and publishes mus for celtic harp. 9 area branches throughout the UK.*

Club for Acts and Actors (incorporating The Concert Artistes' Association). 20 Bedford St, London WC2E 9HP *tel:* 0171 836 3172. Barbara Daniels, sec. *Private Members' Club for artistes in all branches of entertainment with opportunities to perform and meet with other* *professionals. Concert hall may be hired for rehearsals, auditions etc. Membership is also open to those with a strong interest in the performing arts.*

Commercial Radio Companies Association *formerly* The Association of Independent Radio Companies. 77 Shaftesbury Av, London W1V 7AD *tel:* 0171 306 2603 *fax:* 0171 470 0062. Paul Brown, chief exec. *Trade body for UK commercial radio, representing commercial radio to Government, the Radio Authority, Copyright Societies and other organisations involved with radio. Acts as a source of advice to members and a clearing house for radio information. CRCA is a founder member of the Association of European Radios (AER).*

Committee of Principals of Conservatoires. c/o Royal College of Music, Prince Consort Rd, South Kensington, London SW7 2BS *tel:* 0171 589 3643 *fax:* 0171 589 7740. Janet Ritterman, sec. *The association has a membership of the major independent conservatoires of mus in the UK.*

Community and Education Project. Sadler's Wells, Rosebery Av, London EC1R 4TN *tel:* 0171 278 6563. Sheryl Aitcheson, community and educ mgr. *Arranges tours, talks, w/shops, m/classes and outreach projects with educ and community groups.*

Community Education Development Centre (CEDC). The Woodway Park School, Wigstone Rd, Coventry CV2 2RH *tel:* 01203 655700 *fax:* 01203 655701. Phil Street, dir; Kathy Deeth, centre mgr.

Composers' Guild of Great Britain. The Penthouse, 4 Brook St, Mayfair, London W1Y 1AA *tel:* 0171 436 0007 *fax:* 0171 436 1913. Naomi Mostovic, gen sec. *Represents mainly classical mus composers and provides guidance on commission fees and self-publishing. Publications include* Composer News *and* First Performances. *Member of the Alliance of Composer Organisations.*

The Concert Artistes' Association *see* **Club for Acts and Actors.**

Confraternity of Polish Artists in Great Britain. 34 Denmark Rd, London W13 8RG *tel:* 0181 567 1565. Mrs E Rusiecki, sec.

Contemporary Music-Making for Amateurs (COMA). 13 Wellington Way, Bow, London E3 4NE *tel:* 0181 980 1527 *fax:* 0181 980 3330 *email:* 106147.546@compuserve.com. Chris Shurety, dir. *Provides opportunities for amateurs of all abilities to take part in contemporary mus-making. Also developing a high-quality contemporary repertoire for amateur ens through commissions and research.*

Cornet and Trumpet Society (CATS). Dept of Music, University of Huddersfield, Queensgate, Huddersfield HD1 3DH *tel:* 01484 472007 *fax:* 01484 472656.

Corps of Drums Society. 62 Gally Hill Rd, Church Crookham, Hants GU13 0RU *tel:* 01252 614852. Reg Davis, hon sec. *Promotes and preserves the concept and traditions of drum and fife mus, and assists in achieving and maintaining standards of efficiency.*

Covent Garden, Friends of. Royal Opera House, London WC2E 9DD *tel:* 0171 212 9267/9268. Phyllida Ritter, dir. *Events, open rehearsals, m/classes, magazine, advance booking and regular mailings. 19,000 members support opera and ballet at the ROH.*

Critics' Circle. c/o The Stage Newspaper, 47 Bermondsey St, London SE1 3XT *tel:* 0171 403 1818 ext 106 *fax:* 0171 357 9287. Charles Hedges, sec; Catherine Cooper, admin. *Organisation for critics of the performing arts. Membership by invitation only.*

Crotch (William) Society. St Michael's Vestry, Cornhill, London EC3V 9DS *tel:* 0181 658 9428 *also fax;* 0171 626 8841. Jonathan Rennert, hon sec. *Provides information to performers and scholars on the life and mus of the composer, teacher, artist and infant prodigy, Dr William Crotch (1775-1847). No membership.*

The Curwen Institute. 5 Bigbury Close, Coventry CV3 5AJ *tel:* 01203 413010 *also fax.* John Dowding, dir. *Promotes the New Curwen Method which encourages children to listen attentively to mus, to recognise pitch, rhythm and phrasing, develop a musical memory, and sing at sight with confidence.*

Dalcroze Society. 41a Woodmansterne Rd, Coulsdon, Surrey CR5 2DJ *tel:* 0181 645 0714 *also fax.* P Piqué, sec. *Mus educ through movement. Rhythmics, improvisation, ear training and therapy for all age groups. Summer course Jul-Aug.*

Delius Trust. 16 Ogle St, London W1P 8JB *tel:* 0171 436 4816 *fax:* 0171 637 4307. Meredith Davies, chmn; Marjorie Dickinson, sec. *Promotes only the mus of Frederick Delius by giving help towards the cost of performances, recordings and publications.*

Donizetti Society. 146 Bordesley Rd, Morden, Surrey SM4 5LT *tel:* 0181 648 9364. J P Clayton, hon sec. *Promotes interest in the works of Gaetano Donizetti and the mus of his day. Publishes journal and newsletters.*

Dvořák Society for Czech and Slovak Music. 69 Grasmere Rd, London N10 2DH *tel:* 0181 883 7362 *fax:* 0181 245 5591. Graham Melville-Mason, chmn. *Czech and Slovak mus. Journal, newsletters, lectures, concerts, record service, library, yearbook, international reciprocal memberships.*

Early Music Network. Sutton House, 2-4 Homerton High St, London E9 6JQ *tel:* 0181 533 2921 *fax:* 0181 533 2922. Alison Blunt, admin. *To*

generate the development of early mus through the promotion of live performances, educ and the dissemination of information.

Eastern Orchestral Board. 10 Stratford Pl, London W1N 9AE *tel:* 0171 629 9601 *fax:* 0171 495 4710 *email:* eob@compuserve.com. David Richardson, dir; Stuart Bruce, educ mgr; Nancy Buchanan, admin. *A development agency for professional orch mus working with local authorities, orchs and other agencies. Supports concerts, community and educ projects and audience development initiatives.*

Educational Centres Association (ECA). Fareham Adult Education Centre, Wickham Rd, Fareham, Hants PO16 7DA *tel:* 01329 315753 *fax:* 01329 826915. Susan S Dickinson, gen sec. *National adult educ network concerned with furthering the development of adult educ locally, nationally and internationally.*

Educational Institute of Scotland. 46 Moray Pl, Edinburgh EH3 6BH *tel:* 0131 225 6244 *fax:* 0131 220 3151. Ronald A Smith, gen sec. *Scottish teachers' union. Publishes* Scottish Educational Journal, *minimum 6 pa, free to members.*

Elgar Foundation. The Elgar Birthplace Museum, Crown East Lane, Lower Broadheath, Worcester WR2 6RH *tel:* 01905 333224. Melanie Weatherley, curator. *The country cottage where Elgar was born is now a museum dedicated to the composer's life and work.*

The Elgar Society. 29 Van Diemens Close, Chinnor, Oxon OX9 4QE *tel:* 01844 354096 *also fax.* Wendy Hillary, hon sec. *The society exists to foster and encourage a lively interest in and enthusiasm for Elgar's mus as well as to stimulate research into his life and works.*

English Folk Dance and Song Society. 2 Regents Park Rd, London NW1 7AY *tel:* 0171 485 2206 *fax:* 0171 284 0523. Noel Thompson, chief exec; Diana Jewitt, teacher training mgr. *Information service; school supply catalogue, project packs; library including tapes and videos; shop with books, records, cassettes, CDs.*

English National Opera, Friends of. London Coliseum, St Martin's La, London WC2N 4ES *tel:* 0171 836 0111 *fax:* 0171 379 9877. Anne Caldicott, friends mgr; Hattie Naylor, friends admin. *Exists to support new productions and give behind the scenes access for members.*

English Poetry and Song Society. 76 Lower Oldfield Pk, Bath, Avon BA2 3HP *tel:* 01225 313531. Richard Carder, chmn; Joyce Phillips, treasurer. *EPSS is dedicated to the performance, publication and recording of English Art Songs; newsletter and song lists by living composers; competitions.*

English Regional Arts Boards. 5 City Rd, Winchester, Hants SO23 8SD *tel:* 01962 851063 *fax:* 01962 842033 *email:* info.erab@artsfb.org.uk; http://www.poptel.org.uk/arts/. Christopher Gordon, chief exec; Carolyn Nixson, asst. *Information, co-ordination and liaison services for the ten Regional Arts Boards in England and national and international representation of their interests.*

English Sinfonia Friends Association. 1 Wedgwood Ct, Stevenade SG1 4QR *tel:* 01438 350990 *fax:* 01438 350930. Karen Foster, mgr; Jayne Whiteman, sec; Pippa Vaughan, projects mkt mgr. *Supporters of the English Sinfonia receive regular newsletters, attend rehearsals, hold social events and periodically receive other benefits, including discounts on recordings.*

Enterprise Music Scotland. Westburn House, Westburn Pk, Aberdeen AB25 3DE *tel:* 01224 620025 *fax:* 01224 620027. Ronnie Rae, exec dir. *Established to take over from the Scottish Arts Council the administration of funding, tours co-ordination and development of mus clubs and arts guilds in Scotland.*

Ernest Read Music Association (ERMA). 9 Cotsford Av, New Malden, Surrey KT3 5EU *tel:* 0181 942 0318. Noel Long, dir. *Organises and promotes concerts for children, training orch and summer courses.*

European Association of Teachers (EAT/AEDE). 20 Brookfield, Highgate West Hill, London N6 6AS *tel:* 0181 340 9136. Mary Duce, hon sec (UK section). *As the UK branch of a European organisation, works to promote and examine cross-curricular European knowledge in schools and colleges through FCAA approved tests.*

European Conference of Promoters of New Music. c/o Gaudeamus Foundation, Swammerdamstraat 38, NL-1091 RV Amsterdam, Netherlands *tel:* 00 31 20 694 7349 *fax:* 00 31 20 694 7258 *email:* ecpnm@xs4all.nl; http://www.xs4all.n/~ecpnm. H Heuvelmans, sec; S Schaefer, president. *The European union of organisations concerned with the promotion of 20th C mus, festivals and concert organisers.*

European Piano Teachers' Association (UK) Ltd (EPTA). 1 Wildgoose Dr, Horsham RH12 1TU *tel:* 01403 267761 *also fax.* Frances Bryan, admin; Kendall Taylor CBE, president; Frank Martin, chmn. *EPTA now has 34 regional organisations in the UK.*

European String Teachers Association (ESTA). 247 Hay Green La, Bournville, Birmingham B30 1SH *tel:* 0121 475 3345 *also fax.* Olive Goodborn, admin. *Aims to raise the standard of str playing and teaching, provide an international forum for the exchange of ideas, promote w/shops, lectures, discussions and sponsor publications.*

Faculty of Church Music. 27 Sutton Pk, Blunsdon, Swindon SN2 4BB *tel:* 0181 675 0180. Rev G Gleed, registrar. *Promotion of high standards in Church mus through graded exams. Tuition provided in theoretical subjects.*

Farnon (Robert) Society. Stone Gables, Upton La, Seavington St Michael, Ilminster, Somerset TA19 0PZ *tel:* 01460 242226 *also fax.* David Ades, sec. *RFS supports work of Robert Farnon and leading musicians and composers in the light orch and film mus fields.*

Federation Internationale des Jeunesses Musicales *see* **Youth and Music.**

Federation of Recorded Music Societies. 29 Brockenhurst Close, Rainham, Kent ME8 0HG *tel:* 01634 235612. Michael Smith. *To promote the development and extension of societies and organisations using recorded mus as part of their activities.*

Federation of Music Services. Wheatley House, 12 Lucas Rd, High Wycombe, Bucks HP13 6QE *tel:* 01494 439572 *also fax.* Richard Hichman, chief exec; Michael Wearne, chmn. *The Federation aims to offer support and advice to mus services in the provision and development of high quality specialist mus educ to schools and the wider community; to help mus services to maintain and develop access and opportunity; and to promote the work of mus services.*

Fellowship of Makers and Researchers of Historical Instruments. 171 Iffley Rd, Oxford OX4 1EL *email:* jeremy.montagu@music.oxford.ac. uk. Jeremy Montagu, hon sec. *Promotes authenticity in the reconstruction and use of historical insts.*

Flutewise. 9 Beaconsfield Rd, Portslade, E Sussex BN41 1XA *tel:* 01273 702367 *fax:* 01273 888864 *email:* flutewise@i-gadgets.com; http://www.ndirect.co.uk/~flutewise. James Galway, president; Liz Goodwin, ed. *Organisation for all flautists, especially the young. Quarterly magazine with competitions and prizes. Regular events.*

Galpin Society. 2 Quinton Rise, Oadby, Leicester LE2 5PN *tel:* 0116 271 1808 *also fax.* P Holden, sec and admin. *Founded in 1946 for the publication of original research into the history, construction, development and use of mus insts.*

Gamba Music Club. 32 The Burgage, Market Drayton TF9 1EG *tel:* 01630 653802. Cathy Gaskell, admin. *Issues a directory of viol players, teachers and makers; publishes a selection of viol mus annually.*

Gilbert and Sullivan Society. 1 Nethercourt Av, Finchley, London N3 1PS. Margaret Bowden, hon sec. *Aims to encourage an interest in the Gilbert and Sullivan operas.*

Gilbert and Sullivan Society of Edinburgh. 108 Northfield Drive, Edinburgh EH8 7RF. Anne McDonald, hon sec. *Promotes the works of Gilbert and Sullivan through stage productions, concerts and monthly meetings.*

Girls' Public Day School Trust. 100 Rochester Row, London SW1P 1JP *tel:* 0171 393 6666 *fax:* 0171 393 6789. M Oakley, sec.

Girls' Schools Association. 130 Regent Rd, Leicester LE1 7PG *tel:* 0116 254 1619 *fax:* 0116 255 3792 *email:* gsa@dial.pipex.com. Ms S Cooper, gen sec; Mrs W Khan, admin.

Grainger (Percy) Society. 6 Fairfax Cres, Aylesbury, Bucks HP20 2ES *tel:* 01296 28609 *also fax; email:* 101464.2670@compuserve.com; http://www.tisl.co.uk/grainger/grainger.htm. Barry P Ould, sec and mus archivist. *To promote interest in the life and works of the composer Percy Aldridge Grainger (1882-1961).*

Grieg Society of Great Britain. 25 Belgrave Sq, London SW1X 8QD *tel:* 01634 714434. Beryl Foster, sec; Torbjørn Støverud, chmn. *Promotes interest in Grieg and other Norwegian composers amongst performers and audiences in Britain.*

Guild for the Promotion of Welsh Music. 94 Walter Rd, Swansea SA1 5QA *tel:* 01792 464623/464648. Geraint W Walters, hon sec. *Promotes the composition, performance, recording and publication of contemporary Welsh mus. Bi-annual journal, plus catalogue of all known contemporary mus due for publication.*

Guild of Church Musicians. St Katharine Cree, 86 Leadenhall St, London EC3A 3DH *tel:* 01883 741854. John Ewington OBE, gen sec. *Examining body to Archbishops of Canterbury and Westminster: Archbishop's Certificate in Church Music. Fully ecumenical.*

Handbell Ringers of Great Britain. 87 The Woodfields, Sanderstead, South Croydon, Surrey CR2 0HJ *tel:* 0181 651 2663 *also fax.* Sandra Winter, hon sec. *National association for handbell, handchime and belleplate tune ringers.*

Handel at Barn Elms. 30 Torridon Rd, London SE6 1AQ *tel:* 0181 698 6044. Richard Soar, convener. *New society acknowledging links with Barn Elms, near Barnes, and promoting interest in Handel's less often performed works.*

Haydn Society of Great Britain. Music Dept, University of Lancaster, Lancaster LA1 4YW *tel:* 01524 593777 *fax:* 01524 847298 *email:* d.mccaldin@lancaster.ac.uk; http://www.lancs.ac.uk/users/concerts/haydn.html. Denis McCaldin, dir; Stella Buchall, admin. *Promotes the mus of Joseph Haydn and his circle in the form of concerts, recordings and the publication of a yearly journal.*

The Headmasters' Conference. 130 Regent Rd, Leicester LE1 7PE *tel:* 0116 285 4810 *fax:* 0116 247 1167. David Prince, membership sec. *Association of heads of independent schools, with 242 members. Publishes a private members bulletin. Divided into 7 areas, each area meeting regularly to exchange ideas and concerns.*

Headteachers Association of Scotland. University of Strathclyde, Jordanhill Campus, Southbrae Dr, Glasgow G13 1PP *tel:* 0141 950 3298 *fax:* 0141 950 3434. James B O McNair, sec. *Exists to promote educ, particularly secondary educ in Scotland and to safeguard and promote the interests of headteachers and deputy heads.*

House of Commons Culture, Media and Sport Committee. Committee Office, 7 Millbank, London SW1P 3JA *tel:* 0171 219 6120/5739/6188 *fax:* 0171 219 6606 *email:* cmscom@parliament.uk; http://www.parliament.uk. Colin Lee, clerk of the committee. *The committee examines the work of the Department of Culture, Media and Sport and of associated public bodies.*

House of Commons Education and Employment Committee. Committee Office, House of Commons, London SW1A 0AA *tel:* 0171 219 5774/6243/6181/0653 *fax:* 0171 219 6606 *email:* educempcom@parliament.uk. Matthew Hamlyn, clerk of the committee; Kenneth Fox, second clerk. *Monitors activities of Department for Education and Employment and associated public bodies.*

Howells (Herbert) Society. 32 Barleycroft Rd, Welwyn Garden City, Herts AL8 6JU *tel:* 01707 335315. Andrew Millinger, sec. *Promotes interest in performances and recordings of the mus of Herbert Howells.*

The Hurdy-gurdy Society. The Old Mill, Duntish, Dorchester, Dorset DT2 7DR *tel:* 01300 345412 *email:* hurdyplay@aol.com; gurdysmith@aol.com. Michael Muskett, sec; Richard Smith, membership sec; Angela Beaumont, publicity sec.

Hymn Society of Great Britain and Ireland. St Nicholas Rectory, Glebe Fields, Curdworth, Sutton Coldfield B76 9ES *tel:* 01675 470384. Rev Michael Garland, sec. *Society for those interested in the study and application of hymnody.*

Incorporated Association of Organists. 11 Stonehill Dr, Bromyard, Herefordshire HR7 4XB *tel:* 01885 483155 *fax:* 01885 488609. Richard Popple MBE, hon gen sec. *Dedicated to improving org playing at all levels; has over 6000 members worldwide. Publishes* Organists' Review *quarterly.*

Incorporated Association of Preparatory Schools. 11 Waterloo Pl, Leamington Spa, Warwicks CV32 5LA *tel:* 01926 887833 *fax:* 01926

888014 *email:* hq@iaps.org.uk. J H Morris, gen sec. *The main professional association for headteachers of independent preparatory and junior schools throughout the British Isles and overseas.*

Incorporated Society of Musicians. 10 Stratford Pl, London W1N 9AE *tel:* 0171 629 4413 *fax:* 0171 408 1538 *email:* membership@ism.org; http://www.ism.org. Neil Hoyle, chief exec. *Professional body for all musicians. Legal, financial and professional services; conferences, seminars and publications. Full, associate, student and corporate categories.*

Incorporated Society of Organ Builders. Petersfield, Hants GU32 3AT *tel:* 01730 262151 *also fax.* D M van Heck, sec. *Pipe org builders association.*

Independent Schools Association. Boys' British School, East St, Saffron Walden, Essex CB10 1LS *tel:* 01799 523619 *fax:* 01799 524892 *email:* isa@dial.pipex.com. T M Ham, gen sec.

Independent Schools Careers Organisation. 12a Princess Way, Camberley, Surrey GU15 3SP *tel:* 01276 21188 *fax:* 01276 691833 *email:* info@isco.org.uk. G W Searle, national dir. *Provides advice to boys and girls concerning all aspects of higher educ and careers. Support and training is provided for school staff.*

Independent Schools Information Service (ISIS). 56 Buckingham Gate, London SW1E 6AG *tel:* 0171 630 8793 *fax:* 0171 630 5013 *email:* national@isis.org.uk. D J Woodhead, dir. *Information for parents about independent schools, including specialist mus and choir schools and mus scholarships.*

Independent Television Commission. 33 Foley St, London W1P 7LB *tel:* 0171 255 3000 *fax:* 0171 306 7806 *email:* 100731.3515@compuserve.com. *Licenses and regulates non-BBC television services including Channels 3, 4 and 5, cable, satellite and additional services.*

Institute of Contemporary Arts. The Mall, London SW1Y 5AH *tel:* 0171 930 0493 *fax:* 0171 873 0051 *email:* lois@ica.org.uk; http://www.illumin.co.uk/ica/. Lois Keidan, dir, live arts.

Institute of Entertainment and Arts Management. 1 Beatrice Rd, Clacton on Sea, Essex CO15 1JS *tel:* 01255 220081 *also fax. Professional institute for those who work in the management and administration of the performing arts and entertainment industry, providing social and welfare facilities, a monthly newsletter and regular seminars.*

Institute of Leisure and Amenity Management (ILAM). Ilam House, Lower Basildon, Reading, Berks RG8 9NE *tel:* 01491 874222 *fax:* 01491 874059. Alan Smith, dir. *Professional body representing over 7000*

managers throughout the leisure industry. ILAM represents its members both nationally and regionally, offering its own qualification system and a wide range of benefits to members, including educ and training seminars, dissemination of information, publications and conferences.

Institute of Musical Instrument Technology. 8 Chester Ct, Albany St, London NW1 4BU *tel:* 0171 935 8682 *fax:* 0171 224 0957. Julian Markson, hon sec. *Promotes the professional status of members engaged in mus inst design, manufacture and repair.*

International Artist Managers' Association (IAMA) *formerly* British Association of Concert Agents. 41a Lonsdale Rd, London W11 2BY *tel:* 0171 243 2598 *fax:* 0171 792 2655 *email:* iama@easynet.co.uk. Richard Steele, exec dir; Marie-Alice Frappat, projects and development mgr. *International professional association for classical mus artist managers and concert agents.*

International Association for the Study of Popular Music. Graduate Research Centre in Culture and Communication, University of Sussex, Falmer, Brighton BN1 9QT *tel:* 01273 606755 *fax:* 01273 678644 *email:* culcom@sussex.ac.uk. Sarah Thornton, chair; Dave Hesmondhalgh, sec and treasurer. *The association brings together scholars of popular mus from 36 different countries; it includes sociologists, musicologists, anthropologists, educationalists and others.*

International Association of Music Libraries. Archives and Documentation Centres, c/o County Library Headquarters, Walton St, Aylesbury, Bucks HP20 1UU *tel:* 01296 382266 *fax:* 01296 382274. Margaret Roll, gen sec. *Careers information and special students subscriptions available to those working in, or with interest in, mus librarianship.*

International Cultural Desk. 6 Belmont Cres, Glasgow G12 8ES *tel:* 0141 339 0090 *fax:* 0141 337 2271 *email:* icd@dial.pipex.com. Hilde Bollen, development mgr; Anne C Robb, information offr. *Assists the Scottish cultural community to operate more effectively in an international context by providing information and advice. Provides and disseminates info on funding sources, international opportunities and cultural policy development in Europe, and assists with establishing contacts internationally. It is not a funding agency. The Desk publishes* Communication, *a bimonthly update about forthcoming international opportunities, and* InFocus, *a series of specialised guides with an international focus.*

International Federation of the Phonographic Industry. IFPI Secretariat, 54 Regent St, London W1R 5PJ *tel:* 0171 878 7900 *fax:* 0171 878 7950 *email:* info@ifpi.org. Nic Garnett, dir gen and chief exec. *IFPI*

promotes and defends the copyright interests of its members in sound recordings and mus videos.

International Jazz Federation. c/o 2b Gleneagle Mews, Ambleside Av, London SW16 6AE *tel:* 0181 769 7725 *fax:* 0181 677 7128. Charles Alexander, vice-president. *Represents national jazz organisations at the international level and organises the annual European Jazz Competition.*

International Liszt Centre for 19th Century Music. 135 Stevenage Rd, Fulham, London SW6 6PB *tel:* 0171 381 9751 *fax:* 0171 381 2406 *email:* ilc.rabes@mbox318.swipnet.se. J Audrey Ellison, UK representative.

International Piano Teachers' Consultants (IPTEC). 29 Beaumont Rd, Chiswick, London W4 5AL *tel:* 0181 994 4288. Meriel Jefferson, hon sec. *1-day courses. Consultations available in specialist subjects.*

International Shakuhachi Society. Lorien, Wadhurst, Sussex TN5 6PN *tel:* 01892 782045. Dan E Mayers, president; Clive Bell, sec and treasurer. *The society provides information on teachers, methods and recordings to devotees of Shakuhachi worldwide. Also provides Shakuhachi insts and bamboo blanks. Periodically publishes hardback volume,* Annals of the International Shakuhachi Society, *sent free to members.*

International Society for Contemporary Music (ISCM). British Section, c/o SPNM, Francis House, Francis St, London SW1P 1DE *tel:* 0171 828 9696 *fax:* 0171 931 9928. Cathy Graham, admin. *The ISCM British section organises talks, concerts and exhibitions and provides information on the activities of the International Society for Contemporary Music. The ISCM world mus days will be held in Manchester 17-26 Apr 1998.*

International Society for Music Education (ISME). International Centre for Research in Music Education, University of Reading, Bulmershe Ct, Reading RG6 1HY *tel:* 0118 931 8846 *also fax; fax:* 0118 935 2080 *email:* e.smith@reading.ac.uk; http://www.isme.org. Elizabeth Smith, admin. *Aims to promote mus educ throughout the world as an integral part of general educ through conferences, publications, etc. Membership information and details of the next world conference are available from the above address.*

International Society for the Study of Tension in Performance. School of Music, Kingston University, c/o 28 Emperor's Gate, London SW7 4HS *tel:* 0171 373 7307 *fax:* 0171 274 6821. Carola Grindea, chmn; Gordana Petrovic, sec. *Charitable organisation committed to helping musicians afflicted by physical and psychological problems at ISSTIP/London College of Music 'Performing Arts Clinic'. Publishes* ISSTIP journal.

International Viola Society (British Chapter). 36 Seeleys, Harlow, Essex CM17 0AD *tel:* 01279 422567. John White, president and organising sec. *Association for the promotion of va performance and research. Affiliated to the Lionel Tertis International Viola Competition held every 3 yrs at Port Erin, Isle of Man (next competition 2000). The 1998 International Viola Congress will be held at the RSAMD, Glasgow on 16-19 Jul.*

Ireland (John) Trust. 35 St Mary's Mansions, St Mary's Terrace, London W2 1SQ *tel:* 0171 723 6376 *fax:* 0171 724 8362. Mrs M Taylor, hon sec.

The Irish Contemporary Music Centre. 95 Lower Baggot St, Dublin 2, Republic of Ireland *tel:* 00 353 1 661 2105 *fax:* 00 353 1 676 2639 *email:* info@cmc.ie; http://www.cmc.ie. Eve O'Kelly, dir. *Promotes and documents Irish contemporary mus.*

Jazz Services Ltd. Room 518, Africa House, 64 Kingsway, London WC2B 6BD *tel:* 0171 405 0737/47/57 *fax:* 0171 405 0828 *email:* jazz @dial.pipex.com; http://ds.dial.pipex.com/town/square/ad663/. Chris Hodgkins, dir; Celia Wood, information. *Jazz Services promotes the growth and development of jazz within the UK by providing services in marketing, communications, touring, information, educ and jazz newspapers.*

Jewish Heritage Music Trust. PO Box 232, Harrow, Middx HA1 2NN *tel:* 0181 909 2445 *fax:* 0181 909 1030 *email:* jewishmusic@jmht.org. Geraldine Auerbach. *Promotes the study and performance of all aspects of Jewish mus.*

The Josephs (Wilfred) Society. Hill House, Corsiehill, Perth PH2 7BN *tel:* 01738 442079 *also fax.* Philippa Porritt, sec and treasurer. *Promotes Josephs' performances and broadcasts; helps the remaining unpublished works into print; produces and disseminates recordings.*

Karg-Elert Society. 29 Orford Gardens, Twickenham, Middx TW1 4PL *tel:* 0181 894 6859 *fax:* 0171 703 5689. Brian Parsons, sec; Nicholas Choveaux, president. *Promotion of the composer and organist Sigfrid Karg-Elert through encouraging research and publication of his mus.*

Kato Havas Association For The New Approach (KHANA). 3 Beacon View, Marple, Stockport SK6 6PX *tel:* 0161 449 7347. Gloria Bakhshayesh, admin and treasurer. *Kato Havas vn teaching method. KHANA holds w/shops on the alleviation and prevention of physical tensions and anxiety in str playing. 2 journals pa.*

King (Reginald) Trust. 6 Fairfax Cres, Aylesbury, Bucks HP20 2ES *tel:* 01296 28609 *also fax; email:* 101464.2670@compuserve.com. Barry Peter Ould, archivist. *Promotes interest in the life and mus of Reginald King (1904-1991). Mus and sound archives maintained.*

Klavar Music Foundation of Great Britain. 171 Yarborough Rd, Lincoln LN1 3NQ *tel:* 01522 523117. Michael Magnus Osborn, dir. *Educ Trust. Klavar system correspondence courses for pno, org, gui and pno-accordion. Klavar notation printed mus supplies.*

The Kodály Institute of Britain. 133 Queen's Gate, London SW7 5LE *tel:* 0171 823 7371 *fax:* 0171 584 7691. Mary Skone-Roberts, admin; Cecilia Vajda, dir. *Adult educ; 1-yr p/t courses in musicianship. W/end courses on early childhood mus educ, primary and secondary educ. Annual Aug summer school in London. Publications include books, video and audio cassettes.*

Leighton (Kenneth) Trust. 38 McLaren Rd, Edinburgh EH9 2BN *tel:* 0131 667 3113 *email:* j.leighton@napier.ac.uk; http://www.music. ed.ac.uk/pubs/composition/leighton. Mrs J A Leighton, sec. *Promotes British mus in general and Leighton's mus in particular by providing financial assistance for performances (especially by younger performers), recordings and commissions.*

Library Association. 7 Ridgmount St, London WC1E 7AE *tel:* 0171 636 7543 *fax:* 0171 436 7218 *email:* info@la-hq.org.uk; http://www.la-hq. org.uk. Ross Shimmon, chief exec. *Professional body for library and information workers with 25,000 members UK and overseas.*

Light Music Society. Lancaster Farm, Chipping La, Longridge, Preston, Lancs PR3 2NB *tel:* 01772 783646 *fax:* 01772 786026. Ernest Tomlinson, chmn. *The society aims to back up the library of light mus established in 1984 and to keep alive and promote listening to light mus.*

Liszt Society. 9 Burnside Close, Twickenham TW1 1ET *tel:* 0181 287 5518 *also fax; email:* 100707.47@compuserve.com. Jan Hoare, sec. *The Society, through its publications and holding of events such as recitals, m/classes and soirées, exists to promote interest in and appreciation of the works of Franz Liszt.*

London Piano Circle. 30 Southway, London NW11 6RU *tel:* 0181 731 7887 *also fax.* E Gundrey, hon organiser. *For proficient amateurs wishing to play in groups, in one another's homes.*

London Suzuki Group. 96 Farm La, London SW6 1QH *tel:* 0171 386 8006. Christine Livingstone, mus dir; Nicholas Pullinger, admin. *Charitable organisation of teachers, parents and children committed to the Suzuki approach to mus educ for children aged 3-18.*

Lowland and Border Pipers' Society. 6 Garrioch Cres, Maryhill, Glasgow G20 8RR *tel:* 0141 946 8624. Rona MacDonald, membership sec; Gordon Mooney, hon president. *Aims to provide a focus for everyone interested in lowland and border pipes through meetings, concerts, sessions, newsletters and a twice yearly magazine.*

Lute Society. Southside Cottage, Brook Hill, Albury, Guildford GU5 9DJ *tel:* 01483 202159 *fax:* 01483 203088. Christopher Goodwin, sec. *Holds 4 meetings pa in central London with lectures and recitals on all aspects of the lute and related insts and their repertoire. Publishes annual journal* The Lute, *quarterly newsletter* Lute News, *mus, working drawings of lutes. Holds occasional 1 day w/shops. Lutes available for hire.*

The Massenet Society. Flat 2, 79 Linden Gardens, London W2 4EU *tel:* 0171 229 7060. Stella J Wright, founder and dir. *Founded 1972, the society promotes a greater knowledge and understanding of Massenet's works.*

Master Music Printers' and Engravers' Association. 2-10 Plantation Rd, Amersham, Bucks HP6 6HJ *tel:* 01494 725525 *fax:* 01494 432305.

Mayr + Donizetti Collaboration. 8 Cosway Mansions, Cosway St, London NW1 6UE *tel:* 0171 258 1798 *also fax.* Ian Caddy, John Stewart Allitt, founders. *Promotes the work of the two composers, co-ordinates scholarship and performing material; biographies and editions for sale.*

Mechanical-Copyright Protection Society Ltd (MCPS). Elgar House, 41 Streatham High Rd, London SW16 1ER *tel:* 0181 664 4400 *fax:* 0181 769 8792 *email:* webmaster@mcps.co.uk; http://www.mcps.co.uk. Simon Lindsay, customer services adviser. *Membership organisation that acts as a centralised licensing and collection agency for mechanical royalties, whenever its members' musical works are recorded.*

Metier. Glyde House, Glydegate, Bradford, W Yorks BD5 0BQ *tel:* 01274 738800 *fax:* 01274 391566. Claire Pickard, info offr. *Metier is the industry lead body developing standards of competence for a wide range of occupations in the arts and entertainment sector, many of which will underpin new National and Scottish Vocational Qualifications. (NVQ already available in Music Performance at Level 4.) It is an approved Industry Training Organisation acting as a focal point for training matters and representing the interests of employers in the sector to TECs, LECs and government.*

The Music Club of London. 78 Bedford Ct Mansions, Bedford Av, London WC1B 3AE *tel:* 0171 636 2946 *fax:* 0171 267 5619. *Bi-monthly newsletter. Programme of special events, audiences with leading musical personalities and international travel to festivals and important musical events.*

Music Education Council. 54 Elm Rd, Hale, Altrincham, Cheshire WA15 9QP *tel:* 0161 928 3085 *fax:* 0161 929 9648 *email:* ahassan@easynet. co.uk. Anna Hassan, admin. *The major forum for those involved in mus educ and training in the UK.*

Music for Youth. 4 Blade Mews, London SW15 2NN *tel:* 0181 870 9624 *fax:* 0181 870 9935 *email:* http://www.pjpubs.co.uk/mfy. Larry Westland CBE, exec dir. *Charity dedicated to providing regional and national platforms for young musicians.*

Music Industries Association. Grove Ct, Hatfield Rd, Slough, Berks SL1 1QU *tel:* 01753 511550 *fax:* 01753 539200 *email:* mia@dial.pipex.com; http://www.mia.org.uk. Bob Kelley, sec gen. *Trade association representing manufacturers, distributors and retailers of mus insts and accessories. Sponsors UK trade and public exhibitions and promotes British involvement in appropriate overseas trade fairs.*

Music Masters' and Mistresses' Association (MMA). Three Ways, Chicks La, Kilndown, Cranbrook, Kent TN17 2RS *tel:* 01892 890537 *also fax.* Victoria Aldous-Ball, admin. *Furthers all aspects of mus in schools. Membership open to those teaching mus in schools, and those wishing to support the development of mus in schools. Regular regional meetings, courses and an annual conference are held. Termly journal and annual mus scholarship guide.*

Music, Mind and Movement. 28 Glebe Place, London SW3 5LD *tel:* 0171 352 1666 *fax:* 01233 712768. Lucinda Mackworth-Young, Nicola Gaines, Karin Greenhead, dirs. *An association devoted to enhancing the performance and teaching of mus and dance through an integrated multi-arts approach. Courses run for performers, teachers and students in the practical application of psychology, eurhythmics, historical dance and other disciplines to performance, teaching and learning of mus and dance. Courses may be validated by Trinity College of Music as bearing credit to the LTCL (Music Education) or certificate in mus educ.*

Music Publishers' Association Ltd. 3rd Floor, Strandgate, 18-20 York Buildings, London WC2N 6JU *tel:* 0171 839 7779 *fax:* 0171 839 7776 *email:* mpa@mcps.co.uk. Sarah Faulder, chief exec; Peter Dadswell, exec adviser. *Trade organisation representing mus publishers in the UK, advising and assisting members in the promotion and protection of mus copyright.*

Music Trades Benevolent Society. 8 Darsway, Castle Donington, Derby DE74 2RZ *tel:* 01332 811320 *also fax.* J M Smith, sec. *Assists mus industry employees and former employees who through accident, illness, and other stresses of life have been caused deep personal hardship.*

A DONATION TO THE MUSICIANS BENEVOLENT FUND CAN DO SO MUCH TO HELP NEEDY MUSICIANS AND THEIR DEPENDANTS – FOR WHOM ACCIDENT OR ILLNESS CAN LEAD TO DESPAIR AND EVEN SILENCE. PLEASE SEND US A DONATION AND CONSIDER REMEMBERING US IN YOUR WILL.

SILENCE?

MUSICIANS BENEVOLENT FUND, ROOM BMYB2, 16 OGLE STREET, LONDON W1P 8JB

REGISTERED CHARITY NO. 228089

Musicians Against Nuclear Arms (MANA). 71 Greenfield Gardens, London NW2 1HU *tel:* 0181 455 1030. Elizabeth Fraser, chair; Joan R Horrocks, admin. *Organises concerts to assist the peace movement. Professionals, amateurs and non-performing mus lovers welcome. Quarterly newsletter.*

Musicians Benevolent Fund. 16 Ogle St, London W1P 8JB *tel:* 0171 636 4481 *fax:* 0171 637 4307 *email:* helen.faulkner@mbf.sprint.com.uk. Philip Jones CBE, chmn; Helen Faulkner, sec. *Largest charity in the UK helping professional musicians and their dependants in need.*

Musicians Benevolent Fund, Friends of the. 16 Ogle St, London W1P 8JB *tel:* 0171 636 4481 *fax:* 0171 637 4307 *email:* hilary.pentycross @mbf.sprint.com.uk. Hilary Pentycross, co-ord. *The Friends support the Musicians Benevolent Fund which is the largest musical charity in the UK helping professional musicians and their dependants in need.*

Musicians' Social and Benevolent Council. 194 Muswell Hill Rd, London N10 3NG *tel:* 0181 444 0246. *Assists London-based professional musicians in times of sickness and distress. Mainly funded by contributions from London orchestral and theatre musicians. All donations gratefully received.*

Musicians' Union. 60-62 Clapham Rd, London SW9 0JJ *tel:* 0171 582 5566 *fax:* 0171 582 9805. Dennis Scard, gen sec.

NATFHE - The University and College Lecturers' Union. 27 Britannia St, London WC1X 9JP *tel:* 0171 837 3636 *fax:* 0171 837 4403 *email:* natfhe-hq@geo2.poptel.org.uk. *Represents lecturers in post-16 educ. Campaigns for high quality educ opportunities as well as decent pay and conditions for staff. Has active mus section.*

National Association for Gifted Children. Elder House, Milton Keynes MK9 1LR *tel:* 01908 673677 *fax:* 01908 673679 *email:* nagc@rmplc. co.uk. Peter Carey, dir; Michal Hambourg, mus counsellor. *A national charity helping able and talented children to achieve fulfilment and advising those involved in their upbringing and educ.*

National Association for Music Staff in Higher Education. Royal Northern College of Music, 124 Oxford Rd, Manchester M13 9RD *tel:* 0161 273 6283 *fax:* 0161 273 7611 *email:* c.r.timms@bham.ac.uk; colin@fs1.rncm.ac.uk. Colin Timms, chmn. *Professional subject association for mus staff in higher educ. Membership is arranged through mus depts. It is a forum for debate and exchange of information about teaching methodology and admin matters.*

National Association for Primary Education (NAPE). University of Leicester, Queens Building, Barrack Rd, Northampton NN2 6AF *tel:* 01604 36326 *fax:* 01604 36328 *email:* nape@rmplc.co.uk. Emma Wilkinson, hon gen sec. *Membership includes parents, teachers,* governors, school communities and others who share concern for children's educ from 0-13. Festival of voices held annually in London.

The National Association for Special Education Needs. NASEN House, 4-5 Amber Business Village, Amber Close, Amington, Tamworth B77 4RP *tel:* 01827 311500 *fax:* 01827 313005 *email:* welcome@nasen.org. uk. *Promotes the development of children and young people with special educ needs, wherever they are located, offering support to those who work with them.*

National Association of Advisory Officers for Special Education. 32a Pleasant Valley, Saffron Walden, Essex CB11 4AP *tel:* 01799 521257 *also fax. Links inspectors and advisers with responsibility for special educ provision both in mainstream and special schools and those involved in OFSTED inspections with an SEN brief.*

National Association of Careers and Guidance Teachers. Portland House, 4 Bridge St, Usk, Gwent NP5 1BG *tel:* 01291 672985 *fax:* 01291 672090 *email:* http://www.careersoft.co.uk/nacgt. Mrs J G Cook, gen sec. *Professional association for careers teachers and others involved in careers educ and guidance.*

National Association of Choirs. 21 Charmouth Rd, Lower Weston, Bath BA1 3LJ *tel:* 01225 426713. John Robbins, gen sec. *NAC caters exclusively for choirs, providing a wide range of services such as liaison with festivals, insurance, charitable status applications, mus discount, mus loan scheme. Choirs benefit from being placed in groups for local and combined choir activities.*

National Association of Educational Inspectors, Advisers and Consultants. 1 Heath Sq, Boltro Rd, Haywards Heath, W Sussex RH16 1BL *tel:* 01444 441279. William H Wright, gen sec. *Association exclusively dedicated to educ inspection and advice, offering professional advice, legal help and representation and insurance for members.*

National Association of Head Teachers. 1 Heath Sq, Boltro Rd, Haywards Heath, W Sussex RH16 1BL *tel:* 01444 472472 *fax:* 01444 472473. David Hart OBE, gen sec. *NAHT membership is open to heads and deputies of schools of all types serving the educ of pupils aged 3-19.*

National Association of Music Educators. County Music Centre, Westfield Primary School, Bonsey La, Westfield, Woking GU22 9PR *tel:* 01483 728711 *fax:* 01483 725980. Keith Willis, head of Surrey youth mus and perf arts. *National and regional conferences on wide range of subjects organised regularly throughout the country.*

National Association of Musical Instrument Repairers. 2 Arthur Cottages, Frimley Rd, Ash Vale, Surrey GU12 5PD *tel:* 01252 518098 *also fax; email:* rdawson821@aol.com. Richard Dawson. *Individual*

The National Association of Youth Orchestras
President: Sir Simon Rattle CBE
Chairman: Sir John Manduell CBE

Festival of British Youth Orchestras
Saturday 15 August – Sunday 6 September 1998
(1999 dates: 14 August - 4 September)
Central Hall, Tollcross, Edinburgh
RSAMD, 100 Renfrew St, Glasgow
*With the Boosey & Hawkes
Youth Orchestra Award*

Anglo/German	**British Reserve**
Youth Music Week	**Insurance Conducting**
1-10 August 1998 -	**Prize/Seminar**
Oberwesel-am-Rhein	November 1998
	Young Sinfonia
August 1999 - UK	Newcastle upon Tyne

Marion Semple Weir Library of Chamber Music
The Salvesen Baton for Young Conductors
British Reserve Insurance Youth Orchestra Awards
E-mail addresses for member orchestras

NAYO, Ainslie House, 11 St Colme Street,
Edinburgh EH3 6AG; tel: 0131 539 1087, fax: 0131 539 1069
e-mail: admin@nayo.org.uk   Web: http://www.nayo.org.uk
Director: Carol Man   *Administrator:* Jenny Brockie

*Serving 125,000 young instrumentalists in 1,800 youth orchestras and
ensembles throughout the UK*   Registered Charity No 281493

NATIONAL · FEDERATION
OF · MUSIC · SOCIETIES

THE NATIONAL VOICE OF MUSIC MAKERS

NFMS represents 1700 choirs, orchestras and music
clubs and provides financial, artistic and development
services to members

PRINCIPAL SERVICES
Block Insurance Scheme
Music Hire
Conference/Seminars
PRS Licences
Programme Notes
Instrument/Staging Loans
Newsletter
Concert Promoters Network
Information Services
Workshops
Publications

Further details from: Russell Jones, Chief Executive, NFMS,
Francis House, Francis Street, London SW1P 1DE
Tel: 0171-828 7320 Fax: 0171-828 5504
WE'RE HERE TO HELP YOU MAKE MUSIC

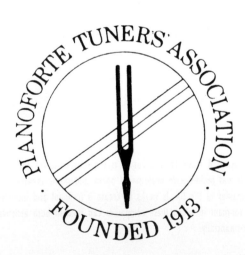

PIANOFORTE TUNERS' ASSOCIATION · FOUNDED 1913

**OUR MEMBERSHIP QUALIFICATION SETS THE
STANDARD FOR THE PROFESSION**

For members in your area, contact the Secretary:
Mrs Valerie Addis,
10 Reculver Road,
Herne Bay,
Kent CT6 6LD
Telephone: (01227) 368808
Facsimile: (01227) 368808

repairers dedicated to maintaining standards of quality in a particular inst. Enables enquirers to contact a local repairer of the appropriate specialism.

National Association of Percussion Teachers. 138 Springbank Rd, London SE13 6SU *tel:* 0181 698 7885 *fax:* 0181 461 5910 *email:* chrski @delphi.com. Christeen Skinner, sec. *To further the knowledge of perc playing and teaching and ensuring the highest standards are maintained.*

National Association of Schoolmasters' Union and Women Teachers (NASUWT). Hillscourt Education Centre, Rose Hill, Rednal, Birmingham B45 8RS *tel:* 0121 453 6150. Nigel de Gruchy, gen sec.

National Association of Youth Orchestras. Ainslie House, 11 St Colme St, Edinburgh EH3 6AG *tel:* 0131 539 1087 *fax:* 0131 539 1069 *email:* admin@nayo.org.uk; http://www.nayo.org.uk. Carol Main, dir; Jenny Brockie, admin. *National association for youth orchs throughout UK. Activities include annual Festival of British Youth Orchestras in Edinburgh and Glasgow, Anglo-German Youth Music Week, British Reserve Insurance Conducting Prize (biennial), British Reserve Insurance Youth Orchestra Awards (annual). Newsletter Full Orchestra 3 pa, free to members. Marion Semple Weir library of chmbr mus, no hire charges to members.*

National Campaign for the Arts. Francis House, Francis St, London SW1P 1DE *tel:* 0171 828 4448 *fax:* 0171 931 9959 *email:* nca@ecna.org. Jennifer Edwards, dir; Laverne Layland, membership offr. *The independent lobby for all arts interests, including mus and mus in educ. Entire funding from membership fees. New members always welcome.*

National Committee of Inquiry into Higher Education. Newcombe House, 45 Notting Hill Gate, London W11 3JB *tel:* 0171 229 1234 *fax:* 0171 243 9486. Sir Ron Dearing, chmn. *Review of higher educ.*

National Council for Vocational Qualifications. 222 Euston Rd, London NW1 2BZ *tel:* 0171 387 9898 *fax:* 0171 387 0978. Mike Heron, chmn; John Hillier, chief exec. *NCVQ provides the framework of National Vocational Qualifications (NVQs) through which everyone at work can be assessed against nationally agreed standards. It also provides the framework of the General National Vocational Qualifications (GNVQs).*

National Early Music Association. 18 High St, Caythorpe, Grantham, Lincs NG32 3BS *tel:* 01400 273795 *also fax; email:* http:// www.brainlink.com/~starmus/unison/nema/nema.html. Elspeth Fraser-Darling, admin. *NEMA publishes the* Early Music Yearbook *incorporating the Register of Early Music and the bi-annual journal* Leading Notes.

National Federation of Music Societies. Francis House, Francis St, London SW1P 1DE *tel:* 0171 828 7320 *fax:* 0171 828 5504 *email:* postmaster@nfms.demon.co.uk. Russell Jones, chief exec. *Provides legal, financial, artistic, training, advocacy and lobbying services for 2000 voluntary member mus societies.*

National Harmonica League. Rivendell, High St, Shirrell Heath, Nr Southampton, Hants SO32 2JN *tel:* 01329 832178. Colin Mort, chmn. *For harmonica enthusiasts; newsletter and events.*

National Institute for Careers Education and Counselling. Sheraton House, Castle Pk, Cambridge CB3 0AX *tel:* 01223 460277 *fax:* 01223 311708 *email:* nicec@crac.org.uk. A G Watts, dir. *Carries out applied research and development work related to careers guidance in educ settings and in work and community settings.*

National Institute of Adult Continuing Education. 21 De Montfort St, Leicester LE1 7GE *tel:* 0116 255 1451 *fax:* 0116 285 4514 *email:* niace @niace.org.uk; http:\\www.niace.org.uk. Louise McGill, snr info offr. *Twice yearly, Jan/Aug, publishes* Time to Learn *at £4.25, detailing a wide range of w/end and 1-wk residential courses held at various centres throughout the UK.*

National Junior Music Club of Great Britain. 23 Hitchin St, Biggleswade, Beds SG18 8AX *tel:* 01767 316521 *fax:* 01767 317221. Douglas Coombes, mus dir; Rose Miles, membership sec; Carole Lindsay-Douglas, ed. *Termly resource magazine for primary and middle school teachers. Membership includes right to photocopy for use within own school, and preferential fees for courses and summer school organised by the club.*

National Music Council. Francis House, Francis St, London SW1P 1DE *tel:* 0181 347 8618 *also fax.* Russell Jones, chmn; Mark Isherwood, deputy chmn; Jennifer Goodwin, admin. *Forum for mus organisations concerned to further the interests of mus and musicians in the UK.*

National Operatic and Dramatic Association (NODA). NODA House, 1 Crestfield St, London WC1H 8AU *tel:* 0171 837 5655 *fax:* 0171 833 0609. Mark Thorburn, chief exec. *Umbrella body for the Amateur Theatre. Services include discounted sales of mus, scripts, make-up, insurance, etc. Also summer school and conferences.*

National Piano Centre. 5 Summerfield Rd, London W5 1ND *tel:* 0181 997 1793 *also fax.* Jonathan Ranger, dir. *Working collection of the history and development of the pno. Courses and training. Resource centre and forum for mus professionals, teachers, students, arts organisations, schools, colleges and individuals. Membership includes meetings, visits, newsletter, discounts, information and advice.*

National Sound Archive (British Library). 96 Euston Rd, London NW1 2DB *tel:* 0171 412 7440 *fax:* 0171 412 7441 *email:* nsa@bl.uk. A Crispin Jewitt, dir. *Largest reference collection of sound recordings in the UK open to the public, full reference library of associated literature. Information on commercial discs, broadcasting, history of recording. Free listening service; groups from schools, universities and colleges welcome to listen by prior arrangement. Free newsletter.*

National Union of Students. 461 Holloway Rd, London N7 6LJ *tel:* 0171 737 2944 *fax:* 0171 924 0890 *email:* waves@mite.co.uk.

National Union of Teachers. Hamilton House, Mabledon Pl, London WC1H 9BD *tel:* 0171 388 6191 *fax:* 0171 387 8458. Doug McAvoy, gen sec; Steve Sinnott, deputy gen sec.

National Youth Jazz Association. 11 Victor Rd, Harrow, Middx HA2 6PT *tel:* 0181 863 2717 *fax:* 0181 863 8685 *email:* bill.ashton@virgin.net. William Ashton, chmn. *NYJA organises two Sat clinics by the National Youth Jazz Orchestra and w/shops throughout Britain usually in conjunction with a concert by NYJO.*

North West Composers' Association. 41 Parklands Way, Poynton, Cheshire SK12 1AL *tel:* 01625 875389 *also fax.* Kevin Malone, sec; David Golightly, chmn. *Comprised of members of the Composers' Guild of Great Britain who live in the north-west region, the association promotes concerts of mus by north-west composers. Aims to increase concert series, be involved in educ w/shops and develop a composers' representative agency.*

Northumbrian Pipers' Society. Morpeth Chantry Bagpipe Museum, Bridge St, Morpeth, Northumberland NE61 1PJ *tel:* 01670 519466 *fax:* 01670 511326. J Richmond, hon sec. *Supports the playing and making of Northumbrian pipes, and the composition of traditional Northumbrian mus.*

Opera and Music Theatre Forum. c/o Association of British Orchestras, Francis House, Francis St, London SW1P 1DE *tel:* 0171 828 8023 *fax:* 0171 931 9959 *email:* abo@orchestranet.co.uk. Jean Nicholson, mgr; Judith Ackrill, chmn. *Represents small and medium-scale opera companies in UK and international links. Information centre for related activities and serves to advance the ideals of its member companies.*

The Operetta Foundation. 27 Cheetham Fold Rd, Hyde, Cheshire SK14 5DU *tel:* 0161 366 1709. Jeffrey Lomas, chmn; Joan Pancott-Lomas, development; John Edwars, finance controller. *Promotes and sponsors operetta.*

Orff Society (UK). 7 Rothesay Av, Richmond, Surrey TW10 5EB *tel:* 0181 876 1944 *also fax; email:* orff@catan.demon.co.uk. Margaret Murray, hon sec. *Through teachers' courses it promotes Orff's creative approach to mus educ, stressing improvisation and using voices, movement and perc insts.*

Organists' Benevolent League. 10 Stratford Pl, London W1N 9AE. Martin Neary, president; Richard Lyne, sec. *Charity to provide assistance for organists or their dependants in cases of need.*

Performing Right Society (PRS). 29-33 Berners St, London W1P 4AA *tel:* 0171 580 5544 *fax:* 0171 306 4050 *email:* http://prs.co.uk. John Hutchinson, chief exec. *Protects, promotes and administers the public performance and broadcasting rights of its composer, songwriter and mus publisher members.*

The Phil, Friends of. Philharmonic Hall, Hope St, Liverpool L1 9BP *tel:* 0151 708 7897 *fax:* 0151 709 0918. Barbara Wall, admin. *Members are entitled to priority booking, discounts on tickets and free rehearsal passes.*

Philatelic Music Circle. 22 Bouverie Gardens, Kenton, Middx HA3 0RQ *tel:* 0181 907 2790 *also fax.* Irene Lawford, president and consultant ed; Geoffrey Datson, hon chmn. *For mus stamp collectors. Magazine* The Baton; *holds meetings, exchanges, competitions, exhibitions. A/v programme on loan, library, worldwide membership.*

Piano Trade Suppliers' Association Ltd. 78-80 Borough High St, London SE1 1XG *tel:* 0171 403 2300 *fax:* 0171 403 8140 *email:* d_m_hart@ compuserve.com. David M Hart, sec.

Piano Trio Society. Stoneville Cottage, Gretton Fields, Cheltenham, Glos GL54 5HH *tel:* 01242 620736 *also fax.* Colin Taylor, chmn; Christine Talbot-Cooper, admin. *Membership organisation for those interested in the pno trio medium.*

Pianoforte Tuners' Association. 10 Reculver Rd, Herne Bay, Kent CT6 6LD *tel:* 01227 368808 *also fax.* Mrs V M Addis, sec. *The association has countrywide membership. An examination is required for entry.*

The Pianola Institute. 6 Southbourne, Hayes, Bromley, Kent BR2 7NJ. Denis Hall, chmn; C L'Enfant, sec. *Journal, concerts, library of rolls, roll and information archive.*

Piobaireachd Society. 20 Otago St, Glasgow G12 8JH *tel:* 0141 334 3587 *fax:* 0141 337 3024. Dugald MacNeill, sec.

Pipers' Guild. 121 Hallam Way, West Hallam, Derbys DE7 6LP *tel:* 0115 930 8323 *email:* margent@rmplc.co.uk; http://www.quantine.co.uk/ ~piper/pgpage.htm. Stephanie Payne, sec; Mary argent, chmn; Betty Roe, president. *Organisation for the making, playing and decorating of bamboo pipes (insts similar to Renaissance recorders).*

Player Piano Group. 93 Evelyn Av, Ruislip, Middx HA4 8AH *tel:* 01895 634288. Tony Austin, hon sec. *Concerned with the mus, mechanical and historic aspects of the player pno and the reproducing pno, organising social meetings, quarterly bulletin and occasional public concerts.*

Polish Cultural Institute. 34 Portland Pl, London W1N 4HQ *tel:* 0171 636 6032 *fax:* 0171 637 2190. Aleksandra Czapiewska, deputy dir. *Promotes Polish arts in Great Britain in general. Assists in arranging Polish-British contacts.*

Pro Corda Trust (National School for Young Chamber Music Players). Leiston Abbey House, Theberton Rd, Leiston, Suffolk IP16 4TB *tel:* 01728 831354 *fax:* 01728 832500. Pamela Spofforth MBE, artistic dir emeritus. *Courses held during school holidays for young str players and pianists under the direction of distinguished musicians see* **Summer Schools and Short Courses.**

Professional Association of Teachers. 2 St James' Ct, Friar Gate, Derby DE1 1BT *tel:* 01332 372337 *fax:* 01332 290310/292431. John R Andrews, gen sec; Richard Fraser, communications offr. *Trade union and a professional association with around 40,000 members from all parts of the UK in both the maintained and independent sectors, teaching at all levels from nursery to tertiary. PAT is non-party political and is not affiliated to the TUC. A publications list is available.*

Rachmaninoff Society. 4 Springfield Cottages, New Rd, Rotherfield, E Sussex TN6 3JR *tel:* 0189285 2265. John Lockyer, admin. *Promotes Rachmaninoff as a composer, pianist and conductor. Publishes quarterly newsletter; annual conference in UK.*

Rawsthorne (Alan) Society. RNCM Library, 124 Oxford Rd, Manchester M13 9RD *tel:* 0161 273 6283. Tony Hodges, chmn. *Promotes the mus of Rawsthorne with recordings, live concerts, publications, etc. Publishes* The Creel *annually.*

Reed Organ Society (UK Branch). York House, Bluntisham Rd, Colne, Huntingdon, Cambs PE17 3LY *tel:* 01487 842722 *fax:* 01223 330388 *email:* brian.styles@mrc-bsu.cam.ac.uk. Brain C Styles, regional counsellor. *International society with headquarters in the USA. Publishes quarterly journal with historical, restoration and performance articles.*

Royal College of Organists. 7 St Andrew St, London EC4A 3LQ *tel:* 0171 936 3606 *fax:* 0171 353 8244. Gordon Clarke, registrar; Robin Langley, librarian. *Educ charity of 3000 members for promotion of org playing and choir training. Exams for Associateship, Fellowship diplomas, choir training and org teaching diplomas and preliminary certificate. Library and programme of lectures, seminars, short courses, overseas tours, m/classes. Also jnr section.*

Royal Liverpool Philharmonic Society. Philharmonic Hall, Hope St, Liverpool L1 9BP *tel:* 0151 709 2895 *fax:* 0151 709 0918. *Promotes the Royal Liverpool Philharmonic Orchestra and Choir, the Merseyside Youth Orchestra as well as managing the Philharmonic Hall itself.*

Royal Musical Association. Dept of Music, University of Leeds, Leeds LS2 9JT *tel:* 0113 233 2579 *fax:* 0113 233 2586 *email:* j.g.rushton@ leeds.ac.uk. Julian Rushton, president. *The RMA holds meetings for the presentation of musicological papers and publishes a scholarly journal, a research chronicle and a series of monographs. It hosts one-day meetings, an annual conference (Apr) and a conference for research students.*

Royal Philharmonic Society. 10 Stratford Pl, London W1N 9AE *tel:* 0171 491 8110 *fax:* 0171 493 7463. Richard Fisher, gen admin. *Arranges annual seasons of concerts and other events. Administers competitions and awards for students in UK; also international Gold Medal and annual RPS Music Awards for outstanding achievement. Membership by application.*

Royal School of Church Music. Cleveland Lodge, Westhumble, Dorking RH5 6BW *tel:* 01306 877676 *fax:* 01306 887260. Harry Bramma, dir. *Training and advisory organisation for the development of church mus. Membership open to all churches, with or without choirs, and to individuals.*

Royal Scottish Country Dance Society. 12 Coates Cres, Edinburgh EH3 7AF *tel:* 0131 225 3854 *fax:* 0131 225 7783. Miss G S Parker, gen sec. *Aims to preserve and further the practice of traditional Scottish country dances and to provide educ and instruction to this end. Has 162 branches throughout the world and more than 500 affiliated groups. Founded 1923.*

Royal Scottish Pipe Band Association. 45 Washington St, Glasgow G3 8AZ *tel:* 0141 221 5414 *fax:* 0141 221 1561. J Mitchell Hutcheson, exec offr. *Association of amateur pipe bands. 12 branches running educ classes. Organises contests and championships. Publishes bi-monthly magazine,* The Pipe Band. *Annual Summer School in last week of Jul at above address.*

Royal Scottish Pipers' Society. 127 Rose St, South La, Edinburgh EH2 4BB *tel:* 0131 552 5231. J J Burnet, sec.

The Royal Society of Musicians of Great Britain. 10 Stratford Pl, London W1N 9AE *tel:* 0171 629 6137. Maggie Gibb, sec. *The Society exists to provide help for professional musicians and their families in need because of illness, accident or old age.*

The RVW Society. c/o The Chantry, Stoney La, Stocklinch, Ilminster, Somerset TA19 9JJ *tel:* 01460 57819 *fax:* 01206 852876 *email:* mason @oup.co.uk; kurwenal@easynet.co.uk. Robin Barber, sec; Stephen Connock, chmn. *Aims to increase knowledge and appreciation of Ralph Vaughan Williams' mus and to encourage performances of lesser known works.*

RVW Trust. 7th Floor, Manfield House, 1 Southampton St, London WC2R 0LR *tel:* 0171 379 6547 *fax:* 0171 240 6333. Bernard Benoliel, admin. *Assists young British composers with premieres and second performances and promotes works by neglected British composers of the past. The Trust also considers applications from the smaller mus festivals who programme mus by young British composers. Does not accept applications towards the cost of recordings, mus insts, degree or summer courses.*

St John's, Smith Square, Friends of. St John's, Smith Sq, London SW1P 3HA *tel:* 0171 222 2168 *fax:* 0171 233 1618. Paul Davies, gen mgr. *Mailing list membership, priority booking, concerts (evening and lunchtime), art exhibitions, ticket discounts. Free entry to Thursday lunchtime concert series.*

Schools Music Association (SMA). 71 Margaret Rd, New Barnet, Herts EN4 9NT *tel:* 0181 440 6919 *also fax.* Maxwell Pryce, hon sec. *Aims to promote the mus educ of young people by encouraging and supporting those who work with them.*

Schubert Institute (UK). Putmans, West Harting, Petersfield, Hants GU31 5PB *tel:* 01730 825574 *also fax.* Brian Newbould, chmn; Patricia Troop, hon sec. *Aims to promote the study of Schubert's life and work and appreciation of his mus. All Schubert lovers welcomed. Affiliated to International Franz Schubert Institute, Vienna. Establishing a Schubert library and research centre in association with Leeds University.*

Schubert Society of Great Britain. Rainbow Farm, Redisham, Beccles, Suffolk NR34 8NE *tel:* 01502 575404 *fax:* 01502 575505. Alan Tabelin, sec. *The Schubert Society presents 'Schubertiades' in London monthly, Oct-May (except Dec), as a forum for young artistes.*

Scottish Amateur Music Association. 18 Craigton Cres, Alva, Clackmannanshire FK12 5DS *tel:* 01259 760249. Margaret W Simpson, hon sec. *Provides national training courses to help and encourage amateur mus-making in Scotland.*

Scottish Community Education Council. Rosebery House, 9 Haymarket Terrace, Edinburgh EH12 5EZ *tel:* 0131 313 2488 *fax:* 0131 313 6800 *email:* scec@scec.dircon.co.uk; http://www.qedl.co.uk. Charlie McConnell, chief exec. *The council helps those active in community education to meet the learning needs of people in communities. This is achieved through influencing public policy and awareness, promoting effective strategies and best practice, and providing information, publications and other services.*

Scottish Music Education Forum. School of Music, Department of Aesthetic Education, Northern College, Hilton Pl, Aberdeen AB24 4FA *tel:* 01224 283558 *fax:* 01224 283900 *email:* j.p.stephens@norcol.ac.uk. Jonathan Stephens, dir of mus, head of aesthetic educ. *Acts as co-ordinating body, providing a point of contact for those involved in mus and mus educ courses, associations and societies. Membership consists of reps from wide range of mus interests: school, higher educ, commerce, industry and special interest groups including Scottish traditional mus. Aims to promote diversity of mus in Scotland, maintain particular strengths, collate and disseminate information and identify and promote good practice.*

Scottish Music Information Centre. 1 Bowmont Gardens, Glasgow G12 9LR *tel:* 0141 334 6393 *fax:* 0141 337 1161 *email:* smic@glasgow. almac.co.uk; http://www.music.gla.ac.uk/htmlfolder/resources/smic/ homepage.html. Kirsteen McCue, gen mgr; Alasdair Pettinger, information offr. *Resource and information centre for mus (especially contemporary) by Scottish and Scottish-based composers. Reference, hire and audio libraries; photocopying service, promotional activities.*

Scottish Musical Instrument Retailers' Association. c/o McCormacks Music, 33 Bath St, Glasgow *tel:* 0141 332 6644 *fax:* 0141 353 3095. *A purchasing group encompassing 15 shops across Scotland. Enquiries welcome from British wholesalers and distributors.*

Scottish Musicians Benevolent Fund. c/o 10 Manse Rd, Bearsden, Glasgow G61 3PT *tel:* 0141 942 1364 *also fax.* Evelyn Bryson, hon sec and treasurer. *Cares for Scottish professional musicians (and their dependants) in need, ill or convalescing. Regular monthly grants and one-off grants. Membership of a trade union/professional organisation is not necessary.*

Scottish Secondary Teachers' Association. 15 Dundas St, Edinburgh EH3 6QG *tel:* 0131 556 5919 *fax:* 0131 556 1419. David Eaglesham, gen sec. *Professional association for secondary teachers in Scotland. Recognised at the Scottish Office Education Dept and represented on the Scottish Joint Negotiating Committee for Teaching Staff in School Education. Publishes bulletins (6 pa) and Secondary Teacher (4 pa) for members only.*

Scottish Society of Composers. Mazagon, 4 Glen Rd, Lennoxtown G65 7JX *tel:* 01360 313217. Thomas Wilson CBE, hon president; Neil Butterworth, chmn; Derek Ball, sec and treasurer. *Promotes wider knowledge of contemporary mus in Scotland through international and local liaison, annual awards to musicians, distribution of catalogues of new mus, sponsorship of new mus recording.*

Secondary Heads Association. 130 Regent Rd, Leicester LE1 7PG *tel:* 0116 299 1122 *fax:* 0116 299 1123. John Sutton, gen sec. *Professional association which caters specifically for principals, heads and deputies in secondary schools and colleges.*

Seeds Ltd (Christian Creative Resource Service). 30 Grasvenor Av, Barnet, Herts EN5 2BZ *tel:* 0181 364 9652 *also fax.* Neil Ruckman, admin and educ; Chris Norris, chmn.

Sibelius Society. 5 Fitzwilliam Rd, London SW4 0DL *tel:* 0171 430 1247; 0171 627 3086 *fax:* 0171 430 1251. E W Clark, president; A Barnett, chmn. *Promotes the works of Sibelius. Quarterly newsletter and awards for best CD and artist.*

The Silvester (Victor) Appreciation Society. 1 Portland Cres, Weymouth, Dorset DT4 0NW *tel:* 01305 784379. Geoff Williams, sec. *Produces 3 newsletters pa.*

Simpson (Robert) Society. 24 Regent Close, Fleet, Hants GU13 9NS *tel:* 01252 614548. Rev B Duke, membership sec. *Promotes study, performance and recording of the mus and writings of Robert Simpson.*

Society for Cooperation in Russian & Soviet Studies. 320 Brixton Rd, London SW9 6AB *tel:* 0171 274 2282 *fax:* 0171 274 3230. J Turner, sec. *Reference library of mus scores, encyclopedias and records pertaining to Russian and Soviet mus and composers.*

Society for Music Analysis. Dept of Music, University of Nottingham, University Pk, Nottingham NG7 2RD *tel:* 0115 951 4755 *fax:* 0115 951 4756. S Britten, admin; R Pascall, president. *Society for the development of all aspects of mus analysis, especially research and teaching. Open to lecturers, students, etc.*

Society for Research in the Psychology of Music and Music Education. c/o Dept of Music, The University of Sheffield, Western Bank, Sheffield S10 2TN *email:* http://www.shef.ac.uk/uni/academic/l-m/mus/staff/ wlw/srpmme.html. Annette Davison, membership sec. *Aims to encourage the exchange of ideas and to disseminate research findings in the fields of psychology of mus and in mus educ.*

Society for the Promotion of New Music (SPNM). Francis House, Francis St, London SW1P 1DE *tel:* 0171 828 9696 *fax:* 0171 931 9928. Cathy Graham, exec dir; Peter Craik, admin; Sarah Gibbon, educ offr. *SPNM promotes concerts and w/shops nationwide with new works by new composers. Education work with young people and their teachers. Also publishes* new notes *monthly concert listings magazine.*

Society of Assistants Teaching in Preparatory Schools. Cherry Trees, Stebbing, Great Dunmow, Essex CM6 3ST *tel:* 01371 856369 *also fax.* Bob Carter, mus sec. *The mus group of an organisation covering all subjects taught in prep schools. It publishes termly broadsheets for members and organises occasional conferences.*

Society of Headmasters and Headmistresses of Independent Schools. Celedston, Rhosesmor Rd, Halkyn, Holywell CH8 8DL *tel:* 01352 781102 *also fax.* I D Cleland, gen sec. *An association of 75 heads of independent secondary schools with VI forms. Most of the schools have boarders and almost all are wholly or partly co-educational. The society represents the smaller independent school offering a balanced educ to pupils of widely varying interests and abilities; also included are two of the specialist mus schools and a ballet school.*

Society of Leisure and Entertainment Consultants and Publishers (SOLECAP). 1 Sandringham Close, Sandringham Pk, Tarleton, Lancs PR4 6UZ *tel:* 01772 816046. J B A Sharples, dir. *Represents consultants and publishers in the field of entertainment and the arts, recreation, marketing, etc.*

Society of Producers and Composers of Applied Music (PCAM). Birchwood Hall, Storridge, Malvern, Worcs WR13 5EZ *tel:* 01886 884204 *also fax; email:* bfromer@netcomuk.co.uk. Bob Fromer, admin.

Society of Recorder Players. 15 Palliser Rd, London W14 9EB *tel:* 0171 385 7321 *email:* secretary@srp.org.uk. A Read, sec. *A national society with international membership offering rcdr players in the UK the opportunity to meet regularly and play in conducted ens. Over 50 groups meet nationwide, mostly on a monthly basis. Members also receive* The Recorder Magazine *quarterly. The Society issues its own certificate to confirm a candidate's ability to conduct and direct rcdr groups and an annual festival, w/shops and other events take place throughout the year.*

Society of Schoolmasters. Doltons Farm, Newport Rd, Woburn MK17 9HX *tel:* 01525 290093. Mrs B Skipper, sec. *Gives assistance to needy schoolmasters, their widows and orphans, provided such masters have been continuously engaged in teaching for not less than 10 years.*

Society of Teachers of the Alexander Technique (STAT). 20 London House, 266 Fulham Rd, London SW10 9EL *tel:* 0171 351 0828 *fax:* 0171 352 1556 *email:* stat@pavilion.co.uk; http://www.pavilion.co.uk/stat/ welcome.html. Angela Price, admin. *The society can provide a list of*

members who teach in the UK and members of affiliated societies throughout the world (please enclose an A5 sae) and information on the technique.

Sonic Arts Network formerly EMAS. London House, 271-273 King St, London W6 9LZ tel: 0181 741 7422 fax: 0181 741 7433 email: samantha @sonicart.demon.co.uk. Samantha Seaborne, exec dir; Paul Wright, educ dir; Rachel Spencer, admin. National association of composers, performers and teachers and others interested in the creative uses of technology in the composition and performance of mus. Campaigns for a national centre for sonic art and initiates educ projects bringing together composers, school pupils and teachers. Also INSET on ways of integrating new technology with other classroom resources.

The Sorabji Archive. Easton Dene, Bailbrook La, Bath BA1 7AA tel: 01225 852323 fax: 01225 852523 email: 100775.2716@compuserve. com; http://www.mcgill.ca/~schulman/sorabji.html. Alistair Hinton, curator and dir. Makes available to the public the mus and literary collection of Sorabji's works. Includes published, manuscript and new edition scores; articles and essays; reviews of books, mus publications, concerts and recordings; correspondence and discography.

Sound Sense, The National Community Music Association. Riverside House, Rattlesden, Bury St Edmunds, Suffolk IP30 0SF tel: 01449 736287 fax: 01449 737649 email: 100256.30@compuserve.com; http:// ourworld.compuserve.com/homepages/soundsense. Kathryn Deane, dir; Floria Hall, admin. Sound Sense is the development agency for participatory, creative mus-making, offering support, advice and training to community musicians and groups as well as other arts and educ organisations. Information services include publications, mus and disability advice and a Lottery help scheme for members.

Spohr Society of Great Britain. 123 Mount View Rd, Sheffield S8 8PJ tel: 0114 258 5420. C H Tutt, sec. Aims to support and promote the mus of Louis Spohr through research, publications and recordings.

Steel Band Adviser. 60 Greenford Gardens, Greenford, Middx UB6 9LZ tel: 0181 578 6485; 0850 650401 fax: 0181 578 6485 email: terry.noel @btinternet.com. Terry Noel, chmn. Provides advice on all aspects of steel bands, getting insts, tuition, upkeep of insts.

Stevens (Bernard) Trust. The Forge, Gt Maplestead, Halstead, Essex CO9 2RE tel: 01787 460315 also fax; email: http:www.cdj.co.uk/cdj/inart/ stevens.htm. Promotes the mus of Bernard Stevens (1916-1983). Recordings, concerts and publications.

The Stevenson (Ronald) Society. 3 Chamberlain Rd, Edinburgh EH10 4DL fax: 0131 229 9298. P Hutton, chmn; C Scott-Sutherland, treasurer; M Lister, sec. Promotes the mus of Ronald Stevenson; sponsors publication, performance and recording of his work. Summer school.

Stolz (Robert), The Friends of. Red Lion Ct, Stalbridge, Sturminster Newton, Dorset DT10 2LR tel: 01963 362999. Robert Keys, founder and sec. Supports and promotes the mus of Robert Stolz, with meetings, bulletins, concerts, lectures and a reference library.

Strauss (Johann) Society of Great Britain. Flat 12, Bishams Ct, Church Hill, Caterham, Surrey CR3 6SE tel: 01883 349681. Mrs V E Coates, hon sec. Promotes the performance, recording, study and deeper appreciation of the mus of the Strauss family and their Viennese contemporaries.

Strauss (Richard) Society. 78 Bedford Ct Mansions, Bedford Av, London WC1B 3AE tel: 0171 636 2946. Mike Coleman, sec. Bi-monthly newsletter. Monthly meetings in Central London. Block opera bookings.

Traditional Music and Song Association of Scotland. 17 Calton Rd, Edinburgh EH8 8DL tel: 0131 557 8484 fax: 0131 557 6519. Elspeth Cowie, national organiser. National organisation promoting the performance and awareness of traditional Scottish mus and song, story-telling and dance. Organises w/shops, m/classes and school curriculum enrichment visits.

Tureck Bach Research Foundation. Windrush House, Davenant Rd, Oxford OX2 8BX tel: 01865 515760 fax: 01865 512620 email: rosalyn. tureck@st-hildas.ox.ac.uk; http://mmm.wwa.com/tbrf. Rosalyn Tureck, dir; Kim Wilson, admin asst. Examines the identities of the fundamental concepts that nourish the arts, sciences and humanities.

UK-Japan Music Society. 27 Heron Close, Great Glen, Leicester LE8 9DZ tel: 0116 259 3891.

Ulster Society of Organists and Choirmasters. 1b Beverley Hills, Bangor, N Ireland BT20 4NA tel: 01247 465222. Rodney Bambrick, hon sec. Provides a forum for church musicians of all denominations; lectures, discussions, recitals, w/shops, org visits, etc.

United Kingdom Harp Association. 35 Vienna Road, Stockport, Cheshire SK3 9QH tel: 0161 474 1148 also fax. Eira Lynn Jones, magazine ed. 600 members worldwide. For professional harpists, students, amateurs, hp makers and retailers. Publishes quarterly magazine and directory of members. Also annual awards for student harpists.

Universities and Colleges Admissions Service (UCAS). Fulton House, Jessop Av, Cheltenham, Glos GL50 3SH tel: 01242 227788 (enquiries);

01242 222444 *fax:* 01242 221622 *email:* enq@ucas.ac.uk. M A Higgins, chief exec; A P McClaren, deputy chief exec. *UCAS is the central agency through which applicants apply for all f/t u/grad first degrees and most DipHE and HND courses at universities and colleges in the UK.*

Universities Association for Continuing Education. School of Continuing Education, University of Leeds, Leeds LS2 9JT *tel:* 0113 233 3184 *fax:* 0113 233 3246 *email:* j.brownridge@leeds.ac.uk; http://www.stir.ac.uk/epd/uace/. Richard Taylor, sec. *The association promotes the interests of continuing educ within higher educ, acts as a forum for the discussion of policy issues, promotes and conducts research and disseminates the results to the public and interested organisations.*

Video Performance Ltd. 14-22 Ganton St, London W1V 1LB *tel:* 0171 437 0311 *fax:* 0171 734 9797. Roger Drage, consultant. *Administers the public performance and broadcast rights in mus videos on behalf of its 680 member companies.*

Viola d'Amore Society of Great Britain. 4 Constable Rd, Felixstowe, Suffolk IP11 7HH *tel:* 01394 285584. Ian White, Annelise Tinlin; Nicholas Neale, dirs; Ian James, sec. *Aims to promote the viola d'amore, and to use it in performance with other insts. Also publishes original works from the 18th C and supplies them on demand.*

Viola da Gamba Society. 56 Hunters Way, Dringhouses, York YO2 2JJ *tel:* 01904 706959. Caroline Wood, admin. *Publishes annual journal and quarterly newsletter* Music for Viols. *Meetings and conferences.*

The Voices Foundation. 21 Earls Court Sq, London SW5 9BY *tel:* 0171 370 1944 *fax:* 0171 370 1874. Susan Digby, principal; Michael Stocks, dir of curriculum and training. *Educ charity specialising in mus curriculum development in primary schools and the professional development of primary teachers. 1-day w/shops for parents/teachers.*

The Wagner Society. 15 David Av, Wickford, Essex SS11 7BG *tel:* 01268 560833 *also fax.* J J Pritchard, chmn. *A charity dedicated to the appreciation and study of Richard Wagner's life and mus.*

Walton (William) Trust. 12 Central Chambers, Wood St, Stratford-upon-Avon CV37 6JQ *tel:* 01789 261573 *fax:* 01789 266467 *email:* sw_artists@msn.com. Stephannie Williams, artistic dir. *The Trust was created to establish the property 'La Mortella' as a study centre for gifted young musicians under the guidance of the world's leading teachers; to organise and administrate educ projects in schools, and to aid research projects related to the life and work of William Walton and closely allied subjects.*

Warlock (Peter) Society. 32a Chipperfield House, Cale St, London SW3 3SA *tel:* 0171 589 9595 *also fax.* Malcolm Rudland, sec. *To increase awareness and knowledge of the composer.*

Welsh Amateur Music Federation. 9 Museum Pl, Cardiff CF1 3NX *tel:* 01222 394711 *fax:* 01222 221447. Keith Griffin, dir. *The Federation offers financial assistance, advice and training to amateur mus organisations in Wales. It founded and now administers the National Youth Brass Band of Wales and the National Youth Choir of Wales.*

The Welsh Association of Ladies' Choirs. 11 The Firs, Newton Burrows, Porthcawl, Mid Glamorgan CF36 5AX *tel:* 01656 782970. L Walker, sec; V Grenfell, chmn. *Promotes ladies' choirs within Wales. Organises choral festivals, mus seminars, courses, and gives advice to conductors and choir officials.*

Welsh Association of Male Choirs. 98 Glannant Way, Cimla Neath, West Glamorgan, SA11 3YN *tel:* 01639 767884; 01639 637932 *also fax.* J J Watkins, organising sec; J Layton Watkins, admin sec. *Offers a legal advice service and mus and insurance at a discount to members. Also organises festival.*

Welsh Folk Dance Society. Ffynnonlwyd, Trelech, Caerfyrddin, Sir Caerfyrddin SA33 6QZ *tel:* 01994 484496. Dafydd M Evans, sec. *Formed in 1949 to promote Welsh folk dancing and dance mus.*

Welsh Folk Song Society. Hafan, Cricieth, Gwynedd *tel:* 0176652 2096. Buddug Lloyd Roberts, sec.

Welsh Jazz Society Ltd. 26 The Balcony, Castle Arcade, Cardiff CF1 2BY *tel:* 01222 340591. Brian Hennessey, mgr dir. *An educ charity devoted to the promotion, educ and presentation of jazz in all its varied forms.*

Welsh Music Information Centre. c/o ASS Library, University of Wales, College of Cardiff, Cardiff CF1 1XL. A J Heward Rees, dir.

Welsh National Opera, Friends of. John St, Cardiff CF1 4SP *tel:* 01222 464666 *fax:* 01222 483050. Maureen Lawrence, admin; Sara Greenwood, asst.

White (Ernest George) Society. 106 Gladstone Rd, South Willesborough, Ashford, Kent TN24 0DD *tel:* 01233 629921. Dorothy Douse, sec. *An educ charity to promote White's voice teaching on the principles described as Sinus Tone Production.*

Whitlock (Percy) Trust. 32 Butcher Close, Staplehurst, Kent TN12 0TJ. Malcolm Riley, hon sec. *Holds archive of scores, diaries, photographs, letters, etc. Hire library of orch works available.*

Whittaker Centenary Fund. Viking Publications, 15 Watcombe Cottages, Kew Green, Richmond, Surrey TW9 3BD *tel:* 0181 948 8132. Jonathan Piers-Pollitzer. *To promote the mus of W G Whittaker (1876-1944).*

Women in Music. BAC, Old Town Hall, Lavender Hill, London SW11 5TF *tel:* 0171 978 4823 *fax:* 0171 978 4823. Lolita Ratchford, admin dir; Wendy Hee, archive and resource co-ord. *Celebrates and raises public awareness of women's work in mus. Advocates, enables and encourages*

women to make mus. Archive resource and information about various aspects of women's involvement in mus. Currently producing a booklet with details of access to orchestral repertoire by women.

Workers' Educational Association. 17 Victoria Park Sq, London E2 9PB *tel:* 0181 983 1515 *fax:* 0181 983 4840 *email:* wea-uk@mcrl.poptel. org.uk. Robert Lochrie, gen sec. *Adult educ charity with 14 districts and over 700 branches in the UK.*

Workers' Music Association. 240 Perry Rise, Forest Hill, London SE23 2QT *tel:* 0181 699 2250. A F Schuman, hon sec; M Cook, chair. *The association believes that music has a bearing on social life and is a means of attaining a brighter and better society; publishes mus, annual summer school of mus; London-based choir.*

Worshipful Company of Musicians. 74-75 Watling St, London EC4M 9BJ *tel:* 0171 489 8888 *fax:* 0171 489 1614. S F N Waley, clerk. *Livery Company of the City of London (founded 1500).*

Young Concert Artists Trust. 23 Garrick St, London WC2E 9AX *tel:* 0171 379 8477 *fax:* 0171 379 8467. Rosemary Pickering, chief exec. *A charity offering career management for young musicians. Annual auditions. Apply to YCAT for application forms and eligibility.*

Young People in Music (YPM). 2 Greystoke Lodge, Hanger La, London W5 1EW *tel:* 0181 998 1176. Yoriko Wakabayashi, founder. *YPM is dedicated to providing the opportunity for children to discover the excitement and phenomenon of mus, encouraging them to develop listening as well as performance skills. Offers lecture recitals, listening classes, summer mus camp, concerts.*

Young Persons Concert Foundation. 95 Wellington Rd, Enfield, Middx EN1 2PW *tel:* 0181 360 7390; 01923 859388 *fax:* 0181 364 0185 *email:* http://www.webcasting.com/stamps/found.htm. William A J Starling, artistic dir; Sally Needleman, special projects co-ord. *Presents w/shops and concerts (from individual str, w/wind, br and perc sections to full orch) by young professional players from the Foundation Philharmonic Orchestra; free to schoolchildren where sponsorship is available.*

Youth and Music. 28 Charing Cross Rd, London WC2H 0DB *tel:* 0171 379 6722 *fax:* 0171 497 0345 *email:* stagepass@dial.pipex.com. Alan Fluck, artistic dir; Katharine Meadows, admin dir. *Operates Stagepass, a nationwide ticket concessionary scheme for young people. British representative of Jeunesses Musicales. Also World Orchestra, World Choir, international mus camps, etc.*

Musicians' Union

Musicians' Union National Office. 60-62 Clapham Rd, London SW9 0JJ *tel:* 0171 582 5566 *fax:* 0171 582 9805. Dennis Scard, gen sec; Stan Martin, Ken Cordingley, asst gen secs; Don Smith, session organiser; Horace Trubridge, mus business adviser, careers adviser.

Musicians' Union London Office and Central London Branch. 60-62 Clapham Rd, London SW9 0JJ *tel:* 0171 582 5566 *fax:* 0171 582 9805. Tony Lucas, branch sec and district organiser.

Musicians' Union Midlands Office. Benson House, Lombard St, Birmingham B12 0QN *tel:* 0121 622 3870 *fax:* 0121 622 5361. Bob Bennett, Midlands district organiser, Birmingham branch sec, br band liaison official and jazz section sec.

Musicians' Union North/North-East Office. 327 Roundhay Rd, Leeds LS8 4HT *tel:* 0113 248 1335 *fax:* 0113 248 1292 *email:* bobwearn@mu. win-uk.net. Bob Wearn, district organiser, Leeds branch sec.

Musicians' Union North West Office. 40 Canal St, Manchester M1 3WD *tel:* 0161 236 1764 *fax:* 0161 236 0159. Bill Kerr, district organiser, Manchester branch sec.

Musicians' Union Scottish Office. 11 Sandyford Pl, Glasgow G3 7NB *tel:* 0141 248 3723 *fax:* 0141 204 3510. Ian D C Smith, Scottish organiser, Glasgow branch sec; Francesca Howell, admin asst.

Musicians' Union South-East Office. 60-62 Clapham Rd, London SW9 0JJ *tel:* 0171 582 5566 *fax:* 0171 582 9805. Alf Clarke, district organiser.

Musicians Union South-West Office. 131 St Georges Rd, Bristol BS1 5UW *tel:* 0117 926 5438 *fax:* 0117 925 3729. Paul Westwell; district organiser.

Music and Disability

Organisations

All Clear Designs Ltd. 3rd Floor, Cooper House, 2 Michael Rd, London SW6 2AD *tel:* 0171 384 2950/1 *fax:* 0171 384 2951 *email:* allclear@easynet.co.uk. James Holme-Siedle, dir. *Specialises in access design and disability equality training, following a format of detailed audits on existing buildings or advice on new designs which produce working documents for the architect and designer. The disability equality training offers customised courses, run by disabled trainers, for design professionals and staff within a range of organisations.*

Arts Council of England. 14 Great Peter St, London SW1P 3NQ *tel:* 0171 333 0100 *email:* http://www.artscouncil.org.uk. Mary Holland, policy officer. *The Arts Council publishes directory of arts and disability contacts, available from the Information Department, price £10. Enquiries about the funding of mus-related projects should be made to the mus dept.*

Arts for Health. Manchester Metropolitan University, All Saints, Manchester M15 6BY *tel:* 0161 236 8916 *fax:* 0161 247 6390 *email:* p.senior@mmu.ac.uk. Peter Senior MBE, dir. *National centre providing practical consultancy, advice and information to all those interested in using any art form as a complimentary aspect of health care.*

Artsline. 54 Chalton St, Camden, London NW1 1HS *tel:* 0171 388 2227 *fax:* 0171 383 2653 *email:* artsline@dircon.co.uk. Pauline Guthrie, development offr. *Minicom available. Information and advice service for disabled people on access to arts and entertainments, including participation in the arts, in London. Open for enquiries Mon-Fri 9.30am-5.30pm. Produces a guide for elderly disabled people and Play, a booklet with details of activities available to disabled children. Also produces other access guides, including those for theatres, cinemas, mus venues and tourist attractions. Also runs a multi-cultural project for disabled people from ethnic minority communities.*

Association of Professional Music Therapists. 38 Pierce La, Fulbourn, Cambs CB1 5DL *tel:* 01223 880377 *fax:* 01223 881679. Diana Asbridge, admin. *Deals with the needs of professional mus therapists in relation to standards of practice, employment, career structure, training, etc.*

Beethoven Fund for Deaf Children. 2 Queensmead, St John's Wood Pk, London NW8 6RE *tel:* 0171 586 8107 *fax:* 0171 722 7981. Ann Rachlin MBE, founder, chmn and trustee; Kevin Maddison, hon treasurer and trustee; Max Ziff, vice-chmn and trustee. *Charity providing specially-designed instruments to help profoundly deaf children to speak. Funds musical speech therapy centres throughout UK for deaf children.*

British Dyslexia Association. 98 London Rd, Reading, Berks RG1 5AU *tel:* 0118 966 8271 (helpline); 0118 966 2677 *fax:* 0118 935 1927 *email:* info@dyslexiahelp-bda.demon.co.uk; http://www.bda-dyslexia.org.uk/. *Provides information and advice relating to the effect of dyslexia on reading and writing mus. Also deals with individual enquiries regarding mus difficulties arising from dyslexia.*

British Society for Music Therapy. 25 Rosslyn Av, E Barnet, Herts EN4 8DH *tel:* 0181 368 8879 *also fax.* Helen Tyler, chair. *The BSMT promotes the use and development of mus therapy in the treatment, education and rehabilitation of children and adults suffering from emotional, physical or mental handicap. Membership is open to all interested in mus therapy. The Society holds meetings, w/shops and conferences. Publishes a journal (jointly with the Association of Professional Music Therapists) and a bulletin for members.*

British Wireless for the Blind Fund. Gabriel House, 34 New Rd, Chatham, Kent ME4 4QR *tel:* 01634 832501 *fax:* 01634 817485 *email:* margaret@blind.org.uk; http://www.blind.org.uk. Mrs M R Grainger, chief exec; Mrs C Ford, fundraiser. *Provides radios and radio cassette recorders on a free permanent loan basis to registered blind people in need in the UK.*

The Chantry Trust. 1a King's Mews, London WC1N 2JA *tel:* 0171 242 8586 *fax:* 0171 831 7914. Rex Montgomery, founder and admin. *Organisation researching therapeutic benefits of mus in education for autistic and handicapped children. Grants not available at present, but occasional gifts of books and manuscript material made to established bodies in similar fields.*

Community Music Wales. 2 Leckwith Pl, Canton, Cardiff CF1 8PA *tel:* 01222 387620 *also fax; email:* cmw@mcr1.poptel.org.uk. Steve Garrett, development offr; Sarah Harman, development offr; Biddy Wells, youth development worker. *Community Music Wales is inspired by the belief that everyone can derive pleasure and satisfaction from playing mus, and that mus projects provide a rich learning environment in which a host of other important skills can be acquired. Resources and expertise in a wide range of mus forms, including mus technology, are made available to people who are typically excluded from opportunities for creative self-expression and personal development for reasons of disability or disadvantage. Also professional training course for community musicians.*

Council for Music in Hospitals. 74 Queens Rd, Hersham, Surrey KT12 5LW *tel:* 01932 252809 *fax:* 01932 252966. Susan Alcock, dir; Diana Greenman, admin. *Over 3000 performances pa given by professional musicians in hospitals, homes and hospices throughout the UK.*

Council for Music in Hospitals (Scotland). 10 Forth St, Edinburgh EH1 3LD *tel:* 0131 556 5848 *fax:* 0131 556 0225. Alison Frazer, dir. *Concerts of live mus given by professional musicians selected for their communication skills. Participation encouraged. Venues include hospitals, hospices, homes for elderly people and day centres.*

Disability Scotland. 5 Shandwick Pl, Edinburgh EH2 4RG *tel:* 0131 229 8632 *fax:* 0131 229 5168. Robert Pickles, social issues offr. *Works with Scottish cultural agencies and institutions to ensure that opportunities are created for people with a disability to become involved in cultural activities.*

Drake Music Project. Christchurch Forum, Trafalgar Rd, London SE10 9EQ *tel:* 0181 305 0580 *fax:* 0181 305 0583 *email:* drake@dircon.co.uk. Adèle Drake, project dir; Brent Barraclough, development dir; Tim Anderson, technology mgr. *The Drake Music Project, in collaboration with the mus technology dept of York University, is involved in research including specialist software development. Enables people with severe disabilities to explore the world of mus through w/shops, and trains professionals in related fields. Also London, Scotland, Midlands, Ireland and Northern England co-ordinators.*

Healing Arts: Isle of Wight. St Mary's, Parkhurst Rd, Newport, Isle of Wight PO30 5TG *tel:* 01983 524081 ext 4253 *fax:* 01983 525157. Guy Eades, arts dir. *Co-ordinates an arts programme across the spectrum of health services on the Isle of Wight.*

Hospice Arts. Forbes House, 9 Artillery La, London E1 7LP *tel:* 0171 377 8484 *fax:* 0171 377 0032. David Frampton, acting dir. *National charity established to develop creative and therapeutic arts activities for hospice patients throughout the UK.*

London Disability Arts Forum. 34 Osnaburgh St, London NW1 3ND *tel:* 0171 916 5484 *fax:* 0171 916 5396. Diane Pungartnik, co-ord; Katherine Walsh, visual arts worker. *Set up to define and promote disability arts; to provide a forum for disabled artists and performers and to further participation and representation of disabled people in the arts. Publishes an annual directory of disabled performers, which includes many musicians and produces a yearly musical performance programme.*

Music for Disabled People. Kirkstyle, The Creek, Lower Sunbury, Middx TW16 6BY *tel:* 01932 765885 *also fax.* Ophra Goetz, dir of mus. *Takes live mus to people who cannot get to concert halls.*

Music for Living. Bentham House, Purton, Wilts SN5 9HZ *tel:* 01793 770269 *fax:* 01793 771782 *email:* mj.musfoliv@pop3.hiway.co.uk. Mark Johnson, dir. *Various activities organised, and facilities available; individually planned mus-making day courses for disabled people and their supervisors (with advice and guidance on further development); conferences, lectures and talks for professionals working with people with learning disabilities; reference library of mus books and recordings for use with people with learning disabilities (selection advice also offered); several places also available for resident clients.*

MusicSpace. The Southville Centre, Beauley Rd, Bristol BS3 1QG *tel:* 0117 963 8000 *fax:* 0117 966 9889. Leslie Bunt, dir. *Provides mus therapy sessions for people of all ages, also w/shops and training sessions, including a p/t mus therapy training course in conjunction with Bristol University.*

National Association for Special Educational Needs (NASEN). NASEN House, 4-5 Amber Business Village, Amber Close, Amington, Tamworth B77 4RP *tel:* 01827 311500 *fax:* 01827 313005 *email:* welcome@nasen. org.uk. C Gallow, exec office admin. *Promotes the interests of children and young people with special educational needs and supports those who work with them.*

National Disability Arts Forum. Mea House, Ellison Pl, Newcastle NE1 8XS *tel:* 0191 261 1628 *fax:* 0191 222 0573 *email:* 100575.3633@compuserve.com; http://www.disabilitynet.co.uk/groups/ndaf. Geoff Armstrong, dir; Sian Williams, information worker. *This organisation was established by disabled people to promote equality of opportunity for disabled people in all aspects of the arts. It is particularly concerned with supporting the development of disability arts locally, nationally and internationally.*

Nordoff-Robbins Music Therapy Centre. 2 Lissenden Gardens, London NW5 1PP *tel:* 0171 267 4496 *fax:* 0171 267 4369. Pauline Etkin, dir. *Centre houses a clinic which children and adults with a variety of needs can attend for mus therapy. Offers a 2-yr Master of Music Therapy training validated by City University. Library holds collection of material including documentation of the work of Dr Nordoff and Dr Robbins.*

Northern Ireland Music Therapy Trust. Graham House, Knockbracken Healthcare Pk, Saintfield Rd, Belfast BT8 8BH *tel:* 01232 705854. David Browne, business mgr. *Promotes interest in and the application of mus therapy throughout Northern Ireland.*

Nottinghamshire Arts Support Service. Eastbourne Centre, Station Rd, Sutton in Ashfield, Notts NG17 5FF *tel:* 01623 556804. John Childs, regional arts co-ord (special needs). *Developing the use of mus and a variety of creative work within schools for children with learning difficulties.*

Research Centre for the Education of the Visually Handicapped. School of Education, University of Birmingham, Edgbaston, Birmingham B15 2TT *tel:* 0121 414 6733 *fax:* 0121 414 4865. *The centre produces programs for very young and less able children and programs for adults wishing to convert braille into text; also programs to enable totally blind adults to have the freedom of using word processors.*

Royal Association for Disability and Rehabilitation (RADAR). 12 City Forum, 250 City Rd, London EC1V 8AF *tel:* 0171 250 3222; 0171 250 4119 (minicom) *fax:* 0171 250 0212. *A national campaigning and information organisation working with and for physically disabled people with an information dept for general enquiries.*

Royal National Institute for the Blind. Music Education Advisory Service, National Education Services, Garrow House, 190 Kensal Rd, London W10 5BT *tel:* 0181 968 8600 *fax:* 0181 960 3593 *email:* szimmermann@rnib.org.uk. Sally-Anne Zimmermann, mus educ adviser. *Offers advice and information on all matters concerning the mus education of visually impaired children and adults.*

Shape London. c/o The London Voluntary Sector Resource Centre, 356 Holloway Rd, London N7 6PA *tel:* 0171 700 0100 *fax:* 0171 700 8143. Maggie Woolley, dir. *Arts development agency working with disabled people for greater access and involvement in all aspects of the arts.*

Sound Sense. National Music and Disability Information Service, Riverside House, Rattlesden, Bury St Edmunds, Suffolk IP30 0SF *tel:* 01449 736287 *fax:* 01449 737649 *email:* 100256.30@compuserve.com; http:// ourworld.compuserve.com/homepages/soundsense. Roni Armstrong, NMDIS adviser. *The National Music and Disability Information Service, run by Sound Sense, gives information and advice on most aspects of mus and disability issues. Publications and a quarterly journal are available.*

Yorkshire and Humberside Association for Music in Special Education. 46 Nunroyd Rd, Leeds LS17 6PF *tel:* 0113 268 4198. Mavis West, sec. *Open to anyone interested in exploring the role of mus with people with special needs for pleasure, education and communication through courses, seminars, w/shops and concerts.*

Professional Training

The courses listed below are mainly designed for able-bodied people who wish to work with people with disabilities.

Anglia Polytechnic University. Division of Music and Performing Arts, East Rd, Cambridge CB1 1PT *tel:* 01223 363271. Helen Odell-Miller, admissions tutor and course dir. *MA and Professional Diploma in Music Therapy covers both university work and placements. Applicants should normally possess a degree or graduate diploma in mus but graduates of other disciplines with an appropriate level of musicianship will be considered. Some practical experience needed, working with people with learning disabilities and/or mental illness. 15 places on course. 38 weeks f/t from Sep-Aug. Fees: £3880.*

Bristol University. Dept for Continuing Education, 8-10 Berkeley Sq, Clifton, Bristol BS8 1HH *tel:* 0117 928 7135; 0117 928 7140 *fax:* 0117 925 4975 *email:* john.pickard@bristol.ac.uk. John Pickard, course organiser in mus. *2-yr p/t diploma in mus therapy. Applicants should possess a mus degree or diploma and be age 25 or above. 20 places on course. Next course Jan 2000.*

Centre for Music Therapy and Related Practices. Northern College, Hilton Pl, Aberdeen AB24 4FA *tel:* 01224 283500 ext 3510 *fax:* 01224 283900 *email:* j.w.robertson@norcol.ac.uk. James Robertson, co-ord of mus therapy practices. *The centre seeks to provide BEd (Hons) mus students with an insight into the nature and value of mus therapy practices. Central to this will be the opportunity for children with a wide range of needs to receive mus therapy provision. It is also envisaged that this work will be developed on a modular basis for existing teachers and related professionals.*

City University. Music Dept, Northampton Sq, London EC1V 0HB *tel:* 0171 477 8284 *fax:* 0171 477 8576. Denis Smalley, head of dept. *Offers one research fellowship in mus therapy for graduate mus therapists wishing to pursue theoretical and academic studies in relation to practical clinical work.*

Colchester Institute. Music Dept, Sheepen Rd, Colchester, Essex CO3 3LL *tel:* 01206 718000 *fax:* 01206 763041. Christopher Turner, module leader. *In the final yr of the mus BA/BA (Hons), there is special honours study entitled Health and Educational Studies for Musicians.*

Guildhall School of Music and Drama. Silk St, Barbican, London EC2Y 8DT *tel:* 0171 628 2571 *fax:* 0171 256 9438. Sarah Hoskyns, head of mus therapy dept; Jackie Robarts, mus therapy lecturer; Elaine Streeter, mus therapy tutor. *Diploma in Music Therapy. 1-yr p/grad mus therapy course validated by the University of York and recognised by the Dept of Health. Applicants must normally have had 3 yrs of f/t higher education. Applications from mature professional musicians are also welcomed. Some experience with disabled, mentally or physically ill or hospitalised people necessary, as is personal therapy prior to or during the course.*

Nordoff-Robbins Music Therapy Centre. 2 Lissenden Gardens, London NW5 1PP *tel:* 0171 267 4496 *fax:* 0171 267 4369. Pauline Etkin, dir and head of training. *Offers a 2-yr Master of Music Therapy training validated by City University. Fees: £4400. Places: max 6 pa. Also one-day conferences for those interested in mus therapy for children and adults and 10-week evening class on Nordoff-Robbins approach to mus therapy.*

Roehampton Institute, London. Dept of Music, Southlands College, 80 Roehampton La, London SW15 5SL *tel:* 0181 392 3432 *fax:* 0181 392 3435 *email:* music@roehampton.ac.uk. John Woodcock, Kay Sobey, mus therapy programme conveners. *Introduction to Music Therapy. A short course in the spring term for those in related professions or who are considering training. Graduate Diploma in Music Therapy (1 f/t; 2-3 p/t), recognised by the Association of Professional Music Therapists) is designed to train musicians as therapists with the ability and flexibility to practise professionally with a wide range of clients within the NHS, education, social services or private sector. Also a research MA. Fees: £3000 plus £75 registration (f/t home), £4668 plus £75 registration (f/t overseas), £250 plus registration per 10 credits (p/t home and overseas). 120 credits required in total.*

Royal Academy of Music. Marylebone Rd, London NW1 5HT *tel:* 0171 873 7373. Graeme Humphrey, course dir. *Optional information and performance opportunities for all f/t students who wish to develop their performing and communication skills for the benefit of schools audiences.*

Royal National College for the Blind. College Rd, Hereford HR1 1EB *tel:* 01432 265725 *fax:* 01432 353478. Greg Barker, head of creative arts. *A course in Braille mus and psychology of teaching the visually impaired (offered to overseas students who are expected to return to their own countries to teach).*

Activities and Courses for People with Disabilities

Artsreach. Jacksons Lane Community Centre, 269a Archway Rd, London N6 5AA *tel:* 0181 340 5226 *fax:* 0181 348 2424. Patricia Place, co-ord. *Offers arts-based w/shops (including mus) to special schools and units, integration work in mainstream schools, primarily in the London Boroughs of Barnet, Camden, Islington and Haringay.*

The Bull. 68 High St, Barnet EN5 5SJ *tel:* 0181 449 0048 *fax:* 0181 364 9037. *Runs occasional art w/shops for adults with learning difficulties.* *Regular programme of mus events, including rock, funk, jazz and Klezmer.*

Carousel. 40 Upper Gardner St, Brighton, E Sussex BN1 4AN *tel:* 01273 570840. Sal Roberts, admin. *Works to promote the active involvement and participation of people with learning difficulties in the arts (including mus) through w/shops, residencies and special events, performances, exhibitions, and training courses run for volunteers and staff.*

Community Music East Ltd. 155 Waterloo Rd, Norwich NR3 3HY *tel:* 01603 628367 *fax:* 01603 767863. *CME has developed a substantial programme of work with a range of special needs clients in East Anglia, establishing long-term educational w/shop programmes.*

Council for Music in Hospitals. 74 Queens Rd, Hersham, Surrey KT12 5LW *tel:* 01932 252809/252811 *fax:* 01932 252966. Susan Alcock, dir; Diana Greenman, admin. *Over 3000 performances pa given by professional musicians for patients in hospitals, homes and hospices throughout the UK.*

Council for Music in Hospitals (Scotland). 10 Forth St, Edinburgh EH1 3LD *tel:* 0131 556 5848 *fax:* 0131 556 0225. Alison Frazer, dir. *Concerts of live mus given by professional musicians selected for their communication skills. Participation encouraged. Venues include hospitals, hospices, homes for elderly people and day centres.*

Creative Young People Together (CRYPT Foundation). Forum Workspace, Stirling Rd, Chichester, W Sussex PO19 2EN *tel:* 01243 786064. *Residencies in the community arranged for young people (age 18-30) with disabilities to further their arts skills, including all aspects of mus.*

Drake Music Project. Christchurch Forum, Trafalgar Rd, London SE10 9EQ *tel:* 0181 305 0580 *fax:* 0181 305 0583 *email:* drake@dircon.co.uk. Adèle Drake, project dir; Brent Barraclough, development dir; Tim Anderson, technology mgr. *Weekly mus w/shops to enable children and adults with physical disabilities to produce and play mus by use of computers and electronic technology. Training of teachers, carers and musicians through seminars and in-service training days. Summer courses and residencies are held in London, Yorkshire, Scotland, Midlands, Ireland and Sarajevo.*

Ebony Steelband Trust. Acklam Playcentre and Adventure, 6 Acklam Rd, London W10 5QZ *tel:* 0181 960 6424 *fax:* 0181 964 4624. Darren Francis, project dir; Pepe Francis, mgr. *Classes and w/shops throughout London to provide relief and personal development through the provision of mus therapy. One to one sessions are also available. Steelpan tutors are available for all educational establishments.*

English Touring Opera. W121 Westminster Business Sq, Durham St, London SE11 5JH *tel:* 0171 820 1131; 820 1141 (minicom and voice) *fax:* 0171 735 7008. Paul Reeve, educ mgr; Nicholas Skilbeck, artistic consultant. *ETO run an extensive programme of work for people with disabilities including w/shops and signed performances for people who are deaf or hard of hearing, w/shops for visually impaired people and creative opera projects with adults and young people with disabilities. Also projects and recital programmes in hospitals and hospices.*

Firebird Trust. 27 Newport, Lincoln LN1 3DN *tel:* 01522 522995 *also fax.* Sibyl Burgess, dir. *The trust carries out a large number of w/shops, residencies, research and training projects.*

Glamorgan Summer School. University of Glamorgan, Pontypridd CF37 1DL *tel:* 01443 482828 *fax:* 01443 482705. Gill Giles, summer school admin. *Combined arts w/shop for people with and without learning difficulties, combining elements of mus, dance, movement, visual arts and drama.*

Heart'n'Soul. c/o Albany Empire, Douglas Way, Deptford, London SE9 4AG *tel:* 0181 694 1632; 0181 694 2988. Mark Williams, dir; Alix Parker, co-dir; Yvette Thelemmont, tour mgr. *Theatrical mus company for people with learning disabilities who tour shows and mus, organised by members within the UK and abroad. Also runs two 1-yr accredited theatre courses for people with learning disabilities. Course entitled Music, Theatre and Workshop Skills and Technical Theatre Skills.*

Lewisham Academy of Music. 77 Watson's St, Deptford, London SE8 4AU *tel:* 0181 691 0307. John Savage. *Runs weekly w/shops for people with disabilities.*

Live Music Now! 4 Lower Belgrave St, London SW1W 0LJ *tel:* 0171 730 2205 *fax:* 0171 730 3641. Virginia Renshaw, dir; Katherine Potter, asst

dir. *Brings live mus performances by selected young professional musicians into community venues, especially those for disadvantaged and disabled people.*

Morley College. 61 Westminster Bridge Rd, London SE1 7HT *tel:* 0171 928 8501 ext 238 *fax:* 0171 928 4074. Robert Hanson, dir of mus. *Offers two specific courses, Music for People with Learning Difficulties and Music for People with Physical Disabilities. Also aims to integrate disabled people into other classes.*

Music and the Deaf. Kirklees Media Centre, 7 Northumberland St, Huddersfield HD1 1RL *tel:* 01484 425551 *fax:* 01484 425560. Paul Whittaker, principal. *An organisation to help hearing-impaired people of all ages to explore the world of mus; to develop their own mus skills and interests in all its forms. W/shops, lectures, residencies, signed song. Various publications available.*

Northampton Footlights Group. c/o 20 Duncan Ct, Wellingborough NN8 2BP *tel:* 01933 229512. Eileen Smith, sec. *Amateur operatic company of disabled and able-bodied people.*

Richard Attenborough Centre for Disability and the Arts. University of Leicester, University Rd, Leicester LE1 7RH *tel:* 0116 252 2455 *fax:* 0116 252 5165 *email:* racentre@le.ac.uk. E Hartley, dir. *Organises taught courses and opportunities to participate in creative arts activities, including mus w/shops. Priority is given to people with disabilities.*

Royal National College for the Blind. College Rd, Hereford HR1 1EB *tel:* 01432 265725 *fax:* 01432 353478. Greg Barker, head of creative arts. *F/t pno tuning and repair course for the visually impaired; course to prepare students for teachers and performers diplomas at mus colleges; BTEC First Diploma Performing Arts; f/t and short courses in mus technology.*

SHARE Music. 15 Deramore Dr, Belfast BT9 5JQ *tel:* 01232 669042 *also fax.* Michael Swallow, admin. *Promotes residential courses in mus and drama with special facilities for people with physical disabilities or sensory impairments.*

SITE at the City Lit. Stukeley St, London WC2B 5LJ *tel:* 0171 831 6908. Janet Wyatt MBE, head of section. *Programme of w/shops and classes for people with learning difficulties. Training course for tchrs, musicians and others in Independence Through Education (mus and other arts).*

Stackpole Centre. Home Farm, Stackpole, Pembroke, Dyfed SA71 5DQ *tel:* 01646 661425 *fax:* 01646 661456. Alison Rees; Adrian Lewis. *Stackpole Centre Theatre. Newly opened theatre with mus and art w/shop spaces. Fully accessible facilities. Courses, w/shops and events including live mus programme (jazz, world, classical and folk). Opportunities for musicians, mus teachers and mus therapists to run courses.*

Strathcona Theatre Company. Unit 13 The Leather Market, Weston St, London SE1 3ER *tel:* 0171 403 9316 *fax:* 0171 403 9587 *email:* stc@strathco.demon.co.uk. Ann Cleary, dir; Roger Farrell, admin. *Theatre company of people with learning difficulties who devise their own productions.*

Wedgwood Memorial College. Barlaston, Stoke-on-Trent, Staffs ST12 9DG *tel:* 01782 372105 *fax:* 01782 372393. Derek Tatton, principal. *Residential adult education college which organises regular mus courses for visually impaired people including one on 'Creative Arts'.*

Wheelchair Dance Association. 43 Thurlby Rd, Wembley, Middx HA0 4RT *tel:* 0181 902 5102. Michael Massey, national sec and tutor. *National body promoting wheelchair dancing. Assistance given and starter packs available.*

Wingfield Trust. 4 Mortlock Ct, 63 Whitta Rd, Manor Park, London E12 5DU. Ms C Woods, gen sec. *Mus activities to assist children and adults with physical or minor-learning handicaps to overcome disabilities by learning to play mus insts. The Wingfield Orchestra, made up of able-bodied and disabled people, gives concerts in and around the outskirts of London.*

Manufacturers and Retailers

Acorn (Percussion) Ltd. Unit 33, Abbey Business Centre, Ingate Pl, London SW8 3NS *tel:* 0171 720 2243 (24 hrs) *fax:* 0171 627 8883. Richard Benson, dir; Marguerite Vetter, dir of sales. *Manufacturer and supplier of a variety of multi-cultural and mainstrean perc insts for special needs education and hospitals. Also insts for general school use.*

Echo City. 7 Mornington Terrace, Camden, London NW1 7RR *tel:* 0171 387 7962 *also fax.* Paul Shearsmith, member. *Designs, builds and installs sound playgrounds; organises inst building and mus w/shops. Office hours 10am-4pm Mon-Thu.*

Music Education Supplies. 101 Banstead Rd South, Sutton, Surrey SM2 5LH *tel:* 0181 770 3866 *fax:* 0181 770 3554. Ray Mason, dir. *Agents of*

Sonor school perc and suppliers of Suzuki handchimes and perc, Nordoff-Robbins reed horns, Aulos recorders, books, insts, etc.

Partially Sighted Society. PO Box 322, Doncaster, S Yorks DN1 2XA *tel:* 01302 323132. *Provides wide-spaced, heavily lined manuscript and a service for enlarging mus.*

REMAP GB (Technical Equipment for Disabled People). Hazeldene, Ightham, Sevenoaks, Kent TN15 9AD *tel:* 01732 883818 *fax:* 01732 886238. John Wright, dir. *Registered charity which designs, manufactures and supplies 'one-off' aids and adaptions that are not commercially available.*

Artists
and
Agents

Symphony and Chamber Orchestras

In this section the conductor or musical director is given, together with the names of the chief administrative staff and the associated chamber groups. A list of officers responsible for booking orchestral players will be found under **Orchestral Contractors**. The number of performers is shown in parenthesis; those of 15 and under are listed in **Ensembles**. An asterisk indicates membership of the **Association of British Orchestras** (*see* **Associations**). Youth orchestras are listed in the **Youth Orchestras and Bands** section.

* **The Academy of Ancient Music** (3-300). 10 Brookside, Cambridge CB2 1JE *tel:* 01223 301509 *fax:* 01223 327377 *email:* administrator@aam. co.uk; http://www.aam.co.uk. Christopher Hogwood CBE, dir; Paul Goodwin, associate cond; Andrew Manze, associate dir and concert master; Chris Lawrence, gen mgr; Fiona Seers, admin. *Associated choir is The Academy of Ancient Music Chorus.*

* **Academy of London** (18-65). Building 250, GEC Estate, East La, Wembley, Middx HA9 7PX *tel:* 0181 908 4348 *fax:* 0181 908 4713. Richard Stamp, artistic dir.

* **Academy of St Martin in the Fields** (8-80). Raine House, Raine St, London E1 9RG *tel:* 0171 702 1377 *fax:* 0171 481 0228. Sir Neville Marriner CBE, mus and artistic dir; Iona Brown OBE, artistic dir; Kenneth Sillito, artistic dir; Mrs George Brown, gen mgr; Gillian Brierley, development mgr; Elise Akseralian, educ co-ord; Lucy Potter, admin; Antony Delmega, financial admin. *Associated chmbr group is Academy of St Martin in the Fields Chamber Ensemble.*

Academy of St Nicolas 21-37. 14 Upper Bar, Newport, Shrops TF10 7EJ *tel:* 01952 825235 *fax:* 01952 814734. John Reid, mus dir; Sandra Day, admin.

Academy of the London Mozarteum (50). 7 Woodland Glade, Farnham Common, Bucks SL2 3RG *tel:* 01753 648113 *fax:* 01753 648114 *email:* 100522.522@compuserve.com. Robert Hamwee, artistic dir; Josefina Stabile, gen mgr.

Aeolian Sinfonia (23-70). 25 Roy Rd, Northwood, Middx HA6 1EQ *tel:* 01923 828055. Philip Gibson, mus dir.

All Souls Orchestra (35-110). All Souls Music Office, St Paul's Church, Robert Adam St, London W1M 5AH *tel:* 0171 487 3508 *fax:* 0171 224 6087. N H Tredinnick, mus dir and principal cond. *Associated chmbr groups are All Souls Sinfonietta, Band and Theatre Orchestra.*

Amadeus Orchestra. Foxholes Farm, Alderley, Wotton-Under-Edge, Glos GL12 7RJ *tel:* 01453 842364; 0171 537 2329 *fax:* 01483 843557. Philip Mackenzie, principal cond; Jason Thornton, associate cond; Alastair King, composer in association.

* **Ambache Chamber Orchestra** (16-30). 9 Beversbrook Rd, London N19 4QG *tel:* 0171 263 4027 *also fax;* 0171 281 7880. Diana Ambache, mus dir; Heather Baxter, gen mgr. *Associated chmbr group is the Ambache Chamber Ensemble.*

Amici. 24 Rae St, Stockport SK3 9LJ *tel:* 0161 474 7657. Raymond Lomax, mus dir; Judith Lomax, admin.

Amici Chamber Orchestra (12-50). 55 Rosedale, Welwyn Garden City, Herts AL7 1DP *tel:* 01707 322448. Nigel Springthorpe, principal cond; Karen Van Poznak, admin. *Associated chmbr group is Amici Wind Ensemble.*

Apollo Chamber Orchestra (25-45). 43 Clifden Rd, London E5 0LL *tel:* 0181 986 4101 *also fax.* David Chernaik, cond; Elizabeth Greaves, leader; Rebecca Dawson, admin.

* **BBC Concert Orchestra** (56). The Hippodrome, North End Rd, Golders Green, London NW11 7RP *tel:* 0171 765 4010 *fax:* 0171 765 4929 *email:* evetta01@bh.bbc.co.uk. Barry Wordsworth, principal cond; Ian Maclay, gen mgr; Adrian Evett, orch mgr; Jan Parr, asst orch mgr; Sarah Biggs, promotions and mkt mgr; Terry Leahy, librarian.

* **BBC National Orchestra of Wales** (88). BBC Broadcasting House, Llandaff, Cardiff CF5 2YQ *tel:* 01222 572524 *fax:* 01222 322575 *email:* jenkib60@wales.bbc.co.uk. Mark Wigglesworth, mus dir; Tadaaki Otaka, cond laureate; Huw Tregelles Williams, dir; Michael George, snr producer; Byron Jenkins, orch mgr; Jeremy Garside, business mgr; Helena Braithwaite, educ offr; Cathi Marcus, mkt offr; Philip Watts, development offr.

* **BBC Philharmonic** (89). New Broadcasting House, Oxford Rd, Manchester M60 1SJ *tel:* 0161 244 4005 *fax:* 0161 244 4010. Yan Pascal Tortelier, principal cond; Vassily Sinaisky, principal guest cond; Sir Peter Maxwell Davies, composer and cond; Sir Edward Downes, cond emeritus; Brian Pidgeon, snr prod; Fiona McIntosh, orch mgr; Alison Auld, business mgr; Amanda Dorr, concert promotions co-ord; Martin Maris, educ and community co-ord.

* **BBC Scottish Symphony Orchestra** (66). BBC Broadcasting House, Queen Margaret Dr, Glasgow G12 8DG *tel:* 0141 338 2606 *fax:* 0141 307 4312 *email:* bbcsso@bbc.co.uk. Osmo Vänskä, chief cond; Martyn Brabbins, associate principal cond; Jerzy Maksymiuk, cond laureate; Tan Dun, associate composer and cond; Hugh Macdonald, dir; Simon Lord, mus producer; Alan Davis, mgr; Marion Caldwell, asst mgr; Stephen Strugnell, mkt offr; Chris Dale, promotions asst.

* **BBC Symphony Orchestra.** BBC Maida Vale Studios, Delaware Rd, London W9 2LG *tel:* 0171 765 5751. Andrew Davis CBE, chief cond; Günter Wand, chief guest cond; Jiri Belohlavek, principal guest cond; Louise Badger, gen mgr; Ann McKay, chief producer; Matias Tarnopolsky, producer; Stephen Revell, orch mgr; Susanna Simmons, asst orch mgr; Marelle McCallum, concert mgr; Kate Finch, mkt mgr.

Belmont Ensemble of London (16-35). The Old School House, St Mary's Road, Aingers Green, Great Bentley, Colchester, Essex CO7 8NF *tel:* 01206 251996; 0976 278476 (mobile) *fax:* 01206 251998. Peter Gilbert-Dyson, mus dir; Rebekah Gilbert-Dyson, admin; Andrea Morris, leader.

Ben Uri Chamber Orchestra (20). 5 Bradby House, Carlton Hill, London NW8 9XE *tel:* 0171 624 1756. Sydney Fixman, cond and mus dir; David Richmond, personnel and orch mgr.

The Bernini Ensemble (12-25). 7 Parkhill Rd, London NW3 2YH *tel:* 0171 586 7910 *also fax.* Alastair Levy, cond. *Associated group is Bernini Opera.*

The Birmingham Ensemble (12). 16 Yew Tree Rd, Edgbaston, Birmingham B15 2LX *tel:* 0121 440 5164 *also fax.* Peter Thomas, artistic dir; Constanza Lezama, admin.

Birmingham Sinfonietta (24-45). 41 St Agnes Rd, Birmingham B13 9PJ *tel:* 0121 449 0225. Jeremy Ballard, mus dir; Susan Savage, orch mgr.

* **Bournemouth Sinfonietta** (30). Bournemouth Orchestras, 2 Seldown La, Poole, Dorset BH15 1UF *tel:* 01202 670611 *fax:* 01202 687235. Alexander Polianichko, principal cond; Anthony Woodcock, mgr dir; Christina Rocca, gen mgr; Bob Cator, orch mgr; Millicent Jones, mkt dir; Nick Simmonds, development dir; Andrew Burn, educ dir; Stewart Collins, head of public affairs.

* **Bournemouth Symphony Orchestra** (81). Bournemouth Orchestras, 2 Seldown La, Poole, Dorset BH15 1UF *tel:* 01202 670611 *fax:* 01202 687235. Yakov Kreizberg, principal cond; Paavo Berglund, cond emeritus; Andrew Litton, cond laureate; Kees Bakels, chief guest cond; Anthony Woodcock, mgr dir; Cristina Rocca, gen mgr; Nick Simmonds, development dir.

* **The Brandenburg Consort** (14-30). 97 Mill La, Lower Earley, Reading RG6 3UH *tel:* 0118 935 2595 *fax:* 0118 935 2627 *email:* roy.goodman@ virgin.net. Roy Goodman, mus dir. *Period insts.*

Brandenburg Opera Orchestra. 57 Kingswood Rd, Merton Pk, London SW19 3ND *tel:* 0181 542 1661 *fax:* 0181 540 1103. Robert Porter, artistic dir; Wendy Warrilow, admin; Pat Unwin, finance dir.

Brandenburg Orchestra. 57 Kingswood Rd, Merton Pk, London SW19 3ND *tel:* 0181 542 1661 *fax:* 0181 540 1103. Robert Porter, artistic dir; Emmanuel Hurwitz CBE, principal cond; Julian Leaper, ens dir; Wendy Warrilow, admin; Pat Unwin, finance dir.

* **The Brandenburg Orchestra** (30-60). 97 Mill La, Lower Earley, Reading, Berks RG6 3UH *tel:* 0118 935 2595 *fax:* 0118 935 2627 *email:* roy. goodman@virgin.net. Roy Goodman, mus dir. *Period insts.*

Brandenburg Sinfonia. 57 Kingswood Rd, Merton Pk, London SW19 3ND *tel:* 0181 542 1661 *fax:* 0181 540 1103. Robert Porter, artistic dir; Emmanuel Hurwitz CBE, principal cond; Julian Leaper, ens dir; Wendy Warrilow, admin; Pat Unwin, finance dir.

Brighton Philharmonic Orchestra (80). 50 Grand Parade, Brighton, E Sussex BN2 2QA *tel:* 01273 622900 *fax:* 01273 697887. Barry Wordsworth, principal cond; Tony Woodhouse, gen mgr; Wilfred Goddard, orch mgr; Ronald Power, chmn; Katherine Blenkinsop, asst mgr and librarian; Patricia Pickett, accounts admin.

Bristol Philharmonic Orchestra *formerly* Philharmonia of Bristol (100). 11 Windsor Ct, Victoria Terrace, Bristol BS8 4LJ *tel:* 0117 929 7597 *fax:* 0117 925 1301. Derek Bourgeois, artistic dir; Kenneth Gibbs, gen mgr; Anthony Pooley, orch mgr; Raefe Shelton, chmn. *Associated chmbr group is Bristol Philharmonic Ensemble.*

British Concert Orchestra (30-80). 147 Haling Park Rd, Croydon, Surrey CR2 6NN *tel:* 0181 688 4605 *fax:* 0181 667 0607. Frank Renton, principal cond; Peter Craen, gen mgr.

British Police Symphony Orchestra. Woodbine House, 148 Crewe Rd, Alsager, Stoke on Trent ST7 2JA *tel:* 01270 884347 *also fax.* Alex Roe, sec; Paul Hilliam, mus dir; Miki Volpe, orch mgr; Martyn Snell, concert mgr; Mike Botley, tour mgr. *Members of the orch are police personnel from all over the UK.*

* **The Britten Sinfonia** (14-50). 6-8 Hills Rd, Cambridge CB2 1JP *tel:* 01223 300795 *fax:* 01223 302092. Nicholas Cleobury, artistic dir; Helen Busbridge, orch mgr; David Butcher, gen mgr; Helen Thompson, concert mgr; Jackie Inverdale, development dir; Glyn Evans, educ consultant; Rachel Leach, educ offr; Charles Barrington, chmn. *Associated chmbr group is the Britten Sinfonia Ensemble directed by Nicholas Daniel, ob, and Pauline Lowbury, vn.*

Brunel Ensemble (4-90). 16 Heol Fair, Llandaff, Cardiff CF5 2EE *tel:* 01222 563676 *also fax.* Christopher Austin, artistic dir; Deborah Keyser, admin; Robert Saxton, president; Malcom Williamson CBE, patron. *Chmbr and symph orch.*

Buxton Spa Orchestra. Riverside House, Chapel-en-le-Frith, High Peak SK23 0QQ *tel:* 01298 813813. Sylvia Goodborn, mgr; John Goodborn, stage mgr. *Associated chmbr groups are Buxton Spa Duo and Buxton Spa Quintet.*

Camerata Roman of Sweden. c/o Neil Chaffey Concert Promotions, 8 Laxton Gardens, Baldock, Herts SG7 6DA *tel:* 01462 491378 *fax:* 01462 895094.

* **CBSO (City of Birmingham Symphony Orchestra)** (101). Paradise Pl, Birmingham B3 3RP *tel:* 0121 236 1555 *fax:* 0121 233 2423 *email:* information@cbso.co.uk. Sir Simon Rattle CBE, mus dir; Edward Smith, chief exec; Richard York, deputy chief exec; Natalie Cruse, concerts admin; Michael Buckley, gen mgr; Sir Michael Checkland, chmn; Judy Dolman, orch mgr; Rob Macpherson, mkt mgr; Caroline Gant, business relations mgr; Ann Tennant, educ mgr. *Associated chmbr group is Birmingham Contemporary Music Group.*

Cerddorion (The Musicians Touring Company) (12-28). Ty-wrth-y-Coed, Cwmystwyth, Aberystwyth, Ceredigion SY23 4AF *tel:* 01974 282631; 01981 250849 *also fax.* Robert Spearing, dir; Joanna Medcalf, admin.

Chamber Orchestra Kremlin. c/o Olivia Ma Artists' Management, 28 Sheffield Terrace, London W8 7NA *tel:* 0171 221 3606 *fax:* 0171 221 3607 *email:* oliviama@omam.u-net.com.

Chamber Orchestra of Europe (50). 8 Southampton Pl, London WC1A 2EA *tel:* 0171 831 2326 *fax:* 0171 831 8248. Claudio Abbado, artistic adviser; Peter Readman, chmn; June Megennis, gen mgr; Simon Fletcher,

personnel and planning mgr; Christopher Smith-Gillard, tour mgr; Julie Pickles, travel and office mgr; Mollie Pearson, press offr. *Associated chmbr group is Wind Soloists of The Chamber Orchestra of Europe.*

Chamber Orchestra of London. c/o COOL Music, 9 Higham Hill Rd, Walthamstow, London E17 6EA *tel:* 0468 570383 (business); 0181 531 4962. Anthony Langrish, gen mgr; Tania Steinbeck, mkt dir. *Opera galas and concert performances. Associated groups include the COOL str quartet and Trilogia (str trio).*

Charivari Agréable Simfonie. 81 Bullingdon Rd, Oxford OX4 1QL *tel:* 01865 723870 *also fax; email:* kah-ming.ng@music.oxford.ac.uk. Kah-Ming Ng, mus dir; Lynda Sayce, artistic dir; Susanne Heinrich, admin dir.

Cheltenham Chamber Orchestra (40). 5 Dean's Quarry, Burleigh, Stroud, Glos GL5 2PQ *tel:* 01453 882268 *fax:* 01453 886772. Robin Proctor, Denise Ham, mus dirs; Dorothy Roberts, press offr; Peter Tomlinson, orch mgr; Peter B Kerr, treasurer; Alison Vlach, sec.

The City of London Chamber Players (3-50). 18 Burnt Hill Way, Farnham, Surrey GU10 4RP *tel:* 01252 795047 *also fax.* Brian Lloyd Wilson, dir.

* **City of London Sinfonia** (16-50). 11 Drum St, London E1 1LH *tel:* 0171 480 7743 *fax:* 0171 488 2700 *email:* info@cls.co.uk. Richard Hickox, mus dir; Andrew Watkinson, leader and dir; Stephen Carpenter, gen mgr; Elaine Baines, admin; Kate Murdoch, educ mgr; Jane Downing, orch mgr; Jacqui Baines, mkt offr; Nicky Goulder, development dir; Liz Knock, development asst; Samantha Lodge, office mgr. *Associated chmbr group is Sinfonia Soloists.*

* **City of Oxford Orchestra** (70). Bury Knowle House, North Pl, Headington, Oxford OX3 9HY *tel:* 01865 744457 *fax:* 01865 744481. Marios Papadopoulos, principal cond; Lindsay Sandison, artistic dir. *Associated chmbr group is the Soloists of the City of Oxford Orchestra.*

City of Peterborough Symphony Orchestra (60). 55 Sapperton, Werrington, Peterborough PE4 5BS *tel:* 01733 576797 *fax:* 01733 755939. Antony Hopkins, president; Norman Beedie, cond; Jackie Over, sec.

Classic East Orchestra (50+). Marriotts Drove Farm, Ramsey Mereside, Huntingdon, Cambs PE17 1UE *tel:* 01733 844603 *also fax.* Norman Beedie, cond; Hilary Stafford-Clark, events co-ord; Robert Reynolds, mkt dir; John Owen, development dir.

Collegium Musicum 90 (3-35). 71 Priory Rd, Kew, Surrey TW9 3DH *tel:* 0181 940 7086 *fax:* 0181 332 0879. Richard Hickox, mus dir; Simon Standage, mus dir; Francesca McManus, gen mgr.

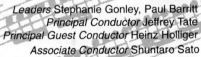

Consort of London (15-30). 36 Minsterley Av, Shepperton, Middx TW17 8QT *tel:* 01932 784925 *fax:* 01932 782589. Robert Haydon Clark, mus dir; Dom Duroux, gen mgr.

Continuum Ensemble. 28 King Edward Gardens, London W3 9RG *tel:* 0181 993 1466. Douglas Finch, pno, co-artistic dir; Philip Headlam, cond, co-artistic dir.

Corelli Chamber Orchestra (12-20). 155 Hewlett Rd, Cheltenham, Glos GL52 6UD *tel:* 01242 570383 *also fax.* Warwick Cole, dir; Rachel Abbess, gen mgr.

Corinthian Orchestra (24+). 80 Hampton La, Solihull, W Midlands B91 2RS *tel:* 0121 704 4450 *fax:* 0121 711 3582. Elaine Donohoe, gen mgr; Peter Donohoe, artistic dir and principal cond.

* **Corydon Orchestra** (40-80). 26 Sutherland Rd, West Croydon, Surrey CR0 3QG *tel:* 0181 665 5626 *fax:* 0181 251 9950. Matthew Best, artistic dir; Rowena Brown, gen mgr.

The Court Chamber Orchestra (42). Harewood, 22 Rooksmead Rd, Sunbury-on-Thames, Middx TW16 6PD *tel:* 01932 781577 *fax:* 01932 789822. Peter Clarke, cond.

Dante Alighieri Orchestra (15-25). East West Arts Ltd, 93b Cambridge Gardens, N Kensington, London W10 6JE *tel:* 0181 960 5889 *fax:* 0181 968 5541. Anup Kumar Biswas, mus dir; Peter A Connell OBE, personnel and orch mgr. *Associated chmbr group is Guadagnini Piano Trio.*

Divertimenti (6-20). 1 Pendley Bridge Cottages, Tring Station, Tring, Herts HP23 5QU *tel:* 01442 822732 *also fax.* Paul Barritt, mus dir; André Harries, finance dir.

* **East of England Orchestra** (40). Derby College - Wilmorton, Pentagon Centre, Beaufort St, Derby DE21 6AX *tel:* 01332 207570 *fax:* 01332 207569. Nicholas Kok, principal cond; Peter Helps, gen mgr; David Hill, chmn; Naomi Wilds, admin; Siân Davies, educ mgr; Nick Cutts, orch mgr; Mimi Errington, development mgr.

Emerald Chamber Players (8-14). 10 Cossins Rd, Bristol BS6 7LY *tel:* 0117 962 4289; 0117 924 3159. Roger Huckle, dir.

English Bach Festival Baroque Orchestra (20-30). 15 South Eaton Pl, London SW1W 9ER *tel:* 0171 730 5925 *fax:* 0171 730 1456. Lina Lalandi OBE, dir.

English Baroque Orchestra (12-37). 57 Kingswood Rd, London SW19 3ND *tel:* 0181 542 1661 *fax:* 0181 540 1103. Leon Lovett, mus dir; Robert Porter, mgr. *Associated chmbr group is English Baroque Players.*

English Baroque Soloists (20-45). Monteverdi Choir and Orchestra Ltd, The Bowring Building, PO Box 145, Tower Pl, London EC3P 3BE *tel:* 0171 480 5183 *fax:* 0171 480 5185 *email:* http://www.monteverdi. org.uk. John Eliot Gardiner, artistic dir; Paul Hughes, gen mgr; Heather Duncan, admin; David Adams, orch mgr.

* **English Camerata** (35). 54 Pegholme Mill, Wharfebank Business Centre, Ilkley Rd, Otley LS21 3JP *tel:* 0113 267 5821 *also fax.* Elizabeth Altman, mus dir; John Harris, admin; Dawn Foulger, PA and office mgr. *Associated ensemble is the English Camerata Soloists.*

English Chamber Orchestra (35). 2 Coningsby Rd, London W5 4HR *tel:* 0181 840 6565 *fax:* 0181 567 7198. Jeffrey Tate, principal cond; Heinz Holliger, principal guest cond; Shuntaro Sato, associate cond; Quintin Ballardie, mgr dir; Pauline Gilbertson, dir.

* **English Classical Players** (15-50). 25b Epsom La South, Tadworth, Surrey KT20 5TA *tel:* 01737 813273 *fax:* 01737 215676. Jonathan Brett, mus dir; Lyn Mumford, admin.

The English Concert (20-36). 8 St George's Terrace, London NW1 8XJ *tel:* 0171 911 0905 *fax:* 0171 911 0904. Trevor Pinnock, artistic dir; Felix Warnock, gen mgr; Sarah Fenn, orch mgr; Victoria Atkinson, admin.

English Concert Orchestra (50). 18 The Rotyngs, Rottingdean, Brighton BN2 7DX *tel:* 01273 300894 *fax:* 01273 308394 *email:* engconilan@ fastnet.co.uk. Roy Wales, mus dir; Christine Wales, admin.

English Festival Orchestra (15-75). 151 Mount View Rd, London N4 4JT *tel:* 0181 341 6408 *fax:* 0181 340 0021. Trevor Ford, gen mgr; Marianne Barton, concerts mgr.

English Haydn Orchestra. The Town House, 14 Upper Bar, Newport, Shropshire TF10 7EJ *tel:* 01952 825235 *fax:* 01952 814734. *Period insts.*

The English Heritage Orchestra (10-100). Hollybank, 5 The Orchard, Kislingbury, Northants NN7 4BG *tel:* 01604 832461 *also fax.* Graham Mayo, mus dir; Jackie Mayo, admin.

* **English National Opera Orchestra** (91). London Coliseum, St Martin's La, London WC2N 4ES *tel:* 0171 836 0111 *fax:* 0171 836 8379. Paul Daniel, mus dir; Michael Lloyd, asst mus dir; Barry Griffiths, orch leader; Dennis Marks, gen dir; Richard Smith, orch mgr; Jonathan Burton, librarian; Anthony Legge, head of mus; Guus Mozart, dir of artistic admin.

* **English Northern Philharmonia** (54). Opera North, Grand Theatre, Leeds LS1 6NU *tel:* 0113 243 9999 *fax:* 0113 244 0418. Richard Mantle, gen dir; Elgar Howarth, mus adviser; Ian Killik, orch and concerts mgr; David Hogan, financial controller; Richard Whitehouse, head of mkt; Douglas Scarfe, chmn, orch committee; Andrew Fairley, snr librarian; Ellen Gallagher, librarian. *Associated chmbr groups are Yorkshire Classic Brass, Music Serenade.*

NEW LONDON ORCHESTRA

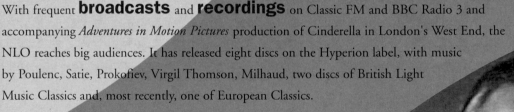

Adventures with
20th century music

Musical Director: Ronald Corp

Ronald Corp is the architect of the NLO's reputation for interesting and accessible programmes. He **talks** to his audiences, bringing performances to life. This, combined with the Orchestra's outreach work, helps to make **classical** music **popular** music.

The New London Orchestra maintains a high profile, performing regularly at St John's, Smith Square as well as all other major London concert venues. The Orchestra is available for concerts, engagements and festivals, bringing with it Ronald Corp and his unique ability to **communicate** with audiences.

With frequent **broadcasts** and **recordings** on Classic FM and BBC Radio 3 and accompanying *Adventures in Motion Pictures* production of Cinderella in London's West End, the NLO reaches big audiences. It has released eight discs on the Hyperion label, with music by Poulenc, Satie, Prokofiev, Virgil Thomson, Milhaud, two discs of British Light Music Classics and, most recently, one of European Classics.

TO FIND OUT MORE ABOUT THE NEW LONDON ORCHESTRA, **talk** TO:-

EMMA CHESTERS, GENERAL MANAGER
TEL 0171-823 5523
FAX 0171-823 6373

NEW LONDON ORCHESTRA
4 LOWER BELGRAVE STREET
LONDON SW1W 0LJ

Patrons;
Gerald Clark CMG
Lord McIntosh
Anne Johnson
Christopher Johnson
Rt Hon John MacGregor OBE MP
Rt Hon David Mellor QC
Luke Rittner

Musical Director: Ronald Corp

* **English Sinfonia** (35). 1 Wedgwood Ct, Stevenage, Herts SG1 4QR *tel:* 01438 350990 *fax:* 01438 350930. Bramwell Tovey, principal cond; Jacek Kaspszyk, principal guest cond; Graham Pfaff, chief exec; Trevor Ford, personnel mgr; Jonathan Hagger, chmn; David Bedford, composer in association; John Lill, president; Janice Graham, leader. *Associated chmbr group is English Sinfonia Ensemble (3-9 of the principal players).*

English Sinfonietta (25). The Barn, Layston Pk, Royston, Herts SG8 9DS *tel:* 01763 242847 *fax:* 01763 248048. Steuart Bedford, principal cond; Graham Pfaff, gen mgr; Trevor Ford, personnel and orch mgr.

* **English String Orchestra** (23) and **English Symphony Orchestra** (48-55). Rockliffe House, 40 Church St, Malvern, Worcs WR14 2AZ *tel:* 01684 560696 *fax:* 01684 560656. William Boughton, artistic and mus dir; The Lord Menuhin OH, cond laureate; David N James CBE, chmn of the board; Elizabeth Wild, admin; Pat Hodgson, finance mgr; Marie Oldland, orch mgr; Christine Woodcock.

Eos (6-45). Broomhill House, 19-21 Powerscroft Rd, Sidcup, Kent DA14 5EE *tel:* 0181 302 6699 *also fax.* Charles Hazlewood, mus dir; Philip Dukes, leader; Mark Dornford-May, producer.

Equinox (45). 29a Barclay Rd, London E11 3DQ *tel:* 0181 556 6348. Richard Farnes, mus dir; Karen Dennison, mgr.

The Esterhazy Orchestra (17). 278 Kew Rd, Richmond, Surrey TW9 3EE *tel:* 0181 948 6140. Philip Trzebiatowski, admin; Martin Loveday, leader.

European Union Chamber Orchestra (15-23). Fermain House, Dolphin St, Colyton, Devon EX13 6LU *tel:* 01297 552272 *fax:* 01297 553744 *email:* 101461.330@compuserve.com. Ambrose Miller, dir gen.

European Women's Orchestra (35+). Toynbee Studios, 28 Commercial St, London E1 6LS *tel:* 0171 247 2950 *fax:* 0171 247 2956. Odaline de la Martinez, cond and mus dir; Derek Warby, admin.

Ex Cathedra Baroque Orchestra (18-25). Suite 303, Jewellery Business Centre, 95 Spencer St, Birmingham B18 6DA *tel:* 0121 523 1025 *fax:* 0121 523 1026. Micaela Comberti, leader; Jeffrey Skidmore, artistic dir; Justin Lee, gen mgr; Andrew Gray, admin; Lyn Collin, business and educ development; Alison Perrier-Burgess, finance.

Fine Arts Sinfonia (40). c/o Thornton Management, 24 Thornton Av, London SW2 4HG *tel:* 0181 671 4408 *fax:* 0181 671 2848. Michael Nebe, mus dir; Peter Fisher, Martin Smith, leaders; Julia de Camillis, admin.

Fiori Musicali. Bank Cottage, Old Forge La, Preston Capes, Northants NN11 3TD *tel:* 01327 361380 *fax:* 01327 361415 *email:* fiori@aol.com. Penelope Rapson, dir; Kerstin Linder-Dewan, leader; Bernard Rapson, treasurer; Jonathan Asquith, chmn.

Foundation Philharmonic Orchestra, Young Persons Concert Foundation (30-80). 95 Wellington Rd, Enfield, Middx EN1 2PW *tel:* 0181 360 7390; 01923 859388 *fax:* 0181 364 0185 *email:* http://www.webcasting.com/stamps/found.htm. William Starling, artistic dir; Sara Neighbour, orch mgr; Sally Needleman, special projects co-ord; David Gallagher, librarian. *Associated group is the Foundation Big Band.*

Gabrieli Consort and Players (12-70). Foresters Hall, 25-27 Westow St, London SE19 3RY *tel:* 0181 771 7974 *fax:* 0181 771 7973 *email:* 101526.3227@compuserve.com. Paul McCreesh, dir; Anita Crowe, gen mgr; Jennifer Smith, admin. *Renaissance and baroque insts.*

The Georgian Camerata (4-40). 85 Pepys Rd, London SE14 5SE *tel:* 0171 277 5048; 0171 381 2175 *also fax.* Jonathan Stallick, artistic dir; Sarah Baxter, orch mgr. *Specialists in baroque and classical repertoire.*

* **Glyndebourne Touring Opera Orchestra.** Lott's End, Highgate, Forest Row, E Sussex RH18 5BE *tel:* 01342 824536 *also fax.* Ivor Bolton, mus dir; Nicholas Logie, orch mgr.

Grieg Festival Orchestra (14-45). c/o Roy Baker Concert Management, 25 Lynors Av, Rochester, Kent ME2 3NQ *tel:* 01634 714434 *also fax.* Roy Baker, mkt dir and publicity; David Burrowes, artistic dir and cond.

* **Guildford Philharmonic Orchestra** (70-75). Millmead House, Millmead, Guildford, Surrey GU2 5BB *tel:* 01483 444666 *fax:* 01483 444732. En Shao, principal cond; Vernon Handley, cond emeritus; Nicola Goold, gen mgr; Peter Holt, mus admin. *Associated chmbr group is Guildford Philharmonic Ensemble.*

* **The Hallé Orchestra** (100). The Bridgewater Hall, Manchester M2 3WS *tel:* 0161 237 7000 *fax:* 0161 237 7029. Kent Nagano, mus dir and principal cond; Alan Dean, chief exec; John Whibley, artistic planning dir; Marian McGrath, orch mgr; Helen Dunnett, acting mkt mgr; Jack Whittaker, dir of finance; Katharine Russell, dir of development; Richard Wigley, dir of educ.

Handel Festival Orchestra (45+). 26 Lamont Rd, London SW10 0JE *tel:* 0171 352 6805 *fax:* 0171 376 3503. Charles Farncombe CBE, mus dir; Rolf Wilson, leader; Sylvia Darley OBE, admin.

* **The Hanover Band.** 45 Portland Rd, Hove, E Sussex BN3 5DQ *tel:* 01273 206978 *fax:* 01273 329636 *email:* 106142.1007@compuserve.com. Caroline Brown, artistic dir; Stephen Neiman, exec dir; Martin Williams, gen mgr. *Agent: OWM.*

Havant Symphony Orchestra (70-90). 152 West St, Havant PO9 1LP *tel:* 01705 483228. Peter Craddock, mus dir; Sandra Craddock, admin; Bill Clarke, librarian. *Associated orch group is Havant Chamber Orchestra.*

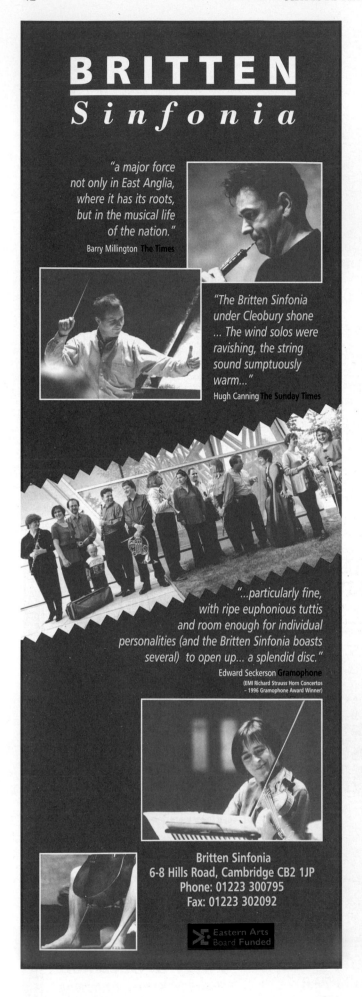

Haydn Orchestra. c/o NFMS, Francis House, Francis St, London SW1P 1DE *tel:* 0171 828 7320 *fax:* 0171 828 5504. Harry Newstone, cond; Russell Jones, admin.

Imperial Chamber Orchestra (35). 1 Imperial Manor, 34 Clifftown Parade, Southend-on-Sea, Essex SS1 1DL *tel:* 01702 338943 *fax:* 01702 340558. Miranda Hanbury, admin; Christopher Wood, principal cond.

Irish Chamber Orchestra. c/o Owen/White Management (OWM), 39 Hillfield Av, London N8 7DS *tel:* 0181 340 9571 *fax:* 0181 340 4056.

Isle of Wight Symphony Orchestra Society (80+). 5 Melcombe House, Queens Rd, Cowes, Isle of Wight PO31 8BW *tel:* 01983 290495 *fax:* 01983 297282. Jean Kirkpatrick, admin; Christopher Manning, chmn; Peter Lipari, mus dir and cond; Malcolm Lawson, press offr.

The King's Consort (15-50). 34 St Mary's Grove, London W4 3LN *tel:* 0181 995 9994 *fax:* 0181 995 2115 *email:* info@the-kings-consort. org.uk; http://www.the-kings-consort.org.uk. Robert King, artistic dir; Philip Cole, gen mgr; Nicky Oppenheimer, development dir; Eugenia Pino, tour mgr; Stephen Metcalfe, admin. *Associated chmbr group and choir.*

Kreisler String Orchestra (17). 57 Sunnyside Rd, Chesham, Bucks HP5 2AR *tel:* 01494 792572 *also fax.* Robert Woollard, mgr; Helen Kamminga, admin. *Associated chmbr groups are Duke String Quartet, Diorama String Quartet and Kreisler String Quartet.*

Langham Chamber Orchestra (15-35). 9 Weylea Av, Burpham, Guildford, Surrey GU4 7YN *tel:* 01483 573705. Peter Holt, gen mgr.

Leicester Symphony Orchestra. 37 Cancell Rd, London SW9 6HP *tel:* 0171 735 1002 *also fax.* Roland Melia, artistic dir.

Little Symphony of London (35). 14 Beaumont Rd, Purley, Surrey CR8 2EG *tel:* 0181 668 5883 *also fax.* Darrell Davison, mus dir.

Liverpool Sinfonia (20-70). 117 Beresford Rd, Birkenhead, Merseyside L43 2JD *tel:* 0151 653 4575 *fax:* 0151 653 5541. G J Ellis, principal cond; Ferdinand Bush, admin; John Bratherton, leader.

London Bach Orchestra (8-40). c/o Malcolm Layfield Management, 1 Rowsley Av, West Didsbury, Manchester M20 2XD *tel:* 0161 446 2170 *also fax.* Nicholas Kraemer, artistic dir. *Associated chmbr group is London Bach Ensemble.*

London Baroque Players (variable). Weavers House, Inkpen, Berks RG17 9DN *tel:* 01488 681131 *fax:* 01488 681671. Roger Norrington, mus dir; Kay Lawrence, mgr dir; Karin Long, admin.

London Camerata (15-35). 51 Feversham Av, Queen's Pk, Bournemouth BH8 9NH *tel:* 01202 251356. Paul Hilliam, mus dir.

London Chamber Orchestra (6-45). c/o The London Chamber Society Ltd, 6 Hambalt Rd, London SW4 9EB *tel:* 0181 772 9741 *fax:* 0181 772 9742 *email:* step.lco@virgin.net; http://freespace.virgin.net/step.lco. Christopher Warren-Green, mus dir; Step Parikian, business mgr; Jonathan Williams, artistic admin.

London Chamber Players (10-32). PO Box 84, London NW11 8AL *tel:* 0181 455 6799 *also fax.* Adrian Sunshine, mus dir; Sheila Genden, admin. *Associated chmbr groups are various ensembles (quartets, quintets, sextets, etc).*

London Chamber Symphony (30+). Toynbee Studios, 28 Commercial St, London E1 6LS *tel:* 0171 247 2950 *fax:* 0171 247 2956. Odaline de la Martinez, cond and mus dir; Sophie Langdon, leader; Derek Warby, admin.

London Chanticleer Orchestra (variable). Tickerage Castle, Pound La, Framfield, Uckfield, E Sussex TN22 5RT *tel:* 01825 890348. Ruth Gipps MBE, mus dir; Robert Baker, gen mgr. *Associated chmbr group is Rondel Ensemble (10 wind).*

London City Chamber Orchestra (25). 3-5 Bridge St, Hadleigh, Suffolk 1P7 6BY *tel:* 01473 822596 *fax:* 01473 824175. T L McIntosh, principal cond; Miranda H V Reckitt, gen mgr and admin; Jane Jarvis, press offr. *Associated chmbr group is London City Chamber Orchestra Ensemble.*

London Concert Orchestra (30-80). 176a High St, Barnet, Herts EN5 5SZ *tel:* 0181 441 8940 *fax:* 0181 441 0887. Cathy Lewis, admin; Raymond Gubbay, dir.

London Concert Sinfonia (13-45). 14 Frampton House, Frampton St, London NW8 8LY *tel:* 0171 724 7222 *also fax.* John Landor, mus dir.

London Concertante (18). 1st Floor, 105 Ferndale Rd, London SW4 7RL *tel:* 0171 207 3564 *fax:* 0171 652 0979 *email:* chris@cgrist.demon.co. uk; http://www.intune.co.uk/cmg. Bjorn Bryn Petersen, cond; Chris Grist, gen mgr.

London Festival Orchestra (15-30). 13 Theed St, London SE1 8ST *tel:* 0171 928 9251 *fax:* 0171 928 9252 *email:* 100105.673@ compuserve.com; http://www.lforch.org. Ross Pople, artistic dir; Ian Pressland, gen mgr; Beccy Jones, educ and development mgr; Katie Woods, orch mgr. *Based at the Warehouse, Waterloo.*

London Gala Orchestra (20-70). 14 Lytton Rd, London E11 1JH *tel:* 0181 556 8294 *also fax.* Phillip Ellis, associate cond; Wilfred Goddard, gen mgr; Lynne Dore, admin. *Associated chmbr group is London Gala Soloists.*

* **London Handel Orchestra** (13-30). 32 Wolverton Gardens, London W6 7DY *tel:* 0181 563 0618 *fax:* 0181 741 5233. Denys Darlow, mus dir; Paul Nicholson, associate mus dir; Ann Senior, admin.

* **London Jupiter Orchestra** (30-35). 57 White Horse Rd, London E1 0ND *tel:* 0171 790 5883 *fax:* 0171 265 9170. Gregory Rose, mus dir; Jo Hills, gen mgr. *Associated chmbr groups are Principal Winds of London Jupiter Orchestra, London Jupiter Brass and London Jupiter Singers.*

London Lyric Orchestra. 4a Harewood Rd, South Croydon, Surrey CR2 7AL *tel:* 0181 688 2430 *also fax.* Judith Wordsworth, orch mgr.

London Metropolitan Orchestra (15-110). Timbers, Woburn Hill, Weybridge, Surrey KT15 2QG *tel:* 01932 853271/853273 *email:* andy @lmo.co.uk; http://www.lmo.co.uk. Andrew Brown, mgr dir; Steven Fox, company sec; Rachel Bennett, orch mgr; Howard Chilvers, business development mgr.

* **London Mozart Players** (19-45). 92 Chatsworth Rd, Croydon CR0 1HB *tel:* 0181 686 1996 *fax:* 0181 686 2187. Matthias Bamert, mus dir; Ian Lush, mgr dir; Howard Shelley, principal guest cond; Fiona Emmerson, admin; David Wilson, orch mgr; Alice Walton, mkt mgr; Margaret Archibald, educ mgr. *Associated chmbr group is London Mozart Players Chamber Ensemble.*

London Musici. Studio 25, Royal Victoria Patriotic Building, Fitzhugh Grove, London SW18 3SX *tel:* 0181 871 0330 *fax:* 0181 871 0440. Mark Stephenson, mus dir; Victoria Millward, business mgr.

* **London Musicians Orchestra** (25-80). 49 Castlebar Rd, London W5 2DA *tel:* 0181 997 6886 *fax:* 0181 997 0588 *email:* mail@lonmus.demon.co. uk. Dave White, mgr dir; Sylvia Addison, orch mgr.

London Orpheus Orchestra (50-60). 2 Tenby Mansions, Nottingham St, London W1M 3RD *tel:* 0171 486 1929. James Gaddarn, principal cond.

London Philanova Orchestra. 43 Briton Hill Rd, Sanderstead, Surrey CR2 0JJ *tel:* 0181 657 1662. Philip Winter, mus dir.

* **London Philharmonic Orchestra** (92). 35 Doughty St, London WC1N 2AA *tel:* 0171 546 1600 *fax:* 0171 546 1601. Bernard Haitink, president; Harrison Birtwistle, composer in residence; Robert St John Wright, chmn; Serge Dorny, artistic dir and chief exec; James Grigor, gen mgr and finance dir; Sally Rogers, concerts admin; Dominique Savelkoul, dir of mkt and development; Jacqueline Barsoux, mkt mgr.

London Pops Orchestra (18-80). Hadfield House, Buckland Common, Tring, Herts HP23 6NH *tel:* 01494 758595 *also fax.* Ian McMillan, principal cond and artistic dir; Quentin Poole, exec dir; John Alexander, mkt offr; Steve Aubrey, finance dir; Paul Elliott, concert mgr; Kevin Dennett, concert mgr; Becca Smithers, concert admin; Stephen Dinwoodie, personnel and orch mgr.

London Pro Arte Baroque Orchestra. 121 Addiscombe Court Rd, Croydon, Surrey CR0 6TX *tel:* 0181 655 3950 *fax:* 0181 654 9137. Murray Stewart, artistic dir; Richard Thomas, mgr.

* **London Pro Arte Orchestra** (14-60). 121 Addiscombe Court Rd, Croydon, Surrey CR0 6TX *tel:* 0181 655 3950 *fax:* 0181 654 9137. Murray Stewart, mus dir; John Cobb, orch mgr. *Associated chmbr groups are London Pro Arte Brass Ensemble and London Pro Arte Percussion Ensemble.*

London Schubert Orchestra (12-70). 105 Woodgrange Av, London N12 0PT *tel:* 0181 445 4091 *also fax.* Brian Smith, personnel and orch mgr.

London Schubert Players (27+). 72 Warwick Gardens, London W14 8PP *tel:* 0171 603 1396 *also fax.* John Gritten, dir; Anda Anastasescu, mus dir; Jonathan Del Mar, principal cond. *Associated chmbr groups are London Schubert Players Piano Trio, Quartet, Quintet; string, wind quintet.*

London Sinfonia Ltd (34). 1 The Bridle Path, Coventry CV5 9PF *tel:* 01203 404696. Gordon Heard, mus dir; Noreen Mason, gen mgr. *Associated chmbr groups are Mozart Orchestra, London Wind Sinfonia.*

* **London Sinfonietta** (variable). Clove Building, 4 Maguire St, London SE1 2NQ *tel:* 0171 378 8123 *fax:* 0171 378 0937. Markus Stenz, principal cond; Paul Meecham, gen mgr; Jane Williams, artistic admin; Sarah Holmes, personnel mgr; Michael Haines, chmn of the council; Christine Bisatt, press and mkt; Victoria Dawes, educ offr; Julia Lawrence, concerts mgr. *Associated chmbr groups are London Sinfonietta Voices and London Sinfonietta Chorus.*

London Soloists' Chamber Orchestra (14-43). 76 Sloane St, London SW1X 9SF *tel:* 0171 235 6378 *fax:* 0171 235 1615. David Josefowitz, principal cond; Nick Bomford, gen mgr; Sue Johnston, sec.

London String Orchestra (16). 37 St Davids Rd, Clifton Campville, nr Tamworth, Staffs B79 0BA *tel:* 01827 373586 *fax:* 01827 373437. James Maddocks, mus dir; Joan Maddocks, mgr. *Associated chmbr group is Concordia Ensemble.*

* **London Symphony Orchestra** (100). Barbican Centre, Barbican, London EC2Y 8DS *tel:* 0171 588 1116 *fax:* 0171 374 0127. Sir Colin Davis CBE, principal cond; Michael Tilson Thomas, principal guest cond; André Previn, cond laureate; Clive Gillinson, mgr dir; John Lawley, chmn; Daniel Burton, concerts mgr; Moira Bennett, head of development; Karen Cardy, head of mkt; Sue Mallet, admin; Dvora Lewis, PR consultant.

London Theatre Orchestra. 210 Burnt Ash Hill, London SE12 0QE *tel:* 0181 857 1297. Peter Civil, cond.

London Viennese Concert Orchestra (27). 52 Helen Av, Feltham, Middx TW14 9LB *tel:* 0181 751 0417 *also fax.* Adrian Brown, mus dir; Keith Harmon, gen mgr.

* **Manchester Camerata** (30). The Bridgewater Hall, Manchester M2 3WS *tel:* 0161 237 7012 *fax:* 0161 237 7014 *email:* 106235.415@ compuserve.com. Sachio Fujioka, principal cond; Richard Howarth, leader; Lucy Potter, gen mgr.

Manchester Concert Orchestra. Raymond Gubbay Ltd, PO Box 48, Manchester M41 0AJ *tel:* 0161 718 9208 *fax:* 0161 718 1501. Christopher Knowles.

The Matrix Ensemble (5-35). 82 Kempshott Rd, London SW16 5LH *tel:* 0181 679 9303 *fax:* 0181 679 9306. Robert Ziegler, mus dir; Nicky Webb, gen mgr.

Mendelssohn Chamber Orchestra (16). c/o J Audrey Ellison International Artists' Management, 135 Stevenage Rd, London SW6 6PB *tel:* 0171 381 9751 *fax:* 0171 381 2406. Peter Kovats, mus dir and soloist.

Millenium Sinfonia (15-70). Twisted Chimney House, Church St, Buckingham, MK18 1BY *tel:* 01280 824191 *fax:* 01280 824811. James Kelleher, artistic dir. *Associated opera company, Millenium Opera.*

* **Milton Keynes City Orchestra** (25-40). Acorn House, 369 Midsummer Boulevard, Central Milton Keynes MK9 3HP *tel:* 01908 692777 *fax:* 01908 230099. Hilary Davan Wetton, mus dir; Luing Cowley, chmn; Ian Brignall, personnel and orch mgr; Sue Smith, operations mgr.

Minsk Chamber Orchestra (20-30). c/o J Audrey Ellison International Artists' Management, 135 Stevenage Rd, London SW6 6PB *tel:* 0171 381 9751 *fax:* 0171 381 2406. *Agent: Ellison*

Moray Chamber Orchestra (20-90). Kildonan, Young St, Elgin, Moray IV30 1TH *tel:* 01343 543531. Peter Zanrè, dir.

* **Mozart Orchestra Ltd** (18-50). Sinfonia, The Bridle Path, Coventry CV5 9PF *tel:* 01203 404696. Gordon Heard, artistic dir; Cyril Horne, chmn.

Music Projects/London (10-50). 11 Elmwood Rd, Chiswick, London W4 3DY *tel:* 0181 994 9528 *fax:* 0181 994 9595. Richard Bernas, Roger Williams, artistic dirs; Nancy Ruffer, concert mgr.

The Musicians of All Saints. 11 Cranedown, Lewes, E Sussex BN7 3NA *tel:* 01273 475544 *fax:* 01273 483561. Andrew Sherwood, mus dir; Jan Stammers, sec; Peter Copley, deputy mus dir.

The National Symphony Orchestra (60-100). Jumps Rd, Churt, Farnham, Surrey GU10 2JY *tel:* 01252 792315 *fax:* 01252 795120. Anne Collis, joint artistic dir and mgr; Perry Montague-Mason, leader and artistic dir; Eileen Wellington, librarian. *Associated chmbr group is National Symphony Orchestra Virtuosi.*

New Chamber Orchestra. 130 High St, Oxford OX1 4DH *tel:* 01865 378514 *fax:* 01865 722953. Andrew Zreczycki, mus dir; Philip Vincent, chmn.

New English Concert Orchestra (35-40). 23 Hitchin St, Biggleswade, Beds SG18 8AX *tel:* 01767 316521 *fax:* 01767 317221. Douglas Coombes, mus dir; Rose Miles, gen mgr; Carole Lindsay-Douglas, concerts mgr. *Agent: Lindsay.*

New English Orchestra (variable). 14 Woodbine Rd, Barbourne, Worcester WR1 3JB *tel:* 01905 613771. Nigel Swinford, artistic dir and principal cond; Alison Hawcutt, gen enquiries; Nick Gerrard, PR; Tony Trotter, friends.

* **New London Orchestra** (15-50). 4 Lower Belgrave St, London SW1W 0LJ *tel:* 0171 823 5523 *fax:* 0171 823 6373. Ronald Corp, artistic dir; Emma Chesters, gen mgr; Andrew Bentley, concerts mgr; Carolyn Pascall, admin.

New London Sinfonia (12-75). 2 Cuckoo Close, North Waltham, Hampshire RG25 2BJ *tel:* 01256 397409 *also fax.* David Gibson, mus dir; Julian Leaper, leader; Lara Taylor, gen mgr.

New Mozart Orchestra (15-35). c/o Westcott House, 54 Walkford Rd, Walkford, Christchurch, Dorset BH23 5QF *tel:* 01425 277128. Clive Fairbairn, principal cond; Andrew Foreman, finance dir; Ronald Swann, chmn and acting sec.

* **New Queen's Hall Orchestra** (80). c/o Manygate Management, 13 Cotswold Mews, 30 Battersea Sq, London SW11 3RA *tel:* 0171 223 7265 *fax:* 0171 585 2830 *email:* manygate@easynet.co.uk. John Boyden, artistic dir; James Thomson, gen admin.

New Wind Symphony Orchestra (8-40). 119 Woolstone Rd, Forest Hill, London SE23 2TQ *tel:* 0181 699 1101 *fax:* 0181 699 2219. Catherine Pluygers, mus dir; Neil Thomson, principal cond; Jonathan Lindridge, admin; Mark Tromans, personnel and orch mgr.

North of England Chamber and Concert Orchestra. Northern Orchestral Enterprises Limited, Room 23, Dean Clough, Halifax HX3 5AX *tel:* 01422 330533 *fax:* 01422 348916. John Pryce-Jones, artistic dir; Barry Collarbone, gen mgr; Jane Oakes, admin asst.

Northern Chamber Orchestra (16-27). 1 Crescent View, Hall Bank, Buxton, Derbys SK17 6EN *tel:* 01298 70395 *fax:* 01298 72289. Nicholas Ward, artistic dir; Jane Davies, gen mgr.

* **Northern Sinfonia** (37). The Sinfonia Centre, 41 Jesmond Vale, Newcastle upon Tyne NE2 1PG *tel:* 0191 240 1812 *fax:* 0191 240 2668. Jean-Bernard Pommier, artistic dir; Richard Hickox, cond emeritus; Heinrich Schiff, hon guest cond; John Casken, composer in association; John Summers, chief exec; A R Pender, chmn. *Associated chmbr group is The Sinfonia Ensemble.*

Northern Symphony Orchestra. PO Box 113, Stockport SK3 9LX *tel:* 0161 474 7657. Raymond Lomax, mus dir.

Oare String Orchestra (24). 25 Church Rd, Oare, Faversham, Kent ME13 0QA *tel:* 01795 535209 *fax:* 01795 533215 *email:* dgoodsel@argonet. co.uk. Peter Aviss, cond; Don Goodsell, mgr.

* **Orchestra da Camera** (25-50). 41 Fishponds Rd, Kenilworth, Warwicks CV8 1EY *tel:* 01926 858187 *also fax.* Kenneth Page, mus dir; Brenda Page, personnel and orch mgr; David Wilkinson, chmn; Margaret Banwell, educ co-ord. *Associated chmbr group is Neue Wiener Ensemble.*

Orchestra of Polyphony. c/o Magenta Music International Ltd, 4 Highgate High St, London N6 5JL *tel:* 0181 340 8321 *fax:* 0181 340 7823 *email:* http://www.polyphony.co.uk. Stephen Layton, cond. *Agent: Magenta.*

* **Orchestra of St John's Smith Square** (12-80). Clove Building, Maguire St, London SE1 2NQ *tel:* 0171 378 1358 *fax:* 0171 403 5620. John Lubbock, artistic dir; David Fisk, gen mgr; Emma Abel, admin; Lucy Heslop, educ and audience development offr; Dominic Muldowney, associate composer, 1997-8; John Woolrich, associate composer, 1998-2000. *Various associated chmbr groups and choir.*

* **Orchestra of The Age of Enlightenment.** Fifth Floor, Westcombe House, 56-58 Whitcomb St, London WC2H 7DN *tel:* 0171 930 0646 *fax:* 0171 930 0626 *email:* oae@premier.co.uk. Marshall Marcus, chmn; David Pickard, gen mgr; Janet Reeve, dir of development; James Ellis, artistic admin; Philippa Brownsword, orch mgr; Jo Newmarch, mkt offr.

The Orchestra of the Swan. 66 West St, Stratford-upon-Avon, Warks CV37 6DR *tel:* 01789 267567 *also fax.* David Curtis, cond, artistic dir; Margaret Lamb, educ offr; Sheila Bligh, sec of Friends.

* **Orchestre Révolutionnaire et Romantique** (45-70). Monteverdi Choir and Orchestra Ltd, Bowring Building, PO Box 145, Tower Pl, London EC3P 3BE *tel:* 0171 480 5183 *fax:* 0171 480 5185. John Eliot Gardiner, artistic dir; Paul Hughes, gen mgr; Heather Duncan, admin; David Adams, orch mgr.

* **Oxford Orchestra da Camera.** 2 Axtell Close, Kidlington, Oxford OX5 1TW *tel:* 01865 842889 *fax:* 01865 842950. Patricia Bavaud, mgr dir; Mike Gold, admin dir; Eve Harris, orch mgr; Chris Caspell, concert mgr.

Parnassus Ensemble of London (4-30). 18 Chimney Ct, 23 Brewhouse La, Wapping E1 9NU *tel:* 0171 480 5145 *also fax.* Peter Sheppard, mus dir; Ruth Slater, Juliet Lewis, co-dirs.

The Percy Grainger Chamber Orchestra (16-30). 22 Brook Ct, Harrow Rd, London E11 3PP *tel:* 0181 539 5933. Joe Conway, mus dir.

Performing Arts Symphony Orchestra (65). c/o Performing Arts Management Ltd, Canal 7, Clarence Mill, Bollington, Macclesfield, Cheshire SK10 5JZ *tel:* 01625 575681 *fax:* 01625 572839 *email:* http://www.performingarts.co.uk. Clare Scott, orch mgr; Nicholas Smith, cond.

* **Philharmonia Orchestra** (93). 76 Great Portland St, London W1N 6HA *tel:* 0171 580 9961 *fax:* 0171 436 5517 *email:* philharmonia@ philharmonia.co.uk. Christoph von Dohnányi, principal cond; Leonard Slatkin, principal guest cond; Keith Bragg, chmn; David Whelton, mgr dir; Fiona Martin, admin; Nikola White, concerts dir; Sarah Coop, development dir; Jill Pridmore, sales and mkt mgr; Michael Elliston, finance dir; Mansel Bebb, personnel mgr. *Philharmonia Orchestra Library, Unit LG10, Linton House, 164 Union St, London SE1 0LH* tel: 0171 928 7692 *fax:* 0171 401 9098. *Jacqui Compton, librarian.*

Philharmonic Concert Orchestra (35). 6 Victoria Grove, Fallowfield, Manchester M14 6BF *tel:* 0161 256 3686 *fax:* 0161 248 4435 *email:* joncordial@msn.com. Edward Peak, mus dir and principal cond; Matthew Scrivener, leader; Jonathan Thackeray, gen mgr.

Philomusica of Aberystwyth (80). Maesarfor, Borth, Ceredigion SY24 5JP *tel:* 01970 871372. David Russell Hulme, cond; Geraint Lewis, chmn of orch; Celia Matthews, sec.

* **Philomusica of London** (14-50). 24 Stormont Rd, London N6 4NP *tel:* 0181 340 9729/2070. David Littaur, co-cond; Neville Dilkes, co-cond; Joyce Fox, admin; Trevor Ford, personnel and orch mgr.

The Phoenix Ensemble (up to 35). 100 Adelaide Av, Ladywell, London SE4 1YR *tel:* 0181 691 6161 *also fax.* Simon Lock, artistic dir.

The Portsmouth New Music Orchestra. The New Theatre Royal, Guildhall Walk, Portsmouth, Hants PO1 2DD *tel:* 01705 351816 *also fax; email:* 101364.1355@compuserve.com. John Webber, dir of mus; Robert Blanken, dir of chmbr mus.

Primavera Chamber Orchestra (13-33). Horseshoe Barn, Cobbarn Farm, Groombridge La, Eridge, Tunbridge Wells TN3 9LA *tel:* 01892 864069 *also fax.* Paul Manley, mus dir. *Associated chmbr group is Primavera Chamber Ensemble.*

Purcell Orchestra (15-35). 86 Park Hill, Carshalton Beeches, Surrey SM5 3RZ *tel:* 0181 669 4358 *also fax.* Robin Page, artistic dir; Elizabeth Andrews, gen mgr; Gayle Scott, orch mgr.

Raglan Baroque Players (9-40). 140 Muswell Hill Rd, London N10 3JD *tel:* 0181 444 2507 *fax:* 0181 444 1795. Nicholas Kraemer, mus dir; Melanie Turner, gen mgr; Vicky Miller, concerts mgr. *Agent: Sykes.*

The Regent Sinfonia of London (14-60). 17 Parliament Hill, London NW3 2TA *tel:* 0171 435 5965. George Vass, artistic dir; Michael Moore, concerts mgr; Charlotte Edwards, leader.

The Rosebery Orchestra (18-70). 51 Stradella Rd, London SE24 9HL *tel:* 0171 274 8214. Clarissa Melville, personnel and orch mgr.

Rossini Chamber Orchestra (13-35). 10a Radipole Rd, London SW6 5DL *tel:* 0171 736 3821. Alexander Bryett, mus dir; Gill Green, gen mgr; John Biggin, concerts mgr; John McCathy, finance dir.

The Royal Ballet Sinfonia, the Orchestra of the Birmingham Royal Ballet (46). Thorp St, Birmingham B5 4AU *tel:* 0121 622 5108 *fax:* 0121 666 6244. Barry Wordsworth, mus dir; John Beadle, mus admin; Hazel Province, orch mgr.

* **The Royal Liverpool Philharmonic Orchestra** (90). Philharmonic Hall, Hope St, Liverpool L1 9BP *tel:* 0151 709 2895 *fax:* 0151 709 0918. Petr Altrichter, principal cond; Junichi Hirokani, principal guest cond; Antony Lewis-Crosby, chief exec; Robert Moon, finance dir; Ian Archer, dir of mkt; Sandra Parr, orch dir; Tom Baxter, orch mgr; Andrew Bentley, Philharmonic Hall dir; Martin Mosley, development dir.

* **Royal Opera House Orchestra** (124). Royal Opera House, Covent Garden, London WC2E 9DD *tel:* 0171 240 1200 *fax:* 0171 836 1762. Mary Allen, chief exec, ROH; Bernard Haitink, mus dir; Edward Downes, associate mus dir and principal cond; Malcolm Warne Holland, orch dir; Clifford Corbett, orch mgr; Keith Cooper, dir of corporate affairs; Andrew Stokes, dir of sales and mkt; Helen Anderson, press offr; Gina Boaks, librarian.

* **Royal Philharmonic Concert Orchestra** *formerly* Pops Orchestra (80). 16 Clerkenwell Green, London EC1R 0DP *tel:* 0171 608 2381 *fax:* 0171 608 1226. Thomas Siracusa, mgr; John Manger, mgr dir; John Bimson, chmn.

* **Royal Philharmonic Orchestra** (85). 16 Clerkenwell Green, London EC1R 0DP *tel:* 0171 608 2381 *fax:* 0171 608 1226. The Lord Menuhin OM KBE, president and associate cond; Daniele Gatti, mus dir; Yuri Temirkanov, principal cond; Sir Peter Maxwell Davies CBE, associate cond and composer; John Manger, mgr dir; John Bimson, chmn.

* **Royal Scottish National Orchestra** (87). 73 Claremont St, Glasgow G3 7JB *tel:* 0141 226 3868 *fax:* 0141 221 4317. Alexander Lazarev, mus dir and principal cond; Simon Crookall, chief exec; Neeme Järvi, cond laureate; Morrison Dunbar, chmn; Mary Jones, head of planning; Simon Crookall, gen mgr; Valerie Carlaw, head of mkt.

St James's Baroque Players (3-50). 200 Broomwood Rd, London SW11 6JY *tel:* 0171 228 6388 *fax:* 0171 738 1706. Ivor Bolton, mus dir; Delia Pye, mgr.

Sarum Chamber Orchestra (20-30). 57 East St, Corfe Castle, Wareham, Dorset *tel:* 01929 481020 *also fax.* Howard Moody, artistic dir; Nancy Strike, admin; Daphne Handford, leader. *Associated chmbr groups are Eberle String Quartet, Banks Piano Trio.*

* **The Scottish Chamber Orchestra** (37). 4 Royal Terrace, Edinburgh EH7 5AB *tel:* 0131 557 6800 *fax:* 0131 557 6933 *email:* http://www.sco.org. uk. Joseph Swensen, principal cond; Sir Charles Mackerras, cond laureate; Sir Peter Maxwell Davies, composer laureate; James MacMillan, affiliate composer; Donald MacDonald, chmn; Roy McEwan, mgr dir; Tim Baker, mkt dir; Judith Colman, concerts dir; Fiona McLeod, business relations dir; Andrea Stafford, orch mgr.

Scottish Early Music Consort (20+). 22 Falkland St, Glasgow G12 9PR *tel:* 0141 334 9229 *also fax; email:* semc@glasgow.almac.co.uk. Warwick Edwards, artistic dir; Gregory Squire, associate dir.

* **Sinfonia 21** (5-40). Office Unit 2, Free Trade Wharf, 350 The Highway, London E1 9HU *tel:* 0171 780 9434 *fax:* 0171 780 9379 *email:* info@ sinfonia21.co.uk. Dennis Stevenson CBE, chmn; Martyn Brabbins, principal cond; Sue Bottomley, gen mgr; Paul Miller, concerts mgr; Tabby Bowers-Broadbent, educ mgr; Jessica Morgan, office admin; Valerie Thorncroft, community programme co-ord.

Sinfonia da Camera (12-60). 105 Woodgrange Av, London N12 0PT *tel:* 0181 445 4091 *also fax.* Brian Smith, artistic dir; L Rosner, finance dir.

Sinfonia of London (20-110). Pigeon House Meadow, 27 Grove Rd, Beaconsfield, Bucks HP9 1UR *tel:* 01494 677934 *fax:* 01494 670443. Peter Willison, exec dir; Sally Birkett, sec; Bruce Broughton, mus dir.

Sinfonia Verdi (21-42). 60 Cowper Rd, Harpenden, Herts AL5 5NG *tel:* 01582 462137 *also fax.* David Murphy, mus dir; Claire Dwyer, admin; Julia Barker, personnel mgr; Enrico Alvares, orch chmn.

Slovene State Symphony Orchestra (60-120). c/o Antony Pristavec Artist and Concert Management, 79 Norbury Cres, London SW16 4JT *tel:* 0181 679 0369 *fax:* 0181 679 9399.

South Yorkshire Symphony Orchestra (5-50). 35 Grove Rd, Totley, Sheffield S17 4DJ *tel:* 0114 235 0277. Paul Scott, mus dir.

Southern Festival Orchestra (30-35). 11 Juniper Av, Bricket Wood, St Albans AL2 3LR *tel:* 01923 670278. Robin White, cond.

Southern Pro Musica. York House, 39 The Avenue, Fareham, Hants PO14 1PF *tel:* 01329 235474 *fax:* 01329 314101. Jonathan Willcocks, principal cond; Bryan Burdett, personnel and orch mgr.

Southern Sinfonia (3-36). 4 Toomers Wharf, Canal Walk, Newbury, Berks RG14 1DY *tel:* 01635 580035 *also fax.* Miranda Wilson, artistic dir; Amanda Richards, gen mgr and educ organiser.

Steinitz Bach Players (c 30). Bach House, 73 High St, Old Oxted, Surrey RH8 9LN *tel:* 01883 717372 *fax:* 01883 715851. Margaret Steinitz, mgr; Shauni McGregor, orch mgr; Simon Standage, leader.

Stockholm Chamber Orchestra. c/o Van Walsum Management, 4 Addison Bridge Place, London W14 8XP *tel:* 0171 371 4343 *fax:* 0171 371 4344 *email:* vwm@vanwalsum.demon.co.uk.

Stockport Festival Orchestra. PO Box 113, Stockport SK3 9LX *tel:* 0161 474 7657. Raymond Lomax, mus dir.

Surrey Chamber Orchestra (27-40). 25b Epsom La South, Tadworth, Surrey KT20 5TA *tel:* 01737 813273 *fax:* 01737 215676. Jonathan Brett, mus dir; Lyn Mumford, admin.

Surrey Sinfonietta (3-50). 18 Teevan Rd, Addiscombe, Croydon, Surrey CR0 6RN *tel:* 0181 654 5854 *also fax.* Richard Milone, artistic dir; Hilary Dennis, orch mgr; Jane Healey, personnel mgr; Chris Gee, treasurer; Sue Shearman, admin.

Sussex Symphony Orchestra (105). 20 Hampton Pl, Brighton, E Sussex BN1 3DD *tel:* 01273 208680 *fax:* 01273 777963 *email:* sso@goodger.demon.co.uk; http://www.goodger.demon.co.uk. P B Ziolkowski, chmn; Mark Andrew-James, mus dir and cond; Greg Brooks, concerts mgr; Allyson Cherry, sec; David Keighley, PR and mkt; Richard Bramwell, librarian. *Associated chamber groups are: Sussex Symphony Chamber Orchestra, Sussex Wind, Regency Wind Ensemble, Sussex Symphony Opera Orchestra.*

Swedish Radio Symphony Orchestra. c/o Van Walsum Management, 26 Wadham Rd, London SW15 2LR *tel:* 0171 371 4343 *fax:* 0171 371 4344 *email:* vwm@vanwalsum.demon.co.uk.

The Symphony of Harmony and Invention (20). First Floor, Enslow House, Station Rd, Enslow, Oxon OX5 3AX, Kidlington *tel:* 01869 331544/331711 *fax:* 01869 331011 *email:* info@thesixteen.org.uk. Harry Christophers, mus dir; Gijs Elsen, gen mgr; Alison Stillman, admin; Peter Burrows, development dir.

Taunton Sinfonietta (15-20). Weaver's Cottage, Hardington Moor, Yeovil, Somerset BA22 9NW *tel:* 01935 862339 *fax:* 01460 75707. Alan Schiller, president; John Edwards, finance dir; Robin Carpenter, chmn; Miranda Lisk, vice chmn; Anne Cleves, sec; Sheila Carpenter, librarian.

* **Taverner Players** (5-60). Ibex House, 42-46 Minories, London EC3N 1DY *tel:* 0171 481 2103 *fax:* 0171 481 2865. Andrew Parrott, artistic dir; Malcolm Bruno, associate dir; Victoria Newbert, admin.

Thames Chamber Orchestra. 41 Shirley Dr, Hounslow, Middx TW3 2HD *tel:* 0181 894 2068. The Lord Menuhin OM KBE, president; Keith Marshall, artistic dir; Anthea Robinson, admin.

Thames Sinfonia (25-60). 86 Park Hill, Carshalton Beeches, Surrey SM5 3RZ *tel:* 0181 669 4358 *also fax.* Robin Page, mus dir and principal cond; Elizabeth Andrews, gen mgr; Gayle Scott, orch mgr.

* **Ulster Orchestra** (64). Elmwood Hall at Queens, 89 University Rd, Belfast BT7 1NF *tel:* 01232 664535 *fax:* 01232 662761. Michael Henson, chief exec; James Stewart OBE, chmn; Lesley Hatfield, leader; Suzi Ashcroft, mkt mgr; Mary O'Beirne, accountant; Lucy Champion, concerts mgr; Liz Fernee, orch mgr; Paul McKinley, librarian. *Associated chmbr groups are Adelphi String Quartet, Ulster Orchestra Jazz Ensemble, Bebb-Mason Duo, Belfast Wind Quintet, 'Big Bad Bass', Carousel, Elmwood Trio, Orion String Quartet, Phoenix Duo/Trio, Ulster Brass Ensemble.*

Virtuosi of England (27). 14 Beaumont Rd, Purley, Surrey CR8 2EG *tel:* 0181 668 5883 *also fax.* Darrell Davison, mus dir.

Vivaldi Concertante. 35 Laurel Av, Potters Bar, Herts EN6 2AB *tel:* 01707 650735 *also fax;* 01707 643366. Joseph Pilbery, cond and mus dir; Maurice Powell, chmn; Mary Pilbery, sec; Audrey Banker, admin and personnel mgr; Robin Selwyn, orch mgr; Roy Baker, promotions. *Associated chmbr group is Giordani Ensemble.*

Welsh Chamber Orchestra (12-42). 100 Ystrad Fawr, Bridgend, Mid-Glamorgan CF31 4HW *tel:* 01656 658891 *also fax.* Anthony Hose, mus dir and principal cond; Barbara Parish, admin.

Welsh National Opera Orchestra (64). c/o Welsh National Opera Ltd, John St, Cardiff CF1 4SP *tel:* 01222 464666 *fax:* 01222 483050. Carlo Rizzi, mus dir; Anthony Freud, gen dir; Geoffrey Rowe, dir of admin; Peter Harrap, orch and concerts mgr; Peter Bellingham, head of mkt and press; Julian Smith, head of mus; John Stein, leader; Anthony Burke, librarian.

Welsh Philharmonic Orchestra (85-95). 40 Tudor Ct, Murton, Swansea SA3 3BB *tel:* 01792 232387. G J Harries, gen mgr; H Benjamin, treasurer. *Associated chmbr ens are Welsh Symphonic Wind Orchestra and Gower Symphonic Wind.*

Western Sinfonia (12-30). Sarum House, Union Rd, Crediton, Devon EX17 3AL *tel:* 01363 773472. Scott Stroman, cond and mus dir; Isolde Summers, admin.

Westminster Chamber Orchestra (c 30). 152 Blackmoor Wood, North Ascot, Berks *tel:* 01344 884155. Peter Davis, mgr.

Worthing Symphony (60). Connaught Theatre, Union Place, Worthing, W Sussex BN11 1LG *tel:* 01903 231799 *fax:* 01903 215337. David Smith, orch admin; John Gibbons, principal cond.

Wren Baroque Orchestra. Wren Music, 8 Park La, Selsey, W Sussex PO20 0HD *tel:* 01243 604281 *fax:* 01243 604387 *email:* starmus@brainlink.com; http://www.brainlink.com/~starmus/unison/wren/wren.html. Martin Elliott, mus dir; Susan Carpenter-Jacobs, leader.

Yorkshire Philharmonic Orchestras (12-61). Torridon House, 104 Bradford Rd, Wrenthorpe, Wakefield WF1 1BR *tel:* 01924 371496. Brian Greensmith, gen mgr; Magdalen Greensmith, company sec. *Incorporating Yorkshire Sinfonietta, Yorkshire Symphony Orchestra, Yorkshire Chamber Orchestra, Yorkshire Concert Orchestra.*

Opera, Dance and Music Theatre

The organisations listed here comprise companies presenting opera, ballet or mixed-media dramatic productions on a professional or mainly professional basis. An asterisk indicates membership of the **Opera and Music Theatre Forum (OMTF)**, Francis House, Francis St, London SW1P 1DE *tel:* 0171 828 8023 *fax:* 0171 931 9959 *email:* abo@orchestranet. co.uk, which represents the interest of small-scale opera and music theatre companies. The youth opera companies are also included in this chapter.

* **Abbey Opera Training.** 68 Queens Gardens, London W2 3AH *tel:* 0171 262 9023 *also fax; email:* emsdata@compuserve.com. Antony Shelley, cond; Mary Hill, artistic dir; Richard Gregson, dir; Maria Koripas, choreographer. *Operatic training and performance. University foundation and diploma courses in association with Birkbeck College.*

Alias Opera. 206 Amelia St, London SE17 3AS *tel:* 0171 701 6963 *email:* sg@mailbox.co.uk. Sabrina George, artistic dir.

* **Almeida Opera.** Almeida Theatre, Almeida St, London N1 1TA *tel:* 0171 226 7432 *fax:* 0171 704 9581 *email:* almeidatheatre@demon.co.uk; http://www.almeida.co.uk. Jonathan Reekie, dir. *Presents premieres of newly-commissioned operas and concerts.*

* **Broomhill.** Broomhill House, 19-21 Powerscroft Rd, Sidcup, Kent DA14 5EE *tel:* 0181 302 6699 (admin) *also fax;* 0181 300 1155 (box office) *email:* broomhill@broomhill.demon.co.uk; http://www.broomhill. demon.co.uk. Mark Dornford-May, gen dir; Charles Hazlewood, mus dir.

Cameo Opera Group. 175 Nether Priors, Basildon, Essex SS14 1LT *tel:* 01268 282221. Martyn Harrison, artistic dir; Susan Graham Smith, mus dir; Caroline Moss, stage mgr; Audrey Harris, auditions sec. *Essex-based touring company. 4-15 singers, chorus and orch available. Educ programme.*

Castleward Opera. 61 Marlborough Park North, Belfast, N Ireland BT9 6HL *tel:* 01232 661090 *fax:* 01232 687081. Ian Urwin, artistic dir; Jack Smith, artistic dir; R L Schierbeek, chmn; Hilda Logan, company mgr. *Principal venue: Castle Ward.*

Central Festival Opera Ltd. 411b Wellingborough Rd, Abington, Northampton NN1 4EY *tel:* 01604 233082 *fax:* 01604 27089. Tom Hawkes, artistic dir; Pierre Aumonier, admin; Jeffrey Greenwell CBE, chmn. *Principal venue: Derngate, Northampton.*

Champagne Opera. Burycroft Farm House, Crawley Rd, Witney, Oxon OX8 5TG *tel:* 01993 708294/708652 *fax:* 01993 708643.

Chelsea Opera Group. 21 Woodlands Rd, Isleworth TW7 6NR *tel:* 0181 568 6104. *Gives concert performances of less familiar operas. Most performances are in major London concert halls.*

* **City of Birmingham Touring Opera.** 205 The Argent Centre, 60 Frederick St, Birmingham B1 3HS *tel:* 0121 246 6644 *fax:* 0121 246 6633. Graham Vick, artistic dir; Andrew Bennett, admin; Simon Halsey, principal cond. *Touring company.*

* **Classical Adventures** *formerly* Compact Opera. 105 Aberdeen House, Aberdeen Centre, 22-24 Highbury Grove, London N5 2EA *tel:* 0171 354 8794 *fax:* 0171 354 5692. Jonathan Alver, artistic dir. *Touring company, small and mid-scale venues.*

Court Opera Productions. Durngate House, 3 Durngate St, Dorchester, Dorset DT1 1JP *tel:* 01305 264420 *fax:* 01305 269005. Margaret Powell, artistic dir; Richard Morris, designer; Terry Mead, production mgr. *Touring company. Auditions and rehearsals held in London area.*

* **Crystal Clear Opera.** The Old Rectory, Grafham, Cambs PE18 0BB *tel:* 01480 810261 *fax:* 01480 812835 *email:* martin.mcevoy@virgin. net. Martin McEvoy, artistic dir; Jane Ford, admin; Anna Arthur, press and publicity. *Mid-scale touring company; spring and autumn seasons; Arts Council funded. European tour 1998; American tour 1999.*

D'Oyly Carte Opera Company. Valley Pk, Cromer Gardens, Wolverhampton WV6 0UA *tel:* 01902 744555; 01902 744414 (mus hire library) *fax:* 01902 744333. Sir Michael Bishop CBE, chmn; Ray Brown, gen mgr; John Owen Edwards, mus dir; Ian Martin, admin mgr; Jon Sherwood, technical mgr; Keith Nicholls, finance controller; Bill Clancy, head of mkt; Ian Brignall, orch mgr; Nick Stockton, librarian. *Touring company. Principal venue (prior to touring): Grand Theatre, Wolverhampton.*

Diva Opera and Concerts. 115 Princes Gardens, London W3 0LR *tel:* 0181 932 8555 *fax:* 0181 723 6357. Bryan Evans MBE, mus dir; Anne Marabini Young, Anne Gerbic, admins. *International touring company, opera, concerts and recitals.*

Dorset Opera. 26 Central Acre, Yeovil, Somerset BA20 1NU *tel:* 01935 479297 *fax:* 01935 412210. Patrick Shelley, mus dir; Gareth Jones, chorus master; Jennifer Coultas, chief repetiteur; Elisabeth Lang Brown, admin; Sir Anthony Wilson, finance dir; Arthur Davies, personnel and orch mgr; Diana Lapping, mkt offr; The Lady Digby, president; Gordon McKechnie, dir; Mark Friend, designer. Gill Vahey, costume designer; Kara McKechnie, stage mgr; Erik Smith, chmn. *Principal venue: Sherborne.*

Duchy Opera. Long View, Hillside Rd, Carharrack, Redruth, Cornwall TR16 5RZ *tel:* 01209 821972. Jenny Gardiner, admin. *Amateur touring company. Principal venue: Truro City Hall.*

English Festival Opera. Unit 11, Gerrard House, Worthing Rd, E Preston, Littlehampton, W Sussex BN16 1AX *tel:* 01903 850432 *also fax.* Pamela Haywood, mgr dir; Simon Gray, mus dir; Paul Hayes, dir of mkt; Elizabeth Wall, finance dir; Ian Gledhill, technical dir; Alison Hoyland, orch mgr. *Touring company.*

English National Opera. London Coliseum, St Martin's La, London WC2N 4ES *tel:* 0171 836 0111 *fax:* 0171 836 8379. Dennis Marks, gen dir; Paul Daniel, mus dir; Guus Mostart, dir of artistic admin; Michael Woolley, dir of business and admin; Laurence Holderness, technical dir; Maggie Sedwards, dir of PR; Jane Livingston, head of press; Maddy Morton, head of mkt. *Principal venue: London Coliseum.*

* **English Touring Opera.** W121 Westminster Business Sq, Durham St, London SE11 5JH *tel:* 0171 820 1131/1141 *fax:* 0171 735 7008. Andrew Greenwood, mus dir; Katharine Herbert, chief exec; Peter Thompson, orch mgr; Trudi Maxwell, mkt mgr; Paul Reeve, educ mgr; Robert Chevara, production dir; Lucy Anderson Jones, development dir; John Haywood, press and publicity offr. *Touring company.*

Essex Opera. 141 Inverness Av, Westcliff-on-Sea, Essex SS0 9DU *tel:* 01702 349009. Isobel Tedstill, gen mgr; Brian Galloway, mus dir. *Opera w/shop, concerts and opera performance.*

European Chamber Opera. 60c Kyverdale Rd, London N16 7AJ *tel:* 0181 806 4231/9996 *fax:* 0181 806 4465. Stefan Paul Sanchez, artistic dir; Andrea Quinn, Jonathan Tilbrook, Peter Selwyn, conds; Peter Freestone, admin and associate artistic dir; Monserrat Caballé, patron; Lara Taylor, orch mgr. *International touring company.*

First Act Opera International. The Thatched House, West Farleigh, Maidstone, Kent ME15 0NJ *tel:* 01622 747762 *fax:* 01622 745276 *email:* figaro@globalnet.co.uk; http://members.tripod.com/~operavox. Elaine Holden, principal; John von Nuding, producer; Ken Roberts, mus dir. *To promote increased appreciation and enjoyment of opera to a wider audience. Performances in theatres, private houses and stately homes.*

The Garden Opera Company. All Saints Church, 100 Prince of Wales Dr, London SW11 4BD *tel:* 0171 720 4627. Peter Bridges, artistic dir; Andrea Spain, admin. *Touring company. Summer season, outdoor performances; winter season, devised and educ work in various venues.*

* **Garsington Opera Ltd.** Garsington Manor, Garsington, Oxford OX44 9DH *tel:* 01865 368201 *fax:* 01865 361545. Leonard Ingrams, chmn; Clare Adams, PR; Simon Sandbach, sponsorship.

* **Gloria.** The Lyric Theatre Hammersmith, King St, London W6 0QL *tel:* 0181 563 9293 *fax:* 0181 563 9294 *email:* 100625.3221@ compuserve.com. Neil Bartlett; Nicolas Bloomfield; Leah Hausman; Simon Mellor, producer; Mavis Seaman, admin. *Touring mus theatre company presenting live mus in theatres rather than arts centres.*

Glyndebourne Festival Opera. Glyndebourne, Lewes, E Sussex BN8 5UU *tel:* 01273 812321 *fax:* 01273 812783. Andrew Davis, mus dir; Graham Vick, dir of productions; Christopher Moulds, chorus master; Anthony Whitworth-Jones, gen dir; Peter Horne, technical dir; Sarah Playfair, artistic admin dir; Christopher Millard, head of press and PR; Louise Flind, auditions sec; Katie Tearle, head of educ and community projects.

* **Glyndebourne Touring Opera.** Glyndebourne, Lewes, E Sussex BN8 5UU *tel:* 01273 812321 *fax:* 01273 812783. Louis Langrée, mus dir; Aidan Lang, dir of production; Sarah Playfair, admin; Christopher Moulds, chorus master; Helen McCarthy, company mgr; Christopher Millard, press and mkt; Nicholas Logie, orch mgr; Katie Tearle, head of educ and community; Jenny KilBride, appeals admin. *Touring company. Principal venue: Glyndebourne.*

Hampstead Garden Opera. 5 Ben Hale Close, Stanmore, Middx HA7 3AQ *tel:* 0181 954 6432. Roy Budden, cond; David Rose, chmn; Keith Martin, treasurer; Simon de Friend, publicity offr; Marilyn Schock, chorus sec; Madeleine Leftwich, tickets sec. *Principal venue: Hampstead Garden Suburb Institute Theatre.*

The Handel Opera Company. 23 Winston Close, Romford, Essex RM7 8LL *tel:* 01708 724544 *also fax;* 0860 452623. Nicolino Giacalone, artistic dir and vocal coach; Ian Hayter, mus dir; Peter Walters, admin dir.

Hatstand Opera Ltd. 3 Heber Rd, Cricklewood, London NW2 6AB *tel:* 0181 452 7042 *also fax;* 0374 133155 *email:* hatstand@halfrunt. demon.co.uk; http://www.halfrunt.demon.co.uk/hatstand. Kirsty Young, dir. *Touring company offering a wide range of innovative opera shows for small and mid-scale venues. Also educ work with schools.*

Hillside Opera. 57 Gordon Av, Portswood, Southampton, Hants SO14 6WH *tel:* 01703 551088 *also fax.* Jill Meager, artistic dir; Kaarina Manzur, business mgr. *Opera training company for singers preparing for a professional career. Principal venue: Nuffield Theatre, Southampton. Also touring company.*

* **Jigsaw Music Theatre** *formerly* JCM Productions. 38 Rectory Grove, London SW4 0EB *tel:* 0171 498 5380 *also fax.* Sarah Jennings, artistic dir; Bruce O'Neil, mus dir; William Pool, company mgr; Cynthia Buckwell, fundraising and tour mkt; Caroline Loeb, admin. *Touring company. Principal venues: Bloomsbury Theatre and Purcell Room. Specialists in 20th C comic mus theatre and opera. Community outreach programme.*

* **London Chamber Opera.** 82 Redcliffe Gardens, London SW10 9HE *tel:* 0171 373 8535. David Wordsworth, mus dir; Geoffrey Colman, artistic dir. *Small-scale touring company. 20th C chmbr opera.*

London Community Opera. 55 Guinness Court, Guinness Estate, Cadogan St, London SW3 2PQ *tel:* 0171 225 3152 *fax:* 0171 720 4627. Peter Bridges, artistic dir.

London Jupiter Opera. 57 White Horse Rd, London E1 0ND *tel:* 0171 790 5883 *fax:* 0171 265 9170. Gregory Rose, mus dir. *Touring company.*

London Opera Players. Broadmeade Copse, Westwood La, Wanborough, Surrey GU3 2JN *tel:* 01483 811004 *fax:* 01483 811721. Peter Gellhorn, mus dir; Elisabeth Parry, mgr dir; Robin Green, mus educ offr; Peter Andrews, mkt offr; Derek and Jennie Chappel, stage and lighting. *Touring company.*

* **Mecklenburgh Opera.** Number Eight, 1 Benjamin St, London EC1M 5QL *tel:* 0171 608 1974 *fax:* 0171 608 2201. Anne Manson, mus dir; John Abulafia, artistic dir; Brian Matcham, gen mgr; Jo Hills, projects mgr. *Touring company, small and mid-scale venues. 20th C opera and mus theatre, including new commissions.*

Mid Wales Opera. Meifod, Powys SY22 6BY *tel:* 01938 500611 *fax:* 01938 500681. Barbara McGuire, dir; Keith Darlington, artistic dir. *Touring company. Tours of Wales, Marches and Border.*

Midland Music Theatre. Ball Hall Farm, Storwood, Melbourne, York YO4 4TD *tel:* 01759 318464 *also fax.* Anna Myatt, dir; Roger Marsh, educ offr. *Touring company. Exclusively 20th C repertoire.*

Midsummer Opera. 90 Grange Rd, London W5 3PJ *tel:* 0181 579 7477; 0181 840 9560 *also fax.* David Roblou, mus dir; Alan Privett, producer; David Skewes, chmn; Lorelle Skewes, admin and artistic dir. *Tours occasionally, often outside UK.*

Millennium Opera. Twisted Chimney House, Church St, Buckingham MK18 1BY *tel:* 01280 824191 *fax:* 01280 824811. James Kelleher, artistic dir. *London and touring, stage productions and large-scale works in concert. Associated orch, Millennium Sinfonia.*

* **Modern Music Theatre Troupe.** 18 St Gerards Close, Clapham, London SW4 9DU *tel:* 0181 675 5365 *also fax; email:* mmtt@globalnet co.uk; http://www.globalnet.co.uk/~mmtt. Caroline Sharman, C Newell, artistic dirs; Sue Hutchison, gen mgr. *Touring company. Principal London venue: Purcell Room. Small and medium-scale touring venues.*

* **Music Theatre London.** Chertsey Chambers, 12 Mercer St, London WC2H 9DQ *tel:* 0171 240 0919 *fax:* 0171 240 0805. Tony Britten, artistic dir; Clare Foden, admin consultant; Andrew Taylor, admin. *Touring company. Mid and large-scale venues, opera and mus theatre.*

* **Music Theatre Wales.** 5 Llandaff Rd, Cardiff CF1 9NF *tel:* 01222 230833 *fax:* 01222 342046. Michael Rafferty, mus dir; Michael McCarthy, artistic dir. *Touring company.*

New Sussex Opera. 22 Bradford Rd, Lewes, E Sussex BN7 1RB *tel:* 01273 471851 *email:* new_sussex_opera@hotmail.com. David Angus, mus dir; John Lloyd Davies, dir of productions; David James, dir of planning; Dick Passmore, treasurer; Richard Pulham, general admin. *Principal venues: The Dome, The Gardner Centre, Brighton; also touring company.*

* **Nexus Opera.** 16 Kennington Park Pl, London SE11 4AS *tel:* 0171 582 0980 *fax:* 0171 582 1444. Lionel Friend, Keith Warner, artistic dirs; Ian R Jarvis, admin; Delia Lindon, artistic dir. *Touring company which runs w/shops for singers and actors. Educ work.*

Northern Opera Ltd. 24 Bankside, Morpeth, Northumberland NE61 1XD *tel:* 01670 514149 *also fax.* Roy Beasley, chmn and admin; Richard Bloodworth, mus dir; James McAvoy, chorus dir; David Nicol, company sec. *Newcastle upon Tyne. Touring concerts and small-scale productions in the Northeast and Cumbria.*

Opera Anglia/Artsanglia Ltd. 3-5 Bridge St, Hadleigh, Suffolk IP7 6BY *tel:* 01473 822596 *fax:* 01473 824175. Thomas McIntosh, artistic dir; M H V Reckitt, admin; Jane Jarvis, asst. *Principal venue: The Old School, Hadleigh.*

* **Opera Box Ltd.** Rhydyberry Cottages, Merthyr Cynog, Brecon, Powys LD3 9SA *tel:* 01874 690339 *fax:* 01874 690254. Brendan Wheatley, dir; Fraser Goulding, mus dir. *Touring company associated with English Heritage, giving outdoor performances of operas at historic venues and touring in theatres.*

Opera Brava. 28 Annett Rd, Walton-on-Thames, Surrey KT12 2JR *tel:* 01932 248874. Susan Graham Smith, mus dir; Bronek Pomorski, artistic dir; Nicola Cutcliffe, PR mgr; Amanda Buckland, company sec; Brunek Pomorski, educ; Sue Warren, admin. *Touring company.*

* **Opera Circus.** 1 Aberdeen House, 22 Highbury Grove, London N5 2EA *tel:* 0171 228 1222 *fax:* 0171 228 1220. Tina Ellen Lee, David Pearl, dirs. *Opera singers trained in mime, commedia and movement.*

* **Opera da Camera.** 7 Meadow Rd, New Costessey, Norwich NR5 0NF *tel:* 01603 744584 *fax:* 01603 507720. Jeffrey Davies, gen dir; Mark Riches, dir admin; Derek Barnes, mus dir and cond; John Aplin, cond. *Touring company.*

Opera Europa. 149 Woodhouse Av, Perivale, Middx UB6 8LQ *tel:* 0181 991 5063 *fax:* 0181 810 7118. John Gibbons, mus dir; Romolo Bruni, artistic dir. *Anglo-Italian opera company.*

Opera Exclusive. 87 Sumatra Rd, London NW6 1PT *tel:* 0171 433 1058 *fax:* 0171 813 5486. C Humphreys, mgr. *Opera concerts, opera dinner cabaret and specialised educ programmes for schools.*

Opera Experience. Marriotts Drove Farm, Ramsey Mereside, Huntingdon, Cambs PE17 1UE *tel:* 01733 844603 *also fax.* Norman Beedie, artistic dir; Diana Stuart, vocal consultant. *Regional touring company in East Anglia.*

* **Opera Factory.** 9 The Leathermarket, Weston St, London SE1 3ER *tel:* 0171 378 1029 *fax:* 0171 378 0185 *email:* 106047.3334@ compuserve.com. David Freeman, artistic dir; Sandy Bailey, admin dir; Claire Shovelton, press and mkt dir. *Touring company.*

* **Opera Holland Park.** Central Library, Phillimore Walk, Kensington, London W8 7RX *tel:* 0171 361 3364 *fax:* 0171 361 2976. John McEachen, head of public services; Ray Bingle, admin. *Principal venue: Holland Park Theatre.*

Opera in Cameo. c/o Roy Baker Management, 25 Lynors Av, Rochester, Kent *tel:* 01634 714434 *also fax.* Matthew Craven, gen dir; Judith Buckle, mus dir. *Performances in a range of venues from private functions to theatres.*

Opera In Concert. 2 Elizabeth Ct, 84 Southgate Rd, London N1 3JD *tel:* 0171 923 9100 *fax:* 0171 923 2432 *email:* garyfbn@aol.com. Gary Brown, dir. *International celebrity concerts, mus theatre concerts and opera galas.*

Opera Ireland. John Player Building, 276-288 South Circular Rd, Dublin 8, Republic of Ireland *tel:* 00 353 1 453 5519/20 *fax:* 00 353 1 453 5521. David Collopy, gen mgr; Kay Keilthy, admin; Dorothy Whelan, mkt consultant; Frank O'Rourke, chmn; Dieter Kaegi, artistic dir. *Principal venue: Gaiety Theatre, Dublin.*

Opera Italiana (incorporating the Rossini Society). 10a Radipole Rd, London SW6 5DL *tel:* 0171 736 3821. Alexander Bryett, mus dir; Richard Black, chorus master; John Biggin, admin dir; Rita Volante, admin; John McCarthy, finance dir. *Principal venue: St James's, Piccadilly.*

* **Opera Live!** 119 The Vineyard, Welwyn Garden City, Herts AL8 7PX *tel:* 01707 325375. Neil Simon, producer; Matthew Hough, mus dir; Susan Wright, educ offr; Chris Cowell, dir. *Provides performance opportunities for young professional singers.*

* **Opera North.** Grand Theatre, 46 New Briggate, Leeds LS1 6NU *tel:* 0113 243 9999 *fax:* 0113 244 0418. Richard Mantle, gen dir; Christine Chibnall, controller of planning; Ian Killik, orch and concerts mgr; James Holmes, head of mus; Martin Fitzpatrick, chorus master; Jane Bonner, company mgr; Pam Bone, head of development; Richard Whitehouse, head of mkt; Shona Galletly, press offr; Ric Green, technical dir. *Principal venues: Grand Theatre, Leeds; touring to Palace Theatre, Manchester; Hull New Theatre; Theatre Royal, Nottingham; Theatre Royal, Newcastle; Lyceum Theatre, Sheffield. Winner of the 1992 and 1993 Prudential Awards for Opera.*

* **Opera Northern Ireland.** 35 Talbot St, Belfast BT1 2LD *tel:* 01232 322338 *fax:* 01232 322291. Stephen Barlow, artistic dir; Tim Kerr, gen mgr; David Stuttard, technical mgr. *Principal venue: Grand Opera House, Belfast.*

Opera Omnibus. c/o Anne's Hatch, Hatch La, Kingsley Green, Haslemere, Surrey GU27 3LJ *tel:* 01428 656605 *also fax.* Jenny Hill, publicity mgr; John Braithwaite, chmn; John Miller, financial dir; Moyra Finlay, controller of opera planning. *Performs grand opera each Feb; also fully staged concerts and recitals. Principal venue: Haslemere Hall, Surrey.*

Opera Project. 2 Cosbycote Av, Herne Hill, London SE24 0DY *tel:* 0171 737 1867. Richard Studer, artistic dir; Jonathan Lyness, mus dir. *Touring company.*

Opera Rara Ltd. 134-146 Curtain Rd, London EC2A 3AR *tel:* 0171 613 2858 *fax:* 0171 613 2261. Patric Schmid, artistic dir.

* **Opera Restor'd.** 54 Astonville St, London SW18 5AJ *tel:* 0181 870 7649 *fax:* 0181 672 6540. Peter Holman, mus dir; Peter Milne, gen mgr; Caroline Anderson, admin; Jack Edwards, stage dir. *Touring company. Specialises in 17th-18th C opera in English, fully staged with small orch.*

Opera on a Shoestring. 13/10 Mavisbank Gardens, Festival Pk, Glasgow G51 1HG *tel:* 0141 427 9896. Christina Dunwoodie, artistic dir. *Current repertoire can offer the choice of a full, or semi-staged opera, small-scale opera highlights or reduced after-dinner opera.*

* **Opera Spezzata.** 36 Abdale Rd, London W12 7ET *tel:* 0181 740 7286 *also fax.* Dominic McGonigal, mus dir; Paul Jepson, dir. *Small opera company using the techniques of physical theatre in opera.*

Opera West. Production Office, 14 Ashgrove St, Ayr KA7 3AQ *tel:* 01292 264489 *fax:* 01292 282424. Raymond Bramwell, Marilyn de Blieck, joint artistic dirs; George Bain, chmn and chief exec. *Productions with professional soloists, orch and quality amateur chorus with high level of community involvement. Project only basis. Young artists' training. Principal venue: The Gaiety Theatre, Ayr.*

Operating Theatre. 47 Balmoral Rd, Colwick, Nottingham NG4 2GF *tel:* 0115 961 4182 *also fax.* Stephen Williams, artistic dir; Michael Palin, mus dir; Kate Pallant, company mgr. *Midlands-based opera and mus theatre specialising in rarely performed and new works. Small or medium venues.*

The Operatory. 5 St Georges Buildings, Bourdon St, London W1X 9JA *tel:* 0171 495 3122. Richard Burgess-Ellis, dir; Derek Nicholson, admin. *W/shop for singers wishing to specialise in bel canto repertoire, based on technique, vocalizi and aesthetic of the castrati.*

Pavilion Opera. Thorpe Tilney Hall, Thorpe Tilney, nr Lincoln LN4 3SL *tel:* 01526 378231 *fax:* 01526 378315. Lesley-Anne Sammons, mus dir; Freddie Stockdale, gen mgr; Christine Baxter, admin.

Pegasus Opera Co Ltd. 12 Paddock Close, Silverdale, Sydenham, London SE26 4SS *tel:* 0181 659 3289 *also fax.* Lloyd Newton, artistic dir; Simon Oliver, admin. *Touring company, small and mid-scale venues. Also educ work.*

* **Pimlico Opera.** 1 Fleet Pl, London EC4M 7WS *tel:* 0171 246 7568 *fax:* 0171 246 7569. Wasfi Kani, artistic dir; Anna Simpson, admin. *Small-scale touring company with own orch. Extensive co-productions with prisons.*

Pisa Opera Group. Flat 2, 79 Linden Gardens, London W2 4EU *tel:* 0171 229 7060. Stella J Wright, dir. *Gives advice concerning repertoire, etc to young singers.*

Pocket Opera. Brixton Opera Centre, Wiltshire Rd, London SW9 7NE *tel:* 01264 737351 *also fax.* David Stewart, mgr; Michael Armitage, artistic dir; Terence Allbright, mus dir. *Touring company.*

Randazzo Opera. 24 Bladon Ct, Barrow Rd, London SW16 5NE *tel:* 0181 677 8821 *also fax.* Arlene Randazzo, stage dir and admin; Janet Haney, mus dir. *On-going w/shops with 12 opera miniature performances pa. London-based.*

* **The Royal Opera.** Royal Opera House, Covent Garden, London WC2E 9DD *tel:* 0171 240 1200 *fax:* 0171 212 9502. Bernard Haitink, mus dir; Nicholas Payne, dir; Peter Mario Katona, artistic admin; Helen Anderson, head of press; Ann Richards, press offr; Sue Banner, company mgr; Richard Sadler, chorus mgr; Terry Edwards, chorus dir.

Scottish Early Music Consort. 22 Falkland St, Glasgow G12 9PR *tel:* 0141 334 9229 *also fax; email:* semc@glasgow.almac.co.uk. Warwick Edwards, artistic dir; Gregory Squire, associate artistic dir; Kate Brown, stage dir. *Early opera, dance and mus theatre. Venues include Tramway, Glasgow and University of Glasgow.*

* **Scottish Opera.** 39 Elmbank Cres, Glasgow G2 4PT *tel:* 0141 248 4567 *fax:* 0141 221 8812 *email:* http://www.arts.gla.ac.uk/tfts/scotop.html. Richard Armstrong, mus dir; Stephen Clarke, head of mus; Ruth Mackenzie, gen dir; David Jones, chorus master; Jenny Slack, head of planning; Jane Macintosh, finance dir; Jay Allen, orch mgr; Roberta Doyle, head of press and mkt; Jane Davidson, educ offr; Penny Lewis, head of sponsorship. *Principal venue: Theatre Royal, Glasgow.*

* **Selfmade Music Theatre.** 16d Hampstead Hill Gardens, London NW3 2PL *tel:* 0171 794 3610 *also fax.* Susannah Self, artistic dir; Michael Christie, admin. *London-based mus theatre company; newly commissioned and devised works.*

South Yorkshire Opera Ltd. 22 Paradise Sq, Sheffield S1 2DE *tel:* 0114 275 4879 *fax:* 0114 270 1125. Nita White, admin; Melvyn White, chmn; Peter King, mgr; Alison King, tickets and patronage. *Grand opera productions in summer season, operetta in winter season, one night concerts, celebrity concerts. Principal venue: The Crucible Theatre, Sheffield.*

* **Spitalfields Market Opera.** 4-5 Lamb St, Spitalfields, London E1 6EA *tel:* 0171 375 2637 *fax:* 0171 247 2559. Philip Parr, artistic dir; Andrew Hammond, gen mgr; David Mann, technical mgr; Tyrrell Burgess, chmn.

Stowe Opera. 1 Poplars Close, Preston Bissett, Bucks MK18 4LP *tel:* 01280 848275 *also fax.* Robert Secret.

Surrey Opera. 71 Gainsborough Rd, Tilgate, Crawley, W Sussex RH10 5LJ *tel:* 01293 532692. Jonathan Butcher, artistic dir; Anthea Hall, gen admin; Ian Clarke, finance dir; John Ingman, sponsorship dir; Mary Parker, publicity offr. *Principal venues: Ashcroft Theatre, Croydon; Harlequin Theatre, Redhill; Stag Theatre, Sevenoaks.*

Travelling Opera. 114 St Mary's Rd, Market Harborough, Leics LE16 7DX *tel:* 01858 434677 *fax:* 01858 463617. Peter Knapp, artistic dir; Sarah Pickering, press and PR offr.

* **Vocem Electric Voice Theatre.** 39 Birnam Rd, London N4 3LJ *tel:* 0171 281 0672 *also fax.* Frances Lynch, artistic dir. *Contemporary mus theatre productions. Major educ projects. Tours in UK, Europe and Scandanavia.*

* **Welsh National Opera.** John St, Cardiff CF1 4SP *tel:* 01222 464666 *fax:* 01222 483050. Anthony Freud, gen dir; Carlo Rizzi, mus dir; Peter Bellingham, head of mkt and press; Geoffrey Rowe, dir of admin; Julian Smith, head of mus; Isabel Murphy, dir of opera planning; Lucy Stout, dir of development; Alan Parr, technical dir; Wendy Franklin, stage mgr. *Principal venue: New Theatre, Cardiff.*

Youth Opera Companies

* **British Youth Opera.** South Bank University, 103 Borough Rd, London SE1 0AA *tel:* 0171 815 6090 *fax:* 0171 815 6094. Timothy Dean, mus dir; Denis Coe, exec chmn; Mikel Toms, orch mgr. *Singers from 22-30, instrumentalists and repetiteurs from 18-30. Auditions Nov-May, Summer season mid Jul-mid Sep; also year round programme.*

* **Live Culture and Live Wires Youth Opera Group.** c/o Baylis Programme, The ENO Works, 40 Pitfield St, London N1 6EU *tel:* 0171 729 8550 *fax:* 0171 379 8928. Tim Yealland, Jo Davies, artistic dirs. *Opera groups meet weekly Sep-Jun during term-time with annual summer school. Not purely singing based but looks at all aspects of opera including design and directing. Informal w/shop auditions in Jul. Live Culture, age 12-16; Live Wires, 8-12.*

National Youth Music Theatre. 5th Floor, The Palace Theatre, Shaftesbury Av, London W1V 8AY *tel:* 0171 734 7478 *fax:* 0171 734 7515 *email:* http:24/www.easynet.co.uk/clearsite/nymt. Jeremy James Taylor, artistic dir; Vivienne Hughes, auditions admin. *Touring mus theatre with 4 major productions pa and open w/shops for singers, actors, dancers (aged 11-19) and instrumentalists (aged 11-22). Open auditions for productions Oct-Dec. Also national and regional open access w/shops throughout the yr.*

* **New Chamber Opera.** 4 Mansfield Rd, Oxford OX1 3TA *tel:* 01865 279526 *fax:* 01865 279590. Gary Cooper, mus dir; Michael Burden, dir; Suzanne Aspden, admin. *Acts as a platform for young singers with 3-4 major productions pa.*

* **Opera Inside Out.** Goblins Hold, Wootton Rivers, Marlborough, Wilts SN8 4NQ *tel:* 01672 811175. Kevin Scott, artistic dir. *Provides a platform for young opera singers and senior students in mus colleges and in private tuition. Fully staged productions with reduced orch.*

Dance and Ballet Companies

Alexander Roy London Ballet Theatre. 69 Eton Av, London NW3 3EU *tel:* 0171 586 2498 *fax:* 0171 722 9942. Alexander Roy, artistic dir; Christina Gallea, associate dir. *Touring company.*

The Birmingham Royal Ballet *formerly* Sadlers Wells Royal Ballet. Birmingham Hippodrome, Thorp St, Birmingham B5 4AU *tel:* 0121 622 2555 *fax:* 0121 622 5038. David Bintley, artistic dir; Derek Purnell, admin dir; John Beadle, mus admin; Su Matthewman, mkt mgr; Keith Longmore, press and PR mgr; Sandy Robertson, dir, BRB trust. *Large-scale classical ballet company.*

City Ballet of London Trust Ltd. International Buildings, 71 Kingsway, London WC2B 6SX *tel:* 0171 405 0044 *fax:* 0171 405 2050. Harold King, artistic dir; Sally Vaughan, gen mgr; Sara Winnington, mkt mgr; Nick Kyle, technical mgr. *Touring neo-classical ballet company.*

The Companie of Dansers and Trabocchetti. 41 Talma Gardens, Twickenham, Middx TW2 7RB *tel:* 0181 892 9638 *also fax.* Madeleine Inglehearn, artistic dir; Jean McCreery, mus dir. *Renaissance, baroque dance and mus.*

Dance For Everyone. 30 Sevington Rd, London NW4 3RX *tel:* 0181 202 7863 *also fax.* Naomi Benari, artistic dir. *To entertain and educate, with special concern for new audiences and the deaf.*

Early Dance Project. Weavers House, Inkpen, Berks RG15 9DN *tel:* 01488 668366 *fax:* 01488 668821. Kay Lawrence, Alison Pooley, dirs; Karin Long, admin. *Dance 1550-1860.*

Earthfall. Chapter, Market Rd, Cardiff CF5 1QE *tel:* 01222 221314 *fax:* 01222 342259. Jessica Cohen, artistic dir; Jim Ennis, artistic dir. *Touring company with a policy to create innovative dance-theatre with live mus.*

English National Ballet. 39 Jay Mews, London SW7 2ES *tel:* 0171 581 1245 *fax:* 0171 225 0827 *email:* marketing@en-ballet.co.uk. Derek Deane, artistic dir; Carole McPhee, exec dir; Richard Shaw, deputy exec dir; Patrick Flynn, mus dir; Jack Haslam, finance dir; Alan Riches, technical dir. *Touring company. Principal venues: London Coliseum; Royal Albert Hall; Mayflower Theatre, Southampton; Palace Theatre, Manchester.*

Glasshouses. Church House, Springfield Rd, Leicester LE2 3BB *tel:* 0116 270 8636; 0116 257 7829 *fax:* 0116 257 7825 *email:* jbreslin@dmu.ac. uk. Jo Breslin, artistic dir. *Contemporary dance, educ projects.*

Ludus Dance Company. Assembly Rooms, King St, Lancaster LA1 1RE *tel:* 01524 389901/35936 *fax:* 01524 847744. Deborah Barnard, dir; Joan Dowthwaite, head of finance and admin; Jacqueline Greaves, head of touring. *Contemporary, touring, educ company.*

MZT Dance Company. 4 Stream Cottages, Main St, Peasmarsh, Rye, E Sussex TN31 6SP *tel:* 01797 230398 *also fax.* Stephen Preston, artistic dir; Sarah Cremer, rehearsal dir; Nikki Fido, admin. *Touring company.*

Northern Ballet Theatre. West Park Centre, Spen La, Leeds LS16 5BE *tel:* 0113 274 5355 *fax:* 0113 274 5381 *email:* press@nbtdance.demon. co.uk. Christopher Gable, artistic dir; John Pryce-Jones, mus dir; Anna M D Izza, press and PR mgr; Helen Rotherforth, head of mkt; Barry Collarbone, orch and concerts mgr. *Dance, drama.*

Rambert Dance Company. 94 Chiswick High Rd, London W4 1SH *tel:* 0181 995 4246 *fax:* 0181 747 8323. Christopher Bruce, artistic dir; Christopher Nourse, exec dir; Malcolm Glanville, technical dir; Alison Whyte, educ mgr. *Touring contemporary dance company.*

Richard Alston Dance Company. The Place, 17 Duke's Rd, London WC1H 9AB *tel:* 0171 387 0324 *fax:* 0171 383 4851. Richard Alston, artistic dir; Chris May, admin dir.

The Royal Ballet. Royal Opera House, Covent Garden, London WC2E 9DD *tel:* 0171 240 1200 *fax:* 0171 836 1762. Mary Allen, chief exec offr; Sir Anthony Dowell CBE, dir; Anthony Russell-Roberts, admin dir; Barry Wordsworth, mus dir; Amanda Jones, head of press; Keith Cooper, dir of corporate affairs. *Touring company. Principal venue: The Royal Opera House, Covent Garden, London.*

Scottish Ballet. 261 West Princes St, Glasgow G4 9EE *tel:* 0141 331 2931 *fax:* 0141 331 2629. Galina Samsova, artistic dir; David Williams, gen mgr; Alan Barker, mus dir; Lucy Shorrocks, mkt dir; Linsey Stuart, dir of development. *Classical (and contemporary) ballet. Principal venue: Theatre Royal, Glasgow.*

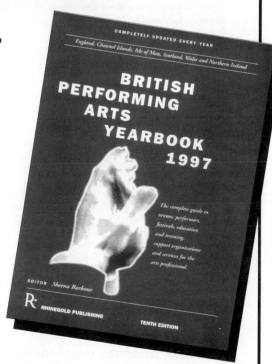

Choirs and Choruses

The following list of choirs includes only professional choirs and choirs with amateur membership which have achieved a national reputation through concerts, recordings and broadcasts.

Other amateur choirs can be contacted through the **National Federation of Music Societies** (Francis House, Francis St, London SW1P 1DE *tel:* 0171 828 7320 *fax:* 0171 828 5504 *email:* postmaster@nfms.demon.co.uk) which operates a mailing service for artists and agents wishing to contact choirs and offers free advice to singers wanting to join a choir in their area. The **National Association of Choirs** (21 Charmouth Rd, Lower Weston, Bath BA1 3LJ *tel:* 01225 426713) represents the interests of amateur choirs in the United Kingdom and the Republic of Ireland.

Abbey Singers (45+). Beckstones, Orton, Penrith, Cumbria CA10 3RG *tel:* 015396 24695. Elizabeth Lamb, cond; Jay Norris, sec.

Academy of St Martin in the Fields Chorus (24-70). Raine House, Raine St, London E1 9RG *tel:* 0171 702 1377 *fax:* 0171 481 0228 *email:* http://www.academysmif.co.uk. Laszlo Heltay, chorus dir; Louise Allen, admin.

The Aeolian Singers (90+). 22 Ben Austins, Redbourn, Herts AL3 7DR *tel:* 01582 792166. Stephen Jones, mus dir; Wendy Morgan, sec.

Aldwyn Consort of Voices (16-20). 42 Worcester Rd, Malvern, Worcs WR14 4AA *tel:* 01684 569721. Andrew Sackett, cond; Peter Smith, dir.

Alldis (John) Choir (16+). 3 Wool Rd, Wimbledon, London SW20 0HN *tel:* 0181 946 4168. John Alldis, cond. *Allied*

The Allegri Singers (30-40). 16 Hall Dr, Sydenham, London SE26 6XB *tel:* 0181 778 4760. Malcolm Gale, hon sec.

Ambrosian Opera Chorus (450). 4 Reynolds Rd, Beaconsfield, Bucks HP9 2NJ *tel:* 01494 680873 *fax:* 01494 680501. John McCarthy OBE, cond.

Ambrosian Singers (450). 4 Reynolds Rd, Beaconsfield, Bucks HP9 2NJ *tel:* 01494 680873 *fax:* 01494 680501. John McCarthy OBE, cond.

Amici 24. 24 Rae St, Stockport SK3 9LJ *tel:* 0161 474 7657. Raymond Lomax, mus dir; Judith Lomax, admin.

The Bach Choir (265). 5 Mountfort Cres, London N1 1JW *tel:* 0171 700 1144 *fax:* 0171 609 4056. Sir David Willcocks, cond (until May 98); David Hill, cond (from May 98); Jennifer Vernor-Miles, concert mgr.

Bath Camerata (25). Birch Tree Cottage, Nettlebridge, Oakhill, Somerset BA3 5AA *tel:* 01749 841086. Nigel Perrin, dir; Pauline Perrin, sec.

BBC National Chorus of Wales (165). BBC, Room E4101, Broadcasting House, Llandaff, Cardiff CF5 2YQ *tel:* 01222 322587 *fax:* 01222 322575. Simon Halsey, artistic dir; Adrian Partington, asst artistic dir; David Lawrence, chorus mgr.

BBC Singers (24). Room 24, BBC Studios, Delaware Rd, London W9 2LG *tel:* 0171 765 4370 *fax:* 0171 765 2762 *email:* stephen.ashley-king@bbc.co.uk. Stephen Cleobury, chief cond; Stephen Ashley-King, mgr.

BBC Symphony Chorus (150). BBC Studios, Delaware Rd, London W9 2LG *tel:* 0171 765 4715 *fax:* 0171 286 3251 *email:* graham.wood@bbc.co.uk. Stephen Jackson, dir; Graham Wood, admin.

Bournemouth Sinfonietta Choir (25). 221 Queen's Park Av, Bournemouth, Dorset BH8 9HD *tel:* 01202 393352. Rupert Jeffcoat, cond; Pat Williams, sec.

Bournemouth Symphony Chorus (150). 37 Harland Rd, Bournemouth BH6 4DW *tel:* 01202 423429 *also fax.* Neville Creed, chorus master; Carolyn Date, sec.

Bradford Festival Choral Society (140). Fairbank, Woodlands Grove, Ilkley, W Yorks LS29 9BX *tel:* 01943 600175 *also fax.* Michael Baker, chorus dir; John C Hammond, sec.

Brighton Festival Chorus (160). 89 Shirley Dr, Hove, E Sussex BN3 6UE *tel:* 01273 504088 *also fax.* Jonathan Grieves-Smith, mus dir; Buster Ashdown, chmn; Eric Thomson, gen mgr; Gill Kay, artistic admin.

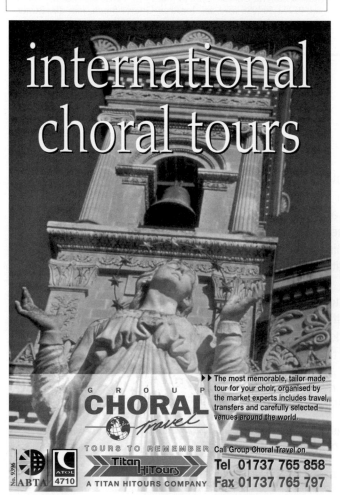

Bristol Choral Society (150). 10 Logan Rd, Bishopston, Bristol BS7 8DT *tel:* 0117 942 2719. Murray Stewart, cond; Carla Murray, hon sec.

Britten Singers *formerly* BBC Northern Singers (16+). Gurnel Beck, Witherslack, Grange-over-Sands, Cumbria LA11 6SG *tel:* 015395 52222 *fax:* 015395 52538. Simon Wright, cond; Jolyon Dodgson, mgr. *Denny Lyster*

Cambridge Taverner Choir (20). 29 Denton House, Bingham Ct, Halton Rd, Islington, London N1 2AE *tel:* 0171 359 5960 *also fax; email:* helen.garrison@bbc.co.uk. Helen Garrison, admin; Owen Rees, dir.

Cambridge University Chamber Choir (30). Clare College, Cambridge CB2 1TL *tel:* 01223 333264 *fax:* 01223 333219. Timothy Brown, cond; David Lowe, associate cond.

Cambridge Voices (16-40). The White Horse, 24 Fair Green, Reach, Cambridge CB5 0JD *tel:* 01638 741366 *fax:* 01223 772828. Ian Moore, dir; Carl Rütti, president.

Cannock Chase Orpheus Male Choir (62). 78 Brooklands Av, Cheslyn Hay, Walsall WS6 6LG *tel:* 01922 412094. Alan D Jones, mus dir; Alan Goodman, chmn; David Robinson, sec.

Canterbury Cathedral Choir (30). Christ Church Cathedral, 6 The Precincts, Canterbury CT1 2EE *tel:* 01227 765219 *fax:* 01227 762897. David Flood, choir master.

Canticum (30). 2 Newton Grove, Chiswick, London W4 1LB *tel:* 0181 994 0938. Mark Forkgen, cond; Laura Corner, admin.

Cantores ad vincula (14-18). 2 Child's Pl, London SW5 9RX *tel:* 0171 373 3638. John Williams, dir.

Canzonetta (12-28). 266 Manor Av, Sale, Cheshire M33 4NB *tel:* 0161 905 1218 *also fax.* Jeffrey Wynn Davies, dir; Fiona Clucas, admin.

Capilla Vocal Hispana. c/o 223 Kingston Rd, Leatherhead, Surrey KT22 7PE *tel:* 01372 375728 *also fax. Michael Harrold*

Cappella Nova (3-18). 172 Hyndland Rd, Glasgow G12 9HZ *tel:* 0141 552 0634 *fax:* 0141 552 4053 *email:* cn003@post.almac.co.uk; http://www.scot-art.org/cappella. Alan Tavener, dir; Rebecca Tavener, mgr.

Cardiff Polyphonic Choir (50). 148 Westbourne Rd, Penarth, Vale of Glamorgan CF64 5BQ *tel:* 01222 707827 *also fax.* Howard Goodfellow, mgr.

The Cecilian Singers (25). 23 Prince Edward Cres, Radcliffe-on-Trent, Nottingham NG12 2DX *tel:* 0115 933 2896 *also fax; email:* clive.holland@btinternet.com. Jeremy Jackman, mus dir; Lynne Holland, sec.

Chameleon Arts Chorus (20-80). Andrew Phillips, chorus master. *Chameleon*

Chandos Chamber Choir (30). 63 Mayford Rd, Balham, London SW12 8SE *tel:* 0973 630990. Piers Maxim, mus dir.

Chantry Singers of Bath 58. 6 Budbury Pl, Bradford on Avon, Wilts BA15 1QF *tel:* 01225 862159. Christine Warner, publicity offr; Elizabeth Bates, mus dir.

Chapelle du Roi (10). 10 Kensington Hall Gardens, Beaumont Av, London W14 9LS *tel:* 0171 385 6489 *email:* chapelle@wolrych.demon.co.uk. Alistair Dixon, dir.

Cheltenham Bach Choir (100). Cotteswold, Brockhampton La, Swindon Village, Cheltenham, Glos GL51 9RS *tel:* 01242 222853. Brian Kay, cond; Lesley Nicholls, sec.

Choir of Christ Church Cathedral, Oxford. Stephen Darlington, dir. *Magenta*

Choir of St Mary's Cathedral, Edinburgh (30). St Mary's Cathedral, Palmerston Pl, Edinburgh EH12 5AW *tel:* 0131 225 6293 *fax:* 0131 225 3181. Timothy Byram-Wigfield, dir.

City Chamber Choir (26). 6 Barnfield Rd, St Albans, Herts AL4 9UP *tel:* 01727 864007 *also fax; email:* 106510.1264@compuserve.com. Stephen Jones, mus dir.

City of Birmingham Choir (180). 3 Fallowfield Rd, Walsall, W Midlands WS5 3BS *tel:* 01922 722602. Christopher Robinson, cond; Mrs S A Emberson, sec.

City of Birmingham Symphony Chorus (200). Paradise Pl, Birmingham B3 3RP *tel:* 0121 236 1555; 0121 236 2461 *fax:* 0121 236 4231 *email:* information@cbso.co.uk. Simon Halsey, chorus dir; Sir Simon Rattle CBE, artistic dir; David Francis, chorus mgr.

The City of Glasgow Chorus (150). 14 Hyndland Rd, Glasgow G12 9UP *tel:* 0141 339 6153; 0141 334 9588 *fax:* 0141 357 2186. Graham Taylor, chorus master.

City of London Choir (c 100). 21 Arundel Gardens, London W11 2LN *tel:* 0171 792 3763. Hilary Davan Wetton, dir of mus; Sonia Renwick, chair; Daniel Mansfield, membership sec.

City of London Sinfonia Singers *formerly* Richard Hickox Singers (28). 11 Drum St, London E1 1LH *tel:* 0171 480 7743 *fax:* 0171 488 2700. Richard Hickox, mus dir; Stephen Carpenter, gen mgr.

Clare College Choir (24). Clare College, Cambridge CB2 1TL *tel:* 01223 333264 *fax:* 01223 333219. Timothy Brown, dir of mus.

Cori Spezzati (6-24). 36 Abdale Rd, London W12 7ET *tel:* 0181 740 7286 *also fax.* Dominic McGonigal, mus dir.

Corydon Singers (35-80). 26 Sutherland Rd, West Croydon, Surrey CR0 3QG *tel:* 0181 665 5626 *fax:* 0181 251 9950. Matthew Best, artistic dir; Rowena Brown, gen mgr.

Crouch End Festival Chorus (135). 57 Crouch Hall Rd, London N8 8HD *tel:* 0181 348 1167 *also fax; fax:* 0181 442 1748. David Temple, cond; John Gregson, chmn.

Croydon Philharmonic Choir (140). 29 Sundown Av, Sanderstead, Surrey CR2 0RQ *tel:* 0181 657 1631. Janet Jalfon, chorus sec.

Croydon SDA Gospel Choir (28). 95-97 Selhurst Rd, South Norwood, London SE25 *tel:* 0956 395203; 0973 665175 *fax:* 0181 656 7748 *email:* 101507.2207@compuserve.com. Ken Burton, Herbie Joseph, dirs.

Cryes of London (40). 41 Greenham Rd, London N10 1LN *tel:* 0181 442 1748 *also fax.* David Temple, mus dir.

Derby Choral Union (110+). 36 Buttermere Dr, Allestree, Derby DE22 2SN *tel:* 01332 550968. Kenneth E Spruce, hon sec; David Fisher, mus dir.

Ditchling Choral Society (150). 11 Barrowfield, Cuckfield, W Sussex RH17 5ER *tel:* 01444 454091 *fax:* 01444 811171. Rosemary Pardey, hon sec; Janet Canetty-Clarke, cond.

Dunedin Consort (4-15). 11c Lauriston Gardens, Edinburgh EH3 9HH *fax:* 0131 228 3410 *also fax.* Ben Parry, mus dir; Susan Hamilton, associate dir.

Dyfed Choir (50-55). 6 Lawnswood, Ragged Staff, Saundersfoot, Dyfed SA69 9HX *tel:* 01834 811588 *also fax.* Christopher Barton, mus dir; Joyce Gallon, hon sec.

East London Chorus (40). 3 Bloomfield Cres, Ilford, Essex IG2 6DR *tel:* 0181 554 2272 *fax:* 0171 225 5796. Murray Stewart, mus dir; John Buckmaster, chair.

Edinburgh Festival Chorus (175). c/o Edinburgh Festival Society, 21 Market St, Edinburgh EH1 1BW *tel:* 0131 473 2001 *fax:* 0131 473 2002 *email:* http://www.go-edinburgh.co.uk. David Jones, chorus master; James Waters, chorus admin; Margery Ramsay, chorus sec.

Edinburgh Royal Choral Union (c 150). 43 Inverleith Gardens, Edinburgh EH3 5PR *tel:* 0131 552 3874 *fax:* 01620 842960. Lilian Davidson, admin sec; John Grundy, chorus master.

The Elysian Singers of London. Top Flat, 30 Undercliff Rd, Lewisham, London SE13 7TT *tel:* 0171 499 8567; 0181 691 7503 *fax:* 0171 499 4795. Matthew Greenall, dir; Rosie Edge, admin.

English Arts Chorale (75). 9a West St, Reigate, Surrey RH2 9BL *tel:* 01737 244407 *fax:* 01737 241153. Leslie Olive, artistic dir; Mary Wilson, hon sec; David Everett, admin.

English Baroque Choir (60). 33 Horniton St, Kensington, London W8 7NR *tel:* 0171 938 1076 *also fax; email:* dmo@globalnet.co.uk; http://www. users.dircon.co.uk. Leon Lovett, mus dir; Debora Mo, concert mgr.

English Chamber Choir (40-45). 8 Alma Sq, London NW8 9QD *tel:* 0171 286 3944 *fax:* 0171 289 9081. Guy Protheroe, cond; Ann Manly, admin.

English Concert Singers/English Concert Chorus (30-150). 18 The Rotyngs, Rottingdean, Brighton BN2 7DX *tel:* 01273 300894 *fax:* 01273 308394 *email:* engconsing@fastnet.co.uk. Roy Wales, dir; Christine Wales, admin.

English National Opera Chorus (68). London Coliseum, St Martin's La, London WC2N 4ES *tel:* 0171 836 0111 *fax:* 0171 836 8379. Stephen Harris, chorus master; Charles Kraus, chorus mgr.

English String Orchestra Choir (40-45). 17 Swinton La, St Johns, Worcester WR2 4JP *tel:* 01905 424789; 01600 890289 *fax:* 01905 420196. Adrian Partington, choir dir; Sue Davis, admin.

Ex Cathedra Chamber Choir (24-32). Suite 303, Jewellery Business Centre, 95 Spencer Street, Birmingham B18 6DA *tel:* 0121 523 1025 *fax:* 0121 523 1026. Justin Lee, gen mgr; Jeffrey Skidmore, artistic dir; Andrew Gray, admin.

Exmoor Singers. 18 Claremont Gardens, Surbiton, Surrey KT6 4TN *tel:* 0181 399 4222 *fax:* 0181 399 0892. James Jarvis, cond.

Farnborough Abbey Choir. c/o 223 Kingston Rd, Leatherhead, Surrey KT22 7PE *tel:* 01372 375728 *also fax.* Michael Harrold

Finzi Singers (12-24). 4 The Close, Lichfield, Staffs WS13 7LD *tel:* 01543 250627 *fax:* 01543 250970 *email:* paul@finzi.idiscover.co.uk. Paul Spicer, dir; Elizabeth Dibben, admin.

Gentlemen of the Chappell (16). North Lodge, Potter Row, nr Gt Missenden, Bucks HP16 9NT *tel:* 01494 868240 *fax:* 01494 868250. Peter Bassano, cond.

Geoffrey Mitchell Choir (variable). 49 Chelmsford Rd, Woodford, London E18 2PW *tel:* 0181 491 0962 *fax:* 0181 491 0956. Geoffrey Mitchell, cond.

Glyndebourne Chorus. Glyndebourne Festival Opera, Glyndebourne, Lewes, E Sussex BN8 5UU *tel:* 01273 812321 *fax:* 01273 812783. Christopher Moulds, chorus master; Louise Flind, auditions sec.

Goldsmiths Choral Union (130). 6 Pembridge Cres, London W11 3DT *tel:* 0171 229 2610 *also fax.* Brian Wright, mus dir and cond; Janet Lowy, sec.

Gonville and Caius College Choir (21). Gonville and Caius College, Cambridge CB2 1TA *tel:* 01223 332448 *fax:* 01223 332456 *email:* gaw25@cam.ac.uk. Geoffrey Webber, dir of mus.

Guildford Choral Society (200). 42 Binscombe Cres, Farncombe, Godalming, Surrey GU7 3RB *tel:* 01483 416325 *fax:* 01483 450597. Hilary Davan Wetton, dir of mus; Nicola Fournel, sec.

Guildford Philharmonic Choir (140). Guildford Borough Council, Millmead House, Millmead, Guildford, Surrey GU2 5BB *tel:* 01483 444666 *fax:* 01483 444732 *email:* http://ourworld.compuserve.com/homepages/rodcuff/gpcfull/htm. Jeremy Backhouse, chorus dir; Nicola Goold, admin.

Halifax Choral Society (150-160). Warren Wells, Woodbottom La, Brighouse, W Yorks HD6 2QW *tel:* 01484 713803 *also fax.* John Pryce-Jones, mus dir; Mrs B S Whitehead, concert admin.

Hallé Choir (145). 92 Brown La, Heald Green, Cheadle, Cheshire SK8 3RA *tel:* 0161 437 5991 *also fax.* William Golightly, admin.

Harlow Chorus (130). 7 Great Hyde Hall, Sawbridgeworth, Herts CM21 9JA *tel:* 01279 726806 *fax:* 01279 726603 *email:* harlowsong@aol.com. Val Brockbank, admin; Sarah Tenant-Flowers, mus dir.

Harrogate Choral Society (154). 4 Langcliffe Av, Harrogate, N Yorks HG2 8JQ *tel:* 01423 563990. Jennifer Goodwin, sec; Jeffrey Wynn Davies, cond; Brian Kay, principal guest cond.

Hertfordshire Chorus (130). 1 Tintern Close, Kinsbourne Green, Harpenden, Herts AL5 3NZ *tel:* 01582 763871 *also fax.* Michael Kibblewhite, mus dir; Shirley Thwaite, admin.

Highgate Choral Society (160). 31 Lanchester Rd, London N6 4SX *tel:* 0181 883 8740 *fax:* 0181 883 5961. Ronald Corp, mus dir; Huw Morgan, chmn; Carolyn Pascall, sec.

Holst Singers (36). PO Box 16090, London EC4Y 7HS *tel:* 0171 936 3836 *also fax email:* holst.singers@tisl.co.uk; http://www.podium.uk.com/holst-singers/. Stephen Layton, cond; Karin Brookes, exec producer; Liz de Lacey, artistic producer.

Huddersfield Choral Society (210). Jane Glover, principal guest cond; Paul Leddington Wright, choral dir; Stephen Brook, sec. *Blythe*

Ionian Singers (c 35). 54 Holmdene Av, London SE24 9LE *tel:* 0171 733 6719 *also fax.* Timothy Salter, cond; Ulla Gray, sec.

John McCarthy Singers (60). 4 Reynolds Rd, Beaconsfield, Bucks HP9 2NJ *tel:* 01494 680873 *fax:* 01494 680501. John McCarthy OBE, cond.

The Joyful Company of Singers (24-30). 452 Kings Rd, London SW10 0LQ *tel:* 0171 352 7050 *fax:* 0171 351 7058. Peter Broadbent, cond; Rosemary Day, chmn.

King's College Choir, Cambridge (16+14). King's College, Cambridge CB2 1ST *tel:* 01223 331224 *fax:* 01223 331890 *email:* 101644.2007@compuserve.com. Stephen Cleobury, dir; Karin Brookes, mgr.

Lancaster Singers (50). Music Dept, Lancaster University, Lancaster LA1 4YW *tel:* 01524 593777 *fax:* 01524 847298 *email:* r.hutchison@lancaster.ac.uk. Denis McCaldin, cond; Ruth Hutchison, sec.

Leeds Festival Chorus (160). 9 Ashleigh Rd, Leeds LS16 5AX *tel:* 0113 275 1628. Simon Wright, chorus master; Marie Holland, sec.

Leeds Philharmonic Chorus (200). 30 Jackman Dr, Horsforth, Leeds LS18 4HS *tel:* 0113 243 3311 (day) *fax:* 0113 242 0507. Countess of Harewood, president; John Brodwell, sec.

Leicester Philharmonic Choir (180). 12 Brinsmead Rd, Knighton, Leicester LE2 3WB *tel:* 0116 270 9934 *also fax.* Michael Jackson, gen sec; Chris Exton, treasurer.

Liverpool Welsh Choral Union (150). 2 Brooklet Rd, Heswall, Wirral, Merseyside L60 1UL *tel:* 0151 342 7543. Gwyn L Williams, dir of mus; Mair Ellis, sec.

London Adventist Chorale (32). Ken Burton, artistic dir and cond; Tina Brooks, dir. *Ellison*

London Choral Society (140). 15 Aldersmead Rd, Beckenham, Kent BR3 1NA *tel:* 0181 659 1108 *fax:* 0181 325 3586 *email:* 106306.3704@compuserve.com; http://www.users.dircon.co.uk/~wjgw/lcs.htm. Jane Glover, principal cond; Ronald Corp, mus dir; Anne Howick, admin.

London Concert Choir (90). 9 Cromwell Rd, Burgess Hill, W Sussex RH15 8QH *tel:* 01444 230779 *fax:* 01444 233699. Mark Forkgen, cond; Helen Houghton, mgr.

London Contemporary Voices (16-24). 19a North Villas, Camden Sq, London NW1 9BJ *tel:* 0171 267 8778 *also fax; email:* 100770.3421@compuserve.com. Andrew Skirrow, cond.

London Handel Choir (18-20). The Coach House, Drury La, Redmarley d'Abitot, Glos GL19 3JX *tel:* 01531 650616. Denys Darlow, cond.

London Jupiter Singers (16). 57 White Horse Rd, London E1 0ND *tel:* 0171 790 5883 *fax:* 0171 265 9170. Gregory Rose, cond.

London Philharmonic Choir (150). 13 Huntspill St, London SW17 0AA *tel:* 0181 947 4355 *also fax; email:* russ@dircon.com. Norma Creed, chorus dir; Jane Hanson, chmn; Barbara Wintersgill, hon sec.

London Symphony Chorus (230). 4 Mews St, London E1 9UG *tel:* 0171 481 0090; 0171 606 7080 *fax:* 0171 606 5113. Richard Hickox, principal cond; Stephen Westrop, chorus dir; David Leonard, chmn.

London Voices. 22 St Mary's Av, London E11 2NP *tel:* 0181 989 4804 *fax:* 0181 989 7389. Terry Edwards, dir; Jacqueline Peet, sec.

THE ROYAL CHORAL SOCIETY

Patron: Her Majesty the Queen
President: HRH the Duke of Kent

Conductor: Richard Cooke

LONDON'S PREMIER CHOIR

The Royal Choral Society which celebrated its 125th Anniversary last season, continues to enhance its reputation as London's Premier Choir. Originally formed for the opening of the Royal Albert Hall, the choir's founder/conductor was the renowned composer Charles Gounod.

Since then, the most eminent musicians of the day have both influenced and contributed to the Royal Choral Society as a leading force in the Great British choral tradition, especially Sir Malcolm Sargent whose appointment with the RCS lasted over forty years. Richard Cooke took over the conductor's baton in 1995.

The 1997/98 season includes performances of oratorio, opera, popular classics and new music at London's major concert halls and in Leeds and Manchester. A highlight of the season is a series of performances of 'Mahler 8'at Canterbury Cathedral, the Royal Albert Hall and the Palais de Congrès, Lille, France. Two new recordings are also due for early release. Annual fixtures include Christmas Carols and the famous, annual Good Friday 'Messiah', both at the Royal Albert Hall.

Rehearsals are at 18.30 on Mondays at the City of London School for Girls, Barbican.

If music is one of your pleasures in life, and in particular the joy of making music, why not consider joining the Royal Choral Society?

*For full details and information,
please contact Graeme Tonge
Royal Choral Society
Studio 9, 92 Lots Rd.
London
SW10 OQD
Tel: 0171 376 3718
Fax: 0171 376 3719*

MALCOLM SARGENT FESTIVAL CHOIR

CHARLES FARNCOMBE CBE
Director of Music

DENIS COLEMAN
Associate Director

SYLVIA DARLEY OBE
Chairman

The Malcolm Sargent Festival Choir always sings in aid of the Malcolm Sargent Cancer Fund for Children. The Choir is 24 years old this coming season and has a standing choir of 450 auditioned voices. They perform regularly at the Royal Albert Hall and many of the Cathedrals in this country, in Europe, as well as visits to Notre Dame, in Paris and St. Peter's, Rome.

The Festival Choir is drawn from members of Choirs from every part of England, from the South Coast to Newcastle in the North, from Bristol in the West to Aldeburgh in the East, after passing an audition. They pay all their own travel and personal expenses to rehearsals in London, however far afield the concerts are scheduled. The Choir performs voluntarily in order to raise magnificent and substantial sums of money for the Fund.

New members always welcome.

**Enquiries for Concerts and Auditions:
The Choir Office
201a Honor Oak Road
London SE23 3RP
Tel: 0171 352 6805 / 0181 699 3309
Fax: 0171 376 3503**

Charity Registration no 1055426

London Welsh Chorale (100). 118 Thurlow Park Rd, London SE21 8HP *tel:* 0171 931 9929. Kenneth Bowen, cond; Helen Downey, sec; Paul Medlicott, chair.

Magnificat (8-24). 64 Ferry Rd, Marston, Oxford OX3 0EU *tel:* 01865 244801 *fax:* 01865 437238 *email:* magnificat@compuserve.com; http://www.magnificat.org.uk. Philip Cave, dir; Neil Bellingham, admin.

Malcolm Sargent Festival Choir (400). 26 Lamont Rd, London SW10 0JE *tel:* 0171 352 6805 *fax:* 0171 376 3503. Sylvia Darley OBE, admin.

Manchester Chorale (50). 98 Jubilee Rd, Middleton, Manchester M24 2LX *tel:* 0161 653 2406. Mark Henderson, chmn; Geoffrey Wynn Davies, mus dir; Clare Dwyer, membership sec.

Monteverdi Choir (20-75). Monteverdi Choir and Orchestra Ltd, Bowring Building, PO Box 145, Tower Pl, London EC3P 3BE *tel:* 0171 480 5183 *fax:* 0171 480 5185. John Eliot Gardiner, artistic dir; Paul Hughes, gen mgr; Heather Duncan, admin.

New College Choir, Oxford. Edward Higginbottom, dir. *Magenta*

New London Chamber Choir (12-50). Bancroft, Rectory La, Fringford, Bicester, Oxon OX6 9DX *tel:* 01869 278392 *also fax; email:* nlcc@brailsford.demon.co.uk; http://www.brailsford.demon.co.uk. James Wood, mus dir.

New London Collegium (30). 52 Finsbury Park Rd, London N4 2JX *tel:* 0171 359 3729. Peter Owens, chorus master; Barry Creasy, chmn; Ann Flett, sec.

New London Singers (c 32). Flat 7, Beechwood Ct, 572 Dunstable Rd, Luton, Beds LU4 8RT *tel:* 01582 575646. Ivor Setterfield, cond; Sali Davies, sec.

Northern Sinfonia Chorus (60). c/o The Sinfonia Centre, 41 Jesmond Vale, Newcastle-upon-Tyne NE2 1PG *tel:* 0191 240 1812 *fax:* 0191 240 2668. Alan Fearon, chorus master.

Opera North Chorus (36). Grand Theatre, 46 New Briggate, Leeds LS1 6NU *tel:* 0113 243 9999 *fax:* 0113 244 0418. Martin Fitzpatrick, chorus master; Helga Richardson, vocal auditions co-ord; Kevin Hollands, chorus mgr.

Oxford Bach Choir (200). Shepherd's Well, Church Hanborough, Oxford OX8 8AB *tel:* 01993 882211 *also fax.* Nicholas Cleobury, cond; Miss M K Arnold, hon admin; Ruth Durbridge, mkt mgr.

Oxford Pro Musica Singers (35). 15 Parkers Hill, Tetsworth, Oxford OX9 7AQ *tel:* 01844 281427 *also fax; email:* m.smedley.opms@lineone.net; http://mcs.open.ac.uk/opms/. Michael Smedley, cond.

Pamplona Cathedral Choir. c/o 223 Kingston Rd, Leatherhead, Surrey KT22 7PE *tel:* 01372 375728 *also fax. Michael Harrold*

The Philharmonia Chorus (180). 1 Pound Close, Eastbourne, E Sussex BN23 6EF *tel:* 01323 721708 *also fax; email:* 100546.1126@compuserve.com. Ron Archer, chmn; David Hill, chorus master (to Apr 98); Hana Tiller, auditions sec.

The Philharmonic Choir (150). Hollybank, 5 The Orchard, Kislingbury, Northants NN7 4BG *tel:* 01604 830679 *also fax.* Graham Mayo, cond; Jackie Mayo, admin.

Polyhymnia (12-16). Richard Lowell Childress, dir. *Chameleon*

Polyphony (10-24) *email:* http://www.polyphony.co.uk. Stephen Layton, cond. *Magenta*

Pro Musica Chorus of London (120). 6 Durham Row, London E1 0NP *tel:* 0171 790 1004 *also fax.* William Ryder, admin.

Reading Bach Choir (50). 2 Church St Cottages, Upton, Oxon OX11 9JB *tel:* 01235 850488 *also fax; email:* info@thesixteen.org.uk. Sarah Tenant-Flowers, cond; Ian Fowler, sec.

Reading Festival Chorus (120). Acorn Cottage, The Old Orchard, Mill La, Kelcot, Reading RG31 7RF *tel:* 0118 941 0720 *also fax.* Jacques Cohen, cond; Mrs T Dodd, sec.

Regent's Singers (30). 32 Angel Rd, Harrow, Middx HA1 1JY *tel:* 0181 427 5409 *also fax.* Bernard Barker, cond.

The Renaissance Singers (30). Woodside, Woodcock Hill, Pleasington, Blackburn BB2 6RB *tel:* 01254 207395 *also fax; email:* lindsey@macdonald.demon.co.uk. Lindsey Macdonald.

Rossica Choir of St Petersburg (26). 12 Warren Dr, Dorridge, Solihull, W Midlands B93 8JY *tel:* 01564 776376 *also fax.* Jean Shearman, mgr.

Royal Choral Society (c 200). Unit 9, 92 Lots Rd, London SW10 0QD *tel:* 0171 376 3718 *fax:* 0171 376 3719. Graeme Tonge, admin; Richard Cooke, cond.

Royal Liverpool Philharmonic Choir (175). Philharmonic Hall, Hope St, Liverpool L1 9BP *tel:* 0151 709 2895 *fax:* 0151 709 0918. Ian Tracey, choir master; Eleanor Wright, admin; Stuart Christie, chmn.

Royal Opera (Covent Garden) Chorus (36). Royal Opera House, Covent Garden, London WC2E 9DD *tel:* 0171 240 1200 *fax:* 0171 212 9444. Terry Edwards, chorus dir; Richard Sadler, mgr.

Royal Scottish National Orchestra Chorus (190). 73 Claremont St, Glasgow G3 7HA *tel:* 0141 226 3868 *fax:* 0141 221 4317 *email:* rsno@glasgow.almac.co.uk; http://www.scot-art.org/rsno. Christopher Bell, chorus master; Jill Mitchell, chorus mgr.

St John's College Choir (16+14). St John's College, Cambridge CB2 1TP *tel:* 01223 338612/338765 *fax:* 01223 337720. Christopher Robinson, choir master.

St Michael's Singers (25). St Michael's Vestry, Cornhill, London EC3V 9DS *tel:* 0181 658 9428 *also fax*; 0171 626 8841. Jonathan Rennert, mus dir.

Schola Cantorum of Oxford (30-40). c/o Faculty of Music, St Aldates, Oxford OX1 1DB *tel:* 01865 276147 *fax:* 01865 276128. Mark Shepherd, cond; Kathryn Whitney, sec.

Scottish Chamber Orchestra Chorus (60). 4 Royal Terrace, Edinburgh EH7 5AB *tel:* 0131 557 6800 *fax:* 0131 557 6933 *email:* http://www. sco.org.uk. Ben Parry, chorus master; Richard Hyder, admin.

Scottish Opera Chorus (34). Scottish Opera, 39 Elmbank Cres, Glasgow G2 4PT *tel:* 0141 248 4567 *fax:* 0141 221 8812. David Jones, chorus master.

Sheffield Philharmonic Chorus (150). 15 Lumley Dr, Tickhill, Doncaster DN11 9QE *tel:* 01302 742049. Paul Tennant, gen sec; Keith Alford, chmn; Darius Battiwalla, chorus master.

The Sinfonia Chorus (60). The Sinfonia Centre, 41 Jesmond Vale, Newcastle upon Tyne NE2 1PG *tel:* 0191 240 1812 *fax:* 0191 240 2668. Alan Fearon, chorus master.

The Sixteen (16+). First Floor, Enslow House, Station Rd, Enslow, Kidlington, Oxon OX5 3AX *tel:* 01869 331544 *fax:* 01869 331011 *email:* info@thesixteen.org.uk. Gijs Elsen, gen mgr; Harry Christophers, cond; Alison Stillman, admin.

South West Chamber Choir (32). Melbury House, The Crescent, Crapstone, Yelverton, Devon PL20 7PS *tel:* 01822 855201 *also fax*. Michael Johnson, cond; Janet Clarke, sec.

Southampton Choral Society (120). Cwch House, Leep La, Alverstoke, Gosport, Hants PO12 2BE *tel:* 01705 528122. Derek Goodger, mus dir; W I M Dow.

Tallis Chamber Choir (15-60). c/o 13 Albury St, London SE8 3PT *tel:* 0181 691 8337 *also fax*. Philip Simms, dir; Deborah Sandringham, admin.

Taverner Choir and Consort (5-30). Taverner Concerts Ltd, Ibex House, 42-46 Minories, London EC3N 1DY *tel:* 0171 481 2103 *fax:* 0171 481 2865. Andrew Parrott, artistic dir; Malcolm Bruno, associate dir; Victoria Newbert, admin.

Thames Philharmonic Choir (90-100). 7a Cromford Rd, London SW18 1NZ *tel:* 0181 870 8154 *also fax*. John Bate, artistic dir.

Thomas Tallis Society (40+). 13 Albury St, London SE8 3PT *tel:* 0181 691 8337 *also fax*. Philip Simms, dir; Deborah Sandringham, sec.

University of Warwick Chorus (350). Music Centre, University of Warwick, Coventry CV4 7AL *tel:* 01203 523799 *fax:* 01203 528136 *email:* musac@warwick.ac.uk; http://www.warwick.ac.uk/~music/. Colin Touchin, cond; Stuart Dunlop, asst cond.

Vasari Singers (25-35). 89 Dovercourt Rd, Dulwich, London SE22 8UW *tel:* 0181 693 5498 *fax:* 0181 690 4462 *email:* http://ourworld. compuserve.com/homepages/rudcuff/vasari.htm. Jeremy Backhouse, cond; Julia Field, admin.

Welsh National Opera Chorus (40). Welsh National Opera, John St, Cardiff CF1 4SP *tel:* 01222 464666. Gareth Jones, chorus master.

Westminster Cathedral Choir (28-32). 42 Francis St, London SW1P 1QW *tel:* 0171 798 9066/9057 *fax:* 0171 798 9091. James O'Donnell, master of mus.

Whitehall Choir (80). 4 North Way, Pinner, Middx HA5 3NY *tel:* 0181 866 4931. Lis Warren, chmn.

Winchester Cathedral Choir (20+12). David Hill, org and choirmaster; Stephen Farr, sub-org. *Chameleon*

The Wooburn Singers (60). 14 Copperfields, Beaconsfield, Bucks HP9 2NS *tel:* 01494 672287 *also fax*. Stephen Jackson, mus dir; J E Robinson, sec.

Worcester Festival Choral Society (206). The Cedars, 171 Oldbury Rd, Worcester WR2 6AR. Adrian Lucas, mus dir; Marjorie Potts, sec.

Wren Singers of London. Wren Music, 8 Park La, Selsey, Chichester, W Sussex PO20 0HD *tel:* 01243 604281 *fax:* 01243 604387 *email:* starmus @brainlink.com. Martin Elliott, artistic dir; Peter Beaven, asst dir.

Yorkshire Bach Choir (35). 11 Bootham Terrace, York YO3 7DH *tel:* 01904 652799 *fax:* 01904 338349. Peter Seymour, cond.

The Zemel Choir (55-60). 5 Gable Lodge, 17-19 Torrington Pk, North Finchley, London N12 9TB *tel:* 0181 343 9819 *fax:* 0181 933 6375. Peter Pollak, business mgr; Robert Max, mus dir.

Military and Brass Bands

Military Bands

Most bands of the armed forces are standard 'military bands' of woodwind, brass and percussion (double bass is usually added when not on the march). The police, fire service and Royal British Legion have military bands and also some bands that follow the format of a conventional brass band. Some of the bands may also be able to provide orchestras. The list below consists of the best-known bands and their music directors, preceded by the address of their particular school of music.

Army

Royal Military School of Music Kneller Hall. Headquarters CAMus, Twickenham, Middx TW2 7DU *tel:* 0181 898 5533 ext 8625 *fax:* 0181 893 8746. Lt Col S A Watts LRAM psm, principal dir of mus.

Household Cavalry
Band of The Life Guards. Combermere Barracks, Windsor, Berks SL4 3DN *tel:* 01753 755209 *fax:* 01753 755281. Maj M J Torrent LTCL LGSM psm, dir of mus.
The Blues & Royals (Royal Horse Guards and 1st Dragoons). Hyde Park Barracks, Knightsbridge, London SW7 1SE *tel:* 0171 414 2525 *fax:* 0171 414 2599. Maj C R C Garrity LTCL psm, dir of mus. *From Apr 1998: Capt R J Owen ARCM psm, dir of mus.*

Royal Artillery
Royal Artillery Band. Royal Artillery Band Rooms, RA Barracks, Woolwich, London SE18 4BB *tel:* 0181 854 1508 *fax:* 0181 781 3178. Maj G A Kingston psm RA, dir of mus.

Royal Engineers
Band of the Corps of Royal Engineers (RE Band). Brompton Barracks, Chatham, Kent ME4 4UG *tel:* 01634 822321 *fax:* 01634 822837. Capt A R Chatburn ARCM psm, dir of mus.

Royal Signals
Band of the Royal Corps of Signals. School of Signals, Blandford Camp, Blandford Forum, Dorset DT11 8RH *tel:* 01258 482425; 01258 482445 *also fax.* Maj D F Wall LTCL BBCM psm, dir of mus.

Infantry: Guards Division
Coldstream Guards. Wellington Barracks, Birdcage Walk, London SW1E 6HQ *tel:* 0171 930 4466 ext 3269; 0171 414 3269 *fax:* 0171 414 3399. Maj D J Marshall ARCM LTCL BBCM psm, dir of mus.
Grenadier Guards. Wellington Barracks, Birdcage Walk, London SW1E 6HQ *tel:* 0171 414 3267 *fax:* 0171 414 3236. Maj P E Hills FLCM psm, dir of mus.
Irish Guards. Chelsea Barracks, London SW1W 8RF *tel:* 0171 414 4519 *fax:* 0171 414 4349. Maj M J Henderson, dir of mus.
Scots Guards Band. Wellington Barracks, Birdcage Walk, London SW1E 6HQ *tel:* 0171 414 3266 *fax:* 0171 414 3011. Lt Col D E Price, dir of mus.
Welsh Guards. Chelsea Barracks, London SW1W 8RF *tel:* 0171 414 4516 *fax:* 0171 414 4530. Maj T S Davis FTLC ARCM psm, dir of mus.

Miscellaneous Staff Bands
Band of the Adjutant General's Corps. Armstrong Block, AGC Centre, Winchester, Hants SO21 2RG *tel:* 01962 887717 *fax:* 01962 887720. Maj C J Reeves LTCL psm, dir of mus.
Band of the Army Air Corps. School of Army Aviation, Middle Wallop, Stockbridge, Hants SO20 8DY *tel:* 01980 674545. Capt P R Clark psm AAC, dir of mus.
Band of the Brigade of Gurkhas. Queen Elizabeth Barracks, Church Crookham, Fleet, Hants GU13 0RJ *tel:* 01252 355171 *also fax.* Capt D D Robertson psm CAMus, dir of mus.

Band of the Corps of Royal Electrical and Mechanical Engineers. Rowcroft Barracks, Arborfield, Reading, Berks RG2 9NL *tel:* 0118 976 3279 *fax:* 0118 976 3466. Capt Ian R Peaple LRSM, dir of mus.
Band of the Royal Lancers. Stanley Barracks, Bovington Camp, Wareham, Dorset BH20 6JB *tel:* 01929 403339/403429 *fax:* 01929 403217. Capt D Burton ARCM psm, dir of mus.
Band of the Royal Logistic Corps. The Princess Royal Barracks, Deepcut, Camberley, Surrey GU16 6RW *tel:* 01252 340628 *also fax.* Maj S J Smith ARCM LRSM psm CAMus, dir of mus.

Regimental Bands
The Band of The Dragoon Guards. Barker Barracks, BFPO 22 *tel:* 00 49 525 110 1225 *also fax.* Capt C C Gray ARCM BBCM psm, dir of mus.
Band of the Hussars and Light Dragoons. York Barracks, BFPO 17 *tel:* 00 49 251 927 2427 *fax:* 00 49 251 927 2426. Capt D W Cresswell BBCM psm, dir of mus.
Band of the Light Division. Sir John Moore Barracks, Winchester, Hants SO22 6NQ *tel:* 01962 888315/888282 *fax:* 01962 888285. Capt G Jones, dir of mus.
Band of the Parachute Regiment. New Normandy Barracks, Aldershot, Hants GU11 2LZ *tel:* 01252 347644 *also fax.* Capt I D McElligott, dir of mus.
The Band of the Prince of Wales's Division (Clive). Clive Barracks, Tern Hill, Market Drayton, Shrops TF9 3QE *tel:* 01630 698270/698273 *fax:* 01630 698233. Capt P D Shannon MBE ARCM LRAM psm, dir of mus.
Band of the Prince of Wales Division (Lucknow). Jellalabad Barracks, Tidworth, Hants SP9 7AB *tel:* 01980 602814/602852/602853 *fax:* 01980 602831. Capt J A C Huggins ARCM psm, dir of mus.
The Band of the Royal Irish Regiment. St Patrick's Barracks, Ballymena, BFPO 808 *tel:* 01266 661122 *fax:* 01266 661262. Capt C C Attrill psm, dir of mus.
Highland Band of the Scottish Division. Dreghorn Barracks, Redford Rd, Edinburgh EH13 9QW *tel:* 0131 310 2735. Capt G D Rodger LRAM ARCM psm, dir of mus.
The King's Division Normandy Band. Weeton Barracks, Preston PR4 3JQ *tel:* 01772 260942 *fax:* 01772 260944. Capt K Hatton FTCL ARCM psm, dir of mus.
King's Division Waterloo Band. Marne Barracks, Catterick, Richmond, N Yorks DL10 7NP *tel:* 01748 875860/1 *fax:* 01748 875862. Capt C E Hicks LRAM ARCM LTCL psm, dir of mus.
Lowland Band of the Scottish Division. Edinburgh Training Centre, Collington Rd, Cavalry Barracks, Edinburgh EH13 0PP *tel:* 0131 310 5325 *fax:* 0131 310 5288. Capt G O Jones MBE ARCM psm, dir of mus.
Minden Band. The Queen's Division, Oakington Barracks, Longstanton, Cambridge CB4 5EJ *tel:* 01223 205555 *fax:* 01223 205559. Capt C R Meldrum LRSM ARCM ALCM psm, dir of mus.
Normandy Band of the Queen's Division. Piave Lines, Leyburn Rd, Catterick Garrison, N Yorks DL9 3LR *tel:* 01748 874805 *fax:* 01748 874900. Capt J W Taylor ARCM ALCM BBCM psm CAM, dir of mus.
Royal Tank Regiment Cambrai Band. Lumsden Barracks, BFPO 38 *tel:* 00 49 5162 6324 *fax:* 00 49 5162 6561. Capt D D Robertson psm CAMus, dir of mus.

Royal Air Force

Headquarters Music Services. RAF Uxbridge, Middx UB10 0RZ *tel:* 01895 237144 ext 6291 *fax:* 01895 810846. Wg Cdr R E Wilkinson LRAM ARCM RAF, principal dir of mus. *All booking enquiries for RAF bands and mus services should be directed to the Engagement Co-ordinator at the above address. This covers the Central Band of the RAF, The Band of the RAF Regiment, the Band of the RAF College, The*

Western Band of the RAF, the RAF Squadronnaires (Big Band), Fanfare Trumpeters and smaller ensembles including the Salon Orchestra of the RAF.
Band of the Royal Air Force College. Cranwell, Sleaford, Lincs NG34 8HB *tel:* 01400 261201 ext 6040/6053. Flt Lt D J G Stubbs ARCM LGSM, dir of mus.

Band of the RAF Regiment. RAF Uxbridge, Middx UB10 0RZ *tel:* 01895 237144 ext 6376 *fax:* 01895 239306. Flt Lt D W Compton, dir of mus.

Central Band of the RAF. Uxbridge, Middx UB10 0RZ *tel:* 01895 237144 ext 6344 *fax:* 01895 810846. Sqn Ldr R K Wiffin, dir of mus.

Western Band of the RAF. RAF Locking, Weston-Super-Mare, N Somerset BS24 7AA *tel:* 01934 822131 ext 7293. Flt Lt G J Bain LRAM ARCM MIL RAF, dir of mus.

Royal Marines

Royal Marines School of Music. HMS Nelson, Queen St, Portsmouth PO1 3HH *tel:* 01705 726161 *fax:* 01705 726169. Lt Col R A Waterer LRAM, principal dir of mus.

Dartmouth: Band of HM Royal Marines. Britannia Royal Naval College, Dartmouth, Devon TQ6 0HJ *tel:* 01803 832141 ext 7189; 01803 835788 *also fax.* Lt P F Watson LRAM ARCM RM, dir of mus.

Exmouth: Band of HM Royal Marines. Commando Training Centre Royal Marines, Lympstone, Devon EX8 5AR *tel:* 01392 414138 *fax:* 01392 414149. Lt A D Henderson LRAM, dir of mus.

Plymouth: Band of HM Royal Marines. HMS *Raleigh*, Torpoint, Cornwall PL11 2PD *tel:* 01752 811297 *also fax.* Capt P J Rutterford LRAM ARCM, dir of mus.

Portsmouth: Band of HM Royal Marines. HMS *Nelson*, Portsmouth, Hants PO1 3HH *tel:* 01705 864069; 01705 876943 *also fax.* Capt D Cole ARAM, dir of mus.

Rosyth: Band of HM Royal Marines Scotland. HMS *Caledonia*, Rosyth, Fife KY11 2XH *tel:* 01383 425418 *also fax.* Lt C J Davis LRAM RM, dir of mus.

Police Force

Band of the Nottinghamshire Constabulary. Public Relations Office, Sherwood Lodge, Arnold, Nottingham NG5 8PP *tel:* 0115 967 2626 *fax:* 0115 967 2642. Gary Glover, sec.

Essex Police Band. Police HQ, PO Box 2, Springfield, Chelmsford, Essex CM2 6DA *tel:* 01245 491491. Bill Brightmore, band sec.

Garda (Irish Police) Band. Garda HQ, Garda Depot, Phoenix Pk, Dublin 8, Republic of Ireland *tel:* 00 353 1 677 1156 exts 2040-2044 *fax:* 00 353 1 679 5180. Superintendent J King, dir of mus.

Greater Manchester Police Band. Police Training School, Sedgley Pk, Manchester M25 8JT *tel:* 0161 856 2243 *fax:* 0161 856 2259. Capt M S Hennis SB St J ARCM, dir of mus.

Royal Ulster Constabulary Police Band. Community Affairs Branch, 42 Montgomery Rd, Belfast BT6 9LD *tel:* 01232 650222 ext 24091 *fax:* 01232 700589. Superintendent T King.

Fire Service

Band of the West Midlands Fire Service. Lancaster Circus, Queensway, Birmingham B4 7DE *tel:* 0121 380 6724 *fax:* 0121 380 7007. Wendy Williams, band mgr.

Suffolk Fire Service Band. Fire Service HQ, Colchester Rd, Ipswich, Suffolk IP4 4SS *tel:* 01473 588888 *fax:* 01473 558999. A Brock, chmn.

Royal British Legion

Central Band of The Royal British Legion. 4 Christopher Way, Emsworth, Hants PO10 7QZ *tel:* 01243 379594 *also fax.* Capt E P Whealing MVO, dir of mus. *For information on other Royal British Legion Bands throughout the country contact the above address.*

Central Band of the Royal British Legion Scotland. New Haig House, Logie Green Rd, Edinburgh EH7 4HR *tel:* 0131 557 2782; 01764 654988 *fax:* 0131 557 5819. Capt B H S Rodgers LRAM ARCM, dir of mus.

Maghull Town Band (The Band of the Royal British Legion in Maghull). Beech Lodge, 51 Burscough Rd, Ormskirk, Lancs L39 2XE *tel:* 01695 572150. Bill Casey, sec.

Poynton Royal British Legion Concert Band. 24 Fawns Keep, Wilmslow Park, Wilmslow, Cheshire SK9 2BQ *tel:* 01625 520243. Peter Leary, mus dir.

Brass Bands

The following bands compete in various championships ('contesting bands'); their competition successes since 1996 and the section in which they will compete in 1998 are shown in italics. The number of members is given in parenthesis. Additional information can be obtained from the **British Brass Band Registry** (c/o PO Box 349, Halifax, W Yorks HX3 5YJ *tel:* 01422 252245, Anthea Whittaker). For details and dates of the brass band competitions *see* **Competitions UK.**

The **British Federation of Brass Bands** (17 Kiln Way, Badgers Dene, Grays, Essex RM17 5JE *tel:* 01375 375831) publishes a directory of British Brass Bands. *The British Bandsman,* a weekly publication, is available form Harold Charles House, 64a London End, Beaconsfield, Bucks HP9 2JD *tel:* 01494 674411 *fax:* 01494 670932. *Brass Band World,* a monthly publication, is available form Caron Publications, Peak Press Building, Eccles Rd, Chapel-en-le-Frith, High Peak SK23 9RQ *tel:* 01298 812816 *fax:* 01298 815220.

Aldbourne Band (34). Mayfield, 18 Lottage Rd, Aldbourne, Marlborough, Wilts SN8 2ED *tel:* 01672 540863. David Williams, mus dir; Mrs J Palmer, sec. *1st section. Milton Keynes (1st); Stroud (1st); Weston Super Mare (1st).*

Armthorpe Elmfield Band (40). 36 Fernbank Dr, Armthorpe, Doncaster DN3 2HB *tel:* 01302 831646. Haydn Griffiths, mus dir. *3rd section. Yorkshire Area.*

The Aveley Band (30). 49 Rowley Rd, Orset, Essex. Robert Nunnery, sec; Melvyn White, mus dir; David Whitson, resident mus dir. *Championship section. 1996: Brighton Spring Festival champions; SCABA Crawley champions.*

Banavallum Brass (Horncastle) Band. Oriana, Bowl Alley Lane, Horncastle, Lincs LN9 54EQ. Miss W Sharp, treasurer; Elizabeth White, cond; Mark Tong, sec. *4th section.*

Barnton Silver Band (35). 1 Rowan Rise, Barnton, Northwich, Cheshire CW8 4WZ *tel:* 01606 40103 *fax:* 01606 724100 *email:* steve@ yatesenterprises.demon.co.uk. S A Yates, mus dir; C Ravenscroft, bandmaster; K Hodgkinson, sec. *1st section.*

Beaumaris and District Silver Band (100). East Lodge, Henllys La, Beaumaris, Gwynedd LL58 8HU *tel:* 01248 811538. R Kingman, sec; G Evans, cond. *Championship section. 1996: N Wales area (1st). 1997: Welsh Regional Qualifiers (1st).*

Bedwas Trethomas and Machen Band (BTM). 30 Hazelhurst Rd, Llandaff North, Cardiff *tel:* 01222 568019. Dewi Jones, sec.

Besses o' th' Barn Band (30). 7 Yew Tree Grove, Lostock Hall, Preston PR5 5NP *tel:* 01772 316908. Jean Heyes, sec; Derek Broadbent, mus dir; Steven Beardmore, resident mus dir. *Championship section. 1996: All England Masters; British Open and South Somerset Entertainment Contest, runners up.*

Black Dyke Mills Band (31). Black Dyke Band (1855) Ltd, Bandroom, Sandbeds, Queensbury, Bradford BD13 1AB *tel:* 01274 814970 *fax:* 01274 882264. James Watson, mus dir; Robert Childs, cond; Geoffrey Whiteley, admin. *1996: National champions.*

Blackburn and Darwen Band (35). 19 Ainsworth Hall Rd, Ainsworth, Bolton, Lancs BL2 5RY *tel:* 01204 526743. C Harrison, contest sec; Mrs C Baxter, band sec; Alan Widdop, cond. *1st section. 1997: area contest; Buxton contest; Rhyl contest.*

Blackley Band (25). 50b Chapelhill Dr, Blackley, Manchester M9 8FJ *tel:* 0161 795 9494; 01625 520243 *also fax.* Peter Leary, mus dir. *3rd section. Manchester and District (3rd); Buxton Contest (1st).*

Blaina Band (48). 40 Abertillery Rd, Blaina, Gwent NP3 3DW *tel:* 01495 290549. Bernard Williams, mus dir; Lesley Bradley, sec. *1st section. Regional Contest at Aberystwth (3rd); Ebbw Vale (2nd).*

The Bodmin Town Band (30). 5 Lower Cleaverfield, Launceston, Cornwall PL15 8ED *tel:* 01566 774903. Howard Taylor, cond; Mrs V A Dobson, sec. *Championship section. 1996: South West Area; Cornwall Brass Band; Grand Shield; Whit Marches; West of England Bandsmans Festival.*

Boldon Colliery Brass Band (35). 20 Penhill Close, Ouston, Chester-le-Street, Co Durham DH2 1SF *tel:* 0191 410 9423. S Malcolm, mus dir; M Burr, sec. *Championship section. Buxton Brass Band Festival; Wansbeck Entertainment contest; Whit Friday Marches.*

Brighton Silver Band (35). 18 Flower Farm Close, Henfield, Sussex BN5 9QA *tel:* 01273 493469 *also fax.* Sian Buss, sec; Estelle Flood, mus dir; Geoffery Enefer, chmn. *1st section. National championships (1st); London and Southern counties, 2nd section.*

Britannia (Foden) Band. c/o 26 Horsefair Av, Chapel-en-le-Frith, High Peak SK23 9SQ *tel:* 01298 812591. Nicholas Childs, mus dir; G Preston, treasurer. *1995: Swiss Open champions.*

British Steel Teesside Band (30). 12 Berkley Dr, Guisborough, Cleveland TS14 7LX *tel:* 01287 635029. Jayne Batemen, gen sec; Colin Johnson, contest sec; John Roberts, professional cond; Alan Boyer, resident cond. *Championship section. 1997: Grand Shield (5th); Isle of Wight Entertainment Contest (1st); Rhyl Entertainment Contest (2nd).*

Broxburn Public Band (40). 40 Station Rd, Broxburn, W Lothian EH52 5QX *tel:* 01506 852144. T White, sec; Michael Marzella, cond; D W Anderson, treasurer; A Chalmers, president. *Championship section. Scottish Championship winners, 1st section.*

Camborne Town Band (28). 1 Harveys Way, Hayle, Cornwall TR27 4PE *tel:* 01736 753779. Ruth Richards, sec; Philip Robinson, chmn. *Championship section. 1996: West of England Bandmen's Festival (2nd).*

Chapeltown Silver Prize Band (35). 66 Glenwood Cres, Chapeltown, Sheffield S35 1YX *tel:* 0114 246 0983. Mrs M Bryan, sec; N Kirk, president; John Kendall, mus dir. *1st section.*

City of Birmingham (28). 65 Beeches Dr, Erdington, Birmingham B24 0DT *tel:* 0121 373 7237. Miss B J Dunscombe, sec and treasurer; Warren Belshaw, mus dir. *2nd section. 1996: Milton Keynes; Stroud; Midlands Region; West Midlands Brass Band Association. 1997: Midlands Region.*

City of Stoke-on-Trent Brass Band (35). 2 Whitnall Dr, Shabington, nr Crewe, Cheshire *tel:* 01270 663286; 01782 332988. Lindsey Laurie, mus dir; Derek Swindel, chmn; Helen Twiss, sec. *2nd section.*

Cosham Concert Brass Band (27). 9 The Tithe, Denmead, Waterlooville, Hants PO7 6XU *tel:* 01705 257867/834040 *fax:* 01705 834076. Brian Partridge, cond; Ted Howard, sec. *2nd section. 1996: Wessex (3rd). 1997: Regionals (2nd).*

Crystal Palace Band (35). 26 Clock House Rd, Beckenham, Kent BR3 4JP *tel:* 0181 658 9659 *email:* angela@cua.ulsop.ac.uk. Rachel Bleach, hon sec; Michael Gray, mus dir. *3rd section. Southern Counties ABA 1st section; London & Southern Counties 3rd section.*

Cwmaman Institute Silver Band (30). 3 Foundry View, Godreaman, Aberdare, Mid Glamorgan CF44 6DW *tel:* 01685 879326. D Jones. *Championship section.*

David A Hall Whitburn Band (40). Cumloden, Fauldhouse, W Lothian EH47 9EL *tel:* 01501 771616. Maj Peter Parkes, mus adviser and hon president; A Simpson, sec. *Championship section. Scottish champions.*

David Urquart Travel Yorkshire Imperial (28). 10 Mitchell Rd, Prescot, Merseyside L34 1LJ *tel:* 0151 430 6520. Bernard Logan, mgr. *Championship section. 1995: Spennymoor champions.*

Denham Brass Band (28). 5 Plover Close, Berkhamstead HP4 2HH *tel:* 01442 870572. Alan Goodall, cond; Lindsey Davies, sec. *1st section. Winners of Harrow contest; Basildon area contest (3rd).*

Dobcross Silver Band (28). 16 Bury St, Mossley OL5 9ND *tel:* 01457 836223. F Hanley, president; Mrs J Lawless, sec; Mark Owen, mus dir. *1st section.*

Dodworth Colliery Band (35). 12 Meadow Croft, Outwood, Wakefield, W Yorks WF1 3TF *tel:* 01924 870981. G O'Conno, cond/mus dir; A Leicester, sec. *Championship section. Amber Valley Entertainment (1st); Grand Shield; Yorkshire Area Contest.*

Easington Colliery Band (35). 3 Brougham Ct, Oakerside Pk, Peterlee, Co Durham SR8 1PS *tel:* 0191 587 2886. Peter Lawson, band sec; Keith Watson, band chmn; John Bell, mus dir. *Championship section.*

Elland Silver Band (34). 7 Elland Hall Farm, Exley La, Elland, W Yorks HX5 0SN *tel:* 01422 370880. Mrs K Harrison, sec; John Harrison, mus dir; K Billington, treasurer. *2nd section. 1996: Yorkshire Area (2nd); Pogson Bray Trust Contest (1st). 1997: Yorkshire area (6th); Pogson Bray Trust Contest (2nd).*

Ever Ready Band (35). 1 Goodrich Close, Lambton Rise, Philadelphia, Houghton-le-Spring, Tyne & Wear DH4 4XJ *tel:* 0191 512 0296 *fax:* 0191 512 0294 *email:* lesp@brkb11-agw.bt.com.uk. L J Palmer, band mgr; S Malcolm, bandmaster. *Championship section. 1996: Camerons Champions; Grimethorpe Entertainment Champions. 1997: Northern Area runners-up; Wansbeck contest champions.*

Friary Guildford Brass Band (30). 131 Arethusa Way, Bisley, Surrey GU24 9BT *tel:* 01483 480518. C Powell, sec; B Wassell, cond; B Gates, chmn. *Championship section. Yeovil Entertainment; Milton Keynes Entertainment; Crawley Entertainment. Folkestone, Brighton, Whit Friday.*

Frickley-South Elmsall Standard Fireworks Band (33). 1 Lincoln Cres, South Elmsall, Pontefract, W Yorks WF9 2TJ *tel:* 01977 643826. D Baxter, sec; B Till, chmn; L Price, mus dir. *3rd section. 1996: British Coal National Championships (1st in 3rd section); Cleethorpes Annual Entertainment Contest (1st in 2nd section).*

Fulham Brass Band (17). 6 Chaldon Rd, London SW6 7NJ *tel:* 0171 385 4092. Guy Dawes, band sec. *4th section. Sole remaining central London brass band.*

Gillingham Imperial Silver Band (37). 37 Bridgeclose, Gillingham, Dorset SP8 4LS *tel:* 01747 823550. N W Perrin, gen sec; R Sansom, contest sec; S F Tranter, mus dir. *1st section.*

Grimethorpe Colliery Band (29). Acorn Centre, 51 High St, Grimethorpe, Barnsley, S Yorks S72 7BB *tel:* 01226 780981 *also fax; email:* webmaster@cjohns43.demon.co.uk. Peter Parkes, mus dir; Garry Cutt, mus dir; Terry Webster, sec. *Championship section. Agent: Allied.*

Hadley Brass Band. c/o John Boddy Agency, 10 Southfield Gardens, Twickenham, Middx TW1 4SZ *tel:* 0181 892 0133; 0181 891 3809 *fax:* 0181 892 4283.

Hatherleigh Silver Band (35). 51 Market St, Hatherleigh, Devon EX20 3JP *tel:* 01837 810414. P Chandler, contest sec; R A Wonnacott, cond; Rachael Green, band sec. *3rd section. Bristol Area; SWBB Annual; Bandsmens Festival.*

Horden Colliery Band. Cliffe Villa, Coastroad, Blackhall Rocks, Hartlepool TS27 4AN. W McDonald; Wilf Beddell, cond; Basil Rice, chmn. *2nd section.*

Hyde Band (35). Latchmore, Furzehill, Fordingbridge, Hants SP6 2PU *tel:* 01425 653266 *fax:* 01425 475044. P Downer; Peter Wise, cond. *1st section. Area qualifying (7th in 1st section); SCABBA (Brighton).*

Ipswich Co-op Band (30). 4 Orchard Grove, Claydon, Ipswich, Suffolk IP6 0BZ *tel:* 01473 832242 *fax:* 01473 211417. Andrew Shipp, membership sec; Stephen Kenna, cond. *1st section. Watford Area; Milton Keynes Entertainment; Folkestone Open.*

JJB Sports Leyland Band *formerly* The BNFL Band (28). 15 Hugh Barn La, New Longton, Preston PR4 4XA *tel:* 01772 613238. Richard Evans, mus dir; Andrew Blackledge, band mgr. *Championship section.*

Kirkby Colliery Welfare Band (28). 31 Burton Rd, Stutton-in-Ashfield, Notts NG17 2EU *tel:* 01623 553715. Mrs V Wilkes, sec; Andrew Dennis, cond. *2nd section. 1997: Midlands area champions, 3rd section.*

Lewis Merthyr Brass Band (35). 24 Ynysfeio Av, Treherbert, Rhondda Cynon Taff CF42 5HE *tel:* 01443 772570. John Lewis, sec; Nigel G Seaman, cond. *Championship section. Aberystwyth Area (7th); SEWBBA competition Ebbw Vale (2nd); Stroud Entertainments Contest (3rd).*

Littleport Brass Band (35). 37 Angoods La, Chatteris, Cambs PE6 6RG *tel:* 01354 692247. Mrs C Frost, sec; Mark Kerridge, chmn; Mrs S Peacock, mus dir. *3rd section. 1996: 3rd section Watford National Area (5th).*

Long Melford Silver Band (25-30). Thorncroft Batt Hall, Bulmer, Sudbury, Suffolk CO10 7EZ *tel:* 01787 372439. M Gore, membership sec; Roger Green, cond.

Lydbrook Band (58). c/o Cheristow, Stowfield, Lydbrook, Glos GL17 9PD *tel:* 01594 860944 *fax:* 01594 860394. R Morgan, sec. *Championship section.*

Lydmet Lydney Band (30). 17 Warren Rd, Aschchurch Gardens, Tewkesbury *tel:* 01684 273184. Julie Jones, sec; Kevin White, mus dir. *Championship section.*

Marple Band (36). 21 Rushton Dr, Marple, Stockport *tel:* 0161 427 3612. Mrs E M Murphy, sec; Garry E Cutt, cond. *Championship section. 1996-7: British Open Champions. 1997-8: French Open Champions.*

Newtongrange Silver Band. 10 Park Rd, Newtongrange, Midlothian EH22 4JU *tel:* 0131 663 1430. Grant O'Connor, sec; Derek Broadbent, cond. *Championship section.*

Oldham Brass 97 (35). 9 The Sycamores, Lees, Oldham, Lancs OL4 3JP *tel:* 0161 620 7434. G Briggs, chmn. *3rd section.*

Ovington Tynedale Band (25). First Cottage, West View, Acomb, Hexham, Northumberland NE46 4PP *tel:* 01434 608469. P Rutherford, sec. *3rd section.*

Pendennis Brass Band (25). 10 Langton Rd, Falmouth, Cornwall TR11 2NH. M Thomas. *3rd section. 1996: West of England champions (4th section); South West champions (4th section); Cornish champions (3rd section); West of England Bandsman's Festival (3rd section).*

RAF St Athan Voluntary Band (40). RAF St Athan, Barry, Vale of Glamorgan CF62 4WA *tel:* 01446 797318; 0378 156568. Alan R Bourne, dir of mus. *2nd section.*

Ratby Co-Operative Band (108). 20 Mill Dr, Ratby, Leics *tel:* 0116 238 6954. Kevin Steward, mus dir; Sheralyn Newman, sec. *Championship section. 1996: North West Leics Brass Band Festival (1st). 1997: Midlands area champions, first section.*

Redbridge Brass (28). 31 Stanway Rd, South Menfleet, Essex SS7 5UX *tel:* 0873 313913 *email:* ajr@nortel.co.uk. Alan Roberts, sec; Graham Wilson, mus dir. *Championsip section. 1996: London & Southern Counties Area champions. Also quintet and 10-piece band available.*

Regent Brass (30). 114 Wheatlands, Heston, Middx TW5 0SD *tel:* 0181 577 1752 *fax:* 0181 937 3484. Karen Hunt, band sec; Paul Fensom, mus dir; Paul Cosh, artistic dir. *Championship section.*

Rigid Containers Group Band (28). 1 Knoll St, Market Harborough, Leics LE16 9QR *tel:* 01858 433408. Mrs L Hume, concert sec; J Berryman, mus dir. *Championship section. All England Masters; British Open; National Championships.*

Rothwell Temperance Band (34). 22 Knightscroft Drive, Rothwell, Leeds, W Yorks *tel:* 0113 282 5715. A Riley, sec; David Roberts, cond. *1st section. 1996: Yorkshire Area Championship 2nd section (1st). 1997: Yorkshire Area Championships 1st section (2nd).*

Runnymede Brass Band (35). 72 Nelson Road, Whitton, Twickenham, Middx TW2 7AU *tel:* 0181 898 5509 *also fax.* David E Loftus, hon sec. *2nd section. 1996: SCABA Spring Contest (2nd); SCABA Entertainment (4th). 1997: SCABA Spring Contest (best horn section).*

St Austell Kernow Band (100+). The Band Hall, East Hill, St Austell, Cornwall PL25 4TR *tel:* 01726 61008 *also fax;* 01726 69990. Trevor Hitchens, sec; Trevor Bedding, chmn. *Third section.*

St Austell Town Band (100+). The Band Hall, East Hill, St Austell, Cornwall PL25 4TR *tel:* 01726 61008 *also fax;* 01726 69990. Trevor Hitchens, sec; Trevor Bedding, chmn. *Championship section.*

St Dennis Band (28). Bayview, 71a Treverbyn Rd, St Austell, Cornwall PL25 4EW *tel:* 01726 64785. A I McAuley, sec; C Toghill, mus dir. *Championship section.*

Seindorf Trefor Band (30). Bethlehem, Trefor, Caernarfon, Gwynedd LL54 5HN *tel:* 01286 660340 *fax:* 01286 660622. D Roberts, sec; Geraint Jones, cond. *3rd section.*

Sellers Engineering Band (36). Sellers & Co (Huddersfield) Ltd, Chapel Hill, Huddersfield, W Yorks HD1 3EH *tel:* 01484 469620 *also fax;* 0410 311771. Alan Morrison, mus dir; David Johnson, treasurer; Paul Walton, sec. *Championship section. 1996: Swiss Open championships (2nd); All England Masters (4th).*

Skipton Brass Band (35). 21 Raikeswood Dr, Skipton, N Yorks BD23 1NA *tel:* 01756 798435/700200 *fax:* 01756 700186. Howard Lorriman, cond; C R Davies, sec. *Championship section. 1996: Cardiff Finals. 1997: Birmingham Finals, 1st section.*

South West Trains Woodfalls Band (30). Mere, Oak Dr, Alderbury, Salisbury, Wilts *tel:* 01722 710074 *email:* woodfallsband@geocities.com; http://www.geocities.com/vienna/2603. Brian Easterbrook, sec; M White, mus dir; D Hayward, resident cond. *Championship section. 1996: Pontins (runners up).*

Southampton Central Band (25). 8 Beechwood Cres, Chandler's Ford, Eastleigh, Hants SO53 5PA *tel:* 01703 254416. A J Hickson, sec; P Marnoch, cond. *2nd section. National Brass Band Championships, S W area finals.*

Staffordshire Building Society Band (35-40). 13 New St, Essington, Wolverhampton WV11 2BU *tel:* 01922 495254 *fax:* 01922 53726. Andy Culshaw, mus dir; Ian T Aulton, sec. *Championship section. Regional Qualifying (4th). 1997: Milton Keynes Entertainment Contest (1st).*

Stocksbridge Engineering Steels Band. 19 Hesley Bar, Thorpe Hesley, Rotheram S61 2PP *tel:* 0114 246 0981. A Goddard, sec.

Tredegar Band (35). 8 Dolwydellan Close, Grove Pk, Blackwood, Gwent NP2 1GG *tel:* 01495 226510. D Powell, band mgr; Nicholas Childs, cond; Nigel Seaman, resident cond. *Championship section. Champion Band of Wales; Radio Wales Band of the Year; South Somerset champions. British Open Welsh Championship, runners-up.*

Treherbert Silver Band (35). 35 Cardiff St, Treorci, Rhondda *tel:* 01443 775804. Mrs M Shewring, gen sec; Miss S Pritchard, contest sec. *2nd section. Welsh Regional Final (8th); Weston Contest (2nd); Ebbw Vale Contest (1st).*

Tylorstown Band - Valley Lines (33). c/o 23 Elizabeth St, Pentre, Mid Glamorgan CF41 7JN *tel:* 01443 442504. Mrs R Evans, sec; W H Taylor, chmn; L Harries, cond. *1st section.*

Uckfield Concert Brass (28). 7 Elm Drive, Hove, E Sussex BN3 7JS *tel:* 01273 882539 *email:* awooler@compuserve.com. Andy Wooler, resident cond. *1st section. National Area Contest; Southern Counties Amateur Bands Association spring contest.*

Unison Kinneil Band. 31 Ochilview Rd, Bo'ness, W Lothian EH51 0LD *tel:* 01506 827761. Robert Doherty, sec. *Championship section.*

Unity Brass Band (50+). 157 Old Ashby Rd, Loughborough, Leics LE11 4PQ *tel:* 01509 233933. Mrs S McEntee. *1st and 4th section.*

Wansbeck's Ashington Colliery Band. 98 Burnside, North Seaton, Ashington, Northumberland NE63 9UF *tel:* 01670 812823. J Dunn. *2nd section.*

Williams Fairey Band (28). Fairey Engineering Ltd, PO Box 41, Crossley Rd, Heaton Chapel, Stockport SK4 5BD *tel:* 0161 432 0281 *fax:* 0161 431 3575. James Gourlay, mus dir; John Cresswell, mgr. *Championship section. 1997: North West area champions.*

Wingates Band. 1 Foxglove Close, Wistaston, Crewe, Cheshire CW2 6UD *tel:* 01270 69183 *also fax.* T R Davies, sec. *Championship section. 1996: Grand Shield (1st). 1997: All England Masters (runners up).*

Yeovil Town Band (45). 71 St Michaels Rd, Yeovil, Somerset BA21 5AH *tel:* 01935 471604. A J Lock, sec; S Syke, mus dir. *1st section. 1996: West of England Champions (3rd section); Western-Super-Mare 3rd Section winners; National Champions of Great Britain 3rd section; Wessex Winter Contest (winners 3rd section). 1997: Milton Keynes Entertainment Contest 2nd section; West of England Champions (2nd section).*

Yiewsley & West Drayton Band (24). 10 Church Rd, W Drayton, Middx *tel:* 01895 420007. I Carter, sec; C Cole, mus dir. *4th section.*

Yorkshire Building Society Band (28). 21 Leafield Dr, Eccleshill, Bradford, W Yorks BD2 3RX *tel:* 01274 632676 *fax:* 01274 627122 *email:* rbuo8@dial.pipex.com; http://www.ybs.co.uk/r_band.htm. David King, principal cond; Richard Hirst, band mgr. *Championship section. 1996: European champions. 1997: European champions.*

Agents and Managers

Artists wishing to register with a concert agency or artist management company should be aware of what services an agent or manager can provide. All those listed below may assist with the administration of engagements already secured by the performer. Additionally, agents may find work on behalf of the artists they represent, and may also undertake to provide an employer (eg opera house, music club) with artists for a given performance. The agencies listed below all represent two or more classical artists or groups within the UK.

The **Incorporated Society of Musicians** at 10 Stratford Pl, London W1N 9AE *tel:* 0171 629 4413 publishes an information sheet, free to members, on the artist/agent relationship and how to approach an agent or manager.

Most artist managers and concert agents are members of the **International Artist Managers' Association** (*formerly* BACA), 41a Lonsdale Rd, London W11 2BY *tel:* 0171 243 2598, indicated here by an asterisk.

Agents' Abbreviations

CDI	Concert Directory International	OCA	Opera and Concert Artists
DCM	Daniels Concert Management	OWM	Owen/White Management
GIA	Georgina Ivor Associates	PA	Performing Arts
HP	Harrison Parrott	PGM	Patrick Garvey Management
JLM	Jonathan Land Management	SS	Simply Singers
KDM	Karen Durant Management	SWA	Stephannie Williams Artists
LA	London Artists	THA	Terry Harrison Artists Management
LM	London Musicians	VWM	Van Walsum Management
NBM	NB Management	WWA	World Wide Artists
NCCP	Neil Chaffey Concert Promotions	YCAT	Young Concert Artists Trust
NWA	N W Artists		

Alexander European Management. 38 Lytton Grove, Putney, London SW15 2HB *tel:* 0181 780 9377 *fax:* 0181 788 1481. David Bartleet, dir.

* **Allied Artists Agency.** 42 Montpelier Sq, London SW7 1JZ *tel:* 0171 589 6243 *fax:* 0171 581 5269. Andrew Rosner, Robert Slotover, partners.

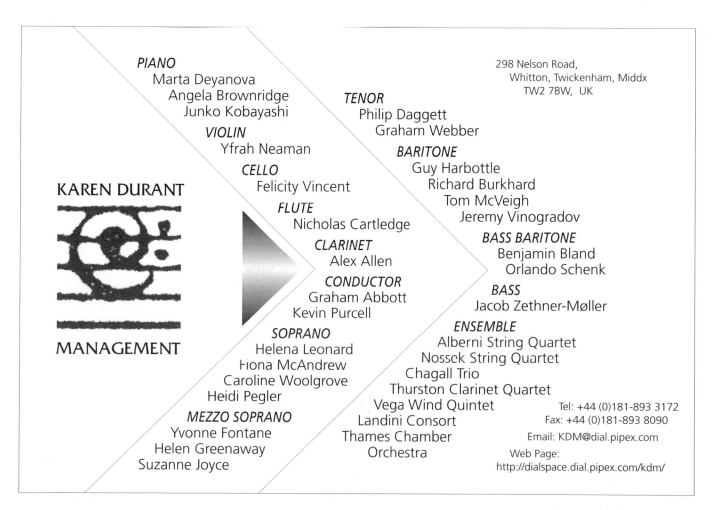

ARTISTS' LIST 1997/98

CONDUCTORS

Dietfried Bernet	W
Noel Davies	W
Simone Fermani	W
Andrew Greenwood	W
Hilary Griffiths	W*
James Kelleher	W
Jiri Kout	W*
Cem Mansur	W
Stewart Robertson	E + Sundry Terr.
Donald Runnicles	□
David Syrus	W

ENSEMBLES

The Gabrieli Consort	W
Concerto Grosso	W
Ensemble 415	W

SOPRANOS

Maria Abajan	W*
Georgina Benza	W
Elena Brilova	W
Eirian Davies	W
Dilber	W*
Giovanna Doñadini	W*
Helen Field	W
Jacquelyn Fugelle	W
Juliette Galstian	W
Cornelia Götz	W
Cynthia Haymon	W
Katerina Kudriavchenko	W
Amy Lawrence	W
Karen Notare	E
Nina Pavlovski	W
Rosalind Plowright	W
Claire Primrose	W
Ashley Putnam	W (ex USA/Can)
Soya Smolyaninova	W
Anita Soldh	W
Penelope Thorn	W
Christine Weidinger	W

MEZZO SOPRANOS

Joanna Campion	W
Angela Hickey	W
Stefania Kaluza	W*
Bärbel Müller	W
Ilia Aramayo Sandivari	W
Natascha Petrinsky	W (ex Ger. & Aust.)
Patricia Spence	W
Nuala Willis	W

W = GENERAL MANAGEMENT

□ = GB/SUNDRY TERRITORIES

E = EUROPE

* = NON EXCLUSIVE

STAGE DIRECTORS

Mike Ashman	W
Tim Coleman	W
John Dew	W
John Lloyd Davies	W
Michael McCaffery	W
John Pascoe	W
Keith Warner	W

TENORS

Ruben Amoretti	W*
Terje Andersen	W
Paolo Barbacini	W*
Evan Bowers	W
John Duykers	E
Francis Egerton	W
Bruce Ford	W (ex USA/Can)
Valentin Jar	W
Stuart Kale	W
Justin Lavender	W
Peter Lindroos	W
Herbert Lippert	W*
Mark Luther	W
Daniel Munoz	W
Jeremy O'Sullivan	W
Michael Pabst	W*
Patrick Power	W* (ex Aust.)
Ian Thompson	W
Kevin West	W
Bradley Williams	E
Alan Woodrow	W
Charles Workman	W
Cesare Zamparino	W
Boiko Zvetanov	W*

BARITONES

Sigmund Cowan	W (ex USA/Can)
Roderick Earle	W
Mark Glanville	W
Piero Guarnera	W*
John Hancock	E
Anthony Marber	W
Francesco Medda	W*
Giovanni Meoni	W*
Stephen Owen	W
Malcolm Rivers	W (ex USA/Can)
Andrew Rupp	W
Andrew Shore	W
Russell Smythe	W
Giovanni Tarasconi	W
David Wakeham	W

BASSES

Alan Ewing	W
Eric Garrett	W
Frode Olsen	W
John Rath	W
Tómas Tómasson	W

**ATHOLE STILL
INTERNATIONAL
MANAGEMENT LTD**

FORESTERS HALL
25-27 WESTOW STREET
LONDON SE19 3RY

TEL: 0181 771 5271 (6 LINES)
FAX: 0181 771 8172
E-MAIL ADDRESS:
ATHOLE@DIAL.PIPEX.COM

ATHOLE STILL
INTERNATIONAL MANAGEMENT LTD

Anglo-Swiss Artists' Management Ltd. Suite 35-37, Morley House, 320 Regent St, London W1R 5AD *tel:* 0171 323 2147 *fax:* 0171 323 1760. Susanne Baumgartner, artists' mgr; Leor Segal, consultant.

Annon Music Services - Anne Hancox. 44 Cromwell Rd, Canterbury CT1 3LE *tel:* 01227 463867 *also fax;* 0973 132402. Anne Hancox, mgr.

Anthony Abbott Music Management. Medlar Cottage, Lodge La, Keymer, Hassocks, W Sussex BN6 8NA *tel:* 01273 843348 *fax:* 01273 846585.

Anthony Purkiss. 35 Fonthill Rd, Hove, E Sussex BN3 6HB *tel:* 01273 774730 *also fax.*

Antony Pristavec Artist and Concert Management. 79 Norbury Cres, London SW16 4JT *tel:* 0181 679 0369 *fax:* 0181 679 9399. Antony Pristavec, dir.

Askonas *see* Lies Askonas Ltd.

* **Athole Still International Management Ltd.** Foresters Hall, 25-27 Westow St, London SE19 3RY *tel:* 0181 771 5271 *fax:* 0181 771 8172 *email:* athole@dial.pipex.com. Athole Still, mgr dir; Isobel Still, deputy mgr dir; Christopher Broom, Florence Brunel, Henry Little, Rosalba di Raimondo, artists mgrs.

Barber *see* Valerie Barber PR & Personal Management Ltd.

Blythe *see* Jennie Blythe Artists' Management.

Brunskill Management Ltd. Suite 8a, 169 Queens Gate, London SW7 5HE *tel:* 0171 581 3388 *fax:* 0171 589 9460 *email:* 101234.2025@ compuserve.com.

* **C & M Craig Services Limited (Mary Craig).** 3 Kersley St, London SW11 4PR *tel:* 0171 228 4855; 0171 978 4715 *fax:* 0171 223 2189.

Camerata Artists (International Artists Management). 4 Margaret Rd, Birmingham B17 0EU *tel:* 0121 426 6208 *also fax.* John Humphreys.

Caroline Ireland Management. Uwchlaw'r Coed, Llanbedr, Gwynedd LL45 2NA *tel:* 01341 241532 *also fax.*

* **Caroline Phillips Management** *formerly* Gonsalves Artists' Management. Tailor House, 63-65 High St, Whitwell, Herts SG4 8AH *tel:* 01438 871828 *fax:* 01438 871838. Caroline Phillips; Nadia Haidar, artists mgr.

Chameleon Arts Management. 32 St Michaels Rd, Sandhurst, Berks GU47 8HE *tel:* 01252 873313 *fax:* 01252 871517 *email:* camarts@dial. pipex.com. Andrew Phillips, Frances Dennys, partners.

Charles McK Finch Artists' Management. 23 Farm Rd, Morden, Surrey SM4 6RA *tel:* 0181 648 8852 *fax:* 0181 687 1741.

Charlton Concert Agency. Flat 2, 228 London Rd, Charlton Kings, Cheltenham, Glos GL52 6HW *tel:* 01242 244200 *also fax.* Richard Sharpe, Alison Sharpe, associates.

Chuck Julian Associates. Suite 51, 26 Charing Cross Rd, London WC2H 0DH *tel:* 0171 437 4248; 0171 240 1301 *fax:* 0171 240 1296. Chuck Julian, Sue Yager, Anita Alraun, associates.

* **Clarion/Seven Muses.** 47 Whitehall Pk, London N19 3TW *tel:* 0171 272 4413/5125/8448 *fax:* 0171 281 9687 *email:* c7m@dircon.co.uk. Nicholas Curry, Caroline Oakes, partners and artist mgrs; Alan Coates, senior artists mgr; Costas Peristianis, artistic asst.

Clifton Wyatt Artists Management. 1 Poets Rd, London N5 2SL *tel:* 0171 354 2050 *also fax; email:* cliftonwyattartistsmanagement@compuserve. com. Jacqueline Clifton, David Wyatt, dirs.

CMG Artists. 1st Floor, 105 Ferndale Rd, London SW4 7RL *tel:* 0171 207 3564 *fax:* 0171 652 0979 *email:* chris@cgrist.demon.co.uk; http://www. intune.co.uk/cmg/.

* **Columbia Artists Management Ltd.** 28 Cheverton Rd, London N19 3AY *tel:* 0171 272 8020 *fax:* 0171 272 8991. Judith Salpeter, dir.

Concert Directory International (CDI). Lyndhurst, Denton Rd, Ben Rhydding, Ilkley, W Yorks LS29 8QR *tel:* 01943 607821 *fax:* 01943 817063. Catherine Scott, dir.

* **Connaught Artists Management Ltd.** 39 Cathcart Rd, London SW10 9JG *tel:* 0171 376 7405 *fax:* 0171 352 7309 *email:* jill@connaught-artists. com. Jill Segal, Patrick Allen, dirs.

Craig *see* C & M Craig Services Limited (Mary Craig).

Cruickshank Cazenove Ltd. 97 Old South Lambeth Rd, London SW8 1XU *tel:* 0171 735 2933 *fax:* 0171 820 1081. Harriet Cruickshank, mgr dir. *Opera producers, choreographers and designers only.*

Daniels Concert Management (DCM). 63 Marlborough Mansions, Cannon Hill, London NW6 1JS *tel:* 0171 794 9108 *also fax.* M Daniels, dir.

* **Denny Lyster Artists' Management.** 25 Courthope Rd, London NW3 2LE *tel:* 0171 485 5932 *fax:* 0171 267 0179. Denny Lyster, dir.

Donald Scrimgeour. 49 Springcroft Av, London N2 9JH *tel:* 0181 444 6248 *fax:* 0181 883 9751. Donald E Scrimgeour; Valerie West.

Dyfel Management. 19 Fontwell Dr, Bromley, Kent BR2 8AB *tel:* 0181 467 9605; 07000 367687 *fax:* 0181 249 1972.

* **ECAM Ltd.** 130 Drayton Park, Highbury, London N5 1LX *tel:* 0171 354 3844 *also fax; fax:* 0171 609 5644 *email:* 100342.1717@compuserve. com; http://www.ecam-limited.com. J Cormac McGettigan, admin.

Ellison *see* J Audrey Ellison International Artists' Management.

Encore Concerts. Caversham Grange, The Warren, Mapledurham, Berks RG4 7TQ *tel:* 0118 948 2751 *fax:* 0118 946 1886. Elizabeth Goldfinch, dir. *In association with CHL Artists, Los Angeles.*

* **Festival Artists.** Danesmoor, Green La, Hemingby, Lincs LN9 5QH *tel:* 01507 578382 *also fax.* Carolyn Wright, admin asst.

Finch *see* Charles McK Finch Artists' Management.

Gallus International. 79 Norbury Cres, London SW16 4JT *tel:* 0181 679 0369 *fax:* 0181 679 9399. Jeff H Pivac, Antony Pristavec, dirs.

GBZ Management. PO Box 11845, London SE21 8ZS *tel:* 0181 761 6565 *fax:* 0181 670 3195 *email:* gbz_mgmt@compuserve.com. Gwenneth Bransby-Zachary, dir.

* **Georgina Ivor Associates (GIA).** 28 Old Devonshire Rd, London SW12 9RB *tel:* 0181 673 7179 *fax:* 0181 675 8058 *email:* givor@aol.com.uk. Georgina Ivor, dir; Karen Price, asst.

Gilder *see* Robert Gilder & Company.

Grant Rogers Musical Artists Management. 64 Wathing St, Radlett, Herts WD7 7NP *tel:* 01923 855753 *fax:* 01923 856877.

Greenan *see* Patricia Greenan.

Grosvenor Management. 79 Henley Rd, Ipswich, Suffolk IP1 3SB *tel:* 01473 213215 *also fax.*

* **Harlequin Agency Ltd.** 203 Fidlas Rd, Llanishen, Cardiff CF4 5NA *tel:* 01222 750821 *fax:* 01222 755971. Doreen O'Neill, mgr dir and artist mgr; Colin Ure, artist mgr and dir.

* **Harold Holt Ltd.** 31 Sinclair Rd, London W14 0NS *tel:* 0171 603 4600 *fax:* 0171 603 0019 *email:* info@holt.co.uk; http://ds.dial.pipex.com/ silvius/holt. Martin Campbell-White, chief exec; Diana Rix, dir; Peter Martin, dir (finance and development); Dom Quinton, dir (tours and projects); Sir Ian Hunter, president.

* **Harrison Parrott Ltd (HP).** 12 Penzance Pl, London W11 4PA *tel:* 0171 229 9166 *fax:* 0171 221 5042 *email:* info@harrisonparrott.co.uk. Jasper Parrott, chmn and joint mgr dir; Linda Marks, joint mgr dir; Lydia Connolly, dir.

Haydn Rawstron (UK) Ltd. 36 Station Rd, London SE20 7BQ *tel:* 0181 659 2659 *fax:* 0181 676 9119 *email:* haydnraw@aol.com. Chris Gray, dir.

* **Hazard Chase Ltd.** Richmond House, 16-20 Regent St, Cambridge CB2 1DB *tel:* 01223 312400 *fax:* 01223 460827 *email:* hazard.chase@dial. pipex.com. James Brown, mgr dir; Juliet Allan, dir; Ally Smale, artist mgr; Rachel Brasier, admin; Nick McMillen, financial controller.

HAYDN RAWSTRON
1997/98 SEASON

Sopranos

Renate Behle
Katarina Dalayman
Gabriele Fontana
Dorothee Jansen
Hillevi Martinpelto
Anne Schwanewilms

Mezzo Sopranos

Kathleen Kuhlmann
Lani Poulson

Tenors

Heinz Kruse
David Kuebler
Thomas Sunnegårdh
Rainer Trost
Roland Wagenführer

Baritones/Basses

Reinhard Dorn
Carlos Feller
Eike Wilm Schulte
Kristinn Sigmundsson
Alexandre Vassiliev

Conductors

Gregor Bühl
Peter Erckens
Johannes Fritzsch
Arnold Östman
Erich Wächter
Heinz Wallberg

Stage
Directors/Designers

Willy Decker
Andreas Homoki
Anthony Pilavachi
Wolfgang Gussmann

ENQUIRIES MAY BE MADE TO HAYDN RAWSTRON (UK) LTD
36 STATION ROAD • LONDON • SE20 7BQ
TELEPHONE: (+44 181) 659 2659 FACSIMILE: (+44 181) 676 9119
E-MAIL: haydnraw@aol.com

IMG *Artists*

IMG ARTISTS IS PROUD TO
ANNOUNCE EUROPEAN REPRESENTATION
OF THE FOLLOWING ARTISTS AND ORCHESTRAS

CONDUCTORS
Kees Bakels
Iona Brown
Justin Brown
Jean-Claude Casadesus *Paris office*
Michael Christie
William Christie
Thomas Dausgaard
Patrick Fournillier *Paris office*
Sachio Fujioka
János Fürst
John Eliot Gardiner CBE
Alan Gilbert
Manfred Honeck *UK, France*
Michiyoshi Inoue *France*
Marek Janowski
Mariss Jansons
Lü Jia
Djansug Kakhidze *Paris office*
Marcel Landowski *Paris office*
Andrew Litton
Jerzy Maksymiuk
Ion Marin *France*
Yehudi Menuhin
John Nelson
Paolo Olmi
Chean See Ooi
Libor Pesek
Luca Pfaff *Paris office*
En Shao
Vassily Sinaisky
Dmitry Sitkovetsky
Pinchas Steinberg
Yuri Temirkanov
Yan Pascal Tortelier
Tamás Vásáry
Franz Welser-Möst

PIANISTS
Dmitri Alexeev
Leif Ove Andsnes
Boris Berezovsky
Barry Douglas
Jeffrey Kahane
Constantin Lifschitz
Vardan Mamikonian *France*
Alexander Melnikov
Eldar Nebolsin *France*
Maria Joao Pires *France*
Mikhail Rudy

Aleksandar Serdar *Paris office*
Jean-Yves Thibaudet *France*
Tamás Vásáry
Eliso Virsaladze *UK*

VIOLINISTS
Joshua Bell
Fabio Biondi *France (by special arrangement)*
Augustin Dumay *France*
Hilary Hahn
Leila Josefowicz
Julian Rachlin *Paris office*
Vadim Repin
Dmitry Sitkovetsky

CELLISTS
Lynn Harrell
Julian Lloyd Webber
Truls Mørk
Jian Wang *UK, France*

FLUTE
Patrick Gallois *Paris office*
James Galway OBE
Jeanne Galway

CLARINET
Michel Lethiec *Paris office*

SAXOPHONE
John Harle

CHAMBER MUSIC
Berlin Philharmonic String Quartet *Paris office*
Augustin Dumay, violin &
Maria Joao Pires, piano *France*
Emerson String Quartet *UK*
Europa Galante (Biondi) *Paris office*
New Helsinki Quartet
Maria Joao Pires, piano,
Augustin Dumay, violin &
Jian Wang, cello *Paris office: in association
with Harold Holt*
Zephyr (Jeanne Galway, flute, Käthe Jarka,
cello & Samuel Sanders, piano)

SOPRANOS
Juliane Banse *UK*
Clarry Bartha *UK*
Barbara Bonney
Kathleen Brett

Laura Claycomb
Elizabeth Connell
Majella Cullagh
Lynne Dawson
Jane Eaglen
Renée Fleming
Elisabeth Futral
Nancy Gustafson
Alison Hagley
Soile Isokoski *UK*
Rosemary Joshua
Yvonne Kenny
Solveig Kringelborn
Catherine Malfitano *UK*
Rosa Mannion
Karita Mattila
Marie McLaughlin
Nelly Miricioiu
Regina Nathan
Christine Schäfer
Cyndia Sieden *UK + Sundry*
Anja Silja
Ana Camelia Stefanescu
Rosalind Sutherland
Julie Unwin
Dawn Upshaw
Carol Vaness
Deborah Voigt *UK*
Louise Walsh
Lillian Watson
Gillian Webster
Deborah York
Ruth Ziesak

MEZZO-SOPRANOS
Stephanie Blythe
Sally Burgess
Alice Coote
Imelda Drumm
Susan Graham *UK + Sundry*
Monica Groop
Charlotte Hellekant
Marilyn Horne *UK*
Lorraine Hunt
Jennifer Larmore
Susanne Mentzer
Nadja Michael
Anne-Sofie von Otter
Anne-Marie Owens
Christine Rice
Elizabeth Vaughan

COUNTER-TENORS
Michael Chance
Lawrence Zazzo

TENORS
Neill Archer
Paul Austin Kelly
Kim Begley
Jan Blinkhof *UK + Sundry*
Benjamin Butterfield
Richard Coxon
John Daszak
Ryland Davies
Gordon Gietz *UK*
Paul Groves *UK*
Jerry Hadley
John Graham Hall
David Kuebler *UK*
Keith Lewis
Alexander Oliver
Thomas Randle
Rafael Rojas
Giuseppe Sabbatini *UK*
Jeffrey Stewart
Kurt Streit
Christopher Ventris
Matthias Zacchariasen

BARITONES
Olaf Bär
Jeffrey Black
Simon Estes *UK*
Matthias Görne *UK*
Hakan Hagegard
Thomas Hampson
Ashley Holland
Jason Howard
Phillip Joll
Anthony Michaels-Moore
Timothy Noble
Brett Polegato
Gino Quilico
Stephen Roberts
Andreas Schmidt *UK*
William Shimell
Riccardo Simonetti
Paul Whelan
Oliver Widmer

BASS-BARITONES/BASS
Clive Bayley
Nathan Berg
Michael Druiett
Gerald Finley

Stephen Gadd
Michael George
Eric Halfvarson
Franz Hawlata *UK*
Ronnie Johansen
Samuel Ramey
Dean Robinson
Willard White

OPERA PRODUCERS
David Alden
Robert Carsen
Jonathan Miller
Francisco Negrin
David Pountney
Johannes Schaaf *UK*
Andrei Serban

STAGE PRODUCER
Jonathan Miller

ACCOMPANISTS
Helmut Deutsch *UK + Sundry*
Julius Drake

DANCE COMPANIES
Bill T. Jones / Arnie Zane Dance Co.
Les Ballets Trockadero de Monte Carlo
David Parsons
Urban Bush Women
Sylvie Guillem *(by special arrangement)*

ORCHESTRAS

General Management:
Oslo Philharmonic / Mariss Jansons
Norwegian Chamber Orchestra / Iona Brown
New European Strings /
Dmitry Sitkovetsky
St Petersburg Philharmonic/ Yuri
Temirkanov / Mariss Jansons
New World Symphony / Michael Tilson
Thomas

Touring Representation
IMG Artists also organises tours and/or appearances for the following orchestras and ensembles in various countries

(* denotes UK representation)

Academy of St Martin in the Fields
American Symphony Orchestra
Bavarian Radio Symphony Orchestra*

Belgian National Orchestra
Berliner Symphoniker
Boys Choir of Harlem
BBC Symphony Orchestra
Budapest Symphony Orchestra
Cincinnnati Symphony Orchestra
Czech National Symphony Orchestra
Czech Philharmonic Orchestra*
Dallas Symphony Orchestra
English String Orchestra
English Symphony Orchestra
European Union Youth Orchestra
Florida Philharmonic Orchestra
Gustav Mahler Jugend Orchester
Houston Symphony Orchestra
Hungarian State Symphony Orchestra
Juiliard Orchestra
The King's Consort Kirov Opera & Ballet
Kirov Orchestra
La Scala Philharmonic Orchestra*
Leipzig Gewandhaus Orchestra*
Lithuanian National Symphony Orchestra*
The London Philharmonic
London Symphony Orchestra
Menuhin Festival Orchestra
Moscow Philharmonic Orchestra*
Moscow Radio Symphony Orchestra*
Moscow State Symphony Orchestra*
National Youth Orchestra of Great Britain
Netherlands Youth Orchestra
Orchestra of the Age of Enlightenment
Orchestre National de France*
Orchestre de Paris*
Orchestre Philharmonique de Radio France*
Pittsburgh Symphony Orchestra
Polish Chamber Orchestra*
Polish National Radio Symphony Orchestra
Residentie Orchestra, The Hague
Rhineland Philharmonic Orchestra
Rotterdam Philharmonic Orchestra
Royal Concertgebouw Orchestra*
Royal Liverpool Philharmonic Orchestra
Royal Philharmonic Orchestra
Russian Philharmonic Orchestra
Russian State Philharmonic Orchestra
Russian State Symphony Orchestra
San Francisco Symphony Orchestra
Sinfonia Varsovia*
Sofia Philharmonic Orchestra
Vienna Radio Symphony Orchestra
Vienna Symphony Orchestra
Ukraine National Symphony Orchestra
Ulster Orchestra
Warsaw Philharmonic Orchestra

IMG Artists, Media House,
3 Burlington Lane, Chiswick
London W4 2TH UK
Tel: (0181) 233 5800
Fax: (0181) 233 5801

Stephen Wright, *Managing Director*
Tom Graham, Director, *Vocal Division*
Diana Mulgan, Director, *Vocal Division*
Nicholas Mathias, Director, *Artist Management*
Anthony Howard, Director, *Orchestral Tours*
Kathryn Enticott, *Associate Director,
Artist Management*

Joan Cruickshank, *Associate Director,
Orchestral Tours*
Gillian Newson, *Associate Director,
Dance Division*

IMG Artists, 2 rue Dufrenoy, 75116
Paris, France
Tel: (1) 4503 8503
Fax: (1) 4504 1067

Stephen Wright, *Managing Director*
Veronique Jourdain, *Director, Artist Management*
Thierry d'Agoubet, *Director, Orchestral Tours*

IMG Artists, 22 East 71st Street
New York, New York 10221-4911, USA
Tel: (212) 541 5640
Fax: (212) 265 5483
Edna Landau, *Managing Director*

IMG Artists in Europe is part of IMG Artists worldwide and a division of the IMG Group of Companies (Mark H. McCormack, Chairman and CEO).

MAGENTA MUSIC
International

SOPRANOS
Catherine Bott
Alison Buchanan
Carole Farley
Rosemary Hardy
Ruth Holton
Emma Kirkby
Claron McFadden
Catherine Pierard
Lynda Russell
Jenny Saunders
Barbara Schlick
Lisa Tyrrell

MEZZO-SOPRANOS
AND CONTRALTOS
Catherine Denley
Deborah Miles-Johnson
Louise Mott

COUNTERTENORS
Ryland Angel
Ricard Bordas
David James
Christopher Robson

TENORS
Paul Agnew
Lynton Atkinson
Joseph Cornwell
Rogers Covey-Crump
Charles Daniels
Stephan Drakulich
Peter Evans
Andrew King
Justin Lavender
Andrew Murgatroyd
James Oxley
Mark Padmore

BARITONES
AND BASSES
Brian Bannatyne-Scott
Peter Harvey
Quentin Hayes
Gordon Jones
Michael Pearce
Paul Robinson
Richard Robson
Jeremy White

CONDUCTORS
Stephen Cleobury
Richard Cooke
Leon Gee
Simon Halsey
Ton Koopman
David Lawrence
Stephen Layton
David Riddell
Thomas Woods

SOLO
INSTRUMENTALISTS
Christopher
Bowers-Broadbent *organ*

James Campbell *clarinet*

Frances Kelly *harp*

Ton Koopman
harpsichord/organ

Philip Mead *piano*

Stephen Montague
animateur/live electronics

John Scott *organ*

Christopher Wilson
lute/vihuela

CHOIRS
Christ Church
Cathedral, Oxford
Stephen Darlington, director

Danish National Radio
Choir
Stefan Parkman, director

New College, Oxford
*Edward Higginbottom,
director*

Polyphony
Stephen Layton, director

The Sixteen
*Harry Christophers,
conductor*

Swedish Radio Choir
Tõnu Kaljuste, conductor

ENSEMBLES AND
ORCHESTRAS
Paul Agnew and
Christopher Wilson

Allegri String Quartet

Catherine Bott and Friends

The Dufay Collective

The Duke Quartet

The Hilliard Ensemble

His Majestys Sagbutts
& Cornetts

Emma Kirkby and
Anthony Rooley

Montague/Mead
Piano Plus

Piano Circus

The Sixteen Choir and
Orchestra
*Harry Christophers,
conductor*

Academia Wind Quintet
of Prague
(Czech Republic)

Amsterdam Baroque
Orchestra
*Ton Koopman, director
(Netherlands)*

Sequentia *(Germany)*

Magenta Music International Limited
4 Highgate High Street, Highgate Village, London N6 5JL
Telephone: +44 181 340 8321 Fax: +44 181 340 7823
E-mail: officemail@magentamusic.com

DIRECTORS	John Bickley	Jill Davies
ARTIST MANAGEMENT	Allan Beavis	Anne-Marie Norman
	Cathy Boyes	Hilary Perrott
	Jane Houchin	Anna Sanders
	Toireasa NicCanna	Rachel Sinfield

McCann *see* Norman McCann Concert Agency Ltd.

Maestoso Musicmakers Ltd. Milestone, St Nicholas Av, Gt Bookham, Surrey KT23 4AY *tel:* 01372 457755 *fax:* 01372 450525. Elizabeth Pryde, dir.

* **Magenta Music International Ltd.** 4 Highgate High St, London N6 5JL *tel:* 0181 340 8321 *fax:* 0181 340 7823 *email:* officemail@magenta music.com; http://www.magentamusic.com. John Bickley, Jill Davies, David James, dirs.

Magnum Opus Management. 76a Norwich Rd, Wymondham, Norfolk NR18 0SZ *tel:* 01953 604342 *also fax.* Helen White, James R H Black, dirs.

Manygate Management. 13 Cotswold Mews, 30 Battersea Sq, London SW11 3RA *tel:* 0171 223 7265 *fax:* 0171 585 2830 *email:* manygate@ easynet.co.uk. James Thomson, mgr dir; John Boyden, chmn; Andrew Johnson, dir, artists' management.

Matthew Tullah Management. 301 Firs La, London N13 5QH *tel:* 0181 807 0343; 0956 318810 *fax:* 0181 807 3800 *email:* 100734.3461@ compuserve.com.

* **Maureen Lunn Management.** Top Farm, Parish La, Hedgerley, Bucks SL2 3JH *tel:* 01753 645008 *fax:* 01753 647431.

Michael Brewer. 8 Edward Ct, 317 Hagley Rd, Birmingham B16 9LQ *tel:* 0121 454 3160; 0121 520 0111 *fax:* 0121 520 5800.

Michael Harrold Artist Management. 223 Kingston Rd, Leatherhead, Surrey KT22 7PE *tel:* 01372 375728 *also fax.*

Mostylea Music Management. Grange Cottage, Grange Rd, Knightley, Staffs ST20 0JX *tel:* 01785 284433 *also fax.*

* **Music International.** 13 Ardilaun Rd, London N5 2QR *tel:* 0171 359 5183 *fax:* 0171 226 9792. Neil Dalrymple, mgr dir; Bernard Dickerson, artistic adviser; John McHugh.

Music Management. PO Box 1105, London SW1V 2DE *tel:* 0171 823 1111 *fax:* 0171 823 1001.

Music Theatre Management. Tailor House, 63-65 High St, Whitwell, Herts SG4 8AH *tel:* 01438 871007 *fax:* 01438 871777 *email:* 100620. 2341@compuserve.com.

Musichall. 6 Windmill St, London W1P 1HF *tel:* 0171 436 8911; 0585 227969 *fax:* 0171 631 4631 *email:* musichall@compuserve.com. Aidan Lang, William Relton, dirs.

* **Musicmakers.** Tailor House, 63-65 High St, Whitwell, Herts SG4 8AH *tel:* 01438 871708 *fax:* 01438 871777 *email:* 100620.2341@ compuserve.com. Christopher Knowles, dir.

N W Artists (NWA). 51 Tresco Rd, London SE15 3PY *tel:* 0171 635 7688 *fax:* 0171 635 6211. Nina Whitehurst.

NB Management (NBM). Ashlea, Oakwood Dr, East Horsley, Surrey KT24 6QF *tel:* 01483 282666 *fax:* 01483 284777 *email:* nick.bomford@ btinternet.com. Nick Bomford.

* **Neil Chaffey Concert Promotions (NCCP).** 8 Laxton Gardens, Baldock, Herts SG7 6DA *tel:* 01462 491378 *fax:* 01462 895094. Neil Chaffey, dir; Liz Barron, asst.

* **Norman McCann Concert Agency Ltd.** The Coach House, 56 Lawrie Park Gardens, London SE26 6XJ *tel:* 0181 659 5955 *fax:* 0181 659 4582.

* **Olivia Ma Artists' Management.** 28 Sheffield Terrace, London W8 7NA *tel:* 0171 221 3606 *fax:* 0171 221 3607 *email:* oliviama@omam.u-net. com. Olivia Ma, dir.

Opera and Concert Artists (OCA). 75 Aberdare Gardens, London NW6 3AN *tel:* 0171 328 3097 *fax:* 0171 372 3537. Judith Newton, Andrew Dugdale.

Oriole Music. 72 Sussex Way, London N7 6RR *tel:* 0171 272 9009 *also fax.* George Weigand, mgr.

upbeat management

"magnificent" "sensational" "stunning" "dazzling"

We represent world-class artists of distinction whose exceptional artistry and imaginative programmes create unique and memorable events.

Nicholas Daniel
oboe
"exceptional polish and brilliance... great expressive range"
Gramophone

Gerard McChrystal
saxophone
"dazzling playing"
The Financial Times

Carlos Bonell
guitar
"a wonderful player"
New York Times

Red Priest
director
Piers Adams
"virtuosic... brilliant...total conviction"
Yorkshire Post

The Joachim Trio
(John Lenehan, Rebecca Hirsch, Caroline Dearnley)
"This Naxos recording is a sensation"
Fonoforum

The Marianne Olyver Gypsy Orchestra
"stunning...the thrill of the week"
The Independent

Leland Chen
violin
"quite magnificent"
Hi Fi News & Record
Review

Maxim Xue Wei
violin
*"glorious melodic
tone and excellent
technical expertise"*
The Times

Yuko Inoue
viola
*"splendid tone
and technique"*
The Daily
Telegraph

Piers Adams
recorders
"stunning"
The Times

Susan Milan
flute
*"magical...
marvellous playing"*
Gramophone

**The Revolutionary
Drawing Room**
director Angela East
*"ravishing...a performance
that was both sensitive and
dynamic"*
The Strad

**Carlos Bonell
Ensemble**
*"a quite special musical
delicacy"*
Weilburger Tageblatt

upbeat
management

Contact: Maureen Phillips

Tel: 0181 773 1223   Fax: 0181 669 6752

E-mail: classic@upbeat.co.uk

Upbeat Management, Sutton Business Centre, Restmor Way, Wallington, Surrey SM6 7AH

MICHAEL HARROLD ARTIST MANAGEMENT

ARTIST REPRESENTATION & CONCERT MANAGEMENT

223, Kingston Road, Leatherhead, Surrey, KT22 7PE, United Kingdom.
Telephone & Fax: 01372 375 728 (UK) / (+44) 1372 375 728 (International)
E-mail: michael.harrold@virgin.net

KEYBOARD

JULIE AINSCOUGH (Organ, Conductor)

ÓSCAR CANDENDO ZABALA (Organ)

GUILLERMO DIEZ ARNÁIZ (Organ)

ANDREW PARNELL (Organ, Harmonium, Harpsichord, Conductor)

MALCOLM BINNS (Piano)

MELANIE SPANSWICK (Piano)

DAVITT MORONEY (Harpsichord, Organ)

HELEN ROGERS (Harpsichord)

WIND/BRASS

ARUNDO CLARINET QUARTET
Janet Spotswood, Jill Sadler, Joanna Estall (Clarinets),
Angela Crispe (Bass Clarinet)

ENGLISH BRASS ENSEMBLE
Paul Archibald (Artistic Director)

INTRADA BRASS ENSEMBLE
Alan Furness (Artistic Director)

ANTHONY AARONS (Trumpet)

GERARD McDONALD (Baroque Flute, Baroque Oboe,
Oboe d'Amore, Oboe da Caccia, Recorders)

GERVASE DE PEYER (Clarinet, Conductor)

STRING

RICHARD CHAPMAN (Guitar)

JENIFER JANSE ('Cello, Baroque 'Cello)

DAVID PARSONS (Lute, Archlute, Guitar)

VOCAL / CHORAL

CAPILLA VOCAL HISPANA
(Schola Cantorum of the Benedictine Abbey of Santa Cruz,
Valle de Los Caidos, near Madrid),
Dom Alfredo Simón, O.S.B. (Director)

SARAH-JANE DALE (Soprano)

CARYS-ANNE LANE (Soprano)

SOPHIA GRECH (Mezzo-Soprano)

BEVERLEY MILLS (Mezzo-Soprano)

ANDREW MORRIS (Tenor)

FARNBOROUGH ABBEY CHOIR

ENSEMBLE

ARABESQUE
Alison Mary Sutton (Mezzo-Soprano),
Maria Beattie (Harp),
Julie-Dawn Lloyd (Flute)

COPERNICUS PIANO TRIO
Rafael Todes (Violin),
Jennifer Janse ('Cello), Virginia Hanslip (Piano)

FROG IN THE THROAT
Sarah-Jane Dale (Soprano), Andrew Morris (Tenor),
Audrey Hyland (Piano)

GRECH, KIRKBRIDE & SPANSWICK
Sophia Grech (Mezzo-Soprano),
Simon Kirkbride (Baritone),
Melanie Spanswick (Piano)

CHRISTOPHER HORNER (Violin) &
JULIE AINSCOUGH (Piano)

JENIFER JANSE ('Cello) &
VIRGINIA HANSLIP (Piano)

JENIFER JANSE (Baroque 'Cello) &
HELEN ROGERS (Harpsichord)

LOKI ENSEMBLE
Heidi Pegler (Soprano),
Gerard McDonald, William Summers (Baroque Woodwind),
Richard Partridge (Viola da Gamba),
Helen Rodgers (Harpsichord).

MELOS ENSEMBLE OF LONDON
Gervase de Peyer (Artistic Director)

ORPHEAN ENSEMBLE
Gabrielle Fisher (Soprano), Anthony Aarons (Trumpet),
Richard Hill, Timothy Bond (Organ), David Wickham (Piano)

PAMPLONA CATHEDRAL CHOIR
Padre Aurelio Sagaseta (Maestro de Capilla)

GERVASE DE PEYER (Clarinet) &
GWENNETH PRYOR (Piano)

COMPOSER/CONDUCTOR

EDWIN ROXBURGH
(also Lecturer)

* **Owen/White Management (OWM).** 39 Hillfield Av, London N8 7DS *tel:* 0181 340 9571 *fax:* 0181 340 4056. John Owen, Trudy White.

* **Patricia Greenan.** 19b Belsize Pk, London NW3 4DU *tel:* 0171 794 5954 *fax:* 0171 431 3503. Patricia Greenan.

* **Patrick Garvey Management (PGM).** Top Floor, 59 Lansdowne Pl, Hove, E Sussex BN3 1FL *tel:* 01273 206623 *fax:* 01273 208484 *email:* patrick@pgmartistmanager.demon.co.uk. Patrick Garvey, dir; Andrea McDermott, asst; Una Marchetti, project dir; Marrianne Bradfield, admin.

* **Performing Arts (PA).** 6 Windmill St, London W1P 1HF *tel:* 0171 255 1362 *fax:* 0171 631 4631. Richard Haigh, proprietor; Samantha Lambourne, mgr.

Phillips *see* Caroline Phillips Management.

* **Portland Wallis Artists' Management.** 50 Gt Portland St, London W1N 5AH *tel:* 0171 636 6785 *fax:* 0171 636 6786. John McMurray, gen mgr; Daniel Stinson, admin.

Pristavec *see* Anthony Pristavec Artist and Concert Management.

Purkiss *see* Anthony Purkiss.

PVA Management. Hallow Park, Worcester WR2 6PG *tel:* 01905 640663 *fax:* 01905 641842. Paul Vaughan, mgr dir; Stephen Pink, company sec; Lisa Ventura-Whiting, sec; Irene Sanderson, mkt mgr.

Rawstron *see* Haydn Rawstron Ltd.

RGO Ltd. Flint Barn Ct, Church St, Old Amersham, Bucks HP7 0DB *tel:* 01494 723700 *fax:* 01494 723800 *email:* rgo-ltd@msn.com. R D Gunner, mgr dir; M A B Harrison, T J Regan, H S Taylor, dirs. Also at: 28 Cathedral Rd, Cardiff CF1 9LJ *tel:* 01222 390130 *fax:* 01222 664891.

* **Robert Gilder & Company.** Enterprise House, 59-65 Upper Ground, London SE1 9PQ *tel:* 0171 928 9008 *fax:* 0171 928 9755. Robert Gilder, dir; Catrin Ley, Chris Loake, artist mgrs; Alexandra Mercer, associate.

* **Robert White Artist Management.** 182 Moselle Av, London N22 6EX *tel:* 0181 881 6914 *fax:* 0181 888 9662 *email:* rwhiteam@aol.com. Robert White, dir.

* **Rostrum Promotions.** 4 Ferniebank Brae, Bridge of Allan FK9 4PJ *tel:* 01786 834449 *fax:* 01786 833949. Fiona Paterson, mgr dir.

Roy Baker Concert Management. 25 Lynors Av, Rochester, Kent ME2 3NQ *tel:* 01634 714434 *also fax.* Audrey Banker, admin.

Scott Mitchell Management. West Byres Cottage, Balmerino, Fife DD6 8SB *tel:* 01382 330883. Scott Mitchell, dir.

Scrimgeour *see* Donald Scrimgeour.

* **Seaview Music.** 28 Mawson Rd, Cambridge CB1 2EA *tel:* 01223 772690 *fax:* 01223 772828. Alison Page, mgr; Selene Mills, asst mgr.

Simply Singers (SS). 23 Freke Rd, London SW11 5PU *tel:* 0171 223 7327 *fax:* 0171 924 5730.

Singers Direct. 39 The Ridings, Surbiton, Surrey KT5 8HG *tel:* 0181 390 5375; 0589 153382 *fax:* 0181 390 9818 *email:* singersdirect@mrb.clara.net. Michael R Bundy.

Stafford Law. 6 Barham Close, Weybridge, Surrey KT13 9PR *tel:* 01932 854489 *fax:* 01932 858521.

Stella Baker. Home Close, Sheep St, Winslow, Buckingham MK18 3HR *tel:* 01296 712411 *also fax.*

* **Stephannie Williams Artists (SWA).** 12 Central Chambers, Wood St, Stratford upon Avon, Warwicks CV37 6JQ *tel:* 01789 266272 *fax:* 01789 266467 *email:* sw_artists@msn.com. Stephannie Williams, mgr; Martin Denny, concerts mgr; Rosalind Humphrey, admin.

Still *see* Athole Still International Management Ltd.

* **Sue Lubbock Artist Management.** 25 Courthope Rd, London NW3 2LE *tel:* 0171 485 5932 *fax:* 0171 267 0179. Sue Lubbock, dir.

Presents
FORTHCOMING SEASON

Anup Kumar Biswas

Solo Cellist/Composer/Conductor

A born communicator...here is an Artist whose physical being, like that of Rostropovich or the young Jacqueline du Pré seems intertwined with instrument and music.
THE GUARDIAN, LONDON

Masterly performance...superb playing by Mr Biswas.
THE TIMES, LONDON

... superb singing quality... a master of dynamics, his energy, vitality, fine delicacy of bowing and a fierce attack, and a more fibrous tone suitable to Brahms produced a magnificent account of the Opus 99 sonata.
THE TELEGRAPH, LONDON

In the prestigious setting of the packed Margravine Opera House, Bayreuth, a delightful theatrical visual experience was owed to the cellist Biswas... he lived the music in his face and handled the cello as if in ecstasies of love.
Frankenpost, Germany

His mellow tone, technical control, and relish of the importance of punctuation, mark him out as an exceptionally gifted player for his years. Everything was there – beauty of tone, natural vibrant intensity and above all, a complete affinity with the gorgeous music.
Music and Musicians

A player of definate and individual talent. He has no technical shortcomings... a cellist of great sensitivity and feeling.
The Strad

THE MATHIESON MUSIC SHCOOL CALCUTTA

An unique charitable music shcool in Calcutta, which gives musical and general education to deprived children of India. The school had arranged successfully an International cultural and educational exchange between India and the UK in 1996 and two major music festivals in Calcutta. The School is seeking volunteer musicians and teachers to help these children in Calcutta. Further exchanges are being planned. For information contact East West Arts Ltd.

GUADAGNINI PIANO TRIO

".. easy-going in its sentiment and charm... had eloquent intensity beneath a smiling surface, the performance took advantage of generous repeats and unhurried assurance to work its melodic Magic".
The Times, London

EAST WEST ENCOUNTER SERIES
East West Music Group
East West Dance Company

TRAVELLING FESTIVAL
OF
india
A Celebration of Indian Classical Music and Dance

The Travelling Festival of India every year is a resounding success. Performances at London's South Bank Cenre, Bayreuth Opera House, Turku Festival Finland and elsewhere were sold out and received critical acclaim.

DANTE ALIGHIERI ORCHESTRA

Chamber 15-25 players, symphony 65 players. This London-based professional orchestra of all nationalities provides a platform for soloists and conductors, under the patronage of the Rt. Hon. Lord St. John of Fawsley, and Kensington MP Dudley Fishburn

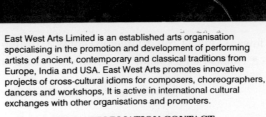

East West Arts Limited is an established arts organisation specialising in the promotion and development of performing artists of ancient, contemporary and classical traditions from Europe, India and USA. East West Arts promotes innovative projects of cross-cultural idioms for composers, choreographers, dancers and workshops, It is active in international cultural exchanges with other organisations and promoters.

FOR FURTHER INFORMATION CONTACT:
EAST WEST ARTS LTD. 93B Cambridge Gardens, North Kensington,
London W10 6JE, United Kingdom Telephone: 0468-720124 or 0181-960 5889 Fax: 0181-968 5541

Susie Wong Artists Management Ltd. 27 Old Gloucester St, London WC1N 3XX *tel:* 0171 633 9878 *also fax;* 0410 380838. Susie Wong, mgr; Iris Tse, sec.

Sykes *see* Helen Sykes Artists' Management.

Sylvia Junge Management (SJM). 7 Elton Close, Kingston upon Thames, Surrey KT1 4EE *tel:* 0181 977 9613.

Sympathetic Developments. 48 Bridle Way, Colehill, Wimborne, Dorset BH21 2UE *tel:* 01202 880331 *fax:* 01202 888037. Graham Stansfield, proprietor.

* **Tennant Artists.** Unit 2, 39 Tadema Rd, London SW10 0PY *tel:* 0171 376 3758 *fax:* 0171 351 0679. Christopher Tennant, mgr dir; Angela Sulivan, dir.

Terry Harrison Artists Management (THA). The Orchard, Market St, Charlbury, Oxon OX7 3PJ *tel:* 01608 810330 *fax:* 01608 811331. Helen Turner, mgr; Lynne Ness, Denise Bucknell, assts.

* **TransArt (UK) Ltd.** 8 Bristol Gardens, London W9 2JG *tel:* 0171 286 7526 *fax:* 0171 266 2687. Hervé Corre de Valmalète, dir; Anne-Marie Simmenauer, Rachel Champion MacPherson, artist mgrs; Niki Cook, company sec.

* **Upbeat Management.** Sutton Business Centre, Restmor Way, Wallington, Surrey SM6 7AH *tel:* 0181 773 1223 *fax:* 0181 669 6752. Maureen Phillips, Liz Biddle, dirs.

* **Valerie Barber PR & Personal Management Ltd.** Suite 300, Mappin House, 4 Winsley St, London W1N 7AR *tel:* 0171 436 1115/6 *fax:* 0171 436 5090 *email:* vbpr@compuserve.com; 106653.1112@compuserve.com.

* **Van Walsum Management (VWM).** 4 Addison Bridge Pl, London W14 8XP *tel:* 0171 371 4343 *fax:* 0171 371 4344 *email:* vwm@vanwalsum.demon.co.uk. Joeske van Walsum, mgr dir.

* **Victoria Smith Management Ltd.** 2 Police Cottages, North End Lane, Droxford, Hampshire SO32 3QN *tel:* 01489 878787 *fax:* 01489 877777.

* **Worldwide Artists (London) Ltd (WWA).** 12 Roseberry Av, Thornton Heath, London CR7 8PT *tel:* 0181 771 3444 *fax:* 0181 771 3445 *email:* wwartists@aol.com.

Wright Music Promotions Limited. 235 Streetsbrook Rd, Solihull, W Midlands B91 1HE *tel:* 0121 705 0098 *fax:* 0121 705 4815 *email:* http://www.classicalmusic.co.uk/wright-music-promotions. Penelope Beaumont-Wright, dir.

* **Young Concert Artists Trust (YCAT).** 23 Garrick St, London WC2E 9AX *tel:* 0171 379 8477 *fax:* 0171 379 8467. Rosemary Pickering, chief exec; Susan Hudson, artists mgr. *Career management for young musicians selected by audition.*

Ensembles

Ensembles listed here are confined to those based in Britain or those bookable through a British concert agent. Agents are shown in italics at the end of the entry (*see* **Agents and Managers**). Entries are in alphabetical order, and where a partnership has no name except those of the individuals, the surnames are given in square brackets. Performers' names are given and the nature of the ensemble (string, vocal, etc) is indicated. A small number of ensembles combine music with the spoken word and these are listed at the end of this chapter under **Words and Music**.

A Man, a Woman and a Double Bass. Warwick House, 34 Warwick Rd, Coulsdon, Surrey CR5 2EE *tel:* 0181 660 7877 *fax:* 0181 763 0492 *email:* silvius@dial.pipex.com; http://ols.dial.pipex.com/silvius/. Lowri Blake, voice, vc; Peter Buckoke, db. Classical Music Cabaret. *Seaview*

A1 Brass Ensemble. 26 Wattleton Rd, Beaconsfield, Bucks HP9 1TS *tel:* 01494 674692/676428. Phillip Pickering, Chris White, tpt; Chris Many, hn; Nigel Barr, trb; John Carr, euph, tb. Concerts, weddings, funerals, educ demonstrations, dinners, garden parties.

Abacus. 20 Spencer Gate, St Albans, Herts AL1 4AD *tel:* 01727 839516 *fax:* 01727 762407. Joanna West, vn; Angela Crispe, cl; Helen Edgar, vc; Karen Suter, pno.

[Abbott, O'Gorman]. Jocelyn Abbott and Laura O'Gorman, pno duo. *GBZ*

Aberdeen Sinfonietta. South House, 17 Kirk Brae, Cults, Aberdeen AB15 9QP *tel:* 01224 869615. Julian Marx, concert mgr; Mary Dargie, sec; Margaret Bremner, sponsorship sec.

Aberdeen Trio. Morven, Crossroads, Strathdon, Aberdeen AB3 68XN *tel:* 019756 51284. Bryan Dargie, vn; Raymond Dodd, vc; Donald Hawksworth, pno.

Academia Wind Quintet of Prague. Jiri Marsalek, fl; Otto Trnka, ob; Petr Donek, cl; Frantisek Pok, hn; Josef Janda, bsn. *Magenta*

The Academy of Ancient Music Chamber Ensemble. 10 Brookside, Cambridge CB2 1JE *tel:* 01223 301509 *fax:* 01223 327377 *email:* administrator@aam.co.uk; http://www.aam.co.uk. Christopher Hogwood CBE, dir; Paul Goodwin, associate cond; Andrew Manze, associate dir and concert master; Christopher Lawrence, mgr; Ivan Rockey, admin.

Academy of St Martin in the Fields Chamber Ensemble. Station House, Staverton, Totnes, Devon TQ9 6AG *tel:* 01803 762670 *fax:* 01803 762451. Kenneth Sillito, dir; Malcolm Latchem, mgr. Ens performs as str quintet, sextet and octet, mixed wind and strings, pno quintet.

Accademia Bizantine. Baroque and modern insts. *Intermusica*

Accademia Wind Ensemble. 61 Queen's Dr, London N4 2BG *tel:* 0181 802 5984 *fax:* 0181 809 7436 *email:* flute@paulrodriguezmus. demon.co.uk. Ann Cherry, fl; Anthony Randall, hn; Brian Wightman, bsn; David Wilson, ob; Peter Thompson, cl.

Act One, Sing Too. 7 Allington Ct, Allington St, London SW1E 5ED *tel:* 0171 828 1335. Eileen Diamond; Stephen Clark, pno, trb. Children's concert w/shops for ages 3-11. Songs, rounds, perc, mus stories. Educ entertainment.

Adam Trio. Eliyahu Shulman, vn; David Sella, vc; Morris Chernorudsky, pno. *Ellison*

Adderbury Ensemble. 17 Whittall St, Kings Sutton, Banbury OX17 3RD *tel:* 01295 810683 *also fax*. Chris Windass, mus dir. Chmbr ens.

Adelphi Saxophone Quartet. 3 Corran Close, Winton Eccles M30 8LP *tel:* 0161 789 2092 *fax:* 0161 477 9835. Sarah Markham, sop sax; Andrew Wilson, alto sax; Martin Kerrigan, ten sax; Alex Mitchell, bar sax. *Chameleon*

Aeolian Reeds. 4 Hillside Way, Bevendean, Brighton, E Sussex BN2 4TR *tel:* 01273 677588; 01293 871251. Sarah Cobby, ob; Nicola Hazelwood, cl; David Burles, bsn.

Aeona Flute Quartet. 87a Queens Rd, E Grinstead, W Sussex RH19 1BG *tel:* 01342 300949 *fax:* 01342 410846 *email:* http://www.egnet.co.uk/ clients/music/rgm.html. Paul Cheneour, Helen Lee, Sinéad McCarthy, Adrian Coucher, fls.

Aerophonic. 49 Gleneldon Rd, London SW16 2AX *tel:* 0181 677 1845 *fax:* 0181 677 1846 *email:* rimbal@dircon.co.uk. Colin Boyle, marimba; Katy Gainham, fls. Contemporary mus and popular arrangements.

[Agnew, Wilson]. Paul Agnew, ten; Christopher Wilson, lute. *Magenta*

Aguado Guitar Duo. c/o 24 Beaumont Park Rd, Beaumont Pk, Huddersfield, W Yorks HD4 5JS *tel:* 01484 540255. Kenneth Heggie, Peter Batchelar, gui.

The Alberni String Quartet. Howard Davis, Peter Pople, vn; Roger Best, va; David Smith, vc. *Blythe/KDM*

Albion Brass Consort. 78 Jacksons Dr, Cheshunt, Waltham Cross, Herts EN7 6HW *tel:* 01992 637180 *also fax*. Paul Thornton, Peter Rudeforth, tpt; Christine Norsworthy, hn; David Whitehouse, trb; Marc Easener, tb.

Albion Ensemble. 29 Alston Rd, Barnet, Herts EN5 4EU *tel:* 0181 441 1107 *also fax*. Philippa Davies, fl; George Caird, ob; Angela Malsbury, cl; Gareth Newman, bsn; Peter Francomb, hn. *SWA*

Alexandra Ensemble. Stella Maris, Anglesea Rd, Kingston-upon-Thames, Surrey KT1 2EW *tel:* 0181 546 8677 *fax:* 0181 541 1448. Janice Chapman, sop; Barbara McGregor, cl; Sally Mays, pno. Mus for all occasions.

Alibas. Halfpenny Cottage, 18 Greenfield Rd, Pulloxhill, Bedfordshire MK45 5EZ *tel:* 01525 714398 *also fax; email:* 100704.1557@ compuserve.com. Chmbr mus for fl.

Allandale Quartet. Torridon House, 104 Bradford Rd, Wrenthorpe, Wakefield, WF1 2AH *tel:* 01924 371496. Brian Greensmith, dir. Str and pno quartet. Mus for all occasions.

Allegri String Quartet. Peter Carter, David Roth, Jonathan Barritt, Bruno Schrecker. *Magenta*

Almira String Quartet. 17 Willow Coppice, Bartley Green, Birmingham B32 3IA *tel:* 0121 475 6491 *also fax*. Simon Chalk, Ian Davidson, vn; David Aspin, va; Sean Gilde, vc. *Encore*

Alpha-Beta-Cello. 33 Romsey Rd, Cambridge CB1 3DD *tel:* 01223 413234 *also fax*. Veronica Henderson, vc; Murray McLachlan, pno. Programmes from baroque to present day built around chosen letters of the alphabet.

Amadé Wind Ensemble. 8 Hob La, Edgeworth, Bolton, Lancs BL7 0PS *tel:* 01204 853776. Robin Proudman, dir. Wind octet; obs, cls, hns, bsns.

Amaryllis Consort. 4 Lebanon Ct, Richmond Rd, Twickenham, Middx TW1 3DA *tel:* 0181 892 3484 *also fax*. Charles Brett, dir, c-ten; Catherine Peacock, Juliet Schiemann, sop; Ian Thompson, ten; Stephen Roberts, bs.

Amati Quartet. *Gilder*

[Amos, Burke]. Lawron House, Wycombe Rd, Stokenchurch, Bucks HP14 3RP *tel:* 01494 483506. Lisa-Maree Amos, fl; Mark Burke, gui. Latin-American mus.

Amsterdam Baroque Orchestra. Ton Koopman, cond. *Magenta*

Angelique String Quartet. *John Boddy*

The Angell Piano Trio. 40 Pattison Rd, London NW2 *tel:* 0171 435 7962 *also fax*. Jan Peter Schmolck, vn; Richard May, vc; Frances Angell, pno. *Connaught*

Anúna. Celtic choir. Michael McGlynn, artistic dir. *Hazard*

Any-Tessitura. 115 Alleyn Pk, London SE21 8AA *tel:* 0181 693 0324 *fax:* 0181 693 7535. Hugh Riddell, dir; Morag McLaren, sop; David Bexon, ten; Iwan Llewelyn-Jones, acc.

Apollo Brass Quintet. 1 Railway Cottages, Holland La, Oxted, Surrey RH8 9AZ *tel:* 01883 723072 *also fax*. Christopher Pigram, Timothy Hayward, tpt; Raul Diaz, hn; Simon Gunton, trb; David Powell, tb.

Apollo Consort. William Thorp, vn and va d'amore; Imogen Seth-Smith, ten and bs viols; Margaret Richards, bs viol; Laurence Cummings, hpd and org. *Chameleon*

Apollo Group of London. Gatekeepers, 77 Gordon Av, Stanmore, Middx HA7 3QR *tel:* 0181 954 4646. Barbara Kendall-Davies, sop; Christopher Davies, bar; Jillian Skerry, pno.

Apollo Saxophone Quartet. c/o Tonia Franklin Management, 12 Taplin Way, Tylers Green, Bucks HP10 8DW *tel:* 01494 815653 *fax:* 01494 817588. Will Gregory, Rob Buckland, Tim Redpath, Andy Scott.

Arabesque. Maria Beattie, hp; Alison Mary Sutton, m-sop; Julie-Dawn Lloyd, fl. *Michael Harrold*

Archaeus Quartet. 29 Chadwick Rd, Peckham, London SE15 4RA *tel:* 0171 639 1203 *also fax*; 0181 855 2851. Ann Hooley, Bridget Davey, vn; Elizabeth Turnbull, va; Martin Thomas, vc.

Archduke Trio. 41 Fishponds Rd, Kenilworth, Warwicks CV8 1EY *tel:* 01926 854040 *fax:* 01926 858187. Kenneth Page, vn; Russell Davis, vc; James Walker, pno. Resident ens at University of Leicester.

[Ardagh-Walter, Jeffrey]. 40 Mossbury Rd, London SW11 2PB *tel:* 0171 223 2408 *also fax*. Catherine Ardagh-Walter, vc; Emily Jeffrey, pno.

Arditti String Quartet. Irvine Arditti, Graeme Jennings, vn; Garth Knox, va; Rohan de Saram, vc. *Lyons*

Arensky Trio. c/o Chetham's School of Music, Long Millgate, Manchester *tel:* 0161 834 9644 *fax:* 0161 839 3609. Martin Milner, vn; Stephen Threlfall, vc; Kathleen Uren, pno.

Arenstein-Hoy Guitar Duo. 78 Ridge Rd, London N8 9NR *tel:* 0181 348 3630. Colin Arenstein, Robert Hoy, gui.

Arethusa Oboe Quartet. Bearsden, 25 Hampstead La, London N6 4RT *tel:* 0181 348 8498 *also fax.* Graham Salter, ob; Emer Calthorpe, vn; Ian Rowbotham, va; Justin Pearson, vc.

Arioso Trio of London. 83 Woodwarde Rd, London SE22 8UL *tel:* 0181 693 5696 *also fax.* Lynda Russell, sop; David Campbell, cl; Andrew Ball, pno.

Arlequinade. Fiona Masters, fl; Hilary Dennis, ob; John Davies, pno. *Purkiss*

Arundo Clarinet Quartet. Woodside, Orestan La, Effingham, Surrey KT24 5SN *tel:* 01372 452513 *also fax.* Janet Spotswood, Jill Sadler, Angela Crispe, Joanna Estall, cl. *Michael Harrold*

Aspidistra. 1 Riverside Mews, Millgate, Thirsk, N Yorks YO7 1AE *tel:* 01845 525207. Jean Hotton, dir. Duo, trio or quartet of strs, w/wind and keyboards.

Athena Ensemble. 91 Brands Hill Av, High Wycombe, Bucks HP13 5PX *tel:* 01494 527826. Robert Jordan, dir. Wind and str ens.

Athenaeum Enesco String Quartet. *Transart*

Atlantic Winds. 10 Adria Rd, Didsbury, Manchester M20 6SG *tel:* 0161 434 6182 *also fax.* Laurence Perkins, mus dir.

Attacca. 37 Mount Pleasant Cres, Crouch Hill, London N4 4HP *tel:* 0171 272 6101 *also fax.* Andrew Pearce, Dale Loth, vn; Michael Blee, va; Joseph Spooner, vc; Helen Fidler, ob; Jessica Rabin, tpt; Rachael Bromlow, fl; Andrew Pink, dir and continuo.

Audubon Quartet. David Ehrlich, David Salness, vn; Doris Lederer, va, Thomas Shaw, vc. *NCCP*

Aurelian Trio. Torridon House, 104 Bradford Rd, Wrenthorpe, W Yorks WF1 2AH *tel:* 01924 371496. Brian Greensmith, dir. Vn or fl, vc and pno. Mus for all occasions.

The Australian String Quartet. Peter Tanfield, Elinor Lea, vn; Keith Crellin, va; Niall Brown, vc. *Ellison*

The Avian Trio. Ob, cl and bsn. *Clifton Wyatt*

[Ax, Stern, Laredo, Ma]. Emanuel Ax, pno; Isaac Stern, vn; Jaime Laredo, va; Yo-Yo Ma, vc. *Holt*

Badinage Ensemble. Paul Carroll, bsn, fl, rcdr; Sally Civval, vc, va da gamba; David Rowland, hpd, org, f-pno: baroque and classical repertoire on period insts. *Music Management*

The Baker Collection. 18 Burnt Hill Way, Wrecclesham, Farnham, Surrey GU10 4RP *tel:* 01252 795047 *also fax.* 17th C mus on period insts. Brian Lloyd Wilson, Diane Terry, vns; Oliver Webber, vn and va; Laurie Ann Macleod, bs vn, 5 str vc, gamba; Alastair Ross, keyboards; Peter Trevelyan, presenter.

Banjo and Piano Duo. 34 Balfour Av, Hanwell, London W7 3HS *tel:* 0181 567 9297 *fax:* 0181 723 0155. Douglas Rogers, banjo; Joanne Last, pno. Victorian and Edwardian classic banjo repertoire.

Barbican Piano Trio. Gabrielle Lester, vn; Robert Max, vc; James Kirby, pno. *Festival*

Bartók Quartet. *Ingpen*

Bartók String Quartet. *Michael Brewer*

Bashava Band. Geroge Weigand, cimbalom; Sharon Lindo, vn; Edward Hession, acc; Simon Russell, db; Alexandra Valavelsky, sop. Gypsy mus from Eastern Europe, operetta, yiddish and klezmer mus. *Oriole/John Boddy*

Bassoon & Beyond. Bsn jazz band. *Michael Brewer*

The Beaufort Ensemble. Clare Bentley, fl; Deborah Rich, ob; Timothy Lines, cl; Elizabeth Mason, bsn; David Bentley, hn. *Chameleon*

Beaumont Reed Trio. 441b Kingsbury Rd, Kingsbury, London NW19 9DT *tel:* 0181 204 6513. Simon Dewhurst, ob; Rachel Elliott, cl; Hazel Granthier, bsn.

Beaux Arts Trio. c/o 35 Victoria Rd, Shoreham by Sea, W Sussex BN43 5LA *tel:* 01273 454310 *also fax.* Menahem Pressler, pno; Ida Kavafian, vn; Peter Wiley, vc.

The Beethoven String Trio of London. 170 Bow Common La, London E3 *tel:* 0181 9812910 *also fax;* 01588 640361 *fax:* 01588 640107. Pavlo Beznosiuk, vn; Jeremy Williams, va; Richard Tunnicliffe, vc.

Bekova Sisters Piano Trio. 76 Honeybrook Rd, London SW12 0DN *tel:* 0181 675 6885 *fax:* 0181 673 8356. Elvira Bekova, vn; Eleonora Bekova, pno; Alfia Bekova, vc.

Bella Opera. Finchingfield House, The Green, Finchingfield, Essex CM7 4JS *tel:* 01371 810289 *also fax.* Lorraine Patient, artistic dir. Opera highlights from popular operas.

[Bennetts, Bowman]. Kathryn Bennetts, Peter Bowman, rcdrs. *Invisible Pilots*

Berg (Alban) Quartet. Guenter Pichler, Gerhard Schulz, vn; Thomas Kakuska, va; Valentin Erben, vc. *Intermusica*

Bernard Roberts Piano Trio. Bernard Roberts, pno; Andrew Roberts, vn; Nicholas Roberts, vc. *Ireland*

[Beyer, Dagul]. 15 Birchmead Close, St Albans, Herts AL3 6BS *tel:* 01727 858485 *also fax; email:* mailbox@classical-artists.com. Isabel Beyer, Harvey Dagul, pno duettists.

[Bibby]. 73 Pirbright Rd, London SW18 5ND *tel:* 0181 874 6886. Alexandra and Nicola Bibby, pno duo. *NBM*

Bingham String Quartet. 4 Elmfield Rd, Walthamstow, London E17 7HH *tel:* 0181 521 7125 *also fax;* 0973 977704 *email:* stephen.bingham @virgin.net; http://freespace.virgin.net/stephenbingham. Stephen Bingham, Sally-Ann Weeks, vn; Brenda Stewart, va; James Halsey, vc. *Purkiss*

Birmingham Contemporary Music Group. c/o CBSO, Paradise Pl, Birmingham B3 3RP *tel:* 0121 616 2616 *fax:* 0121 616 2622. Simon Rattle, artistic adviser; Simon Clugston, artistic dir; Jackie Newbould, admin; Stephen Newbould, development mgr.

[Bishop, Hastings]. 57 Ingleton Rd, Stockport, Cheshire SK3 9NN *tel:* 0161 480 5922; 01625 531240 *also fax; fax:* 0161 291 8974 *email:* t.williams@nwnet.co.uk/psapph-a. Sally Bishop, Anne-Marie Hastings, pno duo.

Black Hair. Ball Hall Farm, Storwood, Melbourne, York YO4 4TD *tel:* 01759 318464 *also fax.* Anna Myatt, dir; Roger Marsh, artistic dir. Contemporary mus ens; vocal, inst and mus theatre.

The Bold Balladiers. 23 King Edward's Rd, Ruislip, Middx HA4 7AQ *tel:* 01895 635737 *also fax.* Michael Goldthorpe, ten, dir; Wendy Eathorne, Roimata Templeton, sops; John Bradbury, Alice Pratley, vns; Christina Shillito, vc; Sam Brookes, fl; Samantha Newbold, pno; Iain Ledingham, pno, org. Victorian and Edwardian ballads.

Borante Piano Trio. Laurence Jackson, vn; Paul Marleyn, vc; Scott Mitchell, pno. *Scott Mitchell*

Borodin String Quartet. *VWM*

[Bradshaw, Bennett]. 55 Compton Rd, London N1 2PB *tel:* 0171 226 8675. Susan Bradshaw, Richard Rodney Bennett, pnos.

Brahms Trio of London. 187c Devonshire Rd, London SE23 3NJ *tel:* 0181 291 2510. Peter Thompson, mus dir, cl; Anne Baker, vc; Timothy Barratt, pno.

Brass Belles. 112 Bargery Rd, Catford, London SE6 2LW *tel:* 0181 697 3005 *also fax.* Marion Wilson, Claire Duncan, tpt; Tracey Golding, hn; Lorraine Temple, tb; Amanda Parkin, tb.

Brass Camerata. 2 Courtfield House, Baldwins Gardens, London EC1N 7SB *tel:* 0171 916 8461 *fax:* 0171 916 8462 *email:* img@msn.com/an. Rhys Owens, John MacDomnic, tpt; Jonathon Bareham, hn; Richard Dickins, tb; Ian Golding, admin, trb.

Brass Pages Quintet. c/o 28 Wingate Rd, Luton, Bedfordshire LU4 8PX *tel:* 01582 576450. Garry Page, Mark Cadman, tpt; Ian Frankland, hn; Ashley Horton, trb; Robin Norman, tb.

Bravura. 32 Chandos Av, London W5 4ER *tel:* 0181 847 0888 *also fax.* Fiona Firth-Spiller, sop; Martin Robson, bs; William Hancox, pno.

Bridge String Quartet. 12 Haslemere Av, London W13 9UJ *tel:* 0181 579 4624 *also fax.* Catherine Schofield, Kaye Barker, vn; Michael Schofield, va; Lucy Wilding; vc.

Brindisi String Quartet. Jacqueline Shave, Patrick Kiernan, vn; Katie Wilkinson Khoroshunin, va; Clive Greensmith, vc. *Columbia*

British Chamber Ensemble. c/o Keown Artists Management, 62 Chestnut Rd, London SE27 9LE *tel:* 0181 761 4221. Celia Chambers, fl; Julian Shaw, va; Rachel Masters, hp.

British Chamber Orchestra. 10 Ivy La, Westgate, Chichester, W Sussex PO20 6RA *tel:* 01243 545007 *also fax.* Crispin Ward, artistic dir; Simon Growcott, mgr.

British String Trio. c/o Keown Artists' Management, 62 Chestnut Rd, London SE27 9LE *tel:* 0181 761 4221. Jagdish Mistry, vn; Julian Shaw, va; Rhydian Shayson, vc.

British Tuba Quartet. Meadowview, 10 Old Forge Rd, Fenny Drayton, Warwicks CV13 6BD *tel:* 01827 711964 *also fax; email:* stevemead@ compuserve.com. Steven Mead, David Thornton, euph; Richard Sandland, Stuart Birnie, tb.

Broadside Band. 20 Leverton St, London NW5 2PJ *tel:* 0171 267 7176 *fax:* 0171 267 0127. Jeremy Barlow, dir.

Brodsky Quartet. Delfina Studios, 50 Bermondsey St, London SE1 3UD *tel:* 0171 378 8033 *fax:* 0171 378 8034 *email:* brodskyquartet@ compuserve.com. Celia Mike, mgr.

Brunel Ensemble. 16 Heol Fair, Llandaff, Cardiff CF5 2EE *tel:* 01222 563676 *also fax.* Deborah Keyser, admin; Christopher Austin, artistic dir.

[Brymer, Lloyd]. Jack Brymer, cl; David Lloyd, pno. *Lunn*

BT Scottish Ensemble. 2 Anchor La, Glasgow G1 2HW *tel:* 0141 221 2222 *fax:* 0141 221 4444. Roger Pollen, mgr; Clio Gould, artistic dir.

Buckingham Duo. 1 Buckingham Rd, Leeds LS6 1BP *tel:* 0113 275 8509; 01227 261975. Anna Shuttleworth, vc; Elizabeth Altman, pno.

Bureau Piano Trio. 120 Belmont Rise, Sutton, Surrey SM2 6EE *tel:* 0181 642 5714. Richard Bureau, vn; Elizabeth Angel, vc; Carlina Carr, pno.

The Burning Bush. 19 Patshull Rd, London NW5 2JX *tel:* 0171 485 3957 *fax:* 0171 267 2957. Lucie Skeaping, voice, rebec, vn; Robin Jeffrey, oud, gui, perc; Roddy Skeaping, vn, accordion; Ben Harlan, cl, darabukka; Stuart Hall, db, bendir, saz. Traditional Jewish music and song.

Calyx. Pno, vn, vc and cl. *JLM*

Cambiata Wind Trio. Lawron House, Wycombe Rd, Stokenchurch, Bucks HP14 3RP *tel:* 01494 483506. Peter Sheridan, fl, picc, alto fl.

The Chamber Music Company. 44 Melrose Av, London NW2 4JS *tel:* 0181 452 8983 *fax:* 0181 450 0546. Mark Troop, artistic dir, pno; Patricia Rozario, sop; Jagdish Mistry, vn; Matthew Barley, vc; Joan-Enric Lluna, cl; Stephen Stirling, hn.

Chameleon Chamber Ensemble. 115 Selsey Rd, Edgbaston, Birmingham B17 8JP *tel:* 0121 434 5440. Rachel Selvidge, fl; Simon Dewhurst, ob; Luan Ford, cl; Robert Percival, bsn; Tim Hill, hn; plus strs, wind and pno as required.

Chandos Baroque Players. St Canice's Cottage, Kilkenny, Ireland *tel:* 00 353 56 61497 *also fax.* Rachel Beckett, fl, rcdr; Lorraine Wood, ob; Jeremy Ward, bsn; Maya Homburger, vn; David Watkin, Daniel Yeadon, vc; Malcolm Proud, hpd.

The Charleston Chasers. 16 Chiswick End, Meldreth, Royston, Herts SG8 6LZ *tel:* 01763 260823 *fax:* 01763 260823. Terry Dash, mgr.

Charlie Barber + Band. 62 Arran St, Roath, Cardiff CF2 3HT *tel:* 01222 497157 *also fax.* Charlie Barber, dir; David Sheppard, admin. Wind, str and perc ens; 12 musicians.

[Charlier, Engerer]. Vn and pno. *Transart*

[Cheetham, Pillinger]. 15 Sitwell Grove, Stanmore, Middx HA7 3NB *tel:* 0181 954 4058. Edward Pillinger, cl; Suzanne Cheetham, pno.

Chesapeake Minstrels. George Weigand, dir. Banjos, mandolin, vn, pno, fl, cornet, trb, tb, db; ragtime ens. *CDI/Oriole*

Chiaroscuro. 71 Priory Rd, Kew, Surrey TW9 3DH *tel:* 0181 940 7086 *fax:* 0181 332 0879. Nigel Rogers, dir; Francesca McManus, mgr. Vocal soloists and baroque inst ens.

Chilingirian Quartet. Levon Chilingirian, Charles Sewart, vn; Asdis Varldimarsdottir, va; Philip De Groote, vc. *Intermusica*

Chinese Festival Ensemble. Chen Dacan, dir and chinese fiddle; Cheng Yu, pipes; Xu Pingxin, dulcimer; Lu Xiaohu, bamboo fl. *Chameleon*

Chinook Clarinet Quartet. 42 Vancouver Quay, Salford Quays, Lancs M8 2TU *tel:* 0976 245762. Teresa Whiffen, Maria Insua-Cao, Emily Gould, Esther Moors, cls.

Chopin Trio. *Finch*

Chris Wood Trio. 37 Cancell Rd, London SW9 6HP *tel:* 0171 735 1002 *also fax.* Chris Wood, Clare Salaman, vn; Roland Melia, vc.

Circa 1500. 86 Avenue Rd, London N15 5DN *tel:* 0181 802 7873 *also fax.* Nancy Hadden dir, fl, rcdr; Erin Headley, va da gamba; Dirk Freymuth, lute; Stephen Player, dancer, gui; Mhairi Lawson, sop. *Upbeat*

Circle. 57 White Horse Rd, London E1 0ND *tel:* 0171 790 5883 *fax:* 0171 265 9170. Gregory Rose, dir. Contemporary inst ens.

The City of London Chamber Players. 18 Burnt Hill Way, Wrecclesham, Farnham, Surrey GU10 4RP *tel:* 01252 795047 *also fax.* Brian Lloyd Wilson, dir and vn. Chmbr mus on period insts.

The City Waites. Lucie Skeaping, Doug Wooton, Roddy Skeaping, Michael Brain. Four voices, lute, cittern, fiddle, viol, shawm, rebecs, etc. *Chameleon/NBM*

[Clark, McMahon]. 31 Velindre Rd, Whitchurch, Cardiff CF4 7JE *tel:* 01222 617180; 0131 447 5386 *email:* mcmahonrb@wcmd.ac.uk. James Clark, vn; Richard McMahon, pno.

[Clarke, Cole]. Grange Cottage, Grange Rd, Knightley, Stafford ST20 0JX *tel:* 01785 284433 *also fax.* Garry Clarke, vn; Warwick Cole, hpd, f-pno. *Mostylea*

The Classic Buskers. Michael Copley, w/winds; Ian Moore, accordion. Arrangements and derangements of the world's mus masterpieces. *Seaview*

Classic Rhythm. Helen O'Connell, fl, picc; Chris Brannick, perc (tuned and untuned); Adrian Sutcliffe, pno, hpd and keyboards. *Chameleon*

Classical Rasumovsky. 13 Cambridge Rd, New Malden, Surrey KT3 3QE *tel:* 0181 949 6621 *also fax.* Frances Mason, Marilyn Taylor, vn; Christopher Wellington, va; Joy Hall, vc.

Classical Wind Quintet. Joanne Clements, fl; Ian Hardwick, ob; Meyrick Alexander, bsn; Michael Whight, cl; Richard Maskell, hn. *GBZ*

Classical Woodwind Trio. 37 Gloucester Dr, London N4 2LE *tel:* 0181 880 1557 *fax:* 0181 211 0734. Patrick Taggart, fl; Dick Ihnatowicz, cl,fl; Graham Lyons, bsn.

Clementi Piano Quartet. Blackland Farm, Stewkley, Leighton Buzzard, Beds LU7 0EU *tel:* 01525 240296 *fax:* 01525 240918 *email:* blacklands @compuserve. Yossi Zivoni, vn; Robert Smissen, va; Martin Loveday, vc; Sally Mellor, pno.

The Clerks' Group. 3 Chadwick Rd, London SE15 4RA *tel:* 0171 277 8742 *also fax.* Edward Wickham, dir. Vocal ens.

[Cohen, Rael]. 38 Keyes Rd, London NW2 3XA *tel:* 0181 452 3493 *also fax.*

Cohen Trio. 38 Keyes Rd, London NW2 3XA *tel:* 0181 452 3493. Raymond Cohen, vn; Robert Cohen, vc; Anthya Rael, pno.

Collegiate Wind Ensemble. David Campbell, cond. Flexible wind ens, 8-16 players. *Janet Hughes*

Collegium Musicum 90. 71 Priory Rd, Kew, Surrey TW9 3DH *tel:* 0181 940 7086 *fax:* 0181 332 0879. Simon Standage, Richard Hickox, mus dirs; Francesca McManus, gen mgr.

Colmore Octet. 8 Court Oak Grove, Harborne, Birmingham, W Midlands B32 2HR *tel:* 0966 463118. Natasha Stallard, Rachel Barber, ob; Emma McKnight, Karen Keay, cl; Sarah Chapple, Tom Simmonds, bsn; Ian Frankland, Luke Woodhead, hn.

Combattimento Consort Amsterdam. Jan Willem de Vriend, dir. *Matthew Tullah*

The Composers Ensemble. 80 Highworth Rd, London N11 2SH *tel:* 0181 368 1211 *also fax.* John Woolrich, Mary Wiegold, dirs; Jenny Goodwin, admin.

Concert Royal. 25 Turners Croft, Heslington, York YO1 5EL *tel:* 01904 410298. Peter Harrison, fl; Margarette Ashton, sop; John Treherne, hpd; Rachel Gray, vc. *Festival*

Concertante di Chicago. *NCCP*

Concertina and Piano Duo. 34 Balfour Av, Hanwell, London W7 3HS *tel:* 0181 567 9297 *fax:* 0181 723 0155. Douglas Rogers, concertina; Joanne Last, pno. Victorian concert works.

Concerto Grosso. *Still*

Les Concerts Royaux. 12 Spenser Rd, Harpenden, Herts AL5 5NN *tel:* 01582 462024 *also fax.* Terence Charlston, dir.

Concordia. 46 Uplands Rd, London N8 9NL *tel:* 0181 348 4295 *fax:* 0181 292 7125. Mark Levy, Joanna Levine, Alison McGillivray, Emilia Benjamin, viols.

Conjunto Ibérico. Elias Arizcureu, dir. Vc octet. *Matthew Tullah*

Consort of Musicke. 54a Leamington Rd Villas, London W11 1HT *tel:* 0171 229 5142 *fax:* 0171 221 1282 *email:* consort@easynet.co.uk. Anthony Rooley, mus dir; Imogen Mitchell, admin.

Contemporary Music Ensemble of Wales. 21 Chamberlain Rd, Cardiff CF4 2LW *tel:* 01222 568392. Gordon Downie, dir.

Contraband. 4 Sunnybank, Shipley, W Yorks BD18 3RP *tel:* 01274 599379 *also fax.* Graham Coatman, dir. 20th C mus and mus theatre.

Contrasts. 799 Chester Rd, Erdington, Birmingham B24 0BX *tel:* 0121 373 0420; 0976 414663. Frank Allen, cl, admin, dir. Cl and str trio; popular classics for concerts, banquets and special occasions.

Convivium. Elizabeth Wallfisch, baroque vn; Richard Tunnicliffe, baroque vc; Paul Nicholson, hpd. Baroque mus on authentic insts. *Sykes*

Cook and Stanley Piano Duet. Greystones, Pyrford Rd, West Byfleet, Surrey KT14 6QY *tel:* 01932 342187 *also fax.* Berendina Cook, Matthew Stanley.

The Copenhagen Trio. Søren Elbaek, vn; Troels Svane, vc; Morten Mogensen, pno. *SWA*

Copernicus Piano Trio. Rafael Todes, vn; Jennifer Janse, vc; Virginia Hanslip, pno. *Michael Harrold*

Cordial Company. 6 Victoria Grove, Fallowfield, Manchester M14 6BF *tel:* 0161 256 3686 *fax:* 0161 248 4435 *email:* joncordial@msn.com. Jennifer Hamilton, m-sop, celtic hp; Andrew Forbes-Lane, ten; Jonathan Thackeray, db; Richard de Volle, pno. Entertainments of mus and words on themes.

Corus Brass Ensemble. 4 Tonge Clough, Bolton BL7 9HR *tel:* 01204 593442 *also fax.* S S Talbot, ens mgr. 11 br, 1 perc.

Coull String Quartet. Roger Coull, Philip Gallaway, vn; David Curtis, va; John Todd, vc. *SWA*

Courtney Kenny and Friends. Kate Flowers, Nuala Willis, Harry Nicoll, Sandra Dugdale. Programmes including Gershwin, Berlin, Coward, Cole Porter. *Musicmakers*

Covent Garden String Quartet. *John Boddy*

[Cox, Latarche]. 33 Sandy La, Lymm, Cheshire WA13 9HP *tel:* 01925 756281. Nicholas Cox, cl; Vanessa Latarche, pno.

The Cremone Trio. 411 Manhattan Building, Bow Quarter, Fairfield Rd, London E3 2UQ *tel:* 0181 981 7413 *also fax.* Jo Shephard, ob; Gregor Laing, cl; Paul Harris, bsn.

The Crimson Twilight. *Mostylea*

Critical Band. Bancroft, Rectory La, Fringford, Bicester, Oxon OX6 9DX *tel:* 01869 278392 *also fax; email:* cb@brailsf.demon.co.uk; http://www. brailsf.demon.co.uk. James Wood, dir; Matthew Brailsford. Specialises in extended contemporary techniques such as microtonality and multiphonics as well as 20th C mus in general.

[Cross, Page]. Fiona Cross, cl; Kathryn Page, pno. *NCCP*

The Crowther Wind Quintet. *Annon*

The Crusell Ensemble. 23 Manor House Rd, Wilsden, Bradford BD15 0EB *tel:* 01535 273033. Sally Robinson, vn; Nick Turner, cl; Sally Ladds, vc. Michael Aston, pno. Chmbr mus for mixed ens.

Csardàs. 2 Falkland Av, Newton Mearns, Glasgow G77 5DR *tel:* 0141 639 3176 *also fax.* Bernard Docherty, vn; Stephen Adam, pno; Sheila Osborne, m-sop, admin. Gypsy, Viennese, Russian, dance and film themes.

!Cuatro! 78 Ridge Rd, London N8 9NR *tel:* 0181 348 3630. Colin Arenstein, dir. Mus for 4, 3, 2 and solo guis.

Cummings String Trio. 44 Gondar Gardens, London NW6 1HG *tel:* 0171 435 6232 *fax:* 0171 431 6843 *email:* trio@gondar.demon.co.uk. Diana Cummings, vn; Luciano Iorio, va; Gerard Le Feuvre, vc.

Da Ponte Ensemble. 27 Kensington Park Gardens, London W11 2QS *tel:* 0171 792 8723; 0385 320068 *fax:* 0171 221 8448. Luigi de Filippi, dir; Miranda Fulleylove, leader.

Da Rocha Pastorale. 31 Minster Ct, Hillcrest Rd, London W5 1HH *tel:* 0181 998 2392. Margaret Morrell, sop; William Morton, fl; Robert Bell, pno.

Dai-Chi and Valentin. 10 Mead Rd, Edgware, Middlesex HA8 6LJ *tel:* 0181 952 8245 *also fax.* Dai-Chi Chiu, Valentin Schiedermair, pno duo and pno duet.

Dallapiccola Ensemble. 23 Lancaster Grove, London NW3 4EX *tel:* 0171 435 8839 *also fax.* Luigi Suvini, mus dir; Daniele Quilleri, artistic dir.

Danish Chamber Ensemble. Hanne Holten, sop; Gitte Sørensen, fl; Kim Bak Dinitzen, vc; Eugene Asti, pno. *Roy Baker*

Dante Quartet. Str quartet. *Connaught*

Dartington Piano Trio. 35 St Marychurch Rd, Torquay, Devon TQ1 3JF *tel:* 01803 297123. Frances Mason, vn; Michael Evans, vc; John Bryden, pno.

Davey String Quartet. 75 Platts La, London NW3 7NL *tel:* 0171 435 0821. Juliet Davey, Jennifer Thorn, vn; Lucy White va; Olga Hegedus vc.

David Campbell and the Bingham String Quartet. 76 Cross Oak Rd, Berkhamsted, Herts HP4 3HZ *tel:* 01442 878654; 0850 667092 *email:* stephen.bingham@virgin.net; http://freespace.virgin.net/stephen. bingham. David Campbell, cl; Stephen Bingham, Sally-Ann Weeks, vn; Brenda Stewart, va; James Halsey, vc. Janet Hughes, admin.

[Davies], Helen and Harvey. 7 Menai Ville, Menai Bridge, Anglesey, North Wales LL59 5ES *tel:* 01248 713336. Pno duo. Helen Davies, Harvey Davies, pnos.

De Saram Clarinet Trio. 40 Greenford Av, London W7 3QP *tel:* 0181 579 0420 *fax:* 0181 567 9832. Rohan de Saram, vc; Angela Malsbury, cl; David Pettit, pno.

The De Voce String Quartet. 10 Trinity Av, London N2 0LX *tel:* 0181 883 8013 *also fax.* Julian Cummings, admin.

Deakin (Richard) Piano Trio. Richard Deakin, vn; Emma Ferrand, vc; Catherine Dubois, pno. *Ellison*

Debussy Trio. Susan Milan, fl; Yuko Inoue, va; Aline Brewer, hp. *Upbeat*

The Defoe String Quartet. 17 Fairfield Close, Harpenden, Herts Al5 5RZ *tel:* 01582 765322 *also fax.* Cimat Askin, Simon Perkins, vn; Andrew Byrt, va; Chris Fish, vc.

del Gesù Piano Trio. One Acre, Farnham Rd, Snape, Saxmundham, Suffolk IP17 1QW *tel:* 01728 689003. Geoffrey Trabichoff, vn; Alexander Volpov, vc; John Stafford, pno.

Deller Consort. 2 Rural Terrace, Wye, Ashford, Kent TN25 5AP *tel:* 01233 812267. Olive Simpson, Elisabeth Priday, sop; Mark Deller, c-ten, dir; Charles Daniels, ten; James Ottaway, bs; Robert Spencer, lute.

Delme String Quartet. 33 Whittingstall Rd, London SW6 4EA *tel:* 0171 736 7316 *fax:* 0171 371 7396; 01787 237970. *NBM*

Delos Quartet. 69 Rodenhurst Rd, London SW4 8AE *tel:* 0181 674 4804 *fax:* 0181 674 9685. Charlotte Edwards, Clare Renwick, vn; Sarah Pope, va; Babette Lichtenstein, vc.

Delta Saxophone Quartet. 109 George La, Lewisham, London SE13 6HN *tel:* 0181 690 6071 *also fax; email:* scottrell@gold.ac.uk. Stephen Cottrell, Chris Caldwell, Peter Seago, Peter Whyman.

Demon Barbers. Paul Thompson, alto; Andrew Phillips, ten; Rob Scales, ten; Anthony Scales, bar; Jeremy Birchall, bs. *Chameleon*

Derbyshire String Quartet. 18 Oaklea Way, Old Tupton, Chesterfield, Derbys S42 6JD *tel:* 01246 863829. Nina Martin, Edward Boothroyd, vn; Patricia Curteis, va; Peter White, vc.

[Derwinger, Pontinen]. Love Derwinger, Roland Pontinen, pno duo. *Gilder*

The Devienne Ensemble. 168 Downs Rd, Hastings, E Sussex TN34 2DZ *tel:* 01424 440929; 0973 734572. Warwick Potter, bn; Joanne Gould, vn; John Murphy, va; Carolyn Richards, vc.

Dittmer/Coulson Baroque to Modern Duo. 10 Pembroke Mews, London W8 6ER *tel:* 0171 937 0684 *also fax.* Petronella Dittmer, vn, sop; Richard Coulson, org, hpd. Mus from plainsong to the present day.

Divertimenti Ensemble. 1 Pendley Bridge Cottages, Tring Station, Tring, Herts HP23 5QU *tel:* 01442 822732 *also fax; email:* 101765.465@ compuserve.com. Paul Barritt, leader: str octet.

Dizzy Lips. 18 Hillfield Pk, Muswell Hill, London N10 3QS *tel:* 0181 444 8587 *fax:* 0181 245 0358 *email:* impulse@styx.cerbernet.co.uk. Geraldine Allen, cl and wind synthesizer; Carol Wells, pno, keyboards and vocals.

Double Image. 20 Standish Rd, London W6 9AL *tel:* 0181 748 0935 *fax:* 0181 748 2144. David Carhart, dir, pno; Erica Dearing, vn; Miriam Lowbury, vc; Andrew Sparling, cl; Carola Nielinger, fl.

Dragonsfire. Nigel Perona-Wright, dir. *Upbeat*

Dramatis Personae. The Old Rectory Coach House, High St, Bourton-on-the-Water, Glos GL54 2AP *tel:* 01451 821481 *also fax.* Lesley-Jane Rogers, sop; Edward Peters, bar; Christopher Ross, pno. Concert-staged recitals on a chosen theme.

Eusebius Piano Trio. 109 Pulborough Rd, London SW18 5UL *tel:* 0181 874 2125 *fax:* 0181 947 9867. Jonathan Rutherford, pno; Nicholas Evans-Pughe, vn; Susanna Wilson, vc.

Eva Meier Company. German cabaret entertainment. *Michael Brewer*

Extempore String Ensemble. George Weigand, dir, lute, mandore; Rosemary Thorndycraft, viols; William Thorp, vn; Sally Owen, hpd, viols; Robin Jeffrey, theorbo, lute; also optional singer, wind insts and dancers. 17th C mus. *CDI/Oriole*

I Fagiolini. 24 Salisbury Close, Princes Risborough, Bucks HP27 0JF *tel:* 01844 344525 *also fax.* Robert Hollingworth, dir; Anna Crookes, Rachel Elliott, Carys Lane, sop; Robin Blaze, Richard Wyn-Roberts, c-ten; Hugh Wilson, Nicholas Smith, ten; Roderick Williams, Matthew Brook, bs. Vocal mus (ens) and solo team for oratorio. *Clarion/Seven Muses*

Fairman Piano Trio. Matthew Fairman, vn; Anne-Isabel Meyer, vc; Peter Croser, pno. *Chameleon*

[Farrall, Drake]. Joy Farrall, cl; Julius Drake, pno. *NCCP*

Fermata. *NBM*

[Ferrand, Hare]. Emma Ferrand, vc; Ian Itare, org and hpd. *Ellison*

The Fibonacci Sequence. 81 Lacy Rd, London SW15 1NR *tel:* 0181 780 3266; 01892 870187 *fax:* 0181 780 0600 *email:* cicfib@easynet.co.uk. Kathron Sturrock, pno; Jonathan Rees, Abigail Young, vn; Yuko Inoue, va; Michael Stirling, vc; Duncan McTier, db; Anna Noakes, fl; Christopher O'Neal, ob; Julian Farrell, cl; Richard Skinner, bsn; Stephen Stirling, hn; Gillian Tingay, hp; Paul Archibald, tpt; Shelley Phillips, mgr.

Fiddlesticks. 10 Mill Rd, Waterbeach, Cambridge CB5 9RQ *tel:* 01223 862232 *also fax.* Ishani Bhoola, Sarah Ewins, vn; Ania Ullman, va; Joy Hawley, vc, Ann Clampit, admin.

Fidelio Trio. 24 Ballater Rd, London SW2 5QR *tel:* 0956 916510 *fax:* 0171 923 1557. Darragh Morgan, vn; Michael Atkinson, vc; Mary Dullea, pno.

Fine Arts Brass Ensemble. 3 Cumbria Close, Coundon, Coventry CV1 3PG *tel:* 01203 779480 *fax:* 01203 779479 *email:* 106232.332@ compuserve.com. Simon Lenton, Bryan Allen, tpt; Stephen Roberts, hn; Simon Hogg, trb; Richard Sandland, tb; Steven Greenall, mgr.

Fiori Musicali. Bank Cottage, Old Forge La, Preston Capes, Northants NN11 3TD *tel:* 01327 361380 *fax:* 01327 361415 *email:* fiori@aol.com. Penelope Rapson, dir; Kerstin Linder-Dewan, leader; Bernard Rapson, treasurer; Jonathan Asquith, chm.

Fioritura. 38 Alric Av, New Malden, Surrey KT3 4JN *tel:* 0181 942 1519; 0467 221138. Lorna Anderson, sop; Jane Booth, cl; Simon Nicholls, f-pno; Sebastian Comberti, vc.

Firebird. Barrie Webb, dir. *KDM*

[Fisher, Lasserson]. Peter Fisher, vn; Nadia Lasserson, pno. *Ellison*

Fitzwilliam Quartet. Lucy Russell, Jonathan Sparey, vn; Alan George, va; Daniel Yeadon, vc. *Manygate*

Florestan Piano Trio. Anthony Marwood, vn; Richard Lester, vc; Susan Tomes, pno. *Tennant*

Florilegium. 53 Tresco Rd, London SE15 3PY *tel:* 0171 639 7376 *also fax; email:* florilegium@compuserve.com. Ashley Solomon, Neal Peres Da Costa, management; Rachel Podger, leader; Helen Whitaker, admin. Baroque and classical chmbr and orch mus on period insts; also choir.

Flute House Trio. *John Boddy*

Flutes Fantastic. Trevor Wye. Fls and pno. Amusing recital with commentary. *Seaview/NCCP*

Forellen Ensemble. 41 Roupell St, London SE1 8TB *tel:* 0171 928 2512 *also fax.* Members of the RPO: David Towse, Christopher Lydon, vn; David Newland, va; Christopher Irby, vc; Roy Benson, db; Vivian Troon, pno.

Four Strings Each. 75 Platts La, London NW3 7NL *tel:* 0171 435 0821. Lucy White, vn; Juliet Davey, pno and vn. Concerts for the sick and elderly. Registered charity.

[Frankl, Pauk, Kirshbaum]. Peter Frankl, pno; György Pauk, vn; Ralph Kirshbaum, vc. *Transart/Ingpen*

Fretwork. 67 King's Rd, Richmond, Surrey TW10 6EG *tel:* 0181 948 1250 *fax:* 0181 332 0415. Wendy Gillespie, Richard Campbell, Richard Boothby, Julia Hodgson, Susanna Pell, William Hunt, viols. *Holt*

Fritz Spiegl and the Spieglers. Fritz Spiegl, dir. *Musicmakers*

Frog in the Throat. Sarah-Jane Dale, sop; Andrew Morris, ten; Audrey Hyland, pno. *Michael Harrold*

Frottola. 79 Humber Doucy La, Ipswich, Suffolk IP4 3NU *tel:* 01473 718811. Jennie Cassidy, m-sop; Jacob Heringman, lute; Philip Thorby, viol, rcdr. Lute song trio, programmes of renaissance mus.

The Gabrieli Consort. Nicholas Morrison, Jennifer Smith, admin; Anita Crowe, gen mgr. *Still*

Gabrieli String Quartet. Yossi Zivoni, vn; Brendan O'Reilly, vn; Ian Jewel, va; Keith Harvey, vc. *Anglo-Swiss*

The Gagliano Trio. The Fountain, Tidebrook, Wadhurst, E Sussex TN5 6PF *tel:* 01892 782220 *also fax.* Roger Garland, vn; Brian Hawkins, va; Roger Smith, vc.

Gainsborough Piano Trio. 27 Leicester Rd, London N2 9DY *tel:* 0181 444 5905 *also fax.* Adrian Levine, vn; Andrew Shulman, vc; Graeme Humphrey, pno.

Galliard Ensemble Wind Quintet. 119 Ashfield St, Stepney, London E1 3EX *tel:* 0171 791 0495; 0976 399828. Wind quintet. Kathryn Thomas, fl; Judi Elphick, ob; Katherine Spencer, cl; Richard Bayliss, hn; Helen Simons, bsn.

Gamelan Sekar Petak. c/o Music Dept, University of York, Heslington, York YO1 5DD *tel:* 01904 432438 *fax:* 01904 432450 *email:* nfis1@ york.ac.uk. Neil Sorrell, mus dir. Complete bronze javanese gamelan, played by past and present members of the York mus department.

Garden Consort. 36 Southside, Clapham Common, London SW4 9BS *tel:* 0171 627 1089 *also fax.* Vocal quartet and pno artists from the Royal Opera House. *Clifton Wyatt*

The Gatsby Saxophone Quartet. 28b Heddington Grove, Islington, London N7 9SY *tel:* 0171 700 5431. Nick White, sop sax; Nicola Baigent, alto sax; James Scannell, ten sax; Susan Gleave, baritone sax.

Gemini. 137 Upland Rd, E Dulwich, London SE22 0DF *tel:* 0181 693 4694 *fax:* 0181 693 4426. Ian Mitchell, cl, dir. Mixed chmbr ens; repertoire from 12th C to present day; regular educ projects.

Gemini Duo. 8 Lloyd St South, Manchester M14 7HY *tel:* 0161 226 8806. Sarah Bull, fl; Wendy Jackson, gui.

The Georgian Camerata. 10 Queensmill Rd, London SW6 6JS *tel:* 0171 737 3591 *also fax.* Jonathan Stallick, artistic dir; Sarah Baxter, orch mgr. Mixed inst ens, 4-40 players, baroque and classical repertoire.

Gershwin & Co. Sarah Poole, sop; Nigel Clayton, pno; David Heyes, db; Chris Gould, drums. *Chameleon*

Gilbert and Sullivan Ensemble. 10 Pembroke Mews, London W8 6ER *tel:* 0171 937 0684 *also fax.* Petronella Dittmer, vn; Christine Blair, pno; also vc. Gilbert and Sullivan, palm court mus, light classics, dinner mus.

Giordani Ensemble. Mary Pilbery, mus dir, ob; Susan Edwards, ob; Glyn Williams, bsn; Stephen Warner, db; Nicholas Durcan, hpd, pno. *Roy Baker*

Giovanni Piano Trio. Tong Lee Head, Marsden HD7 6NJ *tel:* 01484 841868 *also fax.* Katharine Durran, pno; Gina McCormack, vn; Sebastian Comberti, vc.

The Glinka Trio. Spencer Pitfield, cl; Risto Lauriala, pno; Antal Mojzer, bsn. *Ellison*

Goldberg Ensemble. Empress Business Centre, 380 Chester Rd, Manchester M16 9EA *tel:* 0161 872 2455 *fax:* 0161 872 2260. Malcolm Layfield, artistic dir; Stephen Voysey, promotions mgr. Str and chmbr ens, chmbr orch.

[Goldberg, Frith]. 28 Leicester Rd, London N2 9EA *tel:* 0181 444 5891 *fax:* 0181 444 3225. Nigel Goldberg, vn; Benjamin Frith, pno.

[Goldstone, Clemmow]. Walcot Old Hall, Alkborough, N Lincs DN15 9JT *tel:* 01724 720475 *fax:* 01724 721599. Anthony Goldstone, Caroline Clemmow, pno duo.

[Gough, Bottomley]. John Gough, Sally Ann Bottomley, pno duo. *NCCP*

Gould Piano Trio. Lucy Gould, vn; Martin Storey, vc; Gretel Dowdeswell, pno. *Hazard*

[Gowers, Owen]. Katharine Gowers, Charles Owen. Vn and pno. *GBZ*

Graham Fitkin Group. c/o 19 Green St, Chorleywood, Herts WD3 5QS *tel:* 01923 493903 *also fax.* Ann Morfee, vn; Anton Lukoszevieze, vc; Richard Benjafield, perc; Nick Moss, Simon Haram, sax; Graham Fitkin, keyboards.

Grand Union. 14 Clerkenwell Green, London EC1R 0DP *tel:* 0171 251 2100 *fax:* 0171 250 3009. Tony Haynes, dir; Catherine Mummery, admin. Brian Abrahams, drums; Claude Deppa, tpt; Paul Jayasinha, tpt; Louise Elliott, fl, sax; Balu Shrivastav, sitar, table; Vladimir Vega, charango, panpipes; Brenda Rattray, voice, steel pans. Performed by professional musicians from different countries and ethnic backgrounds.

[Grech, Kirkbride, Spanswick]. Sophia Grech, mezzo-sop; Simon Kirkbride, bar; Melanie Spanswick, pno. *Michael Harrold*

Grieg Trio. *Gilder*

[Griffett, Walker]. James Griffett, ten; Timothy Walker, lute, gui. *CDI*

Grosvenor String Quartet. 1 Church View, Ampthill, Bedford MK45 2PZ *tel:* 01525 406456 *fax:* 01525 406451. Andrew Bentley, Andrew Thurgood, vn; Timothy Grant, va; Trevor Burley, vc.

Grupo de Canto Coral. Nestor Andrenacci, dir. *Ellison*

The Guadagnini Piano Trio. East West Arts Ltd, 93b Cambridge Gardens, N Kensington, London W10 6JE *tel:* 0181 960 5889 *fax:* 0181 968 5541. Robert Whysall Gibbs, vn; Anup Kumar Biswas, vn, vc; Stephen Gutman, pno.

Guarneri Quartet. *Ingpen*

Guarneri Trio Prague. Pno trio. *Judith Hendershott*

Guildhall Strings. 7 Durham Rd, London N2 9DP *tel:* 0181 883 4944 *also fax;* 0831 200474 *email:* ian.brignall@virgin.net. Ian Brignall, gen mgr; Robert Salter, mus dir. 11-piece str ens.

Guitaria. 35 Enmore Gardens, London SW14 8RF *tel:* 0181 876 6161 *also fax.* Marylyn Troth, sop; Michael Lewin, gui.

[Guy, Riley, Wachsmann]. 53 Tweedy Rd, Bromley, Kent BR1 3NH *tel:* 0181 290 5917. Phillip Wachsmann, vn; Barry Guy, db; Howard Riley, pno.

Horn Belles. Mill Farm, Farlow, Kidderminster, Worcs DY14 0LP *tel:* 01746 718727 *fax:* 01746 718540 *email:* the.pigpen@dial.pipex. com.uk. Gillian Jones, Stella Disney, Allyson Roper, Nicola Daw, hns.

[Horner, Ainscough]. Christopher Horner, vn; Julie Ainscough, pno. *Michael Harrold*

The Houghton Consort. 9 Cromwell Rd, Burgess Hill, W Sussex RH15 8QH *tel:* 01444 230779 *fax:* 01444 233699. Nicholas Houghton, artistic dir; Helen Houghton, mgr.

Hugo Wolf String Quartet. *Lubbock*

I Musicanti. 82 Manor Rd, Tring, Herts HP23 5DA *tel:* 01442 823796 *also fax; email:* lebosch@compuserve.com. Str, wind and pno chmbr ens.

Icebreaker. 26 Stadium St, London SW10 0PT *tel:* 0171 351 6519; 01306 889057 *also fax.* James Poke, artistic dir; Amy Coffey, admin. Amplified ens combining elements of contemporary mus, rock and jazz. Fl, pan pipes, sax, keyboard, gui, vn, vc, accordion, perc.

The Ictus Ensemble. Contemporary mus. *Lyons*

Ifeka Saunders Duo. Althea Ifeka, ob; Dominic Saunders, pno. *Ellison*

Il Giardino Armonico. *Askonas*

Instant Sunshine. 9 Ashdown Rd, Epsom, Surrey KT17 3PL *tel:* 01372 720727. David Barlow, Peter Christie, Alan Maryon-Davis; Tom Barlow, db. Guis, banjos, db, perc.

Instrumental Quintet of London. Susan Milan, fl; Nicholas Ward, vn; Yuko Inoue, va; John Heley, vc; Aline Brewer, hp. *Upbeat*

Interfusion. 38 Denman Rd, London SE15 5NR *tel:* 0171 701 6438 *also fax; email:* interfusion@brailsf.demon.co.uk. Matthew Brailsford, admin; Judith Mitchell, dir, vc; Clive Williamson, pno, keyboards. Acoustic/elec ensemble performing with sound projection 20th C works for vc and pno, keyboards and electronics.

Intrada Brass Ensemble. Alan Furness, dir. *Michael Harrold*

Isis Piano Trio. 70 Midhurst Rd, Ealing, London W13 9XR *tel:* 0181 579 1740. Kaye Barker, vn; Kevin Faux, vc; Shelley Corkill, pno.

Isos String Quartet. *Lubbock*

Israel Piano Trio. Stoneville Cottage, Gretton Fields, Cheltenham, Glos GL54 5HH *tel:* 01242 620736 *also fax.* Menahem Breuer, vn; Marcel Bergman, vc; Alexander Volkov, pno; Christine Talbot-Cooper, admin.

Israel String Quartet. Yigal Tunch, vn; Elyakum Saltzman, vn; Robert Mozes, va; Alexander Kaganovsky, vc. *Ellison*

[Jackson, McAllister]. Robin Jackson, Maureen McAllister, org duo. *Invisible Pilots*

Janacek String Quartet. *Lubbock*

Jane's Minstrels. 2 Wilton Sq, London N1 3DL *tel:* 0171 359 1593 *fax:* 0171 226 4369. Jane Manning, artistic dir; Roger Montgomery, cond. Mixed ens: 4-18 insts plus occasional vocals and Jane Manning, sop.

[Janse, Hanslip]. Jennifer Janse, vc; Virginia Hanslip, pno. *Michael Harrold*

Japan Music Pool. 27 Heber Rd, London NW2 6AB *tel:* 0181 452 9234 *also fax.* Takako Selby-Okamoto, sop, dir; Lyn McLarin, fl; Yuri Nagai, vn; Julia Walker, vc; Keiko Tokunaga, pno; Harold Lester, pno, hpd; Mike Selby, sec.

Jeux. 30 Woodsome Rd, London NW5 1RY *tel:* 0171 485 1903 *also fax.* Imogen Barford, artistic dir; Gillian Tingay, hp; Ileana Ruhemann, fl; Rebecca Hirsch, vn; Martin Outram, va; Julia Vohralik, vc. Chmbr mus with hp.

[Jewel, Slater]. 49 Exeter Rd, London NW2 4SE *tel:* 0181 452 6843. Carol Slater, vn; Ian Jewel, va.

Jourdan String Quartet. 15 Merton St, Cambridge CB3 9JD *tel:* 01223 517623 *also fax; email:* paj20@cam.ac.uk. Christine Townsend, Paul Jourdan, vn; Kathryn Jourdan, va; Michael Mace, vc.

The Jupiter Ensemble. Cornubia, 16 Edenfield, Orton Longueville, Peterborough PE2 7HY *tel:* 01733 235888 *email:* 100413.1360@ compuserve.com. Graham Casey, admin. Chmbr ens of mixed insts.

Kalengo Percussion Ensemble. 9 Ivy Rd, Poynton, Cheshire SK12 1PE *tel:* 01625 858878 *fax:* 01625 858804. Eryl Roberts, Liz Gulliver, John O'Hara, Andrew Whettam, perc.

[Kalichstein, Laredo, Robinson]. Joseph Kalichstein, pno; Jaime Laredo, vn; Sharon Robinson, vc. *Holt*

Kandinsky String Quartet. 13 Radlet Av, London SE26 4BZ *tel:* 0181 699 9030 *also fax.* Jenny Godson, Jane Carwardine, vn; Rachel Bolt, va; Shuna Wilson, vc.

Karisma. c/o Little Corner, Cross Oak Rd, Berkhamsted, Herts HP4 3NA *tel:* 01442 863263. Christopher Hughes, pno; Marie-Anne Mairesse, vn; Karen Stephenson, vc.

Katin Piano Trio. Krzysztof Smietana, vn; Pal Banda, vc; Peter Katin, pno. *Purkiss*

Kegelstatt Trio. Fiona Cross, cl; Rosemary Sanderson, va; Nigel Clayton, pno. *NCCP*

Keller String Quartet. Andras Keller, Janos Pilz, vn; Zoltan Gal, va; Otto Kertesz, vc. *Tennant*

Kensington Gore Singers. 10 Pembroke Mews, London W8 6ER *tel:* 0171 937 0684 *also fax.* Petronella Dittmer, dir. 3-16 singers. Sacred and secular mus.

Kenwood Ensemble. West Byres Cottage, Balmerino, Fife DD6 8SB *tel:* 01382 330883. Yvonne Howard, m-sop; Duncan Prescott, cl; Ivan McCready, vc; Scott Mitchell, pno.

The King's Consort. 34 St Mary's Grove, London W4 3LN *tel:* 0181 995 9994 *fax:* 0181 995 2115 *email:* info@the-kings-consort.org.uk; http://www.the-kings-consort.org.uk. Robert King, artistic dir; Philip Cole, gen mgr; Nicky Oppenheimer, development dir; Stephen Metcalfe, admin. Baroque and early classical on period insts; can also be with choir and soloists. Chmbr ens 8-14 players.

The King's Singers. Nigel Short, David Hurley, c-ten; Bob Chilcott, ten; Philip Lawson, Gabriel Crouch, bar; Stephen Connolly, bs. *IMG*

Kingsdown Duo. 10 Cossins Rd, Bristol BS6 7LY *tel:* 0117 924 3159; 0117 942 3373. Roger Huckle, vn; John Bishop, pno.

[Kipling, Moore]. Flat 10, Towerside, 144 Wapping High St, London E1 9XF *tel:* 0171 488 3490 *also fax.* Timothy Kipling, fl; Angela Moore, hp.

[Kipling, Packwood]. Flat 10, Towerside, 144 Wapping High St, London E1 9XF *tel:* 0171 488 3490 *also fax.* Timothy Kipling, fl; Mark Packwood, pno.

[Kirby, Parnell]. 22 Chestnut Av, Hornsey, London N8 8NY *tel:* 0181 340 2983 *also fax.* Michael Kirby, cl; Brian-Michael Parnell, pno.

[Kirkby, Rooley]. Emma Kirkby, sop; Anthony Rooley, lute. *Magenta*

Klarinettenharmonie. 24 Clarence Rd, Malvern WR14 3EH *tel:* 01684 575771. Cl quartet. Elizabeth Rozelaar, Richard Percy, Rosemary Harrington, Antony Dean.

Klaviola. Duo. *John Boddy*

Kocian Quartet. Str quartet. *Judith Hendershott*

Kontraste. 8 Pit Farm Rd, Guildford, Surrey GU1 2JH *tel:* 01483 563096. Martin Feinstein, fl; Marina Solarek, vn; Michael Mace, vc; Penelope Cave, hpd.

Kreutzer Quartet. Peter Sheppard, David Le Page, vn; Malcolm Allison, va; Philip Sheppard, vc. *Manygate*

Kroumata. Perc. *Lyons*

Kubelik Trio. Jan Talich jnr, vn; Karel Fiala, vc; Kvita Bilynska, pno. *Ellison*

Kutrowatz Piano Duo. Eduard and Johannes Kutrowatz. *Ellison*

La Petite Bande. *Allied*

[Labèque]. Katia and Marielle Labèque, pno. *Transart*

Lacock Abbey Chamber Ensemble. 10 Pembroke Mews, London W8 6ER *tel:* 0171 937 0684 *also fax.* Group of 4-24 musicians. Petronella Dittmer, dir, vn.

Ladybones. c/o B & B Concert Services, 66 Hyde Way, Hayes, Middx UB3 4PB *tel:* 0181 606 0030 *fax:* 0181 606 0037 *email:* roderick_burnett@ compuserve.com. Roderick Burnett, mgr dir; Sarah Williams, Abigail Newman, Jayne Murrill, Tracy Holloway, trb; Carole Marnoch, sop. Trb quartet and voice. Offers introduction to lower br insts, demonstrations of various mus styles, detailed lecture recitals, children's w/shops.

Lake Piano Trio. 157 Ferndale Rd, London SW4 7RU *tel:* 0171 738 7391 *also fax.* Grigori Zhislin, vn; Douglas Cummings, vc; Ian Lake, pno.

Landini Consort. Rainer Beckmann, Clémence Comte, Lara Morris, rcdrs. *KDM*

The Lark String Quartet. *McCann*

Lecosaldi Ensemble. 27 Prentis Rd, London SW16 1QB *tel:* 0181 769 2677 *also fax;* 0171 606 4986. Peter Lea-Cox, dir; Rev Ronald T Englund, admin. Singers and insts, mainly 18th C mus, specialising in Bach cantatas.

Leda Piano Trio. 107 Woodhall Rd, Edinburgh EH13 0HP *tel:* 0131 441 4247. Kate Thompson, pno, Peter Campbell Kelly, vn; Kevin McCrae, vc.

Legrand Ensemble. James Bowman, Charles Brett, c-ten; John Turner, David Pugsley, rcdr; Jonathan Price, vc; Keith Elcombe, hpd. *Upbeat*

Lehar Schrammel. 68 Lysia St, London SW6 6NG *tel:* 0171 385 0182 *fax:* 0171 381 1155. John Leach, dir, zither; Jake Rea, vn; Rodney Stewart, bs; Laurence Joyce, fl; Colin Courtenay, cl; Judd Procter, gui; Tracey Goldsmith, accordion. *GBZ*

[Lenehan, Page]. 38 Rectory Av, High Wycombe, Buckinghamshire HP13 6HW *tel:* 01494 531862 *fax:* 01494 558045. John Lenehan, Kathryn Page, pno duo.

Leodian String Quartet. 34 Stainburn Cres, Moortown, Leeds LS17 6NS *tel:* 0113 266 0602 *also fax.* Douglas Reid, Raymond Sidebottom, vn; Brian Carlile, va; Roger Ladds, vc.

Leopold String Trio. Marianne Thorsen, vn; Sarah-Jane Bradley, va; Kate Gould, vc. *YCAT*

Les Rossignols. 111c St Mark's Rd, London W10 6NP *tel:* 0181 969 8707 *email:* http://www.intune.co.uk/lesrossignols. Ian Judson, fl; Joseph Asghar, gui. *Clifton Wyatt*

Les Trois. 142 Elmington Rd, London SE5 7RA *tel:* 0171 701 0400 *fax:* 0171 225 5279 *email:* 106325.1302@compuserve.com. Kirsten Spratt, fl; Rachel Bolt, va; Ruth Holden, hp.

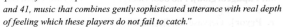

Primavera Chamber Ensemble. Horseshoe Barn, Cobbarn Farm, Groombridge La, Eridge TN3 9LA *tel:* 01892 864069 *also fax.* Paul Manley, artistic dir. 3-8 players in varying combinations.

Priory Concertante of London. 43 Beech Rd, Branston, Lincoln LN4 1PP *tel:* 01522 791662. Frank Stiles, principal cond. 14-40 players.

Pro Arte Guitar Trio. Raymond Burley, Cornelius Bruinsma, Peter Rueffer. *NCCP*

Pro Cantione Antiqua. Timothy Penrose, Robin Blaze, Michael Chance, c-ten; James Griffett, Ian Partridge, Joseph Cornwell, ten; Michael George, Stephen Roberts, Julian Clakson, Adrian Peacock, bar. Vocal ens. *CDI*

Progetto Avanti. Gui duo. *Connaught*

Prospero Chamber Ensemble. 34a Dry Hill Park Rd, Tonbridge, Kent TN9 1LX *tel:* 01732 369041 *also fax.* Jennifer Stinton, fl; Caroline Blading, vn; Judith Busbridge, Susan Knight, va; Alastair Blayden, vc. *KDM*

Purcell Consort of Voices. The Spinney, 5 Park La, Histon, Cambridge CB4 4JJ *tel:* 01223 237317. Grayston Burgess, dir.

Quartet Caravaggio. c/o Conchord Orchestras Ltd, Jumps Rd, Churt, Surrey GU10 2JY *tel:* 01252 792315 *fax:* 01252 795120. Perry Montague-Mason, Rita Manning, vn; Kate Musker, va; Justin Pearson, vc.

Quatuor Ludwig. Str quartet. *Judith Hendershott*

Quatuor Mosaïques. Str quartet. *Judith Hendershott*

Quatuor Parisii. Thierry Brodard, vn; Jean-Michel Berrette, vn; Dominique Lobet, va; Jean-Philippe Martignoni, vc. *Clarion/Seven Muses*

Quatuor Sine Nomine. *Ingpen*

[Queffálec, Cooper]. Anne Queffálec, Imogen Cooper, pno duo. *Tennant*

Quintaria. Flat 2, 2 Great North Rd, Highgate, London N6 *tel:* 0956 431449. Ian Judson, fl; Huw Clement-Evans, ob; Nicola Baigent, cl; Philip Gibbon, bsn; Tom Ainger, hn.

Quintessence. The Little House, 14 Windhill, Bishops Stortford, Herts CM20 2NG *tel:* 01279 651856. Anna Lethieullier, sop; Carol Leatherby, m-sop; James Hay, Alan J Preston, John Terry, ten; Alan Lamb, bar; Carol Wells, pno. Victorian Edwardian drawing room entertainment: opera, operetta and musicals.

Quintessential Opera. Hamilton House, Cobblers Corern, Felsted, Great Dunmow, Essex CM6 3LX *tel:* 01371 820382 *fax:* 01371 821100. Antoine Mitchell, dir.

QuintEssential Sackbut and Cornett Ensemble. 10 King's Highway, Plumstead, London SE18 2NL *tel:* 0181 855 8584 *also fax.* Richard Thomas, dir.

Quintus. 5 voices: programmes from Gesualdo to 20th C. Gerald Place, dir. *Chameleon*

Quintus. 77 Lonsdale Rd, Barnes, London SW13 9DA *tel:* 0181 748 1460. Allan Schiller, pno; Tess Miller, ob; Julia Rayson, cl; Francis Markus, hn; John McDougall, bsn.

Quorum. 21 Allendale Close, London SE5 8SG *tel:* 0171 703 7372. Julia Munn, cl, sax; Martin Pring, vn, va; Hugh McDowell, vc; Andrew Spiceley, pno, perc.

The Rachmaninov Trio. 537 Sauchiehall St, Glasgow G3 7PQ *tel:* 0141 248 1989 *also fax;* 0141 248 1611 *email:* phillipsilver@allegro.demon. co.uk. Lev Atlas, vn and va; Alexander Volpov, vc; Phillip Silver, pno.

Raglan Baroque Players. 52 Goldsmith Av, Acton, London W3 6HN *tel:* 0181 896 2741 *also fax.* Nicholas Kraemer, dir; Melanie Turner, gen mgr; Vicky Miller, concerts mgr. Baroque insts. *Sykes*

Rags to Riches. Helen Crayford, pno. Illustrating the development of ragtime into jazz. *Seaview*

[Ránki, Klukon]. Dezsö Ránki and Edit Klukon, pno duo. *Lubbock*

Raphael Ensemble. Anthony Marwood, Catherine Manson, vn; Timothy Boulton, Louise Williams, va; Andrea Hess, Michael Stirling, vc. *Tennant*

The Rascher Saxophone Quartet. *Lyons*

Rasumovsky String Quartet. 13 Cambridge Rd, New Malden, Surrey KT3 3QE *tel:* 0181 949 6621 *also fax.* Frances Mason, Marilyn Taylor vn; Christopher Wellington, va; Joy Hall, vc.

ReSound. 47 Boscombe Rd, Wimbledon, London SW19 3AX *tel:* 0181 715 8123 *also fax; email:* faure@globalnet.co.uk. Anthony Aarons, tpt; Tim Palmer, perc; Andrew Lovett, electronics.

Red Byrd. John Potter, ten; Richard Wistreich, bs; other voices, insts. Early and contemporary mus. *Robert White*

Regency Wind Ensemble. 1 Hillmead, Gossops Green, Crawley, W Sussex *tel:* 01293 546762 *fax:* 01273 777963. Alison Letschka, fl; Mark James, ob; Andrew Sutton, cl; Alan Newnham, hn; Alison Wills, bsn.

Regular Music II. 13c Grove Pk, London SE5 8LR *tel:* 0171 733 3808 *also fax.* Amplified chmbr ens.

[Reid, Stewart]. 75 Moor End Rd, Mellor, Stockport, Cheshire SK6 5PT *tel:* 0161 427 5482 *also fax; email:* gavinreid@compuserve.com. Gavin Reid, tpt; Gordon Stewart, org.

The Rembrandt Trio. Valerie Tryon, pno; Gerard Kantarjian, vn; Coenraad Bloemendal, vc. *Ellison*

Reservoir. 89 Glenwood Rd, London N15 3JS *tel:* 0181 292 6484 *fax:* 0171 815 6094. Mikel Toms, dir. Contemporary mus ens, largely late 20th C repertoire.

The Revolutionary Drawing Room. 34 Fernwood Av, London SW16 1RD *tel:* 0181 769 4158 *fax:* 0181 677 4157. Adrian Butterfield, Julia Bishop, vn; Peter Collyer, va; Angela East, vc; Judith Evans, db; Rachel Brown, fl; Frank de Bruine, ob; Colin Lawson, cl; Alastair Mitchell, bsn; Roger Montgomery, hn; Nigel North, gui. Chmbr mus on period insts. *Upbeat*

[Riley, Rubenstein]. 9 St George's Av, London N7 0HB *tel:* 0171 609 2976 *email:* 101454.2231@compuserve.com. Catherine Riley and Robin Rubenstein, pno duo and duet.

[Riley, Tippett]. 53 Tweedy Rd, Bromley, Kent BR1 3NH *tel:* 0181 290 5917. Howard Riley, Keith Tippett, pno duo.

The Roger Heaton Group. Cl, gui, perc. Electro-acoustic. *Lyons*

The Rogeri Trio. Yoshiko Endo, pno; Nadia Myerscough, vn; Peter Adams, vc. *GBZ*

Romanesca. Barn House, Holtwood, Hamstead Marshall, nr Newbury, Berks RG20 0JH *tel:* 01635 253073; 00 31 20 6844 322 *fax:* 01635 255255; 00 31 20 6828 799 *email:* hmoens@ dds.nl. Andrew Manze, vn; Nigel North, lute, theorbo; John Toll, hpd, org. Specialising in 17th C inst mus.

The Romantic Chamber Group of London. Brick Kiln Cottages, Hollington, Newbury, Berks RG20 9XX *tel:* 01635 254331 *fax:* 01635 253629. Paul Barritt, vn; Charles Medlam, vc; James Lisney, pno.

The Rondel Ensemble. Tickerage Castle, Pound La, Framfield, Uckfield, E Sussex TN22 5RT *tel:* 01825 890348. Ruth Gipps, cond; Melanie Wall, sop; Leonard Paice, Kathleen Moy, fl, picc; Catherine Pluygers, Marcia Ferran, ob, eh; Catherine Morphett, Angela Crispe, cl, bs-cl; Anna Meadows, Barbara Lake, bsn, double-bsn; Lance Baker, Paul Burnett, hn, tam-tam.

[Roscoe, Donohoe]. Martin Roscoe, Peter Donohoe, pno. *Hazard*

[Rose, Blake]. 90 Ashburnham Rd, London NW10 5SE *tel:* 0181 969 9243 *also fax.* Sally Rose, Michael Blake, pnos.

Rose Consort of Viols. 28 Wentworth Rd, Scarcroft Hill, York YO2 1DG *tel:* 01904 652736 *fax:* 01484 472656; 0181 452 3254. John Bryan, Alison Crum, Sarah Groser, Roy Marks, Peter Wendland, viols.

Rosehill Instruments. 64 London End, Beaconsfield, Bucks HP9 2JD *tel:* 01494 671717 *fax:* 01494 670932. Neville Griffiths, Ken Tinsley, tpt; Emma Roberts, hn; Peter Hinkley, trb; Trevor Austin, tb.

The Rosell Quartet. 64 Linden Rd, Hampton, Middx TW12 2JB *tel:* 0181 979 8112 *also fax.* Angus Gibbon, Liz Van Ments, vn; Stephen Giles, va; Paul Brunner, vc.

Rossetti Cartledge Duo. Dario Rossetti-Bonell, gui; Nicholas Cartledge, fl. *Chameleon*

Rothwell Band (Leeds). Douglas Blackledge, dir. *Chameleon*

Ruskin Trio and Ensemble. 26 Common View, Rusthall, Tunbridge Wells, Kent TN4 8RG *tel:* 01892 540576 *also fax.* Jane Gomm, dir, vn. Mixed chmbr group: strs, wind, pno, gui.

St Andrews Baroque Trio. 29 Airthrey Av, Glasgow G14 9LJ *tel:* 0141 954 5020 *email:* marjorie@music.gla.ac.uk. Christopher Field, baroque vn; Marjorie Rycroft, baroque vc and bs viol; John Kitchen, hpd, org.

St James's Baroque Players. 200 Broomwood Rd, London SW11 6JY *tel:* 0171 228 6388 *fax:* 0171 738 1706. Ivor Bolton, mus dir; Delia Pye, mgr. Period insts.

St Magnus Trio. 61 Clock House Rd, Beckenham, Kent BR3 4JU *tel:* 0181 650 9990. Neil Mackie, ten; Richard Watkins, hn; John Blakely, pno.

Sajori Ensemble. 131 Heol-y-deri, Rhiwbina, Cardiff CF4 6UH *tel:* 01222 620469; 0378 001053 *email:* 100662.2427@compuserve.com. Sara Clethero, m-sop; Richard Wiegold, vc; Jonathan Middleton, pno.

Salomon String Quartet. 71 Priory Rd, Kew, Surrey TW9 3DH *tel:* 0181 940 7086 *fax:* 0181 332 0879. Simon Standage, Micaela Comberti, vn; Trevor Jones, va; Jennifer Ward Clarke, vc; Francesca McManus, mgr.

San Francisco Saxophone Quartet. *Gilder*

[Sanderson, Clayton]. Rosemary Sanderson, va; Nigel Clayton, pno. *NCCP*

Sarband. Vladimir Ivanoff, artistic dir. Ens specialising in links between European, Islamic and Jewish mus. Early mus to avantgarde. *Pristavec*

[Saunders]. Coleford House, Coleford, Bath BA3 5LU *tel:* 01373 812203 *fax:* 01373 813170. Catherine and Helen Saunders, fl and cl.

Saxology Quartet. 110 Wantz Rd, Maldon, Essex CM9 5DE *tel:* 01621 852844 *fax:* 01621 850647. Jeffery Wilson, ten sax; Denis Hill, alto sax; Fiona Dermit, sop sax; Tracey Bridgeman, bar sax.

Saxpak. Peter Davis, Richard Addison, Peter Ripper, Tim Holmes, Stan Sulzman, Andy Findon, Dave White, sax septet; Ted White, mus dir. *LM*

Saxtet. 53 Truro Rd, Wood Green, London N22 4EH *tel:* 0181 881 2515 *also fax;* 0973 692497. Karen Street, sop sax; Chris Gumbley, alto sax; Jamie Anderson, Richard Exall, ten sax; Andrew Tweed, bar sax; Nigel Wood, mus dir.

Schidlof Quartet. 28 Springfield Rd, Stoneygate, Leicester LE2 3BA *tel:* 0116 270 6528 *also fax.* Ofer Falk, Rafael Todes, vn; Graham Oppenheimer, va; Oleg Kogan, vc.

The Scholars. Kym Amps, sop; Angus Davidson, c-ten; Robin Doveton, ten; David van Asch, bs. *Festival*

The Scholars' Baroque Ensemble. David van Asch, dir. *Festival*

Schubert Ensemble of London. c/o 32 Wolverton Gardens, London W6 7DY *tel:* 0181 563 0618 *fax:* 0181 741 5233. William Howard, pno; Simon Blendis, vn; Jane Salmon, vc; Douglas Paterson, va; Peter Buckoke, db.

[Scott, Chard]. c/o 5 Inglis Rd, London W5 3RH *tel:* 0181 992 1571. Andy Scott, gui; Verona Chard, sop and narrator.

Scottish Early Music Consort. 22 Falkland St, Glasgow G12 9PR *tel:* 0141 334 9229 *also fax; email:* semc@glasgow.almac.co.uk. Warwick Edwards, artistic dir. Voices, medieval, renaissance and baroque insts.

Scottish Saxophone Quartet. c/o Music Centre, University of St Andrews, St Andrews, Fife KY16 9AJ *tel:* 01334 462226 *fax:* 01334 462570. Gillian Craig, sec and alto sax; Philip Greene, sop sax; Ken Thompson, ten sax; Ronald Mackie, baritone sax.

Segovia Trio. c/o Montague Music, East Wing, Southwick Hall, Peterborough, Cambs PE8 5BL *tel:* 01832 274790 *also fax; email:* segtrio@aol.com. Alexander MacDonald, dir; Vincent Lindsey-Clark, Roland Gallery.

Sequentia. Barbara Thornton, Benjamin Bagby, and others. 12th and 13th C vocal and inst mus. *Magenta*

Seraphim Ensemble. c/o Jean Calder Concerts Management, 2 Dane Acres, Bishops Stortford, Herts CM23 2PX *tel:* 01279 655715. Iain King, vn; David Greenlees, va; Clive Greensmith, vc; Aaron Shorr, pno; and others.

Seraphim Piano Quartet. c/o Jean Calder Concerts Management, 2 Dane Acres, Bishops Stortford, Herts CM23 2PX *tel:* 01279 655715. Ian King, vn; David Greenlees, va; Clive Greensmith, vc; Aaron Shorr, pno.

Seraphim Trio. M-sop, vn, hp. *CMG*

Serenata. 119 The Vineyard, Welwyn Garden City, Herts AL8 7PX *tel:* 0421 470286. Neil Simon, gui; Susan Wright, sop; Neil Latchman, ten.

Sheherazade. c/o 5 Inglis Rd, London W5 3RH *tel:* 0181 992 1571. Denise Dance, fl; Verona Chard, sop; Fiona Clifton Welker, hp. *Clifton Wyatt*

[Shelley, Littlewood]. 38 York St, London W1H 1FF *tel:* 0171 486 2941; 0181 444 4088 *fax:* 0171 935 7496. Rosamund Shelley, sop; Christopher Littlewood, pno.

[Shelley, Macnamara]. Howard Shelley, Hilary Macnamara, pno. *Intermusica*

Sheridan Brass Ensemble. 35 Norbiton Hall, London Rd, Kingston, Surrey KT2 6RB *tel:* 0171 223 1414; 01372 745584. Ben Lees, Richard Hammond, Nick Baker, Matthew Booth, tpts; Phil Woods, hn; Tony Boorer, Tony Neal, Tracy Holloway, Andy White, trbs; Graham Sibley, tb. *Chameleon*

Shika. 27 Heber Rd, London NW2 6AB *tel:* 0181 452 9234. Philip Booth, pno, dir; Takako Selby-Okamoto, sop; plus various insts.

Shiraz. 139 Churchill Rd, London NW2 5EH *tel:* 0181 459 6462. Nia Harries, vc; Fenella Barton, vn; Pamela Lidiard, pno.

Shiva Nova. Peregrine, Grange Rd, St Michaels, Tenterden, Kent TN30 6TJ *tel:* 01580 764258; 0171 829 8465; 0973 342626 *fax:* 01580 764258; 0171 240 5600 *email:* shivanova@aol.com. Priti Paintal, artistic dir. Euro-asian mus group: Indian, African Jazz, western classical insts, mus theatre.

Silk and Steel. 4 Mayfield Rd, Manchester M16 8FT *tel:* 0161 226 5655 *also fax.* John Powell, euph; Susie Hodder-Williams, fl; Stuart Death, pno.

Silver Duo. 4 May Terrace, Mount Florida, Glasgow G42 9XF *tel:* 0141 569 6319 *fax:* 0141 569 6322 *email:* phillipsilver@allegro.demon.co.uk. Phillip Silver, pno; Noreen Silver, vc.

Singcircle. 57 White Horse Rd, London E1 0ND *tel:* 0171 790 5883 *fax:* 0171 265 9170. Gregory Rose, mus dir. Contemporary vocal ens.

Singers Two. 14 The Crescent, S Harrow, Middx HA2 0PJ *tel:* 0181 864 1802 *also fax.* Lynne Hirst, sop; Kenneth Fraser Annand, bar; Timothy Barratt, acc.

Singers Unlimited. Jennifer Partridge, mus dir; Beryl Korman, sop; Julia Meadows, m-sop. Vocal ens with pno. *Upbeat*

Singphoniker. Alfons Brandl, Christof Rösel, Ludwig Thomas, Berno Scharpf, Gunnar Mühling, Christian Schmidt. *Ellison*

Sirinu. Sara Stowe, sop, keyboards; Henry Stobart, rcdrs, shawm, bagpipes; Jon Banks, hp, dulcimer, sackbut; Matthew Spring, lutes, vihuela, guis, hurdy-gurdy. Early and world mus. *Seaview*

The Sixteen. First Floor, Enslow House, Station Rd, Enslow, Kidlington, Oxon OX5 3AX *tel:* 01869 331544 *fax:* 01869 331011 *email:* info@ thesixteen.org.uk. Harry Christophers, cond. Choir and period orch.

Škampa Quartet. *Barber*

Slowind. *Gallus*

[Smith, Brown]. 8 Heath Close, London NW11 7DX *tel:* 0181 458 4827. Maureen Smith, vn; Ian Brown, pno.

[Smith, Llewellyn-Jones]. Bsn and pno. *Michael Brewer*

[Smith, Rowland-Jones]. 8 Heath Close, London NW11 7DX *tel:* 0181 458 4827. Maureen Smith, vn; Simon Rowland-Jones, va.

[Soames, Higgins]. 77 St Albans Av, East Ham, London E6 4HH *tel:* 0181 472 2057 *also fax; email:* 106240.1350@compuserve.com; http://www.cdj.co.uk/impulse/soames/. Victoria Soames, cl; Jonathan Higgins, pno.

The Songmakers' Almanac. 25 Fournier St, Spitalfields, London E1 6QE *tel:* 0171 247 7219 *fax:* 0171 247 6094. Graham Johnson, dir; Carolyn Humphreys, admin.

Sounds for Silents. Margaret Campbell, fl; David Fuest, cl; Rebecca Hirsch, vn; James Potter, vc; John Lenehan, Kathryn Page, pno. Mus for classic silent films. *Upbeat*

Sounds Positive. 28 Cavendish Av, London N3 3QN *tel:* 0181 349 2317 *fax:* 0181 346 8257. David Sutton-Anderson, cond; Simon Desorgher, fl; Linda Merrick, cl; Edwin Roxburgh, ob; Anthony Aarons, tpt; Sally Mays, pno; Avril Anderson, co-ord.

[South]. 2 Welland Gardens, Welland, Malvern, Worcs WR13 6LB *tel:* 01684 310370 *email:* vz04@dial.pipex.com. Joan and Robert South, pno duo.

Southern Concert Brass. 45 Garibaldi Rd, Redhill, Surrey RH1 6PB *tel:* 01737 763708; 0976 402178. Robin Woollams, Alan O'Dell, tpt; Graham Ivory, hn; Alison Knight, trb; Robin Tweddle, tb.

Spectrum. 8 Alma Sq, London NW8 9QD *tel:* 0171 286 3944 *fax:* 0171 289 9081. Guy Protheroe, Ann Manly, dirs. Contemporary mus ens.

[Spratt, Holden]. 142 Elmington Rd, London SE5 7RA *tel:* 0171 701 0400 *fax:* 0171 252 5279 *email:* 106325.1302@compuserve.com. Kirsten Spratt, fl; Ruth Holden, hp.

Stamic Quartet of Prague. *Gilder*

Stanesby Recorder Trio. 35 Victoria Cres Rd, Glasgow G12 9DD *tel:* 0141 339 5012. Jennifer Hill, rcdr; Marjorie Rycroft, va da gamba; John Kitchen, hpd.

[Stanzeleit, Jacobson]. 217a Milkwood Rd, London SE24 0JE *tel:* 0171 738 5356 *also fax.* Susanne Stanzeleit, vn; Julian Jacobson, pno.

The Stars of Gilbert and Sullivan. Finchingfield House, The Green, Finchingfield, Essex CM7 4JS *tel:* 01371 810289 *also fax.* Lorraine Patient, artistic dir. Highlights from the Gilbert and Sullivan operas.

Status Cymbal. Paul Costin, Mardyah Tucker, vn; Paul Appleyard, va; Maryan Balkwill, vc. *Chameleon*

[Steele, Sherbourne]. 13 Salegate La, Temple Cowley, Oxford OX4 2HQ *tel:* 01865 770272 *also fax; email:* luke.steele@bigfoot.com. Jan Steele, sax, fl, cl; Janet Sherbourne, pno, vocals. Contemporary mus and jazz duo.

[Stenstadvold, Blewett]. Erik Stenstadvold, gui; Brenda Blewett, f-pno. *Ellison*

[Stephens, Bullingham]. Alison Stephens, mandolin; Lauren Bullingham, hp. *Purkiss*

[Stephens, Smith]. Alison Stephens, mandolin; Neil Smith, gui. *Purkiss*

Sterling Quartet. 7 Fernleigh Rd, Winchmore Hill, London N21 3AN *tel:* 0181 886 5290; 01372 273358 *fax:* 01372 278369. Megan Pound, Rebecca Jones, vn; Rachel Walker, va; Brian Mullan, vc.

Steve Martland Band. Steve Martland, cond. Saxes, guis, keyboards, br, drums. *Magenta*

Steve Reich and Musicians. *Allied*

[Stigmer, Lenehan]. Jan Stigmer, vn; John Lenehan, pno. *NCCP*

Stockhausen Group. *Allied*

Storyville Tickle. *NBM*

[Stowe, Spring]. Sara Stowe, sop, keyboards; Matthew Spring, lutes, vihuela, guis, hurdy gurdy. Early to contemporary mus. *Seaview*

String Sound. 15 Hawkhurst Way, West Wickham, Kent BR4 9PE *tel:* 0181 777 6414 *also fax.* Clive Lander, vn; Lesley Shrigley Jones, vc; Max Brittain, gui; Roy Chilton, db.

Stringendo. Str quartet. *Annon*

Sun Music. 51b Dartmouth Rd, London NW2 4EP *tel:* 0181 208 1541 *also fax.* Tony Gray, admin. Ens promoting Australian mus and musicians in the UK.

Sweet and Low. 278 Monega Rd, London E12 6TS *tel:* 0181 552 7149; 0181 559 1696; 0589 988312. Carole Mudie, m-sop; Carol Leatherby, m-con; David Mackie, pno.

The Swingle Singers. *HP*

Sylfanome Quintet. 76 Lower Oldfield Pk, Bath, Avon *tel:* 01225 313531. Richard Carder, dir. Flexible w/wind group of up to 5 fls and cls.

Syrinx Ensemble. 1 Wickham Hall Cottages, Langford Rd, Wickham Bishops, Essex CM8 3JQ *tel:* 01621 892229. Stephen Rumsey, mus dir. Mixed ens from str, wind, perc, keyboard, voice.

Syrinx Wind Quintet. 411 Manhattan Building, Bow Quarter, Fairfield Rd, Bow, London E3 2UQ *tel:* 0181 981 7413 *also fax.* Tracey Stewart, fl; Jane Finch, ob; David Coyle, cl; Paul Harris, bsn; Stephen Flower, hn.

Szabó Quartet. Attila Szabó, Zarko Mickovic, vn; Margit Szabó, va; Gertraud Hajdany, vc. *Ellison*

Tagore String Trio. 16 Stonehill Rd, E Sheen, London SW14 8RW *tel:* 0181 876 3156 *fax:* 01983 852201. Frances Mason, vn; Brian Schiele, va; James Halsey, vc.

Take 2. The Old Station, Kimberley, Wymondham, Norfolk NR18 9HB *tel:* 01953 850711. Sax and pno.

Take Two. c/o Lyric Production, 41 Arkwright Rd, Sanderstead, Surrey CR2 0LP *tel:* 0181 657 5840 *also fax.* Classical and elec gui, mandolin, balalaiki, bazouki, etc.

The Tallis Scholars. Fenton House, Banbury Rd, Chipping Norton, Oxon OX7 5AW *tel:* 01608 644080 *fax:* 01608 643235. Peter Phillips, dir; Shauni McGregor, admin.

Tamarisk. Anthony Abbott, admin; Janet Howd, sop; Dona Lee Croft, vn; Martin Pacey, Alvin Moisey, pno. *Anthony Abbott*

Tambourin. Fiona Masters, fl; Peter Howe, gui. *Purkiss*

Tapestry. 113 High Rd, Wilmington, Dartford, Kent DA2 7BW *tel:* 01322 224085 *fax:* 01322 407282. Sandra Lissenden, sop; Andrew Sparling, cl; Tony Gray, pno.

Taringa String Quartet. *John Boddy*

Tarrega Trio. 32 South Grove, Sale, Cheshire M33 3AU *tel:* 0161 969 5772. Margaret Duffy, vn; Valerie Hayward, vc; Andrew Allen, gui. Classical and light mus for all occasions.

Tate Music Group of London. 101 Queens Park Av, Bournemouth, Dorset BH8 9LJ *tel:* 01202 394955 *also fax.* Richard Studt, dir.

Taverner Consort and Players. Ibex House, 42-46 Minories, London EC3N 1DY *tel:* 0171 481 2103 *fax:* 0171 481 2865. Andrew Parrott, artistic dir; Malcolm Bruno, associate dir; Victoria Newbert, admin. Various medieval, renaissance and baroque insts with voices.

Telemann Players of London. Redwings, Linden Chase, Uckfield, E Sussex TN22 1EE *tel:* 01825 760046 *also fax.* Linda Brand, rcdr, baroque ob; Philip Turbett, baroque bsn; Helena Brown, hpd.

Temps Contre Temps. c/o Diana Hirst Arts Administration and PR, 55 Marmora Rd, London SE22 0RY *tel:* 0181 299 1914 *also fax.* Dominique Hellsten, sop; David Roblou, hpd and pno. 18th and 20th C French vocal and inst mus.

Terroni Piano Trio. Raphael Terroni, pno; John Trussler, vn; Fiona Murphy, vc. *Purkiss/Grant Rogers*

Tetra Guitar Quartet. Stephen Goss, Peter Howe, Richard Storry, Graham Roberts, gui. *Purkiss/Chameleon*

Thames Brass. Br quintet. *Lyons*

Thames Fanfare Brass. 26 Cartmel Rd, Bexleyheath, Kent DA7 5EA *tel:* 01322 430779 *fax:* 01322 448416. Br group, dixie band, herald tpts.

Three Down One Across. 105 Priory Park Rd, London NW6 7UY *tel:* 0171 372 7311 *fax:* 0181 537 9665 *email:* sarafreedman@johnsonarts.demon. co.uk. Sara Freedman, mus dir. W/wind quartet; fl, ob, cl and bsn and doubling insts.

Three Reeds. The Old Meeting House, St James, Shaftesbury, Dorset SP7 8HF *tel:* 01747 854999. Gillian Carter, Elisabeth Jacoby, Jennifer Porcas; concerts include ob, ob d'amore, eh, bs ob, bsn.

Thurston Clarinet Quartet. Alex Allen, John Bradbury, Jon Carnac, Paul Richards, cl. *KDM*

Tokyo String Quartet. Mikhail Kopelman, Kikuei Ikeda, vn; Kazuhide Isomura, va; Sadao Harada, vc. *Intermusica*

Tonus Peregrinus. 5 The Cloisters, Gordon Sq, London WC1H 0AG *tel:* 0171 387 2867 *also fax.* Joanna Forbes, Rebecca Parkyns, sop; Kathryn Oswald, alto; Alexander L'Estrange, c-ten; Mark Anderson, Alexander Hickey, ten; Antony Pitts, bar; Francis Brett, bs. Vocal and inst ens.

Topologies. 411 Forest Rd, Walthamstow, London E17 5LD *tel:* 0181 503 2364 *also fax.* Nancy Ruffer, fls; Andrew Sparling, cls; Ian Pace, keyboards.

Tradewinds Clarinet Quartet. 37 Eden Rd, Walthamstow, London E17 9JS *tel:* 0181 520 8682 *also fax;* 0976 350062; 01636 830881. Sarah Lewington, Clare Williams, James Wolfe, Gary Holdsworth, cl; plus saxes.

Trafalgar Brass. 57 Foxon La, Caterham, Surrey CR3 5SG *tel:* 01883 344775. Dave McCallum, Tony Nash tpt; Alan Jones, hn; Danny Scott, trb; Kevin Morgan, tb. *Charlton*

Triangle Balalaika Trio. 24 Carbery Av, Acton, London W3 9AL *tel:* 0181 723 5384 *fax:* 0181 932 2501. David Nissen, mgr, Prima Balalaika; Gordon Mabbett, alt balalaika and acc; David Pine, contra bs balalaika. Russian folk mus.

Tricontro di Solisti. Pno quartet. *ECAM*

Trio Busoni. Pno, vn, cl.*CMG*

Trio Concordia. 16 Learmonth Terrace, Edinburgh EH4 1PG *tel:* 0131 332 0481. Margaret Aronson, sop; Philip Greene, cl; Lindsay Sinclair, pno.

Trio Gemelli. c/o Diana Lashmore, 35 Lendell Rd, London W12 9RS *tel:* 0181 743 0457 *also fax.* John Bradbury, cl; Adrian Bradbury, vc; Emily Segal, pno.

Trio Holloway, ter Linden, Mortensen. The Old Manse, Leafield, Witney, Oxon OX8 5NN *tel:* 01993 878200 *fax:* 01993 878375. John Holloway, vn; Jaap ter Linden, va da gamba; Lars Ulrik Mortensen, hpd.

Trio Krosta. Mere Cottage, Ashmansworth, nr Newbury, Berks RG20 9SJ *tel:* 01635 253031. Sylvia Bowden, pno; Celia Redgate, fl; Christopher Redgate, ob.

Trio Serenata. 21 Lynn Dr, Eaglesham, Glasgow G76 0JJ *tel:* 01355 302869. Alison Donaldson, sop; George Macilwham, fl; David Murray, pno. Victorian, Viennese, French, Burns and Scottish programmes.

Trio Sonnerie. 71 Priory Rd, Kew, Surrey TW9 3DH *tel:* 0181 940 7086 *fax:* 0181 332 0879. Monica Huggett, vn; Sarah Cunningham, bs viol; Gary Cooper, hpd; Francesca McManus, mgr.

Trio Veracini. The Old Manse, Leafield, Witney, Oxon OX8 5NN *tel:* 01993 878200 *fax:* 01993 878375. Mary Taylor, admin; John Holloway, vn; Lars-Ulrik Mortensen, hpd; David Watkin, vc.

Trio Wanderer. Vincent Coq, pno; Jean-Marc Phillips, vn; Raphael Pidoux, vc. *Hazard*

Trio Zingara. 1 Lincoln Rd, London N2 9DJ *tel:* 0181 444 1723. Elizabeth Layton, vn; Felix Schmidt, vc; Annette Cole, pno.

Triple Echo. 17 Keele Rd, Newcastle-under-Lyme, Staffs ST5 2JT *tel:* 01782 618156. Jane Ginsborg, sop; Philip Edwards, cl; George Nicholson, pno.

Triptych. c/o Little Corner, Cross Oak Rd, Berkhamsted, Herts HP4 3NA *tel:* 01442 863263. Christopher Hughes, pno; Ruth Scott, ob; Sarah Burnett, bsn.

Tryptyque Piano Trio. c/o 27 London Rd, Tonbridge, Kent TN10 3AB *tel:* 01732 353944 *also fax.* Ruth Herbert, pno; Alun Thomas, vn; Jonathan Few, vc.

Tuba Magna. 95 Parklands Av, Leamington Spa CV32 7BP *tel:* 01926 451550. Andrew Stone-Fewings, tpt; Colin Druce, org.

Tubalaté. PO Box 55, Manchester M16 8TJ *tel:* 01625 532932 *also fax;* 0410 311771. John Powell, Paul Walton, euph; Ian Anstee, Ryan Breen, tb.

[Tulacek, Wray]. Tomas Tulacek, vn; Steven Wray, pno. *Chameleon*

Two's Company. 2 Princes Rd, St Leonards on Sea, E Sussex TN37 6EL *tel:* 01424 715167 *fax:* 01424 712214 *email:* 100723.510@compuserve. com. Rhondda Gillespie, Robert Weatherburn, pno duo.

The Umbrella Collection. 175 Malefant St, Cathays, Cardiff CF2 4QG *tel:* 01222 239198. Lynne Plowman, dir. Emphasis on 20th C and contemporary mus.

[Underwood, Wells]. 20 Summerhill Rd, Dartford, Kent DA1 2LP *tel:* 01322 287924 *also fax.* Mark Underwood, fl; Alexander Wells, pno.

Choir of Uppingham School. Neil Page, dir of mus. *SWA*

Uroboros Ensemble. 13 Nevil Rd, Bishopston, Bristol BS7 9EG *tel:* 0117 924 7537 *also fax; email:* gp.ck@virgin.net. Wind, str, hp, pno and perc ens. *Camerata*

Vale Wind Quintet. 50 Parc-y-Coed, Creigiau, Cardiff CF4 8LY *tel:* 01222 892388 *also fax.* Christopher Vale, bsn; Jonathan Burgess, fl; Helen Powell, ob; John Cooper, cl; Angus West, hn.

Vallis-Davies Chamber Music Concerts. PO Box 2242, Poole, Dorset BH14 0YX *tel:* 0181 943 5329 *also fax.* Nicholas and Sian Vallis Davies, fl and ob.

Vanbrugh String Quartet. Gregory Ellis, Elizabeth Charleson, vn; Simon Aspell, va; Christopher Marwood, vc. *NCCP*

Vega Wind Quintet. Duke Dobing, fl; George Caird, ob; Charles Hine, cl; Anthony Gladstone, hn; Nicholas Hunka, bsn. *KDM*

Vellinger String Quartet. Stephanie Gonley, Harvey de Souza, vn; James Boyd, va; Sally Pendlebury, vc. *Tennant*

Vermeer String Quartet. *Allied*

Versability. 7b Hart Grove, Ealing, London W5 3NA *tel:* 0181 932 1815. Ralph Varcoe, bar; Simon Mulligan, pno. Song from Monteverdi to modern jazz.

Versus Ensemble. 17 Roseberry Gardens, London N4 1JQ *tel:* 0181 809 3893 *also fax.* Ian Fawcett, fl; Ian Rowbotham, va; Daniel Sanz, gui.

The Victorians. *Mostylea*

Victoriana. 278 Monega Rd, London E12 6TS *tel:* 0181 552 7149; 0181 559 1696; 0589 988312. Carol Leatherby, dir: Victorian mus entertainment in costume.

Vienna Brahms Trio. Juri Smirnov, pno; Boris Kuschnir, vn; Orfeo Mandozzi, vc. *Anglo-Swiss*

The Vienna Collection. 12 Wren Ct, Ash, Aldershot, Hants GU12 6AX *tel:* 01252 319610 *also fax;* 0831 192772. David Heyes, admin, cond; Sarah Poole, sop. 5 players upwards. Viennese mus.

The Viennese Salon Orchestra. 12 Wren Ct, Ash, Aldershot, Hants GU12 6AX *tel:* 01252 319610 *also fax;* 0831 192772. David Heyes, admin, db; Sarah Poole, sop; Nigel Clayton, pno; Chris Gould, perc; also strs and wind. Viennese mus, including waltzes, polkas and marches by the Strauss family.

Vivaldi Concertante. 35 Laurel Av, Potters Bar, Herts EN6 2AB *tel:* 01707 650735 *also fax;* 01707 643366. Joseph Pilbery, mus dir. Str ens with hpd and wind.

Vocal Chords. Craig Ogden, gui; Claire Bradshaw, m-sop. *Matthew Tullah*

Vocal Diversions. Alison Mary Sutton, m-sop; Maria Beattie, hp. *Charlton*

[Wakeford, Nicholls]. Lucy Wakeford, Alison Nicholls, hp duo. *NBM*

The Wallace Collection. 26 Cartmel Rd, Bexleyheath, Kent DA7 5EA *tel:* 01322 430779 *fax:* 01322 448416. Roy Bilham, gen mgr. Br ens.

Weingarten Ensemble. 13 Ravenscroft Av, London NW11 0SA *tel:* 0181 458 0980 *also fax.* Noa Lachman, concert mgr; Eiko Tanaka, vn; Vicci Wardman, va; David Kenedy, vc; Jane Finch, ob; William Hancox, pno.

Werethina String Quartet. Suzanne Stanzeleit, Ingo Hirsekorn, vn; Andreas Kuhlmann, va; Katja Schaefer, vc. *Encore*

Westminster Glee Singers. Male voices from London Cathedrals. *Sympathetic*

Westminster Piano Trio. c/o Merlin Cottage, 13a Merlin Haven, Wotton under Edge, Glos GL12 7BA *tel:* 01453 521091. Justine Tomlinson.

[Williams, Goss]. Jenevora Williams, sop; Stephen Goss, gui. *Chameleon*

Wind and Company. Bell House, Bell La, Widford, Ware, Herts SG12 8SH *tel:* 01279 842632. Graham Knight, dir; Judith Knight, co-dir. Wind octet and other combinations.

Wind Soloists of The Chamber Orchestra of Europe. *Lubbock*

Winds of the Southern Cross II. Paul Dean, cl; Leesa Dean, bsn; Peter Luff, hn; Kevin Power, pno; Margaret Schindler, sop; Duncan Tolmie, ob. *Ellison*

Wren Baroque Soloists. Wren Music, 8 Park La, Selsey, Chichester, W Sussex PO20 0HD *tel:* 01243 604281 *fax:* 01243 604387 *email:* starmus @brainlink.com; http://www.brainlink.com/~starmus/unison/wren/ wren.html. Lesley-Jane Rogers, Nicola Jenkin, sop; Frances Jellard, alto; Simon Davies, ten; Martin Elliott, bs; Melanie Woodcock, baroque vc; Jan Waterfield, hpd, org, virginals.

Wren Consort. Wren Music, 8 Park La, Selsey, Chichester, W Sussex PO20 0HD *tel:* 01243 604281 *fax:* 01243 604387 *email:* starmus@ brainlink.com. Alison Pearce, sop; Martin Elliott, bs-bar; Steven Keogh, Paul Thomas, tpt; Andrew Lumsden, org, hpd; Christopher Ross, pno.

Wren Singers of London. Wren Music, 8 Park La, Selsey, Chichester, W Sussex PO20 0HD *tel:* 01243 604281 *fax:* 01243 604387 *email:* starmus @brainlink.com. Martin Elliott, artistic dir; Peter Beaven, asst dir.

Yggdrasil Quartet. Henrik Peterson, Per Öman, vn; Robert Westlund, va; Per Nyström, vc. *Clarion/Seven Muses*

York Guitar Quartet. John Mackenzie, requinto; David Ashworth, Andrew Forrest, ten; Dave Scarth, bs. *Invisible Pilots*

The York Waits. 6 Ingleborough Av, Tang Hall, York YO1 3SA *tel:* 01904 432878/431328 *fax:* 01904 432860 *email:* jwm5@york.ac.uk; http:// www.intr.net/bleissa/lists/yorkwait.html. James Merryweather, admin; Tim Bayley, Anthony Barton, Ian and Roger Richardson, William Marshall, shawms, cornetts, curtals, sackbuts, rcdrs, bagpipes, hurdy-gurdies, etc. Ten concert programmes plus additional renaissance entertainments.

Yorkshire Baroque Soloists. 11 Bootham Terrace, York YO3 7DH *tel:* 01904 652799 *fax:* 01904 338349 *email:* ps22@unix.york.ac.uk. Peter Seymour, dir. Voices, str, wind, keyboard.

Yorkshire Classic Brass. 32 Heaton Grove, Heaton, Bradford BD9 4DZ *tel:* 01274 487078 *also fax.* Br sextet with perc.

Zagreb Guitar Trio. Darko Petrinjak, István Römer, Goran Listeš. *GBZ*

The Zagreb Quartet. str quartet. *ECAM*

Zehetmair Quartet. *Lubbock*

Zhar. 87a Queens Rd, E Grinstead, W Sussex RH19 1BG *tel:* 01342 300949 *fax:* 01342 410846 *email:* http://www.egnet.co.uk/clients/music/rgm. html. Paul Cheneour, fls; Dilly Meah, tabla.

Zirayab. Greek and Middle Eastern traditional mus. Rebab, qanun, santouri, oud, saz, perc. *Oriole*

The Zurich String Trio. Boris Livschitz, vn; Zvi Livschitz, va; Pi-Chin Chien, vc. *Ellison*

Words and Music

A Breath of Fresh Air. Station View, St Mary's St, Penistone, Sheffield S30 6AA *tel:* 01226 767759. Catherine Baker, Mark Pollard, Alan Asquith, bsns; Jeremy Fisher, pno; Patrick Moody, narrator.

Airs & Graces. 22a Tavistock Terrace, London N19 4DB *tel:* 0171 281 9364 *also fax; email:* norburnc@dircon.co.uk. Clare Norburn, sop; Richard Black, pno; Patience Tomlinson, actress; David Timson, actor.

All Things English. Blackthorn Lodge, The Common, Happisburgh, Norfolk NR12 0RT *tel:* 01692 583002. Jack Barratt, ten, actor, insts; Marjorie Barratt, pno, actress, sop. Celebration of English life.

An Evening with Queen Victoria. Prunella Scales; Ian Partridge, ten; Richard Burnett, pno. *Clarion/Seven Muses*

Arden Duo. The Old Cricket, Broadheath, Presteigne, Powys LD8 2HG *tel:* 01544 267418. Lynden Rees-Roberts, sop; Gareth Rees-Roberts, gui, lute.

Belle and Two Beaux. 41 Newlands Close, Walton on Thames, Surrey KT12 4PW *tel:* 01932 242805 *also fax.* Janet Shell, mezzo sop; Mark Oldfield, baritone; John Flinders, pno. An evening in the company of Victoria and Albert.

The Carolinian Consort. 14 Queens Ct, Queens Rd, London E11 1BD *tel:* 0181 539 0830 *also fax.* Hedvig Åberg, sop; Liliana Mazzarri, sop; Emma Haines, alto; Scott Pauley, lutes; Carolyn Gibley, hpd.

Cornel Music Group. Orchard House, Orchard St, Blandford Forum, Dorset DT11 7QZ *tel:* 01258 451493. Christine Page, sop; Annabelle Willetts, vn; Richard Willetts, va; Ruth Hozack, vc; Richard Hall, pno, hpd.

The Gentle Art. 41 Newlands Close, Walton on Thames, Surrey KT12 4PW *tel:* 01932 242805 *also fax.* Janet Shell, mezzo sop; Christopher Goldsack, baritone; John Flinders, pno. A portrait of Henry J Wood, founder of the Proms, cond and acc. Also other song recital programmes.

The Georgian Music Room. 33 Hartswood Rd, London W12 9NE *tel:* 0181 749 3365 *fax:* 0181 749 1201. Neil Jenkins, ten; Rachel Beckett, baroque fl, rcdr; Celia Harper, dir, hpd. Concerts in period costume with contemporary readings. *Blythe*

Geraldine McEwan's Jane Austen. Geraldine McEwan; Danielle Perrett, hp. *Clarion/Seven Muses*

I Remember Jane. Smallwood Productions, Bramleys, Tarrant Keyneston DT11 9JE *tel:* 01258 453969 *also fax.* Melanie Armitstead, sop; Julius Drake, pno. A celebration of Jane Austen in words and mus.

Jane Austen and Colette. Maggie Cole, pno with sop and speaker. *Robert White*

Jill Balcon and the Rasumovsky String Quartet. 13 Cambridge Rd, New Malden, Surrey KT3 3QE *tel:* 0181 949 6621 *also fax.* Jill Balcon, speaker; Frances Mason, Marilyn Taylor, vns; Christopher Wellington, va; Joy Hall, vc. Two programmes, 'The Sunlight on the Garden' and 'Know'st thou the land where lemon trees bloom'.

Litmus. 12 Wellfield Av, Muswell Hill, London N10 2EA *tel:* 0181 883 1567 *fax:* 0181 340 2983. Songs, poetry, pno mus, prose on a variety of themes. Christine Bunning, Elisabeth Clarke, sops; Brian-Michael Parnell, pno; John Ringham, actor; various soloists.

Lyricanta. 55 Rosedale, Welwyn Garden City, Herts AL7 1DP *tel:* 01707 322448. Karen Van Poznak, Nigel Springthorpe, artistic dirs.

Music and Sweet Poetry. 53 Upwood Rd, London SE12 8AE *tel:* 0181 318 6187 *fax:* 0181 318 7236. Patricia Williams, dir. Words and mus anthology programmes.

Odyssey. Gwespyr, 6 Hallcroft La, Copmanthorpe, York YO2 3UQ *tel:* 01904 701459; 01502 724020. Yvonne Robert, sop; Maurice Ridge, pno; Graham Roberts, reader.

Opus Anglicanum. 92 St Thomas St, Wells, Somerset BA5 2UZ *tel:* 01749 677903 *fax:* 01749 675131. Stephen Tilton, c-ten; James Gilchrist, William Lee, ten; Roland Robertson, bar; John Rowlands-Pritchard, bs; John Touhey, narrator.

Playing - with Words. Katharina Wolpe and Corin Redgrave, poetry and pno. *Michael Brewer*

Tête à Tête. Flat 21, 5 Elm Pk Gardens, London SW10 9QQ *tel:* 0171 352 8271. Ian Edwards, Jennifer Rice, two voices and gui. Themed entertainments in words and mus; international folk songs and 'nostalgia' of twenties, thirties and forties.

Turner Fish Smith Trio. Brownson House, Grenofen, Tavistock, Devon PL19 9ER *tel:* 01822 615730 *also fax.* Rosemary Turner, sop; Adrian Vernon Fish, pno; Will Smith, narrator. Themed entertainments with appropriate stage sets.

Voice and Verse. 25 Tamar House, Kennington La, London SE11 4XA *tel:* 0171 582 1746. Garry Humphreys, dir. Anthology entertainments on specific themes with 2 speakers, 2 singers and pno.

Voices-go-Round. 8 Ashwood Villas, Leeds LS6 2EJ *tel:* 0113 278 0827 *fax:* 0113 230 6114. Virginia Rushton, sop; David Rowland, hpd, f-pno, pno; Clive Brown, vn. Musical and literary programmes.

Words and Music. 16 Highbury Pk, London N5 2AB *tel:* 0171 359 0707 *also fax.* Sally Bradshaw. Programmes on particular themes involving actors, singer and insts.

Solo Performers

The artists listed in this section are confined to those living in Britain and/or bookable through a British concert agent. Chorus-masters are included under Conductors. Instrumentalists are listed according to instrument in the following order: organ, solo piano, harpsichord, accompanists and coaches, violin, viola and viola d'amore, cello, double bass, woodwind, brass, harp, guitar and lute, percussion and miscellaneous. Singers are sub-divided according to voice.

Where an artist's services may be booked through an agent or manager, that agent or manager is named in abbreviated form. Those which are not self-explanatory are listed below. *The agent is not necessarily that artist's exclusive agent,* however, and may not represent the artist outside Britain. *See* **Agents and Managers** for addresses and telephone numbers. Where the artist is currently or has been associated with a major opera company, then that company is given as the contact, *see* **Opera, Dance and Music Theatre** for addresses and telephone numbers. Reference to an opera company does not necessarily imply that the company has any control of, or present interest in, the availability of the artist. Artists without named agents are either listed with a personal telephone or a number preceded by *c/o* which denotes a personal manager through which the artist may be contacted.

The *Register of Performers and Composers* published by the **Incorporated Society of Musicians** (10 Stratford Place, London W1N 9AE *tel:* 0171 629 4413) gives addresses as well as telephone numbers for its members who may be soloists or members of an ensemble or orchestra. Many other instrumentalists are members of the **Musicians' Union** (60-62 Clapham Rd, London SW9 0JJ *tel:* 0171 582 5566). Many singers are members of the **British Actors' Equity Association** (Guild House, Upper St Martin's La, London WC2H 9EG *tel:* 0171 379 6000). A list of artists represented by artist managers and concert agents who are members of the **International Artist Managers' Association** is available from 41a Lonsdale Rd, London W11 2BY *tel:* 0171 243 2598.

Agents' Abbreviations

CDI	Concert Directory International	OCA	Opera and Concert Artists
DCM	Daniels Concert Management	OWM	Owen/White Management
GIA	Georgina Ivor Associates	PA	Performing Arts
HP	Harrison Parrott	PGM	Patrick Garvey Management
JLM	Jonathan Land Management	SS	Simply Singers
KDM	Karen Durant Management	SWA	Stephannie Williams Artists
LA	London Artists	THA	Terry Harrison Artists Management
LM	London Musicians	VWM	Van Walsum Management
NBM	NB Management	WWA	World Wide Artists
NCCP	Neil Chaffey Concert Promotions	YCAT	Young Concert Artists Trust
NWA	N W Artists		

Conductors

Choral directors and chorus-masters are included in this list.

Abbado, Claudio – *Holt*
Abbott, Graham – *KDM*
Abel, Yves – *Holt*
Adams, John – *HP*
Adey, Christopher – *PA*
Ainscough, Julie – *Michael Harrold*
Ajmone-Marsan, Guido – *Tennant*
Alcantara, Theo – *ICM*
Alldis, John – *Allied*
Alsop, Marin – *Intermusica*
Altman, Elizabeth – 01943 850853 *also fax*
Alwyn, Kenneth – 01403 741348
André, Martin – *Ingpen*
Andreescu, Horia – *McCann*
Andrew-James, Mark – 01273 208680
 fax: 01273 777963
Anissimov, Alexander – *Askonas*
Armstrong, Richard – *Ingpen*
Armstrong, Stephen – 01494 528664 *also fax;*
 email: 106506.1555@compuserve.com
Arnic, Lovrenc – *Pristavec*
Arundel Timms, T – 01237 473887

Asbury, Stefan – *HP*
Ashkenazy, Vladimir – *HP*
Atherton, David – *Holt*
Atzmon, Moshe – *PGM*
Auguin, Philippe – *Askonas*
Backhouse, Jeremy – 0181 690 1278
 fax: 0181 690 4462 *email:* backhouse
 jeremy@msn.com
Badea, Christian – *Transart*
Bainbridge, Simon – c/o 0171 434 0066
 fax: 0171 287 6329
Bakels, Kees – *IMG*
Balcombe, Richard – *LM*
Bale, Matthew – 01225 337722
Balkwill, Bryan – 0181 947 4250
Ball, Christopher – 0171 935 1270
Ball, Timothy – 0181 871 0317 *also fax*
Balzer, Wolfgang – *Connaught*
Bamert, Matthias – *Intermusica*
Barber, Graham – 0113 263 1890 *fax:* 0113
 263 7178
Barenboim, Daniel – *Holt*

Barham, Stuart – 0171 622 8864
Barker, Bernard – 0181 427 5409 *also fax*
Barker, John – 0181 224 0514
Barlow, Alan – 01639 849497
Barlow, Jeremy – 0171 267 7176 *fax:* 0171
 267 0127
Barlow, Stephen – *Gilder*
Barnard, Nick – *Jeffrey Cambell*
Barnes, Richard – 01243 776325 *fax:* 01243
 539604
Barshai, Rudolf – *Askonas*
Barton, Christopher – 01633 266708
Bate, John – 0181 940 8930 *fax:* 0181
 547 7400
Bateman, Paul – 0181 882 5375 *fax:* 0181
 447 9226
Bates, Kevin – 01449 741707
Baudo, Serge – *Manygate*
Beaven, Peter – 01932 788785 *fax:* 01932
 765060 *email:* pmsnet@argonet.co.uk
Bedford, Steuart – *HP*
Beedie, Norman – 01733 844603 *also fax*

Pickett, Philip – 0171 735 8154 *fax:* 0171 820 0801

Pilbery, Joseph – *Ellison*

Pink, Andrew – 0171 272 6101 *also fax*

Pinnock CBE, Trevor – *Holt*

Pittman, Richard – *Sykes*

Pletnev, Mikhail – *Columbia*

Polianichko, Alexander – *Ingpen*

Pommier, Jean-Bernard – *GIA*

Pomphrey, John – 0161 428 5456

Ponsford, David – 01285 651995 *also fax*

Poole, John – *Sykes*

Pople, Ross – 01539 560304 *fax:* 01539 561483

Porcelijn, David – *Olivia Ma*

Potter, Warwick – 01424 440929; 0973 734572

Proost, Walter – *WWA*

Protheroe, Guy – 0171 286 3944 *fax:* 0171 289 9081

Pryce-Jones, John – 01422 825594 *also fax;* 0468 352399

Purcell, Kevin – *KDM*

Quinn, Andrea – *Clarion/Seven Muses*

Rafferty, Michael – c/o 01222 230833 *fax:* 01222 342046

Rahbari, Alexander – *Anglo-Swiss*

Rands, Bernard – *Allied*

Rattle CBE, Sir Simon – *Holt*

Redmond, Timothy – 0161 861 8088 *also fax*

Reed, Michael – *LM*

Renes, Lawrence – *HP*

Rennert, Jonathan – 0181 658 9428 *also fax*

Rennert, Wolfgang – *Allied*

Renzetti, Donato – *Allied*

Rescigno, Joseph – *Gilder*

Reymond, Valentin – *Mus Int*

Reynish, Timothy – 0161 928 8364 *also fax*

Reynolds, Julian – *Portland*

Rhodes, Burt – 0181 371 9896

Rickenbacher, Karl Anton – *Transart*

Riddell, David – *Magenta*

Ridley, Anthony – 0151 677 8708

Rifkin, Joshua – *Clarion/Seven Muses*

Rizzi, Carlo – *Allied*

Robertson, David – *ICM*

Robertson, Stewart – *Still*

Robinson, Christopher – *SWA*

Roblou, David – c/o 0181 299 1914 *also fax*

Rochester, Marc – 01252 783172 *also fax; email:* marcroc@jarings.co.my

Romano, Marco – 0141 551 8789

Romanos, Simon – *ECAM*

Ros-Marbá, Antoni – *Ingpen*

Rose, Gregory – *Connaught*

Roseberry, Eric – 01225 891410

Rosen, Steven – *WWA*

Rostropovich, Mstislav – c/o 0171 794 0987 *fax:* 0171 431 2531

Roth, Alec – 0171 497 3754 *also fax*

Rothstein, Jack – c/o 0181 459 1475 *fax:* 0181 459 1642

Rowe, Matthew – *Musicmakers*

Rowe, Tony – 0161 928 8640 *fax:* 0161 929 6808

Roxburgh, Edwin – *Michael Harrold*

Rozhdestvensky, Gennadi – *Allied*

Rudel, Julius – *PGM*

Rudland, Malcolm – 0171 589 9595 *also fax*

Rumble, Andy – *Brunskill*

Rumsey, Stephen – c/o 01621 892229

Rumstadt, Guido Johannes – *Gilder*

Runnicles, Donald – *Still*

Ruud, Ole Kristian – *VWM*

Saccani, Rico – *Stafford*

Sacher, Paul – *Ingpen*

Sado, Yutaka – *Transart*

Salonen, Esa-Pekka – *VWM*

Salter, Lionel – 0181 458 3568 *also fax*

Salter, Timothy – 0181 318 2031 *also fax*

Sander, Alexander – *Mus Int*

Sanderling, Kurt – *McCann*

Sanderling, Stefan – *WWA*

Sanderling, Thomas – *McCann*

Saraste, Jukka-Pekka – *VWM*

Sato, Shuntaro – c/o 0171 483 2681 *fax:* 0171 586 5343

Schiff, Heinrich – *Intermusica*

Schirmer, Ulf – *HP*

Schmidt, Ole – *PGM*

Schneider, Peter – *Ingpen*

Schønwandt, Michael – *Ingpen*

Schwarz, Gerard – *Columbia*

Scimone, Claudio – *Transart*

Scott, Paul – 0114 235 0277

Seaman, Christopher – *HP*

Secret, Robert – 01280 848275 *also fax*

Segal, Uriel – *Olivia Ma*

Segerstam, Leif – *PGM*

Semkow, Jerzy – *Transart*

Shallon, David – *HP*

Shao, En – *IMG*

Shelley, Howard – *Intermusica*

Shelley, Patrick – *Mus Int*

Shipway, Frank – 01981 580363 *fax:* 01981 580578

Shostakovich, Maxim – *Pristavec*

Shulman, Andrew – 01420 472206 *fax:* 01420 478690

Sidwell, Martindale – 0171 435 9210

Simms, Philip – c/o 0181 692 3037; 0181 691 8337 *also fax*

Simon, Geoffrey – 0181 883 7306 *fax:* 0181 365 3388 *email:* 100336.2446@ compuserve.com; http://www. calarecords.com

Simonov, Yuri – *Allied*

Sinaisky, Vassily – *IMG*

Singer, Malcolm – 0181 992 2318 *fax:* 0181 896 2556

Sitkovetsky, Dmitry – *IMG*

Skidmore, Jeffrey – c/o 0121 523 1025 *fax:* 0121 523 1026

Skrowaczewski, Stanislaw – *Intermusica*

Slageren, Johan van – *Alexander*

Slater, Christopher – 01372 454963 *also fax*

Slatkin, Leonard – *Holt*

Sloane, Steven – *Allied*

Snashall, John – 01983 753527

Snell, Howard – 01889 507221 *also fax*

Spearing, Robert – 01981 250849 *also fax;* 01974 282631

Spicer, Paul – 01543 250627 *fax:* 01543 250970 *email:* paul@finzi.idiscover.co.uk

Springthorpe, Nigel – 01707 322448

Squires, Chris – c/o 0141 248 4567; 0966 416765 *fax:* 0141 221 8812

Stanger, Peter – 0181 398 6611

Stapleton, Robin – *Stafford*

Stark, Peter – 0181 208 1709 *also fax; email:* peterstark_conductor@ compuserve.com

Steadman, Robert – 0115 917 4546 *also fax*

Steen, Jac van – *McCann*

Steinberg, Pinchas – *IMG*

Stenz, Markus – *Ingpen*

Stephens, Richard – 01437 760269 *also fax;* 04325 161890

Stephenson, Mark – c/o 0181 871 0330 *fax:* 0181 871 0440

Stern, David – *ICM*

Stern, Michael – *Transart*

Stones, Joseph – 0113 275 2348

Studt, Richard – 01202 394955 *also fax*

Sturman, Paul – 01703 260342 *also fax*

Summers, Patrick – *Askonas*

Sunshine, Adrian – c/o 0181 455 6799 *also fax*

Sutherland, Iain – 01273 504073

Sutton-Anderson, David – 0181 349 2317 *fax:* 0181 346 8257

Svarovsky, Leos – *McCann*

Swensen, Joseph – *VWM*

Syrus, David – *Still*

Tabachnik, Michel – *PGM*

Talmi, Yoav – *Anglo-Swiss*

Taylor, Graham – 0141 334 9588 *fax:* 0141 339 6153

Taylor, Matthew – 0181 761 8968 *also fax*

Tear CBE, Robert – *Holt*

Temirkanov, Yuri – *IMG*

Temple, David – *Magenta*

Tenant-Flowers, Sarah – 01235 850488 *also fax; email:* info@thesixteen.org.uk

Thorp, Sigmund – *Anthony Abbott*

Tilbrook, Jonathan – 0181 521 7657 *also fax*

Tilson Thomas, Michael – *Columbia*

Tirimo, Martino – *McCann*

Tongue, Alan – *Ellison*

Tortelier, Yan Pascal – *IMG*

Touchin, Colin – 01203 670211 *also fax;* 01203 523799 *fax:* 01203 528136 *email:* musac@warwick.ac.uk

Tovey, Bramwell – *Gilder*

Townend, Richard – 0171 589 1206 *fax:* 0171 589 5925

Tracey, Ian – 0151 708 8471 *fax:* 0151 708 0378

Treacher, Graham – 0117 974 3279

Tredinnick, Noël – 0171 487 3508 *fax:* 0171 224 6087

Trifan, Mariora – *Gilder*

Trory, Robert – *NWA*

Turnovsky, Martin – *McCann*

Vandernoot, Joseph – 0171 385 5432

Vann, Stanley – 01780 782192

Vänskä, Osmo – *Clarion/Seven Muses*

Vardigans, Richard – *Connaught*

Varga, Gilbert – *Intermusica*

Vasáry, Támás – *IMG*

Vass, George – 0171 435 5965

Veis, Daniel – c/o 0181 788 2710 *fax:* 0181 788 4282

Venzago, Mario – *Tennant*

Verdernikov, Alexander – *Askonas*

Vignoles, Roger – *OWM*

Viotti, Marcello – *Askonas*

Volkov, Ilan – *VWM*

Von Dohnányi, Oliver – *Mus Int*

Vonk, Hans – *Intermusica*

Waart, Edo de – *HP*

Wagner, Jan – *PGM*

Wales, Roy – 01273 300894 *fax:* 01273 308394 *email:* musedman@fastnet.co.uk

Wallberg, Heinz – *Rawstron*

Walter, Alfred – *Finch*

Walton, Philip – *KDM*

Warren-Green, Christopher – c/o 0181 772 9741 *fax:* 0181 772 9742

Warren, Edward – 0151 336 4039 *also fax; email:* edwarren@aol.com

Webb, Barrie – *KDM*

Wehner, Nigel – *JLM*

Weil, Bruno – *Ingpen*

Weller, Walter – *HP*

Welser-Möst, Franz – *IMG*

West, Martin – 0181 785 4142 *also fax;* 0966 196996

Wheeler, Dominic – *Musicmakers*

White, Robin – 01923 670278

Wigglesworth, Mark – *Holt*

Willcocks CBE, Sir David – 01223 359559 *fax:* 01223 355947

Willcocks, Jonathan – 01705 631369 *fax:* 01705 631786

Willén, Niklas – *PGM*

Williams, Elwyn – 01222 611435

Williams, Howard – *Tennant*
Williams MBE, John Hywel – 01554 772979
 also fax
Williamson, Julian – 0181 579 5643
Wit, Antoni – *WWA*
Wolff, Hugh – *VWM*
Wood, Christopher – 01702 338943
 fax: 01702 340558
Woods, Thomas – *Magenta*

Woolfenden, Guy – *SWA*
Wordsworth, Barry – *ICM*
Wright, Simon – *Denny Lyster*
Wulstan, David – 01974 241229
 email: dww@aber.ac.uk
Yershon, Gary – *Chuck Julian*
Young, Emanuel – 0181 886
 1144
Yü, Long – *ICM*

Yuasa, Takuo – *PGM*
Zambelli, Marco – *Allied*
Zender, Hans – *Allied*
Ziegler, Robert – c/o 0181 679
 4609/9303 *fax:* 0181 679 9306
 email: ziegler@matrixmuisc.
 u-net.com
Zinman, David – *HP*
Zreczycki, Andrew – *Encore*

Instrumentalists

Organ

The artists marked with an asterisk also perform as accompanists.

Ainscough, Julie – *Michael Harrold*
Alain, Marie-Claire – *Transart*
* Archer, Malcolm – 01749 673526 *also fax*
Arnáiz, Guilliermo Diez – *Michael Harrold*
Ashfield, Robert – 01634 841508
* Aubrey-Drew, Helen – 01824 704582
* Ayres, Paul – 0181 998 2294 *also fax*
* Baden Fuller, Stephen – 01455 552009 *also fax*
* Baker, Alison – 01206 575825 *also fax;* 0850 241637
Baker, Cyril – 01595 692632
* Baldwin, Antony – 0171 483 4262 *fax:* 0171 586 6069
* Ball, Timothy – 0181 871 0317 *also fax*
* Barber, Graham – 0113 263 1890 *fax:* 0113 263 7178
* Barham, Jeremy – 01483 505309 *also fax*
* Barker, Bernard – 0181 427 5409 *also fax*
* Barnes, Gerald – 0181 346 6637
* Barnes, Richard – 01243 776325 *fax:* 01243 539604 *email:* kath.mus@arunet.co.uk
* Barton, Christopher – 01633 266708
Bate, Jennifer – 0181 883 3811 *fax:* 0181 444 3695 *email:* jenniferbate@classical-artists. com; http://www.classical-artists.com/jbate
Beard, Kenneth – 01246 582472
Beaumont, Kerry – 01765 600237 *also fax*
* Beaven, Peter – 01932 788785 *fax:* 01932 765060 *email:* pmsnet@argonet.co.uk
* Beechey, Gwilym – 01482 508910
Bending, Arthur – 01626 890242
Bielby, Jonathan – 01924 378841 *fax:* 01924 215054
* Binnington, Stephen – 01258 820087 *fax:* 01747 854684
* Bishop, John – 0117 942 3373 *fax:* 0117 944 1994
Bonaventure, Michael – 0131 657 4631
Bond, Timothy – 0181 670 3308
Bowen, Geraint – 01437 720128 *also fax*
Bowers-Broadbent, Christopher – *Magenta*
Bowyer, Kevin – *Ellison*
Bramma, Harry – c/o 01306 877676 *fax:* 01306 887260
Bruce-Payne, David – 0121 454 6222
Bunney CVO, Herrick – 0131 337 6494
* Byram-Wigfield, Timothy – 0131 225 6293
* Carter, Roger – 01582 720095
Carter, Stanley – *JLM*
* Charlston, Terence – 01582 462024 *also fax*
Cleobury, Stephen – *Magenta* – 01223 331224 *fax:* 01233 331890
* Coulson, Richard – 01932 229171
* Curley, Carlo – *PVA*
* Curror, Ian – 0171 730 7395
Darlington, Stephen – 01865 276195 *fax:* 01865 794199
* Davies, Stephen Robert – 0181 656 1732
* Dawkes, Hubert – 01264 324467
* Druce, Colin – 01926 451550
Dunnett, David – *Chameleon*
Elcombe, Keith – 0161 445 6661
Ennis, Catherine – *Blythe*
* Farrell, Scott – 01284 725778 *fax:* 01284 768655
* Farrell, Timothy – 0181 694 1528 *also fax*
Filsell, Jeremy – *Clifton Wyatt*
* Fisher, Roger – 01745 561072 *also fax*

* Fletcher, Andrew – 0121 706 5708 *fax:* 0121 608 2990 *email:* a_fletcher@ compuserve.com
* Foreman, Robert – 0116 286 1216
* Gaze, Nigel – 01772 743821
Gifford, Gerald – 01954 250190 *also fax*
Goodwin, Andrew – 01248 714194/354015 *fax:* 01248 353882
Gower, Christopher – 01733 65165 *fax:* 01733 52465
Gower, Robert – *Denny Lyster*
* Green, Gareth David – 01924 376848 *also fax*
Greenway, Kenneth – 01902 754529
* Hale, Paul – 01636 812228 *also fax;* 01636 812649
Hanson, Geoffrey – 0181 444 9214
* Hare, Ian – *Ellison*
* Harries, Clive – 01609 881552 *fax:* 01642 616511
Harris Michael – 01506 410477 *also fax; email:* m.harris@napier.ac.uk
Harverson, Alan – 0181 883 2553
* Heath-Downey, Susan – 0171 231 1423
Hekimova, Yanka – *PVA*
Herrick, Christopher – 0181 546 8966 *fax:* 0181 541 0034
Higginbottom, Edward – 01865 279519 *fax:* 01865 279590 *email:* edward.higginbottom @new.ox.ac.uk
* Hoeg, Michael Erling – 01222 563179 *fax:* 01222 567752
Hollick, Douglas – 01949 861347 *also fax; email:* dwh@globalnet.co.uk
* Hone, Timothy – 0191 232 1939 *fax:* 0191 230 0735
* Horsey, Alan – 01422 203468; 01274 777720 *fax:* 01274 777730
* Houghton, Nicholas – 01444 230779 *fax:* 01444 233699
* Howard, Jeffrey – 01222 549383 *also fax;* 0467 387726
* Howard Duro, Stephen – 01895 232055 *also fax*
* Howell, Alison – 0117 951 4692
Hoyland, David – *Grosvenor*
* Hughes, Trevor – *Lindsay*
* Hunt OBE, Donald – 01905 24067
* Jackson, Carl – 0181 686 4297 *also fax; email:* carl_jackson@ccis.org.uk
Jackson, Graham – 0117 962 3850 *also fax*
Jarvis, Keith – 01484 683159
* John, Keith – 01234 708029
Jones, Jonathan Hellyer – 01223 515688
Jordan, John – 01553 692708/772858
* Kemp-Luck, Edward – 0171 226 1218 *fax:* 0171 919 7644 *email:* e.kemp-luck @gold.ac.uk
Kerry, Nigel – 01553 692665 *also fax*
King, David – 0171 976 6805 *also fax*
* Kitchen, John P – 0131 650 2432 *fax:* 0131 650 2425 *email:* j.kitchen@music.ed.ac.uk
Koopman, Ton – *Magenta*
Kynaston, Nicolas – 0181 878 4455 *fax:* 0181 392 9314
Lancelot, James – 0191 386 4766
Layton, Stephen – *Magenta*
* Ledger CBE, Philip – c/o 0141 332 4101 *fax:* 0141 332 8901
Lehtonen, Maija – *Ellison*

* Leith, Ronald – 01224 634427 *fax:* 01224 639096
Leonhardt, Gustav – *Allied*
* Lester-Cribb, Michael – 0131 552 1224
Liddle, David – 0181 444 4454
* Lindley, Simon – 0113 234 1146 *also fax*
* Longden, Lee – 0161 224 4530 *also fax;* 01426 241423; 0802 583647
Lucas, Adrian – *Chameleon*
* Lucas, Andrew – 0171 236 4257
* Luke, Philip – 01449 711511
* Lumsden, Andrew – 01543 263306 *also fax*
McAllister, Maureen – *Invisible Pilots*
McGreal, John – 0181 771 8508
McGregor, Simon – 0171 987 5110
* McPhee MBE, George – 0141 889 3528 *fax:* 0141 887 3929
* McVicker, William – 0181 299 1971 *also fax; email:* william.mcvicker@port.ac.uk
* Marsden Thomas, Anne – 0171 638 3052 *fax:* 0171 638 8285 *email:* 100413.1352@ compuserve.com
Marshall, Wayne – *Holt*
Massey, Roy – 01432 272011
* Matthews, Charles – 01386 438078
* Medley, Russell – 0161 485 3886
* Missin, Russell – 0191 281 1513
* Moore, Adrian – 01926 883615
Moroney, Davitt – *Michael Harrold*
Morris, Andrew – 01234 365520
Muzzi, Massimiliano – *Ellison*
* Myers, Charles – 01200 423711
Neary, Martin – 0171 222 6923 *fax:* 0171 222 1025 *email:* pneary@westminster.abbey.org
* Nethsingha, Lucian – 01392 277521
* Nevill, Barry StJohn – 01323 417006; 0421 373734 *fax:* 01323 729776
* Newberry, Andrew – 01243 830695
* Nickol, Christopher – 0141 558 6555 *also fax; email:* kingnickol@aol.com
Nolan-Cain, Joseph – *Ellison*
Ogden, David – 0117 946 7456 *fax:* 0117 973 8263
* Overbury, Michael – 01636 702054
* Oxley, Harrison – 01284 787533
Page, Anne, org, harmonium – 01223 240026 *fax:* 01223 573663
Parker-Smith, Jane – 0171 262 9259 *also fax*
Parnell, Andrew – *Michael Harrold*
* Parry, Martyn – 0181 980 9735 *also fax; email:* m.parry@herts.ac.uk
* Parsons, James – 01832 273447 *fax:* 01832 272026
* Partington, Adrian – *PVA*
* Patrick, David Kinnear – 0181 449 4873
Patrick, David M – 01392 275078
Paukert, Karel – *Judith Hendershott*
* Pearce, Geoffrey – 01977 681831
* Perrin, Ronald – 01765 603906
* Phillips, Margaret – 01963 250899 *fax:* 01963 250999
* Pilliner, Richard – 0181 651 3728
Pink, Andrew – 0171 272 6101 *also fax*
* Ponsford, David – 01285 651995 *also fax*
* Popplewell, Richard – 0181 332 7301
Preston, Simon – 01892 862042 *also fax*
* Price, David J C – 01705 730792 *fax:* 01705 295480 *email:* pennyport@aol.com
* Proud, Malcolm – 00 353 56 61497 *also fax*

Photo: Robert Barber

EVA-MARIA ALEXANDRE
Pianist

First Prizewinner
East-West Artists' International Competition, New York
Pro Musicis International Competition, Paris
South East Arts 'Young Musicians' Platform, London

"PATRICIAN OF THE KEYS - qualities that set her apart...
dark foreboding, dreaminess and fiery brilliance with flair"
THE TIMES

"An artist who compels attention. Everything fell into place
with majestic inevitability"
MUSICAL OPINION

"Power in reserve...intimate and engaging performances..."
THE BOSTON GLOBE

"Top notch pianist... dramatic and highly virtuosic..."
THE NEW YORK TIMES

SIVA OKE MUSIC MANAGEMENT
13 RIVERSDALE ROAD THAMES DITTON SURREY KT7 0QL
Tel: 0181-398 1586 Fax: 0181-339 0981

Anda Anastasescu

Pianist and Artistic Director of the London Schubert
Players chamber orchestra

"'Yet another pianist!' you may think. No, of this
calibre the world can never have enough." – Paris

72 Warwick Gardens, London W14 8PP
Tel/Fax: 0171 603 1396
E-mail: schubert@dial.pipex.com

Isabel Beyer & Harvey Dagul

International Piano Duettists

For more than 40 years Isabel Beyer & Harvey Dagul have
delighted audiences worldwide with their unrivalled knowledge
of the piano duet repertoire.

"the couple's refined skills and remarkable talents
made a deep impression" **Mainichi Shinbun – Tokyo**

"the audience had been won over by the virtuosity
of the two musicians."   **Suddeutsche Zeitung**

Live recitals are complemented by many recordings (on the FHM label)

Four Hands Favourites Vols 1 & 2	**FHMD 8045/6**
Carl Czerny 2, 4 & 6 Hands 1/2	**FHMD 881/2**
Jeux d'Enfants (various composers)	**FHMD 9212**
French Duets Alkan, Koechlin etc.	**FHMD 9110**
Mozart Variations and Late Sonatas	**FHMD 9111**
Schubert Complete Duets 8 vols	**FHMD 891-8**
Moszkowski + albums featuring Moszkowski,	
Juon, Dvorak, Brahms & Grieg	**FHMD 9671/2/3**

Isabel Beyer & Harvey Dagul "communicate with enthusiasm the sheer
joy of playing piano duets..a happy blend of elegiac expressivity and
colourful exuberance..the ensemble is impeccable." **Gramophone May 1997**

All enquiries:
15 Birchmead Close, St Albans, Herts AL3 6BS UK
Tel/Fax: 01727 858485
Websites: http://www.classical-artists.com/beydag *(availability)*
http://www.mdt.co.uk *(recordings)*

Racy RAGTIME thru'
to the roaring
TWENTIES rendered
ravishingly by Miss
Helen Crayford

Wearing authentic costumes
from the period 1890-1940,
Helen Crayford performs
virtuoso, syncopated piano
solos by composers ranging
from Scott Joplin and Zez
Confrey to George Gershwin,
'Fats' Waller and Billy
Mayerl. Be entertained and
illuminated by the stories
behind the music, as Helen
traces the history of ragtime,
and its transformation into the
riches of early jazz.

This sparkling show can be
tailored to suit any event:
choose from lecture/recital, or
show.

"(Helen) Crayford's playing took on the joyous
assertiveness of the great stride pianists."
(The Independent).

Contact:
Alison Page
Seaview Music
Tel: 01223-772690
Fax: 01223-772828

RAGS TO RICHES

* Rathbone, Christopher – 0113 274 7716
    also fax
  Rees-Williams, Jonathan – *Musicmakers*
* Rennert, Jonathan – 0181 658 9428 *also fax*
* Riddle, Ian – 01782 661723
* Roblou, David – 0181 299 1914
* Rochester, Marc – 0370 388001 *fax:* 01252
    783172 *email:* marcroc@jarings.co.my
  Rowland, David – *Music Management*
* Rudland, Malcolm – 0171 589 9595 *also fax*
  Saint, David – 0121 454 8529
  Sanger, David – 017687 76628 *also fax*
* Sayer, Roger – 01634 849683 *fax:* 01634
    401410
  Scott, John – *Magenta*
  Seivewright, Andrew – 017687 72172
* Seymour, Peter – 01904 652799 *fax:* 01904
    338349 *email:* ps22@unix.york.ac.uk

  Sidwell, Martindale – 0171 435 9210
* Sieling, Gary – 01400 273795 *also fax*
  Smedley, Peter – 0115 929 1308
* Smith, Michael – 01262 670869 *also fax*
  Souter, Martin – 01865 726553 *fax:* 01865
    243388
  Stewart, Gordon – 01254 51491
  Tebbet, Roger D – 01904 416219 *also fax*
* Thomas, James L – 0181 942 2574
  Titterington, David – *Denny Lyster*
  Townend, Richard – 0171 589 1206 *fax:* 0171
    589 5925
  Townhill OBE, Dennis – 0131 225 1116
    fax: 0131 225 3181
* Tracey, Ian – 0151 708 8471 *fax:* 0151
    708 0378
  Trinkwon, D'Arcy – 0181 746 3425 *also fax*
  Trotter, Thomas – 01753 859265 *also fax*

* Underwood, Philip – 0161 456 9037
* Walsh, Colin – *Chameleon*
* Ward Russell, Gillian – 01621 853237
  Watts, Jane – 01525 222729 *also fax*
  Weir DBE, Dame Gillian – *Denny Lyster*
* White, Martin John – 01861 524110 *fax:*
    01762 394525
  Williams, John – 0171 373 3638
  Williams, Roger Bevan – 01224 272570 *fax:*
    01224 272515
* Williams, Simon – 01923 770543
  Wills OBE, Arthur – 01353 662084 *also fax;*
    0374 680716 *email:* artwill@argonet.co.uk
  Winpenny, Keith – 01204 852466
* Woolley, Robert – 0181 398 6085 *also fax*
* Wright, Simon – *Denny Lyster*
  Zabala, Oscar Candenda – *Michael
    Harrold*

Solo Piano

The artists listed below are soloists; those indicated with an asterisk also perform as accompanists. Other accompanists and coaches are listed in a separate section. This list includes players of the fortepiano, whilst harpsichordists are listed in the following section.

* Aarons, Mignonette – 0181 204 8778
  Achúcarro, Joaquín – *Olivia Ma*
  Adams, John Christopher – *Ellison*
* Adni, Daniel – 0171 794 4076 *also fax*
  Alexandre, Eva-Maria – 0171 289 5114
    also fax
  Alexeev, Dmitri – *IMG*
  Alexeyev, Anya – *HP*
* Alston, Raymond – 0181 348 5506
  Altman, Elizabeth – c/o 0113 267 5821
    also fax
  Alvanis, Louis Demetrius – *JLM*
  Amato, Donna – *Pristavec*
  Ambache, Diana – 0171 263 4027 *also fax;*
    email: ambache@aol.com
  Anastasescu, Anda – 0171 603 1396 *also fax*
  Anderson, Mark – *Jennings*
  Anderszewski, Piotr – *Holt*
* Andrievsky, Alexandra – 0181 459 4654
    also fax
  Andsnes, Leif Ove – *IMG*
  Ang, Linda – *Dyfel*
  Appleton, David – 0181 986 9197
  Ardakov, Alexander – *Ellison/Dyfel* – 01494
    724461 *also fax; email:* chri0562@sable.
    ox.ac.uk
  Ardasev, Igor – *McCann*
  Arkadiev, Mikhail – *Askonas*
  Armstrong, Paul – 0171 603 8431
    also fax
  Ashkenazy, Vladimir – *HP*
  Ax, Emanuel – *Holt*
  Badura-Skoda, Paul – *Connaught*
* Bailie, Eleanor – 0181 788 5270
* Baker, Alison – 01206 575825 *also fax;*
    0850 241637
  Balakleets, Olga – *Gilder*
* Bale, Matthew – 01225 337722
  Ball, Andrew – 0171 732 1405 *fax:* 0171
    635 0709
* Bamford, Stephanie – 0151 652 2033
  Banowetz, Joseph – *Camerata*
  Barenboim, Daniel – *Holt*
* Barham, Stuart – 0171 622 8864
  Barnes, Philippa – 01638 714534
  Barthold, Kenneth van – 01747 838318
    also fax
  Barto, Tzimon – *Olivia Ma*
  Bavouzet, Jean-Efflam – *Gilder*
* Beament, Jane – 01279 436570
  Bebbington, Mark – *SWA*
* Beechey, Gwilym – 01482 508910

  Bekova, Eleonora – 0181 675 6885 *fax:* 0181
    673 8356
  Belinkaya, Noemy – *Ellison*
  Belliere, Krystian – *Purkiss*
  Bellucci, Giovanni – *Transart*
  Ben-Or, Nelly – 01923 822268 *also fax*
  Bennett CBE, Richard Rodney –
    Clarion/Seven Muses
* Benselin, Margaret – 01737 843792
* Benson, Clifford – 01732 364204 *also fax*
* Bentley, Keith – 01642 485207
  Berezovsky, Boris – *IMG*
  Berman, Boris – *Askonas*
  Berman, Lazar – *Transart*
  Béroff, Michel – *Transart*
* Beyer, Isabel – 01727 858485 *also fax*
  Bidini, Fabio – *McCann*
  Bielicki, Richard – *SJM*
* Billington, Vincent – 01723 364241
  Bingham, John – *GBZ* – 0114 230 8113 *also
    fax;* 0181 289 3067
  Binns, Malcolm – *Michael Harrold*
* Black, Richard – 0171 277 7068 *fax:* 0171
    277 8354 *email:* 100115.3701
    @compuserve.com
  Blewett, Brenda – *Ellison*
  Blumenthal, Daniel – *Jennings*
  Bottrill, Andrew – 01367 820067
* Bradshaw, Susan – 0171 226 8675
  Branson, David – 01424 422061
  Bratke, Marcelo – *Connaught*
  Brautigam, Ronald – *Lubbock*
  Brendel KBE, Alfred – *Ingpen*
* Brewster-Franzetti, Allison G – *Ellison*
* Brickman, Miriam – *Jennings*
  Bridges, Peter – 0171 225 3152 *fax:* 0171
    720 4627
  Briggs, Sarah Beth – 01653 648253
    fax: 01653 648519
  Bronfman, Yefim – *ICM*
* Broster, Eileen – 0181 551 0439 *also fax;*
    0585 941695
* Brown, Alan – 01737 354642
  Brown, Ian – *Chameleon*
  Browning, John – *PGM*
  Brownridge, Angela – *KDM*
* Bruce, Margaret – 01422 842275; 0181 940
    0697; 0181 960 0897 *fax:* 0181 969 0820
* Bruzon, John – 0181 800 2430
  Buckley, Geoffrey – 01600 780354 *also fax*
  Burke, Paul – 01226 752504 *also fax*
  Burmester, Pedro – *Gilder*

  Burnett, Richard, f-pno – 01580 211702
    fax: 01580 211007
  Burns MBE, Joan – 0161 998 3715
* Burnside, Iain – *ICM*
  Burwell, Kim – *Purkiss*
* Canetty-Clarke, Janet – 01444 811243
    fax: 01444 811171
  Canino, Bruno – *Allied*
  Carter, Jeremy – *Charlton* – c/o 01452
    857859 *also fax; email:* jjcarter7@aol.com;
    http://members.aol.com/jjcarter7/
  Cascioli, Gianluca – *Ingpen*
* Casén, Petra – 0181 941 9778
  Chen, Shu-Ching Evelyn – *WWA*
* Chiu, Dai-Chi – 0181 952 8245 *also fax*
  Choi, Vivian – *Ellison*
  Ciccolini, Aldo – *SWA*
* Clayton, Nigel – 0181 462 5702 *also fax*
  Clegg, John – *Ellison*
* Clemmow, Caroline – 01724 720475
    fax: 01724 721599
  Cload, Julia – *Grosvenor*
  Cohen, Arnaldo – *Gilder/Grant Rogers*
* Cole, Annette – 0181 444 1723
  Cole, Maggie, f-pno – *Robert White*
  Collard, Jean-Philippe – *Tennant*
  Colvill, Robin – 01727 848123 *fax:* 01727
    854910
* Constable, John – 0171 229 4603
  Coombs, Stephen – 01273 685849 *fax:* 01273
    703850 *email:* scriptory@compuserve.com
  Cooper, Imogen – *VWM*
* Crayford, Helen – *Seaview* – 0181 863 4659
    also fax; email: http://www.brailsford.
    demon.co.uk
* Croser, Peter – 01932 228012
* Crossland, Jill – 0181 579 4394
* Crossland, Neil – *Purkiss*
  Crossley, Paul – *VWM*
* Cuckston, Alan – 01757 638238
  D'Ascoli, Bernard – *Clarion/Seven Muses*
  Dagul, Harvey – 01727 858485 *also fax*
  Dalberto, Michel – *Transart*
  Darnborough, Jonathan – 0181 395 7433
    fax: 0181 543 6735 *email:* midman503a
    @aol.com; http://members.aol.com
    /midman503a
  Davidovich, Bella – *Tennant*
  Davies, Eiluned – 0181 368 8202
* Davies, Helen – 01248 713336
  De Maria, Pietro – *Transart*
  de Quetteville, Timothy – 01534 879082

de Saram, Druvi – *Stella Baker*
de Waal, Rian – *Gilder*
* Deering, Richard – 0181 656 6222 *also fax*
* Deighton, Elizabeth – *Wright*
Demidenko, Nikolai – *GIA*
Desson, Sheila – 0131 556 5979
Dewey, Thomas – *Gilder*
Deyanova, Marta – *KDM*
Dick, James – *Camerata*
* Dickinson, Peter – 01728 454540
Dimitrova, Lora – *Annon*
* Dodd, Jane – 0181 642 5418
Douglas, Barry – *IMG*
* Downes, Derek – 0171 376 8334
Dubravka, Tomsic – *Hazard*
Dupré, Heather – 0181 455 1966
* Durcan, Nicholas – c/o 0181 673 1901
* Durran, Katharine – 01484 841868 *also fax*
* Dussek, Michael – 0181 958 6983 *also fax*
Dyson, Julian – 0181 393 5722
* Earl, David – 01865 728281 *also fax*
* Edwards, Catherine – 0171 732 9399 *also fax*
Elias-José, Vanya – 0181 878 0980 *fax:* 0181 392 9546
Elton, Christopher – 0181 455 6587 *fax:* 0181 381 4797
* Elwin, David – *Purkiss*
Engerer, Brigitte – *Transart*
Entremont, Philippe – *ICM*
Evans, Clifford – 01473 253217
* Evans, Patricia – 01908 542269
* Evans, Peter – 0131 447 6414 *also fax*
Fear, Margaret – 01923 661159
Feghali, José – *Olivia Ma*
Fellner, Till – *Ingpen*
* Fenyö, Gusztáv – 0141 339 2708 *fax:* 0141 337 6923
Fergus-Thompson, Gordon – 0181 202 5861 *also fax*
Ferguson, Robert – 01708 441799
Few, Margerie – 0171 435 1884
Fialkowska, Janina – *Ingpen*
* Filsell, Jeremy – *Clifton Wyatt*
Fingerhut, Margaret – c/o 01444 230779 *fax:* 01444 233699
* Fischer, Raymond – 0181 748 4702 *also fax*
Fisher, Norma – *Ellison*
Fitch, Graham – 0171 731 6826 *also fax*
Fleisher, Leon – *ICM*
Fong, William – *Lyons*
Forey, Edmund – *Mostylea*
Fountain, Ian – *Connaught*
Fowke, Philip – *PGM* – 0171 935 5773 *fax:* 0171 224 6278
Fralovna, Natalia – *NWA*
Francesch, Homero – *Anglo-Swiss*
Franceschetti, Davide – *OWM*
Frankl, Peter – *Transart*
Frantz, Justus – *Anglo-Swiss*
* Freyhan, Michael, f-pno – 0181 459 6825 *also fax*
* Frith, Benjamin – 01909 562395 *also fax*
* Gammon, Philip – 0181 866 3260
Garzon, Maria – *Ellison*
Gasser, Mark – *Camerata*
Gee, Alison – 0161 980 8203
Gelber, Bruno Leonardo – *Transart*
* Gellhorn, Peter – 0181 876 3949
Gergieva, Larissa – *Askonas*
Gibb, James – *Purkiss*
Gibbons, Jack – *NBM/McCann*
Gilad, Jonathan – *ICM*
Gillespie, Rhondda – 01424 715167 *fax:* 01424 712214 *email:* 100723.510@ compuserve.com
Golan, Itamar – *Askonas*
Goldstone, Anthony – 01724 720475 *fax:* 01724 721599
Gómez-Morán, Miriam – *Ellison*
Goode, Richard – *Intermusica*
Gordon, David – *Clifton Wyatt*

* Govier, Geoffrey, f-pno – 0181 922 0587 *also fax*
Graf, Enrique – *Ellison*
Gräsbeck, Folke – *Ellison*
* Gray, Antony – *Blythe*
Green-Armytage, Christopher – 01362 694223
* Greenwood, Richard – *Clifton Wyatt* – 0181 748 6203
Grimaud, Helene – *ICM*
Gruenberg, Joanna – *Intermusica*
* Gulley, Margaret – 01392 874761
Gutierrez, Horacio – *ICM*
Gutman, Stephen – 0171 254 7763
Hadjinikos, George – 0161 928 3329 *fax:* 00 301 361 9373
Haefliger, Andreas – *Intermusica*
* Hall, Garth – 01730 231765 *also fax*
Hamelin, Marc André – *GIA*
Hamilton, Kenneth – *Camerata*
* Hancox, William – 0956 833337 *fax:* 0181 458 0980
Harding, Elizabeth – 01690 710523
* Harmer, Louisa – 0171 603 3602 *also fax*
* Harris, Jeffery – 01737 355245
* Harte, Ruth – 0181 650 2929 *also fax*
Harvey, Jean – 01428 642230
* Hashimoto, Miyako – 0181 882 5032
Hatchard, Mike – *Clifton Wyatt*
* Hattingh, Michael – c/o 0181 802 2719
Haywood, Sam – 0181 964 1493 *also fax*
Hazeldine, Alan – 0181 341 0567 *also fax; email:* 101333.1675@compuserve.com
Hazlehurst, Marjorie – 0121 454 0771
Heisser, Jean-Francois – *ICM*
Hewitt, Angela – *McCann*
Hewson, David – *Dyfel*
* Hewson, James – 01572 767653 *email:* room101@architechs.com
Hickman, Carl – 0121 454 8431
* Hill, Barbara – 0171 435 9210
* Hill, Peter – 0114 230 2309 *fax:* 0114 263 0231
Hind, Rolf – *Clarion/Seven Muses*
Hind O'Malley, Pamela – 01223 247885
Hobson, Ian – c/o 0181 894 0391 *fax:* 0181 287 9428
Horsley OBE, Colin – 01624 813095
Hough, Stephen – *HP*
Houlihan, Phillip – 0181 947 0484
Howard, Leslie – c/o 0181 960 4780 *fax:* 0181 964 5510
Howard, William – 01453 872478 *fax:* 01453 872173
Howat, Roy – *Manygate*
Howells, David – *Sykes*
Hoyland, John – *Grosvenor*
Huang, Helen – *ICM*
* Humphrey, Graeme – 0181 690 6264
Humphreys, John – *Camerata*
Hursey, John – *Annon*
* Hurton, Amanda – 0181 390 6951 *also fax*
* Hutchison, Jean – 0141 334 3763
Hutchison, Nigel – 0181 340 5217 *also fax*
* Ibbott, Daphne – 0181 748 6991
Ilya, Itin – *Holt*
Immelman, Niel – 0181 947 7201 *fax:* 0181 946 8846
* Innes, Audrey – 0131 620 0380 *fax:* 0131 620 0379 *email:* 100777.2721@ compuserve.com
Iruzun, Clélia – *NCCP* – 0171 916 2410 *fax:* 0171 916 2448
Jablonski, Peter – *HP*
* Jacobs, Peter – 0181 943 2918
Jacobson, Julian – 0181 694 9525 *fax:* 0181 692 7065
Jacoby, Ingrid – *GBZ*
Janusz – 01765 605508 *also fax;* 01344 22450
* Jeffrey, Emily – 0171 223 2408 *also fax*
Jekéli, Lotte – *Ellison*
Jones, Martin – *OWM*

Jones, Michael – 01384 393706
Joseph, Julian – *HP*
Kahane, Jeffrey – *IMG*
Kalichstein, Joseph – *HP*
Kaplan, Benjamin – 0181 458 1018 *fax:* 0181 209 0265
Katin, Peter – *NBM*
Kerri – c/o 0181 521 2424 *fax:* 0181 521 4343
Kazakevich, Mikhail – *LM*
Kendall, Marie-Noëlle – *Ellison*
Kenner, Kevin – *Connaught*
Khopinski, Erik – 0171 435 9990 *also fax*
* Kingsley, Colin – 0131 669 2070
Kirby, James – 0181 980 5711 *also fax*
Kissin, Evgeny – *Holt*
Klansky, Ivan – *Judith Hendershott*
Kobayashi, Junko – *KDM*
Kodama, Mari – *OWM*
Kodjabashia, Nikola – *ECAM*
Kopelman, Elizaveta – *YCAT*
Kotok, Carolyn – *Invisible Pilots*
Koumis, Matthew – 01962 864546 *fax:* 01962 864727
Kovacevich, Stephen – *VWM*
Kvapil, Radoslav – *Ellison*
Lane, Piers – *PGM (concertos)/GIA (recitals)*
* Latarche, Vanessa – 0181 847 5363; 0831 656827 *fax:* 0181 560 9224
* Latimer, Mark – *SS*
Lauriala, Risto – *Ellison*
Lawson, Peter – 01457 862555
* Lear, Angela – c/o 0181 590 7380 *fax* 0181 506 1500 *email:* 106775.3237@ compuserve.com
Leberman, Martin – *Clifton Wyatt*
* Ledger CBE, Philip – c/o 0141 332 4101 *fax:* 0141 332 8901
Lee, Dennis – 0181 969 7468 *also fax*
Leek, Helen – 0181 691 4217 *also fax;* 0956 881798
* Lenehan, John – 01494 531862 *also fax*
* Lester-Cribb, Michael – 0131 552 1224
Levin, Muriel – 0181 947 5538
Lewis, Paul – *Ingpen* – c/o 0181 874 3222
Liberg, Hans – c/o 01363 866665 *fax:* 01363 866667
Lifschitz, Constantin – *IMG*
Lill OBE, John – *Holt*
* Lion, Margaret – 0171 263 2365 *fax:* 0171 263 3484
Lisney, James – *SWA*
Litwin, Stefan – *Gilder/Lyons*
Llewellyn-Jones, Iwan – *Ellison*
* Lockett, Mark – c/o 01629 825504 *also fax*
Long, Beatrice – *WWA*
* Long, Shirley – 0171 436 0914
Loriod, Yvonne – *Allied*
* Lowe, Timothy – 01892 535040
Lugansky, Nikolai – *ICM*
Lupu, Radu – *THA*
Lympany, Dame Moura – *Transart*
Lythgoe, Clive – *Grant Rogers*
* McArthur, David – *Maestoso*
McCabe, John – 0181 574 5039 *also fax*
McCawley, Leon – *Holt*
MacGregor, Joanna – *Ingpen*
McIntosh, Thomas – 01473 822596 *fax:* 01473 824175
* McKay, Elizabeth – 01993 881910 *fax:* 01993 881278
* McLachlan, Murray – *Chameleon/Rostrum*
* McMahon, Richard – 01222 617180/342854 ext 245 *email:* mcmahonrb@wcmd.ac.uk
Macnamara, Hilary – 0181 341 2811
Madzar, Aleksandar – *HP*
Magill, Ronan – 0171 584 3795
* Malcolm CBE, George – *Holt*
Mantas, Santiago – *Ellison*
Markham, Richard – 0171 738 2765 *also fax*
Markland, Anna – *Denny Lyster*

NORMAN OLSFANGER
pianist

Future plans include:

21st May 1998
Royal Festival Hall Gala Concert
A celebration of the Bicentenary and Sesquicentenary of **Donizetti (1797–1848).** The programme includes rare Donizetti piano music, Liszt operatic transcriptions and a Mayr piano concerto

Also featuring
Montserrat Caballé
Brodsky Quartet
English Chamber Orchestra

CD to be released

Enquiries:
35 Falkland Rd
London
NW5 2PU.

Tel/Fax:
0171 485 1508

Photo: Clive Barda

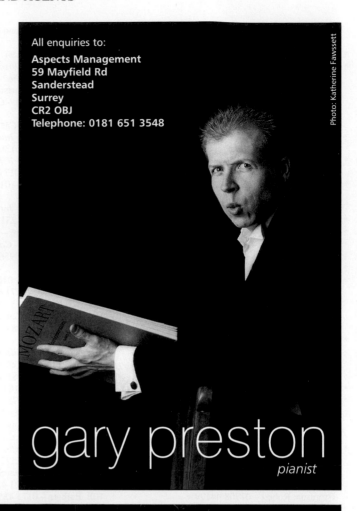

All enquiries to:

Aspects Management
59 Mayfield Rd
Sanderstead
Surrey
CR2 OBJ
Telephone: 0181 651 3548

Photo: Katherine Fawssett

gary preston
pianist

JAMES LISNEY
An artist of distinction and versatility

Recitals
'James Lisney, who was a guest of the Bucharest Philharmonic, offered a Schubert programme... we were able to rediscover Schubert's music in all its diversity as he has a perfectly adapted technique for this repertoire, with a remarkably imaginative sound, springing from a unique sensitivity... a truly original musical personality.'   ***ACTUALITATEA MUZICALA***

Concertos
English Chamber Orchestra, Royal Philharmonic, Rheinische Philharmonie, European Community Chamber Orchestra, Bucharest Filharmonic, City of London Sinfonia, London Mozart Players...

Recordings
Recordings for Olympia and Carlton.

'Lisney clearly has technique to spare, commendable unanimity of co-ordination, an enviable range of articulation and utilises a wide, though never exaggerated dynamic range. He also has the uncanny ability of hitting on just the right tempo and of conjuring up the appropriate mood.'   ***CD REVIEW***

Initiatives
Artistic Director of Newbury Corn Exchange Recital Series.

The Schubert Project (1994-97) – recordings and concerts sponsored by TDK UK Ltd.

Contact Stephannie Williams Artists
Tel: 01789 266272   Fax: 01789 266467

Walker, Elizabeth, renaissance, baroque, classical fl; rcdr – 0171 226 8141 *fax:* 0171 226 9732
Walsh, Kate, fl, alto fl, bs fl, fl d'amore – 0171 588 0195 *also fax;* 0181 533 1372 *email:* rickat@globalnet.co.uk
Waterhouse, William, bsn – 0181 340 8362 *fax:* 0181 341 7616

Weigall, Richard, ob – *Camerata*
Weinberg, Anton, cl – 0181 672 5903
Whight, Michael, cl – *GBZ*
Wiel, Mark van de, cl – 0171 704 8079 *also fax*
Williams, Averil, fl – 0181 946 6857 *also fax*

Williams, Glyn, bsn – 0181 341 3556; 0956 318794
Wilson, David, ob – 0958 651878
Wilson, Jeffery, cl, sax – 01245 450192
Winters, Ross, rcdr – 01263 512605
Wye, Trevor, fl – *NCCP/Seaview*
Zukerman, Eugenia, fl – *ICM*
Zukerman, George, bsn – *Gilder*

Brass

Aarons, Anthony, tpt – 0181 715 8123 *also fax; email:* gaarts@cableinet.co.uk
Adams, Richard, tpt – 01222 495237 *also fax; email:* richard@ricadams.demon.co.uk
Allen, Bryan, tpt – 0121 442 4375 *fax:* 0121 449 6167 *email:* b.allen@rsamd.ac.uk
Antonsen, Ole Edvard, tpt – *Holt*
Ashton, Graham, tpt – *LM*
Ashworth, Robert, hn – 0113 258 1300 *also fax; email:* bob.ashworth@dial.pipex.com
Baker, Julian, hn – 0171 272 6789
Bauer, Wolfgang, tpt – *Pristavec*
Bevan, Clifford, ophicleide, serpent – 01962 864755 *also fax;* 0171 724 3250
Bryant, Jeff, hn – 0181 468 7940
Fulkerson, James, trb – *SJM*
Griffiths, Chris, hn, natural hn – 0191 251 0146
Halstead, Anthony, hn – c/o 01223 352542; 0973 421626 *fax:* 01223 368534
Hazelgrove, Bernard, tpt – 01491 575372
Hogg, Simon, trb – 01926 497887 *fax:* 01926 419701 *email:* warwick_music@compuserve.com

Houghton, William, tpt – 01494 837390
Impett, Jonathan, tpt, natural tpt – 01223 841231 *email:* 101454.2200@compuserve.com
Jenkins, Huw, hn – 0973 268331; 01306 880669
Kenny, John, trb – 0131 447 3707 *also fax*
Laird, Michael, tpt, natural tpt – 0181 946 2700 *fax:* 0181 946 7272
Lindberg, Christian, trb – *Clarion/Seven Muses*
Lumsden, Alan, trb, serpent, ophicleide – 01452 750253 *fax:* 01452 750585
Mason, David, tpt – 0181 864 9056
Mead, Steven, euph – 01827 711964 *also fax;* 0976 437627 *email:* stevemead@compuserve.com
Mowat, Christopher, trb – 0181 398 0057 *fax:* 0181 398 7559
Murphy, Maurice, tpt – 0181 959 1372
Parsons, Anthony, trb – 0181 340 4109 *also fax; email:* lerncurv@aol.com
Picton, Wendy, euph – *Ellison*
Pigneguy, John, hn – 0171 373 8915; 0181 549 1706

Powell, John, euph, ten tb, bs tpt – 0161 226 5655 *also fax*
Pyatt, David, hn – *Holt*
Rhind-Tutt, Mortimer, tpt – 01753 859845 *also fax; email:* 100634.771@compuserve.com
Shifrin, Ken, trb, alto trb, euph, bs tpt – *Chameleon* – 0121 778 4912 *fax:* 0121 778 5569
Smith, Malcolm, tpt, natural tpt – 0181 291 5939 *fax:* 0181 291 2205
Steele-Perkins, Crispian, tpt, natural tpt – *Anglo-Swiss*
Stirling, Stephen, hn – 0181 202 2050 *also fax;* 0181 533 1372; c/o 01892 870187 *also fax*
Thompson, Michael, hn, natural hn – *PGM*
Vlatkovic, Radovan, hn – *Ingpen*
Wallace, John, tpt – c/o 01273 727753 *fax:* 01273 205696
Weale, Malcolm, tpt, cnt – 01202 298795 *also fax*
Webb, Barrie, trb – *KDM*
Whelan, Angela, tpt – *Rostrum*
Wiggins, Bram, tpt – 01280 812408

Harp

Baldry, Elizabeth Jane – 01647 433635; 01243 372253
Barford, Imogen – 0171 485 1903 *also fax*
Beattie, Maria – 0181 519 5474
Bennett, Elinor – *Ellison* – 01286 830010
Bennett, Janet – 0191 276 3019
Bevis, Suzanne, hp, Irish hp – 01703 254238 *also fax*
Boden, Daphne – 0181 346 5706 *also fax*
Brewer, Aline – *OWM*
Clifton-Welker, Fiona – *Clifton Wyatt*
Deere-Jones, Sarah, concert/Celtic hp – 01929 426091 *also fax*
Drake, Susan – *Jennings/Sympathetic*

Ellis CBE, Osian – 0181 445 7896
Gondry, Jeannette – *John Boddy*
Goossens OBE, Sidonie – 01306 611283
Granger, Emma – 0181 747 8171
Holliger, Ursula – *Ingpen*
Jones, Ieuan – c/o 01494 815653 *fax:* 01494 817588
Jones, Rebeca – 0171 924 2436
Kelly, Frances – *Magenta*
Keogh, Miriam, hp, celtic hp – 0181 349 4067 *also fax*
Liston, Jane – *John Boddy*
Master, Rachel – *John Boddy*
Meier, Patrizia – *NCCP*
Moore, Angela – 0181 291 9535

Nicholls, Alison – 01223 843839 *also fax; email:* alisonn@aol.com
Perrett, Danielle – c/o 01883 344300 *fax:* 01883 347712
Robles, Marisa – *Clarion/Seven Muses*
Roth, Rebecca – *John Boddy*
Rothstein, Sue – 0181 202 4769
Salo, Satu – 01753 525249 *also fax*
Seale, Charlotte – 0171 254 0419
Thomas, Caryl – *LM/Harlequin*
Watts, Sheila – *John Boddy*
Webb, Hugh – 0171 837 4954 *fax:* 0171 833 8155
Williams, Sioned – 0181 446 1346 *also fax*

Guitar, Lute, etc

Andresier, Rose – *DCM*
Arenstein, Colin – 0181 348 3630
Asghar, Joseph – *Clifton Wyatt*
Auchterlonie, Domingo, flamenco gui – 01905 424083
Biberian, Gilbert – 01242 581457 *also fax*
Bonell, Carlos – *Upbeat*
Bream CBE, Julian – *Hazard*
Brightmore, Robert – 01455 635851
Brown, Paul – *Dyfel*
Byrne, John – 01928 577596 *also fax*
Byzantine, Julian – *NBM*
Chapman, Richard – *Michael Harrold*
Chateauneuf, Paula, lute, theorbo, early gui – 0181 771 2152 *also fax*
Crawford, Tim, lute – *John Boddy*
Dimakopoulos, Dmitris – *Ellison*
Durrant, Richard – 01273 465371 *also fax; email:* visualmusic@fastnet.co.uk

Eastwell, Martin, early gui, lute – 01434 685733 *also fax; email:* eastwellm@argonet.co.uk
Elsner, Kasia, lute, baroque gui, theorbo – 0171 354 5883 *also fax*
Fierens, Guillermo – *Gilder*
Fisk, Eliot – *Gallus*
Garcia, Gerald, gui, vihuela – 01865 725929 *fax:* 01865 725811 *email:* geraldgarcia@compuserve.com; http://ourworld.compuserve.com/homepages/geraldgarcia
Gibb, Steve, gui, banjo, mandolin, bs, dobro – 0402 648015; 0181 986 5718 *also fax; email:* sgibb@globalnet.co.uk
Gifford, Anthea – 0181 883 3193 *fax:* 0181 442 1005
Gregory, Paul – 01273 564824 *fax:* 01273 882862
Grigoryan, Slava – *Hazard*

Hand, Richard – 0171 724 3806 *also fax*
Harrison, Fiona, gui, lute – 0171 681 0271
Hartman, Thomas, gui, vihuela – 0171 233 5129
Hill, Robin – *Michael Brewer*
Hope, Harvey – 0181 657 5840 *also fax*
Howe, Peter – *Purkiss*
Isbin, Sharon – *McCann*
Jackson, Andy, gui, guitarra portuguesa – 01388 607060; 01670 516997
Jeffrey, Robin, lute – 01892 852878 *also fax*
Kayath, Marcelo – *Jennings*
Keeping, Andrew – *Denny Lyster*
Kenyon, Stephen – 0181 449 0886 *email:* 101602.314@compuserve.com; http://ourworld.compuserve.com/homepages/stevekenyon
Kerstens, Tom – c/o 01494 461177 *fax:* 01494 461188

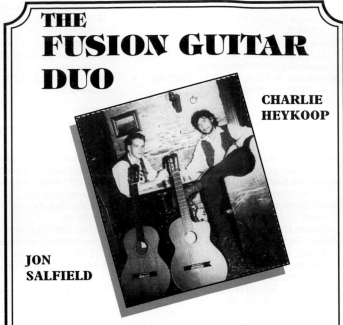

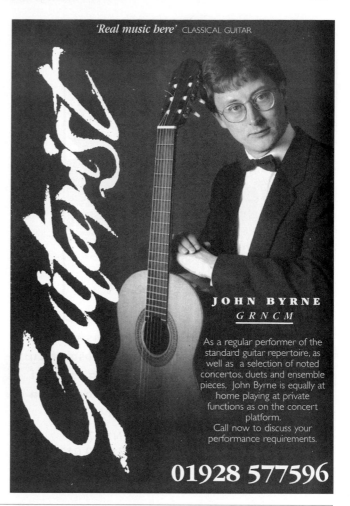

Kilvington, Chris – 01223 276763 *fax:* 01223 277980

Kotzia, Eleftheria – *LM*

Lewin, Michael, gui, lute – 0181 876 6161 *also fax*

Linell, Dorothy, lute, gui, theorbo – 01923 822934; 0171 580 8764 *fax:* 0171 935 5836

Lund, Vegard, gui, lute – *Roy Baker*

Mackenzie, John – 01904 709439

McLaughlin, John – *Transart*

Madeley, Selina, gui, lute – 01785 211218 *also fax*

Marchionda, Stephen – *Camerata*

Marcos, flamenco gui – c/o 01865 243663

Martin, Juan – 0181 346 4500 *fax:* 0171 346 2488 *email:* http://www.flamenco vision.com

Mason, Barry, lute, baroque gui – 0181 992 8973 *also fax*

Meryon, Tom – *Wright*

Mills, John – *Jennings/Sympathetic*

Nockalls, Martin, gui – 01302 772677 *also fax*

Ogden, Craig – *Matthew Tullah*

Parsons, David, gui, lute – *Michael Harrold* – 0171 407 9243

Pells, Timothy, gui – 01473 328881

Perkins, Brian, gui, lute – 01902 333237

Phillips, Freddie – 0181 393 6251

Richards, Jonathan – 01492 544259

Rogers, Douglas, concertina, gui, banjo – 0181 567 9297 *fax:* 0181 723 0155

Romero, Pepe – *Anglo-Swiss*

Rooley, Anthony, lute – 0171 229 5142 *fax:* 0171 221 1282 *email:* consort@ easynet.co.uk

Salameh, Adel, lute, oud – *LA*

Salfield, Ben, lute – 0589 135643

Salfield, Jon, flamenco gui – 01726 883846

Santos, Turibio – *Jennings*

Sayce, Lynda, lute – 01235 816158 *also fax*

Smith, Neil – c/o 0113 239 2222 *fax:* 0113 239 2016

Spooner, Terry – 01279 418015

Spring, Matthew – 01865 61966 *also fax*

Stephens, Alison, mandolin – 0973 111690

Stimpson, Michael – 01722 780671 *also fax*

Taylor, Frances, mandolin – 0181 989 7591

Thodey, Robin, lute – *Ellison*

Thomas, Alan – 0181 690 7576

Vale, Galina – 0161 834 2702

Wade, Graham – 0113 275 2456 *also fax;* 01226 385266

Walker, Timothy, gui, lute – *CDI*

Watson, Malcolm – 0131 447 4951

Weigand, George, lutes, cimbalom, oud, banjos, mandores – *Oriole*

Wheatley, Martin, gui, banjo, ukelele, hawaiian gui – c/o 0181 532 2923

Williams, John – *Holt*

Willmott, Roderick, gui, lute – 01905 427026

Wilson, Christopher, lute – *Magenta*

Wiltchinsky, Peter – *Michael Brewer* – *email:* http://dialspace.dial.pipex. com/hillhouse/

Witoszynskyj, Leo – *Jennings*

Woodhouse, Nigel, mandolin, gui, banjo – 01727 865164 *also fax*

Zaradin, John – 0171 727 7958 *fax:* 0171 460 2409 *email:* 101662.557@compuserve.com

Percussion

Aharon, Yoel – *JLM*

Auchterlonie, Delphine, castanets, platillos, shells – 01905 424083

Boyle, Colin, marimba – 0181 677 1845 *fax:* 0181 677 1846 *email:* rimbal@dircon.co. uk; http://www.users.dirco.co.uk/~rimbal/

Corbett, Heather, tuned perc, cimbalom, timpani – *Upbeat* – 0141 772 3152; 0860 234588

Ganeva, Daniella – *Connaught*

Glennie, Evelyn – *IMG*

Goedicke, Kurt-Hans, timpani – 0181 866 1845

Holland, James – 01494 725854

Johnston, Beverley, marimba, perc – *NCCP*

Limbrick, Simon – 0171 732 4590 *also fax;* 0468 514353

Millar, Jhalib – *Clifton Wyatt*

Shipway, Nigel – 01734 666633

Szakály, Agnes, cimbalom – *Ellison*

van Sice, Robert, marimba – *Lyons*

Warburton, Julian – *YCAT*

Whettam, Andrew, marimba, etc – 01625 858878 *fax:* 01625 858804

Wright, Tim – 0181 986 7655; 0589 410597

Miscellaneous

Broadway, Michael, pianola – 0171 254 6145 *fax:* 0171 249 0130

Crabb, James, accordion – *Ingpen*

Gajic, Djordje, accordion – 01932 864287 *also fax;* 0956 159375

Gupta, Punita, sitar – 0181 427 3530 *fax:* 0181 248 5138

Kalsi, Johnny, dhol – *SJM*

Khan, Imrat, sitar, subahar – 0181 904 2833 *also fax*

Khan, Wajahat, sarod, sitar, surbahar – *NCCP* – c/o 0181 904 2833 *also fax*

Lawther, Ian, bagpipes – *Annon*

Leach, John, zither – 0171 385 0182 *fax:* 0171 381 1155

Leith, Ronald, carillon – 01224 634427 *fax:* 01224 639096

Loriod, Jeanne, ondes martenot – *Allied*

McCabe, Enda, Irish folk gui, mandola, banjo – *Annon*

Malloy, Alasdair, glass harmonica, bag pipes – *LM*

Murray, Owen, classical accordion – *GBZ*

Muskett, Michael, hurdy-gurdy, fujara – 01300 345412 *email:* hurdyplay@ aol.com

Perkins, John, sitar, surbahar – 01626 853387; 01883 344300 *fax:* 01626 854077; 01883 347712

Petric, Joseph, concert accordion – *NCCP*

Rogers, Douglas, concertina, banjo – 0181 567 9297 *fax:* 0181 723 0155

Roth, Alec, Javanese gamelan – 0171 497 3754 *also fax*

Shankar, Ravi, sitar – *Tennant*

Shrivastav, Baluji, sitar – 0171 354 5709; 0956 473454

Spring, Matthew, hurdy-gurdy, sinphonye – 01865 61966 *also fax*

Srikantha Rajah, Arunthathy, veena – 0181 543 2126 *also fax; fax:* 0181 540 3442

Townsend, David, English concertina, bar concertina, bs concertina – 01867 714778

Wilson, Malcolm, handbells – 01786 825387 *also fax*

Xu, Pingxin, Chinese dulcimer – *Ellison*

Singers

Singers with their own accompaniment

Bennett, Janet, hp, celtic hp – 0191 276 3019
Bevis, Suzanne, hp, Irish hp – 01703 254238
also fax
Deere-Jones, Sarah, hp, celtic hp – 01929
426091 *also fax*
Edwards, Jacqueline, m-sop, pno – 01904
763876

Ellis CBE, Osian, hp – 0181
445 7896
Hambleton-Smith, Sandra, gui – 0181
699 8342
Medhurst, Peter, hpd, f-pno – 0181
673 1901
Pearcey, Leonard, gui – 0181 947 2555

Sherry, Rachel, hp, clarsach, Irish hp – 01908
316985 *also fax; email:* johnb@
computrain.co.uk
Vandermeer, Zoe, hpd, hp – 0141 334 5691
email: zoesea@aol.com
Wilkinson, Dee, gui – 0171
401 9320

The singers in the following lists are sub-divided according to voice category.

Sopranos

Aghova, Livia – *Mus Int*
Aikin, Laura – *Ingpen*
Akhurst, Jennifer – *Mus Int*
Aldridge, Anne – 0181 445 7698 *also fax;*
0181 449 1882
Allen, Giselle – *Mus Int*
Allsebrook, Ruth – 01748 823300
Ameling, Elly – *Phillips*
Amit, Sheila – *Annon*
Amou, Akie – *Magenta*
Anderson, Lorna – *Askonas*
Anderson, Valdine – *Ingpen*
Andreyeva, Marina – *Gilder*
Angel, Marie – *Allied*
Angeles, Victoria de los – *Clarion/Seven
Muses*
Archibald, Ann – *Askonas*
Argenta, Nancy – *Holt*
Armitstead, Melanie – *Gilder*
Arthur, Jillian – *Grosvenor* – 0181 948 7966
Ashe, Rosie – *Sykes*
Ashton, Caroline – 0181 740 1567
Astrid, Helen – 0181 993 8822 *also fax*
Atherton, Diane – *Singers Direct* – 0181 896
3492; 0421 007860
Bachmann, Rhonda – *Ellison*
Back, Andrée – *CDI/Mus Int*
Baker, Zena – 01449 760315
Banse, Juliane – *IMG*
Barainsky, Claudia – *Gilder*
Barron, Jacqueline – 0181 886 8521 *also fax*
Barry, Elaine – 0171 928 6291
Barry, Una – *CDI/Ellison* – 0181 981 4648
Barstow, Dame Josephine – *Holt*
Bates, Susan – 0181 208 2272; 0958 616503
Battle, Kathleen – *Askonas*
Bechly, Daniela – *Mus Int*
Behle, Renate – *Rawstron*
Benza, Georgina – *Still*
Berenbau, Helena – *Gilder*
Bern, Jeni – *Musicmakers*
Bisatt, Susan – *Craig*
Bishop, Hilary – 01243 842150
Black, Susan – *CDI*
Blackburn, Olivia – *Sykes*
Blackwell, Harolyn – *Gilder*
Blankenship, Rebecca – *Mus Int*
Bogza, Anda-Louise – *Stafford/Mus Int*
Bonner, Tessa – 0181 676 0270
also fax
Bonney, Barbara – *IMG*
Booth, Juliet – *Portland*
Bott, Catherine – *Magenta*
Bott, Paula – c/o 0181 444 4088; 0181 567
1909 *also fax; fax:* 0181 444 3353
Bovino, Maria – *Musicmakers*
Bowen, Miriam – *Harlequin/CDI*
Boylan, Orla – *HP*

Boynton, Patricia – 01252 629348
Bradshaw, Sally – 0171 359 0707 *fax:* 0171
609 1921
Braga, Sola – *Gilder*
Brathwaite, Maureen – *Harlequin*
Bremar, Jacqueline – *OCA*
Brett, Kathleen – *IMG*
Brewer, Christine – *Askonas*
Bright, Alma – 01527 852806
Brilova, Elena – *Still*
Brister, Penelope – *Sykes*
Brodie, Sarah – *Dyfel*
Broome, Gillian – 01732 461893 *also fax*
Brown, Donna – *HP*
Buchanan, Alison – *Magenta*
Buckle, Judith – *Annon*
Buffle, Christine – *OCA*
Bullock, Susan – *HP*
Bunning, Christine – *Mus Int*
Bureau, Karen – *Gilder*
Burgin Lister, Gabrielle – 01777 702400
fax: 01777 869529
Cahill, Teresa – *NBM* c/o 0181 208 2480
fax: 0181 208 2490
Caine, Rebecca – *Holt*
Cairns, Janice – *Holt*
Callan Clarke, Mary – *Sykes*
Cameron, Fiona – *OWM*
Cantelo, April – 01235 848994
Cardnell, Valerie – 0181 399 9158
Carewe, Mary – *LM*
Carpenter, Jayne – 01625 431450
Carroll, Joan – 01622 745346
Castets, Maryse – *Gilder*
Chadwick, Carolyn – 01743 362015 *also fax*
Chadwick, Suzanne – 01732 366830
Chambers, Sybil – c/o 0113 274 1833
Chard, Verona – 0181 992 1571; 0171 928
8353 *fax:* 0171 928 8505
Charlton-West, Alison – 01487 830521
Chickering, Carol – *Gilder*
Chilcott, Susan – *Ingpen*
Chuchrova, Liubov – *Mus Int*
Ciofi, Patrizia – *OWM*
Clague, Deborah – 01604 710736 *also fax*
Clarke, Elisabeth – 0181 989 6852 *also fax*
Claycomb, Laura – *IMG*
Clemens, Linda – 01622 831782
Close, Shirley – *Gilder*
Coburn, Pamela – *Ingpen*
Coku, Alexandra – *Portland*
Cole, Rosamund – *Mus Int*
Coles, Priti – *Gilder*
Collier, Christina – *Brunskill*
Colwell, Georgina Anne – 01932 244038
fax: 01932 889186 *email:* georgina@
musicair.demon.co.uk
Connell, Elizabeth – *IMG*

Coombes, Susan – 0181 446 6872 *fax:* 0181
201 8071
Cooper, Fiona – c/o 0171 491 0837; 0976
211663 *fax:* 0171 629 5343
Cotterill, Marianne – *Ellison*
Crider, Michèle – *Victoria Smith*
Cullagh, Majella – *IMG*
Cullis, Rita – *Holt*
Cunha, Viola da – 0181 368 4789
d'Aragnes, Maria – *Stafford*
Daguerre, Florence – 0171 737 4403
fax: 0171 326 4961
Dalayman, Katarina – *Rawstron*
Dale, Sarah-Jane – *Michael Harrold* – 01737
249839 *also fax*
Dalton, Julie – *OCA*
Dam-Jensen, Inger – *HP*
Dames-Longworth, Phillippa – *Portland*
Daneman, Sophie – *Phillips*
Davies, Eiran – *Still*
Davies, Lynne – 0171 586 2184 *also fax*
Dawson, Anne – *Portland*
Dawson, Lynne – *IMG*
Deam, Donna – 01483 768790
Dean, Amanda – *SS*
DeFeis, Doreen – *Gilder*
Delahunt, Colette – *Musichall*
Dewhurst, Julia – *Maestoso*
Dimitrova, Ghena – *Stafford*
Dittmer, Petronella – 0171 937 0684 *also fax*
Dives, Tamsin – *Musichall*
Dobie, Fiona – 01865 246718
Donadini, Giovanna – *Still*
Donaldson, Alison – 01355 302869
Driscoll, Sally – *OCA*
Dudley, Bethan – *Sykes*
Dugdale, Sandra – *Mus Int*
Dunwoodie, Christine – 0141 427 9896
fax: 0141 419 0458
Eaglen, Jane – *IMG*
Eckersley, Kate – *Ellison/SJM*
Edwards, Yvonne – *SS*
Ehlert, Sibylle – *VWM*
Eikenes, Adele – *VWM*
Emmanuel, Jane – 0181 694 1528
Enever, Cheryl – *Musicmakers*
Errington, Helen – 0860 164662
Evans, Anne – *Ingpen*
Evans, Rebecca – *Harlequin*
Everall, Shelley – *Singers Direct* – 0181
946 8852
Falcon, Ruth – *Gilder*
Fandrey, Birgit – *Gilder*
Farley, Carole – *Magenta*
Felle, Amelia – *Greenan*
Ferrari, Elena – *Craig*
Ferrarini, Alida – *Stafford*
Field, Helen – *Still*

Carolyn Chadwick
Soprano

Recitalist, oratorio and concert soloist

"...a voice of great beauty." (Birmingham Post)

"...a charming presentation, the voice beautifully even, agile and expressive...with humour as well conveyed as drama."   **(The Recorder Magazine)**

"...her performance throughout was characterised by clear diction in all four languages, imaginative phrasing and sublimely beautiful tone quality."   **(Shropshire Star)**

All enquiries: 20, West Hermitage, Belle Vue,
Shrewsbury, Shropshire SY3 7JP
Tel. & Fax: 01743-362015

Catherine Françoise
Soprano

PROFESSIONAL EXPERIENCE INCLUDES:
Opera, Operetta, Gilbert & Sullivan, West End Musical Theatre, Oratorio, Recital (especially French and Russian Song), Concert work and Gala Events.

...Catherine Françoise was admirable, impressive in her solos..
Trouble in Tahiti – THE INDEPENDENT

There were vocal contributions from first-rate singers. Catherine Françoise sang 'A Fors e Lui' from Verdi's La Raviata with full tone, contrasting strongly with the following 'Sempre Libera'
HERALD EXPRESS TORQUAY

Catherine Françoise sparkled as the Queen of the night...
(The Magic Flute) – SURREY HERALD

Catherine Françoise was most impresive, giving a firm assured performance throughout, but particularly in the very lovely Laudate Dominum.
(Mozart – Solomn Vespers) – CHATHAM, ROCHESTER & GILLINGHAM News

FURTHER INFORMATION & DEMONSTRATION TAPE from

Tel: 01753 882646 / 0850 617 775 Fax: 01753 408089
71 Leachcroft, Chalfront St Peter, Bucks SL9 9LD

Louise Merrett
Coloratura Soprano

Opera, oratorio, concerts and recitals
Noted for her versatality, dramatic range and emotional expression, Loise Merrett is an experienced performer with an international profile

Further details from Sound Management (UK) Limited on 0171 935 1753

GERALD PLACE

SARAH POOLE
– Soprano –

"...a soprano of innocent radiance..." (The Times)

Contact: **Recital Music**
Studio Ten, Farnham Maltings, Farnham, Surrey GU9 7QR
Tel/Fax. 01252-319610
Chameleon Arts Management
Tel. 01252-873313   Fax. 01252-871517

Field, Margaret – 01594 825535
Field, Pamela – 01685 875392
Filip, Felicia – *Stafford*
Firth-Spiller, Fiona – 0181 847 0888 *also fax*
Fisher, Gabrielle – 0181 715 8123 *also fax; email:* gaarts@cableinet.co.uk
Fleming, Renée – *IMG*
Flett, Lydia – 0141 357 1423
Flowers, Kate – *Musicmakers*
Flowers, Suzanne – *CDI*
Focile, Nuccia – *Holt*
Fontana, Gabriele – *Rawstron*
Ford, Sandra – *Mus Int*
Foulkes, Carolyn – *CDI*
Fox, Sarah – *Magnum*
Françoise, Catherine – 01753 882646 *fax:* 01753 408089
Freiberg, Christine – *Mus Int*
Fribo, Louise – *Music Theatre*
Frisani, Rosita – *Askonas*
Frittoli, Barbara – *Holt*
Fuge, Katharine – *Chameleon*
Fugelle, Jacquelyn – *Still*
Futral, Elisabeth – *IMG*
Gale, Elizabeth – *Musichall*
Galstian, Juliet – *Still*
Gannon, Kate – 01327 263887 *also fax; fax:* 01327 262608 *email:* 106714.2057@ compuserve.com
Gasztowt-Adams, Helen – 0171 625 8903 *also fax*
Gerbic, Anne – 0181 932 8555
Gerrard, Linda – *Mus Int*
Gilchrist, Diana – *Sykes*
Gill, Bridgett – 01874 690339 *fax:* 01874 690254
Ginsborg, Jane – 01782 618156
Glanville, Susannah – *Holt*
Glennon, Jean – *Sykes*
Gomez, Jill – 0181 348 4193 *also fax*
Gooding, Julia – *Phillips*
Goodwin, Harriet – *CDI*
Gorchakova, Galina – *Askonas*
Gormley, Clare – *Askonas*
Gotz, Cornelia – *Still*
Gritton, Susan – *Askonas*
Grummet, Adey – *Craig*
Guleghina, Maria – *Askonas*
Gustafson, Nancy – *IMG*
Hagley, Alison – *IMG*
Hammonds, Elaine – 0181 540 5780
Hamvasi, Sylvia – *Ingpen*
Hanley, Regina – *Mus Int*
Hannigan, Barbara – *OWM*
Hardy, Janet – *Mus Int*
Hardy, Rosemary – *Magenta*
Hargreaves, Carolyn – *Grant Rogers*
Harman, Lynne – *Mus Int*
Harper, Catherine – *Ellison*
Harrhy, Eiddwen – *Phillips*
Harries, Kathryn – *Ingpen*
Harrison, Sally – *Gilder*
Harvey, Naomi – *OCA*
Haslam, Micaela – *CDI*
Havas, Mary Jane – *Craig*
Havranova, Jana – *Mus Int*
Hawkins, Cheryl – 01525 261950 *also fax*
Haylett, Jenny – 01736 796247
Haymon, Cynthia – *Still*
Hayward-Segal, Marie – *Ellison*
Heath-Welch, Anne – *Stafford*
Hegarty, Mary – *Holt/Musichall*
Hellgren, Marianne – *Sykes*
Hellsten, Dominique – c/o 0181 299 1914 *also fax*
Hemington Jones, Susan – 01664 822965 *fax:* 01664 823773
Hendricks, Barbara – *Ingpen*
Herman, Natalie – 0181 870 3894
Hetherington, Elizabeth – *Gilder*
Hetherington, Marie-Anne – *SS*

Higham-Bell, Alison – 0181 451 3051 *also fax;* 0468 685469
Hill Smith, Marilyn – *Mus Int*
Hillier, Helen – 0181 675 6172 *fax:* 0181 675 9781
Hjalmtysdottir, Sigrun – *OCA*
Hodges, Anne – 01992 461535 *also fax*
Hogg, Faye – *Sykes*
Hollyman, Nicola – 01222 754032; 0585 951727
Holmes-Drewry, Margaret – c/o 0171 433 1058; 0171 794 3842 *fax:* 0171 794 2700
Holton, Ruth – *Magenta/CDI*
Hooper, Patricia – 0181 858 4293
Horriben, Alison – 01344 883847
Horrocks, Luise – *CDI/Charlton*
Howard, Yvonne – *Stafford/Scott Mitchell*
Howarth, Judith – *Askonas*
Howd, Janet – 0181 747 5072 *also fax*
Hulse, Eileen – 0181 886 6534 *also fax*
Illing, Rosamund – *Harlequin*
Immelman, Elizabeth – *KDM*
Isokoski, Soile – *IMG*
Itami, Naomi – *Mus Int*
James, Catherine – *Camerata*
Jansen, Dorothee – *Rawstron*
Jenisova, Eva – *Mus Int*
Jenkin, Kathryn – *Grant Rogers* – 0181 861 0065
Jenkin, Nicola – 0171 735 7636 *also fax*
Jenkins, Angela – 0181 560 5988 *also fax*
Jenkins, Merril – 0181 579 3108
Jenkins, Susan Anne – 01933 626301 *fax:* 01933 624880
Jo, Sumi – *Holt*
Johansson, Eva – *Allied*
Johnson, Harriet – 01883 652039
Jones, Eldrydd Cynan – *Portland*
Jones, Jayne – *Charlton*
Jones, Natalie – *Craig*
Joshua, Rosemary – *IMG*
Kalinina, Galina – *Stafford*
Kaupova, Helena – *Mus Int*
Kazarnovskaya, Lyuba – *Portland*
Kazimierczuk, Angela – *Camerata*
Keetch, Maureen – 0181 458 4723
Kelly, Janis – *Musichall*
Kemmer, Mariette – *Mus Int*
Kemp, Nicola Jane – *Mus Int*
Kendall-Davies, Barbara – 0181 954 4646
Kennard, Julie – *CDI*
Kennedy, Nicki – *Sykes*
Kennedy-Richardson, Louisa – *Mus Int*
Kenny, Yvonne – *IMG*
Kerr, Virginia – *Gilder*
Kesselman, Maria – *Brunskill*
King, Tracey Anne – *Dyfel*
Kirkby, Emma – c/o 0171 229 5142 *fax:* 0171 221 1282 *email:* consort@easynet.co.uk
Kitchen, Linda – *Musichall*
Kolomyjec, Joanne – *Gilder*
Kompaniyets, Nataliya – *Portland*
Korman, Beryl – *Upbeat*
Kringelborn, Solveig – *IMG*
Kudriavchenko, Katerina – *Still*
Kuhn, Pamela – *Pristavec*
Kwella, Patrizia – *Holt*
Ladner, Kate – *Gilder*
Lane, Carys-Anne – *Michael Harrold*
Lane, Elizabeth – *CDI*
Lapina, Marina – *Gilder*
Lascarro, Juanita – *HP*
Lawrence, Amy – *Still*
Lawrence, Susan – 0121 472 2728
Lawson, Mhairi – *Sykes*
Lax, Janet – *Musicmakers*
Lebedeva, Galina – *Gilder*
Lee, Lynda – *Phillips*
Leeks, Caroline – 01603 618575 *also fax*
Lenton-Ward, Caroline – 0181 299 6866
Leonard, Sarah – *Allied*

Levitt, Marina – *Gilder*
Lil, Elizabeth – *Magnum*
Lind, Eva – *Askonas*
Lindsay-Douglas, Carole – *Lindsay*
Lissenden, Sandra – 01322 224085 *fax:* 01322 407282
Livingstone, Kathleen – 01895 632115 *fax:* 01895 625765
Lloyd, Prudence – 0181 449 4873
Lloyd Davies, Mary – *Harlequin*
Logan, Catriona – 01992 523508 *also fax*
Lorimer, Heather – *OCA*
Lothian, Helen – *Askonas*
Lott DBE, Felicity – *Askonas*
Lucey, Frances – *Mus Int*
Lukianyets, Viktoria – *Askonas*
Lynch, Frances – 0171 281 0672 *also fax*
McAndrew, Fiona – *KDM*
McCarthy, Fionnuala – *Mus Int*
McCulloch, Susan – *Gilder*
McFadden, Claron – *Magenta*
Mackay, Ann – *NBM*
Mackenzie, Jane Leslie – *Mus Int*
McLaren, Morag – c/o 0171 839 4433/4 *fax:* 0171 930 5738
McLaughlin, Marie – *IMG*
McLeod, Linda – *Ingpen*
McNair, Sylvia – *Askonas*
McGreevy, Geraldine – *Askonas*
Malfitano, Catherine – *IMG*
Malmberg, Myrra – *LM*
Malmfrid, Sand – *Gilder*
Maney, Carla – *CDI/Mus Int*
Manly, Ann – 0171 286 3944 *fax:* 0171 289 9081
Manning OBE, Jane – 0171 359 1593 *fax:* 0171 226 4369
Mannion, Rosa – *IMG*
Marc, Alessandra – *Askonas*
Marshall, Margaret – *Allied*
Martin, Clara – *Stafford*
Martinpelto, Hillevi – *Rawstron*
Masterson, Valerie – *Mus Int*
Mathis, Edith – *Ingpen*
Matthews, Dianne – 0161 794 7862
Mattila, Karita – *IMG*
Mayfield, Elizabeth – 01274 826226
Medlyn, Margaret – *Sykes*
Melinek, Julia – c/o 0181 723 6984 *also fax*
Mellor, Alwyn – *Ingpen*
Meloy, Laurie – 0839 682855
Merrett, Louise – 0171 935 1753
Mescheriakova, Marina – *Gilder*
Methven, Jean – 01494 524007
Michael, Beth – *OCA*
Midgley, Maryetta – *Mus Int*
Miles, Gaynor – 0181 452 1336
Miles, Helen – 01908 691487 *also fax*
Mills, Bronwen – *CDI*
Mills, Rachael – 0181 686 2356; 0958 655040
Milne, Lisa – *Askonas*
Minns, Giselle – 0181 964 0920
Miricioiu, Nelly – *IMG*
Monk, Anna-Clare – *Portland*
Moorhouse, Maryrose – 01924 830461
Morgan, Gaynor – *OCA*
Morgan, Nicola – 01222 483063
Morley, Debra – *SS*
Motherway, Fiona – *Craig*
Mulholland, Denise – *Musicmakers*
Munro, Janet – 0181 473 3756
Murphy, Heidi Grant – *Askonas*
Murphy, Suzanne – *Ingpen*
Myers, Deborah – *Sykes*
Nadelman, Noemi – *Mus Int*
Nash, Elizabeth – 01932 857520
Nathan, Regina – *IMG*
Naylor, Joy – 01606 836284
Neave, Harriet – 01725 552336
Nicholson, Evelyn – 01753 821956 *also fax*
Noack, Romana – *Mus Int*

ALISON SMART

Soprano

'exquisitely sung...Her characterisation was without blemish and her fine free-flowing soprano without reproach'   **The Stage**

'Alison Smart...sang brightly' **The Times**

'A lucid tone, strong and rich in all registers, coupled with sensitive characterisation' **Lincolnshire Echo**

'Notable for classical decorative work' **Manchester Evening News**

- wide experience in oratorio, opera, concert, recital
- Baroque, Classical and 20th-century repertoire

For bookings and further details please contact:
Alison Smart at 327 Long Lane, London N2 8JW
Tel: 0181 349 0824 and 0973 350396
or phone Magnum Opus Management on 01582 419 568

Lenka Škorničková

Soprano

All enquiries to her new contact address:
Cees van Dorland
Personal Assistant
'Con Brio', Church Road, Bubbenhall, Warwickshire CV8 3BE
Telephone/Fax 01203 - 306 106

Lesley-Jane Rogers
soprano

An ideal soloist for simple *or* complex programming

Millennium fever?

As the millennium approaches, how are *you* planning to celebrate? Perhaps that extra-special *Messiah*, or a sparkling Poulenc *Gloria* or maybe you fancy the exuberance of David Fanshawe's *African Sanctus*?   Perhaps you are considering commissioning a new work?

Whatever you decide, **Lesley-Jane Rogers** has the necessary flexibility to make your concert special. A highly experienced soloist, she has a vast repertoire of both standard and unusual works, and is praised for her ability to interpret different composers' styles appropriately. From the light and shade of baroque phrasing, to *bel canto*, to freaky modern works, her wide vocal and dynamic range enable her to bring assurity and ease to any concert.

Further details, current bookings, future availability, demo tape, brochure, repertoire list and discography available on request.

To discuss your programming ideas, contact:
The Old Rectory Coach House
High Street
Bourton-on-the-Water
Glos **GL54 2AP**   Tel/fax: **01451 821481**

Norburn, Clare – 0171 281 9364 *also fax;*
email: norburnc@dircon.co.uk
Nordin, Lena – *Allied*
Norman, Jessye – *HP*
Notare, Karen – *Still*
Novis, Constance – *Sykes*
O'Neill, Fiona – *OCA*
O'Neill, Patricia – *Harlequin*
O'Sullivan, Cara – *Harlequin*
O'Sullivan, Paula – *OWM/Magnum*
Oppenheimer, Juliet – *OCA*
Orde, Corinne – 0171 987 9600 *also fax*
Padfield, Jill – *Charlton*
Padmore, Elaine – *SS*
Page, Charlotte – *Mus Int*
Palmerston, Diana – *CDI*
Parker, Jaqueline – *SS*
Parry, Pamela Jane – 0468 362420 *fax:* 0151
708 6091
Passow, Sabine – *Mus Int*
Patrick, Yvonne – 01256 397409; 0468
224576
Pavlovski, Nina – *Still*
Peake-Jones, Deborah – *Grant Rogers*
Pearce, Alison – *CDI/Charlton* – 0171 836
7556 *also fax*
Pearson, Gail – *Harlequin*
Peate, Zoe – *Purkiss*
Pegler, Heidi – *KDM*
Perry, Margaret – 0181 368 5308
Pieczonka, Adrianne – *Allied*
Pierard, Catherine – *Magenta*
Pierce, Judith – 01795 533523
Pilgrim, Shirley – *OCA*
Platt, Rachel – 0181 778 2629; 0958 629337
fax: 0181 325 9098
Plazas, Mary – *OWM*
Plowright, Rosalind – *Still*
Poluektova, Tatyana – *Askonas*
Poole, Sarah – *Chameleon* – 01252 319610
also fax; 0860 251232
Pope, Cathryn – 0193 227191 *also fax*
Preece, Margaret – *Craig*
Price, Janet – 0117 924 8456
Price DBE, Margaret – *Askonas*
Price Jones, Penelope – 01249 812508 *also fax*
Priday, Elisabeth – 01544 230534 *fax:* 01544
231100
Primrose, Claire – *Still*
Pritchett, Bernadine – *Clifton Wyatt*
Putnam, Ashley – *Still*
Quigley, Jennifer – *GBZ*
Rae-Walker, Gillian – 0141 848 5411
Ramage, Adeline – *Grant Rogers*
Randall-Davis, Penelope – *Gilder*
Rautio, Nina – *Askonas*
Rees, Judith – 01707 268576
Richardson, Lynda – 0171 482 0415 *also fax;*
0956 371232
Richardson, Margaret – *Portland*
Riedel, Deborah – *Portland*
Ritchie, Elizabeth – *Grosvenor*
Robert, Yvonne – 01904 701459; 01502
724020
Roberts, Deborah – 01273 833950
email: 101565.3033@compuserve.com
Roberts, Elizabeth – 0181 677 7997 *fax:* 0181
696 9783
Roberts, Susan – *IMG*
Roche, Maureen – *Clifton Wyatt*
Rodgers, Joan – *Ingpen*
Rogers, Lesley-Jane – 01451 821481 *also fax*
Roocroft, Amanda – *Ingpen*
Röschmann, Dorothea – *Askonas*
Rose, Fiona – 0181 870 9591 *also fax*

Rothschild, Charlotte de – 0171 730 4465
fax: 0171 730 0166
Rowley, Laura – *SJM*
Roy, Helen – 01798 874721
Rozario, Patricia – *Holt*
Rudakova, Larissa – *Askonas*
Rushton, Lorna – *Grant Rogers*
Rushton, Virginia – 0113 278 0827; 01423
569820 *fax:* 0113 230 6114
Russell, Lynda – *Magenta*
Rutter, Claire – *Holt*
Salmon Trutz, Caroline – 0181 343 2197
fax: 01572 822943
Sand, Malmfrid – *Gilder*
Saunders, Jenny – *Magenta*
Sauphanor, Simone – *OWM*
Savova, Galina – *Stafford*
Schäfer, Christine – *IMG*
Schiemann, Juliet – *SS*
Schlick, Barbara – *Magenta*
Schuman, Patricia – *Greenan*
Schwanewilms, Anne – *Rawstron*
Scott, Vanessa – 01353 663894
Secunde, Nadine – *Ingpen*
Selby-Okamoto, Takako – 0181 452 9234
also fax
Serra, Luciana – *Allied*
Seymour, Yvonne – *CDI*
Shade, Ellen – *Portland*
Shafajinskaia, Anna – *Gilder*
Shaguch, Marina – *HP*
Shaw, Penelope – *SS*
Shelley, Rosamund – *Charlton*
Shelton, Lucy – *Ingpen*
Shepherson, Sally-Ann – *SS*
Sheppard, Honor – 0161 928 4727
Sheppard, Kerrie – *Harlequin*
Sheridan, Anne – *Connaught*
Sherry, Rachel – 01908 316985 *also fax;*
email: johnb@computrain.co.uk
Sieden, Cynthia – *IMG*
Silja, Anja – *IMG*
Sinclair, Jeannette – 0181 959 6651
Skornicková, Lenka – c/o 01203 306106
also fax
Smart, Alison – *Magnum*
Smith, Carol – *Mus Int*
Smith, Jennifer – *Sykes*
Smolyaninova, Soya – *Still*
Soldh, Anita – *Still*
Stedman, Clarissa – 01227 766335 *email:*
creadl@canterbury.ac.uk
Stefanescu, Ana Camelia – *IMG*
Stowe, Sara – 01865 61966 *also fax*
Strauss, Danielle – *Connaught*
Streeton, Jane – *SS*
Stuart, Diana – 01733 844603 *also fax*
Sullivan, Ghillian – *Portland*
Sutherland, Rosalind – *IMG*
Sweeting, Sarah – *Craig*
Swenson, Ruth Ann – *Askonas*
Taylor, Hilary – *Stafford*
Te Kanawa DBE, Kiri – c/o 0181 233 5800
fax: 0181 233 5801
Teare, Christine – *Stafford*
Thane, Amanda – *Gilder*
Theodoridou, Sonia – *HP*
Thiébaud, Dominique – 01727 848335 *fax:*
01727 847664
Thomas, Caroline – *Gilder*
Thomas, Gwyneth – 01789 763509
Thorn, Penelope – *Still*
Tibbels, Nicole – 0181 961 3773
Tierney, Vivian – *Still*
Tinsley, Pauline – *Mus Int*

Todd Howarth, Anne – 0118 926 4401
Tovey, Rachael – *Phillips*
Trainor, Joan – 0191 267 9164 *also fax; fax:*
0191 267 5366
Tremaine, Sally – *Clifton Wyatt*
Troth, Marylyn – 0181 876 6161 *also fax*
Tsydypova, Valentina – *Askonas*
Tubb, Evelyn – *CDI*
Tucapská, Beryl – 0181 200 5200
Turner, Zoë – *Charlton*
Turri, Ida-Maria – *OCA*
Tuvas, Linda – *Mus Int*
Tynan, Kathleen – *Sykes*
Tyrrell, Lisa – *Magenta*
Unwin, Julie – *IMG*
Upshaw, Dawn – *IMG*
Urbanova, Eva – *Mus Int*
Vaduva, Leontina – *Stafford*
Van Poznak, Karen – 01707 322448
Vaness, Carol – *IMG*
Varady, Julia – *Askonas*
Voigt, Deborah – *IMG*
Voss, Ealynn – *Gilder*
Wainwright, Jeanette – *OCA*
Waite, Nicola – *Gilder*
Walker, Helen – *Magenta*
Wall, Melanie – *Grosvenor/Pristavec*
Walmsley-Clark, Penelope – *Allied*
Walsh, Louise – *IMG*
Watanabe, Yoko – *Stafford*
Waters, Rosalind – 0181 947 5386; 0378
020730
Watson, Janice – *Askonas*
Watson, Lillian – *IMG*
Watts, Karen – *Mus Int*
Watts, Linda – *Dyfel*
Watts, Valerie – 01704 567907 *fax:* 0151
227 5953
Wayman, Lynne – 0115 962 0258
Webster, Gillian – *IMG*
Webster, Jane – *Mus Int*
Weidinger, Christine – *Still*
Wells, Alison – 0181 980 9735 *also fax*
Westwood, Jennifer – 0114 266 6132; 0973
765849
Whaley, Rosemary – *SS*
Wheatley, Rachel – 0171 372 0780
also fax
Whelan, Franzita – *YCAT*
Whittlesey, Christine – *Ingpen*
Wiegold, Mary – 0181 368 1211 *also fax*
Wilkes, Sandra – 0181 979 6266
Williams, Helen – *IMG*
Williams, Jenevora – *Chameleon*
Williams-King, Anne – *Alexander*
Wilson, Elisa – *Craig*
Windsor, Lorna – *Mus Int*
Winter, Sidonie – *Craig*
Witney, Kate – 01673 885058
Wold, Helene – *Roy Baker*
Woodfine, Vanessa – *Harlequin*
Woolgrove, Caroline – *KDM*
Woollett, Elizabeth – *Musicmakers*
Wright, Chloe – *Mus Int*
Wright, Patricia – c/o 0181 969 3579 *fax:*
0181 969 1465
Wright, Susan – 0421 470286
Wyn-Davies, Catrin – *HP*
York, Deborah – *IMG*
Yuen, Nancy – *Sykes*
Zagorinskaia, Natalia – *Gilder*
Zakhartchouk, Tatiana – *Portland*
Zeltzer, Sandra – *Ingpen*
Ziesak, Ruth – *IMG*
Zuel, Veronique – *Charlton*

Mezzo Sopranos and Contraltos

Aarons, Mignonette – 0181 204 8778
Adams, Lynn – 01353 741287
Ager, Jeanette – *CDI*
Anthony, Mary – *Annon*
Araya, Graciela – *Gilder*
Arkhipova, Irina – *Askonas*
Armit, Louise – *Harlequin*
Ash, Pauline – 01207 542832
Asher, Nadine – *Mus Int*
Ashley, Susan – *SS*
Attfield, Helen – *CDI*
Ayers, Angela – 01865 340777
Bainbridge, Elizabeth – *Mus Int*
Balleys, Brigitte – *Mus Int*
Bannister, Phillida – *Grosvenor*
Barber, Kimberley – *Still*
Bardon, Patricia – *Ingpen*
Barton, Alison – 0141 551 8789
Bartram, Claire – 0121 426 4318; 0181 531 6107; 0802 482034
Begg, Heather – *Gilder*
Bellamy, Marcia – *OCA*
Benackova, Marta – *Mus Int*
Berganza, Teresa – *Askonas*
Bickley, Susan – *Allied*
Bishop, Elizabeth – *Harlequin*
Blieck, Marilyn de – *SS*
Blythe, Stephanie – *IMG*
Borodina, Olga – *Askonas*
Botes, Christine – *Gilder*
Bower Kreitzer, Jacalyn – *OCA*
Bramley, Lindsay – 01865 728878
Brice, Shirley – 01438 833145
Brookes, Frances Anne – 0181 521 3818; 01472 874761
Browner, Alison – *Mus Int*
Bruce-Payne, Sally – *Sykes*
Burgess, Sally – *IMG*
Burnett, Yvonne – *Mus Int*
Busby, Joan – 0181 202 1731 *fax:* 01875 341011
Cable, Margaret – *Musicmakers/CDI*
Cairncross, Heather – *SS*
Campbell, Fiona – *Musichall*
Campion, Joanna – *Still*
Cassidy, Jennifer – 01473 718811
Castle, Elizabeth – 01306 730511
Ciurca, Cleopatra – *Stafford*
Clarey, Cynthia – *Holt*
Clennell, Claire – 01624 832713
Clethero, Sara – 0121 454 3087; 0976 388523
Collins, Anne – *Askonas*
Connolly, Sarah – *Askonas*
Cook, Kathryn – *CDI*
Cook MBE, Pamela – 01623 27127 *also fax*
Coote, Alice – *IMG*
Crane, Louise – *Sykes*
Cullen, Susan – c/o 0171 433 1058 *fax:* 0171 813 5486
Cunha, Viola da – 0181 368 4789
D'Intino, Luciana – *Allied*
Daniels, Lorraine – 01371 810289 *also fax*
Davies, Menai – *Harlequin*
Davies, Rebecca de Pont – *Gilder*
De Blieck, Marilyn – *Camerata*
De Young, Michelle – *Askonas*
Debret, Stephanie – 01689 829387
Denley, Catherine – *Magenta/CDI*
Dix, Barbara – 01704 530903
Dolzhenko, Irina – *Gilder*
Doufexis, Stella – *Askonas*
Drumm, Imelda – *IMG*
Duckworth, Margaret – 01709 583461
Duguid, Alison – *Gilder*
Durseneva, Alexandra – *Gilder*
Edmunds, Janet – 01295 711000
Edwards, Jacqueline – *CDI*
Feighan, Therese – *Sykes*

Firestone, Adria – *Stafford*
Fisher, Rachel – *Grosvenor*
Fletcher, Gwynneth – *Clifton Wyatt*
Fontane, Yvonne – *KDM*
Forrester, Oenone – 0181 952 2148
Foster, Beryl – 01727 863477
Foster, Caroline – 0161 226 4098
Fox, Jacqueline – 01932 267607
Frowde, Judi Merri – 01582 840753; 0802 402597 *fax:* 01582 840991
Fryer, Heather – *KDM*
Fryer, Sarah – *Mus Int*
Fulgoni, Sara – *HP*
Gale, Rebecca – *Charlton/Grant Rogers*
Gilbert, Jane – *Still*
Gilmore, Gail – *OCA/Stafford*
Goble, Theresa – *Craig*
Gorton, Susan – *Harlequin*
Graham, Sharon – *Stafford*
Graham, Susan – *IMG*
Gravas, Alexandra – *Grant Rogers*
Grayston, Jean – 0171 286 4133 *fax:* 0171 266 4398
Grech, Sophia – *Michael Harrold*
Greenaway, Helen – *KDM*
Groop, Monica – *IMG*
Grose, Cynthia – *Gilder*
Gushina, Elena – *Gilder*
Hadda, Natanya – c/o 0181 202 7863; 0973 621738
Hatziano, Markella – *Askonas*
Hawksley, Deborah – *Mus Int*
Haydn, Zoe – *Dyfel*
Hellekant, Charlotte – *IMG*
Henry, Claire – *Mus Int*
Henschel, Jane – *Askonas*
Hesse, Ursula – *HP*
Hibberd, Linda – *SS*
Hickey, Angela – *Still*
Higgins, Jennifer – *Singers Direct* – 01438 221918
Higgins, Suzanne – 0181 471 7739
Hillerud, Margareta – *Mus Int*
Hirst, Linda – 0171 481 1345 *fax:* 0171 680 0665 *email:* hirstcraig@compuserve.com
Hoffman, Paula – *Gilder*
Holden, Elisabeth – 0116 270 6430
Horne, Marilyn – *IMG*
Howard, Ann – *Stafford*
Howells, Anne – *Allied*
Hughes, Alexandra – *Mus Int*
Hunt, Lorraine – *IMG*
Hwang, Der-Shin – *Magnum*
Irvine, Carole – *Alexander*
Irwin, Jane – *Ingpen*
Jagusz, Maria – *Musicmakers*
James, Buddug Verona *Sykes*
Januszajtis, Iwona – 01932 229412 *fax:* 0181 871 9416 *email:* 100631.1755@compuserve.com
Jennings, Sarah – 0171 622 4794 *fax:* 0171 498 5380
Jidkova, Elena – *Askonas*
Jones, Della – *Mus Int*
Jones, Leah-Marian – *Holt*
Joyce, Suzanne – *KDM*
Kaluza, Stefania – *Still*
Karnéus, Katarina – *Musicmakers*
Keeble, Gaynor – 01676 533072 *also fax*
Keegan, Liane – *Craig*
Keen, Catherine – *Portland*
Kettlewell, Alison – *Pristavec/KDM*
Kimm, Fiona – *Connaught*
King, Catherine – *CDI*
King, Mary – *Craig*
Knight, Gillian – *Gilder*
Kubrick, Anya – *CMG*
Kuhlmann, Kathleen – *Rawstron*

Lambert, Rachel – *Charlton*
Lanzetter, Nicola – 0171 723 5245
Lapworth, Jane – 01702 711146 *also fax*
Larmore, Jennifer – *IMG*
Lea, Yvonne – *Portland*
Leatherby, Carol – 0181 552 7149; 0589 988312
Legg, Susan – 01243 552389
Lewis, Katharine – *Annon*
Lipovsek, Marjana – *Askonas*
Lofthouse, Susan – 0171 720 4973
Lucas, Claire-Louise – 0181 395 7433 *fax:* 0181 543 6735 *email:* midman503a @aol.com; http://members.aol.com/midman503a
McAdam, Lynne – *SS*
McCafferty, Frances – *Mus Int*
McCarney, Kate – *Musicmakers*
McClymont, Lesley – *Music Theatre*
McCormack, Elizabeth – *Holt*
McDonald, Margaret – *Musicmakers*
Maguire, Margaret – *Stafford*
Mason, Anne – *Phillips*
Meadows, Julia – *Upbeat*
Meek, Clarissa – *Craig/Musichall*
Melnikova, Ekaterina – *Gilder*
Mentzer, Susanne – *IMG*
Michael, Nadja – *IMG*
Michelow, Sybil – 0181 459 2027
Miles-Johnson, Deborah – *Magenta/CDI/Grant Rogers*
Millburn-Fryer, Cherith – *CDI*
Miller, Jenny – *Gilder*
Mills, Beverley – *Mus Int/Michael Harrold*
Minton CBE, Yvonne – *Ingpen*
Montague, Diana – *Portland*
Morloc, Renee – *Gilder*
Mott, Louise – *Magenta*
Müller, Bärbel – *Still*
Murray, Ann – *Askonas*
Newman-Pound, Mary – 0802 446208
Nichiteanu, Liliana – *Gilder*
Nicholls, Hyacinth – *Sykes*
Nichols, Mary – 01263 721552 *fax:* 01263 720349
Nikolova, Zlatomira – *Pristavec*
Norman, Juliet – *Mus Int*
O'Brien, Clara – *Musicmakers*
Olsen, Marion – 01932 874405
Ormiston, Linda – *Mus Int*
Otter, Anne Sofie von – *IMG*
Owens, Anne-Marie – *IMG*
Pantos, Pamela – *Alexander*
Parker, Gloria – *Gilder*
Parry, Susan – *Portland*
Payne, Patricia – *OCA*
Payne, Rachel – *CDI* – 01829 740246
Peel, Ruth – *IMG*
Petrie, Mollie – 01275 830733
Petrinsky, Natascha – *Still*
Philogene, Ruby – *Askonas*
Place, Alison – 0181 941 2684 *also fax*
Powell, Claire – *Holt*
Pring, Sarah – *Musicmakers*
Prüssner, Ariane – *Magnum*
Pullicino, Joanna – *Charlton*
Quittmeyer, Susan – *Askonas*
Quivar, Florence – *Victoria Smith*
Randova, Eva – *Askonas*
Rappé, Jadwiga – *Finch*
Rearick, Barbara – *OWM*
Rees, Diana – 01823 451347
Reid, Valerie – *OCA*
Rice, Christine – *IMG*
Ridehalgh, Helen – 01253 722749; 0402 096891
Rigby, Jean – *Holt*
Robbin, Catherine – *Phillips*

Robinson, Ethna – *OWM*
Roebuck, Janine – *Mus Int*
Romanova, Nina – *Gilder*
Rørholm, Marianne – *Ingpen*
Rowlands, Carol – *Gilder*
Sallay, Linnea – *Gilder*
Sandivari, Ilia Aramayo – *Still*
Schaufer, Lucy – *Musichall*
Schimmack, Susanne – *Askonas*
Schneiderman, Helene – *Gilder*
Sciannimanico, Lucia – *CDI*
Sebron, Carolyn – *Gilder*
Self, Susannah – *Musicmakers*
Selway, Emma – *OWM*
Shaw, Teresa – *Stafford*
Shearer, Clare – *Portland*
Shell, Janet – *Gilder*
Shemchuk, Ludmilla – *Allied*
Shirai, Mitsuko – *Transart*
Simpson, Glenda – 0181 992 8973 *also fax*
Slater, Judy – c/o 0181 876 8666 *fax:* 0181
   876 7594
Slepkoviska, Denisa – *Mus Int*
Small, Margaret – *Charlton*
Soffel, Doris – *Ingpen*
Spence, Patricia – *Still*
Spicer, Susanna – *Singers Direct* – 0181 671
   4112; 0976 4112 *fax:* 0181 671 0210

Squires, Shelagh – 01892 524099
Stafford, Dianne – 01776 870272 *also fax*
Steffan, Katherine – *Sykes*
Steinfeld, Josephine – *SS*
Stene, Randi – *Askonas*
Stephen, Pamela Helen – *Mus Int*
Stilwell, Jean – *Victoria Smith*
Stuart, Debra – *Gilder*
Summers, Hilary – *Ingpen*
Sutton, Alison Mary – *CDI/Charlton*
Sykes, Belinda – 0171 708 3529 *also fax*
Taylor, Ann – *Ingpen*
Taylor, Patricia – 01202 747393
Tchistjakova, Irina – *Askonas*
te Brummelstroete, Wilke – *OWM*
Templeton, Helen – *Chameleon*
Theobald, Ruth – *Mostylea*
Thomas, Margaret – 01768 341437
Thompson, Annette – 0118 926 1480
Toczyska, Stefania – *Stafford*
Tomlinson, Margaret – 01326 241049
Tucker, Louise – *Alexander*
Turton, Patricia – 0181 660 4623
Uleman, Klara – *Stafford*
Unsworth, Beatrice – 01222 765177
Van Nes, Jard – *Askonas*
Vaughan, Elizabeth – *IMG*
Waleson, Susanna – *Gilder*

Walker, Penelope – *Gilder*
Walker CBE, Sarah – *Askonas*
Walker Smith, Nicola – 01484 854407
   also fax
Walton, Michelle – *OWM*
Watkins, Helen – 0181 660 2786
Wendel, Renate Maria – 0171 277 7068
   fax: 0171 277 8354 *email:* 100115.3701@
   compuserve.com
Westbrook, Kate – 01752 830589 *fax:* 01752
   830539
Wilkens, Anne – *Portland*
Wilkinson, Dee – 0171 401 9320
Wilkinson, Kathleen – *Sykes*
Williams, Harriet – *Harlequin*
Williamson, Josephine Ann – *Pristavec*
Williamson, Vanessa – *CDI*
Willis, Nuala – *Still*
Wilson, Christina – *Connaught*
Winkler, Jutta – *Stafford/Alexander*
Winter, Louise – *Askonas*
Wood, Hazel – 0181 878 9714 *also fax*
Woodfield, Ann – *Clifton Wyatt*
Woodhouse, Kim-Marie – *CDI*
Woodruff, Kathryn – *CDI*
Woolford, Delia – 01428 642653 *also fax*
Wyn-Rogers, Catherine – *Askonas*
Zajick, Dolora – *HP*

Counter Tenors and Falsettists

Angel, Ryland – *Magenta*
Asawa, Brian – *Askonas*
Barber, Terrance L – 0171 450 0664
   email: tlbarber@aol.com
Blaze, Robin – *Phillips*
Bordas, Ricard – *Magenta*
Bowman, James – 01737 767520 *fax:* 01737
   779690
Brett, Charles – 0181 892 3484 *also fax*
Bryan, Richard – *Matthew Tullah*
Chance, Michael – *IMG*
Chavner, Robert – 01732 452462 *also fax*
Clapton, Nicholas – *Gilder*
Clifford, Christopher John – 0181 543 7633;
   0468 908486 *fax:* 0181 543 9600
Clulow, Simon – *Musicmakers*
Cordier, David – *Gilder*
Daniels, David – *Askonas*
Esswood, Paul – *CDI/Transart*
Gay, Simon – *Sympathetic* – 0181 761 2779

Giles, Peter – *Annon*
Harper, Michael – *Mus Int*
Harries, Clive – 01609 881552 *fax:* 01642
   616511
Hill, Simon – 0181 995 2757
Howells, Vaughan – 0181 683 1659
Humphries, Charles – *Mus Int*
Huw Jeffries, James – *Ellison/CDI/*
   Chameleon/Magnum
James, David – *Magenta*
Kagan-Paley, Vyatcheslav – *Magenta*
Kenny, Jonathan Peter – *Phillips*
Kusel, Paul – 01255 506377 *fax:* 01255
   503677
Laban, Rénald, male sop – *Musicmakers*
Lakey, Denis – *Connaught*
McLusky, Fergus – 0171 403 7474 *also fax*
Missin, William – *Magnum* – 0181 553 3247
   also fax
Penrose, Timothy – *CDI*

Ragin, Derek Lee – *Askonas*
Robson, Christopher – *Mus Int/Magenta*
Royall, Christopher – 0181 292 5987
   also fax
Sanderson, James – 0171 791 1730 *fax:* 0171
   791 2618 *email:* james@musico.demon.
   co.uk; http://www.musico.demon.co.uk
Scholl, Andreas – *IMG*
Stafford, Ashley – *OCA*
Stefanowicz, Artur – *Sykes*
Tay, Cheng-Jim – 0171 720 6928
Taylor, Daniel – *HP*
Tyson, Robin – *CDI/Chameleon*
Wallace, Stephen – *HP*
Watts, Andrew – *Mus Int*
Whitworth, John – 01509 413327
Wyn Roberts, Richard – 01372 739985
   also fax
Wynne, Owen – 0161 973 3549
Zazzo, Lawrence – *IMG*

Tenors

Adams, Allan – *Magnum*
Agafonov, Mikhail – *Gilder*
Agnew, Paul – *Magenta*
Ainsley, John Mark – *Askonas*
Aler, John – *Holt*
Allen, Stephen – *Portland*
Anderson, Mark – *Magnum*
Anderson-Hall, Alexander – *OCA*
Aragall, Giacomo – *Stafford*
Archer, Neill – *IMG*
Arden-Griffith, Paul – *Brunskill*
Arevalo, Octavio – *Askonas*
Arvidsson, Bjorn – *Sykes*
Aschenbach, Hans – *Musicmakers*
Ashmore-Turner, David – 0181 505 9698
   fax: 0181 281 0318 *email:* dturner@
   thenet.co.uk
Atkinson, Lynton – *Magenta*
Austin-Kelly, Paul – *IMG*
Azocar, Jose – *Stafford*
Bamber, Peter – *CDI*
Banks, Barry – *HP*
Bantick, John – 01438 812761 *also fax*

Barbacini, Paolo – *Still*
Barham, Edmund – *Stafford/Harlequin*
Barratt, Jack – 01692 583002
Barrett, James – *Gilder*
Bartleet, David – *Alexander*
Bartolini, Lando – *Stafford*
Begley, Kim – *IMG*
Berkeley-Steele, Richard – *Gilder*
Berridge, Simon – *CDI*
Beudert, Mark – *Portland*
Biazeck, Simon – *Magnum*
Blinkhof, Jan – *IMG*
Bostridge, Ian – *Askonas*
Bottone, Bonaventura – *Stafford/Harlequin*
Bowen, John – *Phillips*
Bowers, Evan – *Still*
Bowley, John – *Singers Direct* – 0181
   664 6078
Boydall, Steven – *Mus Int*
Bridle, Matthew – *Charlton*
Bronder, Peter – *Allied*
Bruni, Romolo – 0181 992 0527; 0370 303422
Burden, Andrew – *Musicmakers*

Burden, William – *Holt*
Burt, Robert – *OWM*
Busher, Andrew – *SS*
Butterfield, Benjamin – *IMG*
Butterfield, Peter – *Mus Int*
Caley, Ian – *Ingpen*
Carlin, Robert – 0181 968 0485
Carwood, Andrew – *CDI/Singers Direct* –
   0181 723 5337 *fax:* 0181 723 5340
Cave, Philip – 01865 244801 *fax:* 01865
   437238 *email:* magnificat@
   compuserve.com
Chaundy, Stephen – *Gilder*
Clark, Graham – *Ingpen*
Clarke, Paul Charles – *Holt*
Cogram, John – *Craig*
Conrad, Andreas – *Mus Int*
Conyers, David – 017683 41783 *also fax*
Cornwell, Joseph – *Magenta (opera)/CDI*
Covey-Crump, Rogers – *Magenta*
Coxon, Richard – *IMG*
Cresswell, Jeffrey – *CDI*
Croft, Richard – *Askonas*

Crowe, Robert W – 01764 684535 *fax:* 01764 664235
Cupido, Alberto – *Stafford*
Curtis, Mark – *Mus Int*
Daggett, Philip – *SS/KDM*
Daniels, Charles – *Magenta*
Darling, Edward – 0181 669 8483
Daszak, John – *IMG*
Davies, Arthur – *Stafford/Harlequin*
Davies, Maldwyn – *Gilder/CDI*
Davies, Ryland – *IMG*
Davies, Simon – 0171 732 7389 *fax:* 0171 642 5310
del Pozo, Rodrigo – *Sykes*
Dobson, John – *Portland*
Dodd, Geraint – *Harlequin*
Doghan, Philip – 0171 836 3770
Donets, Sergei – *Gilder*
Douglas, Nigel – *Mus Int*
Douse, Stephen – *Chameleon*
Downes, Craig – *Sykes*
Drakulich, Stephan – *Magenta*
Duykers, John – *Still*
Edgar-Wilson, Richard – *Phillips*
Egerton, Francis – *Still*
Elliott, Paul – *CDI*
Elming, Poul – *Ingpen*
Evans, Joseph – *Mus Int*
Evans, Peter – *Magenta*
Evans, Wynford – *OCA/CDI*
Evans, Wynne – *Harlequin*
Evans-Jones, Timothy – *Mus Int/Musichall*
Eve, Philip – 0171 265 1384
Farrington, Paul – *SS*
Fedderly, Greg – *Askonas*
Fieldsend, David – *Musicmakers*
Fleming, Mark – *Matthew Tullah*
Flint, Ivor – 0181 968 9605
Forbes, Rupert Oliver – *Mus Int*
Forbes-Lane, Andrew – *Mus Int*
Ford, Bruce – *Still*
Fouchécourt, Jean Paul – *Askonas*
Frederick, James – 01327 263887 *fax:* 01327 262608 *email:* 106714.2057@ compuserve.com
Fryatt, John – *Mus Int*
Gardner, Lyndon – 01509 236281
Garfield Henry, Antoni – *Mus Int*
Gavin, Julian – *Craig*
Gedda, Nicolai – *Clarion/Seven Muses*
George, Donald – *Stafford*
Giacomini, Giuseppe – *Greenan*
Gibbs, Robert – 01843 842996
    email: bobgibbs@mistral.co.uk
Gietz, Gordon – *IMG*
Gilchrist, James – *Magenta*
Gillett, Christopher – *Portland*
Gimenez, Raul – *Greenan*
Ginty, Eugene – *Phillips*
Goldberg, Reiner – *Allied*
Goldthorpe, Michael – *Grosvenor/Mus Int/CDI*
Goss, Adrian – 01342 312712
Graham-Hall, John – *IMG*
Gray, George – *Portland*
Green, Robin – *CDI/SS*
Griffett, James – *CDI*
Grivnov, Vsevolod – *Askonas*
Groves, Paul – *IMG*
Hadley, Jerry – *IMG*
Hall, Aled – *Harlequin*
Hall, Peter – *CDI*
Hancock, James – *Craig*
Hand, Christopher – 01905 351292
Hands, Edward – *Craig*
Harrison, Martyn – 01268 282221 *also fax*
Hart-Davis, Michael – *Musicmakers*
Hartman, Sidwill – *Gilder*
Haskin, Howard – *Stafford*
Hill, Martyn – *OWM*
Hillman, David – *Ellison*
Hindmarsh, Martin – *CDI*

Hoare, Peter – *Harlequin*
Hobkirk, Christopher – *Gilder*
Hogan, Christopher – *CDI*
Honeyman, Ian – *Robert White*
Horn, Robert – *Mus Int*
Howard, Colin – 01258 860954 *also fax;* 0831 700066 *email:* cph7000@aol.com
Hudson, John – *Ingpen*
Hull, Paul – *Matthew Tullah*
Husband, Bryan – *Charlton*
Ireland, Richard – *CDI*
Jamieson Smith, Michael – *Charlton*
Jar, Valentin – *Still*
Jenkins, Neil – *Mus Int*
Jenkins, Terry – *Mus Int*
Jennings, Rupert – *Chameleon*
Jensen, Julian – *Mus Int*
Johnson, Alan – 01952 550816 *also fax;* 0181 345 8399
Johnston, Robert – *Musicmakers*
Jones, Doug – *Gilder*
Jones, Gwyn Hughes – *Harlequin*
Judson, Colin – *Craig*
Kaasch, Donald – *Portland*
Kale, Stuart – *Still*
Kelen, Peter – *Mus Int*
Kelly, Declan – *Sykes*
King, Andrew – *Magenta/CDI*
Kirk, Vernon – *Craig*
Knowles, Malcolm – *CDI*
König, Klaus – *Allied*
Kruse, Heinz – *Rawstron*
Kuebler, David – *IMG/Rawstron*
La Pierre, John – *Mus Int*
Langridge, Philip – *Allied*
Lauren, Graeme – *SS*
Lavender, Justin – *Still/Magenta*
Lawton, Jeffrey – *Mus Int*
Le Brocq, Mark – *Phillips*
Leggate, Robin – *Askonas*
Lentz, Jeffrey – *Gilder*
Levinsky, Ilya – *Askonas*
Lewis, Keith – *IMG*
Liley, Stephen – *Charlton*
Lima, Luis – *Stafford*
Lincoln, Christopher – *Harlequin*
Lindroos, Peter – *Still*
Lippert, Herbert – *Still*
Lloyd-Roberts, Jeffrey – *Holt*
Lopez-Yanez, Jorge – *Gilder*
Ludha, Ludovit – *Mus Int*
Luther, Mark – *Still*
McCann, Paul – *Gilder*
MacDougall, Jamie – *HP*
MacKenzie, Neil – *Musicmakers*
Mackenzie-Wicks, Andrew – 01273 474635 *also fax*
McKerracher, Colin – 0181 445 6646; 01324 626441
Mackie, Neil – *Askonas*
McLean-Mair, Kevin – *CDI/Sykes/Magnum*
Maisuradze, Badri – *Askonas*
Margita, Stefan – *Mus Int*
Marlton, Hilton – *Craig*
Marsden, John – *Portland*
Martin, Adrian – *Mus Int*
Martinucci, Nicola – *Stafford*
Maxwell Anderson, David – *Allied*
Mayall, Alan – 0181 680 8287 *also fax;* 0973 641305 (mobile)
Meades, Daniel – *Dyfel*
Mee, Anthony – *Harlequin*
Merritt, Chris – *Askonas*
Midgley, Vernon – 01932 853050 *fax:* 01932 829443
Milhofer, Mark – *Mus Int*
Millner, Robert – 0171 503 6280
Milner, Howard – *Craig*
Mitchinson, John – *CDI/Camerata/Mus Int*
Mok, Warren – *Mus Int*
Morgan, Wills – c/o 0181 883 0172

Morris, Andrew James – *Michael Harrold* – 01737 249839 *also fax*
Morton, Richard – 01865 372045
Moser, Thomas – *Askonas*
Moss, Henry – *Allied*
Munoz, Daniel – *Stafford*
Murgatroyd, Andrew – *Magenta*
Mussard, Timothy – *Gilder*
Nagore, Antonio – *Gilder*
Nelson, James – *Mus Int*
Newman, David – *Musicmakers*
Newton, Lloyd B A – 0181 659 3289 *also fax; email:* lloydnewton@pegopera.org
Nicoll, Harry – *Musicmakers*
Nilon, Paul – *Ingpen*
O'Beirne, Gerard – 01923 774485
O'Neill, Dennis – *Ingpen*
O'Sullivan, Jeremy – *Still*
Oakman, John – 0181 368 5308
Oke, Alan – *Musichall*
Oliver, Alexander – *IMG*
Oxley, James – *Magenta*
Pabst, Michael – *Still*
Padmore, Mark – *Magenta*
Partridge CBE, Ian – *Clarion/Seven Muses/CDI*
Paton, Iain – *Holt*
Pike, Julian – *Camerata*
Place, Gerald – 0181 941 2684 *also fax*
Potter, John – *Robert White*
Powell, Michael – 01993 708652 *fax:* 01993 708643 *email:* michael.powell@ btinternet.com
Power, Patrick – *Still*
Prégardien, Christoph – *Askonas*
Preston-Roberts, Michael – *Gilder*
Priday, Huw – *CDI*
Priest, Richard – 0121 643 7553 *fax:* 0121 633 4773 *email:* richard.priest@ allegro.co.uk
Prunell-Friend, Agustin – *Mus Int*
Pullin, Gordon – 01449 741414
Rahme, Edmondo – *Dyfel*
Randle, Thomas – *IMG*
Rankin, Bruce – *OCA*
Reaville, Richard – *CDI/Craig*
Rendall, David – *Portland*
Renshaw, Martin – *Annon*
Roberts, Gareth – 0181 907 3022 *also fax*
Robertson, Terence – *Alexander*
Robinson, Paul – *Magenta*
Robinson, Timothy – *Askonas*
Robson, Nigel – *Ingpen*
Roden, Anthony – *Greenan*
Rogers, Nigel – *Sykes*
Rojas, Rafael – *IMG*
Rolfe Johnson, Anthony – *Askonas*
Rooke, Stephen – *Harlequin*
Russell, Campbell – *Grant Rogers*
Ryan, Barry – *Askonas*
Sabbatini, Giuseppe – *IMG*
Sadé, Gabriel – *Gilder*
Salmon, Philip – *Gilder*
Sanders, Graham – *Victoria Smith*
Sayers, Gavin – *Alexander*
Schade, Michael – *HP*
Schreier, Peter – *Askonas*
Scott, Adrian – *Music Theatre*
Sears, Nicholas – *Holt*
Sharpe, Ivan – *Portland*
Sheffield, Philip – *Musicmakers*
Slane, Philip – *Annon*
Solodovnikov, Vladimir – *Gilder*
Spence, Toby – *Askonas*
Stephenson, Donald – 01597 840204 *fax:* 01597 840608 *email:* 100345.2566@ compuserve.com
Stewart, Jeffrey – *IMG*
Storey, Ian – *OCA*
Streit, Kurt – *IMG*
Sunnegårdh, Thomas – *Rawstron*

JOHN EDWARDS-LOWE

Bass-Baritone

"He sang with an exciting, full, rich voice in bel canto tradition, which one might never tire of hearing. His baritone voice with deep bass resonances must rank him amongst the best in his generation..."
D G Hambleton, Greenwich Festival 1990

"Formerly a student with John Noble among others, Mr Lowe has a handsome bass-baritone voice, and his opening group of Vaughan Williams songs revealed a marked feeling for colour and nuance."
St Mary's Church Recital, Nottingham Evening Post

419 Mansfield Road, Sherwood, Nottingham NG5 2DP
Telephone: 0115 9857167

Vassily Savenko

Bass-Baritone

"The voice is resonant, the legato genuine, the expression sensitive to music and to mood"
John Steane, Opera Now

"A voice so big and dark and deep...the Medtner and Rachmaninov were memorable"
Felix Aprahamian

"Savenko sang the taxing role with real conviction" world premiere review of Yuri Kasparov's mono-opera *Nevermore* **Opera**

"A magnificent voice which would fill the largest opera house"
(Cheltenham debut) **Gloucestershire Echo**

Winner of the MUSSORGSKY competition.
Has sung principal roles for Bolshoi Opera and Kirov Opera.
Experienced in opera, concerts and recitals.

UK based, Vassily Savenko also offers masterclasses and private tuition in Russian vocal repertoire.

Contact:
Margarete Rolle Promotions
Tel: 44 1684 892343 Fax: 44 1684 572734

NICOLINO GIACALONE

Bass-Baritone

Available for:
Opera
Recital
Oratorio, Lieder and Baroque solo repertoire
Masterclasses in singing interpretation
Private and group voice instruction

"The Handel [Cantata Dalla Guerra Amorosa] showed off the virtues of Mr Giacalone's bass baritone register, displaying a warm, resonant sound as rich as creamy chocolate."
David Barber, *The Whig Standard*, Kingston, Canada

"He played with the audience like an accomplished comedian, so that our laughter felt almost forbidden; we experienced the double pleasures of delight and shame."
Peter Pagnall, *The Independent,* London, England

"He is a brilliant and persuasive teacher who combines professional exactness with a charismatic personality."
Keith Taylor, *Stephen Sondheim Society*, Westminster University, London

"He has a magical gift for communicating self-confidence in oneself and his motivation to heal and develop other's ability to sing to their full potential is felt as a profound experience by his students, myself especially."
Elizabeth O'Driscoll, Director of the *Irish International Arts Centre*

Contact:
J Audrey Ellison International Artists' Management
135 Stevenage Road, Fulham, London, SW6 6PB
Tel: 0171 381 9751   Fax: 0171 381 2406

Tear CBE, Robert – *Holt*
Thompson, Adrian – *Phillips*
Thompson, Alastair – 01865 558501
Thompson, Ian – *Still/CDI*
Thompson, Robert – *CDI* – 01765 604775
Tolley, Phillip – c/o 01392 258149
Treleaven, John – *OCA*
Trost, Rainer – *Rawstron*
Trotter, Paul – *CDI*
Tucker, Mark – *HP*
Van Der Plas, Harrie – *Magenta*
Ventris, Christopher – *IMG*

Villars, John – *HP*
Vodicka, Leo-Marian – *Mus Int*
Voinorowski, Vjacheslav – *Gilder*
Wagenführer, Roland – *Rawstron*
Watkin-Holmes, David – *Charlton*
Webb, Barry – 0171 430 1373
Wedd, Peter – *Mus Int*
Welborn, Tracey – *Allied*
West, Jon Fredric – *Gilder*
West, Kevin – *Gilder*
White, Melvyn – 0114 258 0148 *fax:* 0114 270 1125
Wilde, Mark – *Sykes*

Williams, Bradley – *Still*
Williams, Tom Emlyn – 0181 944 1402; 00 31 20 625 1750
Wilson, Gordon – *Portland*
Wilson, Hugh – 01923 237261 *also fax*
Woodrow, Alan – *Still*
Workman, Charles – *Still*
Woroniecki, Robert – *Gilder*
Yemm, Ian – 0181 907 1155; 0958 571892
Zachariassen, Mathias – *IMG*
Zamparino, Cesare – *Still*
Zvetanov, Boiko – *Still*

Baritones, Bass-Baritones and Basses

Abdrazakov, Askar – *Askonas*
Agache, Alexandru – *Stafford*
Albert, Laurence – *CDI*
Alder, Stephen – 0181 540 6795
Aleksashkin, Sergei – *Askonas*
Alexander, Trevor – *Alexander/Grosvenor*
Allan, Lewis – 0141 639 5433; 0585 423214
Allen, Thomas – *Askonas*
Angas, Richard – *Sykes*
Anisimov, Alexander – *Askonas*
Ashman, David – 01273 623164; 0585 622520 *fax:* 01273 676241
Ashworth, James – 01274 499062 *also fax*
Ataneli, Lado – *Allied*
Ayldon, John – *Mus Int*
Bailey, Norman – *Gilder*
Baker, Alisdair – *SS*
Bamford, Alistair – 0181 742 0858
Bannatyne-Scott, Brian – *Magenta*
Bär, Olaf – *IMG*
Barlier, Pierre-Maurice – *Charlton*
Barrell, David – *Allied*
Bateman, Robert – *Charlton*
Bayley, Clive – *IMG*
Beavan, David – *CDI*
Beaven, Peter – 01932 788785 *fax:* 01932 765060 *email:* pmsnet@argonet.co.uk
Beesley, Mark – *Portland*
Belsey, Ian – *Dyfel*
Benson, Lindsay – *Clifton Wyatt*
Berg, Nathan – *IMG*
Berger, Leon – 0171 485 8702
Best, Jonathan – *Mus Int*
Best, Matthew – *Portland*
Bindley, Justin – *SS* – 01242 239049
Birchall, Jeremy – *SS*
Birchall, Simon – *CDI*
Black, Jeffrey – *IMG*
Black, Lynton – *Phillips*
Bland, Benjamin – *KDM*
Boarer, Nigel – *Charlton*
Booth-Jones, Christopher – *Mus Int*
Bork, Robert – *Gilder*
Borowski, Daniel – *Magenta*
Boughton, Ian – 01582 400824
Braun, Russell – *HP*
Braun, Victor – *Ingpen*
Broadbent, Graeme – *Holt*
Brocheler, John – *Ingpen*
Brown, Quentin – *CDI*
Bryson, Roger – *Mus Int*
Bundy, Michael – *Singers Direct* – 0181 390 5375; 0589 153382 *fax:* 0181 390 9818 *email:* mrb@clara.net
Burchuladze, Paata – *Askonas*
Burton, Nigel *fax:* 0118 931 8412
Bussell, Antony – *Annon*
Butler, James Elliot – 01383 872049
Caddy, Ian – *CDI/Mus Int*
Campbell, David – 0171 912 0873; 0378 776876
Campbell, Colin – *Magenta*
Caproni, Bruno – *Portland*

Carl, Jeffrey – *Craig*
Carolis, Natale de – *Holt*
Carpenter Turner, Robert – *CDI*
Carr, Gavin – *Magnum*
Carroli, Silvano – *Stafford*
Cashmore, John – *Alexander*
Cavallier, Nicolas – *Gilder*
Clarke, Adrian – *Musicmakers*
Clarkson, Julian – *CDI*
Cliffe, Nigel – 01603 618575 *also fax*
Cold, Ulrik – *Allied*
Coleman-Wright, Peter – *HP*
Comboy, Ian – *Mus Int*
Connell, John – *Holt*
Cook, Brian Rayner – *CDI* – 0181 368 3010
Corbelli, Alessandro – *Greenan*
Corbett, Joseph – 0171 624 6280
Cowan, Sigmund – *Still*
Croft, Howard Quilla – *Stafford*
Cunningham, Anthony – *Charlton*
D'Arcangelo, Ildebrando – *Askonas*
Dale Forbes, Andrew – *Mus Int*
Danby, Graeme – *Stafford*
Davenport, Glyn – *Music Theatre*
Davies, Christopher – 0181 954 4646
Davies, Gavin – *Charlton*
Davies, Giles – *Musicmakers*
Davies, Meurig – *OWM*
Davies, Neal – *Askonas*
Daymond, Karl – *Holt*
Dazeley, William – *Holt*
De Costa, Michael – *Pristavec*
de Jong, Lucas – *Sykes*
Dean, Mikel – *Mus Int*
Dean, Stafford – *Allied*
Delrez, Gerard – *Annon*
Dewis, Michael – *Harlequin*
Diaz, Justino – *Stafford*
Dolton, Geoffrey – *Allied*
Donnelly, Malcolm – *Gilder*
Donnelly, Patrick – *Gilder*
Dorn, Reinhard – *Rawstron*
Druiett, Michael – *IMG*
Ducarel, Michael – 0171 582 1052 *also fax;* *email:* morrice@cix.co.uk
Duesing, Dale – *Askonas*
Dulieu, John – *Brunskill*
Earle, Roderick – *Still*
Ebrahim, Omar – *Allied*
Edelmann, Peter – *Gilder*
Edwards-Lowe, John – 0115 985 7167
Elliot, Brian Newton – 0161 773 2266
Elliott, Martin – *CDI* – c/o 01243 604281 *fax:* 01243 604387 *email:* starmus@ brainlink.com
Ely, Dean – *Mus Int*
Ens, Phillip – *Portland*
Estes, Simon – *IMG*
Evans, Bryn – 0181 891 1308
Evans, Mark – *Mus Int*
Evans, Richard – *Musicmakers*
Ewing, Alan – *Still*
Fair, Nigel – *OCA*

Fairs, Alan – *OCA/CDI*
Faughey, Steven – *Magnum*
Feller, Carlos – *Rawstron*
Field, Christopher – 0181 858 6510
Finley, Gerald – *IMG*
Finney, Jonathan – *CMG*
Fissore, Enrico – *Gilder*
Fitchew, Michael – 0181 523 1054; 0171 433 1058 *fax:* 0171 813 5486
Flanagan, John Michael – 01273 478268
Fletcher, John – *Sykes*
Folwell, Nicholas – *Gilder*
Foster, Christopher – *Connaught/Singers Direct* – 0181 677 7997 *fax:* 0181 696 9783
Foster, Robert Ivan – 01992 462528
Fox, Tom – *Victoria Smith*
Francke, Donald – 0181 769 0423; 0171 328 0864 *fax:* 0171 328 0684
Fraser Annand, Kenneth – 01209 820890
Fredriksson, Karl-Magnus – *Allied*
Gadd, Stephen – *IMG*
Galla, Jan – *Mus Int*
Gardner, Jake – *Holt*
Garrett, Eric – *Still*
George, Michael – *IMG*
Gerello, Vassily – *Askonas*
Giacalone, Nicolino – *Ellison*
Gilfry, Rodney – *Askonas*
Glanville, Mark – *Still*
Goldsack, Christopher – *Gilder*
Golesorkhi, Anooshah – *Stafford*
Görne, Matthias – *IMG*
Greenan, Andrew – *Gilder*
Greenlaw, Kevin – *Grant Rogers*
Guarnera, Piero – *Still*
Guedes, Hector – *Gilder*
Gunn, Nathan – *Ingpen*
Gunthorpe, Jonathan – *Magnum*
Guy-Bromley, Phillip – *OCA*
Haenen, Tom – *Gilder*
Hagegård, Håkan – *IMG*
Halem, Victor von – *Portland*
Halfvarson, Eric – *IMG*
Halton, Richard – *Portland*
Hammond-Stroud OBE, Derek – 0181 883 2120
Hamon, Deryck – *Craig*
Hampson, Thomas – *IMG*
Hancock, John – *Still*
Hancorn, John – *Sykes*
Hargreaves, Glenville – *CDI/Musichall*
Hargreaves, Matthew – *Phillips*
Harvey, Peter – *Magenta*
Haugland, Aage – *Askonas*
Hawlata, Franz – *IMG*
Hayes, Quentin – *Magenta*
Hayward, Robert – *Ingpen*
Hearne, John – 01651 882274 *also fax*
Held, Alan – *Askonas*
Henry, Didier – *Stafford*
Herford, Henry – *CDI* – 01865 300884 *also fax*
Hodges, Paul – *OCA*

Holl, Robert – *Ingpen*
Holland, Ashley – *IMG*
Holland, Mark – *Gilder*
Holloway, Stephen – *Musicmakers*
Hoult, David – 0161 427 7255
Howard, Jason – *IMG*
Howell, Gwynne – *Ingpen*
Hudson, Paul – *Alexander*
Humphreys, Garry – 0171 582 1746
Hunt, Tom – *CDI*
Hvorostovsky, Dmitri – *Askonas*
Hynninen, Jorma – *Allied*
Jackson, Richard – *Phillips*
Jaffe, Monte – *Ingpen*
Jessop, Jonathan – 01733 574142
Johansen, Ronnie – *IMG*
Johnston, Charles – *Mus Int*
Joll, Philip – *IMG*
Jones, Darren – *Harlequin*
Jones, Gareth – *OCA*
Jones, Gordon – *Magenta*
Kavrakos, Dimitri – *Greenan*
Keenlyside, Simon – *Askonas*
Kempster, David – *Harlequin*
Kennedy, Roderick – *Mus Int*
Keohone, Paul – *Magnum*
Kesselman, Bryan – 0181 422 1379
Keyte, Christopher – *CDI/Mus Int*
Kharitonor, Dimitri – *Allied*
Kirby-Ashmore, David – *OCA*
Kirkbride, Simon – *Allied*
Kit, Mikhail – *Askonas*
Knapp, Peter – 01223 464866 *fax:* 01223 327874
Koc, Jozik – *Craig*
Konstantinov, Julian – *Askonas*
Kovats, Kolos – *Mus Int*
Kubiak, Laurence – *Ellison*
Kusjner, Ivan – *Mus Int*
Lamb, Alan – 01279 651856
Langford, Roger – *Gilder*
Langley, John – 0171 603 8796 *fax:* 0171 602 1257
Latham, Keith – *Stafford*
Leiferkus, Sergei – *Allied*
Liaugminas, Gintaras – *OCA*
Linnenbank, René – *Gilder*
Lloyd, Robert – *Askonas*
Lloyd-Morgan, Richard – *Gilder*
Lochak, Anatoly – *Gilder*
Lowe, John – 0115 985 7167
Ludlow, Ivan – *Askonas*
Mc Intyre, Sir Donald – *Ingpen*
Mackie, William – *CDI (concerts only)*
McElroy, Sam – *Harlequin*
McVeigh, Tom – *Dyfel*
Magee, Garry – *HP*
Maltman, Christopher – *Askonas*
Mann, Noel – *Mus Int*
Mannov, Johannes – *Gilder*
Marsh, David – *Mus Int*
Massis, René – *Gilder*
Masterton-Smith, Simon – *Chuck Julian*
Matorin, Vladimir – *Gilder/Allied*
Matthews, Hubert – *CDI*
Mattison, David – *Victoria Smith*
Maxwell, Donald – *Mus Int*
May, Jonathan – *Stafford*
Mayor, Andrew – *SS*
Mazura, Franz – *Ingpen*
Meanley, Ralph – *SS*
Medhurst, Peter – c/o 0181 673 1901
Meek, James – *Musichall*
Michaels-Moore, Anthony – *IMG*
Mikhailov, Maxim – *Gilder*
Mikulas, Peter – *Mus Int*
Miller, Niven – 01372 275430
Milne, John – 0181 806 1872
Milnes, Sherrill – *Ingpen*
Moll, Kurt – *Askonas*

Morgan, Arwel Huw – *Ingpen*
Morgan, John – *Alexander/Clifton Wyatt*
Morgan, Tim – *Mus Int*
Morris, Colin – *Mus Int*
Morris, James – *Askonas*
Morris, Richard – *OCA*
Morris, Wayne – *Mus Int*
Moses, Geoffrey – *Phillips*
Mosley, George – *Gilder*
Motchalov, Alexei – *Gilder*
Murzaev, Sergei – *Gilder*
Napier-Burrows, Paul – *OCA*
Nelson, Martin – *Chuck Julian*
Nesterenko, Evgeny – *Allied*
Newman, Henry – *Alexander*
Noble, John – *CDI*
Noble, Timothy – *IMG*
Norris, James – *SS*
O'Donnell, Kevin – *LM*
O'Connor, Gerard – *Mus Int*
Ognev, Vladimir – *Gilder*
Ogston, Bruce – *OCA*
Okerlund, David – *Harlequin*
Oldfield, Mark – *Gilder*
Olsen, Frode – *Still*
Ong, Wei Kiat – *Musicmakers*
Opie, Alan – *Allied*
Ottaway, James – *CDI*
Owen, Stephen – *Still*
Page, Steven – *Stafford*
Pape, René – *Allied*
Parfitt, Paul – *Mus Int*
Park, Kenneth – 01205 351733
Patriarco, Earle – *Askonas*
Patston, Timothy – *Craig*
Peacock, Adrian – *CDI*
Peaker, Jeremy – *Mus Int*
Pearce, Michael – *Magenta/CDI*
Peel, William – *Gilder*
Pencarreg, Wyn – *Craig*
Pittman-Jennings, David – *Allied*
Platt, Ian – *Gilder*
Polegato, Brett – *IMG*
Polhamus, John – *Grosvenor/Dyfel*
Poliakovs, Aleksandrs – *Allied*
Polikanin, Evgeny – *Gilder*
Pons-Tena, Ismael – *Stafford*
Pott, Charles – 01923 234669
Poulton, Robert – *Musicmakers*
Prey, Hermann – *Askonas*
Purves, Christopher – *Mus Int*
Putilin, Nicolai – *Askonas*
Quasthoff, Thomas – *Ingpen*
Quilico, Gino – *IMG*
Quinn, Gerard – *OCA*
Raffell, Anthony – 01235 525412 *fax* 01235 559722
Ramey, Samuel – *IMG*
Rath, John – *Still*
Rathbone, Harvey – 0181 340 3693 *also fax;* 01502 578 360
Rea, Sean – *OCA*
Reeves, Paul – 0181 679 1812 *email:* 101554.2750@compuserve.com
Relyea, John – *Askonas*
Rice, Robert – *Chameleon*
Richardson, Mark – *Gilder*
Richardson, Stephen – *HP*
Rivenq, Nicolas – *Gilder*
Rivers, Malcolm – *Still*
Roberts, Eric – *Musicmakers*
Roberts, Stephen – *IMG*
Robinson, Dean – *IMG*
Robson, Martin – *Sykes* – 0181 847 0888 *also fax*
Robson, Richard – *Gilder*
Rock, Philip – *Mus Int*
Roman, Emilio – *Sykes*
Rootering, Jan-Hendrik – *Ingpen*
Rose, Peter – *Askonas*
Rouillon, Philippe – *Allied*

Rowlands-Pritchard, John – 01749 677903 *fax:* 01749 675131
Rowlinson, Mark – 01625 527628 *fax:* 0161 244 4211
Rupp, Andrew – *Still*
Russell, Christopher – 0181 940 4484
Safiulin, Anatoli – *GIA*
St John, Del – *Dyfel*
Saipe, Julian – *Magnum*
Saks, Gidon – *Harlequin*
Salminen, Matti – *Ingpen*
Salters, Stephen – *Magenta*
Sandison, Gordon – *Portland*
Sarrazin, Lionel – *Stafford*
Savenko, Vassily – c/o 01684 892343 *fax:* 01684 572734
Savidge, Peter – *Musicmakers*
Scales, Anthony – *Camerata*
Schagidullin, Albert – *Askonas*
Schenk, Orlando – *KDM*
Schmidt, Andreas – *IMG*
Schöne, Wolfgang – *Ingpen*
Schulte, Eike Wilm – *Rawstron*
Schwets, Stanislaw – *Askonas*
Sedov, Denis – *Allied*
Sharp, Martyn – *OCA*
Shilling, Eric – 0181 989 7093
Shimell, William – *IMG*
Shore, Andrew – *Still*
Sidhom, Peter – *Allied*
Sigmundsson, Kristinn – *Rawstron*
Simonetti, Riccardo – *IMG*
Sims, Toby – 01273 472548
Singer, Malcolm – 01582 27248
Skinner, Philip – *Gilder*
Slater, Andrew – 01246 566243 *also fax*
Smit, Henk – *Gilder*
Smith, Anthony – *OCA*
Smith, Craig – *Portland*
Smythe, Russell – *Still*
Snipp, Peter – *Askonas*
Spagnoli, Pietro – *Greenan*
Stamm, Harald – *Allied*
Steffan, Michael – *Matthew Tullah*
Stephenson, David – *Portland*
Stone, Graham – *Mus Int*
Storojev, Nikita – *Sykes*
Strauch, Jacek – *Grant Rogers*
Struckmann, Falk – *Mus Int*
Stuart-Lloyd, Anthony – *Harlequin*
Suart, Richard – *Gilder*
Summers, Jonathan – *Greenan*
Tattersall, Norman – 01206 867462 *also fax*
Terfel, Bryn – *Harlequin*
Thomas, David – *Allied*
Thomas, Gwion – 0116 271 7887 *also fax*
Thomas, Matthew Elton – *Craig*
Thorpe, Simon – *OWM*
Tian, Hao Jiang – *Gilder*
Todorovic, Nicholas – *Craig*
Tómasson, Tómas – *Still*
Tomlinson, John – *Mus Int*
Tovey, Julian – *CDI/Craig*
Tranter, John – *Mus Int*
Trew, Graham – 0171 275 8260 *also fax*
Tschammer, Hans – *Allied*
Tumagian, Eduardo – *Stafford*
Tumanyan, Barseg – *Askonas*
Turner, Wayne – 01244 679701
Underwood, Christopher – *CDI*
Van Allan, Richard – *Holt*
Van Ast, Jochem – *Mus Int*
Van Dam, Jose – *Askonas*
Varcoe, Ralph – 0181 932 1815
Varcoe, Stephen – *Phillips*
Vassiliev, Alexandre – *Rawstron*
Veira, Jonathan – *Sykes*
Vinogradov, Jeremy – *KDM*
Waddington, Henry – *Ingpen*
Wade, Eddie – *OCA*

Wakeham, David – *Still*
Wakeham, Michael – 0181 567 6302
Washington, Daniel – *Mus Int*
Watson, Keel – *Sykes*
Wegner, John – *Mus Int*
Weikl, Bernd – *Askonas*
Werba, Markus – *Askonas*
Wheatley, Brendan – 01874 690339
  fax: 01874 690254
Whelan, Paul – *IMG*

White, Brian – 01622 756660 *also fax;* 0589
  558797 *email:* drbdwhite@aol.com
White, Jeremy – *Musicmakers/
  Magenta*
White, Willard – *IMG*
Whitehouse, Richard – *Mus Int*
Wickens, Nigel – 01223 248812
Wickham, Henry – 0181 788 0158
  also fax
Widmer, Oliver – *IMG*

Wilding, Simon – *IMG*
Wildman, Mark – *Sympathetic*
Williams, Jeremy Huw – *Stafford*
Williams, Roderick – *Mus Int*
Wilson-Johnson, David – *Askonas*
Windmüller, Yaron – *Anglo-Swiss*
Wistreich, Richard – *Robert White*
Wlaschiha, Ekkehard – *Allied*
Woodall, Richard – *Grant Rogers*
Zancanaro, Giorgio – *Stafford*

172

Opera Producers

Addresses and telephone numbers of agents listed below will be found under **Agents and Managers**.

Abulafia, John – *Craig*
Albery, Tim – *Cruickshank*
Alden, David – *IMG*
Alver, Jonathan – 0171 354 8794 *fax:* 0171 354 5692
Ashman, Mike – *Still*
Bailey, Lucy – c/o 0171 287 4550 *fax:* 0171 287 9128
Bedford, Peter Lehmann – 0181 361 9648
Besch, Anthony – 0181 749 0181
Brown, Adrian – 0171 352 3479
Brown, Kate – *Gilder*
Burden, Michael – 01865 279526 *fax:* 01865 279590
Burge, Stuart – *Cruickshank*
Caird, John – 0181 348 1996 *fax:* 0181 340 5030 *email:* churchhouse@zoo.co.uk
Cairns, Tom – *Cruickshank*
Callow, Simon – *Cruickshank*
Carsen, Robert – *IMG*
Chevara, Robert – *PA*
Cocker, Jonathan – 0171 249 0887 *also fax*
Coleman, Tim – *Still*
Collins, Aletta – *Cruickshank*
Cox, John – *Askonas*
Curran, Paul – *PA*
Dane, John – *Scrimgeour*
de Mallet Burgess, Thomas – *Sykes*
Decker, Willy – *Rawstron*
Dew, John – *Still*
Dooner, Daniel – 01273 476700
Douglas, Nigel – *Mus Int*
Duncan, Martin – *Askonas*
Edwards, David – 0171 625 8903 *also fax*
Fettes, Christopher – *Cruickshank*
Fielding, David – *Cruickshank*
Freeman, David – *Allied*
Fuchs, Olivia – 0171 736 2439 *also fax*
Gilbert, Terry – *Scrimgeour*
Godefroid, Philippe – *Gilder*
Graham, Colin – c/o 0171 727 0601
Gregson, Richard – *Victoria Smith*
Hands, Terry – *Allied*

Hausman, Leah – *PA*
Havergal, Giles – c/o 0141 429 5561 *fax:* 0141 429 7374 *email:* boxoffice@citz.co.uk
Hawkes, Tom – *OCA*
Hayes, Jamie – *Sykes*
Heyland, Michael – c/o 0181 789 0776
Hollander, Julia – *Ingpen*
Homoki, Andreas – *Rawstron*
Hunter, Malcolm – 01452 814089 *also fax*
Hytner, Nicholas – *Askonas*
Ibelhauptaite, Dalia – *Cruickshank*
Jacobs, Sally – *PA*
Judd, Wilfred – c/o 0181 894 2277 *fax:* 0181 894 7952
Judge, Ian – c/o 0171 434 9167 *fax:* 0171 494 2887
Knapp, Peter – 01223 464866 *fax:* 01223 327874
Koenig, Leslie – *IMG*
Kraus, Mary Anne – *PA*
Kupfer, Harry – *Allied*
Lang, Aidan – *Musichall*
Lawless, Stephen – *Askonas*
Lloyd, Matthew – *Cruickshank*
Lloyd, Phyllida – c/o 0171 734 0626 *fax:* 0171 434 2346
Lloyd Davies, John – *Still*
Lowery, Nigel – *Cruickshank*
McCaffery, Michael – *Still*
McCarthy, Michael – c/o 01222 230833 *fax:* 01222 342046
MacDonald, James – *Cruickshank*
McVicar, David – *PA*
Mason, Patrick – c/o 0171 287 5131 *also fax; fax:* 0171 287 5161
Maunder, Stuart – *Craig*
Medcalf, Stephen – *PA*
Meitlis, Rebecca – 01273 477990
Melbye, Mikael – *Askonas*
Miller, Jonathan – *IMG*
Molnár, Nicolette – *PA*
Moore, Jonathan – *Ingpen*

Mound, Vernon – *Gilder*
Mumford, Peter – *Cruickshank*
Negrin, Francisco – *IMG*
Nunn, Trevor – 0171 928 2033 *fax:* 0171 401 3038
Parr, Philip – 0181 555 2154 *also fax*
Pascoe, John – *Still*
Pimlott, Steven – *Cruickshank*
Pountney, David – *IMG*
Prowse, Philip – *Cruickshank*
Ramsay, Alasdair – 01904 338155 *also fax*
Relton, William – *Musichall*
Richardson, Matthew – *Cruickshank*
Ritch, David – c/o 0181 741 3794; 0171 637 0993 *fax:* 0171 836 8379; 0171 637 0985
Russell, Ken – *Victoria Smith*
Schaaf, Johannes – *IMG*
Schut, Henk – 0171 281 0432 *also fax*
Serban, Andrei – *IMG*
Sharman, Caroline – 0181 673 3076 *also fax; email:* caro@mmtt.co.uk
Sinclair, Andrew – *Gilder*
Spink, Ian – *Cruickshank*
Squires, Chris – 0141 248 4567; 0966 416765 *fax:* 0141 221 8812
Sulkin, David – 0171 837 3444 *also fax; email:* 101767.133@compuserve.com
Sutcliffe, Jeremy – c/o 0171 240 1200 *fax:* 0171 212 9549 – *PA*
Tebbutt, Robin – c/o 01222 464666
Tinkler, Mark – 0171 635 8905 – *IMG*
Trevis, Di – *Allied*
Venables, Clare – *Cruickshank*
Vick, Graham – *Ingpen*
von Nuding, John – 01622 747762 *fax:* 01622 745276 *email:* figaro@globalnet.co.uk; http://members.tripod.com/~operavox
Warner, Deborah – c/o 0171 287 0077 *fax:* 0171 287 1940
Warner, Keith – *Still*
Watson, Peter – 0181 985 7712 *also fax*
Watt-Smith, Ian – 0181 693 4009
Wright, Rennie – *Askonas*

Composers

Most of the composers listed belong to the **Composers' Guild of Great Britain** (indicated by an asterisk) or to the **Association of Professional Composers** (indicated by †) *see* **Associations.** Composers living overseas are not included unless they belong to one of these organisations. Each composer's contact address is followed by a listing of his/her music publisher(s) in alphabetical order. Contact information for the publishers listed below can be found under **Music Publishers** and **Subsidiary Music Publishers**.

Publishers' Abbreviations

The following abbreviations of publishing companies are used. Self-explanatory abbreviations are not given. *Sp* indicates that the composer has set up a self-publishing company.

AA	Anglo-American	For	Forsyth Brothers Ltd	Oec	Oecumuse
AAK	Alfred A Kalmus	Free	H Freeman & Co	OUP	Oxford University Press
ABd	Associated Board of the Royal Schools of Music	Gal	Galliard Ltd	PP	Paterson's Publications Ltd
		GMC	Galaxy Music Corp	Ric	G Ricordi & Co Ltd
Arc	Arcadia Music Publishing Co Ltd	GS	G Schirmer Inc	Rob	Roberton Publications St
Asch	Ascherberg, Hopwood and Crew	Hin	Hinrichsen Edition Ltd	RSCM	Royal School of Church Music
B	Bosworth & Co Ltd	IMC	International Music Co	SB	Stainer & Bell Ltd
BC	British and Continental Agencies	IMP	International Music Publications	SMIC	Scottish Music Information Centre
Belwin	Belwin-Mills Ltd	JW	Joseph Williams Ltd	Sou	Southern Music Publishing Co Ltd
BH	Boosey & Hawkes Ltd	KM	Kevin Mayhew Ltd	Sph	Sphemusations
Breit	Breitkopf	KPM	Keith Prowse Music Publishing Co Ltd	Suv	Edizioni Suvini Zerboni
Ches	J & W Chester Ltd			TP	Thames Publishing
CUP	Cambridge University Press	Leng	Alfred Lengnick & Co Ltd	UE	Universal Edition
Elk	Elkin & Co Ltd	LGB	Leonard, Gould & Bolttler	UMP	United Music Publishers Ltd
Eul	Ernst Eulenberg Ltd	ME	Mozart Edition (Great Britain) Ltd	Wein	Josef Weinberger Ltd
F-E	Fraser-Enoch Publications	Mod Ed	Modern Edition	Wolfe	de Wolfe Ltd
Feld	Feldman & Co Ltd	Nov	Novello & Co Ltd	WC	Warner Chappell
Fil	Film Music	NWM	New Wind Music Co	WR	Wright & Round Ltd

Aaron, Bernard. 8 Townfield Gardens, Altrincham, Cheshire WA14 4DT *tel:* 0161 941 1138. *Playwrights Press (Canada), Tayborn Publishing, Waterloo Music (Canada). Classical gui, songs, children's theatre scores.*

Adams, John. c/o Boosey & Hawkes Music Publishers Ltd, 295 Regent St, London W1R 8JH *tel:* 0171 580 2060 *fax:* 0171 637 3490 *email:* composers@boosey.com. *Opera, chmbr, orch, vocal and ens.*

* **Addison, John.** 359 Elm St, Old Bennington, Vermont 05201, USA *tel:* 00 1 802 442 7019 *fax:* 00 1 802 442 7007. *EC Schirmer (Boston USA), Emerson, OUP (UK/USA), SB. Orch concert works, chmbr, ballet, film, TV and theatre mus.*

Aho, Kalevi. c/o Boosey & Hawkes, 295 Regent St, London W1R 8JH *tel:* 0171 580 2060 *fax:* 0171 637 3490 *email:* composers@boosey.com. *Opera, orch, concertos, chmbr.*

Alberga, Eleanor. 166 Bethnal Green Rd, London E2 6DL *tel:* 0171 729 8362 *also fax. OUP. Chmbr mus, choral and orch works, film scores.*

† **Alexander, Christian.** 26 New Rd, Kingham, Oxon OX7 6YP *tel:* 01608 659558 *email:* c.d.alexander@bristol.ac.uk; http://music-uk.com/c-alexnd.html. *Leng. Concert mus.*

Alvarez, Javier. 23 Barrington Rd, London N8 8QT *tel:* 0181 348 4973 *also fax; email:* musqja@herts.ac.uk. *Faber. Chmbr, orch, film, electro-acoustic.*

Amos, Keith. c/o CMA Publications, 10 Avenue Rd, Kingston, Surrey KT1 2RB *tel:* 0181 541 0857 *fax:* 0181 974 8120 *email:* kamos@classical-artists.com; http://www.classical-artists.com/kamos. *CMA. Orch, chmbr mus, wind, br band, choral.*

Anderson, Avril. 28 Cavendish Av, London N3 3QN *tel:* 0181 349 2317 *fax:* 0181 346 8257. *Andresier. Orch, inst, vocal, mus for dance, educ mus.*

Andrews, Mark. c/o Penelope Manuel, 135 Lower Weybourne La, Badshot Lea, Farnham, Surrey GU9 9LQ *tel:* 01252 331174. *BH, Fand. Inst, orch, choral, ens, chmbr, children's.*

Andriessen, Louis. c/o Boosey & Hawkes Music Publishing Ltd, 295 Regent St, London W1R 8JH *tel:* 0171 580 2060 *fax:* 0171 637 3490 *email:* composers@boosey.com. *Opera, works for large ens, theatre, jazz singer and ens, chmbr.*

Anstey, Marjolijn. Belvedere, Seymer Rd, Swanage, Dorset BH19 2AL *tel:* 01929 422908. *Leng. Chmbr mus, oratorio, vocal.*

* **ApIvor, Denis.** 9 Ashurst Av, Saltdean, E Sussex BN2 8DR *tel:* 01273 301587. *Bèrben (Milan), Doorns (USA), Forsythe, Hans Pero (Vienna), Musical New Services (Bimport), OUP, Schott, Sikesdi (Canada). Ballet, opera, inst, symphonic and songs.*

Archer, Malcolm. 15 Vicars Close, Wells, Somerset BA5 2UJ *tel:* 01749 673526. *Hinshaw (USA), KM, OUP. Choral, org, educ and musicals.*

Arenstein, Colin. 78 Ridge Rd, London N8 9NR *tel:* 0181 348 3630.

Argento, Dominick. c/o Boosey & Hawkes Music Publishing Ltd, 295 Regent St, London W1R 8JH *tel:* 0171 580 2060 *fax:* 0171 637 3490 *email:* composers@boosey.com. *Opera, voice and orch, chorus and orch.*

* **Arnell, Richard.** Benhall Lodge, Benhall, Saxmundham, Suffolk IP17 1DJ *tel:* 01728 602014 *fax:* 01728 603256. *Broadbent and Dunn, Leng, Peer-Southern (USA), Peters, Schott. Symphonic and chmbr works, opera, ballet mus, film and TV, electro-acoustic, mus theatre.*

*† **Arnold CBE, Sir Malcolm.** c/o Stan Hibbert, 18 Bloomfield Dr, Unsworth, Bury, Lancashire BL9 8JX *tel:* 0161 766 2909 *also fax. EMI, Emerson, Faber, Leng, Molenaar, Nov, Rob, Studio. Symphonic, wind band, military band, br band, ens, orch and chmbr works; ballet, film and TV scores.*

* **Arnold, Stephen.** Dept of Music, University of Glasgow, 14 University Gardens, Glasgow G12 8QH *tel:* 0141 330 5509 *fax:* 0141 307 8018 *email:* s.arnold@music.gla.ac.uk.

Arundel Timms, T. 10 Moreton Pk Rd, Bideford, N Devon EX39 3AU *tel:* 01237 473887. *EMI, Rob. Vocal, orch, choral, solo inst.*

Ascough, Richard. 118 Summer Rd, Thames Ditton, Surrey *tel:* 0181 398 7863 *email:* r.ascough@directon.alztec-iip.co.uk. *EMC, Frontier.*

* **Aston, Peter.** 9 Bourne Close, Long Stratton, Norwich NR15 2RW *tel:* 01508 530644. *AA, Asch, Banks, Chappell, CUP, Hinshaw, Nov, OUP, Pavane, RSCM, SB, WC. Choral, orch, chmbr, church mus, opera.*

Aubrey-Drew, Helen. Hafod, Llanbedr DC, Ruthin, Clwyd LL15 1YG *tel:* 01824 704582. *PP, Kerygma. Opera, orch, org, choral, church.*

* **Aviss, Peter R F.** 16 Mitcham Rd, Dymchurch, Romney Marsh, Kent TN29 0TH *tel:* 01303 874449. *Shaftesbury Edition (sp). Orch, choral, chmbr, educ.*

* **Ayres, Paul.** Flat 4, 2 Albany Rd, Ealing, London W13 8PG *tel:* 0181 998 2294 *also fax. Gordon Thompson Music (WC), Parkfield Music. Choral, vocal, mus for theatre, inst.*

Back, Peter. 5 St Martin's House, Lewes Rd, Ringmer, E Sussex BN8 5QB *tel:* 01273 812159. *PP. Musicals.*

Bailey, Judith. 1 Stable Flat, Uppark, South Harting, Petersfield GU31 5QB *tel:* 01730 825638. *Composers Library, Da Capo, Goodmusic, Modus, Samuel King, Sarnia Music. Orch, chmbr, inst, br band, vocal, wind band.*

Bailey, Keith McDonald. 194a Straight Rd, Harold Hill, Romford, Essex RM3 8XR *tel:* 01708 371936. *WC. Pno, vocal.*

† **Bainbridge, Simon.** c/o Novello & Co Ltd, 8-9 Frith St, London W1V 5TZ *tel:* 0171 434 0066 *fax:* 0171 287 6329 *email:* music@musicsales.co.uk. *Nov, UMP. Contemporary classical mus.*

* **Baird, John.** 121 St James's Dr, Wandsworth Common, London SW17 7RP *tel:* 0181 672 0423. *Camden. Choral mus, operas.*

Baker, Lance. 2 Cavendish Rd, Woking, Surrey GU22 0EP *tel:* 01483 715474. *(Sp). Wind mus.*

Ball, Christopher. 122 Wigmore St, London W1H 9FE *tel:* 0171 935 1270. *Belwin, Columbia Pictures, E&S Mus, Nova. Chmbr, concertos for wind, symph.*

*† **Ball, Michael.** c/o Novello & Co Ltd, 8-9 Frith St, London W1V 5TZ *tel:* 0171 434 0066 *fax:* 0171 287 6329. *Brass/Wind, For, Maecenas, Nov. Orch, wind and br band, chmbr, choral, educ.*

Ball, Timothy. 12a Sudlow Rd, London SW18 1HP *tel:* 0181 871 0317 *also fax. SB, (sp). Choral, church, songs, mus theatre.*

Bamford, Adrian. 4 Bells End Rd, Walton-on-Trent, Swadlincote, Derbys DE12 8ND *tel:* 01283 712942 *email:* adrian.bamford@ndirect.co.uk. *ACB Notation (sp). Chmbr, choral, solo, orch, vocal.*

Barber, Charlie. 62 Arran St, Roath, Cardiff CF2 3HT *tel:* 01222 497157 *also fax. (Sp). Concert, mus theatre, dance, film.*

Barbour, Freeland. 6 The Steils, Edinburgh EH10 5XD *tel:* 0131 447 0991 *also fax;* 0831 779920. *Traditional and folk mus, educ, film and TV, theatre.*

† **Barker, Paul.** Flat 3, 33 Hopton Rd, London SW16 2EH *tel:* 0181 677 9880 *also fax; email:* paul@mmtt.co.uk; http://www.mmtt.co.uk. *(Sp). Opera, vocal, orch, inst mus, dance, theatre mus. Educ projects.*

Barker, Stan. Inglemead, Waddington Rd, Clitheroe, Lancs BB7 2HN *tel:* 01200 424839. *Jazz, educ.*

Barnard, Keith. 34 Longberrys, Cricklewood La, London NW2 2TE. *Chmbr, orch, pno, vc concerto, vocal, chmbr opera, choral.*

* **Barnes, Bryan.** Sandy, Whitehouse La, W Bergholt, nr Colchester, Essex CO6 3ET *tel:* 01206 240427. *(Sp). Children's cantatas (secular and sacred), choral works, inst ens pieces.*

* **Barnes, Derek.** 56 Further Green Rd, Catford, London SE6 1JH *tel:* 0181 698 8480 *fax:* 0181 698 1673. *BH, (sp). Mus theatre, br band, reduced orchestrations for opera and mus theatre, incidental mus for the theatre.*

Barratt, Jack. Blackthorn Lodge, The Common, Happisburgh, Norwich, Norfolk NR12 0RT *tel:* 01692 583002. *Cadenza. Inst, choral, ens, oratorio, mus theatre.*

* **Barrell, Bernard.** 48 Norwich Rd, Ditchingham, Bungay, Suffolk NR35 2JL *tel:* 01986 896122. *Anglian, Brunton, F-E, Goodmusic, MSM, Nov, Oec, Piper, Ric, Rob, SB, R Schauer, Sph, UE, Wise Owl. Contemporary, schools, adult, church.*

Barrett, Richard. c/o United Music Publishers Ltd, 42 Rivington St, London EC2A 3BN *tel:* 0171 729 4700 *fax:* 0171 739 6549 *email:* ump@compuserve.com; http://ourworld.compuserve.com/homepages/ump. *UMP. Inst, chmbr, vocal, orch, electronic, mus theatre.*

† **Barron, Angela.** 27 Madeira Croft, Coventry, Warwicks CV5 8NX *tel:* 01203 679827 *also fax; email:* angbaron@dircon.co.uk. *BH, Carlin, EMI, Standard Music Ltd, WC. Library mus; film, TV and radio scores; advertisements, theatre, orch, electro-acoustic, educ mus.*

Barry, Gerald. c/o Oxford University Press, Repertoire Promotion, 70 Baker St, London W1M 1DJ *tel:* 0171 616 5900 *fax:* 0171 616 5901 *email:* repertoire.promotion@oup.co.uk. *OUP. Opera, pno, chmbr mus.*

Bartlett, John. c/o Great Stave Publications, Sycamore Lodge, Lower Peryers, E Horsley, Surrey KT24 6SD *tel:* 01483 284207. *(Sp). Vocal, choral, chmbr, orch, org, inst, pno.*

* **Barton, Nicholas.** 14 Clifton Dr, Abingdon, Oxon OX14 1ET *tel:* 01235 527861. *Andresier, Spartan.*

* **Barton-Armstrong, John.** Overdale, Ravenswood Av, Crowthorne, Reading, Berks RG45 6AX *tel:* 01344 777772. *Obelisk, Ramsey, Wessex. Opera, symphonies, film scores, chmbr, sonatas, choral, educ mus, light mus and songs.*

Bate, Jennifer. 35 Collingwood Av, Muswell Hill, London N10 3EH *tel:* 0181 883 3811 *fax:* 0181 444 3695 *email:* jenniferbate@classical-artists.com; http://www.classical-artists.com/jbate. *Banks, Nov. Solo inst (org).*

† **Bauld, Alison.** 6 Dungarvan Av, London SW15 5QU *tel:* 0181 876 3008. *Nov. Opera, chmbr, vocal, radio, theatre.*

Bawden, Rupert. c/o Novello & Co Ltd, 8-9 Frith St, London W1V 5TZ *tel:* 0171 434 0066 *fax:* 0171 287 6329. *Nov.*

* **Bayford, Frank.** 21 Canonbury Rd, Enfield, Middx EN1 3LW *tel:* 0181 363 2663. *Modus, Mayola. Concert works, pno, cl, w/wind, chmbr mus, vocal, str orch, etc.*

* **Bayliss, Colin.** c/o Da Capo Music Ltd, 26 Stanway Rd, Whitefield, Manchester M45 8EG *tel:* 0161 766 5950. *Da Capo, Fentone. Chmbr, orch.*

† **Beamish, Sally.** c/o Scottish Music Information Centre, 1 Bowmont Gardens, Glasgow G12 9LR *tel:* 0141 334 6393 *fax:* 0141 337 1161

email: http://www.music.gla.ac.uk/htmlfolder/resources/smic/html/beamish.html. *Solo, chmbr, orch and vocal mus, TV scores.*

* **Beat, Janet.** c/o Scottish Music Information Centre, 1 Bowmont Gardens, Glasgow G12 9LR *tel:* 0141 334 6393. *Bastet Productions, Ches, Faber, Furore Verlag, Nov, OUP. Classical electro-acoustic and chmbr mus.*

* **Beaumont, Adrian.** 73 Kings Dr, Bishopston, Bristol BS7 8JQ *tel:* 0117 924 8456. *Vanderbeek. Choral, orch, chmbr.*

† **Bedford, David.** 39 Shakespeare Rd, London NW7 4BA *tel:* 0181 959 3165. *Camden, Gand M Brand, Nov, UE, (sp). Concert mus, film and TV.*

Beechey, Gwilym. 15 Hamlyn Av, Hull HU4 6BT *tel:* 01482 508910. *Augsburg, Concordia, Oec, SB. Church, org mus.*

Beeson, Jack. c/o Boosey & Hawkes, 295 Regent St, London W1R 8JH *tel:* 0171 580 2060 *fax:* 0171 637 3490 *email:* composers@boosey.com. *Opera, orch, choral, pno.*

† **Benjamin, George.** c/o Faber Music, 3 Queen Sq, London WC1N 3AU *tel:* 0171 833 7911/2 *fax:* 0171 833 7939. *Faber. Inst, orch, chmbr, vocal mus.*

† **Bennett, Richard Rodney.** c/o Novello & Co Ltd, 8-9 Frith St, London W1V 5TZ *tel:* 0171 434 0066 *fax:* 0171 287 6329 *email:* music@music sales.co.uk. *Nov. Concert works, film and TV.*

Bergman, Erik. c/o Boosey & Hawkes, 295 Regent St, London W1R 8JH *tel:* 0171 580 2060 *fax:* 0171 637 3490 *email:* composers@boosey.com. *Orch, voices and orch, choral.*

Berio, Luciano. c/o Universal Edition (London) Ltd, 48 Gt Marlborough St, London W1V 2BN *tel:* 0171 437 6880 *fax:* 0171 437 6115 *email:* miranda@ue-london.demon.co.uk. *UE.*

*† **Berkeley, Michael.** c/o Oxford University Press, Repertoire Promotion, 70 Baker St, London W1M 1DJ *tel:* 0171 616 5900 *fax:* 0171 616 5901 *email:* repertoire.promotion@oup.co.uk. *OUP.*

Best, Christopher. 60 Tudor Rd, Hinckley, Leics LE10 0EQ *tel:* 01455 618416. *Inst, contemporary dance mus, mus theatre, electro-acoustic mus.*

* **Betro, Denis.** Houseboat Alma, Scotland Bridge Lock, Weybridge, Surrey KT15 3HL *tel:* 01932 350575. *Orch, film and TV scores, concertos, symphonies.*

Bettison, Oscar. 3 Grove House, 66 British Grove, London W4 2NL *tel:* 0181 741 0392 *also fax. Orch, chmbr, vocal, arrangements.*

Bevan, Clifford. 10 Clifton Terrace, Winchester, Hants SO22 5BJ *tel:* 01962 864755 *fax:* 01962 867755. *BC, Carlin, Columbia, Feld, Piccolo. Chmbr mus, pno, vocal, band and choral.*

* **Biberian, Gilbert.** 49 Copt Elm Rd, Charlton Kings, Cheltenham, Glos GL53 8AG *tel:* 01242 581457. *Belwin, Bèrben, Ches, Cramer, Editions Orphée, Nouran Enterprises (sp), Nov, Rob, Van Poppel.*

† **Bicât, Nick.** c/o Marc Berlin, 2-4 Noel St, London W1V 3RB *tel:* 0171 287 9000 *fax:* 0171 287 3236.

* **Biggin, Tony.** 38 Manchester Rd, Southport, Merseyside *tel:* 01704 535740. *SB. Film and TV scores, choral, orch.*

Bingham, Judith. c/o Maecenas Music Ltd, 5 Bushey Close, Old Barn La, Kenley, Surrey CR8 5AU *tel:* 0181 660 4766 *fax:* 0181 668 5273. *Maecenas, Nov.*

Birney, Anthony. 17 The Drive, Gosforth, Newcastle upon Tyne NE3 4AH *tel:* 0191 285 2120. *Oratorios, opera, musicals.*

Biro, Daniel. 6 Maryland Walk, Popham St, London N1 8QZ *tel:* 0171 359 7825 *also fax. Acoustic and electronic chmbr mus; dance, film, theatre, vocal, inst.*

† **Birtwistle, Harrison.** c/o Allied Artists Agency, 42 Montpelier Sq, London SW7 1JZ *tel:* 0171 589 6243 *fax:* 0171 581 5269. *BH, UE. Opera, orch, concertos, ens, chmbr.*

* **Black OBE, Stanley.** 8 Linnell Close, London NW11 *tel:* 0181 458 4082. *Film scores.*

Blake, David. Mill Gill, Askrigg, nr Leyburn, N Yorks DL8 3HR *tel:* 01969 650364. *Nov, OUP, Schott, University of York, Music Press Ltd. Opera, orch, choral, solo cantata, chmbr, children's mus, etc.*

† **Blake OBE, Howard.** c/o Faber Music, 3 Queen Sq, London WC1N 3AU *tel:* 0171 833 7912/8 *fax:* 0171 833 7939 *email:* str@strmmm.com; http://www.fabermusic.co.uk. *Faber, Highbridge, Leng. Concert mus, film and TV scores, choral, opera, ballet, concerto.*

Blake, Michael. c/o Bardic Edition, 6 Fairfax Cres, Aylesbury, Bucks HP20 2ES *tel:* 01296 28609. *Bardic. Chmbr, inst, choral, orch.*

* **Blezard, William.** 2 Beverley Gardens, London SW13 0LZ *tel:* 0181 876 2824 *fax:* 0181 876 1860. *TP.*

* **Blunt, Marcus.** Craigs Cottage, Lochmaben, Lockerbie, Dumfries DG11 1RW *tel:* 01387 811949. *Emerson, Modus.*

* **Blyton, Carey.** Howans, Pytches Rd, Woodbridge, Suffolk IP12 1EY *tel:* 01394 383468. *ABC Book Publishing, AV Music, Bardic, Belwin, Bèrben, BH, Ches, Fand, Fox, F-E, GS, HaMaR, IMP, Kendor, Maurer, Modus Music, Nov, NWM, Oec, OUP, Rob, UE, Wein. Film and TV scores, opera, songs, chmbr, schools mus, orch.*

Bonsor, Brian. 37 Weensland Rd, Hawick, Roxburghshire TD9 9NW *tel:* 01450 372643. *Faber, IMP, Rob, Schott, UE, (sp). Rcdr, educ mus.*

*† **Bourgeois, Derek.** 43 Bute Gardens, London W6 7DR *tel:* 0181 748 6027 *also fax; email:* 10323.2604@compuserve.com; dbourgeo@spgs.mhs. compuserve.com. *Brass Wind, Ches, R Smith, Vanderbeek, Warwick. Symphonies, orch, concertos, br, wind band, choral, chmbr, org; film, TV and stage scores.*

Bousted, Donald. Burnside House, Melbourne, York YO4 4QJ *tel:* 01759 318440 *email:* 101600.3130@compuserve.com. *Composer Press Dist, Goodmusic. Concert mus, mus for stage and TV.*

* **Bower, Neville.** 1 Freeford Gardens, Lichfield, Staffs WS14 9RJ *tel:* 01543 256930. *BH, Frontier, (sp). Orch, chmbr mus, educ mus, choral, org, pno, solo song-cycles.*

Bowers-Broadbent, Christopher. 94 Colney Hatch La, London N10 1EA *tel:* 0181 883 1933 *also fax. Gal, SB. Choral, org, children's mus, operas.*

* **Boyle, Rory.** Firs Cottage, College Green, Malvern, Worcestershire WR14 3HP *tel:* 01684 573710 *also fax. ABd, BH, Ches. Orch, chmbr, choral, TV mus.*

Brandon, Patrick C. 53 Broad St, Ely, Cambs CB7 4BD *tel:* 01353 664253. *Ric. Chmbr, songs, orch and educ mus.*

Branson, David. Rock House, Exmouth Pl, Hastings, E Sussex TN34 3JA *tel:* 01424 422061. *B, Fischer (USA), Helicon (sp), MSM, Nov, SB. Concert works.*

Brindle, Reginald Smith. 219 Farleigh Rd, Warlingham, Surrey CR6 9EL *tel:* 01883 627317. *BH, Bèrben, Oec, Peters, Schott, Suv, UE. Gui solos and concertos, symphonic and chmbr mus, opera.*

Broughton, Julian. c/o GBZ Management, PO Box 11845, London SE21 8ZS *tel:* 0181 761 6565 *fax:* 0181 670 3195 *email:* gbz_mgmt@ compuserve.com. *Choral, orch, pno and chmbr.*

*† **Brown, Christopher.** 6 Station Rd, Catworth, Huntingdon, Cambs PE18 0PE *tel:* 01832 710227 *email:* musography@compuserve.com. *AA, ABd, Ches, Forsyth, Gamut, Musography, OUP, Rob. Choral mus, opera and chmbr.*

Brown, James. 29 Vesper Gate Dr, Leeds LS5 3NH. *Banks, OUP. Choral, org, vocal, pno, chmbr, orch, operetta.*

Brown, James Francis. 99 Frenches Rd, Redhill, Surrey RH1 2HS *tel:* 01737 768597 *also fax. Music Haven. Concert mus.*

Bruce, Stuart. 5 Brook Dr, Kinoulton, Nottingham NG12 3RA *tel:* 01949 81682 *also fax. Film and TV, concert works.*

† **Bryars, Gavin.** c/o Erica Bolton & Jane Quinn Ltd, 8 Pottery La, Holland Park, London W11 4LZ *tel:* 0171 221 5000 *fax:* 0171 221 8100. *Schott.*

† **Buckeridge, Corin.** Flat B, 140 Kennington La, London SE11 4UZ *tel:* 0171 207 6863. *Theatre mus.*

* **Bullard, Alan.** 11 Christ Church Ct, Ireton Rd, Colchester, Essex CO3 3AU *tel:* 01206 562607. *ABd, Banks, BH, Colne (sp), For, Harlequin, Nov, Nova, Oec, OUP, Presser, RSCM, Schott, UE. Concert mus, choral mus for adults and children.*

† **Buller, John.** c/o Oxford University Press, Repertoire Promotion, 70 Baker St, London W1M 1DJ *tel:* 0171 616 5900 *fax:* 0171 616 5901 *email:* repertoire.promotion@oup.co.uk. *OUP.*

† **Burgon, Geoffrey.** c/o Chester Music, 8-9 Frith St, London W1V 5TZ *tel:* 0171 434 0066 *fax:* 0171 287 6329 *email:* music@musicsales.co.uk. *Ches. Concert, opera, film and TV mus.*

Burn, Chris. Garden Flat, 33 Grosvenor Rd, Wanstead, London E11 2EW *tel:* 0181 989 9640. *ACTA. Contemporary mus.*

† **Burrell, Diana.** c/o United Music Publishers, 42 Rivington St, London EC2A 3BN *tel:* 0171 729 4700 *fax:* 0171 739 6549 *email:* ump@ compuserve.com; http://ourworld.compuserve.com/homepages/ump. *UMP. Inst, chmbr, orch, opera, choral and vocal mus.*

* **Burtch, Mervyn.** 5 Oakfield St, Ystrad Mynach, Hengoed, Caerphilly County Borough CF82 7AF *tel:* 01443 812100 *also fax. Ashdown, Banks, Curiad, Griffiths, Gwynn, Rob, Vanderbeek, WC, WMIC. Children's opera, choral, chmbr mus.*

Burton, Jonathan. 12 Corner Green, Blackheath, London SE3 9JJ *tel:* 0181 852 7399.

Burton, Ken. c/o J Audrey Ellison International Artists' Management, 135 Stevenage Rd, London SW6 6PB *tel:* 0171 381 9751 *fax:* 0171 381 2406.

* **Bush, Geoffrey.** 43 Corringham Rd, London NW11 7BS *tel:* 0181 458 3928. *Nov, Ramsey, SB, TP. Songs, choral mus, opera, orch, chmbr.*

Bush, Glyn. 17 Wollaston Rd, Dorchester, Dorset DT1 1EQ *tel:* 01305 266567; 0121 603 0033 *fax:* 0121 603 0060 *email:* diffdrum@dircon. co.uk. *Article Don Music. Theatre, film and TV documentary scores, musicals, jingles, signature, children's, youth radio and TV, electronic mus.*

Butler, Martin. c/o Oxford University Press, Repertoire Promotion, 70 Baker St, London W1M 1DJ *tel:* 0171 616 5900 *fax:* 0171 616 5901 *email:* repertoire.promotion@oup.co.uk. *OUP.*

Butt, James. 12 Northfield Rd, Onehouse, Stowmarket, Suffolk IP14 3HF *tel:* 01449 613388. *BC, Belwin, BH, Cramer, EMI, OUP, SB, Sph, TP, WC. Film, TV, opera, musicals, chmbr, orch, choral, educ, mus for children.*

Butterworth MBE, Arthur. Pohjola, Dales Av, Embsay, Skipton, N Yorks BD23 6PE *tel:* 01756 792968. *BH, Brass Wind, Ches, Comus, Feld, For, Léduc, Molenaar, Nov, Peters, Smith, Vanderbeek. Orch, symphonic, br band, chmbr mus.*

* **Butterworth, Neil.** 1 Roderick Pl, West Linton, Peeblesshire EH46 7ES *tel:* 01968 661112. *Banks, Belwin, Brunton, Cathedral, Chiltern, Fentone, Francis, Garland (US), Nova, Nov, NWM, Oec, Ric, Rob, WC.*

* **Cannon, Philip.** 25 Ansdell St, London W8 5BN *tel:* 0171 937 6768. *Kronos (sp), Seresta, Tech. Opera, symphony, choral, chmbr.*

* **Caradon, Sulyen R.** 76 Lower Oldfield Pk, Bath BA2 3HP *tel:* 01225 313531. *Da Capo, (sp). W/wind, vocal, choral, ecological and spiritual mus.*

* **Carhart, David.** 20 Standish Rd, London W6 9AL *tel:* 0181 748 0935 *also fax. Ric. Orch, pno, chmbr, songs.*

† **Carpenter, Gary.** The Old Bakery, 10 Seaview, Hoylake, Wirral, Merseyside L47 2DD *tel:* 0151 632 6631; 0976 775561 *fax:* 0151 632 3275. *BH, Camden, Donemus, Ric, Sparta Florida, Wein. Brass, ens, inst, band.*

* **Carr, Paul.** 33 Guildford St, Brighton, E Sussex BN1 3LS *tel:* 01273 770392. *Allans Music, Comus, Cramer, Nova Music, Presser (USA), Rob.*

* **Carr, Peter Hutchinson.** 8 Hempstead Rd, Saltdean, Sussex BN2 8QD *tel:* 01273 305213. *Anglia, Corn.*

Carter, Andrew. c/o Oxford University Press, Repertoire Promotion, 70 Baker St, London W1M 1DJ *tel:* 0171 616 5900 *fax:* 0171 616 5901 *email:* repertoire.promotion@oup.co.uk. *OUP.*

Carter, Elliott. c/o Boosey & Hawkes Music Publishing Ltd, 295 Regent St, London W1R 8JH *tel:* 0171 580 2060 *fax:* 0171 637 3490 *email:* composers@boosey.com. *Chmbr mus, orch, vocal, ens and concertos.*

Cashian, Philip. 8 Arthurdon Rd, London SE4 1JU *tel:* 0181 318 6998 *also fax.*

Cashmore, Donald. Cottage End, 27 King Alfred Way, Newton Poppleford, Sidmouth EX10 0DG *tel:* 01395 567923. *Nov, OUP. Cantatas, anthems, songs, carols.*

Casken, John. Craigside, Reservoir Rd, Whaley Bridge, High Peak, Derbyshire SK23 7BW *email:* john.casken@man.ac.uk. *Schott.*

Catán, Daniel. c/o Boosey & Hawkes, 295 Regent St, London W1R 8JH *tel:* 0171 580 2060 *fax:* 0171 637 3490 *email:* composers@boosey.com. *Opera, voice and orch.*

* **Chandler, Mary.** Parson's Cottage, Bisley, Stroud, Glos GL6 7BB *tel:* 01452 770502. *Nova, Phylloscopus. Wind chmbr mus.*

† **Chappell, Herbert.** c/o London Management (Marc Berlin), 2-4 Noel St, London W1V 3RB *tel:* 0171 287 9000 *fax:* 0171 287 3036. *Ches, Clarabella, UE, WC. Film and TV scores, opera, orch, educ.*

† **Chapple, Brian.** 31 Warwick Rd, New Barnet, Herts EN5 5EQ *tel:* 0181 449 8610. *AA, ABd, Ches, OUP. Choral, orch, inst.*

Cheshire, John. 3 Maes Yr Hafod, Llanfairtalhaiarn, Clwyd LL22 8SA *tel:* 01745 720708.

Chilcott, Bob. c/o Oxford University Press, Repertoire Promotion, 70 Baker St, London W1M 1DJ *tel:* 0171 616 5900 *fax:* 0171 616 5901 *email:* repertoire.promotion@oup.co.uk. *OUP.*

Chin, Unsuk. c/o Boosey & Hawkes, 295 Regent St, London W1R 8JH *tel:* 0171 580 2060 *fax:* 0171 637 3490 *email:* composers@boosey.com. *Orch, ens, chmbr, electronic, pno.*

Christie, Michael. Basement Flat, 16d Hampstead Hill Gardens, London NW3 2PL *tel:* 0171 435 0914 *fax:* 0171 794 3610. *Composers' Library. Opera, mus theatre, film scores, inst mus, songs.*

* **Churches, Richard.** c/o 44 Mendip Av, Worle, Weston-super-Mare, Avon BS22 0HW *tel:* 01934 513973. *Andresier, Frontier. Contemporary and educ mus.*

Clark, Philip. 96a Wandsworth Bridge Rd, London SW6 2TF *tel:* 0171 731 0973. *Orch, ens, chmbr, inst, jazz.*

† **Clarke, Nigel.** 7 West St, Ewell Village, Surrey KT17 1UZ *tel:* 0181 393 0873. *Brass Wind, Maecenas, Nov. Contemporary mus.*

Clayton, Kenny. c/o Brunskill Management Limited, Suite 8a, 169 Queen's Gate, London SW7 5HE *tel:* 0171 581 3388 *fax:* 0171 589 9460 *email:* 101234.2025@compuserve.com.

* **Clemson, Gareth.** Tillywhally Cottage, Milnathort, Kinross-shire KY13 7RN *tel:* 01577 864297. *Tillywhally Arts (sp). Chmbr mus, pno, orch, wind band, songs.*

Cliff, Tony. 27 Beccles Rd, Brooklands, Sale, Cheshire M33 3RP *tel:* 0161 962 3269 *also fax. Cascade, Kirklees, Magnolia Manor Ltd (USA), Rosehill, SB, Studio. Choral, inst, orch, jazz and commercial songs, ens, br band, educ mus.*

Cloke, Geoffrey. Dawlish Community College, Elm Grove Rd, Dawlish, Devon EX7 0BY *tel:* 01626 862318 *fax:* 01626 866238. *Orch, chmbr, vocal, opera.*

Clucas, Humphrey. 19 Norman Rd, Sutton, Surrey *tel:* 0181 642 3233. *KM, Oec, OUP. Choral, org mus.*

* **Coates, Leon.** 35 Comely Bank Pl, Edinburgh EH4 1ER *tel:* 0131 332 4553. *Hardie Press. Chmbr, vocal, org, concert band, orch.*

Coatman, Graham. 4 Sunny Bank, Shipley, W Yorks BD18 3RP *tel:* 01274 599379 *also fax. Opera, mus theatre, songs, orch, chmbr, choral, educ.*

* **Coe, Michael.** Karelia, 16 Gorse Ridge Dr, Baslow, Derbyshire DE45 1SL *tel:* 01246 582121. *Chandos, Hope, HRGB. Choral, orch, wind band, hand bells, educ.*

Cole, Keith Ramon. 25 Vale Rd, Ramsgate, Kent CT11 9LT *tel:* 01843 595024. *BH, Camden Music, Clark Inc, Emerson, Sam French, Ganymede (sp). Musicals, educ mus.*

† **Collier, Graham.** 38 Shell Rd, London SE13 7TW *tel:* 0181 692 6250 *fax:* 0181 692 5213 *email:* graham@jazzword.demon.co.uk. *Film and TV scores, jazz.*

Conway, Joe. 22 Brook Court, Harrow Rd, London E11 3PP *tel:* 0181 539 5933. *Bardic, (sp). Inst, chmbr, str orch.*

Cook, Douglas. Bal Row, Boskednan, Newmill, Penzance, Cornwall TR20 8XX *tel:* 01736 363677 *fax:* 01736 366925. *Schott. Pno, fl, br quintet, vc, jazz pieces, film scores.*

* **Cooke, Mervyn.** Music Dept, University of Nottingham, Nottingham NG7 2RD *tel:* 0115 951 4762 *fax:* 0115 951 4756 *email:* mervyn.cooke@ nottingham.ac.uk.

Coombes, Douglas. 23 Hitchin St, Biggleswade, Beds SG18 8AX *tel:* 01767 316521 *fax:* 01767 317221. *BBC, Brass Wind, EMI, Early Learning, Lindsay, Music Sales, OUP, Rob. Orch, opera, musicals, choral, educ, vocal, ens.*

Cooney, John. 86 Bromfelde Rd, London SW4 6PR *tel:* 0171 498 2643 *also fax. Orch, ens, ballet, opera, educ, film scores.*

Cooper, David. 12 Cornmill Cres, Norristhorpe, Liversedge, W Yorks WF15 7DU *tel:* 01924 409051 *fax:* 01132 332583. *Samuel King, (sp). Inst, vocal, electronic, film.*

*† **Cooper, Lindsay.** 6b Burton Pl, London WC1H 9AH *tel:* 0171 388 3539 *fax:* 0171 383 7582. *(Sp). Film, TV, theatre, dance, songs, concertos, chmbr.*

* **Copley, Peter.** 2a Fairlight Pl, Brighton BN2 3AH *tel:* 01273 672222. *Ric, TP. Orch, choral, pno solo, gui, chmbr, film.*

Corp, Ronald. 41 Aberdare Gardens, London NW6 3AL *tel:* 0171 625 4641 *fax:* 0171 625 4876. *Nov, OUP, SB. Choral and orch.*

* **Cowdell, Alexander.** 8 Blendon Terrace, Plumstead Common, London SE18 7RR *tel:* 0181 854 5167. *Frontier Press. Pno, vocal, ens, orch.*

Cowles, Colin E. Keens Barn Cottage, Keens La, Othery, Bridgwater, Somerset TA7 0PU *tel:* 01823 698162. *BH, Cascade, Ches, Chiltern, Cottage Harmony, Fentone, Griffiths, Headline, PP, Polyphonic, Ric, Spartan, Studio, Tyne. Orch, wind mus.*

Cox, David. 5 Downs View Close, Orpington, Kent BR6 7SU *tel:* 01689 854821. *Belwin, Curwen, Elk, Nov, OUP, Ric. Choral, pno, vn and songs.*

Cox, David Harold. Dept of Music, University College Cork, Eire *tel:* 00 353 212 76871 ext 2123 *fax:* 00 353 212 71595. *Seesaw Music Corp.*

Coxon, Christopher. 18 St Julian's Rd, St Alban's, Herts AL1 2AZ.

Crane, Laurence. Flat 4, 17 Harecourt Rd, London N1 2LW *tel:* 0171 704 6541 *also fax.*

* **Crawford, Robert.** 12 Inverleith Terrace, Edinburgh EH3 5NS *tel:* 0131 556 3600. *Chmbr mus, pno, orch.*

*† **Cresswell, Lyell.** 4 Leslie Pl, Edinburgh EH4 1NQ *tel:* 0131 332 9181 *also fax. Wai-te-ta Press. Orch, chmbr, choral and vocal.*

Crosse, Gordon. c/o Oxford University Press, Repertoire Promotion, 70 Baker St, London W1M 1DJ *tel:* 0171 616 5900 *fax:* 0171 616 5901 *email:* repertoire.promotion@oup.co.uk. *OUP.*

* **Crump, Peter.** 21 Kingsway Rd, Evington, Leicester LE5 5TL *tel:* 0116 273 6257. *TP. Chmbr, songs, pno, choral.*

Cunneen, Paddy. c/o Jeffrey Cambell Management, 18 Queen Anne St, London W1M 0HB *tel:* 0171 637 0993 *fax:* 0171 637 0985.

* **Curtis, Matthew.** 152 Granville Rd, London NW2 2LD *tel:* 0181 458 2492. *(Sp). Symphonic, light orch, songs, choral mus.*

Dakin, Charles. Lane Cottage, Norbury, Bishops Castle, Shropshire SY9 5DX *tel:* 01588 650307. *BH, Dorn, Hin, (sp). Orch, chmbr, educ.*

† **Dalby, John.** 63 Gunnersbury La, London W3 8HG *tel:* 0181 992 1269. *WC. Film and TV scores, musicals.*

*† **Dalby, Martin.** 23 Muirpark Way, Drymen, Stirlingshire, Scotland G63 0DX *tel:* 01360 660427 *fax:* 01360 660397 *email:* pescatore@dial. pipex.com. *BH, Ches, Leng, Nov. Concert mus, film and TV.*

Dale, Gordon. 17 White Horse Sq, Hereford HR4 0HD. *EMI, For, Piper. Mus for schools, colleges and amateurs.*

Daltry, Stephen. 8 Tavistock Av, Walthamstow, London E17 6HR *tel:* 0181 531 5362 *also fax. Lantern. Pno, vocal, film scores, musicals.*

* **Dankworth CBE, John.** The Old Rectory, Wavendon, Milton Keynes, Bucks MK17 8LT *tel:* 01908 583151 *fax:* 01908 584414. *Jazz, orch, film scores.*

Darlow, Denys. The Coach House, Drury La, Redmarley, D'Abitot, Glos GL19 3JX *tel:* 01531 650616 *also fax. Banks, Lorenz, Nov, OUP. Choral and orch.*

Darnborough, Jonathan. 503a Kingston Rd, Wimbledon Chase, London SW20 8JP *tel:* 0181 395 7433 *fax:* 0181 543 6735 *email:* midman503a@

aol.com; http://members.aol.com/midman503a. *Solo pno, vocal, chmbr, orch.*

Davies, Eiluned. 40 The Limes Av, New Southgate, London N11 1RH *tel:* 0181 368 8202. *Bardic, Gwynn, Guild for the Promotion of Welsh Music. Solo songs, part songs, pno arrangements.*

Davies, Hugh. 25 Albert Rd, London N4 3RR *tel:* 0171 272 5508. *(Sp). Avant-garde electronic and inst mus.*

Davies, Terry. c/o Jeffrey Cambell Management, 18 Queen Anne St, London W1M 0HB *tel:* 0171 637 0993 *fax:* 0171 637 0985.

† **Davis, Carl.** c/o Faber Music Ltd, 3 Queen Sq, London WC1N 3AU *tel:* 0171 278 7436 *fax:* 0171 278 3817. *EMI, Euston, Faber, Leeds, Threefold. Film, TV, musicals, ballets, concert works.*

Davis, Oliver. 76 Raleigh Rd, London N8 0JA *tel:* 0181 374 1124 *fax:* 0181 374 1125. *Orch, incidental and commercial mus.*

* **Dawes, Julian.** 31 Primrose Hill Rd, London NW3 3DG *tel:* 0171 722 4117. *Concert mus, film, TV scores, musicals.*

de Haan, Stefan. 96 Highgate Hill, London N6 5HE *tel:* 0181 340 4991. *Highgate Music, Music Sales, Schott. Wind, br, educ mus, tpt concerto, chmbr, orch, ens, childrens' records.*

de Souza, Christopher. Westbrook Farm Cottage, Boxford, Newbury, Berks RG20 8DL *tel:* 01488 608503. *Orch, choral, chmbr, radio, TV.*

Deacon, Nigel. 56 Arbor Rd, Croft, Leics LE9 3GD *tel:* 01455 284096 *fax:* 0116 223 1999. *Sutton Elms Publications (Sp). Pno solo, original compositions and folk-tune arrangements.*

Dean, Roger. 23 Westfield Terrace, Longford, Gloucester GL2 9BA *tel:* 01452 522379 *fax:* 00 61 2 527 2139 *email:* r.dean@hri.edu.au. *Open University Press, Soma Recording, Sounds Australian, Red House Tall Poppies Recording. Contemporary, electro-acoustic mus.*

* **Dedman, Malcolm.** 27 Pentland Av, Thornbury, Bristol BS12 2YB *tel:* 01454 413917. *Anglian, Obelisk. Contemporary, children's mus.*

Del Tredici, David. c/o Boosey & Hawkes Music Publishing Ltd, 295 Regent St, London W1R 8JH *tel:* 0171 580 2060 *fax:* 0171 637 3490 *email:* composers@boosey.com. *Solo voice and orch, solo voice and ens, orch, pno.*

Dench, Chris. c/o United Music Publishers Ltd, 42 Rivington St, London EC2A 3BN *tel:* 0171 729 4700 *fax:* 0171 739 6549 *email:* ump @compuserve.com; http://ourworld.compuserve.com/homepages/ump. *Australian Music Centre, BMG (Rome), UMP. Inst, chmbr, vocal and orch.*

† **Dennis, Brian.** 30 Runnemede Rd, Egham, Surrey TW20 9BL *tel:* 01784 436508 *fax:* 01784 439441 *email:* uhwmozi@vms.rhbnc.ac.uk. *Forward, Frontier, Nov, UE, (sp).*

Denny, Louise. Arun House, 58 Seddlescombe Rd South, St Leonards on Sea, Sussex TN38 0TJ *tel:* 01424 714222. *Bandleader. Military, light orch mus.*

* **Denwood, Russell.** 38 Littledale, Pickering, N Yorks YO18 8PS *tel:* 01751 367473. *Cascade, Emerson, ME, Muzika, Phoenix, Phylloscopus. Educ mus, wind ens, w/wind, chmbr.*

Diamond, Eileen. Flat 7, Allington Ct, Allington St, London SW1E 5ED *tel:* 0171 828 1335. *Black, IMP, UE, Ward Lock Educational, WC. Educ, songs, perc, rounds, musicals for children. Schools, radio and TV.*

† **Dickinson, Peter.** Foxborough House, Aldeburgh, Suffolk IP15 5QP *tel:* 01728 454540. *Nov.*

Dillon, James. c/o Peters Edition Ltd, 10-12 Baches St, London N1 6DN *tel:* 0171 553 4030 *fax:* 0171 490 4921 *email:* promotion@edition-peters.com; http://www.edition-peters.com.

Dillon, Shaun. 34 Richmond St, Aberdeen AB25 4TR *tel:* 01224 630954. *Lomond, Music to Measure, SB. All mus including Scottish traditional.*

Dodgson, Stephen. 4 Scarth Rd, London SW13 0ND *tel:* 0181 876 6901. *ABd, Bèrben, BH, Ches, Eschig, Möseler, Nogatz, Nov, OUP, Ric, SB, Schott, WC.*

* **Don, Nigel.** 12 Kelso Pl, Dundee DD2 1SL *tel:* 01382 667251 *fax:* 01382 640775. *Church mus, inst, vocal, concert mus.*

* **Dorward, David.** 10 Dean Park Cres, Edinburgh EH4 1PH *tel:* 0131 332 3002. *Curwen, Gal, GMC, OUP, SB, Scottish Music Publishing. Radio, film, TV, concert works, opera, musicals.*

Douglas, James. c/o Eschenbach Editions, 28 Dalrymple Cres, Edinburgh EH9 2NX *tel:* 0131 667 3633. *Eschenbach.*

Douglas, Johnny. 39 Tadorne Rd, Tadworth, Surrey KT20 5TF *tel:* 01737 812922. *Anglia, EMI, Fil, KPM, Marlyn, Wein, WC. Film, TV, musicals.*

* **Downes, Professor Andrew.** 2 Church St, West Hagley, W Midlands DY9 0NA *tel:* 01562 886625 *fax:* 0121 331 5906. *Lynwood. Orch, choral, chmbr mus, songs, small ens, solo inst, voice.*

Downie, Gordon. 21 Chamberlain Rd, Cardiff CF4 2LW *tel:* 01222 568392. *Editio Musica Budapest.*

Downing, Jaemus. The Allans, Dunheved Rd, Launceston, Cornwall PL15 9JF *tel:* 01566 775742. *Treborne (sp), Trelaske (sp). Choral, chmbr mus, carols.*

* **Drakeford, Richard.** 30 Dovehouse Close, Upper Wolvercote, N Oxford OX2 8BG *tel:* 01865 554836. *Elk, Nov, Oec, Schott. Songs, chmbr (br, wind, str), choral, pno, org, church opera.*

Drayton, Paul. 73 Polmear Parc, Par, Cornwall PL24 2AU *tel:* 01726 813529. *Hinshaw (USA), KS Music, Nov, OUP, Ramsey. Vocal, choral, opera, inst, educ mus.*

† **Druce, Duncan.** Westfield House, 155 West End, Netherthong, Huddersfield HD7 2YJ *tel:* 01484 683158 *fax:* 01484 689408. *Corda Music, For, Nov. Orch, chmbr, choral, reconstructions and transcriptions of classical mus.*

* **Duarte, John.** 25 Brunswick Grove, London N11 1HN *tel:* 0181 361 2731. *Bèrben, Broekmans, Chappell, Ches, Columbia, Criterion, Eschig, Faber, Gendai, Hampton, Lemoine, Margaux, Norsk Musik, Nov, Novascribe, Ric, Schott, UE, Wise, Yolotl, Zanibon, Zimmerman. Gui mus.*

Dubery, David Leigh. 2 Boardman Rd, Higher Crumpsall, Manchester M8 4WJ *tel:* 0161 740 2762. *MSM, Rob, Sunshine Music Co. English song, chmbr, musicals.*

Duro, Stephen. 33 Belmont Close, Uxbridge, Middx UB8 1RF *tel:* 01895 232055 *also fax. ABd, Chappell, Spartan, Stanza. Inst, jazz, band mus, choral.*

Duxbury, Rosemary. 74 Stoneygate Rd, Leicester LE2 2BN *tel:* 0116 270 2255. *Chmbr, pno, vocal, choral, orch and film.*

Earl, David. 21 Kineton Rd, Oxford OX1 4PG *tel:* 01865 728281 *also fax. Nov. Symphonic, ballet, chmbr, film.*

Earle, Melvyn Stuart. 53 The Street, Blundeston, Suffolk NR32 5AA. *Orch, chmbr, inst, ens.*

East, Harold. 11 Bettridge Rd, London SW6 3QH *tel:* 0171 736 6109. *Brass Wind, Ches, Ric, Wolfe.*

Edwards, Paul C. c/o Middle Farm, Oakley, Beds MK43 7RG. *BBMP, Jubilate Hymns, Oec, RSCM. Church mus.*

† **Elias, Brian.** c/o Chester Music, 8-9 Frith St, London W1V 5TZ *tel:* 0171 434 0066 *fax:* 0171 287 6329 *email:* music@musicsales.co.uk. *Ches. Chmbr, orch, vocal.*

† **Ellerby, Martin.** 1 St Hilda's Close, College Gardens, London SW17 7UL *tel:* 0181 767 0081 *also fax. Brass Wind, Maecenas, Rosehill, Studio Music.*

* **Ellis, David.** 14 Patch La, Bramhall, Cheshire SK7 1JB *tel:* 0161 440 9007 *also fax. Birnbach, Da Capo, For, Gal, Leng, Nov, Wein, Yorke. Contemporary classical, educ, jazz orch.*

Ellis, James Antony. 19 South St, Lewes, E Sussex BN7 2BT *tel:* 01273 473745 *also fax; email:* oae@premier.co.uk. *Ric. Opera, vocal, inst.*

* **Elton, Antony.** Badger Bungalow, 41 Findon Av, Witton Gilbert, Durham DH7 6RF *tel:* 0191 371 2522. *Leeds, Nov, Scores, Essex, Toad (sp). Songs, song cycles, pno suites, mus for drama, ballet, choral, chmbr mus including w/wind quartets and str quartet, semi-improvisation.*

* **Elwyn-Edwards, Dilys.** Caerwys, 48 Cae Gwyn, Caernarfon, Gwynedd LL55 1LL *tel:* 01286 672820. *Curiad, Guild for the Promotion of Welsh Music, Gwasg Gwynedd, Gwynn, Pantycelyn, Rob. Songs, choral works.*

* **Emmans, Les.** 23 Welwyn Av, Allestree, Derby DE22 2JR *tel:* 01332 552519 *also fax. DOW, Lindens Music (sp). Ballad operas, schools, church, songs, chmbr and inst.*

† **Emmerson, Simon.** 15 Holligrave Rd, Bromley, Kent BR1 3PJ *tel:* 0181 460 4997 *fax:* 0181 460 0540 *email:* s.emmerson@city.ac.uk. *Live electro-acoustic mus.*

Emsley, Richard. 168 Carlyle Rd, London W5 4BJ *tel:* 0181 847 5074. *(Sp).*

† **Endrich, Archer (Tom).** 12 Goodwood Way, Cepen Park South, Chippenham, Wilts SN14 0SY *tel:* 01249 461361 *email:* tendrich@cix. compulink.co.uk. *Eul, Kunz. Chmbr, electronic, orch, vocal, theatrical.*

Erber, James. 258 Perry Hill, Sydenham, London SE6 4HD *tel:* 0181 291 6121 *also fax. Ric.*

Evans, Colin. 30 Ravensroost, Beulah Hill, London SE19 3LN *tel:* 0181 771 7467 *also fax; email:* vista222@dircon.co.uk. *Belwin, BH, Ches, Nov, OUP, Paxton, Schott. School and educ mus.*

Ewers, Tim. 79 Erlanger Rd, London SE14 5TQ *tel:* 0171 652 4575 *also fax. Forward. Concert mus.*

*† **Fanshawe, David.** Fanshawe Enterprises, PO Box 574, Marlborough, Wilts SN8 2SP *tel:* 01672 520211 *fax:* 01672 521151. *IMC, OUP, WC. Choral, orch, pno, vocal, film, TV, ethnic mus recordings.*

Farnon, Robert. La Falaise, St Martins, Guernsey, Channel Islands *tel:* 01481 38986 *fax:* 01481 38087. *Carlin, Feld, Leeds, R Smith, Rediffusion, WC, Zomba.*

* **Farquhar, David.** 15 Nottingham St, Wellington 5, New Zealand *tel:* 00 64 4 476 8146 *also fax. Bèrben, Nov, Otago, Pro Arte, Waiteata, Yorke. Concert mus, opera and mus for children.*

FeBland, Jonathan. c/o 9 Hendon Hall Ct, Parson St, Hendon, London NW4 1QY *fax:* 0181 951 1005/5219. *Bardic, Samuel King, UE. Contemporary, educ and film mus.*

Feeney, Philip. c/o Robert White Artist Management, 182 Moselle Av, London N22 6EX *tel:* 0181 881 6914 *fax:* 0181 888 9662 *email:* rwhiteam@aol.com. *Concert mus, dance and ballet scores.*

Fenby OBE, Eric. 1 Raincliffe Ct, Stepney Rd, Scarborough, N Yorks YO12 5BT *tel:* 01723 372988. *BH.*

† **Fenton, George.** 1 Barrett St, London W1M 5HG *tel:* 0171 486 6676 *fax:* 0171 486 0789. *Shogun. Film, TV and theatre scores.*

* **Ferguson, Howard.** 51 Barton Rd, Cambridge CB3 9LG *tel:* 01223 359206. *ABd, BH, OUP, SB. Orch, choral, chmbr mus, pno, songs.*

Fernández, Agustín. Dept of Music, University of Newcastle, Newcastle upon Tyne NE1 7RU *tel:* 0191 222 7636 *email:* agustin.fernandez@ newcastle.ac.uk. *Chmbr, orch, electro-acoustic, opera.*

Ferneyhough, Brian. c/o Peters Edition Ltd, 10-12 Baches St, London N1 6DN *tel:* 0171 553 4030 *fax:* 0171 490 4921 *email:* promotion@edition-peters.com; http://www.edition-peters.com.

† **Fiddy, John.** Fruit Farm House, Foxton, Cambridge CB2 6RT *tel:* 01763 208610 *fax:* 01763 208241 *email:* johnfiddymusic@dial.pipex.com. *John Fiddy Music (sp).*

Field, Robin. 4 Ellergreen, Burneside, Kendal, Cumbria LA9 5SD *tel:* 01539 729226. *(Sp). Choral, chmbr, orch, electro-acoustic, vocal.*

Finnerty, Adrian J. 10 Brandon Dr, Bearsden, Glasgow G61 3LN *tel:* 0141 943 1517.

Finnissy, Michael. 11 Mill Rd, Steyning, W Sussex BN44 3LN *tel:* c/o 0171 616 5900 *fax:* c/o 0171 616 5901. *Mod Ed, OUP, Suv, UE, UMP. Opera, pno, chmbr, ecclesiastical choral mus.*

Firsova, Elena. c/o Boosey & Hawkes, 295 Regent St, London W1R 8JH *tel:* 0171 580 2060 *fax:* 0171 637 3490 *email:* composers@boosey.com. *Orch, ens, chmbr, vocal.*

* **Fish, Adrian Vernon.** Brownson House, Grenofen, Tavistock, Devon PL19 9ER *tel:* 01822 615730 *also fax. Brunton, KM, Oec, RSCM.*

* **Fisher, David.** Holly Tree House, 13 Braunstone La East, Leicester LE3 2FD *tel:* 0116 291 8711. *Rob. Choral, vocal, chmbr and mus for children.*

Fitkin, Graham. 4 Lisbon Terrace, St Buryan, W Cornwall *tel:* 01736 810927.

Fleming, Tim. 31 Huddersfield Road, Brighouse, W Yorks HD6 3RQ *tel:* 01484 717173 *also fax. Choral, musicals, oratorios, TV drama, mus for special needs.*

Fletcher, Andrew. 230 The Avenue, Acocks Green, Birmingham B27 6NU *tel:* 0121 706 5708 *fax:* 0121 608 2990 *email:* a_fletcher@compuserve. com. *KM, Oec, OUP (New York), RSCM. Church and org mus.*

* **Fligg, David.** 32 High Moor Cres, Moortown, Leeds LS17 6DU *tel:* 0113 268 7440.

* **Flood, Philip.** 39 Kynaston Rd, Stoke Newington, London N16 0EA *tel:* 0171 249 7208. *CMC, Haven, Warwick. Orch, chmbr, electro-acoustic, dance.*

Floyd, Carlisle. c/o Boosey & Hawkes Music Publishing Ltd, 295 Regent St, London W1R 8JH *tel:* 0171 580 2060 *fax:* 0171 637 3490 *email:* composers@boosey.com. *Opera, mus drama, voice and orch.*

* **Forbes, Sebastian.** Octave House, Boughton Hall Av, Send, Woking, Surrey GU23 7DF *tel:* 01483 211785/259317 *fax:* 01483 259386 *email:* s.forbes@surrey.ac.uk. *ABd, Bosworth, Cathedral, Ches, Nov, OUP, SB, Yorke. Orch, chmbr, choral.*

* **Forshaw, David Campbell.** 40 Howards La, Eccleston, St Helens, Merseyside WA10 5HY *tel:* 01744 28456. *Da Capo. Choral, orch, chmbr, educ, pno.*

Foss, Lukas. c/o Boosey & Hawkes, 295 Regent St, London W1R 8JH *tel:* 0171 580 2060 *fax:* 0171 637 3490 *email:* composers@boosey.com. *Opera, orch, concertos, chmbr, vocal.*

* **Foster, Anthony.** 1 Cawley Rd, Chichester, W Sussex PO19 1UZ *tel:* 01243 780134. *Belwin, Brunton, Epworth, Free, Oec, OUP. Sacred, keyboard, musicals.*

* **Foster, Derek.** 41 Gloucester Ct, Kew Rd, Kew, Richmond, Surrey TW9 3EA *tel:* 0181 940 8373. *Anglian, Modus.*

* **Fowler, Jennifer.** 21 Deodar Rd, London SW15 2NP *tel:* 0181 788 7156 *email:* 100611.2060@compuserve.com. *Sounds Australian, UE.*

Fox, Christopher. 3 Old Moor La, York YO2 2QE *tel:* 01904 704645 *email:* p.c.fox@hud.ac.uk. *Fox Edition.*

*† **Fox, Erika.** 78 Peterborough Rd, London SW6 3EB *tel:* 0171 736 7707. *Chmbr, theatre, solo inst, vocal, opera.*

* **Francis, Alun.** c/o London Artists (LA), 3 Wheelers Ct, Scholars La, Stratford upon Avon, Warwicks CV37 6HE *tel:* 01789 269247. *Bote & Bock, Peters, Wein. Symphony, chmbr mus, film and TV scores.*

* **Fraser, Bruce.** 32 Bankton Pk, Kingskettle, Fife KY15 7PY *tel:* 01337 830974 *fax:* 01337 830653. *Bandleader, Ches, Fortune, Kirklees Music, Lomond Music, Obrasso (Switzerland), Smith & Co, Studio.*

* **Freedman, Latif.** 163 Gwydir St, Cambridge CB1 2LJ *tel:* 01223 322712. *Mercia. Vocal, choral, inst, solo, ens, drama, ballet.*

* **Fribbins, Peter.** 44 Rosecroft Dr, Watford, Herts WD1 3JQ *tel:* 01923 223581 *fax:* 01923 334696. *Edward Kassner Ltd, Music Haven.*

* **Gange, Kenneth.** 129 Dartmouth Av, Cannock, Staffs WS11 1EJ *tel:* 01543 577447. *B, Banks, Cramer, Evans, Gal, Nov, Oec, OUP, Piper, Rob.*

Gardiner, Ian. 11 Hampden Rd, Higher Tranmere, Birkenhead L42 5LH *tel:* 0151 647 8022 *email:* lpaigard@lipa.ac.uk. *Concert mus, mus for silent film, TV mus.*

* **Gardner CBE, John.** 20 Firswood Av, Epsom, Surrey KT19 0PR *tel:* 0181 393 7181 *also fax. AA, BH, CUP, For, Hansen, Hinshaw, Lorenz, Nov, OUP, Schott, SB. Opera, choral, symphonic, chmbr, vocal, inst.*

* **Gardner, Robert Neil.** Slip Cottage, Hawkley, Liss, Hants GU33 6NH *tel:* 01730 827315. *Inst, orch, chmbr mus.*

Gaze, Nigel. Priory House, 35 Priory La, Penwortham, Preston, Lancs PR1 0AR *tel:* 01772 743821. *Brunton, Oec. Choral, org.*

Geddes, John Maxwell. 21 Cleveden Rd, Glasgow G12 0PQ *tel:* 0141 357 2941. *Berben (Italy), Periwinkle (UK), Peterson (California). Chmbr, symphonic, film and TV, orch, band.*

Geesin, Ron. Headrest, Street End La, Broadoak, Heathfield, E Sussex TN21 8TU *tel:* 01435 863994 *fax:* 01435 867027 *email:* geesinr@dean. port.ac.uk; http://www.ice.net/~porta/geesin.htm. *Installations, (Sp). Ballet, opera, film scores, radio mus.*

Gibbs, Alan. 8 St Margaret's Dr, Twickenham, Middx TW1 1QN *tel:* 0181 892 9888 *fax:* 0181 891 2174. *Bardic, B, Lawson-Gould, RSCM, WC. Choral, org, chmbr, orch, radio drama.*

Gibson, Stephen. 40 Campbell Close, Streatham, London SW16 6NG *tel:* 0181 677 8473 *fax:* 0181 877 3494 *email:* 100105.201@ compuserve.com. *Ararat (sp), R Smith. Mus theatre, concert mus.*

Gifford, Keith. 77 Gayton House, Knapp Rd, London E3 4BY *tel:* 0171 987 2887 *also fax. Orch, chmbr.*

*† **Gilbert, Anthony.** Magpies, Teuthill, Tarvin Rd, Alvanley, Cheshire WA6 9AL *tel:* 01928 723476 *fax:* 0161 273 7611 *email:* sallyw@rncm.ac.uk. *For, Schott, UP, University of York Music Press. Mus theatre, orch, chmbr, vocal, ens.*

Gilder, Eric. 21 Fieldend, Twickenham, Middx TW1 4TF *tel:* 0181 892 0742. *Cramer, Curwen, Evans, French, Gay, Manor, Ric. Musicals, orch, choral, chmbr, songs.*

* **Gipps, Ruth.** Tickerage Castle, Pound La, Framfield, Uckfield, E Sussex TN22 5RT *tel:* 01825 890348. *Emerson, For. Symphonies, choral, chmbr, wind mus.*

Glanert, Detlev. c/o Boosey & Hawkes, 295 Regent St, London W1R 8JH *tel:* 0171 580 2060 *fax:* 0171 637 3490 *email:* composers@boosey.com. *Opera, orch, concertos, ens and chmbr.*

Glass, Jennifer. 24 Hill Top, London NW11 6EE *tel:* 0181 455 1106 *also fax. Emerson, Griffiths. Ens, vocal mus.*

*† **Glasser, Stanley.** 8 Pendlebury House, Master Gunner Pl, London SE18 4NQ *tel:* 0181 856 9923. *Bosworth, Essex, Faber, Griffiths, Lemmel, MR, Piers, Ric, Woza. Orch, choral, theatre mus, educ.*

Globokar, Vinko. c/o Allied Artists Agency, 42 Montpelier Sq, London SW7 1JZ *tel:* 0171 589 6243 *fax:* 0171 581 5269.

* **Glyn, Gareth.** Frogwy Fawr, Llangwyllog, Llangefni, Anglesey LL77 7PX *tel:* 01248 750418 *email:* gareth@llonod.demon.co.uk. *Llonnod (sp). Classical, TV and film scores.*

Goddard, Mark. Old Brewery House, Redbrook, Monmouth NP5 4LU *tel:* 01600 71248/712482 *fax:* 01600 712483. *Ric, Spartan, Trinity College London. Educ mus, flexible mus.*

Godman, Robert. 5 Nursery Dr, Sandy Bedfordshire SG19 1DL *tel:* 01767 692161. *Orch, electro-acoustic, educ.*

* **Golightly, David.** Modrana Music Publishers, 41 Parklands Way, Poynton, Cheshire SK12 1AL *tel:* 01625 875389 *also fax; email:* 113027.1502@ compuserve.com. *MM. TV and film, theatre incidental mus.*

Gomelskaya, Julia. 14 Moreton Terrace, Pimlico, London SW1V 2NX *tel:* 0171 834 3318 *also fax. GSMD.*

Goodall, Howard. PBJ Management, 5 Soho Sq, London W1V 5DE *tel:* 0171 287 1112 *fax:* 0171 287 1448 *email:* howardg@argonet.co.uk. *Choral, opera, musicals, TV and film.*

*† **Goodwin, Ron.** Blacknest Cottage, Brimpton Common, Reading, Berks RG7 4RP *tel:* 0118 981 5147 *fax:* 0118 981 0770. *Chandos, EMI, KPM, G & M Brand, WC. Film scores.*

† **Gorb, Adam.** 138 Salcott Rd, London SW11 6DG *tel:* 0171 223 5843 *also fax. Brass Wind, Corda, Leng, Maecenas. Orch, chmbr, wind band, choral, ballet, pno, educ.*

Gordon, Christopher. 22 Ivybridge Close, Twickenham, Middx TW1 1EA *tel:* 0181 892 1833 *also fax. Janus Music (Studio Mus Company). Mus for children, wind and chmbr mus, pno, ens, choral songs, duos, trios, quartets, wind band.*

*† **Gordon, Jerold James.** Hohenfriedbergstr 3, D-10829 Berlin, Germany *tel:* 00 49 30 781 2321 *fax:* 00 49 30 787 5894. *Leng. Ballet, opera, symphonic.*

Gordon, Morgan. 258 Perry Hill, Bell Green, London SE6 4HD *tel:* 0181 291 6121 *also fax. Theatre (incidental mus to plays and songs), concert works.*

Górecki, Henryk Mikolaj. c/o Boosey & Hawkes Music Publishing Ltd, 295 Regent St, London W1R 8JH *tel:* 0171 637 3490 *fax:* 0171 580 2060 *email:* composers@boosey.com. *Works for solo voice and orch, br and str mus, orch, chmbr, choir.*

Graebner, Ric. Music Dept, University of Southampton, Highfield, Southampton SO17 1BJ *tel:* 01703 593558 *fax:* 01703 593197 *email:*

ehg@soton.ac.uk. *(Sp). Electronic, opera, multi-media, vocal, inst, dance.*

Grange, Philip. c/o Maecenas Music, 5 Bushey Close, Old Barn La, Kenley, Surrey CR8 5AU *tel:* 0181 660 4766 *fax:* 0181 668 5273. *Maecenas.*

* **Grant, Julian.** 7 Thackeray House, Herbrand St, London WC1N 1HN *tel:* 0171 278 5263 *also fax. Opera, inst, chmbr, vocal.*

Grant, Robin. 46 Austin St, Whitmore Reans, Wolverhampton WV6 0NW *tel:* 01902 423685. *ABd, BH, Brass Wind, Ches, Faber, Goodmusic. Concert, educ, opera.*

* **Graubart, Michael.** 18 Laitwood Rd, London SW12 9QL *tel:* 0181 265 5504. *Chmbr, vocal, choral, orch.*

Gray MBE, David. 3 Railway Cottages, Ripe La, Firle, Lewes, E Sussex BN8 6NJ *tel:* 01323 811488. *Nov. Orch and educ mus.*

Gray, Simon. 91 Portland St, Southport, Merseyside PR8 6QZ *tel:* 0956 854959 *fax:* 0121 331 5906 *email:* simon@star-one.org.uk. *Mahayana Music. Chmbr, film, video and TV mus.*

* **Greenway, Kenneth.** 6 Buttermere Close, Tettenhall, Wolverhampton WV6 9DN *tel:* 01902 754529. *Rob. Org and choral mus.*

*† **Gregson, Edward.** c/o Royal Northern College of Music, 124 Oxford Rd, Manchester M13 9RD *tel:* 0161 273 6283 *fax:* 0161 273 7611. *BH, Brass Wind, Emerson, Maecenas, Nov, OUP, Smith, Studio Music, WC. Concert mus.*

Grier, Francis. 22 Rydal Gdns, Wembley, Middx HA9 8RZ *tel:* 0181 904 2422. *Banks, OUP. Opera, choral, chmbr, church, inst.*

Gruber, H K. c/o Intermusica Artists' Management Ltd, 16 Duncan Terrace, London N1 8BZ *tel:* 0171 278 5455 *fax:* 0171 278 8434. *BH. Opera, orch, concertos.*

Gruss, René. 2 St Richard's Ct, Ashburnham Rd, Richmond, Surrey TW10 7NS *tel:* 0181 940 3680 *email:* rene.gruss@newklassical.com; http://www.newklassical.com.

Gubaidulina, Sofia. c/o Boosey & Hawkes, 295 Regent St, London W1R 8JH *tel:* 0171 580 2060 *fax:* 0171 637 3490 *email:* composers@boosey.com. *Orch, concerto, ens, chmbr.*

* **Gundry, Inglis.** 11 Winterstoke Gardens, London NW7 2RA *tel:* 0181 959 1744. *BH, Hin, OUP, TP. Opera, song-cycle, hp mus, orch.*

† **Guy, Barry.** Carrickmourne, Thomastown, Co Kilkenny, Ireland. *Nov. Concert mus, chmbr, jazz, film.*

Haines, David Charles. 88 Higher Brimley, Teignmouth, Devon TQ14 8JU *tel:* 01626 779690. *Operas, musicals, children's mus, theatre mus.*

Hall, John. c/o Mrs Kaye, 11 Bleasdale Av, Thornton-Cleveleys, Lancs FY5 3QZ *tel:* 01253 856606. Also at: St Leger de Montbrillais, F-86120 Les Trois Moutiers, France *tel:* 00 33 05 49 22 93 06 *also fax. Yorke.*

Hallett, Sylvia. 33 Summerhill Rd, London N15 4HF *tel:* 0181 802 0094 *also fax. Contemporary dance, film, educ, theatre mus, vocal, inst, electro-acoustic.*

Hallgrimsson, Haflidi. 5 Merchiston Bank Gardens, Edinburgh EH10 5EB *tel:* 0131 447 5752. *Ches, ITM, Ric, SMIC. Orch, solo and chmbr mus, mus theatre.*

Halsey, Louis. 8 Beechcroft Av, New Malden, Surrey KT3 3EG *tel:* 0181 942 7597 *also fax. Encore, Kirklees, OUP, Thames. Choral.*

Hamilton, Iain. Flat 4, 85 Cornwall Gardens, London SW7 4XY *tel:* 0171 589 4788. *AAK (Presser), Schott, UE. Opera, orch, chmbr, choral, solo inst.*

Hand, Colin. 10 St Joan's Dr, Scawby, Brigg, Lincs DN20 9BE *tel:* 01652 655802. *Asch, BH, Curwen, Elk, Eul, Faber, Gal, KM, Nova, Nov, Oec, OUP, Piper, Ric, Schott. Choral, orch, pno, org and rcdr.*

Hankinson, Michael. PO Box 32661, Glenstantia, Pretoria 0010, South Africa *tel:* 00 27 12 47 2192 *fax:* 00 27 12 348 9729 *email:* musicman@smarthet.co.za. *BH (SA), Carlin, Kanda Music (Toronto), WC. Ballet and film scores.*

Hansel, Stanislaw. 38 West Parade, Peterborough, Cambs PE3 6BD *tel:* 01733 341068 *email:* http://eae.netinnov.co.uk/. *(Sp), Writers' Forum. Sound poetry, sound installations, opera, keyboard and pno, ens.*

* **Hanson, Geoffrey.** 89 Fordington Rd, London N6 4TH *tel:* 0181 444 9214. *Rob. Orch, choral and opera.*

*† **Hardy, John.** Ael Y Garth, 3 Iron Bridge Rd, Tongwynlais, Cardiff CF4 7NJ *tel:* 01222 810653 *also fax;* 01222 810655. *Aureus, EMI, Pocket. Opera, mus theatre, orch, concert, chmbr, choral, solo, film and TV, dance, educ, theatre.*

† **Harper, Edward.** 7 Morningside Pk, Edinburgh EH10 5HD *tel:* 0131 447 5366. *OUP. Opera, orch, choral, chmbr.*

* **Harrex, Patrick.** 21 Preston Dr, Brighton, E Sussex BN1 6LA *tel:* 01273 501758. *Schott, (sp).*

Harris, Max. Checkmate, Chequers La, Walton on the Hill, Tadworth, Surrey KT20 7RB *tel:* 01737 812744. *Amphonic Music, ATV Music, Bruton Music, EMI, Essex, Music Sales, WC. Film and TV scores.*

* **Harris, Paul.** 5 Fox Way, Buckingham, Bucks MK18 7EH *tel:* 01280 813144 *also fax; email:* paulharris@easynet.co.uk. *ABd, BH, Camden Music, CUP, Faber, Fentone, Nov, OUP, Ric. Educ mus.*

Harris, Philip. 52 Dean Rd West, Hinckley, Leics LE10 1QB *tel:* 01455 634945 *email:* phil@beacon-hky.demon.co.uk; http://www.beacon-hky.demon.co.uk. *(Sp). Religious mus, Christian worship songs.*

Harris, William Lewarne. 26 Park Ct, Park Hall Rd, London SE21 8DZ *tel:* 0181 761 6460. *Leduc, OUP. Operas, orch, chmbr, songs and choral.*

Hart, Donald. Cottage Farm, The Hollow, Westbury-sub-Mendip, nr Wells, Somerset BA5 1HH *tel:* 01749 870351. *Orch, choral, chmbr, Christian worship songs.*

Hartman, Thomas. 41 Nash House, Lupus St, London SW1V 3HQ *tel:* 0171 233 5129. *Arlington, Bèrben (Italy), Ches. Orch, choral, opera, ballet, gui, film scores, jazz.*

* **Harvey, Frank.** 26 Waite Meads Close, Purton, nr Swindon, Wilts SN5 9ET *tel:* 01793 770139. *School, orch, choral, chmbr.*

† **Harvey, Jonathan.** 35 Houndean Rise, Lewes, Sussex BN7 1EQ *tel:* 01273 471241. *Faber, Nov, Schott. Chmbr, orch, vocal, choral, opera, electronic.*

Harvey, Paul. 36 Alton Gardens, Twickenham TW2 7PD *tel:* 0181 898 4869. *BH, Breit, Ches, Egon, Emerson, Fentone, Harlequin, Kahn & Averill, Kjos, KM, Maurer, Music Sales, Nov, NWM, Ric, Roncorp, Schott, Shallumo, Sou, Studio, Universal, WC. W/wind mus.*

† **Harvey, Richard.** Fireworks Music Ltd, Ickenham Manor, Ickenham, Uxbridge, Middx UB10 8QT *tel:* 01895 672994 *fax:* 01895 633264 *email:* fwx@fireworks.demon.co.uk. *Film and TV scores.*

Hasse, Jean. 12 Woodlands, Clapham Common North Side, London SW4 0RJ *tel:* 0171 622 1607 *fax:* 0171 720 5426. *Visible Music (sp). Chmbr, inst, ens, orch.*

* **Hawes, Jack.** 29 Lynwood Av, Felixstowe, Suffolk IP11 9HS *tel:* 01394 284055. *Banks, Brunton, CF, Emerson, Nov, Oec, Piper, Rob, RSCM. Orch, inst ens, pno, org, hp, hpd, br band, choral (secular and sacred), songs.*

* **Hawkins, John B.** 94 Greenham Rd, London N10 1LP *tel:* 0181 245 7990. *BH. Orch, vocal, chmbr, educ.*

† **Hawkshaw, Alan.** Oakwood, 10 The Warren, Radlett, Herts WD7 7DX *tel:* 01923 856865 *fax:* 01923 852776 *email:* bigal@globalnet.co.uk. *Petal Music, (sp). TV and film scores.*

Haynes, Stanley. 63 Severn Way, London NW10 2UU *tel:* c/o 0171 722 2600. *Electronic, computer mus, inst.*

Haynes, Tony. 14 Clerkenwell Close, London EC1R 0DP *tel:* 0171 278 1929 *fax:* 0171 250 3009. *Large scale works.*

Head, Raymond. The Firs, 10 Worcester Rd, Chipping Norton, Oxon OX7 5XX *tel:* 01608 642025. *(Sp). Inst, choral, wind band, ens.*

* **Hearne, John.** Smidskot, Fawells, Keithhall, Inverurie AB51 0LN *tel:* 01651 882274 *also fax. Adlais, Longship (sp), Sph. Vocal, chmbr, choral, orch, br, org.*

Hedger, Alison. Hinton House, Hinton, Christchurch, Dorset BH23 7EA *tel:* 01425 274993 *also fax. Golden Apple. Children's educ mus.*

* **Hedges, Anthony.** Malt Shovel Cottage, 76 Walkergate, Beverley, Humberside HU17 9ER *tel:* 01482 860580 *email:* ahedges@westfield music.karoo.co.uk; http://www.karoo.net/westfieldmusic/hedges.htm. *Fentone, Rob, Samuel King, UE, Westfield (sp). Chmbr, orch, choral, educ, opera.*

Heininen, Paavo. c/o Boosey & Hawkes, 295 Regent St, London W1R 8JH *tel:* 0171 580 2060 *fax:* 0171 637 3490 *email:* composers@boosey.com. *Opera, orch and ens mus.*

Hellawell, Piers. 94 Carmel St, Belfast BT7 1QF *tel:* 01232 247064 *also fax; email:* p.hellawell@qub.ac.uk. *Maecenas.*

† **Hellewell, David.** M-D Music, 57 Lansdowne Rd, Bournemouth BH1 1RN *tel:* 01202 551440. *Editio Musica Budapest, M-D Music (sp).*

Henshall, Dalwyn James. 35a Northgate, Canterbury, Kent CT1 1BL *tel:* 01227 462305; 0802 719100 *email:* d.j.henshall@canterbury.ac.uk. *Aureus, Curiad. Choral, chmbr, orch.*

* **Hensher, Ray.** 134 Millhouses La, Sheffield S7 2HB *tel:* 0114 235 0096. *Emerson, Fentone. Wind ens, br ens, solo insts.*

* **Henshilwood, Donald.** 130 Frankby Rd, Newton, West Kirby, Wirral L48 9UX *tel:* 0151 625 6742. *Orch, band, chmbr, electronic.*

Henze, Hans Werner. c/o Schott & Co Ltd, 48 Gt Marlborough St, London W1V 2BN *tel:* 0171 494 1487 *fax:* 0171 287 1529 *email:* http://www.schott-music.com. *Schott. Opera, symphony, chmbr.*

* **Herschmann, Heinz.** 32 Ellerdale Rd, London NW3 6BB *tel:* 0171 435 5255 *fax:* 0171 431 0621. *Kunzelmann, Obelisk. Light orch, background.*

* **Higginson, Gary Michael.** Gidleys, 36 Ide La, Alphington, Exeter *tel:* 01392 433196. *Oec. Serious mus.*

Hill, Richard George. 24a North Tolsta, Isle of Lewis HS2 0NW *tel:* 01851 890382 *fax:* c/o 01851 880216. *Vanderbeek and Imrie. Chmbr, choral, ens, orch, incidental mus, film.*

* **Hinchliffe, Robert.** 4 The Jays, Nightingale Wood, Uckfield, E Sussex TN22 5YG *tel:* 01825 767149. *Faber, Fentone, OUP. Chmbr mus.*

Hind O'Malley, Pamela. 23 Nightingale Av, Cambridge CB1 4SG *tel:* 01223 247885. *SB, SJ Music. Pno, chmbr, vocal.*

Hinton, Alistair. The Sorabji Archive, Easton Dene, Bailbrook La, Bath BA1 7AA *tel:* 01225 852323 *fax:* 01225 852523 *email:* 100775.2716@ compuserve.com. *Inst, pno, vocal, org.*

Hiscocks, Wendy. 26 Morden Ct, Morden, Surrey SM4 5HN *tel:* 0181 648 1700 *also fax. Australian Music Centre, Creativity & Music (sp), Currency (Sydney), Frontier, Hovea (Perth). Songs, chmbr, pno mus.*

* **Ho, Edward.** 5 Wallace Fields, Epsom, Surrey KT17 3AX *tel:* 0181 393 6133 *fax:* 0181 786 7630. *Mus for Chinese insts and combinations of Western and Chinese insts.*

*† **Ho, Wai-On.** 25 Wellington Rd, London E11 2AS *tel:* 0181 530 5687 *also fax. Vocal, inst, orch, choral, ens, mus for dance, mus theatre, electro-acoustic, film, cross-cultural and combined arts.*

Hobbs, Christopher. 202 Green Lane Rd, Leicester LE5 4PA *tel:* 0116 246 1556. *Forward, (sp). Concert mus, theatre, electronic.*

Hoddinott, Alun. Maesawelon, 86 Mill Rd, Lisvane, Cardiff CF4 5UG *tel:* 01222 755356. *Aureus, Brass Wind, Leng, OUP, Paraclete. Opera, incidental mus for film, TV, radio, stage, choral, orch, inst, vocal and chambr.*

Hodkinson, Juliana. 11 Hammond Croft Way, Alphington, Exeter EX2 8FZ *tel:* 01392 278217. *Chmbr mus.*

Hofmann-Engl, Ludger. 12 Essenden Rd, Sanderstead, Surrey CR2 0BU *tel:* 0181 651 5832. *Maecenas. Orch, pno, chmbr, vocal.*

Hold, Trevor. Dovecote House, Wadenhoe, Oundle, Northants, via Peterborough PE8 5SU *tel:* 01832 720279 *also fax. Ramsey, TP. Concert mus, opera.*

Höller, York. c/o Boosey & Hawkes Music Publishing Ltd, 295 Regent St, London W1R 8JH *tel:* 0171 580 2060 *fax:* 0171 637 3490 *email:* composers@boosey.com. *Opera, concertos, orch and tape, chmbr.*

Holloway, Laurie. Elgin, Fishery Rd, Bray, Berkshire SL6 1UP *tel:* 01628 37715 *fax:* 01628 776232. *TV and film scores.*

Holloway, Robin. c/o Boosey & Hawkes Music Publishers Ltd, 295 Regent St, London W1R 8JH *tel:* 0171 580 2060 *fax:* 0171 436 5675 *email:* composers@boosey.com. *Opera, orch, concertos, ens and chmbr.*

† **Holmes, Richard.** 18 Baylis Cres, Burgess Hill, W Sussex RH15 8UP *tel:* 01444 257427; 0802 250510. *EMI, (sp). Film and TV, jingles, musicals.*

Holt, Simon. c/o Chester Music Ltd, 8-9 Frith St, London W1V 5TZ *tel:* 0171 434 0066 *fax:* 0171 287 6329 *email:* music@musicsales.co.uk. *AAK, Chester, UE. Contemporary classical mus.*

† **Hooper, Nicholas.** Muffities, The Ridings, Stonesfield, Witney, Oxon OX8 8EA *tel:* 01993 891313 *also fax. BMG, Carlin, EMI, SRTL. Film and TV scores.*

* **Hope, Peter.** Toller Mill, Toller Porcorum, Dorchester, Dorset DT2 0DQ *tel:* 01300 320826 *fax:* 01300 321131. *Anglo, Arc, ME, Wein.*

Hopkins, John. 7 Cherry Hinton Ct, Cherry Hinton Rd, Cambridge CB1 4AL *tel:* 01223 411259. *Ric. Orch, chmbr, vocal, inst, TV, radio and software incidental mus.*

Horder, Mervyn. c/o Bardic Edition, 6 Fairfax Cres, Aylesbury, Bucks HP20 2ES *tel:* 01296 28609 *also fax. Abingdon Press, Bardic, CF, Hin, Leng, Oec, Schott, Williams. Church mus, songs and inst.*

Horne, David. c/o Boosey and Hawkes Music Publishers Ltd, 295 Regent St, London W1R 8JH *tel:* 0171 580 2060 *fax:* 0171 436 5675 *email:* composers@boosey.com. *Chmbr opera, concerto, ens, chmbr.*

*† **Horovitz, Joseph.** 7 Dawson Pl, London W2 4TD *tel:* 0171 229 5333 *also fax. ABd, Belwin, BH, Ches, Molenaar, Nov, OUP, Schott, Smith.*

Hough, Lester. c/o Da Capo Music Ltd, 26 Stanway Rd, Whitefield, Manchester M45 8EG *tel:* 0161 766 5950.

Hoyland, David. c/o Grosvenor Management, 79 Henley Rd, Ipswich, Suffolk IP1 3SB *tel:* 01473 213215 *also fax.*

Hubicki MBE, Margaret. c/o Katharine Lovell, Flat 1, 14 Abbey Gardens, London NW8 9AT *tel:* 0171 624 1031. *B, Braydeston, Faber, Hin, Schott. Vocal, inst (vn, vc, fl, pno), educ.*

* **Hudes, Eric.** The Old White Horse, Parsonage St, Halstead, Essex CO9 2JZ *tel:* 01787 475845. *Anglian, Bosworth, Forsyth, Simrock, (sp). Concert mus, theatre.*

Huehns, Colin. 18 Crundale Av, London NW9 9PL *tel:* 0181 204 7369. *Opera, vocal, inst, chmbr, choral.*

Hughes, Edward Dudley. 11 Brudenell St, Aldeburgh, Suffolk IP15 5DD *tel:* 01728 452252 *also fax; email:* 101761.40@compuserve.com.

Hughes, Eric. 65 Mount Pleasant, S Ruislip, Middx HA4 9HQ *tel:* 0181 841 2880. *Emerson, Griffiths, Harlequin Music, Schauer, Studio, WC. Musicals, arranging (especially br and military bands).*

Hugill, Andrew. De Montfort University, Scraptoft Campus, Leicester LE7 9SU *tel:* 0116 257 7833 *also fax; email:* ahu@dmu.ac.uk. *Cymbalum Pataphysicum, Forward, Rubble. Concert works, mus theatre, TV, film, electronic.*

* **Hugill, Robert C.** 36 Torrens Rd, Brixton, London SW2 5BT *tel:* 0171 274 3600 *email:* hugill@hugill.demon.co.uk; http://www.hugill.demon.co. uk/. *Da Capo. Choral, vocal.*

Humpage, David. The Church, Toft-Next-Newton, Lincolnshire LN8 3NE *tel:* 01673 878719 *email:* david.humpage@zetnet.co.uk. *(Sp).*

Humphris, Ian. 21 Brackley Rd, London W4 2HW *tel:* 0181 747 1025. *Nov. Choral arr, orch, mus for children.*

Hunt, Geoffrey. 52 Wolsey Rd, Ashford, Middx TW15 2RB. *Da Capo. Chmbr, gui, educ.*

Hunt, Oliver. 35 Salisbury Rd, Harrow, Middx HA1 1NU *tel:* 0181 863 8275 *also fax. Goodmusic, Music Sales, Revelo-Cornish, Schott, (sp). Educ, inst, electronic mus.*

Hurd, Michael. 4 Church St, W Liss, Hants GU33 6JX *tel:* 01730 893378. *Nov. Choral, orch, chmbr, opera, film.*

* **Hush, David.** 170 Windsor St, Paddington, Sydney NSW 2021, Australia *tel:* 00 612 328 1685 *also fax; email:* hush@tig.com.au. *Orch, inst, chmbr and concert mus.*

* **Iliff, James.** Eithin Tewion, Cilycwm, Llandovery, Caerfyrddin SA20 0TF *tel:* 01550 720021. *(Sp). Momentum in mus.*

Ingle, Anthony. c/o Jeffrey Cambell Management, 18 Queen Anne St, London W1M 0HB *tel:* 0171 637 0993 *fax:* 0171 637 0985. *Mus theatre, incidental mus for plays, songs, concert works.*

† **Ingman, Nick.** 10 The Gardens, E Dulwich, London SE22 9QD *tel:* 0181 693 5608 *fax:* 0181 693 9576 *email:* 100712.153@compuserve.com. *Film, TV, records.*

* **Ives, Grayston.** Potmans Heath Cottage, Wittersham, Tenterden, Kent TN30 7PU *tel:* 01797 270347. *Banks, Curwen, Faber, Nov, OUP, Ric, Rob, RSCM, SB. Choral mus.*

Jackson, Andy. 13 West Road, Bishop Auckland, Durham DL14 7PP *tel:* 01388 607060. *Durham County Books, Schott, Hampton, Ric. Choral, ens, dance, gui mus, mus theatre, opera, orch, br band, composer in educ, soundtracks.*

* **Jackson OBE, Francis.** Nether Garth, East Acklam, Malton, N Yorks YO17 9RG *tel:* 01904 620632; 01653 658395. *Asch, Banks, Nov, OUP, Paraclete, RSCM. Org, church mus, monodramas.*

Jackson, Gabriel. Basement Flat, 10 Comeragh Rd, London W14 9HP *tel:* 0171 381 4326.

* **Jacques, Michael.** 22 Stephen's Rd, Tunbridge Wells, Kent TN4 9JE *tel:* 01892 537764 *fax:* 01892 511352. *ABd, B, Oec, OUP, Quavers Rest (sp), Ramsey, Ric, Rob, SB. Educ, concert.*

* **Janovicky, Karel.** 18 Muswell Av, London N10 2EG *tel:* 0181 883 6351 *also fax; email:* simsova@simsova.demon.co.uk. *Orch, chmbr, songs, children's mus, opera, org, pno.*

Jenkins, Clive. 9 Fircroft Rd, Beacon Pk, Plymouth, Devon PL2 3JU *tel:* 01752 709236. *Oec, (sp). Light orch, choral, concert band, br band.*

Jenkins, Karl. c/o Boosey & Hawkes, 295 Regent St, London W1R 8JH *tel:* 0171 580 2060 *fax:* 0171 637 3490 *email:* composers@boosey.com. *Orch, choral, chmbr, TV and film.*

*† **Johnson, Christopher.** Holly Cottage, 19 Chapel La, Biddulph Moor, Staffs ST8 7JY *tel:* 01782 515004; 0976 292524. *(Sp). Film and TV scores, educ mus.*

* **Johnson, Laurie.** 10 College Rd, Harrow, Middx HA1 1DA *tel:* 0181 861 1771 *fax:* 0181 861 3759. *(Sp). Mus for films, TV, theatre mus, oratorio, symphony, tone poem.*

* **Jones, Kenneth Victor.** Cleavers, Bishopstone Village, Seaford, E Sussex BN25 2UD *tel:* 01323 894377. *ABd, Ches, Nov. Concert works, film scores.*

* **Jordan, John.** 3 Famet Close, Purley, Surrey CR8 2DX *tel:* 0181 660 1542. *Bardic, Kahn & Averill. Chmbr, orch, choral, songs, opera.*

Joseph, Jeffrey. 11 Maple Mews, London SW16 2AL *tel:* 0181 677 1349. *Orch, vocal, ens, inst, incidental mus, chmbr.*

*† **Josephs, Wilfred.** Flat 3, 156 Haverstock Hill, Belsize Pk, London NW3 2AT *tel:* 0171 722 6889. *BH, ME, Music Haven, Nov, Orpheus, OUP, Pan Educational, Recital, WC, Wein. Film and TV, opera, ballet, org, orch, chmbr, vocal.*

* **Joubert, John.** 63 School Rd, Moseley, Birmingham B13 9TF *tel:* 0121 449 4997. *Nov. Opera, orch, choral, chmbr, vocal, inst.*

Judd, Garry. 30 Kingsway, Ware, Herts SG12 0QT *tel:* 01920 487823 *also fax. Artful Music. Film, TV, radio, concert, musicals.*

Kagel, Mauricio. c/o Peters Edition Ltd, 10-12 Baches St, London N1 6DN *tel:* 0171 553 4030 *fax:* 0171 490 4921 *email:* promotion@edition-peters.com; http://www.edition-peters.com.

Kancheli, Giya. c/o Boosey & Hawkes, 295 Regent St, London W1R 8JH *tel:* 0171 580 2060 *fax:* 0171 637 3490 *email:* composers@boosey.com. *Orch, concerto, ens.*

Kay, Norman Forber. The Summer House, St Donats, nr Llantwit Major, S Wales CF61 1ZB *tel:* 01446 794775 *also fax. Apollo, BH, Emerson, OUP, Polygram. Orch, opera, chmbr, film and TV.*

Keeley, Robert. 38 Wakeman Rd, London NW10 5DE *tel:* 0181 968 3625 *email:* robert.keeley@kcl.ac.uk. *Symph, chmbr, choral, vocal.*

Keeling, Andrew. 15 Marsh Rd, Thornton-Cleveleys, Lancs FY5 2SE *tel:* 01253 825927. *Orch, chmbr, choral, vocal.*

* **Kell, Richard.** 18 Rectory Grove, Gosforth, Newcastle upon Tyne NE3 1AL *tel:* 0191 284 2017. *Solo, small ens, orch.*

Kelly, Bryan. Le Moulin de Sourreau, Velines, F-24230 France *tel:* 00 33 5 5327 3714. *ABd, Alphonse Leduc, Banks, BH, Ches, Emerson, Encore, Fentone, Nov, Oec, OUP, Rob, RSCM, WC, Wein.*

Kendell, Iain. Mousehole Cottage, 1-32 Park Rd, Swanage, Dorset BH19 2AD *tel:* 01929 422739. *Arnold, Ches, (sp). TV and radio, chmbr, songs, pno, choral, orch.*

Kenny, John. 69 Spottiswoode St, Edinburgh EH9 1DL *tel:* 0131 447 3707 *also fax. Tezak Verlag (Cologne), Warwick. Mus theatre, dance, ens, orch, film, TV.*

Kenyon, Stephen. 52 Ashurst Rd, Cockfosters, Herts EN4 9LF *tel:* 0181 449 0886 *email:* 101602.314@compuserve.com; http://ourworld. compuserve.com/homepages/stevekenyon. *(Sp). Gui, chmbr, orch.*

* **Kershaw, David.** 18 Sand Hutton, York YO4 1LB *tel:* 01904 468484. *Chmbr, orch, big band.*

Keyes, Colin. c/o Brunskill Management Limited, Suite 8a, 169 Queen's Gate, London SW7 5HE *tel:* 0171 581 3388 *fax:* 0171 589 9460 *email:* 101234.2025@compuserve.com.

Khan, Wajahat. c/o 141 Carlton Av East, Wembley, Middx HA9 8PU *tel:* 0181 904 2833 *also fax. Agent: NCCP.*

* **Kiernan, Catherine.** 33 Arun Vale, Coldwaltham, Pulborough, W Sussex RH20 1LP *tel:* 01798 872 978. *Planet Music (sp). Inst and vocal mus.*

Kilvington, Chris. 40 Thornton Rd, Cambridge CB3 0NW *tel:* 01223 276763 *fax:* 01223 277980. *Cambridge Music Works, Corda, Edition Transatlantique, Hampton Edition, Kevin Mayhew, Ric, Verlag Nogatz. Gui mus.*

* **Kimpton, Geoffrey.** 52 Hillingdon Rd, Stretford, Manchester M32 8PJ *tel:* 0161 865 1201. *(Sp). Orch, chmbr, choral, solo vocal, and inst mus.*

† **King, Denis.** 55 Parliament Hill, London NW3 *tel:* 0171 794 5110. *Deekers. Film and TV scores.*

King, Geoffrey. c/o Hazel Sheppard, 16 Clerwood Gardens, Edinburgh EH12 8PT *tel:* 0131 539 8877 *fax:* 0131 539 2211.

King, Matthew. Brook Garden Cottage, Troy Town La, Brook, Ashford, Kent TN25 5PQ *tel:* 01233 813066 *also fax. Chmbr, choral, opera, ens, pno, vocal, orch, educ mus theatre and pno.*

King, Steve. 8 Hopeward Mews, Dalgety Bay, Fife KY11 5TB *tel:* 01383 821187. *Opera, ballet, educ, orch, chmbr, film and TV.*

† **Kinsey, Tony.** 5 The Pennards, Sunbury-on-Thames, Middx *tel:* 01932 783160. *BH, KPM. TV and film scores.*

Kirby, Kenneth. 18 Silvertree Close, Walton on Thames, Surrey KT12 1NN *tel:* 01932 228635.

Kirkby-Mason, Barbara. Flat 5, 6 Weymouth Mews, Portland Pl, London W1N 3FS *tel:* 0171 580 1676. *B, Music Sales, OUP, SB. Pno courses.*

Kirkwood, Antoinette. 56 Sutherland St, London SW1V 4JZ *tel:* 0171 828 1683 *fax:* 0171 828 7907. *Andresier, Bardic. Orch, chmbr mus, songs.*

† **Kiszko, Martin.** 29 Wellington Pk, Clifton, Bristol BS8 2UW *tel:* 0117 973 1267 *fax:* 0117 973 8170. *Film and TV, stage.*

* **Knight, Tim.** 24 Lidgett Hill, Roundhay, Leeds LS8 1PE *tel:* 0113 293 7834. *Corda, Phylloscopus, Oec, Parkfield, Sam King. Inst, ens, choral.*

Knotts, David. Flat A, 2 Egmont Rd, Sutton, Surrey SM2 5JN *tel:* 0181 770 3825. *Chmbr, ens, choral, inst, opera.*

Kodjabashia, Nikola. c/o ECAM Ltd, 130 Drayton Pk, Highbury, London N5 1LX *tel:* 0171 354 3844 *also fax; fax:* 0171 609 5644.

Kolb, Barbara. c/o Boosey & Hawkes Music Publishing Ltd, 295 Regent St, London W1R 8JH *tel:* 0171 580 2060 *fax:* 0171 637 3490 *email:* composers@boosey.com. *Orch, chmbr, pno and pre-recorded tapes.*

Kurtág, György. c/o Boosey & Hawkes, 295 Regent St, London W1R 8JH *tel:* 0171 580 2060 *fax:* 0171 637 3490 *email:* composers@boosey.com. *Orch, ens, chmbr, vocal, pno.*

Lack, Graham. 88 Northey Av, Cheam, Sutton, Surrey SM2 7HJ *tel:* 0181 642 7348. *Choir, chmbr, fl, ob, choral, orch, vocal, ens.*

* **Laing, Alan.** Barnham Lodge, Townend Rd, Walkington, E Yorks HU17 8SY *tel:* 01482 870210. *Da Capo, Fentone, Saga, (sp). Theatrical mus, pno, vn, va, orch, chmbr, choral, inst.*

Lamb, Peter. 5 Silchester Close, Bournemouth BH2 6PY *tel:* 01202 295034. *BH.*

Lambros, Simon. Elmina, Old Dashwood Hill, Studley Green, Bucks HP14 3XD *tel:* 01494 483524 *also fax. Charo Pubs, Mayhew Pubs. Film and TV, concert mus, theatre mus.*

* **Lane, Philip.** c/o Goodmusic, 16 Cheltenham Trade Park, Arle Rd, Cheltenham, Glos GL51 8LX *tel:* 01242 226101 *fax:* 01242 573441. *Banks, Bourne, Fentone, Fulcrum, KM, KPM, Lorenz, Nov, OUP, Rob, Smith, Studio, UE, Wein, WR. Orch, choral, chmbr, TV and radio.*

* **Last OBE, Joan.** 11 St Mary's Close, Littlehampton, W Sussex BN17 5PZ *tel:* 01903 713522. *AA, B, BH, Cramer, Curwen, EMI, For, GMC, JW, LGB, Lorenz (USA), MSM, Nov, OUP, SB, WC.*

† **Laurence, Zack.** 1 Glanleam Rd, Stanmore, Middx HA7 4NW *tel:* 0181 954 2025 *also fax. Miriamusic. TV, film scores and jingles.*

Lawrance, Peter A. 7 Reading Av, Nuneaton, Warwicks CV11 6HE *tel:* 01203 373250. *Alders, Arnold, Brass Wind, Ches, Fortune, Frontier, Practical Teacher, Thomas Nelson. Musicals, educ wind mus, br ens, br band, vocal, orch.*

* **Lawrence, Mark.** Garden Flat, 29 West Pk, Clifton, Bristol BS8 2LX *tel:* 0117 974 4666 *also fax. Vocal, choral, children's and community opera, theatre and radio.*

Lawson, Gordon. Braeside, 32 College Pl, Brighton, Sussex BN2 1HN *tel:* 01273 705426. *Cathedral, Emerson, Fraser-Enoch, Kenwood (USA),*

Novello, Oec, RSCM, Selah (USA). Choral, pno, inst, org, songs, chmbr, concertos.

Laycock, Jolyon. Music Dept, University of Bath, Avon BA2 7AY *tel:* 01225 826431 *fax:* 01225 462508. *Opera, chmbr, solo.*

Leach, John. 68 Lysia St, London SW6 6NG *tel:* 0171 385 0182 *fax:* 0171 381 1155. *Bruton, Editio Musica Budapest, KPM, Rob, Studio G, Parry Music (Canada), WC, Wein, Wolfe, Yorke. Film mus.*

Leadbetter, Martin. Ivy Lodge, 2 Priory La, Little Wymondley, Herts SG4 7HE *tel:* 01438 359292 *also fax. Con Moto, Fentone, Mostyn. Inst, vocal, choral, orch.*

* **Lee, Clifford.** 21 Lawn La, Springfield, Chelmsford, Essex CM1 6NP *tel:* 01245 357539. *Melandra (sp). Concert and chmbr mus.*

Lees, Benjamin. c/o Boosey & Hawkes Music Publishing Ltd, 295 Regent St, London W1R 8JH *tel:* 0171 580 2060 *fax:* 0171 637 3490 *email:* composers@boosey.com. *Orch, concertos.*

Lesser, David. 351 Station Rd, Dorridge, Solihull, W Midlands B93 8EY *tel:* 01564 772402 *also fax. Chmbr, inst and vocal.*

*† **Lewis, Jeffrey.** Crafnant, Park Cres, Llanfairfechan, Gwynedd LL33 0AU *tel:* 01248 680776. *Nov, Rob. Orch, chmbr, choral, vocal, solo, church mus.*

Lewis, Paul. Court House, Church St, Martock, Somerset TA12 6JL *tel:* 01935 825100 *also fax. Studio G, De Wolfe. TV, library, concert.*

Liddle, David. 9 Western Rd, East Finchley, London N2 9JB *tel:* 0181 444 4454. *Nov, Randall M Egan. Org mus.*

Lindberg, Magnus. c/o Boosey & Hawkes, 295 Regent St, London W1R 8JH *tel:* 0171 580 2060 *fax:* 0171 637 3490 *email:* composers@boosey. com. *Orch, concertos, ens, chmbr.*

Lindley, Simon. 8 The Chandlers, The Calls, Leeds LS2 7EZ *tel:* 0113 234 1146 *also fax. Banks, Ramsey, RSCM. Church mus.*

Lipkin, Malcolm. Penlan, Crowborough Hill, Crowborough, Sussex TN6 2EA *tel:* 01892 652454. *Ches, (sp). Symphonic, concerto, chmbr, inst, choral, vocal.*

Llewellyn MBE, William. Forecourt, Queens Sq, Colyton, Devon EX13 6JX *tel:* 01297 552414 *also fax. Nov, OUP, RSCM. Choral, educ mus, hymn tunes.*

† **Lloyd, George.** c/o Albany Records (UK) Ltd, PO Box 12, Carnforth, Lancs LA5 9PD *tel:* 01524 735873 *fax:* 01524 736448 *email:* http://www. albanyrecords.demon.co.uk. *BH, Ches, George Lloyd Music Library, Smith, UMP. Symphonic, choral, br, wind, opera.*

Lloyd, Jonathan. c/o Boosey & Hawkes Music Publishers Ltd, 295 Regent St, London W1R 8JH *tel:* 0171 580 2060 *fax:* 0171 436 5675 *email:* composers@boosey.com. *Orch, concertos, chmbr, ens.*

Lloyd, Richard. Refail Newydd, Pentraeth, Anglesey LL75 8YF *tel:* 01248 450220. *Banks, Basil Ramsey, Cathedral, Encore, Kirklees Cathedral Music, KM, Leng, Lorenz, Nov, RSCM. Church mus.*

Lloyd-Howells, David. 24 Kensington Rd, Arundel Pk, Chichester, W Sussex PO19 2XN *tel:* 01243 778740 *email:* http://www.baskerville. cineca.it/netmag/home.html. *DLH Productions, Five Lines. Sonic art mus concept and protoscores all media. I.D.E.A.*

Lloyd Webber, Andrew. The Really Useful Group Ltd, 22 Tower St, London WC2H 9NS *tel:* 0171 240 0880 *fax:* 0171 240 1204. *Really Useful Group.*

Lockett, Mark. 59b The Dale, Wirksworth, Derbys DE4 4EH *tel:* 01629 825504 *also fax. Ens, jazz, keyboards, gamelan, educ, TV.*

Lord, David. c/o Terra Incognita, 1 Walcot Gate, Bath BA1 5UG *tel:* 01225 462286 *also fax; email:* dlord@easynet.co.uk. *Cary, Chapman, Ches, OUP, UE. Film and TV scores.*

† **Lovett, Andrew.** 1 George's Terrace, Halifax Rd, Cambridge CB4 3PY *tel:* 01223 369641. *(Sp). Electro-acoustic mus.*

Lowe, Jez. 60 Maritime Cres, Horden, Peterlee, Co Durham SR8 3SX *tel:* 0191 586 1938 *also fax. Fellsongs, Lowe Life (sp). Folk mus.*

* **Luff, Enid.** 12 Heol Tyn Y Cae, Cardiff CF4 6DU *tel:* 01222 616023. *Primavera (sp). Chmbr, orch, dance and pno.*

* **Lyon, David.** 1 St Rumbolds Rd, Shaftesbury, Dorset SP7 8NE *tel:* 01747 855903. *ABd, Ches, Fulcrum, Hinshaw, IMC, ME, Studio, WC. Orch, choral, chmbr, mus theatre, children's mus events.*

Lyttleton, Trevor. 23 Bryanston Ct, George St, London W1H 7HA *tel:* 0171 402 4810 *fax:* 0171 262 4296. *Light Music Ltd (sp). Film, TV themes.*

McBain, Hugh. 1 Munro Rd, Glasgow G13 1SQ *tel:* 0141 959 1966. *SMIC. Mus theatre, symphony, chmbr, pno, concerto.*

† **McCabe, John.** 49 Burns Av, Southall, Middx UB1 2LR *tel:* 0181 574 5039 *also fax. Nov, OUP.*

McDevitt, Robert. c/o Bardic Edition, 6 Fairfax Cres, Aylesbury, Bucks HP20 2ES *tel:* 01296 28609. *Bardic. Pno, inst.*

* **McDowall, Cecilia.** 58 Abinger Rd, London W4 1EX *tel:* 0181 994 8639. *Gemini, Hunt, Nova, Pan Educational. Children's mus, choral, songs, chmbr mus.*

* **McGowan, Peter.** c/o Caroline Ireland Management, Uwchlaw'r Coed, Llanbedr, Gwynedd LL45 2NA *tel:* 01341 241532 *also fax. Film, ballet scores, chmbr mus, mus theatre.*

McGregor, Richard Ewan. c/o Performing Arts Dept, University College of St Martin, Lancaster LA1 3JD *tel:* 01524 384234/384339 *fax:* 01524 68943 *email:* r.mcgregor@ucsm.ac.uk.

*† **McGuire, Eddie.** 13 Lawrence St, Glasgow G11 5HH *tel:* 0141 334 8580 *email:* http://www.music.gla.ac.uk/htmlfolder/resources/smic/html/ mcguire.html. *Opera, ballet, orch, solo.*

MacIlwham, George. 25 Ravelston Rd, Bearsden, Glasgow G61 1AW *tel:* 0141 942 6779.

McIntosh, John M. Stamford, 55 Royal Cres, Dunoon, Argyll PA23 7AQ *tel:* 01369 703304. *Choral, arrangements.*

Mackey, Steven. c/o Boosey & Hawkes Music Publishing Ltd, 295 Regent St, London W1R 8JH *tel:* 0171 580 2060 *fax:* 0171 637 3490 *email:* composers@boosey.com. *Chmbr, orch, voice and str quartet.*

Mackmin, Norman. 17 Bazehill Rd, Rottingdean, E Sussex BN2 7DB *tel:* 01273 302033. *Film and TV, songs, light classical, musicals.*

McLain, John (J A Lain). 42 Osidge La, Southgate, London N14 5JG *tel:* 0181 368 2759. *Bardic, Copperplate. Vocal, inst, pno, choral, humour.*

† **Maclean, Grahame.** Buttonsnap, 44 Streetly End, West Wickham, Cambridgeshire CB1 6RP *tel:* 01223 893920 *fax:* 01223 890471. *EMI, Sonoton, Sparta (Florida). Film and TV scores, advertising, library.*

McLelland-Young, Thomas. 2 Onslow Gardens, Sanderstead, Surrey CR2 9AB *tel:* 0181 672 3502. *KM, Nov, Oec. Choral, org, song cycles, ballet, orch, pno, chmbr.*

*† **McLeod, John.** Hill House, 9 Redford Cres, Edinburgh EH13 0BS *tel:* 0131 441 3035 *fax:* 0131 441 5218. *Griffin. Choral, orch, chmbr, inst mus, film and TV.*

MacMillan, James. c/o Boosey & Hawkes Music Publisher Ltd, 295 Regent St, London W1R 8JH *tel:* 0171 580 2060 *fax:* 0171 637 3490 *email:* composers@boosey.com. *Opera, orch, concertos, choral, chmbr.*

McNeff, Stephen. 131 Melbourne Grove, London SE22 8RR *tel:* 0181 693 8388 *also fax; email:* stephen_mcneff@msn.com. *Brassworks (Toronto). Opera, mus theatre, theatre songs, chmbr.*

McPhee MBE, George. 17 Main Rd, Castlehead, Paisley, Renfrewshire PA2 6AJ *tel:* 0141 889 3528 *fax:* 0141 887 3929. *Oec. Church and choral mus.*

McQuaid, John. 8 Ardrossan Rd, Saltcoats, Ayrshire KA21 5BW *tel:* 01294 463737. *Chapman, Five Line, JS Burns.*

† **McQueen, Ian.** 159 Newport Rd, Leyton, London E10 6PG *tel:* 0181 926 1867. *Ric. Opera, orch, vocal and chmbr mus.*

Mallett, Charles. c/o Grosvenor Management, 79 Henley Rd, Ipswich IP1 3SB *tel:* 01473 213215 *also fax.*

*† **Maloney, Kevin.** Dept of Arts, Design and Performance, Manchester Metropolitan University, Hassall Rd, Alsager, Cheshire ST7 2HL *tel:* 0161 247 5319 *fax:* 0161 247 6377 *email:* http://www.nwnet.co.uk/ psappha. *Orch, chmbr, electro-acoustic, multimedia, theatre, dance.*

* **Manduell CBE, Sir John.** Chesham, High Bentham, Lancaster LA2 7JY *tel:* 0161 226 8272 *fax:* 0161 226 8144 *email:* mailbox@eoperac.org.uk. *Nov.*

Marsh, Roger. c/o Music Dept, University of York, Heslington, York YO1 5DD *tel:* 01904 432432 *fax:* 01904 432450. *Maecenas, Nov. Orch, ens, vocal, mus theatre.*

Martelli, Carlo. 215 Burrage Rd, London SE18 7JZ *tel:* 0181 316 7905. *Broadbent & Dunn, Leng. Inst, opera and film scores.*

Martin, David Charles. 27 Nimrod Rd, London SW16 6SZ *tel:* 0181 769 6537. *(Sp). Mus theatre, opera.*

* **Martin, Philip.** Chapel House, Theobald's Green, Calstone, nr Calne, Wilts SN11 8QE *tel:* 01249 812508 *also fax. BH, Bosworths, Irish Contemporary Music Centre. Symphonies, concertos, chmbr, choral.*

Martinez, Odaline de la. c/o Lontano Trust, Toynbee Studios, 28 Commercial St, London E1 6LS *tel:* 0171 247 2950 *fax:* 0171 247 2956. *Opera, chmbr, inst, vocal, choral.*

Martland, Steve. c/o Schott & Co Ltd, 48 Gt Marlborough St, London W1V 2BN *tel:* 0171 494 1487 *fax:* 0171 287 1529 *email:* schottcontemporary music@compuserve.com. *Schott.*

Mason, Benedict. c/o Chester Music Ltd, 8-9 Frith St, London W1V 5TZ *tel:* 0171 434 0066 *fax:* 0171 287 6329 *email:* music@musicsales.co.uk. *Ches.*

Matthew-Walker, Robert. 1 Exford Rd, London SE12 9HD *tel:* 0181 857 1582 *also fax. Arena, BH, Leng, OUP, Ramsey.*

† **Matthews, Colin.** 3 Manchuria Rd, London SW11 6AF *tel:* 0171 228 5591 *fax:* 0171 228 2358. *Faber, Nov.*

† **Matthews, David.** 12 Woodlands, Clapham Common North Side, London SW4 0RJ *tel:* 0171 622 1607 *fax:* 0171 720 5426. *BH, Faber.*

† **Maw, Nicholas.** c/o Faber Music Ltd, 3 Queen Sq, London WC1N 3AU *tel:* 0171 833 7911/2 *fax:* 0171 833 7939. *BH, Ches, Faber, Nov, OUP.*

* **Maxwell, Michael.** 29 Riverview Rd, London W4 3QH *tel:* 0181 994 6111. *MME, Schott. Pno, chmbr, songs, arrangements for wind ens.*

† **Maxwell Davies, Sir Peter.** c/o Mrs J Arnold, Flat 3, 50 Hogarth Rd, London SW5 0PU *tel:* 0171 370 2328 *fax:* 0171 373 6730 *email:* j.arnold@maxopus.com. *BH, Ches, Schott.*

Mayer, John. 27 Hermitage Rd, London N4 1DF *tel:* 0181 802 2421. *Leng, Lopes, Preston Stevens, Paragon, Schott, Simrock. Musicals, orch, chmbr, radio and film mus.*

Mellers, Wilfrid. 17 Aldwark Rd, York YO1 2BX *tel:* 01904 638686. *Belwin, CUP, Faber, Gal, Leng, Nov, OUP, Schott.*

Merrell, Crispin. c/o Amphonic, Kerchesters, Waterhouse La, Kingswood, Surrey KT20 6HT *tel:* 01737 832837 *fax:* 01737 833812. *Amphonic. Film and TV.*

* **Messervy, George.** Flat 20, Hautmont Close, Mont Millais, St Helier, Jersey JE2 4XS *tel:* 01534 610055. *Inst.*

Metcalf, John. Ty Yfory, Llanfair Rd, Lampeter, Ceredigion SA48 8JZ *tel:* 01570 493576 *fax:* 01570 493636 *email:* john@metcalf.demon.co.uk.

† **Michelmore, Guy.** 35 Binden Rd, London W12 9RJ *tel:* 0181 740 7727 *fax:* 0181 743 2523. *Music for Television. TV and film scores.*

* **Middleton, John.** 35 Kingswood Av, London NW6 6LR *tel:* 0181 969 4294. *Cramer, (sp).*

Millar, Jhalib. c/o Clifton Wyatt Artists Management, 1 Poets Rd, London N5 2SL *tel:* 0171 354 2050 *also fax; email:* cliftonwyattartists management@compuserve.com.

* **Mills, Alan.** 87 Palmerston Rd, Wood Green, London N22 4QS *tel:* 0181 888 8214. *Material Productions, Music Haven, Warwick. Concert, vocal, choral.*

† **Milner, Anthony.** 147 Heythorp St, London SW18 5BT *tel:* 0181 870 7023. *KM, Nov, Ramsey, UE.*

† **Mitcham, David.** 1 Lyons Green Cottages, Shillinglee Rd, Plaistow, W Sussex RH14 0PH *tel:* 01403 871297 *fax:* 01403 871303 *email:* david@lyonsgreen.demon.co.uk; http://www.lyonsgreen.demon. co.uk. *Carlin, Chappell, Standard, Wein. Film scores and concert mus.*

Mitchell, John. Whisper Cottage, Rectory Lane, Lyminge, Folkestone, Kent CT18 8EG *tel:* 01303 863796. *Mayola, Modus, TP. Handbell mus.*

† **Mitchell-Davidson, Paul.** 25 Bannerman Av, Prestwich, Manchester M25 1DZ *tel:* 0161 798 9604 *also fax. Kamela, Maurice Wray. Chmbr, dance, jazz, orch, radio, theatre, TV, educ.*

Mold, Simon. Farfalla, 48 Roosevelt Av, Wayfield, Chatham, Kent ME5 0EW. *Banks, Cwmni Cyhoeddi Gwynn, Encore, Harper Collins, KM, RSCM. Choral and song (sacred and secular), org.*

* **Monk, Peter Anthony.** Fir Tree House, 169b St James's Rd, Croydon, Surrey CR0 2BY *tel:* 0181 689 9268. *Belpaire (sp), Hampton, Suv. Solo inst and voice, full ens, film mus, chmbr mus, br and songs.*

Montague, Stephen. 2 Ryland Rd, London NW5 3EA *tel:* 0171 267 5416 *also fax; email:* ump@compuserve.com; http://ourworld.compuserve. com/homepages/ump. *Mod Ed, UMP. Concert mus, electro-acoustic mus, dance, ballet.*

Moody, Ivan. c/o Vanderbeek & Imrie Ltd, 15 Marvig, Lochs, Isle of Lewis HS2 9QP *tel:* 01851 880216 *also fax. Vanderbeek. Choral, orch, religious, chmbr, inst.*

* **Moore, Philip.** 1 Minster Ct, York YO1 2JJ *tel:* 01904 642526 *fax:* 01904 654604. *Banks, Kenwood, KM, Nov, RSCM. Choral, org mus, chmbr and orch.*

* **Moore, Timothy.** 86 Chesterton Rd, Cambridge CB4 1ER *tel:* 01223 363711/564933 *fax:* 01223 363731. *Editions BIM, Elkin, For, Frontier Press, Nov, Oriel Library, Schott, Westerleigh. Chmbr, orch, choral, vocal.*

† **Moran, Mike.** Ballinger Lodge, Ballinger Common, Gt Missenden, Bucks HP16 9LQ *tel:* 01494 866161; 01494 890694 *also fax. Film and TV scores.*

Morris, Keith. 5 Bentinck Rd, Newcastle upon Tyne NE4 6UT *tel:* 0191 273 5326. *Br band, choral, jazz, contemporary classical, dance, film and TV, theatre, educ.*

† **Morris, Peter.** 56 Gloucester Pl, London W1H 3HL *tel:* 0171 486 3297. *ATV, Bruton, EMI.*

† **Muldowney, Dominic.** c/o David Japp, Carlin Music Co, Iron Bridge House, 3 Bridge Approach, Chalk Farm, London NW1 8BD *tel:* 0171 734 3251. *Faber, Nov, UE.*

Mullen, Michael. 153 Wilberforce Rd, Finsbury Park, London N4 2SX *tel:* 0171 226 7092.

* **Muncaster, Clive.** 119 Commonwealth Ct, Apt 1, Princeton, NJ 08540, USA *tel:* 00 1 609 452 8257. *BH, Chandos. Film and TV, opera.*

Muskett, Jennie. 53 Cholmeley Pk, London N6 5EH *tel:* 0181 340 1910 *fax:* 0181 347 8027. *TV and film scores.*

Nash, Peter Paul. 1 Birch St, Nayland, Colchester CO6 4JA *tel:* 01206 263550. *(Sp).*

* **Naylor, Peter.** Greenacres, Brady Rd, Lyminge, Folkestone, Kent CT18 8HA *tel:* 01303 863284. *Nov, Oec, Ramsey. Opera, vocal, orch and inst mus.*

Nelson, Peter. Faculty of Music, Edinburgh University, Alison House, Nicolson Sq, Edinburgh EH8 9DF *tel:* 0131 650 2433 *fax:* 0131 650 2425 *email:* p.nelson@music.ed.ac.uk. *SMIC. Orch, chmbr, electro-acoustic.*

* **Nevens, David.** Trengale, Piccadilly, Llanblethian, Cowbridge, Vale of Glamorgan CF71 7JL *tel:* 01446 772930. *Welsh Music Information Centre, Cyhaeddiadau Curiad. TV and film scores, educ mus.*

† **Neville, Paul.** 9 Greenfield Rd, Eastbourne, E Sussex BN21 1JJ *tel:* 01323 640067 *fax:* 01323 644699 *email:* music@greenfield.prestel.co.uk. *Orch, ens, film, TV, theatre.*

† **Newson, George.** Chapel Cottage, Stone in Oxney, nr Tenterden, Kent TN30 7JL *tel:* 01233 758227 *also fax. Leng, Schott.*

Nicholls, David. Dept of Music, Keele University, Keele, Staffs ST5 5BG *tel:* 01782 583462 *fax:* 01782 583295 *email:* mua02@keele.ac.uk. *Chmbr mus.*

† **Nicholson, George.** 17 Keele Rd, Newcastle under Lyme, Staffs ST5 2JT *tel:* 01782 618156 *email:* g.nicholson@sheffield.ac.uk. *Forsyth, University of York. Concert work.*

Noble, Harold. 45 Park Rd, Watford WD1 3QW *tel:* 01923 224199. *Asch, Banks, B, BC, BH, Cramer, Dix, EMI, Leduc, Leng, Max, NWM, Nov, Oec, OUP, Peters, Ric, Schott, Smith, Studio. Vocal, inst, choral, orch, ballet and opera.*

Nockalls, Martin. Charnwood House, High St, Wroot, Doncaster DN9 2BT *tel:* 01302 772677 *also fax. Amber Rose, Hampton, Wise Owl. Gui mus.*

Norris, Michael. 31 Hawthorn Av, Glasgow G61 3NG *tel:* 0141 942 5527. *Camden, Sirron Publications (sp), Yorke. Orch, inst, chmbr mus, mus theatre, vocal.*

* **North, Roger.** 24 Strand on the Green, London W4 3PH *tel:* 0181 995 9174. *Ches, (sp). Film and TV (electro-acoustic), opera, chmbr, orch.*

Nunn, Stephanie. c/o Clifton Wyatt Artists Management, 1 Poets Rd, London N5 2SL *tel:* 0171 354 2050 *also fax; email:* cliftonwyattartists management@compuserve.com.

* **Nutman, Carey.** Rosegarth, Hetton Rd, Houghton-le-Spring, Durham DH5 8JN *tel:* 0191 584 4141 *fax:* 01325 462394 *email:* cnutmanmps@aol. com. *Electro-acoustic, computer mus, chmbr.*

Nye, Richard. c/o Cascade Music Publishing, 30 College Green, Bristol BS1 5TB *tel:* 01454 323608 *also fax; email:* cascademusic@hotmail. com. *Andresier, Attic (sp), Cascade. Choral, inst, chmbr and ens.*

† **Nyman, Michael.** c/o Jane Carter, Chester Music Ltd, 8-9 Frith St, London W1V 5TZ *tel:* 0171 434 0066 *fax:* 0171 287 6329. *Ches. Film, TV, chmbr mus, songs, orch, opera and choral.*

O'Neill, Nicholas B B. 74 New Bond St, London W1Y 9DD *tel:* 0831 751956 *fax:* 0171 629 5205. *Choral.*

Oehring, Helmut. c/o Boosey & Hawkes, 295 Regent St, London W1R 8JH *tel:* 0171 580 2060 *fax:* 0171 637 3490 *email:* composers@ boosey.com. *Chmbr, ens, orch, mus theatre.*

† **Omer, Michael.** 12 Belsize La, London NW3 5AB *tel:* 0171 794 6834; 0836 262457 *fax:* 0171 431 3034 *email:* 100014.1076@compuserve. com; http://ourworld.compuserve.com/homepages/mikemusic/. *A&C Black, Music to Picture Company (sp), TVS Music. TV and film scores, musicals, concert works.*

*† **Orr, Buxton.** Church House Barn, Llanwarne, Hereford HR2 8JE *tel:* 01981 540193 *also fax; fax:* 0181 748 4505 *email:* bdorr@aronet.co. uk. *Gamber, Kunzelman, Leduc, Leng, Nov, OUP, Smith. Film and TV scores, concert mus, opera, mus theatre.*

*† **Orr CBE, Robin.** 16 Cranmer Rd, Cambridge CB3 9BL *tel:* 01223 352858. *AA, Hin, Nov, OUP, Paraclete, Peters, Schott, SMIC, WC. Opera, orch, chmbr and church mus.*

Orton, Richard. 21 West Moor La, Heslington, York YO1 5ER *tel:* 01904 416312 *also fax; email:* ro1@york.ac.uk. *University of York. Inst, electro-acoustic, orch, vocal.*

Osbon, David. The Tithe Barn, Ashwell Farm, Windsor La, Little Kingshill, Bucks HP16 0DZ *tel:* 01494 866462 *email:* dosbon@sas. upenn.edu. *Contemporary concert.*

* **Osborne, Tony.** 42 Parkland Av, Slough, Berks SL3 7LQ *tel:* 01753 541818 *also fax. BH, Faber, Piper, Recital, Yorke. Concert, film and TV, educ mus.*

* **Owen, Albert Alan.** Melindwr, Ponterwyd, Aberystwyth, Dyfed SY23 3JY *tel:* 01970 890603 *fax:* 0171 580 4754. *Amphonic, BTW, Chordsongs, Emeryson (sp), Obelisk and New Experience. Film and TV.*

Owen Thomas, Janet. c/o Maecenas Europe, 5 Bushey Close, Old Barn La, Kenley, Surrey CR8 5AU *tel:* 0181 660 3914 *fax:* 0181 668 5273. *Nov. Concert mus.*

Oxley, Harrison. 1 Conyers Way, Gt Barton, Bury St Edmunds, Suffolk IP31 2RL *tel:* 01284 87533. *KM, Nov, OUP, RSCM, Ramsey, Rob. Church, choral, org mus.*

* **Özdil, Sidika.** 29 Foster Dr, Hitchin, Herts SG4 9EH *tel:* 01462 435198 *also fax. Les Editions de Lestang (France). Orch, chmbr, vocal, choral.*

† **Paintal, Priti.** Peregrine, Grange Rd, St Michaels, Tenterden, Kent TN30 6TS *tel:* 01580 764258 *also fax; email:* ppaintal@aol.com. *Opera, orch, chmbr, solo works and works for Western, Asian, African and jazz insts using improvisation.*

Painter, Christopher. 33 Southminster Rd, Penylan, Cardiff CF2 5AT *tel:* 01222 491585 *fax:* 01222 499970 *email:* painter@dial.pipex.com; http://www.richmondhouse.com. *Vanderbeek. Classical.*

† **Palmer, John.** 70 Western Way, Barnet EN5 2BT *tel:* 0181 275 0693 *also fax; email:* j.palmer@herts.ac.uk. *Inst, orch, chmbr, vocal, electro-acoustic mus.*

*† **Panufnik, Roxanna.** c/o Helen Sykes Artists' Management, 1st Floor, Parkway House, Sheen La, London SW14 8LS *tel:* 0181 876 8276 *fax:* 0181 876 8277. *AAK. Orch, chmbr, vocal, choral, dance, opera, mus theatre, arranging, TV and film.*

Papastávrou, Krinió. Stackwood Cottage, Monks Eleigh, Ipswich, Suffolk IP7 7BD *tel:* 01449 740321. *Bardic, Lyra. Opera, cantatas, pno, w/wind, songs, str mus.*

* **Parfrey, Raymond.** 53 Longley Rd, Harrow, Middx HA1 4TG *tel:* 0181 427 5267. *AV, Bardic, Cascade, Chapman, Cinque Port, Comus, Con Moto, Cramer, Da Capo, Emerson, Griffiths, Harlequin, Kendor, Longley, Oec, Piccolo, Samuel King, Studio. Wind and br ens, pno, str, choral.*

† **Parker, Alan.** Whistler's Wood, The Ridge, Woldingham, Surrey *tel:* 01883 653147. *Amphonic, ASP, De Wolfe, Golden Eagle, KPM, Music House, Themes International. Film and TV scores.*

Parker, Jim. 19 Laurel Rd, London SW13 0EE *tel:* 0181 876 8442 *also fax. BH, Brass Wind Educational, Ches, Faber, IMP, Studio. Film and TV, concert works.*

* **Parkinson, Paul.** 37c Allen Rd, Stoke Newington, London N16 8RX *tel:* 0171 249 5356. *Forward, Maecenas Music, Oec. Concert mus, film and TV scores.*

Parrott, Ian. Henblas Abermad, nr Aberystwyth, Ceredigion SY23 4ES *tel:* 01974 241660. *Banks, BH, Ches, Elk, EMI, Griffiths, Gwynn, Leng, MR, Nov, Oec, Samuel King, Schott, PP, TP, UWP, Weekes.*

* **Parsons, Alan.** 32c Military Rd, Colchester, Essex *tel:* 01206 510784. *Anglian. Concert mus.*

Parsons, Michael. 148 Fellows Rd, London NW3 3JH *tel:* 0171 722 0054. *EMC, Forward. Vocal, inst, electronic.*

Pärt, Arvo. c/o Universal Edition (London) Ltd, 48 Gt Marlborough St, London W1V 2BN *tel:* 0171 437 6880 *fax:* 0171 437 6115 *email:* miranda@ue-london.demon.co.uk. *UE. Contemporary classical.*

Paterson, Wilma. Greystones, 30 Kelvinside Gardens, Glasgow G20 6BB *tel:* 0141 946 2236 *also fax. Vocal, chmbr, incidental.*

*† **Patten, James.** 1 Crown Cottages, Cats Ash, Shepton Mallet, Somerset BA4 5EL *tel:* 01749 344859. *Bosworth Ltd, KM. Orch, inst ens, inst solo, vocal, military band, TV scores, incidental mus and theatre mus.*

† **Patterson, Paul.** 31 Cromwell Av, London N6 5HN *tel:* 0181 348 3711 *fax:* 0181 340 6489 *email:* p.patterson@ram.ac.uk. *UE, Wein.*

Peacock, Bob. 52 Reeth Rd, Linthorpe, Middlesbrough, Cleveland TS5 5JX *tel:* 01642 815943. *Jazz-biased educ, radio drama incidental mus.*

Pearce, Malcolm N. 26 The Warren, Abingdon, Oxon OX14 3XD *tel:* 01235 528444. *Camden.*

Peck, Dennis. 167 Woodstock Rd, Oxford OX2 7NA *tel:* 01865 53694. *Opera, songs.*

† **Pehkonen, Elis.** Lupin Cottage, Church Rd, Theberton, Suffolk IP16 4SF *tel:* 01728 830531. *Corinium, OUP. Choral, orch, chmbr.*

* **Penri-Evans, David.** 23a High St, Esher, Surrey KT10 9RN *tel:* 01732 471193 *also fax; email:* dpe@compuserve.com. *Bryntirion (sp), Da Capo, UMI (USA). Orch, chmbr, opera, film scores, contemporary dance.*

† **Perrin, Glyn.** 4 Rochester House, Rushcroft Rd, London SW2 17R *tel:* 0171 326 1096 *also fax. University of York. Concert, dance, electro-acoustic scores.*

Pert, Morris. The Chalet, 189 Balchrick, Kinlochbervie, Sutherland IV27 4RU *tel:* 01971 521314. *Wein. Orch, symphonic, inst, electronic, educ, jazz and rock.*

Peyton Jones, Jeremy. 13c Grove Pk, London SE5 8LR *tel:* 0171 733 3808 *also fax. Chmbr, dance, film, mus theatre, orch, vocal.*

† **Pheloung, Barrington.** 41 Imperial Av, Westcliff on Sea, Essex SS0 8NQ *tel:* 01702 342404. *Polygram.*

Philips, Julian. The Granary, 19 Green End, Comberton, Cambridgeshire CB3 7DY *tel:* 01223 264210 *also fax; email:* granary@argonet.co.uk. *Choral, ens, inst, vocal, orch.*

Phillips, Freddie. 178 Chessington Rd, West Ewell, Surrey KT19 9XA *tel:* 0181 393 6251. *Weinberger. Film and TV scores.*

Piatti, Polo. 81 Windsor Rd, Forest Gate, London E7 0QY *tel:* 0181 534 6975; 0956 251858. *Film, theatre, dance, elec inst.*

Pickard, John. c/o Bardic Edition, 6 Fairfax Cres, Aylesbury, Bucks HP20 2ES *tel:* 01296 28609 *also fax. Bardic. Orch, choral, inst and chmbr.*

* **Pike, Jeremy.** 84 Southdown Cres, Cheadle Hulme, Cheadle, Cheshire SK8 6HA *tel:* 0161 486 0742. *(Sp). Orch, choral, chmbr, inst and vocal works.*

* **Pitfield, Thomas B.** Lesser Thorns, 21 East Downs Rd, Bowdon, Altrincham, Cheshire WA14 2LG *tel:* 0161 928 4644. *Adlais, Aurora, Banks, Bardic, Belwin, Con Moto, For, Fox, Hin, Leng, Lewis Dyson, ME, Molenaar, Oec, OUP, Piper, RNCM, Rob, TP, WC. Choral.*

Pittas, Christos. 4 Hendham Rd, London SW17 7DQ *tel:* 0181 767 4451. *Theatre and ballet mus.*

Pitts, Antony. 5 The Cloisters, Gordon Sq, London WC1H 0AG *tel:* 0171 387 2867 *also fax; email:* antony.pitts@bbc.co.uk. *Faber Music. Sacred choral, chmbr opera, chmbr, orch, multimedia.*

Plowman, Lynne. 175 Malefant St, Cathays, Cardiff CF2 4QG *tel:* 01222 239198. *Orch, chmbr, inst, vocal, theatre, dance.*

Pont, Kenneth H. Old Mullions, Queen St, Paddock Wood, Kent TN12 6NT *tel:* 01892 835164. *OUP. Inst and vocal arrs for schools, church mus.*

† **Poole, Geoffrey.** Woodlands, 19 Grange Av, Levenshulme, Manchester M19 2EY *tel:* 0161 224 3224 *fax:* 0161 275 4994 *email:* g.poole@man. ac.uk. *For, Maecenas, (sp). Contemporary classical.*

Poppy, Andrew. 22c Breakspears Rd, London SE4 1UW *tel:* 0181 691 8646. *Concert, dance, theatre, film and TV scores.*

* **Pott, Francis.** Thurlows, Main Rd, Littleton, Winchester, Hants SO22 6PS *tel:* 01962 880975. *Cathedral Music, Kirkless, Nov, UMP. Org, pno, religious choral, chmbr, orch.*

† **Powers, Anthony.** c/o Oxford University Press, Repertoire Promotion, 70 Baker St, London W1M 1DJ *tel:* 0171 616 5900 *fax:* 0171 616 5901 *email:* repertoire.promotion@oup.co.uk. *OUP.*

Pratt, Stephen. c/o Music Department, Liverpool Hope University College, Hope Park, Liverpool L16 9JD *fax:* 0151 737 3170 *email:* pratts@ livhope.ac.uk.

Previn, Andre. c/o Columbia Artists Management, 165 W 57th St, New York, NY 10019, USA *tel:* 00 1 212 841 9500 *fax:* 00 1 212 841 9599. *BH, Ches, GS. Orch, chmbr mus, film score, opera.*

Pritchard, Gwyn. 13 Nevil Rd, Bishopstom, Bristol BS7 9EG *tel:* 0117 924 7537 *also fax; email:* gp.ck@virgin.net. *Orch, inst, vocal. Agent: Camerata.*

* **Proctor OBE, Charles.** Bay Tree House, Winchelsea, Sussex TN36 4HB *tel:* 01797 226319. *Leng, Oec, Wein. Org, choral, chmbr.*

* **Proctor, Simon.** 8 Henbane Close, Grove Green, Maidstone, Kent ME14 5UW *tel:* 01622 734003. *Cathedral, Heavy Metal (USA), Musicland, School Sheet Music, Spring Tree (USA), Studio. Concertos, choral, chmbr, musicals.*

Purkiss, Anthony. 35 Fonthill Rd, Hove, E Sussex BN3 6HB *tel:* 01273 774730 *also fax.*

Puumala, Veli-Matti. c/o Boosey & Hawkes, 295 Regent St, London W1R 8JH *tel:* 0171 580 2060 *fax:* 0171 637 3490 *email:* composers@boosey. com. *Orch and ens.*

* **Rabinowitz MBE, Harry.** Yellow Cottage, Walking Bottom, Peaslake, Surrey GU5 9RR *tel:* 01306 730605. *BH, EMI, Essex, Key, KPM, Mood Music, Songways, Sou, Standard, Virgin, Weekend, Wein. TV, radio and film. Mus for children.*

* **Rae, Charles Bodman.** Head of Academic Studies, Leeds College of Music, 3 Quarry Hill, Leeds LS2 7PD *tel:* 0113 243 2491; 01943 602016 *fax:* 0113 243 8798.

* **Ramskill, Robert.** 142 Woodside Av South, Green La, Coventry CV3 6BE *tel:* 01203 410325. *BH, Brass Wind. Concert pieces, educ mus.*

Randalls, Jeremy S. 3 Luss Brae, Hamilton, Lanarkshire ML3 9UW *tel:* 01698 334023 *fax:* 00 39 91 528516 *email:* jrandall@mbox.vol.it; http://www.music.gla.ac.uk. *Caliban Press. Orch, wind band, chmbr, vocal, fl and picc.*

Rathbone, Jonathan. c/o Massey Music, 61 Clarendon Rd, London E17 9AY *tel:* 0181 925 7884 *fax:* 0181 520 0662. *Choral, orch, musicals and film.*

Rautavaara, Einojuhani. c/o Boosey & Hawkes, 295 Regent St, London W1R 8JH *tel:* 0171 580 2060 *fax:* 0171 637 3490 *email:* composers @boosey.com. *Opera, orch and concertos.*

* **Read, Martin.** 7 Gladstone St, Winchester, Hants SO23 8TQ *tel:* 01962 860886. *Banks, Editions A Coeur Joie (Lyon), Fand, Noteworks, (sp). TV and video scores, chmbr, choral, inst, orch.*

Reade, Paul. 30 Platts La, London NW3 7NS *tel:* 0171 435 8535 *fax:* 0171 431 8317. *ABd, Faber, Nova, Simrock, Studio, Wein. Ballet, concert, TV.*

Redgate, Roger. 119a Sternhold Av, Streatham Hill, London SW2 4PF *tel:* 0181 671 9771. *Editions Henry Lemoine, (Paris), UMP.*

Reed, William L. Upper Suite 7, The Quadrangle, Morden College, London SE3 0PW *tel:* 0181 305 0380. *Blandford, Cassell, SB. Chmbr, vocal, orch, musicals, film mus.*

* **Reeman, John.** 6 Grenville Av, Lytham St Annes, Lancs FY8 2RR *tel:* 01253 726681. *Nov, SB, Spartan, Studio Music, UE.*

Reeve, Stephen. 73 Knightsfield, Welwyn Garden City, Herts AL8 7JE *tel:* 01707 331689.

Regan, Michael. 85 Northwood Way, Northwood, Middx HA6 1RT *tel:* 01923 825955 *also fax. Animus, Brunton, Duettino, Phylloscopus, Piccolo, Power, Samuel King, SB, Schott, Spartan, Vanderbeek. Educ, inst, songs, choral.*

Reich, Steve. c/o Allied Artists Agency, 42 Montpelier Sq, London SW7 1JZ *tel:* 0171 589 6243 *fax:* 0171 581 5269. *BH.*

* **Reichard-Gross, Clara.** 17 Finlay St, London SW6 6HE *tel:* 0171 736 1977. *Opera, concertos, ens, orch.*

Rentsch, Veronika. c/o Clifton Wyatt Artists Management, 1 Poets Rd, London N5 2SL *tel:* 0171 354 2050 *also fax; email:* cliftonwyattartists management@compuserve.com.

Reynolds, Peter. 46 Richmond Rd, Roath, Cardiff CF2 3AT *tel:* 01222 482183.

Reynolds, Roger. c/o Peters Edition Ltd, 10-12 Baches St, London N1 6DN *tel:* 0171 553 4030 *fax:* 0171 490 4921 *email:* promotion@edition-peters.com; http://www.edition-peters.com.

* **Rhys, John Marlow.** 26 Cresswell Rd, Twickenham, Middx TW1 2DZ *tel:* 0181 892 0759.

Richman, Eddie. Flat 13, Birchington Ct, West End La, London NW6 4PB *tel:* 0171 328 2205. *Bardic. Vocal, inst.*

Rihm, Wolfgang. c/o Universal Edition (London) Ltd, 48 Gt Marlborough St, London W1V 2BN *tel:* 0171 437 6880 *fax:* 0171 437 6115 *email:* miranda@ue-london.demon.co.uk. *UE. Contemporary classical mus.*

Riley, Colin. 77 Godstone Rd, St Margarets, Twickenham, TW1 1JY *tel:* 0181 891 0143. *Inst, opera, orch, dance.*

Riley, Howard. 53 Tweedy Rd, Bromley, Kent BR1 3NH *tel:* 0181 290 5917. *Notated inst works, jazz for small and large ens.*

* **Rimmer CBE, Frederick.** Manor Farmhouse, 6 Millway, Grantchester, Cambridge CB3 9NB *tel:* 01223 840716. *AA, CF, Hin, IMC, Nov, SMIC.*

Robinson, Paul. 5 Box House, Luddenden, Halifax, W Yorks HX2 6QA *tel:* 01422 883408 *also fax; email:* paul@box-house.demon.co.uk. *Film, orch, chmbr, dance.*

* **Roderick Jones, Richard.** 2 Primrose Ct, Moreton-in-Marsh, Glos GL56 0JG *tel:* 01608 651097. *Opera, choral, ballet, symphonic, concerto, br band, chmbr, TV and theatre mus.*

* **Rodgers, Sarah.** 18 Hillfield Pk, Muswell Hill, London N10 3QS *tel:* 0181 444 8587 *fax:* 0181 245 0358 *email:* impulse@styx.cerbernet.co.uk; http://www.cdj.co.uk/impulse/. *English Music Press (sp), Impulse Edition, Methodist Publishing, SB. Orch, choral, chmbr, film, cross-cultural mus, liturgical mus.*

*† **Roe, Betty.** 14 Barlby Rd, London W10 6AR *tel:* 0181 969 3579. *KM, TP, Yorke. Solo vocal, choral, opera, inst, mus for children, inst and vocal mus for special needs.*

Roe, Helen. Little Greystones, West End, Launton, nr Bicester, Oxon OX6 0DF *tel:* 01869 252658. *Chmbr and orch mus.*

Rogers, Timothy. 22 Tonbridge Rd, Hildenborough, Kent TN11 9BS *tel:* 01732 832783 *fax:* 01732 832706. *Encore, SB. Choral, org.*

* **Roper, Antony.** 72 Doxey, Stafford ST16 1EE *tel:* 01785 253289. *(Sp), Studio. Orch, chmbr, pno, songs.*

Rorem, Ned. c/o Boosey & Hawkes Music Publishing Ltd, 295 Regent St, London W1R 8JH *tel:* 0171 580 2060 *fax:* 0171 637 3490 *email:* composers@boosey.com. *Orch, chmbr, songs.*

Rose, Gregory. 57 White Horse Rd, London E1 0ND *tel:* 0171 790 5883 *fax:* 0171 265 9170. *BH, Nov, OUP. Orch, choral, vocal, inst, ens.*

* **Rose, John.** 42 Killermont Rd, Bearsden, Glasgow G61 2JA *tel:* 0141 942 3089. *Eden Music (sp), Nov. Sacred choral, pno, org, choral, educ, songs, br ens.*

* **Rose, John Luke.** Kalon, 113 Farnham Rd, Guildford, Surrey GU2 5PF. *BH, Gal, JW. Symphonic, operatic, musicals, inst, vocal.*

† **Roth, Alec.** H13 Peabody Buildings, Wild St, London WC2B 4BJ *tel:* 0171 497 3754 *also fax.*

Rothstein, Sue. 37 Sydney Grove, Hendon, London NW4 2EJ *tel:* 0181 202 4769. *Salvi. Inst, songs.*

Rourke, Sean. 296 Hughenden Rd, High Wycombe, Bucks HP13 5PE *tel:* 01494 526052. *Forward.*

Rouse, Christopher. c/o Boosey & Hawkes Music Publishing Ltd, 295 Regent St, London W1R 8JH *tel:* 0171 580 2060 *fax:* 0171 637 3490 *email:* composers@boosey.com. *Orch, concerto, ens.*

Routh, Francis. 68 Barrowgate Rd, London W4 4QU *tel:* 0181 995 1223 *also fax. Leng, Redcliffe.*

Rowland-Jones, Simon. 77 The Vineyard, Richmond, Surrey TW10 6AS *tel:* 0181 948 2345 *fax:* 01227 832418 *email:* tirrel@easynet.co.uk. *(Sp). Va, chmbr mus.*

† **Roxburgh, Edwin.** Springside, Forest Rd, E Horsley, Surrey KT24 5AZ *tel:* 01483 282995 *also fax. IMC, Ric, UMP. Agent: Michael Harrold.*

Rudland, Malcolm. 32a Chipperfield House, Cale St, London SW3 3SA *tel:* 0171 589 9595 *also fax. TP.*

Rumble, Andy. c/o Brunskill Management Limited, Suite 8a, 169 Queen's Gate, London SW7 5HE *tel:* 0171 581 3388 *fax:* 0171 589 9460 *email:* 101234.2025@compuserve.com.

† **Runswick, Daryl.** c/o Faber Music Ltd, 3 Queen Sq, London WC1N 3AU *tel:* 0171 833 7911/7906 *fax:* 0171 639 6007 *email:* drunswick@tcm.ac.uk. *Faber. Opera, concert mus, community works, film, TV.*

* **Rushby-Smith, John.** The Folly, Lower Soudley, Glos GL14 2UB *tel:* 01594 825535. *Chandos, Simrock. Chmbr, choral, vocal, inst, church mus.*

Russell, Colin James. 112 Hamilton Av, Glasgow G41 4EX *tel:* 0141 427 1383; 0171 431 1512. *Pno, orch, film scores, songs, dance, electro-acoustic mus.*

Russell, James. 30 Lithos Rd, London NW3 6EF *tel:* 0171 431 1512. *Member of Scottish Society of Composers. Orch, pno mus and film scores; electro-acoustic mus, songs.*

Rutherford, Jonathan. 10 Burntwood La, London SW17 0JZ *tel:* 0181 947 9867 *also fax.*

† **Rutter, John.** Old Laceys, St John's St, Duxford, Cambridge CB2 4RA *tel:* 01223 832474 *fax:* 01223 836723. *OUP.*

Sackman, Nicholas. 19 Selby Rd, West Bridgford, Nottingham NG2 7BP *tel:* 0115 981 9528; 01602 514759 *fax:* 0115 951 4756. *Schott.*

* **Sager, Sidney.** 90 Church Rd, Bristol BS7 8SE *tel:* 0117 942 5317. *(Sp). Choral, orch, film, TV and radio scores.*

* **Sainsbury, Lionel.** Boot Cottage, Brook End, Chadlington, Chipping Norton, Oxon OX7 3NF *tel:* 01608 676486 *also fax. Nov. Vn concerto, pno mus, str.*

Salter, Lionel. 26 Woodstock Rd, London NW11 8ER *tel:* 0181 458 3568 *also fax. ABd, Asch, BH, Emerson, Faber, Gal, Leng, OUP, Ric, Wein.*

*† **Salter, Timothy.** 26 Caterham Rd, London SE13 5AR *tel:* 0181 318 2031 *also fax. Obelisk, Usk.*

*† **Salzedo, Leonard.** 363 Bideford Green, Leighton Buzzard, Beds LU7 7TX *tel:* 01525 371126. *Amoris, Ches, Lopés. Ballet, film, chmbr mus for perc and br, orch, vocal.*

* **Sander, Peter.** 73 The Avenue, London NW6 7NS *tel:* 0181 459 1781 *fax:* 0181 459 4990. *Bèrben, B, BH, Carlton, Ches, Eul (Zurich), KPM, Kunzelmann, Lemmel, Record Supervision, Schmitt, Sou. Film and TV scores, commercial and serious concert mus.*

Sanders, John. Ridge Cottage, Upton Bishop, Ross-on-Wye, Herefords HR9 7UD *tel:* 01989 780482. *KM, Nov, Oec, Presser, Roger Dean, RSCM. Choral, orch, vocal, church mus.*

*† **Savaskan, Sinan.** 27 Dorchester Ct, Herne Hill, London SE24 9QX *tel:* 0171 737 5777 *also fax;* 0171 963 1123 *email:* s@sav777.demon.co.uk; scs9027@westminster.org.uk. *Independent Composers Catalogue, IMC, Society of New Musics. Contemporary classical, dance, electro-acoustic, incidental mus.*

Sawer, David. c/o Universal Edition (London) Ltd, 48 Gt Marlborough St, London W1V 2BN *tel:* 0171 437 6880 *fax:* 0171 437 6115 *email:* miranda@ue-london.demon.co.uk. *UE. Contemporary classical mus.*

Sawyers, Philip. c/o NWA Artists, 51 Tresco Rd, London SE15 3PY *tel:* 0171 635 7688 *fax:* 0171 635 6211.

* **Saxton, Robert.** c/o Chester Music, 8-9 Frith St, London W1V 5TZ *tel:* 0171 434 0066 *fax:* 0171 287 6329 *email:* music@musicsales.co.uk. *Ches. Orch, chmbr, opera, choral.*

Schlünz, Annette. c/o Boosey & Hawkes, 295 Regent St, London W1R 8JH *tel:* 0171 580 2060 *fax:* 0171 637 3490 *email:* composers@boosey.com. *BH. Chmbr, ens, opera and orch.*

Schnittke, Alfred. c/o Boosey & Hawkes, 295 Regent St, London W1R 8JH *tel:* 0171 580 2060 *fax:* 0171 637 3490 *email:* composers@boosey.com. *Opera, orch, concertos, ens, chmbr, pno.*

Schofield, Ian. c/o Caddy Publishing, 8 Cosway Mansions, Cosway Street, London NW1 6UE *tel:* 0181 995 1753 *fax:* 0181 747 9507.

† **Schurmann, Gerard.** 3700 Multiview Dr, Hollywood Hills, Los Angeles, CA 90068, USA *tel:* 00 1 213 850 0744 *fax:* 00 1 213 850 1242. *Nov.*

Schweinitz, Wolfgang von. c/o Boosey & Hawkes Music Publishing Ltd, 295 Regent St, London W1R 8JH *tel:* 0171 580 2060 *fax:* 0171 637 3490 *email:* composers@boosey.com. *Works for soloists, chorus and orch, vc and orch, ens.*

Schwertsik, Kurt. c/o Boosey & Hawkes Music Publishing Ltd, 295 Regent St, London W1R 8JH *tel:* 0171 580 2060 *fax:* 0171 637 3490 *email:* composers@boosey.com. *Opera, orch, vn concerto, songs.*

* **Scott, Anthony.** 18 Spin Hill, Market Lavington, Devizes, Wilts SN10 4NR *tel:* 01380 813689. *BH, Basil Ramsey, KM. Mus for small chmbr ens, school orchs, concertos, songs.*

* **Scott, Stuart.** 6 Colville Grove, Sale, Cheshire M33 4FW *tel:* 0161 972 0327. *Da Capo, Elbeck, Frontier, MSM, Phylloscopus, Southern (Texas USA), (sp). Choral, orch, chmbr, inst, pno, opera, educ, mus.*

* **Seaman, Barry.** PO Box 11845, London SE21 8ZS *tel:* 0181 761 6565 *fax:* 0181 670 3195 *email:* gbz_mgmt@compuserve.com. *OUP. Inst, orch, chmbr, vocal, choral, mus theatre, dance.*

Segger, Jill.32 Holland Pk, Cheveley, Newmarket, Suffolk CB8 9DL *tel:* 01638 730006. *AV Music, KM, Phylloscopus. Vocal, choral, liturgical, wind mus, pno.*

Seivewright, Andrew. Rest Harrow, Millbeck, Keswick, Cumbria CA12 4PS *tel:* 01768 772172. *Augsberg Fortress (USA), GIA (USA), Kirklees Music, KM, Ramsey, RSCM. Choral, orch, org, vocal.*

Seivewright, Peter. The Old Joinery, Lintfieldbank by Coalburn, Lanarks ML11 0NJ *tel:* 01555 820369 *also fax. For.*

* **Selby, Philip.** Hill Cottage, via Primo Maggio 93, I-00068 Rignano Flaminio, Rome, Italy *tel:* 00 39 761 507945. *Rob, Waterloo. Orch, choral, pno, gui, songs.*

Self, Adrian. 4 Rawlinson St, Dalton-in-Furness LA15 8AL *tel:* 01229 467432. *AA, Nov, Oec, RSCM. Choral, org, inst.*

Self, Geoffrey. 5 Trecarrack Rd, Camborne, Cornwall TR14 7UQ *tel:* 01209 713427. *Animus, Nov. Songs, carols, chmbr, choral, org and orch.*

Self, George. 10 Bassett Close, Southampton SO16 7PE *tel:* 01703 769143. *UE. Tape, computer mus.*

* **Selwyn, David.** 8 Barrow Ct, Barrow Gurney, Bristol BS19 3RW *tel:* 01275 463421. *Opera, vocal, chmbr mus.*

* **Senator, Ronald.** 20 Denbigh Gardens, Richmond, Surrey TW10 6EN *tel:* 0181 940 8831 *also fax. Albert, BH, Cary, GS, Leng, SB. Opera, oratorio, symphonic, concerto, chmbr, pno, TV mus.*

Sharkey, Jeffrey. West Lodge House, The Purcell School, Aldenham Rd, Bushey, Herts WD2 3TS *tel:* 01923 331100 *email:* 101557.3530@ compuserve.com. *Orch, chmbr, vocal and solo.*

Sharma, Elizabeth. 18 Thirlmere Av, Perivale, Middx *tel:* 0181 998 6896. *Multicultural mus w/shops, children's mus stories, inst, vocal.*

† **Shaw, Francis Richard.** 39 Crane Grove, London N7 8LD *tel:* 0171 607 8379 *also fax. Ches, Leng, Music Sales, Nov. Concert mus, film and TV scores.*

* **Shephard, Richard.** The Minster School, Deangate, York YO1 2JA *tel:* 01904 625217 *fax:* 01904 632418. *OUP, RSCM. Orch, church, musicals.*

Sherbourne, Janet. 13 Salegate La, Temple Cowley, Oxford OX4 2HQ *tel:* 01865 770272 *also fax; email:* luke.steele@bigfoot.com. *Practical (sp).*

Sherlaw Johnson, Robert. Malton Croft, Woodlands Rise, Stonesfield, Oxon OX8 8PL *tel:* 01993 891318 *email:* sherlawj@ermine.ox.ac.uk. *OUP. Pno, chmbr, choral, song cycles, orch, opera.*

* **Short, Michael.** Dassells, Priory Rd, Hastings, E Sussex TN34 3JS *tel:* 01424 442729. *Bandleader, BH, Blackwell, Consort, Crouch (sp), Dolmetsch, Goodmusic, Oriel, OUP, Rob, SB, Studio, Thames, WC.*

* **Shrapnel, Hugh.** 27a Shooters Hill Rd, Blackheath, London SE3 7AS *tel:* 0181 858 7123 *email:* http://www.musicnow.co.uk/composers/ shrapnel.html. *Forward. Chmbr mus, songs, pno.*

Sims, Toby. 2 Pelham Terrace, Lewes, E Sussex BN7 2DR *tel:* 01273 472548. *Children's mus, vocal mus.*

*† **Singer, Malcolm J.** 29 Goldsmith Av, London W3 6HR *tel:* 0181 992 2318 *fax:* 0181 896 2556.

Sisson, Richard. 31 The Heath, Breachwood Green, Hitchin, Herts SG4 8PJ *tel:* 01438 833452. *Ballet, chmbr, oratorio.*

Skempton, Howard. Flat 11, 11 Warwick Pl, Leamington Spa, Warwicks CV32 5BS *tel:* 01926 316595. *OUP, UE.*

Skene, Hugh Crawford. Crowhills, Quarter, by Hamilton, Lanarks ML3 7XP *tel:* 01357 300303. *SMIC, member of Scottish Society of Composers. Concerto, symphonic, vocal and inst.*

Smalley, Denis. Dept of Music, City University, Northampton Sq, London EC1V 0HB *tel:* 0171 477 8270 *fax:* 0171 477 8576 *email:* d.smalley@ city.ac.uk. *Electro-acoustic mus.*

Smirnov, Dmitri. c/o Boosey & Hawkes, 295 Regent St, London W1R 8JH *tel:* 0171 580 2060 *fax:* 0171 637 3490 *email:* composers@boosey.com. *Opera, orch, ens, chmbr.*

Smith, Dave. 61a Farleigh Rd, London N16 7TD *tel:* 0171 241 1909. *Pno, inst mus.*

* **Smith, Gavin.** 36 Linden Grove, Hartlepool, Cleveland TS26 9PY *tel:* 01429 260916. *Studio. Br band, wind orch, big band, solo, ens.*

Smith, Geoff. Ash Tree Cottage, Royd Rd, Meltham, W Yorks HD7 3BG *tel:* 01484 854407 *also fax. EMI.*

* **Smith, Peter R.** 20 Northcote Av, Holgate, York YO2 4JD *tel:* 01904 782279. *Classic mus, concertos, chmbr mus, symphonies.*

Smith, Robert. Bodafon Villa, Park Cres, Llanfairfechan, Gwynedd LL33 0BE *tel:* 01248 680572. *Curiad, Gwynn, Hughes, OUP, Rob, UWP, Welsh Music Information Centre.*

Sohal, Naresh. 55 Drakefell Rd, London SE14 5SH *tel:* 0171 635 5132. *Nov, Music Production Company. Orch, chmbr mus, mus theatre, film and TV.*

Spall, Charles William. Flat 3, 8 Inglewood Rd, London NW6 1QZ *tel:* 0171 431 2959.

* **Spearing, Robert.** Ty-wrth-y-Coed, Cwmystwyth, Aberystwyth, Ceredigion *tel:* 01974 282631; 01981 250849 *fax:* 01981 250849. *Faber, Nov, Paraclete. Orch, choral, chmbr mus, solo vocal mus, incidental mus, mus theatre.*

* **Spedding, Frank.** 17 Digby Av, Mapperley, Nottingham NG3 6DS *tel:* 0115 960 5964. *TV, film, symphonic and chmbr mus.*

Spicer, Paul. 4 The Close, Lichfield, Staffs WS13 7LD *tel:* 01543 250627 *fax:* 01543 250970 *email:* paul@finzi.idiscover.co.uk. *Editions Billaudot, For, Nov, Ramsey. Choral, inst, vocal, orch.*

† **Spratling, Huw.** c/o Siva Oke Music Management, 13 Riversdale Rd, Thames Ditton, Surrey KT7 0QL *tel:* 0181 398 1586 *fax:* 0181 339 0981. *Opera, orch, choral, chmbr, vocal, solo, inst.*

Sproston, Darren. 3 Woodhill Close, Wombourne, Wolverhampton, Staffs WV5 0ET *tel:* 01902 326567. *Inst, ens, theatre mus.*

Stacey, Peter. 7 Pitman St, Pontcanna, Cardiff CF1 9DJ *tel:* 01222 641727. *Multi-cultural mus.*

* **Standford, Patric.** 17 Bradford Rd, St John's, Wakefield, Yorks WF1 2RF *tel:* 01924 370454. *Fentone, Leng, Nov, SB, WC. Film and TV.*

Stead, John. 26 Hopwood Close, Hull HU3 1QU *tel:* 01482 225663 *email:* wooler@cix.compulink.co.uk; http://www.compulink.co.uk/~ wooler/. *(Sp). Son et lumières, celebratory openings, electro-acoustic, sacred mus.*

Steadman, Robert. 36 Trafalgar Rd, Beeston Rylands, Nottingham NG9 1LB *tel:* 0115 917 4546 *also fax. Con Moto, Piccolo, TVS, Vanderbeek.*

Steel, Alan. 324 Desborough Av, High Wycombe, Bucks HP11 2TJ *tel:* 01494 528380 *fax:* 01494 464166. *Choral works.*

Steele, Jan. 13 Salegate La, Temple Cowley, Oxford OX4 2HQ *tel:* 01865 770272 *also fax; email:* luke.steele@bigfoot.com. *Practical (sp). Jazz, classical, Indian light mus.*

* **Steer, Maxwell.** 125 Duck St, Tisbury, Wilts SP3 6LJ *tel:* 01747 870070 *fax:* 01747 871451 *email:* mms@enterprise.net. *Nov. Experimental mus drama, educ mus.*

Steinke, Gunter. c/o Boosey & Hawkes, 295 Regent St, London W1R 8JH *tel:* 0171 580 2060 *fax:* 0171 637 3490 *email:* composers@boosey.com. *Orch, ens and chmbr.*

Stephen-Samuels, Patrick. c/o SOTAC, Ty-Coat, Kinlochmoidart by Lochailort, Inverness-shire, PH38 4ND *tel:* 01967 431298 *fax:* 01967 431289. *Camerati. Chmbr, vocal, opera.*

* **Steptoe, Roger.** c/o Alfred Lengnick and Co, Pigeon House Meadow, 27 Grove Rd, Beaconsfield, Bucks HP9 1UR *tel:* 01494 681216 *fax:* 01494 670443. *Leng, SB. Inst, orch mus and concerti, concert mus, opera, chmbr mus, vocal mus.*

† **Stevens, James.** c/o The Association of Professional Composers, 34 Hanway St, London W1P 9DE *tel:* 0171 346 3335. *FDH, ME, Mod Ed. Serious concert works from chmbr to orch; also film and TV scores, musicals, jazz, pop, cabaret mus.*

* **Stevenson, Ronald.** Townfoot House, West Linton, Peeblesshire EH46 7EE *tel:* 01968 60511. *Altarus, BH, EMI, Henmar, Hyperion, Klavar, Marco Polo, Nov, Olympia, OUP, Peters, Rob, Ronald Stevenson Society, Schott, UMP. Vocal, choral, orch and pno.*

* **Stiles, Frank.** 43 Beech Rd, Branston, Lincoln LN4 1PP *tel:* 01522 791662. *Anglian, Cramer, Mixolydian. Orch, choral, inst and opera.*

Stimpson, Michael. Bridge House, Bishopstone, Salisbury, Wilts SP5 4DB *tel:* 01722 780671 *also fax. OUP, Ric.*

* **Stocken, Frederick.** 3 Goodhope House, Poplar High St, London E14 0AQ *tel:* 0171 537 4951 *also fax. Orch, choral, chmbr.*

Stockhausen, Karlheinz. Kettenberg 15, D-51515 Kuerten, Germany *tel:* 00 49 2268 1813 *also fax. Stockhausen-Verlag (Germany), UE (Vienna). Vocal, opera, chmbr, electronic mus, orch.*

† **Stoker, Richard.** 38 Lee Rd, Blackheath, London SE3 9RU *tel:* 0181 852 9608 *also fax; email:* http://cdj.cerbenet.co.uk/cdj/inart/stoker.htm; http://www.poets.com/richardstoker.html. *BH, BCMA, Bèrben, Breit, Brunton, Evans Brass, Fentone, Hin, Leeds, MCA, Merlin, Minerva, Music Sales, Nes de Bur, Oec, OUP, Outposts, Ric, WC. Concert mus, opera, film, TV, musicals.*

† **Stoll, David M.** 4 Cranford Av, London N13 4PA *tel:* 0181 882 1358 *fax:* 0181 886 7095 *email:* stoll.dm@argonet.co.uk. *Four Seasons Music. Concert, film, TV, theatre, children's mus.*

* **Stone, David E.** Lammasbank, 26 Chalk Rd, Godalming, Surrey GU7 3AP *tel:* 01483 423298. *BH, Goodmusic, Nov. Orch, band, chmbr, educ mus.*

Stone, Robin. Kerkyra, Straight Rd, Boxted, nr Colchester, Essex *tel:* 01206 272587.

* **Streatfield, Valma.** Valley View, Sulhamstead Hill, Sulhamstead, Reading RG7 4DE *tel:* 0118 930 2859. *Children's songs, mus comedy, chmbr mus, pno, org, rcdr mus.*

* **Strutt, D A L.** 27 Dunedin Rd, Rainham, Essex RM13 8HA *tel:* 01708 520779 *email:* 10664.2024@compuserve.com. *Roeginga Edition. Chmbr, vocal, inst, choral.*

Stuart, Amanda. ZigZag Music Productions, Croeso, Church La, Hilton, Huntingdon, Cambs PE18 9NH *tel:* 01480 830073 *also fax. Film, TV, video, theatre, radio, ballet, opera, educ.*

Sturman, Paul. 30 Guildford Dr, Chandlers Ford, Hants SO53 3PT *tel:* 01703 260342. *Ashdown, EMI, Feld, Longman. Educ mus, choral, orch, keyboard.*

Summers, Al. 61 Bratton Rd, Westbury, Wiltshire BA13 3ES *tel:* 01373 864721. *Chmbr, incidental.*

Sutton-Anderson, David. 28 Cavendish Av, London N3 3QN *tel:* 0181 349 2317 *fax:* 0181 346 8257. *Andresier, Camden. Orch, chmbr, dance, educ.*

† **Swayne, Giles.** c/o Performing Arts, 6 Windmill St, London W1P 1HF *tel:* 0171 255 1362 *fax:* 0171 631 4631. *Nov. Orch, choral, chmbr, opera.*

Tamblyn, William. Malting Cottage, Church Rd, Peldon, Colchester CO5 7PU *tel:* 01206 735770. *BH, CTS, Chapman, Chiswick, Faber, Jabulani (USA), Nov, OCP (USA), OUP, St Thomas More Group. Liturgical mus.*

* **Tausky CBE, Vilem.** 44 Haven Green Ct, London W5 2UY *tel:* 0181 997 6512.

* **Tavener, John.** c/o Chester Music, 8-9 Frith St, London W1V 5TZ *tel:* 0171 434 0066 *fax:* 0171 287 6329 *email:* music@musicsales.co.uk. *Ches. Orch, choral, chmbr, opera, vocal.*

Taylor, Matthew. 60 Highlands Ct, Highland Rd, London SE19 1DS *tel:* 0181 761 8968 *also fax. Maecenas.*

Taylor, Philip. 6 Scholes Rd, Huddersfield HD2 2PB *tel:* 01484 452506.

* **Taylor, Richard.** 10 Candleford Ct, Candleford Rd, Withington, Manchester M20 3JH *tel:* 0161 446 2163 *also fax. Musicland, Wein. Mus theatre, concert hall.*

* **Taylor, Timothy.** Dept of Music, University of Wales, College of Cardiff, Corbett Rd, Cardiff CF1 3EB *tel:* 01222 874816 *fax:* 01222 874379 *email:* taylortn@cf.ac.uk. *UCC.*

* **Teed, Roy.** 63 Egret Cres, Longridge Pk, Colchester, Essex CO4 3FP *tel:* 01206 870839. *ABd, Ches, Curwen, Ric, Rob. Vocal, chmbr, orch, opera, film, pno.*

* **Teterev, Mikhail.** c/o 50 Bowling Green Rd, Stourbridge, West Midlands DY8 3RZ *tel:* 01384 832264. *Banks. Film mus, orch, musical.*

Thomas, David. Arunvale House, 10 Kingsmead Rd, Broadbridge Heath, W Sussex RH12 3LL *tel:* 01403 269378. *UE. Song cycles, school musicals, cantatas.*

Thomas, Jane. Arunvale House, 10 Kingsmead Rd, Broadbridge Heath, W Sussex RH12 3LL *tel:* 01403 269378. *UE. Song cycles, school musicals, cantatas.*

† **Thomas, John Ashton.** 22a Chesterton Rd, London W10 5LX *tel:* 0181 964 5410. *Bruton. Film and TV, orch.*

Thomas, Wyndham. Dept of Music, University of Bristol, Bristol BS8 1SA *tel:* 0117 954 5028. *Antico, Imrie, Vanderbeek. Org, choral, chmbr mus.*

Thompson, Peter. The Barony, 16 Sandringham Rd, Petersfield, Hants GU32 2AA *tel:* 01730 267341. *Fand. Vocal, chmbr, choral, orch, pno.*

* **Thompson, Terence J.** 58 Willenhall Rd, Bilston, W Midlands WV14 6NW *tel:* 01902 495646. *Schott, Studio, WC. Solo inst, ens, sax quartets, educ, band, orch.*

Thwaites, Penelope. 23 Lyndale Av, Child's Hill, London NW2 2QB *tel:* 0171 794 5090 *also fax. Bardic. Songs, incidental mus, musicals, inst works.*

* **Tipler, Brian.** 24 Catherine Rd, Bredbury Green, Romiley, Stockport, Cheshire SK6 3DH *tel:* 0161 430 6046. *Orch, operetta, ens, choral.*

† **Tippett OM, Sir Michael.** c/o Schott & Co Ltd, 48 Gt Marlborough St, London W1V 2BN *tel:* 0171 494 1487 *fax:* 0171 287 1529 *email:* http://www.schott-music.com.

Tocher, Gordon. 54 Glenburn Dr, Inverness IV2 4NE *tel:* 01463 232345. *Corda. Inst, choral mus, gui quartet.*

Todd, Paul. 3 Rosehart Mews, 165a Westbourne Grove, London W11 3JN *tel:* 0171 229 9776 *also fax. Musicals, theatre mus.*

*† **Tomlinson, Ernest.** Lancaster Farm, Chipping La, Longridge, Preston PR3 2NB *tel:* 01772 783646 *fax:* 01772 786026. *BH, Electrophonic, FDH, ME, Nov, Wein. Light orch, symphonic jazz, library mus, songs, choir mus, br band, wind band and org.*

Toovey, Andrew. 57b Station Rd, Willesden, London NW10 4UX *tel:* 0181 961 1051 *also fax. BH. Orch, opera, chmbr mus. Agent: YCAT.*

Torke, Michael. c/o Boosey & Hawkes Music Publishing Ltd, 295 Regent St, London W1R 8JH *tel:* 0171 580 2060 *fax:* 0171 637 3490 *email:* composers@boosey.com. *Ballet, orch, chmbr, br, keyboard and perc.*

Tormis, Veljo. c/o Boosey & Hawkes, 295 Regent St, London W1R 8JH *tel:* 0171 580 2060 *fax:* 0171 637 3490 *email:* composers@boosey.com. *Vocal and choral.*

* **Torphichen, Pamela.** c/o Bardic Edition, 6 Fairfax Cres, Aylesbury, Bucks HP20 2ES *tel:* 01296 28609 *also fax. Bardic. Vocal, inst.*

Touchin, Colin. 17 Kensington Rd, Earlsdon, Coventry CV5 6GG *tel:* 01203 670211 *also fax. Tomus (sp). Orch, choral, chmbr, wind ens.*

* **Tremain, Ronald.** PO Box 887, Niagara on the Lake, Ontario L0S 1J0, Canada *tel:* 00 1 905 468 3414 *fax:* 00 1 905 468 1971.

* **Tucapsky, Antonin.** 50 Birchen Grove, London NW9 8SA *tel:* 0181 200 5200. *Ed A Coeur Joie, Ric, Rob. Opera, choral, chmbr, orch.*

Turnage, Mark-Anthony. c/o Schott & Co, 48 Gt Marlborough St, London W1V 2BN *tel:* 0171 494 1487 *fax:* 0171 287 1529 *email:* http://www.schott-music.com. *Schott.*

Turner, Barrie Carson. 2 Redbrick Cottages, Little Green, Burgate, Diss, Norfolk IP22 1QG *tel:* 01379 783277 *fax:* 01379 783177. *Educ, mus for children.*

Tüür, Erkki-Sven. c/o Peters Edition Ltd, 10-12 Baches St, London N1 6DN *tel:* 0171 553 4030 *fax:* 0171 490 4921 *email:* promotion@edition-peters.com; http://www.edition-peters.com.

* **Twigg, David.** 15 Wentworth Pk Av, Harborne, Birmingham B17 9QU *tel:* 0121 427 7343. *Oec, Ramsey. Church, org mus, songs, pno mus, musicals.*

* **Tyrrell, Andrew.** 29 Castle Hill, Banwell, Weston-super-Mare, N Somerset BS24 6NX *tel:* 01934 822857.

Underwood, Mark. 20 Summerhill Rd, Dartford, Kent DA1 2LP *tel:* 01322 287924 *also fax. Pan Educational.*

* **Usher, Julia.** 110 Wyatt Park Rd, Streatham, London SW2 3TP *tel:* 0181 674 1711. *Primavera (sp). Chmbr, mus theatre, choral, orch, cross-media.*

Ustvolskaya, Galina. c/o Boosey & Hawkes, 295 Regent St, London W1R 8JH *tel:* 0171 580 2060 *fax:* 0171 637 3490 *email:* composers@boosey.com. *Orch, ens, chmbr.*

* **Vale, Sydney.** 3 Albany Mews, Fourth Av, Hove, Sussex BN3 2PQ *tel:* 01273 775630. *Modus, (sp). Opera, orch, inst, film scores, vocal.*

Vann, Stanley. Holly Tree Cottage, Wansford, Peterborough, Cambs PE8 6PL *tel:* 01780 782192. *AA, Lorenz, KM, Oec, Ramsey, Rob, RSCM. Choral, vocal, org and inst.*

Vaughan, Mike. 36 Windmill Dr, St Audlem, Cheshire CW3 0AH *tel:* 01270 811589 *fax:* 01782 583295 *email:* m.p.vaughan@keele.ac.uk.

* **Veale, John.** 7 Nourse Close, Woodeaton, Oxford OX3 9TJ *tel:* 01865 558156. *Leng. Concert mus, film and TV.*

Venables, Ian. Turrall House, 2 Turrall St, Barbourne, Worcester WR3 8AJ *tel:* 01905 611570. *Enigma, Headline. Orch, chmbr, pno, songs, solo inst, choral, br.*

Vinao, Alejandro. Flat 3, 27 Coolhurst Rd, London N8 8ET *tel:* 0181 340 4664 *fax:* 0181 374 1021 *email:* alej@vinao.u-net.com. *Serious mus, opera, film and TV scores.*

Vincent, Simon. 8 Milton Av, London N6 5QE *tel:* 0181 342 8687. *Vision of Sound (sp). Electro-acoustic, choral, inst.*

* **Vishnick, Martin Lawrence.** 12 Watling St, St Albans, Herts AL1 2PX *tel:* 01727 866507 *also fax; email:* vish@tabia.demon.co.uk. *Corda. Concert, chmbr, film and TV, opera, theatre.*

Volans, Kevin. c/o Chester Music Ltd, 8-9 Frith St, London W1V 5TZ *tel:* 0171 434 0066 *fax:* 0171 287 6329 *email:* music@musicsales.co.uk. *Ches. Orch, pno, chmbr, opera, dance.*

Vriend, Jan. Benwell Coach House, Park La, South Woodchester, Glos GL5 5HW *tel:* 01453 832492 *also fax. Donemus. Orch, inst, vocal.*

† **Wadsworth, Derek.** 22 Gerard Rd, London SW13 9RG *tel:* 0181 748 5868 *also fax. Film, TV, orch, electronic.*

Wakefield, Anthony. 115 Village Way, Ashford, Middx TW15 2JY *tel:* 01784 252958 *also fax. Carlin, Harlequin, KPM, Patterdale, Studio. Orch, inst, chmbr, wind band, br band, big band, arranger and orchestral reductions.*

* **Walker, Eldon.** 1 Ashford Av, off Ashton Rd, Lancaster LA1 5BA *tel:* 01524 39141. *Anglia. Chmbr, orch mus, songs, big band, jazz arrangements.*

Walker, James. The Brooklands, 57 Shottery, Stratford upon Avon CV37 9HD *tel:* 01789 204315. *GS, Polyphonic, Studio Music, Wein. Chmbr, wind, vocal, theatre.*

Walker, Robert. c/o Novello & Co, 8-9 Frith St, London W1V 5TZ *tel:* 0171 434 0066 *fax:* 0171 287 6329. *Nov.*

Wallen, Errollyn. 37 Coltman House, Welland St, London SE10 9DW *tel:* 0181 853 0818 *also fax. Orch, ens, opera, ballet, theatre, popular songs, radio, film and TV.*

Walters, Gareth. 31 Beauchamp Rd, E Molesey, Surrey KT8 0PA *tel:* 0181 979 3202. *AA, BH, Hohner, OUP, Ric, SB.*

* **Walters, Leslie.** 7 Garden Mews, Newtown Rd, Warsash, Southampton SO31 9GW *tel:* 01489 575825. *Brunton, Oec, Rob. Solo songs, choral.*

† **Ward, David.** St Olaf, Sellafirth, Yell, Shetland ZE2 9DG *tel:* 01957 744307. *Vanderbeek, SMIC. Chmbr, opera, orch, vocal.*

* **Ward, Stuart.** c/o Grosvenor Management, 79 Henley Rd, Ipswich, Suffolk IP1 3SB *tel:* 01473 213215 *also fax.*

*† **Warlow, Wayne.** The Haven, Ocean View, West Dr, Porthcawl CF36 3HT *tel:* 01656 773389. *Film, TV scores, orch, ballet, chmbr.*

*† **Warren, Raymond.** 9 Cabot Rise, Portishead, Bristol BS20 9NX *tel:* 01275 844289. *Nov. Operas, symphonic, chmbr mus and cantatas.*

† **Watkins, Michael Blake.** Acacia House, Uxbridge Rd, Hillingdon, Middx UB10 0LF *tel:* 01895 238689 *also fax. Nov.*

Watkins, Roderick. 1 Grove Terrace, Canterbury, Kent CT1 3SZ *tel:* 01227 458456 *also fax; email:* r.watkins@cant.ac.uk. *Orch, chmbr, opera, ens, symphonic.*

* **Watkinson, Fabian.** 8 Stoneleigh Terrace, Dartmouth Park Hill, London N19 5TY *tel:* 0171 561 0576. *New Essex, Saxtet.*

Watson, Stephen. c/o Alfred Lengnick & Co, Pigeon House Meadow, 27 Grove Rd, Beaconsfield, Bucks HP9 1UR *tel:* 01494 681216 *fax:* 01494 670443. *Leng. Cl, symphonic and choral.*

* **Watt, Howard.** Y Graig, 17 Coryton Cres, Whitchurch, Cardiff CF4 7EQ *tel:* 01222 691811.

Webb, John. 30 Coleman Rd, Camberwell, London SE5 7TG *tel:* 0171 701 8038 *also fax. Chmbr, ens, orch, choral.*

Webber, John. 88 Balfour Rd, North End, Portsmouth PO2 0NH *tel:* 01705 351816 *also fax; email:* aas54@dial.pipex.com. *AA, Arsis (USA), Webber. Orch, chmbr and vocal.*

Weeks, John Ralph. 120 Kylepark Dr, Uddingston, Glasgow G71 7DE *tel:* 01698 813723. *Britannia, Oec, Rob. Solo inst, chmbr mus, vocal, org.*

Weiland, Douglas. Lilac Cottage, 38 Hargham Rd, Old Buckenham, Norfolk NR17 1SL *tel:* 01953 860687.

† **Weir, Judith.** c/o Chester Music, 8-9 Frith St, London W1V 5TZ *tel:* 0171 434 0066 *fax:* 0171 287 6329 *email:* music@musicsales.co.uk. *Ches, Nov.*

Wells, Jane. Lion Cottage, 2 High St, Wighton, Wells next the Sea, Norfolk NR23 1AL *tel:* 01526 834526. *Concert mus, mus with dance and film.*

Westbrook, Mike. Brent House, Holbeton, nr Plymouth PL8 1LX *tel:* 01752 830589 *fax:* 01752 830539. *Metisse (Paris). Jazz and classical ens, radio, TV, theatre, opera, dance and cinema.*

Wetherell, Eric. 24 The Crescent, Bristol BS9 4RW *tel:* 0117 962 8652. *Anglo-Continental, Banks, Kirklees, KPM, ME, Molenaar, Rob, Sou, TP.*

*† **Whettam, Graham.** Silverwood House, Woolaston, nr Lydney, Glos GL15 6PJ *tel:* 01594 529026 *fax:* 01594 529027. *Meriden (sp), Theodore Presser (USA). Orch, chmbr, choral mus.*

Whipp, Ivy Mason. c/o Mrs L M Gale, 32 Springfield Close, Elburton, Plymouth, Devon PL9 8QG. *BH. Songs, pno duets, choral, solo inst.*

White, John. c/o Clifton Wyatt Artists Management, 1 Poets Rd, London N5 2SL *tel:* 0171 354 2050 *also fax; email:* cliftonwyattartists management@compuserve.com.

* **Wickens, Dennis.** Candleshoe, Manor Rd, Wantage, Oxon OX12 8NE *tel:* 01235 763598. *Nov, OUP. Choral, orch, chmbr, vocal, br band.*

Wiegold, Peter. 82 Lordship Pk, London N16 5UA *tel:* 0181 802 9646 *also fax. UE. Works including improvisation.*

* **Wiggins, Christopher D.** Tilsdown Lodge, Dursley, Glos GL11 5QQ. *AA, Concordia, Kjos, Neuschel, Oec, Phoenix, Ric, Studio*

Wilby, Philip. c/o Chester Music, 8-9 Frith St, London W1V 5TZ *tel:* 0171 434 0066 *fax:* 0171 287 6329 *email:* music@musicsales.co.uk. *Ches, Nov. Orch, chmbr, wind and br band, choral.*

* **Wilde, David.** c/o J Audrey Ellison International Artists' Management, 135 Stevenage Rd, London SW6 6PB *tel:* 0171 381 9751 *fax:* 0171 381 2406. *Chmbr mus.*

Wildman, Eddie. c/o Da Capo Music Ltd, 26 Stanway Rd, Whitefield, Manchester M45 8EG *tel:* 0161 766 5950.

* **Wilens, Greta.** 333 Russell Ct, Woburn Pl, London WC1H 0NG *tel:* 0171 837 6001. *B, EMI. Military marches, classical mus, vocal.*

† **Wilkins, Margaret Lucy.** 4 Church St, Golcar, Huddersfield HD7 4AH *tel:* 01484 652762 *fax:* 01484 472656 *email:* m.l.wilkins@hud.ac.uk. *For, Satanic Mills (sp). Concert mus, orch, chmbr, solo, contemporary dance, acoustic, electro-acoustic, choral, vocal, br band.*

Wilkinson, Philip. Lyndhurst, Avenue Rd, Cranleigh, Surrey GU6 7LE *tel:* 01483 273813. *Arnold, Asch, Nov, OUP, WC. Educ mus.*

Willcocks, Jonathan. 3 The Square, Compton, W Sussex PO18 9HA *tel:* 01705 631369 *fax:* 01705 631786. *Lorenz, OUP. Classical, vocal, inst.*

* **Willcox, Scott.** 16 Gordon Rd, Shepperton, Middx TW17 8JX *tel:* 01932 228147. *Music in Worship.*

Willett, Susan Anne. 9 Westfield Oval, Yeadon, Leeds, W Yorks LS19 7NR *tel:* 0113 250 4989. *Ballet.*

Williams, Adrian. c/o Editions Max Eschig, 215 Rue du Faubourg Saint Honoré, F-75008 Paris, France *tel:* 00 33 1 4289 1713 *fax:* 00 33 1 4563 6291 *email:* adrian.williams@virgin.net; http://freespace.virgin.net/ adrian.williams/. *Eschig (Paris). Orch, chmbr, choral, vocal, film and TV.* Agent: *NCCP.*

* **Williams, Chris.** 11 Great Bridge Cottages, Headborough Rd, Ashburton, Devon TQ13 7QW *tel:* 01364 653603. *Choral, mus theatre, mus for young people.*

* **Williams, Graham.** 48 Etheldene Av, Muswell Hill, London N10 3QH *tel:* 0181 365 2952 *fax:* 0181 444 5014. *Chmbr, orch.*

Williams, Roger Bevan. c/o University Music, Powis Gate, College Bounds, Old Aberdeen AB24 2UG *tel:* 01224 272570 *fax:* 01224 272515.

† **Williams, Tom.** 18 Copland Meadows, Totnes, Devon TQ9 6ER *tel:* 01803 864316 *email:* tom@twills.demon.co.uk. *Electro-acoustic mus, vocal, chmbr, orch.*

* **Williamson, John Ramsden.** 31a Aberconway Rd, Prestatyn, Denbighshire, N Wales LL19 9HL *tel:* 01745 852067. *Gwynn. Orch, chmbr, pno, vocal, choral, symphonic, concerto.*

* **Williamson CBE AO, Sir Malcolm.** c/o Campion Press, Sandon, Buntingford, Herts SG9 0QW *tel:* 01763 247287 *fax:* 01763 249984. *BH, Campion, Wein.*

† **Wills OBE, Arthur.** 26 New Barns Rd, Ely, Cambs CB7 4PN *tel:* 01353 662084 *also fax;* 0374 680716 *email:* artwill@argonet.co.uk. *ABd, BB, Banks, BH, Bèrben, Brunton, Cramer, Fentone, Nov, Nova, Oec, OUP, Ric, Rob, RSCM, Warwick, WC, Wein. Choral, opera, org, vocal.*

Wilson, Herman. c/o Clifton Wyatt Artists Management, 1 Poets Rd, London N5 2SL *tel:* 0171 354 2050 *also fax; email:* cliftonwyatt artistsmanagement@compuserve.com.

Wilson, Ian. c/o Universal Edition (London) Ltd, 48 Great Marlborough St, London W1V 2BN *tel:* 0171 437 6880 *fax:* 0171 437 6115 *email:* miranda@ue-london.demon.co.uk. *Camden, Irish Contemporary Music Centre, UE. Orch, chmbr mus.*

Wilson, James. 10a Wyvern, Killiney Hill, Co Dublin, Republic of Ireland *tel:* 00 353 1 285 0786 *email:* jwilson@iol.ie. *Preissler, Waterloo. Opera, concertos, songs, orch, chmbr.*

† **Wilson, Jeffery.** 5 Church Green, Boreham Village, Essex CM3 3EH *tel:* 01245 450192 *email:* http://classical-artists.com/camden. *Camden, Environ Music, Hayter & Shone, LCD, Royal Ballet School. Chmbr mus, jazz, opera, orch.*

Wilson, Malcolm C. Claganach, 1a Stirling Rd, Dunblane, Perthshire FK15 9EP *tel:* 01786 825387 *also fax. Agehr, ASCAP, Deeay, Flagstaff, Flammer, Hope Publishing Company, HRGB, Jeffers, Lorenz, National. Handbells.*

* **Wilson CBE, Thomas.** 120 Downhill St, Glasgow, Scotland G12 9DN *tel:* 0141 339 1699 *also fax. Bèrben, Queensgate (sp), SMIC, WC. Operas, symphonies, orch, choral, vocal, chmbr, inst including concertos for gui, pno, va, vn.*

Wilson-Dickson, Andrew. 25 Plasturton Av, Cardiff CF1 9HL *tel:* 01222 228154 *also fax; email:* w-d@baynet.co.uk. *Banks Music. Opera, classical scores, church mus.*

Wimhurst, Karen. c/o Clarke Agency, 39 Birnam Rd, Islington N4 3LJ *tel:* 0171 281 0672 *also fax. Opera, choral, mus theatre, br bands, dance.*

* **Winters, Geoffrey.** Brett Cottage, Ash St, Semer, Ipswich IP7 6QZ *tel:* 01449 740613. *Brett (sp), Ches, For, OUP, Nov, Nova, Simrock, UE, WC.*

† **Wiseman, Debbie.** 31 Kingsley Way, London N2 0EH *tel:* 0181 455 4030 *fax:* 0181 455 2700 *email:* dwiseman@sprynet.co.uk. *Film and TV.*

† **Wishart, Trevor.** 83 Heslington Rd, York YO1 5AX *tel:* 01904 630143. *Realspace (sp), University of York. Voice, electro-acoustics, mus theatre, educ and computer mus.*

* **Witchell, Peter J.** Old School House, Owston Rd, Knossington, Oakham LE15 8LX *tel:* 01664 454469. *RSCM. Musicals, orch, choral, inst, ballet.*

Wood, David. c/o Casarotto Ramsay Ltd, National House, 60-66 Wardour St, London W1V 4ND *tel:* 0171 287 4450 *fax:* 0171 287 9128. *Samuel French. Musical plays for children.*

Wood, Gareth Haydn. 57 Marishal Rd, London SE13 5LE *tel:* 0181 318 3312. *BH, Maecenas, Rosehill, Smith, Warwick Music.*

Wood, James. Bancroft, Rectory La, Fringford, Bicester, Oxon OX6 9DX *tel:* 01869 278392 *also fax; email:* jw@rogosanti.demon.co.uk. *(Sp). Chmbr ens, chmbr orch, vocal, choir, electronic mus, perc solo and ens.*

Wood, Philip. 18 Ash View, E Ardsley, Wakefield, W Yorks WF3 2HY *tel:* 01924 826159. *Da Capo. Solo inst, orch, educ mus, chmbr and wind band.*

*† **Woolfenden, Guy.** Malvern House, Sibford Ferris, Banbury, Oxon OX15 5RG *tel:* 01295 780679 *fax:* 01295 788630. *Ariel, Brass Wind, R Smith, Warwick. Theatre mus, ballet, opera, film and TV, concert, chmbr mus.*

† **Woolrich, John.** c/o Faber Music, 3 Queen Sq, London WC1N 3AU *tel:* 0171 833 7911/2 *fax:* 0171 833 7939. *Faber.*

Worby, Robert. 30a Spencer Pl, Leeds, W Yorks LS7 4BR *tel:* 0113 262 7302 *fax:* 0113 262 2766. *Low Noise Music. Contemporary dance, film, TV, educ, electro-acoustic mus.*

* **Wright, Christopher George.** Greenways, 46 Duke's Dr, Halesworth, Suffolk IP19 8DR *tel:* 01986 872050. *Boosey, Harlequin. Br, w/wind, inst and pno, vocal, choral, symph.*

* **Wright, Geoffrey.** Shrub Wood Cottage, E Barton, Bury St Edmunds, Suffolk IP31 2QY *tel:* 01284 87316. *AA, BC, Ches.*

Wulstan, David. Ty Isaf, Llanilar, nr Aberystwyth, Cardiganshire SY23 4NP *tel:* 01974 241229 *email:* dww@aber.ac.uk. *Ches.*

Wuorinen, Charles. c/o Peters Edition Ltd, 10-12 Baches St, London N1 6DN *tel:* 0171 553 4030 *fax:* 0171 490 4921 *email:* promotion@edition-peters.com; http://www.edition-peters.com.

Yershon, Gary. c/o Chuck Julian Associates, Suite 51, 26 Charing Cross Rd, London WC2H 0DH *tel:* 0171 437 4248; 0171 240 1301 *fax:* 0171 240 1296. *Theatre, TV, radio, educ.*

* **Young, Derek.** 1 Hive Cottages, North St, Cambridge CB4 3QW *tel:* 01223 560067. *Lynwood.*

Young, Douglas. c/o Ricordi, Kiln House, 5th Floor, 210 New Kings Rd, London SW6 4NZ *tel:* 0171 371 7501 *fax:* 0171 371 7270. *Opera, ballet, vocal, orch, chmbr mus, TV and film scores, mus for children.*

Yu, Julian. c/o Universal Edition (London) Ltd, 48 Gt Marlborough St, London W1V 2BN *tel:* 0171 437 6880 *fax:* 0171 437 6115 *email:* miranda@ue-london.demon.co.uk. *UE. Contemporary classical mus.*

Zschenderlein, Holger. c/o Clifton Wyatt Artists Management, 1 Poets Rd, London N5 2SL *tel:* 0171 354 2050 *also fax; email:* cliftonwyattartists management@compuserve.com.

Librettists and Translators

Writers whose operatic work has been professionally performed and/or has been published (in score or libretto form) are listed below. Only those resident in the UK are included, plus some overseas-based translators whose translations are used by British opera companies. Composers who have written librettos only for their own works are excluded. Translators' languages are listed alphabetically in italics after each entry.

Andrews, John. 101 Western Rd, Lewes, East Sussex BN7 1RS *tel:* 01273 473910. *Librettist.*

Apter, Ronnie. 5748 West Brooks Rd, Shepherd, Michigan 48883-9202, USA *tel:* 00 1 517 828 6987 *email:* herman.apter@sensible-net.com. *Librettist and translator. Anglo-Saxon, Czech, French, German, Greek, Italian, Latin, Old Provençal, Russian, Spanish.*

Ashurst, David. 76 Gilbey Rd, London SW17 0QG *tel:* 0181 767 1358 *also fax; email:* d.ashurst@english.bbk.ac.uk. *Librettist.*

Barzetti, Marcella. 8 Hawthorn Rd, Hatfield Peverel, Essex CM3 2SE *tel:* 01245 382349 *fax:* 01245 382223. *Translator. French, German, Italian.*

Black, Leo. 112 Chetwynd Rd, London NW5 1DH *tel:* 0171 485 1211. *Translator. German.*

Branscombe, Peter. 32 North St, St Andrews, Fife KY16 9AQ *tel:* 01334 473367. *Translator. French, German.*

Burton, Jonathan. 12 Corner Green, Blackheath, London SE3 9JJ *tel:* 0181 852 7399. *Translator. Czech, French, German, Italian, Latin, Russian.*

Carstairs, Adam. 19 Highgate Av, London N6 5SB *tel:* 0181 340 0547 *fax:* 0181 347 6733. *Translator. French, German.*

Clarke, Peter. Harewood, 22 Rooksmead Rd, Sunbury-on-Thames, Middx TW16 6PD *tel:* 01932 781577 *fax:* 01932 789822. *Librettist and translator. French, Italian.*

Cooper, Helen. c/o Judy Daish Associates Ltd, 2 St Charles Pl, London W10 6EG *tel:* 0181 964 8811 *fax:* 0181 964 8966. *Librettist and translator. Dutch, French, German, Italian.*

Cruickshank, Marty. c/o Cruickshank Cazenove Ltd, 97 Old South Lambeth Rd, London SW8 1XU *tel:* 0171 735 2933 *fax:* 0171 820 1081. *Librettist.*

Daguerre de Hureaux, Florence. 72 Lowden Rd, London SE24 0BH *tel:* 0171 737 4403 *fax:* 0171 326 4961. *Translator. French.*

Dawson, David. 10 Glen Rd, Eldwick, Bingley, W Yorks BD16 3ET *tel:* 01274 562007 *also fax. Translator. French, Italian.*

Downes CBE, Sir Edward. c/o Ingpen & Williams Ltd, 26 Wadham Rd, Putney, London SW15 2LR *tel:* 0181 874 3222 *fax:* 0181 877 3113. *Translator. Italian, Russian.*

Drew, David. 12 Favart Rd, London SW6 4AZ *tel:* 0171 371 0170 *also fax. Translator. German.*

Dunnett, Roderic. 4 Warwick Ct, Michaelmas Rd, Coventry CV3 6HD *tel:* 01203 502749 *also fax. Librettist and translator.*

Farncombe CBE, Charles. c/o Werner Kühnly, Woerthstr 31, D-70563 Stuttgart, Germany *tel:* 00 49 711 780 2764 *fax:* 00 49 711 780 4403. *Translator. Italian, German.*

Forbes, Elizabeth. Flat 3, 1 Bryanston Sq, London W1H 7FE *tel:* 0171 262 0266 *also fax. Translator. French, German, Italian, Swedish.*

Gledhill, Ian. 29 Over St, Brighton, Sussex BN1 4EE *tel:* 01273 689657. *Translator. Czech, French, German.*

Hancock, Leonard. 18 St Mary's Grove, London N1 2NT *tel:* 0171 226 0724. *Translator. Czech, French, German, Italian.*

Harriott, Ted. Belvedere, Seymer Rd, Swanage, Dorset BH19 2AL *tel:* 01929 422908. *Librettist.*

Hauger, George. Motley, 9 Hollybush Green, Collingham, Wetherby, W Yorks LS22 5BE *tel:* 01937 573101. *Librettist and translator. French, German.*

Herman, Mark. 5748 West Brooks Rd, Shepherd, Michigan 48883-9202, USA *tel:* 00 1 517 828 6987 *email:* herman.apter@sensible-net.com. *Librettist and translator. Anglo-Saxon, Czech, French, German, Greek, Italian, Latin, Old Provençal, Russian, Spanish.*

Hughes, Ted. c/o Faber & Faber Ltd, 3 Queen Sq, London WC1N 3AU *tel:* 0171 465 0045 *fax:* 0171 465 0034. *Librettist.*

Jones, Andrew V. Selwyn College, Cambridge CB3 9DQ *tel:* 01223 335866 *fax:* 01223 335837. *Translator. Italian (Handel operas).*

Kennedy, Paula. 37 Swainstone Rd, Reading, Berkshire RG2 0DX *tel:* 0118 975 0981 *also fax; email:* shortkennedy@compuserve.com. *Translator. French, Hungarian.*

Keys, Robert. Red Lion Ct, Stalbridge, Sturminster Newton, Dorset DT10 2LR *tel:* 01963 362999. *Translator. German, Italian.*

Knapp, Peter. 16 Oxford Rd, Cambridge CB4 464866 *tel:* 01223 464866 *fax:* 01223 327874. *Translator. French, German, Italian.*

Lenz-Mulligan, Gundhild. 15 Sandbourne Av, Merton Pk, London SW19 3EW *tel:* 0181 544 0983 *fax:* 0181 543 8909 *email:* glenz-mulligan@dial.pipex.com. *Translator. German.*

Levy, Jonathan. Mooney Hill Rd, Patterson, New York, NY 12563, USA *tel:* 00 1 914 878 6064 *also fax. Librettist and translator. French, Italian.*

Lindsay CBE, Maurice. 7 Milton Hill, Milton, Dumbarton G82 2TS *tel:* 01389 762655. *Librettist.*

McCann, Norman. 56 Lawrie Park Gardens, London SE26 6XJ *tel:* 0181 778 6474. *Librettist and translator. French, German, Italian, Romanian, Slovak.*

Macdonald, Hugh. c/o Dept of Music, Washington University, St Louis, MO 63130, USA *tel:* 00 1 314 863 6621 *fax:* 00 1 314 863 7231 *email:* hjmacdon@artsci.wustl.edu. *Translator. French, German, Italian.*

Maresova, Eva. 40 Campbell Close, London SW16 6NG *tel:* 0181 677 8473. *Translator. Czech.*

Mertl, Michael. 81 Chambers La, London NW10 2RN *tel:* 0181 459 5023 *also fax; email:* 101620.3265@compuserve.com. *Translator. German.*

Minchin, Leslie. 11 Parkhill Rd, London NW3 2YH *tel:* 0171 722 8022. *Translator. German.*

Mitchell, Adrian. c/o Peters, Fraser & Dunlop Scripts Ltd, 5th Floor, The Chambers, Chelsea Harbour, Lots Rd, London SW10 0XF *tel:* 0171 376 7676. *Librettist and adaptor from foreign language literal translations.*

Morgan, Edwin. 19 Whittingehame Ct, Glasgow G12 0BG *tel:* 0141 339 6260 *fax:* 0141 357 4977. *Librettist and translator. French.*

Morley, Christopher. 16 Melbourne Rd, Halesowen B63 3NB *tel:* 0121 550 4482 *also fax. Translator. French, German, Italian.*

Morris, Gwyn. 62 St Isan Rd, Heath, Cardiff CF4 4LY *tel:* 01222 618763. *Librettist and translator. French, German, Italian, Spanish.*

Mugridge, Pat. 19 Mount Pleasant Dr, Belper, Derbyshire DE56 2TQ *tel:* 01773 824770. *Librettist.*

Novelli, Florence. 8 Townfield Gardens, Altrincham, Cheshire WA14 4DT *tel:* 0161 941 1138. *Librettist.*

Phillips, Gordon. 28 Ridgeway, Fenham, Newcastle upon Tyne NE4 9UL *tel:* 0191 274 7803. *Librettist.*

Platt, Norman. Pembles Cross, Egerton, Ashford, Kent TN27 9BN *tel:* 01233 756237 *also fax. Librettist and translator. French, German, Italian.*

Porter, Andrew. c/o E Snapp Inc, 421 W 57th St, No 49, New York NY 10019, USA *tel:* 00 1 212 489 1889 *email:* esnappinc@aol.com. *Translator.*

Rae, Charles Bodman. Leeds College of Music, 3 Quarry Hill, Leeds LS2 7PD *tel:* 0113 243 2491; 01943 602016 *fax:* 0113 243 8798. *Translator. French, German, Polish.*

Redmond, Patrick. 1 Ashmore Rd, Coundon, Coventry CV6 1LH *tel:* 01203 593931. *Translator. French, German, Italian.*

Rees, Simon. Dramaturg, Welsh National Opera, John St, Cardiff CF1 4SP *tel:* 01222 464666 *fax:* 01222 483050. *Librettist and translator. French, German, Italian. Specialises in Focon surtitle system.*

Roberts, Don. Dale House, Marshborough, nr Sandwich, Kent CT13 0PG *tel:* 0130481 2576. *Librettist.*

Salter, Lionel. 26 Woodstock Rd, London NW11 8ER *tel:* 0181 458 3568 *also fax. Translator. French, German, Italian, Spanish.*

Shaw, Jean. 38 Hazlewell Rd, London SW15 6LR *tel:* 0181 788 0680. *Translator. French, German, Italian.*

Smith, Rosemary. 11 Oxdowne Close, Cobham, Surrey KT11 2SZ *tel:* 01372 844271 *fax:* 01372 843854. *Translator. French, German. Books, concert programmes, texts and pronunciation texts for choral and solo singers.*

Taylor, Philip. 112 Main Rd, Wilby, Northants NN8 2UE *tel:* 01933 223301 *also fax; email:* 100661.1355@compuserve.com. *Translator. Russian.*

Tracey, Edmund. 58 Ripplevale Grove, London N1 1HT *tel:* 0171 607 4116. *Librettist and translator. French, Italian.*

Trickett, Rachel. St Hugh's College, St Margaret's Rd, Oxford OX2 6LE *tel:* 01865 556121. *Librettist.*

Trowell, Brian. Faculty of Music, University of Oxford, St Aldate's, Oxford OX1 1DB *tel:* 01865 276126 *fax:* 01865 276128 *email:* office@music.ox.ac.uk. *Translator. French, German, Italian, Latin, Spanish.*

Tunnicliffe, Stephen. Clairmont, The Square, Clun, Shrops SY7 8JA *tel:* 01588 640398. *Librettist.*

Venables, Clare. c/o Cruickshank Cazenove Ltd, 97 Old South Lambeth Rd, London SW8 1XU *tel:* 0171 735 2933 *fax:* 0171 820 1081. *Librettist.*

Venues
and
Promoters

Concert Halls and Theatres

This section includes concert halls and theatres where at least six professional classical music, opera or ballet performances are held per annum. Schools, places of worship and halls with a capacity of less than 500 are excluded. London venues are listed first followed by the rest of England, Scotland, Wales and Northern Ireland. The venues are listed alphabetically in town order. Detailed information on over 1200 venues is contained in the *British Performing Arts Yearbook 1997/8* which is also available from Rhinegold Publishing Ltd.

Inner London

Barbican Centre. Silk St, Barbican, London EC2Y 8DS *admin:* 0171-638 4141 *box office:* 0171-638 8891 *fax:* 0171-920 9648. John Tusa, mgr dir; Graham Sheffield, arts dir; Ruth Hasnip, dir of public affairs. *Barbican Hall Capacity:* 1989; *Barbican Theatre Capacity:* 1156; *The Pit Capacity:* 200.

Barbican Theatre. Barbican Centre *admin:* 0171-638 4141, 0171-628 3351 *box office:* 0171-638 8891 *fax:* 0171-374 0818. Adrian Noble, RSC: artistic dir; Lynda Farran, exec producer; Graham Sykes, theatre admin. *Barbican Theatre Capacity:* 1156; *The Pit Capacity:* 200.

Bloomsbury Theatre. 15 Gordon St, London WC1H 0AH *admin:* 0171-383 5976 *box office:* 0171-388 8822 *fax:* 0171-383 4080 *email:* blooms. theatre@ucl.ac.uk; http://www.ucl.ac.uk/bloomsburytheatre/. Kath Abrahams, Catriona Lenihan, joint gen mgrs; Ellen Bridgeland, admin; Rachel Howes, FOH mgr. *Capacity:* 550.

Brixton Academy. 211 Stockwell Rd, Brixton, London SW9 9SL *admin:* 0171-274 1525 *box office:* 0171-924 9999 *fax:* 0171-736 4427. Break for the Border Group, management; Tim Chambers, gen mgr; Richard Christie, maintenance mgr. *Capacity:* 2154.

Broadgate Arena/Ice Rink. c/o Exchange House, 12 Exchange Sq, London EC2A 2BQ *admin:* 0171-505 4000 *fax:* 0171-638 5544. Christine Purdie, events mgr; Mark Smith, asst events mgr. *Arena/Ice Rink Capacity:* 3000; *Exchange Sq Capacity:* 3000.

Conway Hall. Red Lion Sq, Holborn WC1R 4RL *admin:* 0171-242 8032 *fax:* 0171-430 1271. Stephen Norley, hall mgr. *Main Hall Capacity:* 500; *Small Hall Capacity:* 100.

Hackney Empire. 291 Mare St, Hackney, London E8 1EJ *admin:* 0181-986 0171 *box office:* 0181-985 2424 (6 lines) *fax:* 0181-985 4781 (admin), 0181-985 9997 (technicians) *email:* cm@hackemp.demon.co.uk. Roland Muldoon, theatre dir; Simon Thomsett, gen mgr. *Capacity:* 1200.

Holland Park Theatre. Kensington High St, London W8 6LU *admin:* 0171-603 1123 *box office:* 0171-602 7856 *fax:* 0171-603 3436; Gabriel West, principal arts offr; Mick Goggin, Robert Warner, arts offrs. *Capacity:* 720.

Labatt's Apollo Hammersmith. Queen Caroline St, Hammersmith, London W6 9QH *admin:* 0181-748 8660 *box office:* 0171-416 6080 *fax:* 0181-846 9320 (admin). Graham Gilmore, gen mgr. *Capacity:* 3485.

Lewisham Theatre & the Studio Theatre. Rushey Green, Catford, London SE6 4RU *admin:* 0181-690 2317 *box office:* 0181-690 0002 *fax:* 0181-314 1716 *email:* 100316.1453@compuserve.com. Chris Hare, Martin Costello, gen mgrs. *Theatre Capacity:* 845; *Studio Theatre Capacity:* 102.

London Coliseum. St Martin's La, London WC2N 4ES *admin:* 0171-836 0111 *box office:* 0171-836 3161 *fax:* 0171-836 8379 *email:* 100064.377 @compuserve.com. Dennis Marks, gen dir; Guus Mostart, dir, artistic admin; Laurence Holderness, technical dir. *Capacity:* 2358.

Lyceum Theatre. 21 Wellington St, Strand, London WC2E 7DA *box office:* 0171-420 8114/3/2 *fax:* 0171-240 4155 (admin); 0171-240 4346 (box office). Debbie Garrick, mgr. *Capacity:* 2000.

Peacock Theatre. Portugal St, Off Kingsway, London WC2A 2HT *box office:* 0171-314 8800. Ian Albery, chief exec; Ivan Wadeson, mkt dir; Nigel Hinds, artistic producer. *Capacity:* 1010.

Royal Albert Hall. Kensington Gore, London SW7 2AP *admin:* 0171-589 3203 *box office:* 0171-589 8212 *fax:* 0171-823 7725. P Deuchar, chief exec; E Hewitt, sales dir; R Flower, show department mgr. *Capacity:* 5205.

Royal Opera House. Covent Garden, London WC2E 9DD *admin:* 0171-240 1200 *box office:* 0171-304 4000 *fax:* 0171-212 9502 *email:* http://www. royalopera.org; http://www.royalballet.org. Lord Chadlington, chmn; Mary Allen, chief exec; Nicholas Payne, dir, Royal Opera.

St John's, Smith Sq. Smith Sq, London SW1P 3HA *admin:* 0171-222 2168 *box office:* 0171-222 1061 *fax:* 0171-233 1618. Paul Davies, gen mgr; Laura Curtis, asst mgr. *Capacity:* 780.

Savoy Theatre. Savoy Ct, The Strand, London WC2R 0ET *admin:* 0171-836 8117 *box office:* 0171-836 8888 *fax:* 0171-379 7322. Kevin Chapple, theatre mgr; Thomas Bondanetzky, gen mgr. *Capacity:* 1158.

South Bank Centre. London SE1 8XX *admin:* 0171-921 0600 *box office:* 0171-960 4242 *fax:* 0171-928 0063 *email:* http://www.sbc.org. uk. Nicholas Snowman, chief exec; Jodi Myers, dir of perf arts; Malcolm Young, dir of planning. *Royal Festival Hall Capacity:* 2895; *Queen Elizabeth Hall Capacity:* 915; *Purcell Room Capacity:* 368.

Spitalfields Market Opera. 4-5 Lamb St, Spitalfields, London E1 6EA *admin:* 0171-375 2637 *box office:* 0171-247 2558 *fax:* 0171-247 2559. Philip Parr, artistic dir; Tyrrell Burgess, chmn. *Capacity:* 500.

Steiner Theatre. 35 Park Rd, London NW1 6XT *admin:* 0171 723 4400 *also box office; fax:* 0171 724 4364. Terry Goodfellow, mgr. *Capacity:* 250.

Westminster Central Hall. Storey's Gate, Westminster, London SW1H 9NH *admin:* 0171-222 8010 *box office:* 0171-222 4163 *fax:* 0171-222 6883; Peter Tudor, mgr. *Gt Hall Capacity:* 2350; *Lecture Hall Capacity:* 500.

Wigmore Hall. 36 Wigmore St, London W1H 0BP *admin:* 0171-486 1907 *box office:* 0171-935 2141 *fax:* 0171-224 3800 (admin); 0171-935 3344 (box office). William Lyne, artistic dir. *Capacity:* 538.

Outer London

Alexandra Palace. Alexandra Palace Way, Wood Green, London N22 4AY *admin:* 0181-365 2121 *fax:* 0181-803 3999 *email:* alexandrapalace@ dial.pipex.com. *Gt Hall Capacity:* 7008; *West Hall Capacity:* 2500.

Ashcroft Theatre. Park La, Croydon, Surrey CR9 1DG *admin:* 0181-681 0821 *box office:* 0181-688 9291 *fax:* 0181-760 6835 *email:* dbarr@ fairfield.co.uk. Derek Barr, chief exec; Colin May, theatre dir. *Capacity:* 763.

Beck Theatre. Grange Rd, Hayes, Middx UB3 2UE *admin:* 0181-561 7506 *box office:* 0181-561 8371 *fax:* 0181-569 1072. Apollo Leisure (UK) Ltd, management; Graham Bradbury, gen mgr. *Main Theatre Capacity:* 600; *Foyer Performance Area Capacity:* 150.

Churchill Theatre. High St, Bromley, Kent BR1 1HA *admin:* 0181-464 7131 *box office:* 0181-460 6677 *fax:* 0181-290 6968 (admin); 0181-460 7043 (technical) *email:* churchill-th@mail.bogo.co.uk; http://www.bogo.co. uk/churchill-th/home.html. Ian Ross, gen mgr; Colin Hilton, mkt and publicity; Liz Gentry, financial controller. *Capacity:* 785.

Crystal Palace Concert Bowl. Crystal Palace Pk, Thicket Rd, Penge, London SE20 8UT *admin:* 0181-778 9612/7148 *fax:* 0181-659 8397. Peter Beale, mkt mgr. *Capacity:* 17,500.

Fairfield Halls. Fairfield (Croydon) Ltd, Park La, Croydon, Surrey CR9 1DG *admin:* 0181-681 0821 *box office:* 0181-688 9291 *fax:* 0181-760 0835 *email:* dbarr@fairfield.co.uk. Derek Barr, chief exec. *Concert Hall Capacity:* 1700.

Greenford Hall. Ruislip Rd, Greenford, Middx UB6 9QN *admin:* 0181-758 5624 *fax:* 0181-566 5008. Mark Hand, halls mgr; Jud O'Connor, hall supervisor. *Capacity:* 580.

Harrow Arts Centre. Uxbridge Rd, Hatch End, Middlesex HA5 4EA *admin:* 0181-428 0123 *box office:* 0181-428 0124 *fax:* 0181-428 0121 *email:* http://www.harrowarts.org.uk/. Ann Dooley, education mgr. *Elliott Hall Capacity:* 585; *Travellers' Studio Capacity:* 130.

Hippodrome. c/o BBC Concert Orchestra, North End Rd, Golders Green, London NW11 7RP *admin:* 0181-765 3976 (Sue MacIntyre) *box office:* 0171-765 3200 *fax:* 0171-765 3201 *email:* concert/orch@bbc.co. uk; paul.townson@bbc.co.uk; http://www.bbc.co.uk/resources. Ian Maclay, gen mgr; Adrian Evett, orch mgr; Jan Parr, asst orch mgr. *Circle Capacity:* 520; *Stage Capacity:* 180.

Queen's Theatre. Billet La, Hornchurch, Essex RM11 1QT *admin:* (01708) 456118 *box office:* (01708) 443333 *fax:* (01708) 452348. Tony Hill, admin dir; Bob Carlton, artistic dir; Steve Lark, theatre mgr. *Capacity:* 506.

Richmond Theatre. The Green, Richmond upon Thames, Surrey TW9 1QJ *admin:* 0181-940 0220 *box office:* 0181-940 0088 *fax:* 0181-948 3601;

Michael Lynas, theatre dir; Geoff Summerton, technical mgr. *Capacity:* 840.

Wembley Grand Hall. Wembley Conference Centre, Empire Way, Wembley, Middx HA9 0DW *admin:* 0181-902 8833 *box office:* 0181-900 1234 *fax:* 0181-585 3879 *email:* wembley-wcec@btinternet. com; http://www.hotelworld.com. Mike Potter, gen mgr; David Thomson, snr operations mgr; Nigel Beaven, mkt exec. *Capacity:* 2636.

Wembley Stadium. Wembley Complex, Wembley, Middx HA9 0DW *admin:* 0181-902 8833 *box office:* 0181-900 1234 *fax:* 0181-900 1045 *email:* wembley.wcrc@btinternet.com; http://www.ilmc.com/db/ wembley.html. Mike Potter, mgr dir. *Capacity:* 83,000.

Wimbledon Theatre. The Broadway, Wimbledon, London SW19 1QG *admin:* 0181-543 4549 *box office:* 0181-540 0362 *fax:* 0181-543 6637. Anthony Radford, gen mgr. *Capacity:* 1500.

England

Aylesbury. Civic Centre. Market Sq, Aylesbury, Bucks HP20 1UF *admin:* (01296) 585858 ext 5526 *box office:* (01296) 86009 *fax:* (01296) 392091. Sam McCaffrey (ext 5541), programming mgr; John Braley (ext 5528), house mgr. *Reg Maxwell Hall Capacity:* 700.

Barnstaple. The Queen's Theatre. Boutport St, Barnstaple, Devon EX31 1SY *admin:* (01271) 327357 *box office:* (01271) 724242 *fax:* (01271) 326412. Rick Bond, dir; Tracy Davison, mgr; Simon Crick, stage mgr. *Capacity:* 688.

Basildon. Towngate Theatre. Towngate Centre, Pagel Mead, Basildon, Esses SS14 1DW *admin:* (01268) 531343 *also box office; fax:* (01268) 525415. Andy Grays, Beryl Spokes, Diana Millwood, dirs. *Main House Capacity:* 550; *Mirren Studio Capacity:* 200.

Basingstoke. The Anvil. Churchill Way, Basingstoke, Hants RG21 7QR *admin:* (01256) 819797 *box office:* (01256) 844244 *fax:* (01256) 331733 (admin); (01256) 329726 (box office) *email:* http://www.winterthur-life. co.uk/anvil.html. Christine Bradwell, chief exec; Matthew Cleaver, mkt dir. *Concert Hall Capacity:* 1400; *The Forge Capacity:* 10.

Bath. Assembly Rooms. Bennett St, Bath, Avon BA1 2QH *admin:* (01225) 477752 *fax:* (01225) 428184 *email:* historic_roomhire@bathnes.gov.uk; http://www.museumofcostume.co.uk. Ruth Warren, sales mgr. *Ballroom Capacity:* 529; *Tea Room Capacity:* 250.

Bath. Theatre Royal. Sawclose, Bath, Avon BA1 1ET *admin:* (01225) 448815 *box office:* (01225) 448844 *fax:* (01225) 444080. Danny Moar, theatre dir; Julia Clotworthy Bird, development dir. *Main House Capacity:* 940; *Studio Capacity:* 142.

Bedford. Corn Exchange. St Paul's Sq, Bedford MK40 1SJ *admin:* (01234) 344813 *box office:* (01234) 269519 *fax:* (01234) 325358. Horell Hazelwood, admin offr; Carl Amos, business mgr, operations; Barbara Brooker, asst operations mgr. *Corn Exchange Capacity:* 820; *Harpur Suite Capacity:* 200.

Bedworth. The Civic Hall. High St, Bedworth, Warwicks CV12 8NF *admin:* (01203) 376705 *box office:* (01203) 376707 *fax:* (01203) 376730. David Matthews, gen mgr and licensee; Colin Whitmore, production and technical mgr. *Main Auditorium Capacity:* 813; *Small Hall Capacity:* 100.

Bexhill-on-Sea. De La Warr Pavilion. The Marina, Bexhill-on-Sea, East Sussex TN40 1DP *admin:* (01424) 787900 *box office:* (01424) 787949 *fax:* (01424) 787940. Caranne Collier, gen mgr; Tony Williams, snr technician. *Capacity:* 1016.

Birmingham. Adrian Boult Hall. Birmingham Conservatoire, Paradise Circus, Birmingham B3 3HG *admin:* 0121-331 5909 *fax:* 0121-331 5908. Marilyn Seeckts, publicity mgr; Sally Frankish, hire and concerts mgr. *Capacity:* 525.

Birmingham. Birmingham Hippodrome. Hurst St, Birmingham B5 4TB *admin:* 0121-622 7437 *box office:* 0121-622 7486 *fax:* 0121-622 1433 (admin); 0121-622 6506 (box office). Peter Tod, theatre dir; Barry Hopson, theatre mgr; James Prescott, theatre accountant. *Capacity:* 1887.

Birmingham. Symphony Hall. Broad St, Birmingham B1 2EA *admin:* 0121-200 2000 *box office:* 0121-212 3333 *fax:* 0121-212 1982 *email:* jo-5003@admin.icc.necvenues.co.uk. Andrew Jowett, dir; Chris Baldock, operations mgr; Michael Rye, technical mgr. *Capacity:* 2200.

Blackburn. King George's Hall. Northgate, Blackburn, Lancashire BB2 1AA *admin:* (01254) 582579 *box office:* (01254) 582582 *fax:* (01254) 667277. Geoff Peake, gen mgr. *The Concert Hall Capacity:* 1853; *Windsor Suite Capacity:* 584; *The Studio.*

Blackpool. Grand Theatre. Church St, Blackpool FY1 1HT *admin:* (01253) 28309 *box office:* (01253) 28372 *fax:* (01253) 751767/752981. Stephanie Sirr, gen mgr. *Main House Capacity:* 1215; *Studio Capacity:* 80.

Blandford Forum. Bryanston Arts Centre. Blandford, Dorset DT11 0PX *admin:* (01258) 484682 *box office:* (01258) 456533 *fax:* (01258) 484657 *email:* djg@bryanston.co.uk. Sarah Moore, admin. *Coade Hall Capacity:* 600.

Bolton. Albert Halls Complex. Room 100, Town Hall, Bolton, Lancashire BL1 1RU *admin:* (01204) 522311 ext 1064 *box office:* (01204) 364333 *fax:* (01204) 399928. Peter Miller, mgr. *Albert Hall Capacity:* 670; *Festival Hall Capacity:* 375.

Borehamwood. The Venue. Elstree Way, Borehamwood, Herts WD5 1NQ *admin:* 0181-207 2575 *box office:* 0181-207 6655 *fax:* 0181-207 3053.

Lance Stanbury, gen mgr; Martin Hutchings, technical mgr. *Capacity:* 716.

Bournemouth. Bournemouth International Centre. Exeter Rd, Bournemouth, Dorset BH2 5BH *admin:* (01202) 456400 *box office:* (01202) 456456. Kevin Sheehan, dir; Rob Zuradzki, ents and events mgr. *Windsor Hall Capacity:* 3500; *Tregonwell Hall Capacity:* 1000.

Bournemouth. Pavilion Theatre. Westover Rd, Bournemouth, Dorset BH1 2BX *admin:* (01202) 456400 *box office:* (01202) 456456. Kevin Sheehan, dir. *Theatre Capacity:* 1518; *Pavilion Ballroom Capacity:* 950.

Bournemouth. Winter Gardens. Exeter Rd, Bournemouth BH2 5BH *admin:* (01202) 456400 *box office:* (01202) 456456 *fax:* (01202) 451024. Rob Zuradzki, ents and events mgr; Kevin Sheehan, dir. *Capacity:* 1818.

Bradford. Alhambra Theatre. Morley St, Bradford, W Yorks BD7 1AJ *admin:* (01274) 752375 *box office:* (01274) 752000 *fax:* (01274) 752185. John Botteley, gen mgr; Iain Bloomfield, hd of community and educ; Gerry Clifford, hd of customer services. *Main House Capacity:* 1464; *Studio Capacity:* 200.

Bradford. St George's Hall. Bridge St, Bradford, W Yorks BD1 1JS *admin:* (01274) 752374 *box office:* (01274) 752000. Gerry Clifford, mgr, St George's. *Capacity:* 1700.

Brentwood. Brentwood Centre. Doddinghurst Rd, Brentwood, Essex CM15 9NN *admin:* (01277) 215151/261111 *box office:* (01277) 262616 *fax:* (01277) 229694. Steve Allen (ext 381), concerts promotion mgr; Lynn Barhan (ext 744), events mgr. *International Hall Capacity:* 1936.

Bridgnorth. Bridgnorth Leisure Centre. North Gate, Bridgnorth, Shropshire *admin:* (01746) 761541/2. M Burnell, mgr. *Capacity:* 650.

Bridlington. Leisure World. The Promenade, Bridlington YO15 2QQ *admin:* (01262) 606715 *fax:* (01262) 673458. Amanda Eustace, PR. *Capacity:* 700.

Bridlington. Spa Royal Hall. South Marine Dr, Bridlington, E Riding YO15 3JH *admin:* (01262) 678257 *box office:* (01262) 678258 *fax:* (01262) 401769. John Ginniver, dir, educ, leisure and libraries; Richard Primmer, asst dir; Pam Naylor, ents offr. *Capacity:* 2000.

Bridlington. Spa Theatre. South Marine Dr, Bridlington, E Riding YO15 3JH *admin:* (01262) 678257 *box office:* (01262) 678258 *fax:* (01262) 401679. John Ginniver, dir, educ, leisure and libraries; Richard Primmer, asst dir; Pam Naylor, ents offr. *Capacity:* 987.

Brighton. The Dome Complex. Brighton, Sussex BN1 1UG *admin:* (01273) 700747 *box office:* (01273) 709709 *fax:* (01273) 707505. Stephen Piper, gen mgr. *Dome Theatre Capacity:* 2102; *Corn Exchange Capacity:* 1200; *Pavilion Theatre Capacity:* 230.

Brighton. Theatre Royal, Brighton. New Rd, Brighton BN1 1SD *admin:* (01273) 327480 *box office:* (01273) 328488 *fax:* (01273) 777156. Roger Neil, gen mgr. *Capacity:* 951.

Bristol. Bristol Hippodrome. St Augine's Parade, Bristol BS1 4UZ *admin:* 0117-926 5524 *box office:* 0117-929 9444 *fax:* 0117-925 1661. Apollo Leisure (UK) Ltd, proprietors; P R Gregg, mgr dir; John Wood, gen mgr. *Capacity:* 1981.

Bristol. Colston Hall. Colston St, Bristol BS1 5AR *admin:* 0117-922 3693/3673 *box office:* 0117-922 3682 *fax:* 0117-922 3681. Ken Lovell, gen mgr; Paul Preager, concert planning; Daniel Wood, house mgr. *Colston Hall Capacity:* 2121.

Bristol. St George's Brandon Hill. Bristol BS1 5PZ *admin:* 0117-929 4929 *box office:* 0117-923 0359 *fax:* 0117-927 6537. Jonathan Stracey, dir; Catherine Eastwood, admin. *Capacity:* 500.

Bristol. Victoria Rooms. Department of Music, Queen's Rd, Clifton, Bristol BS8 1SA *admin:* 0117-954 5035 *fax:* 0117-954 5011. Lesley Mason, client services mgr. *Capacity:* 745.

Burton upon Trent. Burton Town Hall. King Edward Pl, Burton upon Trent, Staffs DE14 2EB *admin:* (01283) 508548 *box office:* (01283) 508000 *fax:* (01283) 50733. John White, hd of leisure; Charles Dean, leisure development offr; Caroline Berwick, FOH mgr. *Main Hall Capacity:* 580; *Rochefort Room Capacity:* 150; *Lingen Room Capacity:* 150.

Buxton. Buxton Opera House. Water St, Buxton, Derbyshire SK17 6XN *admin:* (01298) 72050 *box office:* (01298) 72190 *fax:* (01298) 27563 *email:* admin@buxton-opera.co.uk; http://www.buxton-opera.co.uk. Judith Christian, theatre mgr. *Capacity:* 937.

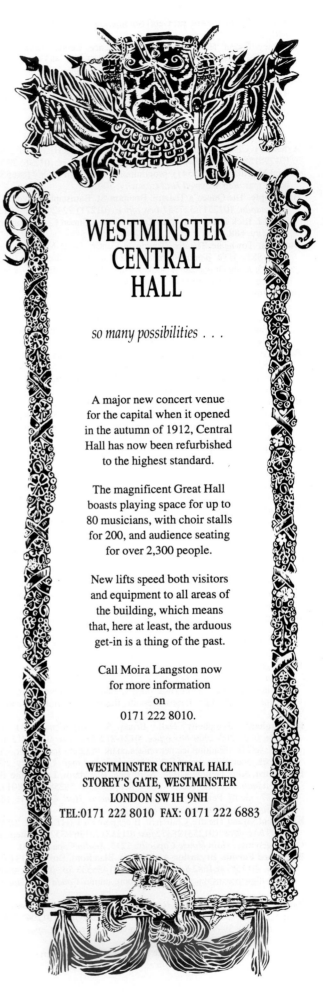

Cambridge. Cambridge Corn Exchange. Wheeler St, Cambridge CB2 3QB *admin:* (01223) 457555 *box office:* (01223) 357851 *fax:* (01223) 457559 *email:* technical.cornex@cambridge.gov.uk; http://www.cambridge. gov.uk/cornex.htm. Robert Sanderson, dir; Graham Saxby, business mgr; Mick Gray, ents and events. *Capacity:* 1462.

Canterbury. The Marlowe Theatre. The Friars, Canterbury, Kent CT1 2AS *admin:* (01227) 763262 *box office:* (01227) 787787 *fax:* (01227) 781802. Mark Everett, theatre dir; Jan de Caux, asst theatre dir; Peter Walker, theatre mgr. *Capacity:* 993.

Carlisle. Sands Centre. The Sands, Carlisle, Cumbria CA1 1JQ *admin:* (01228) 810208 *box office:* (01228) 25222. Jim Douglas, Centre mgr; Nicky Appleby, arts and ents mgr. *Main Hall Capacity:* 1400; *2nd Hall Capacity:* 200.

Chatham. The Central Theatre. 170 High St, Chatham, Kent ME4 4AS *admin:* (01634) 848584 *box office:* (01634) 403868 *fax:* (01634) 827711. Anthea Rathlin-Jones, theatre mgr; Emma Cooper-Hammond, asst mgr; Karl Vosper, FOH mgr. *Capacity:* 945.

Chelmsford. Civic Theatre. Fairfield Rd, Chelmsford, Essex CM1 1JG *admin:* (01245) 606635 *box office:* (01245) 605606. Bernard Mellar, hd, leisure services; Jim Gillies, arts and ents mgr; Andy Chafer, technical. *Capacity:* 525.

Cheltenham. Dean Close School New Theatre. Dean Close School, Cheltenham, Glos GL51 5HE *admin:* (01242) 258002 *also box office; fax:* (01242) 258007. Marian Venn, theatre admin. *Main Auditorium Capacity:* 550; *Orangery Capacity:* 100.

Cheltenham. Everyman Theatre. Regent St, Cheltenham, Glos GL50 1HQ *admin:* (01242) 512515 *box office:* (01242) 572573 *fax:* (01242) 224305 *email:* admin@everymanchel.u-net.com. Richard Hogger, chief exec; Jakki Hall, mkt mgr; Sheila Mander, associate dir. *Main Auditorium Capacity:* 658; *Richardson Studio Capacity:* 60.

Cheltenham. Town Hall. Imperial Sq, Cheltenham, Glos GL50 1QA *admin:* (01242) 521621 *box office:* (01242) 227979 *fax:* (01242) 573902; Jeremy Tyndall, hd of festivals and ents; Tim Hulse, ents and mkt offr. *Capacity:* 1008.

Chesterfield. The Winding Wheel. 13 Holywell St, Chesterfield, Derbys S41 7AY *admin:* (01246) 343533 *box office:* (01246) 345334 *fax:* (01246) 345330. Christine Norcliffe, community ents; Sue Barham, DSO mgr; G Cass, recreation offr. *Auditorium Capacity:* 1000; *Ballroom Capacity:* 200.

Chichester. Chichester Festival Theatre. Oaklands Pk, Chichester, West Sussex PO19 4AP *admin:* (01243) 784437 *box office:* (01243) 781312 *fax:* (01243) 787288 *email:* admin@cftplay.demon.co.uk. Duncan C Weldon, dir; David Bownes, admin; Paul Rogerson, gen mgr. *Main House Capacity:* 1374; *Minerva Theatre Capacity:* 278.

Clacton-on-Sea. Princes Theatre. Town Hall, Station Rd, Clacton-on-Sea, Essex CO15 1SE *admin:* (01255) 425501 *box office:* (01255) 422958/423400 (advance). Bob Foster, ents offr. *Capacity:* 820.

Colchester. Charter Hall. Colchester Leisure World, Cowdray Av, Colchester, Essex CO1 1YH *admin:* (01206) 282946 *box office:* (01206) 282080 *fax:* (01206) 282916. Mike Hill, gen mgr; Claire Jackson, events co-ord. *Event Hall Capacity:* 1200.

Colne. Colne Municipal Hall. Albert Rd, Colne, Lancs BB8 0BP *admin:* (01282) 661216 *box office:* (01282) 661234 *fax:* (01282) 661221. Gary Hood, principal ents offr; Robin Jackson, technical and stage mgr. *Capacity:* 636.

Corby. Festival Hall Complex. George St, Corby, Northants N17 1QB *admin:* (01536) 402551 *box office:* (01536) 402233 *fax:* (01536) 400200. Charles Sanders, mgr; Steve Lloyd, stage mgr. *Festival Hall Capacity:* 1300; *Civic Theatre Capacity:* 500.

Coventry. Warwick Arts Centre. University of Warwick, Coventry CV4 7AL *admin:* (01203) 523734 *box office:* (01203) 524524. Alan Rivett, dep. *Theatre Capacity:* 573; *Studio Capacity:* 150; *Concert Hall Capacity:* 1471.

Crewe. Lyceum Theatre. Heath St, Crewe, Cheshire CW1 2DA *admin:* (01270) 537243 *box office:* (01270) 537333 *fax:* (01270) 537322. Cliff Stansfield, gen mgr; Judith Edwards, mkt mgr. *Capacity:* 693.

Darlington. Darlington Civic Theatre. Parkgate, Darlington DL1 1RR *admin:* (01325) 468006 *box office:* (01325) 486555 *fax:* (01325) 368278 *email:* 100130.404@compuserve.com. Peter Cutchie, theatre dir; Sarah Richards, theatre mgr; Adam Nix, technical mgr. *Capacity:* 909.

Dartford. The Orchard. Home Gardens, Dartford, Kent DA1 1ED *admin:* (01322) 220099 *box office:* (01322) 220000 *fax:* (01322) 227122. Charles Bishop, admin; Robert Wallis, theatre mgr; Andrew Jones, mkt mgr. *Proscenium Capacity:* 959; *In round Capacity:* 1017.

Derby. Assembly Rooms. Market Pl, Derby DE1 3AH *admin:* (01332) 255443 *box office:* (01332) 255800 *fax:* (01332) 255788. Chris Ward-Brown, gen mgr. *Gt Hall Capacity:* 1742; *Darwin Suite Capacity:* 330.

Dewsbury. Dewsbury Town Hall. Wakefield Rd, Dewsbury, West Yorkshire *admin:* (01484) 221900. Julia Robinson, venues mgr; Anna Mesarovic, admin offr. *Capacity:* 690.

Doncaster. Civic Theatre. Waterdale, Doncaster, S Yorkshire DN1 3ET *admin:* (01302) 735600 *box office:* (01302) 342349 *fax:* (01302) 367223. *Capacity:* 511.

Dorking. Dorking Halls. Reigate Rd, Dorking, Surrey RH4 1SG *admin:* (01306) 879200 *box office:* (01306) 881717 *fax:* (01306) 877277. Vanessa Hart, gen mgr. *Grand Hall Capacity:* 801; *Martineau Hall Capacity:* 252.

Dudley. Dudley Town Hall. St James's Rd, Dudley, W Midlands DY1 1HF *admin:* (01384) 815544 *box office:* (01384) 812812 *fax:* (01384) 815534 (admin); (01384) 815599 (technician). David Boyce, mgr; Claire Crone, principal arts offr; Martin Jones, halls and arts technician. *Capacity:* 1060.

Dunstable. Queensway Hall. Vernon Pl, Dunstable, Beds LU5 4EU *admin:* (01582) 609620 *box office:* (01582) 603326 *fax:* (01582) 471190; Yvonne Mullens, gen mgr. *Capacity:* 900.

Eastbourne. Congress Theatre. Carlisle Rd, Eastbourne, East Sussex BN21 4BP *admin:* (01323) 415500 *box office:* (01323) 412000; 411555 (cc) *fax:* (01323) 727369. Ian Alexander, gen mgr; Giles Letheren, operations mgr. *Capacity:* 1689.

Exeter. Exeter University Gt Hall. Stocker Rd, Exeter EX4 4PZ *admin:* (01392) 215566 *fax:* (01392) 263512 *email:* m.v.carter@exeter.ac.uk. Derek Phillips, dir, domestic services; Marilyn Carter, bookings. *Capacity:* 1435.

Exeter. St George's Hall. George St, Exeter, Devon EX1 1BU *admin:* (01392) 265866 *fax:* (01392) 422137. David Lewis, halls mgr; Dave Avery, halls supervisor. *Capacity:* 500.

Fareham. Ferneham Hall. Osborn Rd, Fareham, Hampshire PO16 7DB *admin:* (01329) 824864 *box office:* (01329) 231942. Jane Masterman, gen mgr. *Solent-Meon Hall Capacity:* 1022.

Felixstowe. Spa Pavilion Theatre. Undercliff Rd West, Felixstowe, Suffolk IP11 8AQ *admin:* (01394) 283303 *box office:* (01394) 282126 *fax:* (01394) 278978. Miles Cowburn, gen mgr. *Capacity:* 919.

Frimley Green. Lakeside Country Club. Wharf Rd, Frimley Green, near Camberley, Surrey GU16 6PT *admin:* (01252) 836464 *fax:* (01252) 836777. Bob Potter, mgr dir; Austin Brown, promotional mgr; Rob Goodwin, technical mgr. *Lakeside Cabaret Suite Capacity:* 1170; *Canal Suite Capacity:* 500.

Gloucester. Gloucester Leisure Centre. Bruton Way, Gloucester GL1 1DT *admin:* (01452) 306498 *box office:* (01452) 306788 *fax:* (01452) 310029. Cathy Daley, gen mgr. *Main Hall Capacity:* 2100.

Glyndebourne. Glyndebourne Opera House. Glyndebourne, Lewes, E Sussex BN8 5UU *admin:* (01273) 812321 *box office:* (01273) 813813 *fax:* (01273) 812783 *email:* http://www.demon.co.uk/glyndbn/home. html. Anthony Whitworth-Jones, gen dir; Andrew Davis, mus dir; Graham Vick, dir of productions. *Capacity:* 1200.

Gravesend. Woodville Halls. Civic Centre, Wrotham Rd, Gravesend, Kent *admin:* (01474) 337456 *box office:* (01474) 337459/60/61 *fax:* (01474) 337458 *email:* woodville.halls@gravesham.gov.uk. Brian N Tourle, arts and ents mgr. *Main Hall Capacity:* 835.

Grays. Thurrock Civic Hall. Blackshots La, Grays, Essex RM16 2JU *admin:* (01375) 652397 *box office:* (01375) 383961. M Allinson, gen mgr. *Capacity:* 747.

Great Yarmouth. Wellington Pier Theatre. Marine Parade, Gt Yarmouth, Norfolk NR30 3JF *admin:* (01493) 843635 *box office:* (01493) 842244. Jim Davidson, lessee. *Capacity:* 960.

Guildford. Guildford Civic Hall. London Rd, Guildford, Surrey GU1 4DP *admin:* (01483) 444720/1 *box office:* (01483) 444555 *fax:* (01483) 301982. John Holmes, gen mgr. *Main Hall Capacity:* 1150; *County Suite Capacity:* 160.

Guildford. Yvonne Arnaud Theatre. Millbrook, Guildford, Surrey GU1 3UX *admin:* (01483) 440077 *box office:* (01483) 440000 *fax:* (01483) 564071. James Barber, dir; David Lindsey, gen mgr; John Bostock, finance offr. *Capacity:* 590.

Halifax. Piece Hall. Halifax, West Yorkshire HX1 1RE *admin:* (01422) 358087 *fax:* (01422) 349310. Rebecca Ashworth, events offr. *Capacity:* 2000.

Halifax. The Victoria Theatre. Wards End, Halifax, W Yorks HX1 1BU *admin:* (01422) 351156 *box office:* (01422) 351158. *Main Hall Capacity:* 1585.

Harrogate. Harrogate International Conference Centre. King's Rd, Harrogate, N Yorkshire HG1 5LA *admin:* (01423) 500500 *box office:* (01423) 537230 *fax:* (01432) 537210 (admin); (01432) 537240 (technical). P Lewis, dir; S Quin, dep dir; Colin Weston, hd of operations. *Capacity:* 2009.

Harrogate. Harrogate Theatre. Oxford St, Harrogate, North Yorks HG1 1QF *admin:* (01423) 502710 *box office:* (01423) 502116 *fax:* (01423) 563205. Sheena Wrigley, gen mgr; Phil Day, production mgr; Nick Roberts, finance mgr. *Theatre Capacity:* 500; *Studio Capacity:* 50.

Harrogate. Royal Hall. Ripon Rd, Harrogate, N Yorks H61 2RD *admin:* (01423) 500500 *box office:* (01423) 537230 *fax:* (01432)

537210. P Lewis, dir; S Quin, dep dir; Colin Weston, hd of operations. *Grand Hall Capacity:* 1260.

Hartlepool. Borough Hall. Middlegate, Hartlepool *admin:* (01429) 523803 *box office:* (01429) 266269 *fax:* (01429) 806831. Duncan K Osborne (ext 3803/3859), mgr. *Capacity:* 1300.

Hastings. White Rock Theatre. White Rock, Hastings, E Sussex TN34 1JX *admin:* (01424) 781010 *box office:* (01424) 781000 *fax:* (01424) 781170. G Candler, gen mgr. *Capacity:* 1165.

Hemel Hempstead. The Dacorum Pavilion. Marlowes, Hemel Hempstead, Herts HP1 1HA *admin:* (01442) 228727 *box office:* (01442) 228700 *fax:* (01442) 228735 *email:* http://www.caxton_ carrier.co.uk/time-off. Tom Kealey, gen mgr. *Main Hall Capacity:* 1055; *Small Hall Capacity:* 120.

Hertford. Castle Hall. The Wash, Hertford SG14 1PS *admin:* (01992) 589024 *fax:* (01992) 589025. T Brooke-Auty, admin; Eoin Baird, hall mgr. *Capacity:* 500.

High Wycombe. Wycombe Swan. St Mary St, High Wycombe, Bucks HP11 2XE *admin:* (01494) 514444 *box office:* (01494) 512000 *fax:* (01494) 538080. Stuart Griffiths, gen mgr; Roger Keele, asst gen mgr; Carlos Queiroz, technical mgr. *Theatre Capacity:* 1076; *Town Hall Capacity:* 400; *Oak Room Capacity:* 130.

Horsham. Christ's Hospital Theatre. Christ's Hospital, Horsham, W Sussex RH13 7LW *admin:* (01403) 252709/267005 *box office:* (01403) 252709 *fax:* (01403) 255283. Duncan Noel-Paton, admin; Dominic Gibson, technical mgr; Jackie Davies, publicity. *Capacity:* 500.

Hove. Hove Town Hall. Norton Rd, Hove, East Sussex BN3 4AH *admin:* (01273) 292903 *fax:* (01273) 729330. Chris Jones, gen mgr. *Gt Hall Capacity:* 1400.

Huddersfield. Huddersfield Town Hall. Ramsden St, Huddersfield, W Yorks HD1 2TA *admin:* (01484) 513808/446885/442139 *box office:* (01484) 430808 *fax:* (01484) 446842. Gary Ellis, hall bookings; Julia Robinson, halls development offr. *Capacity:* 1274.

Hull. Hull City Hall. Victoria Sq, Hull HU1 3NA *admin:* (01482) 610610 *box office:* (01482) 226655 *fax:* (01482) 613961. Tony Ridley, operations mgr; Alison Duncan, Marie Burkitt, mkt and publicity; Michael Lister, programming mgr. *Main Hall Capacity:* 1648; *Mortimer Suite (2 galleries) Capacity:* 150.

Hull. The Middleton Hall. University of Hull, Cottingham Rd, Hull, N Humberside HU6 7RX *admin:* (01482) 465012 *fax:* (01482) 465936 *email:* m.bucknall@admin.hull.ac.uk. P Martin, campus services offr; M Bucknall, sec. *Capacity:* 514.

Ilfracombe. Victoria Pavilion Theatre. Wilder Rd, Ilfracombe, Devon EX34 9BE *admin:* (01271) 864118 *box office:* (01271) 862228 *email:* info@northdevon.gov.uk. David Irwin, theatre admin. *Main Theatre Capacity:* 500; *East Wing Capacity:* 150; *Carousel Room Capacity:* 200.

Ilkley. King's Hall and Winter Gardens. Station Rd, Ilkley, W Yorks LS29 8HA *admin:* (01943) 751576; Mark Davies, gen mgr. *King's Hall Capacity:* 745; *Winter Gardens Capacity:* 300.

Ipswich. Corn Exchange. King St, Ipswich IP1 1DH *admin:* (01473) 255851 *box office:* (01473) 215544 *fax:* (01473) 250951 (admin), 262688 (publicity) *email:* corn@ipswich-ents.co.uk; http://www.ipswich-ents. co.uk. Billy Brennan, gen mgr. *Grand Hall Capacity:* 893; *Council Chamber Capacity:* 200.

Ipswich. The Ipswich Regent. 3 St Helen's St, Ipswich, Suffolk IP4 1HE *admin:* (01473) 263555 *box office:* (01473) 281480 *fax:* (01473) 288236 (admin); (01473) 262688 (publicity) *email:* regent@ipswich.ents.co.uk; http://www.ipswich.ents.co.uk. Roy Stephenson, gen mgr; Hazel Clover, publicity. *Capacity:* 1783.

Kendal. Kendal Leisure Centre. Burton Rd, Kendal, Cumbria LA9 7HX *admin:* (01539) 729511 *box office:* (01539) 729702 *fax:* (01539) 731135; R W Gibson, mgr. *Westmorland Hall Capacity:* 932.

King's Lynn. King's Lynn Corn Exchange. Tuesday Market, King's Lynn, Norfolk PE30 1JW *admin:* (01553) 765565 *box office:* (01553) 764864 *fax:* (01553) 762141. Howard Barnes, gen mgr; Amanda McKee, mkt offr; Paul Pomfret, technical mgr. *Capacity:* 738.

Kirkby. Kirkby Suite. Cherryfield Dr, Kirkby, Merseyside L32 1TX *admin:* 0151-443 4064 *box office:* 0151-443 4063. Cathy Weir, mgr. *Main Hall Capacity:* 700; *Hall 2 Capacity:* 140.

Kirkby in Ashfield. Festival Hall. Festival Hall Leisure Centre, Hodgkinson Rd, Kirkby in Ashfield, Notts NG17 7DJ *admin:* (01623) 457101 *box office:* (01623) 457100 *fax:* (01623) 457099. Denis Nicholls, centre mgr; Peter Lamb, asst mgr; Russell Webster. *Capacity:* 520.

Lancaster. Great Hall. Dept of Music, University, Lancaster LA1 4YW *admin:* (01524) 593777 *box office:* (01524) 593729 *fax:* (01524) 847298 *email:* d.mccaldin@lancaster.ac.uk; s.birchall@lancaster; http://www. lancs.ac.uk/users/concerts/. Denis McCaldin, artistic dir; Stella Birchall, admin. *Gt Hall Capacity:* 1100; *Jack Hylton Room Capacity:* 250.

Leamington Spa. Royal Spa Centre. Newbold Terrace, Leamington Spa, Warwicks CV32 4HN *admin:* (01926) 334418 *also box office;*

fax: (01926) 832054. Peter B Nicholson, ents mgr; David F Phillips, asst ents mgr. *Avon Hall Capacity:* 800.

Leatherhead. Leatherhead Leisure Centre. Guildford Rd, Leatherhead, Surrey KT22 9BL *admin:* (01372) 377674/377737 *fax:* (01372) 386749. T Ward, gen mgr. *Sports Hall Capacity:* 1200; *Tyllney Room/Mariners Suite Capacity:* 350; *Mole Barn Capacity:* 600.

Leeds. Civic Theatre. Cookridge St, Leeds LS2 8BH *admin:* 0113-245 6343 *box office:* 0113-245 5505/247 6962 *fax:* 0113-234 7973 *email:* http://www.leeds/gov.uk/tourinfo/attract/theatre/civic.html. Steven Cartwright, gen mgr; Vivien Simpson, asst mgr. *Capacity:* 521.

Leeds. Leeds Grand Theatre and Opera House. 46 New Briggate, Leeds LS1 6NZ *admin:* 0113-245 6014 *box office:* 0113-245 9351/244 0971 *fax:* 0113-246 5906. Warren Smith, gen mgr; Anne Baxendale, house mgr. *Main Auditorium Capacity:* 1550; *Assembly Rooms Capacity:* 600; *Studio Capacity:* 160.

Leeds. Victoria Hall. Town Hall, The Headrow, Leeds LS1 3AD *admin:* 0113-247 7989/8 *fax:* 0113-247 7747. Sue Finnigan, town hall mgr. *Capacity:* 1500.

Leicester. De Montfort Hall. Granville Rd, Leicester *admin:* 0116-233 3113 *box office:* 0116-233 3111 *fax:* 0116-233 3182. Alvin Hargreaves, operations mgr. *Capacity:* 1974.

Leicester. Haymarket Theatre. Belgrave Gate, Leicester LE1 3YQ *admin:* 0116-253 0021 *box office:* 0116-253 9797 *fax:* 0116-251 3310 (admin); 0116-252 9043 (technical) *email:* 100072.1014@compuserve. com; http://www.ourworld.compuserve.com/homepages/ html. Paul Kerryson, artistic dir. *Main Capacity:* 752; *Studio Capacity:* 120.

Liverpool. Methodist Mission Central Hall. Renshaw St, Liverpool L1 2SS *admin:* 0151-709 4435/6. Mr Gardam, gen mgr. *Gt Hall Capacity:* 985; *Lonsdale Hall Capacity:* 250.

Liverpool. Philharmonic Hall. Hope St, Liverpool L1 9BP *admin:* 0151-709 2895 *box office:* 0151-709 3789 *fax:* 0151-709 0918 *email:* spine92@liv.dc.uk; http://www.liv.ac.uk/humananatomy/rlps.html. Antony Lewis-Crosby, chief exec; Petr Altrichter, principal cond, RLPO; Andrew Bentley, hall dir. *Capacity:* 1700.

Liverpool. Royal Court. Roe St, Liverpool L1 1HL *admin:* 0151-709 1808 *box office:* 0151-709 4321 *fax:* 0151-709 2678 *email:* royal.court@ mail.cybuse.co.uk. Simon Geddes, Eddy Grant, gen mgrs. *Capacity:* 1500.

Liverpool. St George's Hall. William Brown St, Liverpool L1 1JJ *admin:* 0151-707 2391 *fax:* 0151-709 2252. John Davies, dir, leisure and recreation; Simon Osborne, hall mgr. *Gt Hall Capacity:* 1000.

Loughborough. Loughborough Town Hall. Market Pl, Loughborough, Leics LE11 3EB *admin:* (01509) 634775 *box office:* (01509) 231914 *also fax.* Geoff Rower, admin; Ian Stephens, gen mgr. *Theatre Capacity:* 528; *Victoria Room Capacity:* 350.

Lowestoft. The Marina Theatre. The Marina, Lowestoft, Suffolk NR32 1HH *admin:* (01502) 523444 *box office:* (01502) 573318 *fax:* (01502) 538179. Sue Webster, principal arts and heritage offr; David Shepheard, theatre offr; Darryl Franklin, technical mgr. *Capacity:* 751.

Manchester. The Bridgewater Hall. Lower Mosley St, Manchester M2 3WS *admin:* 0161-950 0000 *box office:* 0161-907 9000 *fax:* 0161-950 0001 (admin); 0161-907 9001 (box office) *email:* admin@bridgewater-hall.co.uk; box@bridgewater-hall.co.uk. Victoria Gregory, chief exec; Sue Vanden, dir of sales and mkt; Alex Medhurst, dir of operations. *Concert Hall Capacity:* 2330.

Manchester. Dancehouse Theatre. 10 Oxford Rd, Manchester M1 5QA *admin:* 0161-237 1413 *box office:* 0161-237 9753 *fax:* 0161-237 1408. Crispin Radcliffe, theatre mgr. *Capacity:* 430.

Manchester. Manchester Town Hall. Albert Sq, Manchester M60 2LA *admin:* 0161-234 3039/5000 *fax:* 0161-234 3242. Avril Chang, facilities co-ord; John Henstock, buildings mgr. *Gt Hall Capacity:* 500.

Manchester. Palace Theatre. Oxford St, Manchester M1 6FT *admin:* 0161-228 6255 *box office:* 0161-242 2503 *fax:* 0161-237 5746. Apollo Leisure (UK) Ltd, proprietors; Jackie Hinde, gen mgr. *Capacity:* 2000.

Manchester. Royal Exchange Theatre. St Ann's Sq, Manchester M2 7DH *admin:* 0161-833 9333 *box office:* 0161-833 9833 *fax:* 0161-832 0881. Braham Murray, Greg Hersov, artistic dirs; Valerie Hawkin, financial controller. *Capacity:* 740.

Manchester. Royal Northern College of Music. 124 Oxford Rd, Manchester M13 9RD *admin:* 0161-273 6283 *box office:* 0161-273 4504 *fax:* 0161-273 7611. Edward Gregson, principal; Philip Jones, promotions co-ord; Mandy Fiude, events mgr (for hirings). *Opera Theatre Capacity:* 620; *Concert Hall Capacity:* 475.

Mansfield. Palace Theatre. Leeming St, Mansfield, Notts NG18 1NG *admin:* (01623) 663086 *also fax;* *box office:* (01623) 633133. Andrew Tucker, gen mgr; Samantha Hunt, mkt mgr. *Capacity:* 582.

Margate. Winter Gardens. Fort Cres, Margate, Kent CT9 1HX *admin:* (01843) 296111/292795 *box office:* (01843) 292795 *fax:* (01843) 292795. Christopher Wolfe, gen mgr; Steven Davis, food and beverages mgr. *Main Hall Capacity:* 1400; *Queen's Hall Capacity:* 550.

Middlesbrough. Middlesbrough Town Hall. Albert Rd, PO Box 69, Middlesbrough *admin:* (01642) 263848 *box office:* (01642) 242561 *fax:*(01642) 221866. Judith Croft, ents offr; Jean Hewitt, town hall mgr. *Town Hall Capacity:* 1190; *Town Hall Crypt Capacity:* 450.

Newark. Palace Theatre. Appletongate, Newark, Notts NG24 1JY *admin:* (01636) 71636 *box office:* (01636) 71156 *fax:* (01636) 701402. David Piper, theatre dir. *Capacity:* 607.

Newcastle under Lyme. New Victoria Theatre. Etruria Rd, Newcastle under Lyme, Staffs ST5 0JG *admin:* (01782) 717954 *box office:* (01782) 717962 *fax:* (01782) 712885 *email:* http://www.uktw.co.uk/info/newvic. htm. Ludo Keston, gen mgr. *New Victoria Theatre Capacity:* 605; *Stephen Joseph Room Capacity:* 150.

Newcastle upon Tyne. Newcastle City Hall. Northumberland Rd, Newcastle upon Tyne NE1 8SF *admin:* 0191-222 1778 *box office:* 0191-261 2606 *fax:* 0191-261 8102. P J Brennan, gen mgr. *Capacity:* 2133.

Newcastle upon Tyne. Newcastle Playhouse. Barras Bridge, Newcastle upon Tyne NE1 7RH *admin:* 0191-232 3366 *box office:* 0191-230 5151 *fax:* 0191-261 8093 *email:* northern.stage@ncl.ac.uk. Alan Lyddiard, artistic dir; Mandy Stewart, exec dir; David Hayden, dir of productions. *Capacity:* 510.

Newcastle upon Tyne. Theatre Royal. Grey St, Newcastle upon Tyne, NE1 6BR *admin:* 0191-232 0997 *box office:* 0191-232 2061 *fax:* 0191-261 1906. Peter J Aughton, gen mgr. *Capacity:* 1294.

Northampton. Derngate. 19-21 Guildhall Rd, Northampton NN1 1DP *admin:* (01604) 26222 *box office:* (01604) 24811 *fax:* (01604) 250901 (admin); (01604) 233095 (box office) *email:* postbox@derngate. demon.co.uk; http://www.derngate.org. Howard Raynor, gen mgr. *Capacity:* 1400.

Norwich. St Andrew's and Blackfriars Halls. St Andrew's Plain, Norwich, Norfolk NR3 1AU *admin:* (01603) 628477 *fax:* (01603) 762182. Timothy Aldous, gen mgr. *St Andrew's Hall Capacity:* 850; *Blackfriars Hall Capacity:* 400.

Norwich. Theatre Royal. Theatre St, Norwich, Norfolk NR2 1RL *admin:* (01603) 623562 *box office:* (01603) 630000 *fax:* (01603) 762904. Peter Wilson, chief exec; Norman Cullingford, finance mgr. *Main House Capacity:* 1318; *Studio Theatre Capacity:* 150.

Nottingham. The Albert Hall. North Circus St, Nottingham *admin:* 0115-950 0411 *fax:* 0115-947 6512. Sally Robinson, gen mgr. *Gt Hall Capacity:* 700; *Osborne Suite Capacity:* 200; *Balmoral Gallery Capacity:* 60.

Nottingham. Royal Concert and Conference Hall. Theatre Sq, Nottingham NG1 5ND *admin:* 0115-948 3505 *box office:* 0115-948 2626 *fax:* 0115-947 4218 *email:* m.grayson@royalcentre.emnet.co.uk; http://www.netpresence.co.uk/royalcentre. J Michael Grayson, mgr dir; James Ashworth, operations dir; Sally Anne Tye, mkt mgr. *Capacity:* 2496.

Nottingham. Theatre Royal. Theatre Sq, Nottingham NG1 5ND *admin:* 0115-948 3505 *box office:* 0115-948 2626 *fax:* 0115-947 4218 *email:* mgrayson@royalcentre.emnet.co.uk; http://www.netpresence.co. uk/royalcentre. J Michael Grayson, dir; Ken Marshall, technical mgr; James Ashworth, operations dir. *Capacity:* 1186.

Oldham. Queen Elizabeth Hall. PO Box 66, West St, Oldham, Lancashire OL1 1UT *admin:* 0161-911 4070/4071 *box office:* 0161-911 4072 *fax:* 0161-626 9952. Richard Bealing, arts and ents mgr; Jeremy Davies, ents offr; Shelagh Malley, systems and admin mgr. *Queen Elizabeth Hall Capacity:* 832; *Chadderton Suite Capacity:* 250; *Failsworth Suite Capacity:* 160.

Oxford. Apollo Theatre. George St, Oxford OX1 2AG *admin:* (01865) 243041 *box office:* (01865) 244544 *fax:* (01865) 791976. Apollo Leisure (UK) Ltd, proprietors; P R Gregg, mgr dir; Louise Clifford, gen mgr. *Capacity:* 1826.

Oxford. Oxford Playhouse. Beaumont St, Oxford OX1 2LW *admin:* (01865) 247134 *box office:* (01865) 798600 *fax:* (01865) 793748 *email:* admin@oxfordplayhouse.demon.co.uk; http://www.oxford playhouse.demon.co.uk. Tish Francis, Hedda Beeby, joint theatre dirs; Wes Jennings, theatre asst. *Capacity:* 590.

Oxford. Oxford Town Hall. St Aldate's, Oxford OX1 1BX *fax:* (01965) 252388. Rosemary Charlett, bookings; David Clark, town hall mgr. *Main Hall Capacity:* 742; *Assembly Room Capacity:* 200.

Oxford. Sheldonian Theatre. Broad St, Oxford OX1 3AZ *admin:* (01865) 277299 *fax:* (01865) 276708. Sue Waldman, admin. *Capacity:* 1000.

Paignton. Festival Theatre. Torbay Rd, Paignton, Devon TQ4 6ED *admin:* (01803) 666899 *box office:* (01803) 558641 *fax:* (01803) 666681. Apollo Leisure (UK) Ltd, management; P R Gregg, mgr dir; Wendy Hughes, mgr. *Capacity:* 1470.

Plymouth. Plymouth Pavilions. Millbay Rd, Plymouth, Devon PL1 3LF *admin:* (01752) 222200 *box office:* (01752) 229922 *fax:* (01752) 262226 (operations); (01752) 601382 (mkt). Margaret Garcia, hd of operations; Trina Jones, mkt mgr. *Arena Capacity:* 2500.

Plymouth. Theatre Royal. Royal Parade, Plymouth PL1 2TR *admin:* (01752) 668282 *box office:* (01752) 267222 *fax:* (01752) 671179 (admin); (01752) 601382 (mkt) *email:* education@theatreroyal.demon. co.uk. Adrian Vinken, chief exec; Alan Finch, hd of productions. *Theatre Royal Capacity:* 1296; *Drum Theatre Capacity:* 200.

Poole. Poole Arts Centre. Kingland Rd, Poole, Dorset BH15 1UG *admin:* (01202) 665334 *box office:* (01202) 685222 *fax:* (01202) 670016. Ruth Eastwood, chief exec; Don Gent, admin dir; Alistair Wilkinson, programme dir. *Wessex Hall Capacity:* 1473; *Towngate Theatre Capacity:* 669.

Portsmouth. Portsmouth Guildhall. Guildhall Walk, Portsmouth, Hants PO1 2AB *admin:* (01705) 834146 *box office:* (01705) 824355 *fax:* (01705) 834177. Martin Dodd, gen mgr; Daniel Green, dep gen mgr. *Main Hall Capacity:* 2017.

Preston. Guild Hall Centre. Lancaster Rd, Preston, Lancs PR1 1HT *admin:* (01772) 203456 *box office:* (01772) 258858 *fax:* (01772) 881716. John Shedwick, gen mgr. *Charter Theatre Capacity:* 780; *Guild Hall Capacity:* 2020.

Reading. The Hexagon. Queens Walk, Reading RG1 7UA *box office:* 0118-960 6060 *fax:* 0118-939 0028 *email:* hexagon@beta.reading-bc. gov.uk; http://www.reading.gov.uk/hexagon. William Brooker, operations mgr; Paul Kennedy, technical mgr. *Capacity:* 1200.

Redruth. Carn Brea Leisure Centre. Station Rd, Pool, near Redruth, Cornwall TR15 3QS *admin:* (01209) 714766. Malcolm Lear, leisure mgr; Chiz Celani, admin asst. *Main Hall Capacity:* 1250.

Ryde. Ryde Theatre. Lind St, Ryde, Isle of Wight, PO33 2NL *admin:* (01983) 568099 *also fax.* Malcolm Bennett, Sarah Clark, admin. *Capacity:* 502.

St Ives. St Ivo Recreation Centre. Westwood Rd, St Ives, Cambs PE17 4WU *admin:* (01480) 388500 *fax:* (01480) 388513. I C Cousins, Centre mgr. *Burgess Hall Capacity:* 600; *Drama Theatre Capacity:* 250.

Salford. The Lowry Centre. Pier 8, Salford Quays, Trafford Rd, Salford M5 2AZ *admin:* 0161-955 2021 *also fax; email:* info@lowry-centre.org.uk. Stephen Hetherington, chief exec; Felicity Goodey, chmn, Lowry Centre; Chris Hulme, sec, Lowry Centre Trust. *Lyric Theatre Capacity:* 1650; *Flexible Theatre Capacity:* 400; *Open-air Plaza Capacity:* 2000.

Salisbury. City Hall. Malthouse La, Salisbury, Wilts SP2 7TU *admin:* (01722) 334432 *box office:* (01722) 327676 *fax:* (01722) 337059. Phillip Smith, gen mgr. *Auditorium Capacity:* 953; *Alamein Suite Capacity:* 160.

Scarborough. Spa Grand Hall. Spa Complex, South Bay, Scarborough, N Yorks *admin:* (01723) 376774 *also box office:* (01723) 355821. David James, dir of tourism and amenities; Keith Norton, Spa and conference mgr; Sandra Blair, ents and mkt. *Grand Hall Capacity:* 1825.

Scunthorpe. The Baths Hall. 59 Doncaster Rd, Scunthorpe DN15 7RG *admin:* (01724) 297861 *box office:* (01724) 842332 *fax:* (01724) 861341. Terry Wincott, ents mgr. *Main Hall Capacity:* 600; *Apollo Room Capacity:* 200.

Sevenoaks. Stag Theatre. London Rd, Sevenoaks, Kent TN13 1ZZ *admin:* (01732) 451548 *also fax; box office:* (01732) 450175. Terry Shaw, gen mgr. *Capacity:* 700.

Sheffield. Lyceum Theatre. Norfolk St, Sheffield, S Yorks S1 2LA *admin:* 0114-276 0621 (Crucible) *box office:* 0114-276 9922 (Crucible). Grahame Morris, chief exec; Deborah Paige, artistic dir; Rob McKinney, production mgr. *Capacity:* 1099.

Sheffield. Sheffield City Hall. Barkers Pool, Sheffield S1 2JA *admin:* 0114-273 4539 *box office:* 0114-278 9789 *fax:* 0114-276 9866. Maire McCarthy, gen mgr. *Oval Hall Capacity:* 2346; *Memorial Hall Capacity:* 522; *Central Suite Capacity:* 850.

Skegness. Embassy Centre. Grand Parade, Skegness, Lincs PE25 2UN *admin:* (01754) 768444 *box office:* (01507) 768333 *fax:* (01754) 761737. Steve Wattam, mgr. *Capacity:* 1158.

Skegness. Festival Pavilion. Tower Esplanade, Skegness *admin:* (01754) 768444/767820 *box office:* (01754) 768333 *fax:* (01754) 761737. Keith Morrison, publicity mgr; Anne Stocks, admin. *Capacity:* 1200.

Snape. Snape Maltings Concert Hall. c/o Aldeburgh Foundation, High St, Aldeburgh, Suffolk IP15 5AX *admin:* (01728) 452935 *box office:* (01728) 453543 *fax:* (01728) 452715. Steuart Bedford, Oliver Knussen, exec dirs; Jonathan Reekie, chief exec. *Snape Maltings Concert Hall Capacity:* 832; *Britten Pears School Capacity:* 120.

Southampton. Mayflower Theatre. Commercial Rd, Southampton SO15 1GE *admin:* (01703) 711800 *box office:* (01703) 711811 *fax:* (01703) 711801. Dennis L J Hall, dir; Wycliffe Musuku, financial controller; Paul Lewis, hd of mkt and operations. *Capacity:* 2299.

Southampton. Northguild. West Marlands Rd, Southampton, Hampshire SO9 4XF *admin:* (01703) 832451/335555 *box office:* (01703) 632601 *fax:* (01703) 233359 (admin); (01703) 823137 (technical). Sue Cheriton, mgr. *Guildhall Capacity:* 1749; *Solent Suite Capacity:* 250; *Lecture Theatre Capacity:* 118.

Southend on Sea. Cliffs Pavilion. Station Rd, Westcliff on Sea, Essex SS0 7RA *admin:* (01702) 331852 *box office:* (01702) 351135 *fax:* (01702) 433015. Charles Mumford, gen mgr. *Capacity:* 1630.

Southport. Floral Hall. The Promenade, Southport, Merseyside PR9 0DZ *admin:* (01704) 540454 *box office:* (01704) 540404 *fax:* (01704) 536841. Lisa Chu, gen mgr. *Floral Hall Capacity:* 1200.

Southsea. Kings Theatre. Albert Rd, Southsea, Hants PO5 2QJ *admin:* (01705) 811394 *box office:* (01705) 828282 *fax:* (01705) 735242. J N Cooper, I S Barnes, co-lessees; Vanessa Dowling, gen mgr; Steve Charman, chief electrician. *Capacity:* 1450.

Spalding. South Holland Centre. Market Pl, Spalding, Lincs PE11 1SS *admin:* (01775) 725032 *box office:* (01775) 725031 *fax:* (01775) 711253 (South Holland DC). Nigel Hawkins, arts offr; Barbara Gorton, centre mgr. *Spalding Hall Capacity:* 500; *Elloe Hall Capacity:* 153.

Stafford. Stafford Gatehouse. Eastgate St, Stafford, Staffs ST16 2LT *admin:* (01785) 253595 *box office:* (01785) 254653 *fax:* (01785) 225622. Daniel Shaw, mgr and licencee; Lynn Elkin, admin mgr. *Gatehouse Theatre Capacity:* 570; *Malcolm Edwards Theatre Capacity:* 120.

Stevenage. Gordon Craig Theatre. Stevenage Arts and Leisure Centre, Lytton Way, Stevenage, Herts SG1 1LZ *admin:* (01438) 766642/766877 *box office:* (01438) 766866. Bob Bustance, arts and ents mgr. *Theatre Capacity:* 506; *Concert Hall Capacity:* 1500.

Stockport. Davenport Theatre. Buxton Rd, Stockport, Cheshire SK2 7AH *admin:* 0161-483 0683 *box office:* 0161-483 3801/4181 *fax:* 0161-483 7505. Paul Gregg, chmn; Barrie C Stead, divisional mgr; Ted Doan, theatre mgr. *Capacity:* 1702.

Stoke on Trent. King's Hall and Jubilee Hall. PO Box 757, Civic Centre, Glebe St, Stoke-on-Trent, Staffs ST1 1RT *admin:* (01782) 232753 *fax:* (01782) 232592. Tony Meigh, town halls mgr; Simon Tomlins, hallkeeper. *King's Hall Capacity:* 1372; *Jubilee Hall Capacity:* 300.

Stoke on Trent. Victoria Hall. Albion Sq, Hanley, Stoke on Trent, Staffs ST1 1QL *admin:* (01782) 212618 *box office:* (01782) 207777. *Capacity:* 1580.

Sunderland. Sunderland Empire Theatre. High St West, Sunderland SR1 3EX *admin:* 0191-510 0545 *box office:* 0191-514 2517 *fax:* 0191-553 7427 (admin); 0191-553 7428 (publicity). Symon Easton, mgr dir; Stuart Anderson, finance dir; Christabel Smith, operations mgr. *Main Auditorium Capacity:* 1850.

Swindon. Wyvern Theatre. Theatre Sq, Swindon, Wiltshire SN1 1QN *admin:* (01793) 535534 *box office:* (01793) 524481 *fax:* (01793) 480278. Lizzie Jones, gen mgr; David Hollingworth, dep mgr; David Wicks, stage mgr. *Theatre Capacity:* 617.

Telford. Oakengates Theatre. Limes Walk, Oakengates, Telford TF2 6EP *admin:* (01952) 610163 *box office:* (01952) 619020 *fax:* (01952) 610164. Chris Maddocks, theatre mgr. *Capacity:* 650.

Torquay. Babbacombe Theatre. Babbacombe Downs, Torquay, Devon TQ1 3LU *admin:* (01803) 211896 *box office:* (01803) 328385 *fax:* (01803) 296710. Margaret Brooks, theatre mgr; Colin Matthews, dir; Rebecca McDonald, mkt. *Capacity:* 600.

Torquay. Princess Theatre. Torbay Rd, Torquay TQ2 5EZ *admin:* (01803) 666899 *box office:* (01803) 290290 *fax:* (01803) 290170. Apollo Leisure (UK) Ltd, management; P R Gregg, mgr dir; Wendy Hughes, mgr. *Capacity:* 1495.

Torquay. Riviera Centre. Chestnut Av, Torquay, Devon TQ2 5LZ *admin:* (01803) 299992 *box office:* (01803) 295676 *fax:* (01803) 212827 *email:* erc@torbay.goc.uk. Barry Cole, gen mgr; Terry Warne, ents mgr. *Forum Capacity:* 1500; *Arena Capacity:* 1000.

Truro. Hall For Cornwall. Back Qay, Truro, Cornwall TR1 2LL *admin:* (01872) 262465 *box office:* (01872) 262466 *fax:* (01872) 260246. Keith Garrow, chief exec; Chris Warner, artistic and operations dir; Sharon Jackson, mkt mgr. *Capacity:* 1000.

Tunbridge Wells. Assembly Hall Theatre. Crescent Rd, Tunbridge Wells, Kent TN1 2LU *admin:* (01892) 526121 *box office:* (01892) 530613 *fax:* (01892) 525203. Pat Casey, theatre mgr; Sheila Ryall, mkt and publicity mgr. *Capacity:* 940.

Ulverston. Coronation Hall Theatre. County Sq, Ulverston, Cumbria LA12 7LZ *admin:* (01229) 582610 *box office:* (01229) 587120 (TIC) *fax:* (01229) 582610. Jayne Harris, hall mgr; Gordon Crayston, technican; James Croasdale, snr caretaker. *Capacity:* 636.

Wakefield. Theatre Royal and Opera House. Drury La, Wakefield, W Yorkshire WF1 2TE *admin:* (01924) 215531 *box office:* (01924) 211311 *fax:* (01924) 215525 *email:* wkfield-theatre@geo2.poptel.org.uk. Tony Lidington, artistic dir; Simon Baxter, technical mgr; Rose Cuthbertson, admin dir. *Capacity:* 508.

Walsall. Bloxwich Leisure Centre. High St, Bloxwich, Walsall, W Midlands WS3 2DA *admin:* (01922) 710295 *fax:* (01922) 495925. Graham Hill, service mgr; S Wood, snr duty mgr; H Hook, H Malcolm, duty mgrs. *Function Hall Capacity:* 400.

Walsall. Walsall Town Hall. Leicester St, Walsall, W Midlands WS1 1TZ *admin:* (01922) 650000/653170 *box office:* (01922) 653183 *fax:* (01922)

721682. Brian Elwood, curator; Shirley Stone, Julie Sheldon, bookings and admin; Alison Maxam, mkt offr. *Town Hall Capacity:* 1160; *Lily Hall Capacity:* 100.

Warrington. Parr Hall. Palmyra Sq, Warrington, Cheshire WA1 1BL *admin:* (01925) 651178 *box office:* (01925) 634958 *fax:* (01925) 234144. John Perry, mgr; Richard Fleming, hallkeeper; Delphine Corcoran, house mgr. *Capacity:* 950.

Watford. Colosseum. Rickmansworth Rd, Watford, Herts WD1 7JN *admin:* (01923) 445300 *box office:* (01923) 445000 *fax:* (01923) 445225. John Wallace, Paul Scarborough, mgrs; Ollie Smith, dir; James Delanoy, mkt and publicity. *Large Hall Capacity:* 1440.

Watford. Palace Theatre. Clarendon Rd, Watford, Herts WD1 1JZ *admin:* (01923) 235455 *box office:* (01923) 225671 *fax:* (01923) 819664. Giles Croft, artistic dir; Alastair Moir, admin dir; Yvonne Elston, mkt mgr. *Capacity:* 663.

Wellingborough. The Castle. Castle Way, Wellingborough, Northants NN8 1XA *admin:* (01933) 229022 *box office:* (01933) 270007 *fax:* (01933) 229888. Dominic Barber, dir; Pat Souster, admin; Gordon Glass, mkt mgr. *Main House Capacity:* 505; *Studio Theatre Capacity:* 84.

West Bromwich. West Bromwich Town Hall. High St, West Bromwich, W Midlands B70 8DX *admin:* 0121-569 3930 *fax:* 0121-569 3948. Ron Hughes, curator; Joy Thompson, bookings. *Main Hall Capacity:* 700.

Weston super Mare. Playhouse Theatre. High St, Weston super Mare, North Somerset, BS23 1HP *admin:* (01934) 627457 *box office:* (01934) 645544 *fax:* (01934) 622888. Murray Macdonald, gen mgr; Peter Magor, technical mgr; William Pritchard, mkt mgr. *Capacity:* 658.

Weston super Mare. Winter Gardens Pavilion. Royal Parade, Weston super Mare, BS23 1AQ *admin:* (01934) 417117 *box office:* (01934) 645544 *fax:* (01934) 612323; Vivienne Thomson, gen mgr. *Ballroom Capacity:* 550; *Prince Consort Hall Capacity:* 500.

Weymouth. Pavilion Complex. The Esplanade, Weymouth, Dorset DT4 8ED *admin:* (01305) 786732/772444 *box office:* (01305) 783225/765216/7. Harvey Bailey, leisure mgr. *Theatre Capacity:* 1000; *Ocean Room Capacity:* 720.

Whitley Bay. Whitley Bay Playhouse. Marine Av, Whitley Bay NE26 1LZ *admin:* 0191-252 6857 *box office:* 0191-252 3505 *fax:* 0191-251 4949. Tim Flood, gen mgr. *Capacity:* 746.

Windsor. Theatre Royal. Thames St, Windsor, Berks SL4 1PS *admin:* (01753) 863444 *box office:* (01753) 853888 *fax:* (01753) 831673. Bill Kenwright, exec producer; Mark Piper, exec dir; Rob Gale, production mgr. *Capacity:* 633.

Woking. New Victoria Theatre. The Peacocks Arts and Entertainment Centre, Woking, Surrey GU21 1GQ *box office:* (01483) 761144 *fax:* (01483) 770477. David Blyth, chief exec; Richard Wingate, gen mgr; Pat Westwell, mkt mgr. *Capacity:* 1338.

Wolverhampton. Civic Hall and Wulfrun Hall. North St, Wolverhampton, WV1 1RQ *admin:* (01902) 312029 *box office:* (01902) 312030 *fax:* (01902) 713047. Andy Bennett, ents mgr; Dianne Rhodes, admin; Mark Blackstock, gen mgr. *Civic Hall Capacity:* 2040; *Wulfrun Hall Capacity:* 672.

Wolverhampton. Grand Theatre. Lichfield St, Wolverhampton, W Midlands WV1 1DE *admin:* (01902) 428165 *box office:* (01902) 429212 *fax:* (01902) 714030. Brian Goddard, chief exec; Tony Pugh, gen mgr; Gary Postins, financial controller. *Capacity:* 1200.

Worthing. Assembly Hall. Stoke Abbott Rd, Worthing, West Sussex BN11 1HQ *admin:* (01903) 239999 ext 2502/3 *box office:* (01903) 820500 *fax:* (01903) 821124. Peter Bailey, theatre mgr. *Capacity:* 930.

Worthing. Connaught Theatre. Union Pl, Worthing, West Sussex BN11 1LG *admin:* (01903) 231799 *box office:* (01903) 235333 *fax:* (01903) 215337. David Smith, theatre admin; Glenda Harkness, dep theatre admin; Ian Slater, technical mgr. *Main House Capacity:* 514; *Ritz Capacity:* 225.

Worthing. Pavilion Theatre. Marine Parade, Worthing, West Sussex BN11 3PX *admin:* (01903) 239999 ext 2502/2503 *box office:* (01903) 820500 *fax:* (01903) 821124; Peter Bailey, theatres mgr. *Capacity:* 850.

Yeovil. Octagon Theatre. Hendford, Yeovil, Somerset BA20 1UX *admin:* (01935) 422836 *box office:* (01935) 422884 *fax:* (01935) 475281. John G White, gen mgr. *Capacity:* 625.

York. Grand Opera House. Cumberland St, York YO1 1SW *admin:* (01904) 655441 *box office:* (01904) 671818 *fax:* (01904) 671858. Ian Sime, gen mgr; Julian Withers, dep mgr. *Capacity:* 1032.

York. Theatre Royal. St Leonard's Pl, York YO1 2HD *admin:* (01904) 658162 *box office:* (01904) 623568 *fax:* (01904) 611534. Elizabeth Jones, exec dir; Damian Cruden, artistic dir. *Capacity:* 863.

York. York Barbican Centre. Barbican Rd, York YO1 4NT *admin:* (01904) 628991 *box office:* (01904) 656688 *fax:* (01904) 628227 *email:* 100530.1026@compuserve.com. Catherine Asbridge, ents mgr. *Main Hall Capacity:* 1500.

Channel Islands and Isle of Man

St Helier. Fort Regent Leisure Centre. Fort Regent Rd, St Helier, Jersey JE2 4UX, Channel Islands *admin:* (01534) 500200 *box office:* (01534) 500227 *fax:* (01534) 500225. Vic Bourgoise, chief offr. *Gloucester Hall Capacity:* 1974; *Piazza Capacity:* 300; *Queen's Hall Capacity:* 1050.

St Helier. Opera House Theatre. Gloucester St, St Helier, Jersey JE2 3QL, Channel Islands *admin:* (01534) 617521 *box office:* (01534) 22165 *fax:* (01534) 619999. *Capacity:* 700.

St Peter Port. St James. College St, St Peter Port, Guernsey GY1 2NZ, Channel Islands *admin:* (01481) 711360 *box office:* (01481) 711361 *fax:* (01481) 711364. Kirstin R Simon, dir; Jacqueline Bromley, dir's asst. *Capacity:* 580.

Douglas. Gaiety Theatre. Harris Promenade, Douglas, Isle of Man *admin:* (01624) 620046 *box office:* (01624) 625001 *fax:* (01624) 629028 *email:* http://www.iom.com/gaiety-theatre. Mervin Russell Stokes, artistic dir; Seamus Shea, technical contact. *Capacity:* 896.

Douglas. Villa Marina. Harris Promenade, Douglas, Isle of Man *admin:* (01624) 674171 *box office:* (01624) 628855 *fax:* (01624) 612119. *Royal Hall Capacity:* 1500; *Garden Room Capacity:* 250.

Scotland

Aberdeen. Aberdeen Music Hall. Union St, Aberdeen AB10 1QS *admin:* (01224) 632080 ext 220 *box office:* (01224) 641122 *fax:* (01224) 632400 *email:* ab2musichall@dial.pipex.com; http://www.cityscape.co.uk/users/gr62/index.htm. Nigel King, operations mgr. *Capacity:* 1282.

Aberdeen. His Majesty's Theatre. Rosemount Viaduct, Aberdeen *admin:* (01224) 637788 *box office:* (01224) 641122 *fax:* (01224) 632519. Robert Robson, gen mgr, perf arts venues; Peter B Donald, operations mgr. *Capacity:* 1456.

Aberdeen. The Lemon Tree. 5 West North St, Aberdeen AB24 5AT *admin:* (01224) 647999 *box office:* (01224) 642230 *fax:* (01224) 630888. Shona Powell, dir; Andy Shearer, deputy dir; Simon Gane, technical mgr. *Cafe Theatre Capacity:* 200; *Studio Theatre Capacity:* 150.

Ayr. Ayr Pavilion. The Esplanade, Ayr KA7 1DT *admin:* (01292) 265489 *also box office; fax:* (01292) 611614. F Macintyre, gen mgr. *Capacity:* 1000.

Ayr. Ayr Town Hall. New Bridge St, Ayr KA7 1LX *admin:* (01292) 612448 *fax:* (01292) 612143. Graham Peterkin, dir of support services; Andrew Bohan, hallkeeper. *Capacity:* 712.

Ayr. Gaiety Theatre. Carrick St, Ayr *admin:* (01292) 264630 *box office:* (01292) 611222 *fax:* (01292) 288383. Gordon Taylor, gen mgr. *Capacity:* 584.

Dundee. Caird Hall. City Sq, Dundee DD1 3BD *admin:* (01382) 434451 *also fax; box office:* (01382) 434940. *Caird Hall Capacity:* 2429; *Marryat Hall Capacity:* 400.

Dunfermline. Carnegie Hall. East Port, Dunfermline, Fife KY12 7JA *admin:* (01383) 314110 *box office:* (01383) 314127 *fax:* (01383) 314131. J T E McIsaac, principal offr, arts. *Capacity:* 590.

Dunoon. Queen's Hall. Argyll St, Dunoon, Argyll and Bute *admin:* (01369) 702800 *fax:* (01369) 705150. J Anderson, leisure services mgr; Lorna White, asst leisure services mgr. *Main Hall Capacity:* 888.

Edinburgh. Assembly Rooms and Music Hall. 54 George St, Edinburgh EH2 2LR *admin:* 0131-220 4348 *box office:* 0131-220 4349 *fax:* 0131-220 6812 *email:* assemblyrooms@dial.pipex.com; http://www.diaspace.pipex.com/assemblyrooms/. Simon Robson, gen mgr. *Assembly Room Capacity:* 450; *Music Hall Capacity:* 730; *Supper Room Capacity:* 150.

Edinburgh. Edinburgh Festival Theatre. 13/29 Nicolson St, Edinburgh EH8 9FT *admin:* 0131-662 1112 *box office:* 0131-529 6000 *fax:* 0131-667 0744 (admin); 0131-662 1199 (box office) *email:* empire@edfestth. demon.co.uk; http://www.eft.co.uk/. Stephen Barry, gen mgr; Helen Bates, finance mgr. *Capacity:* 1913.

Edinburgh. King's Theatre. 2 Leven St, Edinburgh EH3 9LQ *admin:* 0131-229 4840 *box office:* 0131-220 4349. A Blyth, technical mgr; I Gillespie, stage mgr. *Capacity:* 1336.

Edinburgh. Playhouse Theatre. 18-22 Greenside Pl, Edinburgh EH1 3AA *admin:* 0131-557 2692 *box office:* 0131-557 2590 *fax:* 0131-557 2692. Apollo Leisure (UK) Ltd, proprietors; P R Gregg, mgr dir; Andy Lyst, gen mgr. *Theatre Capacity:* 3056.

Edinburgh. Ross Theatre. Princes Street Gardens, Edinburgh *admin:* 0131-529 4145 *fax:* 0131-220 6813. Joyce Sibbald, admin; Jo Navarro, halls offr. *Capacity:* 1700.

Edinburgh. The Queen's Hall. Clerk St, Edinburgh EH8 9JG *admin:* 0131-668 3456 *box office:* 0131-668 2019 *fax:* 0131-668 2656. Paul Gudgin, gen mgr; Ann Small, mkt and publicity; Beth Cavanagh, hall mgr. *Main Auditorium Capacity:* 800.

Edinburgh. Usher Hall. Lothian Rd, Edinburgh EH1 2EA *admin:* 0131-228 8616 *box office:* 0131-228 1155 *fax:* 0131-228 8848. Moira McKenzie, mgr; Fiona Easton, asst; James Ashford, FOH mgr. *Capacity:* 2215.

Elgin. Elgin Town Hall. 5 Trinity Pl, Elgin, Grampian IV30 1VL *admin:* (01343) 563403 *box office:* (01343) 562600 *fax:* (01343) 562610. Eric McGillivray, mgr; William McCook, caretaker. *Capacity:* 692.

Falkirk. Falkirk Town Hall. c/o Leisure Services Dept, Kilns House, Kilns Rd, Falkirk *admin:* (01324) 506176 *box office:* (01324) 628038/620110. A Craig Murray, ents mgr; Jane Clark, ents offr; Morag Rodgers, asst ents offr. *Main Hall Capacity:* 900; *Lesser Hall Capacity:* 200.

Fort William. Marco's An Aird. An Aird, Fort William PH33 6AN *admin:* (01397) 700707 *fax:* (01397) 700708. Barry I Mason, centre mgr. *An Aird Hall Capacity:* 1117; *Lounge Capacity:* 500.

Galashiels. Volunteer Hall. St John St, Galashiels, Selkirkshire *admin:* (01896) 754751. D Harrison, hall supervisor; John Brotherston, caretaker. *Capacity:* 553.

Glasgow. City Hall. Candleriggs, Glasgow G1 1NQ *admin:* 0141-227 5008/9 *box office:* 0141-227 5014. Robert Palmer, dir, perf arts; S Miller, ticket centre mgr. *Grand Hall Capacity:* 1216.

Glasgow. Henry Wood Hall. RSNO Centre, 73 Claremont St, Glasgow *admin:* 0141-226 3868. Simon Croakall, mgr; Ann Elliott, admin. *Capacity:* 500.

Glasgow. King's Theatre. Bath St, Glasgow G2 4JN *admin:* 0141-287 5429 *box office:* 0141-287 5511 *fax:* 0141-287 5533. Robert Palmer, dir. *Capacity:* 1785.

Glasgow. The Glasgow Royal Concert Hall. 2 Sauchiehall St, Glasgow G2 3NY *admin:* 0141-332 6633 *box office:* 0141-287 5511 *fax:* 0141-333 9123 (admin); 0141-353 4150 (stage dept) *email:* grch@scotnet.co.uk. Louise Mitchell, dir; Arthur Laird, finance and admin; Phil Smith, stage and events production. *Concert Hall Capacity:* 2417; *Strathclyde Suite Capacity:* 500.

Glasgow. Theatre Royal. 282 Hope St, Glasgow G2 3QA *admin:* 0141-332 3321 *box office:* 0141-332 9000 *fax:* 0141-332 4472 *email:* ian@g4fmw.demon.co.uk. Peter Price, theatre mgr; Roberta Doyle, press and mkt dir; Ian Irving, chief electrician. *Capacity:* 1547.

Glasgow. Tramway. 25 Albert Dr, Glasgow G41 2PE *admin:* 0141-287 3921/2/3/4 *box office:* 0141-287 3900 *fax:* 0141-422 2021 *email:* http://www.glasgow.gov.uk/dpav/. Susan Deighan, Steve Slater, perf arts programming; Steve Slater, visual arts programming; Peter Green, technical mgr. *Tramway 1 Capacity:* 600; *Tramway 2 Capacity:* 1500; *Tramway 4 Capacity:* 115.

Glenrothes. Rothes Halls. Kingdom Centre, Rothes Sq, Glenrothes, Fife KY7 5NX *admin:* (01592) 612121 *box office:* (01592) 611101 *fax:* (01592) 612220 *email:* rothes_halls@dial.pipex.com; http://www.dspace.dial.pipex.com/town/plaza/gx70/index.htm. Nick Weeks, technical mgr; Vicki Moffat, box office mgr. *Hall A Capacity:* 720; *Hall B Capacity:* 204.

Inverness. Eden Court Theatre. Bishop's Rd, Inverness IV3 5SA *admin:* (01463) 239841 *box office:* (01463) 234234 *fax:* (01463) 713810 *email:* ecmail@cali.co.uk; http://www.edencourt.uk.com. Jane Grant, programme mgr. *Capacity:* 814.

Kelso. Tait Hall. Edenside Rd, Kelso, Borders. Jim Connor, mgr. *Capacity:* 651.

Kilmarnock. Palace Theatre. 9 Green St, Kilmarnock KA1 3BN *admin:* (01563) 537710 *box office:* (01563) 523590 *fax:* (01563) 573047. *Capacity:* 503.

Kirkwall. Phoenix Cinema. Junction Rd, Kirkwall, Orkney KW15 1AX *admin:* (01856) 873535 ext 2404 *fax:* (01856) 870302. William Scolley, cinema mgr. *Capacity:* 520.

Lerwick. Clickimin Centre. Lochside, Lerwick, Mainland, Shetland Islands, ZE1 0PJ *admin:* (01595) 741000 *also fax.* James Johnston, gen mgr; Shona Robb, centre mgr; Robert Leask, Maurice Haining, asst mgrs. *Capacity:* 1200.

Motherwell. Motherwell Theatre and Concert Hall. PO Box 14, Civic Centre, Motherwell, Lanarkshire ML1 1TW *admin:* (01698) 267515 *also box office; fax:* (01698) 268806. Ann Malloy, hd of cultural services; Lizanne McMurrich, arts and venues mgr; Stuart Archibald, technical mgr. *Concert Hall Capacity:* 1008; *Theatre Capacity:* 395.

Perth. Perth City Hall. King Edward St, Perth, Tayside PH1 5UG *admin:* (01738) 624055 *fax:* (01738) 630566. Anne-Marie McCarthy, gen mgr. *Large City Hall Capacity:* 1624; *Lesser City Hall Capacity:* 300.

Pitlochry. Festival Theatre. Port-na-craig, Pitlochry, Perthshire PH16 5DR *admin:* (01796) 473054 *also fax; box office:* (01796) 472680. Clive Perry, festival dir; Sheila Harborth, festival admin. *Capacity:* 544.

Rothesay. Pavilion. Argyle St, Rothesay, Isle of Bute *admin:* (01700) 504250. D McCombe, theatre mgr; T M McKay, dir, leisure and recreation. *Main Hall Capacity:* 1250.

St Andrews. Younger Graduation Hall. University of St Andrews, North St, St Andrews KY16 9AJ *admin:* (01334) 462226 *fax:* (01334) 462570 *email:* aem@st-and.ac.uk. Alison Malcolm, admin. *Capacity:* 968.

Stirling. Macrobert Arts Centre. University of Stirling, Stirling FK9 4LA *admin:* (01786) 467155 *box office:* (01786) 461081 *email:* http://www.stir.ac.uk/theuni/suinfo/macrobert/. Elizabeth Moran, dir; Liz Wright, deputy dir. *Main Theatre Capacity:* 500; *Studio Capacity:* 140.

Wales

Aberdare. The Coliseum. Mount Pleasant St, Trecynon, Aberdare CF44 8NG *admin:* (01685) 882380 *box office:* (01685) 881188 *fax:* (01685) 883000. Adrian Williams, gen mgr and licensee; Ioan Wynne, technical mgr. *Capacity:* 621.

Aberystwyth. Aberystwyth Arts Centre. University of Wales Aberystwyth, Penglais, Aberystwyth, Ceredigion SY23 3DE *admin:* (01970) 622882 *box office:* (01970) 623232 *fax:* (01970) 622883 *email:* lla@aber.ac.uk; http://www.aber.ac.uk/~arcwww/index.htm. Alan Hewson, dir; Maris Davies, admin. *Theatr y Werin Capacity:* 327; *Gt Hall Capacity:* 900.

Barry. The Memorial Hall Theatre. Gladstone Rd, Barry, S Glamorgan CF64 8NA *admin:* (01446) 738663. I J Harris, exec offr. *Main Hall Capacity:* 1111; *Glamorgan Suite Capacity:* 150.

Cardiff. Cardiff International Arena. Mary Ann St, Cardiff CF1 2QE *admin:* (01222) 234500 *box office:* (01222) 224488 *fax:* (01222) 234501. Paul Latham, divisional mgr; Graham Walters, dep gen mgr; Sharon Phillips, sales mgr. *Arena Capacity:* 5500; *Conference Suite Capacity:* 400; *Novello/Langley Suite Capacity:* 336.

Cardiff. Great Hall and Terminal 396. University Union, Park Pl, Cathays, Cardiff CF1 3QN *admin:* (01222) 781456 *box office:* (01222) 387421 *fax:* (01222) 781407 *email:* ssucw@cf.ac.uk. Sheila Davies, admin mgr; David Pearce, ents mgr; Roy Bryan, finance mgr. *Gt Hall Capacity:* 1350; *Terminal 396 Capacity:* 1600; *Finistere Capacity:* 300.

Cardiff. New Theatre. Park Pl, Cardiff CF1 3LN *admin:* (01222) 878787 *box office:* (01222) 878889 *fax:* (01222) 878788 *email:* new.theatre.com. Judi Richards, hd of arts and cultural services. *Capacity:* 1186.

Cardiff. St David's Hall. The Hayes, Cardiff CF1 2SH *admin:* (01222) 878500 *box office:* (01222) 878444. Judi Richards, hd of arts and cultural services. *Capacity:* 1956.

Carmarthen. Lyric Theatre. King St, Carmarthen, Dyfed SA31 1BD *admin:* (01267) 238685 *box office:* (01267) 232632 *fax:* (01267) 234559. Elizabeth Evans, artistic and theatre dir; David Evans, technical mgr. *Capacity:* 740.

Llandrindod Wells. Grand Pavilion. Spa Rd, Llandrindod Wells, Powys LD1 6DA *admin:* (01597) 823532 *fax:* (01597) 824413 *email:* pavilion@powys.gov.uk. Colin R Edwards, chmn, management committee; Carolyn Flynn, mgr. *Capacity:* 565.

Llandudno. North Wales Theatre and Conference Centre. The Promenade, Llandudno LL30 1BB *admin:* (01492) 879771 *box office:* (01492) 872000 *fax:* (01492) 860790 *email:* info@www.nwtheatre.co.uk; http://www.nwtheatre.co.uk. Nick Reed (ext 202), gen mgr; Bridget Jones (ext 306), operations mgr; Huw Roberts (ext 219), mkt offr. *North Wales Theatre Capacity:* 1500; *North Wales Conference Centre Capacity:* 970.

Llangollen. Royal International Pavilion. Abbey Rd, Llangollen, LL20 8SW *admin:* (01978) 860111 *fax:* (01978) 860046. Jeremy Miles, gen mgr; Christine Griffith, Brian Williams, duty offr team; Damien Tobin. *Arena Capacity:* 2000; *Main Hall Capacity:* 600.

Mold. Theatr Clwyd. Mold, Flintshire CH7 1YA *admin:* (01352) 756331 *box office:* (01352) 755114 *fax:* (01352) 758323 *email:* drama@celtic. co.uk. Terry Hands, dir. *Anthony Hopkins Theatre Capacity:* 578; *Emlyn Williams Theatre Capacity:* 300.

Newport. Newport Centre. Kingsway, Newport NP9 1UH *admin:* (01633) 662660 *box office:* (01633) 662666 *fax:* (01633) 662673. Roger Broome, events offr; Glenys Hawkes, admin; Simon Jones, gen mgr. *Main Hall Capacity:* 2024; *Riverside Suite Capacity:* 400; *Kingsway Room Capacity:* 150.

Newtown. Theatr Hafren. Llanidloes Rd, Newtown, Powys SY16 4HU *admin:* (01686) 625447 *box office:* (01686) 625007 *fax:* (01686) 625446. Sara Clutton, admin; Laurence Hanna, deputy admin. *Capacity:* 568.

Pontardawe. Theatr Cwmtawe. Pontardawe Leisure Centre, Parc Ynysderw, Pontardawe, W Glamorgan SA8 4EG *admin:* (01792) 830111. Paul Walker, gen mgr. *Theatre Capacity:* 350; *Sports Hall Capacity:* 600.

Porthcawl. The Grand Pavilion. The Esplanade, Porthcawl CF36 3YW *admin:* (01656) 783860 *box office:* (01656) 786996 *fax:* (01656) 772111. Jason Crook, mgr. *Main Hall Capacity:* 637.

Rhyl. Coliseum Theatre. West Promenade, Rhyl, Flintshire LL18 1HB *admin:* (01745) 351126 *also box offce.* Aubrey Phillips, theatre dir; D Denver, production and technical mgr; Patrick Newley, press offr. *Capacity:* 630.

Rhyl. Pavilion Theatre. Promenade, Rhyl LL18 3AQ *admin:* (01745) 332414 *box office:* (01745) 330000 *fax:* (01745) 339819. Gareth Owen, theatre mgr; Andrew Hughes, technical mgr. *Capacity:* 1032.

Swansea. Brangwyn Hall. Guildhall, Swansea SA1 4PN *admin:* (01792) 635489. Sean Keir, gen mgr. *Capacity:* 1198.

Swansea. Grand Theatre. Singleton St, Swansea, SA1 3QJ *admin:* (01792) 475242 *box office:* (01792) 475715 *fax:* (01792) 475379. Gary Iles, gen mgr. *Capacity:* 1019.

Swansea. Penyrheol Theatre. Pontarddulais Rd, Swansea, West Glamorgon, SA4 4FG *admin:* (01792) 897039 *fax:* (01792) 894931. David Osborne, mgr. *Penyrheol Theatre Capacity:* 600; *Dance Studio Capacity:* 50.

Treorchy. Park and Dare Theatre. Station Rd, Treorchy, Mid-Glamorgan, CF42 6NL *admin:* (01443) 776689/472461 *box office:* (01443) 773112 *fax:* (01443) 776922. Derek Ward, ents offr; E Bowen, mgr. *Theatre Capacity:* 800; *Theatre Lounge Capacity:* 150.

Northern Ireland

Ballymena. Ballymena Town Hall. Bridge St, Ballymena, Co Antrim BT42 5AH *admin:* (01266) 41284/656262 *fax:* (01266) 46296. Rosalind Lowry, arts offr, Ballymena BC; Denise Reynolds, community services offr. *Main Hall Capacity:* 670; *Minor Hall Capacity:* 200.

Belfast. Belfast Waterfront Hall. Lanyon Pl, Belfast, Co Antrim *admin:* (01232) 334400 *fax:* (01232) 334467 *email:* kylre@belfast city.gov.uk; http://www.belfastcity.gov.uk/bwf4/index.htm. Tim Husbands, gen mgr; Andrew Kyle, sales and mkt mgr; Donne Robertson, operations mgr. *Main Auditorium Capacity:* 2235; *BT Studio Capacity:* 500; *Foyer performance space Capacity:* 100.

Belfast. Elmwood Hall. 89 University Rd, Belfast, Co Antrim BT 7 1NF *admin:* (01232) 664535 *fax:* (01232) 662761. Barbara McKinley, Elmwood hall mgr; Kenneth Dennis, caretaker. *Capacity:* 518.

Belfast. Grand Opera House. Gt Victoria St, Belfast, Co Antrim BT2 7HR *admin:* (01232) 240411 *box office:* (01232) 241919 (ticket shop) *fax:* (01232) 236842. Derek Nicholls, theatre dir. *Capacity:* 1001.

Belfast. Queen's University Concert Halls. University Rd, Belfast, Co Antrim BT7 1NN *admin:* (01232) 245133 ext 3052 *fax:* (01232) 663733. Robert Agnew (ext 4286), festival exec dir; D H Wilson, admin sec; Elizabeth Moore, bookings. *Whitla Hall Capacity:* 1224; *Harty Room Capacity:* 200.

Belfast. Ulster Hall. Bedford St, Belfast, Co Antrim BT2 7FF *admin:* (01232) 323900 *fax:* (01232) 247199. F McCausland, asst mgr. *Capacity:* 1600.

Coleraine. The Diamond. University of Ulster, Cromore Rd, Coleraine BT52 1GA *admin:* (01265) 44141 ext 4572. Sylvia McIlvenna, bookings; David Simpson, technical; Jeremy Lewis, university arts admin. *The Diamond Capacity:* 1250; *The Octagon Capacity:* 500.

Derry. Guildhall. Shipquay Pl, Derry, Co Londonderry, BT48 6DQ *admin:* (01504) 377335 *box office:* (01504) 260516/262567 *fax:* (01504) 379757. John Keanie, town clerk and chief exec; Damien McMahon, city sec and solicitor; Cathal Logue, dir, recreation and leisure. *Main Hall Capacity:* 571; *Minor Hall Capacity:* 100.

Derry. Rialto Entertainment Centre. Market St, Derry, Co Londonderry, BT48 6EF *admin:* (01504) 264177 *box office:* (01504) 260516 *fax:* (01504) 260688 *email:* http://www.mni.co.uk/see/derry/festival. David McLaughlin, venues mgr; Johnny Murray, FOH and box office mgr; Paula Bradley, admin asst. *Capacity:* 988.

Downpatrick. Down Leisure Centre. 114 Market St, Downpatrick, Co Down BT30 6LZ *admin:* (01396) 613426 *fax:* (01395) 616905. Macartan Bryce, gen mgr. *Main Hall Capacity:* 650.

Irvinestown. Bawnwacre Centre. Irvinestown, Co Fermanagh BT794 1EE *admin:* (013656) 21177 *fax:* (013656) 28082. George Beacom, centre mgr. *Main Hall Capacity:* 800; *Minor Hall Capacity:* 250.

Newry. Newry Town Hall. Bank Parade, Newry, Co Down BT35 6HP *admin:* (01693) 66232 *also box office; fax:* (01693) 66177. *Capacity:* 500.

Newtownabbey. Assembly Hall. University of Ulster, Jordanstown, Shore Rd, Newtownabbey, BT37 0QB *admin:* (01232) 366172 *fax:* (01232) 366823 *email:* mb.martin@ulst.ac.uk; http://www.ulst.ac.uk/. M Martin, admin offr. *Assembly Hall Capacity:* 1100; *Dalriada Hall Capacity:* 500.

Local Authority Promoters

This section comprises the local authority promoters in England, Wales, Scotland, Northern Ireland and the Isle of Man. The promoters are listed in county order preceded by London. With the exception of London, county entries are headed by the county council and followed by a list of borough and district councils in alphabetical order.

Inner London

Camden Borough Council. Crowndale Centre, 218 Eversholt St, London NW1 1BD *tel:* 0171-911 1647 *fax:* 0171-911 1615. Wendy Neville, hd of Camden arts and tourism services.

City of Westminster Borough Council. Arts Unit, 17th Floor, City Hall, 64 Victoria St, London SW1E 6QP *tel:* 0171-641 2498/2814 *fax:* 0171-641 3265; m/com: 0171-641 1906. Joanne Gray, Cheryl Haris, arts offrs.

Corporation of London. Barbican Libraries, Silk St, London EC2Y 8DS *tel:* 0171-638 4141. John Tusa, Barbican Centre mgr dir.

Greenwich Borough Council. Greenwich Leisure Services, 151 Powis St, London SE18 6JL *tel:* 0181-854 8888 *fax:* 0181-317 2822. Martin Burgoyne, principal arts and cultural offr.

Hackney Borough Council. Leisure Services, Edith Cavell Building, Enfield Rd, London N1 5BA *tel:* 0171-762 6830. Leslie Good, hd of arts and cultural services.

Hammersmith & Fulham Borough Council. Community Learning & Leisure Service, Town Hall, King St, London W6 9JU *tel:* 0181-748 3020 ext 3606. Elizabeth Adlington, asst dir of education.

Islington Borough Council. Leisure and Library Services, 227-229 Essex Rd, London N1 3PW *tel:* 0171-477 3853 *fax:* 0171-477 3810. Laurence Baylis, hd of arts.

Kensington and Chelsea, Royal Borough of. Central Library, Hornton St, London W8 7RX *tel:* 0171-937 2542 *fax:* 0171-361 2976. C J Koster, dir of libraries and arts.

Lambeth Borough Council. Directorate, Environmental Services, Courtenay House, New Park Rd, London SW2 4DU *tel:* 0171-926 7198. C Holmes, library services mgr.

Lewisham Borough Council. Lewisham Arts Service, 199-201 Lewisham High St, London SE13 6LG *tel:* 0181-297 8521. Norman Goodman, principal arts offr.

London Borough of Southwark. Southwark Arts Service, The Civic, 600-608 Old Kent Rd, London SE15 1JB *tel:* 0171-635 6841 *fax:* 0171-732 5868 *email:* info@artsouthwark.org.uk. Vaughan Aston, hd of arts.

Tower Hamlets Borough Council. Mulberry Pl, 5 Clove Cres, London E14 2BG *tel:* 0171-364 5000. Brian Oakaby, arts and events offr.

Wandsworth Borough Council. Room 224A, Wandsworth Town Hall, London SW18 2PU *tel:* 0181-871 7380. Charlie Catling, snr arts offr.

Outer London

Barking and Dagenham Borough Council. Entertainments Office, Broadway Theatre, Broadway, Barking, Essex IG11 7LS *tel:* 0181-591 9662, also fax. Carol Oatham, theatre mgr.

Barnet Council. Recreation, Leisure and Arts, Educational Services, Friern Barnet La, London N11 3DL *tel:* 0181-359 3152 *fax:* 0181-359 3246 *email:* jb62@dial.pipex.com. Lloyd Gee, arts service development offr.

Bexley London Borough. Leisure Link, Howbury Centre, Slade Green Rd, Slade Green, Kent DA8 2HX *tel:* 0181-303 7777 ext 3919. Janet Stone, leisure development mgr.

Brent Borough Council. Town Hall, Forty La, Wembley, Middx HA9 9HD *tel:* 0181-937 1234. George Benham.

Bromley Borough Council. Central Library, High St, Bromley BR1 1EX *tel:* 0181-460 9955 *fax:* 0181-313 9975. Robbie Stoakes, dir of leisure and community services.

Croydon Borough Council. c/o Croydon Clocktower, Katharine St, Croydon CR9 1ET *tel:* 0181-760 5400 ext 1046. Laura Dyer, principal arts offr.

Ealing, London Borough of. Perceval House, 14/16 Uxbridge Rd, Ealing, London W5 2HL *tel:* 0181-758 5743. Adam Farrar, events mgr.

Enfield, London Borough of. Civic Centre, Silver St, Enfield EN1 0XJ *tel:* 0181-967 8459 *fax:* 0181-982 5497. Claire Chidley, arts and museums development mgr.

Haringey Borough Council. 639 High Rd, Tottenham, London N17 8BD *tel:* 0181-808 1066 ext 5541. Julia Montgomery, cultural development offr.

Harrow Borough Council. PO Box 22, Civic Centre, Harrow, Middx HA1 2UW *tel:* 0181-424 1906. Carol Stewart, arts and leisure service mgr.

Havering Borough Council. Arts Office, Broxhill Centre, Broxhill Rd, Romford, Essex RM4 1XN *tel:* (01708) 773950. Chris Cole, arts offr.

Hillingdon Borough Council. Central Library, 14-15 High St, Uxbridge, Middx UB8 1HD *tel:* (01895) 250711. Joan Gallacher, arts co-ord.

Hounslow Borough Council. Civic Centre, Lampton Rd, Hounslow TW3 4DN *tel:* 0181-862 5847. H Simmons, dir, leisure services.

Kingston, Royal Borough of. Cultural Services, Kingston Library, Fairfield Rd, Kingston upon Thames, Surrey KT1 2PS *tel:* 0181-547 6416 *fax:* 0181-547 6426 *email:* http://www.kingston.gov.uk. Colin Bloxham, arts development offr.

Merton Borough Council. Crown House, Morden, Surrey SM4 5DX.

Newham Borough Council. Arts, Entertainment and Leisure Service, 292 Barking Rd, East Ham, London E6 3BA *tel:* 0181-557 8648 *fax:* 0181-557 8845. David Curtis, arts and ents mgr.

Redbridge, London Borough of. Central Library, Clements Rd, Ilford, Essex IG1 1EA *tel:* 0181-478 7145. Helen Colborne, borough arts offr.

Richmond upon Thames Borough Council. Langholm Lodge, 146 Petersham Rd, Richmond TW10 6UX *tel:* 0181-332 0534 *fax:* 0181-940 7568. Nigel Cutting, principal arts offr.

Sutton Borough Council. Central Library, St Nicholas Way, Sutton, Surrey SM1 1EA *tel:* 0181-770 4602 *fax:* 0181-770 4666. Colin Beech, hd of community lifestyles.

Waltham Forest, London Borough of. Sycamore House, Town Hall, Forest Rd, London E17 *tel:* 0181-527 5544 ext 4798. Helen Tredoux, arts and tourism offr.

England

Bath and North East Somerset

Bath & North East Somerset Council. Pump Room, Bath, Avon BA1 1LZ *tel:* (01225) 477782 *email:* ruth_warren@bathnes.gov.uk. Ruth Warren, sales offr.

Bedfordshire

Bedfordshire County Council. County Hall, Cauldwell St, Bedford MK42 9AP *tel:* (01234) 363222. Stephanie Record, county arts development offr.

Bedford Borough Council. Arts and Leisure Unit, Room 550, Town Hall, St Paul's Sq, Bedford, Beds MK40 1SJ *tel:* (01234) 267422 *fax:* (01234) 221606. Gilly Love, principal arts offr.

Luton Borough Council. Luton Leisure and Cultural Services, 14 Old Bedford Rd, Luton LU2 7HH *tel:* (01582) 876084 *fax:* (01582) 876009. arts and entertainment mgr.

Mid Bedfordshire District Council. 23 London Rd, Biggleswade, Beds SG18 8ER *tel:* (01767) 313137/602404 (direct line). Hilary Webster, arts development offr.

South Bedfordshire District Council. The District Offices, High St North, Dunstable, Beds LU6 1LF *tel:* (01582) 474099 *fax:* (01582) 474009. Catherine Doherty, asst dir: leisure and community department.

Berkshire

Royal County of Berkshire. Cultural Services, Shire Hall, Shinfield Pk, Reading, Berks RG2 9XD *tel:* (01734) 233255 *email:* linda.barlow@berkshire.gov.uk. Linda Barlow, arts, leisure and museums offr.

Bracknell Forest Borough Council. Leisure Department, Easthampstead House, Town Sq, Bracknell, Berks RG12 1AQ *tel:* (01344) 424642. Mark Devon, acting borough leisure offr.

Newbury District Council. Council Offices, Market St, Newbury, Berks RG14 5LD *tel:* (01635) 519558. C R Barlow, dir of recreation services.

Reading Borough Council. c/o the Hexagon, Queen's Walk, Reading, Berks RG1 7UA *tel:* 0118-939 0123 *fax:* 0118-939 0028 *email:* hexagon@beta.reading.bc.gov.uk. c/o Ann Brown, programme co-ord.

Slough Borough Council. Town Hall, Bath Rd, Slough SL1 3UQ *tel:* (01753) 875576. Andrew Lee, arts development promotion offr.

Windsor and Maidenhead, Royal Borough of. Berkshire House, Queen St, Maidenhead, Berks SL6 1NF *tel:* (01628) 796100 *fax:* (01628) 796121. Patricia Cowe, arts development offr.

Wokingham District Council. Council Offices, Shute End, Wokingham RG40 1WL *tel:* (01734) 778650 *fax:* (01734) 778660. R A Fuller, leisure and technical services offr.

Bristol, City of

Bristol City Council. Department of Leisure Services, Colston Hall, Colston St, Bristol BS1 5AR *tel:* 0117-922 3698 *fax:* 0117-922 3681. Paul Preager, concert planning and promotions mgr.

Buckinghamshire

Buckinghamshire County Council. Education Department, County Hall, Aylesbury, Bucks HP20 1UZ *tel:* (01296) 383541. Dick Chamberlain, asst education offr, continuing education.

Aylesbury Vale District Council. Bearbrook House, Oxford Rd, Aylesbury, Bucks HP21 3RJ *tel:* (01296) 585206. Chris Smith, arts development offr.

Chiltern District Council. Council Offices, King George V Rd, Amersham, Bucks HP6 5AW *tel:* (01494) 732020. Jill Mace, hd of client and community services.

Milton Keynes Council. Saxon Ct, Milton Keynes MK9 3HG *tel:* (01908) 253698. Pauline Scott-Garrett, arts development mgr.

South Buckinghamshire District Council. Council Offices, Windsor Rd, Slough, Bucks SL1 2HN *tel:* (01753) 533333 ext 347 *fax:* (01753) 676214. Debbie Stubbs, arts and play offr.

Wycombe District Council. Leisure Dept, Queen Victoria Rd, High Wycombe, Bucks HP11 1BB *tel:* (01494) 421887 *fax:* 421808. Richard Sockett, arts development offr.

Cambridgeshire

Cambridgeshire County Council. Education, Libraries and Heritage, Shire Hall, Cambridge CB3 0AP *tel:* (01223) 318134. Steve Hollier, county arts offr.

Cambridge City Council. Leisure Services, The Guildhall, Cambridge CB2 3QJ *tel:* (01223) 457521 *email:* marketing@cambridge.gov.uk; http://www.cambridge.gov.uk. Tim Holt, mkt and press mgr.

East Cambridgeshire District Council. Arts Development in East Cambridgeshire, Artspace, 15 Fore Hill, Ely, Cambs CB7 4AA *tel:* (01353) 669022 *fax:* (01353) 669052. Leslie Hampson, arts development offr.

Fenland District Council. Fenland Hall, March, Cambs PE15 8NQ *tel:* (01354) 622346. Andrew O'Hanlon, arts development offr.

Huntingdonshire District Council. Pathfinder House, St Mary's St, Huntingdon, Cambs PE18 6TN *tel:* (01480) 388057. Vivien Peters, arts and cultural services mgr.

Peterborough City Council. Norwich Union House, 24 Church St, Peterborough, Cambs PE1 1HZ *tel:* (01733) 454414. Hermin McIntosh, asst dir of community cultural services.

South Cambridgeshire District Council. South Cambridgeshire Hall, 9-11 Hills Rd, Cambridge CB2 1PB *tel:* (01223) 443018 *fax:* (01223) 443149 *email:* tim.freathy@scambs.gov.co.uk. T C Freathy, arts development offr.

Cheshire

Cheshire County Council. Arts Services, Goldsmith House, Hamilton Pl, Chester CH1 1SE *tel:* (01244) 602834. Sue Davies, principal arts offr.

Chester City Council. Dept of Development and Leisure, The Forum, Chester CH1 2HS *tel:* (01244) 402211. C Hardy, dir of leisure services.

Congleton Borough Council. Westfields, Middlewick Rd, Sandbach, Cheshire CW1 1HZ *tel:* (01270) 763231. Natalie Power, arts development offr.

Crewe and Nantwich Borough Council. Victoria Community Centre, West St, Crewe, Cheshire CW1 2PZ *tel:* (01270) 211422 *fax:* (01270) 537960. K Walker, mgr.

Ellesmere Port and Neston Borough Council. Council Offices, Civic Way, Ellesmere Port, Cheshire L65 0BE *tel:* 0151-356 6762. Eleanor Evans, snr development offr.

Halton Borough Council. Arts Development Team, Community Services, Town Hall, Heath Rd, Runcorn, Cheshire WA7 5TD *tel:* 0151-424 2061 ext 4063. Christina Christou, arts development offr.

Macclesfield Borough Council. Leisure Services Dept, Town Hall, Macclesfield, Cheshire SK10 1EA *tel:* (01625) 504506 *fax:* (01625) 504515. Mark Wheelton, snr community activities offr.

Vale Royal Borough Council. Leisure Services, Community Services Directorate, Wyvern House, The Drumber, Winsford, Cheshire CW7 1AH *tel:* (01606) 867533 *fax:* (01606) 862100. Sue Gillett, events and ents offr.

Warrington Borough Council. Community Arts and Leisure Section, West Annexe, Town Hall, Warrington, Cheshire WA1 1UH *tel:* (01925) 442362 *fax:* (01925) 442361. Gail Thorne, arts development offr.

Cornwall

Cornwall County Council. Libraries and Arts, County Hall, Truro, Cornwall TR1 3AY *tel:* (01872) 323465 *fax:* (01872) 323804. Jenefer Lowe, arts offr.

Caradon District Council. Luxstowe House, Liskeard, Cornwall PL14 3DZ *tel:* (01579) 341000 *fax:* (01579) 341024. Derek Fairhall, leisure services mgr.

Carrick District Council. Princess Pavilion, Falmouth, Cornwall TR11 4AR *tel:* (01326) 311277 *fax:* (01326) 315382. R H D Phipps, ents mgr.

Kerrier District Council. Council Offices, Dolcoath Av, Camborne, Cornwall TR14 8SX *tel:* (01209) 712941 *fax:* (01209) 718170. G Johns, leisure services offr.

North Cornwall District Council. Finance and Administration Dept, Higher Trenant Rd, Wadebridge, Cornwall PL27 6TW *tel:* (01208) 812255. David Brown, chief exec.

Penwith District Council. Council Offices, St Clare, Penzance, Cornwall TR18 3QW *tel:* (01736) 62341. D H Hosken, clerk of the council.

Restormel Borough Council. Restormel Borough Offices, 39 Penwinnick Rd, St Austell, Cornwall PL25 5DR *tel:* (01726) 74466 ext 2269 *email:* rest@dial.pipex.co; http://www.ds.dial.pipex.com/restormel/. B E Arthur, dir of economic and community development.

Cumbria

Cumbria County Council. Arroyo Block, The Castle, Carlisle, Cumbria CA3 8UR *tel:* (01228) 607292 *fax:* (01228) 607299 *email:* herithq@dial. pipex.com. Joe Hendry, heritage services offr.

Allerdale Borough Council. Cultural Services Unit, Helena Thompson Museum, Park End Rd, Workington, Cumbria CA14 4DE *tel:* (01900) 62598 *fax:* (01900) 606407. Catherine Coulthard, cultural services offr.

Barrow-in-Furness Borough Council. Arts and Museums Service, Town Hall, Duke St, Barrow-in-Furness, Cumbria LA14 2LD *tel:* (01229) 842353 *fax:* (01229) 432289. Sue Jenkins, arts and museums mgr.

Carlisle City Council. The Sands Centre, The Sands, Carlisle, Cumbria CA1 1JQ *tel:* (01228) 810208 *fax:* (01228) 514547. Nicky Appleby, arts, events and ents mgr.

Copeland Borough Council. Whitehaven Civic Hall, Lowther St, Whitehaven, Cumbria CA28 7SH *tel:* (01946) 67575 ext 24/26. Dorothy Graham, hall mgr.

Eden District Council. c/o Eden Arts Trust, 2 Sandgate, Penrith, Cumbria CA11 7TP *tel:* (01768) 899444 *fax:* (01768) 892947 *email:* eden arts@aol.com; http://www.cumbria.com/edenarts/. Nick Jones, arts development offr.

South Lakeland District Council. Tourism and Amenities, South Lakeland House, Lowther St, Kendal, Cumbria LA9 4UF *tel:* (01539) 733333 *fax:* (01539) 740300. Imelda Winters Lewis, events and promotions offr.

Derbyshire

Derbyshire County Council. Libraries, Arts and Records, County Hall, Matlock, Derbys DE4 3AG *tel:* (01629) 580000 ext 6488. Jaci Brumwell, dep dir, dept of libraries and heritage.

Amber Valley Borough Council. Borough Services, Leisure Development Unit, PO Box 18, Town Hall, Ripley, Derbys DE5 3SZ *tel:* (01773) 841419 *fax:* (01773) 841523. Vicki Campbell, arts development offr.

Bolsover (The District of). Sherwood Lodge, Bolsover, Chesterfield, Derbyshire S44 6NF *tel:* (01246) 242320 *fax:* (01246) 242424 *email:* bolsover@dial.pipex.com; http://www.dspace.dial.pipex.com/town/parade/taf24. Steven Singleton, leisure and tourism offr.

Chesterfield Borough Council. North Lodge, Queen's Pk, Chesterfield, Derbys S40 2LD *tel:* (01246) 345111 *fax:* (01246) 345110. G Cass, borough recreation and leisure offr.

Derby City Council. Leisure Services Dept, Derby City Council, Heritage Gate, Derby DE1 1LS *tel:* (01332) 715515 *fax:* (01332) 716215. Alf Fullerton, asst dir arts and recreation).

Derbyshire Dales District Council. Town Hall, Matlock, Derbys DE4 3NN *tel:* (01629) 580580 ext 2400. A R Yarwood, planning offr.

Erewash Borough Council. Town Hall, Derby Rd, Long Eaton, Notts NG10 1HU *tel:* (01602) 461321 ext 612. R G Walters, leisure development mgr.

High Peak Borough Council. Environmental Health and Leisure Dept, Howard Town House, High St East, Glossop, Derbys SK13 8DA *tel:* (01457) 851635. Bob Hall, chief leisure and services offr.

North East Derbyshire District Council. The Council House, Saltergate, Chesterfield S40 1LF *tel:* (01246) 231111 *fax:* (01246) 212620. Wilf Newton, principal recreation offr.

South Derbyshire District Council. Civic Offices, Civic Way, Swadlincote, Burton-on-Trent, Derbys DE11 0AH *tel:* (01283) 228072 *fax:* (01283) 550128. Alison Foote, arts development offr.

Devon

Devon County Council. Sir Joshua Reynolds Centre, Longcause, Plympton, Plymouth, Devon PL7 1JB *tel:* (01752) 338874 *also fax.* David Whitfield, county arts offr.

East Devon District Council. Council Offices, Knowle, Sidmouth, Devon EX10 8HL *tel:* (01395) 516551. David Pagett, amenities offr.

Exeter City Council. Civic Centre, Dix's Field, Exeter, Devon EX1 1RP *tel:* (01392) 77888 ext 5114. Graham Russell, hd of economic development.

Mid Devon District Council. Leisure Services Division, Ailsa House, Tidcombe La, Tiverton, Devon EX16 4DZ *tel:* (01884) 255255 ext 4367/2330. Paul Clark, leisure services offr.

North Devon District Council. Civic Centre, Barnstaple, Devon EX31 1EA *tel:* (01271) 388325. Rosemarie Lyons, arts mgr.

Plymouth City Council. Dept of Leisure Services, St Andrew's Ct, 12 St Andrew's St, Plymouth, Devon PL1 2AH *tel:* (01752) 307000 *fax:* (01752) 307003. Paul Kelly, principal arts development offr.

South Hams District Council. Follaton House, Plymouth Rd, Totnes, Devon TQ9 5NE *tel:* (01803) 861234 *email:* mike-thomas@south.hams; http://www.zynet.cauk/gold/shdc. Mike Thomas, leisure services mgr.

Teignbridge District Council. Forde House, Newton Abbott, Devon TQ12 4XX *tel:* (01626) 61101 ext 2607 *fax:* (01626) 330162. Doff Pollard, arts development offr.

Torbay Borough Council. Arts and Recreation Dept, Parkfield House, 38 Esplanade Rd, Paignton, Devon TQ3 2NH *tel:* (01803) 546870. Roger Mann, acting dir of arts and recreation.

Torridge District Council. Riverbank House, Bideford, Devon EX39 2QG *tel:* (01237) 476711 *fax:* (01237) 478849. David Pinney, dir of planning and technical services.

West Devon Borough Council. Borough Council Offices, Tavistock, Devon PL19 0BZ *tel:* (01822) 615911. Claire Stein, arts development offr.

Dorset

Dorset County Council. Dorset County Library Headquarters, Colliton Pk, Dorchester, Dorset DT1 1XJ *tel:* (01305) 224455 *fax:* (01305) 266120. Ian Lewis, hd of libraries and arts.

Bournemouth Borough Council. Bournemouth International Centre, Exeter Rd, Bournemouth, Dorset BH2 5BH *tel:* (01202) 456400. Rob Zuradzki, ents mgr.

Christchurch Borough Council. Civic Offices, Bridge St, Christchurch, Dorset BH23 1AZ *tel:* (01202) 495000. Chris Horn, leisure services mgr.

East Dorset District Council. Council Offices, Furzehill, Wimborne, Dorset BH21 4HN *tel:* (01202) 886201 ext 355 *email:* tcooper@ eastdorsetdc.gov.uk. Tracy Cooper, leisure development offr.

North Dorset District Council. Nordon, Salisbury Rd, Blandford Forum, Dorset DT11 7LL *tel:* (01258) 484034. Kate Montefiore, arts development offr.

Poole Borough Council. Civic Centre, Poole, Dorset BH15 2RU *tel:* (01202) 683138 *fax:* (01202) 660896. Polly Hamilton, arts development offr.

Purbeck District Council. Westport House, Wareham, Dorset BH20 4PP *tel:* (01929) 556561 *fax:* (01929) 557348. Debbie Anderson, tourism, mkt and admin offr.

West Dorset District Council. Stratton House, High West St, Dorchester, Dorset DT1 1UZ *tel:* (01305) 251010. N J Thornley, leisure and tourism mgr.

Weymouth and Portland Borough Council. The Pavilion Complex, The Esplanade, Weymouth, Dorset DT4 8ED *tel:* (01305) 786732. Stephen Young, pavilion complex mgr.

County Durham

Durham County Council. County Hall, Durham DH1 5TY *tel:* 0191-384 2214 *fax:* 0191-386 1770. Zoe Channing, arts development mgr.

Chester-le-St District Council. Civic Centre, Newcastle Rd, Chester-le-Street, Co Durham DH3 3UT *tel:* 0191-389 0986. Bill Lightburn, leisure development mgr.

Darlington Borough Council. Civic Theatre, Parkgate, Darlington, Co Durham DL1 1RR *tel:* (01325) 468006. Peter Cutchie, hd of theatre and arts.

Derwentside District Council. The Louisa Centre, Front St, Stanley, Co Durham DH9 0TE *tel:* (01207) 218866 ext 8858 *fax:* (01207) 218866. Martin Weston, arts development offr.

Durham City Council. Directorate of Technical and Leisure Services, 87 Claypath, Durham City DH1 1RG *tel:* 0191-386 6111 *fax:* 0191-386 2338. A Wilson, dep dir, technical and leisure services.

Easington District Council. Community Services Dept, 30 Yoden Way, Peterlee, Co Durham *tel:* 0191-586 9999 ext 254. A Sutherland, arts development offr.

Sedgefield Borough Council. Green La, Spennymoor, Co Durham DL16 6JQ *tel:* (01388) 816166 *fax:* (01388) 815374. Pauline Murray, arts development offr.

Teesdale District Council. 43 Galgate, Barnard Castle, Co Durham DL12 8EL *tel:* (01833) 690000 *fax:* (01833) 637269 *email:* tourism@-teesdale.co.uk. Rosie Cross, arts development offr.

Wear Valley District Council. Leisure and Marketing Department, Civic Centre, Crook, Co Durham DL15 9ES *tel:* (01388) 765555 ext 221. Mary O'Malley, arts development offr.

East Riding of Yorkshire

East Riding of Yorkshire Council. County Hall, Beverley, E Yorks HU17 9BA *tel:* (01482) 887700. June Mitchell, museums and arts offr.

East Sussex

East Sussex County Council. 44 St Anne's Cres, Lewes, E Sussex BN7 1SQ *tel:* (01273) 481871 *fax:* (01273) 480092. Hilary Lane, arts offr.

Brighton & Hove Council. Royal Pavilion, Libraries and Museums, 4/5 Pavilion Buildings, Brighton, E Sussex BN1 1EE *tel:* (01273) 603005. Anne Burrill, hd of mkt and visitor services.

Eastbourne Borough Council. Winter Garden, Eastbourne, E Sussex BN21 4BP *tel:* (01323) 415501. Ian Alexander, gen mgr.

Hastings Borough Council. Tourism and Leisure Department, Robertson Terrace, Hastings, E Sussex TN34 1ET *tel:* (01424) 781154 *fax:* (01424) 781165. Paul Ackerley, arts development offr.

Lewes District Council. Leisure and Community Services Dept, 33 High St, Lewes, E Sussex BN7 2LX *tel:* (01273) 471600 ext 4167 *fax:* (01273) 481008. Carole Buchan, arts offr.

Rother District Council. De La Warr Pavilion, Bexhill-on-Sea, E Sussex TN40 1DP *tel:* (01424) 787900. Caroline Collier, gen mgr.

Wealden District Council. Leisure Services Dept, Pine Grove, Crowborough, East Sussex TN6 1DH *tel:* (01892) 4602560 *email:* sussexcountry@wealden.gov.uk. A T Bartlett, hd of leisure services.

Essex

Essex County Council. Arts Unit, Essex County Council, PO Box 47, County Hall, Chelmsford, Essex CM1 1LD *tel:* (01245) 436825 *fax:* (01245) 436841 *email:* richard.lee@essexcc.gov.uk. Richard Lee, asst county arts offr.

Basildon District Council. Basildon Centre, St Martin's Sq, Basildon, Essex SS4 1DL *tel:* (01268) 533333. Roy Short, leisure mgr.

Braintree District Council. Causeway House, Bocking End, Braintree, Essex CM7 9HB *tel:* (01376) 552525. Nicola Deller Sarah Cook, arts development offrs.

Brentwood Borough Council. Council Offices, Ingrave Rd, Brentwood, Essex CM15 8AY *tel:* (01277) 261111 *fax:* (01277) 200152. Kim Anderson, promotions, community services directorate.

Castle Point Borough Council. Leisure Services, Council Offices, Kiln Rd, Benfleet, Essex SS7 1TF *tel:* (01268) 792711 *fax:* (01268) 882464. S W Crackham, dir, leisure services.

Chelmsford Borough Council. Civic Centre, Duke St, Chelmsford, Essex CM1 1JE *tel:* (01245) 606636. Jim Gillies, arts and ents mgr.

Colchester Borough Council. PO Box 331, Town Hall, Colchester, Essex CO1 1GI. *tel:* (01206) 282946. Clare Jackson, event co-ord.

Epping Forest District Council. Epping Forest Arts, The House, rear of Loughton Pool, Traps Hill, Loughton, Essex IG10 1HR *tel:* 0181-532 1103 *fax:* 0181-532 1106. Gillian Clark, arts offr.

Harlow District Council. Leisure Services, Latton Bush Centre, Southern Way, Harlow, Essex CM18 7BL *tel:* (01279) 446404/446427 *fax:* (01279) 446431. Krizim Feltham and Gill Penney, leisure offrs.

Maldon District Council. District Council Offices, Princes Rd, Maldon, Essex CM9 7DL *tel:* (01621) 854477 ext 431. J J Knight, dir of community services.

Rochford District Council. Council Offices, South St, Rochford, Essex SS4 1BW *tel:* (01702) 546366. D Ellis, dir of community services.

Southend-on-Sea Borough Council. PO Box 6, Civic Centre, Victoria Av, Southend-on-Sea, Essex SS2 6ER *tel:* (01702) 215436 *fax:* (01702) 215110. Rosemary Pennington, principal arts offr.

Tendring District Council. Town Hall, Station Rd, Clacton on Sea, Essex CO15 1SE *tel:* (01255) 253208. Robert Foster, ents offr.

Thurrock Borough Council. Thameside Theatre, Orsett Rd, Grays, Essex RM17 5DX *tel:* (01375) 382555. M Allinson, arts leisure mgr.

Uttlesford District Council. Council Offices, London Rd, Saffron Walden, Essex CB11 4ER *tel:* (01799) 510560. Sarah McLagan, hd of leisure and amenities.

Gloucestershire

Gloucestershire County Council. County Library, Arts & Museums Service, Quayside Wing, Shire Hall, Gloucester GL1 2HY *tel:* (01452) 425079 *email:* clams@gloscc.gov.uk. Helen Owen, arts development offr.

Cheltenham Borough Council. Dept of Entertainment and Festivals, Town Hall, Imperial Sq, Cheltenham, Glos GL50 1QA *tel:* (01242) 521621 *fax:* (01242) 573902. Jeremy Tyndall, hd of festivals and ents.

Cotswold District Council. Corinium Museum, Park St, Cirencester, Glos GL7 2BX *tel:* (01285) 655611 *fax:* (01285) 643286. David Viner, curator of museums and arts advisory offr.

Forest of Dean District Council. Council Offices, Coleford, Glos GL16 8HG *tel:* (01594) 812381 *fax:* (01594) 812314. G Derbyshire, ents offr.

Gloucester City Council. Leisure Services Department, Herbert Warehouse, The Docks, Gloucester GL1 2EQ *tel:* (01452) 396620. Lesley Pritchard, promotions and events offr.

Stroud District Council. Ebley Mill, Westward Rd, Stroud, Glos GL5 4UB *tel:* (01453) 754550/4 *fax:* (01453) 754559. Alan Caig, hd of leisure.

Tewkesbury Borough Council. Council Offices, Gloucester Rd, Tewkesbury, Glos GL20 5TT *tel:* (01684) 295010. Douglas Weldon, hd of leisure and tourism.

Greater Manchester (Metropolitan County Area)

Bolton Metropolitan Borough Council. Arts Unit, Education and Arts Dept, PO Box 53, Paderborn House, Civic Centre, Bolton BL1 1JW *tel:* (01204) 522311 ext 2183 *fax:* (01204) 526356. Tony Hughes, principal arts offr.

Bury Metropolitan Borough Council. Textile Hall, Manchester Rd, Bury, Lancs BL9 0DR *tel:* 0161-253 5869 *fax:* 0161-253 5915. Tony Trehy, arts development offr.

Manchester City Council. Central Library, St Peter's Sq, Manchester M2 5PD *tel:* 0161-234 1915 *fax:* 0161-228 6481. Adrian J P Morgan, gen mgr, Library Theatre.

Oldham Metropolitan District Council. PO Box 40, Civic Centre, West St, Oldham OL1 1XJ *tel:* 0161-911 4080 *fax:* 0161-620 6423. Paul Barnett, hd of arts, education and leisure services.

Rochdale Metropolitan Borough Council. Recreation and Community Services, PO Box 122, Municipal Offices, Smith St, Rochdale, Lancs OL16 1YB *tel:* (01706) 47474 *fax:* (01706) 864104. Andy Wiggans, dir, recreation and community services.

Salford City Council. Vulcan House, Albion Pl, The Crescent, Salford M5 4NL *tel:* 0161-736 9448 *fax:* 0161-736 0429. Edward Tootle, arts and leisure mgr.

Stockport Metropolitan District Council. c/o Rimiley Forum, Compstall Rd, Romiley, Stockport SK6 4EA *tel:* 0161-430 6570. Josephine McGrath, principal arts offr.

Tameside Metropolitan District Council. Leisure Services Dept, Council Offices, Wellington Rd, Ashton-under-Lyne OL6 6DL *tel:* 0161-342 3310 *fax:* 0161-342 3744. Philip Rogerson, hd, arts and development.

Trafford Metropolitan District Council. Leisure Services Dept, PO Box 20, Trafford Town Hall, Talbot Rd, Stretford, Manchester M32 0YT *tel:* 0161-912 1212/912 4057. Christine Keogh, arts offr.

Wigan Metropolitan Borough Council. Department of Leisure Services, Trencherfield Mill, Wallgate, Wigan WN3 4EF *tel:* (01942) 828560. Pete Gascoigne, arts development offr.

Hampshire

Hampshire County Council. County Arts Office, Mottisfont Ct, High St, Winchester, Hants SO23 8ZD *tel:* (01962) 846965 *email:* artsmf@ hants.gov.uk. Michael Fuller, snr arts offr.

Basingstoke & Deane Borough Council. Civic Offices, London Rd, Basingstoke, Hants RG21 4AH *tel:* (01256) 845736 *fax:* (01256) 845642 *email:* diane.hayward@basingstoke.gov.uk. Renee Smithens, arts and heritage mgr.

East Hampshire District Council. Penn's Pl, Petersfield, Hants GU31 4EX *tel:* (01730) 234382 *fax:* (01730) 234285 *email:* gbehcrh@ibmmail. com. Robert Hardy, community development mgr.

Eastleigh Borough Council. Civic Offices, Leigh Rd, Eastleigh, Hants SO50 9YN *tel:* (01703) 622187 *fax:* (01703) 629466. Cheryl Butler, tourism and arts offr.

Fareham Borough Council. Dept of Customer and Community Services, PO Box 14, Civic Offices, Civic Way, Fareham, Hants PO16 7PR *tel:* (01329) 236100 *fax:* (01329) 822732. Jane Masterman, mgr, Ferneham Hall.

Gosport Borough Council. Town Hall, Gosport, Hants PO12 1EB *tel:* (01705) 529129 *fax:* (01705) 511856. Robin Fegan, arts and events offr.

Hart District Council. Civic Offices, Harlington Way, Fleet, Hants GU13 8AE *tel:* (01252) 622122. Paul Dimmock, hd of leisure services.

Havant Borough Council. Leisure and Community Service, Civic Offices, Civic Centre Rd, Havant, Hants PO9 2AX *tel:* (01705) 474174 *fax:* (01705) 480263. Stephen Kerr, hd of leisure and community service.

New Forest District Council. Appletree Ct, Lyndhurst, Hants SO43 7PA *tel:* (01703) 285474. Martin Devine, asst dir leisure services.

Portsmouth City Council. City Arts, Guildhall, Portsmouth, Hants PO1 2AD *tel:* (01705) 834182 *fax:* (01705) 834904. Chris Carrell, city arts offr.

Rushmoor Borough Council. Rushmoor Leisure Services, Council Offices, Farnborough Rd, Farnborough, Hants GU14 7JU *tel:* (01252) 398743 *fax:* (01252) 398765 *email:* rmann@rushmoor.gov.uk; http:// www.rushmoor.gov.uk. Richard Mann, arts and cultural offr.

Southampton City Council. City Culture Directorate, Leisure and City Services, Civic Centre, Southampton, Hants SO14 7LP *tel:* (01703) 832730 *fax:* (01703) 337594. Christine Rawnsley, arts development offr.

Test Valley Borough Council. Leisure Services, Beech Hurst, Weyhill Rd, Andover, Hants SP10 3AJ *tel:* (01264) 343204 *fax:* (01264) 332214. Michael Johnson, arts offr.

Winchester City Council. City Offices, Colebrook St, Winchester, Hants SO23 9LJ *tel:* (01962) 840222 *fax* (01962) 841365. Lorraine Mansfield, arts and community offr.

Hartlepool

Hartlepool Borough Council. Dept of Education and Community Service, Suite 8, Municipal Buildings, Hartlepool TS24 7EQ *tel:* (01429) 266522 ext 3417. John Mennear, cultural services offr.

Hereford and Worcester

Hereford & Worcester County Council. County Hall, Spetchley Rd, Worcester WR5 2NP *tel:* (01905) 763763 *fax:* (10905) 766244. M Messenger, county librarian and arts offr.

Bromsgrove District Council. The Council House, Burcot La, Bromsgrove, Worcs B60 1AA *tel:* (01527) 873232 ext 227 *fax:* (01527) 875660. Liz Bayley, arts development offr.

Hereford City Council. Leisure Services, Garrick House, Widemarsh St, Hereford HR4 9EU *tel:* (01432) 364652 *fax:* (01432) 364602. Natalia Silver, hd of cultural services.

Leominster District Council. PO Box 3, Leominster HR6 8LU *tel:* (01568) 618264. Mark Warren, principal leisure offr.

Malvern Hills District Council. The Council House, Avenue Rd, Malvern, Worcs WR14 3AF *tel:* (01684) 892700/569256. E Nicolas Lloyd, Malvern Festival Theatre.

Redditch Borough Council. Town Hall, Alcester St, Redditch, Worcs B98 8AH *tel:* (01527) 64252 ext 3300. Paul Patten, hd of leisure services.

South Herefordshire District Council. Swan House, Edde Cross St, Ross-on-Wye, Herefordshire HR9 7BZ *tel:* (01432) 346349 *fax:* (01989) 561059. Jenny Goldsbury, leisure offr.

Worcester City Council. Orchard House, Farrier St, Worcester WR1 3BW *tel:* (01905) 722322 *fax:* (01905) 722350. Liz Dart, arts development offr.

Wyre Forest District Council. 99 Coventry St, Kidderminster, Worcs DY10 2BL *tel:* (01562) 820505. A Dickens, hd of leisure services.

Hertfordshire

Hertfordshire County Council. Community Information Directorate, New Barnfield, Travellers La, Hatfield, Herts AL10 8XG *tel:* (01707) 281537 *fax:* (01707) 281548; minicom: (01707) 281528 *email:* margo. ladell@hertscc.gov.uk. Margo Ladell, county arts development co-ord.

Broxbourne Borough Council. Bishops' College, Churchgate, Cheshunt, Herts EN8 9XF *tel:* (01992) 785555 ext 5906 *fax:* (01992) 785578. Sue Thiedeman, development and promotions mgr.

Dacorum Borough Council. Dacorum Pavilion, Marlowes, Hemel Hempstead, Herts *tel:* (01442) 228727 *email:* http://www.caxton-carrier. co.uk time-off. Tom Kealey, gen mgr.

East Hertfordshire District Council. PO Box 103, Wallfields, Pegs La, Hertford, Herts SG13 8EQ *tel:* (01279) 655261 ext 410. Tilly Andrews, leisure development offr.

Hertsmere Borough Council. Hertsmere Leisure, Rudolph Rd, Bushey, Herts WD2 3DU *tel:* 0181-420 4044 *fax:* 0181-420 4621. Chris Rushton, hd of operations.

North Hertfordshire District Council. Council Offices, Gernon Rd, Letchworth, Herts SG6 3JF *tel:* (01462) 474274 *fax:* (01462) 474500. Alan Fleck, arts and museums offr.

St Albans District Council. District Council Offices, Civic Centre, St Peter's St, St Albans, Herts AL1 3JE *tel:* (01727) 866100. Julie Simpson, leisure services mgr.

Stevenage Borough Council. Daneshill House, Danestrete, Stevenage, Herts SG1 1HN *tel:* (01438) 354292. Mark Poppu, client services offr.

Three Rivers District Council. Watersmeet Theatre, 17/23 High St, Rickmansworth, Herts WD3 1HJ *tel:* (01923) 896484 *fax:* (01923) 710121. Russell Davies, gen mgr.

Watford Borough Council. Watford Museum, 194 High St, Watford, Herts WD1 2HG *tel:* (01923) 232297/226803. Andrew Lewis, mgr, culture, museums and art.

Welwyn Hatfield Council. Community Leisure, Campus West Complex, the Campus, Welwyn Garden City, Herts AL8 6BX *tel:* (01707) 357174 *fax:* (01707) 357185 *email:* d.lucas@welhat.gov.uk. Dan Clucas, community arts offr.

Isle of Wight

Isle of Wight Council. Guildhall, Newport, Isle of Wight PO30 1TY *tel:* (01983) 823822. Lorna Brown, arts development offr.

Kent

Kent County Council. County Hall, Maidstone, Kent ME14 1XQ *tel:* (01622) 696948 *fax:* (01622) 694465. John Brazier, hd of arts promotion.

Ashford Borough Council. Civic Centre, Tannery La, Ashford, Kent TN23 1PL *tel:* (01233) 637311 ext 228 *fax:* (01233) 645654. Christina Fuller, arts development offr.

Canterbury City Council. Council Offices, Military Rd, Canterbury, Kent CT1 1YW *tel:* (01227) 763763. Mark Everett, theatre dir.

Dartford Borough Council. Civic Centre, Home Gardens, Dartford, Kent DA1 1DR *tel:* (01322) 343360. Charles Bishop, hd of arts and leisure.

Dover District Council. High St, Dover, Kent CT16 1DL *tel:* (01304) 201200 *fax:* (01304) 201200. Trevor S Jones, gen mgr, Dover Town Hall.

Gillingham Borough Council. Leisure Services Dept, Municipal Buildings, Canterbury St, Gillingham, Kent ME7 5LA *tel:* (01634) 281414 *fax:* (01634) 282629. P C Laverack, borough leisure services offr.

Gravesham Borough Council. c/o Woodfield Halls, Woodfield Pl, Gravesend, Kent DA12 1AU *tel:* (01474) 337456. Robert Allen, ents mgr.

Maidstone Borough Council. Hazlitt Theatre, Corn Exchange Complex, Earl St, Maidstone, Kent ME14 1PL *tel:* (01622) 753922/602178. Mandy Hare, Corn Exchange mgr.

Rochester upon Medway City Council. Civic Centre, Strood, Rochester, Kent ME2 4AW *tel:* (01634) 727777 *fax:* (01634) 732756. Dennis Holmes, city environment mgr.

Sevenoaks District Council. Leisure Client and Property Services, Argyle Rd, Sevenoaks, Kent TN13 1HG *tel:* (01732) 741222 ext 297 *fax:* (01732) 744543. Allison Wright, arts development offr.

Shepway District Council. Civic Centre, Castle Hill Av, Folkestone, Kent CT20 *tel:* (01303) 250589.

Swale Borough Council. Council Offices, Trinity Rd, Sheerness, Kent ME12 2PG *tel:* (01795) 580068 *fax:* (01795) 669097. Janice West, leisure services dept.

Thanet District Council. Council Offices, Cecil St, Margate, Kent CT9 1XZ *tel:* (01843) 296111 *fax:* (01843) 292795. Chris Wolfe, gen mgr, ents and catering.

Tonbridge & Malling Borough Council. Council Offices, The Air Station, West Malling, Kent ME19 6LZ *tel:* (01732) 844522. Peter Wright, borough leisure services offr.

Tunbridge Wells Borough Council. Assembly Hall Theatre, Cres Rd, Tunbridge Wells, Kent TN1 2LU *tel:* (01892) 526121/570971 *fax:* (01892) 525203. Pat Casey, theatre mgr.

Kingston upon Hull

Kingston upon Hull City Council. City Arts Unit, 79 Ferensway, Hull HU2 8LE *tel:* (01482) 615701 *fax:* (01482) 615673. Paul Holloway, city arts offr.

Lancashire

Lancashire County Council. Arts Unit, Library Headquarters, 143 Corporation St, Preston, Lancs PR1 2UQ *tel:* (01772) 263584 *fax:* (01772) 264880. Linda Prue, county arts offr.

Blackburn Borough Council. King George's Hall, Northgate, Blackburn, Lancs BB2 1AA *tel:* (01254) 582579. Geoff Peake, gen mgr.

Blackpool Borough Council. Tourism Dept, 1 Clifton St, Blackpool FY1 1LY *tel:* (01253) 25212 *fax:* (01253) 26368. Jane Seddon, hd of tourism.

Burnley Borough Council. Burnley Mechanics, Manchester Rd, Burnley, Lancs BB11 1JA *tel:* (01282) 430005 *fax:* (01282) 457428. Anthony Preston, arts development offr.

Chorley Borough Council. Chorley Arts and Museums Service, Astley Hall, Astley Pk, Chorley, Lancs PR7 1NP *tel:* (01257) 515555 *fax:* (01257) 515556. Nigel Wright, curator.

Fylde Borough Council. Tourism and Leisure Offices, 290 Clifton Dr South, Lytham St Annes, Lancs FY8 1LH *tel:* (01253) 724141. F Moor, dir of tourism and leisure.

Hyndburn Borough Council. Town Hall, Blackburn Rd, Accrington, Lancs BB5 1LA *tel:* (01254) 380296. Peter Baron, promotions offr.

Lancaster City Council. Arts and Events Department, Palatine Hill, Dalton Sq, Lancaster LA1 1PW *tel:* (01524) 582801 *fax:* (01524) 582323; http://www.juiceuk.com/artevents. Jon Harris, hd of arts and events.

Pendle Borough Council. Bank House, Albert Rd, Colne, Lancs BB8 0BP *tel:* (01282) 661220 *fax:* (01282) 661221. Gary Hood, principal leisure services offr.

Preston Borough Council. Guild Hall and Charter Theatre, Lancaster Rd, Preston, Lancs PR1 1HT *tel:* (01772) 203456. John Shedwick, gen mgr.

Ribble Valley Borough Council. Platform Gallery, Station Rd, Clitheroe, Lancs BB7 2JT *tel:* (01200) 443071 *fax:* (01200) 452556 *email:* tourism@ribblevalley.gov.uk; http://www.ribblevalley.gov.uk. Elaine Sagar, arts development offr.

Rossendale Borough Council. 41/45 Kay St, Rawtenstall, Lancs BB4 7LS *tel:* (01706) 217777 ext 243 (leisure and industrial development office).

South Ribble Borough Council. Civic Centre, West Paddock, Leyland, Preston, Lancs PR5 1DH *tel:* (01772) 421491. Paul Callander, leisure services mgr.

West Lancashire District Council. 52 Derby St, Ormskirk, Lancs L39 2DF *tel:* (01695) 585145. Kim Graham, arts offr.

Wyre Borough Council. Civic Centre, Brack Rd, Poulton-le-Fylde, Lancs FY6 7PU *tel:* (01253) 891000 ext 440 *fax:* (01253) 899000. Vicky Tindall, events mgr.

Leicestershire

Leicestershire County Council. Museums, Arts and Records Service, County Hall, Glenfield, Leicester LE3 8TB *tel:* 0116-265 6787 *fax:* 0116-265 6788.

Blaby District Council. Council Offices, Desford Rd, Narborough, Leics LE9 5EP *tel:* 0116-275 0555 *fax:* 0116-275 0368. E Atkins, leisure development offr.

Charnwood Borough Council. Town Hall, Loughborough, Leics *tel:* (01509) 634775. I Stephens, ents mgr.

Harborough District Council. Council Offices, Adam and Eve St, Market Harborough, Leics LE16 7AG *tel:* (01858) 821286. Clare Hudson, arts development offr.

Leicester City Council. Granville Rd, Leicester LE1 7RU *tel:* 0116-233 3138 *fax:* 0116-233 3182. Alvin Hargreaves, operations mgr.

Melton Borough Council. Council Offices, Nottingham Rd, Melton Mowbray, Leics LE13 0UL *tel:* (01664) 67771 *fax:* (01664) 410283. Paul Evans, mgr, client and leisure services.

North West Leicestershire District Council. Council Offices, Coalville, Leics LE6 3FJ *tel:* (01530) 833333 ext 379 *fax:* (01530) 815841. Lawrence Smith, arts development offr.

Oadby & Wigston Borough Council. Council Offices, Station Rd, Wigston, Leics LE18 2DR *tel:* 0116-288 8961. Jo Dacombe, arts and heritage offr.

Rutland District Council. Catmose, Oakham, Rutland LE15 6HP *tel:* (01572) 758399. Alison Healey, community development offr.

Lincolnshire

Lincolnshire County Council. County Offices, Newland, Lincoln LN1 1YL *tel:* (01522) 552831 *fax:* (01522) 552811 *email:* david.lambert@lincolnshire.gov.uk. David M Lambert, county arts development offr.

Boston Borough Council. Municipal Buildings, West St, Boston, Lincs PE21 8QR *tel:* (01205) 3142000 ext 590 *fax:* (01205) 364604. Barrie Higham, arts development offr.

East Lindsey District Council. Central Services Dept, Tedder Hall, Manby Pk, Louth, Lincs LN11 8UP *tel:* (01507) 601111 *fax:* (01507) 327149. E A Clarke, recreation and arts offr.

Lincoln City Council. City Hall, Beaumont Fee, Lincoln LN1 1BW *tel:* (01522) 511511 ext 514. Liz Wilson, arts offr.

North Kesteven District Council. District Council Offices, Kesteven St, Sleaford, Lincs NG34 7EF *tel:* (01529) 414155 ext 465 *fax:* (01529) 413956. Brenda Cullum, arts team business mgr.

South Holland District Council. Council Offices, Priory Rd, Spalding, Lincs PE11 2XE *tel:* (01775) 761161 *fax:* (01775) 711054. Nigel Hawkins, arts offr.

South Kesteven District Council. Council Offices, St Peter's Hill, Grantham, Lincs NG31 6PZ *tel:* (01476) 591591 *fax:* (01476) 591810. Ken Ross, arts development offr.

West Lindsey District Council. 26 Spital Terrace, Gainsborough, Lincs DN21 2HG *tel:* (01427) 615411 *email:* edu@wldc.telme.com. Louise Samouelle, tourism and arts offr.

Merseyside (Metropolitan County Area)
Knowsley Metropolitan Borough Council. Archway Rd, Huyton, Knowsley, Merseyside L36 9YX *tel:* 0151-443 5617; http://www.knowsley.gov.uk/. Paul Bewick, hd of arts and museum service.

Liverpool City Council. Central Libraries, William Brown St, Liverpool L3 8EW *tel:* 0151-225 5428 *fax:* 0151-708 0143. Phil Taylor, arts offr development and resources.

St Helens Metropolitan District Council. Town Hall, St Helens, Merseyside WA10 1HP *tel:* (01744) 456000. Jenny Lloyd, events offr.

Sefton Metropolitan Borough Council. PO Box 25, Southport, Merseyside PR9 0DZ *tel:* 0151-934 2416 *fax:* 0151-934 2418. P N King, chief tourism and attractions offr.

Wirral, Metropolitan Borough of. Dept of Leisure Services and Tourism, HQ2 the Hamilton Quarter, 43 Hamilton St, Birkenhead, Wirral L41 5AA *tel:* 0151-666 5060 *fax:* 0151-666 5070 *email:* dlstrob@wir-mbc.u-net.com. Rob Smith, arts and creative industries development mgr.

Middlesbrough
Middlesbrough Borough Council. Community Development, Leisure, PO Box 69, Vancouver House, Middlesbrough TS1 1EL *tel:* (01642) 263839 *fax:* (01642) 221866. Judith Croft, hd of arts, ents and events.

Norfolk
Norfolk County Council. Library and Information Service, County Hall, Martineau La, Norwich NR1 2DH *tel:* (01603) 222269 *fax:* (01603) 222422 *email:* mari.martin.lib@norfolk.gov.uk. Mari Martin, county arts offr.

Breckland District Council. Breckland House, St Nicholas St, Thetford, Norfolk IP24 1BT *tel:* (01842) 756453. Gill Heriz-Smith, arts development offr.

Broadland District Council. Thorpe Lodge, Yarmouth Rd, Norwich NR7 0DU *tel:* (01603) 703265. T Johnson, leisure and tourism offr.

Great Yarmouth Borough Council. Town Hall, Gt Yarmouth, Norfolk NR30 2PX *tel:* (01493) 846488 *fax:* (01493) 846332 *email:* jd.seaschange@paston.co.uk; http://www.demon.co.uk/seachange/index.html. Jan Dungey, arts development offr.

King's Lynn & West Norfolk, Borough Council of. Leisure and Tourism Dept, Valentine Rd, Hunstanton, Norfolk PE36 5EZ *tel:* (01485) 532516 *fax:* (01485) 533090. Laura Dyer, arts development offr.

North Norfolk District Council. PO Box 3, Council Offices, Holt Rd, Cromer, Norfolk NR27 9EL *tel:* (01263) 513811 ext 2412 *fax:* (01263) 515042. Jan Legge, arts development offr.

Norwich City Council. Gladstone House, 28 St Giles St, Norwich NR2 1TQ *tel:* (01603) 212147 *fax:* (01603) 213003. Ruth Churchill, arts offr.

South Norfolk Council. South Norfolk House, Long Stratton, Norfolk NR15 2XE *tel:* (01508) 533681 *fax:* (01508) 533695 *email:* snc.swan@gtnet.gov.uk. Alex Andrews, community leisure co-ord.

North East Lincolnshire
North East Lincolnshire Council. Civic Offices, Knoll St, Cleethorpes, N E Lincs DN35 8LN *tel:* (01472) 323000. Liz Lowther, asst hd of leisure.

North Somerset
North Somerset Council. Playhouse Theatre, High St, Weston-super-Mare, North Somerset BS23 1HP *tel:* (01934) 627457. Murray Macdonald, gen mgr.

North Yorkshire
Craven District Council. Council Offices, 9 High St, Skipton, N Yorks BD23 1AB *tel:* (01756) 797172. L Humphry-Williams, arts development offr.

Hambleton District Council. Civic Centre, Stonecross, Northallerton, N Yorks DL6 2UU *tel:* (01609) 779977 *fax:* (01609) 780817. David Goodwin, leisure services offr.

Harrogate Borough Council. Harrogate International Centre, Kings Rd, Harrogate, N Yorks HG1 5LA *tel:* (01423) 500500 *fax:* (01423) 537210. P Lewis, dir.

Richmondshire District Council. Friars Wynd, Richmond, N Yorks DL10 4RT *tel:* (01748) 850222 *fax:* (01748) 850897. Tony Clark, leisure and economic development unit mgr.

Ryedale District Council. Ryedale House, Malton, N Yorks YO17 0HH *tel:* (01653) 600666 ext 240 *fax:* (01653) 696801. Marie-Ann Jackson, hd of arts and museums.

Scarborough Borough Council. Londesborough Lodge, The Crescent, Scarborough, N Yorks YO11 2PW *tel:* (01723) 369151 *fax:* (01723) 376941. David J James, dir of tourism and amenities.

Selby District Council. The Civic Centre, Portholme Rd, Selby, N Yorks YO8 0SB *tel:* (01757) 292005 *fax:* (01757) 292003 (economic development unit).

Northamptonshire
Northamptonshire County Council. Leisure Services, PO Box 149, Guildhall Rd, Northampton NN1 1AU *tel:* (01604) 237117. Lesley Hagger, principal arts offr.

Corby District Council. Civic Halls, George St, Corby, Northants NN17 1QB *tel:* (01536) 402551.

Daventry District Council. Lodge Rd, Daventry, Northants NN11 5AF *tel:* (01327) 302418 *fax:* (01327) 703823. Sonia Hawes, arts offr.

East Northamptonshire Council. East Northamptonshire House, Cedar Dr, Thrapston, Northants NN14 4LZ *tel:* (01832) 742044. Stuart Smerdon, principal leisure offr, community services dept.

Kettering Borough Council. Municipal Offices, Bowling Green Rd, Kettering, Northants NN15 7QX *tel:* (01536) 410333 *fax:* (01536) 410795. Sue Gilby, hd of community services.

Northampton Borough Council. Cliftonville House, Bedford Rd, Northampton NN4 7NR *tel:* (01604) 233500 *fax:* (01604) 29571. D J Arterton, recreation mgr.

South Northamptonshire Council. Council Offices, Springfields, Towcester, Northants NN12 6AE *tel:* (01327) 350211 ext 214 *fax:* (01327) 359219. Anna Hayward, arts mgr.

Wellingborough Borough Council. Council Offices, Swanspool, Wellingborough, Northants NN8 1BP *tel:* (01933) 229777 ext 4425. Peter Morrall, ents offr.

Northumberland
Northumberland County Council. Central Library HQ, The Willows, Morpeth, Northumberland NE61 1TA *tel:* (01670) 511156 *fax:* (01670) 518012. Dave Bonser, dir, libraries, arts and heritage.

Alnwick District Council. Allerburn House, Alnwick, Northumberland NE66 1YY *tel:* (01665) 510505 ext 251 *fax:* (01665) 605099.

Berwick-upon-Tweed Borough Council. Wallace Green, Berwick upon Tweed, Northumberland TD15 1SD. Clare Burrow, amenities mgr.

Blyth Valley Borough Council. Council Offices, Seaton Delaval, Whitley Bay, Northumberland NE25 0DX *tel:* (01670) 542350 *fax:* (01670) 542323. Helen Payne, cultural development offr.

Castle Morpeth Borough Council. Council Offices, The Kylins, Loansdean, Morpeth, Northumberland NE61 2EQ *tel:* (01670) 514351. Jane Hanlon, arts development worker.

Tynedale Council. Prospect House, Hexham, Northumberland NE46 3NH *tel:* (01434) 652200. John Maude, chief leisure, tourism and economic development offr.

Wansbeck District Council. Dept of Contract and Leisure Services, East View, Stakeford, Choppington, Northumberland NE62 1TR *tel:* (01670) 819802 ext 6124.

Nottinghamshire
Nottinghamshire County Council. Leisure Services (Arts), Trent Bridge House, Fox Rd, W Bridgford, Nottingham NG2 6BJ *tel:* 0115-977 4206 *fax:* 0115-977 2428. Tim Challans, asst dir (arts).

Ashfield District Council. Community Leisure Office, Sutton Swimming Pool, Brook St, Sutton in Ashfield, Notts NG17 1ES *tel:* (01623) 457092 *fax:* (01623) 457091. Lulu Johnston, arts development offr.

Bassetlaw District Council. Leisure Services, 27 Grove St, Retford, Notts DN22 6JP *tel:* (01777) 710208. Richard Merrill, acting hd of leisure services.

Broxtowe Borough Council. Directorate, Technical and Leisure, Council Offices, Foster Av, Beeston, Nottingham NG9 1AB *tel:* 0115-925 4891 ext 4626 *fax:* 0115-943 1452 *email:* starr@broxbc.demon.co.uk. Simon Starr, asst dir, leisure.

Gedling Borough Council. Civic Centre, Arnot Hill Pk, Arnold, Nottingham NG5 6UL *tel:* 0115-967 0067/0115-967 5359 *fax:* 0115-967 3747. Alison Clark, arts development offr.

Mansfield District Council. c/o Palace Theatre, 58-60 Leeming St, Mansfield, Notts NG18 1NG *tel:* (01623) 663086. Andrew Tucker, gen mgr.

Newark and Sherwood District Council. Kelham Hall, Newark, Notts NG23 5QX *tel:* (01636) 605111 *fax:* (01636) 708267. Gerry Croad, dir, recreation and tourism.

Nottingham City Council. 24-30 Castle Gate, Nottingham NG1 7AT *tel:* 0115-915 1409 *fax:* 0115-915 1408 *email:* tourism@nottinghamcity.gov.uk. Steven Halls, asst dir, leisure and community services.

Rushcliffe Borough Council. The Civic Centre, Pavilion Rd, West Bridgford, Nottingham NG2 5FE, Notts NG2 5FE *tel:* 0115-981 9911 ext 517 *fax:* 0115-945 5882. Nicola Tompkins, arts development offr.

Oxfordshire
Oxfordshire County Council. County Hall, New Rd, Oxford OX1 1ND *tel:* (01865) 792422 *fax:* (01865) 726155.
Cherwell District Council. Bodicote House, Bodicote, Banbury, Oxon OX15 4AA *tel:* (01295) 252535 ext 4348. Vicky Hope-Walker, arts and tourism mgr.
Oxford City Council. Leisure Dept, 109-113 St Aldate's, Oxford OX1 1DS *tel:* (01865) 252838/232843. Alan Brown, Alison Manning, events orgs.
South Oxfordshire District Council. PO Box 140, Council Offices, Crowmarsh, Wallingford, Oxon OX10 8QX *tel:* (01491) 823717 *fax:* (01491) 823015. Peter Bradstock, community services offr.
Vale of White Horse District Council. The Abbey House, Abingdon, Oxon OX14 3JE *tel:* (01235) 520202 *fax:* (01235) 554960. Graeme Surtees, arts and tourism mgr.
West Oxfordshire District Council. Council Offices, Woodgreen, Witney, Oxon OX8 6NB *tel:* (01993) 770347 *fax:* (01993) 770255. Roger Sheridan, leisure and tourism mgr.

Redcar and Cleveland
Redcar and Cleveland District Council. Leisure and Libraries Dept, Kirkleatham St, Redcar TS10 1XX *tel:* (01642) 444306. Bill Sinclair, arts development offr.

Shropshire
Shropshire County Council. Arts, Information and Community, Winston Churchill Building, Radbrook Centre, Radbrook Rd, Shrewsbury, Shropshire SY3 9BJ *tel:* (01743) 254007 *fax:* (01743) 254047. Jenna Kumiega, hd of arts service.
Bridgnorth District Council. Westgate, Bridgnorth, Shropshire WV16 5AA *tel:* (01746) 765131. Cath Farrell, arts development offr.
North Shropshire District Council. Edinburgh House, New St, Wem, Shrewsbury, Shropshire SY4 5DB *tel:* (01939) 238436. Rod Owens, dir of legal and admin services.
Oswestry Borough Council. Castle View, Oswestry, Shropshire SY11 1JR *tel:* (01691) 671111. Paul F Shevlin.
Shrewsbury and Atcham Borough Council. The Music Hall, The Square, Shrewsbury, Shropshire SY1 1LH *tel:* (01743) 361921. Anne Whitfield, hd of culture and tourism.
South Shropshire District Council. Council Offices, Stone House, Corve St, Ludlow, Shropshire SY8 1DG *tel:* (01584) 874941 *fax:* (01584) 872971. R H Thomas, dep dir, admin and legal services.
Wrekin District Council. Leisure and Community Services Dept, PO Box 211, Darby House, Telford, Shropshire TF3 4LA *tel:* (01952) 202532 *fax:* (01952) 291060. Jean Escott, arts and ents mgr.

Somerset
Somerset County Council. Leisure and Arts Unit, County Hall, Taunton, Somerset TA1 4DY *tel:* (01823) 255718 *fax:* (01823) 326725 *email:* educ.si@somerset.gov.uk. Susan Isherwood, county arts offr.
Mendip District Council. Council Offices, Cannards Grave Rd, Shepton Mallet, Somerset BA4 5BT *tel:* (01749) 343399 ext 335 *fax:* (01749) 344050 *email:* nepps@mendip.gov.uk. Nicola Epps, arts development offr.
Sedgemoor District Council. Bridgwater House, King Sq, Bridgwater, Somerset TA6 3AR *tel:* (01278) 435275. Chris Sidaway, mkt and arts development offr.
South Somerset District Council. Area West Offices, Durstons, Chard, Somerset TA20 1QA *tel:* (01460) 66570 *fax:* (01460) 62416. Mark Etherington, arts development offr.
Taunton Deane Borough Council. The Deane House, Belvedere Rd, Taunton, Somerset TA1 1HE *tel:* (01823) 356356. Simon Jutton, arts development offr.
West Somerset District Council. Council Offices, 20 Fore St, Williton, Taunton, Somerset TA4 4QA *tel:* (01984) 632291. Maureen Winnall, arts development offr.

South Gloucestershire
South Gloucestershire Council. Leisure and Community Resources, Broad La, Engine Common, Yate, Bristol BS17 5PN *tel:* (01454) 868686 *fax:* (01454) 865819.

South Yorkshire (Metropolitan County Area)
Barnsley Metropolitan Borough Council. Dept of Education and Leisure, Berneslai Close, Barnsley *tel:* (01226) 770770. Graham Noble, hd of libraries and cultural services.
Rotherham Metropolitan Borough Council. Central Library and Arts Centre, Walker Pl, Rotherham, S Yorks S65 1JU *tel:* (01709) 382121. Jane Glaister, hd of museums and arts.
Sheffield City Council. Ruskin Gallery, 101 Norfolk St, Sheffield S1 2JE *tel:* 0114-273 4784. D N C Patmore, dir of arts and museums.

Staffordshire
Staffordshire County Council. Arts and Museum Service, Shugborough, Milford, Stafford ST17 0XB *tel:* (01889) 881388 *fax:* (01889) 882461. Rosalind Shipsides, county arts and museums offr.
Cannock Chase District Council. Civic Offices, PO Box 28, Beecroft Rd, Cannock, Staffs WS11 1BG *tel:* (01543) 462621. J P Richards, hd of leisure services.
East Staffordshire, Borough of. Leisure Services Dept, Midland Grain Warehouse, Derby St, Burton-on-Trent, Staffs DE14 2JJ *tel:* (01283) 508515. Catherine Bailes, arts offr.
Lichfield District Council. Civic Hall, Castle Dyke, Lichfield, Staffs WS13 6HR *tel:* (01543) 256505. Richard Dabrowski, Civic Hall mgr.
Newcastle-under-Lyme Borough Council. Civic Offices, Merrial St, Newcastle-under-Lyme, Staffs ST5 2AG *tel:* (01782) 717717. J W Martin, hd of leisure.
South Staffordshire District Council. Council Offices, Codsall, Wolverhampton, Staffs WV8 1PX *tel:* (01902) 696109. Brian Holland, strategic dir (technical).
Stafford Borough Council. c/o Stafford Gatehouse, Eastgate St, Stafford ST16 2LT *tel:* (01785) 253595 *fax:* (01785) 225622. Daniel Shaw, mgr.
Staffordshire Moorlands District Council. Leisure Section, Moorlands House, Stockwell St, Leek, Staffs ST13 6HQ *tel:* (01538) 483732/483451 *fax:* (01538) 483586. Nicola Shipley, arts development offr.
Stoke-on-Trent City Council. Leisure and Cultural Services, PO Box 816, Civic Centre, Glebe St, Stoke-on-Trent, Staffs ST4 1HF *tel:* (01782) 236926 *fax:* (01782) 232544. Clair Birkett, asst cultural development offr.
Tamworth Borough Council. Municipal Offices, Marmion House, Lichfield St, Tamworth, Staffs B79 7BZ *tel:* (01827) 311222; http://www.zipmail.co.uk/tbc/arts. Jules Cadie, arts development offr.

Stockton on Tees
Stockton-on-Tees Borough Council. Leisure Services, 72 Church Rd, Stockton-on-Tees, Cleveland TS18 1YB *tel:* (01642) 393939. J P Warbrook, leisure and tourism offr.

Suffolk
Suffolk County Council. Dept of Libraries and Leisure, St Andrew House, County Hall, Ipswich, Suffolk IP4 1LJ *tel:* (01473) 583000 *fax:* (01473) 584549. Jayne Knight, arts offr.
Babergh District Council. Corks La, Hadleigh, Ipswich, Suffolk IP7 6SJ *tel:* (01473) 825718 *email:* mutum@babergh-south-suffolk.gov.uk. Tim Mutum, asst dir of admin.
Forest Heath District Council. District Offices, College Heath Rd, Mildenhall, Suffolk IP28 7EY *tel:* (01638) 719000. J Squires, principal admin asst.
Ipswich Borough Council. Civic Centre, Civic Dr, Ipswich, Suffolk IP1 2EE *tel:* (01473) 263501. J A Orr, corporate dir.
Mid-Suffolk District Council. Council Offices, Needham Market, Suffolk IP6 8DL *tel:* (01449) 720711 *fax:* (01449) 721946. Chris Fry, hd of leisure.
St Edmundsbury Borough Council. Borough Offices, Angel Hill, Bury St Edmunds, Suffolk IP33 1XB *tel:* (01284) 757070 *fax:* (01284) 757124. David Crowther, principal heritage and culture offr.
Suffolk Coastal District Council. Council Offices, Melton Hill, Woodbridge, Suffolk IP12 1AU *tel:* (01394) 444321 *fax:* (01394) 385100. Tony Osmanski, asst dir (leisure and tourism).
Waveney District Council. Technical and Leisure Services Dept, Mariners St, Lowestoft, Suffolk NR32 1JT *tel:* (01502) 523004. Peter Waring, hd of leisure services.

Surrey
Surrey County Council. County Hall, Penrhyn Rd, Kingston-upon-Thames, Surrey KT1 2DN *tel:* 0181-541 9572. Imogen Haig, arts offr.
Elmbridge Borough Council. Civic Centre, High St, Esher, Surrey KT10 9SD *tel:* (01372) 474474. Maggs Latter, leisure admin.
Epsom and Ewell Borough Council. Epsom Playhouse, Ashley Av, Epsom, Surrey KT18 5AL *tel:* (01372) 742226/739351 *fax:* (01372) 726228. Trevor Mitchell, Playhouse mgr.
Guildford Borough Council. Dept of Leisure Services, Millmead House, Millmead, Guildford, Surrey GU2 5BB *tel:* (01483) 444715 *fax:* (01483) 444717. Nicola Peacock, arts development offr.
Mole Valley District Council. Pippbrook, Dorking, Surrey RH4 1SJ *tel:* (01306) 879200. Vanessa Hart, gen mgr (ents).
Reigate and Banstead Borough Council. The Harlequin, Warwick Quadrant, Redhill, Surrey RH1 1NN *tel:* (01737) 773721 *fax:* (01737) 765549. Robin Battersby, Harlequin mgr.
Runnymede Borough Council. Civic Offices, Station Rd, Addlestone, Surrey KT15 2AH *tel:* (01932) 705445. Ronnie Fleming, hd of leisure services.

Spelthorne, Borough of. Council Offices, Knowle Green, Staines, Middx TW18 1XB *tel:* (01784) 881880. Sandra Bruce-Gordon, gen mgr, Old Town Hall Arts Centre.

Surrey Heath Borough Council. Artslink, Knoll Rd, Camberley, Surrey GU15 3SY *tel:* (01276) 26978. Karen Turner, arts mgr.

Tandridge District Council. Commercial and Leisure Dept, Council Offices, Oxted, Surrey RH8 0BT *tel:* (01883) 722000 ext 457. Paul Clark, leisure and business development mgr.

Waverley Borough Council. The Burys, Godalming, Surrey GU7 1HR *tel:* (01483) 869390 *fax:* (01483) 860643.

Woking Borough Council. Civic Offices, Gloucester Sq, Woking, Surrey GU21 1YL *tel:* (01483) 743807 *email:* wokbc@woking.gov.uk. David Vince, arts development offr.

Tyne and Wear (Metropolitan County Area)

Gateshead Metropolitan District Council. Central Library, Prince Consort Rd, Gateshead NE8 4LN *tel:* 0191-477 3478. Mike White, asst dir (arts).

Newcastle City Council. City Library, Princess Sq, Newcastle upon Tyne NE99 1DX *tel:* 0191-261 0691 *fax:* 0191-261 1435. Andrew Rothwell, city arts offr.

North Tyneside Council. Buddle Arts Centre, 258B Station Rd, Wallsend NE28 8RH *tel:* 0191-200 7132 *fax:* 0191-200 7142 *email:* ntynearts@demon.co.uk. Mike Campbell, principal arts offr.

South Tyneside Metropolitan Borough Council. Central Library, Prince Georg Sq, South Shields NE33 2PE *tel:* 0191-427 1717 ext 2059 *fax:* 0191-427 0469. Richard Jago, snr recreation asst.

Sunderland Metropolitan District Council. Arts Development Unit, Central Library, 28-30 Fowcutt St, Sunderland SR1 1RE *tel:* 0191-514 1235 *fax:* 0191-514 8444. Katherine Pearson, hd of arts.

Warwickshire

Warwickshire County Council. Libraries and Heritage Department, Barrack St, Warwick CV34 4TH *tel:* (01926) 410410 ext 2492 *fax:* (01926) 412165. A Litvinoff, arts development offr.

North Warwickshire Borough Council. Leisure Services Division, Council House, South St, Atherstone, Warwicks CV9 1BD *tel:* (01827) 719207. Barry J McLoughlin, area recreation offr.

Nuneaton and Bedworth Borough Council. Civic Hall, High St, Bedworth, Warwicks CV12 8NF *tel:* (01203) 376705 *fax:* (01203) 376730. David Matthews, ents mgr.

Rugby Borough Council. Town Hall, Rugby, Warwicks CV21 2LB *tel:* (01788) 533533 *fax:* (01788) 533778. Mary Ferrier, principal recreation offr.

Stratford upon Avon Town Council. Civic Hall, 14 Rother St, Stratford upon Avon, Warwicks CV37 6LU *tel:* (01789) 269332 *fax:* (01789) 297072. Mike Simkiss, halls mgr.

Warwick District Council. Royal Spa Centre, Newbold Terrace, Leamington Spa, Warwicks CV32 4HN *tel:* (01926) 334418 *fax:* (01926) 832054. Peter B Nicholson, ents mgr.

West Midlands (Metropolitan County Area)

Birmingham City Council. Museum and Art Gallery, Chamberlain Sq, Birmingham B3 3DH *tel:* 0121-235 2919 *fax:* 0121-236 6227. Anthony Sargent, hd of arts and ents.

Coventry City Council. Leisure Services Department, Spire House, New Union St, Coventry CV1 2PS *tel:* (01203) 832399 *fax:* (01203) 832361. Debbie Kingsley, arts offr.

Dudley Metropolitan Borough Council. Dudley Planning and Leisure Dept, Claughton House, Blowers Green Rd, Dudley, W Midlands DY2 8UZ *tel:* (01384) 815513. Claire Crone, principal arts offr.

Sandwell Metropolitan Borough Council. Arts in Sandwell, Dept of Education and Community, Shaftesbury House, 402 High St, W Bromwich B70 9LT *tel:* 0121-569 4926. J Harris, acting principal arts offr.

Solihull Metropolitan Borough Council. Education, Libraries and Arts Dept, Central Library, Homer Rd, Solihull, W Midlands B91 3RG *tel:* 0121-704 6961 *fax:* 0121-704 6991. Lawrence Smith, arts and ents mgr.

Walsall Metropolitan Borough Council. Leisure and Community Services, PO Box 42, Civic Centre, Darwall St, Walsall WS1 1TZ *tel:* (01922) 653170 *fax:* (01922) 721682. Antonia Pompa, promotions and events mgr.

Wolverhampton Metropolitan District Council. Civic Hall, North St, Wolverhampton, W Midlands WV1 1RQ *tel:* (01902) 312029 *email:* wolvercivicwulfrum@dial.pipex.com. Mark Blackstock, civic halls and outdoor events mgr.

West Sussex

West Sussex County Council. County Hall, Chichester, W Sussex PO19 1RQ *tel:* (01243) 777902 *fax:* (01243) 777952. John Godfrey, asst county sec:

Adur District Council. Civic Centre, Ham Rd, Shoreham-by-Sea, W Sussex BN43 6PR *tel:* (01273) 455566 *fax:* (01273) 454847 *email:* devserv@adurdc.gov.uk. Jacqui Bladen, Louise Brattle, mkt and development offrs.

Arun District Council. Civic Centre, Littlehampton, W Sussex BN17 5LF *tel:* (01903) 716133. John Stride, tourism and leisure services mgr.

Chichester District Council. Council Offices, East Pallant House, East Pallant, Chichester, W Sussex PO19 1TY *tel:* (01243) 785166 *fax:* (01243) 776766. Anne Bone, arts and heritage development mgr.

Crawley Borough Council. The Hawth, Crawley, W Sussex RH10 6YZ *tel:* (01293) 552941 *email:* hawth@enterprise.net. Kevin Eason, theatre and arts mgr.

Horsham District Council. Horsham Arts Centre, North St, Horsham, W Sussex RH12 1RL *tel:* (01403) 259708 *fax:* (01403) 211502. Kevin Parker, Arts Centre mgr.

Mid Sussex District Council. Leisure and Amenities Department, Oaklands, Haywards Heath, W Sussex RH16 1SS *tel:* (01444) 458166 ext 2275 *fax:* (01444) 414669. Sarah Elderkin, community arts offr.

Worthing Borough Council. c/o Pavilion Theatre, Marine Parade, Worthing, W Sussex BN11 3PX *tel:* (01903) 239999 ext 2502. Peter Bailey, theatre mgr.

West Yorkshire (Metropolitan County Area)

Bradford City Council. Recreation Division, Jacob's Well, Bradford, W Yorks BD1 5RW *tel:* (01274) 752646 *fax:* (01244) 754676. Jim Mackay, hd of recreation.

Calderdale Metropolitan Borough Council. The Victoria Theatre, Wards End, Halifax, W Yorks HX1 1BU *tel:* (01422) 351156. Alisa Metcalfe, customer services mgr.

Kirklees Metropolitan Council. Kirklees Cultural Services, Red Doles La, Huddersfield, W Yorks HD2 1YF *tel:* (01484) 226300 ext 6837 *fax:* (01484) 446842. Richard Bealing, museums, arts and town halls.

Leeds City Council. Leisure Services, Leeds Town Hall, the Headrow, Leeds, W Yorks LS1 3AD *tel:* 0113-247 8337. Alwin Knowles, dir.

Wakefield Metropolitan District Council. Museums and Arts, The Elizabethan Gallery, Brook St, Wakefield, W Yorks WF1 *tel:* (01924) 305799 *fax:* (01924) 305793. Adele Firth, snr development offr.

Wiltshire

Wiltshire County Council. Youth and Community Services, Bythesea Rd, Trowbridge, Wilts BA14 8JB *tel:* (01225) 713804 *fax:* (01225) 713807. Gordon Evans, hd of youth and community services.

Kennet District Council. Browfort, Bath Rd, Devizes, Wilts SN10 2AT *tel:* (01380) 724911 ext 674. Ruth Hecht, arts development offr.

North Wiltshire District Council. Leisure Strategy, The Citadel, Bath Rd, Chippenham, Wilts SN15 2AA *tel:* (01249) 443322 ext 496. Kerry Wilkins, arts development offr.

Salisbury District Council. The Council House, Bourne Hill, Salisbury, Wilts SP1 3UZ *tel:* (01722) 434307 *fax:* (01722) 434500. Helen Hale, arts development offr.

Swindon Borough Council. Premier House, Station Rd, Swindon, Wilts SN1 1TZ *tel:* (01793) 466462. Julia Holberry, hd of arts, libraries and museums.

West Wiltshire District Council. Direct Leisure, Civic Hall, St Stephens Pl, Trowbridge, Wilts BA14 8AH *tel:* (01225) 775335. Nicola Clench, arts and ents mgr.

York

York City Council. Leisure Services, 18 Back Swinegate, Swinegate Ct, York YO1 2AD *tel:* (01904) 613161 ext 3387 *fax:* (01904) 553378 *email:* http://www.york.gov.uk. Peter Attwood Boardman, service commissioner, arts and culture.

Channel Islands

Bailiwick of Guernsey. States Arts Committee, Sir Charles Frossard House, PO Box 43, St Peter Port, Channel Islands GY1 1FH *tel:* (01481) 717000 *fax:* (01481) 712520. D M Savident, sec.

Bailiwick of Jersey. States Offices, St Helier, Jersey, Channel Islands *tel:* (01534) 700111.

Isle of Man

Douglas Borough Council. Entertainments Department, Villa Marina, Douglas, Isle of Man *tel:* (01624) 674171. E M Quayle, admin.

Isles of Scilly

Isles of Scilly Council. Town Hall, St Mary's, Isles of Scilly TR21 0LW *tel:* (01720) 423371 *fax:* (01720) 422049 *email:* steve@scilly.demon. co.uk. Steve Watt, tourism, development and maritime offr.

Scotland

Aberdeen City Council. Arts and Recreation Department, St Nicholas House, Broad St, Aberdeen AB10 1XJ *tel:* (01224) 522472 *fax:* (01224) 648256. Brian Woodcock, dir of arts and recreation.

Aberdeenshire Council, Central Division. Gordon House, Blackhall Rd, Inverurie AB5 3WA *tel:* (01467) 620981. Ron Reid, divisional mgr, leisure and recreation.

Angus Council. Cultural Services, County Buildings, Forfar, Angus DD8 3WF *tel:* (01307) 461460 ext 3256 *fax:* (01307) 462590. Gavin N Drummond, dir of cultural services.

Argyll and Bute Council. Council HQ, Kilmory, Lochgilphead PA31 8RT *tel:* (01546) 604121 *fax:* (01546) 604208 *email:* p_weatherall@ cqm.co.uk; http://www.cqm.co.uk/ab_leisure/arts.html. W T Young, principal leisure resources offr.

Clackmannanshire Council. Lime Tree House, Castle St, Alloa FK10 1EX *tel:* (01259) 450000. Rosa Macpherson, team leader, arts and arts education and ents.

Dumfries and Galloway Council. Council Offices, 118 English St, Dumfries DG1 2DE *tel:* (01387) 260027 *fax:* (01387) 260029. Stewart S Atkinson, hd of leisure and sport for community resources.

Dundee City Council. Arts and Heritage Department, McManus Galleries, Albert Sq, Dundee DD1 1DA *tel:* (01382) 432021 *fax:* (01382) 432052. Andrea Stark, chief arts offr.

East Ayrshire Council. London Rd Centre, London Rd, Kilmarnock KA3 7BU *tel:* (01563) 574057 *fax:* (01563) 576500. David Montgomery, chief exec.

East Dunbartonshire Council. Kilmardinny Arts Centre, 50 Kilmardinny Av, Bearsden, Glasgow G61 3NN *tel:* 0141-931 5084 *fax:* 0141-931 5085. Joan Riddell, arts and events mgr.

East Lothian Council. Brunton Hall, Ladywell Way, Musselburgh, E Lothian EH21 6AA *tel:* 0131-665 9900. Lesley Smith, principal arts offr.

East Renfrewshire Council. Council Offices, Eastwood Pk, Rouken Glen Rd, Giffnock, Glasgow G46 6UG *tel:* 0141-577 3103 *fax:* 0141-577 3100. Ken McKinlay, hd of cultural services.

Edinburgh, City of, Council. Directorate of Recreation, 17 Waterloo Pl, Edinburgh EH1 3BG *tel:* 0131-529 7736 *fax:* 0131-529 7846. Roger Jones, dir of recreation.

Falkirk Council. Community and Leisure Services, Kilns House, Kilns Rd, Falkirk FK1 5SA *tel:* (01324) 506070. Loudon Craig, dir of community and leisure services.

Fife Council. Fife House, North St, Glenrothes, Fife KY7 5LT *tel:* (01592) 417816 *fax:* (01592) 417894. Bridget McConnell, service mgr, arts, museums and libraries.

Glasgow, City of, Council. City Chambers, George Sq, Glasgow G2 1DU *tel:* 0141-287 2000 *fax:* 0141-287 3919. John Anderson, chief exec.

Highland Council, Inverness Area. Cultural Leisure Services, Town House, Inverness IV1 1JJ *tel:* (01463) 724261. Adrian Clark, arts offr.

Highland Council, Nairn Area. The Court House, High St, Nairn IV12 4AU *tel:* (01667) 458523 *fax:* (01667) 458533.

Highland Council, Ross and Cromarty Area. Cultural and Leisure Services, Council Offices, Dingwall IV15 9QN *tel:* (01349) 868487. Nick Fearne, arts development offr.

Highland Council, Sutherland Area. Council Offices, Main St, Golspie KW10 6RB *tel:* (01408) 633033.

Inverclyde Council. Education Services, 105 Dalrymple St, Greenock PA15 1HT *tel:* (01475) 882828 *fax:* (01475) 726412. J Monteith, hd of service.

Midlothian District Council. Community Services Division, Caledonian House, 19A Canning St, Edinburgh EH3 8TE *tel:* 0131-221 5691. Robin Strang, leisure services mgr.

Moray Council. District HQ, High St, Elgin IV30 1BX *tel:* (01343) 543451.

North Ayrshire Council. Cunninghame House, Friars Croft, Irvine KA12 8EE *tel:* (01294) 324225 *fax:* (01294) 324244. Judith Rankin, arts and cultural services mgr.

North Lanarkshire Council. Leisure Services, Buchanan Tower, Buchanan Business Pk, Cumbernauld Rd, Stepps, Glasgow G33 6HR *tel:* 0141-304 1846. Ann Malloy, hd of cultural services.

Perth and Kinross Council. Perth Museum and Art Gallery, George St, Perth PH1 5LB *tel:* (01738) 632488. Lynn Baxter, principal offr, community arts.

Renfrewshire Council. Paisley Arts Centre, New St, Paisley *tel:* 0141-887 1010 *fax:* 0141-887 6300. Paul Hogan, principal arts offr.

Scottish Borders Council. Council Headquarters, Newtown St, Newtown St Boswells, Melrose TD6 0SA *tel:* (01835) 824000. Ian Yates, dir of leisure and recreation.

South Ayrshire Council. County Buildings, Wellington Sq, Ayr KA7 1DR *tel:* (01292) 612244 *fax:* (01292) 612261. Nick Lartin, hd of community and cultural enrichment.

South Lanarkshire Council. Council Offices, South Vennel, Lanark ML11 7JT *tel:* (01555) 661331 ext 110 *fax:* (01555) 662546. Colin McAllister, arts development offr.

Stirling Council. Heritage and Cultural Services, Viewforth, Stirling FK8 2ET *tel:* (01786) 443241. Evan Henderson, events offr.

West Dunbartonshire Council. Education and Leisure Services, Arts and Leisure Development, Castle St, Dumbarton G82 1JY *tel:* (01389) 738448 *fax:* (01389) 733244. Gill Graham, snr arts development offr.

West Lothian Council. Education Services, Arts Unit, Howden Pk Centre, Livingston EH54 6AE *tel:* (01506) 433634. Val Bickford, Arts Centre mgr.

Orkney Islands Council

Orkney Islands Council. Council Offices, Kirkwall KW15 1NY *tel:* (01856) 873535 *fax:* (01856) 870302. J J Anderson, dir, education and recreation.

Shetland Islands Council

Shetland Islands Council. Dept of Education and Community Services, Quendale House, Lerwick *tel:* (01595) 696606. James G Halcrow, dir of education and community services.

Western Isles Islands Council

Western Isles Islands Council. Lionacleit Education Centre, Benbecula, Western Isles HS7 5PJ *tel:* (01870) 602043 *fax:* (01870) 602053. Richard J Woolford, asst dir (divisional education offr south).

Wales

Alyn & Deeside District Council. Civic Offices, St David's Pk, Deeside CH5 3PW *tel:* (01244) 525168. R A H Morris, chief planning offr.

Blaenau Gwent County Borough. Leisure and Community Services, Festival House, Victoria Business Pk, Ebbw Vale NP3 6EX *tel:* (01495) 308996, also fax. Geoff Cripps, arts development offr.

Bridgend County Borough Council. Education and Leisure Services, Sunnyside, Bridgend CF31 4AR *tel:* (01656) 642684 *fax:* (01656) 642676. Roger Price, arts and ents offr.

Caerphilly County Borough Council. Blackwood Miners Institute, High St, Blackwood NP2 1BB *tel:* (01495) 224425 *fax:* (01495) 226457. Lyn Evans, leisure development offr.

Cardiff City Council. Sports & Leisure Department, County Hall, Atlantic Wharf, Cardiff CF1 5UW *tel:* (01222) 873936/873904 *email:* http:// www.virtualcardiff.co.uk/cardiff-summer-festival. Paul Jenkins, dir of sports and leisure.

Carmarthenshire County Council. Public Library, St Peters St, Carmarthen, Dyfed SA31 1LN *tel:* (01267) 224834. Phil Alder, arts offr.

Ceredigion District Council. Lisburne House, Terrace Rd, Aberystwyth SY23 2AJ *tel:* (01970) 617911 *fax:* (01970) 626566. Daniel J G Owen, mkt and PR offr.

Conwy County Borough Council. Civic Offices, Bodlondeb, Conwy LL32 8DU *tel:* (01492) 879771 *fax:* 901492) 860790. Nick Reed, gen mgr.

Denbighshire County Council. Russell House, Churton Rd, Rhyl, Denbighshire LL18 3DP *tel:* (01824) 706409 *fax:* 344516. Lloyd Conway, hd of tourism and leisure.

Gwynedd Council. Dept of Education and Culture, Swyddfa'r Cyngor, Caernarfon, Gwynedd LL55 1SH *tel:* (01286) 679089 *email:* garethheulfryn@gwynedd.gov.uk; http://www.gwynedd.gov.uk. Gareth Heulfryn Williams, asst dir, culture.

Merthyr Tydfil, County Borough of. Civic Centre, Castle St, Merthyr Tydfil, Mid Glamorgan CF47 8AN *tel:* (01685) 723201. John Stokes, leisure services mgr.

Neath Port Talbot County Council. Civic Centre, Penllergaer, Swansea SA4 1GH *tel:* (01792) 222601. Andy Eagle, cultural services mgr.

Newport County Borough Council. Education Dept, Civic Centre, Newport NP9 4UR *tel:* (01633) 233431 *fax:* (01633) 233376. Alun D Williams, mus adviser.

Pembrokeshire County Council. Scolton Manor Museum, Spittal, Haverfordwest, Pembrokeshire *tel:* (01437) 731328 *fax:* (01437) 731743. Tracey Morris, arts offr, cultural services division.

Powys County Council. Community Dept, Powys County Hall, Llandrindod Wells, Powys LD1 5LG *tel:* (01597) 826464 *fax:* (01597) 826243. John Greatorex, asst dir.

Rhondda Cynon Taff County Borough Council. Education Department, Grawen St, Porth, Rhondda CF39 0BU *tel:* (01443) 687666 *fax:* (016443) 680286. Julie Jones, county borough librarian.

Swansea, City & County of. The Guildhall, Swansea SA1 4PE *tel:* (01792) 302491. D Evans, dir of leisure services.

Torfaen County Borough Council. Civic Centre, Pontypool, Gwent NP4 6YB *tel:* (01495) 762200 *fax:* (01495) 755513. Tony Roberts, dir of recreation and leisure.

Wrexham County Borough Council. Memorial Hall, Bodhyfryd, Wrexham LL2 7AG *tel:* (01978) 292683. G A Lacy, arts and ents offr.

Ynys Mon County Council. Leisure and Heritage Department, Plas Arthur Leisure Centre, Llangefni, Isle of Anglesey LL77 7NF *tel:* (01248) 752024 *fax:* (01248) 750365. E A Mitcheson, dir of leisure and heritage.

Northern Ireland

Antrim

Antrim Borough Council. c/o Clotworthy Arts Centre, Randalstown Rd, Antrim, Co Antrim *tel:* (018494) 428000 *fax:* (018494) 460360. M Armstrong, arts and heritage development offr.

Ballymena Borough Council. 80 Galgorm Rd, Ballymena, Co Antrim BT42 1AB *tel:* (01266) 44111 ext 279. Rosalind Lowry, arts offr.

Ballymoney Borough Council. Riada House, Charles St, Ballymoney, Co Antrim BT53 6DZ *tel:* (01265) 662280 *fax:* (01265) 667659. W J Paul, chief recreation and amenities offr.

Belfast City Council. Ulster Hall, Bedford St, Belfast, Co Antrim BT2 7FF *tel:* (01232) 323900. F McCausland, asst mgr.

Carrickfergus Borough Council. Tourist Information Office, Heritage Plaza, Carrickfergus, Co Antrim BT38 7DG *tel:* (01960) 366455 *fax:* (01960) 350350. Alan Phair, dir of recreation.

Larne Borough Council. Smiley Buildings, Victoria Rd, Larne, Co Antrim BT40 1RU *tel:* (01574) 272313. H G Francis, sec.

Moyle District Council. Sheskburn House, 7 Mary St, Ballycastle, Co Antrim BT54 6QH *tel:* (012657) 62225. Kevin McGarry, recreation mgr.

Newtownabbey Borough Council. Dept of Leisure Services, Glenmount House, 49 Church Rd, Newtownabbey, Co Antrim BT36 7LG *tel:* (01232) 868751. C Cole, leisure development offr (arts).

Armagh

Armagh City & District Council. c/o Tourist Information Centre, 40 English St, Armagh BT61 7BA *tel:* (01861) 521805 *fax:* (01861) 510180. Kate Bond, Armagh City & District arts committee.

Craigavon Borough Council. Pinebank Arts and Resource Centre, Tullygally Rd, Craigavon, Co Armagh BT65 5BY *tel:* (01762) 341618 *fax:* (01762) 342402. Rosaleen McMullan, arts development offr.

Down

Down District Council. Down County Museum, The Mall, Downpatrick, Co Down BT30 6AH *tel:* (01396) 615218 ext 250 *fax:* (01396) 615590. Jill Holmes, arts offr.

Ards Borough Council. Ards Arts Centre, Conway Sq, Newtownards, Co Down BT23 4DD *tel:* (01247) 810803 *fax:* (01247) 823131 *email:* ards@ards-council.govt.uk. Eilis O Baoill, arts offr.

Banbridge District Council. Council Offices, Downshire Rd, Banbridge, Co Down BT32 3JY *tel:* (018206) 62991 *fax:* (018206) 62595. Pamela Matthews, community relations development offr.

Castlereagh Borough Council. 368 Cregagh Rd, Belfast BT6 9EZ *tel:* (01232) 799021. James D Rose, dir of leisure and community services.

Lisburn Borough Council. Harmony Hill Arts Centre, Clonmore House, 54 Harmony Hill, Lisburn, Co Antrim BT27 4ES *tel:* (01846) 678219 *fax:* (01846) 662679 *email:* 101511.665@compuserve.com. Siobhan Stewart, arts development offr.

Newry and Mourne District Council. Haughey House, Rampart Rd, Greenbank Industrial Estate, Newry, Co Down *tel:* (01693) 67226. R F Turley, dir of district services.

North Down Borough Council. Town Hall, Bangor, Co Down BT20 4BT *tel:* (01247) 270371. Paula Clamp, arts offr.

Fermanagh

Fermanagh District Council. Council Offices, Town Hall, Enniskillen, Co Fermanagh BT74 7BA *tel:* (01365) 325050 *fax:* (01365) 322024. R Connor, dir of environmental services.

Londonderry

Coleraine Borough Council. Council Offices, Cloonavin, 41 Portstewart Rd, Coleraine, Co Londonderry BT52 1EY *tel:* (01265) 52181 *fax:* (01265) 53489. Moira Mann, tourism and arts offr.

Derry City Council. Performing Arts, Rialto Entertainment Centre, 5 Market St, Derry, Co Londonderry BT48 6EF *tel:* (01504) 264177 *fax:* (01504) 260689 *email:* http://www.mni.co.uk/see/derry/festival. David McLaughlin, venues mgr.

Limavady Borough Council. 7 Connell St, Limavady, Co Londonderry BT49 0HA *tel:* (015047) 60304. S T McGregor, chief recreation offr.

Magherafelt District Council. Council Offices, 50 Ballyronan Rd, Magherafelt, Co Londonderry BT45 6EN *tel:* (01648) 32151 *fax:* (01648) 31240. Michael Bryan, development offr.

Tyrone

Cookstown District Council. Council Offices, Burn Rd, Cookstown, Co Tyrone BT80 8DT *tel:* (016487) 62205 *fax:* (016487) 64360. M McGuckin, chief exec.

Dungannon District Council. Council Offices, Circular Rd, Dungannon, Co Tyrone BT71 6DT *tel:* (018687) 25311. Theresa McNicholl, arts admin offr.

Omagh District Council. Council Offices, The Grange, Mountjoy Rd, Omagh, Co Tyrone BT79 7BL *tel:* (01662) 245321 ext 316. Jean Brennan, arts development offr.

Strabane District Council. District Council Offices, 47 Derry Rd, Strabane, Co Tyrone BT82 8DY *tel:* (01504) 382204 *fax:* (01504) 382264. Karen McFarland, community services offr.

Concert Promoters

The following organisations, including the cultural institutes of certain Commonwealth and foreign governments, promote concerts regularly using private funds, money from public funding bodies, or a mixture of the two. They act as principals in selecting, engaging, promoting and paying artists and take financial responsibility for the outcome.

Additional concert promoters are listed in the following sections: **Local Authority Promoters, Music Clubs and Societies** and **Associations.**

Adrian Hopkins Promotions. 24 Fulham Palace Rd, Hammersmith, London W6 9PH *tel:* 0181 741 9910 *fax:* 0181 741 9914.

Alternative Arts. 47a Brushfield St, Spitalfields, London E1 6AA *tel:* 0171 375 0441 *fax:* 0171 375 0484. Maggie Pinhorn, dir. *Jazz, opera, classical, contemporary.*

Anglo-Argentine Society. 2 Belgrave Sq, London SW1X 8PJ *tel:* 0171 235 9505 *also fax; email:* angloarg@demon.co.uk. T J Rumboll, sec. *Argentine mus and composers.*

Anglo-Austrian Music Society. 46 Queen Anne's Gate, London SW1H 9AU *tel:* 0171 222 0366 *fax:* 0171 233 0923. Tony Fessler, gen sec. *Promotes concerts which have a connection with Austria.*

Arthur Davison Family Concerts. 14 Beaumont Rd, Purley, Surrey CR8 2EG *tel:* 0181 668 5883 *also fax.* Darrell Davison, mus dir.

Asian Music Circuit. Unit F (Ground Floor), West Point, 33-34 Warple Way, Acton, London W3 0RG *tel:* 0181 742 9911 *fax:* 0181 749 3948. Kuldeep Jalf, sec; Penny King, tour co-ord. *Promotes mus from the Indian subcontinent, SE Asia, China and the Far East.*

Austrian Cultural Institute. 28 Rutland Gate, London SW7 1PQ *tel:* 0171 584 8653 *fax:* 0171 225 0470 *email:* austrcul@dircon.co.uk. Andrea Rauter, mus offr. *Classical and contemporary, mostly chmbr mus; jazz.*

Brighton & Hove Philharmonic Society. 50 Grand Parade, Brighton, E Sussex BN2 2QA *tel:* 01273 622900 *fax:* 01273 697887. Tony Woodhouse, gen mgr. *Presents annual orch concert series.*

British Music Information Centre. 10 Stratford Pl, London W1N 9AE *tel:* 0171 499 8567 *fax:* 0171 499 4795 *email:* bmic@bmic.co.uk; http://www.bmic.co.uk. Matthew Greenall, dir. *Presents concerts of classical mus (mostly 20th C British) twice weekly; also lectures and discussions.*

Cambridge Music Promotions. 10 Gurney Way, Cambridge CB4 2ED *tel:* 01223 350544 *also fax.* Gillian Perkins, festival admin. *Organisation of occasional festivals every 2 or 3 years. Next 1999/2000.*

China People Promotions. 28 Tonmead Rd, Northampton NN3 8HX *tel:* 01604 412922 *also fax.* Li Jiang, dir; Ket Y-Chiu, admin. *Promotion of Chinese traditional mus and cultural events.*

The Chopin Society. c/o 44 Bassett Rd, London W10 6JL *tel:* 0181 960 6717 *also fax.* Gill Newman, sec. *The Chopin Society gives monthly recitals at the Polish Institute, 20 Prince's Gate, London SW7. Membership enquiries to Mrs M D Caven, 13 Woodside Ct, Abbot's Park, Chester, Cheshire CH1 4BA tel:* 01244 380279.

Clifton Wyatt Artists Management. 1 Poets Rd, London N5 2SL *tel:* 0171 354 2050 *also fax; email:* cliftonwyattartistsmanagement@compuserve.com. Jacqueline Clifton, David Wyatt, dirs. *Promotes a range of events both independently and in collaboration with other organisations.*

La Colombe du Paradis. 16 Church St, S Brent, Devon TQ10 9AB *tel:* 01364 72522. *Mainly charity concerts.*

Danish Cultural Institute. 3 Doune Terrace, Edinburgh EH3 6DY *tel:* 0131 225 7189 *fax:* 0131 220 6162 *email:* fa@dancult.demon.co.uk. Finn Andersen, dir. *Concerts throughout UK for Danish soloists and ens.*

Dartington Arts. The Gallery, Dartington Hall, Totnes, Devon TQ9 6DE *tel:* 01803 865864/863073 (box office) *fax:* 01803 868108. Paul Goddard, arts development; Lewis Riley, mus programmer. *Classical, world mus, folk, jazz, contemporary.*

Early Music Network. Sutton House, 2-4 Homerton High St, London E9 6JQ *tel:* 0181 533 2921 *fax:* 0181 533 2922. Alison Blunt, admin dir. *Young artists. Programmes with strong educ content.*

ECAT (Edinburgh Contemporary Arts Trust). 16 Clerwood Gardens, Edinburgh EH12 8PT *tel:* 0131 539 8877 *fax:* 0131 539 2211. Hazel Sheppard, admin. *Contemporary mus.*

Ernest Read Music Association. 9 Cotsford Av, New Malden, Surrey KT3 5EU *tel:* 0181 942 0318. Noel Long, dir. *Concerts for children.*

Experimental Arts Productions. 63 Severn Way, Willesden, London NW10 2UU *tel:* 0171 722 2600. Stan Haynes, Mrs D Gerber, Mrs M Arditti, dirs. *Promoters of contemporary and electronic mus concerts, publications, recordings, etc.*

Flamencovision. 54 Windsor Rd, London N3 3SS *tel:* 0181 346 4500 *fax:* 0181 346 2488 *email:* http://www.flamencovision.com. Helen Martin, mgr. *Flamenco gui and dance.*

Fun with Music. 2 Queensmead, St John's Wood Pk, London NW8 6RE *tel:* 0171 722 9828 *fax:* 0171 722 7981. Iain Kerr, admin. *Children's and family concerts.*

Hochhauser, Victor. 4 Oak Hill Way, London NW3 7LR *tel:* 0171 794 0987 *fax:* 0171 431 2531.

Influence. Disraeli Mews, 137b Outney High St, London SW15 1SU *tel:* 0181 789 1192 *also fax.* Michael Heyland, events consultant. *The promotion of concerts and international tours, particularly choral and operatic.*

Invisible Pilots Ltd. The Barony, 16 Sandringham Rd, Petersfield, Hampshire GU32 2AA *tel:* 01730 267341. Peter Thompson, proprietor. *Classical recitals; annual Match composition prize.*

Jewish Music Heritage Trust. PO Box 232, Harrow, Middx HA1 2NN *tel:* 0181 909 2445 *fax:* 0181 909 1030 *email:* jewishmusic@jmht.org. Geraldine Auerbach, dir. *Promotes concerts and recitals of mus of Jewish significance.*

Kirckman Concert Society Ltd. The Long House, Arkley La, Barnet, Herts EN5 3JR *tel:* 0181 449 0303. Geraint Jones, artistic dir. *London recitals for young artists chosen at audition.*

LACCS. Latin American and Caribbean Cultural Society. PO Box 30, London N12 0PR *tel:* 0181 446 6416 *fax:* 0181 446 5547. J R Monroy, dir; J L Sylvester, project mgr. *Latin-American, classical, popular and folk mus; also worldwide mus and arts.*

Lancaster Concerts. University of Lancaster, Music Dept, Lancaster, Lancs LA1 4YW *tel:* 01524 593777/593729 (box office) *fax:* 01524 847298 *email:* dmccaldin@lancaster.ac.uk; http://lancs.ac.uk/users/concerts/. Denis McCaldin, dir; Stella Birchall, admin. *Symphony orch, chmbr orch, choral, chmbr mus, chmbr opera, early mus, contemporary mus, jazz.*

Leeds International Concert Season. Leeds Leisure Services, Leeds Town Hall, Leeds LS1 3AD *tel:* 0113 247 8335 *fax:* 0113 247 8397. Matthew Sims, principal mus offr. *Orch, chmbr, jazz, br, org and children's concerts.*

London Bach Society. Bach House, 73 High St, Old Oxted, Surrey RH8 9LN *tel:* 01883 717372 *fax:* 01883 715851. Margaret Steinitz, sec. *Promotes London Bach Festival annually in Oct-Nov as well as other events throughout the year.*

Manchester Midday Concerts Society. 134 Kingsbrook Rd, Manchester M16 8WG *tel:* 0161 882 0753 *also fax.* Carolyn Howlett, admin; Christopher Yates, dir of concerts. *Lunchtime chmbr mus concerts.*

Michael Webber Promotions. The Garden Flat, 19 Netherhall Gardens, London NW3 5RL *tel:* 0171 794 5154 *also fax. Jazz, classical (orch and chmbr), br band and opera.*

Minstrel Productions. 3-5 Bridge St, Hadleigh, Suffolk IP7 6BY *tel:* 01473 822596 *fax:* 01473 824175. *Classical chmbr and symphonic concerts. Solo inst concerts.*

Music at Leicester University. University Rd, Leicester LE1 7RH *tel:* 0116 252 2781 *fax:* 0116 252 2200. Anthony Pither, dir of mus; Margaret Rose, admin. *Evening and lunchtime concerts; symphony orch, chmbr orch, wind band, choral, chmbr mus, early mus, contemporary mus.*

Music at Oxford. Elms Ct, Oxford OX2 9LP *tel:* 01865 242865 *fax:* 01865 242867 *email:* info@musicatoxford.demon.co.uk. Melinda Jordan, gen mgr; Jennifer Johns, artistic planning; Stephen Duck, mkt. *Classical concerts in and around Oxford.*

Music For All Occasions. Torridon House, 104 Bradford Rd, Wrenthorpe, Wakefield, W Yorks WF1 2AH *tel:* 01924 371496. Brian Greensmith, mgr dir; Magdalen Greensmith, company sec.

Musicon. The Music School, Palace Green, Durham DH1 3RL *tel:* 0191 374 3210 *fax:* 0191 374 3219 *email:* karen.scott@durham.ac.uk; http://www.dur.ac.uk/music/musicon.htm. Elizabeth Hudson, admin. *Contemporary emphasis.*

Newcastle City Orchestral Subscription Concerts. City Library, Newcastle upon Tyne NE99 1DX *tel:* 0191 261 0691 *fax:* 0191 261 1435. Andrew Rothwell, arts development offr.

Opera-In-Concert. 2 Elizabeth Ct, 84 Southgate Rd, London N1 3JD *tel:* 0171 923 9100 *fax:* 0171 923 2432. Gary Brown, artistic dir.

Wales

Celyn Music Society. Coed y Celyn Hall, Betws-y-Coed, Gwynedd *tel:* 01690 710280. Barbara Carter, sec.

Dolgellau Music Club. Coleg Meirion-Dwyfor, Dolgellau, Gwynedd LL40 2SW *tel:* 01341 422827 *fax:* 01341 422393 *email:* b.ridler@meirion-dwyfor.ac.uk. Ben Ridler, sec.

Llanidloes Music and Arts Club. Bryn Siriol, Llanidloes, Powys. Mrs C A Hughes, sec.

Maelor Music Society. Walnut House, Bangor-on-Dee, Wrexham LL13 0AY *tel:* 01978 780246. Mrs C Peters, hon sec.

Rhyl Music Club. 15 Park Dr, Rhyl, Sir Ddinbych LL18 4DB *tel:* 01745 334255 *fax:* 01745 344094 *email:* derek_bartley@msn.com. Derek Bartley, concert organiser.

Ruthin Music Club. Hafod Lon, Llandegla, Wrexham, N Wales LL11 3BG *tel:* 01978 790256. B J Bickford, chmn.

Welshpool Music Club. Bodynfoel, Guilsfield, Powys SY21 9BX *tel:* 01938 552350. Mrs G Finney.

Northern Ireland

Belfast Music Society. 7 Highgrove Av, Ballyclare BT39 9XL *tel:* 01960 352912. Margaret Langhammer, concert mgr.

Music in Armagh. c/o Tourist Information Centre, 40 English St, Armagh BT61 7BA *tel:* 01861 521805 *fax:* 01861 510180. Katharine Bond, arts offr.

Whiteabbey Music Club. 33 Collinbridge Pk, Glengormley, Newtown Abbey, Co Antrim BT36. Barry Finnegan, sec.

Music in Places of Worship

This section covers both the use of places of worship for regular concert series, and the integral part played by music within the services of each denomination.

Lunchtime Concert Venues

Some of the following churches have a long-standing tradition of lunchtime or evening concert promotion; others offer occasional performance opportunities. An asterisk indicates that a regular concert series takes place at the church.

Greater London

* **Grosvenor Chapel.** South Audley St, London W1 *tel:* 01923 828522 *also fax;* 0171 499 1684. Richard Hobson, org. *Fortnightly; Tue lunchtime.*

* **St Anne & St Agnes.** Gresham St, London EC2 7BX *tel:* 0171 606 4986 *fax:* 0171 600 8984 *email:* 74434.152@compuserve.com. Peter Lea-Cox, cantor. *Weekly; Mon 1.10pm; token fee; ens preferred (pro, semi-pro). Grand pno, org, power-points, changing room.*

* **St Bride's Church.** Fleet St, London EC4Y 8AU *tel:* 0171 353 1301 *fax:* 0171 583 4867. Matthew Busby, admin. *3 times weekly, 1.15pm; max 40 musicians (students, semi-pro, pro). Org, grand pno, power-points, changing rooms.*

* **St George's Church.** Bloomsbury Way, London WC1E 6DP *tel:* 01225 867865; 0171 405 3044 *fax:* 01225 867505. Anthony Goodchild, concerts consultant; Martin Brookes, church admin. *Tue 1.10pm and Sun 5.20 pm (Sun only in summer). Grand pno. Enquiries in writing to 13 Newtown, Bradford on Avon, Wilts BA15 1NG.*

* **St James's Church.** 197 Piccadilly, London W1V 0LL *tel:* 01225 867865; 0171 734 4511 *fax:* 01225 867505; 0171 734 7449. Anthony Goodchild, dir of concerts; Harmony Hedley-Whyte, concerts admin. *Lunchtime recitals 1.00-1.55pm, Wed-Sat. Evening concerts Wed-Sun. Capacity 100 singers plus orch of 40. Concert lighting, org, chmbr org, grand pno. Facilities include power-points, changing rooms, restaurant and box office.*

* **St John's, Smith Square.** London SW1P 3HA *tel:* 0171 222 1061. *Weekly; Mon and Thu 1pm.*

* **St Lawrence Jewry next Guildhall.** London EC2V 5AA *tel:* 0171 600 9478. Rev David Burgess, admin. *Weekly; Mon 1.00-1.45pm (pno recitals), Tue 1.00-1.45pm (org recitals); expenses; changing facilities. Mus festival in Aug.*

* **St Magnus the Martyr.** Lower Thames St, London EC3R 6DN *tel:* 0171 626 4481. The Venerable K H Gibbons, priest-in-charge; C L Henderson, church warden. *Weekly; Tue 1.05pm. 3-manual org and Obermeier baby grand pno. Open to soloists and ens.*

* **St Margaret Lothbury.** London EC2R 7HH *tel:* c/o 0171 589 1206 *fax:* 0171 589 5925. Richard Townend, artistic dir; John Budgen, chmn. *Lunchtime lecture recitals, Thu 1.10pm; also lectures and tutorials on the org and an annual series of international celebrity org and choral concerts.*

* **St Martin-in-the-Fields Church.** Trafalgar Sq, London WC2N 4JJ *tel:* 0171 839 1930. Shirley Henderson, concerts mgr; Paul Stubbings, master of the mus. *Weekly; Mon, Tue and Fri 1.05pm; large and small ens, soloists (auditions). Org, chmbr org, Blüthner concert grand, power-points, changing facilities, restaurant.*

* **St Martin-within-Ludgate Church.** Ludgate Hill, London EC4 *tel:* 0171 248 6054. Douglas Nurse, mus maker. *Weekly; Tue and Wed 1.15-1.45pm; choirs up to 25, ens up to sextet, soloists (pro, semi-pro); org, Bechstein grand pno.*

* **St Mary Abbots.** Kensington, London W8 4LA *tel:* 0171 937 5136 *fax:* 0171 938 4317. Denny Lyster, concerts mgr. *Fri 1.10-1.50pm. No fees. 4-manual org, grand pno. Singers, instrumentalists, small ens. Young artists preferred.*

St Mary-at-Hill Church. Lovat La, Off Eastcheap, London EC3R 8EE *tel:* 0181 658 9428 *also fax.* Jonathan Rennert, dir of mus. *Monthly, Tue 1pm. Performance of a Bach cantata with the St Mary-at-Hill Baroque Players and Soloists. Other concerts by special arrangement. Grand piano, movable seating.*

* **St Mary-le-Strand.** Strand, London WC2R 1EP. Paul Weaver, dir of mus. *Lunchtime recitals throughout the year except during Lent. Church also available for hire. Semi-pro, pro groups, students and individuals. Org, baby grand pno, power-points, toilet, kitchen area, mus stands.*

* **St Michael's Church.** Cornhill, London EC3V 9DS *tel:* 0171 283 3029; 0171 626 8841. Jonathan Rennert, dir of mus. *Weekly (org recitals), Mon 1pm (except public holidays); other occasional concerts, times by arrangement; organists, specialists in British mus preferred. Org, chmbr org, upright pno, power-points, changing rooms.*

* **St Olave's Church.** 8 Hart St, London EC3R TNB *tel:* 0171 488 4318 *fax:* 0171 702 0811. Revd John Cowling, rector. *Weekly; Wed-Thu 1.05pm; expenses; young pro pianists and ens preferred. Org, power-points.*

* **Southwark Cathedral.** Montague Close, London SE1 9DA *tel:* 0171 407 3708 *fax:* 0171 357 7389. Francoise Small. *Weekly (outside term-time of mus colleges when concerts are given by mus students); Tue 1.10pm-1.50pm; retiring collection. Grand pno, power-points, changing rooms.*

Westminster Abbey. 2 Little Cloister, Westminster Abbey, London SW1P 3PL *tel:* 0171 222 6923 *fax:* 0171 222 1025. *Free org recitals, Sun 5.45pm.*

England, Scotland and Wales

* **Birmingham.** Birmingham Cathedral, Colmore Row, Birmingham B3 2QB *tel:* 0121 236 4333/6323 *fax:* 0121 212 0868. *Weekly org recitals, Mon 1pm. Mus recitals (org, chmbr mus, etc), Fri 1.10pm.*

* **Blackburn.** Blackburn Cathedral, Cathedral Close, Blackburn BB1 5AA *tel:* 01254 51491 *fax:* 01254 689666. *Org recitals, Tue 1pm, from Oct to Jul.*

Bridlington. The Priory, 36 St Columba Rd, Bridlington, E Yorks YO16 5QX *tel:* 01262 670869 *also fax. Summer recital series, Wed 7.30pm, Jul-Aug.*

* **Bristol.** Bristol Cathedral, Bristol BS1 5TJ *tel:* 0117 926 4879 *fax:* 0117 925 3678. *Term-time, Tue 1.15pm.*

Bristol. Clifton Cathedral, Clifton Pk, Bristol BS8 3BX *tel:* 0117 946 7456 *fax:* 0117 973 8263. Monsignor Gabriel Leyden, admin; David Ogden, dir of mus. *Sat 4pm, twice monthly; fees occasionally paid, otherwise hire charge. Rieger 3-manual org, chmbr org, Schiedermayer grand pno, power-points, changing and rehearsal rooms.*

Canterbury. Christ Church Cathedral, 6 The Precincts, Canterbury CT1 2EE *tel:* 01227 765219 *fax:* 01227 762897. *Informal recitals by visiting choirs, many from overseas; a cappella, sacred mus. 12 noon.*

* **Chester.** Chester Cathedral, c/o The Cathedral Office, 12 Abbey Sq, Chester CH1 2HU *tel:* 01244 351015 *fax:* 01244 341110. *Org recitals; Thu 1.10pm.*

* **Chichester.** Chichester Cathedral, 2 St Richard's Walk, Chichester PO19 1QA *tel:* 01243 784790 *fax:* 01243 536190. *Term-time; Tue 1.10pm*

* **Coventry.** Coventry Cathedral, 7 Priory Row, Coventry CV1 5ES *tel:* 01203 227597 *fax:* 01203 631448. *Org recitals; Mon 1.00pm; May-Sep.*

* **Dunblane.** Dunblane Cathedral, Goodiebank, By Thornhill, Stirlingshire *tel:* 01786 870657. *Sat 12 noon; Jun-Sep.*

* **Edinburgh.** St Giles' Cathedral, High St, Edinburgh EH1 1RE *tel:* 0131 225 9442 *fax:* 0131 220 4763. Kirsty Nichol, visitor services mgr. *Apr-Jun; Sep-Oct; Thu 1.10pm, org recitals. Occasional choral recitals, weekdays 12.15pm.*

Gloucester. Gloucester Cathedral, 7 Millers Green, Gloucester GL1 2BN *tel:* 01452 524764 *also fax. Summer org recitals; Sat 1.15pm; monthly May-Oct.*

* **Grimsby.** Grimsby Parish Church, The Parish Office, St James' House, St James' Square, Grimsby, N E Lincs DN31 1EP *tel:* 01472 358610 *fax:* 01472 250751. *Org recitals, first Fri of each month, 1.00pm.*

* **Leamington Spa.** All Saints Parish Church, The Parish Office, PO Box 163, Victoria Terrace, Leamington Spa, Warwicks *tel:* c/o 01926 451550 *fax:* 01926 429169 *email:* http://www.soft.net.uk/brooksbank/allsts. Colin Druce, dir of mus. *Regular (c 20 concerts pa); time by arrangement; performers paid occasionally. 4-manual org, power-points, changing rooms, grand pno.*

* **Leicester.** Leicester Cathedral, St Martin's, Leicester LE1 5FX *tel:* 0116 262 5294 *fax:* 0116 262 5295. *Term-time; Mon 1.05pm; Jul-Aug, Tue 8pm.*

* **Newcastle.** Cathedral Church of St Nicholas, Newcastle-upon-Tyne NE1 1PF *tel:* 0191 232 1939 *fax:* 0191 230 0735. Timothy Hone, admin. *Weekly (between Easter and Autumn); Mon 1pm; expenses; usually organists (students and young professionals). 4-manual Nicholson org, changing rooms, refectory facilities.*

* **Norwich.** St Peter Mancroft, 56a The Close, Norwich, Norfolk NR1 4EH *tel:* 01603 614305. Roger Rayner, sec and publicity. *Fri lunchtime concert series, usually 2nd and 4th of month from May-Oct. Mainly org recitals on outstanding classical org. Refreshments always available.*

Rochester. Rochester Cathedral, 7 Minor Canon Row, Rochester, Kent ME1 1ST *tel:* 01634 849683 *fax:* 01634 401410. *Org recitals, bank holiday Mon 12 noon.*

St Davids. St Davids Cathedral, The Organist's Lodgings, Cathedral Close, St Davids, Pembs SA62 6PE *fax:* 01437 721885. *Weekly org recitals; Tue 8.15pm; Jul-Aug.*

Southwell. Southwell Cathedral, 4 Vicars' Ct, Southwell, Notts NG25 0HP *tel:* 01636 812228 *fax:* 01636 815904. Paul R Hale, mus dir. *Bank holidays; org recitals 3.30pm; Apr-Aug; free admission.*

* **Tewkesbury.** Tewkesbury Abbey, 40 Church St, Tewkesbury, Glos GL20 5SN *tel:* 01684 298177/850959 *fax:* 01684 273113. *Wed 1.00pm; Jul-Sep.*

* **Truro.** Truro Cathedral, 21 Old Bridge St, Truro, Cornwall TR1 2AH *tel:* 01872 276782 *fax:* 01872 277788. *Org recitals; Fri 1.15pm; May-Sep.*

* **Winchester.** Winchester Cathedral, 5 The Close, Winchester SO23 9LS *tel:* 01962 853137 *fax:* 01962 841519. *Tue 1.10pm; Jun-Sep.*

Organisations

Church Music Society. 8 The Chandlers, The Calls, Leeds LS2 7EZ *tel:* 0113 234 1146 *also fax.* Simon Lindley, hon sec.

Friends of Cathedral Music. 26 Dumbrells Ct, North End, Ditchling, W Sussex BN6 8TG. Vincent Waterhouse, hon sec; Alan Thurlow, chmn.

Gregorian Association. 26 The Grove, London W5 5LH *tel:* 0181 840 5832 *email:* http://www.beaufort.demon.co.uk/chant.htm. Grey Macartney, chmn; Peter Wilton, mus dir.

Guild of Church Musicians. Hillbrow, Godstone Rd, Blechingley, Surrey RH1 4PJ *tel:* 01883 741854 *also fax.* John Ewington OBE, gen sec.

Royal School of Church Music. Cleveland Lodge, Westhumble, Dorking RH5 6BW *tel:* 01306 877676. Geoffrey Weaver, dir of studies.

Society of St Gregory. Mair Wen, 8 Hampton Fields, Oswestry SY11 1TJ. Patrick Lee, hon sec.

Anglican Church

Cathedrals and Collegiate Foundations

The following churches maintain the full Anglican 'cathedral' tradition holding weekday as well as Sunday services with salaried choirs normally of boys and men. The address and telephone number are that of the organist in most cases. **Choir Schools** are listed in the **Education** section.

London

Chapel Royal (Hampton Court). Hampton Court Palace, East Molesey, Surrey KT8 9AU *tel:* 0181 781 9598 *fax:* 0181 977 4771 *email:* carl_jackson@ccis.org.uk. Carl Jackson, dir of mus.

Chapel Royal (St James's). St James's Palace SW1 *tel:* 0171 930 3007. Richard Popplewell.

St Paul's Cathedral. 5b Amen Ct, London EC4M 7BU *tel:* 0171 236 6883 *fax:* 0171 248 6868. John Scott, org and dir of mus; Andrew Lucas, sub org.

Southwark Cathedral. Montague Close, London SE1 9DA *tel:* 0171 407 3708 *fax:* 0171 357 7389. Peter Wright, dir of mus.

Westminster Abbey. 2 Little Cloister, Westminster Abbey, London SW1P 3PL *tel:* 0171 222 6923 *fax:* 0171 222 1025 *email:* pneary@westminster. abbey.org. Martin Neary, org and master of the choristers; Martin Baker, sub org; Stephen le Provost, asst org.

Birmingham. Birmingham Cathedral. Colmore Row, Birmingham B3 2QB *tel:* 0121 236 4333/6323 *fax:* 0121 212 0868. Marcus Huxley, org.

Blackburn. Blackburn Cathedral. Cathedral Close, Blackburn BB1 5AA *tel:* 01254 51491 *fax:* 01254 689666 *email:* cathedral@blackburn. anglican.org.uk. Gordon Stewart, dir of mus; Ben Sauders, asst dir of mus.

Bradford. St Peter's Cathedral. 1 Stott Hill, Bradford, W Yorks BD1 4EH *tel:* 01274 777720 *fax:* 01274 777730. Alan Horsey, org and choirmaster.

Bridlington. The Priory. 36 St Columba Rd, Bridlington, E Yorks YO16 5QX *tel:* 01262 670869 *also fax.* Michael T Smith.

Bristol. Bristol Cathedral. Bristol BS1 5TJ *tel:* 0117 926 4879 *fax:* 0117 925 3678. Christopher Brayne, org.

Bury St Edmunds. St Edmundsbury Cathedral. Abbey House, Angel Hill, Bury St Edmunds IP33 1LS *tel:* 01284 754933 *fax:* 01284 768655. James Thomas, dir of mus.

Cambridge. Jesus College. Cambridge CB5 8BL *tel:* 01223 339305 *fax:* 01223 324910. Greg Morris, snr org scholar.

Cambridge. King's College. Cambridge CB2 1ST *tel:* 01223 331224 *fax:* 01223 331890. Stephen Cleobury, org.

Cambridge. St John's College. Cambridge CB2 1TP *tel:* 01223 338600/338765 *fax:* 01223 337720. Christopher Robinson, org.

Canterbury. Christ Church Cathedral. 6 The Precincts, Canterbury CT1 2EE *tel:* 01227 765219 *fax:* 01227 762897. David Flood, org and dir of mus.

Carlisle. Carlisle Cathedral. 6 The Abbey, Carlisle CA3 8TZ *tel:* 01228 26646 *fax:* 01228 48151. Jeremy Suter, org.

Chelmsford. Chelmsford Cathedral. Cathedral Office, New St, Chelmsford, Essex *tel:* 01245 263660 ext 226 *fax:* 01245 496802. Graham Elliott, org.

Chester. Chester Cathedral. The Music Office, 1 Abbey Sq, Chester CH1 2HU *tel:* 01244 351015/351024 *fax:* 01244 341110. Graham Eccles, org; David Poulter, dir of mus.

Chichester. Chichester Cathedral. 2 St Richard's Walk, Chichester PO19 1QA *tel:* 01243 784790 *fax:* 01243 536190. Alan Thurlow, org.

Coventry. Coventry Cathedral. 7 Priory Row, Coventry CV1 5ES *tel:* 01203 227597 *fax:* 01203 631448. Paul Leddington Wright, cathedral mus adviser.

Derby. Derby Cathedral. 3 Cathedral View, Littleover, Derby DE22 3HR *tel:* 01332 366692 *fax:* 01332 203991. Peter Gould, org.

Durham. Durham Cathedral. 6 The College, Durham DH1 3EQ *tel:* 0191 386 4766. James Lancelot, org.

Ely. Ely Cathedral. The Old Sacristy, The College, Ely, Cambs CB7 4JU *tel:* 01353 665669 *fax:* 01353 665658. Paul Trepte, org.

Exeter. Exeter Cathedral. 11 The Close, Exeter EX1 1EZ *tel:* 01392 277521. Lucian Nethsingha, org.

Gloucester. Gloucester Cathedral. 7 Millers Green, Gloucester GL1 2BN *tel:* 01452 524764 *also fax.* David Briggs, dir of mus.

Guildford. Guildford Cathedral. 5 Cathedral Close, Guildford GU2 5TL *tel:* 01483 531693 *fax:* 01483 303350. Andrew Millington, org; Geoffrey Morgan, sub-org.

Hereford. Hereford Cathedral. 1 College Cloisters, Cathedral Close, Hereford HR1 2NG *tel:* 01432 272011. Roy Massey, org.

Hexham. Hexham Abbey. Beaumont St, Hexham, Northumberland NE46 3NB *tel:* 01434 602031 *fax:* 01434 606116. John C Green, dir of mus; Henry Wallace, asst org.

Leeds. St Peter-at-Leeds, Kirkgate (Leeds Parish Church). 8 The Chandlers, The Calls, Leeds LS2 7EZ *tel:* 0113 247 8334/234 1146 *also fax;* 0113 245 4012. Simon Lindley, org and master of mus.

Leicester. Leicester Cathedral. St Martin's, Leicester LE1 5FX *tel:* 0116 262 5294 *fax:* 0116 262 5295. Jonathan Gregory, org and master of mus.

Lichfield. St Chad's Cathedral. 19a The Close, Lichfield, Staffs WS13 7LD *tel:* 01543 256120 *fax:* 01543 416306. Andrew Lumsden, org.

Lincoln. Lincoln Cathedral. 12 Minster Yard, Lincoln LN2 1PJ *tel:* 01522 532877/526469 *fax:* 01522 511307. Colin Walsh, org; Jeffrey Maximson, asst org.

Liverpool. Liverpool Cathedral. 6 Cathedral Close, Liverpool L1 7BR *tel:* 0151 708 8471 *fax:* 0151 708 0378. Prof Ian Tracey, org and master of choristers.

Manchester. Manchester Cathedral. Cathedral Yard, Manchester M3 1SX *tel:* 0161 833 2220 *fax:* 0161 839 6226. Christopher Stokes, org.

Newcastle. St Nicholas' Cathedral. Newcastle upon Tyne NE1 1PF *tel:* 0191 232 1939 *fax:* 0191 230 0735. Timothy Hone, org.

Norwich. Norwich Cathedral. 53a The Close, Norwich NR1 4EG *tel:* 01603 626589 *fax:* 01603 766032. David Dunnett, org and master of the mus.

Oxford. Christchurch Cathedral. Oxford OX1 1DP *tel:* 01865 276195 *fax:* 01865 794199 *email:* stephen.darlington@christ-church.oxford.ac. uk. Stephen Darlington, org.

Oxford. Magdalen College. Oxford OX1 4AU *tel:* 01865 276007 *fax:* 01865 276094. Grayston Ives, dir of mus.

Oxford. New College. Oxford OX1 3BN *tel:* 01865 279519 *fax:* 01865 279590 *email:* edward.higginbottom@new.ox.ac.uk. Edward Higginbottom, org.

Peterborough. Peterborough Cathedral. The Norman Hall, Minster Precincts, Peterborough PE1 1XX *tel:* 01733 65165 *fax:* 01733 52465. Christopher Gower, org; Mark Dythie, asst org.

Portsmouth. Portsmouth Cathedral. The Organist's House, Penny St, Old Portsmouth, Hants PO1 2NL *tel:* 01705 730792 *fax:* 01705 295480. David Price, org.

Ripon. Ripon Cathedral. Minster Rd, Ripon, N Yorks HG4 1QT *tel:* 01765 602072. Kerry Beaumont, org.

Rochester. Rochester Cathedral. 7 Minor Canon Row, Rochester, Kent ME1 1ST *tel:* 01634 849683 *fax:* 01634 401410. Roger Sayer, org; William Whitehead, asst org.

St Albans. St Albans Abbey. 31 Abbey Mill La, St Albans, Herts AL3 4HA *tel:* 01727 851810 *also fax.* Andrew Lucas, master of mus; Andrew Parnell, asst master of mus.

Salisbury. Salisbury Cathedral. Ladywell, 33 The Close, Salisbury, Wilts SP1 2EJ *tel:* 01722 323289 *fax:* 01722 330699. Simon Lole, dir of mus.

Selby. Selby Abbey. The Crescent, Selby, N Yorks YO8 0PU *tel:* 01757 703123. R D Tebbet, dir of mus.

Sheffield. Sheffield Cathedral. Sheffield S1 1HA *tel:* 0114 275 3434 *fax:* 0114 278 0244. Neil Taylor, master of mus.

Southwell. Southwell Cathedral. 4 Vicars' Ct, Southwell, Notts NG25 0HP *tel:* 01636 812649/812228 *also fax; fax:* 01636 815904. Paul Hale, org.

Tewkesbury. Tewkesbury Abbey. 40 Church St, Tewkesbury, Glos GL20 5SN *tel:* 01684 298177/850959 *fax:* 01684 273113. Carleton Etherington, org.

Truro. Truro Cathedral. 21 Old Bridge St, Truro, Cornwall TR1 2AH *tel:* 01872 276782 *fax:* 01872 277788. Andrew Nethsingha, org.

Wakefield. Wakefield Cathedral. Womack Cottage, Heath, Wakefield, W Yorks WF1 5SN *tel:* 01924 378841 *fax:* 01924 215054. Jonathan Bielby, org.

Wells. Wells Cathedral. 15 Vicars' Close, Wells BA5 2UJ *tel:* 01749 677517 *also fax.* Malcolm Archer, org; Rupert Gough, asst org; Marian Shaw, mus dept sec.

Winchester. Winchester Cathedral. 5 The Close, Winchester SO23 9LS *tel:* 01962 853137 *fax:* 01962 841519. David Hill, org.

Windsor. St George's Chapel. 25 The Cloisters, Windsor Castle, Berks SL4 1NJ *tel:* 01753 864529/865538 *fax:* 01753 620165. Jonathan Rees-Williams.

Worcester. Worcester Cathedral. 10a College Green, Worcester WR1 2LH *tel:* 01905 28854 *fax:* 01905 611139. Adrian Lucas, dir of mus; Raymond Johnston, org.

York. York Minster. Church House, Ogleforth, York YO1 2JN *tel:* 01904 642526 *fax:* 01904 654604. Philip Moore, org and master of the mus; John Scott Whiteley, asst org; Jonathan Wainwright, asst choir trainer.

Scotland (Episcopal Church)

Aberdeen. St Andrew's Cathedral (Scottish Episcopal Church). 21a Deemount Rd, Aberdeen AB11 6TY *tel:* 01224 581151 *fax:* 01224 210259 *email:* a.morrisson@rgu.ac.uk. Andrew Morrisson, org.

Dundee. St Paul's Episcopal Cathedral. Castlehill, Dundee DD1 1TD *tel:* 01382 224486. Mark Hindley, org.

Edinburgh. St Mary's Episcopal Cathedral. The Cathedral Office, Palmerston Pl, Edinburgh EH12 5AW *tel:* 0131 225 6293 *fax:* 0131 225 3181. Timothy Byram-Wigfield, master of mus; Carol Wood, cathedral office.

Glasgow. St Mary's Cathedral. 300 Gt Western Rd, Glasgow G4 9JB *tel:* 0141 339 6691 *also fax.* Fridrik Walker, dir of mus.

Inverness. St Andrew's Cathedral. Drumbuie Farm, Drumnadrochit, Inverness-shire *tel:* 01456 450309. Russell Grant, org and choirmaster.

Oban. St John the Divine. Oban *tel:* 01631 710335. Norman Nicholson, org and choirmaster.

Perth. St Ninian's Cathedral. North Methven St, Perth *tel:* 01738 627982/626874. James N Laird, org and master of the choristers.

Wales

Bangor. Bangor Cathedral. The Diocesan Centre, Clos y Gadeirlan, Bangor, Gwynedd LL57 1RL *tel:* 01248 354015 *fax:* 01248 353882. Andrew Goodwin.

Brecon. Brecon Cathedral. Garth Cottage, 29 Pendre, Brecon, Powys LD3 9EA *tel:* 01874 622442 *fax:* 01874 623716. David Gedge, org.

Llandaff. Llandaff Cathedral. 1 St Mary's, The Cathedral Green, Llandaff, Cardiff CF5 2EB *tel:* 01222 565880. Michael Smith, org.

Newport. St Woolos' Cathedral. 7 Macaulay Gardens, Newport, South Wales NP9 3JZ *tel:* 01633 266708. Christopher Barton, org.

St Asaph. St Asaph Cathedral. Bryn Siriol, Mount Rd, St Asaph, Denbighshire LL17 0DB *tel:* 01745 583600 *also fax.* Hugh Davies, org; David Davies, asst org.

St Davids. St Davids Cathedral. The Organist's Lodgings, Cathedral Close, St Davids, Pembs SA62 6PE *tel:* 01437 720128 *fax:* 01437 721885. Geraint Bowen, org; Michael Slaney, asst org.

Northern Ireland

Armagh. St Patrick's Cathedral. 50 Mullaghbane Rd, Armagh BT61 9HW *tel:* 01861 524110 *fax:* 01762 394525. Martin White, org.

Belfast. St Anne's Cathedral. Donegall St, Belfast BT1 2HB *tel:* 01232 328332 *fax:* 01232 238855. David Drinkell, org.

Londonderry. St Columb's Cathedral. 2 Columb's Ct, Londonderry BT48 6PT *tel:* 01504 262412. Timothy Allen, org.

Perth Festival of the Arts. 3-5 High St, Perth PH1 5JS *admin:* (01738) 475295 *also fax; email:* artsfestival@perth.org.uk. Sandra Ralston, admin. *20-31 May 1998.*

Scottish Proms. Royal Scottish National Orchestra, 73 Claremont St, Glasgow G3 7JB *admin:* 0141-226 3868 *fax:* 0141-221 4317. Fiona Brownlee, mkt offr; Alexander Lazarev, artistic dir. *May and Jun 1998.*

Wales

Aberystwyth - Musicfest - International Music Festival & Summer School. Aberystwyth Arts Centre, Penglais, Aberystwyth, Dyfed SY23 3DE *admin:* (01970) 622882 *fax:* (01970) 622883. Louise Amery, mkt mgr; Nicholas Jones, artistic dir. *18-31 Jul 1998.*

Barmouth Arts Festival. 1 Epworth Terrace, Barmouth, Gwynedd LL42 1PN *admin:* (01341) 280392 *also box office.* Mair Jones. *4-12 Sep 1998.*

Beaumaris Festival. Ty'n Coed, Llangaffo, Gaerwen, Anglesey LL60 6NE *admin:* (01248) 440541 *also fax.* Eluned Davies; Anthony Hose, artistic dir. *May-Jun.*

Cardiff Summer Festival. Cardiff County Council, Sports and Leisure Dept, County Hall, Atlantic Wharf, Cardiff CF1 5UW *admin:* (01222) 873913 *fax:* (01222) 873937. Helen Kitchen, events mgr. *Jul-Aug 1998.*

Carmarthen Festival - Gwyl Caerfyrddin. Gwynfa, Nant Taredig, nr Carmarthen, Dyfed SA32 7NA *admin:* (01267) 290343. Jean Williams. *Jun-Jul.*

Fishguard Music Festival. Festival Office, Fishguard, Pembrokeshire SA65 9BJ *admin:* (01348) 873612 *also fax.* Marion Butler, festival co-ord; John S Davies, artistic dir. *25 Jul-1 Aug 1998.*

Gower Festival. 58 Hendrefoilan Rd, Tycoch, Swansea SA2 9LU *admin:* (01792) 207924 *box office:* (01792) 468321. Maurice Broady, publicity mgr. *20 Jul-1 Aug 1998.*

Gregynog - Gwyl Gregynog Festival. Gregynog, nr Newtown, Powys SY16 3PW *admin:* (01686) 650224 *box office:* (01686) 625007 *fax:* (01686) 650656. Anthony Rolfe Johnson, artistic dir. *Jun 1998.*

Llandudno October Festival. Festival Office, Aberconwy Centre, Promenade, Llandudno LL30 1BB *admin:* (01492) 879771 *box office:* (01492) 872000 *fax:* (01492) 860790 *email:* http://www.nwtheatre.co.uk. Anthony Hose, artistic dir. *9-18 Oct 1998.*

Llangollen International Musical Eisteddfod. Eisteddfod Office, Llangollen, Denbighshire LL20 8NG *admin:* (01978) 860236 *box office:* (01978) 861501 *fax:* (01978) 861300 *email:* lime@celtic.co.uk; http://www.llangollen.org.uk. Maureen A Jones, mkt dir; Roy Bohana, artistic dir. *7-12 Jul 1998.*

Llantilio Crossenny Festival of Music and Drama. Treadam Farm, Llantilio Crossenny, Abergavenny, Gwent NP7 8TA *admin:* (01600) 780233 *box office:* (01873) 856928. Charles Farncombe, artistic dir. *14-17 May 1998.*

Lower Machen Festival. 44 Richmond Rd, Roath, Cardiff CF4 3AT *admin:* (01222) 482183. Peter Reynolds, artistic dir. *23-28 Jun 1998.*

Machynlleth Festival. Y Tabernacl, Heol Penrallt, Machynlleth, Powys SY20 8AJ *admin:* (01654) 703355/702128 *fax:* (01654) 702160. Ruth Lambert. *23-30 Aug 1998.*

Presteigne Festival of Music and the Arts. The Old Priory, Titley, nr Kington, Herefordshire HR5 3RR *admin:* (01544) 230681 *box office:* (01544) 267800. Joan Hughes, sec; George Vass, artistic dir. *Aug.*

St Asaph - North Wales Music Festival. Festival Office, High St, St Asaph, Denbighshire LL17 0RD *admin:* (01745) 584508 *also box office and fax.* Jill Mort, admin; Geraint Lewis, artistic dir. *19-26 Sep 1998.*

St Davids Cathedral Festival. 65 Goat St, St Davids, Pembrokeshire SA62 6RQ *admin:* (01437) 720271 *also box office; fax:* (01437) 721885. Llywela Harris, admin; Geraint Bowen, artistic dir. *23-31 May 1998.*

Swansea Festival. 9 Gabalfa Rd, Sketty, Swansea *admin:* (01792) 205318 *box office:* (01792) 475715 *fax:* (01570) 493576. Susan Croall, admin; John Metcalf, artistic dir. *3-24 Oct 1998.*

Vale of Glamorgan Festival. St Donats Arts Centre, St Donats Castle, Llantwit Major, Vale of Glamorgan CF61 1WF *admin:* (01446) 792151 *box office:* (01446) 794848 *fax:* (01446) 794711. David Ambrose, dir; John Metcalf, artistic dir. *Early Sep 1998.*

Wrexham Arts Festival. Memorial Hall, Bodhyfryd, Wrexham LL12 7AG *admin:* (01978) 292683 *box office:* (01978) 292015. G A Lacy, arts and ents offr.

Northern Ireland

Armagh Arts Festival. c/o Tourist Information Centre, 40 English St, Armagh BT61 7BA *admin:* (01861) 521805 *fax:* (01861) 510180. Kate Bond, arts offr. *Mid Oct 1998.*

Belfast - Festival of Early Music. School of Music, Queen's University, Belfast BT7 1NN *admin:* (01232) 335205 *email:* http://www.music.qub.ac.uk. Anthony Carver. *11-15 Oct 1998 (biennial).*

Belfast - Sonorities. School of Music, Queen's University, Belfast BT7 1NN *admin:* (01232) 335105 *fax:* (01232) 247895 *email:* http://www.music.qub.ac.uk. Michael Alcorn, committee chmn. *15-19 May 1998.*

Belfast Festival At Queen's. Festival House, 25 College Gardens, Belfast BT9 6BS *admin:* (01232) 667687 *box office:* (01232) 665577 *fax:* (01232) 663733. Robert Agnew, exec dir. *13-29 Nov 1998.*

Castleward Opera Festival. 61 Marlborough Park North, Belfast BT9 6HL *admin:* (01232) 661090 *also box office; fax:* (01232) 687081. Hilda Logan, company mgr; Ian Urwin and Jack Smith, artistic dirs. *5-27 Jun 1998.*

Derry - Banks of the Foyle Halloween Carnival. Recreation and Leisure Dept, Derry City Council, 98 Strand Rd, Derry, Co Londonderry BT48 7NN *admin:* (01504) 365151 *box office:* (01504) 260516 *fax:* (01504) 370080. Nuala McGee, festivals offr. *28 Oct-7 Nov 1998.*

Derry - Two Cathedrals Festival. 2 St Columb's Ct, Derry, Co Londonderry BT48 6PT *admin:* (01504) 262412 *box office:* (01504) 260516. Timothy Allen and Donal Doherty, artistic dirs. *Oct.*

Portstewart - Flowerfield Arts Festival. Flowerfield Arts Centre, 185 Coleraine Rd, Portstewart, Co Londonderry BT55 7HU *admin:* (01265) 833959. Malcolm Murchison, arts org. *10-17 Oct 1998 (provisional).*

Early Music

EARLY MUSIC

Early Music

This section includes the **Early Music Fora**, **Instrument Manufacturers**, **Ensembles** and **Instrumentalists** specialising in early music. Early Music Festivals are included in the main **Music Festivals** section.

The specialist publications are *Early Music Today*, *Early Music Review*, *Early Music*, *Early Music History*, *Early Music News*, *Leading Notes*, and the *Early Music Yearbook*, details of which will be found in the **Music Periodicals** section.

Additional information can be obtained from **The Early Music Network** (Sutton House, 2-4 Homerton High St, London E9 6JQ *tel:* 0181 533 2921 *fax:* 0181 533 2922), or from the **National Early Music Association** (18 High St, Caythorpe, Grantham, Lincs NG32 3BS *tel:* 01400 273795 *also fax).*

Early Music Fora

Border Marches Early Music Forum (BMEMF). 3 Upper Linney, Ludlow, Shropshire SY8 1EF *tel:* 01584 876175. Jenny Sayer, sec. *Medieval to baroque vocal and inst day w/shops held on Sundays, in Leaminster, Herefordshire. Occasional sponsoring of early mus concerts.*

East Midlands Early Music Forum (EMEMF). 127 Sheepbridge La, Mansfield, Notts NG18 5DT *tel:* 01623 658951 *email:* ememf@ compuserve.com; http:/ourworld.compuserve.com/homepages/ememf. Tony Brett, treasurer, events co-ord. *Quarterly newsletter, w/shops, choral and baroque mus days. What's On diary of early mus concerts, early mus w/shops, courses and summer schools both locally and nationwide. Assists members to make contacts for their own mus-making.*

Eastern Early Music Forum (EEMF). 9 Cliff St, St Peter Port, Guernsey, Channel Islands *tel:* 01481 713037 *fax:* 01481 700502. Jane Trewhella, sec.

Midlands Early Music Forum (MEMF). 21 Oakfield Av, Kingswinford, W Midlands DY6 8HJ *tel:* 01384 295210 *email:* memf@diabolus.abel.

co.uk; http://www.abel.co.uk/~diabolus. Paul Baker, sec. *Regular newsletter, w/shops, social events.*

North East Early Music Forum (NEEMF). 43 Becketts Park Cres, Leeds LS6 3PH *tel:* 0113 278 6886 *fax:* 0113 230 7818 *email:* bmb6jlj@bmb. leeds.ac.uk. Jillian Johnson, hon sec. *Regular one-day w/shops in performance and interpretation, for singers and insts. Residential w/end in Sep.*

North West Early Music Forum (NWEMF). 1 Oak Lea, Standish, Wigan WN6 0SL *tel:* 01257 400018 *email:* http://www.users.globalnet.co.uk /steven02. Rosemary Dewey, sec. *W/shops and summer school for singers and insts.*

South Western Early Music Forum (SWEMF). Little Hampden, Hunnacott, Landkey, Barnstaple, Devon EX32 0NW *tel:* 01271 831092. Susan Madgwick, sec.

Southern Early Music Forum (SEMF). 60 Howard Rd, Allington Pk, Maidstone ME16 0RD *tel:* 01622 762409 *email:* tim.samuelson@hri. ac.uk. Tim Samuelson, ed.

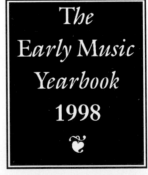

Early Music Instrument Manufacturers

This list of manufacturers of instruments for early music and authentic performance is divided into five broad categories: strings (bowed and plucked instruments); wind (woodwind and brass); keyboard (harpsichord, organ, etc); percussion; materials. Different manufacturers often use different spellings for particular instruments. To avoid confusion, spelling has been standardised in the entries below.

Strings

Ancestral Instruments. Tudor Lodge, Pymoor La, Pymoor, nr Ely, Cambs CB6 2EE *tel:* 01353 698084 *email:* http://www.gmm.co.uk/ai. David Marshall. *Medieval fiddles, rebecs, tromba makina.*

Attwood, Merion David. The North Wing, Himbleton Manor, Himbleton, Droitwich, Worcs WR9 7LE *tel:* 01905 391590 *email:* merion@globalnet.co.uk; http://www.users.globalnet.co.uk/~merion/. *Viols and vns.*

Baker, Paul. 21 Oakfield Av, Kingswinford, W Midlands DY6 8HJ *tel:* 01384 295210 *email:* workshop@diabolus.abel.co.uk; http://www.abel.co.uk/~diabolus. *Medieval and renaissance strs, hurdy-gurdies.*

Border Harps. Waterloo Cottages, Letton, Hereford HR3 6DN *tel:* 01544 327352. M C Saunders, S R Saunders, partners. *Non-pedal hps, hp kits, parts and strings.*

Brescia Student Viols. 68 Jevington Dr, Brighton, E Sussex BN2 4DG *tel:* 01273 605768. Dominic Shann, mgr. *Student viols.*

Bridgewood, Gary D. 146 Stoke Newington Church St, London N16 0UA *tel:* 0171 249 9398 *fax:* 0171 275 9330. *Vas da gamba, violones, baroque vns, vcs, etc.*

Cohen, Brian. Soundpost, The Old Glassworks, Alexandra Pl, Guildford GU1 3QH *tel:* 01483 456422 *also fax; email:* soundpost@compuserve.com. *Guis, lutes, vas da gamba, vns, vcs.*

Coltman, Matthew. 153 Acton La, Chiswick, London W4 5HN *tel:* 0181 742 7934 *also fax. Bowmaker, specialising in baroque and classical. Also strs and accs.*

Crabtree, Charles Hammond. 9 Priestthorpe Rd, Bingley, W Yorks BD16 4LL *tel:* 01274 560350 *fax:* 01274 221714. *Psalteries (bowed, plucked), hammered dulcimers.*

Demetriou, Andrew. 39 Chatsworth Rd, Brighton BN1 5DA *tel:* 01273 550055. *Guis.*

Doe, Roger. Mount St Laurence, High St, Cranbrook, Kent TN17 3EW *tel:* 01580 712330. *Bows for baroque and classical insts, including viols.*

Early Music Shop. 38 Manningham La, Bradford BD1 3EA *tel:* 01274 393753 *fax:* 01274 393516 *email:* sales@earlyms.demon.co.uk; http://www.e-m-s.com. *Viol family, lutes, psalteries (bowed, plucked), medieval fiddles, hourglass dulcimers, hps, hurdy-gurdies; also available in kit form.*

Edgar, Alan. Northwood, 43 Beverley Rd, Hessle, E Yorks HU13 9AE *tel:* 01482 640330. *Small hps, also mus stands.*

Edwards, David Van. The Smokehouse, 6 Whitwell Rd, Norwich, Norfolk NR1 4HB *tel:* 01603 629899. *Medieval, renaissance and baroque lutes, chitarrones and theorbos, renaissance and baroque bows for vn, va da gamba inst families.*

Ellis, Bernard. The Forge, Wigmore, nr Leominster, Hereford HR6 9UA *tel:* 01568 770462 *fax:* 01568 770505 *email:* ellisium@mcmail.com; http://www.ellisium.mcmail.com. Bernard Ellis, Megan Ellis, partners. *Medieval to baroque strs, plucked and bowed.*

Eyland, Robert. 6 Birchwood Close, Totnes, Devon TQ9 5GB *tel:* 01803 864040. Robert Eyland, luthier. *Vas da gamba, violones, baroque dbs and vcs.*

Fleming, Michael. 13 Upland Park Rd, Oxford OX2 7RU *tel:* 01865 512807 *also fax. Viols (wide range, especially early 17th C English), vn family (16th-17th C), viol maintenance and restoration or conservation, fixed-frog and other bows.*

Forrester, Peter S. Sunflower House, 20 Beechwood Av, Aylmerton, Norfolk NR11 8QQ *tel:* 01263 837711. *Early guis, citterns, bandoras, orpharions, mandores, lutes, and associated more exotic plucked strs.*

Frood, Roger. Dove Workshops, Barton Rd, Butleigh, Glastonbury, Somerset BA6 8TL *tel:* 01458 850682 *also fax. Hammered dulcimers and accs.*

Glover, Marcel. Norton Cottage, Colchester Rd, Wivenhoe, Colchester, Essex CO7 9HT *tel:* 01206 826342. *Rebecs, psalteries, fiddles, pochettes.*

Hadaway, Robert. Cwm Meiarth, Bwlch-Llan, Lampeter, Dyfed SA48 8QR *tel:* 01974 821248. Robert Hadaway, luthier, hp maker and organologist. *Renaissance and baroque str insts, special and unusual insts, single and chromatic hps, bandora family, lutes, citterns, lyra, renaissance and early baroque viols, fidel, rebec, cwrth, lutes, early vns, lectures and consultancy.*

Haycock, Martin. 2 Charlton Mill, Charlton, Chichester, W Sussex PO18 0HY *tel:* 01243 811545. *Lutes.*

Heale, Michael. 8 Pit Farm Rd, Guildford, Surrey GU1 2JH *tel:* 01483 563096 *also fax. Baroque and modern str insts (va da gamba, hpd), restoration.*

Jack Hayward Harps. 5 Sun Gardens, Burghfield Common, Reading RG7 3JB *tel:* 0118 983 3922 *fax:* 0118 983 3868. *Celtic hps, hp strings, accs, insurance.*

Jones, Lewis. 18 Mare St, London E8 4RT *tel:* 0181 533 6404 *also fax. Hps, other medieval and renaissance str insts.*

Julier, Jane. Old Trickey's Farmhouse, Blackborough, Devon EX15 2HZ *tel:* 01823 681012 *also fax. Vas da gamba.*

Maynard, Bryan. Teviot House, Fishers Brae, Coldingham, Berwickshire TD14 5NJ *tel:* 01890 771235. *Renaissance and baroque vns, vas, vcs, viols and violones.*

Northern Renaissance Instruments. 6 Needham Av, Chorlton cum Hardy, Manchester M21 8AA *tel:* 0161 881 8134 *email:* esegerman@cityscape.co.uk. E and Mrs Y Segerman, partners. *Medieval, renaissance, baroque lutes, guis, mid-16th C and Jacobean viols, va d'amore, citterns, bandoras, strs and varnish materials.*

Nowak, Steffen. 12 Windsor Terrace, Totterdown, Bristol BS3 4UF *tel:* 0117 977 7141. *Vn, va, vc, baroque and modern.*

O'Kelly, Joseph M. 2 Middleton Rd, London E8 4BL *tel:* 0171 254 7074 *also fax; email:* boxes@globalnet.co.uk. *Baroque lutes, baroque guis, ouds, theorbos, vihuelas, chitarones, calasciones, guis. Also restoration.*

Oakwood Instruments. 8 Ladywood Rd, Leeds LS8 2QF *tel:* 0113 265 8585 *fax:* 0113 293 3011 *email:* oakwood@magpie.demon.co.uk. Martyn Banks, dir. *Hps, hammer dulcimers, guis, citterns, mandolins, banjos, bouzoukis, mandolas.*

Pilgrim Harps. Stansted House, Tilburstow Hill Rd, S Godstone, Surrey RH9 8NA *tel:* 01342 893242 *fax:* 01342 892646. *Non-pedal and pedal hps.*

Plant, Michael. The Coach House, Monyash Rd, Bakewell, Derbys DE45 1FG *tel:* 01629 815294. *Viols.*

Prentice, Ronald. The Mill, Ash Priors, Taunton, Somerset TA4 3NQ *tel:* 01823 432734 *email:* basses@the-mill.co.uk. *Viols, vas d'amore, baroque vns, vas, vcs, dbs.*

Robb, Arthur. 79 Gloucester Rd, Malmesbury, Wilts SN16 0AJ *tel:* 01666 822945 *email:* artlute@argonet.co.uk; http://www.argonet.co.uk/artlute. *Renaissance lutes.*

Rose, Roger. West Dean Musical Inst Workshop, c/o West Dean College, Chichester, W Sussex PO18 0QZ *tel:* 01243 811301/818235. *Viols, baroque vns, vcs and bows.*

Stoppani, George. 6 Needham Av, Chorlton-cum-Hardy, Manchester M21 8AA *tel:* 0161 860 7386 (w/shop); 0161 256 1173 (home). *Period vns, vas, vcs, bass vns, violones.*

Tim Hobrough, Harps. Southview, Back St, Fordyce, Banff AB45 2SU *tel:* 01261 843423. *Historical hps, lyres, psalteries.*

Ward, Alan. St Andrews, 27 Plomer Hill, Downley, High Wycombe, Bucks HP13 5JG *tel:* 01494 523371. *Baroque and modern vns, vas, vcs, also restoration and repairs.*

Williamson, Peter. Oldknow's Cottage, 151 Church La, Marple, Stockport, Cheshire SK6 7LD *tel:* 0161 427 3914. *Viol and vn family historical bows.*

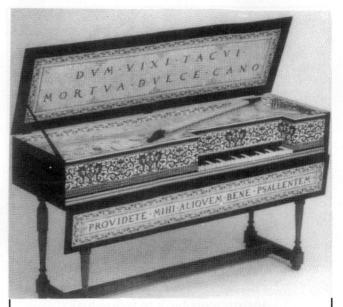

Wind

Ackerman, Brian. 70 Portland Rd, Hove, E Sussex BN3 5DL *tel:* 01273 702444 *also fax; email:* ackerman@mistral.co.uk. *Cls (also mouthpieces), fls, chalumeaux.*

Ancestral Instruments. Tudor Lodge, Pymoor La, Pymoor, nr Ely, Cambs CB6 2EE *tel:* 01353 698084 *email:* http://www.gmm.co.uk/ai. David Marshall. *Reedpipes, hornpipes, medieval and renaissance bagpipes.*

Browning, Stephen. 28 Lawrence Close, Basingstoke, Hants RG24 9DP *tel:* 01256 461507. *Cornetts.*

Dart, Mathew. 45 Bonnington Sq, London SW8 1TF *tel:* 0171 735 0479. *Baroque fls, bsns, classical bsns.*

Dolmetsch Musical Instruments. Unicorn Trading Estate, Weydown Rd, Haslemere, Surrey GU27 1DN *tel:* 01428 643235 *fax:* 01428 654920 *email:* brian@be-blood.demon.co.uk; http://www.be-blood.demon.co.uk. Brian Blood, mgr and sales dir. *Rcdrs.*

Early Brass. 25 Church Path, Merton Pk, London SW19 3HJ *tel:* 0181 542 4942. Frank Tomes. *Eng and Ger baroque and medieval tpts; also sackbutts.*

Early Music Shop. 38 Manningham La, Bradford BD1 3EA *tel:* 01274 393753 *fax:* 01274 393516 *email:* sales@earlyms.demon.co.uk; http://www.e-m-s.com. *Crumhorns, cornamuse, racketts, bagpipes (also available in kit form), sordunes, curtals, baroque bsns.*

Gruar, Philip. Brook Cottage, Burton Rd, Holme, via Carnforth, Lancs LA6 1QN *tel:* 01524 781601. *Northumbrian smallpipes, Scottish smallpipes, Lowland and Border pipes, baroque fls; also restoration work.*

Harding, David. 56 Netherton Rd, Appleton, Abingdon, Oxon OX13 5JZ *tel:* 01865 863673. *Serpents.*

Heriot & Allan. 28 Fairfield Green, W Monkseaton, Whitley Bay, Tyne and Wear NE25 9SD *tel:* 0191 251 3845. *Northumbrian and Scottish small pipes.*

Jones, Lewis. 18 Mare Street, London E8 4RT *tel:* 0181 533 6404 *also fax.* *Renaissance transverse fls.*

Julian Goodacre - Bagpipe Maker. 4 Elcho St, Peebles EH45 8LQ *tel:* 01721 722539 *email:* http://pipes.tico.com/pipes/makers/julian goodacre.html. Julian Goodacre, bagpipe maker. *Historical and folk bagpipes: English medieval bagpipes and Leicestershire small pipes, Cornish double pipes, Scottish bellows, small pipes, Border bagpipes.*

Lewin, Greg. The Hawthorns, Hawthorn Dr, Wheaton Aston, Staffs ST19 9NG *tel:* 01785 840186 *fax:* 01785 840476 *email:* greg@g0nen.demon.co.uk. *Crumhorns, cornamuse, kortholts, racketts, schreierpfeifen (schryarii), sordunes.*

Lyndon-Jones, G & M. 20 Queen St, St Albans, Herts AL3 4PJ *tel:* 01727 853951. *Curtals (dulcians).*

Moeck UK. 38 Manningham La, Bradford, W Yorks BD1 3EA *tel:* 01274 721646 *fax:* 01274 393516. *Crumhorns, cornamuse, dulcians, shawms, cornetts, fls, obs, bsns, racketts, chalumeaux.*

Monk Instruments. 1 Friendly Pl, Lewisham Rd, London SE13 7QS *tel:* 0181 694 1030 *fax:* 0181 325 7638. Jeremy West, Keith Rogers, partners. *Cornetts, serpents, baroque obs.*

Moulder, A Eric. 175 Buxton Rd, Leek, Staffs ST13 6NF *tel:* 01538 385323 *also fax.* *Renaissance reed insts, chorist-fagotts, cornamuse, crumhorns, curtals, shawms, rauschpfeifen, etc.*

Ocarina Workshop, Langley Ocarinas. Fern House, Fern Rd, Buxton, Derbys SK17 9NP *tel:* 01298 26993 *fax:* 01298 79229 *email:* langley@fenetre.co.uk. *Ocarinas, duet ocarinas, poly-ocarinas, gemshorns, songstones, 'Aztec' ocarinas.*

Recorder and Woodwind Centre. 5 Dorset St, London W1H 3FE *tel:* 0171 935 3339. Jane Vickers, rcdr sales specialist. *Rcdrs, baroque fls, various ethnic wind insts.*

Saunders Recorders. 205 Whiteladies Rd, Blackboy Hill, Bristol BS8 2XT *tel:* 0117 973 5149 *also fax.* John Everingham, mgr. *Specialist rcdr dealer.*

Stanley, Barbara. 21 Broad St, Clifton, Beds SG17 5RJ *tel:* 01462 814981 *fax:* 01462 629218 *email:* barbara.stanley@cableol.co.uk. *Baroque bsns, renaissance fls, reeds.*

Theatrum Instrumentorum. 393 Bradford Rd, Huddersfield, W Yorks HD2 2QY *tel:* 01484 427870. John Cousen. *Rcdrs (Virdung and Praetorius), renaissance and baroque fls, chalumeaux.*

Wells, Charles. 32 Manor Rd, Hatfield, Doncaster, S Yorks DN7 6SD *tel:* 01302 846492 *also fax.* *Renaissance, baroque and classical fls, obs, cls, flageolets, tabor pipes, restoration, repairs.*

Keyboard

Anderson, James. The Folly, Eydon, Northants NN11 3PP *tel:* 01327 263887 *fax:* 01327 262608 *email:* 106714.2057@compuserve.com. *Hpds, virginals.*

Bolton, D H. 44 Church La, Acklam, Middlesbrough TS5 7EB *tel:* 01642 817097 *also fax.* *Custom-built hpds, spinets, virginals, clvds, also in kit form with many components sold separately.*

Booth, Colin. Mount Pleasant, Westbury-sub-Mendip, Wells BA5 1HU *tel:* 01749 870516 *also fax.* *Hpds, virginals.*

Coad, Lucy. Workshop 3, Greenway Farm, Bath Rd, Wick, nr Bristol BS15 1RL *tel:* 0117 937 4949 *also fax.* *Square pno conservation and repairs; wound bass strings.*

Cole, Michael. Little Tatchley, 334 Prestbury Rd, Cheltenham Spa, Glos GL52 3DD *tel:* 01242 517192 *fax:* 01242 570383. *Maker of hpds, f-pnos.*

Dolmetsch Musical Instruments. Unicorn Trading Estate, Weydown Rd, Haslemere, Surrey GU27 1DN *tel:* 01428 643235 *fax:* 01428 654920 *email:* brian@be-blood.demon.co.uk; http://www.be-blood.demon.co.uk. Brian Blood, mgr and sales dir. *Hpds, clvds, spinets.*

Early Keyboard Agency. Heyford Galleries, High St, Upper Heyford, Oxon OX6 3LE *tel:* 01869 232282. Martin Robertson, proprietor. *Hpds, virginals, spinets, clvds, restoration, tuning; specialists in all types of early and modern overspun strs.*

Early Music Shop. 38 Manningham La, Bradford BD1 3EA *tel:* 01274 393753 *fax:* 01274 393516 *email:* sales@earlyms.demon.co.uk; http://www.e-m-s.com. *Spinets, clvds, hpds (also in kit form).*

Edgar, Alan. Northwood, 43 Beverley Rd, Hessle, E Yorks HU13 9AE *tel:* 01482 640330. *Hpds, spinets, virginals, clvds, mus stands.*

Garlick, Andrew. Madgeon Wood House, Buckland St Mary, Chard, Somerset TA20 3QF *tel:* 01460 234221. *Hpds, spinets, virginals.*

George Veness Workshop. Stanhope Studio, Donald Way, Winchelsea, E Sussex TN36 4NH *tel:* 01797 225878. *Clvd maker and restorer.*

Glover, Marcel. Norton Cottage, Colchester Rd, Wivenhoe, Colchester, Essex CO7 9HT *tel:* 01206 826342. *Virginals.*

Goetze, Martin and Dominic Gwynn. 5 The Tan Gallop, Welbeck Abbey Estate, Worksop, Notts S80 3LW *tel:* 01909 485635 *also fax.* *Church and chmbr orgs in period styles; also restoration work.*

Gotto, Alan. 5 Bessemer Rd, Norwich NR4 6DQ *tel:* 01603 620102 *also fax.* *Hpds, virginals, spinets.*

Greenhalgh, Malcolm. 48 Lordship Pk, London N16 5UD *tel:* 0181 800 6176.

Handy, Edmund. 9 Shirley Rd, Sidcup, Kent DA15 7JW *tel:* 01322 527366; 0181 300 2715. *Square pno restoration; tuning, maintenance of early keyboard insts. Also reconditioning.*

Hellon, Miles F. Unit B114, 8-10 Creekside, London SE8 3DX *tel:* 0181 694 1477. *Hpds, spinets, virginals.*

Hollick, Douglas. 4 Station Cottages, Harby La, Stathern, Leics LE14 4HJ *tel:* 01949 861347 *also fax; email:* dwh@globalnet.co.uk. *Hpds, virginals, clvds, also restoration work.*

Huggett, Martin. The Old Library, Stour St, Manningtree, Essex CO11 1BE *tel:* 01206 396354 *also fax.* *Hpds, clvds, spinets, also mus stands, chmbr orgs and harmoniums.*

Hugh Craig Harpsichords. Sugarcroft, Lower Southfield La, Bosbury, Ledbury, Herefords HR8 1NH *tel:* 01531 640046. *Hpds, spinets, clvds.*

Jennings, Robin. 16 Hilden Park Rd, Hildenborough, Kent TN11 9BL *tel:* 01892 770821 *also fax.* *Chmbr orgs, early keyboard insts including keyed glockenspiel.*

John Morley, Robert Morley and Co Ltd. 34 Engate St, London SE13 7HA *tel:* 0181 318 5838 *fax:* 0181 297 0720 *email:* http://www.yell.co.uk/sites/morley. *Hpds, clvds, spinets, virginals, celestes. Also repairs, rentals, sales and restoration work.*

John Storrs Workshop. Oakley Court, Benson, Wallingford OX10 6QH *tel:* 01491 832932 *also fax; email:* jsw@storrs.demon.co.uk; http://www.i-way.co.uk/~storrs/. John Storrs. *Hpds, spinets, clvds, kits.*

Jones, Lewis. 18 Mare St, London E8 4RT *tel:* 0181 533 6404 *also fax.* *Hpds, spinets, virginals, clvds, clavicytheria, lute-hpds, also specialist restoration work.*

Keen, Nicholas. Lamel Towers, 81 Hull Rd, York YO1 3JS *tel:* 01904 411873. *Hpds, clvds, spinets, virginals, f-pnos, pedalboard insts and orgs.*

Leigh-Flanders, Xavier. 4 Carbery La, Southbourne-on-Sea, Dorset BH6 3QG *tel:* 01202 428835 *also fax; email:* xl-f@harpsichords.prestel.co.uk; http://www.musiclink.co.uk/harpsichord/xlf.html. *Hpds, virginals, claviorganum.*

Mackinnon & Waitzman. Early Keyboard Workshop, 85 Cholmley Gardens, Fortune Green Rd, London NW6 1UN *tel:* 0171 431 5507.

Donald Mackinnon, Mimi Waitzman. *Hpds, f-pnos; also conservation, repair, courses in early keyboard inst tuning.*

Mander, N P. St Peter's Organ Works, St Peter's Sq, London E2 7AF *tel:* 0171 739 4747 *fax:* 0171 729 4718 *email:* manderuk@compuserve. com; http://www.mander-organs.com. John Pike Mander, mgr dir. *Portatives, regals, chmbr orgs, pipe orgs.*

Marshall, Anthony. Moss View Cottage, Walton, nr Brampton, Cumbria CA8 2DY *tel:* 01697 73718. *Clvds.*

Minns, Michael. 22a Davenant Rd, Oxford OX2 8BX *tel:* 01865 556368 *fax:* 01865 316876. *Hpds, spinets, virginals.*

Mitchell, William. 4 Carbery La, Southbourne on Sea, Dorset BH6 3QG *tel:* 01202 428835 *also fax; email:* wm@harpsichords.prestel.co.uk; http://www.musiclink.co.uk/harpsichord/mitchell.html. *Hpds, virginals, claviorganum.*

Nimblejack Ltd. 24 Alexandra Rd, Windsor, Berks SL4 1HN *tel:* 01753 853724. Alan Whear. *Portable clavicytheria, hpd maintenance, gen inst repairs.*

Peter Collins Ltd. 42 Pate Rd, Melton Mowbray, Leics LE13 0DG *tel:* 01664 410555 *fax:* 01664 410535. Peter Collins, mgr dir; Alan Goulding, gen mgr. *New pipe orgs of all sizes, restoration; continuo org for hire.*

R A J Bower & Co. Wellgrove Organ Manufactory, Weston Longville, Norwich NR9 5JJ *tel:* 01603 881189 *fax:* 01603 881222. *Early orgs, practice orgs, continuo orgs, church and chmbr orgs, pipe orgs.*

Ransom, Mark. 130 Westbourne Terrace Mews, London W2 6QG *tel:* 0171 723 9650 *also fax. Hpds, virginals, spinets.*

Richter, Karin. The Workshop, English Passage, Lewes, E Sussex BN7 2AP *tel:* 01273 481010 *also fax. Clvds, restoration of mus insts.*

Robert Deegan Harpsichords. Tonnage Warehouse, St Georges Quay, Lancaster LA1 1RB *tel:* 01524 60186 *fax:* 01524 33277 *email:* http://

www.kabine.demon.co.uk/harpsichord/. Robert Deegan, proprietor. *Hpds, virginals, spinets, clvds. Also concert hire, tuning, maintenance, restoration and repairs.*

Robert Goble & Son Ltd. Greatstones, Kiln La, Headington, Oxford OX3 8HQ *tel:* 01865 761685 *also fax.* Edward Goble, dir. *Hpds, spinets.*

Robert Shaftoe Organbuilder. 58 High St, Pavenham, Bedford MK43 7PE *tel:* 01234 823609. Robert Shaftoe. *Orgs, spinets, hpds.*

Rogers, Sandy. Warren House, Stone St, Faversham, Kent ME13 8PS *tel:* 01795 532437. *Hpd, clvd (insts and kits).*

Rose, Malcolm. The Workshop, English Passage, Lewes, E Sussex BN7 2AP *tel:* 01273 481010 *also fax. Hpd maker, repairer and conservator. Maker of iron and brass wires for keyboard insts up to 1850.*

Temple, Alex. Platt Lodge, 61 Barton Rd, Worsley, Manchester M28 2GX *tel:* 0161 794 3717 *email:* alextemple@compuserve.com. *Hpds, clvds; also hire and maintenance.*

W P Williams & Co. 2 Boscombe Mews, Boscombe Rd, Southend-on-Sea SS2 5JD *tel:* 01702 610981 *fax:* 01702 352049. *Pipe orgs, reeds and shallots.*

Wells-Kennedy Partnership Ltd. 85-87 Gregg St, Lisburn, Co Antrim BT27 5AW *tel:* 01846 664257 *fax:* 01846 603722. David H McElderry, dir. *Chmbr orgs.*

Whale & Martin. 156 Broadgate, Weston Hills, Spalding, Lincs PE12 6DQ *tel:* 01406 380731. *Hpds, clvds.*

Wooderson, Andrew. 5 Bourne Rd, Bexley, Kent DA5 1LG *tel:* 01322 558326; 01322 525558 *also fax. All types of hpds, spinets, virginals, clvds, early pnos; also tuning, maintenance, restoration, repairs and hire.*

Woolley, Dennis. Tubhole Barn, Dent, Sedbergh, W Riding, Yorks LA10 5RE *tel:* 01539 625361. *F-pno, hpd.*

Percussion

Early Music Shop. 38 Manningham La, Bradford BD1 3EA *tel:* 01274 393753 *fax:* 01274 393516 *email:* sales@earlyms.demon.co.uk; http://www.e-m-s.com. *Timbrels, tabors, nakers, drums and timpani (also in kit form).*

Glover, Marcel. Norton Cottage, Colchester Rd, Wivenhoe, Colchester, Essex CO7 9HT *tel:* 01206 826342. *Nakers, tabors, triangles.*

Materials

Aubrey, A B. 'The Willows', Crudwell, Malmesbury, Wilts SN16 9EL *tel:* 01666 577451 *also fax. Specialist in boxwood and blackwood for mus inst makers.*

Camwood (UK) Ltd. Unit 2, Staden Business Park, Buxton, Derbys SK17 9RZ *tel:* 01298 77407 *fax:* 01298 71156. *Specialists in ebony, blackwood, rosewood and boxwood for all insts.*

Huggett, Martin. The Old Library, Stour St, Manningtree, Essex CO11 1BE *tel:* 01206 396354 *also fax. All early keyboard insts, clvd, hpd, spinet, org and harmonium. Specialist inlaying and marquetry and high-class cabinet making and mus stands.*

Woolrich, A P. Canal Side, Huntworth, Bridgewater, Somerset TA7 0AJ *tel:* 01278 663020. *Ironmogery; tuning hammers, rest pins, itch pins, hpd stop levers, stop mechanisms, etc.*

The magazine for everyone concerned with music education

MUSIC TEACHER

First published in 1909

MUSIC TEACHER will...

* Help you focus your teaching methods

* Guide you on the interpretation of set works for GCSE and the ULEAC Anthology

* Familiarise you with the latest computer hardware and music software for schools

* Advise you on how to engender in your pupils a positive attitude towards instrumental practice

* Inform you about the history and development of the major conservatoires and music colleges

* Keep you up to date on the relevant courses and seminars

* Provide reviews of the sheet music and books published during the year

FREE Music Teacher GUIDES
Music Teacher subscribers are also sent up to six FREE supplementary guides published during the course of the year on subjects such as Notes for the Associated Board Piano and Violin Exams and Summer Schools

Monthly £2.95

ANNUAL SUBSCRIPTION PRICES: United Kingdom £34; airmail Europe £41; airmail outside Europe £47 (N & S America, Africa, Middle East and Hong Kong); £50 (Australia, New Zealand, Japan and Far East); surface mail worldwide £37

To subscribe please send your cheque (in pounds Sterling made payable to Rhinegold Publishing Ltd) to: Rhinegold Publishing Ltd (MT SUBS), Freepost, Gravesend, Kent DA12 2BR

CREDIT CARD SUBSCRIPTIONS
Tel: 01474 334500 (office hours); Fax: 01474 325557

FOR A FREE SAMPLE COPY telephone 0171 333 1720

Fiori Musicali performing Monteverdi's *1610 Vespers* at Stationers' Hall, London during the St Ceciliatide International Festival of Music

Fiori Musicali

Fiori Musicali specialise in 18th-century music on authentic instruments, bridging the gap between historically informed, scholarly performances and music which touches and moves the listener.

Kerstin Linder-Dewan *leader*

"the music's inventiveness hit one between the eyes" *Financial Times*

"a performance that radiated the sheer joy of music" *Daily Express*

METRONOME
1998 releases

MET CD 1019 Bach and Zelenka

Bach *Violin Concerto in D minor, BWV 1052*
Zelenka *Sinfonia in A minor*
Bach *Brandenburg Concerto no 2 in F*

MET CD 1024 Haydn and Wanczura

Haydn *Nelson Mass*
Wanczura *Symphony no 1 (Russian)*

Dr Penelope Rapson *director*

Bank Cottage, Preston Capes, Northamptonshire NN11 3TD Tel: 01327 361380 Fax: 01327 361415
Fiori Musicali Charitable Trust exists to educate the public in the Art and Science of Music. Registered charity no. 802684

Adrian Tribe, cornetts; Abigail Newman, Tom Lees, Adrian France, sackbuts.

Ensemble of the Bela Bartók Centre for Musicians. 6 Frognal Ct, Finchley Rd, London NW3 5HL *tel:* 0171 435 3685. Agnes Kory, dir.

Eroica String Quartet. Peter Hanson, Lucy Howard, Gustav Clarkson, David Watkin. *Magenta*

Estampie. 6 Weetwood Cres, Leeds LS16 5NS *tel:* 0113 275 7793. John Bryan, Graham Derrick, Susan Marshall, John Peel, Ian Richardson, Barrie Webb, Deborah Catterall. Medieval and renaissance ens.

European Union Baroque Orchestra. Hordley, Wootton, Woodstock OX20 1EP *tel:* 01993 812111 *fax:* 01993 812911 *email:* info@eubo.org. uk. Roy Goodman, mus dir; Paul James, gen admin; Emma Wilkinson, orch mgr.

Ex Cathedra Baroque Ensemble. Suite 303, Jewellery Business Centre, 95 Spencer St, Birmingham B18 6DA *tel:* 0121 523 1025 *fax:* 0121 523 1026. Jeffrey Skidmore, artistic dir; Andrew Gray, admin; Justin Lee, gen mgr; Micaela Comberti, leader; Lyn Collin, business and educ development; Alison Perrier-Burgess, finance.

Ex Cathedra Chamber Choir and Consort. Suite 303, Jewellery Business Centre, 95 Spencer St, Birmingham B18 6DA *tel:* 0121 523 1025 *fax:* 0121 523 1026. Jeffrey Skidmore, artistic dir; Justin Lee, gen mgr; Andrew Gray, admin; Lyn Collin, business and educ development; Alison Perrier-Burgess, finance. Consort 12-16 singers, chmbr choir 24-30 singers.

Extempore String Ensemble. George Weigand, dir, lute, mandore; Rosemary Thorndycraft, viols; William Thorp, vn; Sally Owen, hpd, viols; Robin Jeffrey, theorbo, lute. 16th-17th C inst mus with optional singer, dancers and wind insts. *CDI/Oriole*

I Fagiolini. 24 Salisbury Close, Princes Risborough, Bucks HP27 0JF *tel:* 01844 344525 *also fax.* Robert Hollingworth, dir; Anna Crookes, Rachel Elliott, Carys Lane, sops; Richard Wyn Roberts, Robin Blaze, c-ten; Hugh Wilson, Nicholas Smith, ten; Roderick Williams, bar; Matthew Brook, bs. Renaissance and baroque solo-voice ens mus. *Clarion/Seven Muses*

Farnborough Abbey Choir. *Michael Harrold*

Fiori Musicali. Bank Cottage, Old Forge La, Preston Capes, Northants NN11 3TD *tel:* 01327 361380 *fax:* 01327 361415 *email:* fiori@aol.com. Penelope Rapson, dir; Kerstin Linder-Dewan, leader; Bernard Rapson, treasurer; Jonathan Asquith, chmn.

Florilegium. 53 Tresco Rd, London SE15 3PY *tel:* 0171 639 7376 *also fax; email:* florilegium@compuserve.com. Ashley Solomon, Neal Peres Da Costa, management; Rachel Podger, leader; Helen Whitaker, admin. Baroque and classical chmbr and orch mus on period insts. Also choir.

Fretwork. 67 Kings Rd, Richmond, Surrey TW10 6EG *tel:* 0181 948 1250 *fax:* 0181 332 0415 *email:* 100636.1302@compuserve.com; http://www.brainlink.com/~starmus/unison/fretwork/fretwork.html. Wendy Gillespie, Richard Campbell, Richard Boothby, Julia Hodgson, Susanna Pell, William Hunt, viols. 15th-18th C and contemporary mus for viols. *Holt*

Frottola. 79 Humber Doucy La, Ipswich, Suffolk IP4 3NU *tel:* 01473 718811. Jennifer Cassidy, m-sop; Jacob Heringman, lute; Philip Thorby, viol, rcdr. Lute song trio.

The Gabrieli Consort. Anita Crowe, gen mgr; Jennifer Smith, admin. *Still*

Gallery Quartet. The Mill, Woodmancote, Cheltenham, Glos GL52 4QG *tel:* 01242 673636. Kathleen Malet, Eileen Williams, baroque vn; Alison Montgomery, baroque va; Gillian Stevens, baroque vc.

Gassenhauer Trio. 17 Hayesford Pk Dr, Bromley, Kent BR2 9DA *tel:* 0181 464 1645 *fax:* 0181 402 5859. Margaret Archibald, cl; Sebastian Comberti, vc; David Mason, pno.

The Georgian Chamber Orchestra. 25 Turners Croft, York YO1 5EL *tel:* 01904 410298. Peter Harrison, artistic dir; Iona Davies, leader.

The Georgian Music Room. 33 Hartswood Rd, London W12 9NE *tel:* 0181 749 3365 *fax:* 0181 749 1201. Neil Jenkins, ten; Rachel Beckett, baroque fl, rcdr; Celia Harper, dir, hpd. Concerts of 17th-18th C mus in period costume with contemporary readings. *Blythe*

Gilderoy. Sharon Lindo, vn; Keith Thompson, rcdrs, bagpipes; Rosemary Thorndycraft, viols, hurdy gurdy; George Weigand, lutes, dulcimer, hp. Scots, Irish and English traditional mus 16th-18th C. *Magenta*

Gothic Voices. Christopher Page, artistic dir. *Hazard*

[Griffett, Wright]. James Griffett, ten; Brian Wright, lute. *CDI*

[Guimond, Cole]. Claire Guimond, baroque fl; Maggie Cole, hpd. *Robert White*

Hadden/Carolan/Headley Ensemble. 86 Avenue Rd, London N15 5DN *tel:* 0181 802 7873 *also fax.* Nancy Hadden, renaissance and baroque fls; Lucy Carolan, hpd; Erin Headley, va da gamba. Solo, duo and trio programmes.

The Hanover Band. 45 Portland Rd, Hove, E Sussex BN3 5DQ *tel:* 01273 206978 *fax:* 01273 329636. Caroline Brown, artistic dir; Stephen Neiman, exec dir; Martin Williams, gen mgr. *OWM*

The Hanover Harmonie. 45 Portland Rd, Hove, E Sussex BN3 5DQ *tel:* 01273 206978 *fax:* 01273 329636. Principal wind players of The Hanover Band. Wind octet with 18th C period insts.

Harmonious Murmur. 25 Plasturton Av, Cardiff CF1 9HL *tel:* 01222 228154 *also fax; email:* w-d@baynet.co.uk. Lucy Robinson, Alexandra Robinson, Gillian Stevens, viols; Andrew Wilson-Dickson, keyboards; Dylan Fowler, gui with voice.

Hausmusik London. Monica Huggett, Pavlo Beznosiuk, vn; Roger Chase, va; Richard Lester, vc; Chi-chi Nwanoku, db; Antony Pay, cl; Anthony Halstead, hn; Jeremy Ward, bsn. Romantic chmbr repertoire on period insts. *Judith Hendershott*

Haydn Baryton Trio. Waye House, Alston Cross, Ashburton, S Devon TQ13 7ET *tel:* 01364 652114 *also fax.* Oliver Brookes, baryton, dir; Tony Shorrocks, baroque va; Tatty Theo, baroque vc.

Henry's Eight. Jonathan Brown, dir; Declan Costello, William Towers, c-ten; Duncan Byrne, Nick Todd, Nicholas Yates, ten; Damien O'Keefe, Robert Jan-Temmink, bs. *Magenta*

The Hilliard Ensemble. David James, c-ten; Rogers Covey-Crump, John Potter, ten; Gordon Jones, bar. Vocal ens. *Magenta*

His Majestys Sagbutts and Cornetts. Jeremy West, dir. *Magenta*

Holbein Consort. 1 St Vincent Cottage, Swyncombe Av, London W5 4DS *tel:* 0181 568 1445. Tudor wind ens.

[Holmes]. 'Holly Lodge', 231 Worlds End La, Chelsfield Pk, Orpington, Kent BR6 7SS *tel:* 01689 857533. Richard Holmes, vc; Patricia Holmes, hpd.

Hortus Musarum. 18 Mare St, London E8 4RT *tel:* 0181 533 6404 *also fax.* Lewis Jones, dir.

Intrada Brass Ensemble. Alan Furness, dir. *Michael Harrold*

[Janse, Rogers]. Jennifer Janse, baroque vc; Helen Rogers, hpd. *Michael Harrold*

Joglaresa. Belinda Sykes, voice; Ben Davis, Stuart Hall, Paul Clarvis, insts. *Robert White*

Kensington Gore Singers. 10 Pembroke Mews, London W8 6ER *tel:* 0171 937 0684 *also fax.* Petronella Dittmer, dir. 3-16 singers, sacred and secular mus to suit all occasions.

The King's Consort. 34 St Mary's Grove, London W4 3LN *tel:* 0181 995 9994 *fax:* 0181 995 2115 *email:* info@the-kings-consort.org.uk; http://www.the-kings-consort.org.uk. Robert King, artistic dir; Philip Cole, gen mgr; Stephen Metcalfe, admin; Nicky Oppenheimer, development dir. Vocal and inst baroque ens.

[Kirkby, Rooley]. Emma Kirkby, sop; Anthony Rooley, lute. *Magenta*

La Brigata. Billington Manor, Billington, Leighton Buzzard LU7 9BJ *tel:* 01525 372516 *fax:* 01525 851649. Sue Tyson, sop; Kristine Szulik, alto; Philip Leech, ten; Peter Syrus, bass and mus dir. 13th-16th C English, French and Italian mus.

La Serenissima. 23 Burbage Rd, London SE24 9HJ *tel:* 0171 737 4484 *fax:* 0171 326 0712. Adrian Chandler, dir and vn; Giulia Nuti, hpd; Mhairi Lawson, sop. Baroque orch specialising in the mus of Vivaldi and Venice contemporaries.

Ladybones. c/o B & B Concert Services, 66 Hyde Way, Hayes, Middx UB3 4PB *tel:* 0181 606 0030 *fax:* 0181 606 0037 *email:* roderick_burnett@compuserve.com. Sarah Williams, Abigail Newman, Jayne Murrill, Tracey Holloway, trbs; Carole Marnoch, sop. Trb quartet and voice.

Le Nouveau Quatuor. 171 Plowman Close, London N18 1XD *tel:* 0181 803 1260 *also fax.* Utako Ikeda, fl; Catherine Weiss, vn; Mark Caudle, va da gamba, vc; Paul Nicholson, hpd, f-pno.

Lecosaldi Ensemble. 27 Prentis Rd, London SW16 1QB *tel:* 0181 769 2677 *also fax;* 0171 606 4986. Peter Lea-Cox, dir; Rev Ronald England, admin. Singers and insts; mainly 18th C mus, specialising in Bach cantatas.

Legrand Ensemble. James Bowman, Charles Brett, c-tens; John Turner, David Pugsley, rcdrs; Jonathan Price, vc; Keith Elcombe, hpd. *Upbeat*

Les Concerts Royaux. 12 Spenser Rd, Harpenden, Herts AL5 5NN *tel:* 01582 462024 *also fax.* Terence Charlston, dir.

Loki Ensemble. Heidi Pegler, sop; William Summers, transverse fl, rcdr; Gerard Macdonald, transverse fl, baroque ob, rcdr; Richard Partridge, va da gamba; Helen Rogers, hpd. *Michael Harrold*

London Baroque. Brick Kiln Cottage, Hollington, Newbury, Berks RG20 9XX *tel:* 01635 254331 *fax:* 01635 253629. Ingrid Seifert, vn; Irmgard Schaller, Richard Gwilt, vn, va; Charles Medlam, vc, va da gamba; Terence Charlston, keyboard.

London Baroque Soloists. 34 Fernwood Av, London SW16 1RD *tel:* 0181 769 4158 *fax:* 0181 677 4157. Angela East, artistic dir; Adrian Butterfield, Jean Paterson, vn; Angela East, vc; Alastair Ross, hpd. Chmbr ens to small orch; period insts.

London Baroque Trio. 122 Wigmore St, London W1H 9FE *tel:* 0171 935 1270. Christopher Ball, rcdrs; Paul Arden Taylor, ob, rcdr; Alan Wilson, hpd.

London Harpsichord Ensemble. 10 Avenue Rd, London N6 5DW *tel:* 0181 340 5461 *fax:* 0181 347 5907. Sarah Francis, ob; Graham Mayger, fl; Peter Stevens, vn; Margaret Powell, vc; Jane Dodd, hpd.

London Pro Musica. 15 Rock St, Brighton, E Sussex BN2 1NF *tel:* 01273 692974 *fax:* 01273 622792. Bernard Thomas, dir. Shawms, cornetts, sackbuts, etc.

London Serpent Trio. Cantax House, Lacock, Chippenham, Wiltshire SN15 2JZ *tel:* 01249 730648 *also fax.* Alan Lumsden, Clifford Bevan, Philip Humphries, Andrew van der Beek, serpents.

London Wind Consort. Cantax House, Lacock, Chippenham, Wilts SN15 2JZ *tel:* 01249 730468 *also fax.* Andrew van der Beek, dir. Renaissance wind insts.

Ludus Instrumentalis. 32 Gayfield Sq, Edinburgh EH1 3PA *tel:* 0131 556 7996. Jane Norman, leader; Richard Neville-Towle, dir, hpd; Daphne Godson, vn; Simon Milton, ob; Christopher Robson, bsn; Ian Darling, ten. Baroque chmbr orch and choir specialising in mus of 17-18th C on period insts.

McGibbon Ensemble. 25 Forth Reach, Dalgety Bay, Fife KY11 5FF *tel:* 01383 820810. Edna Arthur, vn, Scots fiddle; David Johnson, vc; Bryce Gould, hpd, pno.

[Mackintosh, Cole]. Catherine Mackintosh, baroque vn; Maggie Cole, hpd. *Robert White*

Maggie Cole & Friends. Hpd and f-pno with other insts, or period str and soloists. *Robert White*

The Mellstock Band. 22 Swinbourne Rd, Littlemore, Oxford OX4 4PQ *tel:* 01258 837034; 01865 714778. David Townsend, concertina, vn, dir; Tim Hill, cl; Philip Humphries, serpent; Charles Spicer, ob, vox humana. Authentic performance of early 19th C west-gallery church mus and other village band mus; also available with small choir.

Midland Baroque. 3 Abbey Mill End, St Albans, Herts AL3 4HN *tel:* 01727 843656 *also fax.* Diane Terry, baroque vn; Pam Cresswell, baroque va; Laurie Ann MacLeod, baroque vc, va da gamba; Katharine May, hpd. Baroque mus on original insts.

Minstralsye. Philip Astle, insts; Alison Payne, sop, hp. *Sympathetic*

The Music Collection. 38 Fairhazel Gardens, London NW6 3SJ *tel:* 0171 328 9347 *fax:* 0171 328 4689 *email:* max@musical.demon.co.uk. Susan Alexander-Max, f-pno; Catherine Martin, baroque vn; Alison McGillivray, baroque vc. Ens featuring mus of the late 18th and early 19th C as well as new commissions.

Music is Pleasure. 71 Woodburn Close, London NW4 2NF *tel:* 0181 202 1731 *also fax; email:* joan@buzbee.dem.uk. Joan Busby. Voices and insts; thematic programmes to order.

Musica Antiqua of London. 87 Olive Rd, London NW2 6UR *tel:* 0181 452 3254 *also fax.* Philip Thorby, dir; Alison Crum, admin; John Bryan, Margaret Westlake, viols, rcdrs, crumhorns, shawms, sackbut, hp, fl, etc; Jacob Heringman, lute.

Musica Contexta. 24 Fairfield Rd, Crouch End, London N8 9HG *tel:* 0181 347 9655. Vocal ens.

Musica Dolce. Redwings, Linden Chase, Uckfield, E Sussex TN22 1EE *tel:* 01825 760046 *also fax.* Donna Deam, sop; Linda Brand, rcdr, ob; Joanna Levine, vc; Helena Brown, hpd.

Musica Fiammante. Kate Eckersley, sop; Katharine Sharman, vc; Timothy Roberts, hpd. *Ellison*

Musica Secreta. 9 Chalkers La, Hurstpierpoint, W Sussex BN6 9LR *tel:* 01273 833950 *also fax; email:* 101565.3033@compuserve.com. Deborah Roberts, Tessa Bonner, sops; Mary Nichols, alto; John Toll, hpd, org; David Miller, lute, theorbo. Sacred and secular mus for women's voices and continuo.

Musical Offering. Darnholme, 14 Bristow Close, Westbrook, Warrington, Cheshire WA5 5EU *tel:* 01925 710454. Rachel Brown, baroque fl, rcdr; Pauline Nobes, baroque vn; Jonathan Price, baroque vc; David Francis, hpd.

Musiche Delightes. c/o Lyric Production, 41 Arkwright Rd, Sanderstead, Surrey CR2 0LP *tel:* 0181 657 5840 *also fax.* Lutes, viols, guis, clvds, rcdrs, sackbuts, serpents and crumhorns.

The Musicke Companye. Phillippa Hyde, sop; Timothy Brown, c-ten; Jennifer Janse, baroque vc; Helen Rogers, hpd. *NCCP*

Músicos de Cámara. 19 Linton St, London N1 7DU *tel:* 0171 354 2973 *also fax.* June Yakeley, dir. Baroque mus (especially Spanish) with voices and early guis.

Musikfreunde. 38 Alric Av, New Malden, Surrey KT3 4JN *tel:* 0181 942 1519; 0467 221138. Lorna Anderson, sop; Jane Booth, cl; Simon Nicholls, f-pno.

Myriell Consort. 20 Wolseley Gardens, London W4 3LP *tel:* 0181 995 2757. Simon Hill, dir. Early vocal ens.

New London Consort. 12 Vathouse, Regents Bridge Gardens, London SW8 1HD *tel:* 0171 735 8154 *fax:* 0171 820 0801. Philip Pickett, dir. Medieval, renaissance and baroque insts with solo voices.

Noise of Minstrels. 94 High St, Tring, Herts HP23 4AF *tel:* 01442 825191. Ray Attfield, perc, hurdy-gurdy, voice; Dave Chatterley, symphonie, hurdy-gurdy, gui, lute; Peter Sharp, gui, citole, cittern; James Tribble, vn, vielle; John Grubb, citole, cittern, gittern; Michael Sargeant, bagpipes, w/wind. Early and traditional secular mus.

Norwich Waits. The Old Station, Kimberley, Wymondham, Norfolk NR18 9HB *tel:* 01953 850711. Six musicians, shawms, curtals, rauschpfeifen, crumhorns, hurdy-gurdy, bagpipes, lute, viol, cittern, rcdrs, org.

Costumed entertainments of 16th and 17th C mus on period wind and str insts with readings and dialogue.

Odyssey. Gwespyr, 6 Hallcroft La, Copmanthorpe, York YO2 3UQ *tel:* 01904 701459; 01502 724020. Yvonne Robert, sop; Maurice Ridge, pno; Graham Roberts, reader.

Opera Restor'd. 54 Astonville St, London SW18 5AJ *tel:* 0181 870 7649 *fax:* 0181 672 6540. Peter Holman, mus dir; Jack Edwards, stage dir. Revival and performance of 17th-18th C opera; fully staged, small orch.

Opus Anglicanum. 92 St Thomas St, Wells, Somerset BA5 2UZ *tel:* 01749 677903 *fax:* 01749 675131. Stephen Tilton, c-ten; James Gilchrist, William Lee, ten; Roland Robertson, bar; John Rowlands-Pritchard, bs; John Touhey, narrator.

Orchestra of the Age of Enlightenment. 5th Floor, Westcombe House, 56-58 Whitcomb St, London WC2H 7DN *tel:* 0171 930 0646 *fax:* 0171 930 0626 *email:* oae@premier.co.uk.

Orchestra of the Renaissance. 111 Bulwer Rd, London E11 1BU *tel:* 0181 539 8125 *also fax;* 0171 704 9137 *fax:* 0171 359 1448 *email:* 100422. 3126@compuserve.com. Richard Cheetham, dir; Vicky Miller, mgr.

Orlando Consort. 124 Westway, London SW20 9LS *tel:* 0181 540 1633 *fax:* 0181 542 8215 *email:* donald_greig@compuserve.com; http:// ourworld.compuserve.com/homepages/donald_greig/. Robert Harre-Jones, alto; Charles Daniels, Angus Smith, ten; Donald Greig, bar.

Oxford Baroque. 70 Hayfield Rd, Oxford OX2 6TU *tel:* 01865 559771 *also fax.* Guy Williams, artistic dir, fl; Jean Paterson, vn; Gabriel Amherst, vc; Martin Souter, hpd.

Palladian Ensemble. 51 Thornhill Houses, Fourth Floor, Thornhill Rd, London N1 1PB *tel:* 0171 607 9541. Pamela Thorby, rcdr; Rachel Podger, vn; Susanne Heinrich, va da gamba; William Carter, lutes, gui. Baroque chmbr ens specialising in 17th and 18th C repertoire. *Hazard*

The Parley of Instruments. 42 Owlstone Rd, Newnham, Cambridge CB3 9JH *tel:* 01223 354096 *also fax.* Peter Holman, dir. Baroque and renaissance vns, viols and continuo. *Sykes*

Parnassus Ensemble of London. 18 Chimney Ct, 23 Brewhouse La, Wapping E1 9NU *tel:* 0171 480 5145 *also fax.* Peter Sheppard Skaerved, mus dir; Ruth Slater, Juliet Lewis, co-dirs.

Phantasm. 32 Belsize Park, London NW3 *tel:* 0171 435 5970 *also fax; email:* l.dreyfus@kcl.ac.uk. Laurence Dreyfus, Wendy Gillespie, Jonathan Manson, Markku Luolajan-Mikkold, viols.

Polyhymnia. Richard Lowell Childress. Vocal ens. *Chameleon*

Praetorius Consort of London. 122 Wigmore St, London W1H 9FE *tel:* 0171 935 1270. Christopher Ball, dir, renaissance wind; Paul Arden

Taylor, Philip Thorby, wind; Alan Wilson, spinet; Peter Vel, bs viol; Michael Lewin, lute.

Pro Cantione Antiqua. Vocal ens. *CDI*

Purcell Quartet. Richard Boothby, bs vn, va da gamba, vc; Catherine Mackintosh, vn, va, va d'amore; Catherine Weiss, vn; Robert Woolley, hpd, org. *Hazard*

QuintEssential Sackbut and Cornett Ensemble. 10 King's Highway, Plumstead, London SE18 2NL *tel:* 0181 855 8584 *also fax.* Richard Thomas, dir.

Quintus. Gerald Place, dir. Vocal ens. *Chameleon*

Raglan Baroque Players. 52 Goldsmith Av, Acton, London W3 6HN *tel:* 0181 896 2741 *also fax.* Nicholas Kraemer, dir; Melanie Turner, gen mgr; Vicky Miller, concert mgr. Baroque insts. *Sykes*

Red Byrd. John Potter, ten; Richard Wistreich, bs; and other voices, insts. Early and contemporary mus. *Robert White*

Red Priest. Piers Adams, dir, rcdrs. *Upbeat*

Réjouissance. 14 Belsize Av, London W13 9TF *tel:* 0181 840 7406 *fax:* 0181 840 5406. Suzie Le Blanc, sop; Charles Daniels, ten; Marie Knight, vns; Susanna Pell, va da Gamba; Nicholas Parle, hpd. 17th-18th C vocal and inst chmbr mus, especially French Cantata.

The Revolutionary Drawing Room. Angela East, dir, vc. *Upbeat*

Rose Consort of Viols. 28 Wentworth Rd, Scarcroft Hill, York YO2 1DG *tel:* 01904 652736 *fax:* 01484 472656; 0181 452 3254. John Bryan, Alison Crum, Sarah Groser, Roy Marks, Peter Wendland, viols.

The Rosewood Ensemble. The Old Rectory Coach House, High St, Bourton-on-the-Water, Glos GL54 2AP *tel:* 01451 821481 *also fax.* Lesley-Jane Rogers, sop; Jan Waterfield, hpd; Melanie Woodcock, baroque vc; plus other insts.

Roundelay. Waye House, Alston Cross, Ashburton, Devon TQ13 7ET *tel:* 01364 652114 *also fax; email:* 101522.3644@compuserve.com. Oliver Brookes, early str; Roxana Gundry, voice, lutes, early insts.

St Andrews Baroque Trio. 29 Airthrey Av, Glasgow G14 9LJ *tel:* 0141 954 5020 *email:* marjorie@music.gla.ac.uk. Christopher Field, baroque vn; Marjorie Rycroft, baroque vc, bs viol; John Kitchen, hpd, org.

St James's Baroque Players. 200 Broomwood Rd, London SW11 6JY *tel:* 0171 228 6388 *fax:* 0171 738 1706. Ivor Bolton, mus dir; Delia Pye, mgr.

Salomon String Quartet. 71 Priory Rd, Kew, Surrey TW9 3DH *tel:* 0181 940 7086 *fax:* 0181 332 0879. Simon Standage, Micaela Comberti, vn; Trevor Jones, va; Jennifer Ward Clarke, vc; Francesca McManus, mgr.

San Petronio Players. 119 Canal La, Stanley, Wakefield, W Yorks *tel:* 01924 827337 *fax:* 01484 689408. Duncan Druce, Kenneth Mitchell, vn; Rachel Gray, vc; Keith Elcombe, hpd, org.

Sarabande. 8 Elmslack La, Silverdale, Carnforth, Lancs LA5 *tel:* 01524 701623 *email:* ann@sdale1.demon.co.uk. Ann Bond, hpd; Elizabeth Dodd, va da gamba; Philip Gruar, baroque fl and rcdr. French baroque repertoire, also baroque dance.

Sarband. Vladimir Ivanoff, artistic dir. Ens specialising in links between European, Islamic and Jewish mus. *Pristavec*

Scaramella. 25 Hailstone Close, Rowley Regis B65 8LJ *tel:* 01384 252632 *also fax.* Heather Wastie, Mitchell Phillips, Stewart McCoy, Pamela Smith, Cathy Gaskell, viols, rcdrs, voices, lutes, theorbo, renaissance gui.

The Scholars Baroque Ensemble. David van Asch, dir. *Festival*

Scottish Early Music Consort. 22 Falkland St, Glasgow G12 9PR *tel:* 0141 334 9229 *also fax; email:* semc@glasgow.almac.co.uk. Warwick Edwards, artistic dir. Voices, medieval, renaissance and baroque insts.

Sequentia. Barbara Thornton, Benjamin Bagby, and others, 12th-13th C vocal and inst mus. *Magenta*

Sinfonye. 16 Tillingham Av, Rye, E Sussex TN31 7BA *tel:* 01797 222257 *also fax; email:* 101525.2667@compuserve.com. Stevie Wishart, dir; Judy Greenwell, admin.

Sirinu. Sara Stowe, sop, kybds; Henry Stobart, rcdrs, shawm, bagpipes; Jon Banks, hp, sackbut; Matthew Spring, lutes, vihuela, guis, hurdy-gurdy. Early and world musics. *Seaview*

The Sixteen. First Floor, Enslow House, Station Rd, Enslow, Kidlington, Oxon OX5 3AX *tel:* 01869 331544 *fax:* 01869 331011 *email:* info@thesixteen.org.uk. Harry Christophers, cond. Choral ens performing also with period orch, The Symphony of Harmony and Invention.

[Stowe, Spring]. Sarah Stowe, sop, kybds; Matthew Spring, lutes, vihuela, hurdy-gurdy, guis. *Seaview*

The Symphony of Harmony and Invention. First Floor, Enslow House, Station Rd, Enslow, Kidlington, Oxon OX5 3AX *tel:* 01869 331544 *fax:* 01869 331011 *email:* info@the sixteen.org.uk. Harry Christophers, cond. Period orch.

The Tallis Scholars. Fenton House, Banbury Rd, Chipping Norton, Oxon OX7 5AW *tel:* 01608 644080 *fax:* 01608 643235. Peter Phillips, dir; Shauni McGregor, admin.

Taverner Consort, Choir and Players. Ibex House, 42-46 Minories, London EC3N 1DY *tel:* 0171 481 2103 *fax:* 0171 481 2865. Andrew Parrott, artistic dir; Malcolm Bruno, associate dir; Victoria Newbert, admin. Medieval, renaissance and baroque insts with voices.

Telemann Players of London. Redwings, Linden Chase, Uckfield, E Sussex TN22 1EE *tel:* 01825 760046 *also fax.* Linda Brand, rcdr, ob; Philip Turbett, baroque bsn; Helena Brown, hpd.

Tirata. 4 Heathleigh Cottages, Maidstone Rd, Horsmonden, Kent TN12 8JL *tel:* 01892 723370 *also fax; email:* 101767.2724@compuserve.com. Peter Bowman, Kathryn Bennetts, rcdrs; Laurie Ann MacLeod, vc, va da gamba; Yeo Yat-Soon, hpd. *Invisible Pilots*

Trio Basiliensis. 58 Redhill Dr, Brighton BN1 5FL *tel:* 01273 552548 *also fax.* Marianne Mezger, rcdr and fr flageolet; Ekkehard Weber, va da gamba, Paul Simmonds, hpd. 16th-18th C chmbr mus.

Trio Sonnerie. 71 Priory Rd, Kew, Richmond, Surrey TW9 3DH *tel:* 0181 940 7086 *fax:* 0181 332 0879. Monica Huggett, vn; Sarah Cunningham, bs viol; Gary Cooper, hpd; Francesca McManus, mgr.

Trompette. The Old Station, Kimberley, Wymondham, Norfolk NR18 9HB *tel:* 01953 850711. 2 costumed entertainers of medieval and renaissance mus.

The Troubadours. Tudor Lodge, Pymoor La, Pymoor, nr Ely, Cambs CB6 2EE *tel:* 01353 698084 *email:* http://www.gmm.co.uk/ai. Costumed demonstrations and concerts with medieval and renaissance w/winds, strs, br and perc.

The Wallace Collection. 26 Cartmel Rd, Bexleyheath, Kent DA7 5EA *tel:* 01322 430779 *fax:* 01322 448416. Roy Bilham, gen mgr.

[Wallfisch, Nicholson]. Elizabeth Wallfisch, baroque, classical vn; Paul Nicholson, early keyboards. *Sykes*

Wolsey's Wilde. 25 Hailstone Close, Rowley Regis B65 8LJ *tel:* 01384 252632 *also fax.* Heather Wastie, Pam Smith, Joanna Smith, rcdr, renaissance gui, lute, medieval pipes, windcaps, vn, voice, perc. Costumed Elizabethan entertainment.

Wren Baroque Orchestra. Wren Music, 8 Park La, Selsey, Chichester, W Sussex PO20 0HD *tel:* 01243 604281 *fax:* 01243 604387 *email:* starmus @brainlink.com; http://www.brainlink.com/~starmus/unison/wren/wren.html. Martin Elliott, dir; Susan Carpenter-Jacobs, leader.

Wren Baroque Soloists. Wren Music, 8 Park La, Selsey, Chichester, W Sussex PO20 0HD *tel:* 01243 604281 *fax:* 01243 604387 *email:* starmus @brainlink.com; http://www.brainlink.com/~starmus/unison/wren/wren.html. Lesley-Jane Rogers, Nicola Jenkin, sop, Frances Jellard, alto; Simon Davies, ten; Martin Elliott, bs; Melanie Woodcock, baroque vc; Jan Waterfield, hpd, org, virginals.

Wren Consort. Wren Music, 8 Park La, Selsey, Chichester, W Sussex PO20 0HD *tel:* 01243 604281 *fax:* 01243 604387 *email:* starmus@brainlink.com. Alison Pearce, sop; Martin Elliott, bs-bar; Steven Keogh, Paul Thomas, tpt; Andrew Lumsden, org, hpd.

Wren Singers of London. Wren Music, 8 Park La, Selsey, Chichester, W Sussex PO20 0HD *tel:* 01243 604281 *fax:* 01243 604387 *email:* starmus @brainlink.com. Martin Elliott, artistic dir; Peter Beaven, asst dir.

The York Waits. c/o James Merryweather, 6 Ingleborough Av, Tang Hall, York YO1 3SA *tel:* 01904 432878/431328 *fax:* 01904 432860 *email:* jwm5@york.ac.uk; http://www.intr.net/bleissa/lists/yorkwait.html. James Merryweather, admin; Tim Bayley, Anthony Barton, William Marshall, Ian and Roger Richardson, shawms, cornetts, sackbuts, curtals, rcdrs, bagpipes, hurdy-gurdies, etc. Ten concert programmes plus a host of other renaissance entertainments.

Yorkshire Baroque Soloists. 11 Bootham Terrace, York YO3 7DH *tel:* 01904 652799 *fax:* 01904 338349 *email:* ps22@unix.york.ac.uk. Peter Seymour, dir. Voices, str, wind, keyboard.

Zorzi. 1 St Vincent Cottage, Swyncombe Av, London W5 4DS *tel:* 0181 568 1445. Martin Pope, dir. 17th C chmbr ens. Cornett, sackbut, vn and continuo.

Early Music Instrumentalists

Performers who have made a special study of early instrumental technique and performance practice are listed below under three broad categories: strings (bowed and plucked), wind and keyboard. A telephone number is given for each artist; where an agent is named, details will be found in the **Agents and Managers** section.

Strings (bowed and plucked)

Adams, Peter, va da gamba, treble and bs – 01295 277976 *also fax*

Barford, Imogen, early hp – 0171 485 1903 *also fax*

Chandler, Adrian, baroque vn – 0181 778 5754

Chateauneuf, Paula, lutes, theorbos, early guis – 0181 771 2152 *also fax*

Civval, Sally, va da gamba, baroque vc – *Music Management*

Comberti, Micaela, baroque vn – 0181 349 3580 *fax:* 0181 346 7490

Crum, Alison, viols, violone, hp, early strs, sackbut – 0181 452 3254 *also fax*

Davis, Howard, baroque vn – 01279 431337 *also fax*

Deere-Jones, Sarah, hp – 01929 426091 *also fax*

Dittmer, Petronella, vn – 0171 937 0684 *also fax*

Dolmetsch, Marguerite, bs viol – 01428 651473

East, Angela, classical and baroque vc, va da gamba, bs vn – 0181 769 4158 *fax:* 0181 677 4157

Eastwell, Martin, lute, early guis, theorbo – 01434 683733 *also fax; email:* eastwellm@argonet.co.uk

Elsner, Kasia, theorbo, lute, baroque gui – 0171 354 5883 *also fax*

Harper, Celia, double hp, hpd, chmbr org – 0181 749 3365 *fax:* 0181 749 1201

Heinrich, Susanne, viols, violone – 01865 723870 *also fax*

Hope, Harvey, baroque gui – 0181 657 5840 *also fax*

Janse, Jennifer, baroque vc – *Michael Harrold*

Jeffrey, Robin, lute, theorbo, baroque gui, oud – 01892 852878 *also fax*

Kelly, Frances, hp – *Magenta*

Kuijken, Sigiswald, vn – *Allied*

Kuijkin, Wieland, va da gamba – *Allied*

Lawrence-King, Andrew, early hp – 01481 713037 *fax:* 01481 700502 *email:* theharpconsort@compuserve.com

Levine, Joanna, vc, va da gamba, violone – 0181 348 4295 *fax:* 0181 292 7125

Levy, Mark, va da gamba, violone, lirone – 0181 348 4295 *fax:* 0181 292 7125

Lewin, Michael, lute, archlute, theorbo – 0181 876 6161 *also fax*

Linell, Dorothy, lute, theorbo – 01923 822934; 0171 580 8764 *fax:* 0171 935 5836

Lund, Vegard, baroque gui, lute – *Roy Baker*

MacLeod, Laurie Ann, baroque and classical vc, bs viol, bs vn, ten vn – 01252 795047 *also fax*

Malet, Kathleen, baroque vn – 01242 673636

Marks, Roy, viols, lutes, violone, theorbo – 0181 452 3254 *also fax*

Mason, Barry, lute, baroque gui – 0181 992 8973 *also fax*

Medlam, Charles, baroque vc, va da gamba – 01635 254331 *fax:* 01635 253629

Muskett, Michael, hurdy-gurdy – 01300 345412 *email:* hurdyplay@aol.com

Pallott, Elizabeth, lute – *Mostylea*

Parsons, David, lute, gui, theorbo – *Michael Harrold*

Partridge, Richard, va da gamba – 0181 691 6537

Podger, Rachel, baroque vn – 0181 458 1281 *also fax*

Remnant, Mary, various medieval insts – *Jennings*

Robinson, Lucy, va da gamba – 01222 228154 *also fax; email:* w-d@baynet.co.uk

Rogers, Cornelia, va da gamba, baroque vn – 01323 734207 *also fax*

Rogers, Maurice, viols – 01323 734207

Rooley, Anthony, lute – 0171 229 5142 *fax:* 0171 221 1282 *email:* consort@easynet.co.uk

Sayce, Lynda, lute, baroque gui, theorbos, baroque mandolin – 01235 816158 *also fax*

Skeaping, Roderick, baroque vn, rebecs, viols – 0171 485 6668 *fax:* 0171 267 2957

Spencer, Robert, lute, gui – 0181 504 5639 *fax:* 0181 505 7138

Spring, Matthew, lute, guis, viols, theorbo, hurdy-gurdy – 01865 61966 *also fax*

Stowell, Robin, baroque vn – 01222 752001 *fax:* 01222 874379 *email:* stowell@cardiff.ac.uk

Taylor, Frances, mandolin – 0181 989 7591

Theo, Tatty – 0171 607 0185 *fax:* 01603 763279 *email:* tatty@easynet.co.uk

Wallfisch, Elizabeth, baroque vn – *Sykes*

Weigand, George, lutes, mandores, oud, dulcimers – *Oriole*

Wendland, Peter, viol, violone – 0181 690 1176

Willmott, Roderick, gui, lute – 01905 427026

Wilson, Brian Lloyd, baroque, classical, romantic vn, va, va d'amore – 01252 795047 *also fax*

Wilson, Christopher, lute – *Magenta*

Wright, Brian, lute – *CDI*

Wind

Adams, Piers, rcdr – *Upbeat*

Arden-Taylor, Paul, rcdr, early reeds, ob – 01562 710801 *also fax*

Baker, Paul, rcdrs, hurdy-gurdy, renaissance winds, bagpipes – 01384 295210 *email:* paul@diabolus.abel.co.uk; http://www.abel.co.uk/~diabolus

Ball, Christopher, rcdr, early wind insts – 0171 935 1270

Barlow, Jeremy, fl, rcdr, pipe and tabor – 0171 267 7176 *fax:* 0171 267 0127

Bennetts, Kathryn, rcdr – 01892 723370 *also fax; email:* 101767.2724@compuserve.com

Beznosiuk, Lisa, early fls – 01588 640361; 0181 533 0429 *fax:* 01588 640107

Booth, Jane, cl, chalumeau – 0181 942 1519; 0467 221138

Bowman, Peter, rcdr – 01892 723370 *also fax; email:* 101767.2724@compuserve.com

Carroll, Paul, baroque and classical bsn, baroque fl, rcdr – *Music Management*

Dolmetsch, Marguerite, rcdr – 01428 651473

Donnelly, Christopher, cl – 01296 334272

Halstead, Anthony, natural hn – c/o 01223 352542; 0973 421626 *fax:* 01223 368534

Harris, Paul, baroque and classical bsn – 0181 981 7413 *also fax;* 0181 533 1372

Kemp, Jill, rcdr – *Grant Rogers*

Kuijken, Barthold, transverse fl – *Allied*

Laird, Michael, natural tpt, cornetto – 0181 946 2700 *fax:* 0181 946 7272

Lawson, Colin, cl, chalumeau, basset hn – 0181 866 3557 *also fax*

Lumsden, Alan, sackbut, serpent, ophicleide, rcdr – 01452 750253 *fax:* 01452 750585

Macdonald, Gerard, baroque fl, baroque ob, rcdr – *Michael Harrold*

Merryweather, James, shawms, curtal, medieval and renaissance bagpipes, baroque bsn – 01904 432878/431328 *fax:* 01904 432860 *email:* jwm5@york.ac.uk; http://www.intr.net/bleissa/lists/yorkwait.html

Mezger, Marianne, rcdrs, fr flageolet – 01273 552548 *also fax*

Muskett, Michael, rcdr, cl, musette, hurdy-gurdy – 01300 345412 *email:* hurdyplay@aol.com

Nallen, Evelyn, rcdrs – 01223 561331

Pay, Antony, cl – *Allied*

Petri, Michala, rcdr – *Clarion/Seven Muses*

Pickett, Philip, rcdr – 0171 735 8154 *fax:* 0171 820 0801

Preston, Stephen, cl, romantic and baroque fl – 01797 230398 *also fax*

Puddy, Keith, cl, basset hn, chalumeau – 0171 229 4185 *fax:* 0171 727 2036

Rogers, Cornelia, rcdr – 01323 734207 *also fax*

Schuelein, Rainer, fl, rcdr – 0171 722 5744 *also fax*

Solomon, Ashley, rcdr, baroque and classical fl – 0181 346 2896 *also fax*

Steele-Perkins, Crispian, tpt, natural tpt – *Anglo-Swiss*

Thompson, Michael, natural hn – *PGM*

Thorby, Pamela, rcdr – 0171 607 9541 *also fax – Hazard*

van der Beek, Andrew, sackbut, serpent – 01249 730468 *also fax*

Walker, Elizabeth, renaissance, baroque and classical fl, rcdr – 0171 226 8141 *fax:* 0171 226 9732

Keyboard

Ainscough, Julie, org – *Michael Harrold*
Aldwinckle, Robert, hpd, chmbr org – 01424
    715435 *also fax*
Alexander-Max, Susan, f-pno, clvd – 0171
    328 9347 *fax:* 0171 328 4689 *email:* max@
    musicol.demon.co.uk
Arnáiz, Guilliermo Diez, org – *Michael
    Harrold*
Barber, Graham, hpd, org – 0113 263 1890
    fax: 0113 263 7178
Barlow, Jeremy, hpd – 0171 267 7176
    fax: 0171 267 0127
Barthold, Kenneth van, f-pno – 01747 838318
    also fax
Bate, Jennifer, org – 0181 883 3811 *fax:* 0181
    444 3695 *email:* jenniferbate@classical-
    artists.com; http://www.classical-artists.
    com/jbate
Beechey, Gwilym, hpd – 01482 508910
Black, Virginia, hpd – 01279 431337 *also fax*
Bond, Ann, hpd, org – 01524 701623 *email:*
    ann@sdale1.demon.co.uk
Booth, Colin, hpd – 01749 870516 *also fax*
Burnett, Richard, f-pno – 01580 211702
    fax: 01580 211007
Cave, Penelope, hpd, virginals – 01483
    563096 *also fax*
Chapman, Jane, hpd – 0181 997 7621 *also fax*
Charlston, Terence – 01582 462024 *also fax*
Cole, Maggie, hpd, f-pno – *Robert White*
Cooper, Gary – 01865 242209 *also fax*
Coulson, Richard, hpd, org – 01932 229171
Cuckston, Alan, hpd – 01757 638238
Dawkes, Hubert, hpd – 01264 324467
Elcombe, Keith, hpd – 0161 445 6661
Francis, David, hpd, chmbr org – 01925
    710454
Gordon, David – 01923 239038 *also fax*
Gould, Sharon, hpd – 01722 712449
Griffiths, Clare, Hpd – 01233 663775
    fax: 01233 664547
Harper, Celia, hpd, org – *Blythe*
Harris, Richard Leigh, hpd – 01865 243306
Heilbron, Annette, hpd, f-pno – 01223 315681

Henry, John, hpd – 0171 586 7216
Hill, Robert, hpd – *Michael Brewer*
Hollick, Douglas, hpd, org – 01949 861347
    also fax; email: dwh@globalnet.co.uk
Hoyland, David, hpd – *Grosvenor*
Jones, Stephen, hpd, org, harmonium – 01727
    864007 *also fax;*
    email: 106510.1264@compuserve.com
Kenny, Courtney, hpd – *Grosvenor*
King, Robert, hpd – 0181 995 9994 *fax:* 0181
    995 2115 *email:* info@the-kings-consort.
    org.uk
Klosiewicz, Wladislaw, hpd – *Finch*
Koopman, Ton, hpd, org – *Magenta*
Ledingham, Iain, hpd – *Grosvenor*
Leigh, David, hpd, f-pno – 01865 244197;
    01608 810607
Leonhardt, Gustav, hpd – *Allied*
Lucas, Andrew, hpd, org – 0171 236 4257
Lumsden, Sir David, hpd – 01353 720100
    fax: 01353 720918
Malcolm, George CBE, hpd – *Holt*
Mallett, Charles, hpd – *Grosvenor*
May, Katharine, hpd – 0115 925 7851; 01753
    869103 *also fax*
Medhurst, Peter, hpd, early keyboards – c/o
    0181 673 1901
Mobbs, Kenneth, f-pno, hpd – 0117 973 3613
    also fax
Moroney, Davitt, hpd, org – *Michael Harrold*
Nash, Pamela, hpd – 01270 67895 *also fax*
Ng, Kah-Ming – 01865 723870 *also fax;*
    email: kah-ming.ng@music.oxford.ac.uk
Nicholls, Simon, f-pno – 0181 446 0812
Overbury, Michael, hpd, org – 01636 702054
Parnell, Andrew, harmonium, hpd – *Michael
    Harrold*
Parry, Martyn, hpd, org – 0181 980 9735 *also
    fax; email:* m.parry@herts.ac.uk
Patrick, David Kinnear, hpd – 0181 449 4873
Peacock, Gary, hpd – *Grosvenor*
Phillips, Margaret, org, hpd – 01963 250899
    fax: 01963 250999
Pinnock CBE, Trevor, hpd – *Holt*

Pleasants, Virginia, f-pno, hpd – 0171
    834 5011
Ponsford, David, hpd, org – 01285 651995
    also fax – *Camerata*
Pratley, Geoffrey, hpd – *Grosvenor*
Proud, Malcolm, hpd, org – 00 353 56 61497
    also fax
Pruslin, Stephen, hpd, chmbr org, f-pno, regal
    – 0181 948 7404 *also fax*
Puyana, Rafael, hpd – c/o 0171 722 7142 *fax:*
    0171 911 0904
Rennert, Jonathan, hpd, chmbr org – 0181 658
    9428 *also fax*
Rifkin, Joshua, hpd – *Clarion/Seven Muses*
Roblou, David, hpd, org, pno – c/o 0181 299
    1914 *also fax*
Rogers, Helen, hpd – *Michael Harrold*
Rowland, David, hpd, org, f-pno – *Music
    Management*
Rowland, Gilbert, hpd – 0181 699 2549 – *SJM*
Sawyer, Philip, hpd, org – 0131 455 6200
    fax: 0131 455 6211 *email:*
    p.sawyer@napier.ac.uk
Simmonds, Paul, hpd, clvd, chmbr org –
    01273 552548 *also fax*
Skuce, Peter, early keyboards – 0181 672
    1338 *also fax; email:* 100130.3053@
    compuserve.com
Souter, Martin, hpd, org – 01865 726553
    fax: 01865 243388
Titterington, David, org – *Denny
    Lyster*
Townend, Richard, hpd – 0171 589 1206
    fax: 0171 589 5925
Ward, David, f-pno, hpd – 0181 874 4938
    also fax
Ward Russell, Gillian, org – 01621 853237
Waterfield, Jan, hpd, chmbr org – 0171 834
    4951 *also fax*
Weir, Dame Gillian, org – *Denny Lyster*
Wilson-Dickson, Andrew, hpd, org – 01222
    228154 *also fax*
Zabal, Oscar Candendo, org – *Michael
    Harrold*

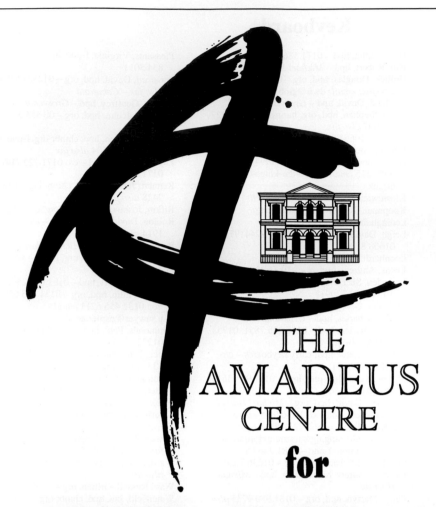

Recording
and
Broadcasting

Radio and Television

British Broadcasting Corporation

BBC Broadcast. Television Centre, Wood La, London W12 7RJ *tel:* 0181 743 8000. Will Wyatt, chief exec, broadcast; Alan Yentob, dir of television; David Docherty, deputy dir of television; Mark Thompson, controller, BBC2.

BBC Corporate Headquarters. Television Centre, Wood La, London W12 7RJ *tel:* 0171 580 4468. Sir Christopher Bland, chmn; John Birt, dir gen.

BBC Local Radio. BBC Regional Broadcasting, Room 704, Henry Wood House, 3 & 6 Langham Pl, London W1A 1AA *tel:* 0171 765 2801 *fax:* 0171 765 5838.

BBC Network Radio. Broadcasting House, London W1A 1AA *tel:* 0171 580 4468.

BBC World Service. Bush House, Strand, London WC2B 4PH *tel:* 0171 240 3456. Jenny Bild, executive producer mus.

BBC Worldwide. Woodlands, 80 Wood La, London W12 0TT *tel:* 0181 576 2000 *fax:* 0181 749 0538. Richard Emery. *Magazines, books, videos, spoken word, audio, multimedia, programme licensing, channels mgt, online services, mus publishing and licensing.*

BBC Radio Principal Music Executives

Radio 1. Yalding House, London W1N 6AJ *tel:* 0171 580 4468. Andy Parfitt, dep controller; Trevor Dann, head of mus entertainment.

Radio 2. 99 Gt Portland St, London W1A 1AA *tel:* 0171 765 0868. Jim Moir, controller; Lesley Douglas, mgr ed; Trevor Dann, head of mus; Brian Stephens, ed of programmes. Stella Hanson, exec producer, live mus and arts.

Radio 3. Broadcasting House, London W1 1AA *tel:* 0171 580 4468. Nicholas Kenyon, controller; Brian Barfield, mgr ed; John Evans, head of mus; William Robson, deputy head of mus. Martyn Westerman, commissioning ed mus (live); Hilary Boulding, commissioning ed mus

(policy): Andrew Kuroski, new mus ed; Graham Dixon, early mus ed; Andrew Lyle, sequence programmes ed; Edward Blakeman, snr producer, BBC Proms; Ann McKay, chief producer, BBC SO; Michael Emery, snr producer, BBC Singers; William Robson, chamber mus ed; Cathy Wearing, head of presentation; Donald MacLeod, ed night-time broadcasts.

Radio 4. Broadcasting House, London W1A 1AA *tel:* 0171 765 4422. James Boyle, controller.

Radio 5 Live. Broadcasting House, London W1A 1AA *tel:* 0171 580 4468. Jenny Abramsky, controller.

BBC Radio Production Centres Outside London

Midlands. BBC Radio 3, Broadcasting Centre, Pebble Mill Rd, Birmingham B5 7QQ *tel:* 0121 414 8888 *fax:* 0121 414 8156. Chris Marshall, exec producer, music unit; Jeremy Hayes, snr producer, music unit; Christina Pritchard, Chris Wines, producers, music unit; Chris Wines, producer -music unit.

North. BBC North, PO Box 27, Oxford Rd, Manchester M60 1SJ *tel:* 0161 200 2020. John Whiston, head of entertainment features; Ernie Rea, head of religious broadcasting; David Holdsworth, head of regional & local programmes, northwest.

Northern Ireland. BBC Radio Ulster, Broadcasting House, 25-27 Ormeau Av, Belfast BT2 8HQ *tel:* 01232 338000 *fax:* 01232 338800. Anna

Carragher, head of programmes; David Byers, snr mus producer; Terry Black, mus producer.

Scotland. BBC Radio Scotland, Broadcasting House, Queen Margaret Dr, Glasgow G12 8DG *tel:* 0141 339 8844 *fax:* 0141 357 1283; 0141 338 2792. Colin Cameron, head of production; Hugh Macdonald, dir BBC SSO.

Wales. BBC Radio Wales and Radio Cymru, Broadcasting House, Llantrisant Rd, Llandaff, Cardiff CF5 2YQ *tel:* 01222 322000 *fax:* 01222 552973. Nick Evans, Aled Glynne Davies, eds; Huw Tregelles Williams, dir of mus; Michael George, snr producer; Phil George, head, arts, music and features.

BBC Staff Orchestras and Choirs

Information on the BBC staff orchestras and choirs can be found under BBC in the **Symphony and Chamber Orchestras** and **Choirs and Choruses**.

BBC Local Radio Stations

The BBC Local Radio Stations are listed below. Additional information can be obtained from **BBC Regional Broadcasting Headquarters**, Room 715, Henry Wood House, 3 and 6 Langham Pl, London W1A 1AA *tel:* 0171 765 2795.

BBC Asian Network. Epic House, Charles St, Leicester LE1 3SH *tel:* 0116 251 6688. Pebble Mill Rd, Birmingham B5 7SD *tel:* 0121 414 8484. Vijay Sharma, ed.

BBC Coventry and Warwickshire. 25 Warwick Rd, Coventry CV1 2WR *tel:* 01203 559911 *fax:* 01203 520080. Caroline Wilson, snr producer; Conal O'Donnell, snr broadcast journalist.

BBC Essex. 198 New London Rd, Chelmsford, Essex CM2 9XB *tel:* 01245 262393 *fax:* 01245 492983 *email:* essex@nc.bbc.co.uk. Margaret Hyde, mgr ed.

BBC GLR. 35c Marylebone High St, London W1A 4LG *tel:* 0171 224 2424 *fax:* 0171 487 2908. Steve Panton, mgr ed.

BBC GMR Talk. PO Box 951, Oxford Rd, Manchester M60 1SD *tel:* 0161 244 3002 *fax:* 0161 236 5804. Karen Hannah, acting ed.

BBC Hereford and Worcestershire. Hylton Rd, Worcester WR2 5WW *tel:* 01905 748320/748485 *fax:* 01905 748006 *email:* 101574.1767@

compuserve.com. Eve Turner, ed; John Hayward-Warburton, classical mus producer.

BBC Radio Bristol. PO Box 194, Bristol BS99 7QT *tel:* 0117 974 1111 *fax:* 0117 923 8323. Michael Hapgood, mgr ed.

BBC Radio Cambridgeshire. Broadcasting House, PO Box 96, Cambridge CB2 1LD *tel:* 01223 259696 *fax:* 01223 460832. Nigel Dyson, mgr ed.

BBC Radio Cleveland. PO Box 95FM, Newport Rd, Middlesbrough TS1 5DG *tel:* 01642 225211 *fax:* 01642 211356. David Peel, mgr ed.

BBC Radio Cornwall. Phoenix Wharf, Truro, Cornwall TR1 1UA *tel:* 01872 275421 *fax:* 01872 240679. Leo Devine, mgr ed.

BBC Radio Cumbria. Annetwell St, Carlisle, Cumbria CA3 8BB *tel:* 01228 592444 *fax:* 01228 511195. John Watson, mgr ed.

BBC Radio Derby. PO Box 269, Derby DE1 3HL *tel:* 01332 361111 *fax:* 01332 290794. Mike Bettison, acting ed.

BBC Radio Devon. PO Box 5, Broadcasting House, Seymour Rd, Mannamead, Plymouth PL1 1XT *tel:* 01752 260323 *fax:* 01752 234599. Robert Bufton, mgr ed.

BBC Radio Foyle. 8 Northland Rd, Londonderry BT48 7JD *tel:* 01504 262244 *fax:* 01504 378666.

BBC Radio Gloucestershire. London Rd, Gloucester GL1 1SW *tel:* 01452 308585 *fax:* 01452 309491. Jenny Lacey, mgr ed.

BBC Radio Guernsey. Commerce House, Les Banques, St Peter Port GY1 2HS, Guernsey, Channel Islands *tel:* 01481 728977 *fax:* 01481 713557. Bob Lloyd-Smith, mgr ed.

BBC Radio Humberside. 9 Chapel St, Hull HU1 3NU *tel:* 01482 323232 *fax:* 01482 326038. Barrie Stephenson, acting ed.

BBC Radio Jersey. 18 Parade Rd, St Helier JE2 3PL, Jersey, Channel Islands *tel:* 01534 870000 *fax:* 01534 62569. Bob Lloyd-Smith, mgr ed.

BBC Radio Kent. Sun Pier, Chatham, Kent ME4 4EZ *tel:* 01634 409644. David Farwig, mgr ed.

BBC Radio Lancashire. 26 Darwen St, Blackburn, Lancs BB2 2EA *tel:* 01254 262411 *fax:* 01254 680821. Steve Taylor, mgr ed.

BBC Radio Leeds. Broadcasting House, Woodhouse La, Leeds LS2 9PN *tel:* 0113 244 2131 *fax:* 0113 242 0652. Ashley Peatfield, acting mgr ed.

BBC Radio Leicester. Epic House, Charles St, Leicester LE1 3SH *tel:* 01162 516688 *fax:* 01162 511463. Liam McCarthy, mgr ed.

BBC Radio Lincolnshire. PO Box 219, Newport, Lincoln LN1 3XY *tel:* 01522 511411 *fax:* 01522 511058. David Wilkinson, mgr ed.

BBC Radio Merseyside. 55 Paradise St, Liverpool L1 3BP *tel:* 0151 708 5500 *fax:* 0151 709 2394 (news); 0151 794 0988 (general). Mick Ord, mgr ed.

BBC Radio Newcastle. Broadcasting Centre, Barrack Rd, Newcastle upon Tyne NE99 1RN *tel:* 0191 232 4141 *fax:* 0191 232 5082. Tony Fish, mgr ed.

BBC Radio Norfolk. Norfolk Tower, Surrey St, Norwich, Norfolk NR1 3PA *tel:* 01603 617411 *fax:* 01603 633692. Tim Bishop, mgr ed.

BBC Radio Northampton. Broadcasting House, Abington St, Northampton NN1 2BE *tel:* 01604 239100 *fax:* 01604 230709. Claire Paul, mgr ed.

BBC Radio Nottingham. York House, Mansfield Rd, Nottingham NG1 3JB *tel:* 0115 955 0500 *fax:* 0115 955 0501. Peter Hagan, news and programmes ed.

BBC Radio Orkney. Castle St, Kirkwall, Orkney KW15 1DF *tel:* 01856 873939 *fax:* 01856 872908.

BBC Radio Scotland. High St, Selkirk TD7 4JX *tel:* 01750 21884 *fax:* 01750 22400. Carol Wightman, snr producer; Ninian Reid, network reporter.

BBC Radio Sheffield. Ashdell Grove, 60 Westbourne Rd, Sheffield S10 2QU *tel:* 0114 268 6185 *fax:* 0114 266 4375 *email:* radio.sheffield@bbc. co.uk. Barry Stockdale, ed.

BBC Radio Shropshire. 2-4 Boscobel Dr, Shrewsbury, Shropshire SY1 3TT *tel:* 01743 248484 *fax:* 01743 271702. Barbara Taylor, mgr ed.

BBC Radio Solent. Broadcasting House, Havelock Rd, Southampton SO14 7PW *tel:* 01703 631311 *fax:* 01703 339648. Chris van Schaick, mgr ed.

BBC Radio Stoke. Cheapside, Hanley, Stoke-on-Trent, Staffs ST1 1JJ *tel:* 01782 208080 *fax:* 01782 289115. Phil Ashworth, mgr ed; Mervyn Gamagé, asst ed.

BBC Radio Suffolk. Broadcasting House, St Matthew's St, Ipswich IP1 3EP *tel:* 01473 250000 *fax:* 01473 210887 *email:* suffolk@nc.bbc.co.uk. Ivan Howlett, mgr ed.

BBC Radio WM. Pebble Mill Rd, Birmingham B5 7SD *tel:* 0121 414 8484 *fax:* 0121 472 3174. Peter Davies, mgr ed.

BBC Radio York. 20 Bootham Row, York YO3 7BR *tel:* 01904 641351 *fax:* 01904 610937. Geoff Sargieson, Jane Sampson, mgr eds; Martin Cooper, asst ed.

BBC Shetland. Brentham House, Lerwick, Shetland ZE1 0LR *tel:* 01595 694747 *fax:* 01595 694307. Mary Blance, snr producer; Brian Flett, producer.

BBC Solent for Dorset. Broadcasting House, Havelock Rd, Southampton SO14 7PW *tel:* 01305 269654. Chris Van Schaick, ed.

BBC Solway. Elmbank, Lovers' Walk, Dumfries DG1 1NZ *tel:* 01387 268008 *fax:* 01387 252568.

BBC Somerset Sound. 14-15 Paul St, Taunton TA1 3PF *tel:* 01823 252437. Michael Hapgood, mgr ed.

BBC Southern Counties Radio. Broadcasting Centre, Guildford GU2 5AP *tel:* 01483 306306 *fax:* 01483 304952. Chris Van Schaick, acting mgr ed; Roger Mahony, snr producer.

BBC Thames Valley FM. 269 Banbury Rd, Oxford OX2 7DW *tel:* 0645 311444 *fax:* 0645 311555. Steve Egginton, mgr ed.

BBC Three Counties Radio. PO Box 3CR, Luton, Bedfordshire LU1 5XL *tel:* 01582 441000 *fax:* 01582 401467. David Robey, mgr ed.

BBC Wiltshire Sound. Broadcasting House, Prospect Pl, Swindon, Wilts SN1 3RW *tel:* 01793 513626 *fax:* 01793 513650 *email:* bbc.wiltshire. sound@dial.pipex.com. Sandy Milne, mgr ed.

Radio nan Gaidheal. Rosebank, Church St, Stornoway HS1 2LS *tel:* 01851 705000 *fax:* 01851 704633.

Radio Wales. The Old School House, Glanrafon Rd, Flintshire CH7 1PA *tel:* 01352 700367 *fax:* 01352 750919. Jane Morris, Gavin McCarthy, Alan Daulby, producers.

National Independent Radio Stations

Atlantic 252. 74 Newman St, London W1P 3LA *tel:* 0171 637 5252 *fax:* 0171 637 3925. Travis Baster, mgr dir; Henry Owens, programme dir; Paul Heaney, sales controller.

Classic FM. Academic House, 24-28 Oval Rd, London NW1 7DQ *tel:* 0171 284 3000 *fax:* 0171 713 2630. Murray Dudgeon, mgr dir; Steve Orchard, programme controller; Simon Ward, sales dir; Ralph Bernard, chief exec.

Talk Radio UK. 74 Newman St, London W1P 3LA *tel:* 0171 343 2222 *fax:* 0171 343 2230/2291. Paul Robinson, gen mgr; Travis Baxter, mgr dir; Steve Johnson, sales dir.

Virgin Radio. 1 Golden Sq, London W1R 4DJ *tel:* 0171 434 1215 *fax:* 0171 434 1197 *email:* virgin@vradio.co.uk; http://www.virginradio.co.uk. David Campbell, chief exec Virgin media group; John Pearson, mgr dir; Ian Grace, programme dir.

Independent Local Radio

Independent Local Radio (ILR) provides a daytime mix of information, education and entertainment, and the evening programmes are frequently of specialist or minority interest. International and national news is supplied by the Independent Radio News. Organisations concerned with independent broadcasting are to be found below and under **Independent Television**. Enquiries and comments concerning individual programmes should be addressed to the Press Office of the local ITV or ILR company. Complaints specifically concerning unfair or unjust treatment, or infringement of privacy should be made to the **Broadcasting Complaints Commission**, 7 The Sanctuary, London SW1P 3JS *tel:* 0171 233 0544.

Commercial Radio Companies Association (CRCA). 77 Shaftesbury Av, London W1V 7AD *tel:* 0171 306 2603 *fax:* 0171 470 0062. Paul Brown, chief exec. *Trade association for commercial radio companies, representing them to the Government, copyright organisations and other bodies with an interface with commercial radio. CRCA provides a forum for the radio companies and co-ordinates industry initiatives.*

Radio Advertising Bureau (RAB). 77 Shaftesbury Av, London W1V 7AD *tel:* 0171 306 2500 *fax:* 0171 306 2505 *email:* http://www.rab.co.uk.

RAB, the marketing company of commercial radio industry, provides an independent information service to advertisers. Also involved in publication of marketing material and organising consumer research.

The Radio Authority. Holbrook House, 14 Gt Queen St, London WC2B 5DG *tel:* 0171 430 2724 *fax:* 0171 405 7062. Tracey Mullins, press offr. *Licenses and regulates all Independent Radio Services. Plans frequencies; appoints licensees with a view to widening listener choice; and regulates programming and advertising.*

Local Radio Stations

The area of transmission of the radio station is shown in italics after each entry.

102.7 Hereward FM. PO Box 225, Queensgate Centre, Peterborough PE1 1XJ *tel:* 01733 460460 *fax:* 01733 281445. Lynda Couch-Smith, mgr dir; Stewart Francis, chmn. *Peterborough.*

103 FM Leicester Sound. Granville House, Granville Rd, Leicester LE1 7RW *tel:* 0116 256 1300 *fax:* 0116 256 1303. Carlton Dale, station dir; Colin Wilsher, programme controller. *Leicester.*

106.6 Star FM. Tristar Broadcasting Ltd, The Observatory Shopping Centre, Slough, Berkshire SL1 1LH *tel:* 01753 551066 *fax:* 01753 512277. Valerie Handley, mgr dir; Nick Ratcliffe, programme and mus mgr; Alan Keen, sales dir. *Slough, Maidenhead and Windsor.*

1152 Xtra AM. Radio House, Aston Rd North, Birmingham B6 4BX *tel:* 0121 359 4481 *fax:* 0121 359 1117 *email:* programmes@brmb.co. uk; sales@brmb.co.uk; news@brmb.co.uk. David Bagley, mgr dir. *Birmingham and Black Country.*

2CR FM/Classic Gold 828. 5-7 Southcote Rd, Bournemouth BH1 3LR *tel:* 01202 259259 *fax:* 01202 255244 *email:* sales@2crfm.musicradio. com; http://www.2crfm.co.uk; http://www.classicgold828.musicradio. com. Ian Andrews, chmn; Jeremy Lewis, mgr dir; Tom Hardy, programme controller 2CR FM; Chris Hopkins, Classic Gold co-ord. *Bournemouth.*

2-Ten FM/Classic Gold 1431. PO Box 2020, Reading, Berks RG3 5RZ *tel:* 0118 925 4400 *fax:* 0118 925 4456. Richard Palmer, chmn; Jeff Lee, station dir; Andrew Phillips, programme controller; Adrian Olney, sales dir. *Reading.*

95.8 Capital Gold FM. 30 Leicester Sq, London WC2H 7LA *tel:* 0171 766 6000 *fax:* 0171 766 6100. Martina King, station dir; Richard Park, programme dir; Fru Hazlitt, sales dir. *Greater London.*

96.3 Q FM. 26 Lady La, Paisley PA1 2LG *tel:* 0141 887 9630 *fax:* 0141 887 0963. Harry McNab OBE, chmn; Carol-Ann Morrison, mgr dir; John Collins, programme dir. *Paisley.*

96.4 FM BRMB. Radio House, Aston Rd North, Birmingham B6 4BX *tel:* 0121 359 4481 *fax:* 0121 359 1117 *email:* programmes@brmb.co. uk; sales@brmb.co.uk; news@brmb.co.uk. David Bagley, mgr dir. *Birmingham.*

96.4 The Eagle. Dolphin House, North St, Guildford GU1 4AA *tel:* 01483 300964 *fax:* 01483 531612. Mike Powell, chief exec and programme dir; Richard Lawley, mgr dir; Alan Keen, sales consultant. *W Surrey and NE Hampshire.*

96.7 City FM/Magic 1548. 8-10 Stanley St, Liverpoool L1 6AF *tel:* 0151 227 5100 *fax:* 0151 471 0330. Terry D Smith, chmn; Tom Hunter, mgr dir; Dave Shearer, programme dir. *Liverpool.*

963 Liberty. Golden Rose House, 26-27 Castlereagh St, London W1H 6DJ *tel:* 0171 706 9963 *fax:* 0171 706 0963. John Ogden, station dir. *Greater London.*

Aire FM. PO Box 2000, 51 Burley Rd, Leeds LS3 1LR *tel:* 0113 245 2299 *fax:* 0113 242 1830 *email:* http://www.airefm.co.uk. Jim Hicks, programmes dir; Stephen King, mgr dir. *Leeds.*

Alpha 103.2. Radio House, 11 Woodland Rd, Darlington, Co Durham DL3 7BJ *tel:* 01325 255552 *fax:* 01325 255551. Brian Lister, mgr dir; Mark Reason, programme controller; Nicola Smith, sales mgr. *Darlington, Newton Aycliffe and Sedgefield.*

Amber Radio. St George's Plain, 47-49 Colegate, Norwich NR3 1DB *tel:* 01603 630621 *fax:* 01603 666353. David Cargill, chmn; Bob Norman, mgr dir; Dave Brown, programme controller. *Norwich and Great Yarmouth, Bury and Ipswich.*

B97 FM. 55 Goldington Rd, Bedford, Beds MK40 3LS *tel:* 01234 272400 *fax:* 01234 218580. Sheila Mallett, mgr dir; Derek Flood, programme controller; Ian Wootton, sales dir.

The Bay. PO Box 969, St George's Quay, Lancaster LA1 3LD *tel:* 01524 848747. Julian Allitt, mgr dir; Kenni James, programme dir and deputy mgr ed; Matthew Allitt, sales dir. *North Lancashire and South Cumbria.*

Beacon Radio. 267 Tettenhall Rd, Wolverhampton WV6 0DQ *tel:* 01902 757211 *fax:* 01902 755163. A Henn, chmn; A V Mullett, mgr dir; P Wagstaff, programming dir. *Wolverhampton and Black Country, Shrewsbury and Telford.*

The Breeze. Radio House, Clifftown Rd, Southend-on-Sea, Essex SS1 1SX *tel:* 01702 333711 *fax:* 01702 345224 *email:* breeze@netforce.net. Rob van Pooss, mgr dir; Paul Chantler, programme dir. *Southend.*

Broadland FM/East Anglian Radio. St George's Plain, 47-49 Colegate, Norwich NR3 1DB *tel:* 01603 630621 *fax:* 01603 666353. Bob Norman, mgr dir; Dave Brown, programme controller; Sheryl Waterland, sales dir. *Norwich and Great Yarmouth.*

Brunel Classic Gold. PO Box 2020, Bristol BS99 7SN *tel:* 0117 984 3200 *fax:* 0117 984 3202. PO Box 2020, Swindon SN4 7EX *tel:* 01793 440300

fax: 01793 440302. Jana Rangooni, programme controller. *Bristol, Swindon, W Wiltshire and Bath.*

Cable Radio Milton Keynes (CRMK). 14 Vincent Av, Crownhill, Milton Keynes MK8 0AB *tel:* 01908 265266 *fax:* 01908 564893. M J Barry, mgr dir; T White, station mgr; N Craske, head of mus; S Wheeler, programme controller. *Milton Keynes.*

Central FM. Stirling Enterprise Pk, Kerse Rd, Stirling FK7 7YJ *tel:* 01786 451188 *fax:* 01786 461883. Grant Millard, mgr dir. *Falkirk, Stirling and Clackmannan districts.*

Century Radio. Century House, PO Box 100, Gateshead NE8 2YY *tel:* 0191 477 6666 *fax:* 0191 477 5660. John Myers, mgr dir; John Simons, programme dir; Sue Mills, head of sales. *North East.*

CFM. PO Box 964, Carlisle, Cumbria CA1 3NG *tel:* 01228 818964 *fax:* 01228 819444. Darrell Thomas, station mgr; Simon Grundy, head of programmes; Gill Garstan, head of news. *Carlisle and West Cumbria.*

Channel 103 FM. 6 Tunnell St, St Helier, Jersey JE2 4LU, Channel Islands *tel:* 01534 888103 *fax:* 01534 887799. Richard Johnson, mgr dir; Jenny Rhodes, sales dir; John Uphoff, head of mus. *Jersey.*

Channel Travel Radio. Main Control Building, Eurotunnel UK Terminal, PO Box 2000, Folkestone, Kent CT18 8XY *tel:* 01303 283873 *fax:* 01303 283874. Lisa Kerr, mgr dir; Michaela Segal, programme co-ord. *Along the M20 towards Folkestone and the Kent Channel ports.*

The Cheltenham Radio Station. The Regent Arcade, Cheltenham, Glos GL50 1JZ *tel:* 01242 699555 *fax:* 01242 699666. Oliver Blizzard, chmn; Mark Bondr, mgr dir; Peter Macfarlane, programme controller. *Cheltenham.*

Chiltern FM. Chiltern Rd, Dunstable, Beds LU6 1HQ *tel:* 01582 666001 *fax:* 01582 661725. Sharon Davies, station dir; Kevin Snowden, sales dir; Trevor James, programme controller.

Choice FM (Birmingham). 95 Broad St, Birmingham B15 1AU *tel:* 0121 616 1000 *fax:* 0121 616 1011. Stuart Reed, mgr dir; Colin Mason, group deputy chmn; Steve Wood, head of sales. *Birmingham.*

Choice FM (London). 16-18 Trinity Gardens, London SW9 8DP *tel:* 0171 738 7969 *fax:* 0171 738 6619. Patrick Berry, mgr dir; Vince Herbert, programme controller. *Brixton.*

Citybeat 96.7 FM. PO Box 967, Belfast BT9 6BN *tel:* 01232 205967 *fax:* 01232 200023. Karen Oyston, mgr dir; John Foley, chmn; Margaret Dunn, head of sales; Phil West, programme controller/head of music. *Belfast.*

Classic Gold 1332 AM. PO Box 225, Queensgate Centre, Peterborough PE1 1XJ *tel:* 01733 460460 *fax:* 01733 281445. Stewart Francis, chmn; Lynda Couch-Smith, mgr dir. *Peterborough.*

Classic Hits 96.6 FM. St Albans & Watford Broadcasting Co, The Broadcast Centre, 7 Hatfield Rd, St Albans AL1 3RS *tel:* 01727 831966 *fax:* 01727 834456. Geoffrey Hunter, chmn; Jeremy Lewis, station dir; Willie Morgan, programme controller. *St Albans and Watford.*

Clyde 1/Clyde 2. Clydebank Business Park, Clydebank, Glasgow G81 2RX *tel:* 0141 306 2200 *fax:* 0141 306 2265. James S Gordon CBE, chmn; Scottish Radio Holdings; Alex Dickson OBE, mgr dir, Radio Clyde. *Glasgow.*

Coast FM. The Studios, 41 Conway Rd, Colwyn Bay *tel:* 01492 534555 *fax:* 01492 535248. Godfrey W Williams, mgr dir and deputy chmn; Terry Underhill, programme dir; Matthew Allitt, sales dir. *North Wales Coast.*

Cool FM. PO Box 974, Belfast BT1 1RT *tel:* 01247 817181 *fax:* 01247 814974 *email:* music@coolfm.co.uk. John Paul Ballantine, head of mus and promotions; Joanne Steen, programming asst. *Belfast.*

County Sound 1476. Dolphin House, North St, Guildford GU1 4AA *tel:* 01483 300964 *fax:* 01483 531612. Mike Powell, chief exec; Peter Gordon, programme controller. *W Surrey and NE Hampshire.*

Downtown Radio. Newtownards, Co Down BT23 4ES *tel:* 01247 815555 *fax:* 01247 815252 *email:* programmes@downtown.co.uk; http://www. downtown.co.uk. James T Donnelly, chmn; David Sloan MBE, mgr dir; John Rosborough, head of programming. *Northern Ireland.*

Eleven Seventy AM. PO Box 1170, High Wycombe HP13 6YT *tel:* 01494 446611 *fax:* 01494 445400. Jim Leftwich, chmn; Keith Francis, mgr dir; Trevor Small, head of sales. *High Wycombe.*

Essex FM. Radio House, Clifftown Rd, Southend-on-Sea, Essex SS1 1SX *tel:* 01702 333711 *fax:* 01702 345224 *email:* essexfm@netforce.net. Rob van Pooss, mgr dir; Paul Chantler, programme dir. *Southend.*

Forth AM/Forth FM. Forth House, Forth St, Edinburgh EH1 3LF *tel:* 0131 556 9255 *fax:* 0131 558 3277 *email:* forth@srh.co.uk. Tom Steele, mgr dir; Jay Crawford, head of mus. *Edinburgh.*

Fortune 1458. PO Box 1458, Quay West, Trafford Park, Manchester M17 1FL *tel:* 0161 872 1458 *fax:* 0161 872 0206. Anthony Goldstone, chmn;

Colin Walters, chief exec; Mark Samaru, mgr dir; Chris Bird, head of sales. *Manchester.*

Fox FM. Brush House, Pony Rd, Cowley, Oxford OX4 2XR *tel:* 01865 871000 *fax:* 01865 871036 *email:* fox@foxfm.co.uk. Mark Flanagan, mgr dir; Julian Blackwell, chmn; Lyn Long, sales dir. *Oxford and Banbury.*

Galaxy 101. PO Box 1010, Bristol *tel:* 0117 901 0101 *fax:* 0117 901 4555. PO Box 1010, Cardiff *tel:* 01222 344101 *fax:* 01222 344111. Tony McVoy, chmn; Steve Parkinson, mgr dir; Simon Dennis, programme controller; Sarah Bernard, sales controller. *South Wales and the West.*

GEM AM. 29-31 Castle Gate, Nottingham NG1 7AP *tel:* 0115 952 7000 *fax:* 0115 912 9333 *email:* prog@gemam.musicradio.com. Chris Hughes, station dir; Paul Robey, programme controller. *Nottingham and Derby.*

Gemini AM. Hawthorn House, Exeter Business Park, Exeter, Devon EX1 3QS *tel:* 01392 444444 *fax:* 01392 444433. David Rodgers, mgr dir; Ivor Stolliday, chmn; Mike Allen, programme mgr; Mike O'Brien, head of sales. *Exeter, E Devon and Torbay.*

Gold Radio. Longmead, Shaftesbury, Dorset SP7 8QQ *tel:* 01747 855711 *fax:* 01747 855722. Tim Butcher, station mgr; David Jeffery, chmn.

Great North Radio. Radio House, Longrigg, Swalwell, Newcastle upon Tyne NE99 1BB *tel:* 0191 420 3040 *fax:* 0191 488 0933. Harry Dunn, mgr dir; Jim Brown, head of programmes; Liz Chapman, sales dir. *Tyne and Wear and Teeside.*

GWR FM (East). PO Box 2000, Swindon SN4 7EX *tel:* 01793 440300 *fax:* 01793 440302. Neil Cooper, station dir and sales dir; Scott Williams, programme controller. *Swindon and Wiltshire.*

GWR FM (West). PO Box 2000, Bristol BS99 7SN *tel:* 0117 984 3200 *fax:* 0117 984 3202. Simon Cooper, station dir; Dirk Anthony, programme controller. *Bristol.*

Hallam FM/Great Yorkshire Gold AM. Radio House, 900 Herries Rd, Hillsborough, Sheffield S6 1RH *tel:* 0114 285 3333 *fax:* 0114 285 3159 *email:* programmes@hallamfm.co.uk. Tony McKenzie, programme controller; Nik Walshe, news mgr. *Sheffield, Rotherham, Barnsley and Doncaster.*

Heart FM. PO Box 1007, 1 The Square, 111 Broad St, Edgbaston, Birmingham B15 1AS *tel:* 0121 626 1007 *also fax.* Viscountess Cobham, chmn; Philip Riley, mgr dir; Don Thomson, sales dir; Paul Fairbairn, programme dir. *West Midlands.*

Heartland FM. Lower Oakfield, Pitlochry, Perthshire PH16 5HQ *tel:* 01796 474040 *fax:* 01796 474007. Michael Dobson, chmn; Martin Hobson, technical dir; Iain Gillespie, programme controller; Brendan Murphy, sales dir. *Pitlochry and Aberfeldy.*

FM 103 Horizon. Broadcast Centre, Crownhill, Milton Keynes, Bucks MK8 0AB *tel:* 01908 269111 *fax:* 01908 564893. Richard Godber, chmn; Richard Robinson, station dir; Steve Fountain, programme controller. *Milton Keynes.*

Invicta FM/Invicta Supergold. Radio House, John Wilson Business Park, Whitstable, Kent CT5 3QX *tel:* 01227 772004 *fax:* 01227 771558. Glen London, station dir; Paul Jackson, programme mgr. *Maidstone, Medway, East Kent, Canterbury, Ashford, Thanet.*

Island FM. 12 Westerbrook St, Sampson, Guernsey *tel:* 01481 42000 *fax:* 01481 49676 *email:* kevin@islandfm.guernsey.net; http://www.islandfm.guernsey.net. Kevin Stewart, mgr dir and programme controller; Fiona Brooks, news ed; Maureen Street, head of promotions. *Guernsey.*

Isle of Wight Radio. Dodnor Pk, Newport, Isle of Wight PO30 5XE *tel:* 01983 822557 *fax:* 01983 821690. Chris Carnegy, mgr dir; Andy Shier, programme dir; Stuart McGinley, head of mus. *Isle of Wight.*

Jazz FM 100.4. The World Trade Centre, Exchange Quay, Manchester M5 3EJ *tel:* 0161 877 1004 *fax:* 0161 877 1005. Richard Wheatley, chief exec; Mick Carter, station mgr. *North West.*

KCBC 1584 AM. Centre 2000, Unit 1, Robinson Close, Telford Way Industrial Estate, Kettering, Northants NN16 8UP *tel:* 01536 412413 *fax:* 01536 517390. Jon Shipton, station mgr; Richard Oliff, news ed; Paul Thompson, programme controller. *Kettering, Corby, Wellingborough.*

Key 103 FM. 127-131 The Piazza, Piccadilly Plaza, Manchester M1 4AW *tel:* 0161 236 9913 *fax:* 0161 228 1503. David Lincoln, mgr dir; John Dash, programme dir; Barbara Gardner, sales dir. *Greater Manchester.*

KFM. 1 East Street, Tonbridge, Kent TN9 1AR *tel:* 01732 369200 *fax:* 01732 369201. Andy Gemmell-Smith, chmn; Andrew Dean, mgr dir and head of sales; Gavin McCoy, programme dir. *Greater London.*

Kiss 100 FM. Kiss House, 80 Holloway Rd, London N7 8JG *tel:* 0171 700 6100 *fax:* 0171 700 3979. Mike Soutar, mgr dir; Lorna Clarke, programme controller. *Greater London.*

Kiss 102. PO Box 102, Manchester M60 1GJ *tel:* 0161 228 0102 *fax:* 0161 228 1020. William Burdett Coutts, chmn; Guy Hornsby, mgr dir; Mike Gray, programme controller; Julian Martin, sales controller. *Greater Manchester.*

Kix 96. PO Box 962, Coventry CV1 4XX *tel:* 01203 525656 *fax:* 01203 551744. Nic Tuff, head of presentation; Ginny Murfin, mgr dir. *Coventry and Warwickshire.*

KL FM. PO Box 77, 18 Blackfriars St, Kings Lynn, Norfolk PE30 1NN *tel:* 01553 772777 *fax:* 01553 767200. Stewart Francis, chmn; John Sanderson, station mgr and sales dir; Craig Morris, programme controller. *Kings Lynn.*

Lantern FM. The Light House, Market Pl, Bideford, North Devon EX39 2DR *tel:* 01237 424444 *fax:* 01237 423333. John Greenstreet, general mgr and programme controller; Paul Hopper, head of mus. *North Devon.*

LBC 1152 AM. 72 Hammersmith Rd, London W14 8YE *tel:* 0171 973 1152 *fax:* 0171 371 2300. Martin Wheatley, mgr dir; Martin Ball, sales mgr. *Greater London.*

Lincs FM 102.2. Witham Pk, Waterside South, Lincoln LN5 7JN *tel:* 01522 549900 *fax:* 01522 549911 *email:* lincsfm@msn.com. Jane Hill, programme controller; Sean Dunderdale, news ed; Eddie Shaw, playlist. *Lincolnshire, former South Humberside and Newark.*

London Greek Radio. Florentia Village, Vale Rd, London N4 1TD *tel:* 0181 800 8001 *fax:* 0181 800 8005. A Yerolemou, mgr dir; G Gregoriou, programme controller; C Harmanda, sales dir. *Haringey.*

London Newstalk Radio/London News Radio. Crown House, 72 Hammersmith Rd, London W14 8YE *tel:* 0171 333 0400 *fax:* 0171 333 2348. Martin Wheatley, mgr dir; Martin Ball, sales mgr. *Greater London.*

Magic 828. PO Box 2000, 51 Burley Rd, Leeds LS3 1LR *tel:* 0113 245 2299 *fax:* 0113 242 1830 *email:* http://www.magic828.co.uk. Steve King, mgr dir; Jim Hicks, programme dir. *Leeds.*

Magic AM. Radio House, 900 Herries Rd, Sheffield S6 1RH *tel:* 0114 285 2121 *fax:* 0114 285 3159. Lynn Wood, mgr dir; Tony Mackenzie, programme dir; Tony Wilkinson, sales dir. *Yorkshire, Lincolnshire.*

Manx Radio. PO Box 1368, Broadcasting House, Douglas, Isle of Man IM99 1SW *tel:* 01624 661066 *fax:* 01624 661411. C Fargher, chmn; Stewart Watterson, mgr dir; Sue Bradshaw, sales mgr; George Ferguson, programme controller. *Isle of Man.*

Marcher Coast 96.3 FM. 41 Conwy Rd, Colwyn Bay, Clwyd LL28 5AB *tel:* 01492 534555 *fax:* 01492 535248 *email:* mfm.radio@ukonline.co.uk. Martin Thomas QC OBE, chmn; Godfrey W Williams, mgr dir and deputy chmn; Terry Underhill, programme dir. *North Wales Coast.*

Marcher Gold. The Studios, Mold Rd, Wrexham, Clywd LL11 4AF *tel:* 01978 752202 *fax:* 01978 759701. Godfrey W Williams, mgr dir and deputy chmn; Kevin Howard, programme controller; Terry Underhill, programme dir. *Wrexham, Deeside and Chester.*

Melody FM. 180 Brompton Rd, Knightsbridge, London SW3 1HF *tel:* 0171 584 1054 *fax:* 0171 581 7000. Sheila Porritt, mgr dir; Peter Black, head of presentation; Gary Johnson, sales dir. *Greater London.*

Mercia FM/Mercia Classic Gold. Hertford Pl, Coventry CV1 3TT *tel:* 01203 868200 *fax:* 01203 868202. Steve Dawson, programme controller. *Coventry.*

Mercury FM. Broadfield House, Brighton Rd, Crawley, W Sussex RH11 9TT *tel:* 01293 519161 *fax:* 01293 565663. Peter McPartland, mgr dir; Carole Straker, programme dir; Neil Macadam, sales dir. *Reigate and Crawley.*

Metro FM. Long Rigg, Swalwell, Newcastle upon Tyne NE99 1BB *tel:* 0191 420 0971 *fax:* 0191 488 9222. Giles Squire, acting mgr dir; Giles Squire, programme dir; Liz Chapman, sales dir.

MFM. The Studios, Mold Rd, Gwersyllt Wrexham, Clwyd LL11 4AF *tel:* 01978 752202 *fax:* 01978 759701 *email:* mfm.radio@ukonline.co.uk. Terry Underhill, programme dir; Kevin Howard, programme controller. *Chester, North Wales, parts of Shropshire, Wirral and Merseyside.*

Minster FM. PO Box 123, York YO1 5ZX *tel:* 01904 488888 *fax:* 01904 488878. Lynn Bell, station mgr; Howard Presman, programme controller. *York.*

Mix 96. Friars Square Studios, 11 Bourbon St, Aylesbury, Bucks HP20 2PZ *tel:* 01296 399396 *fax:* 01296 398988 *email:* mix@mix96.demon.co.uk. Richard Morris-Adams, chmn; Mark Flanagan, dir; Henry Aubrey-Fletcher, dir; Erika Sorby-Firth, mgr dir. *Aylesbury.*

Moray Firth Radio Ltd. PO Box 271, Inverness IV3 6SF *tel:* 01463 224433 *fax:* 01463 243224. Thomas Prag, mgr dir; Ray Atkinson, programme controller; Tich McCooey, head of mus. *North Scotland.*

Nevis Radio. Inverlochy, Fort William, Inverness-shire PH33 6LU *tel:* 01397 700007 *fax:* 01397 701007 *email:* nevisradio@lochaber.co. uk. Ray Sutherland, chmn; Ian Sykes, vice-chmn; Raymond Hervo, mgr dir; Gina Kennedy, sales. *Fort William.*

North East Community Radio. Town House, Aberdeenshire AB51 0US *tel:* 01467 632878 *fax:* 01467 632969. Colin Strong, chmn and mgr dir; John Dean, programme controller; Margaret MacNaughton, head of sales. *Inverurie.*

Northants 96/Classic Gold 1557. 19-21 St Edmunds Rd, Northampton NN1 5DY *tel:* 01604 795600 *fax:* 01604 795601 *email:* reception@ northants96.musicradio.com. Robert Moore, chmn; Mark Lee, mgr dir; Terry Doyle, programme controller. *Northampton.*

Northsound One/Northsound Two. 45 King's Gate, Aberdeen AB15 4EL *tel:* 01224 632234 *fax:* 01224 633282 (news); 01224 637289. John Martin, programme dir; Fiona Stalker, head of news; Gary Stein, head of mus, Northsound One; Gerry Burke, head of mus, Northsound Two. *Aberdeen.*

Ocean FM. Radio House, Whittle Av, Segensworth West, Fareham, Hants PO15 5PA *tel:* 01489 589911 *fax:* 01489 589453. Sally Oldham, station dir; Nik Martin, programme controller; Jane Finden, sales mgr. *Portsmouth, Southampton and Winchester.*

Orchard FM. Haygrove House, Shoreditch, Taunton, Somerset TA3 7BT *tel:* 01823 338448 *fax:* 01823 321044. Howard Bowles, gen mgr; Phil Easton, programme controller; Lindsey Ashwood, newsroom mgr. *Yeovil and Taunton.*

Piccadilly 1152/Key 103. 127-131 The Piazza, Piccadilly Plaza, Manchester M1 4AW *tel:* 0161 236 9913 *fax:* 0161 228 1503. John Dash, programme dir; Christian Smith, head of mus; Dave Lincoln, mgr dir. *Greater Manchester.*

Pirate FM. Cam Brea Studios, Wilson Way, Redruth, Cornwall TR15 3XX *tel:* 01209 314400 *fax:* 01209 314345. James St Aubyn, chmn; Joseph Swain, mgr dir; Stephen Roan, programme and operations mgr. *Cornwall, Plymouth and West Devon.*

Plymouth Sound. Earl's Acre, Alma Rd, Plymouth PL3 4HX *tel:* 01752 227272 *fax:* 01752 670730. Graham Gilbert, mgr dir; Louise Churchill MBE, chmn; Linda Horswell, sales dir. *Plymouth.*

Power FM. Radio House, Whittle Av, Segensworth West, Fareham, Hants PO15 5SH *tel:* 01489 589911 *fax:* 01489 589453. Sally Oldham, station dir; Anthony Brook, chmn; Jane Finden, sales mgr. *Portsmouth, Southampton and Winchester.*

Premier Radio. Glen House, Stag Pl, London SW1E 5AG *tel:* 0171 233 6705 *fax:* 0171 233 6706. Peter Kerridge, station dir; David Heron, mgr dir. *Greater London.*

The Pulse. PO Box 3000, Bradford BD1 5NE *tel:* 01274 731521 *fax:* 01274 307774. Neil S Robinson, chmn; John I Josephs, mgr dir; Steve Martin, programme dir; Sue Timson, sales dir. *Bradford, Huddersfield and Halifax.*

Q102.9. The Old Waterside Railway Station, Duke St, Waterside, Londonderry BT47 1DH *tel:* 01504 44449 *fax:* 01504 311177 *email:* frank@q102-fm.com. Raymond Cowan, chmn; Frank McLaughlin, mgr dir; Trevor Thomas, programme controller; Joan O'Connor, head of sales. *Londonderry.*

Q103. PO Box 103, The Vision Park, Chivers Way, Histon, Cambridge CB4 4WW *tel:* 01223 235255 *fax:* 01223 235161. Craig Morris, programme controller; Alistair Wayne, station dir. *Cambridge and Newmarket.*

RTL Country 1035 AM. 76 Oxford St, London W1N 0TR *tel:* 0171 546 1035 *fax:* 0171 546 1020. Travis Baxter, mgr dir; Paul Robinson, gen mgr; David Atkey, operations dir. *Greater London.*

Radio Borders. Tweedside Pk, Galashiels, Selkirkshire TD1 3TD *tel:* 01896 759444 *fax:* 01896 759494. Rod Webster, station mgr; Danny Gallagher, head of mus. *Borders, North Northumberland.*

Radio Broadland. St George's Plain, 47-49 Colegate, Norwich, Norfolk NR3 1DB *tel:* 01603 630621 *fax:* 01603 666353. Bob Norman, mgr dir; Dave Brown, programme controller; Julian Smith, head of news. *Great Yarmouth and Norwich.*

Radio Ceredigion. Yr Hen Ysgol Gymraeg, Ffordd Alexandra, Aberystwyth SY23 1PE *tel:* 01970 627999 *fax:* 01970 627206. Ellen ap Gwynn, gen mgr; Geraint Davies, chmn; Victor Edwards, head of sales. *Aberystwyth.*

Radio Maldwyn. The Studios, The Park, Newtown, Powys SY16 2NZ *tel:* 01686 623555 *fax:* 01686 623666. Kenn Morris, programme controller and station mgr; Mary Davies, sales; Sue Charles, news ed. *Montgomeryshire.*

Radio Tay. PO Box 123, 6 North Isla St, Dundee DD1 9UF *tel:* 01382 200800 *fax:* 01382 593252. Alex Wilkie, mgr dir; Arthur Ballingall, programme dir. *Dundee and Perth.*

Radio Wyvern plc. Barbourne Terrace, Worcester WR1 3JS *tel:* 01905 612212 *fax:* 01905 612849. Norman Bilton, mgr dir and programme controller; Mike Morgan, head of sales. *Hereford and Worcester.*

Radiowave. 965 Mowbray Dr, Blackpool, Lancs FY3 7JR *tel:* 01253 304965 *fax:* 01253 301965. John Barnett, mgr dir; Simon Tats, programme dir; John Chapman, sales dir. *Blackpool.*

Ram FM. The Market Place, Derby DE1 3AA *tel:* 01332 292945 *fax:* 01332 292229. Phil Dixon, mgr dir; Rev Ben Lewes, chmn; Rob Wagstaff, programme controller. *Derby.*

Red Dragon FM. Radio House, West Canal Wharf, Cardiff CF1 5XJ *tel:* 01222 384041 *fax:* 01222 384014. Phil Roberts, mgr dir; Beverly Cleall-Harding, sales dir; Glynne Clay, chmn. *Cardiff and Newport.*

Red Rose Gold/Red Rose FM. PO Box 301, St Paul's Sq, Preston, Lancs PR1 1XR *tel:* 01772 556301 *fax:* 01772 201917. Tom Finney, chmn; Tom Hunter, mgr dir. *Preston and Blackpool.*

RTL Country 1035 AM. 76 Oxford St, London W1A 1PP *tel:* 0171 546 1000 *fax:* 0171 546 1030. Travis Baxter, mgr dir; Stan Park, sales dir. *Greater London.*

RTM (Independent Radio Thamesmead). The Company Offices, Harrow Manor Way, Thamesmead South, London SE2 9XH *tel:* 0181 311 3112 *fax:* 0181 312 1930. Rodney Collins, mgr dir; Ken Murray, station co-ord; Sammy Bell, head of mus; Eddie Startup, sales dir. *Thamesmead.*

Scot FM. Number 1 Shed, Albert Quay, Leith, Edinburgh EH6 7DN *tel:* 0131 554 6677 *fax:* 0131 554 2266. Michael J Connolly, chmn; Norman L Quirk, mgr dir; Jeff Graham, programme controller. *Central Scotland.*

Severn Sound/Severn Sound Supergold. Broadcast Centre, 67 Southgate St, Gloucester GL1 2DQ *tel:* 01452 423791 *fax:* 01452 423008. Penelope Holton, station dir; Andy Westgate, programme controller. *Gloucester and Cheltenham.*

SGR Colchester. Abbeygate Two, 9 Whitewell Rd, Colchester CO2 7DE *tel:* 01206 575859 *fax:* 01206 561199. Russell Stuart, mgr dir; Danny Cox, station mgr; Robb Young, sales dir. *Colchester.*

SGR FM (Bury). PO Box 250, Bury St Edmunds, Suffolk IP33 1AD *tel:* 01284 702622 *fax:* 01473 741200. David Cargill, chmn; Russell Stuart, mgr dir; Mike Stewart, programme dir; Robb Young, sales dir. *Bury St Edmunds.*

SGR FM (Ipswich). Radio House, Alpha Business Park, White House Rd, Ipswich, Suffolk IP1 5LT *tel:* 01473 461000 *fax:* 01473 741200. David Cargill, chmn; Russell Stuart, mgr dir; Mike Stewart, programme dir; Robb Young, sales dir. *Ipswich.*

Shetland Islands Broadcasting Company (SIBC). Market St, Lerwick, Shetland ZE1 0JN *tel:* 01595 695299 *fax:* 01595 695696. Inga Walterson, head of mus.

Signal Cheshire. Regent House, Heaton La, Stockport SK4 1BX *tel:* 0161 285 4545 *fax:* 0161 285 1010. Barry Machin, mgr dir; Paul Allen, programme dir. *South Manchester and Cheshire.*

Signal Gold/Signal One. Stoke Rd, Stoke-on-Trent ST4 2SR *tel:* 01782 747047 *fax:* 01782 744110. Barry Machin, mgr dir; John Evington, programme dir; Glyn Owen, sales dir. *Staffordshire and Cheshire.*

Sound Wave. Swansea Sound Ltd, Victoria Rd, Gowerton, Swansea SA4 3AB *tel:* 01792 893751 *fax:* 01792 898841. Terry Mann, mgr dir; Charles Braham, chmn; Rob Pendry, head of programmes. *Swansea.*

South Coast Radio. Radio House, Whittle Av, Segensworth West, Fareham, Hants PO15 5PA *tel:* 01489 589911 *fax:* 01489 589453. Radio House, PO Box 2000, Brighton BN41 2SS *tel:* 01273 430111 *fax:* 01273 430098. Bob Hoad, Sally Oldham, station dirs (Brighton and Portsmouth); Mark Sadler, programme controller. *Portsmouth, Southampton, Winchester, Brighton.*

South West Sound. Campbell House, Bankend Rd, Dumfries DT1 4TH *tel:* 01387 50999 *fax:* 01387 65629. Joseph Campbell, mgr dir; Gordon McArthur, programme dir; Colin Thorne, sales dir. *Dumfries and Galloway.*

Southern FM. Radio House, PO Box 2000, Brighton BN41 2SS *tel:* 01273 430111 *fax:* 01273 424783. Mark Sadler, programme controller; Bob Hoad, station dir. *Sussex.*

Spectrum Radio 558 FM. Ingate Place, 204-206 Queenstown Rd, London SW8 3NR *tel:* 0171 627 4433 *fax:* 0171 627 3409 *email:* 106066. 2375@compuserve.com. Wolfgang Bucci, mgr dir; Franco Baitwa, production engineer. *Greater London.*

Spire FM. City Hall Studios, Malthouse La, Salisbury, Wiltshire SP2 7QQ *tel:* 01722 416644. Peter MacFarlane, head of mus; Chris Carnegy, mgr dir; Gary Haderfield, head of sales. *Salisbury.*

Spirit FM. Dukes Ct, Bognor Rd, Chichester PO19 2FX *tel:* 01243 773600 *fax:* 01243 786464 *email:* spiritfm@townchoice.co.uk. Stephen Oates, mgr dir; Kevin Dyball, programme mgr; Jacqui Kavanagh, local sales mgr; Adam Porter, news ed. *Chichester, Bognor Regis, Littlehampton, Arundel and Sussex.*

Stray FM. Stray Studios, PO Box 972, Station Parade, Harrogate HG1 5YF *tel:* 01423 522972 *fax:* 01423 522922. Erik Thompson, chmn; Ann Dyson, mgr dir; Steve Parsley, news ed; Ray Stroud, programme controller. *North Yorkshire.*

Sun City 103.4. PO Box 1034, Sunderland SR1 3YZ *tel:* 0191 567 3333 *fax:* 0191 567 0888. Bruce Davidson, station mgr; John Foster, head of presentation; Robin Griffiths, head of mus. *Sunderland.*

Sunshine 855. Waterside, Ludlow, Shropshire SY8 1GS *tel:* 01584 877855 *fax:* 01584 875900. Graham Symonds, mgr dir; Mark Edwards, programme controller. *Ludlow.*

Swansea Sound/SoundWave. Victoria Rd, Gowerton, Swansea, W Glamorgan SA4 3AB *tel:* 01792 511170/511964 *fax:* 01792 511171/511965. Terry Mann, mgr and programme dir; Andy Griffiths, FM programme mgr; Lynn Courtney, head of news; Sue Timson, sales and mkt dir. *Swansea.*

Tay FM. 6 North Isla St, Dundee DD3 7JQ *tel:* 01382 200800 *fax:* 01382 593252. Alex Wilkie, mgr dir; Arthur Ballingall, programme dir; Ian F Reilly, sales dir. *Dundee and Perth.*

Ten 17. Latton Bush Centre, Southern Way, Harlow, Essex CM18 7BU *tel:* 01279 432415 *fax:* 01279 445289. Eric Moonman, chmn; David Lucas, mgr dir; Peter Kerridge, station mgr and programme controller; Rob van Pooss, head of sales. *Harlow.*

TFM. Yale Cres, Thornaby, Stockton-on-Tees, Cleveland TS17 6AA *tel:* 01642 615111 *fax:* 01642 674402. Harry Dunne, mgr dir; Graham Ledger, programme dir. *Teesside.*

Touch AM. PO Box 99, Cardiff CF1 5YJ *tel:* 01222 237878 *fax:* 01222 373011. Phil Roberts, mgr dir; Beverly Cleall-Harding, sales dir; Simon Walkington, programme controller; Nick Davidson, promotions and sponsorship mgr. *Cardiff and Newport.*

Townland Radio. PO Box 828, Cookstown, Co Tyrone BT80 9LQ *tel:* 016487 64828 *fax:* 016487 63828. John O'Hagan, mgr; Donagh McKeown, production and programme controller. *Mid Ulster.*

Trent FM. 29-31 Castle Gate, Nottingham NG1 7AP *tel:* 0115 952 7000 *fax:* 0115 958 8614. Chris Hughes, station dir; Rob Wagstaff, programme controller. *Nottingham.*

Viking FM. Commercial Rd, Hull HU1 2SG *tel:* 01482 325141 *fax:* 01482 587067. Phil White, programme dir; Lynn Bell, sales dir; Dee Ford, mgr dir. *East Riding of Yorkshire and North Lincolnshire.*

WABC. Box 303, 267 Tettenhall Rd, Wolverhampton WV6 0DQ *tel:* 01902 757211 *fax:* 01902 755163. A V Mullett, mgr dir; P Wagstaff, programming dir. *Wolverhampton and Black Country, Shropshire.*

Wessex FM. Radio House, Trinity St, Dorchester, Dorset DT1 1DJ *tel:* 01305 250333 *fax:* 01305 250052. Stephen Oates, mgr dir; John Baker, general mgr; Peter Bolton, chmn; Jane Soole, news ed. *Weymouth and Dorchester.*

West Sound Radio plc. Radio House, Holmston Rd, Ayr KA7 3BE *tel:* 01292 283662 *fax:* 01292 283665. Paul Cooney, mgr dir; Gordon McArthur, programme dir and head of news; Kenny Campbell, head of mus. *Ayrshire, Dumfries and Galloway.*

West Yorkshire's Classic Gold. Forster Sq, Bradford BD1 5NE *tel:* 01274 203040 *fax:* 01274 203130 *email:* general@pulse.co.uk. John J Josephs, mgr dir; Steve Martin, programme dir; Paul Thornton, sales dir; Geoff Hemming, programme mgr. *West Yorkshire.*

Wey Valley Radio. Prospect Pl, Mill La, Alton, Hants GU34 2SY *tel:* 01420 544444 *fax:* 01420 544044 *email:* wvr@dial.pipex.com. David Way, mgr dir and programme controller; Kim Robson, head of news; Kevin Huffer, commercial production.

Yorkshire Coast Radio. PO Box 962, Scarborough, North Yorkshire YO12 5YX *tel:* 01723 500962 *fax:* 01723 501050 *email:* http://www.yorkshirecoast.co.uk/ycr. Thomas Pindar OBE, chmn; Jerry Scott, station mgr and programme controller; Lynn Bell, head of sales; Howard Nurse, head of news. *Scarborough.*

BBC Television Principal Music Executives

BBC Television. Television Centre, Wood La, London W12 7RJ *tel:* 0181 743 8000. *Will Wyatt, chief exec, broadcast; Alan Yentob, dir of television; David Docherty, deputy dir of television; Mark Thompson,* *controller BBC2; Keith Samuel, controller, press and PR, broadcast; Kim Evans, head of arts; Trevor Dann, head of mus entertainment; Roger Wright, head of classical mus; Avril MacRory, head of classical mus TV.*

Independent Television

Organisations concerned with independent television broadcasting are listed below, followed by the independent television and production companies. The area of transmission is indicated in italics.

Independent Television Commission. 33 Foley St, London W1P 7LB *tel:* 0171 255 3000 *fax:* 0171 306 7800 *email:* 100731.3515@ compuserve.com. Sir George Russell CBE, chmn; The Earl of Dalkeith, deputy chmn; Peter Rogers, chief exec; Clare Mulholland, deputy chief exec. *Under the terms of the Broadcasting Act 1996, the ITC is the public body responsible for licensing and regulating all commercially-funded television in the United Kingdom through codes on programme content, advertising, sponsorship and technical standards.*

Independent Television Network Centre. 200 Gray's Inn Rd, London WC1X 8HF *tel:* 0171 843 8000 *fax:* 0171 843 8158. Marcus Plantin, network dir; Barry Cox, dir of ITV Association; Mike Southgate, commercial dir.

ITC East of England. 24 Castle Meadow, Norwich NR1 3DH *tel:* 01603 623533 *fax:* 01603 633631. Peter Monteith, regional exec.

ITC Midlands and East. 10-11 Poultry, Nottingham NG1 2HW *tel:* 0115 952 7333 *fax:* 0115 952 7353. Lyndon House, 62 Hagley Rd, Birmingham B16 8PE *tel:* 0121 693 0662 *fax:* 0121 693 2753. Janet Wootton, regional offr; Sally Laverack, Peter Monteith, regional execs.

ITC North-East England, The Borders and Isle of Man. 3 Collingwood St, Newcastle upon Tyne NE1 1JS *tel:* 0191 261 0148 *fax:* 0191 261 1158. Robert Conlon, regional exec.

ITC North of England. The Workstation, 15 Paternoster Row, Sheffield S1 2BX *tel:* 0114 276 9091 *fax:* 0114 276 9089. Michael Fay, regional offr.

ITC North-West England. Television House, Mount St, Manchester M2 5WT *tel:* 0161 834 2707 *fax:* 0161 835 3513. Louise Bennett, exec.

ITC Northern Ireland. Albany House, 75 Gt Victoria St, Belfast BT2 7AF *tel:* 01232 248733 *fax:* 01232 322828.

ITC Scotland. 123 Blythswood St, Glasgow G2 4AN *tel:* 0141 226 4436 *fax:* 0141 226 4682. Brian Marjoribanks, offr for Scotland; Alan Stewart, regional exec; Veronica McDowall, asst offr for Scotland.

ITC South and The Channel Islands. Kings Worthy Ct, Kings Worthy, Winchester SO23 7QA *tel:* 01962 883950 *fax:* 01962 848631. Jean Young, regional offr.

ITC South-West England. Royal London House, 153 Armada Way, Plymouth PL1 1HY *tel:* 01752 663031 *fax:* 01752 662490. Nicholas Bull, regional exec.

ITC Wales and West of England. 2nd Floor, Elgin House, 106 St Mary St, Cardiff CF1 1PA *tel:* 01222 384541 *fax:* 01222 223157. Stella Mair Thomas, offr.

Producers Alliance for Cinema and Television (PACT). 45 Mortimer St, London W1N 7TD *tel:* 0171 331 6000 *fax:* 0171 331 6700. *Trade association and employers' body for film and independent TV producers.*

Royal Television Society (RTS). Holborn Hall, 100 Gray's Inn Rd, London WC1X 8AL *tel:* 0171 430 1000 *fax:* 0171 430 0924 *email:* publication@ royaltvsociety.demon.co.uk. Peter Fiddick, ed; Louise Bishop, deputy ed; Sue Griffith, production ed. *Independent forum for discussions of all aspects of television open to all working in or with an interest in television. Magazine published 8 times a year.*

Television and Radio Industries Club. Drake House, 2 Duckling La, Sawbridgeworth, Herts CN21 9QA *tel:* 01279 721100 *fax:* 01279 723100. George Stone, dir and sec.

Independent Television Companies

National Companies

British Sky Broadcasting. Grant Way, Isleworth, Middx TW7 5QD *tel:* 0171 705 3000 *fax:* 0171 705 3030. Rupert Murdoch, chmn; Sam Chisholm, chief exec and mgr dir; Mo Darbyshire, head of mus.

Channel Four Television Corporation. 124 Horseferry Rd, London SW1P 2TX *tel:* 0171 396 4444 *fax:* 0171 306 8366. Sir Michael Bishop CBE, chmn; Michael Grade, chief exec. *National.*

GMTV Ltd. London Television Centre, Upper Ground, London SE1 9TT *tel:* 0171 827 7000 *fax:* 0171 827 7009. Charles Allen, chmn; Christopher Stoddart, mgr dir; Peter McHugh, dir of programmes. *National breakfast-time.*

ITN. 200 Gray's Inn Rd, London WC1X 8XZ *tel:* 0171 833 3000 *fax:* 0171 430 4305. Sir David English, chmn; Stewart Purvis, chief exec. *ITN has been nominated by the ITC to provide a high quality national and international news service to Channel 3, Channel 4 and Channel 5.*

Regional Companies

Anglia Television Ltd. Anglia House, Norwich, Norfolk NR1 3JG *tel:* 01603 615151 *fax:* 01603 631032 *email:* http://www.anglia.tv.co.uk. 48 Leicester Sq, London WC2H 7FB *tel:* 0171 389 8555. Graham Creelman, mgr dir. *East of England.*

Border Television plc. The Television Centre, Durranhill, Carlisle, Cumbria CA1 3NT *tel:* 01228 25101 *fax:* 01228 41384. James Graham OBE, chmn; Peter Brownlow, mgr dir; Neil Robinson, head of programmes; Kath Worrall, dir of broadcasting. *Scottish Borders, Isle of Man and most of Cumbria.*

Carlton Television Ltd. 101 St Martin's La, London WC2N 4AZ *tel:* 0171 240 4000 *fax:* 0171 240 4171. Nigel Walmsley, chmn; Clive Jones, chief exec. *London weekday.*

Central Broadcasting. Central Ct, Gas St, Birmingham B1 2JT *tel:* 0121 643 9898. 35-38 Portman Sq, London W1A 9AH *tel:* 0171 486 6688. Ian Squires, chmn and mgr dir. *East, West and South Midlands.*

Channel Television. The Television Centre, La Pouquelaye, St Helier, Jersey, Channel Islands JE1 3ZD *tel:* 01534 816816 *fax:* 01534 816817. John Henwood, mgr dir; Michael Lucas, dir of television; Roy Manning, dir of operations; Bob Jones, dir of sales and mkt. *Channel Islands.*

Commercial Additional Services Licence. Data Broadcasting International Ltd, Allen House, Station Rd, Egham, Surrey TW20 9NT *tel:* 01784 477711 *fax:* 01784 477722 *fax:* Harry Roche. chmn, Justin Cadbury, Peter Mason; mgr dirs. *Sends data to closed user groups for channel 3.*

Grampian Television. Queens Cross, Aberdeen AB15 4XJ *tel:* 01224 846846 *fax:* 01224 846800 *email:* gtv@grampiantv.co.uk. Calum Macleod, chmn; Donald Waters, chief exec and deputy chmn. *North Scotland to Shetland and Western Isles.*

Granada Television plc. Granada TV Centre, Manchester M60 9EA *tel:* 0161 832 7211 *fax:* 0161 953 0297. 36 Golden Sq, London W1R 4AH *tel:* 0171 451 3000. Gerry Robinson, chmn; Charles Allen, chief exec. *North-West England.*

HTV (Cymru) Wales. The Television Centre, Culverhouse Cross, Cardiff CF5 6XJ *tel:* 01222 590590 *fax:* 01222 597183. Louis Sherwood, chmn; Chris Rowlands, chief exec. *Wales and West England.*

HTV Ltd. The Television Centre, Bath Rd, Bristol BS4 3HG *tel:* 0117 972 2722 *fax:* 0117 972 2400 *email:* http://www.htv.co.uk/. Jeremy Payne, dir of programmes. *Avon, parts of Gloucestershire, Somerset and Wiltshire.*

LWT (Holdings) plc. The London Television Centre, Upper Ground, London SE1 9LT *tel:* 0171 620 1620. Charles L Allen, chmn; Eileen Gallagher, mgr dir. *London Weekend.*

Meridian Broadcasting Ltd. Television Centre, Southampton SO14 0PZ *tel:* 01703 222555 *fax:* 01703 335050 *email:* http://www.meridian.tv.co. uk. Bill Cotton OBE, chmn; Mary McAnally, mgr dir. *South and South-East England.*

S4C (Sianel Pedwar Cymru). Welsh Fourth Channel Authority, Parc Ty Glas, Llanishen, Cardiff CF4 5DU *tel:* 01222 747444 *fax:* 01222 754444. *Wales, parts of Gloucestershire. S4C is the broadcasting service transmitted on the fourth channel in Wales. It broadcasts c 32 hrs in Welsh and for the remainder of the time reschedules Channel 4's English language programmes.*

Scottish Television. Cowcaddens, Glasgow G2 3PR *tel:* 0141 300 3000 *fax:* 0141 300 3030. 20 Lincoln's Inn Fields, London WC2A 3ED *tel:* 0171 446 7000 *fax:* 0171 446 7010. Gus Macdonald, chmn; Andrew Flanagan, mgr dir. *Central Scotland.*

Simple Active Ltd. Allen House, Station Rd, Egham, Surrey TW20 9NT *tel:* 01784 471515 *fax:* 01784 438732. Peter Mason, chmn; Justin Cadbury, deputy chmn. *Sends data to closed user groups for Channel 4.*

Teletext Ltd. 101 Farm La, Fulham, London SW6 1QJ *tel:* 0171 386 5000 *fax:* 0171 386 5751 *email:* e-mail@teletext.co.uk. Sir David English, chmn; Peter Van Gelder, mgr dir; Graham Lovelace, ed.

Tyne Tees Television Ltd. Television Centre, City Rd, Newcastle upon Tyne NE1 2AL *tel:* 0191 261 0181 *fax:* 0191 261 2302. 15 Bloomsbury Sq, London WC1A 2LJ *tel:* 0171 312 3700. Sir Ralph Carr-Ellison, chmn; Tony Brill, mgr dir. *North-East England.*

Ulster Television plc. Havelock House, Ormeau Rd, Belfast BT7 1EB *tel:* 01232 328122 *fax:* 01232 246695. Television Sales and Marketing (TSMS), West World, Westgate, Ealing, London W5 1EH *tel:* 0181 991 6666. John B McGuckian, chmn; Desmond Smyth, mgr dir. *Northern Ireland.*

Westcountry Television Ltd. Western Wood Way, Langage Science Pk, Plymouth PL7 5BG *tel:* 01752 333333 *fax:* 01752 333444. Clive Jones, chmn; Mark Haskell, mgr dir. *South-West England.*

Yorkshire Television Ltd. The Television Centre, Leeds LS3 1JS *tel:* 0113 243 8283 *fax:* 0113 244 5107. 15 Bloomsbury Sq, London WC1A 2LJ *tel:* 0171 312 3700. Ward Thomas, chmn; Bruce Gyngell, group mgr dir and chief exec. *Yorkshire.*

Independent Production Companies

Classic Arts Productions Ltd. The Old Farmhouse, Wilcox Farm, Moreton Morrell, Warwicks CV35 9AN *tel:* 01926 651247 *fax:* 01926 651886. Wendy Thompson, exec dir. *Specialist in classical mus and arts-related productions.*

Heavy Entertainment Ltd. 222 Kensal Rd, London W10 5BN *tel:* 0181 960 9001/2 *fax:* 0181 960 9003 *email:* info@heavy-entertainment.co.uk. Nick St George, David Roper, company dirs; Matthew Thompson, production mgr. *TV and radio production company specialising in arts and mus.*

Peartree Productions. PO Box 325, Worcester WR5 2YR *tel:* 01905 351748 *also fax; email:* scott@peartree.softnet.co.uk. David Scott, audio and programme mgr; Shirley Scott, exec producer.

Symphony Films. Flat 2, 38 Russell Rd, London W14 8HT *tel:* 0171 603 7279 *also fax.* Martin Phillips. *Promotional videos, video press releases, tour videos, concert and recital videos.*

Stockport
Cavalier Sound and Vision Ltd. 280 Wellington Rd South, Stockport, Cheshire SK2 6ND *tel:* 0161 480 6073 *fax:* 0161 429 8492. Arny Sage, studio mgr. *1 studio, 24 track, analogue, digital mastering, Cubase, Yamaha grand pno; capacity 10.*

Cornwall
Penzance
Brio Music Ltd. Cot Valley Lodge, Cot Valley, St Just, Penzance, Cornwall TR19 7NT *tel:* 01736 787788 *fax:* 01736 788335. *Br and military band specialists. Also location facilities, voice work, soundtrack compilation, MIDI editing suite, sound duplication.*

Devon
Newton Abbot
K G Engineering Ltd. Unit 6, Ipplepen Business Park, Edgelands La, Ipplepen, Newton Abbot TQ12 5UG *tel:* 01803 813833 *fax:* 01803 813141. Keith Gould, mgr dir; Jackie M Turner, production mgr. *600 sq ft, 8 track direct to hard disc.*

Dorset
Poole
Active Music Recording Studio. 7c Bank Chambers, Penn Hill Av, Lower Parkstone, Poole, Dorset BH14 9NB *tel:* 01202 746049. *Ampex 1200 24 track, Ampex ATR 100, Raindirk series 3 desk, ATC 100A monitors, digital editing available, large selection of mics.*

East Sussex
Eastbourne
* ICC Studios. 4 Regency Mews, Silverdale, Eastbourne, E Sussex BN20 7AB *tel:* 01323 643341 *fax:* 01323 649240. H Kaufmann, mgr dir; Marilyn Benson, bookings. *3 studio complex. Studio 1: 24-track residential. Studio 2: Budget 24-track 1″ or A-dat Digital. Studio 3: Digital editing and CD mastering.*

Peacehaven
Claudio Records Ltd. Studio 17, The Promenade, Peacehaven BN10 8PU *tel:* 01273 580250 *fax:* 01273 583530. Colin Attwell, William Attwell, studio mgrs. *Studio recording, digital editing and CD production.*

Essex
Chelmsford
SMS. 28 Manor Rd, Chelmsford, Essex CM2 0EP *tel:* 01245 351552. Steve Morris, studio mgr. *1 studio, capacity 5, 8 tracks, analogue.*

Frinton-on-Sea
East Anglian Productions. 21-23 Walton Rd, Frinton-on-Sea, Essex CO13 0AA *tel:* 01255 676252 *fax:* 01255 850528.

Hereford and Worcester
Kempsey
The Old Smithy Recording Studio. 1 Post Office La, Kempsey, Worcester WR5 3N5 *tel:* 01905 820659 *fax:* 01905 820015 *email:* http://www. demon.co.uk/mmi. Jan Allsop, bookings. *3 studios, 24 tracks, digital, analogue, video production, cassette duplication, full MIDI sequencing and sampling hardware; capacity 24. Visual broadcast facilities. Accommodation.*

Hertfordshire
Knebworth
* Select Sound Studio. Big M House, 1 Stevenage Rd, Knebworth, Herts SG3 6AN *tel:* 01438 814433 *fax:* 01438 815252.

Rickmansworth
London Studio Exchange. The Studios, Rickmansworth, Herts WD3 2XD *tel:* 01923 772351 *fax:* 01923 774713. *24 track.*

Watford
EQ Studios. 10 Stanley Rd, Watford, Herts *tel:* 01923 247879 *fax:* 01923 210917. *1 studio, 16 track (MIDI-based).*

Kingston upon Hull
Hull
Fairview Studios. Gt Gutter La West, Willerby, Hull HU10 6DP *tel:* 01482 653116 *fax:* 01482 654667 *email:* keith@fairview-music.demon.co.uk. *1 studio, 24 track; capacity 10.*

Lancashire
Leeds
Lion Studios. 31-34 Aire St Workshops, Leeds LS1 4HT *tel:* 0113 245 8809 *also fax.* Brendan Louis. *Control room and 2 separate recoding spaces. 16 track Pascam or available ADATs, Cubase audio, sound designer, comprehensive outboard and MIDI rig. Mastering to DAT or to CD.*

Leicestershire
Leicester
The Sound Studio. Q Broadcast, 1487 Melton Rd, Queniborough, Leicester LE7 3FP *tel:* 0116 260 8813 *fax:* 0116 260 8329 *email:* 101551.3707@ compuserve.com. Rob Nugent, studio mgr. *2 studios, one for 50+ players, the other for overdubs and vocals; soundcraft DC2000 32F mixing desk; mastering with various DATs. S/Craft 400W active nearfield monitoring. Limited location facilities (stereo only).*

Merseyside
Liverpool
Parr Street Studios. 35-45 Parr St, Liverpool L1 4JN *tel:* 0151 707 1050 *fax:* 0151 707 1813 *email:* parr.street@dial.pipex.com; http://www. connect.org.uk/merseymall/parr. Anne Lewis, mgr; Paul Lewis, bookings mgr. *Residential studio complex, 3 studios, located in Liverpool city centre. Tracking and mixing facilities to suit all budgets. Professional assistants and 2 full-time maintenance engineers.*

Nottinghamshire
Nottingham
* Network Studios (Nohponex Ltd). 22a Forest Rd West, Nottingham NG7 4EQ *tel:* 0115 978 4714 *fax:* 0115 942 4183. *1 studio, 24 track; capacity 35.*

Oxfordshire
Oxford
Snellgrove Studio. 3 Third Acre Rise, Botley, Oxford OX2 9DA *tel:* 01865 862733.

Skipton-on-Cherwell
* Manor Mobiles. The Manor, Skipton-on-Cherwell, Near Kidlington, Oxon OX5 1OL *tel:* 01865 377552 *fax:* 01865 377116.

Staffordshire
Keele
Clock House Recording Studio. Keele, Staffs ST5 5BG *tel:* 01782 583301 *also fax; email:* muaoo@keele.ac.uk; http://www.keele.ac.uk/depts/mu/ index.htm. Cliff Bradbury, studio mgr. *2 studios, 24 track. Digital, analogue, digital mastering and editing, CD preparation, capacity 20.*

Surrey
Dorking
* Ridge Farm Studios. Rusper Rd, Capel, Dorking, Surrey RH5 5HG *tel:* 01306 711202 *fax:* 01306 711626 *email:* info@ridgefarmstudio. com; http://www.ridgefarmstudio.com. Frank Andrews, mgr dir; Ann Needham, bookings and admin. *Main recording area 48 sq metres. SSL 9000J console. 2 Studer A800 MkII multi-track recorders.*

Farnham
* Jacobs Studios Ltd. Ridgway House, Runwick La, Farnham, Surrey GU10 5EE *tel:* 01252 715546 *fax:* 01252 712846. Andy Fernbach, studio mgr. *2 studios (fully residential), 1 Neve VR and 1 SSL.*

Keynote Audio Services. Wishanger La, Churt, Farnham, Surrey *tel:* 01252 794253 *fax:* 01252 792642 *email:* keynote@dial.pipex.com. *1 studio, 24 track; capacity 10, digital, analogue, digital mastering, audio post production, sound to picture sync. 24 track, digital editing.*

Guildford
Performing Arts Technology Studios. University of Surrey, Guildford GU2 5XH *tel:* 01483 259317 *fax:* 01483 259386. Ken Blair, studio mgr. *2 studios, with control rooms, 32 track Neve; capacity 75 and 10-12.*

Kenley
Doodlehums. 30 Cullesden Rd, Kenley, Surrey CR8 5LR *tel:* 0181 668 4833. *24 track Soundcraft Desk/t-machine. Creator with S1000, Proteus 1 and 2 JV880. Professionally designed live room. Ams, Bel, Alesis.*

Ripley
Black Barn Studios. 3 Dunsborough Cottages, The Green, Ripley, Surrey GU23 6AL *tel:* 01483 222600. *1 studio, 24 track; 48 track analogue and digital.*

Woldingham
* The Factory. Toftrees, Church Rd, Woldingham, Surrey CR3 7JH *tel:* 01883 652386 *fax:* 01883 652457 *email:* 10721.3514@compuserve. com. *1 studio, 48 track, digital sync to video; capacity 15.*

Tyne and Wear
Wallsend
Impulse Sound Recording Studios. 71 High St East, Wallsend, Tyne and Wear NE28 7RJ *tel:* 0191 262 4999 *fax:* 0191 263 7082. *24-track studio, 32 input desk, DAT mastering.*

West Midlands
Birmingham
Grosvenor Recording Studios. 16 Grosvenor Rd, Birmingham B20 3NP *tel:* 0121 356 9636 *also fax. 2 studios, 16 track; capacity 40 and 15.*

The Music Station. Pacific Buildings, 7 Mary St, St Pauls, Birmingham B3 1UD *tel:* 0121 200 1838 *fax:* 0121 236 8639. *Advanced digital sound recording facilities for audio and post-production video work. Music and sound effects libraries, plus in-house creative team.*

Ninth Wave Audio. PO Box 5517, Birmingham B13 8QW *tel:* 0121 442 2276; 0370 364464 *fax:* 0121 689 1902 *email:* ninthwave@dial.pipex. com. Tony Wass, studio mgr. *Studio specialising in classical mus for CD*

and radio broadcast. Full BBC broadcast facilities and mastering including short run CD production.

The Sound and Picture House. 2 Greenfield Cres, Edgbaston, Birmingham B15 3BE *tel:* 0121 456 1429 *fax:* 0121 454 6427 *email:* spictureh@aol. com. *1 studio, 16 track.*

Kingswinford
Diabolus in Musica Recording Services. 21 Oakfield Av, Kingswinford, West Midlands DY6 8HJ *tel:* 01384 295210 *email:* studio@diabolus. abel.co.uk; http://www.abel.co.uk/~diabolus. Paul Baker. *Specialist digital recording of soloists and ens in studio or on location. DAT mastering for CD and cassette.*

Scotland

Glasgow, City of
Glasgow
The Audiomobile. 49 Derby St, Glasgow G3 7TU *tel:* 0141 334 5099 *fax:* 0141 339 0271. Helen Clark, admin. *48 or 24 track continuous, fully air-conditioned, sync to picture. Full interface with all standard broadcast applications.*

Ca Va Sound Workshops. 49 Derby St, Glasgow G3 7TU *tel:* 0141 334 5099/6330 *fax:* 0141 339 0271. Helen Clark, admin. *4 studios; 48 and 24*

track analogue plus 16 tracks of hard disc recording on Digidesign Protools III, 24 track demo studio, 16 track programming studio, digital editing and mastering with Digidesign Protools III, CAP 50-100 (ST1). Sync to picture facilities in studios 1, 2 and 3.

* Scotty's Sound Studio. Newtown St, Kilsyth, Glasgow G65 0JX *tel:* 01236 823291 *fax:* 01236 826900 *email:* nscott@scotdisc.co.uk. *1 studio, 24 track and 2 track, digital, analogue.*

Wales

Gwynedd
Bangor
Cantor Music Department. Main Arts Building, University of Wales, Bangor, Gwynedd LL57 2DG *tel:* 01248 383827 *fax:* 01248 370297. Bryn Jones, studio dir. *1 studio, 2 concert halls, 12 tracks digital, AT mastering, digital editing, video post-production, Bösendorfer and Steinway pnos, Apple Mac, Atari; capacity 600.*

Caernarfon
Sain (Recordiau) Cyf. Llandwrog, Caernarfon LL54 5TG *tel:* 01286 831111 *fax:* 01286 831497 *email:* music@sain.wales.com; http://www.sain. wales.com. *2 studios, 24 track; capacity 30. Digital editing, video duplicating. CD-Rom authoring, CD pre-mastering. Also location recording.*

Studio Capel Mawr. Llun y Felin, Capel Mawr, Llanrug, Caernarfon, Gwynedd LL55 4AE *tel:* 01286 678102 *fax:* 01286 677410. Dilwyn

Roberts, studio mgr. *2000 sq ft sound stage. Fully sound-proofed with lighting grid and 3-phase supply.*

Monmouthshire
Caerleon
Loco Studios. Plas Lecha, Llanhennock, Caerleon, Newport, Monmouthshire NP6 1LU *tel:* 01633 450603 *fax:* 01633 450666.

Monmouth
* Rockfield Studios. Amberley Ct, Monmouth, South Wales NP5 4ET *tel:* 01600 712449 *fax:* 01600 714421.

Wrexham
Wrexham
* The Windings. Ffrwd Valley, Wrexham LL12 9TH *tel:* 01978 720420 *fax:* 01978 720503.

Northern Ireland

County Down
Newtownards
Downtown Radio. Newtownards, Co Down BT23 4ES *tel:* 01247 815555 *fax:* 01247 818913 *email:* music@coolfm.co.uk; http://www.downtown.

co.uk. David Sloan, mgr dir. *Soundcraft TS12 console, Orban 8TK digital editor, Sony DATs, Studer A80 quarter inch, compressors, gates and effects, Neuman and AKG mics, ISDN PRIMA 120 & APT X, control room 29 sq m, studio 23 sq m. Speciality audio for radio and TV commercials.*

Record Pressing, Cassette Duplication, CD Mastering

* **Ablex Audio Video Ltd.** Halesfield 14, Telford, Shropshire TF7 4QR *tel:* 01952 680131 *fax:* 01952 583501. Martine Tatman, sales mgr. *Cassette duplication; CD replication and pre-mastering.*

* **Accurate Sound Ltd.** Queniborough Industrial Estate, Melton Rd, Queniborough, Leicester LE7 3FP *tel:* 0116 260 2064 *fax:* 0116 260 0108. Irena Mason, dir and admin. *All aspects of audio cassette duplication and CD replication.*

Adrenalin Records Ltd. 252-253 Argyll Av, Slough, Berks SL1 4HA *tel:* 01753 523200 *fax:* 01753 692243.

AWL Compact Disc Co Ltd. 356 Scraptoft La, Leicester LE5 1PB *tel:* 0116 241 3979 *fax:* 0116 243 3760. Andrew W Lipinski, mgr dir. *CD mastering and replication.*

Channel 5 Audio Visuals. 5 St Wilfrids Rd, New Barnet, Herts EN4 9SB *tel:* 0181 441 4219 *also fax. Location recording for classical mus; also offers video duplication from any format to VHS.*

* **Damont Audio Ltd.** Blyth Rd, Hayes, Middx UB3 1BY *tel:* 0181 573 5122 *fax:* 0181 561 0979. Chris Rose, production dir; Ian Ramsden, finance dir; Malcolm Pearce, sales mgr. *Manufacture vinyl 7" and 12" records; audio cassette duplication.*

Euphonia. Trinity Mews, Cambridge Gardens, London W10 6JA *tel:* 0181 960 8128 *fax:* 0181 968 0341. *Digital editing and mastering services for cassette and CD. CD-R and DAT. Analogue and digital format transfers. Real-time cassette duplication.*

Filterbond Ltd (JBS Records Division). 19 Sadlers Way, Hertford SG14 2DZ *tel:* 01992 500101 *also fax.* John B Schefel, mgr dir; David F J Reeve, dir and sec. *Quality cassette duplication and blanks 1-1000. Computer printed cassette labels. Solo, 1/4" reel, Sony Betamax or R-DAT recording.*

Fine Tuning. Curls Farmhouse, Ripe, Lewes, E Sussex BN8 6AS *tel:* 01323 811604; 0831 614292 *fax:* 01323 811136 *email:* piers@finetuning. demon.co.uk; http://www.finetuning.demon.co.uk. Piers Bishop. *Digital location recording and post-production.*

Finesplice Ltd. 1 Summerhouse La, Harmondsworth, W Drayton, Middx UB7 0AW *tel:* 0181 564 7839 *fax:* 0181 759 9629 *email:* finespl@ dircon.co.uk; http://www.finesplice.co.uk. Ben Turner, mgr dir; Julia Thomas, snr engineer. *Studios for hard disk editing, audio restoration, CD pre-mastering to U-matic or CD-R. One-off CDs.*

Forward Sound and Vision. 4-10 North Rd, London N7 9HN *tel:* 0171 865 3800 *fax:* 0171 865 3803 *email:* fsv@cassette.win-uk.net; http:// www.fsv.co.uk. Keith Lloyd, mgr dir; Marianna Virides, sales mgr. *Cassette duplication, CD replication and vinyl pressing.*

Ginn, Jeffrey. 11 Haycroft, Wootton, Bedford, Beds MK43 9PB *tel:* 01234 765602; 0378 896721 *fax:* 01234 765367 *email:* jeff@ginn-mus.demon. co.uk; http://www.ginn-mus.demon.co.uk. *Location recording service and post-production studios. Classical recording, digital editing and SADIE mastering. SADIE hard disk editor, DAT, CDR.*

* **ICC Duplication.** Silverdale Rd, Eastbourne, E Sussex *tel:* 01323 647880 *fax:* 01323 643095 *email:* duplication@icc.org.uk; http://www.icc.org. uk. Geoff Durrant, customer service mgr; Andy Thorpe, sales and development mgr; Andy Hooper, production mgr. *Professional cassette duplication, blank cassettes, CD replication, CD pre-mastering, video duplication, video blanks.*

* **Isis Duplicating Co Ltd.** Unit 11, Shaftesbury Industrial Centre, The Runnings, Cheltenham, Glos GL51 9NH *tel:* 01242 571818 *fax:* 01242 571315. Glyn Ellis Evans, sales mgr. *Recording, editing, mastering, high-speed cassette duplication.*

* **ITD Cassettes.** Unit 21 Faraday Rd, Rabans La, Aylesbury, Bucks HP19 3RY *tel:* 01296 27211 *fax:* 01296 392019. R P Jackson-Moore, mgr dir; M A McLoughlin, technical dir. *Audio and video cassette duplication.*

James Yorke Ltd. Yorke House, Corpus St, Cheltenham, Glos GL52 6XH *tel:* 01242 584222 *fax:* 01242 222445. Ken Leeks, sales dir. *Loop-bin duplication for cassettes.*

Keynote Cassettes. Wishanger La, Churt, Farnham, Surrey GU10 2QJ *tel:* 01252 794253 *fax:* 01252 792642 *email:* keynote@dial.pipex.com. Tim Wheatley. *Cassette duplicators and CD brokers.*

* **KG Engineering Ltd.** Unit 6, Ipplepen Business Pk, Edgelands La, Ipplepen, Newton Abbot TQ12 5UG *tel:* 01803 813833 *fax:* 01803 813141. Keith Gould, mgr dir; Jackie M Turner, production mgr. *CD mastering, cassette duplication.*

* **London Tape Company.** Woodman Works, 204 Durnsford Rd, Wimbledon, London SW19 8DR *tel:* 0181 944 9477 *fax:* 0181 944 9466 *email:* 100523.1057@compuserve.com. Eddy Wilcox, gen mgr; Simon Howell, production mgr.

* **Nimbus Manufacturing (UK) Ltd.** Llantarnam Pk, Cwmbran, Gwent NP44 3AB *tel:* 01633 465000 *fax:* 01633 876131. Howard Nash, mgr dir; John Denton, commercial dir; Emil Dudek, dir CD-Rom. *Pre-mastering, mastering and manufacture of all CD, CD-Rom, CDI and other optical discs. Also MPEG video compression, full printing and packaging services.*

The Old Smithy Recording Studio. 1 Post Office La, Kempsey, Worcester WR5 3NS *tel:* 01905 820659 *fax:* 01905 820015. Janet Allsopp, bookings mgr. *Cassette duplication, MIDI sequencing and sampling hardware.*

Portfolio CDs - Brochures in Sound. PO Box 2288, Glastonbury BA6 9YJ *tel:* 0181 943 5329 *also fax.* Nicholas Vallis-Davies; Sian Vallis-Davies. *Organisation specialising in putting audition pieces on CD with full production, artwork and distribution services.*

* **PR Records Ltd.** 204 Durnsford Rd, Wimbledon, London SW19 8DR *tel:* 0181 241 2244 *fax:* 0181 241 2227. Ray Young, mgr dir.

Raymer Sound. Apsley House, Courtland Rd, Wellington, Somerset TA21 8ND *tel:* 01823 662160 *fax:* 01823 663000. Neil Raybould, recording engineer. *Mobile recording, CD mastering, cassette duplication for classical mus.*

Reflex Audio Systems Ltd. Unit 5, Cirrus, Glebe Rd, Huntingdon, Cambs PE18 7DX *tel:* 01480 434333 *fax:* 01480 411441. John Garrad, dir; Keith Crooks, production mgr.

Rhinosaurus Records Limited. 7 Springfields, Somerset Rd, New Barnet, Herts EN5 1SG *tel:* 0181 440 0183 *fax:* 0181 440 8169. Colin Middleton, producer; Richard Jacobs, chief sound engineer. *Mastering, cassette duplication.*

Richmond Sound. 24 Sheen Pk, Richmond TW9 1UW *tel:* 0181 948 4339 *also fax.* A Bull, mgr. *Cassette duplication and transcription service.*

* **RTS Ltd.** Units M1 and M2, Albany Rd, Prescot, Merseyside L34 2SH *tel:* 0151 430 9001 *fax:* 0151 430 7441.

Selecta Sound. 5 Margaret Rd, Romford, Essex RM2 5SH *tel:* 01708 453424 *fax:* 01708 455565. John and Carol Smailes. *Audio and video duplication; CD replication; blank tape supply.*

* **Sounds Good Ltd.** 12 Chiltern Enterprise Centre, Station Rd, Theale, Berks RG7 4AA *tel:* 0118 930 2600 *fax:* 0118 930 3181 *email:* http://www. sounds-good.co.uk. Martin Maynard, dir. *Cassette duplication, CD mastering and digital editing, CD pressing, inlay print.*

Speech Plus Recordings. Unit 32, 19 Pages Walk, London SE1 4SB *tel:* 0171 231 0961.

SRL Cassettes. 47 High St, Pinner, Middx HA5 5PJ *tel:* 0181 868 5555 *fax:* 0181 866 5555 *email:* srl@btinternet.com. J Bales, production mgr.

* **SRT Sound Recording Technology Ltd.** Edison Rd, Audio House, St Ives, Cambridge PE17 4LF *tel:* 01480 461880; 0181 446 3218 *fax:* 01480 496100. Matthew Dilley, classical mgr; James Dickinson, operations mgr. *CD manufacturer and 6 studios. Full classical service including restoration and multisession discs.*

Warren Recordings. 59 Hendale Av, London NW4 4LP *tel:* 0181 203 0306. Stanley Warren. *Cassette duplication, small recording studio.*

* **WNE, Unit 7.** Sovereign Centre, Lichfield Rd Industrial Estate, Tamworth, Staffs B79 7AX *tel:* 01827 310052 *fax:* 01827 60868. *Cassette duplication, min run 250.*

Sound Recovery and Restoration

Euphonia. Trinity Mews, Cambridge Gardens, London W10 6JA *tel:* 0181 960 8128 *fax:* 0181 968 0341. Simon Heyworth, chief sound engineer. *Sonic Solutions No-Noise TM and de-clicking systems. Restoration of old and damaged recordings from all sources. Full range of digital and analogue processing and format transfer equipment available. Specialist services for legal and forensic work and film sound restoration.*

Friary Music Services. 142b Friary Rd, London SE15 5UW *tel:* 0171 277 7068 *fax:* 0171 277 8354 *email:* 100115.3701@compuserve.com. Richard Black, producer. *Highest quality transcription of all 78, 45 and 33 rpm records and analogue tape recordings.*

John R T Davies. 1 Walnut Tree Cottage, Burnham, Bucks SL1 8DH *tel:* 01628 604811. *Recovery and restoration of sound from ancient and defective recordings.*

Specialist Record Dealers

Many record shops carry recordings of classical music as a small proportion of their total stock. In the following list, retailers with exclusive or large sections devoted to classical music or jazz are grouped alphabetically by county. Greater London is listed first followed by the rest of England. Scotland and Wales are located at the end of this section.

Greater London

Arcade Music Shop. 13-14 Grand Arcade, Tally Ho Corner, Finchley, London N12 0EH *tel:* 0181 445 6369 *also fax. Cassettes, CDs, video.*

Barbican Music Shop. Cromwell Tower, Silk St, Barbican, London EC2Y 8DD *tel:* 0171 588 9242 *fax:* 0171 628 1080. *Mus, CDs, inst accessories, books.*

Bargain Records. 9 The Arcade, High St, Eltham, London SE9 1BE *tel:* 0181 859 5836. *Second-hand classical records, CDs.*

Cassettes Plus. 12 Earlham St, London WC2H 9LN *tel:* 0171 836 8514. *Cassettes, CDs.*

Consort Records. 34 St Mary's Grove, London W4 3LN *tel:* 0181 995 9994 *fax:* 0181 995 2115 *email:* info@the-kings-consort.org.uk; http://www. the-kings-consort.org.uk. *M/order early mus recordings.*

Dillons the Bookstore. 82 Gower St, London WC1E 6EQ *tel:* 0171 636 1577. *Cassettes, CDs, videos.*

Dress Circle. 57-59 Monmouth St, London WC2H *tel:* 0171 240 2227 *fax:* 0171 379 8540 *email:* online@dresscircle.co.uk; http://www. dresscircle.co.uk. *CDs, cassettes, books, videos.*

ENO Shop, MDC Classic Music. 31 St Martin's La, London WC2N 4ER *tel:* 0171 240 0270 *email:* classic@mdcmusic.co.uk; http://www. mdcmusic.co.uk. *CDs, videos and gifts. Books on opera, dance and ballet.*

Farringdons Records. 64-72 Leadenhall Market, London EC3V 1LT *tel:* 0171 623 9605 *fax:* 0171 626 2891.

Farringdons Records. Royal Festival Hall, South Bank Centre, London SE1 8XX *tel:* 0171 620 0198 *fax:* 0171 928 0063. *Classical CDs, cassettes, videos, jazz films, shows and world mus.*

HMV Shop (HMV UK Ltd). 150 Oxford St, London W1N 0DJ *tel:* 0171 631 3423 *fax:* 0171 580 6648. *Audio recordings (all formats), videos, computers and video games, music merchandise and accs.*

HMV Shop. 363 Oxford St, London W1R 2BJ *tel:* 0171 629 1240 *fax:* 0171 495 0261.

HMV Shop. 81 (Unit 66) The Mall, Broadway Shopping Centre, Bexleyheath DA6 7JJ *tel:* 0181 298 0876.

HMV Shop. Unit Y11A, Brent Cross Centre, Brent Cross, London NW4 3FG *tel:* 0181 201 5430.

HMV Shop. 90-92 High St, Bromley BR1 1EY *tel:* 0181 313 0727.

HMV Shop. 137 North End, Croydon CR0 1TN *tel:* 0181 686 5557.

HMV Shop. 2 Waterglade Centre, Ealing Broadway, London W5 2ND *tel:* 0181 566 2590. *CDs, cassettes and videos.*

HMV Shop. 11 Church St, Enfield EN2 6AF *tel:* 0181 363 0184; 0181 366 8544. *CDs, cassettes and videos.*

HMV Shop. 332-334 North End Rd, Fulham, London SW6 1NF *tel:* 0171 386 5256. *CDs, cassettes, vinyl and videos.*

HMV Shop. Units 11/12, 1st Floor, Bentalls Centre, Clarence St, Kingston KT1 1TR *tel:* 0181 974 8037.

HMV Shop. 70-72 George St, Richmond, Surrey TW9 1HE *tel:* 0181 940 9880 *fax:* 0181 332 6706.

HMV Shop. Trocadero, Coventry St, London W1V 7FD *tel:* 0171 439 0447.

Jewish Music Distribution. PO Box 2286, Hendon, London NW4 3UW *tel:* 0181 203 8046 *also fax; email:* rad74@dial.pipex.com. *Retail and wholesale suppliers of Jewish recorded and printed mus from around the world. Main agents for all of Israel's major recording and sheet mus companies.*

Koolman Records. 7 Gilmore Rd, London SE13 5AD *tel:* 0181 852 5727 *fax:* 0181 297 9214. *Rare and bargain classical LPs in mint condition.*

Magnum Opus. 90 Deans La, Edgware, Middx HA8 9NP *tel:* 0181 959 4280 *also fax . M/order only. Second-hand LPs and CDs. Total stock 75,000. Standard and unusual repertoire: orch, inst, vocal. Many rarities.*

Mole Jazz. 311 Gray's Inn Rd, London WC1X 8PX *tel:* 0171 278 0703 *fax:* 0171 833 1029. *Jazz specialists, new and second-hand CDs, LPs, books. M/order worldwide, free mailing lists, auctions of rare LPs.*

Music Discount Centre. 124 Camden High St, London NW1 0LU *tel:* 0171 482 7097.

Music Discount Centre. 1 Creed La, St Paul's, London EC4V 5BR *tel:* 0171 489 8077. *Records, cassettes, CDs.*

Music Discount Centre. 33-34 Rathbone Pl, London W1P 1AD *tel:* 0171 637 4700. *Classical CDs, opera videos, live and historical opera.*

Music Discount Centre. 437 Strand, London WC2R 0QN *tel:* 0171 240 2157. *Cassettes, CDs.*

Music Discount Centre. 46 Thurloe St, London SW7 2LT *tel:* 0171 584 3338.

Ray's Jazz Shop. Incorporating Ray's Blues & Roots, 180 Shaftesbury Av, London WC2 8JS *tel:* 0171 240 3969 *fax:* 0171 240 7375 *email:* rays.jazz@dial.pipex.com. *Jazz, blues, world and folk CDs, records (vinyl) new and second-hand, cassettes, 78s, books, magazines, videos.*

Reckless Records. 30 Berwick St, London W1V 3RF *tel:* 0171 437 4271 *email:* rarities@reckless.co.uk; http://www.users.dircon.uk/~reckless/. *CDs.*

Reckless Records. 79 Upper St, London N1 0NU *tel:* 0171 359 0501; 0171 359 2222 *fax:* 0171 359 9509 *email:* rarities@reckless.co.uk; http://www.users.dircon.uk/~reckless/. *Buy, sell and exchange CDs, vinyl, tapes. Rock, soul, pop, dance. Rarities by m/order.*

Thomas (Michael G). 5a Norfolk Pl, London W2 1QN *tel:* 0171 723 4935. *Records, cassettes, CDs, m/order. Archive documents. Mengelberg Edition.*

Tower Records. 62-64 Kensington High St, London W8 4PE *tel:* 0171 937 3511 *fax:* 0171 937 5024. *Records, cassettes, CDs.*

Tower Records. 17 Fife Rd, Kingston KT1 1SB *tel:* 0181 974 6990 *fax:* 0181 974 6995.

Tower Records. Swan & Edgar Building, 1 Piccadilly Circus, London W1R 8TR *tel:* 0171 439 2500 *fax:* 0171 434 2766 *email:* tower@easynet.co. uk. *Classical, opera, jazz, international, new age, folk, country, blues, rock & pop, alternative, soul, rap, swing. CD singles, films and shows, easy listening and vocals, comedy, books and magazines, laser discs, videos.*

Tower Records. Whiteleys of Bayswater, Unit 001b, London W2 4YR *tel:* 0171 229 4550 *fax:* 0171 792 0075. *Cassettes, CDs and videos.*

Trehantiri. 365-367 Green Lanes, London N4 1DY *tel:* 0181 802 6530 *also fax; email:* trehanti@greekmus.demon.co.uk; http://www.greekmus. demon.co.uk. *Specialists in Greek and Arabic mus.*

Vinyl Connections. 22 Hilltop Rd, London NW6 2PY *tel:* 0171 625 8966 *also fax. Specialists in original 1950s-1970s classical LP records: symph, chmbr, inst, operatic, vocal etc. Most labels. Collections for cash exchange; record cleaning service; quality vintage turntables and cartridges supplied.*

Virgin Megastore. 14-16 Oxford St, London W1N 9FL *tel:* 0171 631 1234. *Books, records, cassettes, CDs, sheet mus.*

England

Bath and North East Somerset
Bath

Bath Compact Discs. 11 Broad St, Bath, Avon BA1 5LJ *tel:* 01225 464766 *fax:* 01225 482275. *Classical CDs and videos, also m/order.*

HMV Shop. 13-15 Stall Street, Bath BA1 1QE *tel:* 01225 466681 *fax:* 01225 330820.

Bedfordshire
Luton

HMV Shop. 73 The Mall, Arndale Centre, Luton LU1 2TG *tel:* 01582 21368/418835.

Berkshire
Reading

Hickies Ltd. 153 Friar St, Reading, Berks RG1 1HG *tel:* 0118 957 5771 *fax:* 0118 957 5775. *Cassettes, CDs.*

HMV Shop. 138-141 Friar St, Reading RG1 1EY *tel:* 0118 956 0086 *fax:* 0118 958 3523. *Records, cassettes, CDs, books, videos, accs.*

Bristol, City of
Bristol

Bristol Classical Discs. 59 Broad St, Bristol BS1 2EJ *tel:* 0117 927 6536. *CDs, classical specialist.*

HMV Shop. 21-23 Broadmead, Bristol BS1 3HF *tel:* 0117 929 7467/926 0781. *Records, cassettes, CDs.*

Rayners Compact Discs. 84 Park St, Bristol BS1 5LA *tel:* 0117 927 3936. *CDs and cassettes.*

Cambridgeshire
Cambridge

CMS Records. 1a All Saints' Passage, Cambridge CB2 3LT *tel:* 01223 460818 *fax:* 01223 464178 *email:* cmsrecs@cambridge.dungeon.com. *Classical CDs, cassettes, videos, m/order.*

Garon Records. 70 King St, Cambridge CB1 1LN *tel:* 01223 62086. *Records, cassettes, CDs, classical, jazz, folk, blues, ethnic, second-hand and new.*

HMV Shop. 12-15 Lion Yard, Cambridge CB2 3NA *tel:* 01223 319090. *CDs, cassettes and videos.*

Peterborough

HMV Shop. 4 Cathedral Sq, Peterborough, Cambs PE1 1XH *tel:* 01733 347642. *CDs and cassettes.*

Cheshire
Wilmslow

Rare Records Ltd. 13 Bank Sq, Wilmslow, Cheshire SK9 1AN *tel:* 01625 522017 *fax:* 01625 536101 *email:* dimus@aol.com. *Records, cassettes, CDs; classical, jazz, opera, nostalgia, spoken word, classical videos, m/order.*

Cornwall
Lostwithiel

Music Masters. 28 Fore St, Lostwithiel, Cornwall PL22 0BL *tel:* 01208 873525. *Classical CDs, cassettes. M/order postage free on full price CDs.*

Derbyshire
Derby

HMV Shop. 2 Albion St, Derby DE1 2AL *tel:* 01332 201902.

MDT Classics. 6 Old Blacksmiths Yard, Sadler Gate, Derby DE1 3PD *tel:* 01332 368251 *fax:* 01332 383594 *email:* info@mdt.co.uk; http://www.mdt.co.uk. *CDs (classical only), m/order.*

Devon
Exeter

HMV Shop. 191 High St, Exeter EX4 3DU *tel:* 01392 420190. *Records, cassettes, CDs, books.*

Opus Classical. 14a Guildhall Centre, Exeter, Devon EX4 3HW *tel:* 01392 214044 *fax:* 01392 496196. *CDs, cassettes, books, videos.*

Plymouth

HMV Shop. 30-32 New George St, Plymouth PL1 1RW *tel:* 01752 228181. *Records, cassettes, CDs.*

Sidmouth

Acorn Music Inc (Peter Russell's Hot Record Store). PO Box 17, Sidmouth, Devon EX10 9EH *tel:* 01395 578145 *fax:* 01395 578080. *Records (jazz, blues, big band, dance bands, nostalgia, Latin-American, stage and screen), m/order only.*

Dorset
Bournemouth

HMV Shop. 5-6 The Avenue, Commercial Rd, Bournemouth BH2 5RP *tel:* 01202 556297. *CDs, cassettes and videos.*

East Sussex
Brighton

Classics. 28a Tidy St, Brighton, E Sussex BN1 4EL *tel:* 01273 694229. *Second-hand records, cassettes, CDs videos (classical, opera, jazz, stage shows, vocal, big bands, rock, pop, etc), bought and sold.*

HMV Shop. 61-62 Western Rd, Brighton BN1 2HA *tel:* 01273 747223.

Eastbourne

C G Robson Imports. 39 Winchcombe Rd, Eastbourne, E Sussex BN22 8DE *tel:* 01323 725376 *also fax. Customer order only. American and UK CDs, cassettes, laser discs and videos; Rococo records. Worldwide postal service. Supply American Schwann Opus, Fanfare, Spectrum and Artist catalogues, also Fanfare review.*

Seaford Music. 24 Pevensey Rd, Eastbourne, E Sussex BN21 3HP *tel:* 01323 732553 *fax:* 01323 417455 *email:* mail@gic.co.uk; http://www.gic.co.uk/sm. *Classical CDs, cassettes, videos.*

Hove

Fine Records. 32 George St, Hove, E Sussex BN3 3YB *tel:* 01273 723345 *fax:* 01273 748717. *Classical specialist; many rare deletions on cassette, record and CD.*

Essex
Chelmsford

HMV Store. Unit 2 High Chelmer Shopping Centre, Chelmsford, Essex CM1 1XG.

Epping

Chew & Osborne. 148 High St, Epping, Essex CM16 4AG *tel:* 01992 574242. *CDs, classical specialists.*

HMV Shop. Unit 281 Lakeside Shopping Centre, West Thurrock Way, West Thurrock, Grays, Essex RM16 1WT *tel:* 01708 860110.

Saffron Walden

Chew & Osborne. 26 King St, Saffron Walden, Essex CB10 1ES *tel:* 01799 523728. *CDs, classical specialists and hi-fi.*

Southend

HMV Shop. 8-14 Queens Rd, Southend, Essex SS1 1LU *tel:* 01702 435158.

Gloucestershire
Cheltenham

HMV Shop. 111-113 High Street, Cheltenham GL50 1DW *tel:* 01242 230930.

Sounds Good. 26 Clarence St, Cheltenham, Glos GL50 3NU *tel:* 01242 234604 *fax:* 01242 253030. *Classical CDs, cassettes, and videos. Also folk, world, and jazz.*

Gloucester

Audiosonic (Gloucester) Ltd. 6 College St, Gloucester GL1 2NE *tel:* 01452 302280. *Cassettes, CDs, m/order. Classical mus specialists.*

Folktracks (Audio and Video) Cassettes. International Traditions Library, 16 Brunswick Sq, Gloucester GL1 1UG *tel:* 01452 415110 *email:* folktrax@demon.co.uk. *Peter Kennedy, Beryl Kennedy, mgrs. Cassettes and videos of traditional music of the world.*

HMV Shop. 18 Kings Walk, Gloucester GL1 1RW *tel:* 01452 302231/302229. *Records, cassettes, CDs, videos.*

Greater Manchester
Manchester

Forsyth Bros Ltd. 126 Deansgate, Manchester M3 2GR *tel:* 0161 834 3281 *fax:* 0161 834 0630 *email:* forsythmus@aol.com. *Classical, jazz, world, spoken word. CDs, cassettes, mus videos, m/order.*

HMV Store. 90-100 Market St, Manchester M1 1PD *tel:* 0161 834 8550. *CDs, cassettes, videos.*

Virgin Megastore. 52-56 Market St, Manchester M1 1PW *tel:* 0161 833 1111 *fax:* 0161 832 2765. *CDs, cassettes, records, videos, books, games, clothing.*

Hampshire
Basingstoke

HMV Shop. 2 Old Basing Mall, Basingstoke RG21 1AW *tel:* 01256 816707.

Portsmouth

HMV Shop. 183-187 Commercial Rd, Portsmouth PO1 1EA *tel:* 01705 829678. *Records, cassettes, CDs.*

Southampton

HMV Shop. 56-58 Above Bar St, Southampton SO14 7DS *tel:* 01703 338398. *Records, cassettes, CDs and videos.*

Southsea

Orpheus Records. 27 Marmion Rd, Southsea, Hants *tel:* 01705 812397 *fax:* 01705 865421. *Records, cassettes, CDs (classical, big band and jazz), new and second-hand.*

Winchester

Whitwams Music. 70 High St, Winchester, Hants SO23 9DE *tel:* 01962 865253 *fax:* 01962 842064 *email:* quality@whitwams.telme.com. *CD, cassettes, video; classical specialists, m/order.*

Hereford & Worcester
Hay-on-Wye

Hancock & Monks. 15 Broad St, Hay-on-Wye, Herefordshire HR3 5DB *tel:* 01497 821784 *fax:* 01497 851262. *Specialists in classical cassettes, CDs, video. Second-hand books on mus; sheet mus.*

Worcester

HMV Shop. 88-89 High St, Worcester WR1 2EX *tel:* 01905 24567.

Isle of Wight
Newport
HMV Shop. 62 High St, Newport PO39 1BA *tel:* 01983 522533.

Kent
Maidstone
HMV Shop. 34 Week St, Maidstone ME14 1RP *tel:* 01622 751 650.
West Wickham
Showells Record Centre. 94 High St, West Wickham, Kent BR4 0NF *tel:* 0181 777 5255. *Records, cassettes, CDs, videos.*

Kingston upon Hull
Hull
HMV Shop. 45 Whitefriargate, Hull HU1 2HN *tel:* 01482 226160/320993. *CDs, cassettes and videos.*

Lancashire
Blackpool
HMV Shop. Unit 1, Tower Shopping Centre, Bank Hey St, Blackpool FY1 4RZ *tel:* 01253 291393. *Records, cassettes, CDs, books.*
Bolton
HMV Shop. 3-5 Exchange St, Bolton BL1 1RS *tel:* 01204 394934 *fax:* 01204 522547. *CDs, cassettes and videos, computer games, books, clothing.*
Oldham
HMV Shop. 29 Town Sq Shopping Centre, Oldham OL1 1XE *tel:* 0161 633 7332.
St Annes on Sea
Squires Gate Music Centre. 13 St Andrew's Road South, St Annes on Sea, Lancs FY8 1SX *tel:* 01253 782588 *fax:* 01253 782985. *Cassettes, CDs.*

Leicestershire
Leicester
Classic Tracks. 21 East Bond St, Leicester LE1 45X *tel:* 0116 253 7700 *fax:* 0116 252 3553. *Classical mus, film soundtracks, shows and musicals.*
HMV Shop. 9-17 High St, Leicester LE1 4FP *tel:* 0116 253 9638. *Records, cassettes, CDs, books.*
Virgin Megastore. 8 Churchgate, Leicester LE1 4AJ *tel:* 0116 242 5969 *fax:* 0116 253 0136.

Merseyside
Liverpool
HMV Shop. 22-36 Church St, Liverpool L1 3AW *tel:* 0151 709 1088. *Records, cassettes, CDs, video games.*

Middlesbrough
Middlesbrough
HMV Shop. 79 Linthorpe Rd, Middlesbrough TW1 5BU *tel:* 01642 226957. *CDs, cassettes and videos.*

Milton Keynes, City of
Milton Keynes
Chappell of Bond Street. 21 Silbury Arcade, The Shopping Centre, Central Milton Keynes MK9 3AG *tel:* 01908 663366 *fax:* 01908 606414. *CDs, mus.*

Norfolk
Norwich
HMV Store. 21 Gentleman's Walk, Norwich NR2 1NA *tel:* 01603 622 329.
Ives Records. Above St Benedicts Market, 21 St Benedicts Market, Norwich, Norfolk NR2 4PF *tel:* 01603 620272 *also fax. Second-hand records, CDs (classical and jazz specialist).*
Prelude Records. 25b St Giles St, Norwich, Norfolk NR2 1JN *tel:* 01603 628319 *also fax; fax:* 01603 620170 *email:* sales@prelude-records.co. uk. *CDs, cassettes, videos, classical specialist.*

Northamptonshire
Kettering
HMV Shop. 32a Newlands Centre, Kettering NN16 8JB *tel:* 01536 519101. *Cassettes, CDs and videos.*
Northampton
HMV Shop. 2-6 Princes Walk, Grosvenor Centre, Northampton, NN1 2EL *tel:* 01604 232662.
Spinadiscs. 75a Abington St, Northampton NN1 2BH *tel:* 01604 31144. *CDs, cassettes, records.*

Nottinghamshire
Mansfield
HMV Shop. 38 Four Seasons Centre, Mansfield NG18 1FU *tel:* 01623 420568. *Cassettes, CDs and videos.*
Nottingham
HMV Shop. 38 Listergate, Nottingham, Notts NG1 7EE *tel:* 0115 950 2841; 0115 958 6326 *fax:* 0115 950 4785. *Records, cassettes, CDs, books.*
HMV Shop. 134 Victoria Centre, Nottingham NG1 3QE *tel:* 0115 941 5525/950 8164. *Cassettes, CDs, videos.*
Virgin Megastore. 6-8 Wheelergate, Nottingham NG1 2NB *tel:* 0115 947 6126 *fax:* 0115 948 3857.

Oxfordshire
Oxford
HMV Store. 43-46 Cornmarket St, Oxford OX1 3HA *tel:* 01865 728190. *CDs, cassettes.*

South Yorkshire
Doncaster
HMV Shop. 10 Frenchgate, Doncaster DN1 1QQ *tel:* 01302 340484.
Sheffield
HMV Shop. 24 High Street, Sheffield S1 2GE *tel:* 0114 273 9738. *CDs, cassettes and videos.*
HMV Store. 34 High St, Meadowhall Centre, Sheffield S9 1EN *tel:* 0114 256 8138/256 8143. *CDs, cassettes.*
HMV Shop. 121-123 Pinstone St, Sheffield S1 2HL *tel:* 0114 275 1445/275 1668.
Virgin Megastore. 3 Orchard Sq, Fargate, Sheffield S1 2FB *tel:* 0114 273 1175 *fax:* 0114 275 1831.

Staffordshire
Hanley
HMV Store. 212 The Potteries Shopping Centre, Market Sq, Hanley ST1 1PS *tel:* 01762 283 232.

Suffolk
Aldeburgh
Galleon Music. High St, Aldeburgh, Suffolk IP15 5AX *tel:* 01728 453298 *fax:* 01728 452715. *CDs, cassettes, scores, m/order. Britten specialist.*
Felixstowe
Ian's Music and Video. 111 Hamilton Rd, Felixstowe IP11 7BL *tel:* 01394 279442 *also fax; email:* ianmusic@anglianet.co.uk. *CDs. M/order rarities.*
Ipswich
Amberstone Bookshop. 49 Upper Orwell St, Ipswich, Suffolk IP4 1HP *tel:* 01473 250675 *fax:* 01473 226980. *Books, classical CDs, cassettes.*
Andy's Records. Unit 8, The Buttermarket Centre, St Stephens La, Ipswich IP1 1DW *tel:* 01473 258933.
HMV Shop. 20 Tavern Street, Ipswich IP1 3AY *tel:* 01473 213127.
Ipswich Record and Tape Exchange. 34 Upper Orwell St, Ipswich *tel:* 01473 230207. *New and second-hand records and CDs.*
Sudbury
Compact Music. 17 North St, Sudbury, Suffolk CO10 6RB *tel:* 01787 881160 *fax:* 01787 880909. *CDs, cassettes, vinyl, videos, mini disc; classical, jazz and easy listening. Order service.*

Surrey
Cobham
Threshold Compact Discs. 53-55 High St, Cobham, Surrey KT11 3DP *tel:* 01932 865678 *also fax. Classical, jazz, blues, soul, R&B, dance, rock, pop, country, films and shows, easy listening.*
Godalming
Record Corner. Pound La, Godalming, Surrey GU7 1BX *tel:* 01483 422006 *also fax. Records, cassettes, CDs, mus books, styli, videos.*
Guildford
HMV Shop. 75-79 The Friary Centre, Guildford GU1 4YU.
Sound Barrier Compact Disc Centre. 24 Tunsgate, Guildford, Surrey GU1 3QS *tel:* 01483 300947 *fax:* 01483 575153. *CDs.*
Kingston
Tower Records. 17 Fife Rd, Kingston KT1 1SB *tel:* 0181 546 2500 *fax:* 0181 974 6993. *CDs and books.*
Gateshead
HMV Shop. 22 (68a) Cameron Walk, Metro Centre, Gateshead NE11 9YR *tel:* 0191 460 3883.

Tyne and Wear

Newcastle upon Tyne

HMV Shop. 50 Northumberland St, Newcastle NE1 7AE *tel:* 0191 230 0626.

J G Windows Ltd. 1-7 Central Arcade, Newcastle upon Tyne NE1 5BP *tel:* 0191 232 1356. *Records, cassettes, CDs, m/order.*

Virgin Megastore. Monument Mall, 15-21 Northumberland Street, Newcastle NE1 7AE *tel:* 0191 230 5959/5956 *fax:* 0191 230 2218.

Sunderland

HMV Shop. 61 High St West, Sunderland, Tyne and Wear SR1 3DP *tel:* 0191 514 1267.

West Midlands

Birmingham

HMV Shop. 134 New St, Birmingham B2 4NP *tel:* 0121 643 7029. *CDs, cassettes and videos.*

HMV Store. 38 High St, Birmingham B4 7SL *tel:* 0121 643 2177. *Records, CDs, cassettes, videos.*

Tower Records. 5 Corporation St, Birmingham B2 4LP *tel:* 0121 616 2677 *fax:* 0121 616 2686. *CDs, videos, books, magazines, accs.*

Virgin Megastore. 96-98 Corporation St, Birmingham B4 6SX *tel:* 0121 236 2523. *CDs, cassettes, computer games, videos and accs.*

Sutton Coldfield

HMV Shop. 60 The Parade, Sutton Coldfield B72 1PD *tel:* 0121 355 3264. *CDs, cassettes and videos.*

Wolverhampton

HMV Shop. 8 The Gallery, Mander Sq, Wolverhampton WV1 3NJ *tel:* 01902 29978. *CDs, cassettes and videos.*

West Yorkshire

Bradford

HMV Shop. Unit 2, 18 Broadway, Bradford BD1 1EY *tel:* 01274 394900. *CDs, cassettes and videos.*

Leeds

HMV Shop. 1 Victoria Walk, Headrow Centre, Leeds LS1 6JD *tel:* 0113 245 5548. *Cassettes, CDs and videos.*

Wakefield

HMV Shop. 2 Kirkgate, Wakefield WF1 1SP *tel:* 01924 291281. *CDs, cassettes and videos.*

Wiltshire

Devizes

Heritage Records. 39 Woodland Rd, Patney, nr Devizes, Wilts SN10 3RD *tel:* 01380 840362 *also fax. Second-hand 78s and LPs.*

Salisbury

The Collector's Room (at Sutton's Music Centre). 3 Endless St, Salisbury, Wilts SP1 1DL *tel:* 01722 326153. *Classical and jazz records, cassettes, CDs (new and second-hand).*

Swindon

HMV Shop. 16-17 Regents St, Swindon SN1 1JQ *tel:* 01793 420963.

York, City of

York

Banks & Sons (Music) Ltd. 18 Lendal, York YO1 2AU *tel:* 01904 658836 *fax:* 01904 629547 *email:* tad40@dial.pipex.com. *Classical recordings.*

HMV Shop. 10a Coney St, York YO1 1NA *tel:* 01904 640218 *fax:* 01904 640318. *Cassettes, CDs, videos, laser discs, CDI.*

Scotland

Aberdeen City

Aberdeen

HMV Shop. 247-251 Union St, Aberdeen AB1 2BQ *tel:* 01224 575323. *Cassettes, CDs, books, magazines, video, laser disc, computer games.*

Virgin Megastore. 133 Union St, Aberdeen AB12 2BH *tel:* 01224 213050/212908 *fax:* 01224 213568.

Dundee City

Dundee

HMV Shop. 71-77 Murraygate, Dundee DD1 2EA *tel:* 01382 225383.

Edinburgh, City of

Edinburgh

Bauermeister Booksellers. 19 George IV Bridge, Edinburgh EH1 1EH *tel:* 0131 226 5561 *fax:* 0131 220 0679. *Cassettes, CDs, classical specialists.*

HMV Shop. 129 Princes St, Edinburgh EH2 4AH *tel:* 0131 226 3466. *CDs, cassettes, videos.*

HMV Shop. 43-44 St James Centre, Edinburgh EH1 3SL *tel:* 0131 556 1236. *CDs, cassettes and videos.*

Virgin Megastore. 125 Princes St, Edinburgh EH2 4BD *tel:* 0131 220 2230 *fax:* 0131 220 1757.

Fife

Dunfermline

Silver Service CD. 24 Touch Wards, Dunfermline, Fife KY12 7TG *tel:* 01383 738159 *email:* silverservicecd@btinternet.com. *CDs, m/order.*

Glasgow, City of

Glasgow

HMV Shop. 154-160 Sauchiehall St, Glasgow G2 3DH *tel:* 0141 332 6631.

HMV Shop. 72 Union St, Glasgow G1 3QS *tel:* 0141 221 1850. *Records, cassettes, CDs, books, videos.*

Tower Records. 217-221 Argyle St, Glasgow G2 8DL *tel:* 0141 204 2500 *fax:* 0141 248 3640.

Virgin Megastore. 28-32 Union St, Glasgow G1 3QX *tel:* 0141 221 0103. *CDs, cassettes and videos.*

Wales

Cardiff County Borough

Cardiff

HMV Shop. 51 Queen St, Cardiff CF1 4AS *tel:* 01222 227147. *Records, cassettes, CDs.*

Pembrokeshire

Haverfordwest

Swales Music Centre Ltd. 2-6 High St, Haverfordwest, Pembs SA61 2DJ *tel:* 01437 762059 *fax:* 01437 760872. *Records, cassettes, CDs, m/order.*

Swansea County

Swansea

HMV Shop. 21-23 Queens Arcade, The Quadrant Centre, Swansea SA1 3QW *tel:* 01792 462094 *fax:* 01792 455138. *LPs, CDs, video, accessories.*

Competitions
and
Scholarships

Competitions

Competitions are annual unless otherwise stated and are listed in alphabetical order of title. Some of these, such as the Kathleen Ferrier Award, have their final stages as public events like competitions and are listed in both **Scholarships and Grants** and **Competitions**.The closing date for applications is usually several months in advance of the competition date.

Competitions for Performers and Conductors

Admira Young Guitarist of the Year Competition. c/o Bath International Guitar Festival, PO Box 3697, London NW3 2HQ *tel:* 0171 831 0345 *fax:* 0171 831 0346. Philip Castang, mgr. *Aug 1998, applications by 15 Jun 1998. For age 20 and under. Application fee £30. First prize £1000.*

Albert Augustine Memorial International Guitar Competition. c/o Bath International Guitar Festival, PO Box 3697, London NW3 2HQ *tel:* 0171 831 0345 *fax:* 0171 831 0346. Philip Castang, mgr. *Aug 1998, applications by 15 Jun. For age 30 and under. Application fee £50. First prize £3000.*

Anglo-Czechoslovak Trust. 23 Stonefield St, London W1 0HW *tel:* 0171 278 8459 *also fax.* N Newton, treasurer. *Apr-May 1998, applications by 24 Feb 1998. 6 classes: str, w/wind and br, keyboard, singers, gui, ens. For young professional musicians and mus students. Works by Czech and Slovak composers only. No age limit. Application fee £12 (solo), £20 (ens). First prize: 2 return flights to Prague, accommodation for 4 people, and possibility of performance in Prague.*

Bayreuth Bursary Competition. c/o The Wagner Society, 45 Frankfield Rise, Tunbridge Wells, Kent TN2 5LF *tel:* 01892 539781. Roger Temple, admin. *Travel bursary to Bayreuth Festival awarded annually, for young Wagnerian singers of all voices who are British and Commonwealth citizens. Max age 35. Annual auditions held in London during Jan, applications by 24 Dec. First prize of tickets for performances at Bayreuth Festival with travel and accommodation. Half-recital in London during 1998-9 season.*

BBC Radio 3 Young Artists' Forum. Young Artists' Forum, Room 4002 BHXX, BBC Broadcasting House, London W1A 1AA *tel:* 0171 765 0139 *fax:* 0171 765 4317. Tracey Baumann-Wrotny. *Scheme devised to give opportunity to young insts, singers and ens to perform on the network. 18 places available. Closing date for applications May 1998. Solo performers and duos must be aged 18-25 in Jul; singers and accompanists must be aged 18-28 in Jul; ens of 3-8 members must be average age between 18 and 25 in Jul. Successful applicants offered shared recital in a concert series in autumn.*

BBC Young Musicians. BBC Music and Arts, EG30 East Tower, Television Centre, Wood La, London W12 7RJ *tel:* 0181 895 6143/4 *fax:* 0181 895 6146 *email:* young.musicians@bbc.co.uk. Jessica Brennan, admin. *Jul 1999-Mar 2000. Str, w/wind, br, perc, keyboard. Open to UK citizens aged 19 and under (performers), aged 24 and under (composers). Stage one auditions for the next competition held in Jul 1999, entries by 1 Apr 1999. £2000 prize for each concerto finalist, plus Lloyds Bank Travel Award for the winner.*

Birmingham International Piano Competition. 11 Peartree Dr, Pedmore, Stourbridge, W Midlands DY8 2LB *tel:* 01384 379306 *also fax.* Barbara Healey, admin. *Biennial competition for pianists of any nationality aged 18-30. 1999-2000. Fee: £75 (£25 refunded on attending 1st stage). First Prize: £3000, London debut recital, London Steinway recital, engagements and management; second prize: £2000; third prize: £1000; recital prize: £500; 4 Steinway awards.*

British Contemporary Piano Competition. 31 Lingholme Close, Cambridge CB4 3HW *tel:* 01223 357431. Philip Mead, ARAM founder and artistic dir. *Triennial. Open to British pianists aged 18-40. Repertoire entirely 20th C. Application fee £25. First prize £1200 and 10 engagements.*

British Reserve Insurance Conducting Prize/Seminar. National Association of Youth Orchestras, Ainslie House, 11 St Colme St, Edinburgh EH3 6AG *tel:* 0131 539 1087 *fax:* 0131 539 1069 *email:* nayo.office@virgin.net; http://pobox.com/~nayo. Carol Main, dir. *Biennial, next 1999. Age range 18-26. First prize £500.*

Bromsgrove Festival Young Musicians' Platform. c/o 10 Evertons Close, Droitwich Spa, Worcs WR9 8AE *tel:* 01527 575441 *fax:* 01527 575366 *email:* lgharris@compuserve.com. Andrew Harris, hon organiser. *1-3 May 1998, applications by 28 Feb. For young performers of any nationality aged 17-25 (any inst or voice) of gr 8 distinction standard. First prize £750, second prize £350, third prize £200. Application fee £15.*

Cardiff Singer of the World Competition. BBC Wales, Broadcasting House, Llandaff, Cardiff CF5 2YQ *tel:* 01222 572888 *fax:* 01222 552973. Anna Williams, admin. *Biennial competition organised by BBC Wales. Jun, applications by Sep. Singers aged 18 and above must be nominated by broadcasting organisations. First prize £10,000.*

Clonter Opera Farm Inter-Conservatoire Opera Prize. Clonter Opera Farm, Swettenham Heath, Congleton, Cheshire CW12 2LR *tel:* 01260 224638 *fax:* 01260 224742. Josie Aston, asst to gen mgr. *Feb-Mar 1998. Annual inter-conservatoire opera prize worth £1500. Open to singers of UK residence aged 20-35 nominated by heads of conservatoires for audition.*

Croydon Symphony Orchestra Soloists Award. 383 Addiscombe Rd, Croydon CR0 7LJ. Alma Burcombe, admin. *Jun-Jul 1998 at Goldsmiths College, London. Professional and amateur solo instrumentalists or singers aged 29 and under on 31 May 1998. Applications by May-Jun. Entry fee: £12-15. Prize: cash award and performance at Fairfield Halls, Croydon with Croydon Symphony Orchestra.*

Donatella Flick Conducting Competition. 47 Brunswick Gardens, London W8 4AW *tel:* 0171 792 2885 *fax:* 0171 792 2574. Judy Strang, admin. *Biennial. Next competition 30 May-2 Jun 1998, applications by 16 Jan. Award of £15,000 to subsidise period of up to one year as assistant conductor with London Symphony Orchestra, specialist study and concert engagements. Open to European Community nationals under 35. Application fee £20. Final at the Barbican with the LSO.*

Early Bird Opera. PO Box 5, 220 Penarth Rd, Cardiff CF2 3XD. Chris Searle, dir. *Biennial, applications by Jun 1998. For composers, performers and conductors. Awards of £1000 (composers) and £350 (insts and singers).*

Eastbourne Symphony Orchestra Young Musician Awards. 7 Prideaux Rd, Eastbourne, East Sussex BN21 2NW *tel:* 01323 724763. Brian Knights, awards admin. *Concerto competition for young soloists of any nationality. Jnr section (under 18) held Jan 1998; snr section (under 23) held Feb-Mar 1998, applications by 8 Dec 1997. First prize in snr competition £300 and an opportunity to play a concerto with the orchestra; jnr competition first prize £150. Application fee £10 (jnr), £20 (snr).*

Essex Young Musician of the Year. Ongar Music Club, Corbetts House, Norwood End, Fyfield, Chipping Ongar, Essex CM5 0RW *tel:* 01277 899337 *also fax.* Jean Hall, admin. *27-28 Jun 1998, applications by 31 May. Total prize money £1725. Winner receives £500, plus recitals for Ongar Music Club and others, and an invitation to appear at a leading London venue. Age limit 25, with two prizes for those aged 18 and under. Open to instrumentalists (except organists) and singers who were born, live or attend school or college in the Essex postal area. Application fee £25.*

E T Bryant Memorial Prize. Music Library, University of Huddersfield, Queensgate, Huddersfield HD1 3DH *tel:* 01484 472009 *fax:* 01484 517987 *email:* rnbuxton@hud.ac.uk. Richard Buxton, mus librarian. *Prize of £200 to be awarded annually for a significant contribution to the literature of mus librarianship. Entries are invited from students of Library and Information Science and librarians within their first 5 yrs in mus librarianship. Entries by 31 Jan.*

Gerald Moore Award. Courtyard House, Neopardy, Crediton, Devon EX17 5EP. Katie Avey, admin. *Biennial prize for UK pno accompanists (residents or studying full-time) of the song repertoire. Next competition Spring 1998, applications by Dec 1997. Majority of entrants are nominations from colleges. A few outside places for pianists residing or studying full-time in the UK under the age of 29. Auditions in London. Independent candidates selected from written applications. Award £2000.*

Great Elm Music Festival Vocal Award. Bridge House, Great Elm, Frome, Somerset BA11 3NY *tel:* 01373 812383 *fax:* 01373 812083. Maureen Lehane Wishart, organiser. *25-27 Aug 1998, entries by 31 Jul. Age limit 22-32. Application fee £20. First prize £2000.*

Grimsby International Singers Competition. 23 Enfield Av, New Waltham, Grimsby, N E Lincs DN36 5RD *tel:* 01472 812113. Anne Holmes, joint chair. *Triennial. Next 4-8 Oct 1998, applications by 30 Mar. Competition open to all nationalities, voice categories and accompanists. Age range: 20-30 (singers), 20-27 (accompanists). Four prizes of £2500, four of £1250, four of £750, five independent song prizes*

Richard Tauber Prize for Singers 1998

A prize of £2,500 and a London Recital

Open to young singers resident in UK or in Austria

Preliminary auditions in London and Vienna – March 1998
Public Final Audition – Wigmore Hall – 11 June 1998

**Full details and application forms from Hedwig Swan
Anglo-Austrian Music Society
46 Queen Anne's Gate, London SW1H 9AU
Tel: 0171-222 0366**

London International String Quartet Competition

10 - 16 April 2000

Goldsmiths' Hall
All stages of Competition (10 - 15 April)

Barbican Centre
Awards Ceremony and Gala Concert (16 April)

Preliminary details from
The Administrator : Dennis Sayer, 62 High Street, Fareham,
Hampshire PO16 7BG
Tel : (01329) 283603 Fax : (01329) 281969

Invitation

To Aspiring Oboists Worldwide
Compete in Great Britain's
INTERNATIONAL OBOE COMPETITION

Isle of Wight International Oboe Competition

Thursday 4th - Sunday 9th May 1999

Lady Barbirolli OBE
Artistic Director and Chairman of International Jury

Application Final Date: 1st December 1998

PRIZES
First: £1000, Trophy and London Debut Concert
Second: £800 · **Third:** £500 · **Fourth:** £250

For Competitor's Brochure
Julia Holofcener, Inc., Event Producers
Alpine House, 13 Alpine Road, Ventnor, Isle of Wight PO38 1BT, United Kingdom
Tel: +44 (0) 1983 853411 · Fax: +44 (0) 1983 856411
e-mail: oboecomp@islandpartners.co.uk
web site: www.wightonline.co.uk/oboecomp

THE KATHLEEN

FERRIER

AWARDS

PATRON: HRH THE DUCHESS OF KENT GCVO

The 43rd Competition
20 -24 April 1998
at the Wigmore Hall
Semi-final and final auditions
open to the public

Full details from
The Administrator,
Kathleen Ferrier Memorial Scholarship Fund,
52 Rosebank, Holyport Road, London SW6 6LY

Please enclose an SAE.

of £250, accompanists prize of £750. Application fee £40 (singers), £25 (accompanists).

Haverhill Sinfonia Soloist Competition. 8 Templars Ct, Haverhill, Suffolk CB9 9AJ *tel:* 01440 763799 *also fax.* Kevin Hill, mus dir; Deena Shypitka, sec. *26 Sep 1998, applications by end Aug. W/wind, br, str, pno and singers. No age limit and any nationality. Administration fee £10. Six prizes totalling £885 including a first prize of £425, solo performance with orch in May 1999 and solo recital in Jul 1999 to be broadcast by BBC Radio Suffolk. Four other performance prizes. Send sae for details from Apr.*

International Early Music Network Young Artists' Competition. The Early Music Network, Sutton House, 2-4 Homerton High St, London E9 6JQ *tel:* 0181 533 2921 *fax:* 0181 533 2922. *Biennial. Next Jul 1999, applications by early Jan 1999. Open to vocal and inst ens (min 3 persons) aged 17-30 (aged 17-35 for singers) who specialise in repertoire from the Middle Ages to the 19th C and use the playing techniques and stylistic conventions of early mus. Part of the York Early Music Festival.*

International Young Instrumentalist of the Year Competition. Eisteddfod Office, Llangollen, Denbighshire LL20 8NG *tel:* 01978 860236 *fax:* 01978 869047 *email:* lime@celtic.co.uk; http://www.llangollen.org.uk. Mrs E Davies, mus admin. *11 Jul 1998, applications by 15 Apr. Amateur insts aged 25 and under. Competition is part of Llangollen International Eisteddfod in Jul. Application fee £2 for UK competitors, no fee for overseas competitors. First prize £200 and trophy.*

International Young Singer of the Year Competition. Eisteddfod Office, Llangollen, Denbighshire LL20 8NG *tel:* 01978 860236 *fax:* 01978 869047 *email:* lime@celtic.co.uk; http://www.llangollen.org.uk. Mrs E Davies, mus admin. *11 Jul 1998, applications by 15 Apr. Competition for amateur singers aged 16-32 as part of Llangollen International Eisteddfod in Jul. Application fee £2 for UK competitors, no fee for overseas competitors. First prize £200 and trophy.*

Isle of Wight International Oboe Competition. Alpine House, 13 Alpine Rd, St Lawrence, Ventnor, Isle of Wight P038 1BT *tel:* 01983 853411 *fax:* 01983 856411 *email:* oboecomp@islandpartners.co.uk; http://www.wightonline.co.uk/oboecomp. Julia Holofcener, event producer. *Biennial. Next 4-9 May 1999, entries by 1 Dec 1998. For oboists who have not won an international competition and are aged 30 or under on date of finals (9 May 1999). Competition includes chmbr mus at semi-final stage. First prize is a London debut and £1000, second prize £800, third prize £500, fourth prize £250. Application fee £30.*

Julius Isserlis Scholarship. Royal Philharmonic Society, 10 Stratford Pl, London W1N 9AE *tel:* 0171 491 8110 *fax:* 0171 493 7463. Richard Fisher, gen admin. *Scholarship worth £20,000 over two years to fund study abroad. Awarded biennially by competition to students aged 15-25 of any nationality permanently resident in the UK. Selected performing categories: fl and ob spring 1999. Entry fee £20.*

Kathleen Ferrier Awards. Kathleen Ferrier Memorial Scholarship Fund, 52 Rosebank, Holyport Rd, London SW6 6LY *tel:* 0171 381 0985 *also fax.* Shirley Barr, admin. *20-24 Apr 1998, entries by 1 Mar. Open to British singers (and those from the British Commonwealth and Republic of Ireland) aged 21-28. Application fee £25. First prize: £10,000 (from total prize money of £17,500), and Wigmore Hall recital.*

Leeds Conductors' Competition. Music Dept, Leeds Leisure Services, Leeds Town Hall, Leeds LS1 3AD *tel:* 0113 247 8335/6 *fax:* 0113 247 8397. Matthew Sims, dir. *Triennial, next date to be finalised. British-born conductors aged under 35. Application fee £50. First prize £1500 and numerous prestigious engagements.*

Leeds International Pianoforte Competition. The Piano Competition Office, University of Leeds, Leeds LS2 9JT *tel:* 0113 244 6586 *also fax;* 0113 244 6586 *also fax.* Françoise Logan, hon admin. *Triennial. Next Sep 2000, applications by 15 Mar. Competition for pianists of all nationalities aged 32 and under. Application fee £40. First prize £10,000 from total prize money c £57,000.*

Lionel Tertis International Viola Competition. The Secretariat, Erin Arts Centre, Victoria Square, Port Erin, Isle of Man IM9 6LD *tel:* 01624 835858 *fax:* 01624 836658. Martin Norbury, admin. *Triennial. Next 19-26 Aug 2000, entries by 31 Mar 2000. Open to any nationality aged 30 and under. First prize £3000 and Wigmore Hall recital. Application fee £54.*

London International String Quartet Competition. 62 High St, Fareham, Hants PO16 7BG *tel:* 01329 283603 *fax:* 01705 321080. Dennis Sayer, admin. *Triennial. Next 10-16 Apr 2000, entries by 1 Dec 1999. Open to str quartets of all nationalities, max average age 30 and total age of players not exceeding 120 yrs. Application fee £50 per quartet. First prize £8000.*

Maggie Teyte Prize Competition. 2 Keats Grove, London NW3 2RT *tel:* 0171 435 5861 *fax:* 0171 431 5706. Felicity Guinness, admin. *Annual. Next Jan 1998, applications by 1 Dec 1997. Registration fee £18. Prize of £2000 awarded together with a recital in association with the Friends of the Royal Opera House and the Covent Garden Festival. Open*

to female singers aged 30 and under. Application fee £18. Also Megan Foster Accompanists Prize £250. Send sae for application form.

Musicale Young Instrumentalist Competition. Musicale plc, 20 Salisbury Av, Harpenden, Herts AL5 2QG *tel:* 01582 460978 *fax:* 01582 767343. Gillian and David Johnston, dirs. *Biennial, next 1998. Young instrumentalists aged 10-15. Cash prize plus concerto performance with the National Children's Chamber Orchestra of Great Britain.*

National Concert Band Festival. BASBWE, 7 Dingle Close, Tytherington, Macclesfield SK10 2UT *tel:* 01625 430807 *also fax.* Liz Winter, festival admin. *5 symphonic wind band categories: beginners (aged 14 and under), school, youth (aged 19 and under), community, open. 3 big band categories: school, youth, open. Regionals Nov-Dec, finals held Apr 1998 at the RNCM, Manchester.*

National Mozart Competition. 66 Talbot St, Southport, Merseyside PR8 1LU *tel:* 01704 530903. Barbara Dix, sec. *Nov, applications by Oct. Annual competition for singers of any nationality aged under 28 (female), or under 30 (male). Preliminary rounds Oct in London, Manchester, Cardiff, Glasgow and Dublin. Application fee £25. Prize money of £2500 plus engagements. Also Verdi/Wagner prize of £250 for best performance by a male singer of a Verdi or Wagner aria.*

Newport International Competition for Young Pianists. Civic Centre, Newport, Gwent NP9 4UR *tel:* 01633 232888 *fax:* 01633 232808. Vincent Paliczka, hon sec. *Triennial. Next 2000, entries by May. Open to professional pianists of any nationality, aged under 25. Application fee £30. First prize £2000, recording opportunity and concert series.*

NFMS/Young Concert Artists Award. Francis House, Francis St, London SW1P 1DE *tel:* 0171 828 7320 *fax:* 0171 828 5504. Kate Fearnley, award admin. *Entries Jan 1998, auditions spring 1998. Four yearly cycle: 1998 instrumentalists; 1999 men's voices; 2000 pianists; 2001 women's voices. Age limits: men's and women's voices under 30, instrumentalists under 28. Prize of concerts nationwide shared between different artists.*

Norfolk Young Musician Competition. Music at Saint George's, Wahnfried, 4 Church Close, Buxton, Norwich NR10 5ER *tel:* 01603 279742. Ivor Hosgood, chmn and sec. *Nov, entries by 30 Sep. For gr 8+ singers and instrumentalists aged 21 and under who either work, receive tuition or are resident in Norfolk. Three cash prizes plus sponsorship for a public concert later the same year as well as one in the Norfolk and Norwich Festival the following year.*

Parkhouse Award. c/o GBZ Management, PO Box 11845, London SE21 8ZS *tel:* 0181 761 6565 *fax:* 0181 670 3198 *email:* gbz-mgmt@compuserve.com. Gwenneth Bransby-Zachary, admin. *Biennial, next spring 1999, then 2001. Open to pno-based str ens, duos, trios and pno quartets only, age range 18-32. Applications by 1 Dec. First prize, three concerts in prestigious London venues. Application fee £25.*

Richard Tauber Prize. Anglo-Austrian Music Society, 46 Queen Anne's Gate, London SW1H 9AU *tel:* 0171 222 0366 *fax:* 0171 233 0293. Tony Fessler, gen sec. *Biennial. Next spring 1998, applications by 6 Feb 1998. Travel bursary and public London recital. Open to British and Austrian singers aged 21-30 (women), 21-32 (men). Application fee £20. First prize £2500.*

Robert William and Florence Amy Brant Pianoforte Competition. 83 Windsor Rd, Oldbury, W Midlands B68 8PB. Miss G L Brant. *Next 4, 5 and 11 Jul 1998, applications by 2 May. Awarded to pianists of any nationality, aged 20-30. Entry fee £30. First prize £1000, second £500, third £250.*

Royal Over-Seas League Music Competition. Royal Over-Seas League, Park Pl, St James's St, London SW1A 1LR *tel:* 0171 408 0214 ext 219 *fax:* 0171 499 6738. Roderick Lakin, dir of cultural affairs. *Feb-Mar, applications by 16 Jan. Open to commonwealth or former commonwealth citizens. Max age 28 (insts), 30 (singers), also ens. Application fee £20 (insts and ens). £4000 first prize and gold medal; £4000 for ens. £25,000 in prizes including awards for overseas students.*

Sainsbury's Choir of the Year Competition. c/o Kallaway Ltd, 2 Portland Rd, Holland Pk, London W11 4LA *tel:* 0171 221 7883 *fax:* 0171 229 4595. Kate Jones, mgr. *Biennial. Next Nov 1998, entries by Dec 1997. Open to amateur choirs of 20-100 members. No age limit. Three categories: youth choirs; men's or women's choirs; mixed voice choirs. Auditions Mar-May, finals held in Nov and televised on BBC 2. First prize in each category of £2000; overall winner receives a further £1000 plus £1000 to commission a new piece of choral mus.*

St Albans International Organ Festival Competition. PO Box 80, St Albans AL3 4HR *tel:* 01727 844765 *also fax.* Anne Collins, admin. *Biennial. Next 7-17 Jul 1999, applications by 12 Mar 1999. Open to organists of all nationalities born after 7 Jul 1968 for interpretation competition and 7 Jul 1964 for Tournemire Prize. Two competitions: Interpretation Competition and Tournemire Prize for Improvisation. Entry fee £35 per competition or £60 for both. Interpretation first prize £4000 plus recitals; second prize £2500 plus recitals; third prize £1500. Tournemire prize £2000 plus recitals.*

SHELL LSO MUSIC SCHOLARSHIP

One of the most prestigious annual awards for young instrumentalists, the Shell LSO Music Scholarship features a different group of instruments each year working in a four-year cycle.
Forthcoming Scholarships are:

1998 Strings
1999 Brass

Regional auditions and workshops are held early in the year, and the National Final takes place at the Barbican in London in the summer.
The Scholarship is open to candidates from all parts of the UK, aged between 14 and 22. The award of £6,000 is provided for the musical development of the winner and further cash prizes are available.

Detailed information and application forms are available in the previous October for any Scholarship year from: The Administrator, Shell LSO Music Scholarship, London Symphony Orchestra, Barbican Centre, London EC2Y 8DS.

TUNBRIDGE WELLS INTERNATIONAL YOUNG CONCERT ARTISTS COMPETITION
in association with Mazda Cars (UK) Ltd

2nd to 5th JULY 1998

Total cash prizes £11,000

Overall winner £4000

Are you ready for this?

For competitors born after 5th July 1974
Advanced students or professionals

3 Sections:
Piano, Strings, Wind

Rules and Entry Form from:
The Entries Co-ordinator
TWIYCA Competition Office
77, Mount Ephraim, Tunbridge Wells
Kent, TN4 8BS, England
Tel: (01892) 510088 or Fax: (01892 538547)
From outside UK dial International Access Code + 44 + 1892 + last 6 numbers

Closing date for receipt of entries: 23rd Feb. 1998

Tunbridge Wells International Young Concert Artists Competition is a Registered Charity

---

In association with CLASSIC *f*M

Royal Over-Seas League

46th Annual Music Competition 1998

Chairman of Adjudicators
Lady Barbirolli OBE

The Competition has four solo classes: Strings; Woodwind/Brass; Keyboard and Singers. There is also a major award for Chamber Ensembles.

The Competition is open to Commonwealth citizens (including the UK) and also citizens of former Commonwealth countries.

Age limit:
Instrumentalists 28; Singers 30

Over £25,000 in prizes.

Auditions in London February and March 1998.

Deadline Applications: 16th January 1998

Further information and prospectus:

Roderick Lakin,
Director of Cultural Affairs,
Royal Over-Seas League,
Over-Seas House,
Park Place,
St James's Street,
London SW1A 1LR.

Tel: 0171 408 0214 ext. 219
Fax: 0171 499 6738

Scottish International Piano Competition. c/o RSAMD, 100 Renfrew St, Glasgow G2 3DB *tel:* 0141 332 4101 ext 243; 01389 830218 *fax:* 0141 332 8901. Robin Barr, hon sec. *Triennial. Next competition held at RSAMD, Glasgow, 10-19 Sep 1998, applications by 31 Mar. Open to pianists of all nationalities. Max age 32. Application fee £30. First prize £10,000.*

Shell LSO Music Scholarship. c/o The Scholarship Administrator, London Symphony Orchestra, Barbican Centre, Barbican, London EC2Y 8DS *tel:* 0171 272 4032 *fax:* 0171 263 1831 *email:* shell@lso.co.uk; http://www.lso.co.uk. Helen Smith, admin. *Information available Oct, entries by mid-Dec. Orch instrumentalists aged 14-22. Insts vary; 1998 strings. £6000 annual scholarship. Auditions, w/shops and m/classes with LSO principals.*

South East Musicians' Platform. South East Music Schemes, 19 Bourne Rd, London N8 9HJ *tel:* 0181 340 4116. Deborah Rees, admin dir. *Next competition Jul 1998, entries by 22 May. Ens, insts and singers up to the age of 30. Funded by South East Arts. First prize, concerts in the South East and funds to commission a new work. Application fee £15. Send SAE for applications from Mar 1998.*

Texaco Young Musician of Wales. 1 Westferry Circus, Canary Wharf, London E14 4HA *tel:* 0171 719 3000; 0181 549 7660 *fax:* 0171 719 5175. June P McCullough. *Biennial event organised in partnership with Côr Meibion De Cymru, (South Wales Male Choir). Final Mar 1999, entries by 31 Jul 1998. Open to instrumentalists aged 14-19 who have lived or studied in Wales for a minimum of 3 years. The final is broadcast on TV and the winner receives the Texaco Young Musician of Wales trophy and a prize of £1000. Refundable application fee of £10. Second prize £750, third prize £500, 3 other prizes of £250.*

Thames Valley Young Musicians' Platform. Kencot Lodge, Kencot, Lechlade, Glos GL7 3QX *tel:* 01367 860588 *fax:* 01367 860619 *email:* 100067.2013@compuserve.com. Chris Yapp, dir. *Sep-Oct 1998, applications by 30 Jun. Age limit 20-26 (instrumentalists), 28 (singers). Candidates born, educated, living or working in Oxfordshire or Berkshire. First prize £250 plus recitals.*

Tunbridge Wells International Young Concert Artists Competition. TWIYCA, Competition Office, MCL Group 77, Mount Ephraim, Tunbridge Wells, Kent TN4 8BS *tel:* 01892 510088 *fax:* 01892 538547. Arthur Boyd, chmn. *Biennial. Next 2-5 Jul 1998, entries by 23 Feb 1998. Aged under 24 on date of final. 3 sections: pno, str, wind. Total prize money available £10,500 plus London recital. Application fee £45.*

West Belfast Classical Bursary Award. 56 Oakhurst Av, Blacks Rd, Dunmurry, Belfast BT10 0PE *tel:* 01232 626269 *also fax.* Una Downey, sec. *15-18 Apr 1998. Annual Easter event in Belfast for musicians born in Northern or Southern Ireland. Instrumentalists aged 17-23, singers aged 18-30 on 10 March 1998. Applications by 14 Feb. Application fee £6. Prizes of £9000, BBC and RTE studio recordings, trophy and various concert and recital opportunities.*

World Piano Competition London. 28 Wallace Rd, London N1 2PG *tel:* 0171 354 1087 *fax:* 0171 704 1053 *email:* ldn-ipc@dircon.co.uk. S Aronovsky, chmn and artistic controller. *Triennial. Next 2000, entries by Jan. Pianists of all nationalities aged 29 and under. Application fee £50 (provisional). First prize in 1997 was £10,000.*

Yehudi Menuhin International Competition for Young Violinists. 8 St Georges Terrace, London NW1 8XJ *tel:* 0171 911 0901 *fax:* 0171 911 0903. Kim Gaynor, admin. *Next 10-18 Apr 1998, applications by 31 Oct 1997. 2 sections: under 16 (jnr), under 22 (snr). Application fee: 450FF. First prizes 20,000FF (jnr) and 30,000FF (snr) plus performance at gala concert conducted by Yehudi Menuhin for the winner of each section.*

Young Artists Platform. Tillett Trust, Courtyard House, Neopardy, Crediton, Devon EX17 5EP. Katie Avey, admin. *Entry forms available in Oct, applications by Nov, auditions in Jan-Feb. Open to musicians residing or studying f/t in the British Isles. Age limits: inst soloists 20-25, singers 23-28, ens of up to 6 players all members must be within same age limits. Application fee £10, returned at audition. No cash prizes, successful candidates given concerts including Fairfield, Croydon and the St David's Hall, Cardiff, plus a demo tape, publicity photos and a publicity brochure.*

Young Welsh Singers' Competition. Arts Council of Wales, 9 Museum Pl, Cardiff CF1 3NX *tel:* 01222 394711 *fax:* 01222 221447. Roy Bohana, mus dir. *Biennial. Next Jun 1998, entries by 1 Jan. Open to those born and educated in Wales or living and/or working in Wales. For singers at the beginning of their professional careers. First prize £2000.*

Competitions for Composers

Clements Memorial Chamber Music Competition. Fernside, Copthall Green, Upshire, Waltham Abbey, Essex EN9 3SZ. Raymond Cassidy, hon sec. *Biennial. Next 1998, entries by 1 Oct. Chmbr composition (3-8 players); min length 15 mins. Entry fee £4. First prize £750. Send sae for details.*

Early Bird Opera. PO Box 5, 220 Penarth Rd, Cardiff CF2 3XD. Chris Searle, dir. *Biennial, applications by Jun 1998. For composers, performers and conductors. Awards of £1000 (composers) and £350 (insts and singers).*

The Galliard Ensemble Composition Competition. c/o 13 Ashbourne Av, South Woodford, London E18 1PQ *tel:* 0171 791 0495. Kathryn Thomas. *Spring 1998, entries by 1 Feb. Compositions for wind quintet (fl, ob, cl, hn, bsn plus standard orch doublings) in any style invited from professional, amateur and student composers of any age and nationality (school age section available for age 18 and under in full-time educ). Entries should comprise full score plus parts and may include a tape if desired. Recommended duration up to 15 mins. Winning pieces in both categories to be performed at the Woodford and Wanstead Festival of Chamber Music and composers will receive a trophy.*

Gregynog Composers' Award of Wales. Festival Office, Gregynog, Newtown, Powys SY16 3PW *tel:* 01686 621493 *fax:* 01686 650656. Julie Turner, festival organiser. *Entries by 4 Apr 1998. Open to all nationalities, no age limits. Special award available for composers aged 22 and under. Application fee £5. First prize £1000, 2 week residency at Gregynog and performance at 1998 Gregynog Festival. Application fee £5. Composition criteria to be confirmed.*

Dr Harold Smart Competition. Royal School of Church Music, Cleveland Lodge, Westhumble St, Westhumble, Dorking RH5 6BW *tel:* 01306 877676 *fax:* 01306 887260. Harry Bramma. *Competition for short anthem; deadline for applications Jan. Prize of £100 plus publication by RSCM.*

Lloyds Bank Young Composer Workshop. BBC Young Musicians, Room EG 30, East Tower Television Centre, Wood La, London W12 7RJ *tel:* 0181 895 6143/4 *fax:* 0181 895 6974 *email:* young.musicians@bbc.co.uk. Jessica Brennan, admin. *Open to UK citizens aged 16-24. Age limit 16-24. Applications by 1 Apr 1999 to be returned with one example of recent composition not exceeding 15 minutes in duration.*

Masterprize International Competion for Composition. PO Box 12713, London NW6 6WR *tel:* 0171 624 5859; 0181 991 2819 *fax:* 0171 624 7606. Louise Price, competition mgr; Madeleine Milne, asst mgr. *Registration 30 March 1999. Completed manuscripts by end July 1999. Gala concert spring 2000. New composition of between 8 and 12 minutes scored for normal symphonic forces; works including voice or in concerto form will not be accepted. No age or geographical limit. First prize £25,000 and recording release. Multiple radio broadcasts world-wide at semi-final stage. CD covermount with BBC Music Magazine at final stage.*

The Match Composition Prize. Burnside House, Melbourne, York YO4 4QJ *tel:* 01759 318440 *email:* 101600.3130@compuserve.com. *Annual. Next 1998. No age limit. Application fee £15. First prize £1000.*

Royal Philharmonic Society Composition Prize. 10 Stratford Pl, London W1N 9AE *tel:* 0171 491 8110 *fax:* 0171 493 7463. Richard Fisher, gen admin. *Annual award. Application by mid-November for award in December. Open to registered students past or present of any conservatoire or university within the UK, aged 28 and under on closing date. Application fee £20.*

Stephen Oliver Prize. Stephen Oliver Trust, c/o P W Productions, 7 Leicester Pl, London WC2H 7BP. *Biennial, next 1998. The Trust was set up in 1993 in memory of Stephen Oliver and aims to encourage young people working in contemporary opera. Entrants aged 35 and under. First prize of £10,000 awarded for the composition of a chmbr opera set from a given libretto (format may change with next competition). Registration fee £10 should not be sent with enquiries.*

Vivian Ellis Prize. The King's Head Theatre, 115 Upper St, London N1 1QN *tel:* 0171 226 8561 ext 21 *fax:* 0171 226 8507. Abigail Anderson, admin. *A national competition to encourage new composers, lyricists and librettists for the musical theatre. Entries by spring for summer/autumn w/shop and showcase. Application fee £15. Supported by PRS, Stoll Moss Theatres, Warner/Chappell Music Ltd and Rose-Morris.*

Dr William Baird Ross Prize for Composition in Church Music. 10 Strathalmond Pk, Barnton, Edinburgh EH4 8AL *tel:* 0131 339 1113. Mr K Hatton, trustee. *Triennial. Next 1999, entries accepted Mar-May. Open to composers of any age, resident and working in Scotland. First prize £250, second prize £175, third prize £100.*

Peter Whittingham Trust. c/o Musicians Benevolent Fund, 16 Ogle St, London W1P 8JB *tel:* 0171 636 4481 *fax:* 0171 637 4307. *Annual award of £5000 open to individuals for projects in popular mus or jazz. Applications for course fees not accepted. Applications from Jul-Aug, interviews Nov.*

Pocklington Apprenticeship Trust. Town Clerk and Chief Executive, RB of Kensington and Chelsea, Town Hall, Hornton St, London W8 7NX *tel:* 0171 361 2239. Julia Carroll, admin offr. *Small educ awards for young people aged 21 and under in financial need, born and/or living in the Royal Borough for 10 yrs. Max grant awarded £300.*

PRS/NFMS Awards for Enterprise. Francis House, Francis St, London SW1P 1DE *tel:* 0171 828 7320 *fax:* 0171 828 5504 *email:* postmaster@ nfms.demon.co.uk. Russell Jones, chief exec. *Awards made Jul for voluntary mus societies, choirs and orchs that show enterprise in concert programming. Application forms available Jan. Applications by 31 Mar.*

Sir Richard Stapley Educational Trust. PO Box 57, Tonbridge, Kent TN9 1ZT. *Small grants worth £250-1000 for graduates aged over 24 on 1 Oct of the proposed academic year with a first or upper second degree studying for higher degrees at a university in the UK and who are not in receipt of local authority, research council, British Academy or other similar public bodies awards. Send sae for application form. Applications by 31 Mar, with two academic references in sealed envelopes.*

Royal College of Organists. 7 St Andrew St, Holborn, London EC4A 3LQ *tel:* 0171 936 3606 *fax:* 0171 353 8244. Gordon Clarke, registrar. *A number of trusts available to organists who are members of the College (non-members considered in exceptional circumstances). Applications by 30 Apr 1998.*

RVW Trust. 7th Floor, Manfield House, 1 Southampton St, London WC2 0LR *tel:* 0171 379 6547 *fax:* 0171 240 6333. Bernard Benoliel, admin and sec. *Founder, Ralph Vaughan Williams. Corporate Trustee, Musicians' Benevolent Fund. Assists with the cost of first Master's Degrees in mus composition (non electro-acoustic) for British applicants or those of British residency. Does not consider applications towards cost of other degrees, summer courses or PhDs. Applications by mid-May.*

Ryan Davies Memorial Awards. 1 Squire Ct, The Marina, Swansea SA1 3XB *tel:* 01792 301500 *also fax.* Michael Evans, sec. *Awards worth £500-2000 to assist young Welsh performers aged 16-30 in mus and drama. Applications by 30 May.*

Schools Music Association Founder's Fund. 71 Margaret Rd, New Barnet, Herts EN4 9NT *fax:* 0181 440 6919. Maxwell Pryce, hon sec. *Small awards made to help with purchase costs of mus insts and summer schools available to British school pupils and students aged 18 and under in further and higher education.*

Scottish Arts Council Travel and Training Bursaries. Performing Arts Dept (Music), 12 Manor Pl, Edinburgh EH3 7DD *tel:* 0131 226 6051 *fax:* 0131 225 9833 *email:* helen.jamieson.sac@artsfb.org.uk. Helen Jamieson, mus offr. *Bursaries of up to £1500 for instrumentalists, singers, composers and conductors to extend skills (f/t study excluded). Applicants of any age must be based in Scotland and have worked in the profession for 2 yrs. Applications by Feb 1998. Full details and application forms from the mus offr.*

Scottish International Education Trust. 22 Manor Pl, Edinburgh EH3 7DS *tel:* 0131 225 1113 *also fax.* J F McClellan, dir. *Grants to promote individual Scottish talent or for projects contributing to the quality of life in Scotland. Applications in writing to above address.*

Shell LSO Music Scholarship. London Symphony Orchestra, Barbican Centre, Barbican, London EC2Y 8DS *tel:* 0171 588 1116 *fax:* 0171 374 0127 *email:* shell@lso.co.uk; http://www.lso.co.uk. Helen Smith, admin. *Annual competition with a first prize of £6000 for orch instrumentalists aged 14-22. Auditions, w/shops and m/classes with LSO principals. 1998 (strings). Applications by Dec.*

South East Music Schemes. 19 Bourne Rd, London N8 9HJ *tel:* 0181 340 4116. Deborah Rees, admin dir. *Awards of up to £1000 for p/grad singers, instrumentalists and composers based in the SE Arts region, who may not receive mandatory awards towards further study in the UK or abroad. Age limit 30. Applications by 22 May 1998, send SAE for application form from Mar 1998. Funded by South East Arts. Application fee £15.*

Stephen Arlen Memorial Fund. London Coliseum, St Martin's La, London WC2N 4ES *tel:* 0171 836 0111 ext 355 *fax:* 0171 240 7730. Teresa Howell, exec asst to dir of business and admin. *Annual award of £3000 (may be split) to a UK resident aged 18-30, following a career in opera, mus, dance or drama for a specific project. This is specifically not intended for the funding of study or research of any kind. Next award autumn 1998, applications by end of Feb.*

Sybil Tutton Awards. c/o Musicians Benevolent Fund, 16 Ogle St, London W1P 8JB *tel:* 0171 636 4481 *fax:* 0171 637 4307. *Awards to assist exceptionally talented opera students aged 18-30 with the cost of training on a recognised course. Applications from Nov-Apr for auditions in spring. Application fee £10.*

Sydney Perry Foundation Award. KPMG/Martin Musical Scholarship Fund, Lawn Cottage, 23a Brackley Rd, Beckenham, Kent BR3 1RB

tel: 0181 658 9432 *also fax.* Martyn Jones, admin. *Specifically for p/grad study. Two scholarships awarded annually. Applications by 1 Dec for award the following year; auditions in Jan. Send SAE for application form.*

Tait Memorial Trust. 4/80 Elm Park Gardens, London SW10 9PD *tel:* 0171 351 0561 *fax:* 0171 349 0531. Isla Baring, chmn. *Bi-annual, May-Jun and Nov-Dec. Awards to provide training and performance opportunities and generally to help further the careers of young professional Australian musicians in the UK. Age limit 30. Apply with CV, two references and project budget. Please send SAE and tape if possible.*

Thalben-Ball Memorial Awards. St Michael's Vestry, Cornhill, London EC3V 9DS *tel:* 0181 658 9428 *also fax;* 0171 626 8841. Jonathan Rennert, trustee and hon sec. *Annual funds ranging from £100-1600 for young organists and church musicians of any nationality studying in the UK. Age limit usually 26. Applications by 1 Apr annually. Also funds available for annual scholarship for Assistant Organist at St Michael's Church, Cornhill.*

Sir Thomas Beecham Trust. Denton House, Denton, Harleston, Norfolk IP20 0AA *tel:* 01986 788780. Lady Beecham, trustee. *Scholarships, tenable for 3 yrs, established in partnership with certain universities. Available to 1st year students studying for a mus degree and nominated by the university.*

Sir Thomas White's Educational Foundation. General Charities City of Coventry, Old Bablake, Hill St, Coventry CV1 4AN *tel:* 01203 222769 *also fax. Mus scholarship, tenable in a higher education institution approved by Trustees. For students with local connections only.*

Tillett Trust. Courtyard House, Neopardy, Crediton, Devon EX17 5EP. Katie Avey, admin. *Limited financial assistance to young professional musicians, usually aged under 30, of exceptional talent, to further their performing careers. British or residing f/t in British Isles. No application forms available but write giving full CV, references and details of budget for project. Funds not available for the purchase of insts, for normal u/grad or p/grad courses, or for funding commissions.*

Trevor Snoad Award. KPMG/Martin Musical Scholarship Fund, Lawn Cottage, 23a Brackley Road, Beckenham, Kent BR3 1RB *tel:* 0181 658 9432 *also fax. Open to outstanding va player aged 25 and under of p/grad standard. Preference given to UK citizens. Award of £500 pays for tuition fees and/or maintenance. Auditions held in London. Application forms available early summer. Applications by 1 Dec annually. Auditions Jan. Application fee £10.*

W T Best Memorial Scholarship. Worshipful Company of Musicians, 74-75 Watling Street, London EC4M 9BJ *tel:* 0171 489 8888 *fax:* 0171 489 1614. S F N Waley, clerk. *Provides financial assistance (£3000 a year) to an organ scholar showing exceptional promise for a maximum of 3 yrs. Nominations from certain professors or principals of mus colleges. Applications through nominators only.*

William Cox Memorial Fund for Young Singers. Badger Bungalow, 41 Findon Av, Witton Gilbert, Durham DH7 6RF. Antony Elton, hon admin. *Grants to help very talented advanced students of professional solo singing to purchase scores, etc. For age 19-24. Trustees meet late Mar, mid Jun and late Sep. Enquiries and applications by post only; those not sending sae will be ignored.*

William Rushworth Memorial Trust. c/o Rushworths of Liverpool Ltd, 42-46 Whitechapel, Liverpool L1 6EF *tel:* 0151 709 9071 *fax:* 0151 709 9073. W D C Rushworth, sec. *Small awards for instrumentalists within 60-mile radius of Liverpool.*

Wingate Scholarships. 38 Curzon St, London W1Y 8EY. Jane Reid, admin. *Awards of up to £10,000 pa made to people undertaking original work in almost any field and to outstanding musicians for advanced training. Open to citizens of the UK, Commonwealth, Ireland or Israel resident in British Isles during period of application, and to EU citizens who have been resident in the UK for at least 5 years. All applicants should be aged 24 and over on 1 Sep 1998. Applications by 1 Feb 1998. Shortlisted candidates auditioned/interviewed in London during May and results announced in Jun 1998.*

Yamaha Music Foundation of Europe. Yamaha-Kemble Music (UK) Ltd, Sherbourne Dr, Tilbrook, Milton Keynes MK7 8BL *tel:* 01908 366700 *fax:* 01908 368872. Karen Watts. *3 scholarships of £2000 each; disciplines rotate annually.*

Young Concert Artists Trust. 23 Garrick St, London WC2E 9AX *tel:* 0171 379 8477 *fax:* 0171 379 8467. Rosemary Pickering, chief exec. *Career management for young soloists and chmbr musicians at the beginning of their careers. Preliminary auditions in Mar with semi-finals Apr and final auditions Jun 1998. Applications by 24 Jan. Insts and singers normally resident in UK. Under age 28 (insts) and 32 (singers) on 1 Jan 1998. No grants available. Categories vary from year to year.*

Young Musicians' Recording Trust. 26 Cleveland Sq, London W2 6DD *tel:* 0171 262 9066 *fax:* 0171 262 3235. Mark Sutton, admin. *Student recording scheme open to final year inst and singing students. Nominations from heads of mus colleges only.*

Scholarships for Study Abroad

Organisations

It is advisable to contact the Embassy or High Commission in Britain of the country in which you wish to study. The organisations below can provide information on opportunities in certain countries.

Association of Commonwealth Universities. Publications Department, John Foster House, 36 Gordon Sq, London WC1H 0PF *tel:* 0171 387 8572 *fax:* 0171 387 2655 *email:* pubinf@acu.ac.uk; http://www.acu.ac. uk. Sue Kirkland, mgr ed directory publishing. *Students and staff wishing to study in a country other than their own, primarily, but not exclusively, within the Commonwealth, should refer to the following publications available from the above address: Awards for First Degree Study at Commonwealth Universities; Awards for Postgraduate Study at Commonwealth Universities; Awards for University Teachers and Research Workers; Awards for University Administrators and Librarians.*

British Council. Overseas Appointments Services, Bridgewater House, 58 Whitworth St, Manchester M1 6BB *tel:* 0161 957 7383 *fax:* 0161 957 7397. Mark Hepworth, applications offr. *The British Council itself does not offer scholarships to attend courses outside the UK. The funds administered by the British Council are channelled through schemes which enable overseas students to study in Britain. It does, however, administer a certain number of scholarships which are offered by the Chinese government.*

Czech Ministry of Culture. Foreign Relations Dept, Valdstejnska 10, CZ-118 11 Praha 1, Czech Republic *tel:* 00 420 2 513 2628 *fax:* 00 420 2 245 10346. Renata Romanova. *Czech artists, agents or representatives may seek support directly from the Ministry of Culture of the Czech Republic. The Ministry of Culture liaises with the Embassy's Cultural Dept, seeking their advice.*

Embassy of Brazil. 32 Green St, London W1Y 4AT *tel:* 0171 499 0877 *fax:* 0171 493 5105 *email:* http://www.demon.uk/itamaraty. Ademar Seabra da Cruz Junior, head of cultural section. *All requests for support should be addressed to the head of the Cultural Section at the Brazilian Embassy which has a budget for support towards Brazilian cultural activity in the UK. The type and level of support is determined by each application. Proposals should be presented in writing or by fax and interviews will be arranged where appropriate. The cultural section of the Embassy can advise on sponsorship opportunities.*

Embassy of Mexico. 42 Hertford St, London W1Y 7TF *tel:* 0171 499 8586 *fax:* 0171 495 4035. Alejandra de la Paz, minister for cultural affairs. *The Mexican Embassy has a limited budget to support the UK presentation of Mexican arts. However as appropriate the Embassy forwards requests to the Department of Cultural Affairs at the Ministry in Mexico or to the National Council for Culture and Arts in Mexico City. Applications should only be sent to the cultural attaché at the Embassy in London and not direct to the cultural authorities in Mexico. The Embassy is able to offer advice on sponsorship sources. The Mexican Embassy will also provide information about the Mexican Government Scholarships Programme with Great Britain. It is a yearly programme offering 8-10 scholarships to carry out research or p/grad studies in Mexico. Entries must be submitted by 15 May.*

Embassy of Peru. 52 Sloane St, London SW1X 9SP *tel:* 0171 235 2545 ext 20 *fax:* 0171 235 4463. Carmen Azurin, second sec. *The Peruvian Embassy does not have a budget to support the UK presentation of arts from Peru but can offer limited support, such as publicity in the Embassy's press releases, to selected projects. It cannot offer financial assistance direct to the promoter. However, it can offer selective advice on sponsorship opportunities. The Instituto Nacional de Cultura (INC) at Jiron Ancash 390, Lima 1, Peru, and the Ministry of Foreign affairs can also advise on potential sources of private funding and sponsorship opportunities.*

Embassy of Venezuela. Cultural Centre, 58 Grafton Way, London W1P 5LB *tel:* 0171 388 5788. Gloria Carnevali, cultural attaché. *UK promoters seeking advice or support for projects should contact the Cultural Centre which can liaise with the relevant Ministry in Venezuela. The Cultural Centre has a small budget to supplement some of the costs of projects involving the presentation of the Venezuelan arts in the UK. In order to qualify for a grant the project must be supported by an institution or an official body.*

The Italian Institute. The Bursary Dept, 39 Belgrave Sq, London SW1X 8NX *tel:* 0171 235 1461 *fax:* 0171 235 4618 *email:* italcultur@martex. co.uk. *Provides information on advanced training and scholarships in Italy (including study at some opera centres attached to principal opera houses).*

Japan Information and Cultural Centre. The Embassy of Japan, 101-104 Piccadilly, London W1V 9FN *tel:* 0171 465 6500 *fax:* 0171 491 9347 *email:* jicc@jicc.demon.co.uk; http://www.embjapan.org.uk. Jane Anthony, educ offr. *The Embassy deals directly with the Japanese Ministry of Education (Monbusho) scholarship which is annual and open to all UK passport holders aged under 35 who have a first degree in any discipline. Scholarships are held for 18 months to 2 yrs, tenable from Apr or Oct. Participants spend the first 6 months on an intensive Japanese course, then pursue their specialist subject. Living expenses, a return air ticket and university fees are covered by the Japanese Government. Application forms available from Mar for scholarships taken up the following year. A maximum of 20 scholarships offered annually.*

Open Society Institute. 888 Seventh Av, New York, NY 10106 *tel:* 00 1 212 757 2323 *fax:* 00 1 212 974 0367 *email:* osnews@soros.org. Michael Vachon, dir of public affairs. *The network of Soros foundations supports Central and Eastern European projects and people. Where non-indigenous organisations and people receive grants, Central and Eastern European projects and individuals must be direct beneficiaries.*

The Polish Embassy. 34 Portland Pl, London W1N 4HQ *tel:* 0171 636 6032 *fax:* 0171 637 2190 *email:* pci-lond@pcidir.demon.co.uk. Education Officer. *Provides details of study in Poland and administers the Polish Government Postgraduate Scholarship scheme. This scheme enables exchanges to take place in the fields of sciences, humanities and arts, lasting from 3-9 months. The scholarship provides exemption from tuition fees, free medical care and book grants, but does not cover travel costs between the UK and Poland. Candidates must be British citizens aged under 35, and should hold at least a BA, BSc or equivalent degree. Application forms must be submitted by the end of Dec for the following year. Short visits to Poland are also available for individuals under age 50 wishing to visit Poland for professional academic purposes. Visits normally last 2-3 weeks and proposals should be submitted not later than 12 weeks prior to the proposed arrival date. Funding covers internal travel, accommodation and daily subsistence costs, but does not cover travel to and from Poland.*

Scholarships

Grants and Scholarships for Commonwealth students are listed in the *Awards for Postgraduate Study at Commonwealth Universities,* available from the Publications Dept, Association of Commonwealth Universities (*see* **Organisations for Study Abroad**). Some principal scholarships for study abroad are listed below, along with certain British educational trusts which provide scholarships for those wishing to study abroad.

American Foundation Harriet Hale Woolley Scholarships. 15 Boulevard Jourdan, F-75690 Paris Cedex 14, France *tel:* 00 33 1 5380 6888 *fax:* 00 33 1 4580 6899. *Annually awards four to five $8500 scholarships to instrumentalists for the study of art and mus in Paris. Must be a single American graduate aged 21-29, with evidence of artistic or mus accomplishment, and enrolled at an institute of higher learning in Paris. Applications by 31 Jan annually.*

Anna Instone Memorial Award. Capital Radio, PO Box 958, London NW1 3DR. Kevin Appleby, admin. *Award of £5000 for a p/grad student at a London mus college who must be nominated by the principal.*

Applications through nominators only by 1 Mar. Award may be used for study abroad.

Arts Council of Wales Awards for Advanced Study in Music. Music Dept, 9 Museum Pl, Cardiff CF1 3NX *tel:* 01222 394711 *fax:* 01222 221447. Roy Bohana, mus dir. *Awards made to musicians aged 28 and under, born and educated in Wales. Also open to those now permanently resident in Wales and normally having lived in Wales for 2 yrs. May be used for study in UK or abroad. Applications by 1 Feb annually.*

Australian Music Foundation. 17 Lewes Rd, Haywards Heath, W Sussex RH17 7SP *tel:* 01444 454773 *fax:* 01444 456192. G T E Parsons, admin. *Major award for Australian singers and insts of p/grad or equivalent standard for advance course of study in Europe. Max age 30 on 31 Dec prior to application in Apr.*

Countess of Munster Musical Trust. Wormley Hill, Godalming, Surrey GU8 5SG *tel:* 01428 685427 *fax:* 01428 685064. Gillian Ure, sec. *Tuition and maintenance grants for UK and Commonwealth mus students, tenable at home and abroad. Age range: 18-25 for insts, 18-27 for female singers, 18-28 for male singers. Auditions Apr-Jul. Applications by 31 Jan.*

Emanuel Hurwitz Chamber Music Charitable Trust. 44 Church Cres, London N3 1BJ. Miriam Keogh, founder and admin. *Bursaries for str players to further their studies in chmbr mus at home or abroad (college/university fees will not be paid). Applications will only be accepted in writing with sae. Applications by 1 Jun. UK citizens only.*

English Speaking Union Scholarships. The English Speaking Union, Dartmouth House, 37 Charles St, London W1X 8AB, UK *tel:* +44 171 493 332 *fax:* +44 171 495 6108. Phil Ward, cultural affairs. *The ESU offers the following mus scholarships, varying from 3 to 9 weeks, to musicians of outstanding ability to study at summer schools in North America, Canada and Europe: Aspen Music School, Steans Institute (Ravinia Festival), Tanglewood Music Center, Dallas Symphony/Conservatory Music in the Mountains (Colorado), Yale University School of Music (Norfolk Chamber Music Festival), Banff Centre for the Arts, Académie Internationale de Musique Maurice Ravel (France) and International Kodály Seminar (Hungary). Applications in Nov for placements the following year.*

Fulbright Awards. US-UK Fulbright Commission, Fulbright House, 62 Doughty St, London WC1N 2LS *tel:* 0171 404 6880 *fax:* 0171 404 6834 *email:* http://www.fulbright.co.uk. Lisa Davey, programme dir. *For 1st year of p/grad academic study and research in the US, covering round-trip travel and maintenance allowance. Any discipline, must have or expect a 2:1 degree, possess UK citizenship and be able to demonstrate leadership qualities; deadline for submission of application forms is Nov. These awards cover 9 months of academic year only. A number of awards are also available for research and lecturing for a minimum stay of 3 months in the US; £1750 (inclusive of round trip travel). Application forms should be submitted in the spring. Send large (A4) sae (for 100g) to British Programme Administrator for application form, stating clearly the award for which details are required.*

Harriet Cohen Memorial Music Awards Trust. Manches & Co, Aldwych House, 81 Aldwych, London WC2 *tel:* 0171 404 4433 *fax:* 0171 430 1133. John Rubinstein, admin trustee. *Annual awards to young British National professional musicians which may be used for study or performances abroad. Max age 30. Trust invites nominations from main mus institutions in rotation. No individual applications considered. Candidates will be interviewed.*

Ian Fleming Music Education Awards. c/o Musicians Benevolent Fund, 16 Ogle St, London W1P 7LG *tel:* 0171 636 4481 *fax:* 0171 637 4307. *Awards for mus educ and help with inst purchase to outstanding young musicians beginning a career. May be used for study abroad. Max age 25 (insts), 29 (singers). Application fee £10. Applications from Nov, auditions Apr.*

Julius Isserlis Scholarship. Royal Philharmonic Society, 10 Stratford Pl, London W1N 9AE *tel:* 0171 491 8110 *fax:* 0171 493 7463. Richard Fisher, gen admin. *Awarded biennially by competition to students aged 15-25, of any nationality, permanently resident in the UK, in selected performing categories (spring 1999, fl and oboe) for study abroad. Value £20,000 over 2 yrs. Entry fee £20.*

KPMG/Martin Musical Scholarship Fund. Lawn Cottage, 23a Brackley Rd, Beckenham, Kent BR3 1RB *tel:* 0181 658 9432 *also fax.* Martyn Jones, admin. *Annual awards for insts aged 25 and under to study in UK or abroad. Fund aims to assist exceptional talent with specialist and advanced study and to help bridge the gap between study and fully professional status. Not open to organists, singers, conductors, composers or academic students. Includes tuition fees and subsistence grants. Application fee £10. Selection of candidates is by audition. Auditions held in Jan. Applications by 1 Dec. Awards payable from 1 Apr.*

Nadia and Lili Boulanger International Foundation. 11 Rue de Saint-Simon, F-750007 Paris, France *tel:* 00 33 1 4548 2801. Cecile Armagnac, Alexandra Laederich, secs. *Scholarships are awarded to musicians of all nationalities and to scholars who propose research into the history or theory of mus who have shown ability for musical achievement and creativity. Open to those aged 20-35.*

Nannie Jamieson Nutshell Fund. 6 Ember La, Esher, Surrey KT10 8ER *tel:* 0181 398 4691. Sylvia Palmer, admin. *European String Teachers Association, British Branch. Modest bursaries awarded annually for students and teachers of str insts (ESTA members) for help to attend w/shops, conferences and teaching courses. May be used abroad. Applications by 1 May.*

Richard Tauber Prize. Anglo-Austrian Music Society, 46 Queen Anne's Gate, London SW1H 9AU *tel:* 0171 222 0366 *fax:* 0171 233 0293. Tony Fessler, gen sec. *Travel bursary and public recital in London open to British or Austrian singers. Next prize awarded in spring 1998.*

Scottish Arts Council Travel and Training Bursaries. Performing Arts Dept (Music), 12 Manor Pl, Edinburgh EH3 7DD *tel:* 0131 226 6051 *fax:* 0131 225 9833 *email:* helen.jamieson.sac@artsfb.org.uk. Helen Jamieson, mus offr. *Bursaries to professional insts, singers, composers and conductors to extend expertise through study in UK or abroad. Bursaries cannot be made in connection with f/t study or training. Applicants must be Scottish based and have worked in the profession for 2 yrs. Applications by Feb 1998. Awards unlikely to exceed £1500.*

South East Music Schemes. 19 Bourne Rd, London N8 9HJ *tel:* 0181 340 4116. Deborah Rees, admin dir. *Awards for p/grad singers, insts and composers who live (or have lived) in the South East Arts region and who may not receive mandatory awards towards further study in the UK or abroad. Age limit 30. Applications available from Mar 1998 with SAE, closing date 22 May 1998. Funded by South East Arts. Application fee (non-refundable) £15.*

Sybil Tutton Awards. c/o Musicians Benevolent Fund, 16 Ogle St, London W1P 8JB *tel:* 0171 636 4481 *fax:* 0171 637 4307, admin. *Awards to assist exceptionally talented opera students aged 18-30 on recognised operatic study courses; intended primarily for maintenance. May be used for study abroad. Applications from Nov for auditions in Apr. Application fee £10.*

Trevor Snoad Award. Martin Musical Scholarship Fund, Lawn Cottage, 23a Brackley Rd, Beckenham, Kent BR3 1RB *tel:* 0181 658 9432 *also fax.* Martyn Jones, admin. *An award granted to an outstanding va player aged 25 and under of p/grad standard. Preference to UK citizens. To finance tuition fees and/or maintenance. May be used for study abroad.*

Winston Churchill Memorial Trust. 15 Queen's Gate Terrace, London SW7 5PR *tel:* 0171 584 9315 *fax:* 0171 581 0410. Miss R Conner, mgr. *Travelling fellowships in arts subjects, not necessarily mus. Applications Sep-Oct.*

Yamaha Music Foundation of Europe. Yamaha-Kemble Music (UK) Ltd, Sherbourne Dr, Tillbrook, Milton Keynes MK7 8BL *tel:* 01908 366700 *fax:* 01908 368872. K Watts. *3 scholarships of £2000 each; disciplines rotate annually.*

Education

Choir Schools

The schools listed below provide choristers for cathedral choirs and some parish church choirs. They are primarily independent schools and most are members of the **Choir Schools' Association** (The Minster School, Deangate, York YO1 2JA *tel:* 01904 624900, Wendy Jackson, admin).

Preparatory Schools (age 7-13)

Abbey School. Church St, Tewkesbury, Glos GL20 5PD *tel:* 01684 294460 *also fax.* J H Milton, head; Andrew Sackett, dir of mus.

Bramdean School. Richmond Lodge, Exeter, Devon *tel:* 01392 273387 *fax:* 01392 439330. Diane Stoneman, head; Glen Miller, master of choristers; Tony Connett, dir of mus.

Cathedral Choir School. Whitcliffe La, Ripon, N Yorks HG4 2LA *tel:* 01765 602134 *fax:* 01765 608760. R H Moore, head; R W Marsh, dir of mus.

Cathedral School (Salisbury). 1 The Close, Salisbury, Wilts SP1 2EQ *tel:* 01722 322652. C J A Helyer, head; David Halls, dir of mus.

The Chorister School. Durham DH1 3EL *tel:* 0191 384 2935. Stephen Drew, head; Mrs J Tasker, dir of mus.

Christ Church Cathedral School. 3 Brewer St, Oxford OX1 1QW *tel:* 01865 242561 *fax:* 01865 202945. Allan Mottram, head; Simon Whalley, dir of mus.

Exeter Cathedral School. The Chantry, Palace Gate, Exeter, Devon EX1 1HX *tel:* 01392 55298 *fax:* 01392 491910. Mrs J T Attar, G J Pike, acting heads; S W Tanner, dir of mus.

King's College School. West Rd, Cambridge CB3 9DN *tel:* 01223 365814 *fax:* 01223 461388. A S R Corbett, head; Charmian Farmer, dir of mus.

King's School Junior School. Ely, Cambs CB7 4DB *tel:* 01353 662491. M Anderson, head; N Porter-Thaw, head of mus.

Lanesborough School. Maori Rd, Guildford, Surrey GU1 2EL *tel:* 01483 502060 *also fax.* S Deller, head; S Watts, dir of mus.

Lichfield Cathedral School (St Chad's). The Palace, Lichfield, Staffs WS13 7LH *tel:* 01543 263326. A F Walters, head; R W Dingle, dir of mus.

Lincoln Minster School. Eastgate, Lincoln LN2 1QG *tel:* 01522 523769 *fax:* 01522 514778 *email:* lms@legend.co.uk. Clive Rikart, head; Linda Hepburn-Booth, mus dir; Colin Walsh, master of the choristers.

Llandaff Cathedral School. Cardiff Rd, Llandaff, Cardiff CF5 2YH *tel:* 01222 563179 *fax:* 01222 567752. Lindsay Gray, head; Michael Hoeg, dir of mus.

The Minster School. Deangate, York YO1 2JA *tel:* 01904 625217 *fax:* 01904 632418. Richard Shephard, head; Jill Bowman, dir of mus.

New College School. Savile Rd, Oxford OX1 3UA *tel:* 01865 243657. J Edmunds, head; R W Allen, dir of mus.

The Pilgrims' School. 3 The Close, Winchester, Hants SO23 9LT *tel:* 01962 854189. M E K Kefford, head (to Sep 97); Miss Hilary Brooks, dir of mus.

Polwhele House School. Truro, Cornwall TR4 9AE *tel:* 01872 73011 *also fax.* Richard White, head and dir of mus.

The Prebendal School. 53 West St, Chichester, W Sussex PO19 1RT *tel:* 01243 782026. Revd Canon G C Hall, head; James Thomas, dir of mus.

Queen Elizabeth Grammar Junior School. 158 Northgate, Wakefield, W Yorks WF1 3QY *tel:* 01924 373821. M M Bisset, head; David Turmeau, dir of mus.

St Edmund's Junior School. Canterbury, Kent CT2 8HU *tel:* 01227 454575 *fax:* 01227 471083. R G Bacon, head; Ian Sutcliffe, dir of mus.

St George's School. Windsor Castle, Berks SL4 1QF *tel:* 01753 865553 *fax:* 01753 842093. Revd R P Marsh, head; J C Young, dir of mus.

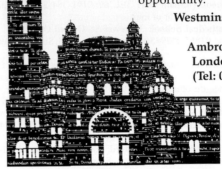

St John's College School. 73 Grange Rd, Cambridge CB3 9AB *tel:* 01223 353532 *fax:* 01223 315535. K L Jones, head; E P Bryan, dir of mus.

St Mary's Preparatory and Choir School. Chart La, Reigate, Surrey RH2 7RN *tel:* 01737 244880 *fax:* 01737 221540. J A Hart, head; Simon Dinsdale, dir of mus; Charles Thompson, master of choristers.

St Paul's Cathedral School. 2 New Change, London EC4M 9AD *tel:* 0171 248 5156 *fax:* 0171 329 6568. Stephen A Sides, head; John Scott, Cathedral dir of mus.

Westminster Abbey Choir School. Dean's Yard, London SW1P 3NY *tel:* 0171 222 6151 *fax:* 0171 222 1548. Gordon Roland-Adams, head; Martin Neary, organist, master of choristers; Stephen Le Prevost, mus master.

Independent and Voluntary Aided Schools (age 7-18)

Bristol Cathedral School. College Sq, Bristol BS1 5TS *tel:* 0117 929 1872 *fax:* 0117 930 4219. K J Riley, head; Simon Holt, dir of mus.

Hereford Cathedral School. Old Deanery, Cathedral Close, Hereford HR1 2NG *tel:* 01432 363522 (snr school) *fax:* 01432 363525. H C Tomlinson, head of snr school; T R Lowe, head of prep school; J M Williams, dir of mus.

King's School (Gloucester). Pitt St, Gloucester GL1 2BG *tel:* 01452 521251. Peter Lacey, head; Ian Fox, dir of mus.

King's School (Peterborough). Park Rd, Peterborough PE1 2UE *tel:* 01733 751541. G L Longman, head; N C Kerrison, dir of mus.

King's School (Rochester). Satis House, Boley Hill, Rochester, Kent ME1 1TE *tel:* 01634 843913 *fax:* 01634 832493. I R Walker, head; G R Williams, dir of mus.

King's School (Worcester). College Green, Worcester WR1 2LH *tel:* 01905 23016 *fax:* 01905 25511. J M Moore, head; D E Brookshaw, dir of mus.

Lincoln Minster School *see* **Preparatory Schools (age 7-13).**

Magdalen College School. Cowley Pl, Oxford OX4 1DZ *tel:* 01865 242191 *fax:* 01865 240379. P M Tinniswood, head; C J G Ives, organist; M N Pearce, dir of mus.

Minster School. Nottingham Rd, Southwell, Notts NG25 0HG *tel:* 01636 814000 *fax:* 01636 815646. P J Blinston, head; Gill Baker, dir of mus.

Norwich School. The Close, Norwich NR1 4DQ *tel:* 01603 623194. C D Brown, head; Colin Dowdeswell, dir of mus.

St James' School. 22 Bargate, Grimsby, S Humberside DN34 4SY *tel:* 01472 362093/4 *fax:* 01472 351437. D J Berisford, head; Adrian King, dir of mus.

St Mary's Music School. Coates Hall, 25 Grosvenor Cres, Edinburgh EH12 5EL *tel:* 0131 538 7766 *fax:* 0131 467 7289. Jennifer Rimer, head; John Grundy, dir of mus; T Byram-Wigfield, master of choristers.

Wells Cathedral School. Wells, Somerset BA5 2ST *tel:* 01749 672117 *fax:* 01749 670724 *email:* wellscs@rmplc.co.uk. J S Baxter, head; Roger Durston, dir of mus.

Roman Catholic Choir Schools

Bramdean School *see* **Preparatory Schools (age 7-13).**

St Edward's College. Sandfield Park, Liverpool L12 1LF *tel:* 0151 228 3376 *fax:* 0151 252 0219. J E Waszek, head; John Moseley, dir of mus.

St John's College. College Green, Newport Rd, Old St Mellons, Cardiff CF3 9YX *tel:* 01222 778936 *fax:* 01222 360688. D J Neville, head; S J Maxson, dir of mus.

Westminster Cathedral Choir School. Ambrosden Av, London SW1P 1QH *tel:* 0171 798 9081 *fax:* 0171 798 9090. C Foulds, head; J O'Donnell, master of mus.

Independent Schools Offering Music Scholarships

All the schools listed below offer music scholarships on the basis of musical ability. Some also participate in the government assisted places scheme which provides assistance towards tuition fees. For full information on scholarships offered and all musical activities see the *Music Education Yearbook 1997/98* also available from Rhinegold Publishing Ltd.

Abbots Bromley (School of S Mary and S Anne) (Girls). Abbots Bromley, Staffs WS15 3BW *tel:* 01283 840232 *fax:* 01283 840988 *email:* 106342.440@compuserve.com. A J Grigg, head.

Abbotsholme School (Co-Ed). Rocester, Uttoxeter, Staffs ST14 5BS *tel:* 01889 590217 *fax:* 01889 591001. Timothy Moon, dir of mus.

Abingdon School (Boys). Abingdon, Oxon OX14 1DE *tel:* 01235 521563 *fax:* 01235 559851. M St John Parker, head; Michael Stinton, dir of mus.

Ackworth School (Co-Ed). Ackworth, Pontefract, W Yorks WF7 7LT *tel:* 01977 611401 *fax:* 01977 616225 *email:* 100021.3420@ compuserve.com. Martin Dickinson, head; Richard Ellis, dir of mus.

Aldenham School (Boys). Elstree, Hertfordshire WD6 3AJ *tel:* 01923 858122 *fax:* 01923 854410. S R Borthwick, head; G J Barker, J Wyatt, dirs of mus.

Alleyn's School (Co-Ed). Townley Rd, Dulwich, London SE22 8SU *tel:* 0181 693 3422 *fax:* 0181 299 3671. C H R Niven, head; A T Kermode, dir of mus.

Allhallows College (Co-Ed). Rousdon, Nr Lyme Regis, Dorset DT7 3RA *tel:* 01297 626110 *fax:* 01297 626114. K R Moore, headmaster; Mrs M L Banting, dir of mus.

Ampleforth College (Boys). York YO6 4ER *tel:* 01439 788000 *fax:* 01439 788330. Rev G F L Chamberlain, head; Ian Little, dir of mus.

Ardingly College (Co-Ed). Haywards Heath, W Sussex RH17 6SQ *tel:* 01444 892577 *fax:* 01444 892266. J W Flecker, head; Robert Hammersley, dir of mus.

Ashford School (Girls). East Hill, Ashford, Kent TN24 8PB *tel:* 01233 625171 *fax:* 01233 647185. Mrs P Metham, head; J Fehr, dir of mus.

Badminton School (Girls). Westbury on Trym, Bristol BS9 3BA *tel:* 0117 962 3141 *fax:* 0117 962 8963 *email:* badminton.office@dial.pipex.com. J Scarrow, head; C Francis, dir of mus.

Bancroft's School (Co-Ed). Woodford Green, Essex IG8 0RF *tel:* 0181 505 4821 *fax:* 0181 559 0032 *email:* staff@bancrofts.netkonect.co.uk. P R Scott, head; R M Bluff, dir of mus.

Barnard Castle School (Co-Ed). Barnard Castle, Co Durham DL12 8UN *tel:* 01833 690222 *fax:* 01833 638985 *email:* barnyscl@rmplc.co.uk. F S McNamara, head; Paul Harrison, dir of mus.

Bearwood College (Co-Ed). Wokingham, Berks RG41 5BG *tel:* 0118 978 6915 *fax:* 0118 977 3186. R J Belcher, head; A R Cummings, dir of mus.

Bedales School (Co-Ed). Church Rd, Steep, Petersfield, Hants GU32 2DG *tel:* 01730 300100 *fax:* 01730 300500 *email:* registr@bedales.org.uk. Alison Willcocks, head; Nicholas Gleed, dir of mus.

Bedford School (Boys). De Parys Av, Bedford MK40 2TU *tel:* 01234 353436. I P Evans, head; Andrew Morris, dir of mus.

Bedgebury School (Girls). Bedgebury Pk, Goudhurst, Cranbrook, Kent TN17 2SH *tel:* 01580 211954 *fax:* 01580 212252. Mrs L J Griffin, head; Bryan Gipps, dir of mus.

Bedstone College (Co-Ed). Bucknell, Shropshire SY7 0BG *tel:* 01547 530303 *fax:* 01547 530740. Michael Symonds, head.

Benenden School (Girls). Cranbrook, Kent TN17 4AA *tel:* 01580 240592 *fax:* 01580 240280 *email:* schooloffice@benenden.kent.sch.uk. Mrs G duCharme, head; Neil Vanburgh, dir of mus.

Berkhamsted School (Boys). Castle St, Berkhamsted, Hertfordshire HP4 2BE *tel:* 01442 863236 *fax:* 01442 877657. Adrian Davis, dir of mus.

Bethany School (Co-Ed). Goudhurst, Cranbrook, Kent TN17 1LB *tel:* 01580 211273 *fax:* 01580 211151. W M Harvey, head; A R Morris, dir of mus.

Birkdale School (Boys). Oakholme Rd, Sheffield S10 2DH *tel:* 0114 266 8408 *fax:* 0114 267 1947. Revd M D A Hepworth, head; Andrew Sanderson, dir of mus.

Bishop's Stortford College (Co-Ed). Bishop's Stortford, Herts CM23 2QZ *tel:* 01279 838575 *fax:* 01279 836570. J G Trotman, head.

Bloxham School (Boys). Banbury, Oxon OX15 4PE *tel:* 01295 720222 *fax:* 01295 721897. David K Exham, head; Christopher Fletcher-Campbell, dir of mus.

Colfe's School (Boys). Horn Park La, London SE12 8AW *tel:* 0181 852 2283 *fax:* 0181 297 1216. D J Richardson, head; P J Hopkins, dir of mus.

Colston's Collegiate School (Co-Ed). Stapleton, Bristol BS16 1BJ *tel:* 0117 965 5207 *fax:* 0117 958 5652. D G Crawford, head; K A Morgan, dir of mus.

Colston's Girls' School (Girls). Cheltenham Rd, Bristol, Avon BS6 5RD *tel:* 0117 942 4328 *fax:* 0117 942 6933. Judith Franklin, head; Alistaire McKenzie, dir of mus.

Cranbrook School (Co-Ed). Waterloo Rd, Cranbrook, Kent TN17 3JD *tel:* 01580 712163/712554. P A Close, head; Malcolm K Riley, dir of mus.

Cranleigh School (Boys). Cranleigh, Surrey GU6 8QQ *tel:* 01483 273666 *fax:* 01483 267398. Guy Waller, head.

Croft House School (Girls). Shillingstone, Blandford, Dorset DT11 0QS *tel:* 01258 860295 *fax:* 01258 860552. M P Hawkins, head.

Culford School (Co-Ed). Bury St Edmunds, Suffolk IP28 6TX *tel:* 01284 728615 *fax:* 01284 728631. John Richardson, head; John Humphries, registrar; James Recknell, dir of mus.

Dauntsey's School (Co-Ed). W Lavington, Nr Devizes, Wilts SN10 4HE *tel:* 01380 818441 *fax:* 01380 813620. C R Evans, head; C B Thompson, dir of mus.

Dean Close School (Co-Ed). Shelburne Rd, Cheltenham, Glos GL51 6HE *tel:* 01242 522640 *fax:* 01242 258003. C J Bacon, head; R O Knight, dir of mus.

Denstone College (Co-Ed). Uttoxeter, Staffs ST14 5HN *tel:* 01889 590484 *fax:* 01889 591295. D M Derbyshire, head; John York Skinner, dir of mus.

Douai School (Co-Ed). Upper Woolhampton, Reading, Berks RG7 5TH *tel:* 0118 971 5200 *fax:* 0118 971 5241 *email:* douai1@aol.com. Dom E Power, head (to Sep 97); Peter McLaughlin, head (from Sep 97); David Bishop, head of mus.

Dover College (Co-Ed). Dover, Kent CT17 9RH *tel:* 01304 205969 *fax:* 01304 242208. M P G Wright, head; Roderick Spencer, dir of mus.

Downe House (Girls). Cold Ash, Hermitage Rd, Thatcham, Berks RG18 9JJ *tel:* 01635 200286. Miss S R Cameron, head; A Cain, dir of mus.

Downside School (Boys). Stratton on the Fosse, Bath, Somerset BA3 4RJ *tel:* 01761 232513 *fax:* 01761 233575. Dom Antony Sutch, head; David Lawson, dir of mus.

Dulwich College (Boys). Dulwich Common, London SE21 7LD *tel:* 0181 693 3601; 0181 299 9256/8 *also fax*. G G Able, master; M Ashcroft, dir of mus.

Durham School (Boys). Durham City, Co Durham DH1 4SZ *tel:* 0191 384 7977; 0191 386 6572 (mus school) *fax:* 0191 383 1025. M A Lang, head; Roger Muttitt, dir of mus.

Eastbourne College (Co-Ed). Old Wish Rd, Eastbourne, E Sussex BN21 4JX *tel:* 01323 452320 *fax:* 01323 452327. C M P Bush, head; Graham Jones, dir of mus.

Edgbaston High School for Girls (Girls). Westbourne Rd, Birmingham B15 3TS *tel:* 0121 454 5831 *fax:* 0121 454 2363. Mrs S J Horsman, head; Miss P M Jelf, dir of mus.

The Edinburgh Academy (Boys). Henderson Row, Edinburgh EH3 5BL *tel:* 0131 556 4603. J V Light, rector; P N Coad, dir of mus.

Elizabeth College (Boys). Guernsey, Channel Islands *tel:* 01481 726544 *fax:* 01481 714839. J H F Doulton, head; P C Harris, dir of mus.

Ellesmere College (Co-Ed). Ellesmere, Shrops SY12 9AB *tel:* 01691 622321 *fax:* 01691 623286. B J Wignall, head; Christopher Deakin, dir of mus.

Emanuel School (Co-Ed). Battersea Rise, London SW11 1HS *tel:* 0181 870 4171 *fax:* 0181 877 1424. T Jones-Parry, head; M T C Strover, dir of mus (to Jul 97); J S Holmes, dir of mus (from Sep 97).

Epsom College (Co-Ed). Epsom, Surrey KT17 4JQ *tel:* 01372 723621 *fax:* 01372 726277. Anthony Beadles, head; Ian Holiday, dir of mus.

Eton College (Boys). Windsor, Berks SL4 6DW *tel:* 01753 671000 *fax:* 01753 671159. J E Lewis, head; R Allwood, dir of mus.

Exeter School (Co-Ed). Exeter, Devon EX2 4NS *tel:* 01392 273679 *fax:* 01392 498144. N W Gamble, head; S D Foxall, dir of mus.

Farlington School (Girls). Strood Pk, Horsham, Sussex RH12 3PN *tel:* 01403 254967 *fax:* 01403 272258. P Mawer, head; Coralie Moult, dir of mus.

Felsted School (Co-Ed). Dunmow, Essex CM6 3JJ *tel:* 01371 820258/ 820497 (mus school) *fax:* 01371 821179. Stephen Roberts, head; Jasper Thorogood, dir of mus.

Fettes College (Co-Ed). Carrington Rd, Edinburgh EH4 1QX *tel:* 0131 332 2281 *fax:* 0131 332 3081 *email:* fettes.sch.uk. M T Thyne, head; David Thomas, dir of mus.

Forest Girls' School (Girls). Snaresbrook, London E17 3PY *tel:* 0181 521 7477 *fax:* 0181 520 7381. Mrs R Martin, head; M D Palmer, dir of mus.

Forest School (Boys). Snaresbrook, London E17 3PY *tel:* 0181 520 1744 *fax:* 0181 520 3656. A G Boggis, warden; M D Palmer, dir of mus.

Framlingham College (Co-Ed). Framlingham, Suffolk IP13 9EY *tel:* 01728 723789 *fax:* 01728 724546. G M Randall, head; R Rogers, dir of mus.

The GODOLPHIN School

Independent Boarding and Day School for 400 girls aged 11-18

Music Scholarships

Music scholarships are offered to talented musicians for entry at 11+, 12+, 13+ & Sixth Form

Major performing arts centre

Choirs, orchestras, bands, ensembles

Professional workshops & masterclasses

Foreign music tours

The director of Music, Mrs Eileen Sharp, is always pleased to meet and advise prospective pupils and their parents.

For further information please contact:
The Admissions Secretary (MYB),
The Godolphin School, Milford Hill,
Salisbury, Wiltshire, SP1 2RA

Tel: 01722 333059 Fax: 01722 411700

The Godolphin School is a registered charity which exists for the education of girls

---

GUILDFORD HIGH SCHOOL

(Church Schools Company. Registered Charity No. 1016538)

The Music Department offers:

✱ Music Scholarships at 11+ and Sixth Form

✱ Structured courses leading to GCSE, A level and university/college entrance, with encouragement of composing

✱ New facilities including Concert Hall and Music Technology Studio

✱ Choirs, orchestras, bands and smaller instrumental ensembles. Performance of choral works and large-scale musicals with Parents' Choir and school orchestra. Foreign tours. National competitions

✱ An experienced staff of instrumental teachers

For further details and a prospectus, contact the Admissions Secretary,
Guildford High School, London Road, Guildford, Surrey.
01483 450240

Highgate School

Music Scholarships

● Two Music Scholarships offered annually

● 50% fees and 33% fees

● More awards available under exceptional circumstances

● FREE tuition on instrument or voice

● Close to central London with all its musical opportunities

● A tradition of musical and academic excellence

● Many choral and orchestral activities for boys of all ages

● The Director of Music, John March, will be pleased to receive enquiries and meet prospective candidates at any time.

Full details and entry forms from :
Admissions Registrar,
Highgate School, London N6 4AY
Tel: (0181) 340 1524

Ibstock Place School

Clarence Lane, Roehampton, London SW15 5PY
Telephone: 0181 876 9991   Fax: 0181 878 4897
I.S.A. Co-educational Day School

Ibstock Place, founded in 1894 has high academic standards and excellent results.

A successful and expanding school, set in spacious grounds next to Richmond Park for boys and girls aged 3-16 years. The School has 580 pupils with a maximum class size of 24.

Music Scholarships & Exhibitions

Music Scholarships and Exhibitions are awarded annually, to pupils entering the Senior School (co-ed pupils, 11-16 years). There is a strong musical tradition, an orchestra, choir, chamber ensembles, jazz and rock groups.

Music scholars can be offered modified academic timetables, providing practice within the school day.
We welcome Junior Academy, Guildhall, College musicians for whom Saturdays can usually be kept free.

The Director of Music, Mr C M Artley BA Hons ARCM would be pleased to meet prospective applicants. Please telephone the Headmistress' Secretary on 0181 876 9991 for full details or fax: 0181 878 4897

The School is part of the Incorporated Educational Institute. Charity No. 312930 R

Frensham Heights (Co-Ed). Rowledge, Farnham, Surrey GU10 4EA *tel:* 01252 792134 *fax:* 01252 794335. Peter M de Voil, head; Edwin Rolles, dir of mus.

George Watson's College (Co-Ed). Colinton Rd, Edinburgh EH10 5EG *tel:* 0131 447 7931 *fax:* 0131 452 8594 *email:* n.mitchell@watsons.edin.sch.uk. F E Gerstenberg, principal; Norman Mitchell, dir of mus.

Giggleswick School (Co-Ed). Giggleswick, Settle, N Yorks BD24 0DE *tel:* 01729 823545 *fax:* 01729 824187. A P Millard, head; Tim Harvey, dir of mus.

Glenalmond College (Co-Ed). Glenalmond, Perthshire PH1 3RY *tel:* 01738 880442 *fax:* 01738 880410 *email:* registrar@glencoll.demon.co.uk. Ian Templeton, warden; Christopher Tambling, dir of mus.

The Godolphin School (Girls). Milford Hill, Salisbury, Wilts SP1 2RA *tel:* 01722 333059 *fax:* 01722 411700. Jill Horsburgh, head; Eileen Sharp, dir of mus.

Gordonstoun School (Co-Ed). Elgin, Morayshire IV30 2RF *tel:* 01343 830445/830264 (mus dept) *email:* jdthomas@rmplc.co.uk; http://www.gordonstoun.org.uk. M C S-R Pyper, head; M J Appleford, dir of mus.

Gresham's School (Co-Ed). Holt, Norfolk NR25 6EA *tel:* 01263 713271. John Arkell, head; Mark Jones, dir of mus.

Guildford High School (Girls). London Rd, Guildford, Surrey GU1 1SJ *tel:* 01483 561440 *fax:* 01483 306516. Mrs S H Singer, head; Graham Thorp, dir of mus.

Haberdashers' Aske's School (Boys). Butterfly La, Elstree, Borehamwood, Herts WD6 3AF *tel:* 0181 207 4323 *fax:* 0181 236 0282. J W R Goulding, head; R Dunster-Sigtermans, dir of mus.

The Haberdashers' Aske's School for Girls (Girls). Aldenham Rd, Elstree, Herts WD6 3BT *tel:* 0181 953 4261. Mrs P Penney, head; Alexander Mitchell, dir of mus.

Haileybury (Boys). Hertford, Herts SG13 7NU *tel:* 01992 463353 *fax:* 01992 467603. S A Westley, master; Alexander Anderson, dir of mus.

Hampton School (Boys). Hanworth Rd, Hampton, Middx TW12 3HD *tel:* 0181 979 5526 *fax:* 0181 941 7368. B R Martin, head; Iain Donald, dir of mus.

Harrogate Ladies' College (Girls). Harrogate, Yorks HG1 2QG *tel:* 01423 504543 *fax:* 01423 568893 *email:* enquire@hlc.org.uk; http://www.rmplc.co.uk/eduweb/sites/g0hca. Margaret J Hustler, headmistress; David Andrews, dir of mus.

Harrow School (Boys). Harrow on the Hill, Middx HA1 3HW *tel:* 0181 869 1231 *fax:* 0181 423 3112 *email:* harrow@rmplc.co.uk. N R Bomford, head; R H Walker, dir of mus.

Hereford Cathedral School (Co-Ed). Old Deanery, Cathedral Close, Hereford HR1 2NG *tel:* 01432 363522 *fax:* 01432 363525. H C Tomlinson, head; J M Williams, dir of mus.

Highgate School (Boys). North Rd, London N6 4AY *tel:* 0181 340 1524 *fax:* 0181 340 7674. R P Kennedy, head; John March, dir of mus.

Howells School (Girls). Denbigh, Clwyd, N Wales LL16 3EN *tel:* 01745 813631 *fax:* 01745 814443. Mary Steel, head; Geoff Coward, dir of mus.

Hurstpierpoint College (Co-Ed). Hassocks, W Sussex BN6 9JS *tel:* 01273 833636 *fax:* 01273 835257. S D A Meek, head; R A Burton, dir of mus.

Hutchesons' Grammar School (Co-Ed). 21 Beaton Rd, Glasgow G41 4NW *tel:* 0141 423 2933 *fax:* 0141 424 0251. David Ward, head; Keith Hamilton, dir of mus.

Ibstock Place (Co-Ed). Clarence La, Roehampton, London SW15 5PY *tel:* 0181 876 9991 *fax:* 0181 878 4897. Franciska Bayliss, headmistress; Chris Artley, dir of mus.

Ipswich High School for Girls (Girls). Woolverstone, Ipswich IP9 1AZ *tel:* 01473 780201 *fax:* 01473 780985. Miss V C MacCuish, headmistress; Robin Highcock, dir of mus.

Ipswich School (Co-Ed). Henley Rd, Ipswich, Suffolk IP1 3SG *tel:* 01473 255313 *fax:* 01473 213831 *email:* registrar@ipswich.suffolk.sch.uk. I G Galbraith, head; A D Leach, dir of mus.

James Allen's Girls' School (Girls). East Dulwich Grove, London SE22 8TE *tel:* 0181 693 1181 *fax:* 0181 693 7842. Marion Gibbs, head; Rupert Bond, dir of mus.

The John Lyon School (Boys). Middle Rd, Harrow, Middx HA2 0HN *tel:* 0181 422 2046 *fax:* 0181 422 5008. T J Wright, head; Stuart Miles, dir of mus.

Kelly College (Co-Ed). Tavistock, Devon PL19 0HZ *tel:* 01822 613005 *also fax; email:* 100432.3050@compuserve.com. M Turner, head; Andrew Wilson, dir of mus.

Kent College (Co-Ed). Canterbury, Kent CT2 9TD *tel:* 01227 763231 *fax:* 01227 764777 *email:* kcollege@rmplc.co.uk. E Halse, head; A J Lowen, dir of mus.

Kent College Pembury (Girls). Old Church Rd, Pembury, Tunbridge Wells TN2 4AX *tel:* 01892 822006 *fax:* 01892 820221 *email:* kentcoll@rmplc.co.uk. Barbara Crompton, head; Jenifer Horbury, dir of mus.

King Edward VI School (Co-Ed). Kellett Rd, Southampton SO15 7UQ *tel:* 01703 704561 *fax:* 01703 705937 *email:* kessoton@rmplc.co.uk. P B Hamilton, head; M C Hall, dir of mus.

King Edward's School (Co-Ed). Witley, Wormley, Godalming, Surrey GU8 5SG *tel:* 01428 683960 (mus dept). R J Fox, head; S C Pedlar, dir of mus.

Claremont Fan Court School

Principal:
Mrs. P.B. Farrar 1994

Claremont Drive,
Esher,
Surrey,
KT10 9LY
01372 467841

SHMIS
Co-Ed
Christian
608 Pupils

Fees 1997/8
Senior School
Per term:
£1,970,00–£2,090.00

MUSIC DEPARTMENT
Christopher Dendy BA 1995
Robert Langston MA FRCO ARCM LRAM
James Rae AGSM, Rachel Gee B.Ed (Cantab)
17 visiting teachers.   Extra tuition: Available on all orchestral instruments
Fees: £113 per term. Group lessons available.

SCHOLARSHIPS
Four scholarships of up to 50% fees plus free instrumental tuitioin are available at Senior School level.
Expectations: To make a major contribution to the school's happy, enthusiastic and expanding Music Department. Potential is assessed as much as achievement
Exam Date & Audition: 17th January, 1998. Closing Date: 31st December, 1997

ACADEMIC MUSIC
'A' Level: 1/1 (London) G.C.S.E. 10/6 SEG)

PRACTICAL MUSIC
Orchestra, String Group, various wind ensembles, Swing Band, Choir

FACILITIES
Purpose built music block with two teaching/rehearsal rooms, seven practice rooms and music technology/recording studio, Concert Hall with Steinway 'D' grand piano.

ENTRY PROCEDURE
Contact the Admissions Secretary. Requirements: entrance examination. For visits, contact the Admissions Secretary by telephone at any time. Information arrangement with the Director of Music by telephone. Emphasis is placed on ethical and spiritual values and the expectation of high moral standards. The pupil's ability to use knowledge rightly and to be an influence for good is fundamental to the ethos of the school.

GEOGRAPHICAL
The school is situated 16 miles from London, in 96 acres of parkland which is part of the historic Claremont Estate.

Claremont Fan Court School is a registered charity providing quality education for girls and boys. Charity No. 274664.

Westminster School

Several awards up to the value of half the current boarding or day fee, including free music tuition, are offered annually. The closing date for entries for both 1998 and 1999 will be in mid-January and the auditions will be held early in February in each year. Candidates, who must be under 14 years of age on 1st September of the year of entry, must subsequently qualify for a place through Westminster's Scholarship Examination, The Challenge, or the Common Entrance. The Director of Music, Guy Hopkins, is happy to give informal advice to prospective applicants.

For further details contact:
The Registrar (0171 963 1003, fax 0171 963 1006)
or
The Director of Music (0171 963 1017)
Westminster School, Little Dean's Yard,
London SW1P 3PF

*Westminster School is a charity (number 312728)
established to provide education.*

WYCLIFFE COLLEGE

✓ 400 pupils aged 13-18
✓ Fully co-educational – 2/3 boarding
✓ Up to 50% Scholarships
✓ Additional bursaries available
✓ Free instrumental tuition
✓ Excellent purpose-built facilities
✓ Cathedral evensongs & Continental tours

Visit, phone (01453 822432) or Fax (01453 827634)
The Director of Music, Christopher Swain,
or the Registrar at:

Wycliffe College
Stonehouse, Glos. GL10 2JQ
$2^{1}/_2$ miles from J13, M5 - $2^{1}/_2$ miles from Stroud
1hr 40 mins from London Paddington

Wycliffe College Inc. is a Registered Charity and exists for education.

TONBRIDGE SCHOOL

Up to **NINE Music Scholarships** of up to **half fees**, with free tuition in music, are offered in February 1998 to candidates of suitable calibre. Music may also be offered as an option in the School's Academic Scholarship Examination in May. The value of any Award may be increased, by any amount up to the full school fee, if assessment of the parents' means indicates a need.

Choral Exhibitions worth **one-sixth fees** are also available without examination to choristers of Cathedral and Collegiate Schools. Choristers can hold these awards and Music Scholarships simultaneously. The Chapel Choir maintains an exceptional choral tradition; the magnificent rebuilt Chapel with an outstanding 4 manual organ by Marcussen was re-dedicated in 1995. Substantial **Choral Scholarships** are also awarded to the trebles of the Chapel Choir who attend either Hilden Grange or Yardley Court Preparatory Schools in Tonbridge.

Boys holding Music Awards are given extra time for practising within the curriculum. More than half the School receive music tuition from 6 full time and 30 visiting staff. Two orchestras, three bands, a large choral society and a vast array of smaller ensembles provide a wide panorama of opportunity for high quality music making, both within and beyond the School. An extensive Arts/Technology centre opened in 1996; it adds a specialist recording studio, a computer suite (with Sibelius 7) and extra teaching, practice and recital rooms to the substantial Music School built in 1926.

The Director of Music, **Hilary Davan Wetton,** is always happy to meet informally with parents and their sons in advance of the Scholarship Auditions.

**Full details of all Scholarships are available from The Admissions Secretary,
Tonbridge School, Kent TN9 1JP Telephone (01732) 365555**

*Tonbridge School is a charitable foundation for the education of boys
Registered Charity No. 307099*

Woodbridge School (Co-Ed). Woodbridge, Suffolk IP12 4JH *tel:* 01394 385547 *fax:* 01394 380944. Stephen H Cole, head; John R Penny, dir of mus.

Woodhouse Grove School (Co-Ed). Apperley Bridge, Bradford BD10 0NR *tel:* 0113 250 2477 *fax:* 0113 250 5290. D C Humphreys, head; Mrs J Johnston, dir of mus.

Worksop College (Co-Ed). Worksop, Notts S80 3AP *tel:* 01909 537127 *fax:* 01909 537102. R A Collard, head; D R Evans, dir of mus.

Worth School (Boys). Paddockhurst Rd, Turners Hill, W Sussex RH10 4SD *tel:* 01342 710200 *fax:* 01342 710201. Father Christopher Jamison, head; Michael Oakley, dir of mus.

Wrekin College (Co-Ed). Wellington, Telford, Shrops TF1 3BG *tel:* 01952 242305 *fax:* 01952 240338. Peter Johnson, head; Michael Davey, dir of mus.

Wycliffe College (Co-Ed). Stonehouse, Glos GL10 2JQ *tel:* 01453 822432 *fax:* 01453 827634 *email:* wycliffecollegesenior@campus.bt.com; http://www.campus.bt.com/campusworld/orgs/org1656/index.html. D C M Prichard, head; C G Swain, dir of mus.

Wycombe Abbey School (Girls). High Wycombe, Bucks HP11 1PE *tel:* 01494 520381 *fax:* 01494 473836. Mrs J M Goodland, head; Judith Connett, dir of mus.

Yarm School (Boys). The Friarage, Yarm, Cleveland TS15 9EJ *tel:* 01642 786023 *fax:* 01642 789216. R N Tate, head; Michael Trotter, dir of mus.

FIDE ET LITERIS

ST PAUL'S SCHOOL

Lonsdale Road, Barnes, London SW13 9JT
Tel: 0181 748 9162 fax: 0181 748 9557
e-mail: pmt@stpauls.richmond.sch.uk

At St Paul's we aim to provide a lively and stimulating environment for the all-round development of the gifted musician. The music department, which is staffed by three full-time academic teachers and thirty part-time instrumental tutors, runs a full weekly programme of musical activites. These include orchestras, a concert band, many early music and chamber ensembles, three jazz groups and brass, saxophone, flute and clarinet ensembles as well as four choirs ranging in size from a large all-comers' chorale to a small close harmony group. There are regular opportunities for performance in one of the thirty or so concerts put on each year. A new purpose-built Music School and Recital Hall is due for completion in August 1999.

We offer a number of Foundation and other Music Scholarships each year for London based boys aged 13+ and 16+. The value of these awards depends upon parental circumstances and can amount to the value of the full fee. Auditions for entry in autumn 1998 will take place on February 4th. Candidates should show evidence of outstanding ability on their main instrument supported by a range of other musical skills. One award at 16+ may be available for a suitably qualified organist. Awards are made subject to candidates' satisfying the school's academic entrance requirements.

The Director of Music, Mark Tatlow, is always willing to meet prospective music scholars and their parents well in advance of any application to talk further about the music at St Paul's and to give informal advice about the scholarship audition.

St Paul's Preparatory School, Colet Court, offers one or two instrumental awards at 10+/11+ and three South Square Choral Scholarships for boys aged 7+, 8+, 10+ or 11+.

For general information about entrance requirements please contact The High Master's Secretary.

St Paul's School exists as a Registered Charity (No: 312749) to provide education for boys

Junior Departments at the Conservatoires

In most cases partial or full local authority funding is available for especially talented children to attend their nearest conservatoire; travelling expenses may also be payable.

Birmingham Conservatoire. Junior School, Paradise Pl, Birmingham B3 3HG *tel:* 0121 331 5905 *fax:* 0121 331 5906. Heather Slade-Lipkin, head of jnr school; snr conservatoire staff, and CBSO players; Katherine Tomlinson, sec.

Guildhall School of Music and Drama. Junior School, Barbican, London EC2Y 8DT *tel:* 0171 382 7160 *fax:* 0171 382 7212. Derek Rodgers, head of jnr school; Robert Pell, head of middle school; Valerie Kampmeier, head of lower school; Frederick Applewhite, head of orch studies; Detlef Hahn, head of strs; Robert Porter, head of w/wind and perc; John Clark, head of br; Susan Tomes, head of keyboard studies; Mollie Petrie, head of singing; Faith Whiteley, head of prep course; Margaret Powell, head of chmbr mus.

London College of Music at Thames Valley University. Junior Music School, St Mary's Rd, Ealing, London W5 5RF *tel:* 0181 231 2304/2677 *fax:* 0181 231 2546. Peter Cook, dir; Peter Turton, head of strs; Christina Bailey, head of w/wind; Jean Reynolds, head of vocal studies; Jeremy Davis, head of keyboard; Martin Vishnick, head of composition; Philip Cunningham, head of GCSE/A-level; Russell Hepworth-Sawyer, head of mus technology.

Royal Academy of Music. Junior Academy, Marylebone Rd, London NW1 5HT *tel:* 0171 873 7380 *fax:* 0171 873 7374. Jonathan Willcocks, dir.

Royal College of Music. Junior Dept, Prince Consort Rd, London SW7 2BS *tel:* 0171 591 4334 *fax:* 0171 589 7740 *email:* phewitt@rcm.ac.uk; http://www.rcm.ac.uk. Peter Hewitt, dir; Elisabeth Cook, asst dir; Clare Morgan, admin asst; John Mitchell, orch mgr and librarian.

Royal Northern College of Music. The Junior School of Music, 124 Oxford Rd, Manchester M13 9RD *tel:* 0161 273 6283; 0161 907 5264. Shirley Blakey, admin of jnr school.

Royal Scottish Academy of Music and Drama. Junior Academy of Music, 100 Renfrew St, Glasgow G2 3DB *tel:* 0141 332 4101 *fax:* 0141 353 0372. Anne Strachan, head of dept; Sharon McGuire, sec.

Trinity College of Music. Junior Dept, Mandeville Pl, London W1M 6AQ *tel:* 0171 935 5773 *fax:* 0171 224 6278 *email:* hjones@tcm.ac.uk. Harold Jones, head of jnr dept; Christopher Caine, snr asst; Lettice Stuart, creative mus consultant; Jennifer Reckless, registrar; Janet Lasky, concerts mgr.

Welsh College of Music and Drama. Junior Music and Access Studies Department, Castle Grounds, Cathays Pk, Cardiff CF1 3ER *tel:* 01222 394665 *fax:* 01222 237639. Edmond Fivet, principal; Malcolm Goldring, dir of mus; James Walker, head of jnr mus; Sally Craven, admin mgr, jnr mus.

Colleges of Further Education

Aberdeen College. Ruthrieston Centre, Holburn St, Aberdeen AB9 2YT *tel:* 01224 640366 ext 4317 *fax:* 01224 573758. Dorothy Carnegie, course leader.

Accrington and Rossendale College of FE. Division of Professional Services and Leisure, Rawtenstall Centre, Haslingden Rd, Rawtenstall, Lancs *tel:* 01254 354202/3. Paul Smith, head of division; Naomi Taylor, team leader performing arts.

Alton College. Old Odiham Rd, Alton, Hants GU34 2LX *tel:* 01420 88118 *fax:* 01420 80012 *email:* altoncollege@campus.bt.com. Martin Read, head of mus; Sylvia Harper, concerts co-ord.

Anglia Polytechnic University. East Rd, Cambridge CB1 1PT *tel:* 01223 63271 *fax:* 01223 352973 *email:* pbritton@bridge.anglia.ac.uk. P Britton, head of mus.

Barking College. Dagenham Rd, Romford, Essex RM7 0XU *tel:* 01708 766841 ext 247 *fax:* 01708 731067. Peter Brown, head of mus.

Boston College. Sam Newsom Music Centre, South St, Boston, Lincs PE21 6HT *tel:* 01205 313227 *fax:* 01205 311478. P E Maher, head of mus.

Bournemouth and Poole College of FE. North Rd, Parkstone, Poole, Dorset BH14 0LS *tel:* 01202 205733/747600 *fax:* 01202 205952. Mark Bellis, dir of mus.

Brockenhurst College. Lyndhurst Rd, Brockenhurst, Hants *tel:* 01590 623565. M C Newton, head of performing arts and media.

Bury College. Peel Centre, Parliament St, Bury, Lancs BL9 0TE *tel:* 0161 820 8300 *fax:* 0161 820 8302. Rob Nash, mus co-ord.

Chichester College of Arts, Science and Technology. Visual and Performing Arts, Dept of Music, Westgate Fields, Chichester, W Sussex PO19 1SB *tel:* 01243 786321 *fax:* 01243 775783 *email:* mdobson@chichester.ac.uk. Martin Seath, head of dept; Mike Dobson, head of school of mus.

City of Liverpool Community College *formerly* Sandown College. School of Performing Arts, Greenbank Centre, Mossley Av, Liverpool L18 1JB *tel:* 0151 733 5511 *fax:* 0151 734 2525. Brian Wishaw, head of mus; Glyn Williams, HND.

Clarendon College. Pelham Av, Mansfield Rd, Nottingham NG5 1AL *tel:* 0115 960 7201. A H Allcock, H Gelhaus, programme mgrs.

Cleveland Tertiary College. Corporation Rd, Redcar, Cleveland TS10 1E2 *tel:* 01642 473132 *fax:* 01642 490856. K Bentley, leader performing arts section.

Colchester Institute. Faculty of Music and Art, School of Music, Sheepen Rd, Colchester, Essex CO3 3LL *tel:* 01206 718000 *email:* colinst@rmplc.co.uk; http://www.eduweb/sites/colinst. Bill Tamblyn, professor and head of dept.

Coventry University Performing Arts. Leasowes Av, Coventry CV3 6BH *tel:* 01203 418868 *fax:* 01203 692374. Patricia Thompson, subject leader.

Cricklade College. Charlton Rd, Andover, Hants SP10 1EJ *tel:* 01264 363311 *fax:* 01264 332088 *email:* info@cricklade.ac.uk; http://www.cricklade.ac.uk. Mark Ray, dir of mus; Mark Osborne, lecturer in mus; Janet Weston, lecturer in mus.

Croydon College. Fairfield, College Rd, Croydon CR9 1DX *tel:* 0181 686 5700 *fax:* 0181 760 5880. John Parkes, programme mgr.

Exeter College. Hele Rd, Exeter EX4 4JS *tel:* 01392 384154. Iorwerth Pugh, head of mus.

Fareham College. Bishopsfield Rd, Fareham, Hants PO13 1NH *tel:* 01329 815000 *fax:* 01329 822483. Shirley Taylor, head of performing arts.

Gorseinon College. Belgrave Rd, Gorseinon, Swansea SA4 6RD *tel:* 01792 890723 *fax:* 01792 898729 *email:* p.ryan.@gorseinon.ac.uk; http://www. gorseinon.ac.uk. Penelope Ryan, principal; Leslie Ryan, mus; John Quirk, mus.

Guildford School of Acting. Millmead Terrace, Guildford, Surrey GU2 5AT *tel:* 01483 560701 *fax:* 01483 35431. Gordon McDougall, principal.

Gwent Tertiary College (Newport). Crosskeys Centre, Newport, Gwent NP1 7ZA *tel:* 01495 333438 *fax:* 01495 333386. Martin Hodson, dir of mus and head of performing arts.

Gwent Tertiary College (Pontypool) *formerly* Pontypool College. Pontypool Campus, Blaendare Rd, Pontypool, Gwent NP4 5YE *tel:* 01495 762242. Mrs S Griffiths, head of mus.

Huddersfield Technical College. New North Rd, Huddersfield HD1 5NN *tel:* 01484 536521 *fax:* 01484 511885 *email:* htcstaff@htcflex8.demon.co.uk. Mark Ellis, head of mus.

Joseph Chamberlain College. Balsall Heath Rd, Highgate, Birmingham B12 9DS *tel:* 0121 440 4288 ext 63. David Henson, dir of performing studies.

Kensington and Chelsea College. Faculty of Performing Arts, Sports, Health and Food, Hortensia Rd, London SW10 0QS *tel:* 0171 573 5233 *fax:* 0171 351 0956. Tim Downs, lecturer in mus.

Kidderminster College. Dept of Community Studies, Hoo Rd, Kidderminster, Worcs DY10 1LX *tel:* 01562 820811. J Shepherd, lecturer in mus; J Bates, lecturer in mus and audio engineering.

Kingsway College. Clerkenwell Centre, Sans Walk, London EC1R 0AS *tel:* 0171 306 5849/5864 *fax:* 0171 306 5850. Colin McDonald, head of mus.

Langside College. 50 Prospecthill Rd, Glasgow G42 9LB *tel:* 0141 649 4991 *fax:* 0141 632 5252. Anna Young, head of school, languages and communication.

Leeds College of Music. Cookridge St, Leeds LS2 8BH *tel:* 0113 243 2491 *fax:* 0113 243 8798 *email:* http://www.netlink.co.uk/users/zappa/clcm/ clcm.html. Peter Whitfield, head of FE programmes; Ian Smith, asst head of FE programmes.

Lewes Tertiary College. East Sussex Academy of Music, Fisher St, Lewes. Roy Wales, dir.

Lewisham College of FE *formerly* South East London College. Lewisham Way, London SE4 1UT *tel:* 0181 692 0353 *fax:* 0181 692 6258. D Moses, mus course tutor.

Middlesbrough College. Acklam Campus, Hall Drive, Acklam, Middlesbrough, Cleveland TS5 7DY *tel:* 01642 333398 *fax:* 01642 333310. L Harrison, mus co-ord and lecturer; E Round, lecturer in mus.

Neath College. Dwr Y Felin Rd, Neath, W Glamorgan SA10 7RF *tel:* 01639 634271 ext 253 *fax:* 01639 637453 *email:* alan.good@neath.ac.uk. Alan Good, course co-ord.

Nelson and Colne College of FE. Scotland Rd, Nelson, Lancs BB9 7YT *tel:* 01282 440200 *fax:* 01282 440274. Peter Young, foundation course dir; Alison Birkinshaw, course tutor, A-Level mus; Rosemary White, lecturer in mus.

Newcastle College. Faculty of Visual and Performing Arts, Maple Terrace, Newcastle upon Tyne NE4 7SA *tel:* 0191 200 4000 *fax:* 0191 272 4020. Ian Spencer, head of faculty.

North Devon College. Sticklepath, Barnstaple, Devon *tel:* 01271 388164 *fax:* 01271 388121. Steve Edwards, head dept of arts and sciences.

North East Surrey College of Technology. Reigate Rd, Ewell, Surrey KT17 3DS *tel:* 0181 394 1731. P Batterham, head of humanities.

North East Worcestershire College. Blackwood Rd, Bromsgrove, Worcs B60 1PQ *tel:* 01527 572813/572824 *fax:* 01527 572900. Alastair Greig, head of mus studies.

North Hertfordshire College. Cambridge Rd, Hitchin, Herts SG4 0JD *tel:* 01462 424242 *fax:* 01462 424380. Steve Sarson, head of section.

North Shropshire College. College Rd, Oswestry, Shrops SY11 2SA *tel:* 01691 653067 *fax:* 01691 679148. Odilon Marcenaro, head of mus.

North Warwickshire College of Technology and Arts. Hinckley Rd, Nuneaton, Warwicks CV11 6BH *tel:* 01203 349321 *fax:* 01203 329056. Judith Norden, head of f/t mus studies.

Norwich City College of FE and HE. Ipswich Rd, Norwich NR2 2LJ *tel:* 01603 773001. David Morgan, head of dept.

Oldham College. Rochdale Rd, Oldham OL9 6AA *tel:* 0161 624 5214 ext 4243; 0161 785 4243 (direct) *fax:* 0161 627 3635. Nick Middleton, head of mus.

Perth College. Faculty of Arts, School of Music and Audio Engineering, Crieff Rd, Perth PH1 2NX *tel:* 01738 621171 *fax:* 01738 440050. Pamela McLean, head of faculty of arts.

Peter Symonds' College. Owens Rd, Winchester, Hants SO22 6RX *tel:* 01962 852764 *fax:* 01962 849372. Anna Bennetts, head of specialist mus; Derek Beck, head of college course.

Peterborough Regional College. Park Cres, Peterborough, Cambs PE1 4DZ *tel:* 01733 67366. Ian Burton, dir of mus.

Preston College. Park School, Moor Park Av, Preston, Lancs PR1 6AP *tel:* 01772 254145. C H Pollington, head of mus; E Proctor, executive offr.

Queen Mary's College. Cliddesden Rd, Basingstoke, Hants RG21 3HF *tel:* 01256 20861. David Coggins, head of mus.

Richmond upon Thames College. Egerton Rd, Twickenham, Middx TW2 7SJ *tel:* 0181 607 8223/4. Chris Mitchell, head of mus; Peter Garvey, Paul Jenkins, lecturers in mus.

Rotherham College of Arts and Technology. Eastwood La, Rotherham S65 1EG, S Yorks *tel:* 01709 362111. Heather Sargeson, course leader in popular mus.

Rugby College of FE. Rugby, Warwicks CV21 3QS *tel:* 01788 541666 *fax:* 01788 538575. Valerie Brodie, curriculum mgr, performing arts.

South Cheshire College. Dane Bank Av, Crewe, Cheshire CW2 8AB *tel:* 01270 69133. J R Pyatt, head of mus dept.

South Devon College. Newton Rd, Torquay TQ2 5BY *tel:* 01803 386235/386381 *fax:* 01803 386403. T Keen, principal.

South Downs College. College Rd, Purbrook Way, Havant, Hants *tel:* 01705 257011. Peter Rhodes, head of mus.

South East Derbyshire College. Cavendish Centre, Ilkeston, Derbys DE7 5AN *tel:* 0115 930 2942 *fax:* 0115 944 7181. Steve McAlone, programme co-ord, mus and the performing arts.

South East Essex College. Carnarvon Rd, Southend-on-Sea, Essex SS2 6LS *tel:* 01702 220400/220639 *fax:* 01702 432320. Mark Vinall, head of media and performing arts.

Southgate College. High St, Southgate, London N14 6BS *tel:* 0181 886 6521 *fax:* 0181 982 5051. Neil Cloake, head of school of performance; Paul Goodey, co-ord jnr arts centre.

Stevenson College of FE. Carrickvale Centre, Stenhouse St West, Edinburgh EH11 3EP *tel:* 0131 535 4621 *fax:* 0131 535 4622. A D Knight, snr lecturer; Morag Campbell, head of section.

Stoke-on-Trent College. Art, Design and Performing Arts, Burslem Campus, J Block, Moorland Rd, Burslem, Stoke-on-Trent ST6 1JJ *tel:* 01782 208208 *fax:* 01782 603103. Richard Longden, programme mgr (mus).

Stratford upon Avon College. The Willows, Alcester Rd, Stratford upon Avon CV37 9QR *tel:* 01789 266245. Will Allen, head of mus.

Strode College. Church Rd, Street, Somerset BA16 0AB *tel:* 01458 844400 *fax:* 01458 844411. Tess Baber, section head; James Phippen, lecturer in charge of mus.

Taunton's College. Hill La, Southampton SO15 5RL *tel:* 01703 511811 *fax:* 01703 511991. Jane Higgins, head of mus and performing arts.

Wakefield District College. Margaret St, Wakefield WF1 2DH *tel:* 01924 789874 *fax:* 01924 789875. Tony Davis, dir of mus; Andy Cholerton, Kevin Dearden, lecturers.

West Cheshire College. Handbridge Centre, Eaton Rd, Handbridge, Chester CH4 7ER *tel:* 01244 677677 *fax:* 01244 680131. Rosalind Rice, head of mus.

West Herts College. Watford Campus, Hempstead Rd, Watford, Herts WD1 3EZ *tel:* 01923 240311 *fax:* 01923 247525. G Warner, mus lecturer.

West Kent College. Brook St, Tonbridge, Kent *tel:* 01732 358101. Nigel Scaife, head of mus.

Wigan and Leigh College. Leigh Campus, Railway Rd, Leigh, Lancs WN7 4AH *tel:* 01942 501726 *fax:* 01942 501720. Mrs A J Boardman, head of mus.

Wirral Metropolitan College. Performing Arts and Media Studies, Borough Rd, Birkenhead, Wirral, Merseyside L42 9QD *tel:* 0151 551 7583 *fax:* 0151 551 7401 *email:* greg.williams@wmc.ac.uk. Greg Williams, head of school, arts and design.

Yale College (Coleg Iâl). Grove Park Rd, Wrexham, Clwyd LL12 7AA *tel:* 01978 311794 *fax:* 01978 291569. Emlyn R Jones, principal; Mike Stevens, head of school of art and design.

Yeovil College. Ilchester Rd, Yeovil, Somerset BA21 3BA *tel:* 01935 23921 ext 312. Stephen Knight, head of mus.

Music Degrees and Diplomas

The following are generally recognised music qualifications. It should be noted that some refer to institutions which are no longer in existence.

University Degrees

AMusM	*master of musical arts of Nottingham University*	MEd	*master of education*
AMusD	*doctor of musical arts of Nottingham University*	MLitt	*master of letters*
BA	*bachelor of arts*	MMus	*master of music*
BA(QTS)	*bachelor of arts (qualified teacher status)*	MMusRCM	*master of music of the Royal College of Music*
BEd	*bachelor of education*	MPhil	*master of philosophy*
BHum	*bachelor of humanities*	MusB	*bachelor of music*
BMus	*bachelor of music*	MusBac	*bachelor of music*
BPhil	*bachelor of philosophy*	MusD	*doctor of music*
DMus	*doctor of music*	MusDoc	*doctor of music*
DPhil	*doctor of philosophy*	MusM	*master of music*
MA	*master of arts*	PhD	*doctor of philosophy*

Diplomas of Graduate Status

Several institutions have power to grant 'graduate diplomas', as they are usually styled. The following selection is of those diplomas most commonly awarded.

DipMusEd (RSAM)	*diploma in musical education of the Royal Scottish Academy of Music and Drama*	GGSM	*graduate of the Guildhall School of Music and Drama*
FRCO	*fellow of the Royal College of Organists*	GLCM	*graduate of the London College of Music*
GBSM	*graduate of the Birmingham School of Music*	GNSM	*graduate of the (former) Northern School of Music*
GCLCM	*graduate of the City of Leeds College of Music*	GRNCM	*graduate of the Royal Northern College of Music*
GDBM	*graduate diploma in Band Musicianship, University College, Salford*	GRSM	*graduate of the Royal Schools of Music*
		GTCL	*graduate of Trinity College of Music*

Other Diplomas

These are usually awarded for either performing or teaching, and cover a wide range of subjects and instruments. Special qualifications may be additionally designated, e.g. TD for 'teaching diploma'.

ABCA	*associate of the British College of Accordionists*	FNCM	*fellow of the National College of Music*
ABSM	*associate of the Birmingham School of Music*	FRCO(CHM)	*fellow of the Royal College of Organists, choirmaster's diploma*
ADCM	*Archbishop's Diploma in Church Music*	FRMCM	*fellow of the (former) Royal Manchester College of Music*
AGSM	*associate of the Guildhall School of Music and Drama*	FTCL	*fellow of Trinity College of Music*
ALCM	*associate of the London College of Music*	FTSC	*fellow of the Tonic Sol-Fa College of Music*
AMusLCM	*associate in general musicianship of the London College of Music*	LBCA	*licentiate of the British College of Accordionists*
AMusNCM	*associate in theory of mus of the National College of Music*	LGSM	*licentiate of the Guildhall School of Music and Drama*
AMusTCL	*associate in compositional techniques of Trinity College of Music*	LLCM	*licentiate of the London College of Music*
AMusTS	*associate in general musicianship of the Tonic Sol-Fa College of Music*	LMusLCM	*licentiate in general musicianship of the London College of Music*
ANCM	*associate of the National College of Music*	LMusNCM	*licentiate in theory of mus of the National College of Music*
ANSM	*associate of the (former) Northern School of Music*	LMusTCL	*licentiate in compositional techniques of Trinity College of Music*
ARCM	*associate of the Royal College of Music*	
ARCO	*associate of the Royal College of Organists*	LMusTSC	*licentiate in general musicianship of the Tonic Sol-Fa College of Music*
ARCO(CHM)	*associate of the Royal College of Organists, choirmaster's diploma*	LNCM	*licentiate of the National College of Music*
ARMCM	*associate of the (former) Royal Manchester College of Music*	LRAM	*licentiate of the Royal Academy of Music*
		LRSM	*licentiate of the Royal Schools of Music*
ARNCM	*associate of the Royal Northern College of Music*	LTCL	*licentiate of Trinity College of Music*
ATCL	*associate of Trinity College of Music*	LTCL (GMT)	*licentiate in general musicianship (teachers) of Trinity College of Music*
ATSC	*associate of the Tonic Sol-Fa College of Music*	
Dip Ed	*diploma in education*	LTSC	*licentiate of the Tonic Sol-Fa College of Music*
Dip Mus Ed	*diploma in musical education*	PDBM	*professional diploma in band musicianship, University College, Salford*
Dip RAM	*recital diploma of the Royal Academy of Music*	
DipTMus	*Scottish music teaching diploma*	PDBM (PMR)	*professional diploma in band musicianship (popular music with recording),University College, Salford*
DPLM	*diploma of proficiency in light music of the City of Leeds College of Music*	
		PGCC (Band)	*post-graduate higher certificate in band conducting, University College, Salford*
DRSAM	*diploma in music of the Royal Scottish Academy of Music and Drama*	
		PPRNCM	*professional performer of the Royal Northern College of Music*
FLCM	*fellow of the London College of Music*	

Conservatoires

Applications for places are made directly to the registrar of the establishment concerned who will forward the necessary forms.

Birmingham Conservatoire. Faculty of the University of Central England in Birmingham, Paradise Pl, Birmingham B3 3HG *tel:* 0121 331 5901/2 *fax:* 0121 331 5906. Prof George Caird, principal; Prof David Brock, associate dean (external affairs); Prof Alastair Pearce, associate dean (academic); Prof Janet Hilton, head of w/wind; Prof Keith Darlington, head of vocal studies; Prof Malcolm Wilson, head of keyboard studies; Reginald Reid, head of br; Prof Andrew Downes, head of composition and creative studies; Prof Jacqueline Ross, head of strs; James Strebing, head of perc; Mark Racz, BMus course dir.

Guildhall School of Music and Drama. Silk St, Barbican, London EC2Y 8DT *tel:* 0171 628 2571 *fax:* 0171 256 9438. Ian Horsbrugh, principal; Damian Cranmer, dir of mus; Peter Gane, head of wind and perc; Johanna Peters, head of vocal studies; Iain Burnside, head of keyboard studies; Robert Saxton, head of composition; Scott Stroman, head of jazz; Clive Timms, head of opera studies; Yfrah Neaman, head of advanced studies; David Takeno, head of strs.

Leeds College of Music. 3 Quarry Hill, Leeds LS2 7PD *tel:* 0113 222 3400 *email:* http://www.netlink.co.uk/users/zappa/clcm.html. David Hoult, principal; Graham Hearn, p/grad certificate course leader; Jonathan Stockdale, head of HE programmes; Peter Whitfield, head of FE programmes; Philip Greenwood, head of technology programmes; Roger Ladds, head of p/t programmes; David Smith, head of performance studies; Charles Rae, head of academic studies and development.

London College of Music and Media at Thames Valley University. St Mary's Rd, Ealing, London W5 5RF *tel:* 0181 231 2304 *fax:* 0181 231 2546. Alastair Creamer, dir; Donald Ellman, pathway leader, p/grad studies; Linda Merrick, pathway leader, u/grad studies; Nigel Clarke, head of w/wind, br and perc; Pamela Bowden, head of vocal studies; Raphael Terroni, head of keyboard; Peter Sheppard, head of strs; Martin Ellerby, head of composition.

National Opera Studio. Morley College, 61 Westminster Bridge Rd, London SE1 7HT *tel:* 0171 928 6833; 0171 261 9267 *fax:* 0171 928 1810.

Richard Van Allan, dir; Roy Laughlin, head of mus; Isobel Flinn, head of studies; Hugh Lloyd, admin.

Royal Academy of Music. Marylebone Rd, London NW1 5HT *tel:* 0171 873 7373 *fax:* 0171 873 7374. Curtis Price, principal; Jonathan Freeman-Attwood, dir of studies; John Wallace, head of br; David Strange, head of strs; Christopher Elton, head of keyboard studies; Paul Patterson, head of composition; Mark Wildman, head of vocal studies; Sebastian Bell, head of w/wind; Terence Charlston, head of historical performance.

Royal College of Music. Prince Consort Rd, London SW7 2BS *tel:* 0171 589 3643 *fax:* 0171 589 7740 *email:* http://www.rcm.ac.uk. Janet Ritterman, dir; Nicholas King, vice-dir, dir of studies; Ruth Gerald, head of keyboard studies; Brian Hawkins, head of strs; Neil Mackie, head of vocal studies; Jeremy Dale Roberts, head of composition; Jeremy Cox, dean of p/grad studies; Graham Caldbeck, head of u/grad studies; Roderick Swanston, head of academic studies; Robert Woolley, adviser for early mus; Edwin Roxburgh, adviser for 20th C mus; Colin Bradbury, head of w/wind; Peter Passano, head of br.

Royal Northern College of Music. 124 Oxford Rd, Manchester M13 9RD *tel:* 0161 273 6283 *fax:* 0161 273 7611. Edward Gregson, principal; Christopher Yates, vice-principal; Colin Beeson, dir of development; Geoffrey Jackson, head of academic studies; Rodney Slatford, head of strs; Renna Kellaway, head of keyboard studies; Patrick McGuigan, acting head of vocal studies; Timothy Reynish, head of wind and perc; David Young, academic registrar.

Royal Scottish Academy of Music and Drama. 100 Renfrew St, Glasgow G2 3DB *tel:* 0141 332 4101 *fax:* 0141 332 8901; 0141 353 0372. Philip Ledger CBE, principal; Rita McAllister, vice-principal and dir of mus; Christopher Underwood, head of vocal studies; Philip Jenkins, head of keyboard studies; Michael Calder, head of strs; David Davies, head of w/wind; Bryan Allen, head of br; Peter Inness, head of academic studies; Walter Blair, associate dir of mus; Timothy Dean, head of opera.

College

- High quality individual tuition. Performance of contemporary and unusual works alongside the standard repertoire

- 4-year BMus (TCM) 'Music Plus' degree*

- MA (Music Education)*

- MMus in Performance Studies**
  (a new degree beginning in Sept 1997)

- Post Graduate Certificate

*   Validated by the University of Westminster
** Validated by the University of Sussex

Music Education

- Short and vacation courses leading to professional qualifications held throughout the UK. Of particular interest to music teachers.

- Consultancy service available to respond to identified needs of institutions and individuals.

Junior Department

- Saturday School offering talented children individual lessons and group activities.

Trinity College of Music
Mandeville Place
London W1M 6AQ
Telephone: 0171. 935 5773
Facsimile: 0171. 224 6278

Patron: HRH The Duke of Kent KG
Principal: Gavin Henderson

Trinity, with a long and innovative tradition of performance-based training, prepares students for a professional career in music
Registered Charity No. 309998

Trinity College of Music. 11-13 Mandeville Pl, London W1M 6AQ *tel:* 0171 935 5773 *fax:* 0171 224 6278 *email:* info@tcm.ac.uk. Gavin Henderson, principal; Derek Aviss, deputy principal; Roger Pope, warden; David Wright, academic registrar and dir of p/grad studies; John Stephens, head of mus educ; Simon Young, head of performance studies; Philip Fowke, dir of keyboard studies; Linda Hirst, dir of vocal studies; Michael Purton, dir of wind, br and perc studies; Elizabeth Turnbull, dir of str studies; Philip Meaden, dir of academic studies; Felicity Young, course dir.

Welsh College of Music and Drama. Castle Grounds, Cathays Pk, Cardiff CF1 3ER *tel:* 01222 342854/640054 *fax:* 01222 237639. Edmond Fivet, principal; Malcolm Goldring, dir of mus; Jeremy Ward, head of performance studies; Richard Adams, head of w/wind, br and perc studies; Chris Powell, head of academic studies; Roger Butler, head of mus technology; Peter Esswood, head of str studies and orch training; Richard McMahon, head of keyboard studies; John Mitchinson, head of vocal studies; James Walker, head of jnr mus and access studies.

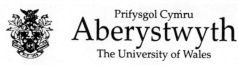

Universities

Degree courses in music are offered at the following universities. Applications for admission to undergraduate courses at all of the following except the Open University are made through the **Universities and Colleges Admission Service (UCAS)**, Fulton House, Jessop Avenue, Cheltenham, Glos GL50 3SH *tel:* 01242 222444/227788.

Anglia Polytechnic University. Music and Performing Arts Division, East Rd, Cambridge CB1 1PT *tel:* 01223 63271 *fax:* 01223 352935 *email:* pbritton@bridge.anglia.ac.uk. Peter Britton, head of division; Robert Reeve, dir of extended curriculum; David Crilly, MA mus course leader; Richard Hoadley, lecturer in composition; David Crilly, MA mus course leader; Richard Hoadley, lecturer in composition, BA mus course leader; Alan Rochford, admissions tutor; Nicholas Toller, foundation course leader; Paul Jackson, dir of practical studies; Helen Odell-Miller, course leader, MA mus therapy.

Bangor, University of Wales. Dept of Music, College Rd, Bangor, Gwynedd LL57 2DG *tel:* 01248 382181 *fax:* 01248 370297 *email:* s.collick@bangor.ac.uk. John M Harper, head of dept; Stephen Rees, admissions tutor; Bruce Wood, snr lecturer; David Evans, dir of studies.

Birmingham University. Dept of Music, Barber Institute of Fine Arts, Edgbaston, Birmingham B15 2TT *tel:* 0121 414 5782 *also fax; email:* http://www.bham.ac.uk. Stephen Banfield, head of dept; John Whenham, dir of p/grad studies.

Brighton University. Grand Parade, Brighton BN2 2JY *tel:* 01273 600900. Billie Cowie, course leader (mus).

Bristol University. Dept of Music, Victoria Rooms, Queens Rd, Clifton, Bristol BS8 1SA *tel:* 0117 954 5028 *fax:* 0117 954 5027 *email:* http://www.bris.ac.uk/depts/music/. Wyndham Thomas, head of dept; T J Samson, prof of mus; A Beaumont, reader in composition; W G Jenkins, snr lecturer in mus; J Irving, J Cross, lecturers in mus; A G Rump, special lecturer in mus.

Brunel University. Faculty of Arts, Twickenham Campus, 300 St Margaret's Rd, Twickenham TW1 1PT *tel:* 0181 891 0121 *fax:* 0181 891 0487. Peter Rudnick, head of mus; John Myhill, head of foundation.

Cambridge University. University Music School, West Rd, Cambridge CB3 9DP *tel:* 01223 335176 *fax:* 01223 335067. Alexander Goehr, prof of mus; Roger Bowers, chmn of faculty board; Dean Sutcliffe, sec of faculty board; Ian Cross, sec of degree committee; John Butt, Laura Davey, Ruth Davis, Martin Ennis, Iain Fenlon, Robin Holloway, Andrew Jones, Susan Rankin, Hugh Wood.

Cardiff, University of Wales. Dept of Music, Cardiff CF1 3EB *tel:* 01222 874816 *fax:* 01222 874379. Robin Stowell, acting head of dept; Stephen Walsh, reader; David Wyn Jones, Richard Elfyn Jones, snr lecturers; Derek Carew, Dexter Edge, Kenneth Gloag, David Humphreys; Caroline Rae, Timothy Taylor, lecturers; Sarah McCleave, research fellow; Stephen Price, tutor.

University of Central England in Birmingham *see* Birmingham Conservatoire under **Conservatoires.**

City University. Dept of Music, Northampton Sq, London EC1V 0HB *tel:* 0171 477 8284 *fax:* 0171 477 8576 *email:* http://www.city.ac.uk/music. Denis Smalley, head of dept; Steve Stanton, BMus/BSc admissions tutor; Jim Grant, Dip/MIT dir; Annegret Fauser, MA dir; Simon Emmerson, research dir.

Derby University *formerly* Derbyshire College of HE. School of Art and Design, Western Rd, Mickleover, Derby DE3 5GX *tel:* 01332 622222 *fax:* 01332 514323. Richard Hodges, head of mus.

Durham University. Dept of Music, The Music School, Palace Green, Durham DH1 3RL *tel:* 0191 374 3221 *fax:* 0191 374 3219. Robert Provine, chmn of dept; Jonathan Stock, co-ord combined courses.

University of East Anglia. School of Music, Norwich NR4 7TJ *tel:* 01603 592452 *fax:* 01603 250454. Peter Aston, prof of mus; Ian Biddle, lecturer in mus; David Chadd, snr lecturer in mus; Sharon Choa, lecturer in mus; Simon Waters, lecturer in mus.

Edinburgh University. Faculty of Music, Alison House, Nicolson Sq, Edinburgh EH8 9DF *tel:* 0131 650 2422/1011 *fax:* 0131 650 2424. D R B Kimbell, head of dept and prof; N Osborne, prof; E J Harper, R J Monelle, readers; J P Kitchen, P W Nelson, T N O'Regan, T M Turnbull, snr lecturers; L Coates, E Sheinberg, lecturers; A M Trewin, ethno-musicology; G G O'Brien, organology.

Essex University. Wivenhoe Pk, Colchester, Essex CO4 3SQ *tel:* 01206 873333 *fax:* 01206 873702. Christopher Holden, arts offr.

Exeter University. Music Dept, Knightley, Streatham Dr, Exeter EX4 4PD *tel:* 01392 263810 *fax:* 01392 264377. Nicholas Sandon, prof of mus and head of dept; Peter C Allsop, lecturer in mus; Philip R Grange, reader in composition; Timothy Jones, lecturer; Alan Street, lecturer and admissions tutor; Richard Langham-Smith, reader; Paul Morgan, p/t lecturer.

University of Exeter. School of Education, Heavitree Rd, Exeter EX1 2LU *tel:* 01392 264797 *fax:* 01392 264736. Sarah Hennessy, subject chair.

Glasgow University. Dept of Music, 14 University Gardens, Glasgow G12 8QH *tel:* 0141 330 4093 *fax:* 0141 330 8018 *email:* marjorie@music.gla. ac.uk; http://www.music.gla.ac.uk. Graham Hair, composition; Marjorie Rycroft, head of dept, baroque and classical mus; Warwick Edwards, medieval and renaissance mus; Eduardo Miranda, mus technology; Stephen Arnold, contemporary composition, computer mus; Stuart Campbell, Russian and Soviet mus.

Goldsmiths. University of London, New Cross, London SE14 6NW *tel:* 0171 919 7640 *fax:* 0171 919 7644. Peter Dickinson, head; Roger Wibberley, admissions tutor.

Huddersfield University. Dept of Music, Queensgate, Huddersfield HD1 3DH *tel:* 01484 472003 *fax:* 01484 472656. Peter Clare, head of dept; Peter Lawson, dir of studies; Michael Holloway, admissions offr; John Bryan, performance leader; Richard Steinitz, composition leader; Michael Clarke, electro-acoustic mus leader; Graham Cummings, musicology leader.

Hull University. Dept of Music, Hull University, Hull HU6 7RX *tel:* 01482 465998. Brian Newbould, prof of mus; Ian Denley, head of w/wind; Pauline Chadwick, head of vocal studies; Valerie Hall, head of keyboard studies; Gillian Dyson, head of strs.

Keele University. Dept of Music, Keele University, Keele, Staffs ST5 5BG *tel:* 01782 583295 *also fax; email:* mua09@keele.ac.uk. David Nicholls, prof and head of dept; Dmitri Smirnov, Elena Firsova, visiting profs and composers in residence; Jane Manning, Julian Rushton, hon profs; Raymond Fearn, Rajmil Fischman, Philip Jones, Barbara Kelly, Sohrab Uduman, Michael Vaughan, Alastair Williams, lecturers.

King's College, London. Dept of Music, Strand, London WC2R 2LS *tel:* 0171 873 2029 *fax:* 0171 873 2326 *email:* irene.auerbach@kcl.ac.uk. Laurence Dreyfus, head of dept; Michael Fend, mus history, dir of u/grad studies; Sir Harrison Birtwistle, professor composition; John Deathridge,

professor of mus, mus history; Daniel Chua, mus analysis; Tim Crawford, applied computing and mus; Cliff Eisen, mus history; Robert Keeley, composition; Silvina Milstein, composition and mus analysis; David Trendell, gen musicianship, mus history; Irene Auerbach, departmental sec.

Kingston University. School of Music, Kingston Hill Centre, Kingston on Thames, Surrey KT2 7LB *tel:* 0181 547 7149 *fax:* 0181 547 7118 *email:* http://www.kingston.ac.uk/~ed-s450/school_of_music/welcome.html. Edward Ho, head of school of mus; Roger Beeson, principal lecturer; Kevin Jones, reader; John Bate, principal lecturer; Carol Gartrell, principal lecturer; Gloria Toplis, snr lecturer; Michael Searby, snr lecturer; Maria Busen-Smith, snr lecturer.

Lancaster University. Music Dept, Bailrigg, Lancaster LA1 4YW *tel:* 01524 65201 *fax:* 01524 63806. Anthony Pople, prof and head of dept.

Leeds Metropolitan University. Calverley St, Leeds LS1 3HE *tel:* 0113 283 5912 *fax:* 0113 283 3110.

University of Leeds. Dept of Music, Leeds LS2 9JT *tel:* 0113 233 2583 *fax:* 0113 233 2586. Julian Rushton, prof of mus; Graham Barber, head of dept and dir of performance studies; David Cooper, dir of electronic studio; Richard Rastall, musicology; Philip Wilby, composition; Steven Sweeney-Turner, research fellow.

Liverpool University. Music Dept, PO Box 147, Liverpool L69 3BX *tel:* 0151 794 3096 *fax:* 0151 794 3141 *email:* music@liv.ac.uk; http://www.liv.ac.uk/~music/. John Williamson, head of dept; Robert Orledge; David Horn, popular mus dir; Colin Iveson, head of vocal studies; James Wishart, head of composition and electronic studio; John Gough, head of keyboard studies; Tony Shorrocks, head of performance studies.

University of London Institute of Education. Dept of Music, 20 Bedford Way, London WC1H 0AL *tel:* 0171 612 6740 *fax:* 0171 612 6741. Keith Swanwick, chair of dept.

Manchester University. Dept of Music, Denmark Rd, Manchester M15 6HY *tel:* 0161 275 4987 *fax:* 0161 275 4994. John Casken, prof of mus; Keith Elcombe, head of dept; David Fallows, reader/admissions offr; Julie Bray, lecturer; Barry Cooper, snr lecturer, p/grad admissions; David Fanning, snr lecturer; Crawford Howie, lecturer; Geoffrey Poole, snr lecturer.

Middlesex University. Trent Park, Bramley Rd, London N14 4YZ *tel:* 0181 362 5684 *also fax.* Michael Bridger, head of mus.

Youth Orchestras and Bands

This section is divided into lists of orchestras, wind bands and brass bands. Each list is subdivided under international, national, and regional and local headings. This subdivision is based upon the method and scope of the audition procedure, and from where the majority of players are drawn. Other orchestras which hold annual courses, but who do not audition and whose personnel change every year are listed under **Summer Schools and Short Courses.** School, music college and university groups are not listed unless membership of the group is open to external applicants. Details of county youth orchestras administered by local education authorities and which are not listed here can be obtained from the Local Music Education Adviser.

An asterisk indicates membership of the **National Association of Youth Orchestras**, Ainslie House, 11 St Colme St, Edinburgh EH3 6AG *tel:* 0131 539 1087 *fax:* 0131 539 1069, which draws its members from amongst both independent and LEA-run orchestras.

Youth Orchestras

International

European Union Baroque Orchestra. Hordley, Wootton, Woodstock OX20 1EP *tel:* 01993 812111 *fax:* 01993 812911 *email:* info@eubo.org. uk. Roy Goodman, mus dir; Paul James, gen admin; Emma Wilkinson, mgr.

European Union Youth Orchestra. 65 Sloane Street, London SW1X 9SH *tel:* 0171 235 7671 *fax:* 0171 235 7370. Bernard Haitink, mus dir; Joy Bryer, gen sec.

National

Britten-Pears Orchestra and Baroque Orchestra. Britten-Pears School for Advanced Musical Studies, High St, Aldeburgh, Suffolk IP15 5AX *tel:* 01728 452935 *fax:* 01728 452715. Elizabeth Webb, school dir.

* **Camerata Scotland.** NYOS, 13 Somerset Pl, Glasgow G3 7JT *tel:* 0141 332 8311 *fax:* 0141 332 3915 *email:* nyos@cqm.co.uk. Richard Chester, dir.

ESO Youth Orchestra. Rockliffe House, 40 Church St, Malvern, Worcs WR14 2AZ *tel:* 01684 560696 *fax:* 01684 560656. Marie Oldland, orch mgr.

Guildhall School of Music and Drama, Junior Guildhall Symphony Orchestra. Junior School, Guildhall School of Music and Drama, Silk St, Barbican, London EC2Y 8DT *tel:* 0171 382 7160 *fax:* 0171 382 7212. Derek Rodgers, head; Frederick Applewhite, cond.

Jewish Youth Orchestra of Great Britain. 5 Bradby House, Carlton Hill, London NW8 9XE *tel:* 0171 624 1756. Sidney Fixman, dir of mus.

The London Philharmonic Youth Orchestra. 35 Doughty St, London WC1N 2AA *tel:* 0171 546 1600. Maria Smith, admin.

Methodist Association of Youth Clubs Orchestra. 2 Chester House, Pages La, London N10 1PR *tel:* 0181 444 9845 *fax:* 0181 365 2471. Craig McLeish, dir.

National Children's Chamber Orchestra of Great Britain. The Bourne, 20 Salisbury Av, Harpenden, Herts AL5 2QG *tel:* 01582 760014 *fax:* 01582 767343. Gillian Johnston, David Johnston, mus dirs; Caroline Marriott, admin.

* **National Children's Orchestra.** 157 Craddocks Av, Ashtead, Surrey KT21 1NU *tel:* 01372 276857 *fax:* 01372 271407. Elisabeth Humphreys, admin; Vivienne Price MBE, dir of mus.

* **The National Children's Orchestra of Scotland.** NYOS, 13 Somerset Pl, Glasgow G3 7JT *tel:* 0141 332 8311 *fax:* 0141 332 3915 *email:* nyos@ cqm.co.uk. Richard Chester, dir.

National Youth Jazz Orchestra of Great Britain. 11 Victor Rd, Harrow, Middx HA2 6PT *tel:* 0181 863 2717 *fax:* 0181 863 8685 *email:* bill. ashton@virgin.net. Bill Ashton, dir of mus.

* **National Youth Jazz Orchestra of Scotland.** NYOS, 13 Somerset Pl, Glasgow G3 7JT *tel:* 0141 332 8311 *fax:* 0141 332 3915 *email:* nyos@ cqm.co.uk. Richard Chester, dir.

National Youth Music Theatre Orchestra. Fifth Floor, Palace Theatre, Shaftesbury Av, London W1V 8AY *tel:* 0171 734 7478 *fax:* 0171 734 7515 *email:* http://www.nymt.org.uk. Jeremy James Taylor, artistic dir; Felicity Bunt, gen mgr; Vivienne Hughes, auditions admin.

* **National Youth Orchestra of Great Britain.** 32 Old School House, Britannia Rd, Bristol BS15 2DB *tel:* 0117 960 0477 *fax:* 0117 950 0376 *email:* nyo@btinternet.com. Jill White, dir of mus; Michael de Grey, chief exec.

* **National Youth Orchestra of Scotland.** 13 Somerset Pl, Glasgow G3 7JT *tel:* 0141 332 8311 *fax:* 0141 332 3915 *email:* nyos@cqm.co.uk. Richard Chester, dir.

* **National Youth Orchestra of Wales.** Welsh Joint Education Committee, 245 Western Av, Cardiff CF5 2YX *tel:* 01222 265247 *fax:* 01222 575894. Beryl Jones, admin; Pauline Crossley, expressive arts offr.

National Youth String Orchestra and String Training Orchestra of Scotland. Scottish Amateur Music Association, 18 Craigton Cres, Alva, Clackmannanshire FK12 5DS *tel:* 01259 760249. Margaret Simpson, hon sec; Iain M White, dir of mus; Mark Duncan, dir of mus, training orch.

Pro Corda (The National School For Young Chamber Music Players). Leiston Abbey House, Theberton Rd, Leiston, Suffolk IP16 4TB *tel:* 01728 831354 *fax:* 01728 832500. Pamela Spofforth MBE, president and dir emeritus.

Royal College of Music Junior Dept Symphony Orchestra. Junior Dept, Royal College of Music, Prince Consort Rd, London SW7 2BS *tel:* 0171 591 4334 *fax:* 0171 589 7740 *email:* phewitt@rcm.ac.uk; http://www. rcm.ac.uk. Peter Hewitt, jnr dept dir; Neil Thomson, cond.

* **Royal Scottish Academy of Music and Drama Junior Academy Orchestra.** Junior Academy, Royal Scottish Academy of Music and Drama, 100 Renfrew St, Glasgow G2 3DB *tel:* 0141 332 4101 *fax:* 0141 353 0372. Anne Strachan, head of jnr academy.

Young Musicians' Symphony Orchestra. 11 Gunnersbury Av, London W5 3NJ *tel:* 0181 993 3135; 0181 440 6927 *fax:* 0181 993 2635 *email:* ymso@dircon.co.uk. James Blair, mus dir; Theresa Bampton-Clare, development dir.

Regional and Local

* **Bedfordshire County Youth Orchestras.** Artbeat, Raleigh Lower School, Ampthill Rd, Bedford MK42 9HE *tel:* 01234 213439 *fax:* 01234 363516. Ian G Smith, county mus offr.

Brentwood Cathedral Youth Orchestra. Cathedral Office, Brentwood Cathedral, Ingrave Rd, Brentwood CM15 8AT *tel:* 01277 261310 *fax:* 01277 214060. Angela Harris, admin; Andrew Wright, cond.

* **Brighton Youth Orchestra.** University of Brighton, Falmer, Brighton BN1 9PH *tel:* 01273 643450 *fax:* 01273 643534. Andrew Sherwood, dir and cond; Natasha Atthill, admin.

* **Bromley Youth Chamber Orchestra.** Bromley Youth Music Trust, Southborough La, Bromley, Kent BR2 8AA *tel:* 0181 467 1566 *fax:* 0181 468 7595. Nicholas Woodall.

* **Bromley Youth Symphony Orchestra.** Bromley Youth Music Centre, Southborough La, Bromley BR2 8AA *tel:* 0181 467 1566 *fax:* 0181 468 7595. Peter M Mawson, principal.

* **Cambridgeshire County Youth Orchestra.** CIMA, The Old School, Papworth Everard, Cambs CB3 8RH *tel:* 01480 831695 *fax:* 01480 831696. Peter Britton, dir.

Cardiff County and Vale of Glamorgan Youth Orchestra. The Friary Centre, The Friary, Cardiff CF1 4AA *tel:* 01222 640950/1 *fax:* 01222 227471. Eric Phillips, mus dir; Stuart Burrows, president.

Cheshire Youth Orchestra. Cheshire School of Music, Woodford Lodge Professional Centre, Woodford Lane West, Winsford, Cheshire CWY 4EH *tel:* 01606 557328. Valerie Hayward, Marilyn Shearns, orch dirs; Tim Redmond, principal cond.

* **City of Coventry Youth Orchestra.** Performing Arts Service Office, Leasowes Av, Coventry CV3 6BH *tel:* 01203 692348 *fax:* 01203 692717. Brian Chappell, dir.

* **City of Hull Youth Symphony Orchestra.** The Albemarle Music Centre, Ferensway, Hull HU2 8LZ *tel:* 01482 223941 *fax:* 01482 320565. Chris Maynard, cond.

* **City of Sheffield Youth Orchestra.** The Cottage, Park Head, Birds Edge, Huddersfield HD8 8XW *tel:* 01484 606114 *also fax; email:* csyo @moffatt.demon.co.uk/; http://www.moffatt.demon.co.uk/. Edward Woodhead, dir; Christopher Gayford, cond.

* **Colchester Youth Chamber Orchestra.** Weltevreden, Mount Pleasant, Hundon, Nr Sudbury, Suffolk CO10 8DW *tel:* 01440 786337. George Reynolds, dir of mus; Edna Robson, hon sec.

* **Dorset Youth Orchestras.** c/o Dorset Music Services, Jademanor Ct, West Quay Rd, Poole BH15 1JG *tel:* 01202 221490/2/4 *fax:* 01202 221493. David Norton, David Kenyon, dirs.

* **Dudley Schools Symphony Orchestra.** Dudley Music Centre, Lawnwood Rd, Wordsley, Stourbridge DY8 5PQ *tel:* 01384 813865 *fax:* 01384 813866 *email:* kan13@dial.pipex.com. Gerald Johnson, head of service; Keith Horsfall, deputy head of service; Clive Kempton, mus inspector.

* **Dundee Schools Symphony Orchestra.** Dundee City Council, Gardyne Rd, Dundee DD5 1NY *tel:* 01382 462857 *fax:* 01382 462862 *email:* advisers@educational-development-service.dundeecity.sch.uk. Charles Maynes, dir.

* **Edinburgh Youth Orchestra.** 92 St Alban's Rd, Edinburgh EH9 2PG *tel:* 0131 667 4648 *fax:* 0131 662 9169 *email:* eyo@ednet.co.uk; http://www.ednet.co.uk/~eyo. Marjory Dougal, admin; Christopher Adey, cond.

Enfield Young Symphony Orchestra. Enfield Arts Support Service, Aylward School, Windmill Rd, Edmonton, London N18 1NB *tel:* 0181 807 8881 *fax:* 0181 807 8213. Debbie Goldman, orch mgr; John Forster, cond.

* **Ernest Read Symphony Orchestra.** 9 Cotsford Av, New Malden, Surrey KT3 5EU *tel:* 0181 942 0318. Noel Long, dir; Peter Stark, principal cond.

* **Fife Youth Jazz Orchestra.** Beath High School, Cowdenbeath, Fife *tel:* 01383 512114 *fax:* 01383 610589. Richard Michael, cond; Jim O'Malley, Carlo Madden, Denis Boyd, asst conds.

* **Fife Youth Orchestra.** Auchterderran Centre, Woodend Rd, Cardenden KY5 0NE *tel:* 01592 414785 *fax:* 01592 414641. Graeme Wilson, cond and admin.

* **Goldsmiths' Youth Orchestras.** Dept of Advanced and Continuing Education, Goldsmiths College, University of London, Lewisham Way, London SE14 6NW *tel:* 0171 919 7171 *fax:* 0171 919 7223. Elinor Corp, cond.

* **Grimsby, Cleethorpes and District Youth Orchestra.** 1 Maple Grove, New Waltham, Grimsby DN36 4PU *tel:* 01472 824463. Leo Solomon, chmn; Mrs S Parr, sec.

* **Hackney Youth Orchestras.** 1 Frobisher House, Dolphin Sq, London SW1V 3LL *tel:* 01582 503555 *email:* hyot@fjopp.demon.co.uk. Nicholas Ridout, dir.

Hemsted Forest Youth Orchestra. Music Dept, Benenden School, Cranbrook, Kent TN17 4AA *tel:* 01580 242030 *fax:* 01580 240280. Patricia M Gane, dir of mus and cond.

* **Hull Junior Philharmonic Orchestra.** 11 Lynwood Av, Anlaby, Hull HU10 7DP *tel:* 01482 651128. J B Harston, sec; D Scotney, dir of mus.

Jordan Junior Strings. 17 Meadow Cottages, Little Kingshill, Great Missenden, Bucks HP16 0DX *tel:* 01494 862861. Elaine Jordan, dir.

London Schools Symphony Orchestra. Centre for Young Musicians, Morley College, 61 Westminster Bridge Rd, London SE1 7HT *tel:* 0171 928 3844 *fax:* 0171 928 3454. Oliver Butterworth, dir of courses.

* **Lydian Orchestra.** 1 Molyneux Park Gardens, Tunbridge Wells, Kent TN4 8DL *tel:* 01892 530548. Victor Clements, chmn.

* **Malden Young Strings.** 242a Tolworth Rise South, Tolworth, Surrey KT5 9NB *tel:* 0181 330 7876. George Steven, dir.

* **Merseyside Youth Orchestra.** Philharmonic Hall, Hope St, Liverpool L1 9BP *tel:* 0151 709 2895 *fax:* 0151 709 0918. L Clark Rundell, mus dir; Andrew Bentley, dir of community educ.

* **Midland Youth Orchestra.** 23 Hazelton Rd, Marlbrook, Bromsgrove, Worcs B61 0JG *tel:* 01527 876928. Stephen Williams, mus dir and chmn; Anthony Bradbury, associate cond; Caroline Jephcott, hon sec.

Milton Keynes Youth Orchestra. Milton Keynes Music Centre, Stantonbury Campus, Stantonbury, Milton Keynes MK14 6BN *tel:* 01908 224250 *fax:* 01908 224201. Nancy Duncan, sec; Graham Reid, cond; Nigel Mainard, head of mus service.

* **Newcastle Youth Chamber Orchestra.** 58 Lansdowne Gardens, Jesmond, Newcastle upon Tyne NE2 1HH *tel:* 0191 281 1034. Layton Ring, dir of mus; Stephen McWeeney, mgr.

* **North Lincolnshire Schools Orchestras.** North Lincolnshire Music Support Service, c/o John Leggott College, West Common La, Scunthorpe DN17 1DS *tel:* 01724 297157 *fax:* 01724 863907. S Fareham, head of service; E Hardy, deputy head of service; S Russell, co-ord.

* **North Norfolk Youth Orchestra.** 11 Cromwell Close, Cromer, Norfolk NR27 0DE *tel:* 01263 511433/512129 *fax:* 01263 515378. Richard Baker, dir of mus; Keith Paterson, treasurer.

Northamptonshire County Youth Orchestra. Northamptonshire County Music Service, 125-129 Kettering Rd, Northampton NN1 4AZ *tel:* 01604 37117 *fax:* 01604 603070. Peter Dunkley, cond and head of mus service.

* **Nottingham Youth Orchestra.** 1 Arlington Dr, Mapperley Park, Nottingham NG3 5EN *tel:* 0115 960 6723 *email:* djfwoodhouse@ enterprise.net; http://www.innots.co.uk/jackw/nyo/derek.html. Alwyn Foster, chmn; Colin Tuck, sec; Derek Williams, cond; Chris Castleden, admin.

Reading Youth Orchestra. 69 Bulmershe Rd, Reading RG1 5RP *tel:* 0118 926 1506/1828 *fax:* 0118 926 3070. Rupert D'Cruze, dir.

The Rehearsal Orchestra. 4 Lucerne Ct, Abbey Pk, Beckenham, Kent BR3 1RB *tel:* 0181 663 1927 *fax:* 0181 658 6261 *email:* bwhyte@rehearsal-orchestra.org. Bridget Whyte, admin; Alistair Scott, hon sec; Harry Legge OBE, artistic dir.

Ripon Youth String Ensemble. Ashley House, Ure Bank, Ripon, N Yorks HG4 1JG *tel:* 01765 602856. Xenophon Kelsey, mus dir.

* **Solihull Youth Orchestras.** Education Dept, Council House, Solihull B91 3QU *tel:* 0121 704 6619 *fax:* 0121 704 8065. Joyce Rothschild, mus inspector; Tony Veal, head of mus service; Richard Hart, mgr of youth orch.

* **South East Surrey Area Youth Orchestra.** South East Surrey Music Centre, Furzefield Primary School, Delabole Rd, Merstham, Surrey RH1 3PA *tel:* 01737 643310 *fax:* 01737 645463. Christopher Pratt, cond.

Southampton Youth Orchestra. Southampton Music Service, 5th Floor Frobisher House, Nelson Gate, Southampton SO15 1GX *tel:* 01703 833635 *fax:* 01703 833324. Keith Smith, mus dir and cond.

* **Stoneleigh Youth Orchestra.** 52 Manor Rd, Teddington, Middx TW11 8AB *tel:* 0181 943 2661. Christine Blake, admin.

Strathclyde Youth Jazz Orchestra. Dept of Applied Arts, University of Strathclyde, Jordanhill Campus, 76 Southbrae Dr, Glasgow G13 1PP *tel:* 0141 950 3476 *fax:* 0141 950 3314. Bobby Wishart, mus dir and admin.

Suffolk Youth Orchestra. County Music Service, Northgate Arts Centre, Sidegate La West, Ipswich, Suffolk IP30 9HG *tel:* 01473 281866 *fax:* 01473 286068. Philip Shaw, cond.

* **Sussex Youth Chamber Orchestra.** 168 Downs Rd, Hastings, East Sussex TN34 2DZ *tel:* 01424 440929; 0973 734572. Warwick Potter, mus dir; Derek Norcross, patron.

Thames Vale Youth Orchestra. Lane House, Eynsham Rd, Farmoor, Oxford *tel:* 01865 862877. Mrs J Cumming, sec; M Stinton, dir of mus.

* **Ulster Youth Orchestra.** Chamber of Commerce House, 22 Gt Victoria St, Belfast BT2 7LX *tel:* 01232 667500 *fax:* 01232 661715. Helen Henson, gen mgr.

Vacation Chamber Orchestras. Ashley House, Ure Bank, Ripon, N Yorks HG4 1JG *tel:* 01765 602856. Xenophon Kelsey, mus dir.

* **Wakefield Youth Symphony Orchestra.** County Hall, Wakefield. Geraldine Gaunt, mus adviser/inspector.

Warrington and District Youth Orchestra. 338 London Rd, Appleton, Warrington, Cheshire WA4 5PW *tel:* 01925 265456. Mrs J Bingham, chmn.

* **Warwickshire County Youth Orchestra.** Education Office, 22 Northgate St, Warwick CV34 4SR *tel:* 01926 412172 *fax:* 01926 412803. Ray Hutchinson, dir.

* **West Norfolk Jubilee Youth Orchestra.** The Dairies, Stoney Rd, Roydon, King's Lynn, Norfolk. S Corbett, sec; Howard Rooke, head of orch; Robin Norman, head of band.

West of England Schools' Symphony Orchestra. Bristol Education Centre, Sheridan Rd, Horfield, Bristol BS7 0PU *tel:* 0117 931 1111 *fax:* 0117 931 1619. V R Ford.

Weston super Mare Youth Orchestra. 367 Locking Rd, Weston super Mare BS22 8NH *tel:* 01934 622519 *fax:* 01934 641649. Dennis Cole, cond; Mrs S Philpott, admin.
* **Wirral Schools' Orchestras.** Education Centre, Acre Lane, Bromborough, Wirral L62 7BZ *tel:* 0151 343 1783 *fax:* 0151 343 9352. Philip Chapman, dir.

* **York Area Schools Symphony Orchestra.** Staff Development Centre, Park Grove, Dudley St, York YO3 7ED *tel:* 01904 553917 *also fax.* Alison Goffin, head of mus centre.
* **Young Sinfonia.** The Sinfonia Centre, 41 Jesmond Vale, Newcastle upon Tyne NE2 1PG *tel:* 0191 240 1812 *fax:* 0191 240 2668. Emma Welton, admin; Ilan Volkov, cond.

Wind Bands

National

National Children's Wind Orchestra of Great Britain. The Bourne, 20 Salisbury Av, Harpenden, Herts AL5 2QG *tel:* 01582 760014 *fax:* 01582 767343. Gillian Johnston, David Johnston, mus dirs; Caroline Marriott, admin.
National Youth Concert Band. 54 St Nicholas Rd, Plumstead, London SE18 1HH *tel:* 0181 854 6492. Mrs Z Bowness Smith, course dir; Mrs I Sharman, hon treasurer; Miss S Cox, hon sec.

National Youth Wind Ensemble and Wind Band of Scotland. Scottish Amateur Music Association, 18 Craigton Cres, Alva, Clackmannanshire FK12 5DS *tel:* 01259 760249. Margaret Simpson, hon sec; Brian Duguid, dir of mus.
* **National Youth Wind Orchestra of Great Britain.** 32 Park Lawn, Church Rd, Farnham Royal, Bucks SL2 3AP *tel:* 01753 642223 *also fax.* Kit Shepherd, exec dir.

Regional and Local

Ashford Youth Wind Orchestra. c/o Kent Music School, Gower House, 32 Maidstone Rd, Ashford, Kent TN24 8UB *tel:* 01233 646269. Tony Spencer, dir.
* **Bedfordshire County Bands.** Artbeat, Raleigh Lower School, Ampthill Rd, Bedford MK42 9HE *tel:* 01234 213439 *fax:* 01234 363516. Ian G Smith, county mus offr.
Birmingham Schools Wind Orchestra. Music Centre, Martineau Education Centre, Balden Rd, Harborne, Birmingham B32 2EH *tel:* 0121 428 1175 *fax:* 0121 428 3755. John Wesley-Barker, cond and admin.
Bodmin Community College Band. Lostwithiel Rd, Bodmin, Cornwall PL31 1DD *tel:* 01208 72114 *fax:* 01208 78680. Adrian Evans, dir of mus.
* **Bromley Youth Concert Band.** Bromley Youth Music Centre, Southborough La, Bromley BR2 8AA *tel:* 0181 467 1566 *fax:* 0181 468 7595. Peter Mawson, cond.
Cardiff County and Vale of Glamorgan Youth Wind Band. The Friary Centre, The Friary, Cardiff CF1 4AA *tel:* 01222 640950/1 *fax:* 01222 227471. Peter Knight, mus dir.
City of Leeds Youth Concert Band. 83 Wakefield Rd, Gildersome, Leeds LS27 7HA *tel:* 0113 252 8100. Aubrey Beswick, dir.
Derbyshire County Youth Wind Band. Area Education Office, 27 St Mary's Gate, Derby DE1 3NN *tel:* 01332 340251. P J King, admin.
Enfield Youth Wind Band. Enfield Arts Support Service, Windmill Rd, Edmonton, London N18 1NB *tel:* 0181 807 8881 *fax:* 0181 807 8213. Ruth Summers, activities co-ord.
* **Fife Youth Concert Band.** Auchterderran Centre, Woodend Rd, Cardenden KY5 0NE *tel:* 01592 414785 *fax:* 01592 414641. Graeme Wilson, admin.
Harrogate and Skipton Area Schools Concert Band. 3 Royd Pl, Cononley, Keighley, W Yorks BD20 8JT *tel:* 01535 636823. Bernard G Tierney, dir of mus.
High Wycombe Music Centre Concert Band. Sands Middle School, Mill End Rd, High Wycombe, Bucks *tel:* 01494 445947 *fax:* 01494 442773. John Davie, cond.
Highbury Area Band. 19 Brunswick Gardens, Bedhampton, Havant, Hants PO9 3HZ *tel:* 01705 462614 *fax:* 01705 595799. B H Strugnell, chmn; J Clelford, mgr.
Isle of Wight Youth Concert Band. 9 Elm Close, Ryde, Isle of Wight PO33 1ED *tel:* 01983 565675. Martyn Stroud, dir of mus.
* **Kent Youth Wind Orchestra.** Kent Music Centre, College Rd, Maidstone, Kent ME15 6YQ *tel:* 01622 688914 *fax:* 01622 661318. Alan Hutt, dir of mus.
Mancunian Winds. Zion Arts Centre, Stretford Rd, Manchester M15 5ZA *tel:* 0161 226 4411/22. Allan Jones, head of mus service.
Milton Keynes Music Centre Youth Band. Milton Keynes Music Centre, Stantonbury Campus, Stantonbury, Milton Keynes MK14 6BN *tel:* 01908 224250 *fax:* 01908 225271. Nancy Duncan, sec; James Howson, cond.

North Tyneside Concert Wind Band. c/o Advice and Inspection, Stephenson House, Stephenson St, North Shields NE30 1QA *tel:* 0191 257 5544 *fax:* 0191 296 2439. R Harrison, cond.
Northallerton Area Wind Orchestra. Northallerton Music Centre Office, c/o Bedale High School, Fitzalan Rd, Bedale, N Yorks DL8 2EQ *tel:* 01677 422070. Trevor Wilson, dir.
Northamptonshire County Youth Concert Band. Northamptonshire County Music Service, 125-129 Kettering Rd, Northampton NN1 4AZ *tel:* 01604 37117 *fax:* 01604 603070. Adele Sellers-Peck, cond; Peter Dunkley, head of mus service.
Shrewsbury Concert Band. 9 Greyfriars Rd, Longden Coleham, Shrewsbury SY3 7EN *tel:* 01743 367482 *fax:* 01743 340412. Mike Dutton, chmn; Shelley Holloway, sec.
* **Solihull Youth Wind Band.** Lyndon Music Centre, Daylesford Rd, Solihull, W Midlands B92 8EJ *tel:* 0121 743 2483 *fax:* 0121 743 5682. Tony Veal, head of mus service; Clive Allsopp, inst teacher.
* **South East Surrey Area Wind Band.** South East Surrey Music Centre, Furzefield Primary School, Delabole Rd, Merstham, Surrey RH1 3PA *tel:* 01737 643310 *fax:* 01737 645463 *email:* 101630.7149@compuserve.com. Hugh Craig, cond.
Suffolk Youth Wind Band. County Music Service, Northgate Arts Centre, Sidegate La West, Ipswich, Suffolk IP30 9HG *tel:* 01473 281866 *fax:* 01473 286068. Suzanne Dexter-Mills, cond.
* **Surrey County Youth Wind Orchestra.** South East Surrey Music Centre, Furzefield Primary School, Delabole Rd, Merstham, Surrey RH1 3PA *tel:* 01737 643310 *fax:* 01737 645463 *email:* 101630.7149@compuserve.com. Hugh Craig, cond.
Swale Youth Wind Orchestra. Swale Music Centre, Highsted School, Highsted Rd, Sittingbourne, Kent ME10 4PT *tel:* 01795 420586. Alan Parris, head of Swale mus centre.
Tutbury Junior Band. 62 Station Rd, Rolleston on Dove, Burton upon Trent DE13 9AA *tel:* 01283 814703. Malcolm Heywood, cond; Barbara Harvey, sec.
* **Warwickshire County Youth Wind Band.** 22 Northgate St, Warwick *tel:* 01926 412803 *fax:* 01926 412746. Jim Norden, dir.
West Kent Youth Wind Band. Kent Music School, The Master's House, College Rd, Maidstone, ME15 6YQ *tel:* 01622 765072. Alun Cook.
* **West Wiltshire Concert Band.** 113 Gloucester Rd, Trowbridge, Wiltshire BA14 0AE *tel:* 01225 753175 *also fax.* V S Blay, mus dir.
West of England Schools' Symphonic Wind Band. Bristol Education Centre, Sheridan Rd, Horfield, Bristol BS7 0PU *tel:* 0117 931 1111 *fax:* 0117 931 1619. V R Ford.
* **Wirral Schools' Concert Band.** Education Office, Hamilton Building, Conway St, Birkenhead L41 4FD *tel:* 0151 666 4324 *fax:* 0151 666 4207. David Straughan, school mus inspector.
* **York Area Schools Concert Band.** City of York Council, Educational Services, PO Box 404, 10-12 George Hudson St, York YO1 1ZG *tel:* 01904 553917 *also fax.* Alison Goffin, head of mus centre.

Brass Bands

National

National Youth Brass Band of Great Britain. 21 The Coppice, Impington, Cambridge CB4 4PP *tel:* 01223 234090 *also fax.* Roy Newsome, dir of mus; Philip Biggs, sec.

National Youth Brass Band of Scotland. Scottish Amateur Music Association, 18 Craigton Cres, Alva, Clackmannanshire FK12 5DS *tel:* 01259 760249. Margaret Simpson, hon sec; Neil Cross, dir of mus.

National Youth Brass Band of Wales. c/o Welsh Amateur Music Federation, 9 Museum Pl, Cardiff CF1 3NX *tel:* 01222 394711 *fax:* 01222 221447. Keith Griffin, admin; Edward Gregson, president; James Watson, mus adviser.

Regional and Local

Beaumaris and District Youth Band. East Lodge, Henllys La, Beaumaris, Gwynedd L58 8HU *tel:* 01248 811538. R Kingman.

* **Bedfordshire County Brass Band.** Artbeat, Raleigh Lower School, Ampthill Rd, Bedford MK42 9HE *tel:* 01234 213439 *fax:* 01234 363516. Ian G Smith, county mus offr; Terry Hext, cond.

Cardiff County and Vale of Glamorgan Youth Brass Band. The Friary Centre, The Friary, Cardiff CF1 4AA *tel:* 01222 640950/1 *fax:* 01222 227471. Keith Griffin, mus dir.

Cheshire Youth Brass Band. Cheshire School of Music, The Professional Centre, Woodford Lodge, Woodford Lane West, Winsford, Cheshire CW7 4EH *tel:* 01606 557328 *fax:* 01606 862113. Sandy Blair; David Lancashire, conds.

Dobcross Youth Band. 42 Sandy La, Dobcross, Oldham, Lancs OL3 5AG *tel:* 01457 870895. Jenny Wood, sec.

East Riding Youth Brass Band. South Cattleholmes, Wansford, Driffield, E Riding of Yorks YO25 8NW *tel:* 01377 254293.

Greater Gwent Youth Brass Band. Gwent Music Support Service, Melfort Rd, Newport, South Wales NP9 3FP *tel:* 01633 223196 *fax:* 01633 252051. Alun F Williams.

Guildhall School of Music and Drama Brass Band. Junior School, Silk St, Guildhall School of Music and Drama, Barbican, London EC2Y 8DT *tel:* 0171 382 7160 *fax:* 0171 382 7212. Derek Rodgers, head; John Miller, cond.

* **Hampshire County Youth Band.** County Music Centre, Gordon Rd, Winchester, Hants SO23 7DD *tel:* 01962 861502 *fax:* 01962 863690 *email:* edhqmslr@hantsnet.hants.gov.uk. Leighton Rich, cond.

Hathern Youth Band. 10 St Peters Av, Hathern, Loughborough, Leics LE12 5JL *tel:* 01509 842813. Mrs M Spencer, sec.

Ipswich Junior Co-op Band. 59a Blackbourne Rd, Elmswell, Suffolk IP30 9UH *tel:* 01359 242545. Andrew Shipp; Stephen Kenna, cond.

North Ayrshire Youth Band. 5 Daltoil Ct, Ralston, Paisley PA1 3AH *tel:* 0141 882 4242. R McNeil; H Brennan.

Northamptonshire County Youth Brass Band. Northamptonshire County Music Service, 125-129 Kettering Rd, Northampton NN1 4AZ *tel:* 01604 37117 *fax:* 01604 603070. Rachel Coles, cond; Peter Dunkley, head of mus service.

Oldham Music Centre Youth Band. Oldham Music Centre, Lyceum Building, Union St, Oldham, Lancs OL1 1QG *tel:* 0161 627 2332 *fax:* 0161 620 0259. M Evans.

Poynton Youth Brass Band. 21 Hollymount Gardens, Offerton, Stockport, Cheshire SK2 7NE *tel:* 0161 487 1989. F Cox.

Ratby Co-operative Junior Band. 12 Oxford Rd, Desford, Leics LE9 9JN *tel:* 01455 823883. Mrs L Plant.

* **Rotherham Schools Youth Brass Band.** Parkhurst Teachers Centre, Doncaster Rd, Rotherham, S Yorks S65 2BL *tel:* 01709 828191 *fax:* 01709 379601. Jeremy Wade, cond.

St Helens Youth Brass Band, Training Band and Beginners Band. 20 Birchwood Dr, Lower Peover, Knutsford, Cheshire WA16 9QJ *tel:* 01565 722590. Miss L Nicholson, cond.

Spennymoor Youth Band. 12 Co-operative Terrace, Coxhoe, Co Durham DH6 4DQ *tel:* 0191 377 0454. Mrs E M Jackson.

Stantonbury Brass Band. Milton Keynes Music Centre, Stantonbury Campus, Stantonbury, Milton Keynes MK14 6BN *tel:* 01908 224250 *fax:* 01908 224201. Nancy Duncan, sec; Paul Coveney, cond; Nigel Mainard, head of mus service.

Stockport Schools' Senior and Intermediate Bands. 6 Oakland Av, Dialstone La, Stockport SK2 6AX *tel:* 0161 285 0869 *also fax.* Gill Scourfield, admin.

Wakefield Metropolitan Band and Schools Band. Band Room 1-2, Manygates Adult Education Centre, Manygates La, Wakefield *tel:* 01924 257643. R Busby, mgr.

* **Wirral Schools' Brass Band.** Professional Development Centre, Acre La, Bromborough, Wirral L62 7BZ *tel:* 0151 343 1783. A Milnes, head of br teaching.

Youth Choirs

The Youth Choirs listed below are divided under national, regional and local headings, depending on the method and scope of the audition procedure and from where the majority of performers are drawn. A list of **Youth Opera and Music Theatre** companies appears at the end of the section.

National

British Methodist Youth Choir. 35 Westwood Rd, Sutton Coldfield, W Midlands B73 6UP *tel:* 0121 353 5909 *also fax; email:* gjones9526@aol. com. Gilbert Jones, admin; Christopher Bridges, cond.

Laudibus - The National Youth Chamber Choir. c/o Chameleon Arts Management, 32 St Michael's Rd, Sandhurst, Berks GU47 8HE *tel:* 01252 873313 *fax:* 01252 871517 *email:* camarts@dial.pipex.com. Mike Brewer, mus dir; Pete Csemiczky, promotions mgr.

National Youth Choirs of Great Britain. PO Box 67, Holmfirth, Huddersfield, W Yorks HD7 1GQ *tel:* 01484 687023 *fax:* 01484 681635. Carl Browning, exec dir; Michael Brewer OBE, mus dir; Danny Curtis, choir admin.

National Youth Choir of Scotland and Chamber Choir. 18 Polmont Pk, Falkirk FK2 0XT *tel:* 01324 711749 *fax:* 01324 713746. Robert Tait, admin; Christopher Bell, artistic dir and cond.

National Youth Choir of Wales. Welsh Amateur Music Federation, 9 Museum Pl, Cardiff CF1 3NX *tel:* 01222 394711 *fax:* 01222 221447. Keith Griffin, admin; Bryn Terfel, president; Ralph Allwood, cond.

The Rodolfus Choir. The Shepherd's Cottage, Gt Shelford, Cambridge CB2 5JX *tel:* 01223 845685 *fax:* 01223 841980 *email:* rallwood@ netcomuk.co.uk. Ralph Allwood, cond; Lydia Smallwood, admin.

Regional and Local

Alicia Bardsley Singers. 22 Greek St, Stockport SK3 8AB *tel:* 0161 429 7413. K Mullen, admin; Alicia Bardsley, cond.

Berkshire Boys' Choir. Berkshire Young Musicians Trust, 25 Whiteknights Rd, Reading, Berks RG6 7BY *tel:* 0118 966 5015. Gillian Dibden, cond.

Berkshire Girls Choir. Berkshire Young Musicians Trust, 25 Whiteknights Rd, Reading, Berks RG6 7BY *tel:* 0118 966 5015. Gillian Dibden, dir.

Berkshire Youth Choir. Berkshire Young Musicians Trust, 25 Whiteknights Rd, Reading, Berks RG6 7BY *tel:* 0118 966 5015. Gillian Dibden, choral dir.

Boden Show Choir. 6-12 Windmill Hill, Enfield, Middx EN2 6SA *tel:* 0181 367 2692 *fax:* 0181 367 1836. Adam Boden, choir dir; Robert Hyman, choirmaster.

The Bradford Choristers. 8 Moorcroft, Eldwick, Nr Bingley, Yorkshire BD16 3DR *tel:* 01274 774758. Ann Foster, sec; Richard Darke, mus dir.

Bridgwater Young People's Choir. 11 Morgans Rise, Bishops Hull, Taunton, Somerset TA1 5HW *tel:* 01823 252658 *also fax.* Andrew Maddocks, cond; Ann Fisher, sec.

Caerphilly Childrens Choir. Llaregyb, Ysgubor Fach, Machen, Caerphilly NP1 8QE *tel:* 01633 440277. Nigel Jones, mus dir.

Calne Girls' Choir. 18 Wyvern Av, Calne, Wilts SN11 8NZ *tel:* 01249 817470 *also fax.* Geoffrey Field, dir.

Cambridgeshire Boys' Choir. 35 Acorn Av, Bar Hill, Cambridge CB3 8DT *tel:* 01954 780307 *also fax; fax:* 0385 597837 *email:* cambridge shire.boys.choir@dial.pipex.com; http://dialspace.dial.pipex.com/ cambridgeshire.boys.choir/. Nicholas Bergstrom-Allen, dir.

Cantamus. c/o Camerata, 4 Margaret Rd, Birmingham B17 0EU *tel:* 0121 426 6208 *also fax.* Sheila Haslam, sec; Pamela Cook MBE, dir.

Cantate Youth Choir. 16 Lambert Cross, Saffron Walden, Essex CB10 2DP *tel:* 01799 527212 *also fax; email:* cantate.choir@virgin.net. Michael Kibblewhite, mus dir; Sean Brady, gen mgr; Dawn Helder, sec.

Cantores Novae. 269 Dobcroft Rd, Sheffield S11 9LG *tel:* 0114 235 0993 *fax:* 0114 235 1883. Vivien Pike, cond.

Capital Arts Children's Choirs. 225 Shurland Av, East Barnet, Herts EN4 8DG *tel:* 0181 449 2342 *also fax.* Kathleen Shanks, mus dir; Pamela Horsepool, sec.

Capital Arts Show Choir. 225 Shurland Av, East Barnet, Herts EN4 8DG *tel:* 0181 449 2342. Kathleen Shanks, mus dir; Pamela Horsepool, sec.

Cardiff County and Vale of Glamorgan Youth Choir. The Friary Centre, The Friary, Cardiff CF1 4AA *tel:* 01222 640950/1 *fax:* 01222 227471. Kelvin Thomas, mus dir; Stuart Burrows, president.

Central Berkshire Girls' Choir. Central Berkshire Music Centre, 25 Whiteknights Rd, Reading, Berks RG6 7BY *tel:* 0118 966 6914 *fax:* 0118 935 3419. Michael Wood, dir and cond; Mrs E Bartley, admin.

Chamber Choir of The Arts Educational School. Tring Pk, Tring, Herts HP23 5LX *tel:* 01442 824255 *fax:* 01442 891069. Vaughan Meakins, cond.

Chelmer Youth Choir. 34 Longmead Av, Gt Baddow, Chelmsford CM2 7EG *tel:* 01245 471649. Eric Withams, cond.

Chelmsford Star Children's Choir. 34 Longmead Av, Gt Baddow, Chelmsford CM2 7EG *tel:* 01245 471649. Eric Withams, cond.

Cheshire Youth Chamber Choir. Hadfield House, County Hall, Chester CH1 1SQ *tel:* 01244 602319 *fax:* 01244 603813. Beverley Stanton, admin; Mervyn Williams, dir.

Cheshire Youth Choir. Hadfield House, County Hall, Chester CH1 1SQ *tel:* 01244 602319 *fax:* 01244 603813. Beverley Stanton, admin; Mervyn Williams, Martin Cooke, dirs.

Children's Voices. 20 Brycedale Cres, Southgate, London N14 7EY *tel:* 0181 882 0630 *also fax.* June Keyte, dir.

City of Birmingham Symphony Youth Chorus. Paradise Pl, Birmingham B3 3RP *tel:* 0121 236 1555/2461 *fax:* 0121 236 4231 *email:* information @cbso.co.uk. Simon Halsey, chorus dir; David Francis, chorus mgr; Hilary Parfitt, vocal coach; Shirley Court, cond jnr chorus; Adrian Partington, cond snr chorus.

City of Sheffield Young Choirs. 269 Dobcroft Rd, Sheffield S11 9LG *tel:* 0114 235 0993 *fax:* 0114 235 1883. Vivien Pike, cond.

Durham County Youth Choir. Darlington Music Centre, Borough Rd, Darlington DL1 1SG. John Allen, admin; Matthew Grehan-Bradley, cond.

Ealing Youth Choir. 169 Murray Rd, Ealing, London W5 4DD *tel:* 0181 560 4532. John Compton, chmn; Paul Ayres, cond.

Farnham Youth Choirs. 21 Firgrove Hill, Farnham, Surrey GU9 8LH *tel:* 01252 723406 *also fax.* David Victor-Smith, dir.

Fife Youth Choir. Auchterderran Centre, Woodend Rd, Cardenden KY5 0NE *tel:* 01592 414785 *fax:* 01592 414641. Graeme Wilson, cond and admin.

Finchley Children's Music Group. 69 Etchingham Park Rd, Finchley, London N3 2ED *tel:* 0181 343 3847 *also fax.* John Langley, admin; Nicholas Wilks, mus dir.

Glasgow Youth Choir. 30 Haggswood Av, Pollokshields, Glasgow G41 4RH *tel:* 0141 427 9921. Agnes F Hoey MBE, founder and cond.

Guildford Chorale. 11 Kingfisher Ct, Merrow Pk, Guildford, Surrey GU4 7EW *tel:* 01483 572208. Andrew Wilson, cond and admin.

Hampshire County Youth Choir. County Music Centre, Gordon Rd, Winchester, Hants SO23 7DD *tel:* 01962 861502 *fax:* 01962 863690. Keith Smith, mus dir and cond.

Hartlepool Youth Choir. 9 Granville Av, Hartlepool TS26 8ND *tel:* 01429 261124. Christopher Simmons, mus dir; Daniel Raine, mgr.

High Wycombe Music Centre Youth Choir. Sands Middle School, Mill End Rd, High Wycombe, Bucks HP12 4BA *tel:* 01494 445947 *fax:* 01494 442773. Clem Virgo, cond; Eric Parsons, acc.

Hywel Girls' Choir and Hywel Boy Singers. 6 Harries Av, Llanelli, Carmarthenshire SA15 3LF *tel:* 01554 772979 *also fax; email:* hywel-williams@msn.com. John Hywel Williams MBE, dir of mus; Lady Mary Mansel Lewis OBE, president; Stuart Burrows, vice-president.

Ipswich Girls' Choir. County Music Service, Northgate Arts Centre, Sidegate La West, Ipswich, Suffolk IP4 3DF *tel:* 01473 281866 *fax:* 01473 286068. David Bramhall, cond.

Jersey Boys' Choir. Professional Development Centre, c/o PO Box 142, Jersey, Channel Islands, JE4 8QJ *tel:* 01534 509491 *fax:* 01534 509300. Malcolm Whittell, dir.

Jewish Heritage Youth Choir. PO Box 232, Harrow, Middx HA1 2NN *tel:* 0181 909 2445 *fax:* 0181 909 1030 *email:* singing@jmht.org. Geraldine Auerbach, dir, Jewish Music Heritage Trust.

Kent Youth Chamber Choir. Kent Music Centre, The Masters House, College Rd, Maidstone ME15 6YQ *tel:* 01622 688914 *fax:* 01622 661318 *email:* kmsho@cix.compulink.co.uk. Andrew Larner, dir of mus.

Kent Youth Choir. Kent Music Centre, The Masters House, College Rd, Maidstone ME15 6YQ *tel:* 01622 688914 *fax:* 01622 661318 *email:* kmsho@cix.compulink.co.uk. Andrew Larner, dir of mus.

Kent Youth Singers. Kent Music Centre, The Masters House, College Rd, Maidstone ME15 6YQ *tel:* 01622 688914 *fax:* 01622 661318 *email:* kmsho@cix.compulink.co.uk. Andrew Larner, dir of mus.

The Manchester Boys' Choir. Zion Arts Centre, Stretford Rd, Manchester M15 5ZA *tel:* 0161 226 4411 *fax:* 0161 226 1010. Adrian P Jessett, founder dir.

Manchester Boys' Chorus. M E C Music Service, Medlock School, Wadeson Rd, Manchester M13 9UR *tel:* 0161 273 3630. Adrian P Jessett, founder dir.

Manchester Grammar School Choir. The Manchester Grammar School, Old Hall La, Manchester M13 0XT *tel:* 0161 224 7201 *fax:* 0161 257 2446. Andrew Dean, cond.

Manx Youth Choir. Music Centre, Lord St, Douglas, Isle of Man IM1 1LE *tel:* 01624 686555 *fax:* 01624 686557.

Maureen Hunter Singers. 14 Vine Close, Cottingham, E Yorks HU16 5RF *tel:* 01482 843344 *also fax.* Maureen Hunter, mus dir.

Methodist Association Youth Club Singers. 2 Chester House, Pages La, London N10 1PR *tel:* 0181 444 9845. Craig McLeish, dir.

New London Children's Choir. 41 Aberdare Gardens, London NW6 3AL *tel:* 0171 625 4641 *fax:* 0171 625 4876. Ronald Corp, cond.

Northants County Youth Choirs. c/o Music Services, 125-129 Kettering Rd, Northampton NN1 4AZ *tel:* 01604 37117 *fax:* 01604 603070. Peter Dunkley, head of mus service.

Nottingham Choral Trust Youth Choir. 18 Hobart Dr, Stapleford, Notts NG9 8PX *tel:* 0115 939 0511. Angela Kay, cond; Susan Hatherly, sec.

Oakdale Youth Choir. Oakdale Community College, Penmaen, Blackwood, Gwent NP2 0DT *tel:* 01495 225110 *fax:* 01495 224580. Nigel Jones, mus dir.

Oldham Boys' Choir. Oldham Metropolitan Borough Music Centre, The Lyceum Building, Union St, Oldham OL1 1QG *tel:* 0161 627 2332 *fax:* 0161 620 0259. Eileen Bentley, cond.

Oldham Girls' Choirs. Oldham Metropolitan Borough Music Centre, The Lyceum Building, Union St, Oldham OL1 1QG *tel:* 0161 627 2332 *fax:* 0161 620 0259. Eileen Bentley, cond snr choir; Jacqui Hamlett, cond jnr choir.

Oxford Girls' Choirs. The Old Manse, Leafield, Witney, Oxon OX8 5NN *tel:* 01993 878200 *fax:* 01993 878375. Mary Taylor, admin.

Royal Scottish National Orchestra Junior Chorus. Royal Scottish National Orchestra, 73 Claremont St, Glasgow G3 7HA *tel:* 0141 226 3868 *fax:* 0141 221 4317 *email:* rsno@glasgow.almac.co.uk; http://www.scot-art.org/rsno. Christopher Bell, chorus master; Jill Mitchell, chorus mgr.

St Catherine's Chamber Choir. St Catherine's School, Bramley, Guildford, Surrey *tel:* 01483 893363 *fax:* 01483 893003. Robert Gillman, cond and admin.

St Margaret's Senior Choir Exeter. St Margaret's School, Magdalen Rd, Exeter *tel:* 01392 273197. Miranda Lisk, cond.

Southend Boys' Choir. PO Box 6, Civic Centre, Southend on Sea, Essex *tel:* 01702 215436 *fax:* 01702 215110. Roger Humphrey, cond.

Southend Girls' Choir. PO Box 6, Civic Centre, Southend on Sea, Essex *tel:* 01702 215436 *fax:* 01702 215110. Roger Humphrey, cond.

Stockport Youth Choirs and The Maia Singers. 23 Buttermere Rd, Gatley, Cheadle, Cheshire SK8 4RH *tel:* 0161 428 5456. John Pomphrey, dir; Lynda Whitney, admin.

Suffolk Jubilee Choir. County Music Service, Northgate Arts Centre, Sidegate La West, Ipswich, Suffolk IP4 3DF *tel:* 01473 281866 *fax:* 01473 286068. David Bramhall, cond.

Vivace Girls' Choir. c/o 7 Park La, Charvil, Reading, Berks RG10 9TR *tel:* 0118 934 0589. Miss S Newman, mus dir.

The Voice Squad. Fish and Bell Management, PO Box 175, Bury St Edmunds, Suffolk IP32 7DY *tel:* 01284 756204 *email:* fishbell@aol.com. Brigitta Kenyon, dir.

West Sussex Girls' Choir. Crawley Area Music Centre, c/o Hazelwick School, Hazelwick Mill La, Three Bridges, Crawley, W Sussex RH10 1SX *tel:* 01293 537197. Janet McCleery, cond.

Worcester Festival Junior Chorus. 40 The Hill Av, Worcester WR5 2AW *tel:* 01905 351292 *also fax.* Christopher Hand, cond.

Youth Opera and Music Theatre

British Youth Opera. South Bank University, 103 Borough Rd, London SE1 0AA *tel:* 0171 815 6090 *fax:* 0171 815 6094. Timothy Dean, mus dir; Denis Coe, exec chmn; Mikel Toms, orch mgr.

Hillside Opera. 57 Gordon Av, Portswood, Southampton SO14 6WH *tel:* 01703 551088 *also fax.* Jill Meager, artistic dir; Kaarina Manzur, business mgr.

Live Culture and Live Wires Youth Opera Groups. Baylis Programme, English National Opera, The ENO Works, 40 Pitfield St, London N1 6EU *tel:* 0171 739 5808 *fax:* 0171 729 8928. Johanne Davies, artistic dir, Live Culture; Tim Yealland, artistic dir, Live Wires.

Music Box Children's Opera Group. Garden Flat, 29 West Park, Clifton, Bristol BS8 2LX *tel:* 0117 974 4666 *also fax.* Mark Lawrence, mus dir; Deborah Cranston, drama dir; Sue Hannam, membership sec.

National Youth Music Theatre. 5th Floor, Palace Theatre, Shaftesbury Av, London W1V 8AY *tel:* 0171 734 7478 *fax:* 0171 734 7515 *email:* http://www.nymt.org.uk. Jeremy James Taylor, artistic dir; Felicity Bunt, gen mgr; Vivienne Hughes, auditions admin.

Opera Inside Out. Goblins Hold, Wootton Rivers, Marlborough, Wilts SN8 4NQ *tel:* 01672 811175. Kevin Scott, artistic dir; Clive Andrews, chmn.

Organisations for Young Performers

The organisations listed below exist to promote excellence in performance for school-age musicians and singers.

Association of British Choral Directors (ABCD). 46 Albert St, Tring, Herts HP23 6AU *tel:* 01422 825859. Howard Layfield, chair; Marie-Louise Petit, gen sec. *The national organisation and forum for choir leaders, teachers, students and choral conductors promotes the interests of all who work with young singers to lay a foundation for a life-long interest in choral singing. Courses, conventions, advice and discussion groups. International study and performing tours.*

Boosey & Hawkes Youth Orchestra Award. Promotion Dept, Boosey & Hawkes, 295 Regent St, London W1R 8JH *tel:* 0171 291 7229 *fax:* 0171 637 3490 *email:* composers@boosey.com. Lloyd Moore. *A major award worth £1000 open to all participating orchs in the Edinburgh and Glasgow Festival of British Youth Orchestras held during the Edinburgh Festival. The prize is aimed at encouraging youth orchs to programme works by many of this century's greatest composers. Applicants must be members of NAYO and perform one work from the Boosey & Hawkes selected list. Designed to provide funds towards a recording, a concert in a major venue or to help towards a foreign or UK tour.*

British Choral Institute. 18 The Rotyngs, Rottingdean, Brighton BN2 7DX *tel:* 01273 300894 *fax:* 01273 308394 *email:* britchorinst@fastnet.co.uk. Roy Wales, dir; Christine Wales, admin. *A national organisation established as an advisory, promotional, educational and training body for choral singers, conductors, choral administrators and organisers from all sectors of the choral community with a special emphasis on developing international choral projects.*

British Federation of Young Choirs (BFYC). Devonshire House, Devonshire Sq, Loughborough, Leics LE11 3DW *tel:* 01509 211664 *fax:* 01509 260630. Susan Lansdale, dir; Andrew Fairbairn, hon sec. *Choral events for young people and training courses for teachers, conductors and singers. 450 members (180 choirs and 270 individuals). Choral animateurs in Scotland, Northern Ireland, East Anglia, London, West and East Midlands.*

British Reserve Insurance Youth Orchestra Awards. NAYO, Ainslie House, 11 St Colme St, Edinburgh EH3 6AG *tel:* 0131 539 1087 *fax:* 0131 539 1069 *email:* nayo.office@virgin.net; http://pobox.com/~nayo. Carol Main, dir. *5 awards of £500 each will be made to youth orchs within NAYO's membership towards a project to enhance the orchestras' activities. Deadline for applications Apr. Previous winners may reapply after an interval of one year.*

Music for Youth. 4 Blade Mews, London SW15 2NN *tel:* 0181 870 9624 *fax:* 0181 870 9935 *email:* http://www.pjbpubs.co.uk/mfy. Larry Westland CBE, exec dir. *Platform for young musicians.*

National Association of Choirs. 21 Charmouth Rd, Lower Weston, Bath BA1 3LJ *tel:* 01225 426713. John Robbins, gen sec.

National Association of Youth Orchestras. Ainslie House, 11 St Colme St, Edinburgh EH3 6AG *tel:* 0131 539 1087 *fax:* 0131 539 1069 *email:* admin@nayo.org.uk; http://www.nayo.org.uk. Carol Main, dir. *Has members from independent and LEA run orchs. Organises the Festival of British Youth Orchestras in Edinburgh and Glasgow, Anglo-German Youth Music Week, British Reserve Insurance Youth Orchestra Awards and the British Reserve Insurance Conducting Prize. NAYO also organises various Silver Baton award schemes in association with business sponsors, eg Salvesen Baton for young conductors. NAYO publishes a newsletter* Full Orchestra *three times pa. Also the Marion Semple Weir library of chmbr mus, free hire to members.*

Sing for Pleasure. 25 Fryerning La, Ingatestone, Essex CM4 0DD *tel:* 01277 353691 *also fax.* Lynda Parker, dir. *Wide variety of day and residential courses for young singers and conductors. Singing day for children and INSET courses for teachers. Choir repertoire is available from above address.*

Young People in Music. 2 Greystoke Lodge, Hanger La, London W5 1EW *tel:* 0181 998 1176. Yoriko Wakabayashi. *Lecture recitals, listening classes, summer mus camp and concert opportunities for children, with particular emphasis laid on developing the ability to listen.*

Festivals for Young Performers

Aberdeen International Youth Festival. 3 Nutborn House, Clifton Rd, London SW19 4QT *tel:* 0181 946 2995 *fax:* 0181 944 6507. Nicola Wallis, festival dir. *5-15 Aug 1998. Youth orchs, choirs, jazz and rock groups, dance and theatre groups from all over the world. Mainly amateur, but some professional input.*

The Festival of British Youth Orchestras in Edinburgh and Glasgow. NAYO, Ainslie House, 11 St Colme St, Edinburgh EH3 6AG *tel:* 0131 539 1087 *fax:* 0131 539 1069 *email:* nayo.office@virgin.net; http://pobox.com/~nayo. Carol Main, dir. *15 Aug-5 Sep 1998; 14 Aug-4 Sep 1999. RSAMD box office tel: 0141 332 5057; Central Hall box office tel: 0131 229 7937 (during Festival period only).*

Harrogate International Youth Music Festival. Perform Europe (Incoming), Deepdene Lodge, Deepdene Av, Dorking, Surrey RH5 4AZ *tel:* 01306 744360 *fax:* 01306 744361 *email:* smb.peurope@kuoni.co.uk. Sharon Brewster, festivals mgr. *10-17 Apr 1998. Celebrating its 26th year in 1998, the festival features varied and exciting performances from local and international choirs, bands, orchs and dance groups.*

Music for Youth's National Festivals. 4 Blade Mews, London SW15 2NN *tel:* 0181 870 9624 *fax:* 0181 870 9935. Larry Westland CBE, exec dir. *Up to 20,000 young musicians will perform at Symphony Hall, Birmingham, the Bridgewater Hall, Manchester and the Royal Festival Hall, London.*

Schools' Prom. Music for Youth, 4 Blade Mews, London SW15 2NN *tel:* 0181 870 9624 *fax:* 0181 870 9935 *email:* http://www.pjbpubs.co.uk/mfy. Larry Westland CBE, exec dir.

West Sussex International Youth Music Festival. Perform Europe (Incoming), Deepdene Lodge, Deepdene Av, Dorking, Surrey RH5 4AZ *tel:* 01306 744360 *fax:* 01306 744361 *email:* mjl.peurope@kuoni.co.uk. Maria Llinares, festival mgr. *9-13 Apr 1998. Celebrating its 7th year in 1998. Non-competitive festival taking place in various venues throughout West Sussex and on the South coast, including Arundel Cathedral and Worthing Assembly Hall. Attracts both local and international bands, orchs, choirs and dance groups.*

Summer Schools and Short Courses

Courses held in the holidays, at weekends and in the evenings are listed here with the address for applications and the venue (if different from the first address). The **Benslow Music Trust** (*see entry below*) maintains a permanent short-term residential centre and presents courses throughout the year for amateur musicians of all types and standards.

A detailed list of music courses held throughout the year can be found in the February issue of *Music Teacher* and a summer school supplement is published in a January issue of *Classical Music*. Both magazines are available from Rhinegold Publishing Ltd. The **National Institute of Adult Continuing Education** (21 De Montfort St, Leicester LE1 7GE *tel:* 0116 255 1451 *fax:* 0116 285 4514) produces a bi-annual publication *Time To Learn* detailing a wide range of residential courses.

Alexander Technique for Pianists. 50 Weston Way, Weston Favell, Northampton NN3 3BN *tel:* 01604 401862 *also fax.* John Naylor, admin. *Residential courses on the application of Alexander Technique to pno study and performance. Individual and group tuition in both pno and Alexander Technique. Details tbc. Benslow Music Trust Summer School, Aug.*

Alston Hall College. Alston La, Longridge, Preston, Lancs PR3 3BP *tel:* 01772 784661 *fax:* 01772 785835. Graham Wilkinson, principal. *1998: Opera appreciation 23-25 Jan; a pianist's journey through the 19th C 13-15 Mar; chmbr mus for str, wind and pno 6-8 Apr; chmbr mus for str quintets 21-23 Nov; also day courses. Fees: from £75 (residential), £14 (day). For those aged 18 and over.*

The Amadeus Chorus and Orchestra Summer School. 41 Cahir St, London E14 3QR *tel:* 0171 537 2329 *fax:* 01453 843557. Philip Mackenzie, dir. *For players aged 18-30 min gr 8 (higher for wind, br and perc). Also places for 2 composers and 2 conductors (u/grads). Repertoire includes Shostakovich, cello concerto no 1; Berlioz, Sinfonie Fantastique; Rossini, Thieving Magpie Overture. Fees: £75 (half-price bursaries are available). 19-26 Jul 1998 in Gloucestershire.*

Amadeus Summer Course. 100 Harvist Rd, London NW6 6HL *tel:* 0181 960 4780 *fax:* 0181 964 5510. Robin Anderton, admin. *For p/grad and young professional str quartets. 1-2 weeks concentrated study of the quartet repertoire, with members of the Amadeus Quartet. 26 Jul-8 Aug 1998 at the RAM, applications by May (some scholarships available).*

The Andover Harp Course. 44 Church Cres, London N3 1BJ *tel:* 0181 349 4067 *also fax.* Miriam Keogh, admin. *Classes in technique, repertoire and ens groups; aspects of orch hp playing, plus care and maintenance of the hp. Held at Farleigh School, Red Rice, Andover in Aug. Residents aged 14-25, non-residents aged 12-14. Fees: £225.*

Anglo-German Youth Music Week. NAYO, 2 Gilberyn Dr, Worle, Weston-super-Mare, Somerset BS22 0TR *tel:* 01934 512380 *also fax;* 0802 437919 *email:* malcolm.goodman@nayo.org.uk; http://www.nayo. org.uk. Malcolm Goodman, NAYO course admin. *1-10 Aug 1998 in Oberwesel-am-Rhein, Germany. Annual residential mus week, alternately in Germany and the UK. Wide range of orch and chmbr mus with students from other European countries. Full symphony orch also forming 2 chmbr orchs. For age 15-25 of gr 7-8+ standard on first inst. Fees: £240.*

Association for Cultural Exchange - Study Tours. Babraham, Cambridge CB2 4AP *tel:* 01223 835055 *fax:* 01223 837394. Hugh Barnes. *Programme of study tours, residential courses in UK and worldwide, including visits to Haydn Festival in Eisenstadt, Music in Bamberg, Schubert at Feldkirch, Verdi and the Spirit of Italy. Average age 40-75. Fees: £600-1000.*

Ayton Castle Summer School. Music-Makers, 17 North Gardner St, Glasgow G11 5BU *tel:* 0141 339 2708 *fax:* 0141 337 6923. Gusztáv Fenyö, artistic dir. *7-19 Jul 1998. Applications by 1 May. Courses for strs, pno and chmbr mus. Combines with 2-week festival (Summer Music*

Solennelle at the Warwick Arts Centre. Some bursaries available. 10-11 Oct 1998.

The City Lit. Music Dept, Keeley House, Keeley St, London WC2B 4BA *tel:* 0171 430 0546 *fax:* 0171 831 8508. Moira Hayward, head of mus section; Della Rhodes, jazz co-ord. *Adult educ courses from elementary to advanced level in inst, vocal, choral, operatic, musicianship, composition, chmbr mus, ens, jazz, pop, world mus, mus appreciation and mus technology. Enrolment Sep for year courses. Also runs a series of short summer courses in Jul, details available on request.*

Clarinetwise. Pengribyn, Cilrehydn, Llanfyrnach, Pembs SA35 0AA *tel:* 01239 698602. Jacqueline Browne, events organiser; Michael Collins, president. *Regular cl w/shops, courses and m/classes. Quarterly journal available.*

Classic FM Masterclass Schools' Music Festival. Masterclass, Academic House, 24-28 Oval Rd, London NW1 7DQ *tel:* 0171 713 2639 *email:* susannw@classicfm.co.uk. Susannah Wainman. *65-piece orch made up of individuals aged 11-18 from youth orchs countrywide. Festival culminates in a concert at Cabot Hall, Canary Wharf, which includes mus by Gershwin, Beethoven, Shostakovich and Elgar. Festival held at Eltham College, London Jul 1998.*

Clonter Opera Farm. Swettenham Heath, Congleton, Cheshire CW12 2LR *tel:* 01260 224638 *fax:* 01260 224742. Jeffery Lockett, artistic dir; Leonard Hancock, mus dir. *Two residential opera studios culminating in public performances for singers aged 20-35. Apr 1998 (Humperdinck, Hansel & Gretel); Jul 1998 (Bizet, Carmen or Mozart, Marriage of Figaro), applications by end Sep for the following year. Performance fees and travel costs paid; free board and lodging.*

Coleg Harlech. Harlech, Gwynedd LL46 2PU *tel:* 01766 780363 *fax:* 01766 780169 *email:* ifans@harlech.ac.uk. M Ifans. *Orch mus summer school for ages 16 and above. Aug 1998, applications by 31 May. Fees: £275 (concessions for students).*

Colla Voce Summer School. Ridgeside, Eastfield Rd, Redhill, Surrey RH1 4DY *tel:* 01737 763292 *also fax; email:* scook@netcomuk.co.uk. Sue Cook, admin. *Jul-Aug, 1998, for singers and acc. Week of m/classes and w/shops taking holistic approach to all aspects of performance. Topics range from oratorio and French song to sessions on posture and opera direction. Final performance held at Leighton Park in Berkshire.*

Colourstrings/Colourkeys Course for Teachers. The Szilvay Foundation, 4 Ullswater Close, Kingston Vale, London SW15 3RF *tel:* 0181 547 3073; 0181 340 4534 *also fax.* Pat Wislocki, Deborah Harris, dirs. *Annual residential/day course which includes mus kindergarten, primary school*

mus (4-7), vn, vc, mini-bass, pno and gui methods. Kodály-based, using relative sol-fa to train the inner ear prior to learning an inst and continuing this approach in inst tuition. Musicianship and Dalcroze Eurhythmics classes included. All 5-day courses are credit bearing for the LTCL (MusEd) and Cert (MusEd). Aug 1998, applications by end Jul. Other dates available for mus kindergarten. Teacher training course for primary school and kindergarten teachers in Feb and Apr.

The 3rd Conspiracy of Flutes. 41 Devon Av, Twickenham TW2 6PN. Julie Wright. *A booster course for adult flautists of all levels held at Bloxham School, near Oxford. Hosted by Atarah Ben-Tovim MBE and directed by Julie Wright.*

Contemporary Music Making for Amateurs (COMA). 13 Wellington Way, Bow, London E3 4NE *tel:* 0181 980 1527 *fax:* 0181 980 3330 *email:* 106147.546@compuserve.com. Chris Shurety, dir; Frances Pace, admin. *Residential summer school, 25 Jul-1 Aug at Bretton Hall, Yorkshire. W/shops for age 18 and above in composition, improvisation, contemporary inst, vocal and electro-acoustic techniques, ens and orchs, concerts of commissioned and students' works, recording and computer facilities, core creative mus project. Fees: £360 (£200 concessions). Reductions for early applications.*

Countrywide Holidays Association. Grove House, Wilmslow Rd, Didsbury, Manchester M20 2HU *tel:* 0161 448 7112; 0161 446 2226 (reservations) *fax:* 0161 448 7113 *email:* 101573.1452@compuserve. com. Patricia Percival, reservations mgr. *Jul-Aug.*

Creative Dance Artists Trust. 15b Lauriston Rd, London SW19 4TJ *tel:* 0181 946 3444 *fax:* 0181 879 0642. Gale Law, admin. *International course for professional choreographers and composers. Fosters creative collaboration between essential elements of dance, mus and movement. Participants are selected by committee. No age restriction, but evidence of talent in a professional context required. 2 weeks in Jul, applications by Mar.*

Curwen Institute. 56 Creffield Rd, Colchester, Essex CO3 3HY *tel:* 01206 572411. Yvonne Lawton, sec. *New Curwen method. Recommended for class mus teachers. Specially arranged local courses on application.*

Dalcroze Society. 41a Woodmansterne Rd, Coulsdon, Surrey CR5 2DJ *tel:* 0181 645 0714 *also fax.* Mrs P Piqué, sec. *Summer course of mus educ through movement for all ages. Rhythmics, improvisation, ear training and therapy for all age groups. Jul-Aug.*

Dartington International Summer School. Dartington Hall, Totnes, Devon TQ9 6DE *tel:* 01803 865988/867068 *fax:* 01803 868108. Gavin Henderson, artistic dir; Justine Peberdy, admin. *18 Jul-29 Aug 1998.*

Summer course for those of any age, with opportunity for advanced tuition and m/classes, informal mus-making, plus concerts, talks, etc. Composer in residence; mus-theatre, masque and opera. Fees: £160-660 per week.

Dillington House. Ilminster, Somerset TA19 9DT *tel:* 01460 52427/55866 *fax:* 01460 52433. *W/end courses throughout the year. 1998 courses: an alphabet of mus, 2-4 Jan; three ages of opera 1900-2000, 30 Jan-1 Feb; rediscovering the hpd, 6-8 Mar; mus in Vienna 1890-1945, 27-29 Mar; Wagner and Parsifal, 3-5 Apr; playing the rcdr 1-3 May; plus day schools and concerts every month.*

Dolmetsch Summer School. Heartsease, Grayswood Rd, Haslemere, Surrey GU27 2BS *tel:* 01428 643235/651473 *fax:* 01428 654920/651473 *email:* brian@be-blood.demon.co.uk; http://www.be-blood.demon.co.uk. Dr Blood, course sec. *Royal School, Haslemere, Surrey. Rcdr, early keyboard, viols, chmbr choir, c/room techniques; also optional classes for choir, rcdr, conducting, composition. For any age group, 9-15 Aug 1998, applications by 1 Aug. Fees: c £370 (residential); c £190 (non-residential).*

Double Bass Summer Holiday Course *see* **Oxford Cello School.**

Double Bass Summer School. 7 St Clair Dr, Worcester Pk, Surrey KT4 8UG *tel:* 0181 330 3188 *also fax; email:* peter.emery@kcl.ac.uk. P W Emery, hon sec. *Separate courses for beginners, intermediate and advanced db players aged 8-25. Ens playing, m/classes, technique classes and chmbr mus. Aug, applications by 1 Aug. Fees: £150.*

Early Music Wales. Welsh College of Music and Drama, Castle Grounds, Cathays Park, Cardiff CF1 3ER *tel:* 01222 342854 *fax:* 01222 237639 *email:* w-d@baynet.co.uk. Andrew Wilson-Dickson, Lucy Robinson, dirs. *Courses for age 17 and above. Places for singers, lutenists, baroque guis, keyboard players, vns, fls, rcdr and str players who are keen to specialise in renaissance and baroque mus. Period insts essential. Jul, applications by end Jun. Fees: c £300.*

The Earnley Concourse. Earnley, Chichester, W Sussex PO20 7JL *tel:* 01243 670392 *fax:* 01243 670832 *email:* earnley@interalpha.co.uk. *W/end and week-long study courses for age 16 and above, featuring mus history, chmbr and jazz w/shops. Ages 16 and over. Fees: c £150+ (w/end); c £380+ (week).*

East Anglia Summer Music School. c/o Opera da Camera, 7 Meadow Rd, New Costessey, Norwich NR5 0NF *tel:* 01603 744584 *fax:* 01603 507720. Jeffrey Davies, organiser and dir. *Residential and w/end classes for adults at the University of East Anglia, covering concert repertoire, opera and technique. M/classes, opera w/shops and w/shops for singers. 21-30 Aug 1998, applications by mid-Jul. Fees: £110 (residential), £60 (non-residential).*

Edinburgh University Centre for Continuing Education. 11 Buccleuch Pl, Edinburgh EH8 9LW *tel:* 0131 650 4400 *fax:* 0131 667 6097. Bridget Stevens, admin dir. *Music at the Edinburgh Festival, 15 Aug-4 Sep 1998; piano w/shop, 10-28 Aug 1998. Also weekly classes in mus theory and appreciation. For age 18 and above. Fees: 9 weekly classes c £35, summer courses £140-250 per wk. Applications taken until one month before start date.*

Edrom House Summer Schools. Edrom House, Duns, Berwickshire TD11 3PX *tel:* 0189 081 8277; 0181 340 0897 *fax:* 0181 341 5292. Christopher Cowan, Lucy Cowan, Penelope Lynex. *Chmbr mus, vn and vc courses, for age 11 upwards. Apr, Jul, Aug and Sep. Fees: £198.*

Elizabeth College (Guernsey) Summer Orchestral Course. Shalom, Les Marettes Villas, St Martin's, Guernsey *tel:* 01481 38980. Miles Attwell, admin; Richard Dickins, principal cond. *Gr 5+. Age 9-19. All orch and wind insts; 3 orchs, 3 bands. 17-22 Aug 1998, applications by 1 Jul. Fees: £130 Including accommodation.*

Emanuel Hurwitz Chamber Music Course. 44 Church Cres, London N3 1BJ *tel:* 0181 349 4067 *also fax.* Miriam Keogh, admin. *Held at Farleigh School, Red Rice, Andover, Hants. Aug. M/classes, str orch, ens coaching. Age 15-27, gr 8+. Serious students only, not for amateurs. Aug. Fees: £260. Bursaries available.*

Emscote Lawn Music School. Emscote Rd, Warwick *tel:* 01926 428135. Paul Russell. *Orch course for young musicians aged 8-14. Mar-Apr.*

Ernest Read Music Association (ERMA). 9 Cotsford Av, New Malden, Surrey KT3 5EU *tel:* 0181 942 0318. Noel Long, dir. *Summer school for age 16 and above. Orch courses (orch I advanced; orch II gr 6-8+), perc course, chmbr choir (advanced), listeners' study group.*

Eton Choral Courses. The Shepherd's Cottage, Gt Shelford, Cambridge CB2 5JX *tel:* 01223 845685 *fax:* 01223 841980 *email:* rallwood@netcomuk.co.uk. Ralph Allwood, dir; Lydia Smallwood, admin. *3 courses at Eton College 4-30 Jul 1998; 3-11 Aug 1998, applications by Apr. Age 16-20. Fees: £325.*

European Federation of Young Choirs. 9 Fairmount Dr, Loughborough, Leics LE11 3JR *tel:* 01509 263954 *fax:* 01509 232310. Mrs S E Rastall, sec. *Loughborough Singing Week for age 16 and above. Next 1999.*

European Piano Teachers' Association UK (EPTA). 1 Wildgoose Dr, Horsham RH12 1TU *fax:* 01403 267761. Frances Bryan, admin; Kendall Taylor CBE, president; Frank Martin, chmn. *EPTA has 34 regional centres throughout UK which organise regular seminars, w/shops,*

m/classes, pupils' and teachers' concerts. Annual pno pedagogy courses. Annual residential summer conference end Aug with m/classes, pno teaching, recitals, lectures. Open to non-members. Ages 18 and above. EPTA UK International Conference 25-29 Aug 1998 in York with lectures, demonstrations and m/classes. Pedagogy course Jan-May.

European String Teachers' Association (ESTA). 247 Hay Green La, Bournville, Birmingham B30 1SH *tel:* 0121 475 3345 *also fax.* Olive Goodborn, admin. *Summer school 14-20 Aug 1998. For str teachers.*

European Youth Summer Music. Festivals House, 198 Park La, Macclesfield, Cheshire SK11 6UD *tel:* 01625 428297 *fax:* 01625 503229 *email:* festivals@compuserve.com; http://ourworld.compuserve.com/homepages/festivals/eysm.htm. Liz Whitehead, course organiser. *A summer orch course for young musicians aged 11-17 and 18-21 at Haileybury College, Herts. 26 Jul-2 Aug 1997, applications by 1 Jul. Fees c £265.*

Fantasia Music School. 5 Aspen Way, Middleton on Sea, W Sussex PO22 6PW *tel:* 01243 586068. Mrs M Sutton, admin. *3 summer courses held at Dorset House School, nr Arundel for young musicians aged 8-18. Residential and day; Aug. Fees: £115-145 (day), £220-240 (boarding).*

Fawley Court Music Courses. 9 Hall Close, Godalming, Surrey GU7 3PW *tel:* 01483 417927. Pippa Dice, admin; Michael Procter. *W/end courses near Henley on Thames. Also late Jul, Beauchamp House, Glos: mus for voices and insts.*

Fife Summer Jazz Course. Arts in Fife, The Tower Block, ASDARC, Woodend Rd, Cardenden KY5 0NE *tel:* 01592 414714 *fax:* 01592 414727. Anne Chalk, publicity and development offr. *Jazz Course directed by Richard Michael. For all ages. Jul 1998, applications by 12 Jun.*

Gathering of the Clans. c/o The Villa, Tollerson, York YO6 2EQ *tel:* 01347 838273. *Courses and m/classes for cellists aged 14 and above. Various venues around the country.*

Glamorgan Summer School. Welsh Jazz Society Ltd, 26 The Balcony, Castle Arcade, Cardiff *tel:* 01222 340591. Brian Hennessey, dir. *A jazz educ summer course held at University of Glamorgan, Treforrest. Jul-Aug.*

Glasgow University. Dept of Adult and Continuing Education, 57-61 Oakfield Av, Glasgow G12 8LW *tel:* 0141 339 8855 ext 4394 *fax:* 0141 307 8025. J G Macdonald, deputy dir. *Joint study days with Scottish Opera. Mus appreciation and theory, 8, 10 and 20 week courses from Oct. For age 18 and above. Fees: from £30 for 10 week courses.*

Gloucestershire Choral Weekend. Cotswold House, Naunton, Cheltenham, Glos GL54 3AA *tel:* 01451 850796. Geoffrey Mitchell, mus dir; Cedric Virgin, organiser. *Study of classical and contemporary choral works for mixed voices at Wycliffe College in Gloucestershire. No age limit. 3-5 Apr 1998, applications by 15 Mar. Fees: c £88 (residential), c £58 (non-residential). Easter course 1999 in Gloucestershire.*

Gloucestershire Summer Orchestral Course. Colwell Centre for Arts in Education, Derby Rd, Gloucester GL1 4AD *tel:* 01452 330300. Brenda Whitwell, office mgr. *Residential orch summer course for insts aged 9-18. Caters for all grades, but min gr 1 required for entry. 26 Jul-1 Aug 1998, applications by 26 Jun.*

Goldsmiths. University of London, Continuing and Community Education, Lewisham Way, London SE14 6NW *tel:* 0171 919 7200/7229 *fax:* 0171 919 7223 *email:* gcce@gold.ac.uk. Lisa Peat, conference offr; Jane Metcalfe, lecturer in mus. *Courses for musicians and teachers, of 10 weeks duration: Afro-Latin perc; African drumming; jazz improvisation for singers; principles and practices of teaching. Also Afro-Latin perc w/shop, 9-10 May 1998; jazz improvisation for singers, 20-21 Jun 1998; jazz pno w/end w/shop, 27-28 Jun 1998; listening, composing, performing, 28-31 Jul 1998.*

Guildhall Summer School. Guildhall School of Music and Drama, Silk St, Barbican, London EC2Y 8DT *tel:* 01702 714733 (eves). Heather Swain, mgr. *2 week jazz, rock, studio and world mus summer school in Jul 1998 for age 12 and above. Fees: £60 (intro to jazz w/end), £80 (mus technology w/end), £180 (week), £330 (jazz, rock and studio 2 weeks), £150 (singers week).*

H F Holidays Ltd. Imperial House, Edgware Rd, London NW9 5AL *tel:* 0181 905 9556; 0181 905 9388 (24 hr brochure line) *fax:* 0181 205 0506. Laura Livingston, admin. *Wide variety of mus-making and appreciation holidays with expert tuition throughout the year. Courses include Elgar in the Dales, Composers of Gloucestershire, Monteverdi to Mozart, Songs from the Shows, Choral Music in England, Singing for Beginners, Gilbert and Sullivan.*

Harrogate Woodwind/Horns Chamber-Music Course. c/o Lindsey Music, 42 St Mary's Pk, Louth, Lincs LN11 0EF *tel:* 01507 605244. Jacqueline Browne, events organiser. *Mid Aug 1998.*

Hawkwood Short Courses. Hawkwood Residential College, Painswick Old Rd, Stroud, Glos GL6 7QW *tel:* 01453 759034 *fax:* 01453 764607. *W/end courses for str, chmbr mus, mus appreciation. Summer orch week (wind and str). Various w/end and mid-week courses throughout year. Hawkwood chmbr orch for str, w/wind and br players of moderate ability.*

Kato Havas One-Day Workshop for Strings. 72 Victoria Rd, Oxford OX2 7QE *tel:* 01865 514094 *also fax. Release of Tension and Stage Fright in Performance held at St Edmund Hall, Oxford. 25 Jul 1998. Fees: £8 (Khana members); £28 (non-members).*

Keele Summer Schools. Centre for Continuing and Professional Education, Keele University, Keele, Staffs ST5 5BG *tel:* 01782 583436 *fax:* 01782 583248 *email:* ada09@keele.ac.uk. Heather Mason, course sec. *Chamber Music Summer School, for amateurs, students and teachers aged 18 and above, 22-29 Aug 1998. Applications by 26 Jun.*

Kenneth van Barthold Intensive Piano Workshop. Arvenis, Stour La, Stour Row, Shaftesbury, Dorset SP7 0QJ *tel:* 01747 838 318 *also fax.* Kenneth van Barthold. *2 tutors for 12 students, 12 practice rooms, recording facilities, final public recitals on Steinway concert grand. Presented in association with the University of Edinburgh Music Faculty and Centre for Continuing Education. Aug.*

The Knack. Baylis Programme at English National Opera, ENO Works, 40 Pitfield St, London N1 6EU *tel:* 0171 739 5808. Mary King, course dir; Steve Moffitt, head of the Baylis Programme. *For singers aged 18-40 developing skills in mus and singing, text and drama, movement and dance. Taught in evening sessions Oct-Jun, auditions in May. No previous formal qualifications needed. Fees: £500 per term.*

Knuston Hall. Irchester, Wellingborough, Northants NN29 7EU *tel:* 01933 312104 *fax:* 01933 357596. John Herrick, principal. *Various w/end and week adult residential courses throughout year. For age 16 and above. Fees: £89.50.*

The Kodály Institute of Britain. 133 Queen's Gate, London SW7 5LE *tel:* 0171 823 7371 *fax:* 0171 584 7691. Mary Skone-Roberts, admin. *Summer school Aug 1998 at Queen's Gate School, London. Courses for kindergarten, primary, secondary and tertiary educators, singers, pno and vc teachers. Musicianship training for all. M/classes and recitals. 1-yr p/t courses in musicianship according to the Kodály Principles at 3 levels: elementary, intermediate, advanced, late Sep, credit bearing for Trinity College LTCL (Music Ed) Cert and Dip. W/end courses in early childhood, primary and secondary mus educ, London, Jan-Feb 1998.*

Lacock Summer School. Cantax House, Lacock, Chippenham, Wilts SN15 2JZ *tel:* 01249 730468 *also fax.* Andrew van der Beek. *19-24 Jul, 26-31 Jul 1998. For singers and players of renaissance and baroque insts. All ages. Fees: £230, £140 (age 25 and under).*

Lake District Summer Music. Stricklandgate House, 92 Stricklandgate, Kendal, Cumbria LA9 4PU *tel:* 01539 733411 *fax:* 01539 724441. *Classes and individual coaching by international artists for ens, str*

players and pianists on this residential chmbr mus course. 1-11 Aug 1998, applications by Jul. Children's w/shops (age 6-12) and Young String Venture (age 6-16) are non-residential. Fees: £100 (Young String Venture); £285 (snr summer school).

Lambent Books. 4 Coombe Gardens, New Malden, Surrey KT3 4AA *tel:* 0181 715 2560 *also fax; email:* lambent@well.com. Joseph O'Connor. *Courses and individual consultations for performers and teachers on performance anxiety, communication skills and psychology of learning.*

Lancaster Rehearsal Orchestra. Dept of Music, University of Lancaster, Lancaster LA1 4YW *tel:* 01524 593777/593013 *fax:* 01524 847298 *email:* d.mccaldin@lancaster.ac.uk. Denis McCaldin; Ronald Adelson, sec. *1-day symphony orch courses 3 times pa. R Strauss, 1 Feb 1998; Prokofiev, 26 Apr 1998; Mahler, 8 Nov 1998. Entry by audition, age 16 and above. Applications by one month before event. Fees: £5 per event.*

Latour International Festival of Music and the Arts (France). c/o Mananan Festival Office, Erin Arts Centre, Port Erin, Isle of Man IM9 6LD *tel:* 01624 835858 *fax:* 01624 836658. John Bethell, dir. *Vocal and opera study courses with Jeffrey Lawton for professionals and amateurs aged 19-35. Opportunity to appear in opera performance. 26-30 Jul 1998, applications by 1 May.*

Lauderdale House Society. 22 Gresley Rd, London N19 3JZ *tel:* 0171 272 5664 *also fax.* Murray Gordon, mus chmn. *M/classes for pno, voice, vc, vn, fl, tpt. Concerts, gui society, Singers Guild, Suzuki, etc.*

Learn at Leisure (Educational Breaks). University of Nottingham, 14 Shakespeare St, Nottingham NG1 4FJ *tel:* 0115 951 6526 *fax:* 0115 947 2977 *email:* ce.residential@nottingham.ac.uk. David Bodger, residential courses dir. *Educational holidays for adults. 1998: CBSO Weekend in Birmingham, 24-26 Apr; Malvern Festival, 22-25 Apr; Welsh National Opera in Llandudno, 26-28 Jun; Beethoven in Oxford, 3-5 Jul; Nottingham University Summer School, 18-25 Jul; Three Choirs Festival, 15-22 Aug; Introduction to Chamber Music, 4-6 Sep; Introduction to Contemporary Music, 18-20 Sep.*

Lights, Music, Action. Fish & Bell Management, PO Box 175, Bury St Edmunds, Suffolk IP32 7DY *tel:* 01284 756204 *email:* fishbelluk@aol. com. *Annual residential summer school held in Aug. Auditions by arrangement. Held in Suffolk. Ages 9-18. Jazz musicians (grade 4+); drama, dance and music theatre (all standards, grouped by experience); backstagers training (make-up, scenery, costume). Large scale final production.*

Lionel Tertis International Viola Workshop. Erin Arts Centre, Victoria Sq, Port Erin, Isle of Man IM9 6LD *tel:* 01624 835858 *fax:* 01624 836658 *email:* http://www.enterprise.net/arts/tertis.htm. John Bethell, dir. *Study courses and m/classes for professional and amateur va players of all ages. Next 2000, applications by 31 Mar 2000. Fees £90 plus £15 registration.*

Llandaff Summer Music Course. 50 Parc-y-Coed, Creigiau, Cardiff CF4 8LY *tel:* 01222 892388 *also fax.* Jenny Vale, admin; Christopher Vale, course dir. *Aug. Orch course for age 10-17.*

MAC (Midlands Arts Centre). Cannon Hill Pk, Birmingham B12 9QH *tel:* 0121 440 4221 *fax:* 0121 446 4372. Gabrielle Oliver, educ programmer. *Specialist mus w/end courses for all ages including jazz and early mus. Mus courses for adults and children (Western and Asian insts and styles) during term-time and holidays.*

Manchester University. Centre for the Development of Continuing Education (CDCE), Humanities Building, Oxford Rd *tel:* 0161 275 3290 *fax:* 0161 275 3300. Glyn Davies, mus tutor. *Learning for pleasure - a term's course on variety of mus topics; Certificate programme (humanities), weekly meeting over 2 years (modular) on jazz and popular mus. Residential w/end courses at Chancellors: choral, orchestral and mus appreciation.*

Marlborough College Summer School. Marlborough, Wilts SN8 1PA *tel:* 01672 892388 *fax:* 01672 892476. Alex Scott, sec. *12 Jul-1 Aug 1998. Weekly courses for residents and non-residents of all ages: singing, pno for beginners and improvers, musical masterpieces, gui, choral w/shop, conducting and directing mus w/shop, vn, gamelan, unlock your voice, jazz improvisation and Alexander technique for musicians. Plus over 140 different courses for all the family. Fees: from £84 (5 half days); accommodation from £100.*

Mayer-Lismann Opera Centre. 106 Gordon Rd, London W13 8PJ *tel:* 0181 998 7854 *fax:* 0181 991 2105. Jeanne Henny, dir. *Opportunity for young singers, accompanists and conductors to gain practical experience of the operatic and concert repertoire. Four operas are staged every year.*

Mid-Pennine Arts. Yorke St, Burnley BB11 1HD *tel:* 01282 421986 *fax:* 01282 429513 *email:* midpen@globalnet.co.uk. Nick Hunt, dir; Jacky Riddell, project co-ord. *Arts Development Agency for Burnley, Hyndburn, Pendle, Rossendale, Todmorden. Various mus in educ projects.*

Missenden Abbey. Gt Missenden, Bucks HP16 0BD *tel:* 01494 890295/6 *fax:* 01494 863697 *email:* enquiries@missendenabbey.ac.uk. Rosa Maria Welsh, curriculum co-ordinator. *W/end courses all year round including mus appreciation, singing and jazz. Age 16 and above. Fees: £159.20 (residential); £69.20 (non-residential). Summer school 2-29 Aug 1998. Fees: £499 (residential); £223 (non-residential).*

Morland Choristers' Camp. Garden Flat, Morland, Penrith, Cumbria CA10 3AZ *tel:* 01931 714654. Revd Canon Gervase W Markham, camp chief. *A residential course approved by the Royal School of Church Music for age 9-18 who are members of church choirs or school choirs. Church mus, secular mus and outdoor activities. 26 Jul-2 Aug 1998. Fees: £165.*

Morley College. 61 Westminster Bridge Rd, London SE1 7HT *tel:* 0171 928 8501 ext 238 *fax:* 0171 928 4074. Robert Hanson, dir of mus. *Large range of adult educ courses, including ens, solo performance, singing, electronic mus, history and theory; all levels from beginners to advanced. Special theme days held regularly.*

Mostly Music. 28 Carlisle Close, Mobberley, Knutsford, Cheshire WA16 7HD *tel:* 01565 87265. Roger Wilkes. *Courses and events throughout the year, in Greater Manchester and NW England: choral, rcdr, early mus, study courses, church mus, private and correspondence tuition. Singing holidays abroad (spring, summer).*

Music at Madingley. Board of Continuing Education, University of Cambridge, Madingley Hall, Madingley, Cambs CB3 8AQ *tel:* 01954 210636 *fax:* 01954 210677. Linda Fisher, programmes mgr. *Various w/end and week-long residential practical courses for ages 18 and above. Alberni m/classes, 10-17 Apr 1998, 24-31 Jul 1998. Fees: £390 (residential), £278 (non-residential).*

Music Summer School. Wedgwood Memorial College, Barlaston, Stoke-on-Trent ST12 9DG *tel:* 01782 372105 *fax:* 01782 372393. D Tatton. *Short courses throughout the year.*

Music Theatre Summer School. Cumbria College of Art and Design, Brampton Rd, Carlisle CA3 9AY *tel:* 01228 25333 *fax:* 01228 514491 *email:* cum@cumbriacollart.ac.uk; http://www.cumbriacollart.ac.uk. Judith Todd, mkt. *Aug. One week summer school for students, practitioners and teachers of composition, inst, singing, dance, acting and design. Fees: £250-275 (non-residential), £400-439 (residential).*

Musicale Holidays. The Bourne, 20 Salisbury Av, Harpenden, Herts AL5 2QG *tel:* 01582 460978 (24 hrs) *fax:* 01582 767343. David Johnston, Gillian Johnston, dirs. *Residential course at Harpenden for high standard orch and symphonic wind orch players, plus other non-residential courses held at venues throughout UK during 21 Jul-15 Aug 1998. Caters for insts aged 5-18 of all standards and non-insts aged 5-9 in the form of a mus activity course. Applications welcome until opening date of course.*

Musicfest International Summer School. Aberystwyth Arts Centre, Penglais, Aberystwyth, Ceredigion SY23 3DE *tel:* 01970 622882 *fax:* 01970 622883 *email:* lla@aber.ac.uk; http://www.aber.ac.uk/~arcwww/index.htm. Louise Amery, mkt mgr. *Runs in conjunction with Musicfest, Aberystwyth International Music Festival. Provides the opportunity for children over 14, mus students, professional and amateur adults to work on chmbr mus and solo repertoire and to play in orchs with a team of British chmbr musicians of international standing. 18-31 Jul 1998, applications by Jul.*

Musicosophia United Kingdom. PO Box 3030, Littlehampton, W Sussex BN16 2QT *tel:* 01903 786745 *also fax.* Catherine Brophy, dir; A Haizel, sec. *Organises courses for listeners as part of an international movement of music lovers. The Listener's Bruckner, 27-28 Jul 1998; Shakespeare and Mendelssohn, 4 Nov 1998. Other short courses available. Fees £25-125 (concessions available). Applications by one month before course begins.*

National Chamber Music Course. 3 Grand Av, London N10 3AY *tel:* 0181 883 2275 *fax:* 0181 372 6465. Caroline Stone, admin; Elisabeth Waterhouse, dir. *2-8 Aug 1998, applications by end Mar. Held at Temple Dinsley, Herts. Chmbr mus course for str players aged 10-18. (2 chmbr ens, inst classes, orch and choir). Fees: £310.*

The National Children's Chamber Orchestra of Great Britain. The Bourne, 20 Salisbury Av, Harpenden, Herts AL5 2QG *tel:* 01582 760014 *fax:* 01582 767343. Gillian and David Johnston, dirs; Caroline Marriott, admin. *For str players aged 10-16 at gr 7 and above. The players will play in quartets and in a chmbr orch combining with wind players from the National Children's Wind Orchestra of Great Britain. Entry is by audition during the autumn term for a residential course at Easter - concerts at major venues around the country later in the year. Also training str orch for promising younger players.*

National Children's Music Camps. 61 Crown Rd, Sutton, Surrey SM1 1RT *tel:* 0181 715 4048 *also fax; email:* david@edcrown.demon.co.uk. Avril Dankworth, founder-president; David Edwards, campers' admin. *Annual mus camps for age 8-17 in the grounds of the Old Rectory, Wavendon, Bucks. Jul-Aug, applications by Feb. Fees: £178 (teenage), £163 (jnr).*

National Children's Orchestra. 157 Craddocks Av, Ashtead, Surrey KT21 1NU *tel:* 01372 276857 *fax:* 01372 271407. Elisabeth Humphreys, admin. *Easter and summer holidays. Auditions in autumn. 5 orchs divided into age groups: under 14, under 13, under 12, under 11 (2 orchs).*

The National Children's Wind Orchestra of Great Britain. The Bourne, 20 Salisbury Av, Harpenden, Herts AL5 2QG *tel:* 01582 760014 *fax:* 01582 767343. Gillian and David Johnston, dirs; Caroline Marriott, admin. *For w/wind, br and perc players aged 10-15 at gr 5 and above. 2 orchs are formed. Entry by audition during the autumn term for a residential course at Easter and concerts at major venues around the country later in the year. Study includes standard repertoire, new commissions and chmbr mus.*

National Isis Strings Academy. 7 Scot Grove, Pinner, Middx HA5 4RT *tel:* 0181 428 7174. Viviane Ronchetti, mus dir. *High-quality chmbr orch training for str players gr 7+ from snr independent schools. Residential courses and w/ends at Queenswood School, Hatfield. Feb, Apr, Jul-Aug. Fees: £23.50 (w/ends), £105 (5-day residential).*

National Junior Music Club of Great Britain. 23 Hitchin St, Biggleswade, Beds SG18 8AX *tel:* 01767 316521 *fax:* 01767 317221. Douglas Coombes, dir; Carole Lindsay-Douglas, organiser. *Summer school for primary teachers at Burwell House, Cambs, Jul-Aug. 1-day courses in mus games for primary teachers at various venues nationwide. Fees: £20-44.*

National Operatic and Dramatic Association (NODA). NODA House, 1 Crestfield St, London WC1H 8AU *tel:* 0171 837 5655 *fax:* 0171 833 0609. Mark Thorburn, chief executive. *Residential week-long theatre training course for age 18 and above. University of Warwick in Coventry, 8-15 Aug 1998.*

National Scout and Guide Symphony Orchestra Course. c/o Youth Activities Section, Guide Association, 17-19 Buckingham Palace Rd, London SW1W 0PT *tel:* 0171 834 6242 *fax:* 0171 828 8317. Karen Rogers, exec asst. *Jul-Aug 1998, applications by Jan. Applicants must be aged 13-26, members of the Scout or Guide Associations and proficient in at least 1 orch inst. Fees: c £280.*

National Youth Choir of Great Britain. PO Box 67, Holmfirth, Huddersfield, W Yorks HD7 1GQ *tel:* 01484 687023 *fax:* 01484 681635. Carl Browning, exec dir; Michael Brewer OBE, mus dir; Danny Curtis, choir admin. *Residential courses for members of the National Youth Choir. Auditions held annually in Oct and Nov for age ranges 12-18 and 16-21. Courses at Christmas and New Year. Fees: £240-300 (course), £20 (audition).*

National Youth Jazz Orchestra of Scotland. 13 Somerset Pl, Glasgow G3 7JT *tel:* 0141 332 8311 *fax:* 0141 332 3915 *email:* nyos@cqm.co.uk. Richard Chester, dir. *Residential summer course with tuition from experienced tutors and public performances. Ages 12-21. Applicants must be resident in Scotland.*

National Youth Music Theatre. 5th Floor, The Palace Theatre, Shaftesbury Av, London W1V 8AY *tel:* 0171 734 7478 *fax:* 0171 734 7515 *email:* bird@clearsite.com; http://www.clearsite.com/nymt/. Jeremy James Taylor, artistic dir; Felicity Bunt, gen mgr. *Application throughout year for open access mus theatre w/shops and regional satellite projects. Auditions Oct-Dec for singer/actor/dancers and insts for 4 major mus theatre productions pa. Courses are residential and non-residential, usually during school holidays and w/ends.*

National Youth Orchestra of Great Britain. 32 Old School House, Britannia Rd, Bristol BS15 2DB *tel:* 0117 960 0477 *fax:* 0117 960 0376 *email:* nyo@btinternet.com. Michael de Grey, chief exec; Jill White, dir of mus. *Residential courses 3 times pa. In 1999 the NYO will perform in major venues throughout the UK and abroad, including Barbican Hall, London; Symphony Hall, Birmingham; and The Bridgewater Hall, Manchester. Auditions annually for players aged 10-19 (gr 8 dist standard, applicants need not have taken exams). Applications for 1999 orch by 31 Jul 1998. Fees: £225.*

National Youth Orchestra of Scotland. 13 Somerset Pl, Glasgow G3 7JT *tel:* 0141 332 8311 *fax:* 0141 332 3915 *email:* nyos@cqm.co.uk. Richard Chester, dir. *Winter and summer residential courses providing tuition from professional musicians and rehearsals with internationally renowned conductors and soloists prior to concert tours. Easter residential training course. Ages 12-21. Annual auditions. Applicants must be resident in Scotland.*

National Youth Wind Orchestra of Great Britain. 32 Park Lawn, Church Rd, Farnham Royal, Bucks SL2 3AP *tel:* 01753 642223 *also fax.* Kit Shepherd, exec dir. *Autumn auditions for residential courses held at Easter and in summer. Chmbr mus m/classes, ens courses and w/shops. Age 15-21 at gr 8+.*

Nelly Ben-Or Piano Courses Incorporating the Alexander Technique. 23 Rofant Rd, Northwood, Middx HA6 3BD *tel:* 01923 822268 *also fax.* Roger Clynes, course sec. *11-15 Jul 1998, 1-3 Jan 1999. Courses at the Guildhall School of Music and Drama, London, for pianists, teachers and advanced students. Individual sessions at the keyboard and in the Alexander Technique. The courses incorporate the principles of the Alexander Technique in details of pno playing and creative study of mus for performance.*

Nonsuch Summer Schools. 101 St Stephens Rd, Canterbury CT2 7JT *tel:* 01227 462871. Sian Jones, admin. *30 Jul-9 Aug 1998 at Hockerill School, Bishops Stortford. W European court dances of 12th-19th C. Fully residential. Age 16 and above. Fees: £90-450.*

North East Early Music Forum (NEEMF). 43 Beckett's Park Cres, Leeds LS6 3PH *tel:* 0113 278 6886 *fax:* 0113 230 7818 *email:* bmb6jlj@bmb. leeds.ac.uk. Jillian Johnson, hon sec. *Day w/shops throughout year in performance and interpretation of early mus for age 16 and above. Residential w/end at the University of Leeds for singers and insts. Monteverdi Vespers. Fees: £130-145.*

North Wales Summer School of Music. Capcoch, Tal-y-bont, Bangor, Gwynedd LL57 3UU *tel:* 01248 351186 (after 7pm). Pat Morrell, course admin. *Vocal m/class, 10-12 Jul 1998; choral course, 3-5 Jul 1998; wind group, 10-12 Jul 1998. For age 16 and above.*

Northern Junior Philharmonic Orchestra Course. Moorcroft, South Rd, Prudhoe, Northumberland NE42 5LB *tel:* 01661 832605 *fax:* 01661 833526. Peter Swan, organising sec. *Orch course for instrumentalists aged 12-23 of gr 8 standard. Sir Michael Tippett Award (£500) available for the most promising musician(s) on the course.*

Northern Recorder Course. 41 Grosvenor Rd, Sale, Cheshire M33 6WL *tel:* 0161 973 2050. D A Bamforth. *Held at University College, Chester, 1 Apr. St Matthews Hall, Stretford, 24 Oct. Any age.*

Northern Sax Course (Harrogate). c/o Lindsey Music, 42 St Mary's Pk, Louth, Lincs LN11 0EF *tel:* 01507 605244. Jacqueline Browne, events organiser. *14-17 Apr 1998.*

Northumbrian Recorder and Viol School (NORVIS). 5 Birchgrove Av, Gilesgate Moor, Durham DH1 1DE *tel:* 0191 386 4782 *email:* marlene. austin@durham.ac.uk. Marlene Austin, admin. *Held at College of St Hild and St Bede, Durham, Aug. Course for any age covers all aspects of early mus: rcdrs, viols, baroque strs, renaissance insts, plucked insts, keyboard, singing and dancing.*

Nottingham University Dept of Adult Education. Cherry Tree Buildings, University Pk, Nottingham NG7 2RD *tel:* 0115 951 3715 *fax:* 0115 951 3711 *email:* philip.olleson@nottingham.ac.uk. Philip Olleson, lecturer in mus. *Day and eve courses in mus appreciation and history. 2 choirs. Holiday courses and mus courses from Feb-Nov.*

The Old Rectory Music Courses. Fittleworth, Pulborough, W Sussex RH20 1HU *tel:* 01798 865306 *also fax; email:* oldrectory@mistral.co.

uk; http://www3.mistral.co.uk/oldrectory/index.html. Tony and Sue Dawkins, principals. *Week, w/end and mid-week courses in singing, hpd, mus appreciation, w/wind, handbells, strs, rcdr and va da gamba. 1998: 20th C English song, 22-25 Jan; Singing/Get Started Now, 9-13 Feb; Viola da Gamba in Consort, 23-27 Feb, 5-9 Oct; Jazz Singing, 13-15 Mar; hpd w/shop, 1-3 May, 20-22 Nov; Music Appreciation, 18-22 May, 11-13 Sep; Singers Summer School, 29 May-5 Jun; Singers Workshop, 4-11 Sep, 23-27 Nov; Singing Course, 23-25 Oct.*

Opera School Wales. Rhydyberry Cottages, Merthyr Cynog, Brecon, Powys LD3 9SA *tel:* 01874 690339; 01874 690254 *also fax.* Bridgett Gill. *Intensive 3-week spring course combining stage and vocal training, make-up and stage-lighting instruction, culminating in several fully-staged performances with orch ens, touring theatres in Wales. Auditions Nov. Fees: £320-380.*

Orff Society (UK). 7 Rothesay Av, Richmond, Surrey TW10 5EB *tel:* 0181 876 1944 *also fax; email:* orff@catan.demon.co.uk. Margaret Murray, hon sec. *Introductory course, Apr 1998; Accent on Rhythm, 6-7 Jun 1998; Hands on Music, 25-31 Jul at University of Warwick. Creative mus courses mainly for teachers in primary and middle schools.*

Oundle International Festival and Summer School for Young Organists. The Old Crown, Glapthorn, Oundle, Peterborough PE8 5BJ *tel:* 01832 272026 *also fax.* James Parsons, dir; Patricia Ryan, admin. *Summer school for up to 50 organists based in Oundle, Northants. Age range 13-23. Four courses offered, with valuable recital awards and week of festival events, professional concerts, exhibitions, etc. 12-19 Jul 1998, applications by 1 Apr. Fees: c £365.*

Oxenfoord International. 71 Woodburn Close, London NW4 2NF *tel:* 0181 202 1731 *also fax; email:* joan@buzbee.dem.uk. Joan Busby, course dir; Sarah Sills, admin. *Opera, mus theatre, early mus, French song, Lieder, vocal technique, etc for solo singers and accompanists aged 17 and above, plus cantata course for soloists and chorus. St Leonards School, St Andrews, Fife. Aug 1998.*

Oxford Cello School. 67 Oxford Rd, Abingdon, Oxon OX14 2AA *tel:* 01235 530572 *fax:* 01235 555952. Marianne Gottfeldt, dir. *Summer holiday courses in vc and db, residential and non-residential. All aspects of technique with use of video camera, ens playing, orch, choir, AEB exams and possibility for solo performance. Various courses covering range of standards from beginners to performers, lasting between 6 and 14 days each. Db summer course for all standards (8 days). Visiting professors for 1998, Maud Tortelier (vc) and Thomas Martin (db).*

Oxford Chamber Music Courses. 80 St Bernard's Rd, Oxford OX2 6EJ *tel:* 01865 553892. Tom Patterson. *Two 3-day meetings each in Apr and Aug. Fees: £155 (residential), £120 (non-residential), reduction for students in f/t educ. For any age group.*

Oxford Flute Summer School. 12 Jesse Terrace, Reading RG1 7RT *tel:* 0118 950 7865 *fax:* 01865 514409 *email:* ofss@carfax.primex.co.uk. Clive Conway, Janet Way, dirs; Katie Bycroft, admin. *Annual course for fl players of all standards age 16 and over, held at The Queen's College, Oxford. Concerts, classes, ens and individual tuition for ages 16 and above. 9-16 Aug 1998, applications by 18 Jul. Three options offered: general course for players of all ages and standards; performance course, daily individual lesson and public performance; audition course for students aged 16-18 auditioning for mus colleges and universities. Fees: £195 (general), £295 (performance and audition).*

Oxford Summer Sessions. d'Overbroeck's College, Beechlawn House, Park Town, Oxford OX2 6SN *tel:* 01865 310000 *fax:* 01865 552296 *email:* doverb@rmplc.co.uk. Sami Cohen, dir. *Aug 1998. Non-residential mus summer school organised by d'Overbroeck's College, Oxford, for str players of grade 5+ standard. Strings in solo, chmbr mus and orch forces are brought to concert pitch by principals of Oxford's New Chamber Orchestra under the direction of Andrew Zreczycki, culminating in a public concert at the Holywell Music Room. Ages 11-21. Auditions.*

Oxford University Department for Continuing Education. 1 Wellington Sq, Oxford OX1 2JA *tel:* 01865 270360 *fax:* 01865 270309. Anna Sandham, co-ord; Jonathan Darnborough, associate tutor in mus. *Wide ranging programme of weekly courses and day schools in Oxford and surrounding area. Fees: from £24. Also runs a number of residential summer schools for adults 18 Jul-22 Aug 1998. Fees from £250.*

Pendrell Hall College. Codsall Wood, Wolverhampton, Staffs WV8 1QP *tel:* 01902 434112 *fax:* 01902 434113. David Evans, principal; Linda Reeve, admin offr. *Mus study w/ends for ages 18-80. Early mus, 12-14 Dec 1997; rcdr playing, 20-22 Feb 1998, 12-14 May 1998 (mid week); Sibelius, 20-22 Mar 1998; English mus, 1-3 May 1998; exploring chmbr mus, 27-29 Jul 1998.*

Pipers' Guild. 121 Hallam Way, West Hallam, Derbys DE7 6LP *tel:* 0115 930 8323 *email:* margent @rmplc.co.uk; http://www.quantine.co.uk/~piper/pgpage/htm. Stephanie Payne, sec; Mary Argent, chmn; Betty Roe, president. *Summer school, 6-11 Aug 1998 at Royal School for the Deaf in Derby.*

Practical Psychology for Instrumental Music Teachers. Music, Mind and Movement, 28 Glebe Pl, London SW3 5LD *tel:* 0171 352 1666. Lucinda Mackworth-Young, dir. *Jul 1998, applications by 31 May. Practical psychology for inst mus teaching and performing, including teacher-pupil-parent relationships, emotions and motivation, teaching styles and learning strategies, communication and anxiety in performance. Also Alexander Technique, Kodály, Eurhythmics, historical dance and improvisation. The course bears credit towards LTCL (mus educ) or Certificate of Music Education of Trinity College, London. Also shorter courses.*

Pro Corda Trust (National School for Young Chamber Music Players). Leiston Abbey House, Theberton Rd, Leiston, Suffolk IP16 4TB *tel:* 01728 831354 *fax:* 01728 832500. Pamela Spofforth MBE, founder; R Max, T Boulton, M Parrington, A Butterfield, course dirs. *Residential courses during school holidays for young str players and pianists aged 8-18 attending twice yearly at preparatory, primary, jnr, intermediate and snr levels. Specialist ens tuition under the direction of distinguished musicians. Entry by audition. Application forms from Administrator at above address. 1998 courses: Preparatory, 23-30 May; primary, 22-29 Jul and 25-31 Oct; jnr, 11-18 Apr and 1-8 Aug; intermediate, 28 Dec 1997-4 Jan 1998 and 9-16 Aug; snr, 4-10 Apr and 19-29 Aug.*

Randazzo Opera. 24 Bladon Ct, Barrow Rd, London SW16 5NE *tel:* 0181 677 8821; 0181 309 1309. Arlene Randazzo, admin and stage dir; Janet Haney, mus dir. *On-going w/shops with 12 performances pa throughout London. All ages. Auditions. Fees: £50 per month.*

Rathbone-Dickson Chamber Music Course. 31 Chepstow Pl, London W2 4TT *tel:* 0171 229 0219 *also fax.* Joyce Rathbone, David Waterman, dirs. *Held at Westonbirt School, Tetbury, Glos. Pno and str players aged 16-26, Aug.*

Recorder Summer School. 113 Birchwood Rd, Marton, Middlesbrough TS7 8DE *tel:* 01642 310628. Miss S Foxall, sec. *Classes and ens for rcdr players aged 16 and above (age 15 accepted if accompanied by an adult on the course). All grades including beginners. Renaissance groups, baroque chmbr mus, concert and mus w/shops. Aug 1998 at Bretton Hall, Wakefield.*

The Rehearsal Orchestra. 4 Lucerne Ct, Abbey Pk, Beckenham, Kent BR3 1RB *tel:* 0181 663 1927 *fax:* 0181 658 6261 *email:* bwhyte@rehearsal. orchestra.org. Harry Legge OBE, artistic dir; Bridget Whyte, admin; William Webb, associate artistic dir. *Advanced orch training for students and young professionals, teachers and experienced players. Wide range of orch repertoire studied, including new mus. 1 and 2-day sessions throughout the year, plus residential week in Edinburgh during the festival. Min gr 8, age 16+ with good sight-reading. Student and non-student rates given on application.*

Royal School of Church Music. Cleveland Lodge, Westhumble, Dorking RH5 6BW *tel:* 01306 877676 *fax:* 01306 887260. Geoffrey Weaver, dir of studies. *1-day and longer residential courses for singers and insts aged 10-25 at many locations around the country. Training events for choristers of all ages during Easter, applications by 1 Mar and summer holidays, applications by 1 Jun. Fees: £120-190.*

Royal School of Church Music Harwich Summer Courses. Cherry Trees, 23 Stanley Rd, Wivenhoe, Essex CO7 9EN *tel:* 01206 824036. Graham Wadley, admin. *Boys' course Jun 1998; girls' course Sep 1998; students' course Oct 1998.*

Royal Scottish Pipe Band Association. 45 Washington St, Glasgow G3 8AZ *tel:* 0141 221 5414 *fax:* 0141 221 1561. J Mitchell Hutcheson, exec offr. *Organises educ classes run by 12 branches. Annual summer school, last week of Jul. All ages.*

Schools Music Association. 71 Margaret Rd, New Barnet, Herts EN4 9NT *tel:* 0181 440 6919 *also fax.* Maxwell Pryce, hon sec. *Annual residential course and conference on mus in schools, Oct. Courses for mus teachers at regional centres throughout year.*

Scottish Amateur Music Association. 18 Craigton Cres, Alva, Clackmannanshire FK12 5DS *tel:* 01259 760249. Margaret Simpson, hon sec. *Summer courses include chmbr mus w/end at Queen Margaret College, Edinburgh, 3-5 Apr 1998; traditional fiddle school, National Youth Wind Ensemble of Scotland, National Youth Brass Band of Scotland 3-8 Aug 1998; National Youth String Orchestra of Scotland (and Training School), 10-15 Aug 1998 at St Andrew's College, Bearsden; National Recorder School of Scotland, 11-13 Sep 1998.*

Sheffield University Division of Adult Continuing Education. 196-198 West St, Sheffield S1 4ET *tel:* 0114 282 5400. Adam White, mus co-ord. *Courses in mus theory, pop mus, women in mus, mus appreciation, improvisation, composition, Sep-May, applications by Sep. Particularly suited to those over age 17 who wish to study mus without the need to give up work. Modules are accredited and validated by the University of Sheffield. Fees: £30-120 per 20 credit modules (24 wks), or £360 pa (concessions also available).*

The Shell Expro Music School. 3 Nutborn House, Clifton Rd, London SW19 4QT *tel:* 0181 946 2995 *fax:* 0181 944 6507. Nicola Wallis, festival dir. *Part of Aberdeen International Youth Festival. Provides*

advanced level tuition and w/shops for individual insts, chmbr ens and singers. Ages 16-23 for inst course, 18-30 for singers. 3-15 Aug 1998, applications by end May.

Sing for Pleasure. 25 Fryerning La, Ingatestone, Essex CM4 0DD *tel: 01277 353691 also fax.* Lynda Parker, dir. *Residential and day courses for children, teachers, singers and choral conductors of all ages, throughout the country. 1998: Superweek singing holidays for ages 10-14, 10-19 Aug and 20-29 Aug; youth singing week for ages 14-18, 26 Jul-2 Aug; summer school for singers, conductors and teachers, 25-30 Aug; primary teachers and choral week, 15-22 Aug. International festivals through the 'A Coeur Joie' movement. Publishes repertoire suitable for schools and choral groups.*

Southampton University. Dept of Adult Education, Southampton SO9 5NH *tel:* 01703 592833. Ann Hayter, mkt co-ord. *Mus courses for the general public in Southampton and throughout Hampshire, Dorset and W Sussex. Opera study days, interdisciplinary courses, jazz w/shop, beginners courses. There is an accredited mus pathway within the Certificate of Higher Education: Humanities. Courses available through the academic year.*

Southend Summer School for the Performing Arts. PO Box 63, Southend-on-Sea, Essex SS21 6FE *tel:* 01702 588700/541595/586790 *also fax.* Roger Humphrey, dir; Rosemary Pennington, co-dir. *Intensive week-long summer school for ages 8-16, 17-21 Aug 1998. Mus, drama, dance, arts and crafts. Mus with specialist tutors includes strs, w/wind groups, perc, composition, keyboard. All activities culminate in a final public performance and demonstration. Fees: £40.*

Spode Music Week. 66 Cornish House, Green Dragon La, Brentford, Middx TW8 0DF *tel:* 0181 568 1072 *email:* ims@moose.co.uk. Ian Saxton, bursar. *Choir, orch, children's orch, lectures, recitals. Informal mus making encouraged and families welcomed; children under 14 must be accompanied by an adult. Creche facilities and bursaries available. 20-27 Aug 1998, applications by 7 Aug. Fees: £250 (adults); £160, aged 12-15; aged 11 and under free.*

Stratford-upon-Avon Flute Festival. PO Box 7, Stratford upon Avon CV37 9GB *tel:* 01789 269247 *fax:* 01789 269843. Elena Durán, dir; Michael Emmerson, chmn. *Annual m/classes for flautists of gr 8 standard at King Edward VI School, Stratford upon Avon. Emphasis on performance; special sessions for young flautists. 17 Jul-1 Aug 1998, applications by 1 Jul. Fees: £450 (including accommodation).*

Stringwise. 3 Dresden Rd, London N19 3BE *tel:* 0171 561 0864. *A team of specialists, led by Sheila Nelson, offering professional development courses for all str teachers with emphasis on musicianship and freedom of movement in playing. Residential course in London, late Aug 1998. 4-day courses in London for young str players aged 6-13, Apr and Jul.*

Summer Flute Academy. Oak Cottage, Elmsted, nr Ashford, Kent TN25 5JT *tel:* 01233 750272 *also fax.* Ann Nichols, sec; Trevor Wye, Clifford Benson, m/class teachers. *Annual week held at Wye College, Kent for age 16 and above. Fl and pno duo repertoire.*

Summer School for Piano Teachers. Dept of Music, Napier University, Craighouse Campus, Queens Craig, Edinburgh EH10 5LG *tel:* 0131 455 6200 *fax:* 0131 455 6211 *email:* a.butterworth@napier.ac.uk. Anna Butterworth, dir. *Lectures, m/classes and survey of ABRSM pno syllabus 1998-9. 9-14 Aug 1998.*

Sussex University. Centre for Continuing Education, Education Development Buildings, Falmer, Brighton, E Sussex BN1 9RG *tel:* 01273 678527/678040/678025 *fax:* 01273 678848. F Gray, dir. *P/t certificate in mus; day schools and weekly classes for adults throughout the year.*

Talbot Lampson Choral School. 18 Amersham Ct, Craneswater Pk, Southsea, Hampshire PO4 0NX *tel:* 01962 867682 *also fax.* Rupert D'Cruze, course dir; Kathleen Edwards, hon sec. *Course for conductors, accompanists and choral singers at University of Greenwich, Avery Hill Campus, Eltham, London. Ages 14 and over. 27-30 Aug 1998, applications by 25 Jun. Brochure available from 1 Feb. Fees: £220 (residential).*

Temple Dinsley Summer School. 86 Cromwell Av, London N6 5HQ *tel:* 0181 340 8362 *fax:* 0181 341 7616. Elisabeth Waterhouse, dir. *Suzuki camp in Herts for children aged 4-11 playing vn, vc or pno. Inst lessons, group lessons and related activities. 9-12 Aug 1998, applications by 1 Jul.*

Trinity College of Music. Music Education Dept, 11-13 Mandeville Pl, London W1M 6AQ *tel:* 0171 935 5773; 0171 224 1626 *fax:* 0171 487 5717. John Stephens, head of mus educ. *Vacation course for teachers. Week one: 20-24 Jul 1998, provides specialist opportunities for study*

appropriate for class mus teachers in primary and secondary schools, teachers in special schools and private inst teachers. Week two: 27-31 Jul 1998, specialist summer school for mus teachers dealing with world mus. Applications by Jun 1998. Fees: £150 (non-residential).

Urchfont Manor. Devizes, Wilts SN10 4RG *tel:* 01380 840495 *fax:* 01380 840005. Patricia Howell, dir. *Courses for adults. 1998: Brahms: An Indian Summer, 31 Jan-2 Feb; A Pianist's Journey through the 19th C, 3-5 April.*

Wansfell College. Theydon Bois, Epping, Essex CM16 7LF *tel:* 01992 813027 *fax:* 01992 814761. Marilyn Taylor, principal. *Week and w/end courses throughout year in all subjects including mus, mus appreciation, history and performance. Age 18 and above. Fees: from £81.*

Wavendon Allmusic Plan. Wavendon Courses, The Stables, Wavendon, Milton Keynes MK17 8LT *tel:* 01908 582522 *fax:* 01908 281024. John Dankworth, Cleo Laine, presidents; Jacky Scott, gen mgr; Chris Loney, admin offr. *W/shops, m/classes and courses running all year for all types of mus and all ages. Mus summer camps and courses for those aged 8-16. Adult summer jazz course Aug. Beginners and advanced improvisation courses throughout year.*

Wessex Youth Band Courses. 7 High Bank, Thurlstone, Sheffield S36 9QH *tel:* 01226 765579 *also fax.* John Grinnell, Margaret Grinnell, organisers. *Courses held at Sturminster Newton, Dorset, for br and wind band players aged 7-21. Snr (max age 21) and jnr (pre gr 3-4 standard). Jul-Aug. Fees: £32.*

West Dean College. West Dean, Chichester, Sussex PO18 0QZ *tel:* 01243 811301 *fax:* 01243 811343 *email:* westdean@pavilion.co.uk. Rosemary Marley, mus course organiser. *1998 courses include: The Three Ages of Opera II (1800-1900), 9-11 Jan; Renaissance mus w/end, 30 Jan-1 Feb; w/end for solo singers wishing to improve technique and increase repertoire, 27 Feb-1 Mar; The Three Ages of Opera III (1900-2000), 27-29 Mar; Summer School in Early Music Performance, 15-20 Aug; Classical Guitar Festival of Great Britain, 21-28 Aug; New Vocal Repertory w/end for singers and composers, dates tbc; Chilingarian str quartet course, dates tbc. Age 16 and above. Further information on application which should be 6 weeks before start of course.*

William Bennett Flute Summer School. 50 Lansdowne Gardens, London SW8 2EF *tel:* 0171 498 9807 *fax:* 0171 498 1155. Michie Bennett, sec. *Course I, 15-23 Jul 1998; course II, 23-31 Jul 1998. Fees: £295 (performer), £275 (participant), £235 (auditor), plus £140 residential fee.*

Winchester Summer Music Course. 37 St David's Rd, Clifton Campville, nr Tamworth, Staffs B79 0BA *tel:* 01827 373586 *fax:* 01827 373437. James Maddocks, dir; Joan Maddocks, sec. *1-8 Aug 1998, applications by 4 Jul.*

Workers' Music Association Summer School. 17a Newton Rd, London NW2 6PS *tel:* 0181 450 4958. Jacqui Selby, hon organiser. *Participatory courses held at Wortley Hall, Yorks, for amateur musicians of any age and standard. Br band, orch, chmbr mus, folk, jazz, wind band, conducting, composition, harmony, rudiments, sight reading, choral, solo and ens singing. 1-8 Aug 1998, applications by Feb. Fees: £275 (residential), £195 (day student), £115 (external student).*

Wycombe Music Summer School. c/o New London Music Society, 83a Vincent Gardens, Dollis Hill, London NW2 7RH *tel:* 0181 452 8739. Philip Meaden, dir; Cynthia Gomme, admin; Peggy Lewis, sec. *Symphony and intermediate orchs, choir, late learner ens, br course, all held at Wycombe Abbey School, Aug 1998. For age 16 and above. Applications by 31 May. Fees: c £130-295.*

Young People in Music. 2 Greystoke Lodge, Hanger Lane, London W5 1EW *tel:* 0181 998 1176. Yoriko Wakabayashi, founder. *Summer mus camp, a non-competitive festival of mus for age 12 and under. Children make own insts and play them.*

Youth Music Centre Summer School. 58 Cyprus Av, Finchley, London N3 1SR *tel:* 0181 343 1940 *fax:* 0181 343 1595. Jane Barnett, sec. *26 Jul-2 Aug 1998, applications by end of May. Held at Farleigh School, Andover, Hants. For str and wind players aged 9-16, orch and chmbr mus. Principal teacher Emanuel Hurwitz CBE. Fees: £225.*

Youthful Promise. 278 Gillott Rd, Edgbaston, Birmingham B16 0RU *tel:* 0121 454 3087/4214; 0976 388523. Sara Clethero, artistic dir; Denise Cutting, hon chair. *Trains individual student singers of all ages to as near professional standards as possible. Provides dramatic and vocal training in a group setting. W/end w/shops and classes in movement, singing technique, Alexander Technique and staging operatic productions, choral work and m/classes. Fees: £40 (w/end).*

* **St Austell.** Cornwall County Music and Drama Library. 2 Carlyon Rd, St Austell, Cornwall PL25 4LD *tel:* 01726 61702 *fax:* 01726 71214. Jonathan L Roberts, principal librarian mus and drama. *Large general coll of mus scores, including performance sets (vocal and orch); Cornish mus (folk, dance, carols); classical CDs, books on all aspects of mus for lending and reference.*
* **Shrewsbury.** Shropshire Music and Drama Library. Lending Library, Castle Gates, Shrewsbury, Shropshire SY1 2AS *tel:* 01743 255341 *fax:* 01743 255309 *email:* lp97@dial.pipex.com. Kate Woodward, librarian. *General colls including classical, popular, folk and world mus. Inter-library loan.*
* **Warwick.** Warwickshire County Council. Barrack St, Warwick CV34 4TH *tel:* 01926 412168 *fax:* 01926 412471 *email:* warcolib@dial.pipex.com. Kathleen Collins, mus and drama librarian. *16,000 mus scores, including vocal sets and sets of part-songs. Books on mus and some orch sets in the schools mus library.*

* **Worcester.** Hereford and Worcester County Libraries. County Hall, Spetchley Rd, Worcester WR5 2NP *tel:* 01905 763763 *fax:* 01905 766244 *email:* mmessenger@hereford-worcester.gov.uk; http://www.hereford-worcester.gov.uk/homepage. Michael Messenger, county librarian and arts officer. *Choral sets, vocal scores, etc, at Worcester City Library. Sound recordings at all branch libraries; some single scores at larger branches.*
  Wrekin. Wrekin Music Library. Wellington Library, Walker St, Wellington TF1 1DB, Wrekin *tel:* 01952 244013 *fax:* 01952 256960. Carol Woolard, snr librarian. *General collections including classical, popular, folk and world mus. Inter library loan.*
* **Yeovil.** Somerset County Library. County Music and Drama Library, King George St, Yeovil, Somerset BA20 1PY *tel:* 01935 472020 *fax:* 01935 431847 *email:* rdtaylor@nildram.co.uk. Roger Taylor, county mus and drama librarian.

Church and Cathedral Libraries

These libraries are private but are usually open to bona fide scholars. Applications for admission are advisable.

London
Lambeth Palace Library. London SE1 7JU *tel:* 0171 928 6222. *A few mss (including early 16th C choir books) and some printed books including church mus.*
St Paul's Cathedral Library. London EC4M 8AE *tel:* 0171 246 8325; 0171 236 4128 *fax:* 0171 248 3104. Joseph Wisdom, librarian; Elizabeth Norman, asst librarian. *17th-18th C ms part-books; a number of autograph scores of services and anthems, some by former organists, mainly 19th and 20th C.*
Westminster Abbey Library. East Cloister, London SW1P 3PA *tel:* 0171 222 5152 *fax:* 0171 222 6391. T A Trowles, asst librarian. *Includes 16th-19th C mss and printed mus.*

Bristol. Baptist College Library. Woodland Rd, Bristol BS8 1UN *tel:* 0117 926 0248 *fax:* 0117 927 7070. *Special coll of Baptist hymn books (mostly words only).*
Bristol. Methodist Church Music Society Library. Wesley College, Henbury Rd, Westbury on Trym, Bristol BS10 7QD *tel:* 0117 959 1200 *fax:* 0117 950 1277. Janet Henderson, librarian. *Coll of hymn books, psalters, etc, and books with special emphasis on hymnody and church mus, 17th-20th C.*
Canterbury. Cathedral Archives. The Precincts, Canterbury CT1 2EH *tel:* 01227 463510 *fax:* 01227 762897. Michael Stansfield, archivist. *Medieval mus mss, 17th-18th C choir mus mss; printed choir mus.*
Canterbury. Cathedral Library. The Precincts, Canterbury CT1 2EH *tel:* 01227 458950 *fax:* 01227 762897 *email:* s.m.hingley@ukc.ac.uk. Sheila Hingley, librarian. *18th-19th C printed choral mus. Ms and printed vocal and orch mus of Canterbury Catch Club 18th-19th C. Ms and printed mus of Canterbury Amateur Harmonic Society 18-19th C.*
Durham. Dean and Chapter Library. The College, Durham DH1 3EH *tel:* 0191 386 2489 *email:* r.c.norris@durham.ac.uk. Roger Norris, deputy chapter librarian. *17th-19th C cathedral choir and organists mss;*

17th-19th C printed mus from Bamburgh Castle; Philip Falle coll of 17th C printed mus. 2 wks notice needed to visit. Open Mon-Fri 9am-1pm, 2.15-5pm only, closed Aug.
Hereford. Cathedral Library. Hereford HR1 2NG *tel:* 01432 359880 *fax:* 01432 355929. J Williams, librarian. *Chained library. 18th-20th C printed and mss mus, including Roger North, Wesley and Elgar mss. Hereford Breviary, with mus, c 1270.*
Lichfield. Cathedral Library. 14 The Close, Lichfield, Staffs *tel:* 01543 256120. Pat Bancroft, hon mus librarian; Percy M Young. *Catalogue of 18th-early 19th C mss. Catalogue of 17th to mid-19th C printed mus in preparation.*
Lincoln. Cathedral Library. Lincoln LN2 1PZ *tel:* 01522 544544 *fax:* 01522 511307. Nicholas Bennett. *Including medieval mss and early printed mus. 17th-19th C ms part books.*
Ripon. Cathedral Library. Ripon, N Yorks HG4 1QT *tel:* 01765 602072 *fax:* 01765 603462. *16th C liturgical printed books; Higgin bequest (now on deposit at Brotherton Library, Leeds University).*
Wimborne. Minster Church of St Cuthburga Library. High St, Wimborne, Dorset BH21 1HT *tel:* 01202 884753. *Chained library of early mus.*
Winchester. Cathedral Library. 5 The Close, Winchester, Hants SO23 9LS *tel:* 01962 853137. *Coll of 18th C printed church mus, including Handel and Haydn.*
Windsor. St George's Chapel Chapter Library. Windsor Castle, Windsor, Berks SL4 1NJ *tel:* 01753 865538 *fax:* 01753 620165. Eileen Scarff, librarian and archivist. *Including mss of Tallis and William Child.*
Worcester. Cathedral Music Library. Worcester WR1 2LH *tel:* 01905 28854 *fax:* 01905 611139. *17th-18th C part books, mss and printed church mus.*
York. York Minster Library. Dean's Pk, York YO1 2JD *tel:* 01904 625308/611118 *fax:* 01904 611119. Mrs D M Mortimer, asst librarian; Mrs A L Hampson, archivist. *Including 16th-20th C mss and printed mus.*

University and College Libraries

Primarily available to staff and students of the institution, but visiting scholars may also be admitted. Applications in writing are advisable.

London
* Goldsmiths College Library. New Cross, London SE14 6NW *tel:* 0171 919 7168 *fax:* 0171 919 7165 *email:* lbs0lpm@gold.ac.uk. Peter Morris, asst librarian. *Includes the A L Lloyd coll (scores, books and offprints of folk and traditional mus, especially Eastern Europe) and the Ewan MacColl/Peggy Seeger coll (books and scores, especially English and Scottish folksong).*
* Guildhall School of Music and Drama. Barbican, London EC2Y 8DT *tel:* 0171 382 7178 *fax:* 0171 786 9378. Kate Royce, snr librarian; Adrian Yardley, mus librarian. *Includes Appleby gui coll, Alkan Society coll and Goossens ob mus coll.*
* Imperial College of Science, Technology and Medicine. Haldane Music Library, London SW7 2AZ *tel:* 0171 594 8812 *fax:* 0171 584 3763 *email:* j.m.smith@ic.ac.uk. Janet M Smith, Haldane librarian. *Haldane mus coll. Recordings, scores, books.*

* King's College London Library. Strand, London WC2R 2LS *tel:* 0171 873 2394 *fax:* 0171 872 0207 *email:* evelyn.cornell@kcl.ac.uk; http://www.kcl.ac.uk/kis/support/lib/top.html. Evelyn Cornell, mus readers' adviser.
London College of Music. Thames Valley University LRC, St Mary's Rd, London W5 5RF *tel:* 0181 231 2648 *fax:* 0181 231 2631 *email:* colin.steele@tvu.ac.uk. Colin Steele, mus librarian. *Scores, books, journals, LPs, CDs, listening facilities, CD-Rom multimedia.*
London School of Economics. Shaw Library, Houghton St, London WC2A 2AE *tel:* 0171 955 7171 (pm only). Alan D Lowson, Shaw librarian and mus dir. *Books, scores, periodicals and recordings.*
Morley College Library. 61 Westminster Bridge Rd, London SE1 7HT *tel:* 0171 928 8501 *fax:* 0171 928 4074. Lise Foster, librarian. *Scores, sheet mus, books, records, CDs.*
* Royal Academy of Music Library. Marylebone Rd, London NW1 5HT *tel:* 0171 873 7323 *fax:* 0181 873 7322 *email:* library@ram.ac.uk.

Katharine Hogg, librarian. *Including Sir Henry Wood library of orch mus, Sir Arthur Sullivan archives, English Bach Society Library, R J S Stevens Library, David Munrow Library.*

* Royal College of Music Library. Prince Consort Rd, London SW7 2BS *tel:* 0171 591 4325 *fax:* 0171 589 7740 *email:* pthompson@rcm.ac.uk; http://www.rcm.ac.uk. Pam Thompson, chief librarian. *Includes libraries of Sacred Harmonic Society, Concerts of Ancient Music, Heron-Allen coll.*

Royal College of Organists. 7 St Andrews St, London EC4A 3LQ *tel:* 0171 936 3606 *fax:* 0171 353 8244. Robin Langley, librarian. *Mainly org mus and books on the org, primarily for reference during college opening hrs.*

* School of Oriental and African Studies Library. University of London, Thornhaugh St, Russell Sq, London WC1H 0XG *tel:* 0171 323 6105 *fax:* 0171 436 3844 *email:* yyl@soas.ac.uk; http://www.soas.ac.uk/ library/guides/recordings.html. Y Yasumura, asst librarian. *Books, sound recordings (and video) of Oriental and African mus.*

Trinity College of Music. The Library, Academic Studies Centre, 10-11 Bulstrode Pl, London W1M 5FW *tel:* 0171 935 5773 *fax:* 0171 224 6278 *email:* library@tcm.ac.uk. Kate Sloss, chief librarian. *Including 16th-17th C printed mus.*

* University of London Library Music Collection. Senate House, Malet St, London WC1E 7HU *tel:* 0171 636 8000 ext 5038 *fax:* 0171 436 1494 *email:* ull@ull.ac.uk. Ruth Darton, mus librarian. *Including library of Royal Musical Association; Tudor Church Music coll, Littleton coll.*

* **Aberdeen.** Aberdeen University Library. Queen Mother Library, Meston Walk, Aberdeen AB24 3UE *tel:* 01224 272592 *fax:* 01224 487048 *email:* r.turbet@abdn.ac.uk. Richard Turbet, mus librarian. *Including libraries of Gavin Greig and Forbes Leith; Stationers' Hall coll (18th-19th C printed mus obtained under copyright).*

Aberystwyth. University of Wales (Hugh Owen Library). Aberystwyth, Dyfed SY23 3DZ *tel:* 01970 622391 *fax:* 01970 622404 *email:* library@aber.ac.uk. R B Brinkley, humanities adviser. *Including David de Lloyd mss; Mendelssohn letters and autographs; George Powell bequest (19th C scores and some 18th-19th C mss).*

* **Belfast.** Queen's University. Belfast BT7 1NN *tel:* 01232 335020 *fax:* 01232 323340 *email:* nrussell@qub.ac.uk. N J Russell, librarian. *Including Bunting mss of Irish folk mus; Hamilton Harty library.*

* **Birmingham.** Barber Music Library. University of Birmingham, Edgbaston, Birmingham B15 2TS *tel:* 0121 414 5852 *fax:* 0121 414 5853 *email:* a.greig@bham.ac.uk; http://www.bham.ac.uk/isg/. Anna Greig, mus librarian. *Including Granville Bantock, Gloria Rose and Shaw-Hellier colls, Elgar diaries.*

* **Birmingham.** Birmingham Conservatoire. Information Services' Library, Paradise Pl, Birmingham B3 3HG *tel:* 0121 331 5914/5 *fax:* 0121 331 5906 *email:* mu.library@uce.ac.uk. Robert Allan, faculty librarian. *Birmingham Flute Society coll.*

Bristol. University Library. Tyndall Av, Bristol BS8 1TJ *tel:* 0117 928 9000 *fax:* 0117 925 5334 *email:* http://www.anglia.ac.uk/fes/library/home. htm.

* **Cambridge.** Anglia Polytechnic University Library. East Rd, Cambridge CB1 1PT *tel:* 01223 363271 ext 2302 *fax:* 01223 363271 *email:* http:// www.anglia.ac.uk/fes/library/home.htm. Rhiannon Jones, subject librarian, humanities and arts.

Cambridge. Cambridge University Library *see* **National Copyright Libraries.**

Cambridge. Cambridge University Musical Society. c/o University Music School, West Rd, Cambridge CB3 9DP *tel:* 01223 335180/3. Andrew Bennett. *Including approx 400 sets of orch parts.*

Cambridge. Clare College. Cambridge CB3 9AJ *tel:* 01223 333202/ 333228 *fax:* 01223 357664. Elizabeth A Keith, asst librarian. *Including mss of Cecil Sharp's folksong colls; mss of W C Denis-Browne; mss of F P Haines.*

Cambridge. Gonville and Caius College. Cambridge CB2 1TA *tel:* 01223 332419 *fax:* 01223 332430 *email:* glh22@cus.cam.ac.uk; http://www. cai.cam.ac.uk/library/. J H Prynne, librarian. *Including mss and fragments of mus from the 10th-18th C (mostly 11th-14th C); also papers and materials relating to Charles Wood (1866-1926).*

Cambridge. King's College. Rowe Music Library, Cambridge CB2 1ST *tel:* 01223 331252. Mrs M V Cranmer, librarian. *Including libraries of L T Rowe, A H Mann and A H King; also E J Dent papers.*

Cambridge. Magdalene College. Cambridge CB3 0AG *tel:* 01223 332100 *fax:* 01223 332187. R Luckett, Pepys librarian. *Pepys Library (personal library of Samuel Pepys (1633-1703): mss, ballads, printed mus); library open chiefly during term-time (appointment necessary). Catalogued in R C Latham, ed The Pepys Library at Magdalene College, Cambridge (11 vols), IV.*

Cambridge. Pembroke College. Cambridge CB2 1RF *tel:* 01223 338100 *fax:* 01223 338163 *email:* pajlool@cus.cam.ac.uk. T R S Allan, librarian. *Including 17th C ms part-mus; 18th C chmbr mus.*

Cambridge. Pendlebury Library of Music. University Music School, West Rd, Cambridge CB3 9DP *tel:* 01223 335182 *fax:* 01223 335067. Andrew Bennett, librarian. *Library of the university mus faculty.*

Cambridge. Peterhouse. Trumpington St, Cambridge CB2 1RD *tel:* 01223 338200 *fax:* 01223 337578. R W Lovatt, Perne librarian. *Including 16th-17th C part-books (permanently deposited at University Library).*

Cambridge. St John's College. Cambridge CB2 1TP *tel:* 01223 338662 *fax:* 01223 337035 *email:* library@joh.cam.ac.uk. Amanda Saville, librarian. *Samuel Butler coll, Rootham compositions.*

Cambridge. Trinity College. Cambridge CB2 1TQ *tel:* 01223 338488 *fax:* 01223 338532 *email:* trin-lib@lists.cam.ac.uk; http://www.trin. cam.ac.uk/tc/wren.html. D J McKitterick, librarian. *Including roll of 15th C English carols, two 15th C Greek mss with mus, lute tablatures of Bacheler, Greaves, Johnson and Taylor, autographs of Gray, Parry and Stanford; early printed mus of Byrd, Mace, Playford and Purcell.*

* **Cardiff.** University of Wales College of Cardiff. Music Dept, Corbett Rd, Cardiff CF1 3EB *tel:* 01222 874000 ext 4387 *email:* musicliby@cardiff. ac.uk; http://www.cf.ac.uk/uwcc/liby/music.html#finding. Gillian Jones, mus librarian. *Mackworth coll: early 18th C printed and mss scores. Aylward coll: printed editions of 18th and 19th C scores.*

* **Cardiff.** Welsh College of Music and Drama Library. Castle Grounds, Cathays Pk, Cardiff CF1 3ER *tel:* 01222 342854 *fax:* 01222 237639 *email:* agusjam@wcmd.ac.uk. Judith Agus, librarian.

* **Colchester.** Colchester Institute Library. Sheepen Rd, Colchester, Essex CO3 3LL *tel:* 01206 718641/718644 *fax:* 01206 718643. Miss J Benfield, subject librarian (mus). *Liturgical mus, wind band and jazz band scores, collected works.*

Durham. University Library. Palace Green Section, Durham DH1 3RN *tel:* 0191 374 3001. Elizabeth Rainey, sub-librarian. *Britten correspondence and related mss, Dame Ethel Smyth mss, medieval liturgical mss.*

Edinburgh. Edinburgh University Library: Main Library. George Sq, Edinburgh EH8 9LJ *tel:* 0131 650 3384 *fax:* 0131 667 9780 *email:* library@edinburgh.ac.uk. I R M Mowat, university librarian. *Gen and special book colls include books of Scottish song; special colls include early Scottish mss (surviving leaves of 14th C Inchcolm Antiphoner, and colls of lute and pipe-tunes, etc); English madrigal books; Marjorie Kennedy-Fraser coll of Hebridean folk-song recordings and books on Highland mus and dance; archives of the Scottish Students' Song Book Committee (1901-1991). Main mus colls are held in the Reid Music Library (see below).*

* **Edinburgh.** Edinburgh University Library: Reid Music Library. Alison House, 12 Nicolson Sq, Edinburgh EH8 9DF *tel:* 0131 650 2436 *fax:* 0131 650 2425 *email:* reid.library@ed.ac.uk. J Upton, mus librarian. *Mus section of Edinburgh Uuniversity Library. Colls of scores, books and periodicals on Western mus. Special colls include Sir Donald Tovey archive; Niecks bequest of books on the theory of mus; Weiss coll of Beethoven literature; Kenneth Leighton mss.*

Edinburgh. New College Library. Mound Pl, Edinburgh EH1 2LU *tel:* 0131 650 8957 *fax:* 0131 650 6579. Mrs P M Gilchrist, librarian. *The Divinity section of Edinburgh University Library. Special colls including James Thin Hymnology Collection.*

Edinburgh. School of Scottish Studies. University of Edinburgh, 27 George Sq, Edinburgh EH8 9LD *tel:* 0131 650 3060/4159. Francesca Hardcastle, librarian; Rhona Talbot, archive asst. *Book colls include Scots and Gaelic song since the 18th C, folk mus and ethnomusicology of Ireland, England, N America and the world. Archives include traditional and national Scottish mus field recordings, the John Levy coll of ethnomusicological recordings (mostly oriental), the Peter Cooke coll of African mus recordings, the Will Forret coll of Scottish national, popular, folk revival mus, and smaller colls (Chilean, Irish, Indian).*

* **Egham.** Royal Holloway, University of London, Music Library. Egham Hill, Egham, Surrey TW20 0EX *tel:* 01784 443560/443759 *fax:* 01784 439441 *email:* c.grogan@rhbnc.ac.uk; http://www.lb.rhbnc.ac.uk. C P Grogan. *Includes library of Dom Anselm Hughes.*

* **Exeter.** University Library. Stocker Rd, Exeter, Devon EX4 4PT *tel:* 01392 263860 *fax:* 01392 263871 *email:* j.a.crawley@exeter.ac.uk. Julie Crawley. *Including special coll of American mus.*

* **Glasgow.** Royal Scottish Academy of Music and Drama. 100 Renfrew St, Glasgow G2 3DB *tel:* 0141 332 4101 *fax:* 0141 332 5924 *email:* ibs01pm@gold.ac.uk. Kenneth F Wilkins, librarian.

* **Glasgow.** University Library. Hillhead St, Glasgow G12 8QE *tel:* 0141 330 6797 *fax:* 0141 330 4952 *email:* library@gla.ac.uk. *Includes Euing Music coll; Drysdale, Farmer, Lamond, McEwen, MacCunn, Zavertal colls. Incorporates Trinity College library and Mearns coll of hymnology.*

Guildford. George Edwards Library. University of Surrey, Guildford, Surrey GU2 5XH *tel:* 01483 300800 ext 3322 *fax:* 01483 259500. Glenda Davies, mus librarian.

Hull. Brynmor Jones Library. The University of Hull, Cottingham Rd, Hull, N Humberside HU6 7RX *tel:* 01482 465274 *fax:* 01482 466205 *email:*

Museums and Other Collections

Hours of opening may vary considerably, and should be checked before a visit is organised. Some collections may be viewed only after written application to the curator.

London

Fenton House. Hampstead Grove, London NW3 6RT *tel:* 0171 435 3471. Joy Ashby, National Trust custodian. *Early keyboard insts.*

The Handel House Trust Ltd. 10 Stratford Pl, London W1N 9AE *tel:* 0171 495 1685 *fax:* 0171 495 1759 *email:* handel.house@virgin.net. Julie Anne Sadie, dir; Jacqueline Young, development offr. *Charity engaged in establishing a museum to Handel in his home at 25 Brook St, Mayfair, London W1.*

Horniman Museum and Gardens. 100 London Rd, London SE23 3PQ *tel:* 0181 699 1872 *fax:* 0181 291 5506 *email:* palmer@horniman. demon.co.uk; allen@horniman.demon.co.uk. Frances Palmer, keeper of mus insts; D W Allen, librarian. *Large coll of mus insts from all over world (6000 insts, 1500 on display) including Adam Carse coll, Percy A Bull coll, L Wayne coll of concertinas and Dolmetsch coll. Library includes sections on mus insts. Also educ service.*

Museum of London. London Wall, London EC2Y 5HN *tel:* 0171 600 3699 *fax:* 0171 600 1058. Rory O'Connell, curator. *Str, keyboard and wind insts; small coll only, 1950s fittings from Dobell's Jazz shop, printed ephemera on theatres and mus in London, (closed Mon). Small number of paper rolls, vinyl discs, cylinders, c1900-70s.*

Musical Museum (Charitable Trust). 368 High St, Brentford, Middx TW8 0BD *tel:* 0181 560 8108. Richard Cole, curator. *Keyboards, automatic mus insts, player-pnos, orchestrions, Wurlitzer Fotoplayer, Welte Philharmonic Reproducing Pipe Organ, Aeolian Residence Duo-Art Pipe Organ, etc. Open w/ends Apr-Oct 2pm-5pm, Weds Jul-Aug 2-4pm.*

Royal College of Music. Prince Consort Rd, London SW7 2BS *tel:* 0171 589 3643; 0171 591 4346 *fax:* 0171 589 7740; 0171 591 4340 *email:* ewells@rcm.ac.uk. Mrs E P Wells, museum curator; O H Davies, keeper of portraits. *Museum of insts (keyboard, str, wind), including Tagore, Donaldson, Hipkins, Ridley and Hartley colls; 600 insts (500 European, 100 Asian and African). Dept of Portraits and Performance History: paintings, prints, photographs, concert programmes, etc.*

Theatre Museum. Tavistock St, Covent Garden, London EC2E 7PA *tel:* 0171 836 7891 *fax:* 0171 836 5148. Margaret Benton, head of museum. *National mus of performing arts including theatre, mus, pop, melodrama, ballet and opera. Public research facilities.*

Victoria and Albert Museum. Cromwell Rd, South Kensington, London SW7 2RL *tel:* 0171 938 8500/8287 *fax:* 0171 938 8283. James Yorke. *Comprehensive exhibition coll of decorative mus insts; mus insts and mus iconography included in National Art Library at the V & A.*

Belfast. Ulster Museum. Botanic Gardens, Belfast BT9 5AB *tel:* 01232 383000 *fax:* 01232 383013. Mrs W Glover, curator of ethnography; T Wylie, curator of history. *Small coll of ancient and modern mus insts. Ethnographic mus insts includes 2 sets of Chimu pottery pan pipes, 2 Bronze Age horns, 3 pairs of Uillean pipes, 4 harps, 2 fifes, 4 Lambeg drums.*

Birmingham. Museum of Science and Industry. Newhall St, Birmingham B3 1RZ *tel:* 0121 235 1661 *fax:* 0121 233 9210. *Mechanical mus insts; coll of mus boxes.*

Bradford. Bolling Hall Museum. Bowling Hall Rd, Bradford, W Yorks BD4 7LP *tel:* 01274 723057 *fax:* 01274 726220 *email:* abickley@ legend.co.uk. Anthea Bickley, snr keeper, history. *Coll of mus insts dispersed among various museums in Bradford Metropolitan area. Mostly at Cliffe Castle Museum.*

Cambridge. Fitzwilliam Museum. Trumpington St, Cambridge CB2 1RB *tel:* 01223 332900 *fax:* 01223 332923. Duncan Robinson, dir. *A few guis, lutes and keyboard insts and a pitch pipe.*

Cambridge. University Museum of Archaeology and Anthropology. Downing St, Cambridge CB2 3DZ *tel:* 01223 333516 *fax:* 01223 333503. D W Phillipson, dir and curator. *Coll of insts of anthropological interest.*

Cardiff. National Museums and Galleries of Wales: Museum of Welsh Life. St Fagans, Nr Cardiff CF5 6XB *tel:* 01222 573500 *fax:* 01222 573490 *email:* http://www.cardiff.ac.uk/nmgw/stfagans.html. Emma Lile, research asst. *Str, keyboard and wind insts.*

Carlisle. City Museum and Art Gallery. Tullie House, Castle St, Carlisle, Cumbria CA3 8TP *tel:* 01228 34781 *fax:* 01288 810249. Nick Winterbotham, dir. *Str and wind insts, including Andrea Amati vn of 1564 and str insts by Forster family.*

Cheltenham. Holst Birthplace Museum. 4 Clarence Rd, Pittville, Cheltenham, Glos GL52 2AY *tel:* 01242 524846 *fax:* 01242 262334. Helen Brown, Mary Greensted, keepers of museum. *Unique coll of Holst material including printed mus, pictures, concert programmes, books, personal possessions. Open to public all yr (closed Sun-Mon), small admission charge, enquiries to information offr, Cheltenham Art Gallery, Clarence St, Cheltenham tel: 01242 237431.*

Chester. Grosvenor Museum. 27 Grosvenor St, Chester CH1 2DD *tel:* 01244 402008 *fax:* 01244 347587. Sophie Fowler, keeper of local and social history. *Unique set of Bressan rcdrs (recording available).*

Douglas. Manx National Heritage. Manx Museum and National Trust, Douglas, Isle of Man IM1 3LY *tel:* 01624 648000 *fax:* 01624 648001. Stephen Harrison, dir. *Str, keyboard and wind insts.*

Edinburgh. Edinburgh University. Collection of Historic Musical Instruments, Reid Concert Hall, Bristo Sq, Edinburgh EH8 9AG *tel:* 0131 650 2423/2 *fax:* 0131 650 2425 *email:* a.myers@ed.ac.uk; http://www. music.ed.ac.uk/euchmi/. Arnold Myers, curator. *University coll of over 1000 historic mus insts spanning 400 yrs. Open Wed pm, Sat am, (Mon-Fri throughout Edinburgh Festival). Admission free.*

Edinburgh. National Museums of Scotland. Chambers St, Edinburgh EH1 1JF *tel:* 0131 225 7534 *fax:* 0131 220 4819 *email:* http://www.nms.ac.uk. *International and Scottish collections of str, keyboard and wind insts, including Glen and Ross bagpipe coll, coll of pipe-making tools. Jean Jenkins coll of sound recordings (ethnomusicological), also photographic slides and mus insts.*

Edinburgh. St Cecilia's Hall (Edinburgh University). Niddry St, Cowgate, Edinburgh EH1 1LJ *tel:* 0131 650 2805 *fax:* 0131 650 2812 *email:* russell.collection@music.ed.co.uk; http://www.music.ed.ac.uk/russell/ index.html. Grant O'Brien, curator. *Russell Coll of Early Keyboard Insts: hpds, virginals, spinets, clvds, early pnos and chmbr orgs from 1586-1840.*

Edinburgh. Scottish United Services Museum. The Castle, Edinburgh EH1 2NG *tel:* 0131 225 7534 *fax:* 0131 225 3848. *Military wind and perc insts from 18th C. Sound archives on tape of European and N American military mus (appointment necessary).*

Glasgow. Art Gallery and Museum. Kelvingrove, Glasgow G3 8AG *tel:* 0141 221 9600 *fax:* 0141 287 2690. E Maitland, information offr. *Coll of historical mus insts.*

Goudhurst. Finchcocks Living Museum of Music. Finchcocks, Goudhurst, Kent TN17 1HH *tel:* 01580 211702 *fax:* 01580 211007. William Dow, curator. *Richard Burnett coll of historic keyboard insts. Open Sun and Bank Holidays Easter-Sep; Wed and Thu in Aug; other times by prior arrangement. Musical tours whenever open.*

Hailsham. Michelham Priory. Upper Dicker, Hailsham, East Sussex BN27 3QS *tel:* 01323 844224 *fax:* 01323 844030. Allex Jenkinson, dir. *Includes Alice Schulmann Frank coll of world mus insts (formerly Mummery coll).*

Halifax. Shibden Hall. Listers Rd, Halifax, W Yorks HX3 6XG *tel:* 01422 352246 *fax:* 01422 348440. Ros Westwood, museums offr. *General coll of mus insts, particularly 18th C chmbr. Also 19th C scores.*

Holdenby. Holdenby House. Holdenby, Northants NN6 8DJ *tel:* 01604 770074 *fax:* 01604 770962. Mrs S Park, educ mgr. *Non-player pno exhibition, old pnos from 1790. 11 pnos from British Piano Museum. House parties by appointment, min 25.*

Huddersfield. Tolson Memorial Museum. Ravensknowle Pk, Wakefield Rd, Huddersfield HD5 8DJ *tel:* 01484 223830 *fax:* 01484 223843. John Rumsby, snr museums offr. *Br, wind and str insts.*

Ipswich. Christchurch Mansion. Christchurch Pk, Ipswich IP4 2BE *tel:* 01473 253246 *fax:* 01473 210328. Jane Sedge, snr asst curator. *Str, wind and keyboard insts. Enquiries and correspondence to Ipswich Museum, see below.*

Ipswich. Ipswich Museum. High St, Ipswich IP1 3QH *tel:* 01473 213761 *fax:* 01473 281274. D L Jones, keeper, human history. *Ethnographic insts.*

Keighley. Cliffe Castle Art Gallery and Museum. Keighley, W Yorks BD20 6LH *tel:* 01535 618230 *fax:* 01535 610536. Anthea Bickley, snr keeper, history. *General coll of mus insts.*

Liverpool. Liverpool Museum. William Brown St, Liverpool L3 8EN *tel:* 0151 207 0001 *fax:* 0151 478 4390. Pauline Rushton, curator of costume and textiles. *Coll of 17th-19th C insts including former Rushworth and Dreaper coll.*

Maidstone. Museum and Art Gallery. Maidstone, Kent ME14 1LH *tel:* 01622 754497 *fax:* 01622 602193. Veronica Tonge, keeper of fine and applied art. *Str, keyboard and wind insts, includes Handel's portable clvd.*

Manchester. Royal Northern College of Music. 124 Oxford Rd, Manchester M13 9RD *tel:* 0161 273 6283. Anthony Hodges, chief librarian. *Henry Watson coll of historic and ethnic insts.*

Merthyr Tydfil. Cyfarthfa Castle Art Gallery and Museum. Merthyr Tydfil, Merthyr Tydfil County Borough CF47 8RE *tel:* 01685 723112 *also fax; fax:* 01685 722146. Stephen Done, curator. *Mid 19th C coll of insts, ms mus, photographs and ephemera relating to the Cyfarthfa Band; also ethnographic inst coll.*

Northleach. Keith Harding's World of Mechanical Music. Oak House, High St, Northleach, Glos GL54 3ET *tel:* 01451 860181 *fax:* 01451 861133 *email:* http://www.leisurehunt.com/womm.htm. Keith Harding. *Demonstrations of antique clocks, musical boxes, automata, reproducing pnos and mechanical mus insts presented as live entertainment. Restoration work done.*

Norwich. St Peter Hungate Museum (Norfolk Museums Service). Princes St, Norwich NR3 1AE *tel:* 01603 667231. *Str, keyboard and wind insts formerly used in churches.*

Norwich. Strangers' Hall Museum (Norfolk Museums Service). Charing Cross, Norwich NR2 4AL *tel:* 01603 667229. Helen Rowles, asst. *Str, keyboard, perc and mechanical wind insts. Gramophones, printed and ms mus in store. Viewing by arrangement.*

Oxford. Ashmolean Museum. Beaumont St, Oxford OX1 2PH *tel:* 01865 278000 *fax:* 01865 278042. *Hill coll of str insts and bows (photographs and measured drawings of str insts available for research).*

Oxford. Bate Collection of Musical Instruments. Oxford University Faculty of Music, St Aldate's, Oxford OX1 1DB *tel:* 01865 276139 *fax:* 01865 276128 *email:* bate.collection@music.oxford.ac.uk. H La Rue, curator. *W/wind, br, early keyboards and a Javanese gamelan; also a bow makers w/shop. Open Mon-Fri 2-5pm, admission free. Open Sat during University full term, 10am-12pm.*

Oxford. University of Oxford, Pitt Rivers Museum. South Parks Rd, Oxford OX1 3PP *tel:* 01865 270927 *fax:* 01865 274725 *email:* pitt@vax.ox.ac. uk. H La Rue, curator. *Important worldwide coll of more than 6000 mus insts. New gallery Music Makers in the Balfour Building, 60 Banbury Rd, Oxford tel: 01865 274726, including a sound guide and a/v booth.*

St Albans. Organ Museum. 320 Camp Rd, St Albans, Herts AL1 5PB *tel:* 01727 851557 *also fax. Mechanical insts and theatre orgs; open Sun 2.15-4.30pm. Other times by arrangement. Correspondence and enquiries to the Secretary, c/o 326 Camp Rd, St Albans, Herts AL1 5PB.*

Shipley. Victorian Reed Organ and Harmonium Museum. Victoria Hall, Victoria Rd, Saltaire Village, Shipley, W Yorks *tel:* 01274 585601 (after 5pm). Phil Fluke, curator. *Private collection of 95 reed organs. Players encouraged to play. Also mechanical reed organs. Open to the public Sun-Thu 11am-4pm.*

Worcester. The Elgar Birthplace Museum. Crown East La, Lower Broadheath, Worcester WR2 6RH *tel:* 01905 333224. Melanie Weatherley, curator. *Unique coll of Elgarian material including scores, books, photographs, insts and personal possessions.*

York. York Castle Museum. York YO1 1RY *tel:* 01904 653611 *fax:* 01904 671078. Stephen Feber, dir. *Social history museum of everyday life. General coll of mus insts, with good w/wind, keyboard and mechanical sections (some on display).*

Tom Petzal and Associates

Consultants - 25 years in arts, sports and charities

We Know the Score

Pantiles Chambers, 85 High Street, Tunbridge Wells, Kent TN1 1YG England
Telephone: (0) 1892 506968   Fax: (0) 1892 547120
e-mail: PantilesBC@CompuServe.com

Thomas F Petzal MA Hons (Cantab)

Marketing, Fundraising and Related Services

This section provides information on the resources necessary to the successful marketing of music and musicians, and on fundraising, whether in the form of patronage or sponsorship.

Marketing and Organisational Management

Entrants listed here usually offer a comprehensive service which may include guidance on market research, marketing planning, advertising, public and media relations, design and print, sales and sales promotion, pricing, personnel selection and training; some offer an event management service and some will provide an interim management service for organisations. There are also some organisations, closely allied in terms of their function, who specialise in arranging and promoting concerts; these are Concert Managements and are listed in the next sub-section. Readers seeking a service should first look here and then move on to the specialist sub-sections which follow. If uncertain as to which service is required, do not hesitate to make preliminary enquiries by telephone. There now exists a membership organisation for practitioners in arts marketing, the **Arts Marketing Association,** Helen Robbins, Bolton's Warehouse, 23 Tenison Rd, Cambridge CB1 2DG *tel:* 01223 578078 *fax:* 01223 578079.

AEA Ltd. 57d Hatton Garden, London EC1N 8JD *tel:* 0171 242 3133 *fax:* 0171 242 3422 *email:* office@aeaone.demon.co.uk. Adrian Ellis, Caroline Kay, Steven Foster, David Hall, snr consultants; Magnus Wistinghausen, Sophie Garnham, consultants. *Management consultancy specialising in the arts and heritage sectors, with some work in the educ and entertainment sectors. Strategic and business planning, fundraising strategies, change management and feasibility work. Recent extensive work on capital projects, many related to the National Lottery.*

Allegro Arts Marketing. Spa House, Worple Rd, Wimbledon, London SW19 4JS *tel:* 0181 944 5800 *fax:* 0181 947 9042. Bob Moffat; Cheryl Lawrence. *Full service marketing and PR agency. Considerable experience in opera and choral mus.*

Anderton, Robin. 100 Harvist Rd, London NW6 6HL *tel:* 0181 960 4780 *fax:* 0181 964 5510. *Administration for w/shops and courses. Career counselling for musicians. Concert management.*

Anna Hassan Arts Marketing. 54 Elm Rd, Hale, Altrincham, Cheshire WA15 9QP *tel:* 0161 928 3085 *fax:* 0161 929 9648 *email:* ahassan@easynet.co.uk. *Freelance arts marketing consultant.*

Arts About Manchester. 23 New Mount St, Manchester M4 4DE *tel:* 0161 953 4035 *fax:* 0161 953 4106 *email:* arts-mcr@mcrl.poptel.org.uk; http://www.aam.org.uk/. Andrew McIntyre, mkt mgr. *Professional print distribution, direct mail, telemarketing and market research, UK-wide at not-for-profit rates.*

Arts Connect. Spa House, 11-17 Worple Rd, London SW19 4JS *tel:* 0181 879 3033 *fax:* 0181 947 9042. Richard Price, mgr dir; Robert Moffatt.

Arts Management Services. Bolton's Warehouse, 23 Tenison Rd, Cambridge CB1 2DG *tel:* 01223 578078 *fax:* 01223 578079. Anne Roberts. *Management of arts projects.*

Arts Marketing East. 50 The Street, Melton, Woodbridge, Suffolk IP12 1PW *tel:* 01394 388029 *fax:* 01394 386511 *email:* ame@anglianet.co.uk. Eric Orme, dir; Mary Ann Bartlet, publicity mgr. *Arts marketing services and consultancy for concert promoters. Clients include local authorities, RABs and many different arts organisations.*

Arts Marketing Hampshire. Mottisfont Ct, High St, Winchester, Hants SO23 8ZD *tel:* 01962 865383 *fax:* 01962 841644 *email:* artsnh@hantsnet.hants.gov.uk. Nicki Hayes, mkt mgr. *Marketing consultants.*

Bill Clancy Arts Marketing. 67 Broadbottom Rd, Mottram-in-Longdendale, Cheshire SK14 6JA *tel:* 01457 765877 *also fax.* Bill Clancy, Adrienne Pye, dirs. *Arts marketing consultants; promoters (mus and literary events).*

Business in the Arts (an ABSA initiative). ABSA, Nutmeg House, 60 Gainsford St, Butler's Wharf, London SE1 2NY *tel:* 0171 378 8143 *fax:* 0171 407 7527. Tim Stockil, dir. *A network of offices throughout Britain whose aim is to encourage business people to help arts managers develop their managerial capacity.*

Cardiff Arts Marketing Ltd. 98 Cardiff Rd, Llandaff, Cardiff CF5 2DT *tel:* 01222 575739 *fax:* 01222 562180. Charles Wilde, chief exec; Peter Reynolds, mkt mgr. *Market research, database services, print distribution, project management, consultancy and marketing services.*

Chadwick Jones Associates. 2 Kelvedon Road, London SW6 5BW *tel:* 0171 731 6012 *fax:* 0171 736 7271. Ana Isabel Gaio, Ian Jones, dirs. *Feasibility studies, planning, marketing, management, market research, fundraising.*

Chuck Julian Associates. Suite 51, 26 Charing Cross Rd, London WC2H 0DH *tel:* 0171 437 4248 *fax:* 0171 240 1296. C Julian, S Yager, A Alraun, associates. *Management and marketing.*

Coopers & Lybrand. 1 Embankment Pl, London WC2N 6NN *tel:* 0171 213 8412 *fax:* 0171 213 2443. Sue Mackenzie Gray, principal associate. *Project appraisal, project review, project management, business planning, funding for new build projects. Advice on property issues relating to business problems.*

CSS International Holdings Plc. CSS House, 12 Gt Newport St, London WC2H 7JA *tel:* 0171 379 7989 *fax:* 0171 414 0304.

David Allthorpe Management Services. 21 Launcelyn Close, North Baddesly, Romsey, Hants SO52 9NP *tel:* 01703 737505. *Market research and management consultancy.*

David Jackson and Associates. Crowlin Cottage, Little London Rd, Cross In Hand, nr Heathfield, E Sussex TN21 0LT *tel:* 01435 868808 *fax:* 01435 868889. David Jackson, dir. *Arts management consultancy, audience development, box office organisation, marketing schemes, customer care, events planning and management, gala concerts.*

European Marketing Consultants Ltd. Spa House, 11-17 Worple Rd, London SW19 4JS *tel:* 0181 879 3033 *fax:* 0181 947 9042. Richard Price, mgr dir. *PR agency with specialist arts expertise.*

Helen Fraser Arts Management. Normansland, Dymock, Glos GL18 2BE *tel:* 01531 890589 *also fax; email:* hf@artsland.demon.co.uk. *Business planning, funding, organising events, concert management.*

Kallaway (Consultants and Management) Ltd. 2 Portland Rd, Holland Park, London W11 4LA *tel:* 0171 221 7883 *fax:* 0171 229 4595. William Kallaway, mgr dir. *Communications and marketing through sponsored arts events. Services include consultancy, event production and management, promotion and media planning.*

Kivity, Sharon. 19b Albert Rd, Teddington, Middx TW11 0BD *tel:* 0181 977 2961 *fax:* 0181 977 6281. Sharon Kivity, snr consultant; Lucia Reynolds, consultant. *Training, promotion, publicity and PR services. Festival programming and organisation.*

McCann Matthews Millman Ltd. Marine House, 23 Mount Stuart Sq, Cardiff Bay, Cardiff CF1 6DP *tel:* 01222 462121 *fax:* 01222 462122 *email:* office@mcmatmil.co.uk. John Matthews, dir. London office: Friars' House, 157-168 Blackfriars' Rd, London SE1 8EZ *tel:* 0171 401 2225 *fax:* 0171 401 3773. Roger McCann, dir. *Specialist consultants in strategic planning, feasibility studies, research and training for the arts.*

Maestsoso Musicmakers Ltd. 'Milestone', St Nicholas Av, Gt Bookham, Surrey KT23 4AY *tel:* 01372 457755 *fax:* 01372 450525. Elizabeth Pryde, dir. *Consultants in arts management and sponsorship.*

The Management Centre. 366 Kennington Rd, London SE11 4DB *tel:* 0171 820 1100 *fax:* 0171 820 3828 *email:* tmc@tmcuk.demon.co.uk. Bernard Ross, Clare Segal, dirs. *Provides management training, fundraising and sponsorship, open and in-house programmes for not-for-profit organisations. Also carries out consultancy.*

Manygate Management. 13 Cotswold Mews, 30 Battersea Sq, London SW11 3RA *tel:* 0171 223 7265 *fax:* 0171 585 2830 *email:* manygate@easynet.co.uk. *Sponsorship and fundraising for orchs, recordings, festivals and concerts. Concert management, marketing strategies, concepts, research.*

The Marketing Office. 9 Chiswick High Rd, London W4 2ND *tel:* 0181 994 0066 *fax:* 0181 994 4499 *email:* tmo@vossnet.co.uk. Lynne Burton, mgr dir. *Marketing consultancy and services, PR and promotion, design and print, research, audits and strategies.*

Michael Webber Promotions. The Garden Flat, 19 Netherhall Gardens, London NW3 5RL *tel:* 0171 794 5154 *fax:* 0171 794 5154. *Mus adviser to English Heritage; general arts consultant.*

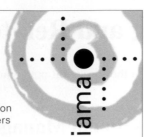

Midlands Arts Marketing. 4 Russel Pl, Nottingham NG1 5HJ *tel:* 0115 948 3344 *fax:* 0115 948 3343. Heather Maitland, chief exec. *Comprehensive arts marketing consultancy service, including design and print, audience development, distribution and market analysis.*

Millward Brown Market Research Ltd. Olympus Av, Tachbrook Pk, Warwick CV34 6RJ *tel:* 01926 452233 *fax:* 01926 833600. Bob Barnes, charts dir. *Specialists in market research for arts, sponsorship, audience development. Compilers of the official record industry mus charts for CIN.*

Nicky Webb Associates. 82 Kempshott Rd, London SW16 5LH *tel:* 0181 679 9303 *fax:* 0181 679 9306. Nicky Webb, Beverley Etkin, Maggie Jones. *Specialist marketing and PR for the arts.*

Organisation for Arts and Media. 5 Dryden St, London WC2E 9NW *tel:* 0171 829 8456 *fax:* 0171 240 5600 *email:* jackieartsorg@msn.com. Jackie Elliman. *Admin, development, marketing and event services for the arts and media.*

Positive Solutions. 6 Bluecoat Chambers, School La, Liverpool L1 3BX *tel:* 0151 709 6511 *fax:* 0151 709 2575. David Fishel. *An organisation specialising in research consultancy and training in the arts and cultural industry.*

Reed, Douglas. 30 Beresford Rd, Kingston upon Thames, Surrey KT2 6LR *tel:* 0181 546 5802 *fax:* 0181 547 3420. *Management, promotion, sponsorship, special events.*

Simon Blake and Co. 52 Manor Rd, Teddington, Middx TW11 8AB *tel:* 0181 943 2661. *Direct marketing and mailing consultancy.*

Spero Communications Ltd. Grampian House, Meridian Gate, Marsh Wall, London E14 9XT *tel:* 0171 538 9946 *fax:* 0171 538 4747 *email:* spero@sperocom.co.uk. Connie Brighton, dir. *Interactive marketing programmes which combine innovation with sound business objectives.*

State of the Art Consultancy (SOTAC). Ty-Coat, Kinlochmoidart, By Lochailort, Inverness-shire, PH38 4ND *tel:* 01967 431298 *fax:* 01967 431289. Patrick Stephen-Samuels, dir; Radford James. *Business administration and marketing advice for small theatre companies and individual artists.*

STR Music Marketing and Management. 296 Hughenden Rd, High Wycombe, Bucks HP13 5PE *tel:* 01494 461177 *fax:* 01494 461188 *email:* admin@strmmm.com; http://www.strmmm.com. Sean Rourke, mgr dir. *Strategic planning, comprehensive marketing campaigns and sponsorship consultant, lottery assessments.*

Taylor, Sally. 17 Grove Terrace, Teddington, Middx TW11 8AU *tel:* 0181 977 4869 *also fax. General arts consultancy.*

The Team (Arts Marketing Consortium on Merseyside). Studio 2, Bluecoat Chambers, School La, Liverpool L1 3BX *tel:* 0151 709 6881 *fax:* 0151 707 2555 *email:* team@agency-net.co.uk; http://www.connect.org.uk/merseyworld/team. David Jackson, dir; Beverley Evans, mkt offr. *Print distribution, primary and secondary research, project management, marketing audits and planning, skills audits.*

Theatre Projects Consultants Ltd. 3 Apollo Studios, Charlton Kings Rd, London NW5 2SW *tel:* 0171 482 4224 *fax:* 0171 284 0636. D Staples, A Russell, J Godden, A Field, L Fleming, I Mackintosh, dirs. *Theatre and leisure consultancy including feasibility, planning, design, project development and implementation. Also offices in the USA.*

Tom Petzal and Associates. Pantiles Chambers, 85 High St, Tunbridge Wells, Kent TN1 1YG *tel:* 01892 506968 *fax:* 01892 547120. Tom Petzal, mgr dir. *Management, promotion, fundraising advice, PR services, feasibility studies and National Lottery application expertise.*

Vineall, Michael G. Edge Side House, Hebden, nr Skipton, N Yorks BD23 5DB *tel:* 01756 753013 *fax:* 01756 752954. *Marketing management consultant. Marketing strategy, research and consultancy on communications. Not fundraising.*

Web Projects Ltd. The Studio, 78 Croydon Rd, Reigate, Surrey RH2 0NH *tel:* 01737 222008 *fax:* 01737 225600 *email:* mwalmsley@webprojects.co.uk; http://www.webprojects.co.uk. Mark Walmsley, mgr dir; Ben Sauer, mkt mgr. *Internet marketing consultancy.*

Concert and Personal Management

This sub-section includes organisations specialising in the marketing and overall management of concerts, tours, festivals and music for special occasions; the service offered will frequently include booking of venues, concert programme production, organisation of press and other receptions. The sub-section also includes organisations providing a personal PR service and/or a representation/agency service for musicians. Concert Managements do not act as principals, i.e. they are not risk-takers. *See also* **Marketing and Organisational Management**.

Anglo-European Arts. 25 Fournier St, Spitalfields, London E1 6QE *tel:* 0171 247 7219 *fax:* 0171 247 6094. Carolyn Humphreys, dir. *Concert, event and festival management, PR consultant.*

Anthony Abbott Music Management. Medlar Cottage, Lodge La, Keymer, Hassocks, W Sussex BN6 8NA *tel:* 01273 843348 *fax:* 01273 846585. *Concert, tours and event management, plus personal representation.*

Antony Pristavec Artist and Concert Management. 79 Norbury Cres, London SW16 4JT *tel:* 0181 679 0369 *fax:* 0181 679 9399. Antony Pristavec, dir. *Personal, concert, festival and tour management.*

B & B Concert Services. 66 Hyde Way, Hayes, Middx UB3 4PB *tel:* 0181 606 0030 *fax:* 0181 606 0037 *email:* roderick_burnett@compuserve.com. Roderick Burnett, mgr dir.

Bullamore, Tim. 25 Brock Street, Bath BA1 2LN *tel:* 01225 330037 *also fax;* 0836 617030.

Caroline Ireland Management. Uwchlaw'r Coed, Llanbedr, Gwynedd LL45 2NA *tel:* 01341 241532 *also fax. Personal and concert management.*

Chase Promotions. Richmond House, 16-20 Regent St, Cambridge CB2 1DB *tel:* 0181 746 2080 *also fax.* Rachel Fisher. *Concert, event and tour management, PR for events, solo artists and ensembles.*

Classic Music Management. 35 Cannonside, Fetcham, Leatherhead, Surrey KT22 9LE *tel:* 01372 375939 *fax:* 01372 379095. Graham Bolton, mgr. *Musicians' management service, contracting freelance musicians for concerts, charity galas, opera and ballet.*

Fox Jones & Associates. 54 Crofton Rd, London SE5 8NB *tel:* 0171 701 3107 *fax:* 0171 701 6918 *email:* foxjones@compuserve.com; foxjones@inforamp.net. Paulo Tardãd, principal; Jeremy Fox, president; Ted Kalaboukis, consultant; Margaret Barkman, mgr. *Management consulting, artist management.*

GBZ Management. PO Box 11845, London SE21 8ZS *tel:* 0181 761 6565 *fax:* 0181 670 3195 *email:* gbz_mgmt@compuserve.com. Gwenneth Bransby-Zachary, dir. *PR, personal and concert management.*

Helen Fraser Arts Management. Normansland, Dymock, Glos GL18 2BE *tel:* 01531 890589 *also fax; email:* hf@artsland.demon.co.uk. *Organises events, tour co-ordination, concert management.*

Impulse. 18 Hillfield Pk, Muswell Hill, London N10 3QS *tel:* 0181 444 8587 *fax:* 0181 245 0358 *email:* impulse@styx.cerbernet.co.uk; http://www.cdj.co.uk/impulse/. Geraldine Allen, Sarah Rodgers. *Mus consultants offering expert assessment, advice and management skills for professional music-making in every context. Internet specialists.*

Influence. Disraeli Mews, 137b Putney High St, London SW15 1SU *tel:* 0181 789 0776; 0181 789 1192 *also fax.* Michael Heyland, events consultant. *Events consultant, specialising in charity.*

Jonathan Land Management (JLM). 95 Oxford Gardens, London W10 6NF *tel:* 0181 993 8350 *fax:* 0181 969 5364. Joëlle Partner, asst dir. *Concert management, career consultation and promotion. Profile enhancement.*

Judith Hendershott Arts Management. 4 Bennett Pk, London SE3 9RB *tel:* 0181 852 0823 *fax:* 0181 852 0016 *email:* 106364.440@compuserve.com. *PR, personal management, press service. Concert, event and project management.*

Kantor Concert Management and Public Relations. 67 Teignmouth Rd, London NW2 4EA *tel:* 0181 208 2480 *fax:* 0181 208 2490. Denise Kantor, proprietor. *PR and publicity, concert management, mus secretariat.*

Ken Chaproniere Arts and Events Management. 3 The Clock House, Little Brickhill, Milton Keynes MK17 9NR *tel:* 01908 692777; 01525 261670 *fax:* 01525 261291 *email:* kenchaproniere@compuserve.com. *Music and arts consultancy, specialising in PR, promotion, marketing and sponsorship. Also artist management.*

Keown Artists' Management. 62 Chestnut Rd, London SE27 9LE *tel:* 0181 761 4221. Sarah Keown. *Concert and personal management.*

Lisa Peacock Concert Management. 27 Elsham Rd, London W14 8HB *tel:* 0171 602 1416 *fax:* 0171 371 2726. Lisa Peacock. *Concert management.*

Suppliers and Services

* **Faber Music Ltd.** 3 Queen Sq, London WC1N 3AU *tel:* 0171 278 7436; 0171 833 7906 (sales) *fax:* 0171 833 7939 *email:* info@fabermusic.co. uk; http://www.fabermusic.co.uk. Trade orders: Burnt Mill, Elizabeth Way, Harlow, Essex CM20 2HX *tel:* 01279 417134 *fax:* 01279 429401. *Contemporary concert and media composers, choral, educ, jazz, tutors/repertoire for pno, keyboard, strs, w/wind, br, etc.*

Fand Music Press. Blumleins, 7a Dragon St, Petersfield GU31 4JN *tel:* 01730 266605 *fax:* 01730 262961. *Pno, vocal, chmbr, choral and orch mus.*

* **Fentone Music Ltd.** Fleming Rd, Earlstrees, Corby, Northants NN17 4SN *tel:* 01536 260981 *fax:* 01536 401075. *Educ, solo, pno, vocal, w/wind, br, gui, strs (especially quartet). Cat available.*

* **Fireworks Music Ltd.** Ickenham Manor, Ickenham, Uxbridge, Middx UB10 8QT *tel:* 01895 672994 *fax:* 01895 633264 *email:* fwx@ fireworks.demon.co.uk. *Film, TV, library, classical.*

Folktracks and Soundpost Publications. 16 Brunswick Sq, Gloucester GL1 1UG *tel:* 01452 415110 *email:* peter@folktrax.demon.co.uk. *Trad mus.*

* **Forsyth Brothers Ltd.** 126-128 Deansgate, Manchester M3 2GR *tel:* 0161 834 3281 *fax:* 0161 834 0630 *email:* forsythmus@aol.com. *Educ, classical.*

Fortune Music Publications. 12 Church Walk, Areley Kings, Stourport-on-Severn, Worcs DY13 0AP *tel:* 01299 825895 *also fax. Solo, ens.*

Forward Music Ltd. 72 Verdant La, London SE6 1LF *tel:* 0181 461 5353 *fax:* 01494 461188. *Contemporary mus publishers.*

Fretwork. 67 Kings Rd, Richmond, Surrey TW10 6EG *tel:* 0181 948 1250 *fax:* 0181 332 0415. *Mus for viols.*

Friendly Music. PO Box 53, Cranbrook, Kent TN17 3ZX *tel:* 01580 713281. *Collections of solos and duets for w/wind insts; also quartets and quintets.*

* **Friendly Overtures Ltd.** 345 West Wycombe Rd, High Wycombe, Bucks HP12 4AD *tel:* 01494 442285 *also fax. Pop mus, traditional and contemporary folk mus.*

Frontier Press. c/o 30 Buckingham Rd, Petersham, Richmond, Surrey TW10 7EQ *tel:* 0973 978014. *Contemporary mus, British Contemporary Music Anthology.*

Fulcrum Music Publications. c/o Goodmusic, 16 Cheltenham Trade Pk, Cheltenham, Glos GL51 8LX *tel:* 01242 239793 *fax:* 01242 573441. *Orch, br band, chmbr and educ mus.*

G & M Brand Publications Ltd. PO Box 367, Aylesbury, Bucks HP22 4LJ *tel:* 01296 682220 *fax:* 01296 681989.

* **Gee Music Group.** 7 Fleetsbridge Business Centre, Upton Rd, Poole, Dorset BH17 7AF *tel:* 01202 686368 *fax:* 01202 686363. *Including Music Forte, Music Gifts Co and Musigraphic Publishers. Edwin F Kalmus Orchestral, Music Gifts, Masters, Southern, Peanuts Piano Course, Wynn School Orchestral and Band.*

* **Golden Apple Productions.** Chester Music, 8-9 Frith St, London W1V 5TZ *tel:* 0171 434 0066 *fax:* 0171 287 6329. Distribution: Newmarket Rd, Bury St Edmunds, Suffolk IP33 3YB *tel:* 01284 702600 *fax:* 01284 768301. *Children's mus, educ mus.*

* **Goodmusic.** 16 Cheltenham Trade Pk, Arle Rd, Cheltenham GL51 8LX *tel:* 01242 239793 *fax:* 01242 573441. *Educ, inst, orch, choral.*

Grail Publications. Grail Centre, 125 Waxwell La, Pinner, Middx HA5 3ER *tel:* 0181 866 2195; 0181 866 0505 *fax:* 0181 866 1408 *email:* waxwell@compuserve.com. *Gelineau psalmody; children's musical, religious dramas.*

Grainger Society Edition. 6 Fairfax Cres, Aylesbury, Bucks HP20 2ES *tel:* 01296 28609 *email:* 101464.2670@compuserve.com. *Mus by Percy Grainger, original compositions and arrangements by others.*

Gregg International. The Old Hospital, Ardingly Rd, Cuckfield, W Sussex RH17 5JR *tel:* 01444 445070 *also fax; email:* umi@ipiumi.demon.co.uk. *Scholarly mus reprints, facsimiles of early scores.*

Griffin Music. Hill House, 9 Redford Cres, Edinburgh EH13 0BS *tel:* 0131 441 3035 *fax:* 0131 441 5218. *Works by John McLeod and contemporary composers.*

Griffiths Edition. 21 Cefn Coed, Bridgend, Mid Glamorgan CF31 4PH *tel:* 01656 649351 *also fax. Pno, strs, hp, w/wind, br, br band, orch, choral and church mus.*

* **Gwynn Publishing Co (Cwmni Cyhoeddi Gwynn Cyf).** Y Gerlan, Heol-y-Dwr, Penygroes, Caernarfon, Gwynedd LL54 6LR *tel:* 01286 881797. *Vocal and choral.*

* **Halcyon Music Ltd.** 11 Howitt Rd, London NW3 4LT *tel:* 0171 586 0288. *Popular.*

Hallamshire Music. Bank End, N Somercotes, Louth, Lincs LN11 7LN *tel:* 01507 358141 *fax:* 01507 358034 *email:* hallamshire-music@msn. com. *Solo, ens, br band, wind band and school band.*

The Hardie Press. 17 Harrison Gardens, Edinburgh EH11 1SE *tel:* 0131 313 1383 *fax:* 0131 313 1388. *Publish Scottish mus: solo inst, vocal and baroque. Publishers for The Liszt Society.*

Harlequin Music. 69 Eversden Rd, Harlton, Cambridge CB3 7ET *tel:* 01223 263795 *fax:* 01223 263795. *Br and wind mus, solo, ens, wind band, perc.*

Harper Collins Religious. 77-85 Fulham Palace Rd, Hammersmith, London W6 8JB *tel:* 0181 741 7070 *fax:* 0181 307 4440. *Christian mus, hymn books.*

Hawkshaw (Alan) Music Ltd. Oakwood, 10 The Warren, Radlett, Herts WD7 7DX *tel:* 01923 856865 *fax:* 01923 852776 *email:* bigal@ globalnet.co.uk. *S/publishing company for Alan Hawkshaw (see* **Composers**).

Hawthorns Music. The Hawthorns, Hawthorn Dr, Wheaton Aston, Staffs ST19 9NG *tel:* 01785 840186 *fax:* 01785 840476 *email:* hawthorn@ g0nen.demon.co.uk; http://www.g0nen.demon.co.uk/. *Specialising in editions of early mus, particularly medieval mus and rcdr ens.*

Hayter & Shone Ltd Music Publishers. 19 Grove Hill, South Woodford, London E18 2JB *tel:* 0181 989 3706 *fax:* 0181 491 0898 *email:* 106277. 3673@compuserve.com. *Orch (incl hire library material), vocal, choral, inst (incl small ens and solo).*

Helicon Publications. PO Box 9, Hastings, E Sussex TN34 3UU. *S/publishing company for David Branson (see* **Composers**). *Pno, vocal, inst, orch, mainly concert.*

Hughes A'i Fab. c/o S4C, Parc Ty Glas, Llanishen, Cardiff CF4 5DU *tel:* 01222 747444 *fax:* 01222 754444. *Traditional and hymn mus, Welsh language.*

Hunt Edition. 40 Portland Rd, London W11 4LG *tel:* 0171 727 5965. *Wind mus for recreation and learning.*

Hymns Ancient & Modern Ltd. St Mary's Works, St Mary's Plain, Norwich NR3 3BH *tel:* 01603 612914 *fax:* 01603 624483. *Hymn books.*

* **International Music Publications Ltd.** Woodford Trading Estate, Southend Rd, Woodford Green, Essex IG8 8HN *tel:* 0181 551 6131 *fax:* 0181 551 3919. *Popular, classical, educ mus, mus instruction videos, show mus.*

Isa Music. 27-29 Carnoustie Pl, Scotland St, Glasgow G5 8PH *tel:* 0141 420 1881 *fax:* 0141 420 1892 *email:* lismor@lismor.co.uk. *Traditional Scottish pipe mus; all other styles.*

* **J & C Richard Enterprises.** 17 Finlay St, London SW6 6HE *tel:* 0171 736 1977. *Classical mus.*

James Pass & Co Ltd. 71 Smallbrook Queensway, Birmingham B5 4HX *tel:* 0121 643 7623 *also fax. Choral mus.*

Janus Music. 22 Ivybridge Close, Twickenham, Middx TW1 1EA *tel:* 0181 892 1833 *also fax. W/wind, rcdr, choral, pno, mus for youth orchs and wind band.*

Jazzwise Publications. 2b Gleneagle Mews, Ambleside Av, London SW16 6AE *tel:* 0181 769 7725 *fax:* 0181 677 7128. *Publisher and distributor of printed mus and study materials for jazz.*

Jessica Kingsley Publishers. 116 Pentonville Rd, London N1 9JB *tel:* 0171 833 2307 *fax:* 0171 837 2917 *email:* post@jkpbooks.demon.co.uk. *Mus therapy books.*

John Fiddy Music. Fruit Farm House, Foxton, Cambridge CB2 6RT *tel:* 01763 208610 *fax:* 01763 208241 *email:* johnfiddymusic@dial. pipex.com. *Production mus library.*

* **Josef Weinberger Ltd.** 12-14 Mortimer St, London W1N 7RD *tel:* 0171 580 2827 *fax:* 0171 436 9616. *Mus theatre, contemporary classical, educ and religious mus.*

Jubilate Hymns. 13 Stoddart Av, Southampton SO19 4ED *tel:* 01703 441884 *fax:* 01703 442323. *Hymns, psalms and worship song material.*

Karaoke Classics Ltd. PO Box 2242, Poole, Dorset BH14 0YX *tel:* 0181 943 5329 *also fax. Classical mus books with recorded accompaniment packages for fl, ob, cl, bsn, vn, vc.*

K B Productions. 72 Waverley Rd, Rayners La, Harrow, Middx HA2 9RD *tel:* 0181 866 4158. *Choral service mus, org mus.*

Kerroy Music (Division of Kerroy Group Ltd). 2 Queensmead, St John's Wood Pk, London NW8 6RE *tel:* 0171 722 9828 *fax:* 0171 722 9886.

Kevin Mayhew Ltd. Rattlesden, Bury St Edmunds, Suffolk IP30 0SZ *tel:* 01449 737978 *fax:* 01449 737834. *Church, org and choral mus; pno and inst; educ materials; recordings.*

King's Music GMC. Redcroft, Banks End, Wyton, Huntingdon, Cambs PE17 2AA *tel:* 01480 52076 *fax:* 01480 450821 *email:* cbkings@ibm. net. *Facsimiles and editions of early mus.*

Kingsway's Thankyou Music Ltd. PO Box 75, Eastbourne, E Sussex BN23 6NW *tel:* 01323 410930 *fax:* 01323 411970 *email:* schamp@ kingsway.co.uk. *Christian mus.*

* **Kirklees Music.** 609 Bradford Rd, Bailiff Bridge, Brighouse HD6 4DN *tel:* 01484 722855 *also fax. Br and wind band, educ mus.*

Kronos Press. 25 Ansdell St, London W8 5BN *tel:* 0171 937 6768. *S/publishing company for Philip Cannon (see* **Composers**).

LE Music. Nelson House, Castle Hill, Hindley, Wigan WN2 4BH *tel:* 01942 55500 *fax:* 01942 517151.

* **Leosong Copyright Services Ltd.** Independent House, 54 Larkshall Rd, Chingford, London E4 6PB *tel:* 0181 523 9000 *fax:* 0181 523 8888.

* **Light Music Ltd.** 23 Bryanston Ct, George St, London W1H 7HA *tel:* 0171 402 4810 *fax:* 0171 262 4296. *S/publishing company for Trevor Lyttleton (see* **Composers***).*

* **Lindsay Music.** 23 Hitchin St, Biggleswade, Beds SG18 8AX *tel:* 01767 316521 *fax:* 01767 317221. *Educ, choral, songbooks, mus giftware.*

Lipkin, Malcolm. Penlan, Crowborough Hill, Crowborough, Sussex TN6 2EA *tel:* 01892 652454. *S/publishing company of Malcolm Lipkin (see* **Composers***).*

Llonnod. Frogwy Fawr, Llangwyllog, Llangefni, Anglesey LL77 7PX *tel:* 01248 750418 *email:* gareth@llonnod.demon.co.uk. *S/publishing company for Gareth Glyn (see* **Composers***).*

Logorhythm Music. 6-10 Lexington St, London W1R 3HS *tel:* 0171 734 7443/4 *fax:* 0171 439 7057. *Film and TV scores.*

* **Lomond Music.** 32 Bankton Pk, Kingskettle, Fife KY15 7PY *tel:* 01337 830974 *fax:* 01337 830653. *Br band, wind band mus; educ, ens mus (br, w/wind, str), choral.*

London Gabrieli Brass Edition. PO Box 1825, London N20 9NU *tel:* 0181 445 3016 *also fax. Rare, mainly 19th C br.*

London Pro Musica Edition. 15 Rock St, Brighton BN2 1NF *tel:* 01273 692974 *fax:* 01273 622792. *Medieval, renaissance and baroque mus.*

London Studio Exchange. The Studios, Rickmansworth, Herts WD3 2XD *tel:* 01923 772351 *fax:* 01923 774713. *Popular mus.*

Longship Music. Smidskot, Fawells, Keith Hall, Inverurie AB51 0LN *tel:* 01651 882274 *also fax. S/publishing company for John Hearne (see* **Composers***).*

* **Lopés Edition Ltd.** 363 Bideford Green, Leighton Buzzard, Beds LU7 7TX *tel:* 01525 371126. *Contemporary mus.*

Lorna Music Company. 127 Charing Cross Rd, London WC2H 0EA *tel:* 0171 434 2131. *Owned by EMI Music Publishing Ltd.*

Lovely Music. 17 Westgate, Tadcaster, N Yorks LS24 9JB *tel:* 01937 832946 *fax:* 01937 835696. *Educ mus and books. Agents for Holdstock & Mayflower publications.*

Lynwood Music. 2 Church St, West Hagley, W Midlands DY9 0NA *tel:* 01562 886625. *Mus of contemporary British and European composers.*

McCrimmon Publishing Co Ltd. 10-12 High St, Gt Wakering, Essex SS3 0EQ *tel:* 01702 218956 *fax:* 01702 216082. *Hymn books, psalm collections, mus for schools.*

McTier Music. 106 Hounslow Rd, Twickenham, Middx TW2 7HB *tel:* 0181 894 5381 *fax:* 0181 898 4591. *Db mus.*

* **Maecenas Europe.** 5 Bushey Close, Old Barn La, Kenley, Surrey CR8 5AU *tel:* 0181 660 3914 *fax:* 0181 668 5273. *Educ, solo, ens, choral, wind band, orch and pno, org, gui, jazz, jazz ens, str, wind, perc, vocal, choral.*

* **Maecenas Music Ltd.** 5 Bushey Close, Old Barn La, Kenley, Surrey CR8 5AU *tel:* 0181 660 3914 *fax:* 0181 668 5273. *Educ, classical, gui, keyboard, perc, wind, jazz, jazz, str, br, orch, wind band, br band, marching band, jazz ens, choral, vocal, textbooks.*

Mahayana Music. 91 Portland St, Southport, Merseyside PR8 6QZ *tel:* 01704 548737; 0121 555 5103 *fax:* 0121 331 5906 *email:* simon@mahayana.demon.co.uk. *Contemporary and educ. Specialists in young composers.*

Makepeace Music. 36 Kingsway, Coventry CV2 4FE *tel:* 01926 612540.

Mansel Thomas Trust. 15 Millfield Pk, Magor, Gwent NP6 3LF *tel:* 01633 880345. *Publishes the works of the late Mansel Thomas.*

* **Mansem Music.** 13 Bank Sq, Wilmslow, Cheshire SK9 1AN *tel:* 01625 527844 *fax:* 01625 536101 *email:* dimus@aol.com. *Recorded mus library.*

Mapa Mundi. 15 Marvig, Lochs, Isle of Lewis, Scotland HS2 9QP *tel:* 01851 880216 *also fax. Renaissance choral mus.*

Masterclass Music. 12 Kelso Pl, Dundee DD2 1SL *tel:* 01382 667251 *fax:* 01382 640775. *Educ mus for secondary schools.*

* **Mautoglade Music Ltd.** 22 Denmark St, London WC2H 8NA *tel:* 0171 836 5996 *fax:* 0171 379 5205.

* **MCA Music Ltd.** Unit 9, Elsinore House, 77 Fulham Palace Rd, London W6 8JA *tel:* 0181 741 8686 *fax:* 0181 741 8646. *Stage musicals and popular mus.*

Memory Lane Music Ltd. 22 Denmark St, London WC2H 8NA *tel:* 0171 240 5349 *fax:* 0171 379 5205.

Mercury Music Company. 127 Charing Cross Rd, London WC2H 0EA *tel:* 0171 434 2131. *Owned by EMI Music Publishing Ltd.*

* **Meriden Music.** Silverwood House, Woolaston, nr Lydney, Glos GL15 6PJ *tel:* 01594 529026 *fax:* 01594 529027. *S/publishing company for Graham Whettam (see* **Composers***).*

Merton Music. 8 Wilton Grove, London SW19 3QX *tel:* 0181 540 2708. *Str chmbr mus.*

Methodist Publishing House. 20 Ivatt Way, Peterborough PE3 7PG *tel:* 01733 332202 *fax:* 01733 331201. *Hymn books, choral mus, religious musical dramas.*

Mister D Music (Publications). 57 Landsdowne Rd, Bournemouth BH1 1RN *tel:* 01202 551440. *Solo, ens, str orch, school orch; also electric keyboard mus. S/publishing company for David Hellewell (see* **Composers***).*

Corby, Northants NN18 9ES. *20th C, choral, orch, educ, easy and tutorial, opera, inst, church, etc.*

* **Oxford University Press/New Music Promotion.** 70 Baker St, London W1M 1DJ *tel:* 0171 616 5900 *fax:* 0171 616 5901 *email:* repertoire. promotion@oup.co.uk. *Also Early Music journal and hymn copyright.*

Pan Educational Music. 40 Portland Rd, London W11 4LG *tel:* 0171 727 5965. *Specialists in wind mus.*

Panache Music Ltd. 2nd Floor, Twyman House, 31-39 Camden Rd, London NW1 9LF *tel:* 0171 267 6899 *fax:* 0171 267 6746.

Parkfield Music. 24 Lidsett Hill, Roundhay, Leeds LS8 1PE *tel:* 0113 293 7834. *Church, org, part songs.*

Pathway Music. 2a Grosvenor Av, London N5 2NR *tel:* 0171 359 0970 *fax:* 0171 226 8958. *Popular and jazz.*

* **Paul Rodriguez Music Ltd.** 61 Queen's Dr, London N4 2BG *tel:* 0181 802 5984 *fax:* 0181 809 7436 *email:* paul@paulrodriguezmus.demon.co.uk. *Classical, pop, jazz.*

Pendragon Press. Crag House, Witherslack, Grange-over-Sands, Cumbria LA11 6RW *tel:* 01539 552286 *fax:* 01539 552013 *email:* musicbks@ rdooley.demon.co.uk. *Facsimiles of 18th-19th C French operas.*

Perfect Songs Ltd. 42-46 St Luke's Mews, London W11 1DG *tel:* 0171 221 5101 *fax:* 0171 221 3374.

* **Peters Edition Ltd.** 10-24 Baches St, London N1 6DN *tel:* 0171 553 4000 *fax:* 0171 490 4921 *email:* info@edition-peters.com; http://www. edition-peters.com. *Classical.*

* **Phoenix Music.** Bryn Golau, Saron, Denbighshire LL16 4TH *tel:* 01745 550317 *fax:* 01745 550560 *email:* phoenixmus@aol.com. *Wind band, mainly educ, jazz band, variable ens including educ.*

Photoplay Music Ltd. 23 Bryanston Ct, George St, London W1H 7HA *tel:* 0171 402 4810 *fax:* 0171 262 4296. *Library mus.*

Phylloscopus Publications. 92 Aldcliffe Rd, Lancaster LA1 5BE *tel:* 01524 67498. *Chmbr mus for wind insts.*

Piccolo Press. 10 Clifton Terrace, Winchester, Hants SO22 5BJ *tel:* 01962 864755 *also fax;* 0171 724 3250. *Mainly mus for unusual ens and soloists. Also books on insts.*

Piers Press. Overthorpe Hall Lodge, Banbury, Oxon *tel:* 01295 257722 *fax:* 01295 263733. *Classical sheet mus.*

* **Pink Floyd Music Publishers Ltd.** 27 Noel St, London W1V 3RD *tel:* 0171 734 6892 *fax:* 0171 439 4613.

Piper Publications. Dochroyle Farm, Barrhill by Girvan, Ayrshire KA26 0QG *tel:* 01465 821377 *email:* piperpub@dircon.co.uk; http://www. users.dircon.co.uk/~piperpub. *Educ, vocal (including cantatas and musical plays), inst (solo and ens), orch; text books and mus linked project packs; Steelpan handbook; Piper New Classics.*

Portsmouth Publications. c/o Clifton Cathedral Music Dept, Clifton Cathedral House, Clifton Pk, Bristol BS7 9QR *tel:* 0117 946 7456 *fax:* 0117 973 8263. *Publishers of religious mus.*

* **Power Music Ltd (Arrensdorff Edition).** 1 Station Rd, Harecroft, Wilsden, Bradford BD15 0BS *tel:* 01535 272905 *fax:* 01535 270905 *email:* http://www.btinternet.com/~power.music. *Educ and w/wind mus specialists. Jazz, sax quartet, br quartet, fl/cl quartet, str quartet and ens series.*

Practical Music. 13 Salegate La, Temple Cowley, Oxford OX4 2HQ *tel:* 01865 770272 *also fax; email:* luke.steele@bigfoot.com. *S/publishing company for Janet Sherbourne, Jan Steele (see* **Composers***).*

Pressit Music. 12 Stanley Rd, Leicester LE2 1RE *tel:* 0116 270 3839.

Primavera. 110 Wyatt Park Rd, London SW2 3TP *tel:* 0181 674 1711. *Contemporary mus. Also solo, str, orch, choir, ABRSM pieces.*

Quavers Rest Music. 22 Stephen's Rd, Tunbridge Wells, Kent TN4 9JE *tel:* 01892 537764 *fax:* 01892 511352. *Pno, choral inst. S/publishing company for Michael Jacques (see* **Composers***).*

* **The Really Useful Group Ltd.** 22 Tower St, London WC2H 9NS *tel:* 0171 240 0880 *fax:* 0171 240 1204 *email:* reallyuseful.co.uk. *Musicals.*

Realspace Music. 83 Heslington Rd, York YO1 5AX *tel:* 01904 630143. *Inst, vocal, electro-acoustic, educ mus games, multi media participatory projects. S/publishing company for Trevor Wishart (see* **Composers***).*

Recital Music. Studio Ten, Farnham Maltings, Bridge Sq, Farnham, Surrey GU9 7QR *tel:* 01252 319610 *also fax. Specialist publications for db.*

Redcliffe Edition. 68 Barrowgate Rd, London W4 4QU *tel:* 0181 995 1223 *also fax. British composers.*

Redgold Music. 14 Clerkenwell Cl, EC1R 0DP *tel:* 0171 251 2100 *fax:* 0171 250 3009. *S/publishing company for Tony Haynes (see* **Composers***) and Grand Union.*

Revelo-Cornish Music. 35 Salisbury Rd, Harrow, Middx HA1 1NU *tel:* 0181 863 8275 *also fax. Elec, inst, educ. S/publishing company for Oliver Hunt (see* **Composers***).*

* **Ricordi & Co (London) Ltd.** Kiln House, 5th Floor, 210 New Kings Rd, London SW6 4NZ *tel:* 0171 371 7501 *fax:* 0171 371 7270 *email:* ricordi@bmg.co.uk. *Opera, ballet, inst, ens, br band, orch, vocal, choral, school mus.*

Roanna Music. 141 Manor Rd North, Thames Ditton, Surrey KT7 0BQ *tel:* 0181 224 6493. *Popular, easy listening.*

* **Roberton Publications.** The Windmill, Wendover, Aylesbury, Bucks HP22 6JJ *tel:* 01296 623107. *Standard classical, vocal, choral and inst mus.*

Rosehill Music Publishing Co Ltd. Harold Charles House, 64a London End, Beaconsfield, Bucks HP9 2JD *tel:* 01494 674411 *fax:* 01494 670932. *Br.*

Rosewood Music Publications. 61 Oak Hill, Surbiton, Surrey KT6 6DY *tel:* 0181 390 3236 *email:* michael@bryant14.demon.co.uk. *Previously un-published or rare chmbr mus for wind and pno, wind, strs and pno, wind and str and wind alone.*

Routledge Ltd. 11 New Fetter La, London EC4P 4EE *tel:* 0171 583 9855 *fax:* 0171 842 2298. *Authorship and copyright, history of mus and of British Publishing, rock and popular mus, world mus, mus therapy.*

* **Royal School of Church Music.** Publications Dept, Cleveland Lodge, Westhumble St, Westhumble, Dorking RH5 6BW *tel:* 01306 877676 *fax:* 01306 887240. *Choral mus, plus reference material for the church musician.*

RTS Music Partnership. 17 Bradford Rd, St Johns, Wakefield, W Yorkshire WF1 2RF *tel:* 01924 370454 *also fax. British composers, educ, light, publishers for Patric Standford.*

St Gregory Publishing Co. 64 Pineheath Rd, High Kelling, Holt, Norfolk NR25 6RH *tel:* 01263 712288. *Church, org, vocal, educ mus.*

Salvationist Publishing & Supplies Ltd. 117-121 Judd St, London WC1H 9NN *tel:* 0171 387 1656 *fax:* 0171 383 3420. *Religious vocal for children and adults, br band mus.*

Salvi Publications. 58 Hopton St, London SE1 9JH *tel:* 0171 928 8451 *fax:* 0171 928 8284. *Hp mus only.*

Samuel French Ltd. 52 Fitzroy St, London W1P 6JR *tel:* 0171 387 9373 *fax:* 0171 387 2161 *email:* http://www.samuelfrench.btinternet.com. *Musical plays and school mus.*

* **Samuel King Music Publishers.** PO Box 17, Cardigan, Ceredigion SA43 1HZ *tel:* 01239 621292 *also fax. W/wind, br, wind band, choral and vocal, str orch. Cat and demo tapes available.*

Satanic Mills Press. 4 Church St, Golcar, Huddersfield HD7 4AH *tel:* 01484 652762 *fax:* 01484 472656 *email:* m.l.wilkins@hud.ac.uk. *S/publishing company for Margaret Lucy Wilkins (see* **Composers***). Orch, chmbr, solo, inst, vocal, choral.*

Saxtet Publications. 15 Paignton Rd, Edgbaston, Birmingham B16 0JX *tel:* 0121 565 5484 *also fax. Sax, cl, fl mus.*

Sceptre Publishers. 97 Elton Rd, Stibbington, Peterborough PE8 6JX *tel:* 01780 782093 *fax:* 01780 783159. *Solo, elec org.*

* **Schauer & May Ltd.** Simrock House, 220 The Vale, London NW11 8HZ *tel:* 0181 731 6665 *fax:* 0181 731 6667. *Classical and educ mus.*

* **Schirmer (G) Ltd.** 8-9 Frith St, London W1V 5TZ *tel:* 0171 434 0066 *fax:* 0171 287 6329.

* **Schott & Co Ltd.** Marketing and Sales Dept, Brunswick Rd, Ashford, Kent TN23 1EH *tel:* 01233 628987 *fax:* 01233 610232 *email:* http://www. schott-music.com. *Solo, ens, wind band, str orch, school orch, choir; also rcdr, Orff-Schulwerk; contemporary.*

Sea Dream Music. PO Box 13533, London E7 0SG *tel:* 0181 534 8500. *Legal texts on mus, christian songs.*

* **SGO Music Publishing Ltd.** The Old Brewery, Church St, Tisbury, Wilts SP3 6NH *tel:* 01747 871653 *fax:* 01747 871654 *email:* 100605.473@ compuserve.com. *Complete spectrum of popular mus.*

Shaftesbury Edition. 16 Mitcham Rd, Dymchurch, Kent TN29 0TH *tel:* 01303 874449. *S/publishing company for Peter Aviss (see* **Composers***).*

* **SJ Music.** 23 Leys Rd, Cambridge CB4 2AP *tel:* 01223 314771 *fax:* 01223 560353. *Str and chmbr mus.*

Snell & Sons. 68 West Cross La, West Cross, Swansea SA3 5LU *tel:* 01792 405727. *Welsh mus.*

Soar Valley Music. 15 Prince William Rd, Loughborough, Leics LE11 6GU *tel:* 01509 269629 *fax:* 01509 269206. *Folk mus, educ mus.*

Sontel Music Ltd. Suite 7, 60 Gt Russell St, London WC1B 3BE *tel:* 0171 242 8525.

Spanish Guitar Centre. 44 Nottingham Rd, New Basford, Nottingham NG7 7AE *tel:* 0115 962 2709 *fax:* 0115 962 5368 *email:* spanish_guitar @compuserve.com. *Specialist classical gui mus.*

The Sparta Florida Music Group. 8-9 Frith St, London W1V 5TZ *tel:* 0171 434 0066; 0171 432 4240 *fax:* 0171 439 2848. *Film, TV and theatre scores and popular songs.*

* **Spartan Press Music Publishers Ltd.** Old Brewery House, Redbrook, Monmouth NP5 4LU *tel:* 01600 712482 *fax:* 01600 712483 *email:* spartanpress@compuserve.com. *Solo, duets, flexible ens, str orch, br ens, pno, group teaching.*

Sphemusations. 12 Northfield Rd, Onehouse, Stowmarket, Suffolk IP14 3HF *tel:* 01449 613388. *Contemporary mus including choral, orch and chmbr mus.*

Spin Publications. 24 Beresford Rd, Wallasey, Merseyside L45 0JJ *tel:* 0151 639 3559.

Springpark Music. 10 Princess Mews, London NW3 5AP *tel:* 0171 431 1771 *fax:* 0171 431 8422.

Springthyme Music. Balmalcolm House, Kingskettle, Fife KY15 7TJ *tel:* 01337 830773 *fax:* 01337 831773 *email:* springthyme@zetnet. co.uk; http://www.springthyme.co.uk. *Folk and traditional mus.*

* **Stainer & Bell Ltd.** PO Box 110, Victoria House, 23 Gruneisen Rd, London N3 1DZ *tel:* 0181 343 3303 *fax:* 0181 343 3024 *email:* post@stainer. demon.co.uk; http://www.stainer.demon.co.uk. *Solo, ens, wind band, str orch, school orch, choral.*

Stanley Thornes (Publishers) Ltd. Ellenborough House, Wellington St, Cheltenham, Glos GL50 1YW *tel:* 01242 228888 *fax:* 01242 221914 *email:* cservice@thornes.co.uk. *Sounds of Music, Silver Burdett mus, Blueprints Music. Curriculum mus materials. Also Music File providing annual subs service for secondary school teachers.*

Stanza Music. 11 Victor Rd, Harrow, Middx HA2 6PT *tel:* 0181 863 2717 *fax:* 0181 863 8685. *Big band and small jazz ens; also standard-type songs. Full cat available on request.*

* **State Music Ltd.** 20 Watford Rd, Radlett, Herts WD7 8LE *tel:* 01923 857792 *fax:* 01923 858052.

Studio G. Ridgway House, Gt Brington, Northampton NN7 4JA *tel:* 01604 770511 *fax:* 01604 770022. *Library mus.*

* **Studio Music Co.** 77-79 Dudden Hill La, London NW10 1BD *tel:* 0181 459 6194; 0181 830 0110 (sales) *fax:* 0181 451 6470. *General educ (inst and vocal); br, wind, jazz band mus, orch.*

Sun Pacific Music (London) Ltd. PO Box 5, Hastings, E Sussex TN34 1HR *tel:* 01424 721196 *fax:* 01424 717704. *Stage and film musicals.*

Sutton Elms Publications. 56 Arbor Rd, Croft, Leics LE9 3GD *tel:* 01455 284096. *Mus of Nigel Deacon.*

Sweet and Maxwell Ltd. Customer Services, c/o ITPS, Cheriton House, North Way, Andover, Hants SP10 5BE *tel:* 01264 332424. *Copyright, EC Directive on rental and lending rights and on piracy, entertainment law, legal books on mus and video private copying.*

* **Sweet 'n' Sour Songs Ltd.** 2-3 Fitzroy Mews, London W1P 5DQ *tel:* 0171 383 7767 *fax:* 0171 383 3020. *Musicals, pop.*

Take Note Publishing Ltd. 54 Lincolns Mead, Lingfield, Surrey RH7 6TA *tel:* 01342 836689 *also fax. Mus for w/wind, strs, gui, pno and keyboard.*

Tecla Editions. PO Box 7567, London NW3 2LJ *tel:* 0171 435 5077 *also fax; email:* tecla@tecla.com; http://www.users.dircon.co.uk/~tecla/index.htm. *Solo.*

* **Television Music Ltd.** Television Centre, Kirkstall Rd, Leeds LS3 1JS *tel:* 0113 243 8283 *fax:* 0113 244 5107.

Thames Publishing. 14 Barlby Rd, London W10 6AR *tel:* 0181 969 3579 *fax:* 0181 969 1465. *Serious solo vocal, choral and inst.*

Tinderbox Music. 93 Stradella Rd, London SE24 9HL *tel:* 0171 274 5314. *Resource material for specialist and non-specialist teachers; primary, song books, rcdr.*

Tobin Music/Helicon Press. The Old Malthouse, Knight St, Sawbridgeworth, Herts CM21 9AX *tel:* 01279 726625. *Educ.*

Tomus Publications. 17 Kensington Rd, Earlsdon, Coventry CV5 6GG *tel:* 01203 670211 *also fax. Rcdr and wind mus.*

Tristan Music Ltd. 22 Denmark St, London WC2H 8NA *tel:* 0171 836 5996 *fax:* 0171 379 5205.

Tyne Music. 38 Westmorland Rd, Newcastle-upon-Tyne NE1 4EN *tel:* 0191 232 2479 *fax:* 0191 232 2479. *Br band, choir, musical plays (8-15 yrs), br, w/wind, ens; also modern original musicals for adults and new Christmas songs.*

* **United Music Publishers Ltd (UMP).** 42 Rivington St, London EC2A 3BN *tel:* 0171 729 4700 *fax:* 0171 739 6549 *email:* ump@compuserve. com; http://ourworld.compuserve.com/homepages/ump. *Classical mus.*

* **Universal Edition (London) Ltd/Alfred Kamus Ltd.** London W1V 2BN, 48 Gt Marlborough St *tel:* 0800 525566 *fax:* 0800 525567. Also at: 38 Eldon Way, Kent TN12 6BE *tel:* 01892 833422 *fax:* 01892 836038.

Useful Music. Old Brewery House, Redbrook, Monmouth NP5 4LU *tel:* 01600 712482 *fax:* 01600 712483 *email:* spartanpress@ compuserve.com. *Distributed by Spartan Press.*

Utopia Music Ltd. 7 Chalcot Rd, London NW1 8LH *tel:* 0171 586 3434 *fax:* 0171 586 3438. *Pop, folk, jazz.*

* **Valentine Music Group Ltd.** 7 Garrick St, London WC2E 9AR *tel:* 0171 240 1628 *fax:* 0171 497 9242. *MOR and country mus.*

* **Valley Music Ltd.** Elsinore House, 77 Fulham Palace Rd, London W6 8JA *tel:* 0181 741 8686 *fax:* 0181 741 8646. *Popular mus.*

* **Vanderbeek & Imrie Ltd.** 15 Marvig, Lochs, Isle of Lewis HS2 9QP *tel:* 01851 880216 *also fax. Renaissance choral mus and 20th C mus.*

Viking Publications (Whittaker Centenary Fund). 15 Watcombe Cottages, Kew Green, Richmond, Surrey TW9 3BD *tel:* 0181 948 8132. *Mus by WG Whittaker (1876-1944).*

Virgo Music Publishers. PO Box 1068, Knowle, Solihull, W Midlands B94 6DT *tel:* 0121 778 5569 *fax:* 0121 778 5569. *Specialists in br, sax, easy jazz and educ mus.*

Visible Music. c/o Studio Music Company, 77-79 Dudden Hill La, London NW10 1BD *tel:* 0181 830 0110 *fax:* 0181 451 6470. *S/publishing company for Jean Hasse (see* **Composers***).*

W W Norton & Co Ltd. 10 Coptic St, London WC1A 1PU *tel:* 0171 323 1579 *fax:* 0171 436 4553. *Norton Critical Scores; Norton Introduction to Music History; Norton History of Music, musicology titles and Grout: A History of Western Music.*

* **Warner Chappell Music Ltd.** 129 Park St, London W1Y 3FA *tel:* 0171 514 5200 *fax:* 0171 514 5201. *Popular, standard and show mus.*

Warwick Music. Holloway House, The Market Place, Warwick CV34 4SJ *tel:* 01926 497887 *fax:* 01926 419701 *email:* warwick_music @compuserve.com; http://ourworld.compuserve.com/homepages/ warwick_music/. *Specialists in trb, tpt and br mus.*

Waterloo Music (UK). c/o Margaret Brace Copyright Bureau, Independent House, 54 Larkshall Rd, Chingford, London E4 6AD *tel:* 0181 523 9000 *fax:* 0181 523 8888.

Welsh Music Information Centre. c/o ASSL, Cardiff University, Cardiff CF1 1XL. *Mus by Welsh composers (in limited editions) otherwise unavailable.*

Westfield Music. Malt Shovel Cottage, 76 Walkergate, Beverley, Humberside HU17 9ER *tel:* 01482 860580 *email:* ahedges@westfield music.karoo.co.uk; http://www.karoo.net/westfieldmusic/hedges.htm. *S/publishing company for Anthony Hedges (see* **Composers***).*

* **William Elkin Music Services.** Station Rd Industrial Estate, Salhouse, Norwich NR13 6NY *tel:* 01603 721302 *fax:* 01603 721801. *Distributors.*

* **Wilson Editions.** 13 Bank Sq, Wilmslow, Cheshire SK9 1AN *tel:* 01625 527844 *fax:* 01625 536101 *email:* dimus@aol.com. *Classical, jazz, MOR.*

Wind Mail Associates. The South Wing, Lullingstone Castle, Eynsford, Kent DA4 0JA *tel:* 01322 862455 *fax:* 01322 866154. *Distributors and m/order company. Publishers of The Wind Band Cat and The Jazz and Stage Band Cat.*

Woodwind Plus. 42 St Mary's Pk, Louth, Lincs LN11 0EF. *Publishers of specialist mus mainly for w/wind.*

Woza Music. 8 Pendlebury House, Master Gunner Pl, London SE18 4NQ *tel:* 0181 856 9923 *fax:* 0181 318 7417. *S/publishing company for Stanley Glasser (see* **Composers***).*

Wright Greaves. 11 Goose Green, Altrincham, Cheshire WA14 1DW *tel:* 0161 929 6949 *fax:* 0161 926 8280. *Sheet mus; m/order service available.*

Wright & Round Ltd. The Cornet Office, PO Box 157, Gloucester GL1 1LW *tel:* 01452 523438 *fax:* 01452 385631. *Br band, solo, ens.*

* **Yorke Edition.** 31 Thornhill Sq, London N1 1BQ *tel:* 0171 607 0849 *fax:* 0171 700 4577. *Db.*

Orchestral Hire Libraries

Listed below are the main commercial libraries that deal in the hire of orchestral scores and parts. The works of most well known composers are available from nearly all the libraries, and the information after each entry indicates the specific composers and editions which are only available from that library. Some orchestral sets of works that are no longer in copyright may be available from larger music libraries.

Alfred A Kalmus Ltd Hire Library *see* **Music Distribution Services Hire Library.**

Banks Music Publications Hire Library. The Old Forge, Sand Hutton, York YO4 1LB *tel:* 01904 468472 *fax:* 01904 468679. Rosemary Goodwin, editorial asst; Margaret Silver, accounts clerk. *Mus of James Brown, Gerald Finzi, Francis Jackson, Philip Marshall.*

Bardic Edition. 6 Fairfax Cres, Aylesbury, Bucks HP20 2ES *tel:* 01296 28609 *also fax; email:* 101464.2670@compuserve.com. *Mus of Percy Grainger, Christopher Headington, John Pickard.*

Baroque Publications Ltd Hire Library. Treadam Farm, Llantilio-Crossenny, Abergavenny, Gwent NP7 8TA *tel:* 01600 780233. Sally Farncombe, hire library mgr. *Mainly mus of Handel (orch parts and vocal scores of operas, separate arias available). Reduced orchestration (10 insts) of some Mozart operas.*

Boosey & Hawkes Music Publishers Ltd Hire Library. 295 Regent St, London W1R 8JH *tel:* 0171 580 2060 *fax:* 0171 580 5815. Bruce MacRae, hire library mgr; Adam Harvey, office admin. *Mus of: Adams (since 1986), Andriessen, Bartók (some), Bernstein, Blacher, Britten (until 1963), Birtwistle (since 1994), Carter (since 1981), Copland, Delius (some), Druckman, Einem, Finzi, Firsova, Floyd, Gerhard (until 1960), Ginastera, Glanert, Goldschmidt, Górecki, Gubaidulina, Gruber, Holloway, Höller (since 1983), Jenkins, Kodály (some), Kurtág, Lindberg (since 1996), MacMillan, Martinu (some), Maxwell Davies (some), Panufnik, Prokofieff, Rachmaninoff (until 1917), Rautavaara, Reich, Rouse, Schnittke, Schwertsik, Shostakovich, Strauss, Stravinsky, Torke, Xenakis (until 1969), Yun. Editions: Bote & Bock/Berlin, Carisch/Milan, Carl Fischer/USA, Dilia/Czech Republic, EMB/Budapest, Gehrmans Musikforlag/Sweden, Margun Music/USA, Moscow State Edition, Roberto Barry/South America, Warner Chappell/Scandinavia, Zen-on Music/Japan.*

Chandos Music Ltd. Chandos House, Commerce Way, Colchester, Essex CO2 8HQ *tel:* 01206 225200 *fax:* 01206 225201.

Chester Music Ltd Hire Library (division of Music Sales Limited). Newmarket Rd, Bury St Edmunds, Suffolk IP33 3YB *tel:* 01284 705705 *fax:* 01284 703401. Paul Narey, hire library mgr; Peter Whitlock, hire librarian. *Editions: Associated Music Publishers, Chester Music, J Curwen & Sons Ltd, Dunvagen, Edwin Ashdown Ltd, Fazer, A Lengnick & Co, MCA, Nordiska, Norsk Musikforlag As, Really Useful Group plc, Ricordi, G Schirmer Inc, G Schirmer (Australia) Pty Ltd, Union Musical Ediciones, Wilhelm Hansen Edition, Zanibon.*

Concord Music Hire Library. 5 Bushey Close, Old Barn La, Kenley, Surrey CR8 5AU *tel:* 0181 660 4766 *fax:* 0181 668 5273. Ray Lee, hire library mgr. *Mus of Judith Bingham, Martin Ellerby, Philip Grange, Piers Hellawell, Daniel Jones, Clark McAlister, Geoffrey Poole, Matthew Taylor, Gareth Wood. Editions: Maecenas Music, Maecenas Contemporary Composers Ltd, Warner Chappell Music Hire Library.*

Faber Music Hire Library. 3 Queen Sq, London WC1N 3AU *tel:* 0171 833 7907 *fax:* 0171 837 8668. Chris Norris, performance and hire library mgr; Hannah Luxton, asst hire librarian. *Mus of T Adès, J Anderson, M Arnold (some), G Benjamin, H Blake, Britten (some), M Daugherty, C Davis, J Harvey (late works), O Knussen, C Matthews, D Matthews (some), N Maw (late works), D Muldowney (some), P Sculthorpe, R Smalley, J Woolrich. Editions: Alkor, Bärenreiter, Highbridge Music, Peer Southern, Threefold Music.*

Fentone Music Ltd Hire Library. Fleming Rd, Earlstrees, Corby, Northants NN17 4SN *tel:* 01536 260981 *fax:* 01536 401075. Mark Coull, hire library mgr. *Editions: Berben, London Orchestral Series, Norsk Musikforlag, Real Musical, XYZ International.*

Josef Weinberger Ltd Hire Library. 12-14 Mortimer St, London W1N 7RD *tel:* 0171 927 7312 *fax:* 0171 436 9616. Christopher Moss, hire library mgr; Timothy Seddon, ed. *Mus of Emmérich Eálmán, Wilfred Josephs (some), Paul Patterson (some), Morris Pert (some), André Tchaikovsky, Ernst Von Dohnanyi (some), Malcolm Williamson (some), Ermanno Wolf-Ferrari (some).*

Music Distribution Services Hire Library. 38 Eldon Way, Paddock Wood, Kent TN12 6BE *tel:* 01892 838083 *fax:* 01892 836038 *email:* rod.taylor@schott-ue-hire.demon.co.uk. Rod Taylor, hire library mgr; Nicky Adamson, Jonathan Penny, hire assts. *Mus of Birtwistle, Bryars, Casken, Goehr, Henze, Holt, Ligeti, Orff, Roxanna Panufnik, Takemitsu, Tippett, Turnage. Editions: Boelke Bomart, Breitkopf & Härtel, Czech Music Fund, European American Music/Helicon Inc, Israel Music Institute, PWM, Schott/London/Mainz/Japan, Theodore Presser, Universal Edition/London/Vienna).*

Novello Co Ltd Hire Library (division of Music Sales Ltd). Newmarket Rd, Bury St Edmunds, Suffolk IP33 3YB *tel:* 01284 705705 *fax:* 01284 703401. Paul Narey, hire library mgr; Leslie Dimsdale, hire librarian; Brenda Fiske, hire librarian. *Mus of Malcolm Arnold (some), Arthur Bliss, Richard Rodney Bennett, Herbert Howells, Tristan Keuris, John McCabe, Thea Musgrave, Stephen Oliver, Aulis Sallinen, Giles Swayne, Judith Weir (some). Editions: Arnold, Belwin Mills, Donemus, Elkin, EMI, Goodwin & Tabb, Paterson, Paxton.*

Oxford University Press Hire Library. Gt Clarendon St, Oxford OX2 6DP *tel:* 01865 267699 *fax:* 01865 267767 *email:* music.hire@oup.co.uk. Simon Wright, hire library mgr; Angharad Evans, hire library asst; Cheryl Hitchman, accounts clerk. *Mus of Eleanor Alberga, Gerald Barry, Michael Berkeley, John Buller, Martin Butler, Bob Chilcott, Gordon Crosse, Michael Finnissy (from 1988), Edward Harper, William Mathias, Anthony Powers, John Rutter, Robert Sherlaw Johnson, Howard Skempton, Ralph Vaughan Williams (from 1926), William Walton.*

Peters Edition Ltd Hire Library. 10-12 Baches St, London N1 6DN *tel:* 0171 553 4020 *fax:* 0171 490 4921 *email:* peters_edition@compuserve.com. Fiona Flower, dir, hire and copyright; Stephen Murphy, hire library mgr; Helen Dunne, hire library asst. *Mus of John Cage, George Crumb, James Dillon, Morton Feldman (some), Brian Ferneyhough, Alan Hovhaness, Mauricio Kagel, György Ligeti (some), Roger Reynolds, Erkki-Sven Tüür. Editions: M P Belaieff, Edition Kunzelmann, Edition Schwann, Heinrichshofen, Henry Litolff, Hinrichsen Edition, C F Kahnt, F E C Leuckart, Robert Lienau, Lyche, C F Peters/London/New York/Frankfurt/Leipzig, Tischer & Jagenberg, Christian Vieweg, Zimmermann.*

Queensgate Music Hire Library. 120 Dowanhill St, Glasgow G12 9DN *tel:* 0141 339 1699 *also fax. Mus of Thomas Wilson only.*

Richard Schauer Hire Library. Simrock House, 220 The Vale, London NW11 8HZ *tel:* 0181 731 6665 *fax:* 0181 731 6667. T R Gill, hire library mgr; Irene Retford, mgr dir. *Editions: Anton J Benjamin, Bartolf Senff, Brockhaus/Germany, Musicus/USA, McNaughtan (David)/Germany, Mannheimer Musikverlag/Germany, D Rahter, Reift (Mark) Editions/Switzerland, N Simrock, Wrede (Otto)/Germany.*

Schott & Co Ltd Hire Library *see* **Music Distribution Services Hire Library.**

Stainer & Bell Ltd Hire Library. PO Box 110, Victoria House, Gruneisen Rd, London N3 1DZ *tel:* 0181 343 3303 *fax:* 0181 343 3024 *email:* post@stainer.demon.co.uk; http://www.stainer.demon.co.uk. Erica Jeal, hire library mgr. *Agents for UK and rest of Europe for the hire library of ECS Publishing, Boston, USA.*

United Music Publishers Ltd Hire Library. 42 Rivington St, London EC2A 3BN *tel:* 0171 729 4700 *fax:* 0171 739 6549 *email:* ump@compuserve.com; http://ourworld.compuserve.com/homepages/ump. Helen Wood, hire library mgr; Shirley Ranger, accounts mgr. *Mus of Simon Bainbridge (some), Richard Barrett, Havergal Brian, Diana Burrell (some), Chris Dench (some), Stephen Montague (some), Edwin Roxburgh (some). Editions (all France unless otherwise stated): Amphion, Billaudot, Bornemann, Carus-Verlag/Germany, Chant du Monde, Chantraine (Belgium), Choudens, Combre, Costallat, Dominis (Canada), Durand, EFM, Elkan-Vogel/USA, Enoch, Eschig, Hamelle, Henn/Switzerland, Heugel, Jobert, Leduc, Lemoine, Marais, R Martin, Ouvrières, Rideau-Rouge, Salabert, Schola Cantorum, SEDIM, Transatlantiques, UMP/UK, Wiscasset/USA, Zurfluh.*

Warner Chappell Music Ltd Hire Library. 5 Bushey Close, Old Barn La, Kenley, Surrey CR8 5AU *tel:* 0171 660 4766 *fax:* 0171 668 5273. Ray Lee, librarian. Administered by the Concord Music Hire Library. *Editions: Asherberg Hopwood and Crew, Chappell, Warner Brothers. Mus of Arnold Bax, Eric Coates and George Gershwin.*

William Elkin Music Services Hire Library. Station Rd Industrial Estate, Salhouse, Norwich NR13 6NY *tel:* 01603 721302 *fax:* 01603 721801. Cindy Hazard, hire library mgr; N Everett, accounts clerk. *Editions: Braydeston Press, Curwen, Hofmeister, Lawson-Gould, Sikorski.*

Copyright

Listed below are the main organisation concerned with musical copyright in the UK. The Copyright Laws are extremely complex and details should be checked carefully with the institution concerned.

British Academy of Songwriters, Composers & Authors. 34 Hanway St, London W1P 9DE *tel:* 0171 629 0992 *fax:* 0171 629 0993. *Represents the copyright interests of its songwriter members within the mus industry.*

Butterworths. Halsbury House, 35 Chancery La, London WC2A 1EL *tel:* 0171 400 2500 *fax:* 0171 400 2842. *Legal texts, copyright.*

Christian Copyright Licensing (Europe) Ltd. PO Box 1339, Eastbourne, E Sussex BN21 4YF *tel:* 01323 417711 *fax:* 01323 417722 *email:* info@ ccli.co.uk. *CCL issue and administrate the Church Copyright Licence. Formerly under the Christian Music Association, the licence allows reproduction of the words of copyright songs and hymns to schools, churches and Christian organisations. Also, by exclusive arrangement with MCPS, video and audio cassette recordings, including the Private Function Filming license and 'dubbings' licenses.*

International Federation of the Phonographic Industry. IFPI Secretariat, 54 Regent St, London W1R 5PJ *tel:* 0171 878 7900 *fax:* 0171 878 7950. *Promotes and defends the copyright interests of its members in sound recordings and music videos.*

Leosong Copyright Service Ltd. Greenland Pl, 115-123 Bayham St, Camden Town, London NW1 0AG *tel:* 0171 446 7400 *fax:* 0171 446 7410. *Leosong administers the rights of mus publishers and writers who form their own companies. The service includes songwriters' agreements, registering the copyrights with societies all over the world and preparing writers' royalties on behalf of publishing companies.*

Margaret Brace Copyright Bureau Ltd *see* **Leosong Copyright Service Ltd.**

Mechanical-Copyright Protection Society Ltd (MCPS). Elgar House, 41 Streatham High Rd, London SW16 1ER *tel:* 0181 664 4400 *fax:* 0181 769 8792 *email:* webmaster@mcps.co.uk; http://www.mcps.co.uk. *MCPS is an organisation of mus publishers and composers, which collects and distributes mechanical royalties due from the recording of their copyright musical works.*

Music and Copyright. FT Telecoms and Media Publishing, Maple House, 149 Tottenham Court Rd, London W1P 9LL *tel:* 0171 896 2237 *fax:* 0171 896 2256 *email:* claired@pearson-pro.com. *Annual subscription £595 (US$952) for 24 issues. Information on legislation, corporate analysis, industry news, contracts, piracy, national trends, market structures and technical developments.*

Music Publishers' Association Ltd. 3rd Floor, Strandgate, 18-20 York Buildings, London WC2N 6JU *tel:* 0171 839 7779 *fax:* 0171 839 7776 *email:* mpa@mcps.co.uk. *Represents mus publishers in the UK. Advises and assists members in the promotion and protection of mus copyright.*

Performing Right Society. 29-33 Berners St, London W1P 4AA *tel:* 0171 580 5544 *fax:* 0171 306 4050 *email:* http://prs.co.uk. John Hutchinson, chief exec. *Protects, promotes and administers the public performance and broadcasting rights of composers, songwriters and mus publishers.*

Phonographic Performance Ltd (PPL). Ganton House, 14-22 Ganton St, London W1V 1LB *tel:* 0171 437 0311 *fax:* 0171 734 2986. Colleen Hue, head of external affairs. *Collecting society licensing the broadcast and performance of sound recordings in the UK on behalf of record companies and performers.*

Sweet & Maxwell Ltd. Customer Services, Sweet and Maxwell Ltd, 100 Avenue Rd, Swiss Cottage, London NW3 3HF (from Jan 1998) *tel:* 0171 393 7000. *Copyright, EC directive on rental and lending rights and on piracy, entertainment law, legal books on mus and video private copying.*

Music Journalism

Newspapers

The following list of major newspapers all carry regular coverage of classical music. The editor, the chief music critics and additional music and arts critics are listed below.

The Birmingham Post. 28 Colmore Circus, Queensway, Birmingham B4 6AX *tel:* 0121 236 3366 *fax:* 0121 233 0271. Nigel Hastilow, ed; Terry Grimley, arts ed; Christopher Morley, chief mus critic. Stephen Daw, David Hart, David Williams, Clare Mackney, John Bradshaw, mus critics.

The Daily Telegraph. 1 Canada Sq, Canary Wharf, London E14 5DT *tel:* 0171 538 5000 *fax:* 0171 538 7650. Charles Moore, ed; Geoffrey Norris, chief mus critic; Sarah Crompton, arts ed. Norman Lebrecht, mus correspondent; Rupert Christiansen, opera critic.

The European (52). The European, 200 Gray's Inn Rd, London WC1X 8NE *tel:* 0171 418 7777 *fax:* 0171 713 1840. Andrew Neil, ed; Anna Pimms, arts ed. *75p.*

Evening Express (Mon-Sat). PO Box 43, Lang Stracht, Mastrick, Aberdeen AB15 6DF *tel:* 01224 690222 *fax:* 01224 699575 *email:* editor@ee.ajl. co.uk. Geoff Teather, ed; Raymond Anderson, features ed. *25p.*

The Evening Standard. Northcliffe House, 2 Derry St, Kensington, London W8 5EE *tel:* 0171 938 6000 *fax:* 0171 937 2648. Max Hastings, ed; Michael Owen, arts ed.

The Financial Times. 1 Southwark Bridge, London SE1 9HL *tel:* 0171 873 3000 *fax:* 0171 407 5700. Richard Lambert, ed; Max Loppert, mus and opera critic; Richard Fairman, mus critic; Annalena McAfee, arts ed. *70p. Arts section daily plus in the Weekend FT.*

The Guardian. 119 Farringdon Rd, London EC1R 3ER *tel:* 0171 278 2332 *fax:* 0171 837 2114. Alan Rusbridger, ed; Claire Armitstead, arts ed; Andrew Clements, chief mus and opera critic. Adrian Searle, art critic; Dan Glaister, arts correspondent.

The Herald (Mon-Sat). 195 Albion St, Glasgow G1 1QP *tel:* 0141 552 6255 *fax:* 0141 552 2288. Harry Reid, ed; Michael Tumelty, chief mus critic. *45p.*

The Independent. Newspaper Publishing plc, 1 Canada Sq, Canary Wharf, London E14 5DL *tel:* 0171 293 2000 *fax:* 0171 293 2182. Andrew Marr, ed; Mark Pappenheim, arts ed; Bayan Northcott, chief mus writer.

Edward Seckerson, chief opera critic. The Independent on Sunday: Michael White, chief mus critic.

The News (Mon-Sat). The News Centre, Hilsea, Portsmouth, Hants PO2 9SX *tel:* 01705 664488 *fax:* 01705 673363 *email:* http://www.thenews. co.uk. Geoff Elliott, ed; Mike Allen, mus critic. *28p.*

The Observer (Sun). 119 Farringdon Rd, London EC1R 3ER *tel:* 0171 278 2332 *fax:* 0171 713 4225. Will Hutton, ed; Andrew Porter, mus critic; Jane Ferguson, arts ed.

The Scotsman. 20 Northbridge, Edinburgh EH1 1YT *tel:* 0131 225 2468 *fax:* 0131 226 7420. Martin Clarke, ed; Jane Johnson, assistant ed (features); Mary Miller, mus critic. Barry Didcock, rock and pop critic. *42p.*

The Sunday Telegraph. 1 Canada Sq, Canary Wharf, London E14 5DT *tel:* 0171 538 5000 *fax:* 0171 538 6242. Dominic Lawson, ed; John Preston, arts ed; Michael Kennedy, opera critic.

The Sunday Times. 1 Pennington St, London E1 9XW *tel:* 0171 481 4100 *fax:* 0171 782 5776. John Witherow, ed; Hugh Canning, Paul Driver, mus critics; Helen Hawkins, arts ed.

The Times. 1 Pennington St, London E1 9XW *tel:* 0171 782 5000 *fax:* 0171 782 5748. Richard Morrison, arts ed; Rodney Milnes, chief opera critic; Barry Millington, Hilary Finch, John Allison, Gerald Larner, mus critics.

The Times Educational Supplement. Admiral House, 66-68 East Smithfield, London E1 9XY *tel:* 0171 782 3000 *fax:* 0171 782 3200. Caroline St John-Brooks, ed; Heather Neill, arts and literature ed; Philippa Davidson, chief mus critic. *£1.*

Yorkshire Evening Press (Mon-Sat). PO Box 29, 76-86 Walmgate, York YO1 1YN *tel:* 01904 653051 *fax:* 01904 612853. Liz Page, ed; Charles Hutchinson, mus ed. *30p. Evening paper serving York and North Yorkshire.*

Yorkshire Post. Yorkshire Post Newspapers Ltd, Wellington St, Leeds LS1 1RF *tel:* 0113 243 2701 *fax:* 0113 238 8537. Tony Watson, ed.

Music Periodicals

Periodicals devoted to classical music or of specific music interest are listed alphabetically, followed by the number of issues per annum and the name of the editor.

ABO News (12). Francis House, Francis St, London SW1P 1DE *tel:* 0171 828 6913 *fax:* 0171 931 9959 *email:* abo@orchestranet.co.uk. Sarah Gee, ed. *Issued free to Association of British Orchestras members.*

Acoustic Guitar (6). Ashley Mark Publishing, 43 Sackville Rd, Newcastle NE6 5TA *tel:* 0191 276 0448. Jeffrey Pepper Rodgers, ed. *£2.95.*

BBC Music Magazine (12). Room A1004, Woodlands, 80 Wood La, London W12 0TT *tel:* 0181 576 3283 (ed); 0181 576 2022 (ad) *fax:* 0181 576 3292. Graeme Kay, ed. *£3.75; subs £45.00 pa (UK).*

Braille Music Magazine (12). Royal National Institute for the Blind, 224 Gt Portland St, London W1N 6AA *tel:* 0171 388 1266 ext 2318 *fax:* 0171 388 2034 *email:* rfirman@rnib.org.uk. Roger Firman, ed.

Brass Band World (10). Caron Publications, Peak Press Building, Eccles Rd, Chapel-en-le-Frith, High Peak SK23 9RQ *tel:* 01298 812816 *fax:* 01298 815220 *email:* info@bbworld.u-net.com; http://www.brass bandworld.com. Robert Mulholland, ed; Debbie Herbert, ad mgr; Gillian Smith, head of subs. *£2.95; £29.50 pa. Illustrated magazine with informative coverage of the br band scene, with articles by leading authorities and up-to-date news.*

Brio (2). Music Library, Central Library, Harpur St, Bedford MK40 1PG *tel:* 01234 350931 *fax:* 01234 342163. Paul Andrews, ed; Christopher Grogan, reviews ed; Linda Anthony, ad mgr. *Membership £30 (individual), £44 (institutions). Journal of International Association of Music Libraries, Archives and Documentation Centres UK Branch.*

British Bandsman (52). Harold Charles House, 64a London End, Beaconsfield, Bucks HP9 2JP *tel:* 01494 674411 *fax:* 01494 670932. Peter Wilson, ed. *60p.*

British Institute of Organ Studies, Journal of the (1). c/o 17 Wheeleys Rd, Edgbaston, Birmingham B15 2LD *tel:* 0121 440 5491 *also fax. £20. Scholarly research into the history of the org.*

British Journal of Music Education (3). Journals Dept, CUP, Edinburgh Building, Shaftesbury Rd, Cambridge CB2 2RU *tel:* 01223 312393 *fax:* 01223 315052 *email:* http://www.cup.cam.ac.uk. John Paynter, Keith Swanwick, eds. *£49 institutions, £30 individuals, £23 students pa. Aims to provide clear, stimulating and readable accounts of current issues in mus educ worldwide. Covers classroom mus teaching, individual inst teaching and group teaching, mus in higher educ, international comparative mus educ, and teacher educ.*

British Journal of Music Therapy (2). 25 Rosslyn Av, East Barnet, Herts EN4 8DH *tel:* 0181 368 8879. Nicky Barber, Jackie Robarts, eds. *£50.*

British Music Yearbook (1). Rhinegold Publishing Ltd, 241 Shaftesbury Av, London WC2H 8EH *tel:* 0171 333 1760 (ed); 0171 333 1733 (ad) *fax:* 0171 333 1769 (ed); 0171 333 1736 (ad) *email:* bmyb@rhinegold. co.uk. Felicity Rich, ed; Laura Dollin, Karen Harman, asst eds. *£23.95 post free. The directory of the classical mus industry.*

British Performing Arts Yearbook (1). Rhinegold Publishing, 241 Shaftesbury Av, London WC2H 8EH *tel:* 0171 333 1762 (ed); 0171 333 1733 (ad) *fax:* 0171 333 1769 (ed); 0171 333 1736 (ad) *email:* bpay@ rhinegold.co.uk. Sheena Barbour, ed. *£23.95 post free. Annual directory of performing arts in Britain. Includes venues, companies, solo performers, symphony and chmbr orchs, jazz and light mus, arts festivals, educ and training, arts councils, regional arts boards, support associations, local authorities, suppliers and services.*

Cambridge Opera Journal (3). Journals Dept, CUP, The Edinburgh Building, Shaftesbury Rd, Cambridge CB2 2RU *tel:* 01223 312393 *fax:* 01223 315052 *email:* http://www.cup.cam.ac.uk. Roger Parker, Arthur Groos, eds. *£51 institutions, £31 individuals pa. Articles across the whole opera repertoire.*

Cerddoriaeth Cymru *see* **Welsh Music.**

Choir & Organ (6). Orpheus Publications Ltd, 7 St John's Rd, Harrow, Middx HA1 2EE *tel:* 0181 863 2020 *fax:* 0181 863 2444. Basil Ramsey, ed; Shirley Ratcliffe, asst ed; Matthew Power, ad mgr. *£2.75. Features and news on choral mus and singing, orgs and org mus.*

Church Music Quarterly (4). 151 Mount View Rd, London N4 4JT *tel:* 0181 341 6408 *fax:* 0181 340 0021. Trevor Ford, ed; Marianne Barton, associate ed; Anne Hastings, ad mgr. *No cover price, issued to Royal School of Church Music members only.*

Classic CD (13). Beauford Ct, 30 Monmouth St, Bath, Avon BA1 2BW *tel:* 01225 442244 *fax:* 01225 732353 *email:* nevans@futurenet.co.uk. Neil Evans, ed; Daniel Jaffé, reviews ed; Mark Finnell, news and production ed. *£3.95; £45 pa. Features, news and reviews of classical mus releases and concerts, with a covermounted CD of extracts.*

Classic FM Magazine (12). Academic House, 24-28 Oval Rd, London NW1 7DQ *tel:* 0171 284 3000 *fax:* 0171 385 6946. Felicity Hawkins, ed. *£3.75.*

Classical Guitar (12). Ashley Mark Publishing Co, Olsover House, 43 Sackville Rd, Newcastle upon Tyne NE6 5TA *tel:* 0191 276 0448 *fax:* 0191 276 1623 *email:* classicalguitar@ashleymark.co.uk. Colin Cooper, ed. *£2.75; £38.50 pa.*

Classical Music (26). Rhinegold Publishing Ltd, 241 Shaftesbury Av, London WC2H 8EH *tel:* 0171 333 1742 (ed); 0171 333 1733 (ad) *fax:* 0171 333 1769 (ed); 0171 333 1736 (ad) *email:* classical.music@ rhinegold.co.uk. Keith Clarke, ed; Rebecca Agnew, deputy ed. *£2.95; £56 pa.*

The Conductor (4). Marrey, 7 Carr View Rd, Hepworth, Huddersfield HD7 7HN *tel:* 01484 683793 *fax:* 01484 608512. Jeffrey Turner, ed. *£2. Journal of the NABBC.*

The Consort (European Journal of Early Music) (2). Dolmetsch Foundation, 3 Kelmarsh Rd, Arthingworth LE16 8JZ *tel:* 01858 525596. Jonathan Le Cocq, ed. *£22.50 pa (overseas), £18 (UK), £7 (student) including general membership and newsletter 'Bulletin' (3).*

Contemporary Music News (3). Peters Edition Ltd, 10-12 Baches St, London N1 6DN *tel:* 0171 553 4030 *fax:* 0171 490 4921 *email:* promotion@edition-peters.com; http://www.edition-peters.com. Julia Haferkorn, ed. *Free. Activities of contemporary composers published in Edition Peters.*

Contemporary Music Review (6). Harwood Academic Publishers, PO Box 90, Reading, Berks RG1 8JL *tel:* 0118 956 0080 *fax:* 0118 956 8211. Nigel Osborne, Peter Nelson, eds. *£200 (plus p&p) to libraries and institutions, £60 to individuals.*

Early Music (4). Oxford University Press, 70 Baker St, London W1M 1DJ *tel:* 0171 616 5902; 0171 352 6400 (ad) *fax:* 0171 616 5901 *email:* jnl.early-music@oup.co.uk; http://www.oup.co.uk/earlyj. Tess Knighton, ed; David Roberts, asst ed. *£10; £40 pa (individuals), £58 (institutions). Articles on medieval, renaissance, baroque and pre-classical mus with special reference to performance practice. Book, mus and recording reviews.*

Early Music History (1). Journals Dept, CUP, Edinburgh Building, Shaftesbury Rd, Cambridge CB2 2RU *tel:* 01223 312393 *fax:* 01223 315052 *email:* http://www.cup.cam.ac.uk. Iain Fenlon, ed. *£56 institutions, £37 individuals. Devoted to the study of mus from the early Middle Ages to the 17th C.*

Early Music News (11). Forever Green, 3 Onslow House, Castle Rd, The Common, Tunbridge Wells, Kent TN4 3BY *tel:* 01892 511652 *also fax.* Robin Hillier, ed. *Free in the UK. Listings of concerts, broadcasts and CD releases.*

Early Music Review (10). King's Music, Redcroft, Bank's End, Wyton, Huntingdon PE17 2AA *tel:* 01480 52076 *fax:* 01480 450821 *email:* cbkings@ibm.net. Clifford Bartlett, ed; Brian Clark, associate ed; Elaine Bartlett, admin. *£1.50; £10 pa. For all concerned with the performance, study and enjoyment of early mus throughout the world.*

Early Music Today (6). Rhinegold Publishing Ltd, 241 Shaftesbury Av, London WC2H 8EH *tel:* 0171 333 1744 (ed); 0171 333 1733 (ad) *fax:* 0171 333 1769 (ed); 0171 333 1736 (ad) *email:* emt@rhinegold.co.uk. Lucien Jenkins, ed. *£2.40; £14.40 pa. News magazine reporting on performers, insts, broadcasting, events, books, mus, CDs and the early mus scene in the UK and abroad.*

Early Music Yearbook (1). National Early Music Association, 18 High St, Caythorpe, Grantham, Lincs NG32 3BS *tel:* 01400 273795 *also fax.* *£14.50 (plus postage and packing). List of individuals and ens, directory of useful addresses, buyers' guide.*

EGTA (UK) Journal (1). 52 Ashurst Rd, Cockfosters, Herts EN4 9LF *tel:* 0181 449 0886 *email:* 101602.314@compuserve.com; http:// ourworld.compuserve.com/homepages/stevekenyon. Stephen Kenyon, ed. *European Guitar Teachers' Association (UK) journal with articles and reviews pertaining to the gui teaching profession. Free to members, £3 to non-members, £5 overseas.*

The First National Directory of Community Music. Sound Sense, c/o The Arts Business, 2 Cotswold Mews, Battersea Sq, London SW11 3RA *tel:* 0171 585 3075 *fax:* 0171 924 2924. Peter Budge, publications mgr. *£5.95 plus £2 postage and packing.*

Flutewise (4). 9 Beaconsfield Rd, Portslade By Sea, E Sussex BN41 1XA *tel:* 01273 702367 *fax:* 01273 888864 *email:* flutewise@i-gadgets.com; http://www.ndirect.co.uk/-flutewise. James Galway, president; Liz Goodwin, ed. *£14 pa. Quarterly magazine for all fl players, especially the young, featuring articles, quizzes, competitions and events.*

Folk Music Journal (1). English Folk Dance and Song Society, 2 Regents Pk Rd, London NW1 7AY *tel:* 0171 485 2206 *fax:* 0171 284 0523. Michael Heaney, ed. *£7.50, £21 including individual membership of EFDSS.*

Footloose in London Magazine (52). 119 Ashfield St, Stepney, London E1 3EX *tel:* 0171 791 0945. Malcolm Galloway. *Free. Arts and Entertainments and review magazine. Highlights classical mus CDs and concerts.*

The Full Score (4). Chester Music Limited, 8-9 Frith St, London W1V 5TZ *tel:* 0171 434 0066 *fax:* 0171 287 6329 *email:* music@musicsales.co.uk. Nick Kimberley, ed; Catherine Manners, head of promotion. *Free. Quarterly newsletter for Chester Music, Novello & Co, Edition Wilhelm Hansen and G Schirmer Inc.*

Galpin Society Journal (1). Ashdown Cottage, Chapel La, Forest Row, E Sussex RH18 5BS *tel:* 01342 822044 *also fax;* *email:* http://www.music. ed.ac.uk/euchmi/galpin/. David Rycroft, ed; Pauline Holden, sec; Arnold Myers, website mgr. *£18 (UK), £24 (Europe), £28 (elsewhere), £30 (institutions and non-members), inclusive of Journal and Bulletins (study of mus insts).*

Gramophone (12). Gramophone Publications Ltd, 135 Greenford Rd, Sudbury Hill, Harrow, Middx HA1 3YD *tel:* 0181 422 4562 *fax:* 0181 869 8400 *email:* editor@gramophone.co.uk. James Jolly, ed; C Pollard, editorial dir. *£3.20. Monthly; features and CD reviews.*

Hallmark (4). Hallé Concerts Society, The Bridgewater Hall, Manchester M2 3WS *tel:* 0161 237 7000 *fax:* 0161 237 7029. Steve Wainwright, ed. *Free to members, press and sponsors. News of fundraising, sponsorship, educ and other activities of the society.*

Haydn Society Journal (1). Music Dept, Lancaster University, Lancaster LA1 4YW *tel:* 01524 593777 *fax:* 01524 847298 *email:* dmccaldin@ lancaster.ac.uk; http://www.lancs.ac.uk/users/concerts/haydn.html. Denis McCaldin, dir; Stella Birchall, admin. *£5 pa.*

Hi-Fi News & Record Review (12). Link House Magazines Ltd, Link House, Dingwall Av, Croydon CR9 2TA *tel:* 0181 686 2599 *fax:* 0181 760 0973. Steve Harris, ed; Christopher Breunig, mus ed. *£3.00; £35.40 pa (UK), $80 (US), £43.10 (Europe and Eire).*

The Horn Magazine (3). 15 Hailey Croft, Chinnor, Oxon OX9 4TS *tel:* 01844 353025 *also fax;* *email:* 101353.1656@compuserve.com. Ian Wagstaff, publisher and ed. *A magazine for horn players by horn players, published for the British Horn Society.*

International Arts Manager (10). Arts Publishing International Ltd, 4 Assam St, London E1 7QS *tel:* 0171 247 0066 *fax:* 0171 247 6868 *email:* editorial@api.co.uk. Marika Thorogood, ed; Jane Morris, staff writer. *£39 pa, or £59 for two years.*

International Journal of Music Education (2). ISME, International Centre for Research in Music Education, University of Reading, Bulmershe Ct, Reading RG6 1HY *tel:* 0118 931 8846 *also fax; fax:* 0118 935 2080 *email:* e.smith@reading.ac.uk; http://www.isme.org. Jack Dobbs, Anthony Kemp, eds; Elizabeth Smith, ISME admin. *£7.50. Articles covering a wide range of issues concerning mus educ worldwide and book reviews.*

ISM Register of Musicians in Education (1). Incorporated Society of Musicians, 10 Stratford Pl, London W1N 9AE *tel:* 0171 629 4413; 0171 278 3686 (ad) *fax:* 0171 408 1538 *email:* membership@ism.org. Elizabeth Poulsen, admin, educ and development; Kim Davenport Gee, production; Ivan Stutchbury, ad sales. *£10. Directory and classified lists of ISM members working in or for educ establishments.*

ISM Register of Professional Private Music Teachers (1). Incorporated Society of Musicians, 10 Stratford Pl, London W1N 9AE *tel:* 0171 629 4413; 0171 278 3686 (ad) *fax:* 0171 408 1538 *email:* membership@ism. org. Elizabeth Poulsen, admin, educ and development; Kim Davenport Gee, production; Ivan Stutchbury, ad sales. *£16. Classified directory, by insts and geographical location, of ISM registered private teachers.*

ISM Yearbook (1). Incorporated Society of Musicians, 10 Stratford Pl, London W1N 9AE *tel:* 0171 629 4413; 0171 278 3686 (ad) *fax:* 0171 408 1538 *email:* membership@ism.org. Neil Hoyle, chief exec and ed; Kim Davenport Gee, production; Ivan Stutchbury, ad sales. *£26. Gives contact details for the ISM's 4500 members, reports on the previous year's activities and describes the Society's services.*

ISSTIP Journal (1). School of Music, Kingston University, c/o 28 Emperor's Gate, London SW7 4HS *tel:* 0171 373 7307 *fax:* 0171 274 6821. Carola Grindea, ed. *£3.50 (including postage); free to ISSTIP members.*

Jazz Journal International (12). 1-5 Clerkenwell Rd, London EC1M 5PA *tel:* 0171 608 1348/1362 *fax:* 0171 608 1292. Eddie Cook, publisher and ed in chief; Janet Cook, company sec and associate publisher; Ivan Etherington, circulation mgr. *£3; £34 pa (UK). A magazine for jazz record collectors.*

Jazz UK (6). c/o Exeter and Devon Arts Centre, Gandy St, Exeter EX4 3LS *tel:* 01392 218368 *fax:* 01392 420442. Kevin Buckland, regional ed; Rosie Jarvis, listings ed. *£10 including membership of National Jazz Card Scheme. Comprehensive listings of forthcoming concerts and events. Editorial commentary on jazz in the UK.*

Jazzwise Magazine (10). Jazzwise Publications, 2b Gleneagle Mews, London SW16 6AE *tel:* 0181 769 7725 *fax:* 0181 677 6128. Stephen Graham, ed. *£2.50; £25 pa (UK). Covers all styles and periods of jazz, with emphasis on current activity. Includes features, news, CD reviews, concert reviews, technical articles.*

Journal into Melody (4). Stone Gables, Upton La, Seavington St Michael, Ilminster, Somerset TA19 0PZ *tel:* 01460 242226 *also fax. £10 pa (Robert Farnon Society).*

Journal of the Music Masters' and Mistresses' Association (3). Three Ways, Chicks La, Kilndown, Cranbrook, Kent TN17 2RS *tel:* 01204 308969. Victoria Aldous-Ball, admin. *Members only.*

Keyboard Cavalcade (12). Sceptre Promotions, 97 Elton Rd, Stibbington, Peterborough PE8 6JX *tel:* 01780 782093 *fax:* 01780 783159. Grant Neal, ed. *£1; £12 pa.*

Leading Notes (2). National Early Music Association, 18 High St, Caythorpe, Grantham, Lincs NG32 3BS *tel:* 01400 273795. Richard Lawrence, ed. *£5, free to NEMA members.*

The Lute (1). c/o The Lute Society, Southside Cottage, Brook Hill, Albury, Guildford, Surrey GU5 9DJ *tel:* 01483 202159 *fax:* 01483 203088. Christopher Goodwin, sec and ed. *£25. The Lute Society also publishes the quarterly newsletter Lute News. Covers all aspects of the lute and related insts and their mus.*

The Mix (12). Alexander House, Forehill, Ely, Cambs CB7 4AF *tel:* 01353 665577 *fax:* 01353 662489. Chris Kempster, ed. *£3.95. Mus production magazine with covermount CD. Interviews with musicians, producers and sound engineers. Reviews of mus recording equipment.*

Museums & Arts Appointments. Rhinegold Publishing Ltd, 241 Shaftesbury Av, London WC2H 8EH *tel:* 0171 333 1720 (subs); 0171 333 1733 (ad) *fax:* 0171 333 1736. Julian Caedmon. *Recruitment medium for the museums and arts world.*

Music Analysis (3). Blackwell Publishers, 108 Cowley Rd, Oxford OX4 1JF *tel:* 01865 791100 *fax:* 01865 791347. Anthony Popple, ed.

Music and Letters (4). Music Dept, Royal Holloway, and Bedford New College, Egham, Surrey TW20 0EX *tel:* 01784 443532 *fax:* 01784 439441. Nigel Fortune, Tim Carter, Katharine Ellis, eds. *UK/Europe £39 (individuals), £53 (institutions).*

Music and Liturgy (5). 33 Brockenhurst Rd, Addiscombe, Croydon CR0 7DR *tel:* 0181 654 3379 *also fax.* Ann Moynihan, ed. *£20 pa (concessions £15), UK; £21 (Europe); £23 (rest of world).*

Music Business (11). Park View House, Woodnesborough, Sandwich, Kent CT13 0PN *tel:* 01304 812586 (ed); 0181 950 4984 (ad) *fax:* 01304 813580 (ed); 0181 950 0302 (ad) *email:* musicbiz@cityscape.co.uk. Jerry Uwins, ed; Sandie Smith, ad mgr. *£15 pa. Trade magazine for mus inst industry, including annual directory (published in Jul).*

Music Education Yearbook (1). Rhinegold Publishing Ltd, 241 Shaftesbury Av, London WC2H 8EH *tel:* 0171 333 1761 (ed); 0171 333 1733 (ad) *fax:* 0171 333 1769 *email:* meyb@rhinegold.co.uk. Felicity Rich, ed; Laura Dollin, asst ed. *£14.*

Music in British Libraries (1). A Directory of Resources, Library Association Publishing, 7 Ridgmount St, London WC1E 7AE *tel:* 0171 636 7543 *fax:* 0171 636 3627 *email:* lapublishing@la.hq.org.uk. Barbara Penney, ed. *£40; LA members £32.*

Music Journal (12). Incorporated Society of Musicians, 10 Stratford Pl, London W1N 9AE *tel:* 0171 629 4413; 0171 278 3686 (ad) *fax:* 0171 408 1538 *email:* membership@ism.org. Neil Hoyle, ed; Kim Davenport Gee, production; Ivan Stutchbury, ad sales. *£2.50, £25 pa. Details of ISM members' activities and the ISM's work, plus news, views and reviews from the world of professional mus.*

Music, Opera, Dance and Drama in Asia, the Pacific and North America. Arts Publishing International Ltd, 4 Assam St, London E1 7QS *tel:* 0171 247 0066 *fax:* 0171 247 6868 *email:* editorial@api.co.uk. Martin Huber, publisher; Tsuyashi Urayama, ed; Wiebke Müller, publishing mgr. *£33.*

Music Review (4). Black Bear Press, King's Hedges Rd, Cambridge CB4 2PQ *tel:* 01223 424571. A F Leighton Thomas, ed. *£15.25; £52.50 pa.*

Music Scholar (1). Rhinegold Publishing Ltd, 241 Shaftesbury Av, London WC2H 8EH *tel:* 0171 333 1747 (ed); 0171 333 1733 (ad) *fax:* 0171 333 1769 (ed); 0171 333 1736 (ad) *email:* music.scholar@rhinegold .co.uk. Lucien Jenkins, ed. *£3. Features on educ choices facing 11 to 19 year olds; mus schools and scholarships, conservatoire and university courses, youth orch courses, exam techniques.*

Music Teacher (12). Rhinegold Publishing Ltd, 241 Shaftesbury Av, London WC2H 8EH *tel:* 0171 333 1747 (ed); 0171 333 1733 (ad) *fax:* 0171 333 1769 *email:* music.teacher@rhinegold.co.uk. Lucien Jenkins, ed; Sara Cunningham, asst ed. *£2.95; £34 pa. News and features on mus technology, A-level history and analysis, insts and teaching choices; book, mus and video reviews. Regular special topic guides.*

Music Week and Music Week Directory (52). Spotlight Publications Ltd, 245 Blackfriars Rd, London SE1 9UR *tel:* 0171 620 3636 *fax:* 0171 401 8035. Steve Redmond, ed in chief. *Mus industry trade publication, including news, new release listings and official CIN charts. £3.10; £120 pa including Music Week Directory.*

Musical Opinion (4). 2 Princes Rd, St Leonards-on-Sea, E Sussex TN37 6EL *tel:* 01424 715167 *fax:* 01424 712214 *email:* 100723.510@ compuserve.com. Denby Richards, ed. *Also 8 supplements. £3.50; £24 pa (UK), £36 pa (overseas).*

Musical Performance (4). Harwood Academic Publishers, 197 Knightsbridge, 8th Floor North, London SW7 1RB. Basil Tschaikov, ed in chief. *£12 (paper); £50 pa (paper); £182 pa (cloth). International journal for composers, musicians and their audiences.*

The Musical Times (12). 63b Jamestown Rd, London NW1 7DB *tel:* 0171 482 5697 (ed) *also fax;* 0171 613 0717 (ad). Antony Bye, ed; Brian R Hook, ad mgr. *£2.50.*

New Music News (3). Irish Contemporary Music Centre, 95 Lower Baggot St, Dublin 2, Ireland *tel:* 00 353 1 661 2105 *fax:* 00 353 1 676 2639 *email:* info@cmc.ie; http://www.cmc.ie. Eve O'Kelly, ed. *Free.*

New Notes (11). c/o SPNM, Francis House, Francis St, London SW1P IDE *tel:* 0171 828 9696 *fax:* 0171 931 9928. Peter Craik, ed. *Free. New mus concerts listings plus SPNM news.*

NODA National News (4). NODA House, 1 Crestfield St, London WC1H 8AU *tel:* 0171 837 5655 *fax:* 0171 833 0609. Mark Thorburn, mgr ed. *£1.80; free to members of National Operatic and Dramatic Association.*

Opera (13). 1a Mountgrove Rd, London N5 2LU *tel:* 0171 359 1037 *fax:* 0171 354 2700. Rodney Milnes, ed. *£2.35. Advertising managers:* Cabbell Publishing Ltd *tel:* 0181 395 3808.

Opera Now (6). Rhinegold Publishing Ltd, 241 Shaftesbury Av, London WC2H 8EH *tel:* 0171 333 1740 (ed); 0171 333 1733 (ad) *fax:* 0171 333 1769 (ed); 0171 333 1736 (ad) *email:* opera.now@rhinegold.co.uk. Ashutosh Khandekar, ed; Antonia Couling, deputy ed. *£4.95; £29.70 pa.*

The Organ (4). 5 Aldborough Rd, St Leonards-on-Sea, E Sussex TN37 6SE *tel:* 01424 422225 *fax:* 01424 712214. Brian Hick, ed. *£3.50; £17 pa (UK), £23 (elsewhere). Magazine for organists, org builders and general listeners, covering all types of org mus and orgs.*

Organ Club Journal (6). Flat 1, 34 Shakespeare Rd, Worthing, Sussex BN11 4AS *tel:* 01903 217676. Philip Bailey, ed. *Issued free to members of the Organ Club only.*

Organists' Review (4). 4 Vicars' Ct, Southwell, Notts NG25 0HP *tel:* 01636 812228 *also fax;* 01245 259120. Paul Hale, ed; Marcus Knight, advertising mgr. *£3.75. Articles on orgs, org and choral mus, org playing. Major review section.*

Organised Sound (3 +CD). Journals Dept, CUP, Edinburgh Building, Shaftesbury Rd, Cambridge CB2 2RU *tel:* 01223 312393 *fax:* 01223 315052 *email:* http://www.cup.cam.ac.uk. Ross Kirk, Leigh Landy, Tony Myatt, Richard Orton, eds. *£63 institutions, £35 individuals, £25 students. Issues arising from the use of contemporary technology in fields of multimedia, performance art, sound sculpture and electronic composition.*

Performing Arts Yearbook for Europe (PAYE) (1). Arts Publishing International Ltd, 4 Assam St, London E1 7QS *tel:* 0171 247 0066 *fax:* 0171 247 6868 *email:* editorial@api.co.uk. Martin Huber, publisher; Wiebke Müller, ed; Karin Junker, deputy ed. *£42.*

Piano (6). Rhinegold Publishing Ltd, 241 Shaftesbury Av, London WC2H 8EH *tel:* 0171 333 1724 (ed); 0171 333 1733 (ad) *fax:* 0171 333 1769 (ed); 0171 333 1736 (ad) *email:* piano@rhinegold.co.uk. Madeline Cohen, ed. *£2.40; £14.40 pa.*

Piano Journal (3). 28 Emperor's Gate, London SW7 4HS *tel:* 0171 373 7307 *fax:* 0171 244 0904. Malcolm Troup, ed; Carola Grindea, consultant. *£8 (including postage) or $15 (annual overseas subscription rate). Free to members of the European Piano Teachers Association (UK) and associate members (outside Europe). Interviews, articles on repertoire, pno teaching, technique, etc; book, mus and CD reviews.*

Piano Tuners Quarterly (4). RNIB, PO Box 173, Peterborough PE2 6WS *tel:* 01733 370777 *fax:* 01733 371555 *email:* rfirman@rnib.org.uk. Roger Firman, mus services mgr. *£1.25 (UK); £1.85 (overseas). News and articles about pno tuning.*

Plainsong and Medieval Music (2). Journals Dept, CUP, Edinburgh Building, Shaftesbury Rd, Cambridge CB2 2RU *tel:* 01223 312393 *fax:* 01223 315052 *email:* http://www.cup.cam.ac.uk. Joseph Dyer, Christopher Page, eds. *£42 institutions, £26 individuals. Liturgical chant of any period, monophonic and polyphonic in East and West.*

Popular Music (3). Journals Dept, CUP, The Edinburgh Building, Shaftesbury Rd, Cambridge CB2 2RU *tel:* 01223 312393 *fax:* 01223 325959 *email:* http://www.cup.cam.ac.uk. Lucy Green, Dave Laing, co-ord eds. *£62 institutions; £36 individuals; £28 students. A multi-disciplinary journal covering all aspects of popular mus.*

Radio Times (51). BBC Worldwide Ltd, Woodlands, 80 Wood La, London W12 0TT *tel:* 0181 576 3999 *fax:* 0181 576 3160 *email:* radio.times@ dial.pipex.com. Sue Robinson, ed. *75p.*

The Record Collector (4). 111 Longshots Close, Broomfield, Chelmsford CM1 7DU *tel:* 01245 441661 *fax:* 01245 443642. Larry Lustig, ed. *£18 by subscription.*

The Recorder Magazine (4). 52 Woking Rd, Cheadle Hulme, Cheadle, Cheshire SK8 6NU *tel:* 0161 485 6477 *fax:* 01422 886157 *email:* ruth@recordermail.demon.co.uk. Andrew Mayes, ed. *£2.75.*

Rhythm (12). Alexander House, Forehill, Ely, Cambs CB7 4AF *tel:* 01353 665577 *fax:* 01353 662489 *email:* rhythm@musicians-net.co.uk. Ronan Macdonald, ed; Louise King, design and production ed; Martin Pointon, staff writer. *£2.50. Magazine for drummers and percussionists, covering a wide range of mus from jazz to world mus.*

The Ringing World (52). Ringing World Ltd, Penmark House, Guildford, Surrey GU1 1BL *tel:* 01483 569535 *fax:* 01483 567876 *email:* ringingw @luna.co.uk; http://www.luna.co.uk/~ringingw. Miss T R Stoecklin, ed. *£1.10; £38 pa.*

Royal Musical Association, Journal of the (2). Journals Dept, Oxford University Press, Gt Clarendon St, Oxford OX2 6DP *tel:* 01865 267907 *fax:* 01865 267485. Andrew Wathey, ed. *£53 pa (UK and EU), US$95 (elsewhere).*

Royal Musical Association Research Chronicle (1). Dept of Music, University of York, Heslington, York YO1 5DD *tel:* 01904 661016 *fax:* 01904 432450 *email:* jpw6@york.ac.uk. Jonathan Wainwright, ed. *Approx £25. Emphasis on the raw materials of musicology; indexes, categories, inventories, etc.*

Scottish Folk Directory (1). Scottish Folk Arts Group, Blackfriars Music, 49 Blackfriars St, Edinburgh EH1 1NB *tel:* 0131 557 3090 *also fax; email:* 101325.13@compuserve.com. Willie Haines, ed. *£2.95. A contact resource for all involved in Scottish folk mus and arts.*

Sheet Music (4). Press House, Godinton Rd, Ashford, Kent TN23 1LJ *tel:* 01233 643574 *fax:* 01233 641816. Paul Smith, ed; Andrew Standing, commercial dir. *For musicians, teachers and all who buy and sell sheet mus.*

Showcase International Music Book (1). Showcase Publications Ltd, 38c The Broadway, London N8 9SU *tel:* 0181 348 2332 *fax:* 0181 340 3750 *email:* http://www.showcase-music.com. Kay Chestnutt, ed; Tony Tillmanns, ad sales and mkt. *£35 (EEC), £42 (other). The mus production guide for the UK and Europe published annually in Jan.*

Sing to the Lord (3). Salvationist Publishing and Supplies Ltd, 117-121 Judd St, London WC1H 9NN *tel:* 0171 387 1656 *fax:* 0171 383 3420. Richard Phillips, ed. *£1. Contains approx nine works for Christian four-part choirs. Also childrens' voices, female voices and male voice issues.*

The Singer (6). Rhinegold Publishing Ltd, 241 Shaftesbury Av, London WC2H 8EH *tel:* 0171 333 1746 (ed); 0171 333 1733 (ad) *fax:* 0171 333 1769 (ed); 0171 333 1736 (ad) *email:* the.singer@rhinegold.co.uk. Antonia Couling, ed. *£2.40; £14 pa. For anyone with a serious, wide-ranging enthusiasm for vocal mus, from choral and lieder to opera, cabaret and mus theatre.*

Sounding Board (4). Sound Sense, Riverside House, Rattlesden, Bury St Edmunds IP30 0SF *tel:* 01449 736287 *fax:* 01449 737649 *email:* 100256. 30@compuserve.com; http://ourworld.compuserve.com/homepages/ soundsense. Kathryn Deane, ed. *Quarterly journal for those interested in participatory mus-making. Subscription ranges from £10 to £65 pa and includes membership of Sound Sense.*

Sounds Great! (10). Bright Horizons Publications, PO Box 1572, Ascot, Berks SL5 0PF *tel:* 01344 291398 *fax:* 01344 623575 *email:* 106 163.2305@compuserve.com; http://www.telesys.com/concert. Joan Brightwell, ed. *£18.50 pa. Guide to live classical events in London and the Home Counties.*

South West Jazz Newsletters. South West Jazz, c/o Exeter & Devon Arts Centre, Gandy St, Exeter, Devon EX4 3LS *tel:* 01392 218368 *fax:* 01392 420442. Kevin Buckland, ed; Rosie Jarvis, listings. *Three newsletters quarterly:* Bands Bulletin; Promoters Newsletters; Workshop Newsletter.

The Stage (52). Stage House, 47 Bermondsey St, London SE1 3XT *tel:* 0171 403 1818 *fax:* 0171 403 1418. Brian Attwood, ed. *80p.*

The Strad (12). Orpheus Publications, 7 St John's Rd, Harrow, Middx HA1 2EE *tel:* 0181 863 2020 *fax:* 0181 863 2444 *email:* editors@thestrad. demon.co.uk. Joanna Pieters, ed; Juliette Barber, deputy ed; Naomi Sadler, asst ed. *£3.25. For performers, teachers, students, makers and enthusiasts of bowed str insts.*

Studio Sound (12). 8 Montague Close, London Bridge, London SE1 9UR *tel:* 0171 620 3636 *fax:* 0171 401 8036. Tim Goodyer, ed. *£2. Controlled circulation journal serving professional recording, post-production and broadcast industry.*

Tempo (4). Boosey & Hawkes Ltd, 295 Regent St, London W1R 8JH *tel:* 0171 580 2060 *fax:* 0171 436 5675 *email:* http://www.boosey.com. Calum MacDonald, ed; Arthur Boyers, ad mgr; Sue Rose, subs mgr. *£3, £15 pa.*

Trumpet and Cornet. 15 Hailey Croft, Chinnor, Oxon OX9 4TS *tel:* 01844 353025 *also fax; email:* 101353.1656@compuserve.com. Murray Greig, ed; Ian Wagstaff, publisher. *Published for the Cornet and Trumpet Society.*

Unknown Public (4). PO Box 354, Reading RG2 7JB *tel:* 0118 931 2580 *fax:* 0118 931 2582 *email:* walters@gn.apc.org; http://www.guardian. co.uk/guardian/up. John L Walters, ed; Laurence Aston, publisher. *£55 (individual), £90 (institutions). Audio journal of contemporary creative mus on CD or MC.*

Welsh Music (2). 17 Penyrheol Dr, Llanelli, Carmarthenshire SA15 3NX *tel:* 01554 774188. A J Heward Rees, ed. *£2.*

What Hi-fi? (13). Haymarket Magazines Ltd, 60 Waldegrave Rd, Teddington, Middx TW11 8LG *tel:* 0181 943 5000 *fax:* 0181 943 5798. Jez Ford, ed; Andrew Clough, deputy ed; Andrew Everard, technical ed. Frank Foster, art ed. *£2.60. Hi-fi buyers guide with reviews of hi-fi and home cinema equipment plus hi-fi news and related features. Now incorporating Audiophile magazine.*

What's On In London (52). 182 Pentonville Rd, London N1 9LB *tel:* 0171 278 4393 *fax:* 0171 837 5838. Michael Darvell, ed; Danny Scott, mus ed. *£1.20. Rock, pop, jazz, folk, world mus as well as classical. Weekly listings of all mus in London including features, previews, album reviews, opera reviews among other entertainment coverage of the arts.*

The White Book (1). Bank House, 23 Warwick Rd, Coventry CV1 2EW *tel:* 01203 559658 *fax:* 01203 252241. Tony Boffey, ed. *£55 (UK). Production directory to the entertainment industry.*

Winds (4). c/o David Kenyon, Dorset Music Service, Jademanor Ct, West Quay Rd, Poole, Dorset BH15 1TG *tel:* 01202 221491 *fax:* 01202 221493 *email:* basbowe@interbs.demon.co.uk; http://www.interbs.demon.co. uk. David Kenyon, chmn ed committee; Liz Winter, advertising and subs mgr. *£2.30. Journal of the British Association of Symphonic Bands and Wind Ensembles, free to members.*

300
SERIES

professional features for beginners who wish to progress faster

VINCENT BACH
INTERNATIONAL LTD
UNIT 71
CAPITOL PARK
INDUSTRIAL ESTATE
CAPITOL WAY
LONDON NW9 0EW
TEL: 0181 905 9505
FAX: 0181 905 9149

Vincent
Bach ®

Centrepiece Music. PO Box 1601, Newport Pagnell, Bucks MK16 8PN *tel:* 01908 218003 *fax:* 01908 211828. *Wholesaler and distributor of speciality accs for w/wind: mouthpieces, reeds, etc; Neotech sax and gui slings and straps; m/order.*

Chappell Piano Co Ltd *see* **Kemble & Co Ltd.**

The Clarke Tin Whistle Co Ltd. The Old Joinery, Whetsted Rd, Five Oak Green, Kent TN12 6RS *tel:* 01892 835632 *fax:* 01892 838086 *email:* clarke@whistles.kentnet.co.uk; http://www.kentnet.co.uk/whistles. *Manufacturers of the 'Clarke' tin whistle.*

Cohen, Brian. Soundpost, The Old Glassworks, Alexandra Pl, Guildford, Surrey GU1 3QH *tel:* 01483 456022 *also fax; email:* soundpost@compuserve.com. *Guis, vns, vcs.*

Copeman Hart & Company Ltd. Finedon Rd, Irthlingborough, Northants NN9 5TZ *tel:* 01933 652600 *fax:* 01933 652288 *email:* info@copeman hart.co.uk; http://www.copemanhart.co.uk. E C Hart, G H Blyth, C C Hart, I J Rees, dirs. *Church org builders.*

David Wells Organ Builders. Cathedral Works, South West Brunswick Dock, Liverpool L3 4BD *tel:* 0151 709 6146 *fax:* 0151 707 0625. *Pipe org builder and restorer.*

Derek Roberts Violins. 185 Leam Terrace, Leamington Spa, Warwicks CV31 1DW *tel:* 01926 428313 *also fax. Modern and baroque vn, va, vc maker and restorer.*

Doe, Roger. Mount St Laurence, High St, Cranbrook, Kent TN17 3EW *tel:* 01580 712330. *Silver and gold mounted bows. French styles and English Hill pattern bows.*

Dolmetsch Musical Instruments. Unicorn Trading Estate, Weydown Rd, Haslemere, Surrey GU27 1DN *tel:* 01428 643235 *fax:* 01428 654920 *email:* brian@be-blood.demon.co.uk. *Viols, rcdrs, hpds, clvds and spinets.*

Eaton, Peter. Woodside, Orestan La, Effingham, Surrey KT24 5SN *tel:* 01372 452513 *also fax. Cls and cl mouthpieces.*

Edgar, Alan. 43 Beverley Rd, Hessle, N Humberside *tel:* 01482 640330. *Hpds, clvds, hps.*

Elysian Pianos. Robert Morley & Co Ltd, 34 Engate St, London SE13 7HA *tel:* 0181 318 5838 *fax:* 0181 297 0720 *email:* http://www.yell.co.uk/sites/morley. *Grand and upright pnos; also stools.*

F H Browne & Sons (Organ Builders). Old Cartwright School, The Street, Ash, Canterbury, Kent CT3 2AA *tel:* 01304 813146. *Orgs.*

Farfisa (UK) Ltd. 12 Churchill Way, Lomeshaye Industrial Estate, Nelson, Lancs BB9 6RT *tel:* 01282 606600 *fax:* 01282 606660. *Pnos, elec orgs, elec keyboards.*

Fazioli. The Music Studios, 29 Marylebone La, London W1M 5FH *tel:* 0171 486 0025 *fax:* 0171 935 8454.

FCN Music. Morley Rd, Tonbridge, Kent TN9 1RA *tel:* 01732 366421/365271.

Flutemakers Guild Ltd. 10 Shacklewell Rd, London N16 7TA *tel:* 0171 254 7175 *also fax. W/wind (fls, piccs, etc).*

Forest Pianos. 101 Ilkely Rd, Otley, W Yorks LS21 3JP *tel:* 01943 465350. *Pnos (Lawrence and Nash); also tuning and repairs.*

Gordon Stevenson Violins. 6 Barclay Terrace, Bruntsfield, Edinburgh EH10 4HP *tel:* 0131 229 2051 *fax:* 0131 229 9298. *Vns.*

Green, Miranda. 21 Wathen Rd, Dorking, Surrey RH4 1JY *tel:* 01306 886199. *Vns and vas.*

Grotrian-Steinweg Pianos. Robert Morley & Co Ltd, 34 Engate St, London SE13 7HA *tel:* 0181 318 5838 *fax:* 0181 297 0720 *email:* http://www.yell.co.uk/sites/morley. *Grand and upright pnos.*

Harrison & Harrison Ltd. St John's Rd, Meadowfield, Durham DH7 8YH *tel:* 0191 378 2222 *fax:* 0191 378 3388 *email:* h.h@btinternet.com. Mark Venning, mgr dir. *Pipe orgs.*

Hawkins (Organ Builders) Ltd. Unit 6, Greenhough Rd, Lichfield, Staffs WS13 7AU *tel:* 015432 55135.

Hele & Co Ltd. The Tower, Lower Port View, Saltash, Cornwall PL12 4BY *tel:* 01752 842027. *Org builders.*

Henry Willis & Sons Ltd. 87-91 Rushes Rd, Petersfield, Hants GU32 3AT *tel:* 01730 263141; 01730 262151 *also fax.* D M van Heck, mgr dir. *Pipe orgs.*

Sir Herbert Marshall & Sons Ltd. 154 Clapham Park Rd, London SW4 7DE *tel:* 0171 978 2444 *fax:* 0171 978 2347. *Pnos.*

Herrburger Brooks. Meadow La, Long Eaton, Nottingham NG10 2FG *tel:* 0115 973 5218 *fax:* 0115 973 0944. *Pno actions, hammers, keys, etc.*

Hibernian Violins. 24 Players Av, Malvern Link, Worcs WR14 1DU *tel:* 01684 562947. Padraig Ó Dubhlaoidh. *Vn and viol family insts, bows.*

Hill, Norman & Beard. Manor Works, Orange St, Thaxted, Great Dunmow, Essex CM6 2LH *tel:* 01371 830338 *fax:* 01371 831225. *Org builders.*

Holywell Music Ltd. 58 Hopton St, London SE1 9JH *tel:* 0171 928 8451 *fax:* 0171 928 8284 *email:* holywell@netcomuk.co.uk. *Salvi and Lyon & Healy concert and non-pedal hps.*

Impact Percussion. 120-122 Bermondsey St, London SE1 3TX *tel:* 0171 403 5900 *fax:* 0171 403 5910 *email:* impactperc@msn.com. *Tubular bells, bass bells, bass drums, custom manufacture of perc insts and touring trolleys.*

Irish Organ Co. Steeple Rd Industrial Estate, Antrim, Co Antrim BT41 1AB *tel:* 018494 67954. *Pipe orgs.*

J P Guivier & Co Ltd. 99 Mortimer St, London W1N 7TA *tel:* 0171 580 2560 *fax:* 0171 436 1461. *Restorers and dealers of insts, bows and accs of the vn family.*

J W Walker & Sons Ltd. Wimbledon Av, Brandon, Suffolk IP27 0NF *tel:* 01842 810296 *fax:* 01842 813124 *email:* organs@jwwalker.co.uk. *Pipe orgs.*

J Wood & Sons Ltd. 38 Manningham La, Bradford BD1 3EA *tel:* 01274 307636 *fax:* 01274 393516 *email:* sales@earlyms.demon.co.uk. *Orgs, celestas, pnos, keyboards, early w/wind insts.*

Jack Hayward Harps. 5 Sun Gardens, Burghfield Common, Reading RG7 3JB *tel:* 0118 983 3922 *fax:* 0118 983 3868. *Celtic and concert hps, accs, insurance, gut and nylon strings.*

Jacques Samuel Pianos Ltd. 142 Edgware Rd, London W2 2DZ *tel:* 0171 723 8818 *fax:* 0171 224 8692. *Pnos, repairs, removals, sale and hire.*

John Brinsmead Pianoforte Manufacturers Ltd *see* **Kemble & Co Ltd.**

John Hornby Skewes & Co Ltd. Salem House, Parkinson Approach, Garforth, Leeds LS25 2HR *tel:* 0113 286 5381 *fax:* 0113 286 8515. *Manufacturer, wholesaler and distributor of mus insts, associated accs, inst amplification and pro-audio equipment.*

John Oakes & Son. Meir Heath, Stoke on Trent ST3 7PB *tel:* 01782 392142. *Pipe orgs, overhaul and rebuilding.*

Justin Sillman & Co. 6 Tomlins Grove, Bow, London E3 4NX *tel:* 0181 981 9800 *fax:* 0181 981 2800 *email:* justin@justin.idiscover.co.uk. *Orgs.*

Kemble & Co Ltd. Mount Av, Bletchley, Milton Keynes MK1 1JE *tel:* 01908 371771 *fax:* 01908 270448 *email:* 100601.2045@ compuserve.com. *Upright pnos, silent pnos.*

KGB Musical Instruments. 61 Derby Rd, Tranmere, Birkenhead, Merseyside L42 7HA *tel:* 0151 647 3268. *Guis and fretted insts; parts and accs.*

Lodge, J M. Fiddlers Folly, Baughurst Rd, Ramsdell, Basingstoke, Hants *tel:* 01256 850140. *Vn, va, vc, db, gui, bows.*

Lowes Woodwind. 102 Greenwich South St, London SE10 8UN *tel:* 0181 691 6944 *fax:* 0181 694 2503. Jeremy Lowe, proprietor; Michael Edwards, repairer. *Cl extensions, mouthpieces, barrels, tuning and alterations.*

Lyons Musicale Ltd. The Bourne, 20 Salisbury Av, Harpenden, Herts AL5 2QG *tel:* 01582 460978 *fax:* 01582 767343. David Johnston, mgr dir. *Lyons 'c' cl.*

McQueens Musical Instruments. Sunset Business Centre, Manchester Rd, Kearsley, Bolton BL4 8RT *tel:* 01204 794600 *also fax.* *Bugles, cavalry tpts, post horns, herald tpts. Also repairs. Contractors to MOD.*

Makin Organs Ltd. Compton House, Franklin St, Oldham, Lancs OL1 2DP *tel:* 0161 626 5666 *fax:* 0161 665 2284 *email:* david@makinorgans. co.uk. David Clegg, dir and gen mgr. *Classical orgs, digital pnos, MIDI expanders. Also distributors and nationwide hire service.*

Michael Johnson Violin Maker/Restorer/Dealer. Upper Sunnyside, Lowther St, Penrith, Cumbria CA11 7UW *tel:* 01768 864424 *also fax.* *Vns, vas, vcs and basses. Visitors by appointment.*

Moeck UK. 38 Manningham La, Bradford, W Yorks BD1 3EA *tel:* 01274 721646 *fax:* 01274 393516. *Rcdrs and historical w/wind.*

Monington and Weston Pianos. Robert Morley & Co Ltd, 34 Engate St, London SE13 7HA *tel:* 0181 318 5838 *fax:* 0181 297 0720 *email:* http://www.yell.co.uk/sites/morley. *Upright pnos.*

N P Mander Ltd. St Peter's Organ Works, St Peter's Sq, Warner Pl, Hackney Rd, London E2 7AF *tel:* 0171 739 4747 *fax:* 0171 729 4718. *Pipe orgs.*

Nicholls, Colin. 316 Church Rd, Northolt, Middx UB5 5AP *tel:* 0181 845 1092 *also fax.* *Vns, vas and vcs.*

Nicholson & Co (Worcester) Ltd. 80 Quest Hills Rd, Malvern, Worcs WR14 1RN *tel:* 01684 574670 *fax:* 01684 567716. A D Moyes, mgr dir. *Pipe and church orgs.*

Norman Hall & Sons Organ Builders. 39 Sturton St, Cambridge CB1 2QG *tel:* 01223 350516 *also fax.*

Northern Renaissance Instruments. 6 Needham Av, Chorlton cum Hardy, Manchester M21 8AA *tel:* 0161 881 8134 *also fax; email:* esegerman@ cityscape.co.uk. *Strs, varnishing materials.*

Norwich Organs. Bidwell Rd, Rackheath, Norfolk NR13 6LH *tel:* 01603 720360/404459 (24 hrs) *fax:* 01603 720746. *Classical elec orgs.*

Nowak, Steffen. 12 Windsor Terrace, Totterdown, Bristol BS3 4UF *tel:* 0117 977 7141. *Baroque and modern vn, va and vc.*

Oakwood Instruments. 8 Ladywood Rd, Leeds LS8 2QF *tel:* 0113 265 8585 *fax:* 0113 293 3011 *email:* oakwood@magpie.demon.co.uk. *Electric vns, mandolins, mandolas, bouzoukis, citterns, guis, banjos, hammer dulcimers, hps, melodeons.*

Ocarina Workshop. PO Box 56, Kettering, Northants NN15 5LX *tel:* 01536 485963 *fax:* 01536 485051 *email:* ocarina@compuserve.com. *Ocarinas, duet ocarinas, poly-oc, ocarina mus (also m/order).*

The Orchestration Workshop. Springwood Music Workshops, Water St, Huddersfield HD1 4BB *tel:* 01484 422300 *fax:* 01484 305303 *email:* musick@netlink.co.uk. David R Leach, proprietor. *Mechanical org design, manufacture and restoration, fine wood pipework and perforated card mus.*

Paxman Musical Instruments Ltd. Linton House, 164-180 Union St, London SE1 0LH *tel:* 0171 620 2077 *fax:* 0171 620 1688 *email:* paxman horn@compuserve.com. *Hns.*

Peavey Electronics Ltd. Great Folds Rd, Oakley Hay, Corby, Northants NN18 9ET *tel:* 01536 461234 *fax:* 01536 747222. *Guis, drums, keyboards, amps and sound equipment.*

Percussion Plus. The Mill, Gt Bowden Rd, Market Harborough, Leics LE16 7DE *tel:* 01858 433124 *fax:* 01858 462218. *Perc inst manufacturer and distributor.*

Percy Daniel & Co Ltd. Beach Av, Clevedon, Somerset BS21 7XX *tel:* 01275 873273 *fax:* 01275 342747. *Orgs.*

Peter Collins Ltd. 42 Pate Rd, Melton Mowbray, Leics LE13 0DG *tel:* 01664 410555 *fax:* 01664 410535. *Pipe org builders and restorers.*

Peter Conacher & Co Ltd. Springwood Organ Works, Water St, Huddersfield HD1 4BB *tel:* 01484 530053 *fax:* 01484 305303 *email:* admin@musiclink.co.uk; http://www.musiclink/co.uk/. *Orgs, harmoniums, reed orgs; repair, restoration and tuning.*

Phil Parker Ltd (Wholesale). 106a Crawford St, London W1H 1AL *tel:* 0171 723 6909 *fax:* 0171 935 6686. *W/wind, br, educ strs, gig bags and accs.*

Phil Rees Music Tech. Unit 2 Clarendon Court, Park St, Charlbury, Oxford OX7 3PT *tel:* 01608 811215 *fax:* 01608 811227. Sheila Cantlay, sales mgr; Philip Rees. *Manufacturers of electronic mus accs. Specialists in MIDI.*

The Piano Workshop. 41 Wharf St, Sowerby Bridge, Halifax *tel:* 01422 835095. Paul E Rayner, proprietor. *Pno restoration, removals, tuning, sales, casework refinishing and valuations.*

Pilgrim Harps. Stansted House, Tilburstow Hill Rd, S Godstone, Surrey RH9 8NA *tel:* 01342 893242 *fax:* 01342 892646. *Pedal and non-pedal hps.*

Premier Percussion Ltd. Blaby Rd, Wigston, Leics LE18 4DF *tel:* 0116 277 3121 *fax:* 0116 277 6627 *email:* info@premier-drums.com. *Perc insts and accs.*

Prentice, Ronald. The Mill, Ash Priors, Taunton, Somerset TA4 3NQ *tel:* 01823 432734 *email:* basses@the-mill.co.uk. *Str (db specialist, keyed E-string extension).*

R A J Bower & Co. Wellgrove Organ Manufactory, Weston Longville, Norwich NR9 5JJ *tel:* 01603 881189 *fax:* 01603 881222. *Orgs, pedal pnos.*

Richard Smith Musical Instruments. 110 The Vale, London N14 6AY *tel:* 0181 882 1580 *fax:* 0181 447 8567 *email:* smithwatkins@rsmi.u-net. com; http://www.rsmi.u-net.com/. *Designers and makers of Smith-Watkins tpts, cornets and flugel hns.*

Robert Morley & Co Ltd. 34 Engate St, London SE13 7HA *tel:* 0181 318 5838 *fax:* 0181 297 0720 *email:* http://www.yell.co.uk/sites/morley. *Pnos, hpds, spinets, clvds, virginals and celestes.*

Roger Hansell Violins. Ulshaw House, Coverbridge, Middleham, Leyburn, N Yorks DL8 4PU *tel:* 01969 623048; 01969 624416 *also fax.* *Modern and baroque vns, vas, vcs; visitor's centre.*

Roland (UK) Ltd. Atlantic Close, Swansea Enterprise Pk, Swansea, W Glamorgan SA7 9FJ *tel:* 01792 702701 *fax:* 01792 700130; 01792 799644 (sales). *Distributor and manufacturer of elec mus insts and computer mus software.*

Rosetti Ltd. 4 Tamdown Way, Springwood Industrial Estate, Braintree, Essex CM7 2QL *tel:* 01376 550033 *fax:* 01376 550042. *Str, br, w/wind, guis, perc, gui accs, amps.*

Rotosound Marketing Ltd. Unit 3b, Morewood Close, Sevenoaks, Kent TN13 2HU *tel:* 01732 450838/9 *fax:* 01732 458994. *Strings for gui, bs gui, vn and db.*

Rushworth & Dreaper Ltd (incorporating Compton Pipe Organs). 72 St Anne St, Liverpool L3 3DY *tel:* 0151 207 5252 *also fax.* Alastair J M Rushworth, chmn and mgr dir. *Pipe orgs; cathedral, church and concert hall.*

Schimmel Pianos. Forsyth Bros Ltd (Distributor), 126 Deansgate, Manchester M3 2GR *tel:* 0161 834 3281 ext 225 *fax:* 0161 834 0630 *email:* forsythmus@aol.com. Kathryn Howard. *Pno.*

Simon Watkin Violins. 2 North Green, Coates, Peterborough PE7 2BQ *tel:* 01733 840235 *email:* scdw@cix.compulink.co. *Vns.*

Soar Valley Music. 15 Prince William Rd, Loughborough, Leics LE11 0GU *tel:* 01509 269629 *fax:* 01509 269206. *Folk inst wholesaler (w/wind, perc), Latin and African perc.*

Solid State Logic Organ Systems. Unit 21-22 Putney Close, Brandon, Suffolk IP27 0PA *tel:* 01842 814814 *fax:* 01842 813802 *email:* organs@ solid-state-logic.com. *Elec switching and piston capture systems for the pipe org.*

Stagg, John W. 10 Christmas Steps, Bristol BS1 5BS *tel:* 0117 925 4538 *also fax. Bow maker and restorer.*

Steinway & Sons (UK). Steinway Hall, 44 Marylebone La, Wigmore St, London W1M 6EN *tel:* 0171 487 3391 *fax:* 0171 935 0466. *Pnos.*

Stentor Music Co Ltd. Albert Rd North, Reigate, Surrey RH2 9EZ *tel:* 01737 240226 *fax:* 01737 242748 *email:* stentor@stentor-music. com. *Str, br, w/wind and gui wholesaler.*

Stoppani, George. 6 Needham Av, Chorlton-cum-Hardy, Manchester M21 8AA *tel:* 0161 860 7386; 0161 256 1173. *Str family insts, db.*

Strings & Things Ltd. Unit 2, 202-210 Brighton Rd, Shoreham-by-Sea, W Sussex BN43 6RJ *tel:* 01273 440442 *fax:* 01273 440278 *email:* strings@stringsandthings.co.uk. *Str, accs.*

Summerfield Bros. Olsover House, 43 Sackville Rd, Newcastle-upon-Tyne NE6 5TA *tel:* 0191 276 0448 *fax:* 0191 276 1623 *email:* summer field@ashleymark.co.uk. *Guis and fretted insts.*

T W Howarth & Co Ltd. 31-35 Chiltern St, London W1M 1HG *tel:* 0171 935 2407 *fax:* 0171 224 2564 *email:* howarth_ltd@msn.com. Nigel Clark, mgr dir. *Cls, obs, ob d'am, ehs, bsns.*

Taylor, Eric J. 17 Orton Dr, Witchford, Ely, Cambs CB6 2JG *tel:* 01353 667422. *Pnos, repairs.*

Technics Musical Instruments. Panasonic UK, Panasonic House, Willoughby Rd, Bracknell, Berks RG12 8FP *tel:* 01344 853177 *fax:* 01344 853389 *email:* emio@mail.panasonic.co.uk. *Elec orgs, digital pnos, keyboards.*

Thibouville-Lamy & Co Ltd. Gilbert House, 406 Roding La South, (Off Woodford Av), Woodford Green, Essex IG8 8EY *tel:* 0181 551 1282 *fax:* 0181 550 8377. *Importer and wholesaler of mus insts and accs.*

Trevor J James & Co. 4-6 Buckland Rd, Maidstone, Kent ME16 0SL *tel:* 01622 692119 *fax:* 01622 692438 *email:* tjjco@kentnet.co.uk. *W/wind, br and accs manufacture and distribution.*

Vincent Bach International Ltd. Unit 71, Capitol Park Industrial Estate, Capitol Way, Edgware Rd, London NW9 0EW *tel:* 0181 905 9505 *fax:* 0181 905 9149. *W/wind, br, orch str insts and related accs.*

W P Williams & Co. 2 Boscombe Mews, Boscombe Rd, Southend on Sea SS2 5JD *tel:* 01702 610981 *fax:* 01702 325049. *Pipe orgs, br shallots.*

Ward, Alan. St Andrews, 27 Plomer Hill, Downley, High Wycombe, Bucks HP13 5JG *tel:* 01494 523371. *Modern and baroque vn, va, vc maker, restorer, repairer.*

Ward & Winterbourn. 75 Alexandra Rd, London NW4 2RX *tel:* 0181 203 2678. *W/wind.*

Wells-Kennedy Partnership Ltd. 85-87 Gregg St, Lisburn, Co Antrim BT27 5AW *tel:* 01846 664257 *fax:* 01846 603722. David H McElderry, dir. *Orgs.*

Welmar Pianos Ltd. 154 Clapham Park Rd, London SW4 7DE *tel:* 0171 978 2444 *fax:* 0171 978 2347. *Pnos.*

Whelpdale, Maxwell & Codd Ltd. 154 Clapham Park Rd, London SW4 7DE *tel:* 0171 978 2444 *fax:* 0171 978 2347. *Pnos. Also manufacture under the names of Rogers, Hopkinson, Gerh Steinberg and Rich Lipp & Sohn, and distributor for Blüthner.*

Wood of Huddersfield. St Andrews Rd, Huddersfield, W Yorks HD1 6RZ *tel:* 01484 533374 *also fax.* Philip Wood; David Wood. *Org builders.*

Woolrich, A P. Canal Side, Huntworth, Bridgwater, Somerset TA7 0AJ *tel:* 01278 663020. *Manufacturer of ironmongery for keyboard insts.*

Wyvern Classical Organs Ltd. Station Rd, Chobham, Woking, Surrey GU24 8AQ *tel:* 01276 856363 *fax:* 01276 855241 *email:* 101674.234@ compuserve.com. *Orgs.*

Yamaha-Kemble Music (UK) Ltd. Sherbourne Dr, Tilbrook, Milton Keynes MK7 8BL *tel:* 01908 366700 *fax:* 01908 368872. *Br, w/wind, elec keyboards, hi-tech, pro audio, pnos, guis, cymbals and drums.*

Young Chang Pianos. The Piano Warehouse, 30a Highgate Rd, London NW5 1NS *tel:* 0171 267 9229. *Distributor of Young Chang pnos.*

Retailers

This list is arranged by county, with Greater London first, followed by England, Channel Islands, Isle of Man, Scotland, Wales and Northern Ireland. Shops listed consist of dealers in printed music and musical instruments. The list does not claim to be exhaustive and excludes multiple stores whose larger branches occasionally stock instruments or accessories. A list of record shops specialising in classical recordings will be found under **Specialist Record Dealers**. Many **Music Publishers** also have a retail counter.

Greater London

Acoustic Centre. 131 Wapping High St, London E1 9NQ *tel:* 0171 265 1366 *fax:* 0171 488 3530. *Acoustic guis, amps, accs, books and videos. Valuations and appraisals, experts on vintage guis.*

All Flutes Plus. 5 Dorset St, London W1H 3FE *tel:* 0171 935 3339 *fax:* 0171 224 2053. *Fl specialists; w/wind, mus, rcdrs, repairs, rentals.*

ASM Music. 318a Kennington Rd, London SE11 4LD *tel:* 0171 735 1932 *fax:* 0171 582 6128. *Keyboards, hi-tech, home recording.*

Baldrey's Music Centre. 19 Cheam Common Rd, N Cheam, Surrey KT4 8TL *tel:* 0181 337 6283. N F Baldrey, proprietor. *Insts, mus, accs.*

Barbican Music Shop. Cromwell Tower, Silk St, Barbican, London EC2Y 8DD *tel:* 0171 588 9242 *fax:* 0171 628 1080. *Books, mus, insts, CDs, accs.*

The Bass Cellar. 21 Denmark St, London WCH2 8NA *tel:* 0171 240 3483. *Bs guis, bs amps, effects and accs.*

The Bass Centre Ltd. 131 Wapping High St, London E1 9NQ *tel:* 0171 265 1567 *fax:* 0171 488 3530. *Bs gui, bs amps, accs.*

Bell Percussion Ltd. 6 Greenock Rd, London W3 8DU *tel:* 0181 896 1200 *fax:* 0181 896 0100. *Perc retail and repairs.*

Bill Lewington Ltd. 144 Shaftesbury Av, London WC2H 8HN *tel:* 0171 240 0584 *fax:* 0171 240 2919 *email:* 106032.2774@compuserve.com. *Books, insts, mus. Also wholesalers.*

Blackburn Stringed Instruments. 75 Harrington Gardens, London SW7 4JZ *tel:* 0171 373 2474 *fax:* 0171 373 5141. *Vns, vas, vcs; also restoration and evaluation. Bows, buying and selling of str insts.*

Blanks Music Store. 271-273 Kilburn High Rd, London NW6 7JR *tel:* 0171 624 7777 *fax:* 0171 624 1260. *Guis, amps, drums, sax, fls, mandolins, perc, servicing (within 24 hrs), books, etc.*

Blüthners. 8 Berkeley Sq, London W1X 5HE *tel:* 0171 753 0533 *fax:* 0171 753 0535. *Leading makes of grand and upright pnos, tuning and repairs.*

Blüthners. 154 Clapham Park Rd, London SW4 7DE *tel:* 0171 978 2444 *fax:* 0171 978 2347. *Pnos.*

Books Etc. Royal Festival Hall, Belvedere Rd, South Bank, London SE1 8XX *tel:* 0171 620 0403 *fax:* 0171 620 0426. *Biographies, analyses, histories, libretti, scores.*

Boosey & Hawkes Music Shop. 295 Regent St, London W1R 8JH *tel:* 0171 291 7255 *fax:* 0171 436 2850. *Books, mus, accs; m/order (cat), credit cards.*

Bridgewood and Neitzert. 146 Stoke Newington Church St, London N16 0UH *tel:* 0171 249 9398 *fax:* 0171 275 9330. *Vn, va, vc, db, bows; maker, restorer and dealer.*

Britten's Music Ltd. 136 George La, South Woodford, London E18 1AY *tel:* 0181 530 6432. K Moorcraft, mgr. *Mus, insts, accs.*

Bush Books & Records. 113 Shepherds Bush Centre, London W12 8PP *tel:* 0181 740 5342 *fax:* 0181 749 7652. *Books, cassettes, CDs.*

Chandler Guitars. 300-302 Sandycombe Rd, Kew, Richmond, Surrey TW9 3NG *tel:* 0181 940 5874 *fax:* 0181 948 8203. *Fretted insts, amps, effects; sales and repairs.*

Chappell of Bond Street. 50 New Bond St, London W1Y 9HA *tel:* 0171 491 2777 *fax:* 0171 491 0133. *Insts, mus, pnos, keyboards, books, school mus.*

Chas E Foote Ltd. 10 Golden Sq, London W1R 3AF *tel:* 0171 437 1811 *fax:* 0171 734 3095. *W/wind, br, str and perc.*

Chimes Music Shop. 44 Marylebone High St, London W1M 3AD *tel:* 0171 935 1587; 0171 486 1303 *fax:* 0171 935 0457 *email:* musicman@

marcus.fnet.co.uk. Ling Sam, mgr. *Books, insts, mus, CDs, sheet mus (comprises majority of stock), bargain books. Also m/order.*
Cramer Music Ltd. 23 Garrick St, London WC2E 9AX *tel:* 0171 240 1612 *fax:* 0171 240 2639.
Dalston Sound and Light. 40-42 Dalston La, Dalston Junction, London E8 3AZ *tel:* 0171 923 3846. *Sale and hire of insts, PA equipment and disco systems.*
Dillons The Bookstore. 82 Gower St, London WC1E 6EQ *tel:* 0171 636 1577 *fax:* 0171 580 7680 *email:* enquiries@gower.dillons.org.uk. Angela Stone. *Books, mus, CDs, video and all related expertise.*
Discurio. 9 Gillingham St, London SW1V 1HN *tel:* 0171 828 7963 *also fax. Books, records, CDs.*
Don Mackrill's Music. 3-5 Station Rd, Edgware, Middx *tel:* 0181 952 5813 *fax:* 0181 951 5248. *Br, w/wind, guis, amps, educ insts, school rentals.*
The Drum Cellar. 23 Denmark St, London WCH2 8NJ *tel:* 0171 240 3483. *Acoustic and electric drums, wide range of ethnic perc.*
The Dulwich Music Shop. 2 Croxted Rd, Dulwich, London SE21 8SW *tel:* 0181 766 0202 *fax:* 0181 766 8689. *Sheet mus, books, CDs, gifts, inst sales and repairs.*
E Withers Ltd. 2 Windmill St, London W1P 1HF *tel:* 0171 916 7840 *fax:* 0171 916 7846. *Vn restorers, makers and experts. Also vas, vcs, bows and accs.*
Ealing Strings. 4 Station Parade, Uxbridge Rd, London W5 3LD *tel:* 0181 992 5222/3993. *Books, str insts, accs. Suppliers and restorers.*
Ebony & Ivory. 11 Varley Parade, Edgware Rd, Colindale, London NW9 6RR *tel:* 0181 200 5510 *fax:* 0181 205 1907. *New and second-hand pnos. Concert hire services.*
Electrohill. 124-126 Green Lanes, London N13 5UN *tel:* 0181 886 9426 *fax:* 0181 886 9356 *email:* sales@electrohill.co.uk. *Specialists in guis, amps, effects and PA equipment.*
ENO Shop. MDC Classic Music, 31 St Martin's La, London WC2N 4ER *tel:* 0171 240 0270 *email:* classic@mdcmusic.co.uk; http://www.mdcmusic.co.uk. *Books on opera, dance and ballet. CDs, videos and gifts.*
Eric Lindsey Ltd. 20-22 Rushey Green, Catford, London SE6 4AS *tel:* 0181 690 8621 *fax:* 0181 690 7064. *Guis, drums, keyboards, recording and PA equipment.*
Fazioli. The Music Studios Ltd, 29 Marylebone La, London W1M 5FH *tel:* 0171 486 0025 *fax:* 0171 935 8454. *Distributor of Fazioli pnos, retail, restoration of fine makes.*

Folk Shop. Cecil Sharp House, 2 Regent's Pk Rd, London NW1 7AY *tel:* 0171 428 9060 *fax:* 0171 284 4255. *Books, records, folk and acoustic insts.*
Frederick Phelps Ltd, Violins. 67 Fortess Rd, London NW5 1AG *tel:* 0171 482 0316 *fax:* 0171 813 4589. Rachel Douglas, dir. *Vns, vas, vcs, accs; also restoration and bow repairs.*
Freedmans Musical Instruments. 631 Leytonstone High Rd, London E11 4PA *tel:* 0181 539 0288 *also fax. Group and elec insts, perc, PA, w/wind insts, guis, amps, books.*
Gigsounds Ltd. 86-88 Mitcham La, Streatham, London SW16 6NR *tel:* 0181 769 6496 *fax:* 0181 769 9530. *Elec and acoustic insts, wind and br insts, accs.*
Hampstead Pianos. 131 Abbey Rd, London NW6 4SL *tel:* 0171 624 8895 *fax:* 0181 245 4653. Mark Ransom, mgr. *Acoustic pnos, restoration, tuning, removals and unique pno designs.*
Hanks Acoustics. 24 Denmark St, London WC2H 8NE *tel:* 0171 379 1139. *Acoustic and semi-acoustic insts, harmonica specialists.*
Harpsichord Workshop. 130 Westbourne Terrace Mews, London W2 6QG *tel:* 0171 723 9650 *also fax.* Mark Ransom, mgr. *Tuning, repair and renovation, short and long-term hire, insts for sale and an agent for well-known makers.*
Harrods Ltd (Piano and Musical Instruments Department). Knightsbridge, London SW1X 7XL *tel:* 0171 730 1234 *fax:* 0171 225 6565. Jeff Charlton, buyer. *Upright and grand pnos, w/wind and br insts, elec keyboards, sheet mus, guis and accs.*
Holywell Music Ltd. 58 Hopton St, London SE1 9JH *tel:* 0171 928 8451 *fax:* 0171 928 8284 *email:* holywell@netcomuk.co.uk. David Williams, gen mgr; Rebecca Jones, mus dept. *Salvi and Lyon & Healy concert and non-pedal hps, hp mus, str, recordings and accs.*
Impact Percussion. 120-122 Bermondsey St, London SE1 3TX *tel:* 0171 403 5900 *fax:* 0171 403 5910 *email:* impactperc@msn.com. Paul Hagen, proprietor. *Orch and latin perc and kits; also repairs and hire.*
Islington Music. 6 Shillingford St, off Cross St, London N1 2DP *tel:* 0171 354 3195 *also fax. Sheet mus, tapes, accs, gifts, insts sales and hire, m/order.*
Ivor Mairants Musicentre. 56 Rathbone Pl, London W1P 1AB *tel:* 0171 636 1481 *fax:* 0171 580 6272. Phil Lusher, mgr. *Fretted insts, mus, accs, m/order, repairs.*
J P Guivier & Co Ltd. 99 Mortimer St, London W1N 7TA *tel:* 0171 580 2560; 0171 636 6499 *fax:* 0171 436 1461. Richard White, Robin

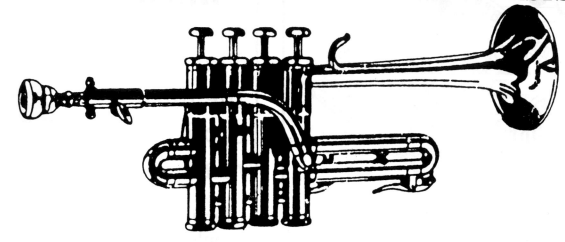

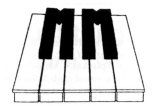

Cheshire

Atrincham

Concert Systems. Unit 4d, Stag Industrial Estate, Atlantic St, Atrincham, Cheshire WA14 5DW *tel:* 0161 927 7700 *fax:* 0161 927 7722 *email:* http://www.concertsys.co.uk. *Sound equipment, PA, repairs and m/order.*

Cheadle

Sounds Great. 182 Wilmslow Rd, Heald Green, Cheadle, Cheshire SK8 3BG *tel:* 0161 436 4799 *fax:* 0161 436 1307. *Insts, br, w/wind, guis, amps, keyboards, mus.*

Chester

Bookland Music Shop. 12 Bridge St, Chester CH1 1NQ *tel:* 01244 313281 *fax:* 01244 341868 *email:* music@bookland.co.uk; http://www.bookland.co.uk. *Printed mus, books, mus gifts, accs.*

Colte Music. 99 Brook St, Chester CH1 3DX *tel:* 01244 312633 *fax:* 01244 343383. *Guis, amps, PA, drums, accs, mus.*

Curzon Music (Mail Order). 82b Hough Green, Chester CH4 8JW *tel:* 01244 683457 *also fax. Educ and classical mus, m/order.*

Knutsford

Mostly Music. 28 Carlisle Close, Noberley, Knutsford, Cheshire WA16 7HD *tel:* 01565 872650. *M/order of books, mus, recordings, tapes, CDs.*

Macclesfield

Macclesfield Organ Centre. 15 Mill La, Macclesfield, Cheshire SK11 7NN *tel:* 01625 427062 *fax:* 01625 619507. *Keyboards, digital pnos, orgs and mus insts.*

Margin Music. 3 Market Pl, Macclesfield, Cheshire SK10 1EB *tel:* 01625 619013 *fax:* 01625 269015. *Keyboards, guis, br, w/wind, amps, records, books, accs.*

Neston

Barrett & Scott: Music for Singers. 6 Hinderton Rd, Neston, S Wirral, Cheshire L64 9PQ *tel:* 0151 260 9641; 0151 336 6235. *M/order retailers, specialists in vocal and choral mus; also all types of sheet mus and books.*

Stockport

Dawsons Music Ltd. 1a Princes St, Stockport, Cheshire SK1 1SL *tel:* 0161 477 1210. *Insts, mus.*

Music Exchange. 9 St Petersgate, Stockport, Cheshire SK1 1EB *tel:* 0161 474 7104 *fax:* 0161 480 0900. *Insts, mus, accs.*

Warrington

Dawsons Music Ltd. 65 Sankey St, Warrington, Cheshire WA1 1SU *tel:* 01925 632591 *fax:* 01925 417812. *Books, insts, mus, hi-tech equipment, pnos.*

Cornwall

Camborne

Trevada Music. 9 Chapel St, Camborne, Cornwall TR14 8ER *tel:* 01209 714353 *fax:* 01209 718708. *Pnos, br, w/wind, perc, str, sheet mus, repairs, rental scheme.*

Launceston

Tottle's Music Shop. 30 Westgate St, Launceston, Cornwall PL15 7AE *tel:* 01566 772512. *Books, mus, records; w/wind, br, str, perc insts; gui, amps, orgs, keyboards, pnos.*

Redruth

John Oliver. 33 Fore St, Redruth, Cornwall TR15 2AE *tel:* 01209 216494 *fax:* 01209 213999. *Records, CDs, Laserdisc, cassettes, mus, small insts, accs, videos.*

St Austell

The Old Baccy Shop (Music Dept). 17 Duke St, St Austell, Cornwall PL25 5PQ *tel:* 01726 73018 *also fax. Strs, accs.*

Truro

Tottles Music Shop. 2 Highshore House, Newbridge St, Truro, Cornwall TR1 2AA *tel:* 01872 78501/2. *W/wind, br, str insts; mus, orgs, pnos, rental scheme.*

Cumbria

Alston

Jacks, Pipes & Hammers. Bridge View, Garrigill, Alston, Cumbria CA9 3DU *tel:* 01434 381583 *also fax. Mus for keyboard, org, vocal, trio sonatas, quadros, solos. Facsimile editions. Specialists in 17th-18th C mus and books. Publishers of 18th C mus in facsimile.*

Barrow in Furness

The New Kelly's Music Shop. 101 Church St, Barrow in Furness, Cumbria LA14 2HW *tel:* 01229 822973. *Books, mus, cassettes, CDs, guis, br, wind, str, perc, keyboards, accs.*

Brampton

Omega Music. Town Foot Estate, Brampton, Cumbria CA8 1SW *tel:* 016977 3067 *fax:* 016977 41018. *Insts, perc, pno showroom.*

Penrith

Creighton & Tweedie Ltd. Poets Walk, Penrith, Cumbria CA11 7HJ *tel:* 01768 864331 *fax:* 01768 899778. *Pno specialists (acoustic and digital), orgs.*

Derbyshire

Chesterfield

C E Hudson & Son Ltd. 5 Market Pl, Chesterfield, Derbys S40 1TJ *tel:* 01246 271177 *fax:* 01246 211631. *Keyboards, guis (elec and acoustic), amps, sheet mus, elec pnos; br, w/wind, str insts. CDs, cassettes, videos, records.*

Palfreymans Music. 171 Chatsworth Rd, Chesterfield, Derbys S40 2AU *tel:* 01246 271737. *Keyboards, drums, guis, digital pnos, sheet mus, rcdrs, harmonicas, folk insts and amps. Repairs and hire. Teaching.*

Derby

Chas Foulds & Son (Derby) Ltd. 40 Irongate, Derby DE1 3GA *tel:* 01332 344842/342654 *fax:* 01332 294415. *Pnos, insts, sheet mus, guis.*

Neville Bros. 74 Babington La, Derby DE1 1SX *tel:* 01332 290762 *also fax. Guis, amps, br, w/wind, repairs.*

Play It Again Sam. 77-79 Osmaston Rd, Derby DE1 2JH *tel:* 01332 348156 *fax:* 01332 341414. *Keyboards, elec, guis, accs, basses, records, computers, amps, PA.*

Ilkeston

Zebra Muzik. 336 Nottingham Rd, Ilkeston, Derbys DE7 5BD *tel:* 0115 930 8362 *fax:* 0115 944 1936. *Peavey, Marshall, Yamaha, Fender. All leading brands.*

Devon

Barnstaple

Soundpad. Rolle Quay House, Rolle Quay, Barnstaple, Devon EX31 1JE *tel:* 01271 23686 *also fax.*

Exeter

Bill Greenhalgh Ltd. 125-127 Fore St, Exeter, Devon EX4 3JQ *tel:* 01392 430008. *Insts, keyboards, mus, pnos, amps.*

LMS Music Supplies. 154 Sidwell St, Exeter EX4 6RT *tel:* 01392 428108 *fax:* 01392 412521 *email:* lmsmusic@compuserve.com. *Educ m/order mus insts and books.*

Music Lines. 1 Bartholomew St West, Exeter, Devon EX4 3AJ *tel:* 01392 433748 *also fax. Sheet mus and m/order.*

The Music Store *formerly* Bell & Crane Music Ltd. 154 Sidwell St, Exeter EX4 6RT *tel:* 01392 436258 *fax:* 01392 423581. *Mus, books, orch insts, keyboards, pnos, orgs, guis, accs, tuition, m/order.*

South Molton

Studio Music Shop. 11 George Hotel Mews, South Molton, Devon EX36 3AB *tel:* 01769 574346 *also fax.*

Tavistock

Maestros (including Mainly Music). 19 Market St, Tavistock, Devon PL19 0DE *tel:* 01822 614074. *Insts, books, repairs, accs, m/order.*

Dorset

Bournemouth

Eddie Moors Music Ltd. 679 Christchurch Rd, Boscombe, Bournemouth, Dorset BH7 6AE *tel:* 01202 395135 *fax:* 01202 397622. *Hi-tech recording studio equipment, classical insts, guis, perc.*

Poole

Achille Roma. 456 Ashley Rd, Parkstone, Poole, Dorset BH14 0AD *tel:* 01202 743654 *also fax. All insts, sheet mus, accs, MIDI, PA equipment.*

Music Store. Unit 14 Towngate Centre, High St, Poole, Dorset BH15 1ER *tel:* 01202 682700 *fax:* 01202 660755. *Printed mus, Yamaha keyboards and guis, Technics pnos, keyboards and orgs, Hohner guis and harmonicas.*

Sherborne

Dorset Music House. 22 Cheap St, Sherborne, Dorset DT9 3PX *tel:* 01935 816332/812914. *Sheet mus, CDs, cassettes, mus gifts.*

County Durham

Darlington

Williams. Blackwellgate, Darlington, Co Durham DL1 5HH *tel:* 01325 466224 *fax:* 01325 383644. *Mus, keyboards, pnos, orgs, insts, guis.*

East Riding of Yorkshire

Beverley

Beverley Music Centre. 14 Norwood, Beverley, East Yorks HU17 9EZ *tel:* 01482 881584 *fax:* 01482 867653. *Dealers and restorers of vns, vas, vcs, bows and accs. Br, w/wind, guis. Educ insts. Printed mus. Postal service.*

East Sussex

Battle

Amadeus Performance Equipment Ltd. Great Beech Barn, Kane Hythe Rd, Battle, E Sussex TN33 9QU *tel:* 01424 775867 *fax:* 01424 775866. *Mus stands, musician posture chairs, inst racks, portable staging, acoustically designed rehearsal rooms, other performing arts furniture and accs.*

Northumberland
Bedlington
Dennis Todd Music. 86 Front St, Bedlington, Northumberland NE22 5AE tel: 01670 822085 fax: 01670 820592. *Br, w/wind, perc, elec keyboards, guis, sheet mus, educ mus, rental plan, repairs.*
Corbridge
John Ross (Pianos). St Helen's St, Corbridge, Northumberland NE45 5BE tel: 01434 632968 fax: 01434 632245. *Insts, mus, accs.*

Nottinghamshire
Long Eaton
Take-2-Music. 116a Derby Rd, Long Eaton, Notts NG10 4LS tel: 0115 973 5468. *Insts, mus, teaching studios.*
Mansfield
Music Scene. 9a Albert St, Mansfield, Notts NG18 1EA tel: 01623 631174 *also fax. Keyboards, orgs, pnos, digital pnos, br, w/wind, guis, amps, mus, accs.*
Newark
Trent Music Centre. 1a Pelham St, Newark, Notts NG24 4XD tel: 01636 77626. *Mus, books, insts, amps, keyboards, repairs, tuition; goods made to order, guild and jazz gui stockist.*
Nottingham
Academy of Sound. 9-13 Hockley, Nottingham NG1 1FH tel: 0115 958 1888 fax: 0115 958 0033. *Multi-media equipment, keyboards, recording, guis, drums, PA.*
Farnsworth Musical Supplies Ltd. 126 Nottingham Rd, Sherwood Rise, Nottingham NG7 7AH tel: 0115 960 8955. *Insts, mus, accs.*
Fox's Music. 246 Victoria Centre, Nottingham NG1 3QQ tel: 0115 947 4221 fax: 0115 924 3292. *Clavinovas, elec orgs, pnos, mus, accs, guis, amplification, br, w/wind, teaching.*
S & E M Turner Violins. 1-5 Lily Grove, Beeston, Nottingham tel: 0115 943 0333. *Vns, dbs, vas, vcs, accs; repairs, valuations, rentals, export, commission.*
Spanish Guitar Centre. 44 Nottingham Rd, New Basford, Nottingham NG7 7AE tel: 0115 962 2709 fax: 0115 962 5368 email: spanish_guitar@ compuserve.com. *Guis, gui mus, accs, m/order, tuition.*
Windblowers. 75-77 Derby Rd, Nottingham NG1 5BA tel: 0115 941 0543 fax: 0115 947 4433. *Mus, br and w/wind insts and accs, all types of sheet mus.*
Worksop
Berry's Music. 23 Bridge Pl, Worksop, Notts S80 1DT tel: 01909 473532 fax: 01909 530609. *Mus, insts, accs.*

Oxfordshire
Bicester
Early Keyboard Agency. Heyford Galleries, High St, Upper Heyford, Bicester, Oxon OX6 3LE tel: 01869 232282. *Hpds, spinets, virginals, clvds, stools, tuners, covers, wound strings, humidification equipment; also reconditioning, maintenance.*
Henley-on-Thames
Peter W Salisbury Ltd. 24 Duke St, Henley-on-Thames, Oxon RG9 1UP tel: 01491 413019 fax: 01491 411361. *Pnos.*
Oxford
Blackwell's Music Library Services. Hythe Bridge St, Oxford OX1 2ET tel: 01865 792792 fax: 01865 261395 email: lbdmus@blackwell.co.uk. *M/order suppliers to mus libraries, colleges and orchs; books, printed mus, recordings.*
Blackwell's Music Shop. 38 Holywell St, Oxford OX1 3SW tel: 01865 792792 fax: 01865 248833. *New and second-hand books and mus, CDs, cassettes, videos, gifts, also m/order, concert tickets.*
Lighting Sound and Equipment. 118 Cowley Rd, Oxford OX4 1JE tel: 01865 722027 fax: 01865 202454. *PA, lighting, hire and sales.*
Oxford University Press Bookshop. 116-117 High St, Oxford OX1 4BZ tel: 01865 242913 fax: 01865 241701 email: bookshop@oup.co.uk. *Books, sheet mus.*
Russell Acott Ltd. 124 High St, Oxford OX1 4DE tel: 01865 241195 fax: 01865 798256. *Insts, mus, pnos.*

Redcar and Cleveland
Guisborough
Greensleeves. 21 Chaloner St, Guisborough, Redcar and Cleveland TS14 6QD tel: 01287 636028 also fax. *Mus, insts, str, w/wind, br, perc, pnos, keyboards, CDs, cassettes, accs.*

Shropshire
Oswestry
Hidersine Co Ltd. Middleton Rd, Oswestry, Shropshire SY11 2RB tel: 01691 657921 fax: 01691 679403 email: barnhide@enterprise.net. *Rosin and strs.*
Shrewsbury
Brattons Pianos Ltd. Bratton House, 23 Dogpole, Shrewsbury, Shropshire SY1 1ES tel: 01743 362133. *Books, insts, mus; m/order.*
Salop Music Centre. St Michaels St, Shrewsbury, Shropshire SY1 2ES tel: 01743 365561/364111. *Sheet mus, br, w/wind, keyboards, orch str, educ perc, gui specialists, hi tech, PA, folk, schools discount.*
Windband. 9 Greyfriars Rd, Shrewsbury, Shropshire SY3 7EN tel: 01743 367482 also fax; email: windband@cableinet.co.uk. *W/wind and br specialist, educ perc, folk and early insts, mus and accs m/order, rental purchase, inst hire schemes, repairs.*
Telford
Telford Musical Instruments Ltd. 7 Bell St, Wellington, Telford, Shropshire TF1 1LS tel: 01952 255310 fax: 01952 223138. *Insts, mus.*

Somerset
Frome
Sounds of Frome. 5 Bath St, Frome, Somerset BA11 1DH tel: 01373 462083. *Orgs, keyboards, guis, amps, synthesizers, multi-track recorders.*
Taunton
Gillian Greig Music. 44 Kingston Rd, Taunton, Somerset TA2 7SG tel: 01823 333317 fax: 01823 338454. *Books, mus, cassettes, CDs.*
John Packer Ltd. 1 Portland St, Taunton, Somerset TA1 1UY tel: 01823 282386 fax: 01823 337653. *Suppliers and repairers of wind and br insts. Educ contractor.*
Westside Music Centre. 24-26 Bridge St, Taunton, Somerset TA1 1UB tel: 01823 283307. *Electronic orgs, keyboards, guis, amps, drums, hi-tech.*

South Yorkshire
Carcroft
Carcroft Organs. Old Co-Op, 39a Skellow Rd, Carcroft, Doncaster, S Yorks DN6 8HQ tel: 01302 338445; 01302 727974 also fax.
Doncaster
Dodds of Doncaster Ltd. 55 Christ Church Rd, Doncaster, S Yorks tel: 01302 366008 fax: 01302 816000. *Strs, br, w/wind, keyboards, perc, mus, accs, repairs.*
E Smedley & Sons. 19 Printing Office St, Doncaster, S Yorks DN1 1TS tel: 01302 323248 also fax. *Mus, portable keyboards, guis, accs.*
Fox's Music. 2-3 Upper Mall, Frenchgate Centre, Doncaster, S Yorks DN1 1SX tel: 01302 367333 fax: 01302 340472. *Sheet mus, keyboards, pnos, insts, etc.*
Sheffield
Fox's Music. 29a The Arcade, Meadowhall, Sheffield S9 1EH tel: 0114 256 9344 fax: 0114 256 9221.
Wilson Peck Ltd. 13 Rockingham Gate, Sheffield S1 4JD tel: 0114 275 0808 fax: 0114 278 7795. *Acoustic pnos, digital pnos (Korg main dealer), insts, sheet mus, classical CDs and cassettes.*

Staffordshire
Burton-on-Trent
Eric Reynolds Ltd. 88 High St, Burton-on-Trent, Staffs DE14 1LJ tel: 01283 565869/565086/517997 fax: 01283 512330. *New and rebuilt pnos, elec orgs and keyboards, guis, sheet mus and accs. Repairs and hire. Also wholesaler of imported used pnos.*
Normans Ltd. Unit 1, Moor St, Burton-on-Trent, Staffs DE14 3SU tel: 01283 535333 fax: 01283 515572. *Books, band and orch insts, mus, m/order.*
Lichfield
Chas Foulds & Son Ltd. Unit 4, Titan Way, Britannia Enterprise Park, Lichfield WS14 9TT tel: 01543 415222. *Pnos.*
Stoke-on-Trent
Kays Music. 8 Hope St, Hanley, Stoke-on-Trent, Staffs ST1 5BS tel: 01782 212183. *Perc specialists, guis, amps. Large stock of harmonicas.*
Music Control Ltd. Chapel Mews, 68 Crewe Rd, Alsager, Stoke-on-Trent, Staffs ST7 2HA tel: 01270 883779 fax: 01270 883847. *Professional audio equipment, specialising in selling and locating second-hand analogue synths.*

N J Tostevin & Son. 491 Hartshill Rd, Hartshill, Stoke-on-Trent, Staffs ST4 6AA *tel:* 01782 617081. *Pnos.*

Stockton-on-Tees, City of
Stockton on Tees
Perfect Acoustics Ltd. Hughes Building, Boathouse La, Stockton on Tees TS18 3AW *tel:* 01642 603395 *fax:* 01642 618176. *PA, disco sound and lighting.*

Suffolk
Aldeburgh
Galleon Music. Aldeburgh Foundation, High St, Aldeburgh, Suffolk IP15 5AX *tel:* 01728 453298 *fax:* 01728 452715. *CDs, cassettes, scores, m/order. Britten specialist.*
Beccles
Morlings Ltd. 18 New Market, Beccles, Suffolk NR34 9HB *tel:* 01502 713143. *Mus, records, cassettes, CDs, video.*
Bury St Edmunds
Balaam's Music. 103 Risbygate St, Bury St Edmunds, Suffolk IP33 3AA *tel:* 01284 766933 *fax:* 01284 701605 *email:* music@balaam.dungeon. com.uk. *Mus, insts, books, repairs, insurance.*
Elmswell Organ Store. Ashfield Rd, Elmswell, Bury St Edmunds, Suffok IP30 9HJ *tel:* 01359 241270 *fax:* 01359 242844. *Orgs, keyboards, digital pnos.*
Jack White Music (East Anglia). 63-64 St John's St, Bury St Edmunds, Suffolk IP33 1SJ *tel:* 01284 764991. *Keyboards, orgs, pnos, mus, guis, amplification, tuition.*
Mail Order Music. Newmarket Rd, Bury St Edmunds, Suffolk IP33 3YB *tel:* 01284 703097/725725 *fax:* 01284 702592 *email:* mailorder@music sales.co.uk; http://www.musicsales.co.uk. *Sheet mus: c/room, solo, ens, choral, musical shows, new media. Catalogues include Chester Music, Novello, Golden Apple, Shawnee Press, G Schirmer, UME and Youngsongs.*
Music In Print (Head Office). Newmarket Rd, Bury St Edmunds, Suffolk IP33 3YB *tel:* 01284 767019 *fax:* 01284 723235. *Printed mus, insts and mus accs franchisers.*
Framlingham
Amadeus Ho (Geoffrey Acton Woodwind Insts). Church St, Framlingham, Woodbridge, Suffolk IP13 9BE *tel:* 01728 723687. *W/wind insts.*
Ipswich
Amberstone Bookshop. 49 Upper Orwell St, Ipswich, Suffolk IP4 1HP *tel:* 01473 250675 *fax:* 01473 226980 *email:* amber@anglianet.co.uk. *Books, classical CDs, cassettes.*
East End Bargains. 142 Felixstowe Rd, Ipswich *tel:* 01473 725961. *Insts, amps (new and second hand).*
Haven Keyboards. 486 Felixstowe Rd, Ipswich *tel:* 01473 710051. *Keyboards, digital pnos, orgs, sheet mus.*
Jack White Music. 92 Fore Hamlet, Ipswich IP3 8AF *tel:* 01473 257223 *also fax. Orgs, keyboards, pnos, synthesizers, MIDI, modules, guis, accs, tuition.*
Keysounds. 37 Upper Orwell St, Ipswich, Suffolk IP4 1HP *tel:* 01473 213494. *Keybaords, digital pnos, amps, orgs, guis, mus books, repairs and m/order.*
Music World. 16 Queens St, Ipswich *tel:* 01473 253666 *fax:* 01473 213091. *Insts, sheet mus.*
Lowestoft
Morlings Ltd. 149-151 London Rd North, Lowestoft, Suffolk NR32 1NG *tel:* 01502 565491/2 *fax:* 01502 589839. *Books, insts, mus, keyboards.*
Sudbury
Bösendorfer Pianos. South Suffolk Business Centre, Alexandra Rd, Sudbury, Suffolk CO10 6ZY *tel:* 01787 313766 *fax:* 01787 313801. *Grands and uprights.*

Surrey
Cobham
Sheargold Pianos Ltd. 162 Anyards Rd, Cobham, Surrey, KT11 2LH *tel:* 01932 866577 *fax:* 01932 868178 *email:* graham@sheargold.demon. co.uk. *Uprights, grands (new and reconditioned); digital pnos, pno rental, removals, sheet mus, tuning and repairs.*
Coulsdon
Just Flutes/Jonathan Myall (Musical). 36 Chipstead Valley Rd, Coulsdon, Surrey CR5 2RA *tel:* 0181 668 4444 *fax:* 0181 668 7262 *email:* justflutes@i-gadgets.com; http://www.i-gadgets.com/justflutes/. *Mus, books, insts, recordings, cassettes, accs; also m/order and repairs.*
Croydon
H & R Cloake Ltd. 29 High St, Croydon, Surrey CR0 1QB *tel:* 0181 686 1336; 0181 686 3965. *Large classical dept, CDs.*
H Lane & Son Pianos. 326 Brighton Rd, South Croydon, Surrey CR2 6AJ *tel:* 0181 688 3513.

Martin Phelps Music Ltd. 9 South End, Croydon, Surrey CR0 1BE *tel:* 0181 680 9747 *also fax. Pnos, orgs, digital pnos, keyboards, guis. Sheet mus, amps, accs, computer mus software.*
Willson & Newman. High Bank, Hook Hill, Sanderstead, Croydon CR2 0LA, Surrey *tel:* 0181 657 5817. *Pno tuning and repairs.*
Dorking
Albert's Music Shop Ltd. 190 High St, Dorking, Surrey RH4 1QR *tel:* 01306 883898 *fax:* 01306 743771. *Insts, mus, keyboards.*
Royal School of Church Music. Cleveland Lodge, Westhumble, Dorking RH5 6BW *tel:* 01306 877676 *fax:* 01306 887240. *Org and choral mus.*
Epsom
Bootleg Musical Instruments. 5-7 South St, Epsom, Surrey KT18 7PJ *tel:* 01372 724528 *fax:* 01372 729703. *Mus insts, educ suppliers.*
Esher
ABC Music Ltd. 85 High St, Esher, Surrey KT10 9QA *tel:* 01372 466195 *fax:* 01372 470445 *email:* abc@enterprise.net; http://www.abcmusic.co. uk. *Insts, mus, CDs, pnos.*
Farnham
Lloyd & Keyworth Music. 6-7 Downing St, Farnham, Surrey GU9 7PE *tel:* 01252 710666. *Pnos, Roland pnos, keyboards, w/wind, br, strs, sheet mus, Roland Music Learning Centre.*
Godalming
T Andrews & Co (Farncombe) Ltd. 62 Meadrow, Godalming, Surrey GU7 3HT *tel:* 01483 422459. *Pnos and pno stools.*
Guildford
Albert's Music Shop Ltd. 9 Market St, Guildford, Surrey GU1 4LB *tel:* 01483 440188 *fax:* 01483 440823. *Mus insts, accs and sheet mus.*
Andertons Music Co. 58-59 Woodbridge Rd, Guildford, Surrey GU1 4RF *tel:* 01483 456777 (sales); 01483 456888 (educ) *fax:* 01483 456722. *Guis, keyboards, perc, computers, recording equipment, educ equipment, hire, PA, repairs, amps, accs.*
Haslemere
Chamberlain Music. 89 Weyhill, Haslemere, Surrey GU27 1HN *tel:* 01428 658806 *fax:* 01428 658807. *Strs, w/wind, br, Yamaha pnos; specialists in sheet mus and school supplies; Grove dictionaries.*
Dolmetsch Musical Instruments. Unicorn Trading Estate, Weydown Rd, Haslemere, Surrey GU27 1DN *tel:* 01428 643235 *fax:* 01428 654920 *email:* brian@be-blood.demon.co.uk; http://www.be-blood.demon.co. uk. *Rcdrs, early keyboard insts, accs, viols.*
Kew Gardens
ABC Music Ltd. 9 Royal Parade, Station Approach, Kew Gardens, Surrey TW9 3QD *tel:* 0181 940 1892 *fax:* 01372 470445 *email:* abc@enterprise. net; http://www.abcmusic.co.uk.
Kingston-upon-Thames
Hands Music. 5 The Griffin Centre, Market Pl, Kingston-upon-Thames, Surrey KT1 1HL *tel:* 0181 546 9630 *fax:* 0181 546 1771. *Sheet mus, albums etc.*
Hands Music. 39-40 Market Pl, Kingston-upon-Thames, Surrey KT1 1JQ *tel:* 0181 546 9156 *fax:* 0181 546 7771. *Insts, new and second hand, mus, rental, repairs.*
Hands Keyboards. 14 Eden Street, Kingston-upon-Thames, Surrey KT1 1BB *tel:* 0181 547 0944 *fax:* 0181 549 4151. *Electric pnos and keyboards.*
Merstham
David Newton Violins at Potters Music Shop (Croydon) Ltd. 12-16 High St, Merstham, Surrey RH1 3EA *tel:* 01737 645065 *fax:* 01737 645808. *Str insts, repairs, bow-makers; and Music In Print Ltd tel:* 01737 645334. *Sheet mus, w/wind, br insts, guis. Also hire of most insts.*
Emma Newton Electric Violins at Potters Music Shop (Croydon) Ltd. 12-16 High St, Merstham, Surrey RH1 3EA *tel:* 01737 645065 *fax:* 01737 645808. *Electric vns and vas.*
Reigate
Eric Lindsey Ltd. 12 West St, Reigate RH2 9BS *tel:* 01737 221481 *fax:* 01737 223584. *Guis, drums, keyboards, recording and PA equipment.*
Stentor Music Co Ltd. Albert Rd North, Reigate, Surrey RH2 9EZ *tel:* 01737 240226 *fax:* 01737 242748 *email:* stentor@stentor-music. com. *Wholesale specialist str inst supplier; also br, w/wind and guis.*
Touchstone Tonewoods Ltd. 44 Albert Rd North, Reigate, Surrey RH2 9EZ *tel:* 01737 221064 *fax:* 01737 242748. *Supplier to makers and repairers.*
Richmond
Chandler Guitars. 300-302 Sandycombe Rd, Kew, Richmond, Surrey TW9 3NG *tel:* 0181 940 5874 *fax:* 0181 948 8203. *Electric and acoustic guis, amps and accs.*
Sanderstead
Willson & Newman. High Bank, Hook Hill, Sanderstead, S Croydon CR2 0LA *tel:* 0181 657 5817. *Pno tuning and repairs.*
Surbiton
Bell & Crane Music Ltd. 157-159 Ewell Rd, Surbiton, Surrey KT6 6AR *tel:* 0181 399 1166 *fax:* 0181 390 8796. *Accordions, drums, digital pnos, acoustic pnos, keyboards, guis, amps, w/wind.*

The Piano Workshop. 111-113 Ewell Rd, Surbiton, Surrey KT6 6AL *tel:* 0181 399 4110. *Upright and grand pnos, Yamaha grand centre, digital pnos.*

Music Store. 157 Ewell Rd, Surbiton, Surrey KT6 6AR *tel:* 0181 399 1166. *Elec pnos, orgs, keyboards, accordions, drums, guis, amps, br, w/wind, perc, accs.*

Sutton

Music Education Supplies. 101 Banstead Rd South, Sutton, Surrey SM2 5LH *tel:* 0181 770 3866 *fax:* 0181 770 3554. *Agents of Sonor school perc and suppliers of Suzuki handchimes and perc, Nordoff-Robbins reed hns, Aulos rcdrs, books, insts, etc.*

Sutton Music Centre. 64 Haddon Rd, Sutton, Surrey SM1 1RN *tel:* 0181 642 2838. *Insts, mus.*

Tadworth

Tadworth Music Shop. Ashurst Rd, Tadworth, Surrey KT20 5PU *tel:* 01737 813091. *Insts, mus, guis, pnos.*

West Byfleet

Britten's Music Ltd. 3-4 Station Approach, West Byfleet, Surrey KT14 6NG *tel:* 01932 351165/351614. *Sheet mus, insts, accs, digital pnos, m/order.*

Woking

Surrey Music Store. 76 High St, Horsell, Woking, Surrey GU21 4SZ *tel:* 01483 729319 *fax:* 01483 747719. *Insts, to rent or buy, accs, mus books including ABRSM exam mus, classical CDs.*

Tyne and Wear

Blaydon-on-Tyne

George Harrison Organs. 7 The Precinct, Blaydon-on-Tyne, Tyne and Wear NE21 5DT *tel:* 0191 414 4333 *fax:* 0191 414 5158.

Gateshead

Williams the Music People. 13 Russell Way, Metro Centre, Gateshead, Tyne and Wear *tel:* 0191 493 2244 *fax:* 0191 460 2422. *Mus, insts, keyboards, pnos, orgs.*

Newcastle upon Tyne

Andy Lee Woodwind. 195 Osborne Rd, Jesmond, Newcastle upon Tyne *tel:* 0191 281 3585 *also fax. W/wind repairs, second-hand refurbished stocks of all w/wind insts specialising in sax.*

Warwickshire

Leamington Spa

Derek Roberts Violins. 185 Leam Terrace, Leamington Spa, Warwicks CV31 1DW *tel:* 01926 428313 *also fax. Orch strs, cases, bows, accs; also maker and restorer.*

Presto Music. 23 Portland St, Leamington Spa, Warwicks CV32 5EZ *tel:* 01926 334834. *Insts, mus, CDs, cassettes, m/order.*

R B Mew. 1 Park St, Leamington Spa, Warwicks CV32 4QN *tel:* 01926 424949. *Pnos, keyboard insts and accs, tuning and repairs.*

Nuneaton

Abbey Music Studios. 114 Abbey St, Nuneaton, Warwicks CV11 5BX *tel:* 01203 641915. *Orgs, pnos, keyboards, mus, insts, tuition.*

Leisure Music (Head Office). 43-44 Abbey St, Nuneaton, Warwicks CV11 5BT *tel:* 01203 348702 *also fax. Orgs, pno, keyboards, guis, w/wind, br; educ insts; m/order.*

Rugby

Freeman & Neale's Music Shop. 40-42 Lawford Rd, Rugby, Warwicks CV21 2DY *tel:* 01788 577064 *also fax. Insts, mus.*

Stratford-upon-Avon

The Music House. 27 Greenhill St, Stratford-upon-Avon, Warwicks CV37 6LE *tel:* 01789 268515 *also fax. Mus, insts, accs.*

West Midlands

Bearwood

Classical Guitar Centre Ltd. 51a St Mary's Rd, Bearwood, W Midlands B67 5DH *tel:* 0121 429 7446 *fax:* 0121 434 4200. *Guis, mus and accs.*

Birmingham

Allegro Music. 82 Suffolk St, Queensway, Birmingham B1 1TA *tel:* 0121 643 7553 *fax:* 0121 633 4773 *email:* sales@allegro.co.uk. *Books, mus, m/order.*

Birmingham Piano Warehouse/Moseley Pianos. Unit L, 68 Wyrley Rd, Witton, Birmingham B6 7BN *tel:* 0121 327 2701 *also fax;* 0831 560518. *Wholesale and retail. Second-hand upright and grand pnos. Restoration, removal, hire and valuations.*

James Pass & Co Ltd. 71 Smallbrook Queensway, Birmingham, W Midlands B5 4HX *tel:* 0121 643 7623 *also fax. Books, insts, mus, educ videos and cassettes, m/order.*

Midland Music. 1070 Stratford Rd, Hall Green, Birmingham, W Midlands B28 8AD *tel:* 0121 777 3188 *fax:* 0121 702 2683. *Mus, books, br, w/wind, str insts, keyboards, accs and novelties, educ mus; m/order; tuition centre.*

Musical Exchanges. 89 Old Snow Hill, Birmingham, W Midlands B4 6HX *tel:* 0121 236 7544 *fax:* 0121 233 9127. *Guis, keyboards, drums, br, PA, w/wind and repairs.*

Sydney Evans Ltd. 45 Regent Pl, Birmingham B1 3NB *tel:* 0121 233 1741 *fax:* 0121 233 1220. *Accs for str insts.*

Coventry

MB Sunderland (Music). 62 Earlsdon St, Coventry CV5 6EJ *tel:* 01203 714272 *also fax. Insts, mus, classical CDs, cassettes.*

Halesowen

Musical Instrument Repairs & Sales. Hereward Rise, Halesowen Industrial Pk, Halesowen, W Midlands B62 8AN *tel:* 0121 550 9707 *fax:* 0121 501 3873 *email:* mir@cableinet.co.uk. *New and second-hand insts, repairs.*

Solihull

Presto Music. 130 Station Rd, Knowle, Solihull B93 0EP *tel:* 01564 773100. *Insts, mus, CDs, m/order.*

Sutton Coldfield

Colbecks. 26-28 Chester Rd, New Oscott, Sutton Coldfield, Birmingham B73 5DA *tel:* 0121 321 3909 *fax:* 0121 321 1815. *Pnos, keyboards, insts, sheet mus.*

Walsall

TR Music. 233-236 Stafford St, Walsall, W Midlands WS2 8DF *tel:* 01922 613101. *Guis, PA, amps, electric repairs, str insts, cl, fl, drums, mus books, accs, recording equipment, lighting, pyrotechnics.*

Wolverhampton

Band Box (Wolverhampton) Ltd. 5 Worcester St, Wolverhampton WV2 4LD *tel:* 01902 421420. *Books, mus, insts, repairs.*

Graeme Hawkins Organ Studios Ltd. 122-123 Salop St, Wolverhampton WV3 0RX *tel:* 01902 425900 *fax:* 01902 424094.

Roden's Music. 88-89 Darlington St, Wolverhampton WV1 4EX *tel:* 01902 428459/425600. *Books, mus, insts.*

Wolverhampton Organ & Piano Centre. 29-30 Victoria St, Wolverhampton WV1 3PN *tel:* 01902 425284. *Orgs, pnos, keyboards, printed mus.*

West Sussex

Burgess Hill

The Rock Shop. 21 Junction Rd, Burgess Hill, W Sussex RH15 0HR *tel:* 01444 241167. *Guis, amps, keyboards, w/wind insts, repairs, mus, m/order, accs.*

Chichester

Berns Music. 42 West St, Chichester, W Sussex PO19 1RP *tel:* 01243 781844 *also fax; email:* bernsmusic@btinternet.com. *Sheet mus; classical, popular and educ. W/wind, br, str insts, rental with option to buy, repairs, accs, gifts.*

Chichester Music. Maudlin House, Westhampnett, Chichester, W Sussex PO18 0PB *tel:* 01243 776325 *fax:* 01243 539604. *Mus (m/order); visitors by appointment.*

Music Store Group Ltd. 4 Eastgate Sq, Chichester, W Sussex PO19 1ED *tel:* 01243 780536 *fax:* 01243 783499. *Insts, mus.*

Crawley

The Guitar Makers. 87 Gales Dr, Three Bridges, Crawley, W Sussex RH10 1QA *tel:* 01293 543055. *Custom-made guis, accs, amps, repairs, Gibsons dealers.*

Hobgoblin Music. 17 The Parade, Northgate, Crawley, W Sussex RH10 2DT *tel:* 01293 515858 *fax:* 01293 561602. *Folk insts.*

Haywards Heath

Peter Voigt Ltd. 71 High St, Lindfield, Haywards Heath, W Sussex RH16 2HN *tel:* 01444 483206. *Vn family insts and accs.*

Horsham

Musique. 36a East St, Horsham, W Sussex RH12 1HL *tel:* 01403 254880 *fax:* 01403 259800. *Sheet mus, accs, insts, repairs, hire and m/order.*

Rustington

Macaulay Library Supply Co Ltd. The Studio, Waverley Rd, Rustington, W Sussex BN16 2DY *tel:* 01903 785966 *fax:* 01903 775950. *Suppliers of books and recorded mus to libraries and schools.*

Steyning

Macdonald Music Service (MMS). 14 High St, Steyning, W Sussex BN44 3GG *tel:* 01903 816120. *Books, mus, speciality org mus.*

Worthing

Music Supplies Ltd. 33 Warwick St, Worthing, W Sussex BN11 3DQ *tel:* 01903 208692 *fax:* 01903 239004. *Books, mus, insts, br, w/wind, keyboards, studio equipment, PA, computers, accs, m/order, educ supplier, rental.*

West Yorkshire

Bradford

A to G Woodwind & Brass. 68 Morley St, Bradford BD7 1AQ *tel:* 01274 307207 *also fax. W/wind and br insts sales and repairs.*

Early Music Shop. 38 Manningham La, Bradford BD1 3EA *tel:* 01274 393753 *fax:* 01274 393516 *email:* sales@earlyms.demon.co.uk; http://e-m-s.com. *Insts, inst kits, rcdrs, mus.*

J Wood & Sons Ltd. 38 Manningham La, Bradford BD1 3EA *tel:* 01274 307636 *fax:* 01274 393516 *email:* sales@earlyms.demon.co.uk. *Insts, mus, pnos, orgs, keyboards, strs, sheet mus and CDs.*

Michael Rath Brass Sales and Repairs. 38 Manningham La, Bradford BD1 3EA *tel:* 01274 721894 *fax:* 01274 393516. *Br sales and repairs. Also manufacture trbs.*

Minstrel Music Shop. 38 Sunbridge Rd, Bradford BD1 2AA *tel:* 01274 390847 *also fax; email:* 106142.651@compuserve.com. *Acoustic and electric guis, vns, w/wind, harmonicas, printed mus and videos, repairs.*

The Woodwind Exchange. 38 Manningham La, Bradford BD1 3EA *tel:* 01274 721831.

Brighouse
Treble Clef. 38 Park St, Brighouse, W Yorks HD6 1JL *tel:* 01484 715417 *email:* treblecl@netcomuk.co.uk. *Keyboards, guis, amps, br, w/wind, computers, PA, sheet mus, accs.*

Castleford
Rock Factory. Wheldon Rd, Castleford, W Yorks WF10 2SD *tel:* 01977 513643 *fax:* 01977 513644. *Guis, amps, drums, PA, group equipment.*

Halifax
GSG Pianos. Grove House, Wade House Rd, Shelf, Halifax HX3 7PX *tel:* 01274 677450 *fax:* 01274 677450. *New and reconditioned pnos.*

Maestro Music. 25 The Piece Hall, Halifax HX1 1RE *tel:* 01422 349359. *Guis, keyboards, mus books, w/wind, br, accs, effects (zoom).*

Huddersfield
Normans Ltd. 9 Mini Pk, Leeds Rd, Huddersfield, W Yorks HD1 6PA *tel:* 01484 514961 *fax:* 01484 514963. *Br and w/wind insts, perc, repairs, mus, accs, also m/order.*

R E Wood & Sons Ltd. 11 Market St, Huddersfield, W Yorks *tel:* 01484 427455 *fax:* 01484 427355. *Insts, mus, records, pnos, orgs, hi-fi, keyboards.*

Ilkley
Time and Tune. 10 The Grove, Ilkley, W Yorkshire LS29 9EG *tel:* 01943 817301 *fax:* 01943 817301. *Mus, CDs, insts.*

Leeds
Fox's Music. 54-58 The Headrow, Leeds LS1 8EQ *tel:* 0113 245 0350. *Guis, PA, hi-tech, keyboards, accs, mus, pnos, digital pnos.*

J Scheerer & Sons Ltd. 88-90 Merrion Centre, Leeds LS2 8NG *tel:* 0113 244 9592/0444; 0113 243 2401. *Insts, br, w/wind, strs, mus, perc and electric guis.*

Knock on Wood. Granary Wharf, Leeds LS1 4BR *tel:* 0113 245 9878 *also fax. Multicultural supplies of insts, recordings, books and teaching resources.*

Ossett
Music for Brass Ltd. Unit 1, Warneford Av, Dewsbury Rd, Ossett, W Yorks WF5 9NJ *tel:* 01924 261154 *fax:* 01924 280310. *Own titles (br and wind band).*

Wakefield
R E Wood & Son Ltd. 20 Cross St, Wakefield, W Yorks WF1 3BW *tel:* 01924 374446 *fax:* 01924 291807.

Wiltshire
Melksham
In Tune Music. Unit G21, Avonside Enterprise Pk, Melksham, Wilts SN12 8BS *tel:* 01225 709710. *Elec orgs and keyboards, digital pnos, sheet mus, repairs.*

Pewsey
Warblers. Embrook House, Hilcot, Pewsey, Wilts SN9 6LE *tel:* 01672 851317 *also fax. M/order vocal mus.*

Salisbury
Percy Prior's Music. 5 Catherine St, Salisbury SP1 2DF *tel:* 01722 322278; 01722 328181 (sheet mus dept) *fax:* 01722 337272. *Electric pnos, keyboards, insts, sheet mus specialists, repairs.*

Swindon
Duck Son & Pinker Ltd. 59-60 Bridge St, Swindon, Wilts SN1 1BT *tel:* 01793 522018/522220. *Mus, books, insts, pnos, orgs, hire, educ mus, CDs, cassettes, records.*

Holmes Music. 21-23 Faringdon Rd, Swindon, Wilts SN1 5AR *tel:* 01793 520948/534095 *fax:* 01793 542436. *Mus, elec orgs, keyboards, pnos, synthesizers, guis, amps, drums, records, educ insts.*

Kempster & Son (The Music Shop). 98 Commercial Rd, Swindon, Wilts SN1 5PL *tel:* 01793 535523 *fax:* 01793 526375. *Group and PA gear, multi-track recording and educ insts.*

Make Music Leisure Centres. 22-23 Victoria Rd, Swindon, Wilts SN1 3AW *tel:* 01793 644181 *also fax. Group equipment, disco and club.*

York, City of
York
Banks & Son (Music) Ltd. 18 Lendal, York YO1 2AU *tel:* 01904 658836 *fax:* 01904 629547 *email:* tad40@dial.pipex.com. *Mus, insts, recordings, books.*

Classical Harpsichords and Classical Organs. Lamel Towers, 81 Hull Rd, York YO1 3JS *tel:* 01904 411873. *Mainly demo insts and work done to order.*

Philip Martin Music Books. 38 Fossgate, York YO1 2TF *tel:* 01904 670323 *fax:* 01904 636111. *Books, mus; also m/order.*

York Music Services. 9 Museum St, York YO1 2DT *tel:* 01904 636721 *fax:* 01904 672392. *Books, mus, accs, insts, CDs.*

Channel Islands
Jersey
Easy Play Music. 11-13 New St, St Helier, Jersey, Channel Islands *tel:* 01534 879570 *fax:* 01534 878901 *email:* offsure@itl.net.

Isle of Man
Douglas
Peter Norris Music. Villa Marina Arcade, Douglas, Isle of Man IM1 2HN *tel:* 01624 661794 *fax:* 01624 622540. *Insts, mus, amplification.*

Scotland

Aberdeen City
Aberdeen
Bruce Millers. 363 Union St, Aberdeen AB9 1EN *tel:* 01224 592211 *fax:* 01224 580085. *Insts, keyboards, pnos, mus, recordings, books, tuning, repairs, hi-fi, accs, TV videos.*

Dundee, City of
Dundee
Rainbow Music. 35 Cowgate, Dundee DD1 2JF *tel:* 01382 201405 *fax:* 01382 225183. *Insts, PA and recording equipment, sheet mus.*

East Ayrshire
Kilmarnock
RGM. 24 Nelson St, Kilmarnock KA1 1BA *tel:* 01563 537711 *fax:* 01563 530209. *Guis, perc, mus, insts, lighting, repairs.*

Edinburgh, City of
Edinburgh
Edinburgh Organ Studio. 98 Canongate, The Royal Mile, Edinburgh EH8 8DD *tel:* 0131 556 3005 *fax:* 0131 556 8445. *Orgs, church orgs, keyboards, elec pnos, accs, books.*

Gordon Stevenson Violin Maker and Restorer. 6 Barclay Terrace, Bruntsfield, Edinburgh EH10 4HP *tel:* 0131 229 2051 *fax:* 0131 229 9298. *Str insts for sale and restoration of vns.*

John Barnes. 3 East Castle Rd, Edinburgh EH10 5AP *tel:* 0131 229 8018. *W/shop drawings and information for builders of early keyboard insts, clvd kits (portable 18th C design), hpd and spinet kits. Covered strings for clvds and square pnos.*

Mev Taylor's Music Shop. 212 Morrison St, Edinburgh EH3 8AE *tel:* 0131 229 7454 *fax:* 0131 228 5913. *Br and w/wind specialists.*

Music Shop. 22 Grindlay St, Edinburgh EH3 9AP *tel:* 0131 229 8392. *Insts, elec.*

Rae Macintosh Music Ltd. 6 Queensferry St, Edinburgh EH2 4PA *tel:* 0131 225 1171 *fax:* 0131 225 9447. *Insts, mus, videos, m/order.*

Scayles Music. 40-42 West Crosscauseway, Edinburgh EH8 9JP *tel:* 0131 667 8241 *fax:* 0131 558 7575. *Guis (elec, acoustic, bass), PA, br, w/wind, drums, perc, bouzoukis, mandolas, mandolins, books, spares, repairs, hires, used equipment, vintage items.*

Sheena McNeil. 7 Barclay Terrace, Edinburgh EH10 4HP *tel:* 0131 228 3666 *fax:* 0131 228 3966. *Books, mus.*

Falkirk, City of
Falkirk
Normans Ltd. The Studio, Burnfoot La, Falkirk *tel:* 01324 611895 *fax:* 01324 634611. *Br, w/wind, str, perc.*

Fife
Dunfermline
Sound Control. The Elgin Works, Dunfermline, Fife KY12 7SD *tel:* 0800 525260 *fax:* 01383 725733. *Hi-tech, recording, PA, guis, keyboards.*

St Andrews

The Musicmongers. 151 South St, St Andrews, Fife KY16 9UN *tel:* 01334 478625. *Classical CDs, cassettes, sheet mus, inst accs (including cl reeds, gui and vn strs).*

Glasgow, City of
Glasgow

Band Supplies (Scotland). 5 Old Dumbarton Rd, Glasgow G3 8QY *tel:* 0141 339 9400 *fax:* 0141 334 8157. *Sax specialists, insts (br, w/wind, perc), mus, recordings; also repairs.*

Biggars - Music for All. 273 Sauchiehall St, Glasgow G2 3HH *tel:* 0141 332 8676 *fax:* 0141 352 7408. *Orgs, pnos, digital pnos, keyboards, orch and band insts, mus, synthesizers, guis, sheet mus.*

Drum Shop. 15 Blackie St, Glasgow G3 8TN *tel:* 0141 339 4497. *Perc.*

McCormack's (Music) Ltd. 29-33 Bath St, Glasgow G2 1HT *tel:* 0141 332 6644 *fax:* 0141 353 3095. *Guis, drums, keyboards, br and w/wind, banjos, mandolins, books, amps, PA systems, microphones, karaoke, accs.*

Highland
Beauly

Serenade for Strings. South Teavarran, Foxhole, Kiltarlity, Beauly, Inverness-shire IV4 7HT *tel:* 01463 741651 *also fax. Specialises in sheet mus for strs, including current syllabuses for the exam boards. Post-free service for any mus not in stock.*

Dingwall

Maitland Music Co Ltd. George St, Dingwall, Ross-shire IV15 9SN *tel:* 01349 63191 *also fax. Acoustic, electric guis, keyboards, sheet mus, amps, accs.*

Inverness

The Music Shop. 27 Church St, Inverness IV1 1DY *tel:* 01463 233374 *fax:* 01463 713983. *Books, insts including bagpipes and bodhrans, mus.*

Perth and Kinross
Perth

Wilkie's Music House. Charterhouse La, Canal Cres, Perth PH2 8HT *tel:* 01738 623041 *fax:* 01738 633173. *Mus, guis, pnos, keyboards, insts, accs.*

Renfrewshire
Paisley

Music Centre. 8 Wellmeadow St, Paisley PA1 2EF *tel:* 0141 848 1033. *Keyboards, guis, mus, insts.*

Scottish Borders
Galashiels

Waverley Piano Co. 4 Chapel St, Galashiels, Selkirkshire TD1 1BU *tel:* 01896 752308. *Upright and grand pnos; also restoration, tuning and reconditioning.*

South Ayrshire
Ayr

Billy McEwen Organ Ltd. Keyboard and Piano Centre, 31-35 Fort St, Ayr KA7 1DG *tel:* 01292 269667 *fax:* 01292 289597. *Orgs, pnos, digital pnos, keyboards, synthesizers, guis, accs, amps.*

Frontline Music. 2 Arthur St, Ayr, South Ayrshire KA7 1QJ *tel:* 01292 265252 *also fax. Insts, accs, books.*

Mackay Music. 3 Cathcart St, Ayr KA7 1BJ *tel:* 01292 289562 *also fax. Books, insts, mus, accs, novelties, inst hire, computer software.*

South Lanarkshire
Auldhouse

Just Music. 246 Auldhouse Rd, Auldhouse, E Kilbride G75 9DX *tel:* 01355 245674 *fax:* 01355 231020 *email:* just_music_scotland@compuserve.com. *Mus (m/order), br and wind band specialist.*

Hamilton

Music Centre. 48 Campbell St, Hamilton ML3 6AS *tel:* 01698 283325 *fax:* 01698 283330. *Insts, amps.*

Stirling, City of
Stirling

Roadshow. 64 Upper Craigs, Stirling FK8 2DS *tel:* 01786 471323 *also fax. PA, guis, amps, drums, lighting; also sales, hire and repairs.*

West Dunbartonshire
Wishaw

Magnum Sound. 67 Stewarton St, Wishaw ML2 8AG *tel:* 01698 358761 *fax:* 01698 359745. *PA, insts, installation, accs, mus.*

Wales

Cardiff County Borough
Cardiff

Cranes Musical Instruments. 5A High St, Cardiff CF1 2AW *tel:* 01222 398215 *fax:* 01222 667017. *Pnos, guis, amps, keyboards, br, w/wind, str, mus.*

Eric Lewin Pianos. 147 Crwys Rd, Cardiff CF2 4NH *tel:* 01222 644558. *Grand and upright pnos, new and second-hand. Repairs and hire.*

G M Music. 2 Wharton St, Cardiff *tel:* 01222 231606 *also fax. Orch and group insts, equipment.*

Gamlin's Music Centre. 56 St Mary St, Cardiff CF1 1FE *tel:* 01222 231290/220828 *fax:* 01222 237616. *Sheet mus, br, w/wind, str, pno, keyboards, guis, amps, hire and repairs.*

Music Direct. 33 Tydfil Pl, Roath Pk, Cardiff CF2 5HP *tel:* 01222 496080 *fax:* 01222 457760. *Printed mus and books; specialist catalogues on request. UK and export.*

Musicland and Sound Centre. 148-154 North Rd, Cardiff CF4 3BH *tel:* 01222 621715 *fax:* 01222 621285.

Normans Ltd (including E Alexander). 5 Lady Margaret Ct, Colchester Av, Cardiff CF3 7AW *tel:* 01222 486486. *Insts, br and w/wind specialists, m/order. Br inst repairs, overhauls and renovations.*

Rowlands Music Ltd. 19 High St, Arcade, Cardiff CF1 2QR *tel:* 01222 226935. *Sheet, exam, choral and educ mus and m/order.*

San Domenico Stringed Instruments. 175 Kings Rd, Cardiff CF1 9DF *tel:* 01222 235881 *fax:* 01222 344510. *Fine vns, vcs, bows and accs. Bow repairs, restoration, insurance and expert appraisals.*

Cwmbran

Soundwave Music Centre. Units 51-52 Inshops, Cwmbran, Gwent NP44 1PX *tel:* 01633 482501. *Books, insts, records, cassettes, CDs.*

Ceredigion
Aberystwyth

Music Warehouse. 10 Northgate St, Aberystwyth, Ceredigion SY23 2JS *tel:* 01970 612349. *Books, insts, mus, recordings.*

Conwy
Colwyn Bay

Music Makers. 12 Penrhyn Rd, Colwyn Bay, Clwyd LL29 8LG *tel:* 01492 534834. *Orgs, keyboards, pnos, guis, str, br, w/wind insts, sheet mus, accs, educ products, inst repair and hire, m/order.*

Llandudno

Rushworths Music Ltd. 11 Vaughan St, Llandudno LL30 1AB *tel:* 01492 876649 *also fax.*

Newport District
Abergavenny

Abergavenny Music. 23 Cross St, Abergavenny, Gwent NP7 5EW *tel:* 01873 853394 *fax:* 01873 859525 *email:* abermusic@compuserve.com; http://ourworld.compuserve.com/homepages/abermusic. *Sheet mus, books, CDs, tapes, videos, gifts, accs, m/order.*

Newport

G M Music. 14 Upper Dock St, Newport, Gwent *tel:* 01633 840606. *Orch and group insts, equipment.*

Speed Music Cool Blue Enterprise Ltd. 177 Upper Dock St, Newport, S Wales NP9 1DY *tel:* 01633 220390 *fax:* 01633 266636.

Pembrokeshire
Haverfordwest

Swales Music Centre Ltd. 2-6 High St, Haverfordwest, Pembrokeshire *tel:* 01437 762059 *fax:* 01437 760872. *Mus, books, cassettes, CDs, insts, accs.*

Pembroke

Music Options. 12 Main St, Pembroke, Dyfed SA71 4NP *tel:* 01646 686297 *fax:* 01646 622425. *Jazz, blues, folk CDs and tapes.*

Newtown

Mid Wales Music Centre. Lion Works, Pool Rd, Newtown, Powys SY16 3AG *tel:* 01686 622161 *also fax. Guis, amps, PA specialists, perc, br, w/wind, keyboards, printed mus.*

Musician Services

Accessory Distributors

American Percussion. 120-122 Bermondsey St, London SE1 3TX *tel:* 0171 403 3200 *fax:* 0171 403 5910. *Distributor of drums, sticks and accs.*

Britannia Reeds and Regency Reeds. PO Box 530, St Albans, Herts AL1 4HR *tel:* 01727 846055 *fax:* 01727 811164. *Specialist manufacturers and sales of ob reeds, cane and accs, m/order world-wide.*

Centrepiece Music. PO Box 1601, Newport Pagnell, Bucks MK16 8PD *tel:* 01908 218003 *fax:* 01908 211828. Glenda Smith. *Wholesaler and distributor of accs for w/wind; mouthpieces, reeds, etc; Neotech sax and gui slings and straps; m/order.*

Impact Percussion. 120-122 Bermondsey St, London SE1 3TX *tel:* 0171 403 5900 *fax:* 0171 403 5910 *email:* impactperc@msn.com. Paul Hagen. *Importer of orch perc and accs.*

Riverside Reeds. 49 Fairway, Raynes Pk, London SW20 9DN *tel:* 0181 540 0670 *fax:* 0181 241 1280 *email:* brisew@globalnet.co.uk; pbeew@ globalnet.co.uk. Brian Sewell, Peter Williams. *Bsn reeds and cane supplied at all stages. Bespoke shapes specialists.*

Rosetti Ltd. 4 Tamdown Way, Springwood Industrial Estate, Braintree, Essex CM7 2QL *tel:* 01376 550033 *fax:* 01376 550042. *Str, br, w/wind, guis, perc, gui accs.*

T W Howarth & Co Ltd. 31 Chiltern St, London W1M 1HG *tel:* 0171 935 2407 *fax:* 0171 224 2564 *email:* howarth_ltd@msn.com. *Manufacturers and wholesale importers of w/wind accs.*

Accountancy and Taxation Services

Bruton Charles Chartered Accountants. 60 Valley Rd, Henley on Thames RG9 1RR *tel:* 01491 411322 *fax:* 01491 410951 *email:* 101565.2202@compuserve.com. Jonathan Lawrence-Archer. *Tax and accounts, VAT returns and personal financial planning.*

Bruton Charles Chartered Accountants. Ashland House, 20 Moxon St, Marylebone High St, London W1M 3JE *tel:* 0171 935 7872 *fax:* 0171 486 7639. *Tax and accounts, VAT returns and personal financial planning.*

Carnmores Royalties Consultants. Suite 350 The Linen Hall, 162-168 Regent St, London W1R 5TB *tel:* 0171 734 0053 *fax:* 0171 734 4827. Andrew Tristram, partner; Nicholas Myles. *Specialist independent services and advice on royalty auditing, contract negotiation, royalty statement review, litigation support, expert witness services, catalogue valuation.*

Chantrey Vellacott. Derngate Mews, Derngate, Northampton NN1 1UE *tel:* 01604 39257 *fax:* 01604 231460 *email:* http://www.chantrey-vellacott.co.uk. Elliot Harris. *Auditing and accounting services; personal financial planning and taxation.*

Chantrey Vellacott. Russell Sq House, 10-12 Russell Sq, London WC1B 5LF *tel:* 0171 436 3666 *fax:* 0171 436 8884. Eric Longley; Chris Jones. *Auditing and accounting services; personal financial planning and taxation.*

David Smith & Co. 41 Welbeck St, London W1M 8HH *tel:* 0171 224 1004 *fax:* 0171 486 8705. D C Smith, practitioner; R Shah, qualified snr. *Accounts preparation and taxation advice to self-employed musicians and teachers. Clients need not be local.*

Guy Rippon & Partners. 24 Pepper St, London SE1 0EB *tel:* 0171 928 9777 *fax:* 0171 928 9222. Guy Rippon, snr partner. *Chartered certified accountants. Comprehensive accountancy services to the mus industry. Also registered auditors.*

Ivan Sopher & Co. 5 Elstree Gate, Elstree Way, Borehamwood, Herts WD6 1JD *tel:* 0181 207 0602 *fax:* 0181 207 6758.

John Seeley & Co. 1 Upper Saint Mary's Rd, Bearwood, Warley, W Midlands B67 5JR *tel:* 0121 429 1504 *fax:* 0121 429 3121. John Seeley, principal. *Full range of accountancy and taxation services for the mus industry. Free financial guide for musicians available on request.*

Lloyd Piggott Chartered Accountants. Blackfriars House, Parsonage, Manchester M3 2JA *tel:* 0161 833 0346 *fax:* 0161 832 0045. Colin Lomas, snr partner; Gary Dodds, Christopher Swallow, partners. *Accountancy and taxation services for musicians throughout the UK.*

Martin Greene Ravden. 55 Loudoun Rd, St John's Wood, London NW8 0DL *tel:* 0171 625 4545 *fax:* 0171 625 5265 *email:* mgr@mgr.co.uk. Lionel Martin, David Ravden, Steve Daniel, Ed Grossman, Harish Shah, partners. *Business management, tour accounting and admin, inter-nation tax clearances, VAT, royalty examinations, litigation support and other financial services.*

Nyman Libson Paul Chartered Accountants. Regina House, 124 Finchley Rd, London NW3 5JS *tel:* 0171 794 5611 *fax:* 0171 431 1109. *Specialist knowledge of the entertainment and mus industry.*

Pearson & Co (Chartered Accountants). Faircross House, 116 The Parade, High St, Watford, Herts WD1 2AX *tel:* 01923 238140 *fax:* 01923 210991. Richard Pearson, partner. *Accountancy, audits, taxation and financial management services.*

Pryor, Begent, Fry & Co. The Great Barn Studio, Cippenham La, Slough SL1 5AU *tel:* 01753 554613 *fax:* 01753 553520. *Accountants.*

Trevor Ford & Co. 151 Mount View Rd, London N4 4JT *tel:* 0181 341 6408 *fax:* 0181 340 0021. *Client list full at present.*

Willott Kingston Smith and Associates. 10 Bruton St, London W1X 7AG *tel:* 0171 304 4646 *fax:* 0171 304 4647. Cliff Ireton, Bob Willott, Mandy Merron, partners. *Financial management, contract reviews, litigation support, international tax, personal financial planning, audit and accounting, taxation and VAT.*

Computer Systems Consultants

ARA Music Technology Services. 28 Longhurst Rd, Lewisham, London SE13 5LP *tel:* 0181 355 4402 *email:* ara@dircon.co.uk; http://www. users.dircon.co.uk/~ara. Andrew Aird, proprietor. *Internet services for musicians including web page design; consultancy on all types of mus software.*

Artifax Software Ltd. 38 Ridgeway, Epsom, Surrey KT19 8LB *tel:* 01372 810081 *fax:* 01372 743390 *email:* http://www.artifaxsoftware.com. Timothy Nathan, Nina Kaye, dirs; Bob Chase, sales; Ben Curthoys, development. *Computer programs: Show Room for venue management to handle bookings, technical resources, personnel management, etc; Artifax, designed for concert agents to handle all office admin.*

Business Industrial Management. 11 Mayfields Close, Wembley, Middx HA9 9PP *tel:* 0181 904 2310 *also fax.* Joseph Roth, principal. *Independent computer consultancy with specialist experience of orch management and associated systems. Services include feasibilty studies, training, systems design and procurement.*

The Control Room. 12 Jasmine Ct, Cambridge CB1 4BG *tel:* 01223 564176 *fax:* 01223 564182 *email:* control.room@direct.co.uk; http:// www.ndirect.co.uk/control.room. Michael Price, consultant; Alan Haigh, consultant. *Mus technology consultancy: advice and project management service for individuals and organisations*

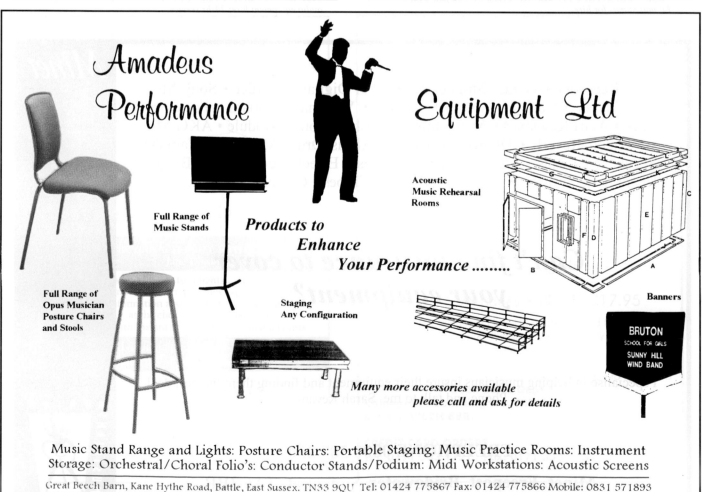

FX Rentals Ltd. 38-40 Telford Way, London W3 7XS *tel:* 0181 746 2121 *fax:* 0181 746 4100. Nick Harris, operations dir; Roger Evan, technical dir. *Professional audio and inst equipment hire. Open 24 hours every day of the year.*

John Henry Enterprises. 16-24 Brewery Rd, London N7 9NH *tel:* 0171 609 9181 *fax:* 0171 700 7040. John Henry, mgr dir. *Musical equipment and sound reinforcement rental.*

Laser Magic. LM House, No 2 Church St, Seaford, E Sussex BN25 1HD *tel:* 01323 890752 *fax:* 01323 898311 *email:* 100563.325@compuserve.

com; http://www.lasermagic.com. Malcolm Harvey, sales dir; Steve Harvey, mgr dir. *Laser display consultants; laser lighting specialists, fireworks, special effects, pyrotechnics displays, video projection, sound systems, large format slide projection.*

Whitwams SV. 70 High St, Winchester, Hants SO23 9DE *tel:* 01962 870408 *fax:* 01962 842064 *email:* quality@whitwams.telme.com. David Harding, dir; Steve Birnage, mgr. *Sound and vision equipment, hire and sales.*

Equipment Manufacturers

Amadeus Performance Equipment Ltd. Great Beech Barn, Kane Hythe Rd, Battle, E Sussex TN33 9QU *tel:* 01424 775867 *fax:* 01424 775866. Anne Holliday, mgr dir. *Musician posture chairs, inst racks, mus stands, portable staging, acoustically designed rehearsal rooms, mus stand banners, performing arts furniture, accs.*

Camwood (UK) Ltd. UK Sawmill, Unit 2, Staden Business Park, Buxton, Derbys SK17 9RZ *tel:* 01298 77407 *fax:* 01298 71156. *Specialise in ebony, rosewood and boxwood for all types of mus inst.*

Covernote. 17 Lime Av, Alton, Hants GU34 2AD *tel:* 01420 84449. Lindy Wiltshire. *Custom-made covers and cases for insts and related equipment.*

George Veness Workshop. Stanhope Studio, Donald Way, Winchelsea, E Sussex TN36 4NH *tel:* 01797 225878. *Wooden mus stands.*

Hostess Furniture. Vulcan Rd, Bilston, W Midlands WV14 7JR *tel:* 01902 493681 *fax:* 01902 353185. *Produces a range of orch seating, ergonomically designed to address the postural and health problems suffered by musicians.*

John Henry Enterprises. 16-24 Brewery Rd, London N7 9NH *tel:* 0171 609 9181 *fax:* 0171 700 7040. John Henry, mgr dir; Robert Harding, audio mgr. *Mus equipment, staging, flight cases and mus stands.*

Midland Flight Cases. Unit 17, Enterprise Workshops, 76 Linden St, Leicester LE5 5EE *tel:* 0116 273 3035 *fax:* 0116 249 0845. Stuart Ashby, proprietor. *Custom-built flight cases for all types of equipment. Also rack cases, perc cases.*

Musisca Ltd. 20 Wellington La, Montpelier, Bristol BS6 6AX *tel:* 0117 924 0934 *also fax. Mus stands, conductor stands, pno stools.*

Mutronics Ltd. 27 Britton St, Farringdon, London EC1M 5NQ *tel:* 0171 608 3636; 0171 251 2376 *fax:* 0171 490 0474. Mark Lusard.

Paxman Cases. 3 Tudor Ct, Harold Ct Rd, Romford RM3 0AE *tel:* 01708 345415 *also fax.*

Promenade Music. St Aubyns, 404 Marine Rd East, Morecambe, Lancs LA4 5AR *tel:* 01524 410202 *fax:* 01524 410802. David Wood, snr partner; Keith Harris, gen mgr. *Aluminium flight cases.*

RAT (Music Stands) Ltd. 16 Melville Rd, London SW13 9RJ *tel:* 0181 741 4804 *fax:* 0181 741 8949. A C Michell, dir. *Mus stands.*

Freight Forwarding

Anglo Pacific International plc. Unit 1, Bush Industrial Estates, Standard Rd, London NW10 6DF *tel:* 0181 965 1955 *fax:* 0181 965 4954. Steve

Perry, dir. *Forwarders to the performing arts: air/sea freight, documentation services.*

Information Services

Jazz Services Ltd. Room 518, Africa House, 64 Kingsway, London WC2B 6BD *tel:* 0171 405 0737/47/57 *fax:* 0171 405 0828 *email:* jazz@dial. pipex.com. Celia Wood, publications mgr. *Information on all jazz matters.*

The Music Information Consultancy. 13 York St, Harborne, Birmingham, B17 0HG *tel:* 0121 427 9376 *also fax; email:* musicinfo@clara.net. Ian Ledsham, dir. *Offers training and professional development courses, cataloguing services, music bibliography, stock editing and advice.*

The National Instrument Registry. PO Box 46, Waterlooville PO8 9RZ *tel:* 01705 348725. *Register of insts and their rightful owners held on computer to act as a national reference point. Liaises with the police and retailers.*

National Piano Centre and Information Service. 5 Summerfield Rd, London W5 1ND *tel:* 0181 997 1793 *also fax.* Jonathan Ranger, dir. *Impartial advice and information on pnos, ownership, use and maintenance.*

South West Jazz. c/o Exeter and Devon Arts Centre, Gandy St, Exeter EX4 3LS *tel:* 01392 218368 *fax:* 01392 420442. Rosie Jarvis, admin; Kevin Buckland, regional development offr. *Information services to amateur and professional musicians, promoters, educators, public, local authorities and business.*

Instrument Auctioneers

Bonhams. Montpelier St, London SW7 1HH *tel:* 0171 393 3958 *fax:* 0171 393 3905. Peter Horner; Dagmar Welle.

Christies. 8 King St, St James's, London SW1Y 6QT *tel:* 0171 839 9060. Frances Gillham, dir.

Phillips Fine Art Auctioneers. 101 New Bond St, London W1Y 0AS *tel:* 0171 468 8380; 0171 629 6602 *fax:* 0171 465 0223 *email:* http://

www.phillips-auctions.com. Philip A Scott, dir, mus insts. *Auctions of vns, vas, vcs and bows; and antique and modern pnos.*

Sotheby's. Musical Instrument Dept, 34-35 New Bond St, London W1A 2AA *tel:* 0171 408 5344 *fax:* 0171 408 5942 *email:* jlaredo@bigfoot. com; http://www.maestronet.com. Graham Wells, dir mus insts.

John Henry Enterprises. 16-24 Brewery Rd, London N7 9NH *tel:* 0171 609 9181 *fax:* 0171 700 7040. John Henry, mgr dir. *Insts and PA.*

Jones, Stephen. 6 Barnfield Rd, St Albans, Herts AL4 9UP *tel:* 01727 864007 *also fax; email:* 106510.1264@compuserve.com. *Hpd, harmonium.*

Justin Sillman & Co. 6 Tomlins Grove, Bow, London E3 4NX *tel:* 0181 981 9800 *fax:* 0181 981 2800 *email:* justin@justin.idiscover.co.uk. *Orgs.*

Ken Smith Music Services Ltd. 6 The Maltings, High St, Henlow, Beds SG16 6AQ *tel:* 01462 811244 *fax:* 01462 851801. Kenneth Smith, mgr dir; Alyda Smith, company sec. *Suppliers, tuners and transporters of hpds, pipe orgs, f-pnos and harmoniums.*

Makin Organs Ltd. Compton House, Franklin St, Oldham, Lancs OL1 2DP *tel:* 0161 626 5666 *fax:* 0161 665 2284 *email:* davidc@makinorgans. co.uk. David Clegg, dir and gen mgr. *Classical orgs, digital pnos, MIDI expanders, nationwide hire service.*

Markson Pianos. 36-38 Artillery Pl, Woolwich, London SE18 4AB *tel:* 0181 854 4517. Julian Markson, Simon Markson, partners. *Pno sale, hire option to buy, concert and recording hire, tuning and repairs, restoration, free advice.*

Maxima Music. 20 Wolseley Gardens, London W4 3LP *tel:* 0181 995 2757. Simon Hill. *Chmbr org.*

Neal, Simon. 10 Hamilton Rd, London NW10 1NY *tel:* 0181 452 1556 *fax:* 0181 452 3467. *Early keyboard insts (hpds, f-pnos, chmbr orgs); also transport and tuning.*

Oxford Harpsichord Hire. The Folly, Eydon, Northants NN11 3PP *tel:* 01327 263887 *fax:* 01327 262608 *email:* 106714.2057@ compuserve.com. James Anderson. *Single-manual hpds for sale.*

Peter Conacher & Co Ltd. Springwood Organ Works, Water St, Huddersfield, W Yorks HD1 4BB *tel:* 01484 530053 *fax:* 01484 305303

email: admin@musiclink.co.uk/; http://www.musiclink.co.uk/. J Sinclair Willis, mgr dir. *Pipe orgs for hire UK only, tunings and stand-by for concerts and recordings.*

Peter Salisbury Concert Services. Units 2, Brook House, Duke St, Henley-on-Thames, Oxon RG9 1UP *tel:* 01491 577530 *fax:* 01491 411361. Lynette Salisbury, admin. *Concert grand hire and tuning service.*

Ransom, Mark. 130 Westbourne Terrace Mews, London W2 6QG *tel:* 0171 723 9650 *also fax. Hpd hire, tuning, maintenance and transport.*

Robert Deegan Harpsichords. Tonnage Warehouse, St Georges Quay, Lancaster LA1 1RB *tel:* 01524 60186 *fax:* 01524 33277 *email:* http://www.kabine.demon.co.uk/harpsichord/. Robert Deegan, proprietor. *Hpd maker, hpd concert hire, tuning, maintenance, restoration and repairs.*

Robert Morley & Co Ltd. 34 Engate St, London SE13 7HA *tel:* 0181 318 5838 *fax:* 0181 297 0720 *email:* http://www.yell.co.uk/sites/morley. *Long-term home rental of pnos, f-pnos, hpds, spinets, clvds, virginals and celestes.*

Shackell Pianos. Burford Rd, Minster Lovell, Witney, Oxon OX8 5RB *tel:* 01993 703375 *fax:* 01993 700867. *Steinway concert grands available for hire.*

T W Howarth & Co Ltd. 31 Chiltern St, London W1M 1HG *tel:* 0171 935 2407 *fax:* 0171 224 2564 *email:* howarth_ltd@msn.com. *Hire scheme for student w/wind insts and short-term hire of w/wind for orch concerts.*

Temple, Alex. Platt Lodge, 61 Barton Rd, Worsley, Manchester M28 2GX *tel:* 0161 794 3717 *email:* alextemple@compuserve.com. *Hpd, clvd concert hire.*

Wooderson, Andrew. 5 Bourne Rd, Bexley, Kent DA5 1LG *tel:* 01322 558326/525558 *fax:* 01322 525558. *All types of hpds, spinets, virginals, clvds, early pnos. Construction, repair, restoration, tuning, hire.*

Instrument Technicians

Those listed below offer a more specialised service than the general repairers listed in the **Retailers** section.

Allen Organs. Trada Business Campus, Stocking La, Hughenden Valley, High Wycombe, Bucks HP14 4ND *tel:* 01494 563833 *fax:* 01494 563546.

Bishop and Son. 38 Bolton La, Ipswich, Suffolk IP4 2BT *tel:* 01473 255165. *Org builders.*

Booth, Colin. Mount Pleasant, Westbury sub Mendip, Wells BA5 1HU *tel:* 01749 870516 *also fax. Early keyboard insts: tuning, maintenance, repair, restoration.*

The Bridge Fiddler. Riverside House, Chapel Milton, Chapel-en-le-Frith, High Peak SK23 0QQ *tel:* 01298 813813. John Goodborn, proprietor. *Str inst and bow repairer and supplier of str insts and accs. Specialists in restoration.*

Cambridge Pianola Co & J V Pianos. The Limes, Landbeach, Cambridge CB4 4DR *tel:* 01223 861348 *fax:* 01223 441276. F T Poole, proprietor. *Pno and pianola restoration, sales and rentals.*

Cambridge Reed Organs. 18 Hill Close, Newmarket, Suffolk CB8 0NR *tel:* 01638 660531. Bruce Dracott, proprietor. *Harmonium restoration, repair, tuning and hire.*

Cavalier Music. 145 Barncroft Way, Havant, Hampshire PO9 3AF *tel:* 01705 475923. B L Boughton. *Br and w/wind repairs, specialist alterations. Insts bought and sold.*

Chandler Guitars. 300-302 Sandycombe Rd, Kew, Richmond, Surrey TW9 3NG *tel:* 0181 940 5874. Charlie Chandler, dir. *Repairs.*

Clive Morley Harps. Goodfellows, Filkins, Nr Lechlade, Glos GL7 3JG *tel:* 01367 860493 *fax:* 01367 860659. *Hp servicing and repair.*

Coad, Lucy. Workshop 3, Greenway Farm, Bath Rd, Wick, Nr Bristol BS15 1RL *tel:* 0117 937 4949 *also fax. Square pno repairs and conservation.*

Cochrane, Maurice. Coach House, Chetwynd Rd, London NW5 1BH *tel:* 0171 267 1710 *also fax;* 0860 297970. *Early keyboard maintenance, preparation and gen advice.*

David Corey Piano Tuning & Repairs. 32 Briar Rd, Ainsdale, Southport, Merseyside PR8 3RB *fax:* 01704 574610. David Corey. *Member of Pianoforte Tuners' Association. Concert tuning, full re-stringing and restoration.*

Davies, Peter. The Woodwind Workshop, 36 Byram Arcade, Westgate, Huddersfield HD1 1ND *tel:* 01484 533053 *also fax. Specialist repair and restoration of ob family of insts. Repairs, insurance, sales (new and second-hand), accs and mus for w/wind.*

Derek Roberts Violins. 185 Leam Terrace, Leamington Spa, Warwicks CV31 1DW *tel:* 01926 428313 *also fax. Vn maker and restorer.*

Dunkley, Clive. 25 Foxenden Rd, Guildford, Surrey GU1 4DL *tel:* 01483 37685. *Repair, tuning and maintenance of hpds, virginals and clvds.*

Frith, Stephen C. 22 Ewhurst Close, W Green, Crawley, Sussex RH11 7EZ *tel:* 01293 543055. Stephen Frith, luthier; Sherrie Frith, mgr. *Maker and repairer of classical concert guis. Custom built electric guis and advisory service.*

George Morris and Sons. 41 Palmerston Rd, Buckhurst Hill, Essex IG9 5PA *tel:* 0181 502 9988; 0402 803433. Anthony Morris, head technician. *Pno tuning, maintenance, repairs and restoration.*

Gittins, Roy. Hollebeke House, Gore End Rd, Ball Hill, Newbury, Berkshire RG20 0PD *tel:* 01635 253566 *also fax. Brass mus insts repairs and overhauls.*

Gordon Stevenson Violins. 6 Barclay Terrace, Bruntsfield, Edinburgh EH10 4HP *tel:* 0131 229 2051 *fax:* 0131 229 9298. *Maker and restorer of vns.*

Hammett, Claire. 19 Buxton Rd, E Sheen, London SW14 8SY *tel:* 0181 876 1496 *also fax;* 0973 659212 *email:* dan.moore@ic.ac.uk. *Hpd tuner and technician; also clvds and f-pnos.*

Handy, Edmund. 5 Bourne Rd, Bexley, Kent DA5 1LG *tel:* 01322 527366; 0181 300 2715. *Tuning, maintenance and repair of hpds, clvds and early pnos. Celeste maintenance and repair. Square pno restorations. Reconditioned insts for sale.*

Hansford, Neil. The Bristol Violin Shop, 12 Upper Maudlin St, Bristol BS2 8DJ *tel:* 0117 925 9990 *also fax. Viols; Eng, Fr, Ger, It baroque vcs.*

Harmonium Services. 6 Albert Terrace, Saltaire, Shipley, W Yorks BD18 4PS *tel:* 01274 585601; 0976 535980. Phil Fluke, proprietor. *Restoration, hiring, parts and reeds, buying and selling.*

The Harpsichord Workshop. 130 Westbourne Terrace Mews, London W2 6QG *tel:* 0171 723 9650 *also fax.* Mark Ransom. *Tuning, repair, renovation and hire.*

Hassle, Derek. 26 Andrew St, Mossley, Lancs OL5 0DN *tel:* 01457 835656. *W/wind inst restoration.*

Hibernian Violins. 24 Players Av, Malvern, Worcs WR14 1DU *tel:* 01684 562947. Padraig O Dubhlaoidh, proprietor. *W/shop for str insts and bows.*

Hickies Ltd. 153 Friar St, Reading, Berks RG1 1HG *tel:* 0118 957 5771 *fax:* 0118 957 5775. *Pno repairs and restoration.*

Huggett, Martin. The Old Library, Stour St, Manningtree, Eseex CO11 1BE *tel:* 01206 396354 *also fax. Repairer, restorer, tuner of historic and modern keyboard insts. Also cabinet work.*

Impact Percussion. 120-122 Bermondsey St, London SE1 3TX *tel:* 0171 403 5900 *fax:* 0171 403 5910 *email:* impactperc@msn.com. *Repair and custom manufacture of perc insts and stands. Also hire and sales.*

J & A Beare Ltd. 7 Broadwick St, London W1V 1FJ *tel:* 0171 437 1449 *fax:* 0171 439 4520. *Str inst restoration, valuation and sale.*

John Coppen Woodwind Repairs. 50 Kipling St, London SE1 3RU *tel:* 0171 378 1952 *fax:* 0171 357 7615. *Hand made keywork, extensions to all cls, tuning for all w/wind, new and commission sales.*

Kreis, Bill. 46 Goldington Av, Bedford MK40 3BZ *tel:* 01234 267896 *fax:* 01234 309877. *Pno restoration, tuning and concert preparation.*

Lowes Woodwind. 102 Greenwich South St, London SE10 8UN *tel:* 0181 691 6944 *fax:* 0181 694 2503. Jeremy Lowe, proprietor. *Cl, sax and fl repairs.*

M and J Healey Violins. 12 Rosehill, Sutton, Surrey SM1 3EU *tel:* 0181 644 4700 *also fax;* 0181 644 3419. *Strs.*

Markson Pianos. 8 Chester Ct, Albany St, London NW1 4BU *tel:* 0171 935 8682 *fax:* 0171 224 0957. Simon Markson, Julian Markson. *Pno sale, hire, restoration, repair, tuning and maintenance. Concert and recording hire; hire with option to buy.*

Marshall McGurk Musical Services. Elm House Farm, Crosby, Maryport, Cumbria CA15 6SH *tel:* 01900 813200 *also fax.* Allison McGurk, Steve Marshall, partners. *W/wind specialists, especially sax, cl, etc. Also other insts and pno servicing.*

Martyn Booth Guitar Services. Unit 4, Old Brickworks, Chapel La, Little Cornard, Sudbury, Suffolk CO10 0PB *tel:* 01787 370192 *also fax. Repairs and customisation of all types of gui.*

Music For You. 12 High St, Waltham, Grimsby, S Humberside, DN37 0LL *tel:* 01472 828524 *fax:* 01472 828681. Roger and Elaine Huggett, proprietors. *Vn maker and repairer.*

Musicparts (UK). PO Box 25, Tyldesley, Manchester M29 7GJ *tel:* 01942 889024; 0802 204669 *fax:* 01942 889452. Peter Pollard, maker. *W/shop at 426 Worsley Rd, Winton, Eccles, Manchester M30 8HQ. Br and w/wind repairs; custom manufacture of br insts, mouthpieces and tpt bells. Design, modification, restoration.*

National Association of Musical Instrument Repairers. 2 Arthur Cottages, Frimley Rd, Ash Vale, Aldershot GU12 5PD *tel:* 01252 518098 *also fax; email:* rdawson821@aol.com. *Can provide contact information for members of the association.*

Nimblejack Ltd. 24 Alexandra Rd, Windsor, Berks SL4 1HN *tel:* 01753 853724. Alan Whear. *Pno and hpd tuning, maintenance and repair. Gen repairs.*

Odell, Nick. The Music Workshop, PO Box 45, Upwell, Wisbech PE14 9AZ *tel:* 01945 772423 *also fax.* Nick Odell. *Repairer of str insts: vn family; guis, early and folk.*

Peter Salisbury Concert Services. 24 Duke St, Henley-on-Thames, Oxon RG9 1UP *tel:* 01491 577530 *fax:* 01491 411361. Lynette Salisbury, admin. *Technical advice and repairs for concert grands.*

Ranger, Jon (Pianos and Harpsichords). 5 Summerfield Rd, London W5 1ND *tel:* 0181 997 1793 *also fax.* Jonathan Ranger. *Repairer, restorer and tuner of historic and modern pnos, hpds, squares, f-pnos, spinets, clvds, virginals. Information service.*

Ransom, Mark. 130 Westbourne Terrace Mews, London W2 6QG *tel:* 0171 723 9650 *also fax. Tuning, maintenance, hire, transport of hpds.*

Reg Thorp Woodwind Repair. 13 Pinewood Way, Midhurst, W Sussex GU29 9LN *tel:* 01730 814782. Reg Thorp, proprietor. *W/wind repair and renovation. Keymaking, tuning, customising, alterations, mouthpiece refacing, silver plating, etc.*

Robert Morley & Co Ltd. 34 Engate St, London SE13 7HA *tel:* 0181 318 5838 *fax:* 0181 297 0720 *email:* http://www.yell/co.uk/sites/morley. *Repair, restoration and tuning of pnos, f-pnos, hpds, spinets, clvds, virginals, celestes.*

Royal National College of the Blind. College Rd, Hereford HR1 1EB *tel:* 01432 265725 *fax:* 01432 353478. *Pno tuning and repairs.*

Stevens, Mike. 272 Louth Rd, Scartho, Grimsby DN33 2LF *tel:* 01472 824138. *Repairs for str, w/wind, br, etc. Replacements made for any part of any inst, modifications for the disabled. Rebuilt second-hand insts for sale.*

T W Howarth & Co Ltd. 31 Chiltern St, London W1M 1HG *tel:* 0171 935 2407 *fax:* 0171 224 2564 *email:* howarth_ltd@msn.com. *Specialist repair of all w/wind insts, including restoration of old and authentic insts.*

Temple, Alex. Platt Lodge, 61 Barton Rd, Worsley, Manchester M28 2GX *tel:* 0161 794 3717 *email:* alextemple@compuserve.com. *Hpd, clvd, tuning, repairs and hire.*

Top Wind. 2 Lower Marsh, London SE1 7RJ *tel:* 0171 928 8181 *fax:* 0171 401 8788 *email:* jon@topwind.com. Jon Dodd. *Specialist fl and picc repairs.*

Trainor, Brian. 15 Stanmore Cres, Lanark ML11 7DF *tel:* 01555 664024. *Br, str and w/wind inst repairs.*

Ward, Alan. St Andrews, 27 Plomer Hill, Downley, High Wycombe, Bucks HP13 5JG *tel:* 01494 523371. *Str restorer and repairer.*

Whitham, J S. Faraway, Llandegla, Denbighshire LL11 3BG *tel:* 01978 790238 *also fax; email:* jswhit@ptfoods.demon.co.uk. *Repairs to all orch insts, also mobile service.*

Whittaker, Helen. Dawsons Music Ltd, 30 Pepper St, Chester CH1 1DF *tel:* 01244 348606. Helen Whittaker, repairer. *W/wind, str, br inst repairs.*

Wooderson, Andrew. 5 Bourne Rd, Bexley, Kent DA5 1LG *tel:* 01322 558326/525558 *fax:* 01322 525558. *Tuning, maintenance, repair and restoration of early keyboard insts. Handbuilt insts made to order.*

Woolley, Dennis. Tubhole Barn, Dent, Sedbergh, W Yorks LA10 5RE *tel:* 015396 25361. *F-pno, hpd. Tuning, regulation and restoration of early keyboard insts.*

Woolrich, A P. Canal Side, Huntworth, Bridgwater, Somerset TA7 0AJ *tel:* 01278 663020. *Reproduction ironmongery for keyboard insts.*

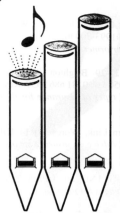

Music Copyists, Setters, Engravers and Printers

Acoustic Art. 2 Milton House, 25 Short St, Waterloo, London SE1 8LH *tel:* 0171 928 1216 *fax:* 0171 976 5408 *email:* less@enterprise.net. James Burden. *Professional computerised mus copying and processing. Full production service. Transposition, orchestration and arranging services available.*

Acuta Music. Hambrook, Ledbury, Herefordshire HR8 2PX *tel:* 01531 670634 *also fax.* Robert Kay. *Computerised mus setting, hand-copying, proof-reading.*

Allan, John. 75 Ealing Rd, Brentford, Middx TW8 0LQ *tel:* 0181 847 1449 *fax:* 0181 400 1952. *Computerised copyist.*

Allegro Reproductions. 33 Belmont Close, Uxbridge, Middx UB8 1RF *tel:* 01895 232055 *also fax.* Stephen Duro, Beryl Duro, dirs. *Computerised mus engraving. Also editing, arranging, orchestrating, transposing, part extraction.*

Animus. 4 Rawlinson St, Dalton-in-Furness, Cumbria LA15 8AL *tel:* 01229 467432. Adrian and Pamela Self. *Computerised mus setting. Transposition, arranging. Choral and organ mus a speciality.*

Arnold Reproduction Co. 77 Dudden Hill La, London NW10 1BD *tel:* 0181 459 6194 *fax:* 0181 459 1184. Peter Hunt, print mgr. *Sheet mus printers.*

Barnes Music Engraving Ltd. Sheepwash Farm, Sheepwash La, Blackboys, E Sussex TN22 4HA *tel:* 01825 830751 *fax:* 01825 830311. Simon Mortimer, dir. *Mus setting, mus and text origination, arranging, transcription, programming and editorial services.*

Barry Peter Ould Music Services. 6 Fairfax Cres, Aylesbury, Bucks HP20 2ES *tel:* 01296 28609 *also fax.* Barry Peter Ould. *Computerised mus setting, design, typesetting and photocopying service.*

Biggin, John R. 23 Boundary Brook Rd, Oxford OX4 4AJ *tel:* 01865 249730. *Mus copying, transposing.*

Boase, Bernard. 38 Mansfield Rd, London NW3 2HP *tel:* 0171 485 3366 *email:* h153@bcs.org.uk. Bernard Boase. *Transcription of manuscript mus to high quality print or computer file using Sibelius software.*

Bowden, Elizabeth. 4 Pitt Ct, Nymet Rowland, Crediton, Devon EX17 6AN *tel:* 01363 83515. *Mus copyist, computer setting; Sibelius 7.*

Brison, R. 75 Enborne Rd, Newbury, Berks RG14 6AP *tel:* 01635 43583. *Mus copying and processing.*

Cabot Music Productions. 29 Long Mead, Brimsham Park, Yate, Bristol BS17 5YT *tel:* 01454 326509. David Kear. *Computerised mus typesetting using Coda Finale. Arranging and transcription services available (PVGs, gui tablature, rock and pop scores, big band transcriptions).*

Caligraving Ltd. Brunel Way, Thetford, Norfolk IP24 1HP *tel:* 01842 752116 *fax:* 01842 755512, Oliver W Makings, sales and mkt dir. *Mus printing and book binding. Full note setting and studio facilities available.*

Camden Music. 19a North Villas, Camden Sq, London NW1 9BJ *tel:* 0171 267 8778 *also fax; email:* http://www.printed-music.com/camden. Andrew Skirrow, dir. *Specialist computerised mus typesetting service.*

Chalmers Enterprises. 48 Bonaly Rise, Edinburgh EH13 0QX *tel:* 0131 441 3488 *fax:* 0131 441 6029. *Computerised mus typesetting using Coda Finale.*

Composit Software. 10 Leasowe Green, Lightmoor, Telford, Shropshire TF4 3QX *tel:* 01952 595436. Andy Murray. *Computer programme for writing mus.*

Craig-McFeely, Julia. 41 Freelands Rd, Oxford OX4 4BS *tel:* 01865 241323 *fax:* 01865 437582 *email:* julia.craig-mcfeely@music.oxford. ac.uk. Julia Craig-McFeely. *Typesetting of all types of mus, specialising in unusual notational requirements: editing includes early mus notations. Proof-reading and copy-editing.*

Criswick, Mary. 94 Kidmore Rd, Reading RG4 7NB *tel:* 0118 947 2627 *email:* mary.criswick@hol.fr. *Computerised mus engraving. French to English translation.*

Crofton, Robin. 8 Wynbury Dr, Totteridge, High Wycombe, Bucks HP13 7QB *tel:* 01494 533775. *Computerised mus setting using Sibelius 7 software.*

Curiad. Unit 6, The Enterprise Centre, The Industrial Estate, Pen-y-Groes, Caernarfon, Gwynedd LL54 6DB *tel:* 01286 882166 *fax:* 01286 881375. *Full mus publishing consultancy by computerised mus copying with editing, design and print service.*

Da Capo Music Ltd. 26 Stanway Rd, Whitefield, Manchester M45 8EG *tel:* 0161 766 5950. *Computer technology able to print mus of engraved quality.*

Dale, Simon. 26 Leicester Rd, Lewes, E Sussex BN7 1SX *tel:* 01273 486389 *also fax; email:* simondale@compuserve.com. *Computer typesetting and hand-copying. Orchestration, arranging, pno reductions.*

Discantus Music. 83 Oakfield Rd, London N14 6LT *tel:* 0181 882 5976. Blaise Compton, mgr. *Gen mus copying, early mus editions to order, archive research.*

Donald Bousted Studio. Burnside House, Melbourne, York YO4 4QJ *tel:* 01759 318440 *email:* 101600.3130@compuserve.com. Donald Bousted, dir. *Computer engraving using Finale software.*

Enigma Music Production Services. 44 Grove Rd, Amersham, Bucks HP6 6NE *tel:* 01494 431663 *also fax.* B R Wilson. *Mus engraving using Sibelius 7.*

Falchion Music. 55 Borough Rd, Darlington, Co Durham DL1 1SR *tel:* 01325 464609 *also fax.* Peter Lawrence, proprietor; Hazel Lawrence. *Computerised mus setting (Sibelius 7), laser printing, binding, recording.*

Fand Music Press. Blumleins, 7a Dragon St, Petersfield GU31 4JN *tel:* 01730 266605 *fax:* 01730 262961. *Pno, vocal, chmbr, choral and orch mus.*

Final Score. Cecilia Cottage, 47 Brighton Rd, Horsham, W Sussex RH13 6EZ *tel:* 01403 264798 *also fax.* Michael and Helen McCabe. *Mus typesetting and printing; publication layout and graphic design; CRC or full-scale production service.*

Friary Music Services. 142b Friary Rd, London SE15 5UW *tel:* 0171 277 7068 *fax:* 0171 277 8354. Richard Black. *Computerised mus copying, editing of pno scores.*

Frontier Music Services. c/o 30 Buckingham Rd, Petersham, Richmond, Surrey TW10 7EQ *tel:* 0973 978014. Jennifer Churches, proprietor. *Computerised typesetting service.*

Galliard (Printers) Ltd. Barith Works, Queen Anne's Rd, Southtown, Gt Yarmouth, Norfolk NR31 0LL *tel:* 01493 604281 *fax:* 01493 655454 *email:* 101602.320@compuserve.com. T J Harrison, mgr dir. *Specialist mus printers.*

GFA Publications. 5 Kirkintilloch Rd, Lenzie, Glasgow G66 4RW *tel:* 0141 776 5056 *also fax.* Charles Ketteringham. *Professional mus copying service using latest technology and software.*

Gibson, Stephen. 40 Campbell Close, London SW16 6NG *tel:* 0181 677 8473 *fax:* 0181 877 3494 *email:* 100105.201@compuserve.com. *Mus typesetting, orchestration, arranging, vocal reductions.*

Ginn, Jeffrey. 11 Haycroft, Wootton, Bedford, Beds MK43 9PB *tel:* 01234 765602; 0378 896721 *fax:* 01234 765367 *email:* jeff@ginn-mus.demon. co.uk; http://www.ginn-mus.demon.co.uk. *Mus typesetting to laser or film. Sibelius 7 recording service.*

Global Music Solutions. 163 Stafford Rd, Wallington, Surrey SM6 9BT *tel:* 0181 773 0953 *fax:* 0181 669 1869 *email:* boss@cmyk.co.uk. Ben Parker, dir. *Computer mus setting, mus arranging and transcription, full colour digital print, graphics with notation, mus and text origination, short-run print and finishing facility.*

Gordon, Christopher. 22 Ivybridge Close, Twickenham, Middx TW1 1EA *tel:* 0181 892 1833 *also fax.* Christopher Gordon. *Computerised mus setting, hand copying. Special rates for educ clients.*

Hagues, Robin. 36 Westbrooke Rd, Sidcup, Kent DA15 7PH *tel:* 0181 309 9308. *Computerised mus copying, arranging and transcribing.*

Halstan & Co Ltd. Plantation Rd, Amersham, Bucks HP6 6HJ *tel:* 01494 725525 *fax:* 01494 432305. Peter Chisholm, sales dir. *Mus process engraving, computerised mus setting, design service, mus printing and binding.*

Harman, Mrs M. 48 Huxley Rd, Welling, Kent DA16 2EW. *Preparation for printing of mastercopies of mus from composers' manuscripts.*

Hinkins, Chris and Gail. 66 Spilsby Rd, Horncastle, Lincs LN9 6AW *tel:* 01507 526531 *also fax. High quality computer mus engraving.*

Johnny Douglas Enterprises Ltd. 39 Tadorne Rd, Tadworth, Surrey KT20 5TF *tel:* 01737 812922. Norma Camby, dir.

King's Music. Redcroft, Banks End, Wyton, Huntingdon, Cambs PE17 2AA *tel:* 01480 52076 *fax:* 01480 450821 *email:* cbkings@ibm.net. Clifford Bartlett, Brian Clark. *Photocopying, mus and text typesetting, programme production (including writing and printing notes).*

Langley, John. 16 Glazbury Rd, London W14 9AS *tel:* 0171 603 8796 *fax:* 0171 602 1257. *Copying/library services, computer setting, transposing, transcribing, proofing and editing.*

Laser Music Ltd. 6 Lytham Close, Chippenham, Wilts SN15 3XW *tel:* 01249 444858 *also fax.* Gareth Bennett, principal associate. *Computerised mus setting and mus copying.*

Linda Lancaster Music Setting. 19 Far View, Almondbury, Huddersfield HD5 8ER *tel:* 01484 546490 *also fax.* Paul Lancaster, partner. *Computerised setting of mus and text.*

Lipkin, Malcolm. Penlan, Crowborough Hill, Crowborough, Sussex TN6 2EA *tel:* 01892 652454. *Mus setting, artwork and editing.*

Loft Music. 103 Stubbington Av, North End, Portsmouth, Hants PO2 0JE *tel:* 01705 690894 *also fax. Computer mus transcription, mus editing.*

Lowdell, Robert. 29 Montana Rd, London SW17 8SN *tel:* 0181 672 8020.

McCreadie, Mary. 8 Willow Close, Brightlingsea, Colchester, Essex CO7 0LD *tel:* 01206 305027. *Computerised mus setting, proof reading.*

Maestro Music Services. Chapel Cottage, High St, Thorpe-le-Soken, Essex CO16 0DY *tel:* 01255 860502. Sarah Williams. *Computerised mus copying from ms or MIDI files; part extractions, transposition, score reduction, arrangements.*

MME (Marrington Musical Enterprises). Flat 1, 16 Bentcliffe La, Moortown, Leeds LS17 6QF *tel:* 0113 226 5943. Mark Marrington. *Computerised mus typesetting (Sibelius 7), transposition, transcription and arranging.*

MSS Studios. Rhiwlas, Cae Deintur, Dolgellau, Gwynedd LL40 2YS *tel:* 01341 422115 *fax:* 01341 422127 *email:* 100273.673@compuserve.com. Mr King, snr partner. *Mus engravers with 20 years experience.*

Music By Design. 8 Lloyd St South, Manchester M14 7HY *tel:* 0161 226 8806. Ian Flower; Wendy Jackson.

Music Reprographics. 34 Hollingworth Ct, Ashford Rd, Maidstone, Kent ME14 5PP *tel:* 01622 683884 *fax:* 01622 661919. R Shipley, dir. *Full range of printing and publishing services.*

Music To Measure. New House, Ballachulish, Argyll PA39 4JR *tel:* 01855 811507 *also fax; email:* 100272.2253@compuserve.com. Mary Anne Alburger, dir. *Computerised mus typesetting to print and film; DTP services.*

The Music Workshop. 17 Bradford Rd, St John's, Wakefield, W Yorkshire WF1 2RF *tel:* 01924 370454 *also fax.* Patric Standford, dir. *Composition, arranging, computer copying, editing, revision and tutorial support for concerts, TV, studios, schools and amateur orgs. EEC and USA service.*

Musicleigh Inklined. 35 Kirtle Rd, Chesham, Bucks HP5 1AD *tel:* 01494 771872/782007. Jackie Leigh. *Computerised mus typesetting, artwork productions and laser printing.*

Musography. 6 Station Rd, Catworth, Huntingdon, Cambs PE18 0PE *tel:* 01832 710227 *email:* musography@compuserve.com. Christopher Brown. *Computerised mus type-setting using SCORE, specialising in complex contemporary scores and baroque mus.*

New Notations. 2 Triangle House, Broomhill Rd, Wandsworth, London SW18 4HX *tel:* 0181 875 0429 *fax:* 0181 877 3494 *email:* new @notation.demon.co.uk; http://www.notation.demon.co.uk. Stephen Gibson, partner; Stephen Ferre, partner. *Advanced computerised mus typesetting, mus and text integration, etc. Specialists in large projects, fast turnaround. Consultancy and hardware and software sales. Linotronic printing service.*

Offline Music Typesetting Services. 52 Ashurst Rd, Cockfosters, Herts EN4 9LF *tel:* 0181 449 0886 *email:* 101602.314@compuserve.com; http://ourworld.compuserve.com/homepages/stevekenyon. Stephen Kenyon. *Mus engraving service using Graphite Music Press, also improvement of Finale files. Specialist in gui mus.*

Parfrey, Raymond. 53 Longley Rd, Harrow, Middx HA1 4TG *tel:* 0181 427 5267. *High class notation by hand.*

Phillips, Sally. 10 Quayside Close, Nottingham NG2 3BP *tel:* 0115 986 3386 *email:* sally.phillips@ntu.ac.uk. *Hand copying, transposition, binding, secretarial services.*

Pilkington, Michael. 268 Coulsdon Rd, Old Coulsdon, Surrey CR5 1EB *tel:* 01737 556346 *also fax. Computerised mus copying, transposition, part extraction.*

Richmond House Music. 33 Southminster Rd, Penylan, Cardiff CF2 5AT *tel:* 01222 499970 *also fax; email:* painter@dial.pipex.com. Chris Painter. *Computerised typesetting using Coda Finale on Power Macintosh, brochure design and printing and web page design.*

RM Music. Ivydene, 37 West Pastures, Fallowfield, Ashington, Northumberland NE63 *tel:* 01670 521570 *also fax. Specialist in br and wind band.*

Rob Danter Computer Music Typesetting. 18 Clydesdale Rd, Box, Corsham, Wilts SNB 8EN *tel:* 01225 742424. Rob Danter. *Computerised mus typesetting on Sibelius 7. Special interest in church and org mus.*

RTS Music Partnership. 17 Bradford Rd, St John's Wood, Wakefield, W Yorks WF1 2RF *tel:* 01924 370454 *also fax.* Patric Standford, dir. *Computer setting with editing and revision.*

Scoreprint. 12b Anstey Way, Cambridge CB2 2JE *tel:* 01223 841721. *Mus process engraving.*

SFZ Professional Music Arranging & Typsetting Services. 86 Newark St, Whitechapel, London E1 2ES *tel:* 0171 426 0340. Jason Glover, dir. *Computerised mus typesetting.*

Sibelius Software Ltd. 75 Burleigh St, Cambridge CB1 1DJ *tel:* 01223 302765 *fax:* 01223 351947 *email:* info@sibelius-software.com. Ben Finn, mgr dir; Jonathan Finn, development mgr. *Developer and distributor of the Sibelius 7 mus processing expert system.*

Silverfen. 57a St Philip's Rd, Cambridge CB1 3DA *tel:* 01223 461143 *also fax; email:* mtargent@silverfe.demon.co.uk. Timothy Argent, dir. *Design, typesetting.*

SJ Music. 23 Leys Rd, Cambridge CB4 2AP *tel:* 01223 314771 *fax:* 01223 560353. Judith Rattenbury, principal; Susan Otty, associate. *Computerised mus typesetting and transposition.*

Smith, Andrew. c/o 27 Reeth Rd, Richmond, N Yorks DL10 4EH *tel:* 01748 823948. *Hand and computer transcription.*

Snell, Piers. 1a All Saints' Passage, Cambridge CB2 3LT *tel:* 01223 460818 *fax:* 01223 464178 *email:* piers@cambridge.dungeon.com. Piers Snell. *Advanced computerised mus engraving.*

John Henry Enterprises. 16-24 Brewery Rd, London N7 9NH *tel:* 0171 609 9181 *fax:* 0171 700 7040. John Henry, mgr dir. *Rehearsal studios.*

London Buddhist Arts Centre. Eastbourne House, Bullards Pl, London E2 0PT *tel:* 0181 983 4473 *also fax; email:* postbox@lbac.demon.co.uk. Srivati, admin; Karen Oram, bookings. *Rehearsal room with pno for hire, sliding scale.*

The Music Room. 49 Gt Ormond St, London WC1N 3HZ *tel:* 0171 405 9848. Alec Forshaw.

The Music Room. Littlefield, 39-39a Parkwood Av, Esher, Surrey KT10 8DE *tel:* 0181 398 8541 *fax:* 0181 339 0625. Susan Garratt. *Garden room with Steinway grand, up to 6 players.*

Music Services (MSA). The Chalet, 75 Claremont Rd, Tunbridge Wells, Kent TN1 1TE *tel:* 01892 52790. David Ebbage, dir. *Studio with two pnos for hire.*

The Music Studios. 29 Marylebone La, London W1M 5FH *tel:* 0171 486 0025 *fax:* 0171 935 8454. *International pno showroom with 5 floors of building devoted to practice/mus rooms.*

St Mary Abbots Church Hall. Vicarage Gate, Kensington, London W8 4HN *tel:* 0973 642710. *Large rehearsal hall, small rehearsal room. Grand pno. Suitable for orch and ens rehearsals, auditions, receptions.*

Terminal 24 Rehearsal Ltd. 4-10 Lamb Walk, London Bridge, London SE1 3TT *tel:* 0171 403 3050 *fax:* 0171 407 6123. Charlie Barrett, dir. *Large Turbosound-equipped studios, central London, parking. Comprehensive equipment hire on site, showcase and production rooms. Café and production office. Storage cages.*

The Warehouse Waterloo. London Festival Orchestra, 13 Theed St, London SE1 8ST *tel:* 0171 928 9251 *fax:* 0171 928 9252. *2 rehearsal halls; large hall up to 60 players, small hall up to 35 players. Steinway and Rönich grand pnos.*

Wigmore Hall. 36 Wigmore St, London W1H 0BP *tel:* 0171 486 1907 *fax:* 0171 224 3800. Marion Friend, gen admin. *Contact the management office. Rehearsal room with upright Bösendorfer pno. Main hall available for rehearsal auditions. Bechstein Room available for talks and receptions.*

Programme and Sleeve Notes

Ades, David. Stone Gables, Upton La, Seavington St Michael, Ilminster, Somerset TA19 0PZ *tel:* 01460 242226 *also fax. Compiler and sleeve note writer.*

Allen, Kevin. 23 Benbow Close, Malvern Wells, Worcs WR14 4JJ *tel:* 01684 569643.

Avis, Peter Graham. 91 Cambridge Rd, New Malden, Surrey KT3 3QP *tel:* 0181 336 1656 *fax:* 0181 336 1742. *Programme and sleeve notes, more anecdotal than technical.*

Bartlett, Clifford. Redcroft, Banks End, Wyton, Huntingdon, Cambs PE17 2AA *tel:* 01480 52076 *fax:* 01480 450821 *email:* cbkings@ibm.net. *Programme notes.*

Bishop, David. Curls Farmhouse, Ripe, Lewes, E Sussex BN8 6AP *tel:* 01323 811654. *Programme and sleeve notes.*

Bryant, Michael. 61 Oak Hill, Surbiton, Surrey KT6 6DY *tel:* 0181 390 3236 *email:* michael@bryant14.demon.co.uk. *Specialising in Czech and Slovak mus, chmbr and wind repertoire.*

Bullamore, Tim. 25 Brock St, Bath BA1 2LN *tel:* 01225 330037 *also fax;* 0836 617030.

Burton, Anthony. 19 Capel Rd, E Barnet, Herts EN4 8JD *tel:* 0181 440 4380. *Programme and sleeve notes.*

Carroll, Brendan. 2 Southbank Rd, Grassendale, Liverpool, L19 9AR *tel:* 0151 427 1181; 0151 281 6810 *fax:* 0151 494 3589 *email:* 101526.

Morley, Christopher. 16 Melbourne Rd, Halesowen B63 3NB *tel:* 0121 550 4482 *also fax. Programme and sleeve notes.*

Newman, Bill. 90 Deans La, Edgware, Middx HA8 9NP *tel:* 0181 959 4280 *also fax. Programme and CD liner notes. Artists' profiles. Articles, record and concert reviews.*

Notes in Edge-Wise. 38 Heyes La, Alderley Edge, Cheshire SK9 7JY *tel:* 01625 585378 *fax:* 01625 590175. Lynne Walker. *Agency for commissioning all types of programme material; also editing.*

Pott, Francis. Thurlows, Littleton, Winchester, Hants SO22 6PS *tel:* 01962 880975. *Regular contributor of concert programme notes and sleeve notes to record companies.*

Purkiss, Anthony J. 35 Fonthill Rd, Hove, E Sussex BN3 6HB *tel:* 01273 774730 *also fax. Programme notes and record sleeves.*

Rast, Nicholas. 47 Borrowdale Dr, Norwich NR1 4LY *tel:* 01603 433935 *fax:* 01603 403400. *Especially Franz Schubert.*

Ravens, Simon. 8 Barbieston Courtyard, Dalrymple, Ayr KA6 6EJ *tel:* 01292 560840 *also fax. Programme and sleeve notes.*

Saba, Thérèse Wassily. 6 Thirlmere Rd, Muswell Hill, London N10 2DN *tel:* 0181 442 1489 *also fax; email:* 106665.3500@compuserve.com. *Programme and sleeve notes, especially Arabic, Spanish and Latin-American mus, gui mus.*

Standford, Patric. 17 Bradford Rd, St John's, Wakefield, W Yorkshire WF1 2RF *tel:* 01924 370454 *also fax.*

Steadman, Robert. 36 Trafalgar Rd, Beeston Rylands, Nottingham NG9 1LB *tel:* 0115 917 4546 *also fax. Including reviews, specialising in 20th C repertoire.*

Stewart, Andrew. 46 Schoolbell Mews, Arbery Rd, London E3 5BZ *tel:* 0181 983 0011 *also fax; email:* 101334.577@compuserve.com. *Specialist in choral, song and early vocal mus.*

Stowell, Robin. 43 Woodvale Av, Cyncoed, Cardiff CF2 6SP *tel:* 01222 752001. *Programme and sleeve notes, especially mus for strs.*

Taylor, Philip. 112 Main Rd, Wilby, Northants NN8 2UE *tel:* 01933 223301 *also fax; email:* 100661.1355@compuserve.com. *Specialist on Russian mus.*

Third Millenium Music Ltd. 22 Avon, Hockley, Tamworth, Staffs B77 5QA *tel:* 01827 286086 *also fax.* Neil Williams, mgr dir. *Programme and sleeve notes, especially for composers, conds and musicians; also picture archive.*

Thomas, Janet Owen. Flat 3, 88 Holgate Rd, York YO2 4AB *tel:* 01904 654283. *Programme and sleeve notes. Record, concert and book reviews, especially contemporary mus and mus educ.*

Ward Russell, Gillian. 10 New Street, Maldon, Essex CM9 6AQ *tel:* 01621 853237. *Programme and sleeve notes.*

Wheeler, Michael. 20 Sudbury St, Derby DE1 1LU *tel:* 01332 362194. *Programme and sleeve notes.*

Wright, Simon. 6 Warneford Pl, Moreton-in-Marsh, Glos GL56 0LR *tel:* 01608 651409. *Programme and sleeve note writing (especially French and Latin-American mus).*

Solicitors

Howell-Jones & Partners. 19a Wimbledon Bridge, London SW19 7NH *tel:* 0181 946 7679 *fax:* 0181 947 8725. Peter Scott, partner.

Marshall Hatchick Solicitors. 17 Bentinck St, London W1M 5RL *tel:* 0171 935 3272 *fax:* 0171 224 1592 *email:* mhat@compuserve.com. Keith Hatchick, Nicholas Marshall, partners. *General arts law advice, particularly sponsorship and lottery applications.*

Nicholas Morris. 70-71 New Bond St, London W1Y 9DE *tel:* 0171 493 8811 *fax:* 0171 491 2094. Leonard Lowy, partner. *Specialists in all aspects of the mus industry.*

Teacher Stern Selby. 37-41 Bedford Row, London WC1R 4JH *tel:* 0171 242 3191 *fax:* 0171 242 1156. Roger Selby; Catherine Fehler; Greig Morrison. *Specialists in the entertainment, mus, film and TV industries, including production and distribution, licences, recording, management, agency, publishing, copyright, multi-media agreements; litigation in all areas.*

Tods Murray WS. 66 Queen St, Edinburgh EH2 4NE *tel:* 0131 226 4771 *fax:* 0131 467 7280 *email:* richard.findlay@todsmurray.co.uk. Richard Findlay, entertainment law partner. *Specialist entertainment and media lawyers.*

Tour and Travel Companies

ABC Executive Travel. Tower Bridge Piazza, Butlers Wharf, London SE1 2LH *tel:* 0171 357 8322 *fax:* 0171 357 8323 *email:* 106026.530@compuserve.com. Andreas Schwalbe, gen mgr. *Complete tour management for individuals, orchs and choirs, including travel arrangements, aircraft charter, ground handling, accommodation and transfers.*

ACFEA Tour Consultants. 12-15 Hanger Green, London W5 3EL *tel:* 0181 991 2200 *fax:* 0181 998 7965 *email:* information@specialised-travel.co.uk. Matthew Grocutt, operations mgr. *Organise concert tours in UK, Europe, the Baltic States, S Africa, USA, Australia and Japan for youth and adult choirs, bands and orchs.*

Aircraft Chartering Services Ltd. 7 High St, Ewell, Epsom, Surrey KT17 1SG *tel:* 0181 394 2795 *fax:* 0181 393 6154. Mark Hugo, mgr dir; Philip Mathews, Andrew Richley, touring mgrs. *The charter of aircraft for the touring orch.*

The Albatross Travel Group. Albatross House, 31 Rochester Rd, Aylesford, Kent ME20 7TT *tel:* 01622 790700 *fax:* 01622 790701. Caron Phillips, dir. *Travel consultants to the entertainment industry.*

Club Europe Concert Tours. Fairway House, 53 Dartmouth Rd, London SE23 3HN *tel:* 0181 699 7788 *fax:* 0181 699 7770 *email:* music@club-europe.co.uk. Alison Moore, concert tours mgr; David Drummond, mus dir. *International concert tours for adult, youth and school groups.*

Congress Travel. 13 Newtown, Bradford on Avon, Wilts BA15 1NE *tel:* 01225 867865 *fax:* 01225 867505. Anthony Goodchild, UK representative. *Performing tours, exchanges, festivals worldwide. Specialises in USA and Canada.*

Edwin Doran Music Travel. 54 King St, Twickenham, Middlesex TW1 3SH *tel:* 0181 288 2921/3 *fax:* 0181 288 2959. Edwin Doran, dir; Philippa Newnham, sales mgr. *Mus and drama tours to and from UK for schools and youth groups. Specialist concert tour operations for choirs, orchs and bands.*

Edwin Doran Music Travel. Gardale House, Gatley Rd, Gatley, Cheadle, Cheshire SK8 4AU *tel:* 0161 491 6969 *fax:* 0161 428 9754. Edwin Doran, dir. *Specialist in mus and educ tours.*

Euro-Academy Ltd. 77a George St, Croydon, Surrey CR0 1LD *tel:* 0181 686 2363 *fax:* 0181 681 8850. Mrs M B Malone. *Mus tours to Germany, Holland and Austria for schools, youth orchs and choirs, br bands, folk groups, etc.*

Gower Music International. 2 High St, Studley, Warwicks B80 7HJ *tel:* 01527 854822 *fax:* 01527 857236 *email:* gower@gowstrav.demon.co.uk. Peter Cook, gen mgr; Julian Edwards, sales and mkt. *Specialist tour operator arranging performance tours and festivals abroad for choirs, bands and orchs.*

HF Holidays. Imperial House, Edgware Rd, London NW9 5AL *tel:* 0181 905 9388 (brochure line) *fax:* 0181 205 0506. *Wide range of mus holidays including orch and choral weeks, opera w/shops and mus appreciation and festivals.*

Hotelink (UK) Ltd. Silver House, Church La, Lower Fyfield, Marlborough, Wilts SN8 1PY *tel:* 01672 861111 *fax:* 01672 861100 *email:* 106513. 724@compuserve.com. Jean R Grant, John Silver, dirs. *Specialists in negotiating best quality hotel accommodation at lowest rates for orchs and other groups on tour in the UK or abroad.*

Interchange. Interchange House, 27 Stafford Rd, Croydon, Surrey CR0 4NG *tel:* 0181 681 3612 *fax:* 0181 760 0031. Gordon Burnett, mgr dir. *Specialists in group tours worldwide catering to individual group requests.*

International Arts and Music. PO Box 1, St Albans, Herts AL1 4ED *tel:* 01727 841115 *fax:* 01727 851676. Stuart Harding, mgr dir. *Central booking point for theatre (opera, music and art), travel and accommodation UK and worldwide.*

Legato Music Tours. 8 Meadow La, Alvechurch, Birmingham B48 7LH *tel:* 0121 445 4938. Christine Read, Nigel Morley, dirs. *Specialist mus tours throughout Europe for schools, youth groups, choirs, bands and orchs.*

Maestro Travel & Touring Company. 6th Floor, 32 Hanover St, Liverpool L1 4AA *tel:* 0151 707 1234 *fax:* 0151 707 1747 *email:* 100437.3622@ compuserve.com. *International travel arrangements for the classical mus business from individual artists to ens and full scale orch touring.*

Martin Randall Travel Ltd. 10 Barley Mow Passage, Chiswick, London W4 4PA *tel:* 0181 742 3355 *fax:* 0181 742 7766. Martin Randall, dir. *Operators of special lecture tours to European festivals and opera houses.*

Music and Travel Ltd. 32 Merlin Grove, Beckenham, Kent BR3 3HU *tel:* 0181 663 3037 *fax:* 0181 663 3012. David Horsburgh, dir. *Travel and tour arrangements specialising in Europe and N America. Tailor-made tours, festivals and exchanges.*

Musica Europa. 7a Farm Rd, Maidenhead, Berks SL6 5HX *tel:* 01628 776795 *fax:* 01628 32112. Ben Gunner, dir. *Organises concert tours, w/shops, courses, exchanges and visits to the European festivals for both performers and listeners.*

Nst Music Tours. Chiltern House, 181 Bristol Av, Blackpool, Lancs FY2 0FA *tel:* 01253 352525 *fax:* 01253 356955 *email:* nst@nstgroup.co.uk. Sarah Foden, mus tours mgr. *Tailor-made performance tours for bands, choirs and orchs throughout Europe. Arrangements for travel and accommodation only are also available.*

Onyx International Travel Services Ltd. 26 Woodford Close, Caversham, Reading, Berks RG4 7HN *tel:* 0118 947 2830 *fax:* 0118 946 3104. *Specialists in orch and choir travel including flight, hotel bookings worldwide, air charter and tailor-made tours.*

Perform Europe. Deepdene Lodge, Deepdene Av, Dorking, Surrey RH5 4AZ *tel:* 01306 744360 *fax:* 01306 744361 *email:* peurope@kuoni.co. uk. Maria Llinares, Sharon Brewster, operations. *Specialists in performing arts tours for amateur groups in the UK and Ireland. Agents for the Bournemouth Music Makers Festival. Organisers of the Harrogate and W Sussex International Youth Music Festivals.*

Progressive Tours Ltd. 12 Porchester Pl, London W2 2BS *tel:* 0171 262 1676 *fax:* 0171 724 6941 *email:* 101533.513@compuserve.com. L R Temple, mgr. *Specialists in travel to former USSR, most European countries, Cuba and South Africa for choirs, orchs, cultural groups, etc. Exchange enquiries welcome.*

Rayburn Tours Ltd. Rayburn House, Parcel Terrace, Derby DE1 1LZ *tel:* 01332 347828 *fax:* 01332 371298. Paul Sibert, Rebecca Jefferies, mus tours orgs; Daniel Carriett, mus tours mgr. *Tailor-made mus tours for all types of amateur youth and adult bands, choirs, orchs and ens.*

St Albans Travel Service. 4a Spencer St, St Albans, Herts AL3 5EQ *tel:* 01727 842276 *fax:* 01727 847418. Sarah Hayes, mgr. *UK and international travel service, hotel bookings, many discounts.*

School Rail. PO Box 1, St Albans, Herts AL1 4ED *tel:* 01727 834475 *fax:* 01727 851676. Pat Kearley, mgr. *Educ tours, reduced rail travel, overnight accommodation, ticket bookings, lecture and tour arrangements. Theatre and mus events. Worldwide tours for choirs, orch, etc.*

Specialised Travel Ltd. 12-15 Hanger Green, Park Royal, London W5 3EL *tel:* 0181 998 1761 *fax:* 0181 998 7965 *email:* information@specialised-

travel.co.uk; http://www.specialised-travel.co.uk. Richard Savage, chmn. *ABTA, IATA and CAA bonded travel consultants to the mus industry since 1955. Competitive quotes for travel to any part of the world. Concert tours organised to E and W Europe, USA and Canada, Japan and South Africa.*

Travel for the Arts. 117 Regent's Park Rd, London NW1 8UR *tel:* 0171 483 4466 *fax:* 0171 586 0639. Clare Temple, mgr. *Operates a programme of visits to opera houses and summer festivals for opera, ballet and mus lovers.*

Upbeat Tours. 10 Orchard St, Llandovery, Carms SA20 0DG *tel:* 01550 720978 *also fax.* Meryl Goodwin, Hugh Thomas, dirs. *Specialists in concert tours of Brittany for choirs, orchs and chmbr musicians.*

Wyvern Schooltours Ltd. 28 Westbourne Gardens, Trowbridge, Wilts BA14 9AW *tel:* 01225 766346 *fax:* 01225 777936. Ashley Scarlett, operations dir. *Tailor-made tours to Western Europe for orch, inst and choral groups.*

Young Travellers Ltd. Dept Music and Leisure, Travel House, 34 Station Rd, London SE20 7BQ *tel:* 0181 778 6850 *fax:* 0181 778 9754 *email:* musicleisure@young-travellers.co.uk. S Williamson, dir; A McIntyre, programme consultant. *Transportation by coach of orchs and choirs in the UK and abroad including accommodation arrangements if required.*

Video Companies

Colmar Video Productions. 36 Planton Way, Brightlingsea, Colchester, Essex CO7 0LB *tel:* 01206 303764 *fax:* 01206 305027. Colin Sadler, partner. *Concert and recital videos.*

Documentary Video Associates Ltd. 7 Campbell Ct, Bramley, Tadley, Hants RG26 5EG *tel:* 01256 882032 *fax:* 01256 882024.

Heavy Entertainment Ltd. 222 Kensal Rd, London W10 5BN *tel:* 0181 960 9001/2 *fax:* 0181 960 9003 *email:* info@heavy-entertainment.co.uk. Nick St George, David Roper, company dirs; Matthew Thompson, production mgr. *TV and radio producers. Radio features and commercials, direct-mail CDs and cassettes, promotional video and audio, electronic press kits, video news releases, media training, event staging.*

Music Mall. 14-22 Ganton St, London W1V 1LB *tel:* 0171 734 6411; 0171 287 6411 *fax:* 0171 734 9797; 0171 287 5597 *email:* post@musmall. demon.co.uk. Roger Drage, mgr dir; Ross Penney, gen mgr. *Sourcing, tracing, clearance, duplication, programme development for mus video.*

Symphony Films. Flat 2, 38 Russell Rd, London W14 8HT *tel:* 0171 603 7279 *also fax.* Martin Phillips. *Full programme production. Promotional videos, video press-releases, tour videos, demo tapes, self-observance videos, audition tapes, concert and recital videos.*

Time Machine Communications Ltd. Penhow Castle, Penhow, nr Newport, Gwent NP6 3AD *tel:* 01633 400800 *fax:* 01633 400990. Stephen Weeks, mgr dir; Peter Taylor, mkt mgr. *Historic mus production and presentation.*

Word Processing and Editorial Services

Better English. Suite 22, Sparkford House, Battersea Church Rd, Battersea, London SW11 3NQ *tel:* 0171 350 0661 *also fax; email:* infomike@dial. pipex.com; http://ds.dial.pipex.com/worldwide/infocom/dd72. Michael Thorne, mgr dir. *Proof-reading and sub-editing services.*

Cadenza Consultants. 40 Shorrolds Rd, London SW6 7TP *tel:* 0171 385 9171 *fax:* 0171 381 4691. *High quality letters, mailings, reports, theses, CVs, etc and business computing.*

Complete Secretarial Services. Milestone, St Nicholas Av, Great Bookham, Surrey KT23 4AY *tel:* 01372 457755 *fax:* 01372 450525. Elizabeth McArthur. *Service includes typing letters, mailings, reports, theses, CV preparation, address labels for mailshots, accounts and book-keeping for artists and small businesses, the organisation of conferences, special events, travel arrangements etc.*

Compro. 63 Charles St, Epping, Essex CM16 7AX *tel:* 01992 572805 *also fax.* Genevieve Pearson, dir. *Laser address labels of concert promoters, UK and abroad. Complete mailshots and mailmerge.*

Davros Services. 12 Rosebery Av, Thornton Heath CR7 8PT *tel:* 0181 771 3444 *fax:* 0181 771 3445 *email:* wwartistaol.com. *Word processing, brochure design and printing.*

Edgerton Publishing Services. 30 Edgerton Rd, Huddersfield HD3 3AD *tel:* 01484 519462 *fax:* 01484 451396 *email:* penfold@eps-edge.demon. co.uk. David Penfold, dir. *Editorial and production services for programmes, newsletters, etc. Consultancy on publications (electronic and conventional).*

Friary Music Services. 142b Friary Rd, London SE15 5UW *tel:* 0171 277 7068 *fax:* 0171 277 8354 *email:* 100115.3701@compuserve.com. Richard Black. *DTP, editorial services, proof-reading (English and German).*

Jackie's Musicians Answering Service Word Processing Service. 42a Shenley Rd, Borehamwood, Herts WD6 1DR *tel:* 0181 207 0007 *fax:* 0181 207 4554. Jackie and David Millman. *Address labels for N America and Europe.*

Lees, Tracy. 35 Hamilton Rd, Wimbledon, London SW19 1JG *tel:* 0181 540 9857 *also fax.* *Secretarial and admin service.*

Maestro Music Services. Chapel Cottage, High St, Thorpe-le-Soken, Essex CO16 0DY *tel:* 01255 860502. Sarah Williams. *CVs, reports, theses, dissertations and general word processing.*

Manly, Ann. 8 Alma Sq, London NW8 9QD *tel:* 0171 286 3944 *fax:* 0171 289 9081. *DTP, design, word-processing, programme notes, PR and marketing.*

Monica Bloxam T/A Take a Note Translations and Transcriptions. 13 Glasslyn Rd, London N8 8RJ *tel:* 0181 348 5137 *fax:* 0181 348 5101 *email:* 106025.30@compuserve.com. *Translations, interpreting, reports, theses, dissertations, etc.*

SMG Secretarial Services. 39 Parkwood Av, Esher, Surrey KT10 8DE *tel:* 0181 398 8541 *fax:* 0181 339 0625. Susan Garratt, proprietor. *Typing of general correspondence, CV preparation, reports, theses, mailshots, laser printing, photo-copying and fax.*

Sprint. 10 Quayside Close, Nottingham NG2 3BP *tel:* 0115 986 3386 *email:* sally.phillips@ntu.ac.uk. Sally Phillips, mgr. *Typing, reports, CV preparation, mailshots, laser printing, data processing, binding, leaflets, HTML coding.*

Wessex Music Services. 19 Ruskin Dr, Warminster, Wilts BA12 8HS *tel:* 01985 300900 *also fax.* John Bickerton, proprietor. *Word processing and typing services, especially text with mus examples.*

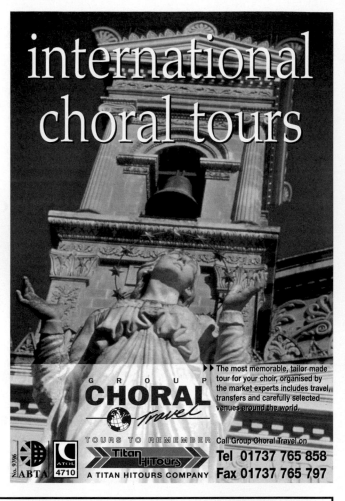

International
Directory
1998

Fourth Edition

Rhinegold Publishing Limited
241 Shaftesbury Avenue
London WC2H 8EH
United Kingdom

Editorial: +44 171 333 1760
Book Sales: +44 171 333 1721 Advertising: +44 171 333 1733
Fax: +44 171 333 1769 E-Mail: bmyb@rhinegold.co.uk

II. Festival Brežice '98
18.7. – 1.8.

*A marvellous series of Early Music concerts
by Europe's most eminent artists
in the most beautiful hall in Slovenia.*

18 July 1998
Adel Singers

19 July 1998
Le Parlement de Musique

21 July 1998
Lynne Dawson & La Stagione Frankfurt

23 July 1998
Musica Florea

25 July 1998
The Harp Consort

26 July 1998
I Fagiolini

28 July 1998
Nancy Argenta & The Purcell Quartett

29 July 1998
**Stephen Wallace, William Purefoy
& Ensemble Musica Poetica**

30 July 1998
Micrologus

31 July 1998
Amsterdam Loeki Stardust Quartet

1 August 1998
Il Diletto Moderno

*Institute of Arts, Marketing, Promotion,
and Investment*
ARS RAMOVŠ
*1000 Ljubljana, Slovenska cesta 1, Slovenia
Tel. (00 386 61) 125 33 66
Fax. (00 386 61) 13 13 067
www.k-ramovs.si/
E-mail: ars.ramovs@net.zaslon.si*

new station and includes African classical music performers like the Soweto String Quartet in its line-up. Many listeners were expected to come from the more than one million choir members which Johannesburg boasts, and research showed that classical music was a preference among higher-education and higher-income South African groups, both black and white.

Australia had a similar story to South Africa, with the Australian Broadcasting Corporation shedding its orchestras to make ends meet. Under Paul Keating's Labor government, the Sydney Symphony had been pushed out of the nest but with a handsome cheque in the bank to encourage it towards international flagship orchestra status. But with some £27m lopped from the ABC's budget by the conservative government which followed Keating's administration, it was forced to ring the changes with its orchestras in Melbourne, Adelaide, Brisbane, Perth and Hobart. During the handover, the orchestras' grants were transferred to independent boards, but it was made clear that future funding will need to be found locally.

Some 200 arts managers formed the Arts Management Group of Western Australia and set up a seminar on The Business of Arts Sponsorship. The message from business was clear: arts organisations throughout Australia needed to get their fingers out if they were to get their hands on the money. In ten years, the proportion of Australia's corporate sponsorship netted by the arts plunged from 13% to 5%. Australia's arts managers needed to pick up a few tips from their counterparts in the sports field, they were told, and understand the nature of the partnership.

And if Australia was having to learn sponsorship, marketing was on the agenda, too. The Australia Council, once purely a distributor of grants, turned into a business-minded outfit in the face of declining funds and published a report on marketing, backing it up with workshops.

Greatly in need of some marketing - or at least some public relations help - was the Sydney Organising Committee for the Olympic Games, whose proposed four-festival programme for the 2000 Games was reported to be in a state of great confusion and unreadiness as the deadline approached.

But there was cheerier news in Melbourne with the return of Trevor Green, former manager of the BBC Philharmonic. The BBC's loss was Melbourne's gain, and the man who once had the responsibility for all the ABC orchestras set about the task of establishing the new Australian National Academy of Music. The academy was set up in 1995 to be a super-conservatoire for the whole country.

In Europe, work neared completion on the rebuilding of the Liceu in Barcelona, destroyed by fire, but at La Fenice, which suffered the same fate, renewal was

Swedish ambassadors Elisabeth Söderström and Christian Lindberg helped to develop Sweden's reputation as a rich source of musical talent

delayed by investigations into the blaze. The evidence of La Fenice's official photographer quickly established that arson was to blame. He photographed the fire from the early stages and experts were able to establish from the pictures that the fire had two separate seats, which made it highly unlikely that it had been accidental. The finger of suspicion pointed variously at the Mafia and at local firms who had been doing restoration work. The suggestion was made that a fire could have been a neat escape from penalty clauses for late-running work.

While battles raged over plans to rebuild the theatre as an exact replica of the one that was destroyed, the company was performing in a tent in an industrial part of Venice.

There was the whiff of further scandal in

the air of Rome, where the new general manager of the Teatro dell'Opera discovered a further deficit of some £6.3m. With the job of restructuring the opera house's finances made that much more difficult, only 46 performances were scheduled for 1997.

In Austria, the all-male Vienna Philharmonic finally summoned up the courage to let down the portcullis which had excluded women from their ranks for 155 years. They did so under threat from American women's groups, who spoke of disrupting performances, but it was probably the arm twisting of the fund-holding Austrian government which finally did the trick.

Sweden went on the road with Sounds of Sweden, a two-week festival in Birmingham. It was seen as a further step towards giving Scandinavian music its due, a process which started in 1992 with the Barbican's Tender is the North festival. Topping the bill at the Birmingham festival was Sweden's most celebrated musical ambassador, Elisabeth Söderström, along with Nicolai Gedda and Swede-in-exile Ulrika Jonsson, who introduced a starry royal gala which opened the event.

Other Swedes flying the flag were the Swedish Radio Symphony Orchestra, the Yggdrasil Quartet (four young Swedes enjoying a successful residency at Aberdeen University) and 1995 winner of the Cardiff Singer of the World competition Katarina Karnéus. In a gesture of support to the visitors, the City of Birmingham Symphony Orchestra were conducted by Paavo Järvi in a Berwald symphony, having discovered that the Swedish composer had never featured in its concert programmes before.

Also in Birmingham was Sweden's trombone superstar, Christian Lindberg, giving world premieres of pieces by Xenakis and Swedish composer Folke Rabe. He was back in Britain again for the premiere of Benedict Mason's trombone concerto and then again to premiere a work by another fellow countryman, Pär Lindgren. With some 60 premieres under his belt, a bulging diary and a shelf-load of CDs to his credit, Lindberg has brought the trombone to the front of the concert stage in no uncertain terms, and is booked for the 2000 Proms.

Plans were made for a European Opera Centre to start work in Manchester in the autumn. The centre was launched in March at the Royal Opera House, with the backing of several European opera houses and a million ecus courtesy of Brussels. The project is the brainchild of Sir John Manduell, former principal of the Royal Northern College of Music, with the Royal Opera's departing general director Sir Jeremy Isaacs and former European Commission deputy secretary general Sir Christopher Audland as his co-trustees.

The aim of the centre is to redress what it sees an an imbalance caused by the influx of North American-trained singers in

Former BBC Philharmonic manager Trevor Green left Manchester for Melbourne, where he took on the task of establishing the new Australian National Academy of Music

European opera houses. It was felt that by providing an advanced training programme, European singers would stand a better chance at getting the jobs. The centre planned to field a performing ensemble, Opera for Europe, which was due to begin its programme with five performances of *Tosca* in Manchester, Derby and Sheffield during December 1997, with Kent Nagano conducting the Hallé Orchestra. In 1998 it plans fully-staged new productions of Mozart's *Lucio Silla* and Stravinsky's *The Rake's Progress*. The centre also has the long-term aim of providing opportunities for technicians, designers, administrators and repetiteurs.

Hard on the heels of the European Opera Centre, along came European Union Opera, another new project. Like the No 11 bus, you wait for ages then two come along together. The EUO was launched with 53 of the most talented singers from the 15 member states of the European Union in a performance-based training programme. The scheme plans to provide singers at the outset of their careers with training and performance opportunities and will also extend the work of the European Union Youth Orchestra by providing young musicians with the chance to play the operatic repertoire.

Like the EOC, it plans to provide training for production personnel, through apprenticeships in stage management, stagecraft, electrics, wigs and make-up, costumes and music administration. The scheme is directed by Brian Dickie, former

general administrator of Glyndebourne Festival Opera and more recently general director of the Canadian Opera Company, with Felicity Jackson as general manager. It is the brainchild of chairman and trustee Lionel Bryer and Joy Bryer, secretary-general of the International Youth Foundation of Great Britain. It will be based in London, as is the European Union Youth Orchestra, whose graduates will form the opera orchestra. Its first project will be performances of *Eugene Onegin* under Gennadi Rozhdestvensky and *Béatrice et Bénédict* conducted by Yan Pascal Tortelier.

As technology continued to forge links across the globe, musicians were not slow to seize the opportunities provided by the world wide web. Many international musical organisations swelled the numbers of those with web sites, and a British firm, Classical Artists Worldwide, launched a service which brought the benefits of the technology within the pockets of impecunious freelance musicians. Many had already seen the benefits of email for arranging bookings, dealing with pro-moters abroad or keeping in touch with their agents, but the new service also provides them with their own web page, giving them an easily accessible world-wide presence, with links to record companies or other organisations if relevant.

While music continued to fulfil the needs of entertainment and spiritual enrichment throughout the world, in troubled areas it served a therapeutic purpose, helping to rebuild lives torn apart by war. It was a story full of unsung heroes. One such was Edward Huws Jones, a peripatetic violin teacher from York, who in 1995 took 20 half-size violins to Mostar in Bosnia to set up the Mostar Children's Violin Project and has since made eight further visits to keep the scheme going. When he arrived, only one violin teacher remained. Musicians had simply fled or been killed. Instruments were also thin on the ground, many of them having been used to stoke winter fires. Starting with a group of refugees who had spent the better part of two years living in cellars, Huws Jones gave lessons which became a life-line to his young pupils. He won the support of local humanitarian organ-isations, who saw his work in the long term as a way of bringing together children from both sides of the city.

Bringing people together was a thorny issue. Simon Mundy, vice-president of the European Forum for Arts and Heritage, visited Vukovar in Croatia, and said, 'Persuading people to sit in the same audience, let alone play in the same orchestra, will be hard. Almost everybody in Vukovar (or in exile from it) has lost family or home. Nevertheless, as War Child has proved further south in Mostar, music can help to begin the process of reconciliation.'

Music Information Centres and Organisations

The entries marked with an asterisk are members of the **International Association of Music Information Centres** (Contemporary Music Centre, 95 Lower Baggot St, Dublin 2, Republic of Ireland *tel:* +353 1 661 2105 *fax:* +353 1 676 2639 *email:* iamic@cmc.ie) which is a worldwide network of organisations promoting new music. Music Information Centres are open to the public and have extensive resources: large libraries of sheet music and sound archives, and up-to-date collections of biographical and research material. Many issue publications and recordings, while all serve as a focus of musical activity.

The other organisations listed below also disseminate information about music and musical activities in their respective countries. Many take particular interest in living composers and contemporary music. These may include composers' societies, associations and national music committees of International Music Council.

Albania
The Albanian New Music. Rr Mine Peca P87 sh 3-21, Tirana, Albania.
National Music Committee (Albania). Union of Writers and Artists, Tirana, Albania. Vasil S Tole, president.

Argentina
Fundación Cultural Coliseum - Harmonia. Marcelo T de Alvear 1125, 1058 Buenos Aires, Argentina *tel:* +541 325 8457 *fax:* +541 325 3789. Agostino Rocco, president; Rawa Jasinski, artistic dir.
National Music Committee (Argentina). Casilla de Correos 5532, Correo Central, 1000 Buenos Aires, Argentina. Alicia Terzian, president.

Australia
* **Australian Music Centre Ltd.** 1st Floor, Argyle Centre, 18 Argyle St, The Rocks, NSW 2000, Australia *tel:* +61 2 9247 4677 *fax:* +61 2 9241 2873 *email:* info@amcoz.com.au; http://www.amcoz.com.au/amc. John Davis, gen mgr. *Over 10,000 works are represented in the AMC library. The commercial arm of the AMC sells recordings, scores, teacher resource materials and publications on Australian mus. Many unpublished scores are available for sale under license from the composers through a facsimile score service. Sales catalogues are available on request. Also London office: object is to perform and increase awareness of Australian mus in Britain. Library of scores and recordings.*
International Society for Contemporary Music. c/o University of Sydney Music Department, Sydney NSW 2006, Australia *tel:* +61 29 692 2923.
National Music Committee (Australia). 12-23 McLeod St, Mosman, NSW 2088, Australia. Richard Letts, chair.

Austria
Austrian Society for New Music. Ungargasse 9-3, A-1030 Wien, Austria *tel:* +222 713 7040 *fax:* +222 715 2977. Lothar Knessl.
International Music Centre Vienna. Speisinger Str 121-127, A-1230 Wien, Austria *tel:* +43 1 889 0315 *fax:* +43 1 889 031577 *email:* imz@magnet.at; http://www.imz.magnet.at/imz/. Avril MacRory, president; Monika Gelbman, ed. *International association of a/v producers of arts programmes with an emphasis on classical and contemporary mus, jazz, world mus and dance. Organises congresses, seminars, w/shops and screenings on topical issues. Also organises festivals and competitions for a/v dance and mus theatre productions. Operates a database for TV programmes and publishes a trilingual trade magazine* Music in the Media.
* **Musik Informations Zentrum Österreich (MICA).** Stiftgasse 29, A-1070 Wien, Austria *tel:* +43 1 52 1040 *fax:* +43 1 52 10459 *email:* mica@mica.at; http://www.mica.at. Matthias Finkentey, mgr dir.
National Music Committee (Austria). Osterreichischer Musikrat, Hanuschgasse 3, A-1010 Wien, Austria. Matthias Finkentey, sec gen.
Österreichische Gesellschaft für Musik. 1 Hanuschgasse 3, A-1010 Wien, Austria *tel:* +43 1 512 3143 *fax:* +43 1 512 4299. Harald Goertz, chmn. *Information, promotion (especially of contemporary mus), publications.*

Bangladesh
National Music Committee (Bangladesh). I/1 Purana Paltan, Dacca, Bangladesh. Mustafa Zaman Abbasi, president.

Belgium
Artist Service. Postbus 1, B-8460 Oudenburg, Belgium *tel:* +32 17 99 76 60 *fax:* +32 15 23 63 13 *email:* artistserv@club.innet.be. Jean-Paul Steenmans, president. *Publish Music Yearbook for Belgium:* 'Guidebook for musicians, artists and showbusiness'.
Azymuth Government Foundation, Association for Public Benefit. Torenstr 13, B-9160 Lokeren, Belgium *tel:* +32 9 348 8000 *fax:* +32 9 348 9974. Jean Pierre Van Avermaet, mgr dir; Agnes Goeman, Peter Van

Poucke, Vessela Dyakova, Michèle De Vry. *Operates an extended database containing musicological information, biographical data and a list of local organisers throughout Europe. Provides translations of mus related texts in Russian, Bulgarian, Dutch, English, German and French.*
* **Centre Belge de Documentation Musicale (CeBeDeM).** Rue d'Arlon 75-77, B-1040 Bruxelles, Belgium *tel:* +32 2 230 9430 *fax:* +32 2 230 9437 *email:* 101573.3644@compuserve.com. Diana von Volborth-Danys, dir. *The centre is a non-profit-making association which aims to promote the performance of the works of Belgian contemporary composers. Available facilities include a sheet mus library, recording library, reading and listening room, loan-dept, publishing and reproduction, promotion dept.*
International Federation of Jeunesse Musicales. 10 rue Royale, B-1000 Bruxelles, Belgium. Dag Franzen, sec gen.
National Music Committee (Belgium). Palais des Beaux Arts, Rue Royale 10, B-1000 Bruxelles, Belgium.

Bolivia
National Music Committee (Bolivia). Centre Pedagogico y Cultural de Portales, Av Potosi N-1450, Casilla 544, Cochabamba, Bolivia. Luz Maria Calvo, sec gen.

Brazil
* **CDMC-Brasil/Unicamp (Universidade Estadual de Campinas - Etat de Sao Paulo).** Cx P 6136, 13083-970 Campinas SP, Brazil *tel:* +55 19 239 1503 p 29 *fax:* +55 19 239 5806 *email:* cdmuisca@turing.unicamp.br. José Augusto Mannis, dir.
National Music Committee (Brazil). Rua Pres Carlos de Campos No 115 B, 2/902, 22231-080 Laranjeiras, Rio de Janeiro RJ, Brazil. Maria-Luiza Corker-Nobre, sec gen.
Sociedade Brasileira de Musica Contemporanea. Av Tocantins 776, 74015-010 Golania, Golas, Brazil *tel:* +55 62 223 1272 *fax:* +55 62 225 7556. Belkiss S Carneiro de Mendonca, president.
Sociedade de Cultura Artistica. Rua Nestor Pestana 196, 01303-010 São Paulo SP, Brazil *tel:* +55 11 256 0223; +55 11 231 4271 *fax:* +55 11 258 3595. Gerald Perret.

Bulgaria
National Music Committee (Bulgaria). Union of Bulgarian Composers, 2 Rue Iv Vazov, Sofia 1000, Bulgaria. Victor Tchoutchkov, sec gen.

Canada
American Federation of Musicians of the United States and Canada. 75 The Donway West, Suite 1010, Don Mills, Ont M3C 2E9, Canada *tel:* +1 416 391 5161 *fax:* +1 416 391 5165 *email:* canoff@afm.org; http://www.afm.org. David Jandrisch, vice-president; Alan Willaert, international rep. *Membership is open to all professional musicians and vocalists in the USA and Canada.*
The Canada Council for the Arts/Conseil des Arts du Canada. PO Box 1047, 350 Albert St, Ottawa, Ont K1P 5V8, Canada *tel:* +1 613 566 4414 *fax:* +1 613 566 4390 *email:* http://www.canadaccouncil.ca. *Provides grants and services to professional Canadian artists and arts organisations.*
* **Canadian Music Centre/Centre de Musique Canadienne (CMC).** Chalmers House, 20 St Joseph St, Toronto, Ont M4Y 1J9, Canada *tel:* +1 416 961 6601 *fax:* +1 416 961 7198 *email:* cmc@interlog.com; http://www.culturenet.ca/cmc. Simone Auger, exec dir. *The CMC collects, reproduces, promotes, records and distributes the music and recordings of its associate composers. Also operates a free lending library of printed music.*
International Association of Music Libraries, Archives and Documentation Centres. Carleton University Library, 1125 Colonel By Drive, Ottawa, Ont K1S 5J7, Canada. Alison Hall, sec gen.

International Society for Music Education. 71 Empress Drive, Regina SK, S4T 6M7, Canada. Joan Therens, sec gen.

National Music Committee (Canada). 5505 Bd St-Laurent, Bureau 4202, Montreal H2T 1S6, Canada. Andree Girard, dir.

Chile

National Music Committee (Chile). Casilla 52.582, Correo Santiago 1, Santiago, Chile. Gabriel Matthey, president.

China

Chinese Musicians' Association. Nong zhanguan Nan Li, No 10, Beijing 100026, China *tel:* +861 500 4524. Lu Ji He Lu-Ting, hon chmn.

National Music Committee (China). Agricultural Exhibition Hall, Nan Li No 10, Chaoyang District, Beijing, China. Yao Wen, sec gen.

Colombia

* **Centro de Documentación Musical.** Calle 24, No 5-60, 4 Piso, Santafé de Bogotá 1, Colombia *tel:* +57 1 342 2097 *fax:* +57 1 243 5994 *email:* colcultura@presidencia.gov.co; http://www.presidencia.gov.co/ colcultura/home.htm. Jaime H Quevedo, dir; Ana Maria Ochoa, research division. *Classical, contemporary, popular and folk colombian mus on scores, recordings, videotapes, newspaper articles, concert programs, etc.*

Instituto Colombiano de Cultura - Colcultura. Calle 11, No 5-51, 2nd Floor, Bogotá, Colombia *tel:* +57 2 341 5161 *fax:* +57 2 282 0854. Blanca Cecilia Carreno, admin asst.

National Music Committee (Colombia). Centro Cultural Gimnasio Moderno, Carrera 9 No 74-99, Sanatafe de Bogota, Colombia. Cecilia Casa Ceron, president.

Costa Rica

National Music Committee (Costa Rica). c/o Comision Costarricense de Cooperación con la UNESCO, Apartado Postal 393, 2050 San Pedro de Montes de Oca, San Jose, Costa Rica. Carmen Mendez, permanent sec.

Cote d'Ivoire

National Music Committee (Cote d'Ivoire). PO Box 49, Abidjan 08, Cote d'Ivoire. Paul Dagri, president.

Croatia

Croatian Composers' Society. Berislaviceva 9, HR 10000 Zagreb, Croatia *tel:* +385 1 423463 *fax:* +385 1 422850. Ivo Josipovic, sec gen; Lidija Parac, admin sec. *Organises festivals of Croatian mus; publishes contemporary and ancient Croatian mus.*

Croatian Music Institute. Gunduliceva 6, 41000 Zagreb, Croatia *tel:* +385 41 424533 *fax:* +385 41 271066. Janko Kichl.

Culturelink, Institute for International Relations (IRMO). Ul Ljudevita Farkasa Vukotinovicá 2, PO Box 303, 10000 Zagreb, Croatia *tel:* +385 1 455 4522 *fax:* +385 1 444 059 *email:* clink@mairmo.irmo.hr; http:// www.culturelink.hr. Biserka Cvjeticanin, co-ord; Zrinjka Perusko-Culek, researcher. *Culturelink is an information network established by UNESCO and the Council of Europe. It is devoted to promoting research into cultural development, cultural policies and cultural and artistic cooperation. It also aims to collect, process and disseminate information. The* Culturelink Bulletin *is issued 4 times a year providing updated information on current activities and projects to its members.*

Cuba

National Music Committee (Cuba). Instituto Cubano de la Musica, Calle F y 15 N 452, El Vedado, La Habana, Cuba. Guido Lopez Gavilan.

Cyprus

National Music Committee (Cyprus). Prince Charles 21, Ayios Dometios, PO Box 4326, Nicosia, Cyprus *tel:* +357 2 462837 *fax:* +357 2 441213. Lenia Serghi, president.

Czech Republic

* **Music Information Centre.** Besední 3, CZ-11800 Praha 1, Czech Republic *tel:* +420 2 573200 08 *fax:* +420 2 539720/534234 *email:* czmic@ login.cz; http://www.vol.cz/sdmusic/czmic. Mirosláv Pudlák, dir; Adam Klemens, ed of Czech Music. *Holds information on the life and work of contemporary Czech composers, classical mus ens, musicians, events, mus institutions, competitions, etc in the Czech Republic. Mus and sound library. Publishes the periodical* Czech Music.

National Music Committee (Czech Republic). Institute of Musicology, Academy of Sciences, Puskinovo nam 9, 160 00 Praha 6, Czech Republic. Lenka Dohnalova, sec gen.

Society for New Music. Terronska 64-878, CZ-160 00 Praha 6, Czech Republic *tel:* +420 2 31 16913 *fax:* +420 2 31 67180. Ivan Bierhanzi, president.

Democratic Republic of Congo

National Music Committee (Democratic Republic of Congo). 5151 Av President Kasa-Vubu, Zone de Kalamu, PO Box 16505 KIN I, Kinshasa, Democratic Republic of Congo. Basunga Mundele, sec gen.

Denmark

Danish Cultural Institute. Kultorvet 2, DK-1175 København K, Denmark *tel:* +45 33 135448 *fax:* +45 33 151091 *email:* d-k-i@inet.uni-c.dk. *Promotes dissemination of information on Denmark and international cultural exchanges.*

Danish Music Council. Vesterbrogade 24, 4, DK-1620 Kobenhavn V, Denmark *tel:* +45 33 251055 *fax:* +45 33 242242. Lennart Ricard, chmn. *Advises and assists public authorities and institutions in mus related matters. Promotes musical life in Denmark and Danish mus abroad.*

* **Danish Music Information Centre.** Graabroedre Torv 16, DK-1154 Kobenhavn K, Denmark *tel:* +45 33 112066 *fax:* +45 33 322016 *email:* mic@mic.bibnet.dk; http://www.bibnet.dk/mic/. Anette Faaborg, dir; Bendt Viinholt Nielsen, chief librarian; Bodil Høgh, export and promotion. *Promotion of Danish music worldwide, plus documentation of all aspects of music and musical life in Denmark. Library of books, printed music and autograph copies, magazines, newspaper cuttings and recordings. Computer database listing more than 10,000 contemporary Danish works.*

International Jazz Federation. Borupvej 66, DK-4683 Ronnede, Denmark. Arnvid Meyer, president.

National Music Committee (Denmark). Vesterbrogade 24, 1620 Kobenhavn V, Denmark. Erik Skovgaard Pederson, sec gen.

Egypt

National Music Committee (Egypt). Gamal-el-Afgany St, Pyramids Av, Giza, Cairo, Egypt. Samha El Kholy.

Equador

National Music Committee (Equador). Conservatorio Nacional de Musica, Calle Madrid No 1159, y Andalucia (La Floresta), Casilla de Correos 3358, Quito, Equador. Eduardo Granja, rector.

Estonia

National Music Committee (Estonia). Estonian Academy of Music, Vabaduse pst 130, EE-0009 Tallinn, Estonia. Peep Lassmann, president.

Finland

Finland Festivals. Uudenmaankatu 36 D 21, FIN-00120 Helsinki, Finland *tel:* +358 9 621 4224 *fax:* +358 9 612 1007 *email:* info@mail.festivals.fi; http://www.festivals.fi/. Tuomo Tirkkonen, gen dir; Riitta Kerman, mkt sec. *Produces and distributes a catalogue containing dates, addresses and a short description of 58 different Finnish festivals.*

* **Finnish Music Information Centre.** Lauttasaarentie 1, FIN-00200 Helsinki, Finland *tel:* +358 9 6810 1313 *fax:* +358 9 682 0770. Pekka Hako, exec dir; Leena Salakari, information service co-ord. *A non-profit institution which promotes Finnish composers and compositions. The information service publishes brochures, essays and booklets on various aspects of music. Also a library of over 20,000 compositions.*

Finnish Performing Music Promotion Centre (ESEK). Pieni Roobertinkatu 16, FIN-00120 Helsinki, Finland *tel:* +358 9 6803 4040 *fax:* +358 9 6803 4010 *email:* http://personal.eunet.fi/pp/gramex/. Leena Hirvonen, sec gen. *Supports Finnish Performing Music and provides information about Finnish artists. Manages Finnish mus export projects.*

France

* **Centre de Documentation de la Musique Contemporaine.** Cité de la Musique, 16 Place de la Fontaine aux Lions, F-75019 Paris, France *tel:* +33 1 47 15 49 81 *fax:* +33 1 47 15 49 89. Marianne Lyon, dir; Corinne Monceau, documentation dept. *Documentation and information on composers, performers, organisations, etc. Scores, recordings, books, theses, articles, reviews of contemporary mus.*

Centre d'Information et de Resource pour les Musiques Actuelles. 21 Bis, Rue de Paradis, F-75010 Paris, France *tel:* +33 1 44 83 10 30 *fax:* +33 1 44 83 10 40 *email:* http://www.euromusic.com/irma. Gilles Castagnac, mgr dir; Marie-Josée Sallaber, co mgr dir. *IRMA offers access to databases, publications, advice and training programmes to all involved in mus.*

* **Centre Européen de Documentation et d'Information des Maitrises d'Enfants (CEDIME).** 30-34 Boulevard Bambetta, F-06130 Grasse, France *tel:* +33 93 40 19 50 *fax:* +33 93 36 55 84. Jacques Menet, dir.

Comité National de la Musique (CNM). 252 Rue du Faubourg St Honoré, Salle Pleyel, F-75008 Paris, France *tel:* +33 1 45 63 48 58 *also fax.* Pierre Henry, president; Masson-Forestier Jacques, gen sec. *The CNM is the French section of the International Council of Music of UNESCO, including 40 musical unions covering all sectors of music.*

European Assocation of Conservatoires, Academies de Musique and Musikhochschulen. Conservatoire National de Région, 26 av Montaigne, F-49100 Angers, France. John Richard Lowry, sec gen.

Fédération Nationale de la Musique. 62 Rue Blanche, F-75009 Paris, France *tel:* +33 1 48 74 09 29 *fax:* +33 1 42 81 19 87. Pierre Henry, president.

International Federation of Musicians. 21b rue Victor Massé, F-75009 Paris, France. Jean Vincent, sec gen.

International Music Council (UNESCO). 1 Rue Miollis, F-75732 Paris Cédex 15, France *tel:* +33 1 45 68 25 50 *fax:* +33 1 43 06 87 98 *email:* imc_cim@compuserve.com. Guy Huot, sec gen. *Exists to support mus education, research, contemporary composers, traditional mus and young professional musicians, to promote the exchange of amateur and professional musicians, mus (written and recorded) and information, and to foster appreciation of mus by the public.*

International Music Critics Association. Press Club de France, 11 Avenue d'Lena, F-75016 Paris, France. Antoine Livio, president.

National Music Committee (France). 252 rue du Faubourg Saint-Honore, F-75008 Paris, France. Jacques Masson-Forestier.

Germany

Deutscher Musikrat eV (German Music Council). Weberstr 59, D-53113 Bonn, Germany *tel:* +49 228 20910 *fax:* +49 228 209 1200. Franz Müller-Heuser, president; Andreas Eckhardt, gen sec. *As the central organisation for all fields of music, the main aim of the council is to secure an adequate role and place for mus in education and society, and to contribute to the further development of music culture.*

European Association of Concert Managers. Landschaftstr 6, D-30159 Hannover, Germany. Andre Pietrek, sec gen.

Fortbildungszentrum für Neue Musik. An der Münze 7, D-21335 Luneberg, Germany *tel:* +49 4131 309390 *also fax.* Helmut W Erdmann.

* **Internationales Musikinstitut Darmstadt (IMD).** Nieder-Ramstädter Str 190, D-64285 Darmstadt, Germany *tel:* +49 615 113 2416/7 *fax:* +49 615 113 2405. Solf Schäfer, dir; William Schlüter, chief librarian.

Music in Europe/European Association of Concert Agents. c/o Konzertbüro Andreas Braun, Sülzgürtel 86, D-50937 Köln, Germany *tel:* +49 221 9 420430 *fax:* +49 221 9 420 4319. Andreas Braun, editor. *Music in Europe is the worldwide edition of the European artist list of the European Association of Concert Agents.*

National Music Committee (Germany). Deutscher Musikrat, Weberstr 59, D-53113 Bonn, Germany. Andreas Eckhardt, sec gen.

Ghana

National Music Committee (Ghana). International Centre for African Music and Dance, School of Performing Arts, PO Box 19, Legon, Accra, Ghana. Kwabena Nketia.

Greece

National Music Committee (Greece). 38 rue Mitropoleos, GR-105 63 Athens, Greece. Apostolos Kostios, sec gen.

Hong Kong

Cultural Services Section (Headquarters Office). Regional Services Department, 14/F Regional Council Building, 1 Pai Tau St, Sha Tin, Hong Kong *tel:* +852 2 601 8700 *fax:* +852 2 602 0047. Bessie Tong, snr cultural services mgr. *The cultural services section is responsible for the management of performing facilities and the presentation of programmes.*

Hong Kong Arts Development Council. 38 Russell St, 11/F, Causeway Bay, Hong Kong *tel:* +852 2827 8786 *fax:* +852 2519 9301. Anita Yu, info offr; Lillian Hau, exec offr (mus and dance). *Aims to increase access to and knowledge of Hong Kong arts and artists. Offers free arts information and enquiries services. Maintains database on local arts organisations and societies, artists, venues, festivals, competitions, awards, funding and education. Publishes the Hong Kong Arts Directory, a quarterly HKADC newsletter and a monthly circular ArtsFax.*

Urban Council and Regional Council Music Office. 25/F Wanchai Tower, 12 Harbour Rd, Wanchai, Hong Kong *tel:* +852 2582 5328 *fax:* +852 2802 8440 *email:* sscheung@hk.super.net. Samson Cheung, chief mus offr. *Promotes mus among general public in Hong Kong. Inst mus training scheme for approx 4000 individuals aged 6-23; manages and trains 14 youth bands, orchs and choirs. Organises a variety of mus activities including festivals and youth orchestra exchange programmes.*

Hungary

Hungarian Music Society. Pusztaszeri ut 30, H-1025 Budapest, Hungary *tel:* +36 1 325 7313 *also fax. Aims to foster cultivation of Hungarian mus, to promote the interests of musical artists, to educate young people's musical taste, and to preserve Hungarian mus past and present.*

* **Magyar Zenei Tanács Zenei Információs Központ (Hungarian Music Information Centre).** Hungarian Music Council, PO Box 47, H-1364 Budapest, Hungary *tel:* +36 1 117 9598 *fax:* +36 1 117 8267 *email:* hmic @mail.c3.hu. Eszter Vida, dir. *The centre collects and provides information on all aspects of Hungarian musical life, especially for contemporary mus. Large collection of contemporary mus, scores, recordings and books.*

National Music Committee (Hungary). Vorosmarty ter 1, PO Box 47, H-1364 Budapest, Hungary. Eva Csebfalvi, sec gen.

Iceland

* **Iceland Music Information Centre.** Sídumúli 34, IS-108 Reykjavík, Iceland *tel:* +354 568 3122 *fax:* +354 568 3124 *email:* icemic@vortex.is; http://www.vortex.is/islenska/fyrirtaeki/itm/. Ásta Hrönn Maack, dir. *Information about Icelandic music, sound recordings and printed material. Music library with sheet music, hire material and catalogues. Information and services to the public and composers.*

India

National Music Committee (India). 12 K Dubash Marg, Bombay 400 023, India. Arvind Parikh, sec gen.

Iran

National Music Committee (Iran). Iranian Music Centre, Ministry of Culture and Islamic Orientation, Av Hafez - Av Arfa, Salle Vahdat, Teheran, Iran. Ali Moradkhani, dir gen.

Iraq

National Music Committee (Iraq). Ministry of Culture and Information, PO Box 6150 (Mansour), Baghdad, Iraq. Bassim Hanna Petros, sec gen.

Israel

* **Israel Music Institute.** 144 Hayarkon St, 63451 Tel Aviv, Israel *tel:* +972 3 544 0219; +972 3 524 6475 *fax:* +972 3 524 5276. Paul Landau, dir.

National Council for Culture and the Arts. Kanfei Nesharim St 22, Ministry of Education and Culture, 91911 Jerusalem, Israel *tel:* +972 2 560 1741 *fax:* +972 2 560 1722. Raaya Simran, mus dept dir. *A government institution supporting musical institutions and professional activities across the country. Commissions new compositions, holds choir w/shops and awards prizes for performance.*

National Music Committee (Israel). Ministry of Education and Culture, Music Department, Jerusalem 91911, Israel. Ofer Turiel, sec gen.

Italy

Associazione Culturale Archivi del Sud. Via Giovanni Spano 5, I-07041 Alghero, Italy *tel:* +39 79 986585. Enzo Faveta.

Centro Ricerche Musicali (CRM). Via Lamarmora 18, I-00185 Roma, Italy *tel:* +39 6 446 4161 *fax:* +39 6 446 7911 *email:* crm@wmail.axnet. it; http://www.axnet.it.crm. Laura Bianchini, dir; Michelangelo Lupone, art dir. *Advanced technology centre for mus research in Europe. CRM has made significant contributions to the fields of musical composition, psycho-acoustics, musicology and musical informatics, including the design and construction of original devices for analysis, synthesis and processing in real time. Collaborates with important inst groups and musical institutions. CRM realises complex electro-acoustic works in concerts and w/shops, conferences worldwide.*

National Music Committee (Italy). Centro Italiano di Iniziative Musicale, Via Vittoria Colonna 18, I-00193 Roma, Italy. Francesco Agnello, president.

Jamaica

National Music Committee (Jamaica). Ministry of Information and Culture, 2a Devon Rd, Kingston, Jamaica. Pearl Anderson, permanent sec.

Japan

* **Documentation Centre of Modern Japanese Music.** 8-14 Azabudai 1-chome, Minato-ku, Tokyo 106, Japan *tel:* +81 3 3224 1584 *fax:* +81 3 3224 1654. Kazuyuki Toyama, dir.

The Japan Foundation. Performing Arts Division, Ark Mori Building, 1-12-32 Akasaka, Minato-ku, Tokyo 107, Japan *tel:* +81 3 5562 3530 *fax:* +81 3 5562 3500. Kazumasa Nishida, dir. *Semi-government organisation designed to promote cultural exchange between Japan and the rest of the world by awarding grants towards artists' international travel costs. Applications by 20 Dec annually. Occasionally organises Japanese music related events.*

National Music Committee (Japan). c/o Kunitachi College of Music, 5-5-1 Kashiwa-cho, Tachikawa-shi, Tokyo 190, Japan. Jinko Katsumura, sec gen.

Jordan

National Music Committee (Jordan). The National Music Conservatory, PO Box 926687, Amman, Jordan. Kifah Fakhouri.

Kenya

National Music Committee (Kenya). PO Box 43844, Nairobi, Kenya. Wahington Omondi, president.

Latvia

International New Music Centre. Jelgavas 25, LV-1004 Riga, Latvia *tel:* +371 288 28538. Egils Straune, dir.

Lebanon

National Music Committee (Lebanon). PO Box 14/5213, Beirut, Lebanon. Tawfik El-Basha, president.

Lithuania

Lithuanian Cultural Foundation. Jaksto 9, LT-2600 Vilnius, Lithuania *tel:* +370 2 617634 *fax:* +370 2 620508. J Dvarionas, president.

Lithuanian Music Information and Publishing Centre. A Mickeviciaus 29, LT-2600 Vilnius, Lithuania *tel:* +370 2 726986 *also fax; email:* center@mipc.vno.osf.lt. Daiva Parulskiene, dir. *Prepares, collects and distributes documentation on Lithuanian contemporary mus, composers and events.*

Luxembourg

National Music Committee (Luxembourg). 2 Rue Sosthène Weis, L-2722, Luxembourg-Grund. Henri Schumacher, president.

Union Europeénne des Musiciens. 2 Rue Sosthène-Weis, L-2722, Luxembourg-Grund *tel:* +352 462 536 *fax:* +352 471 440. Henri Schumacher, president. *European mus association.*

Union Grand-Duc Adolphe Asbl (Fédération Nationale de Musique du Grand-Duché de Luxembourg). 2 Rue Sosthène-Weis, L-2722, Luxembourg-Grund *tel:* +352 462 536 *fax:* +352 471 440. Henri Schumacher, president. *National Music Federation of Luxembourg.*

Madagascar

National Music Committee (Madagascar). 107 Rue Rainandriamampandry, 1001 Antananarivo, Madagascar. Emilie Radaody-Ralarosy, president.

Mexico

* **Centro Nacional de Investigación, Documentación e Información Musical (CENIDIM).** Centro Nacional de las Artes, Torre de Investigación 7 Piso, Calz de Tlalpan y Rio, Churubusco Col Country Club, 04220 Mexico DF, Mexico *tel:* +52 2 420 4415 *fax:* +52 2 420 4454. José Antonio Robles Cahero, dir; Selvio Carrizosa Ontiveros, subdir. *Researches and documents Mexican concert and folk music from pre-hispanic times to the 20th C. The Centre produces books, journals, scores and recordings and aims to promote interest and research into Mexican music.*

National Music Committee (Mexico). Paseo del Cantil 6, Cantil del Pedregal, Coyoacan, CP 04730, Mexico. Manuel de Elias, president.

Moldova

National Music Committee (Moldova). c/o Union of Composers of Moldova, Str 31 August 153, 277 004 Chisinau, Moldova. Ghenadie Ciobanu, president.

Monaco

National Music Committee (Monaco). 8 Rue Louis Notari, 98000 Monte Carlo, Monaco.

Mongolia

National Music Committee (Mongolia). Science and Cultural Building, 5th Floor, Sukhebaatar Sq 3, Ulaanbaatar-11, Mongolia. D Luvsansharav, president.

Netherlands

Centre Netherlands Music (CNM). PO Box 1634, NL-1200 PB Hilversum, Netherlands *tel:* +31 35 624 0957 *fax:* +31 35 621 0570. J W ten Broeke, mgr dir.

* **Donemus.** Paulus Potterstraat 16, NL-1017 CZ Amsterdam, Netherlands *tel:* +31 20 676 4436 *fax:* +31 20 673 3588 *email:* donemus@pi.net; http://www.pi.net/~donemus. Bèr Deuss, mgr dir. *Scores, books, journals, reviews, brochures, CDs, tapes, videos, biographies, etc for Dutch composers since 1945. Also some information on Dutch composers 1890-1945.*

European Conference of Promoters of New Music. Swammerdamstr 38, NL-1091 RV Amsterdam, Netherlands *tel:* +31 20 694 7349 *fax:* +31 20 694 7258 *email:* ecpnm@xsyall.nl; http://www.xsyall.nl/~ecpnm. Solf Schaefer, president; Henk Heuvelmans, sec. *Umbrella organisation for concert and festival organisers and mus information centres in the field of contemporary mus. Publishes a calendar of new mus events. Information services through a bulletin board database.*

* **Gaudeamus Foundation.** Swammerdamstraat 38, NL-1091 RV Amsterdam, Netherlands *tel:* +31 20 694 7349 *fax:* +31 20 694 7258 *email:* gaud@xs4all.nl; http://www.xs4all.nl/~gaud. Henk Heuvelmans, dir. *Centre for contemporary music. Library of scores, records and CDs. General information about contemporary music; organisation of concerts and festivals.*

International Society For Contemporary Music. Swammerstadt 38, N-1091 RV Amsterdam, Netherlands. Henk Heuvelmans, sec gen.

Muziek Netwerk Nederland. Drift 23, NL-3512 BR Utrecht, Netherlands *tel:* +31 30 232 2046 *fax:* +31 30 231 2641 *email:* http://www.mnn.nl. Frans A Vodegál, dir. *From May 1998 this will be the electronic information service of and for the Dutch musical world, collecting current bibliographic, educational, commercial and documentary information and aiming to link and integrate related subjects. The website address is a trial site, available until its full inauguration.*

National Music Committee (Netherlands). c/o Donemus, Paulus Potterstraat 16, 1071 CZ, Amsterdam, Netherlands. Ber Deuss, sec gen.

* **Stichting Repertoire Informatiecentrum Muziek (RIM).** Drift 23, NL-3512 BR Utrecht, Netherlands *tel:* +31 30 232 2046 *fax:* +31 30 231 2641. Frans A Vodegál, dir. *A foundation which aims to promote innovation in the musical repertoire of the Netherlands. Music library of 70,000 works for ens, choirs and orchs. RIM also holds a large collection of educational material and more than 80 repertoire lists. The centre also provides workshops, repertoire courses and concerts.*

New Zealand

* **The Centre for New Zealand Music Ltd (SOUNZ New Zealand).** PO Box 10 042, Wellington, Level 3, 15 Brandon St, Wellington, New Zealand *tel:* +64 4 495 2520 *fax:* +64 4 495 2522 *email:* sounz@actrix.gen.nz; http://www.sounz.org.nz. Nicholas McBryde, exec dir; Scilla Askew, exec asst. *Exists to promote the creation, performance, publication, recording and broadcast of New Zealand music, by working with and on behalf of composers. Library holds over 2000 scores and recordings, plus details of c 5000 works on computer database. Users can buy, hire and borrow music that is not readily available from commercial sources. Listening suite and study area.*

Nigeria

National Music Committee (Nigeria). Federal Ministry of Culture, National Theatre, Private Mailbag 12524, Lagos, Nigeria. A O Olusesi, asst dir of culture.

North Korea

National Music Committee (North Korea). Otan Gangan Gori, Central District, Pyongyang, North Korea. Kim Won Gyun, president.

Norway

National Music Committee (Norway). Rikskonsertene, PO Box 7613, Skillebekk, 0205 Oslo, Norway. Einar Solbu, exec dir.

* **Norwegian Music Information Centre (Norsk Musikkinformasjon).** 28 Tollbugata, N-0157 Oslo, Norway *tel:* +47 2242 9090 *fax:* +47 2242 9091 *email:* nmic@notam.uio.no; http://www.notam.uio.no/nmi/. Jostein Simble, gen mgr; Hilde Holbaek-Hanssen, head of information. *Provides information on Norwegian music; arranges exhibitions, seminars and courses. Resources include manuscript library, orchestral rental materials, reference library with study and listening rooms, Norwegian jazz archives, archives for folk and popular song, plus other music institutions. Produces a music magazine* Listen to Norway *.*

Pakistan

National Music Committee (Pakistan). Pakistan National Music Council of the Arts, Block No 6/c, F-7, Markaz, Islamabad, Pakistan. Kishwar Naheed, president.

Peru

National Music Committee (Peru). Peruvian National Committee for UNESCO, Ministry of Education, Piso 9 - Ofcina 301, Apartado Postal 4681, Correo Central, Lima, Peru. Judith Reyes, permanent sec.

Phillippines

Cultural Centre of the Phillippines. Cultural Centre Complex, Roxas Blvd, Pasay City 1300, Metro Manila, Phillippines *tel:* +632 832 1125 *fax:* +632 832 3683 *email:* ccp@portalinc.com; crobles@ccpap. admu.edu.ph; http://www.admu.edu.ph.ccpap/ccp. Baltazar N Endriga, president; Nestor O Jardine, deputy dir; Melissa Mantaring, dir, music division. *The Musical Arts Division plans, co-ordinates and supervises musical events produced by the Cultural Centre of the Phillippines. Co-operates with foreign embassies on visiting artists.*

National Music Committee (Philippines). National Commission for Culture and the Arts, 633 Gen Luna St, Intramuros, Manila, Philippines. Vilma S Felipe, president.

Poland

National Music Committee (Poland). Fredry 8 Room 305, PL-00-097 Warszawa, Poland. Jan Steszewski, president.

* **Polskie Centrum Muzyczne (Polish Music Centre).** Ul Fredry 8, Room 305, PL-00097 Warszawa, Poland *tel:* +48 2 635 2230 *also fax.* Barbara Zwolska-Stesewska, mgr. *Polish Music Information Centre at the Polish Music Council is temporarily suspended.*

Portugal

* **Fundaçao Calouste Gulbenkian.** Avenida de Berna 45, P-1067 Lisboa, Portugal *tel:* +351 1 793 5131 *fax:* +351 1 793 7296 *email:* musica@ gulbenkian.pt; http://www.estado-arte.pt/gulbenkian. Luis Pereira Leal, dir. *The Foundation supports culture within Portugal and can also provide aid for Portuguese culture in other countries.*

National Music Committee (Portugal). Rua Rosa Araujo 6-3, 1200 Lisboa, Portugal. Alvaro Salazar, president.

Portugese Music Council. Rua Rosa Araújo 6, 3, P-1200 Lisboa, Portugal *tel:* +351 1 355 7118. Alvaro Salazar, president.

Republic of Georgia

* **Georgian Music Information Centre.** David Agmashenebeli Av 123, 380064 Tbilisi, Republic of Georgia *tel:* +995 8832 954861/968678 *fax:* +995 32 958016. Natela Mamaladze, dir; Svetlana Kervalishvili, chief editor. *Aims to promote Georgian music in Georgia and abroad. Organises recitals, exchange concerts and festivals of contemporary music. Publishes information bulletin in Georgian and in English.*

Republic of Ireland

* **Irish Contemporary Music Centre.** 95 Lower Baggot St, Dublin 2, Republic of Ireland *tel:* +353 1 661 2105 *fax:* +353 1 676 2639 *email:* info @cmc.ie; http://www.cmc.ie. Eve O'Kelly, dir. *Promotes and documents Irish contemporary music.*

Romania

National Music Committee (Bucarest). Strada Esarçu 2, Sector 1, Bucarest, Romania. Petre Codreanu, sec.

Russia

International Centre of Culture of the Russian Federation. Ministry of Culture, Kitajgorodskij proezd 7, 103074 Moscow, Russia *tel:* +7 095 220 4620 *fax:* +7 095 248 0755/095 925 8723. Suren Shaumian, dir gen. *Cultural exchange programmes. Organises international festivals, competitions, tours of theatrical companies, mus groups and individual performers on a commerical basis.*

National Music Committee (Russia). c/o Pax Sonoris, Krumsky val 8, 117049, Moscow, Russia. Margarita Karatyghina, sec gen.

Saudi Arabia

National Music Committee (Saudi Arabia). United Arab Music, Arab Music Academy, PO Box 4623, Jeddah, Saudi Arabia. Tariq A Hakeem, president.

Senegal

National Music Committee (Senegal). Conservatoire National Douta Seck, PO Box 3111, Dakar, Senegal. Moustapha Ndiaye, president.

Serbia

* **Yugoslav Music Information Centre (SOKOJ).** Union of Yugoslav Composers' Organisations, Misarska St 12-14, 11000 Beograd, Serbia *tel:* +381 11 324 5192 *fax:* +381 11 323 6168. Vesna Koric, dir.

Slovak Republic

* **Music Information Centre of the Music Fund.** Medená 29, 811 02 Bratislava, Slovak Republic *tel:* +421 75 331 380 *fax:* +421 75 333 569 *email:* his@his.sanet.sk; http://www.sarba.sk/logos/mca/mic.html. Olga Smetanová, head of centre; Jarmila Sykorová, library documentor. *Documents the activity of Slovak composers, musicologists and performers. The information service stores sound recordings, musicological works, press reviews and cuttings.*

National Music Committee (Slovak Republic). c/o SlovKoncert, Michalska 10, 815 36 Bratislava, Slovak Republic. Agnes Zoliomiova, sec gen.

Slovenia

Muzina. Rutarjeva 5, Ljubljana, Slovenia *tel:* +386 61 213972. Brina Jez-Brezavscek. *An association for contemporary music, especially for the promotion of Slovene composers born after 1950.*

South Korea

National Music Committee (South Korea). c/o The Music Association of Korea, Building 1-117, Dongsung-dong, Chongro-gu, Seoul, South Korea. Jai Kook Kwack, sec gen.

Spain

* **Centro de Documentación Musical y de la Danza.** Torregalindo 10, E-28016 Madrid, Spain *tel:* +34 1 350 8600 *fax:* +34 1 359 1579 *email:* cdmyd@sarenet.es. Antonio Alvarez Canibano, dir. *Directory and database of mus and dance resources in Spain.*

Centro Para la Difusion de la Musica Contemporanea. Santa Isabel 52, E-28012 Madrid, Spain *tel:* +34 1 468 2310 *fax:* +34 1 530 8321. Tomas Marco, dir.

International Society for Contemporary Music. Avda de America 58-5, E-28028 Madrid, Spain *tel:* +34 1 356 3621. Luis De Pablo.

National Music Committee (Spain). Ministry of Culture, INAEM, Plaza del Rey 1, 28004 Madrid, Spain. Tomás Marco, president.

Sweden

International Confederation for Electroacoustic Music. Kocksgaten 1, S-116 23 Stockholm, Sweden. Sten Hanson, president.

International Federation for Choral Music. Klockargårdsv 18, S-135 68 Tyresö, Sweden. Christian Ljunggren, sec gen.

National Music Committee (Sweden). c/o Kungl Musikaliska Akademien, Blaisieholmstorg 8, S-111 48 Stockholm, Sweden. Bengt Holmstrand, sec gen.

* **Swedish Music Information Centre.** Box 27327, 79 Sandhamnsgatan, S-102 54 Stockholm, Sweden *tel:* +46 8 783 8800 *fax:* +46 8 783 9510 *email:* swedmic@stim.se; http://www.mic.stim.se. Roland Sandberg, exec dir. *Hire library and m/order service for unpublished, copyright-protected sheet mus. Hire library of electro-acoustic mus, historical popular sheet mus collection, listening room with published sheet mus, commercial and tape recordings, literature about Swedish mus and musical life, information service about composers and works. Own publishing house: Edition Suecia. Record society: Phono Suecia.*

Switzerland

European Association of Festivals. CH-1202 Geneve, Switzerland. Henri Siegwart, sec gen.

European Music Council of International Music Council (UNESCO). Bahnhofstr 78, CH-5000 Aarau, Switzerland *tel:* +41 62 822 9423 *fax:* +41 62 822 4767 *email:* musikrat@mail.spiderweb.ch. Ursula Bally-Fahr, sec gen. *The European Music Council is a platform for representatives of the National Music Councils and all organisations involved in the field of music education, creation, performance and heritage from all European countries.*

* **Fondation SUISA pour la musique.** Rue de l'Hôpital 22, CH-2001 Neuchâtel, Switzerland *tel:* +41 32 725 2536 *fax:* +41 32 724 0472. Claude Delley, dir. *The foundation encourages the composition of all styles of Swiss music. Offers financial support to composers and their publishers; promotes internationally the music of Swiss composers.*

International Confederation of Music Societies. Hammerstr 37, CH-4058 Basel, Switzerland. Hans Schaad, sec gen.

Swiss Council of Music. Bahnhofstr 78, CH-5000 Aarau, Switzerland *tel:* +41 62 822 9423 *fax:* +41 62 822 4767 *email:* musikrat@mail. spiderweb.ch. Jakob Stämpfli, president; Ursula Bally-Fahr, sec gen. *Represents the whole of Swiss musical life in its capacity as an umbrella organisation for all national organisations and associations.*

World Federation of International Music Competitions. 104 Rue de Carouge, CH-1205 Geneve, Switzerland. Jacques Haldenwang, sec gen.

Tunisia

National Music Committee (Tunisia). Ministry of Culture and Information, Rue du 2 Mars 1934, La Kasbah, Tunis, Tunisia. Fehti Zghonda, sec gen.

Turkey

National Music Committee (Turkey). c/o Turkish National Commission for UNESCO, Göreme Sokak No 7, Kavaklidere, Ankara, Turkey.

Ukraine

* **Music Information Centre of the Ukraine Composers Union.** Ul Sofiuska 16/16, 252001 Kiev 1, Ukraine *tel:* +380 44 228 3304 *fax:* +380 44 229 6940. Volodymyr Simonenko, dir.

National Music Committee (Ukraine). 32 Puschkin Str, 252 004 Kiev, Ukraine. Nina Gersimova, sec gen.

Uruguay

National Music Committee (Uruguay). Rio Negro 1228, 11100 Montevideo, Uruguay. Tania Siver, delegate.

Centro Cultural de la Música. Apdo 5 Av 18 de Julio 1006, 6th Floor, Montevideo, Uruguay. Jorge Calvetti, dir.

USA

Americans for the Arts. 1 E 53 St, New York, NY 10022-4201, USA *tel:* +1 212 223 2787 *fax:* +1 212 980 4857 *email:* info@artsusa.org; http://www.artsusa.org. Robert Lynch, president. *National organisation for groups and individuals dedicated to advancing the arts and culture across the USA. Founded by the ACA, it represents a broad network of arts supporters, patrons, business leaders and community arts organisations.*

American Federation of Musicians of the United States and Canada. 1501 Broadway, Suite 600, New York, NY 10036, USA *tel:* +1 212 869 1330 *fax:* +1 212 764 6134 *email:* http://www.afm.org. Steve Young, president. *Union representing the professional interests of musicians. Membership of the federation is open to all professional musicians and vocalists in the USA and Canada.*

* **American Music Center.** 30 West 26th St, Suite 1001, New York, NY 10010-2011, USA *tel:* +1 212 366 5260 *fax:* +1 212 366 5265 *email:* center@amc.net; http://www.amc.net/amc. Nancy M Clarke, exec dir;

Stacie Johnston, dir of information services. *Promotes the creation, performance and appreciation of American contemporary music, through information services, a collection of scores and recordings, grant programmes, and advocacy on behalf of American music.*

Music Associates of America (MAA). 224 King St, Englewood, NJ 07631, USA *tel:* +1 201 569 2898 *fax:* +1 201 569 7023 *email:* maasturm@sprynet.com. George Sturm, exec dir. *Serves a limited number of music publishers and distributors in administrative and promotional activities. Publishes a music journal* MadAminA! *which is distributed to libraries and performing organisations throughout North America. Acts as an agency for a select number of composers.*

National Music Committee (USA). Kingsborough College, Department of Music, 2001 Oriental Boulevard, Brooklyn, NY 11235, USA. Dean Stein, president.

United States Information Agency, Arts America Program. 301 Fourth St, SW, Room 568, Washington DC 20547, USA *tel:* +1 202 619 4779 *fax:* +1 202 619 6315. Robin Barrington.

Uzbekistan

National Music Committee (Uzbekistan). c/o National Commission of Uzbekistan for UNESCO, 54 Buyak Ipak Yuli, Tashkent 700 137, Uzbekistan. Zakhid Haknazarov, president.

Vietnam

National Music Committee (Vietnam). 32 Nguyen Thai Hoc, Hanoi, Vietnam. Pham Dinh Sau, president.

Zambia

National Music Committee (Zambia). Centre of the Arts, University of Zambia, PO Box 32279, Lusaka, Zambia. M I Mapoma, president.

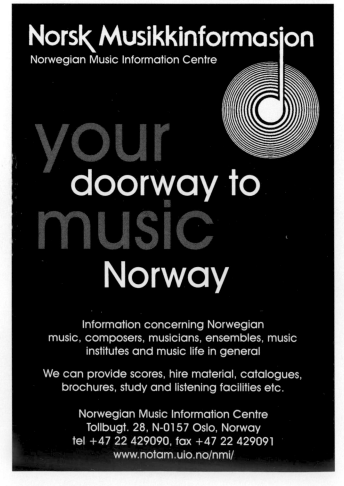

Agents and Promoters

The agents listed below provide representation for individual artists, ensembles and orchestras; many also promote concerts, concert series and festivals.

Andorra

RIAL Andorra Ltd. 24 Av de Tarragona, Andorra la Vella, Principality of Andorra *tel:* +376 860686 *fax:* +376 860992. Pascal Lair, mgr dir. *Artist management and tour promotion. Classical and jazz.*

Argentina

Arte Producciones. Bulnes 44 - 2* R, 1176 Buenos Aires, Argentina *tel:* +54 1 958 2368 *fax:* +54 1 982 3186. Horacio Ceballos, mgr. *Artist representation.*

Barry Editorial. Av Roque Sáenz Peña 1185-8 "N", 1035 Buenos Aires, Argentina *tel:* +54 1 383 0745/382 3230 *fax:* +54 1 383 3946 *email:* barry @satlink.com. Roberto F Barry, mgr. *Artist representation and concert promotion.*

Conciertos Gama. Corrientes 1665, 3rd Fl Room A, 1042 Buenos Aires, Argentina *tel:* +54 1 374 4257/6288/5403 *fax:* +54 1 112260. Alejandro Szterenfeld. *Artist representation and concert promotion.*

Daniel Artist Management. Dragones 1929, 1428 Buenos Aires, Argentina *tel:* +54 1 788 4308 *fax:* +54 1 786 3325 *email:* lumpui@ba.net. Rosario Bauza de Quesada. *Artist representation and concert promotion.*

Werner S Wagner. Casilla de Correo 5293, Correo Central, 1000 Buenos Aires, Argentina *tel:* +54 1 777 7667 *fax:* +54 1 774 7962. *Artist representation: opera, conductors, soloists.*

Australia

Adelaide Festival Centre Trust. King William Rd, Adelaide, SA 5000, Australia *tel:* +61 88 216 8600 *fax:* +61 88 212 7849. Andrew Bleby, program dir. *Concert promotion.*

Andrew McKinnon Concert Presentations Pty Ltd. 450 Elizabeth St, Suite 22, Surry Hills, Sydney, NSW 2010, Australia *tel:* +61 29 310 4204 *fax:* +61 29 698 5778. *Concert promoter; opera, classical mus, jazz.*

Arts Management Pty Ltd. Station House, Rawson Pl, 790 George St, Sydney, NSW 2000, Australia *tel:* +61 2 9212 5066 *fax:* +61 2 9211 7762 *email:* vbraden@ozemail.com.au. Virginia Braden, mgr dir; Clio Calodoukas, Hanne Larsen, associate dirs. *Artist representation for conductors, instrumentalists, singers, ensembles, lighting designers and directors.*

Avere Artists. 26 Oxley Dr, Bowral, NSW 2576, Australia *tel:* +61 48 621688 *fax:* +61 48 621686 *email:* averepl@tpgi.com.au. Raymond Myers, dir. *Artist representation.*

Cameron's Management. Suite 5, Edgecliff Court, 2 New McLean St, Edgecliff, Sydney, NSW 2027, Australia *tel:* +61 2 9362 0500 *fax:* +61 2 9363 3317. Judith Alexander. *Artist representation of opera and concert singers.*

Chris John Management. GPO Box 1289, Adelaide, SA 5001, Australia *tel:* +61 88 231 8017 *fax:* +61 88 231 5003 *email:* cjm@peg.pegasus. oz.au. Chris John, mgr. *Concert promoter.*

Jenifer Eddy Artists' Management. The Clivedon Suite 11, 596 St Kilda Rd, Melbourne, Victoria 3004, Australia *tel:* +61 3 9525 2700 *fax:* +61 3 9529 5410 *email:* 100231.334@compuserve.com. Jenifer Eddy, dir. *Representation of singers and conductors.*

Kevin Jacobsen Productions. 98 Glebe Point Rd, Glebe, Sydney, NSW 2037, Australia *tel:* +61 2 9692 9399 *fax:* +61 2 9552 3629. Kevin Jacobsen, mgr dir. *Concert promotion.*

Performers Management. PO Box 210, Fitzroy, Victoria 3065, Australia *tel:* +61 3 9419 9477 *fax:* +61 3 9416 1492. Vincent Ciccarello, agent. *Artist representation; opera and classical mus.*

Symphony Australia. GPO Box 9994, Sydney, NSW 2001, Australia *tel:* +61 2 9333 1677 *fax:* +61 2 9333 1678 *email:* dixon.samuel@a2.abc. net.au. Nathan Waks, dir of mus; Samuel C Dixon, artistic admin. *Concert promotion.*

Victoria Arts Centre Trust. 100 St Kilda Rd, Melbourne, Victoria 3004, Australia *tel:* +61 3 9281 8000 *fax:* +61 3 9281 8282. Brett Randall, chief exec offr. *Concert promotion.*

Weaver Artist Management. PO Box 7670, St Kilda Rd, Melbourne, Victoria 3004, Australia *tel:* +61 3 9529 2869 *also fax; email:* weaver@ rainbow.nct.au. Jeff Weaver, dir; Mark Matthews. *Representation of singers, conductors, directors, instrumentalists, chmbr mus and ensembles.*

Austria

Agentur Kleinheisterkamp. Rechte Lande 10, 6820 Frastanz, Austria *tel:* +43 5522 52193 *also fax;* +43 664 2529790. *Artist representation.*

AOP Music Agency Vienna. Wurzbachgasse 22/16, A-1150 Wien, Austria *tel:* +43 1 982 8278 *fax:* +43 1 985 1464. Markus Bachmann, chief offr. *Artist representation and concert promotion, especially orchs and ens.*

Ars Media Konzertservice GmbH. Bergstr 22/38, A-5020 Salzburg, Austria *tel:* +43 662 873335 *fax:* +43 662 874752. Freimuth Teufel, dir. *Cultural programme organisation for galas, conventions, events, etc.*

Artsprojects. Meytensgasse 14/3, A-1130 Wien, Austria *tel:* +43 1 876 6728 *fax:* +43 1 876 0755. Kristel Josel, gen mgr. *Representation of instrumentalists and conductors.*

Austroconcert International. Gluckgasse 1, A-1010 Wien, Austria *tel:* +43 1 513 2657 *fax:* +43 1 512 6154. Prof Wolfgang Hartl, gen mgr. *General artistic representation for conductors, singers and orchestras.*

Esther Schollum Artists' Management. Guntramsdorferstr 12/2, A-2340 Mödling B, Wien, Austria *tel:* +43 2236 41004 *fax:* +43 2236 29068. *Artist representation.*

Gerhard Schroeder Konzertdirektion. Am Steinbruch 20, A-4020 Linz-Puchenau, Austria *tel:* +43 732 221523 *fax:* +43 732 221952. *Concert promotion.*

Gerhild Baron International Artists Management. Dornbacher Strasse 41/3/2, A-1170 Wien, Austria *tel:* +43 1 489 6154 *fax:* +43 1 485 6711. Gerhild Baron, mgr dir. *Artist representation.*

Goodmusic Artists' Management and Consulting Künstlervermittlung KEG. Dopschstr 20/3, A-1210 Wien, Austria *tel:* +43 1 259 2027 *fax:* +43 1 259 6124. John Goodman. *Artist representation.*

Kammermusik-Vereinigung Wien. Ganglbauergasse 38-6, A-1160 Wien, Austria *tel:* +43 1 492 3684 *fax:* +43 1 493 3927. Yossi Gutman, mus dir; Anna Vonneman, mgr. *Artist representation and concert promotion.*

Konzertagentur Susanne Wimmer. Burgstall 11, A-3034 Maria Anzbach, Austria *tel:* +43 2772 55927 *fax:* +43 2772 56371. Susanne Kaip- Wimmer.

Konzertdirektion Schlote GmbH. Danreitergasse 4, A-5020 Salzburg, Austria *tel:* +43 662 622174 *fax:* +43 662 629 9645. Joachim and Michael Schlote. *International management for soloists, opera, operetta, ballet, drama, musicals and orchestras.*

Künstleragentur Dr Raab & Dr Böhm. Plankengasse 7, A-1010 Wien, Austria *tel:* +43 512 0501 *fax:* +43 512 7743. Horst Böhm, company dir; Franz Hainzl, dir opera division. *Artist representation.*

Künstleragentur Hollaender-Calix. Grinzinger Allee 46, Haus 2, A-1190 Wien, Austria *tel:* +43 1 320 5317 *fax:* +43 1 318 4733. Ariane Hollaender-Calix, mgr dir. *Artist representation for opera, operetta and concerts.*

Künstlersekretariat Buchmann GmbH. Schachnerstr 27, A-1220 Wien, Austria *tel:* +43 1 203 6357 *fax:* +43 1 203 7483 *email:* buchmann@ m.xpoint.at. *Artist representation and concert promotion.*

Künstlervermittlung Klaus Eisenberger. Peter Jordan Str 8, PO Box 3, A-1183 Wien, Austria *tel:* +43 1 368 1363 *fax:* +43 1 369 2323. Klaus Eisenberger, gen mgr; Eva Eisenberger, asst mgr. *Artist representation specialising in chmbr mus, soloists, early mus, contemporary mus.*

Martin C Turba Arts Management. Franz-Josef-Kai 7, A-5020 Salzburg, Austria *tel:* +43 662 846578 *fax:* +43 662 847556. Martin C Turba, dir. *Artist representation. Specialising in orch tours.*

Mayler Artist Management (MAM). Langenfeldgasse 26-7-33, A-1120 Wien, Austria *tel:* +43 1 815 3733 *fax:* +43 1 812 7167. Keith Hoare-Mayler, owner. *General management and artist representation. Special interest in early mus and soloists.*

Melos Konzerte Wien. Postfach 210, A-1112 Wien, Austria *tel:* +43 1 749 2494 *fax:* +43 1 749 6222. Christian May, chmn; Juan Mendoza, Eleonore Schmidt. *Artist management for instrumentalists, conductors, chmbr mus ens. Orch tours. Local office in Munich.*

Metropolitan Artists' Management. Operngasse 36-38, A-1040 Wien, Austria *tel:* +43 1 586 4909 *also fax.* Aristid von Würtzler, dir.

Morawitz Music Management. Pramergasse 6, A-1090 Wien, Austria *tel:* +43 1 317 1871 *fax:* +43 1 317 1872 *email:* mmm@appleservice. com; http://www.mmmagency.com. Rudolf Morawitz, dir; Christa Redik, artists dept. *Artist representation and concert promotion, especially for orchs, chmbr mus, inst soloists and conds. Festival consulting.*

Musikalische Jugend Osterreichs-Jeunesse. Taubstummengasse 15-10, A-1040 Wien, Austria *tel:* +43 1 505 2949 *fax:* +43 1 504 6361. Matthias Naske, gen mgr. *Promotion of concerts for young people. 350 classical concerts per year.*

Musikverein für Steiermark. Landhausgasse 12, A-8010 Graz, Austria *tel:* +43 316 829924 *fax:* +43 316 829924/3. Mag Uta Werner. *Concert promotion.*

Opera Vladarski Bühnenvermittlung Internationaler Saenger. Reithlegasse 12, A-1190 Wien, Austria *tel:* +43 1 368 6960/1 *fax:* +43 1 368 6962. Lotte Vladarski, dir. *Artist representation.*

Belgium

Ariën International Concert and Teaterbureau. De Boeystr 6, B-2018 Antwerp, Belgium *tel:* +32 3 218 6975/6 *fax:* +32 3 230 3523. Albrecht Klora, mgr; Pascale Montaubau, mgr. *Artist representation of opera singers, instrumentalists, conductors and orchestras.*

Azymuth Government Foundation. Centre of International Cultural Relations, Association for Public Benefit, Torenstraat 13, B-9160 Lokeren, Belgium *tel:* +32 9 348 8000/3836/4344 *fax:* +32 9 348 9974. Jean Pierre Van Avermaet, mgr dir; Agnes Goeman, staff member. *Institution dedicated to international cultural exchanges; organisation of concert tours in co-operation with cultural societies and small towns, concerts of Belgian and European artists, and choir festivals in France, Lettony, Poland and Switzerland.*

Bureau de Concerts Jacques Mauroy. 1 Rue Jules Lejeune, B-1050 Bruxelles, Belgium *tel:* +32 2 345 3935 *fax:* +32 2 347 5928. Jacques Mauroy; Marianne Gérard. *Artist representation, specialising in soloists, str quartets, chmbr and symphonic orchs.*

European Artists Management. Av Alexandre Bertrand 52, B-1190 Bruxelles, Belgium *tel:* +32 2 343 2612 *fax:* +32 2 344 1335. Micheala Tache Ganea, dir. *Artist representation.*

ITM Artists Management. 27 Rue Bassenge, B-4000 Liege, Belgium *tel:* +32 42 230627 *also fax.* Nathalie Hosay, mgr. *Concert promotion.*

Joy Mebus Artists' Management. Waterstr 43, B-3770 Zussen (Riemst), Belgium *tel:* +32 12 457236 *fax:* +32 12 457234 *email:* joy.mebus@ping. be. Joy Mebus, dir. *Artist representation.*

Koninklijke Kring der Winterconcerten. Kraaiaard 2, B-9031 Gent (Drongen), Belgium *tel:* +32 92 262709 *also fax.* Hubert de Kemmeter, president. *Concert promotion.*

Liliane Weinstadt Bureau de Concerts. 69 Rue Langeveld, B-1180 Bruxelles, Belgium *tel:* +32 2 374 2138 *fax:* +32 2 375 7382. Liliane Weinstadt, executive dir; Luc Van Loocke, mgr dir. *Artist representation.*

Maestro Music Productions. Leeuwerikstraat 20, B-3680 Maaseik, Belgium *tel:* +32 89 567557 *fax:* +32 89 561117 *email:* maestro.brosse@ skynet.be. Eric Langie, gen mgr.

Music Hall. Zelliksestenweg 12, B-1080 Bruxelles, Belgium *tel:* +32 2 468 1300 *fax:* +32 2 468 2211. Geert Allaert, mgr dir. *Promotion of ballet, opera, operetta, classical mus, musicals and special events.*

Music Management FEW. 2 Albert Av, Bte E 15, B-1190 Bruxelles, Belgium *tel:* +32 2 345 2225 *fax:* +32 2 346 4647. Francois-Emmanuel de Wasseige, mgr. *Artist representation and concert promotion, mostly chmbr mus.*

Promorga Sprl. Villalaan 26, B-1630 Linkebeek, Belgium *tel:* +32 3 380 9860 *fax:* +32 3 380 8876 *email:* mhe@infoboard.be. Michel Hellawell, mgr. *Concert promoter.*

Société Philharmonique de Bruxelles. Rue Baron Horta 11, B-1000 Bruxelles, Belgium *tel:* +32 2 507 8410 *fax:* +32 2 511 7977. Paul Dujardin, gen dir; Christian Renard, production mgr. *Concert organiser.*

Brazil

Gaby Leib Produções Culturais. Rua Otávio Correia 420/6, 22291-180 Urca, Rio de Janiero RJ, Brazil *tel:* +55 21 295 0730 *fax:* +55 21 295 0580. Gabriele Ilse Leib, dir. *Artist representation and concert promotion.*

Interarte Produções Artisticas S/C Ltda. Rua Mourato Coelho 299, CJ 04 Sao Paulo S P, Brazil *tel:* +55 11 881 1911 *fax:* +55 11 883 1056 *email:* roring@dialdata.com.br. Roberto Ring, Sergio Melardi, mgrs. *Artist representation and concert promotion. Festivals and orch touring.*

Non Plus Ultra-Artes. Rua Donatucio Dotaviano 55, 13094-310 Campinas, Sao Paulo SP, Brazil *tel:* +55 19 254 2069 *email:* acamgucu@sanet.com. br. Adriana Camargo Cangucu, dir. *Concert tour agent.*

Organizacion de Conciertos Gerard srl. Rua Otávio Correia 420, Apt 6 Urca, 22291-180 Rio de Janeiro RJ, Brazil *tel:* +55 21 295 0730 *fax:* +55 21 295 0580. Gabriele Ilse Leib, dir. *Artist representation and concert promotion.*

Schlochauer & Associados. Consultoria e Representaçoes Ltda, Caixa Postal 21151, 04602-970 Sao Paulo SP, Brazil *tel:* +55 11 247 6631 *fax:* +55 11 547 0715. Hans Schlochauer, mgr dir. *Artist representation and concert promotion.*

Studio Serrano. Rua Santa Cristina 127, Santa Teresa, 20241-250, Rio de Janiero RJ, Brazil *tel:* +55 21 508 5220/7505 *fax:* +55 21 253 2815 *email:* serrano@marlin.com.br. Marne Serrano Caldera, president. *Artist representation and concert promotion.*

Bulgaria

Apollonia Art Foundation & Art Agency. 23a Shipchenski Prohod Blvd, BG-1111 Sofia, Bulgaria *tel:* +359 2 723131 *also fax.* Dimo Dimov, president; Margarita Dimitrova, artistic dir. *Artist representation and concert promotion.*

Bulgarian Artistic Agency Sofiaconcert. P Volov Str 3, BG-1527 Sofia, Bulgaria *tel:* +359 2 442914 *fax:* +359 2 445136. Jeanna Mollova, dir. *Artist representation.*

Music Agency Festival Concert. 128 Vasil Aprilovstr, PO Box 545, BG-4000 Plovdiv, Bulgaria *tel:* +359 32 556493 *fax:* +359 32 262626. Jivko Jekov, chief offr. *Artist representation and concert promotion.*

Nelly Lalova Management. Udovo Str 10, Bx 2, BG-1463 Sofia, Bulgaria *tel:* +359 2 235577 *also fax.* Nelly Lalova, mgr dir. *Artist representation, specialising in soloists and choirs.*

Canada

Andrew Kwan Artists Management Inc. 1315 Lawrence Av East, Suite 515, Toronto, Ont M3A 3R3, Canada *tel:* +1 416 445 4441 *fax:* +1 416 445 7744 *email:* akam@compuserve.com. Andrew J Kwan, dir. *Artist representation.*

B C Fiedler Management. 40 Alexander St, Penthouse 6, Toronto, Ont M4Y 1B5, Canada *tel:* +1 416 967 1421 *fax:* +1 416 967 1991 *email:* bcf@the-wire.com. Bernie Fiedler, president; Elisa Amsterdam, partner. *Artist representation and concert promotion. Specialising in classical cross-over, theatre production and recording.*

Campbell Webster Management. 181 Water St, Charlottetown, PE, C1A 1A9, Canada *tel:* +1 902 566 3346 *fax:* +1 902 892 1044 *email:* cwebster@peinet.pe.ca. Campbell Webster, mgr. *Artist representation.*

Classical Canada Concert Management. 23 Kenway Rd, Toronto, Ont M8Z 4W7, Canada *tel:* +1 416 239 1747 *fax:* +1 416 237 0973. Ruth Taylor, president, exec dir. *Artist representation and concert promotion.*

Colwell Arts Management. RR 1 New Hamburg, Ont N0B 2G0, Canada *tel:* +1 519 662 3499 *fax:* +1 519 662 2777 *email:* jcolwell@hookup.net. Jane Colwell, dir; Mary Ingraham, asst. *Specialist representation for singers; also some instrumentalists and ensembles.*

Dean Artists Mangement. 186 Dupont St, Toronto, Ont M5R 2E6, Canada *tel:* +1 416 969 7300 *fax:* +1 416 960 2314. Bruce Dean, president; Carrol Anne Curry, mgr dir. *Artist representation for singers and conductors only.*

Diane Kadota Arts Management. 1014 Homer St, Suite 103, Vancouver, BC, V6B 2W9, Canada *tel:* +1 604 683 8240 *fax:* +1 604 683 7911 *email:* dkam@istar.ca. Diane Kadota. *Represents artists in fields of world music, jazz, New Music, Musique Actuelle.*

EML International Artist Management. 219 Baseline Rd E, London, Ont N6C 2N6, Canada *tel:* +1 519 672 5850 *fax:* +1 519 672 2208. Judith Romyn, exec asst. *Artist representation of singers and conductors.*

Fleming Artists Management. 5975 avenue du Parc, Montréal (QC), H2V 4H4, Canada *tel:* +1 514 276 5605 *fax:* +1 514 276 4642 *email:* fleming@ globale.net. Heidi Fleming, dir. *Represents mainly jazz and folk artists. Concert promotion.*

Fox, Jones and Associates. 2nd Fl, 243 College St, Toronto, Ont M5T 1R5, Canada *tel:* +1 416 586 1302 *fax:* +1 416 586 0287 *email:* foxjones@ inforamp.net. Jeremy Fox, president; Margaret Barkman, mgr. *Artist representation.*

Genovese Vanderhoof and Associates. 77 Carlton St, Suite 1103, Toronto, Ont M5B 2J7, Canada *tel:* +1 416 340 2762 *fax:* +1 416 340 6276. Margaret Genovese, Dory Vanderhoof, snr partners. *Management consultants for the performing arts.*

Hart/Murdock Artist Management. Suite 100, 7b Pleasant Blvd, Toronto, Ont M4T 1K2, Canada *tel:* +1 416 922 5020 *fax:* +1 416 922 6686 *email:* hartmond@interlog.com; http://www.culturenet.ca/hm. Joanne Hart, Anne Murdock, partners. *Artist representation and management for opera and concert soloists, instrumentalists and early mus artists.*

Latitude 45 Arts Promotion. 109 St Joseph Blvd W, Montreal, PQ, Canada *tel:* +1 514 276 2694 *fax:* +1 514 276 2696 *email:* scalesb@aol.com; lat45arts@aol.com; http://www.eggcite.com/latitude.45. Barbara Scales, dir; Helen Fortin, booking. *Artist representation. Specialising in contemporary mus as well as classical, jazz and theatre.*

Marie Rakos Concert Management. 14 Palsen St, Nepean, Ont K2G 2V8, Canada *tel:* +1 613 224 6750 *fax:* +1 613 727 1626. Marie Rakos, dir. *Artist representation for instrumentalists and concert promotion.*

Novater Artists Inc. PO Box 69, 31 Adelaide St E, Toronto, Ont M5C 2H8, Canada *tel:* +1 416 214 2288 *fax:* +1 416 214 2290 *email:* novater@ novater.com; http://www.novater.com. David Julien, artistic dir; Judith Alltree, mgr dir. *Artist representation and concert promotion for classical, jazz and world mus.*

Renée Simmons Artists Management. 117 Ava Rd, Toronto, Ont, Canada *tel:* +1 416 782 7712 *fax:* +1 416 256 7657. Renée Simmons, dir. *Artist representation of instrumentalists and chmbr ens; concert promotion.*

Richard von Handschuh. 411 Duplex Av, Suite 2202, Toronto, Ont M4R 1V2, Canada *tel:* +1 416 489 2762 *fax:* +1 416 483 9840. *Artist representation, especially pianists.*

Robert Missen Artists Management. 156 Front St W, Suite 303, Toronto, Ont M5J 2L6, Canada *tel:* +1 416 971 4839 *fax:* +1 416 971 4841. Robert Missen, president. *Artist representation.*

The Tanglewood Group. 900 - 2 Sheppard Av East, Willowdale, ON, M2N 5Y7, Canada *tel:* +1 416 787 8687 *fax:* +1 416 787 8647 *email:* mail@tanglewood.com; http://www.tanglewood.com. Bruce Davidsen, president; Eileen Melnick, dir, concert productions. *Concert promotion.*

VKD International Artists. 2304 Towne Blvd, Oakville, Ont L6H 5J5, Canada *tel:* +1 905 257 5279 *also fax.* V K DuBois, exec dir. *Artist representation.*

China

China Performing Arts Agency. A25, 10 St Dongsi, Beijing 100007, China *tel:* +86 1 403 2704 *fax:* +86 1 401 5802. Li Deyu, gen dir. *Artist representation for Chinese artists; also presents foreign musicians in China.*

Colombia

Ismael Arensburg Artist & Concert Management. Carerra 6a No 67-09 Ofc 103, PO Box 53490, Bogotá 2, Colombia *tel:* +57 1 211 3626; +57 1 310 0345 *fax:* +57 1 310 0452. *Artist representation and concert promotion.*

Sociedad Musical Daniel. Carrera 6 No 67-09, Ofc 103, PO Box 53490, Bogotá DE, Colombia *tel:* +57 1 211 3626; +57 1 310 0345 *fax:* +57 1 310 0452. Ishmael Arensburg. *Artist representation and concert promotion.*

Costa Rica

Sociedad Musical Universal SA. Universal Artists, Apartado 779, Centro Colon, San José 1007, Costa Rica *tel:* +506 255 1753 *fax:* +506 255 0985. Bruno Schoenberg, Dory Steinberg, exec dirs. *Artist representation and concert promotion.*

Croatia

Koncertna Direkcija Zagreb. Kneza Mislava 18, 41000 Zagreb, Croatia *tel:* +385 41 446011 *fax:* +385 41 443022. Erika Krpan, dir. *Artist representation and concert promotion.*

Koncertna Dvorana Vatroslav Lisinski. Trg Stjepana Radica 4, 41000 Zagreb, Croatia *tel:* +385 1 612 1111 *fax:* +385 1 530023. Lovro Lisicic, gen mgr; Dubravko Madnaric, programme mgr. *Concert promotion.*

Czech Republic

Ars/Koncert Management Ltd. Komenského 8, CZ-602 00 Brno, Czech Republic *tel:* +420 5 4221 5116 *fax:* +420 5 4221 1358. Miroslav Stehlik, mgr dir. *Artist representation.*

Art Productions Praha. Ke Skalkam 2450, CZ-106 00 Praha 10, Czech Republic *tel:* +420 2 762221 *also fax.* Jiri Kovac, dir. *Concert promotion.*

B-Arts Ltd. Moravská 35, CZ-120 00 Praha 2, Czech Republic *tel:* +420 2 258540 *fax:* +420 2 257140. Olga Kokosková, dir. *Artist representation.*

Concert Agency Prague Lupulus. Ovocny Trh 573/12, 11000 Praha 1, Czech Republic *tel:* +420 2 21 637160/637176 *fax:* +420 2 21 637177. Dagmar Vlckova, dir; Oldrich Vlcek, art dir. *Artist representation and concert promotion.*

Czech Artists Agency Dr Bechyne. V Olsinách 114, CZ-100 00 Praha 10, Czech Republic *tel:* +420 2 782 0633 *fax:* +420 2 781 3801 *email:* bechyne@terminal.cz. Václav Bechyne, dir. *Artist representation, especially orchs, opera and soloists.*

Eurosound Artist Agency. Modranská 23, 147 00 Praha 4, Czech Republic *tel:* +420 2 402 2576 *also fax.* Katerina Novotná, general mgr. *Artist representation and concert promotion.*

Jan Drasky Künstlersche Agentur/Art Agency. Ovcí Hájek 2162, CZ-15500 Praha 5, Czech Republic *tel:* +420 2 561 0372 *also fax.* *Artist representation for singers, instrumentalists, conductors, directors and designers. Concert promotion.*

Moravia Artist Management. Anenská 10, CZ-602 00 Brno, Czech Republic *tel:* +420 5 4321 2417 *fax:* +420 5 4321 1266. Jirí Sajtar, dir. *Artist representation.*

Musart Prag. Kaplická 35, CZ-140 00 Praha 4, Czech Republic *tel:* +420 2 438774 *fax:* +420 2 437081. Zinaida Hortková, dir. *Artist representation. Classical, opera, ballet, choirs etc.*

Music Agency Martin Zyka. Dominikánské nám 6/7, 602 00 Brno, Czech Republic *fax:* +420 5 422 13421. Martin Zyka. *Artist representation and concert promotion, specialising in orchs, chmbr ens and singers.*

Music Agency of the Prague Symphony Orchestra. Kostel Sv Simona a Judy, Dusní Ulice, CZ-110 00 Praha 1, Czech Republic *tel:* +420 2 2321068 *fax:* +420 2 2319389 *email:* fok@login.cz. Daniel Sobotka, dept mgr. *Concert promoter.*

Panart Arts Management. Jungmannova 5, CZ-110 00 Praha 1, Czech Republic *tel:* +420 2 242 15781 *also fax.* Tatyána Czechowská. *Artist representation.*

Posh Co Art. Lublanská 13, Praha 2, CZ-120 00, Czech Republic *tel:* +420 2 858 4729 *fax:* +420 2 269 8776 *email:* posh@bajt.cz. Petr Spolc, asst artistic dir; Bohumil Pospiech, dir. *Artist representation for classical, choral, ballet, operetta. Operetta promotion.*

Pragokoncert - Czech Arts Agency. Celetná 17, Praha 1, Czech Republic *tel:* +420 2 2481 1690/1659 *fax:* +420 2 23 203 53. Ivo Letov, artistic dir; Vera Eksteinova, mgr. *Artist representation and concert promotion. Jazz, pop and rock artists as well as classical.*

Richard Kolár Management Ltd. Komenského 112, CZ-252 28 Cernosice 1, Czech Republic *tel:* +420 2 24 224351/7989 *also fax.* Richard Kolár, dir. *Artist representation and concert promotion.*

Sonus Artists Management. Pod Smukyrkou 1049, CZ-150 00 Praha 5, Czech Republic *tel:* +420 2 526583 *also fax.* Zdenek Vokurka, gen dir. *Artist representation and concert promotion. Specialising in chmbr mus and singers.*

VIA Praga. Zatecka 1, CZ-110 00 Praha 1, Czech Republic *tel:* +420 2 232 2536; +420 2 232 4189 *also fax.* J Dvorák, PR dir; T Heinzel, mgr. *Concert promotion.*

Denmark

Arte. Hvidkildevej 64, DK-2400 Copenhagen, Denmark *tel:* +45 38 884900 *fax:* +45 38 332083. Kjeld Hansen, mgr. *Artist representation.*

Dr Gösta Schwarck International Concert Management. Dalgas Blvd 48, PO Box 13, DK-2000 Copenhagen F, Denmark *tel:* +45 31 877010 *fax:* +45 31 877011. Dr Gösta Schwarck, mgr dir. *Artist representation and concert promotion.*

International Personal Management. St Kongensgade 46, DK-1264 Copenhagen K, Denmark *tel:* +45 33 115225 *fax:* +45 33 131950. Steen Witrock, mgr dir. *Artist representation and concert promotion.*

Rohr Artists Management. Grøndalsvej 47, DK-2000 Copenhagen F, Denmark *tel:* +45 31 873223 *also fax.* Joyce Rohr, dir. *Artist representation.*

Tivoli Festival Agency. Vesterbrogade 3, DK-1630 Copenhagen V, Denmark *tel:* +45 33 750400 *fax:* +45 33 155646. Tom Kristensen, mgr. *Artist representation.*

Wilhelm Hansen Concert & Theatre Management. Gothersgade 11, 4th Floor, DK-1123 Copenhagen K, Denmark *tel:* +45 33 143710 *fax:* +45 33 144428. Hanne Wilhelm Hansen, mgr.

Estonia

Eesti Kontsert. State Concert Institution, 4 Estonia Av, EE-0001 Tallinn, Estonia *tel:* +372 2 442901; +372 2 444618 *also fax; fax:* +372 6 314171 *email:* concert@netexpress.ee; http://www.bcs.ee/concert. Enno Mattisen, gen dir; Aivar Mäe, vice-dir. *Artist representation and concert promotion; especially for festivals.*

Finland

Allegro Artist Management. Tapiolan Keskustorni Tap-House, 11th Fl, FIN-02100 Espoo, Finland *tel:* +358 9 462 007 *fax:* +358 9 616 50155. Pekka K Pohjola, mgr dir. *Artist representation.*

Fazer Artists' Management Inc. Nervanderinkatu 5 E 46, FIN-00100 Helsinki, Finland *tel:* +358 9 4542470 *fax:* +358 9 446841. Tuula Sarotie, gen mgr. *Artist representation.*

Festium Oy. Partiotie 34, FIN-00370 Helsinki 37, Finland *tel:* +358 9 556024 *fax:* +358 9 557020. Mirja Salomaa, mgr dir. *Artist representation and concert promotion.*

FinnConcert. Paivolantie 12, FIN-73770 Sayneinen, Finland *tel:* +358 49 279455 *fax:* +358 17 610285. Raija Helena, president. *Artist representation.*

Konserttikeskus r.y./Konsertcentralen. Malmgatan 24 D 38, FIN-00100 Helsinki, Finland *tel:* +358 9 6943 348 *fax:* +358 9 6943 427 *email:* konserttikeskus@pp.kolumbus.fi; http://koti.kolumbus.fi/~konsertk/. Jorma Kesseli, concert sec; Ms Satu Sormunen, clerk. *Arranges and promotes concerts and workshops in schools.*

Orfeo Oy Ltd. Rauhankatu 7, FIN-00170 Helsinki, Finland *tel:* +358 9 135 8993 *fax:* +358 9 622 73400 *email:* orfeo@pp.kolumbus.fi. Erkki Alste, exec mgr; Maarit Mattala, asst. *Artist representation specialising in singers.*

Rockadillo. Keskustori 7 A, FIN-33100 Tampere, Finland *tel:* +358 3 2131 260 *fax:* +358 3 2131 297 *email:* agency@rock.pp.fi. Tapio Korjus, mgr dir. *Artist representation and concert promotion. Mainly rock, jazz and world mus, occasionally classical.*

Show Consults Company Ltd (A C Concert Promotion & Consulting Artist Management). Iso Roobertinkatu 24 A 3, FIN-00120 Helsinki 12, Finland *tel:* +358 9 641023 *fax:* +358 9 603239. Antti Einio, mgr dir. *Concert promotion.*

Sibelius Academy Concert Agency. PO Box 86, FIN-00251 Helsinki, Finland *tel:* +358 9 405 4662 *fax:* +358 9 405 4603. Anja Frosen, mgr; Vesa Ruotonen, mgr. *Concert promotion.*

StillArt. Annegatan 6B, FIN-00120 Helsingfors, Finland *tel:* +358 9 641 771 *fax:* +358 9 607 319. Maj-Britt Still, sec. *Artist representation.*

WellDone. Sorvaajankatu 9 A4, 4 krs, FIN-00810 Helsinki, Finland *tel:* +358 0 755 3100 *fax:* +358 0 755 3131 *email:* http://www.welldone. fi. Risto Juvonen, mgr dir; Jim Mckee, promoter. *Concert promotion.*

France

Agence Artistique Eliane Ribet. Rue Ledion 9, F-75014 Paris, France *tel:* +33 1 45 43 26 07 *fax:* +33 1 45 43 58 25. *Artist representation.*

Agence Artistique Ludmila Lincy. 27 Rue de Marignan, F-75008 Paris, France *tel:* +33 1 45 62 02 93 *fax:* +33 1 45 62 02 92. Ludmila Lincy. *Artist representation.*

Agence Bourbon-Briant. 27 Rue de l'Echiquier, F-75010 Paris, France *tel:* +33 1 47 70 42 93 *fax:* +33 1 45 23 41 36. Michel Chouanard. *Represents jazz artists.*

Agency Jacques Thelen. 252 Rue de Faubourg St Honoré, F-75008 Paris, France *tel:* +33 1 45 61 47 47 *fax:* +33 1 45 61 90 70. *Artist representation.*

Artistic Organisation. 63 Cours Balguerie, BP 146, F-33027 Bordeaux Cedex, France *tel:* +33 56 81 25 61 *fax:* +33 56 48 22 29. Christian Chartier, mgr dir. *Artist representation of jazz musicians.*

Artists International Management Ltd. 10 Rue des Acacias, F-75017 Paris, France *tel:* +33 1 45 74 16 24 *fax:* +33 1 45 74 33 20. Claude-Franck Boisson, mgr dir. *Artist representation, especially conductors; orch tours.*

Artservice International. 30 Rue du Chateau d'Eau, F-75010 Paris, France *tel:* +33 1 42 39 14 00 *fax:* +33 1 42 39 14 02. Benedicte Pesle. *Artist representation, specialising in contemporary composers.*

B/A (Billard Azaïs) Musique. BP 14, 37 Rue de Vilmorin, F-45290 Nogent sur Vernisson, France *tel:* +33 2 38 97 6004 *fax:* +33 2 38 97 6406. Julien Azaïs, dir. *Artist representation.*

Bureau de Concerts Marcel de Valmalète. 7 rue Hoche, 92300 Levallois, France *tel:* +33 1 47 59 8759 *fax:* +33 1 47 59 8750. Mme Pochet de Valmalète, gen dir. *Artist representation and concert promotion.*

Bureau de Concerts Maurice Werner. 7 Rue Richepance, F-75008 Paris, France *tel:* +33 1 40 15 92 80 *fax:* +33 1 42 60 30 49. Maurice Werner, dir; Dominique Werner, dir. *Artist representation.*

Bureau International de Concerts. 252 Rue du Faubourg St Honoré, F-75008 Paris, France *tel:* +33 1 45 63 79 55 *fax:* +33 1 45 62 24 17. Camille Kiesgen, president. *Artist representation.*

Classical Artist Management. 16 Rue du Regard, F-75006 Paris, France *tel:* +33 1 45 44 49 45 *fax:* +33 1 45 44 48 82. Eliza Jamin, dir. *Artist representation and concert and festival promotion*

Classics International Management (CIM). 54 Av d'Iena, F-75116 Paris, France *tel:* +33 1 47 20 55 53 *fax:* +33 1 47 20 37 51. Jacqueline Guélis, dir. *Artist representation of orchestras, soloists, conductors and chmbr mus.*

Dorothée Bonhomme. 31 Rue Laplace, F-75005 Paris, France *tel:* +33 1 43 36 82 11 *fax:* +33 1 47 07 86 55. *Concert and event promotion.*

Dr Gösta Schwarck International. 14 Rue de Clichy, F-75009 Paris, France *tel:* +33 1 45 26 00 75 *fax:* +33 1 45 26 01 14. Yan Brian Schwarck, mgr dir.

Harry Lapp Organisation. 9 Av de la Liberté, F-67000 Strasbourg, France *tel:* +33 3 88 15 29 29 *fax:* +33 3 88 24 03 16. Harry Lapp. *Concert promotion and artist representation, specialising in classical mus, opera, jazz, rock and ballet.*

IMG Artists. 2 Rue Dufrenoy, F-75116 Paris, France *tel:* +33 1 45 03 47 38 *fax:* +33 1 45 04 12 85. Véronique Jourdain, dir; Isabelle de Brion, Marianne Ducsay, assts. *Artist representation, specialising in conductors and instrumentalists.*

Jeanine Roze Production. 17 Rue du Colisée, F-75008 Paris, France *tel:* +33 1 42 56 90 10 *fax:* +33 1 43 59 54 37. *Concert promotion.*

Laurence Doublet Agence Artistique. 63 Rue St Sabin, F-75011 Paris, France *tel:* +33 1 43 38 50 58 *fax:* +33 1 47 00 83 85. *Artist representation.*

Living Art - Impresariat. 9 Blvd Montmartre, F-75002 Paris, France *tel:* +33 1 42 36 49 44/36 32 *fax:* +33 1 42 33 6491. Angelika Belamaric, dir. *Artist representation of opera singers and conductors only.*

Management Artistique Professionnel. 51 Rue Le Marois, F-75016 Paris, France *tel:* +33 1 46 51 85 56. Alain Gramola, president.

Mondial Musique. 15 Av Montaigne, F-75008 Paris, France *tel:* +33 1 47 23 56 50 *fax:* +33 1 47 23 33 66. Robert Alfonsi, dir. *Artist representation.*

Monique Cazeneuve Agence Artistique. 5-7 Av Mac-Mahon, F-75017 Paris, France *tel:* +33 1 43 80 15 86 *fax:* +33 1 46 22 58 76. Monique Cazeneuve. *Artist representation of conductors, instrumentalists and ens. Also local tours for international orchs.*

Musica Gyr. 79 Quai André Citroën, F-75015 Paris, France *tel:* +33 1 45 75 51 88 *fax:* +33 1 45 75 02 73. Santiago Gyr. *Artist representation and concert promotion. Festivals.*

Musicaglotz. 11 Rue Le Verrier, F-75006 Paris, France *tel:* +33 1 42 34 53 40 *fax:* +33 1 40 46 93 77. Michel Glotz, gen dir. *Artist representation of conductors, instrumentalists and opera singers.*

Musilyre. 1 Square de Châtillon, 75014 Paris, France *tel:* +33 1 45 42 65 00 *fax:* +33 1 45 42 65 01. Véronique Réaud, mgr; Florence Affeltranger, asst. *Representation of baroque artists and concert promotion.*

Organisation Internationale Opéra et Concert. 1 Rue Volney, F-75002 Paris, France *tel:* +33 1 42 96 18 18 *fax:* +33 1 42 96 18 00. Charles Fabius, dir; Paule Fabre, Jacqueline Chollet, admin. *Artist representation.*

Productions Claude Giraud. 26 Rue Berlioz, F-75116 Paris, France *tel:* +33 1 45 00 41 87 *fax:* +33 1 44 17 93 52. Claude Giraud.

Productions Dominique Werner. 7 Rue Richepance, F-75008 Paris, France *tel:* +33 1 40 15 92 80 *fax:* +33 1 49 26 05 07. Dominique Werner, dir. *Artist representation and concert promotion. Specialising in orch, opera and ballet.*

Sarah Turner Communication. 24 Rue du Buisson Richard, F-78600 Le Mesnil le Roi, France *tel:* +33 1 39 12 11 91 *fax:* +33 1 39 62 07 22. *Artist representation, especially choirs and instrumentalists.*

Germany

Accento-Künstlersekretariat Alte Musik. Kiesseestr 57a, D-37083 Göttingen, Germany *tel:* +49 551 77930 *fax:* +49 551 77932 *email:* accento-loepthien@t-online.de. Wolfgang Loepthien, dir. *Representation of early music artists and concert promotion.*

Agentur Kleinheisterkamp. Welsheimerstr 28a, D-70188, Germany *tel:* +49 711 483247 *fax:* +49 711 485796. *Artist representation.*

Agentur Ocklenburg Buehnenvermittlung. Hartungstr 15, D-20146 Hamburg, Germany *tel:* +49 40 418656 *fax:* +49 40 410 4668. Guenter Ocklenburg; Wolfgang Schmitt. *Representation of opera singers.*

Arte Music Konzertagentur. Gabelsbergerstr 48/b, D-80333 München, Germany *tel:* +49 89 523 3461 *fax:* +49 89 523 1259. Bettina Braun-Angott, chief offr. *Artist representation.*

Artists International. Am Kreispark 32, D-51379 Leverkusen, Germany *tel:* +49 2171 42663 *fax:* +49 2171 43981. Linda Abberton, dir. *Sponsorship, orch touring and special events.*

Artists Management Hartmut Hasse. Aalgrund 8, D-31275 Lehrte, Germany *tel:* +49 5175 953232 *fax:* +49 5175 953233. *Artist representation of singers and conductors.*

Augsburger Konzertdirektion Georg Hörtnagel. Josef Priller Str 10, D-86159 Augsburg, Germany *tel:* +49 821 593835 *fax:* +49 7313 3425. *Concert promotion.*

Barthelmess Consulting. Grüneburgweg 37, D-60322 Frankfurt am Main, Germany *tel:* +49 73 253207 *also fax.* Stephan Barthelmess, dir. *Artist representation and concert promotion.*

Bayerische Konzertdirektion Karl Gensberger. Marienplatz 1, D-80331 München, Germany *tel:* +49 89 227488 *fax:* +49 89 225311. Paul Kreye, dir. *Artist representation and concert promotion; specialising in choirs.*

Berliner Konzertagentur 3-Klang. Raoul Wallenbergstr 44, D-12679 Berlin, Germany *tel:* +49 30 933 2014 *fax:* +49 30 933 1821. Horst Gutteck, owner. *Artist representation.*

Berliner Konzertagentur Monika Ott. Dramburgerstr 46, D-12683 Berlin, Germany *tel:* +49 30 514 4858 *fax:* +49 30 514 2659. Monika Ott, mgr. *Artist representation, especially conductors and instrumentalists.*

C Intveen GmbH. Kaufhausstr 5, D-78315 Radolfzell/Bodensee, Germany *tel:* +49 7732 54184 *fax:* +49 7732 58836. *Artist representation and concert promotion with emphasis on young musicians.*

Christian Lange Personal Artist Management. Ludwig Behrstr 7, D-82327 Tutzing, Germany *tel:* +49 8158 1832 *fax:* +49 8158 8521. Christian Lange, president. *Artist representation and concert promotion. Festivals.*

Classical Music and Media. Steinlestrasse 27, D-60596 Frankfurt, Germany *tel:* +49 9636 0792 *fax:* +49 9636 0793. Medi A Gasteiner-Girth, mgr dir. *Artist representation and public relations; mainly conductors and singers.*

Concert Team. Düsseldorf, Jägerhofstr. 19-20, 40479 Düsseldorf, Germany *tel:* +49 2 1149 15990 *fax:* +49 2 1149 159999 *email:* concert team@compuserve.com. Bernhard Lenkowicz, dir. *Local concert promotion.*

Concertino Agentur Rita de la Chevallerie. Nerotal 24, D-65193 Wiesbaden, Germany *tel:* +49 611 599559 *fax:* +49 611 522263. *Artist representation.*

Concertino Jutta Jochimsen. Luzernerstr 14b, D-12205 Berlin, Germany *tel:* +49 30 817 3364 *fax:* +49 30 817 9527. *Concert promotion.*

Concerto Winderstein Gmbh. Postfach 440446, D-80753 München, Germany *tel:* +49 89 3838 4611 *fax:* +49 89 337938. Hans-Dieter Goehre, dir. *Artist representation and concert promotion.*

Contour, Büro für Concert und Gastspieltourneen GmbH. PO Box 250152, D-40093 Düsseldorf, Germany *tel:* +49 211 934 8486 *fax:* +49 211 345235. *Artist representation and concert promotion.*

Crescendo Artists Management. Eckbergstr 27, D-76534 Baden-Baden, Germany *tel:* +49 722 199801 *fax:* +49 722 199802. Alec Band, president, CEO. *Artist representation and concert promotion.*

Dagmar von Vietinghoff-Scheel Personal Artists Management. Lange Furche 44, D-72072 Tübingen, Germany *tel:* +49 707 1 73566 *fax:* +49 707 1 76612. *Artist representation.*

Daniela Wiehen Artists Management. Falkenried 7, D-20251 Hamburg, Germany *tel:* +49 40 4231 3121 *fax:* +49 40 4231 3120 *email:* daniela. wiehen@hamburg.netsurf.de. Daniela Wiehen. *Artist representation string quartets, soloists, conductors.*

Elisabeth Meister. Mallertshofener Str 8, D-85716 Unterschleissheim, Germany *tel:* +49 89 3177 0924 *fax:* +49 89 3177 0925. *Artist representation for conductors.*

Floria Productions. Gutleutstr 123, D-60327 Frankfurt, Germany *tel:* +49 60 239848 *fax:* +49 69 236581 *email:* floria@xs4all.nl. Gerardo Ibargüen, dir. *Artist representation, especially for ballet and modern dance.*

Frankfurter Konzertdirektion. Ulmenstr 37, D-60325 Frankfurt/Main, Germany *tel:* +49 69 722341 *fax:* +49 69 722417. Gerd Reul, chief exec. *Artist representation and concert promotion.*

Hello Concerts GmbH. Schiessgrabenstr 2 1/2, D-86150 Augsburg, Germany *tel:* +49 8 2115 4027 *fax:* +49 8 2115 4020. Walter Czermak, Lothar Schlessmann, mgr dirs. *Artist management.*

Herwald Artists' Management. Strasse des Roten Kreuzes 64, D-76228 Karlsruhe, Germany *tel:* +49 721 947647 *fax:* +49 721 473579. Thomas Herwald, dir; Rolf Fath, asst. *Artist representation.*

Hoffmann Konzerte GmbH. Rathenaustr 19, D-68165 Mannheim, Germany *tel:* +49 621 42620 *fax:* +49 621 426 2222. Matthias Hoffmann, gen mgr; Desi Hoffmann, mgr dir. *Concert promotion.*

HP Musik Management. Ainmillerstr 11, D-80801 München, Germany *tel:* +49 89 380 1977 *fax:* +49 89 339065. *Artist representation and concert promotion.*

Johannes Adams. Stadtwaldgürtel 44b, D-50931 Köln, Germany *tel:* +49 221 401538 *fax:* +49 221 408243. Johannes Adams.

Koko Entertainment. Bruder-Turm-Gasse 4a, Postfach 101063, D-78410 Konstanz, Germany *tel:* +49 7531 90880 *fax:* +49 7531 908888. Dieter Boes, mgr dir. *Concert promotion.*

Konzert-Management Jochum. Rotenbühler Weg 28a, 66123 Saarbrücken, Germany *tel:* +49 681 397359 *fax:* +49 681 372310. *Artist representation, specialising in pianists, violinists, organists and conductors.*

Konzert und Werbe GmbH. Julienstrasse 34, 45130 Essen, Germany *tel:* +49 2 0179 2059 *fax:* +49 2 0177 9328. Walter Gommers. *Concert promotion.*

Konzertagentur Andrea Hampl. Prenzlauer Promenade 189, D-13189 Berlin, Germany *tel:* +49 30 478 2699 *fax:* +49 30 478 3792. *Artist representation for instrumentalists, chmbr mus and orchs.*

Konzertagentur Erika Esslinger. Spittlerstr 6, D-70190 Stuttgart, Germany *tel:* +49 711 28 3276 *fax:* +49 711 26 1421. *Artist representation, especially chmbr mus and early mus.*

Konzertagentur Eva Maria Kaufmann. Pillnitzer Landstr 7, D-01326 Dresden, Germany *tel:* +49 351 2687212 *fax:* +49 351 2640585 *email:* konzertagentur@kaufmann.dd. Eva-Maria Kaufmann, dir; Thomas Kaufmann. *Artist representation.*

Konzertagentur Fahrenholtz. Oberweg 51, D-60318 Frankfurt am Main, Germany *tel:* +49 69 597 1479 *also fax.* Wolfgang Fahrenholtz, dir. *Artist representation.*

Konzertagentur Ingrid Hellmann. Birnenweg 12, D-06112 Halle/Saale, Germany *tel:* +49 345 560 3041 *fax:* +49 345 560 3654. *Artist representation and concert promotion, especially chmbr mus, soloists, orchs and ens.*

Konzertagentur Jörg Hannemann. Husumerstr 16, D-20251 Hamburg, Germany *tel:* +49 40 480 7575 *fax:* +49 40 486 281. Jörg Hannemann. *Artist representation.*

Konzertagentur GmbH Marek Lieberberg. Mörikestrasse 14, 60320 Frankfurt/M, Germany *tel:* +49 69 9562020 *fax:* +49 69 568199 *email:* http://www.mlk.com. *Concert promotion.*

Konzertagentur Matthias Vogt. Kaulbachstr 62, D-80539 München, Germany *tel:* +49 89 391 545 *fax:* +49 89 342 683. Matthias Vogt, proprietor; Boris Orlob, collaborator. *Artist representation and concert promotion; opera and orch tours.*

Konzertbüro Andreas Braun. Sülzgürtel 86, D-5093 Köln 17, Germany *tel:* +49 221 9420 430 *fax:* +49 221 9420 4319. Andreas Braun, dir. *Artist representation for early mus, chmbr mus, soloists, singers, choirs, conductors.*

Konzertbüro Richard Weber. Haupstr 66, D-77652 Offenburg, Germany *tel:* +49 781 72041 *fax:* +49 781 23406 *email:* konzertbuero.weber@

baden-online.de. Irma Weber, mgr. *Artist representation, specialising in Russian folk mus and church mus.*

Konzertdirektion Dr Rudolf Goette. Colonnaden 70, D-20354 Hamburg, Germany *tel:* +49 40 346018 *fax:* +49 40 342715. Hans Werner Funke, mgr dir; Egbert Zinner, mgr. *Artist representation and concert promotion.*

Konzertdirektion Drissen. Postfach 1205, D-55478 Kirchberg, Germany *tel:* +49 6763 2024 *fax:* +49 6763 2061. Stuart Farnborough, mgr. *Artist representation; also orch tours.*

Konzertdirektion Fischer GmbH. Joh-Phil-Palm-Str 21, 73614 Schorndorf, Germany *tel:* +49 71 8160 00-0 *fax:* +49 71 8160 0050. Dieter Fischer. *Artist representation and concert promotion.*

Konzertdirektion Franz Günther Büscher. Postfach 101424, D-69004 Heidelberg, Germany *tel:* +49 6223 40695 *fax:* +49 6223 47135. Franz G Büscher. *Artist representation, especially chamber mus.*

Konzertdirektion Fritz Dietrich. Eckenheimer Landstr 483, D-60435 Frankfurt am Main, Germany *tel:* +49 69 545658/544504 *fax:* +49 69 548 4107. Fritz Dietrich, mgr. *Artist representation.*

Konzert-Direktion Hans Adler. Auguste-Viktoria-Str 64, D-14199 Berlin, Germany *tel:* +49 30 895 9920 *fax:* +49 30 826 3520. Witiko Adler. *Artist representation and concert promotion.*

Konzertdirektion Hans Ulrich Schmid. Schmiedestr 8, D-30159 Hanover, Germany *tel:* +49 511 366 0739/27 *fax:* +49 511 366 0734. Hans Ulrich Schmid, chmn; Cornelia Schmid, mgr dir. *Artist representation and orch tours.*

Konzertdirektion Heinz Bertsch. Berg-gasse 62, 72762 Reutlingen, Germany *tel:* +49 71 212 2799. Heinz Bertsch. *Concert promotion.*

Konzertdirektion Jürgen Erlebach. Grillparzerstr 24, D-22085 Hamburg, Germany *tel:* +49 40 229 3059; +49 171 640 2980 *fax:* +49 40 227 9661; +49 40 220 9896. Jürgen Erlebach. *Artist representation.*

Konzertdirektion Karsten Janke. Hallerstrasse 72, 20146 Hamburg, Germany *tel:* +49 40 414788-0 *fax:* +49 40 443597. Karsten Janke, mgr dir; Hauke Tedsen, head of artists booking; Matthias Boensel, head of classic mkt. *Concert and tour promotion.*

Konzertdirektion Kurt Collien. Spielbudenplatz 29/30, 20359 Hamburg, Germany *tel:* +49 40 313901/2 *fax:* +49 40 3191919. Kurt Collien; Michael K Collien, mgr. *Concert promotion.*

Konzertdirektion Meuer. Geislinger Weg 28, D-89522 Heidenheim, Germany *tel:* +49 7321 55 381 *also fax.* Martha Munz. *Concert promotion.*

Konzertdirektion Rainer Haas. Postfach 1240, D-69247 Schonau b Heidelberg, Germany *tel:* +49 6228 1375 *fax:* +49 6228 8455. *Artist representation for soloists and chmbr mus.*

Konzertdirektion Rosemarie und Dr Herbert Tobischek. Schiefenberg 34, D-45239 Essen, Germany *tel:* +49 201 840 5175 *fax:* +49 201 840 5176. *Artist representation for conductors, soloists, singers, chmbr mus and orch.*

Kulturbüro Köln. Engelbertstr 32, D-50674 Küln, Germany *tel:* +49 221 240 3133 *fax:* +49 221 240 3247. Jürgen Ruppert, dir. *Artist representation, especially music theatre.*

Künstler Sekretariat am Gasteig. Rosenheimer Str 52, D-81669 München, Germany *tel:* +49 89 482086 *fax:* +49 89 448 9522. Elisabeth Söling-Ehlers, Lothar Schacke, dirs. *Artist representation.*

Künstlersekretariat Astrid Schoerke. Mönckebergallee 41, D-30453 Hanover, Germany *tel:* +49 511 401048/49 *fax:* +49 511 407435. Astrid Schoerke, dir. *Artist representation for conductors, chmbr mus ens and instrumentalists.*

Künstlersekretariat Rolf Sudbrack. Gösselkoppel 54a, D-22339 Hamburg, Germany *tel:* +49 405 382165 *fax:* +49 405 387220. Rolf Sudbrack, chief exec offr. *Artist representation, specialising in chmbr mus.*

Künstlersekretariat Stefan Trhal. Loehrkamp 7, D-30900 Wedemark, Germany *tel:* +49 5130 7473 *fax:* +49 5130 8342. *Artist representation and concert promotion; also orch tours.*

La Vergne Verlag und Musikproduktion. Ulvenbergstr 16, D-64297 Darmstadt, Germany *tel:* +49 6151 57761 *fax:* +49 6151 594332. Pasal Amann, gen mgr. *Artist representation and concert promotion.*

Lothar Stein Management. Am Rothenbüsch 3, D-66113 Saarbrücken, Germany *tel:* +49 681 73854 *fax:* +49 681 730165. *Artist representation.*

Lothar Wolfgang Theater u Konzertdirektion. Bismarckstr 6, D-14109 Berlin, Germany *tel:* +49 30 803 8506 *fax:* +49 30 803 7351. *Concert promotion.*

Marguerite Kollo Bühnenvermittlung. Mehringdamm 69, D-10961 Berlin, Germany *tel:* +49 30 693 2062 *fax:* +49 30 692 7747. *Artist representation, especially opera.*

Michael Herrmann Konzert & Künstleragentur. Thorwaldsenanlage 74, Postfach 3033, D-65195, Wiesbaden, Germany *tel:* +49 611 599998 *fax:* +49 611 599895. *Artist representation.*

Monika Bundschu Opern und Konzertagentur. Tal 15, D-80331 München, Germany *tel:* +49 89 2916 1663 *fax:* +49 89 2916 1667. *Artist representation.*

Music Circus Concertbüro GmbH. Charlottenplatz 17, 70173 Stuttgart, Germany *tel:* +49 7 1122 1105 *fax:* +49 7 1129 2705. Hans-Peter Haag, dir. *Concert promotion.*

Nentwig Internationale Musikagentur. Freiherr vom Steinstr 1, D-63526 Erlensee, Germany *tel:* +49 6183 3087 *fax:* +49 6183 74339. Dieter Nentwig, mgr. *Represents jazz artists and gospel choirs.*

Norddeutsche Konzertdirektion Melsine Grevesmühl. Postfach 310265, D-27538 Bremerhaven, Germany *tel:* +49 471 88068 *fax:* +49 471 88060. *Artist representation and concert promotion, specialising in ballet companies.*

Ocklenburg, Guenter. Hartungstr 15, D-20146 Hamburg, Germany *tel:* +49 40 418656 *fax:* +49 40 4104668. Guenter Ocklenburg; Wolfgang Schmitt. *Representation for opera singers.*

Opernagentur Inge Tennigkeit. Ottweilerstr 22, D-40476 Düsseldorf, Germany *tel:* +49 211 466750 *fax:* +49 211 463702. Inge Tennigkeit. *Artist representation for opera singers.*

Opernagentur Lore Blümel. Postfach 1725, D-82159 Gräfelfing, Germany *tel:* +49 89 859 3864 *fax:* +49 89 859 3759. Lore Blümel. *Artist representation.*

Paradise Media. Schwibbogengasse 27a, D-86150 Augsburg, Germany *tel:* +49 821 33336 *fax:* +49 821 33309 *email:* paradise@t.online.de. Hubert G. Fell. *Artist management and PR.*

pARThenon. Bismarckstr 105, D-90491 Nurnberg, Germany *tel:* +49 911 598 0849 *also fax; email:* schauspiel@nuernberg. Thomas Parr, dir. *Management and marketing for theatre, dance and music.*

PMI (Paradise Management International). Postfach 2180, D-63243 Neu-Isenburg, Germany *tel:* +49 610 252696 *fax:* +49 610 252696. R Klug, mgr dir. *Artist representation and concert promotion.*

Podium Ahrensburg Konzertburo. Ahrensfelder Weg 32a, D-22927 Grosshansdorf, Germany *tel:* +49 41 02 61781 *fax:* +49 41 02 61997. Klaus Hartmann. *Artist representation and concert promotion.*

PR2 Classic. Kreuznacherstr 63, D-50968 Köln, Germany *tel:* +49 221 381063 *fax:* +49 221 383955. Gabriele Schiller, dir; Ulrike Jessel, Eva Luise Roth, assts. *Artist representation and PR.*

Rafael Concerts GmbH. Frauenberg 4, 97980 Bad-Mergentheim, Germany *tel:* +49 79 3197 90 0 *fax:* +49 79 3197 90 20. Rafael Brown, mgr dir; Corinna Mehrer, Ilona Schmiel, project mgrs. *Concert promotion for opera.*

Reinald Heissler-Remy Theater Agentur. Drakestr 2, PO Box 110931, D-40545 Düsseldorf, Germany *tel:* +49 211 578051 *fax:* +49 211 553498. Reinald Heissler-Remy; Neill Thornborrow, asst. *Artist representation, especially opera.*

Roschlau, Edith. Agentur für Musiktheater und Konzert, Samuel-Schmidt-Str 7, D-96450 Coburg, Germany *tel:* +49 9561 37146 *fax:* +49 9561 32549. *Artist representation*

Shooter Promotions and Classics GmbH. Gartenstr 6, D-60594 Franfurt am Main, Germany *tel:* +49 69 6109390 *fax:* +49 69 61093988 *email:* shooterpromotions@t-online.de. Willi Engelhorn, mgr dir; Christa Wenzl, tour co-ordinator. *Artist representation and concert promotion, especially ballet and dance.*

Sigrid Rostock. Eugen Schönhaarstr 1, D-10407 Berlin, Germany *tel:* +49 30 425 7514 *fax:* +49 30 423 9136. *Artist representation for singers.*

Sonia Simmenauer Impresariat. Folkenried 7, D-20251 Hamburg, Germany *tel:* +49 40 42313111 *fax:* +49 40 42313113. Sonia Simmenauer; Swantje Baxmann. *Artist representation; especially string quartets.*

Südwestdeutsche Konzertdirektion Erwin Russ. Charlottenplatz 17, D-70173 Stuttgart, Germany *tel:* +49 711 163 5311/6 *fax:* +49 711 163 5330. Michael Russ, chief exec offr. *Artist representation and concert promotion.*

Theater und Concertagentur. Orlandostr 8, D-80331 München, Germany *tel:* +49 89 290 4766 *fax:* +49 89 290 4765. Lydia Storle. *Artist representation.*

Theater und Konzertagentur Hermann and Astrid G Winkler. Grillparzerstr 46, D-81675 München, Germany *tel:* +49 89 470 5857 *fax:* +49 89 470 7123. *Artist representation.*

Theateragentur Dr Carl F Jickeli. Nymphenburgerstr 62, D-80335 München, Germany *tel:* +49 89 12 392626 *fax:* +49 89 12 392627. *Artist representation for singers and conductors.*

Theateragentur Glado von May. Steinweg 4, D-60313 Frankfurt am Main, Germany *tel:* +49 69 283347 *fax:* +49 69 295513. Glado von May, head. *Representation of singers (opera and concert), and conductors.*

Theateragentur Hannagret Bueker. Fuhsestr 2, D-30419 Hannover, Germany *tel:* +49 511 271 6910 *fax:* +49 511 271 7873. Hannagret Bueker. *Artist representation and concert promotion.*

Theateragentur Luisa Petrov. Glauburgstr 95, D-60318 Frankfurt am Main, Germany *tel:* +49 69 597 0377 *fax:* +49 69 597 4808. Luisa Petrov. *Artist representation, especially opera.*

Theateragentur Werner Kühnly. Wörthstr 31, D-70563, Stuttgart, Germany *tel:* +49 711 780 2764 *fax:* +49 711 780 4403. Herta Kühnly,

mgr; Vermi Tlerin. *Artist representation for opera and concert singers and conductors.*

Theateragentur Wolfgang Stoll. Mitarbeiter Karl-Erich Haase, Martiusstr 3, 80802 München, Germany *tel:* +49 89 333 162 *fax:* +49 89 342 674. Karl-Erich Haase. *Artist representation.*

Tourneemanagement Berlin. Immanuelkirchstr 5, D-10405 Berlin, Germany *tel:* +49 30 441 5299 *also fax.* Lutz-Rainer Seidel. *Artist representation.*

Volker Schmidt-Gertenbach. Charlottenstr 53155, D-10117 Berlin, Germany *tel:* +49 30 891 6016 *fax:* +49 30 893 1133. *Artist representation.*

ZBF Agentur Berlin. Ordensmeisterstr 15, D-12099 Berlin, Germany *tel:* +49 30 757600 *fax:* +49 30 75 760249.

ZBF Agentur Hamburg. Mittelweg 41, D-20148 Hamburg, Germany *tel:* +49 40 414 7970 *fax:* +49 40 445593. Harald Axtner, chief dir; Bettina Reith, asst dir. *Artist representation for musicians working in the theatre.*

ZBF Agentur Leipzig. Schillerweg 34a, D-04155 Leipzig, Germany *tel:* +49 341 5 80880 *fax:* +49 341 5 5808850.

ZBF Agentur München. Leopoldstr 19, D-80802 München, Germany *tel:* +49 89 38 17070 *fax:* +49 89 38 170738.

Zentrale Bühnen-, Fernseh- und Filmvermittlung (ZBF) General-agentur Frankfurt am Main. Feuerbachstr 42-46, D-60325 Frankfurt am Main, Germany *tel:* +49 69 711 1348 *fax:* +49 69 711 1592.

Greece

Lavris Ltd, Cultural Events Agency. 3 Marasli St, GR-106 76 Athens, Greece *tel:* +30 1 72 58510 *fax:* +30 1 72 58513 *email:* lavris@hol.gr. Georgia Iliopoulou, mgr dir. *Artist representation and concert promotion, specialising in contemporary mus and dance, jazz and street theatre as well as classical mus.*

Petros Linardos Concert Management. Mesogion 501, GR-153 43 Ag Paraskevi, Greece *tel:* +30 1 600 4417 *fax:* +30 1 601 1544 *email:* plinar @compulink.gr. *Artist representation and event management.*

PIA Agency (Promote International Arts). 15 Amerikis Str, GR-106 72 Athens, Greece *tel:* +30 1 362 6274 *fax:* +30 1 361 9373. Pia Hadjinikos-Angelini, dir; Elpida Temarel, sec. *Concert promotion.*

Hungary

Budapest Artists Management. Somlói ut 39, H-1118 Budapest, Hungary *tel:* +36 1 186 6790 *also fax.* Ildikó Gedényi, dir. *Artist representation for conductors, soloists and chamber mus.*

Clemens Concerts Ltd. Attila út 61, H-1013 Budapest, Hungary *tel:* +36 1 212 20 45/+36 20 345 823 *fax:* +36 1 175 81 62. Pál Kelemen, dir; Adam Bikfalvy, mgr. *Artist representation and concert promotion.*

Gergely Arts Ltd. Hollán Erno u 25 I/1, H-1136 Budapest, Hungary *tel:* +36 1 129 4064 *also fax;* +36 1 270 0846. Mária Gergely, mgr dir; Erzsebet Nemeth, mgr. *Artist representation.*

Hungarokoncert Oszk. Városligeti fasor 38, H-1068 Budapest, Hungary *tel:* +36 1 322 0641 *fax:* +36 1 322 5412. László Szirmai, dir; D A Starnfeld, Ferenc Szénási, impresarios. *Artist representation and concert promotion.*

Interkoncert Budapest Arts Corp. Vorosmarty tér 1, H-1051 Budapest, Hungary *tel:* +36 1 118 4542 *fax:* +36 1 118 4767 *email:* corp@ interconcert.alba.hu; http://www.alba.hu/interconcert. Zoltán Sa'nta, gen mgr. *Artist representation and concert promotion, including festivals, folk mus and dance.*

Pentaton Artists & Concerts Management Ltd. Rákóczi ut 65, H-1081 Budapest, Hungary *tel:* +36 1 133 2337 *fax:* +36 1 133 2075. Zsófia Zimányi; György Lörinlzy, exec dir. *Artist representation and concert promotion, including opera and music theatre.*

Premier Theatre and Music Agency. Premier Bt, Kossuth L Sgt 27, H-6722 Szeged, Hungary *tel:* +36 62 482518 *also fax. Artist representation and concert promotion, including operetta and theatre.*

Sotto Voce. József A sgt 67/A, H-6723 Szeged, Hungary *tel:* +36 62 486764 *also fax.* Ervin Bonecz, gen mgr; Mrs Istvánné. *Represents, promotes and develops the careers of young and talented artists. Organises masterclasses.*

India

Bombay Madrigal Singers' Organisation. Oak Chambers, 9 Oak La, Fort, Bombay 400023, India *tel:* +91 22 267 4218 *fax:* +91 22 265 6556. Adi B Sagar, hon sec. *Presentation of artists and concerts.*

Israel

Ambassador Enterprise. 2 Tnuat Hameri St, 55286 Kiryat Ono, Israel *tel:* +972 3 635 3418 *fax:* +972 3 535 2726. Roni Abramson, mgr dir.

Artis Ltd. 17 Ben Yehuda St, 63802 Tel Aviv, Israel *tel:* +972 3 517 0605/9025 *fax:* +972 3 516 0045. Pinhas Postel. *Concert promotion for opera, ballet, classical music and jazz.*

Bloch Artists Management Inc (Israel). POB 261, Sha'a Rei, Tikvah, PN Efraim, Israel 44810 *tel:* +972 3 936 3114 *fax:* +972 3 936 3275 *email:* ileneblo@netmedia.net.il. Joel Bloch, dir; Bernard Margolis, mgr asst. *Artist representation for vocalists, opera and oratorio singers.*

Ruth Shahar Concert Management. 16 Sapir St, 64359 Tel Aviv, Israel *tel:* +972 3 528 7975/7968 *fax:* +972 3 528 8382 *email:* r-s-c-h@netvision.net.il. Ruth Shahar, gen dir. *Artist representation and concert promotion.*

Shmuel Zemach. 108 Dizengof St, 64397 Tel Aviv, Israel *tel:* +972 3 524 7722 *fax:* +972 3 527 9967. *Artist representation and concert promotion.*

Italy

ACOM - Organizzione Concertistica Internazionale. Piazza Buonarroti 29, I-20149 Milano, Italy *tel:* +39 2 4800 1924 *also fax;* +39 2 460636 *email:* conacom@mbox.vol/it; http://www.vol.it/concertacom. Luigi La Pegna, owner. *Artist representation.*

AMP - Artists' Management and Productions. Corso di Porta Romana 122, I-20122 Milano, Italy *tel:* +39 2 5831 4791 *fax:* +39 2 5831 4661. Ettore F Volontieri, mgr dir; Fiorenza Scholey, asst. *Artist representation for singers, conductors and soloists.*

Artists Management Company. Via Marconi 3, I-37060 Castel d'Azzano-Verona, Italy *tel:* +39 45 852 0718 *fax:* +39 45 852 0434 *email:* amc@amcmusic.com. Franco Pio Panozzo. *Artist representation for soloists and orchs.*

Associazione Musica Libera. Via Ciro Menotti 147, I-61100 Pesaro, Italy *tel:* +39 721 414341 *also fax; email:* musicalibera@eventosuono.it; http://www.eventosuono.it. Paolo Giaro, artistic dir; Antonio Cioffi, co-dir. *Festival promotion for world mus and jazz.*

Change Performing Art. Via V Monti 12, I-20123 Milano, Italy *tel:* +39 2 4819 4494 *fax:* +39 2 4819 5178. Franco Laera, president; Yasunori Gunji, dir. *Artist representation.*

Concerto Management. Via Roma 107, I-84084 Fisciano (SA), Italy *tel:* +39 89 958565 *fax:* +39 89 891819. Teresa Tortora, mgr dir; Domenico Spetrini, artistic dir. *Artist representation, especially for orchs, chamber ens and soloists.*

Dell'Amore Management. Via Zeffirino Re 2c, I-47023 Cesena (Forlí), Italy *tel:* +39 547 611690 *fax:* +39 547 25895 *email:* amor@linknet.it. Franco Dell'Amore, artistic dir; Carla Dell'Amore, admin. *Artist representation and concert promotion for early mus, world mus and contemporary mus.*

Dradi, Mario. Via Irnerio 12/4, I-40126 Bologna, Italy *tel:* +39 51 253030/253132 *fax:* +39 51 252726. Mario Dradi, head; Irene Gall, asst. *Artist representation for opera singers and conductors; some concert promotion.*

Fedeli Opera International di Virginio Fedeli, Roberto Gherardi e Giorgio Bruno. Via Montegrappa 3, I-40121 Bologna, Italy *tel:* +39 51 232169/264056 *fax:* +39 51 230766. Virginio Fedeli, Roberto Gherardi, Giorgio Bruno, mgrs; Marta Bellini, Serena Marchi, Elisa Marchi, asst mgrs. *Artist representation of opera singers and conductors.*

Girard, Elisa. Via Luciano Manara 57, I-00153 Roma, Italy *tel:* +39 6 589 9479 *fax:* +39 6 581 0245. Laura Donati, tour mgr; Gaia Girarol, asst. *Artist representation.*

Grompone, Aldo 195 Via Giulia, I-00186 Roma, Italy *tel:* +39 6 687 6495 *fax:* +39 6 686 4605. Alessandra Ferrando, asst. *Production and promotion for theatre, contemporary mus and dance.*

IBA Promotions. Via Bergognone 27, I-20144 Milano, Italy *tel:* +39 2 5810 3583 *fax:* +39 2 5810 0149 *email:* ibapromo@mbox.vol.it. Piero Massari, mgr dir. *Artist representation.*

Italartist SaS di Giulia Frosi & C. Via Museo 33, I-39100 Bolzano, Italy *tel:* +39 471 981 143 *fax:* +39 471 980 041. Giulia Frosi, mgr; Elisabetta Hartl, asst mgr. *Artist representation for singers, conds and orchs.*

IUMA Management. Via Emanuele Filiberto 125, I-00185 Roma, Italy *tel:* +39 6 7045 2328/7003 3766 *fax:* +39 6 7720 5607. Chris F Catena, gen artist mgr. *Artist representation and concert promotion, especially for operas, concerts and ballet.*

Laifer Artists International. Via Maddalena 45/c, I-37138 Verona, Italy *tel:* +39 45 562950 *also fax. Artist representation.*

Luigi Pignotti SrL Promotional Culture Consulting. Via Ponte Seveso 39, I-20125 Milano, Italy *tel:* +39 2 6707 5204/7 *fax:* +39 2 6707 4310. *Artist representation.*

Music Center SnC di Giuseppe Oldani & Co. Viale Legioni Romane 26, I-20147 Milano, Italy *tel:* +39 2 4870 2828/0258 *fax:* +39 2 4870 0692. *Artist representation.*

Musical Dorica. Castella Postale nr 29, I-60021 Camerano (An), Italy *tel:* +39 71 801181 *fax:* +39 71 801235. Silvano Frontalini. *Artist representation and concert promotion, especially lyric opera, ballet and orch.*

ORIA di Maria Bruzzese, Denise Petriccione. Via Cimarosa 26, I-20144 Milano, Italy *tel:* +39 2 466216/4071281 *fax:* +39 2 466238. Maria Bruzzese, Denise Petriccione, partners. *Artist representation.*

Ornella Cogliolo. Via del Babuino 76, I-00187 Roma, Italy *tel:* +39 6 320 7627 *fax:* +39 6 320 7628 *email:* cogliolo@eut.it/pwd; http://www.eurotrade.it/cogliolo. Manuela Baroncini; Antonia Tessitore. *Artist representation.*

OSCAR - Agenzia Spettacoli Musicali. Via Martiri della Liberta 16, Postbox 1, I-47023 Cesena (FO), Italy *tel:* +39 547 29175 *also fax.* Alieto Pieri. *Artist representation.*

Ouverture di Orta Leonardo & C sas. Via Bracciancse Claudia 44 Km 20, I-00062 Bracciano (Roma), Italy *tel:* +39 6 998 6602 *fax:* +39 6 998 6603. Marzia Maramici, asst; Franziska Kurth. *Artist representation for opera singers and conductors.*

Preludio. Via Paolo Martini 38H, I-40134 Bologna, Italy *tel:* +39 51 614 2295 *also fax.* Daniela Berti; Alessandra Scheda. *Artist representation.*

Propoganda Musicale SRL. Via Po 43, I-00198 Roma, Italy *tel:* +39 6 884 2218/2221 *fax:* +39 6 884 2222. Sonia Quercia; Adelano Manfrini. *Artist representation.*

Resia. Via Manzoni 31, I-20121 Milano, Italy *tel:* +39 2 654161/2/3/4 *fax:* +39 2 659 7851 *email:* resiasrl@mbox.vol.it; http://www.vol.it/concorsomicheli/. Patrizia Garrasi, Luisa Panarello, partners. *Artist representation.*

Ricercare. Progetti Artistici Internazionali. Via E Filberto 4, I-20052 Monza, Italy *tel:* +39 39 744703 *fax:* +39 39 744797 *email:* ricercar@askesis.it. Gabriella Castelli, dir; Kim Sommerschield, dir. *Artist representation; specialising in early music.*

Sofia Amman. Piazzetta Bossi 1, I-20121 Milano, Italy *tel:* +39 2 869 3316 *fax:* +39 2 864 64751. *Artist representation; will not accept new artists.*

Stage Door Srl di Angelo Gabrielli. Via Scaglia Est 134, I-41100 Modena, Italy *tel:* +39 59 342135 *fax:* +39 59 343685 *email:* stgdoor@mbox.vol.it. Daniela Barbieri; Angelo Gabrielli. *Artist representation.*

Thomas Arndt - International Management. Via Rubattino 6/6, I-00153 Roma, Italy *tel:* +39 6 57 83 784 *fax:* +39 6 57 42 888. Thomas Arndt.

Trident Agency. Via Lentasio 7, I-20122 Milano, Italy *tel:* +39 2 5830 3311 *fax:* +39 2 5830 3170. Maurizio Salvadori, pres. *Artist representation.*

Walter Beloch Artists Management SrL. Via Melzi d'Eril 26, I-20154 Milano, Italy *tel:* +39 2 33 101922/101605 *fax:* +39 2 33 13643 *email:* belochartists@iol.it. Walter Beloch, president; Marcus Carl, Paola Comerio, opera mgrs. *Artist representation.*

Japan

Allegro Music Tokyo Inc. 7-17-20-502 Roppongi, Minato-ku, Tokyo 106, Japan *tel:* +81 3 3403 5871 *fax:* +81 3 3403 5721. Kazuhiko Ogawa, mgr dir. *Artist representation; concert promotion for early mus.*

Camerata Tokyo. Aoyama Ten-X 8F, 5-50-6 Jingumae, Shibuya-ku, Tokyo 150, Japan *tel:* +81 3 3498 5890 *fax:* +81 3 3498 6239. Hiroshi Isaka, president. *Artist representation and concert promotion.*

Japan Arts Corp. 2-1-6 Shibuya, Shibuya-ku, Tokyo 150, Japan *tel:* +81 3 3499 8090 *fax:* +81 3 3499 8092. Yasuo Nakato, chmn; Masayuki Sekita, president. *Artist representation and concert promotion.*

Japan Orchestral Society Ltd. 4F Cl-Building, 1-3-6 Ebisu-minami, Shibuya-ku, Tokyo 150, Japan *tel:* +81 3 5721 4621 *fax:* +81 3 5721 4624. Hiroshi Kobayashi, chmn. *Artists' agent and concert promoter, specialising in orchs, chmbr orchs and soloists.*

Japan Performing Arts Foundation. 5-1-20 Yakumo, Meguro-ku, Tokyo 152, Japan *tel:* +81 3 3725 8000 *fax:* +81 3 3718 0858. Tadatsugu Sasaki, exec dir. *Concert promotion for mus, opera, ballet and other performing arts.*

Kajimoto Concert Management Company Ltd. Kahoku Building, 8-6-25 Ginza, Chuo-ku, Tokyo 104, Japan *tel:* +81 3 3574 0969 *fax:* +81 3 3574 0980. Naoyasu Kajimoto, chmn; Masahide Kajimoto, president. *Artist representation and concert promotion, specialising in international classical artists, ens and orchs requiring representation in Japan.*

Kambara Music Office Ltd. Urban Life Building, Room 101, 9-2-14 Akasaka, Minato-ku, Tokyo 107, Japan *tel:* +81 3 3403 8011 *fax:* +81 3 3479 6577. Yoshiro Kambara, president; Masahiro Nishizawa, dir. *Artist representation and concert promotion for orchs, chmbr ens, insts and singers, ballet and flamenco dance.*

Million Concert Company Ltd. No 2 Mori Building, 1-10-8 Nishi Shimbashi, Minato-Ku, Tokyo 105, Japan *tel:* +81 3 3501 5638 *fax:* +81 3 3501 5620. Akira Obi, president. *Artist representation, concert promotion and management.*

Music-Culture Enterprises Centre. Castle-River 5F, 5-11 Tanimichi, 1-Chome, Chuo-ku, Osaka 540, Japan *tel:* +81 6 443 1350 *fax:* +81 6 443 7777. Hiroshi Nishio, president. *Artist representation and concert promotion.*

Nippon Artists Management Inc. 2-11-16-502 Kanda Surugadai, Chiyoda-ku, Tokyo 101, Japan *tel:* +81 3 3293 1951 *fax:* +81 3 3293 1960 *email:* namiarts@mxd.meshnet.or.jp. Yusuke Terada. *Artist representation and concert promotion.*

Noah Corp Ltd. Shinjuku-ku Shimoochial 1-5-10-1011, Tokyo 161, Japan *tel:* +81 3 53 86 7000 *fax:* +81 3 52 86 7060.

Ohba Ongaku Jimusho (Ohba Music Promotion). 3516 Hisaishi, Kugino-mura, Aso-gun, Kumamoto 869-14, Japan *tel:* +81 9676 7 2611 *fax:* +81 9676 7 2062. Teruko Ohba, president. *Concert promotion.*

Sautille Company Ltd. Music Office, 2-11-19 Jingumae, Shibuya-ku, Tokyo 150, Japan *tel:* +81 3 3470 2727 *fax:* +81 3 3470 2740. Takao Kasahara, exec dir. *Artist representation and concert promotion; especially baroque and gui mus.*

Station Co Ltd. 201 Sakuma Bldg, 11 Araki-Cho, Shinjuku-Ku, Tokyo 160, Japan *tel:* +81 3 3358 1901 *fax:* +81 3 3353 4830 *email:* lh1m-tmr@ asahi-net.or.jp; http://www2.infoweb.or.jp/paja/presenter/index-e.html. Mitso Tamura. *Concert promotion.*

Korea

Fine Artists Management. 219-8 Pulkwang-dong, Eunpyong-ku, Seoul 122-041, Korea *tel:* +82 2 353 7538 *fax:* +82 2 358 6074 *email:* fam 410@nownuri.nowcom.co.kr. Chung Hoon-sang Thomas, president. *Artist representation and concert promotion.*

Joong-ang Ilbo Management. 7 Soonhwa-dong, Choong-ku, Seoul, Korea *tel:* +82 2 751 9610 *fax:* +82 2 751 9640. Jin-Seok Han, dir. *Concert promotion.*

Michooholl Artists Management Inc. Buwon Building 403, Puahm-dong 175-1, Chongro-gu, Seoul, Korea *tel:* +82 2 391 2822 *fax:* +82 2 391 4623. Kyung-Wha Jun, president.

Pakos Enterprise. 3F Pakos B/D, 116-1 Yong Kang-Dong, Mapo-Ku, Seoul 120-070, Korea *tel:* +82 2 706 5858 *fax:* +82 2 715 2478 *email:* pakos@gmk.co.kr; peterpark@gmk.co.kr. Peter K Park, president. *Artist representation and concert promotion for Korean artists. Record company.*

Latvia

Baltic Concerts Ltd. Strelnieku iela 9, LV-1010 Riga, Latvia *tel:* +371 783 0501 *also fax.* Gatis Darzins, exec dir. *Artist representation and concert promotion.*

Liechtenstein

Artists Management Company Est. Postfach 1131, Austrasse 1, FL-9490 Vaduz, Liechtenstein *tel:* +41 75 232 1444 *fax:* +45 75 232 2085. Andreas von Bennigsen, dir; Daniel Zulauf, co-dir. *Artist representation and concert promotion specialising in orch tours.*

Lithuania

Concert Agency Partitura. Asigalio 21-10, 3043 Kaunas, Lithuania *tel:* +370 7 227500/722726 *fax:* +370 7 227500. Jonas Jucas, dir. *Artist representation and concert promotion.*

Touring Concert Company Arks. PO Box 1272, 2056 Vilnius, Lithuania *tel:* +370 2 629460 *fax:* +370 2 626989. Arunas Simaska, dir; Romualdas Kondrotas, concert mgr. *Concert promotion.*

Luxembourg

SARL Mauroy. 13 Rue des Primevères, L-2351, Luxembourg *tel:* +352 459490 *also fax.* Jacques Mauroy; Marianne Gérard. *Artist representation.*

Mexico

Conciertos Daniel. Av Horacio 1725-PH, 11510 México D F, Mexico *tel:* +52 5 280 5592 *fax:* +52 5 280 9477. Ernesto De Quesada, mgr; Janine de Quesada, mgr. *Artist representation.*

Conciertos Guadalajara AC. Av Jaurez 638 Altos, Ex Convento del Carmen, 44100 Guadalajara, Jalisco, Mexico *tel:* +52 36 132024. Teresa Casillas, dir; Martha Gonzalez de Hernandez Allande, dir. *Concert promotion.*

London Artists. Santisimo 27, Col San Angel, 01000 México D F, Mexico *tel:* +52 5 550 9449 *also fax.* Michael Emmerson, dir. *Artist representation and concert promotion.*

Monaco

Bureau de Concerts Pierre-Edouard Ornella. 49 Rue Plati, 98000 Monte-Carlo, Monaco *tel:* +377 93 15 04 44 *fax:* +377 93 15 94 84. Pierre-Edouard Ornella, dir. *Artist representation and concert promotion.*

Vivienne H Taylor. Le Soleil D'Or, 20 Blvd Prince Rainier III, Monte-Carlo, Monaco *tel:* +33 93 15 03 81; +33 6 07 93 16 47 *fax:* +33 93 25 62 51 *email:* vtaylor@monaco.com. *Personal representation.*

Netherlands

Amstel Artists Muziek Produkties. Ruysdaelkade 155 hs, NL-1072 AS Amsterdam, Netherlands *tel:* +31 20 664 4865 *fax:* +31 20 676 3706. Jelle Kikkert. *Artist representation.*

Ariëtte F C Drost Artists Representative. Prins Bernhardweg 18, NL-6862 ZH Oosterbeek, Netherlands *tel:* +31 26 339 0187 *fax:* +31 26

334 1349. Ariëtte Drost, dir. *Artist representation, especially singers; opera, oratorio, orch and chmbr mus concerts.*

Artivis. Escamplaan 555, NL-2547 EC Den Haag, Netherlands *tel:* +31 70 323 4403 *also fax.* Ferdinand Visser, dir. *Artist representation.*

CNM Centrum Nederlandse Muziek. PO Box 1634, NL-1200 BP Hilversum, Netherlands *tel:* +31 35 6240 957 *fax:* +31 35 6210 570 *email:* cnm@pi.net. J W ten Broeke, mgr dir. *Promotion of Dutch classical music.*

Concertdirectie Samama BV. Weteringschans 130, NL-1017 XV Amsterdam, Netherlands *tel:* +31 20 421 1611 *fax:* +31 20 421 1747. Niels Veenhuijzen, mgr dir. *Artist representation and concert promotion.*

Concertmanagement Rob Groen. W G Plein 206, NL-1054 SE Amsterdam, Netherlands *tel:* +31 20 616 8096 *fax:* +31 20 616 9652. Rob Groen, mgr dir.

Euro Stage. Lijnbaansgracht 292-11, NL-1017 RM Amsterdam, Netherlands *tel:* +31 20 620 6556 *fax:* +31 20 623 7951. Peter Ultee, mgr dir. *Concert promotion especially opera, classical ballet and African mus.*

Herzberger Artists. 't Woud 1, NL-3862 PM Nijkerk, Netherlands *tel:* +31 342 472255 *fax:* +31 342 475275. Marianne Herzberger, dir. *Artist representation.*

Impresariaat Jacques Senf & Partners. PO Box 42, NL-3155 ZG Maasland, Netherlands *tel:* +31 1059 23155 *fax:* +31 1059 15159. Jacques Senf, dir. *Artist representation; shows, musicals, opera, concerts and ballet.*

Impresariaat John de Crane. Rijperwaard 46, NL-1824 JJ Alkmaar, Netherlands *tel:* +31 72 625300 *fax:* +31 72 622440. Marga Wagenaar, dir; Sonia Veel, asst. *Concert promotion and representation of pianists.*

Impulse Art Management. Singel 308-Sous, NL-1016 AE Amsterdam, Netherlands *tel:* +31 20 626 6944 *fax:* +31 20 622 7118. Martijn Jacobus, dir. *Artist representation and concert promotion.*

Interartist Holland BV. Keizersgracht 584, NL-1017 EN Amsterdam, Netherlands *fax:* +31 20 620 9876. Jeannine Salomons, mgr dir. *Artist representation for soloists and conductors; orch tours.*

International Music Productions (IMP). Paviljoensgracht 76, NL-2512 BR Den Haag, Netherlands *tel:* +31 70 363 8778 *fax:* +31 70 360 8114 *email:* musicimp@pi.net. Michaël Hanekroot; David Blake. *Artist representation.*

International Performing Arts Desk. Lutmastraat 184b, NL-1073 HG Amsterdam, Netherlands *tel:* +31 20 671 0749 *also fax.* *Artist representation and concert promotion for contemporary mus and dance.*

Interpresario. Zeekant 102c, NL-2586 JH Den Haag, Netherlands *tel:* +31 70 354 3411 *fax:* +31 70 355 7265. Kees van Liempt, dir; Lucien Dufais, dir. *Artist representation and concert promotion.*

Ivy Artists bv. PO Box 592, NL-1200 AN Hilversum, Netherlands *tel:* +31 35 6282 270/6233 133 *fax:* +31 35 6236 619. Loes Aalders. *Artist representation and concert promotion.*

Marianne Brinks. Graaf Willemlaan 52, NL-1181 EH Amstelveen, Netherlands *tel:* +31 20 643 2043 *fax:* +31 20 640 3961. *Artist representation and director of Delft Chamber Music Festival.*

Marijke Klinkhamer Artists Management. Willemsparkweg 114, NL-1071 HN Amsterdam, Netherlands *tel:* +31 20 675 4061 *fax:* +31 20 675 4771. Marijke Klinkhamer, dir. *Artist representation.*

Murielle Lucie Clément Company. Postbus 95256, NL-1090 HG Amsterdam, Netherlands *tel:* +31 20 692 8246 *fax:* +31 20 663 5040. *Concert promotion, especially opera productions.*

Nederlands Impresariaat. Paulus Potterstr 12, NL-1071 CZ Amsterdam, Netherlands *tel:* +31 20 573 0300 *fax:* +31 20 675 1206. *Artist representation and concert promotion, especially chmbr mus, jazz and children's concerts.*

The Office Performing Arts Management. Keizersgracht 261, NL-1016 EC Amsterdam, Netherlands *tel:* +31 20 622 6979 *fax:* +31 20 622 9081 *email:* kantoor@euronet.nl. J de Heer; L Schipper. *Specialises in contemporary mus.*

Pieter G Alferink Artists Management. Apollolaan 181, NL-1077 AT Amsterdam, Netherlands *tel:* +31 20 664 3151 *fax:* +31 20 675 2426 *email:* alferink@worldonline.nl. Pieter G Alferink, mgr dir; Helga Blaimschein, associate.

Riaskoff Concert Management. Concertgebouwplein 15, NL-1071 LL Amsterdam, Netherlands *tel:* +31 20 664 5353 *fax:* +31 20 671 5106. Marco Riaskoff, mgr dir; Jeroen Tersteeg, artists mgr. *Artist representation and concert promotion.*

Stadsschouwburg en Concertgebouw De Vereeniging. Postbus 364, 6500 AJ Nijmegen, Netherlands *tel:* +31 024 322 8344 *fax:* +31 024 322 2465 *email:* schouwburg.nijmegen@inter.nl.net; http://www.dunamis. nl/schouwburg. Sandor Joó, gen dir. *Concert promotion.*

Supierz Artist Management. Linnaeus-serre 17, NL-3823 DL Amersfoort, Netherlands *tel:* +31 33 455 5656 *fax:* +31 33 455 5433 *email:* supierz@worldaccess.nl. Zdzislaw Supierz, mgr dir. *Agent and concert promotion for opera, ballet, operetta and folk mus.*

Norway

Impresario A/S. Tollbugata 3, N-0152 Oslo, Norway *tel:* +47 22 426379 *fax:* +47 22 332238. Vibeke Gottschalk, mgr dir. *Artist representation and concert promotion for orch and ballet.*

Oslo Arts Management. Den Gamle Logen, Grev Wedels Plass 2, N-1051 Oslo 1, Norway *tel:* +47 22 425350 *fax:* +47 22 426612. Per Boye Hansen, mgr dir; Marit Wathne, artist mgr. *Artist representation for singers, conductors, stage directors and instrumentalists.*

Oslo Konsertdireksjon As. Bjerkebakken 1, N-0756 Oslo, Norway *tel:* +47 22 522 546 *fax:* +47 22 730 103. Ruth Klungsøyr, dir. *Artist representation and concert promotion.*

Pro Arte International Artists Management. Fosswinckelsgt 9, N-5007 Bergen, Norway *tel:* +47 55 319 435 *fax:* +47 55 960 765. Kjell Wernoe, dir. *Artist representation.*

Paraguay

Ruben Franco Producciones. Nuestra Senora de la Asuncion 1155, Asuncion, Paraguay *tel:* +595 21 496548/448820/445169 *fax:* +595 21 442797/27220. Ruben Dario Franco Alcaraz, dir. *Artist representation for conductors and opera singers.*

Phillippines

National Philharmonic Society. MCPO Box 2650, Makati, Metro Manila, Phillippines *tel:* +63 2 817 2601; +63 2 815 2651; +63 2 810 7988 *fax:* +63 2 815 3483. Redentor L Romero, mus dir; Theresa Veloso, concert mgr. *Concert promotion of chosen artists.*

Poland

The Artists Management of the National Theatre. Plac Teatralny 1, PL-00-950, Warszawa, Poland *tel:* +48 22826 3001/7001 ext 282; +48 22 6920755/8267429 *fax:* +48 22826 0423/5012. *Artist representation.*

Classic Management Marek Strasz. Ul Goscincowa 37, PL-05-092 Lomianki, Warszawa, Poland *tel:* +48 82 751 8633 *also fax.* Marek Strasz, president. *Artist representation.*

Concert Agency Rondo. PO Box 77, PL-70334 Szczecin 4, Poland *tel:* +48 91 845242 *fax:* +48 91 846193 *email:* rondo@ubique.com.pl. Jan Szyrocki, mus dir; Stanislaw Zaborowski, mgr dir. *Concert promotion. International Choral Song Festival in Miedyzdroje.*

ESPO Artists Management. ul Pogodna 21 a, k Warszawy, PL-05-077 Wesola, Poland *tel:* +48 22 773 1759 *also fax; email:* espo.art@zigzag. pl. Igor Pogorzelsu, mgr. *Promotes Polish music abroad, especially classical music. Organises concerts, marketing, artists promotion, etc. Specialises in chmbr and symphony orchs.*

Jacek Nedzynski Artists Management. Os Jagiellonskie 12/71, PL-61-227 Poznan, Poland *tel:* +48 61 8765801 *also fax; fax:* +48 61 536947. Jacek Nedzynski, dir. *Artist representation; especially chmbr mus, dance, singers, choirs.*

Music Productions. ul Dereniowa 13-76, PL-02-776 Warszawa, Poland *tel:* +48 22 6410901 *also fax; email:* musicprod@supermedia.pl. Wojciech Nowak, dir. *Concert promotion and classical mus recording.*

Nowak & Szwed Artists Management. Ul Zgoda 12-19, PL-00-012 Warszawa, Poland *tel:* +48 22 8265711; +48 22 8273859 *also fax; fax:* +48 22 641 0901. Wojciech Nowak, Andrzej Szwed, dirs. *Artist representation and concert promotion.*

PWM Artist Management. ul Fredry 8, PL-00-097 Warszawa, Poland *tel:* +48 22 267097 *also fax; fax:* +48 22 269780. Aldona Pruchnicka, gen mgr; Hanna Kozlowska, asst mgr. *Artist representation.*

Warsaw Artists Management Ltd. Kazimierzowska 47/5, PL-02-572 Warszawa, Poland *tel:* +48 602 272115 *fax:* +48 22 487666. Andrzej Haluch, president. *Artist representation and concert promotion.*

Portugal

Interartes-Agencia Artistica de Representacoes Ltd. Avda Marques de Tomar 87, 1st Fl, 1000 Lisboa, Portugal *fax:* +351 1 793 5251. Carlos Pires, gen mgr. *Artist representation.*

Republic of Ireland

International Concert Management. 23 Farmleigh Av, Stillorgan, Co Dublin, Ireland *tel:* +353 1 288 6251 *also fax.* Ashley Pringle, dir. *Artist representation and concert promotion. Local and international touring arrangements for choirs, ens and instrumentalists.*

Young European Strings Promotion Ltd. 21 The Close, Cypress Downs, Dublin 6 W, Republic of Ireland *tel:* +353 1 490 5263 *fax:* +353 1 492 0355 *email:* yes@aol.ie. Maria Kelemen, dir. *Concert promotion.*

Romania

Artexim. Piata Victorei Nr 155, Bl D1 Sc 8 Et 2, 71012 Bucharest, Romania *tel:* +40 1 650 1806/12 *fax:* +40 1 311 0200/659 7523 *email:* artexim@ com.pcnet.ro. Mihai Constantinescu, mgr. *Artist representation and concert promotion.*

Russia

Art Time Corp. 8 Treokhprudny Lane, 103001 Moscow, Russia *tel:* +7 095 209 9414 *fax:* +7 095 209 9417. Svetlana Antyukhina, president. *Artist representation and concert promotion.*

Artistic Association Vivaldi's House. Maly Vlasievsky per 4/1, 121002 Moscow, Russia *tel:* +7 095 244 0653 *also fax.* Vladimir Youriev, dir. *Concert promotion.*

Concert Agency Russian Philharmonic Society. ul B Nikitskaya 14/2, 103009 Moscow, Russia *tel:* +7 095 290 0001; +7 095 229 5905 *also fax.* Sergey Usanov, president. *Artist representation for soloists, instrumentalists, vocalists, chamber orchs, symphony orchs, choirs and dancers.*

Duo Zikr. Zhukovskogo St 19/38, Flat 1, St Petersburg 191014, Russia *tel:* +7 812 279 5983 *fax:* +7 812 279 5650. Vaida Simchoni, asst mgr. *Artist representation.*

Gosconcert. Neglinnaya 15, 103051 Moscow, Russia *tel:* +7 095 921 3578 *fax:* +7 095 288 9588. Panchenko Vladimir, president. *Artist representation and concert promotion.*

Music & Theatre Centre. 26 Bakinsky Komissarov Str 12-3-245, 117526 Moscow, Russia *tel:* +7 095 433 7035 *also fax; fax:* +7 095 238 2260. Andrei Korobeinikov, exec dir. *Artist representation.*

Nectary Music Company Ltd. PO Box #3, 121359 Moscow, Russia *tel:* +7 095 149 9776 *also fax; email:* dr_serge@ore.ru. Svetlana Zharova, mgr; Serge V Drouzhinine, president. *Artist representation and concert promotion, classical and folk.*

ROSInterFest. 12 Sadovaya Triumfalnaya Str, 103006 Moscow, Russia *tel:* +7 095 200 6585 *fax:* +7 095 903 2689. Igor S Gurevich, president, gen mgr; Alexander N Antonov, deputy gen mgr. *Artist representation and concert promotion; also festival organisation.*

Russian State Concert Company (Sodruzhestvo). Arbat 35, 121835 Moscow, Russia *tel:* +7 095 248 3494 *fax:* +7 095 230 2427. Nikolai Butov, producer; Shamil Zakinov, dir.

Sovinart. 18 Murmansky Proezd, App 77, 129075 Moscow, Russia *tel:* +7 095 215 7571 *fax:* +7 095 215 2274 *email:* sovinart.mos@23.relcom.ru. Eilina Tikhomirova, gen dir. *Artist representation.*

Starlet. Nevsky pr 86, Office 96, 191025 St Petersburg, Russia *tel:* +7 812 275 1305 *fax:* +7 812 275 1598. Inga Kutianskaya, gen mgr; Elena Kostiuchenko, art mgr. *Artist representation and concert promotion.*

Zima Concert Agency. PO Box 629, 199053 St Petersburg, Russia *tel:* +7 812 235 5529 *also fax; fax:* +7 812 219 6133 *email:* winter@zima. spb.sn. Nick Winter, dir. *Artist representation and concert promotion.*

Serbia

Sava Centar. Milentija Popovica 9, 11070 Beograd, Serbia *tel:* +381 11 222 2277 *fax:* +381 11 222 1156. George Milutinovic, chief exec. *Concert promotion.*

Slovak Republic

Akord Art Agency. E Culinka, Gessayova 15, 85103 Bratislava, Slovak Republic *tel:* +421 7 815335 *also fax. Artist representation and concert promotion, specialising in br soloists and ens. Also jazz and folk.*

Art Agency Ltd. Nam 1 Maja 7, 81106 Bratislava, Slovak Republic *tel:* +421 7 361451 *fax:* +421 7 361808. *Artist representation.*

Concert Agency Dr Tichy. Clementisova 4, 04022 Kosice, Slovak Republic *tel:* +421 95 717317. *Artist representation; especially pianists and singers.*

Interartists Bratislava. Bajzova 4, 82108 Bratislava, Slovak Republic *tel:* +421 7 526 7170 *also fax.* Jana Kováciková, dir. *Representation for soloists, chmbr mus, choirs and orchs.*

Intermedia. Jakubovo nam 12, 811 09 Bratislava, Slovak Republic *tel:* +421 7 363700/363707 *fax:* +421 7 363296. Peter Horak, gen mgr. *Mainly concert promotion.*

Pip-Art Music Art Agency. Zarnovicka 1, 83106 Bratislava, Slovak Republic *tel:* +421 7 287150 *also fax. Artist representation.*

Slovkoncert - Artists Management. Michalská 10, 81536 Bratislava, Slovak Republic *tel:* +421 7 5334561/5334538 *fax:* +421 7 5332652 *email:* slovkonc@mbox.bts.sk. Marian Lapsansky, dir. *Artist representation and concert promotion.*

Slovenia

Ars Ramovs Institute of Arts Marketing, Promotion and Investment. Slovenska cesta 1, 1000 Ljubljana, Slovenia *tel:* +386 61 125 3366 *fax:* +386 61 131 3067 *email:* http://www.k-ramovs.si/. Klemen Ramovs, president; Petra Barboric, sec. *Artist representation and concert promotion, especially early mus.*

Brina Jez-Brezavscek. Rutarjeva 5, Ljubljana, Slovenia *tel:* +386 61 213972. Brina Jez-Brezavscek, president; Myriam Zgevec, sec. *Artist representation and concert promotion, especially for Slovene composers.*

Cankarjev dom Cultural & Congress Centre. Presernova 10, 1000 Ljubljana, Slovenia *tel:* +386 61 1258121/212492 *fax:* +386 61 224279 *email:* cankarjev.dom@cd-cc.si. Mitja Rotovnik, gen dir; Monika Kartin, mus programme dir. *Artist representation and concert promotion for classical and jazz artists.*

Gallus International. Krakovski nasip 6, 1000 Ljubljana, Slovenia *tel:* +386 61 125 7008 *fax:* +386 61 125 7194 *email:* jeffo13@hotmail. com. Jeff H Pivac, dir. *Artist representation and concert promotion for jazz, blues and world mus as well as classical.*

South Africa

Free State Performing Arts Council (PACOFS). PO Box 1292, Bloemfontein 9300, Orange Free State, South Africa *tel:* +27 51 477 931 *fax:* +27 51 305 523. A J J Ebersohn.

Nico Theatre Centre. PO Box 4107, Cape Town 8000, South Africa *tel:* +27 21 215 470 *fax:* +27 21 215 448 *email:* http://www.millenia.co. za/nico. Michael Maas, chief exec offr. *Concert promotion for mus, opera and ballet.*

Pim Broere Promotions CC. PO Box 55401, Northlands, Johannesburg 2116, South Africa *tel:* +27 11 788 4690 *fax:* +27 11 788 8274. Pim Broere, mgr; Paul Mercer, Lisa Smith, asst mgrs. *Artist representation and concert promotion for classical mus, jazz and contemporary dance.*

State Theatre Pretoria. PO Box 566, Pretoria 0001, Transvaal, South Africa *tel:* +27 12 322 1665 *fax:* +27 12 322 3913 *email:* truk@iafrica. com. Alan Joseph, chief exec offr. *Promoters of the performing arts.*

Spain

Arte Tripharia. Apdo 14622, E-28080 Madrid, Spain *tel:* +34 1 522 1715 *fax:* +34 1 521 4742. Rudesindo Soutelo, dir. *Artist representation.*

Conciertos Augusto SL. Calle Viento N15, 2-B Majadahonda, E-28220 Madrid, Spain *tel:* +34 1 634 0205 *fax:* +34 1 634 0250. Gonzalo Augusto, dir. *Artist representation and concert promotion, especially mus festivals.*

Donald Scrimgeour. Apartado 905, 41080 Seville, Spain *tel:* +34 5 434 3802 *fax:* +34 5 434 3807. Donald Scrimgeour. *Artist representation for classical ballet.*

EMJ Art et Musique SL. Playa de Sitges 27, Punta Galea, 28290 Madrid, Spain *tel:* +34 1 630 30 70 *fax:* +34 1 630 21 98. Elisabeth Michot de Jowers, mgr dir. *Artist representation and concert promotion for chmbr mus, ens and early mus.*

Espectáculos Musicales Espanoles. c/ Sagasta 3-5 Ext Izda, E-28004 Madrid, Spain *tel:* +34 1 594 3773 *fax:* +34 1 594 4337. *Artist representation.*

EuroArte Management. Felipe III 4, 1 Izq, 28012 Madrid, Spain *tel:* +34 1 365 8404/05 *fax:* +34 1 364 0018. Luis Vivo, dir. *Concert promotion for ballet, opera and special events.*

Euroconcert. Rambla de Catalunya 10, 2n, 4a, E-08007 Barcelona, Spain *tel:* +34 3 318 5158 *fax:* +34 3 412 4114. Antoni Sábat, dir. *Artist representation and concert promotion.*

Fusic (Fundacio Societat i Cultura). Consell de Cent 347, Sobreatic, E-08007 Barcelona, Spain *tel:* +34 3 215 7411 *fax:* +34 3 215 7932. Argi Ibanez, mgr. *Concert promotion.*

Ibercamera SA. Gran Via de les Corts Catalanes 636, 08007 Barcelona, Spain *tel:* +34 3 317 9050 *fax:* +34 3 302 6189. Josep Ma Prat, dir. *Artist representation and concert promotion.*

IberMúsica. Costa Rica 32, Bajo B, E-28016 Madrid, Spain *tel:* +34 1 350 1911; 00 34 1 359 5296 *fax:* +34 1 345 2489. Alfonso Aijón, dir.

Joana Danés. Escoles Pies 11, 4-2a, E-08017 Barcelona, Spain *tel:* +34 3 201 4040 *fax:* +34 3 201 4302. *Artist representation.*

Mercedes Sanchez del Rio 'Musica Clasica'. C/Cafeto n 5, E-28007 Madrid, Spain *tel:* +34 1 501 9150 *fax:* +34 1 551 6153. *Artist representation for conductors, soloists, orchestras and chmbr mus.*

Miguel Lerín-Vilardell. Bruc 125, 08037 Barcelona, Spain *tel:* +34 3 301 7548 *fax:* +34 3 301 7486. Michael Lerín, dir; Víctor Flores, asst. *Artist representation for singers and conductors.*

MusiEspana. Zurbano 34, 4 D, 28010 Madrid, Spain *tel:* +34 1 308 4724 *fax:* +34 1 310 1065. Juan Cambreleng, dir. *Artist representation.*

Musiespaña. c/ Zurbano 34, 4-dcha, E-28010 Madrid, Spain *tel:* +34 1 308 4724 *fax:* +34 1 310 1065. Humberto Oran, dir.

Organización Espanola de Conciertos "Sanzkonzert". Pau Claris 113, 08009 Barcelona, Spain *tel:* +34 3 487 3833 *fax:* +34 3 487 7892. Alfonso Sanz Lopez, dir. *Artist representation for symphonic and chmbr orchs, opera and ballet.*

Primusic. Fernan Gonzalez 37, E-28009 Madrid, Spain *tel:* +34 1 574 9051 *fax:* +34 1 573 1077. Carmen Prieto. *Artist representation and concert promotion for early mus.*

Sociedad Musical Armonia. Pl del Principe 2 Entlo, 39003 Santander, Spain *tel:* +34 42 361880 *fax:* +34 42 361969. Sorin Melinte, president; Belen Alonso, mgr dir. *Artist representation and concert promotion.*

Tritó Concerts. Carrer dels Arcs 8, 08002 Barcelona, Spain *tel:* +34 1 302 27 22/301 95 55 *fax:* +34 1 302 26 70. *Artist representation.*

Sweden

Konsertbolaget AB (Scandinavian Artists Management). Vasagatan 52, S-111 20 Stockholm, Sweden *tel:* +46 8 245815 *fax:* +46 8 245595. Thomas Boltenstern, mgr dir; Helena Friberg, Katarina Boltenstern, artist mgrs. *Artist representation.*

Nordic Artist AB. PO Box 12881, S-11298 Stockholm, Sweden *tel:* +46 8 562 62 050 *fax:* +46 8 562 62 060 *email:* info@nordicartist.se; http://www.nordicartist.se. Johan Englund, impresario; Martin Englund, dir. *Artist representation and concert promotion.*

Scandinavian Artists Management Konsertbolaget AB. Vasagatan 52, S-111 20 Stockholm, Sweden *tel:* +46 8 245815 *fax:* +46 8 245595. Thomas Boltenstern, mgr dir. *Artist representation.*

Svensk Konsertdirektion AB. Box 5076, S-402 22 Göteborg, Sweden *tel:* +46 31 830095 *fax:* +46 31 408011. Henrik Lodding, mgr; Gunilla Lodding-Ruijsenaars, asst mgr. *Artist representation and concert promotion.*

Svenska Konsertbyran AB (Swedish Concert Bureau). Jungfrugatan 45, S-114 44 Stockholm, Sweden *tel:* +46 8 665 8088 *fax:* +46 8 665 8066. Kerstin Hammarström, mgr dir; Ann Braathen, artist mgr. *Artist representation.*

Switzerland

Agence Jack Yfar. 7 Rue da la Fontaine, CH-1204 Genève, Switzerland *tel:* +41 22 311 4002 *fax:* +41 22 311 4436. Jack Yfar, dir. *Concert promotion.*

Agency Inter Media. Zwinglistr 35, CH-8004 Zürich, Switzerland *tel:* +41 1 241 1739 *fax:* +41 1 242 3297. Maria Zehnder. *Artist representation and concert promotion, specialising in contemporary music and drums.*

Anne Petkov Artists Management. 6 Rue du Conseil-General, CH-1205 Genève, Switzerland *tel:* +41 22 321 3226 *fax:* +41 22 321 3227. *Artist representation for opera singers and conductors.*

Artists Management Zürich. Rütistr 52, CH-8044 Zürich-Gockhausen, Switzerland *tel:* +41 1 821 8957 *fax:* +41 1 821 0127. Rita Schütz, dir. *Artist representation for opera.*

Artists Personal Representative Claudia Bloechlinger. Gatterstr 1b, CH-9010 St Gallen, Switzerland *tel:* +41 71 222 3980 *fax:* +41 71 222 3889. *Artist representation.*

Balmer & Dixon Management AG. Granitweg 2, CH-8006 Zürich, Switzerland *tel:* +41 1 363 6280 *fax:* +41 1 361 9355. Ritha Dixon, dir; Rudolf Balmer, dir. *Artist representation and personal management.*

Bureau de Concerts Wismar-Casetti. CP 63, CH-1222 Vesenaz, Switzerland *tel:* +41 22 752 5368 *fax:* +41 22 752 5372. Monique Wismer, dir; Eliane Hammerli, co-dir. *Artist representation.*

Circolo Musicale. Emilia Tonolla-Rosa Rappresentanza Artisti, Vignon, CH-6558 Lostallo, Switzerland *tel:* +41 91 830 1288 *fax:* +41 91 830 1555. Emilia Tonolla-Rosa, mgr. *Artist representation.*

Columbia Artists Management AG. Kapuzinerweg 7, CH-6006 Luzern, Switzerland *tel:* +41 41 4207758 *fax:* +41 41 4207759. Beatrice Vesper, mgr; Till Janczukowicz, artist mgr. *Artist representation and orch tours.*

Good News Agency. Frohburgstr 46, Postfach, CH-8033 Zürich, Switzerland *tel:* +41 1 363 4949 *fax:* +41 1 363 0600. André Béchir, dir. *Concert promotion.*

Il Ventaglio Management. Unterdorfstr 74, CH-5505 Brunegg, Switzerland *tel:* +41 64 56 2552 *also fax;* +39 45 623 0297 *also fax.* Clara Ventaglio. *Artist representation; opera.*

Inter-Media International Arts Management. CH-2514 Ligerz-Schernelz, Switzerland *tel:* +41 32 315 27 58 *fax:* +41 32 315 27 59. Hannes Strasser, dir. *Artist representation.*

Interclassica. 4 Rue Jean Jacques Rousseau, CH-1800 Vevey, Switzerland *tel:* +41 21 922 4016 *fax:* +41 21 922 4018. Martin T:son Engstroem, dir; Jean Jacques Indermühle, president. *Artist representation and concert promotion.*

International Booking Agency. Av Florimont 3, CH-1820 Montreux, Switzerland *tel:* +41 21 963 5031 *fax:* +41 21 963 8895. Willy Leiser, dir; Christiane de Dompierre, asst. *Representation for jazz, blues and gospel artists.*

Internationale Konzertagentur Pio Chesini. Aeschenvorstadt 24, Postfach, CH-4010 Basel, Switzerland *tel:* +41 61 272 2229 *also fax; fax:* +41 61 272 2291.

Konzertdirektion Bern. Münzgraben 2, CH-3011 Bern, Switzerland *tel:* +41 31 311 2515 *fax:* +41 31 311 8531. Rolf Hamberger, dir. *Artist representation and concert promotion, especially for chmbr mus.*

Konzert-Agentur Suzanne Gfeller GmbH. Homelstrasse 34, CH-4114 Hofstetten, Switzerland *tel:* +41 61 733 0373 *fax:* +41 61 733 0374 *email:* konzert.sg@magnet.ch. *Artist representation and concert promotion.*

Künstlersekretariat Silviane Mattern-Cuendet. Sichternstr 35, CH-4410 Liestal, Switzerland *tel:* +41 61 921 1644 *fax:* +41 61 921 1081. *Concert promotion.*

Musa Promotion. PO Box 56, CH-3000 Berne 23, Switzerland *tel:* +41 31 371 0049 *fax:* +41 31 372 2248. Alexandru Lucianu, mgr. *Artist representation.*

Music Management. Untere Zelg 30, CH-3145 Berne-Obersherli, Switzerland *tel:* +41 31 849 2323 *fax:* +41 31 849 1719. Dina Thoma-Tennenbaum, president. *Concert promotion.*

Prestige Artists. 16 Rue Du-Roveray, CH-1207 Genève, Switzerland *tel:* +41 22 786 4521 *fax:* +41 22 786 5221. Elisabeth Christeler, mgr dir. *Artist representation and concert promotion, especially chmbr mus.*

Pro Musicis. Rütistr 38, CH-8032 Zürich, Switzerland *tel:* +41 1 251 6533 *fax:* +41 1 252 2914. Silvia Ackermann, dir; Andrea Frehner, asst. *Artist representation for soloists and chmbr mus.*

Saenger-Sekretariat Heidi Wiedmer. Brambergerstr 30, CH-3176 Neuenegg, Switzerland *tel:* +41 31 741 1845 *also fax. Artist representation for singers.*

Sardis Agenzia di Concerti. Via Generale Guisan 7, CH-6900 Lugano-Massagno, Switzerland *tel:* +41 91 966 5034 *fax:* +41 91 967 2256. Yvonne Brodetti, president. *Artist representation and concert promotion.*

Schlaepfer & Partner, ASAM. Hottingerstr 44, Postfach, CH-8030 Zürich, Switzerland *tel:* +41 1 261 0000 *fax:* +41 1 251 4342. Ulrich Schlaepfer, dir. *Artist representation.*

Taiwan

The Management of New Arts. 7F-1,170, Ta-An Rd, Sec 1, Taipei 106, Taiwan *tel:* +886 2 702 5131 *fax:* +886 2 700 4992. Niu Hsiao-Hwa, president. *Concert promotion.*

Pro Musica Artists Management. 4F, 45 Alley 13, Lane 512, Mintzu E Rd, Taipei 10487, Taiwan *tel:* +886 2 508 3851 *fax:* +886 2 502 5551. Chen Yih-Shyong, gen mgr. *Artist representation and concert promotion.*

Turkey

AMM Concerts. Arjantin Caddesi 13, Gaziosmanpasa, 06700 Ankara, Turkey *tel:* +90 312 428 1608 *fax:* +90 312 467 7799. N Kazim, dir. *Concert agent and public relations for artists.*

Ukraine

National Philharmonia of Ukraine. Volodmyrsky Uzviz 2, Kiev, Ukraine *tel:* +7 44 229 6251 *fax:* +7 44 228 0330. V A Loukashev, general and artistic dir. *Promotion of all concerts by National Philharmonia of Ukraine.*

Ukrainian Artists Management. Tchystyakivska St 6-10, Apt 47, 252062 Kiev, Ukraine *tel:* +380 044 442 4561 *fax:* +380 044 442 4541. Irena Stecura, dir. *Artist representation and concert promotion.*

Uruguay

Martin Vivo, Personal Artist Management. Misiones 1305, Piso 1, 11000 Montevideo, Uruguay *tel:* +598 2 951 287 *fax:* +598 2 962 755 *email:* martinv@adinet.com.uy. *Artist representation for conductors and soloists.*

USA

Aaron Concert Management Inc. 729 Boylston St, Suite 600, Boston MA 02116, USA *tel:* +1 617 262 2724; +1 800 394 2766 *fax:* +1 617 267 6539. Jon Aaron, president. *Artist representation.*

AIM - Artists International Management (AIM). 48 Harter Rd, Morristown, NJ 07960, USA *tel:* +1 201 538 0302 *fax:* +1 201 734 1737; +1 908 221 0411 *email:* aimartists@aol.com; http://www.artists international.com. Birgit Schmid-Salm, exec dir; Vincent L Scwenk, programs and contracts. *Artist representation, specialising in chamber music.*

Albert Kay Associates Inc. 58 W 58 St, No 31E, New York, NY 10019-2510, USA *tel:* +1 212 593 1640 *fax:* +1 212 759 7329. Albert Kay, president; Grace Avrick Lawrence, vice-president. *Artist representation and concert promotion.*

Alexander Kedrov Interconcerts Associates. 6563 S Poplar Woods Circle No 7, Germantown, TN 38138, USA *tel:* +1 901 753 5553 *fax:* +1 901 753 5179.

Alkahest Agency Inc. PO Box 12403 Northside Sta, Atlanta GA 30355, USA *tel:* +1 404 315 0709 *fax:* +1 404 636 0844 *email:* alkagency@aol. com. Scott A Bridges, president. *Artist representation.*

American Artists Management Inc. 801 West End Av, Suite 12-A, New York, NY 10025, USA *tel:* +1 212 222 3770 *fax:* +1 212 222 3774 *email:* aami801@aol.com. Sophy Haynes, president. *Artist representation.*

American International Artists. 315 East 62nd St, 6th Floor, New York, NY 10021, USA *tel:* +1 212 715 0470 *fax:* +1 212 715 0461 *email:* 74771.3034@compuserve.com. Cynthia Herbst, dir; Isabelle Deconinck, asst. *Artist representation, especially composers, soloists and ens.*

Amy Blum Personal Representation. 144 Village Landing, Suite 190, Fairport, NY 14450, USA *tel:* +1 716 425 1864 *also fax; email:* prmaven 352@aol.com. Amy Blum, president. *Artist representation and publicity.*

Andes Management. PO Box 55219, Madison, WI 53705, USA *tel:* +1 608 263 1913 *fax:* +1 608 262 8876 *email:* jfcalder@facstaff.wisc.edu; http://hum.lss.wisc.edu/guitar/jcalderon.html. Javier Calderon. *Artist representation.*

Anita R Kurland Associates. 129 Payson Rd, Chestnut Hill, MA 02167, USA *tel:* +1 617 469 0656 *fax:* +1 617 469 4988. Anita Kurland.

Anthony George Artist Management. 250 W 77 St, New York, NY 10024, USA *tel:* +1 212 580 1306/2405 *fax:* +1 212 721 9144. Anthony George, chief offr; Penny Luedtke, associate. *Artist representation, especially opera, theatre and music theatre.*

Arthur H Roach Artists Management. 1749B S Hayes St, Arlington, VA 22202-2714, USA *tel:* +1 703 685 5275 *fax:* +1 703 685 5176 *email:* arthurhr@aol.com. Arthur Roach, dir. *Artist representation for opera and oratorio singers. Also contract negotiation.*

Arthur Shafman International Ltd. PO Box 352, Pawling, NY 12564, USA *tel:* +1 914 855 3005 *fax:* +1 914 855 3167 *email:* ashafman@ aol.com; http://www.performingarts.net/shafman. Arthur Shafman, president; Virginia Pfaff, tour dir. *Artist representation and concert promotion, specialising in physical theatre, dance, jazz and family entertainment.*

Artists' Alliance Management. 28818 NE Hancock Rd, Camas, WA 98607, USA *tel:* +1 360 834 7022 *fax:* +1 360 834 9680 *email:* 105167. 2562@compuserve.com. Peter Christ, mgr. *Artist representation, especially w/wind and br.*

Artra Artists Management Inc. 555 W Madison St, Suite 2110, Chicago, IL 60661, USA *tel:* +1 312 648 4100 *fax:* +1 312 648 0600. Robert Bauchens, president; Terryl Jares, vice-president. *Artist representation.*

Barbara Serage Artist Management. 7419 Hogarth St, Springfield, VA 22151, USA *tel:* +1 703 941 3445 *fax:* +1 703 941 3909 *email:* bserage 451@aol.com. Barbara Serage, president. *Artist representation.*

Baylin Artists Management. 2210 Mt Carmel Av, Suite 202, Glenside, PA 19038, USA *tel:* +1 215 887 7870 *fax:* +1 215 887 7873 *email:* bayam@aol.com. Marc Baylin, president. *Artist representation.*

Bennett Morgan & Associates Ltd. 1282 Rt 376, Wappingers Falls, NY 12590, USA *tel:* +1 914 227 6065 *fax:* +1 914 227 4002. Bennett Morgan, Becky Morgan, artists reps. *Artist representation, especially jazz.*

Bess Pruitt & Associates Inc. 819 E 168 St, Bronx, NY 10459, USA *tel:* +1 718 589 0400 *fax:* +1 718 617 4551. Bessie J Pruitt, president. *Artist representation, especially recitalists and opera singers.*

Betsy M Green Associates Inc. 36 Hampshire Rd, Wayland, MA 01778, USA *tel:* +1 508 358 2939 *fax:* +1 508 358 5556 *email:* bmga@aol.com; http://www.bmga.com. Betsy M Green, president; Rose Raduziner, exec sec. *Artist representation, specialising in classical, perc, pno, world and new mus.*

Beverly Wright & Associates. 157 W 57 St, Suite 1100, New York, NY 10019, USA *tel:* +1 212 333 7735 *fax:* +1 212 333 7734 *email:* bev wright@aol.com; http://www.napama.org. Beverly Wright, dir. *Artist representation, concert promotion and publicity. Specialises in conductors, composers, instrumentalists, chmbr mus and early mus.*

Bill Fegan Attractions/AIM. Shuler Theater, 131 N Second St, Raton, NM 87740, USA *tel:* +1 505 445 5528 *fax:* +1 505 445 8572 *email:* aimbfa@ raton.com. Sue Fleming, CEO; Marvin Fleming, president. *Artist representation; specialising in musicals and children's shows.*

Bravo Artist Management Inc. 14045 Greenwood Av N#103, Seattle, WA 98133, USA *tel:* +1 206 547 0433 *fax:* +1 206 547 2906. Lauren Anderson, president. *Artist representation and concert promotion; especially chmbr mus and recitals.*

The Bresner Management Inc. Hotel des Artistes, 1 W 67 St, Suite 2E, New York, NY 10023, USA *tel:* +1 212 877 0788 *fax:* +1 212 769 1722. Carol Bresner, president; Lizabeth Skalski, vice-president.

Bret Adams Ltd. 448 W 44 St, New York, NY 10036, USA *tel:* +1 212 765 5630 *fax:* +1 212 265 2212. Bret Adams, mgr. *Artist representation.*

Bridge Records Inc, (Management Division). JAF Box 1864, New York, NY 10116-1864, USA *tel:* +1 914 654 9270 *fax:* +1 914 636 1383 *email:* bridgerec@aol.com. Becky Starobin, dir. *Artist representation and recording label, specialising in classical gui.*

By Arrangement With Matthew Sprizzo. 477 Durant Av, Staten Island, NY 10308, USA *tel:* +1 718 948 5402 *fax:* +1 718 984 8996. *Artist representation for vocalists and instrumentalists.*

California Artists Management. 41 Sutter St, Suite 723, San Francisco, CA 94104-4903, USA *tel:* +1 415 362 2787 *fax:* +1 415 362 2838 *email:* camdon@aol.com; http://members.aol.com/camdon/cam.html. Susan Endrizzi, Donald E Osborne, dirs. *Artist representation, especially early and baroque mus, chmbr, choral and world mus.*

Carol Gerson. 145 W 71 St, New York, NY 10023, USA *tel:* +1 212 362 4375 *also fax.* Carol Gerson, president. *Artist representation, especially hpd, clvd, f-pno.*

Robert Gewald Management Inc. 58 W 58 St, New York, NY 10019, USA *tel:* +1 212 753 0450 *fax:* +1 212 935 3706. Robert M Gewald, president. *Artist representation.*

Robert Guralnik Management. Box 116, Mountainville, NY 10953, USA *tel:* +1 914 534 3281 *also fax; email:* robgur@aol.com. Robert Guralnik, dir. *Artist representation, especially chmbr mus.*

Robert Lombardo Associates. 61 W 62 St, Suite 6F, New York, NY 10023, USA *tel:* +1 212 586 4453 *fax:* +1 212 581 5771 *email:* robertjl@ix.netcom.com. Robert Lombardo, president; Michael Rosen, Lewis Ehlers, artist mgrs. *Artist representation, especially opera.*

Rosalie Calabrese Management. Box 20580, New York, NY 10025, USA *tel:* +1 212 663 6620 *fax:* +1 212 663 5941. *Personal representation for composers.*

Sally Sanfield Artist Management. 31550 Stonewood Court, Farmington Hills, MI 48334, USA *tel:* +1 248 626 0948 *fax:* +1 248 626 0904 *email:* ssanfield@aol.com. Sally Sanfield, dir. *Artist representation.*

Sandra Elm Management. 411 W 21 St, No 2, New York, NY 10011, USA *tel:* +1 212 741 0011. Sandra Elm. *Artist representation, especially chmbr and new mus.*

Santa Fe World Music Agency. 609 Onate Place, Santa Fe, NM 87501, USA *tel:* +1 505 988 8037 *fax:* +1 505 988 3168. Kristina Melcher, dir. *Artist representation.*

Sardos Artist Management Corp. 180 West End Av, New York, NY 10023, USA *tel:* +1 212 874 2559 *fax:* +1 212 721 7815. James Sardos, president; Rita Sardos, vice-president. *Artist representation, especially opera singers.*

Schwalbe & Partners. 170 E 61st St, II 5 N, New York, NY 10021, USA *tel:* +1 212 935 5650 *fax:* +1 212 935 4754 *email:* 75124.302@compuserve.com. Douglas Schwalbe, president; Carrie Sykes, artistic admin. *Artist representation.*

Seegers Artists Management Inc. 2004 Swanee Pl, Olypia, WA 98501, USA *tel:* +1 360 956 0585 *fax:* +1 360 956 1045. Raymond Seegers, president; Sharon Seegers, vice-president. *Artist representation.*

Seidel Artists Management. 2092 W Greenleaf Av, Chicago, IL 60645, USA *tel:* +1 773 761 7001 *fax:* +1 773 761 2025 *email:* seidelam@aol.com. Jean Seidel, exec dir. *Artist representation for oratorio, opera, mus theatre.*

Sempre Musica. 11260 Overland Av, Suite 15B, Culver City, CA 90230, USA *tel:* +1 310 287 1031 *fax:* +1 310 815 8133 *email:* sempremus@aol.com. Valerie Bernstein, president; Ina Jo Scheid, vice-president. *Artist representation, especially chmbr and early mus, and soloists.*

Shaw Concerts Inc. 1900 Broadway, 2nd Fl, New York, NY 10023-7098, USA *tel:* +1 212 595 1909 *fax:* +1 212 580 1911. Harold Shaw, chmn; Hugh Kaylor, president.

Sheldon Soffer Management Inc. 130 W 56 St, New York, NY 10019, USA *tel:* +1 212 757 8060 *fax:* +1 212 757 5536 *email:* shelsoffer@aol.com; http://www.napama.org. Sheldon Soffer, president. *Artist representation.*

Shirley Kirshbaum & Associates Inc. 711 West End Av, Suite 5KN, New York, NY 10025, USA *tel:* +1 212 222 4843 *fax:* +1 212 222 7321 *email:* http://www.skassoc.com. Shirley Kirshbaum, exec dir; Susan Demler, booking dir. *Artist management and publicity.*

Shupp Artist Management. 202 Michigan Av, Port Jefferson, NY 11777, USA *tel:* +1 516 928 1531 *fax:* +1 516 474 5071. Erica Shupp. *Artist representation.*

Siegel Artist Management. 1416 Hinman Av, Evanston, IL 60201, USA *tel:* +1 847 475 4224 *fax:* +1 847 475 0440 *email:* lizsam@aol.com. Liz Silverstein, associate dir; Jane Lawrence Curtiss, dir. *Artist representation, especially dance and early mus.*

Sondra Ross Associates Inc. 2705 McGee Av, Middletown, OH 45044, USA *tel:* +1 513 423 3023 *fax:* +1 513 423 4342 *email:* fross@erinet.com. Sondra Ross, president. *Artist representation.*

Springwood Artist Management. Box 622, Hershey, PA 17033, USA *tel:* +1 717 838 9813 *fax:* +1 717 838 4521 *email:* springwd@aol.com; http://members.aol.com/springwd. Roger Gale, dir. *Representation for classical vocalists.*

Stanley Weinstein Arts Management. 408 Charlestown Rd, Hampton, NJ 08827, USA *tel:* +1 908 537 6832 *also fax; email:* stanweinstein@sprintmail.com. Stanley Weinstein, president; Ilene Beckerman, vice-president. *Artist representation for chmbr mus, dance and cabaret artists. Arts management consultancy.*

Steorra Public Relations. 243 West End Av, Suite 907, New York, NY 10023, USA *tel:* +1 212 799 5783 *fax:* +1 212 799 1121 *email:* steorrapr@aol.com. Lynda Ciolek, president. *Artist representation, especially pno, voice, chmbr mus.*

Stephen Cloud Presentations. PO Box 4774, Santa Barbara, CA 93140, USA *tel:* +1 805 962 6682 *fax:* +1 805 965 5945. Stephen Cloud, president. *Artist representation.*

Sutton Artists Corp. 20 W Park Av, Suite 305, Long Beach, NY 11561-2019, USA *tel:* +1 516 432 1790 *fax:* +1 516 869 1855. Frank Modica, president. *Artist representation and concert promotion.*

Thea Dispeker Inc. 59 E 54 St, New York, NY 10022, USA *tel:* +1 212 421 7676 *fax:* +1 212 935 3279 *email:* dispeker@aol.com. Thea Dispeker, president. *Artist management.*

Timothy Gilligan Artists Management. 222 W 23 St, Suite 1500, New York, NY 10011, USA *tel:* +1 212 647 0525 *fax:* +1 212 924 0109. Timothy Gilligan, dir; Berkley Young, artists' rep. *Artist representation, some concert promotion, especially chmbr mus and recitals.*

Tornay Management Inc. 155 West 72 St, New York, NY 10023, USA *tel:* +1 212 580 8696 *fax:* +1 212 580 8698 *email:* stornay@aol.com. Sara Tornay, president. *Artist representation, specialising in vocalists.*

Trawick Artists Management Inc. 1926 Broadway, New York, NY 10023, USA *tel:* +1 212 874 2482 *fax:* +1 212 874 2866. Brenda Trawick, president. *Artist representation.*

TRM Management Inc. 825 S Lazelle St, Columbus, OH 43206, USA *tel:* +1 614 444 0039 *fax:* +1 614 444 0699. Tittica Roberts Mitchell, president. *Artist representation.*

Victoria Brandys Artists Management. 3824 S Fraser, Aurora, CO 80014-4022, USA *tel:* +1 303 693 6267 *fax:* +1 303 766 9332 *email:* rigw@aol.com. Victoria Brandys, dir. *Artist representation, especially gui, pno and world mus.*

Vivace Artistic Representation. 110 Union St, Suite 510, Seattle, WA 98101, USA *tel:* +1 206 340 2557 *fax:* +1 206 583 2726. Roz Benaroya, exec dir. *Artist representation and concert promotion. Specialises in vocal artists and chmbr mus.*

Vladimir Baranov Inc. 301 E 69 St, No 9-E, New York, NY 10021, USA *tel:* +1 212 496 6452 *also fax.* Faina Baranov, dir; Vladimir Baranov, president. *Artist representation for opera singers.*

Warden Associates Inc. 5626 Deer Run Rd, Doylestown, PA 18901, USA *tel:* +1 215 794 3767 *fax:* +1 215 794 8627 *email:* michael@ispa-as.com; http://www.ispa-os.com. Diana Warden, president; Michael Lowell Larsen, vice-president. *Artist representation.*

William Knight. Grant House, 309 Wood St, Burlington, NJ 08016, USA *tel:* +1 609 386 3933 *fax:* +1 609 386 8703. William Knight, president; Nancy Gorman, vice-president. *Artist representation for American vocalists and conductors. No instrumentalists.*

William Morris Agency Inc. 151 El Camino Dr, Beverly Hills, CA 90212, USA *tel:* +1 310 274 7451 *fax:* +1 310 859 4460. Norman Brokaw, chmn. *Artist representation.*

Wolf Artists Management. 788 Columbus Av, No 15a, New York, NY 10025-5936, USA *tel:* +1 212 531 1514 *fax:* +1 212 531 1610 *email:* wolfartist@aol.com. Isabel Wolf, dir. *Artist representation for singers, conductors and directors.*

World Artists. 3126 Bolero Dr, Atlanta, GA 30341, USA *tel:* +1 770 939 4343 *fax:* +1 770 908 1231 *email:* lynnmc@mindspring.com; http://www.mindspring.com/~slideway. Lynn McConnell. *Artist representation.*

WSA Artist Management. PO Box 740564, Dallas, TX 75374, USA *tel:* +1 214 341 1911 *also fax.* Greta Critchlow Scobie, admin dir. *Artist representation, specialising in community outreach programs.*

YACAI Artist Management Inc. 1 E Lexington St, Suite 501, Baltimore, MD 21202, USA *tel:* +1 410 332 8406 *fax:* +1 410 332 1029. Helen Antebi, dir. *Artist representation and concert production; specialising in chmbr and modern mus.*

Young Concert Artists Inc. 250 W 57 St, Room 1222, New York, NY 10019, USA *tel:* +1 212 307 6655 *fax:* +1 212 581 8894 *email:* yca@yca.org; http://www.yca.org. Susan Wadsworth, dir. *Representation for exceptional young artists; artists chosen through international auditions.*

Young Organists Cooperative Ltd. PO Box 103, Worcester, MA 01602, USA *tel:* +1 508 285 5697. Frank Corbin, mgr dir. *Artist representation.*

Zajonc/Valenti Management Inc. PO Box 7023, Ann Arbor, MI 48107, USA *tel:* +1 800 650 8742 *fax:* +1 313 662 8733 *email:* dzmm@aol.com. Donna Zajonc, Judy Valenti, mgrs. *Artist representation for traditional and contemporary jazz, folk and musical theatre, ballet and children's entertainment.*

Venezuela

Asociacíon Cultural Pro Musica de Cámara. Apartado 51494, Caracas 1050 A, Venezuela *tel:* +58 2 239 4761 *also fax.* Florian Ebersberg, dir. *Concert promotion; specialising in chmbr mus.*

Conciertos Avila. Apartado 51494, Caracas 1050 A, Venezuela *tel:* +58 2 239 4761 *also fax.* Florian Ebersberg, dir. *Artist representation.*

Symphony Orchestras

The orchestras listed below perform regularly and operate on a professional, or mainly professional basis. The number of performers is shown in parenthesis, and the conductor or musical director is listed, together with the names of the chief administrative staff.

Argentina

Orquesta Filarmónica de Buenos Aires. Cerrito 618, Teatro Colón, 1010 Buenos Aires, Argentina *tel:* +54 1 383 5199 *fax:* +54 1 383 6167/382 2389. Elias Khayat, cond; Horatio Ceballos, mgr.

Orquesta Sinfónica Nacional. Córdoba 1155, 1055 Buenos Aires, Argentina *tel:* +54 1 45 4252.

Armenia

Armenian Philharmonia Orchestra (120). Mashtotz 46, 375019 Yerevan, Armenia *tel:* +37 885 256 4965 *fax:* +37 885 258 1142. Loris Tjeknavoriav, artistic dir and principal cond; Gevorg Avedisian, gen mgr.

Armenian State Symphony Orchestra (180). Mesropa Mashtotz Av 46, Erevan, Armenia *tel:* +37 42 567438 *fax:* +37 42 151055. Loris Tjeknavorian, principal cond; Gevorg Avedisian, mgr.

Australia

Adelaide Symphony Orchestra (68). GPO Box 2121, Adelaide SA 5001, Australia *tel:* +61 8 8343 4820 *fax:* +61 8 8343 4808. David Porcelijn, chief cond and artistic dir; Robert Clarke, gen mgr; James Ferguson, orch mgr; Yvonne Schwerdt, artistic co-ord.

Canberra Symphony Orchestra (100). GPO Box 1919, Canberra, Act 2601, Australia *tel:* +61 6 247 9191 *fax:* +61 6 247 9026. Barbara George, gen mgr.

Melbourne Philharmonic Orchestra. BOX 102, Glen Iris, Vic 3146, Australia *tel:* +61 3 885 8500.

Melbourne Symphony Orchestra (102). GPO Box 9994, Melbourne, Vic 3001, Australia *tel:* +61 3 9626 1110 *fax:* +61 3 9626 1101. Hiroyuki Iwaki, cond laureate; Steven Porter, gen mgr.

Queensland Symphony Orchestra (71). GPO Box 9994, Brisbane, Queensland 4001, Australia *tel:* +61 7 3377 5000 *fax:* +61 7 3377 5001 *email:* qso@your.abc.net.au. Libby Anistis, acting gen mgr; Muhai Tang, principal cond; Alan Smith, concert master.

State Orchestra of Victoria (69). 100 St Kilda Rd, Melbourne, Vic 3004, Australia *tel:* +61 3 9281 8000 *fax:* +61 3 9281 8282. Peter Garnick, admin; Luke Shaw, mgr.

Sydney Symphony Orchestra (100). GPO Box 4972, Sydney, NSW 2001, Australia *tel:* +61 2 9334 4644 *fax:* +61 2 9334 4646 *email:* symphony@sso.com.au; http://www.symphony.org.au. Mary Vallentine, mgr dir; Edo de Waart, chief cond and artistic dir; Mary Jo Capps, dir of development; Ann Hoban, dir of operations.

Symphony Australia. GPO Box 9994, Sydney NSW 2001, Australia *tel:* +61 2 9333 1677 *fax:* +61 2 9333 1678 *email:* dixon.samuel@a2.abc.net.au. Nathan Waks, dir of mus; Samuel C Dixon, artistic admin.

Tasmanian Symphony Orchestra (47). GPO Box 9994, Hobart, Tas 7001, Australia *tel:* +61 03 6235 3646 *fax:* +61 03 6235 3651. Julie Warn, gen mgr; David Porcelijn, chief cond and artistic dir.

West Australian Symphony Orchestra (90). GPO Box 9994, Perth, WA 6001, Australia *tel:* +61 8 9220 2604 *fax:* +61 8 9220 2551. Henk Smit, gen mgr; N Kegie, concert admin; M Lancaster-Allen, orch mgr; Vernon Handley, chief cond; Vladimir Verbitsky, principal guest cond.

Austria

Austrian Hungarian Haydn Orchestra. Raffaelgasse 20/1/32, A-1200 Wien, Austria *tel:* +43 1 334 6356 *also fax.* Adam Fischer, dir.

Bruckner Orchester Linz (110). Promenade 39, A-4020 Linz, Austria *tel:* +43 70 761 1195 *fax:* +43 70 761 1315. Martin Sieghart, chief cond; Carl F Steiner, gen sec.

The Haydn Academy. Wiener Strasse 14, A-2100 Korneuburg, Austria *tel:* +43 2262 72662 *also fax.* Anton Gabmayer, dir.

Mozarteum Orchester (91). Erzbischof-Gebhard Str 10, A-5020 Salzburg, Austria *tel:* +43 662 843571 *fax:* +43 662 84357123. Hubert Soudant, mus dir; Mag. Erwin Niese, financial dir.

Symphonieorchester Vorarlberg/Camerata Bregenz (90). Römerstr 15, A-6900 Bregenz, Austria *tel:* +43 5574 43447 *fax:* +43 5574 43448. Christoph Eberle, chief cond; Bertram Grass, president; Michael Löbl, mgr.

Vienna Chamber Orchestra (30-40). Schachnerstr 27, A-1220 Wien, Austria *tel:* +43 1 203 6357 *fax:* +43 1 203 7483 *email:* buchmann@m.xpoint.at. Christian Buchmann, gen mgr.

Vienna Mozart Orchestra (30). Brucknerstr 4, A-1040 Wien, Austria *tel:* +43 1 505 77660 *fax:* +43 1 505 9720 *email:* concerts@mozart.co.at; http://www.mozart.co.at/concerts/. Gerald Grünbacher, dir; Josefa Haselböck, international tours and sales; Manuel Hernandez-Silva, Konrad Leitner, principal conds.

Wiener Philharmoniker (149). Bösendorferstr 12, A-1010 Wien, Austria *tel:* +43 1 505 6525. Clemens Hellsberg, president.

Wiener Symphoniker (127). Lehágasse 11/ Stg 2, A-1060 Wien, Austria *tel:* +43 1 591 8916. Rainer Bischof, gen sec; Rafael Frühbeck de Burgos, chief cond.

Belarus

State Academic Symphony Orchestra of Byelorussia (112). Pr Skoriny 50, 220005 Minsk, Belarus *tel:* +17 2 315547 *fax:* +17 2 319050. Vladimir Ratobylsky, dir; Vladimir Grib, orch dir; Misha Katz, chief cond; Yuri Gildiuk, artistic dir; Victor Sobolev, principal cond.

Belgium

BRTN - Filharmonisch Orkest (96). Magdalenazaal, Duquesnoystraat 14, B-1000 Bruxelles, Belgium *tel:* +32 2 548 0170 *fax:* +32 2 548 0177. Frank Deleu, dir; Frank Shipway, chief cond.

Collegium Instrumentale Brugense (15-30). Vijversdreef 96, B-8310 Bruges, Belgium *tel:* +32 50 353717 *fax:* +32 50 362717. Lieve Geerolf, admin; Patrick Peire, mus dir.

Orchestre National de Belgique (90). 23 Rue Ravenstein, B-1000 Bruxelles, Belgium *tel:* +32 2 552 0464 *fax:* +32 2 552 0468. Alain Pierlot, dir; Van Kerckhove Agnes, production mgr; Yuri Simonov, mus dir.

Orchestre Philharmonique de Liège et de la Communaté Francaise (94). Rue Forgeur 11, B-4000 Liège, Belgium *tel:* +32 41 236360 *fax:* +32 41 237065. Roger Pernay, admin dir; Pierre Bartholomée, sec gen.

Orchestre Symphonique de la Monnaie (110). Rue Leopold 4, B-1000 Bruxelles, Belgium *tel:* +32 2 229 1218 *fax:* +32 2 229 1386. Ingrid De Backer, orch mgr.

Royal Philharmonic Orchestra of Flanders (97). Britselei 80, B-2000 Antwerp 1, Belgium *tel:* +32 3 231 3737 *fax:* +32 3 231 9126 *email:* admin@kfovv; http://kfovv.be. Luc Vanackere, mgr; Grant Llewellyn, principal cond.

Brazil

Orquestra Filarmônica do Rio de Janeiro (80). Rua das Marrecas 25, Sala 901, Centro 20031-040 Rio de Janeiro, Brazil *tel:* +55 21 240 7354 *fax:* +55 21 262 4269. Florentino Dias, mus dir and cond; Regina Helena Macedo, mgr.

Orquestra Sinfónica Brasileira (85). Av Rio Branco 135, Rm 918, 20040 Rio de Janeiro RJ, Brazil *tel:* +55 21 222 5842/4592; +55 21 252 6330 *fax:* +55 21 242 5754. João Carlos Alvim Corrêa, gen mgr; Sergio Nepomuceno, admin mgr; Isaac Karatchewsky, mus dir; Roberto Tibiriça, principal guest cond.

Bulgaria

Bulgarian National Radio Symphony Orchestra (110). 4 Dragan Tsankov Blvd, BG-1040 Sofia, Bulgaria *tel:* +359 2 661812 *also fax.* Milen Natchev, mus dir.

Sofia Philharmonic Orchestra (115). 1 Benkovski Str, BG-1000 Sofia, Bulgaria *tel:* +359 2 883197/883195 *fax:* +359 2 874072. Emil Tabakov, mus dir and principal cond; Bedros Papazian, exec dir.

Vratza State Philharmonic Orchestra (60). 1 Christo Botev Sq, BG-3000 Vratza, Bulgaria *tel:* +359 92 23434/23261 *fax:* +359 92 60053 *email:* vratzaphil@mbox.digsys.bg. Dimitar Panov, dir; Valeri Vatchev, chief cond.

Canada

Calgary Philharmonic Orchestra (64). 205 Eighth Av SE, Calgary, Alta T2G 0K9, Canada *tel:* +1 403 571 0270 *fax:* +1 403 294 7424 *email:* http://www.#tn.com/cpo. Hans Graf, mus dir; Leonard Stone, exec dir.

Edmonton Symphony Orchestra (56). Winspear Centre, #4 Sir Winston Churchill Sq N W, Edmonton, AB T5J 4X4, Canada *tel:* +1 403 428 1108 *fax:* +1 403 425 0167. Grzegorz Nowak, artistic dir and principal cond; Robert McPhee, mgr dir.

International Symphony Orchestra. 774 London Rd, Sarnia, Ont N7T 4Y1, Canada *tel:* +1 519 337 7775. Anne Brown, gen dir.

Kingston Symphony. PO Box 1616, Kingston, Ont K7L 5C8, Canada *tel:* +1 613 546 9729 *fax:* +1 613 546 8580. Tricia Baldwin, gen mgr.

Kitchener-Waterloo Symphony (52). Centre in the Square, 101 Queen St, N Kitchener, Ont N2H 6P7, Canada *tel:* +1 519 745 4711 *fax:* +1 519 745 4474. Chosei Komatsu, mus dir and cond; George Lange, acting mgr dir.

Montréal Chamber Orchestra (14-32). 1200 Av McGill, Suite 1100, Montréal, QC H3B 4G7, Canada *tel:* +1 514 871 1224 *fax:* +1 514 393 9069. Wanda Kalyzny, mus dir; Betty Wallbank, treasurer and exec admin.

Montréal Symphony Orchestra. 85 Ste-Catherine W Suite 900, Montréal, PQ H2X 3P4, Canada *tel:* +1 514 842 3402 *fax:* +1 514 842 0728.

National Arts Centre Orchestra of Canada (46). PO Box 1534, Station B, Ottawa, Ont K1P 5W1, Canada *tel:* +1 613 996 5051 *fax:* +1 613 943 1400. Trevor Pinnock, artistic adviser; Christopher Deacon, orch mgr dir; Franz-Paul Decker, principal guest cond.

Newfoundland Symphony Orchestra (60). Arts and Culture Centre, PO Box 1854, Prince Philip Dr, St John's, NF A1C 5P9, Canada *tel:* +1 709 753 6492 *fax:* +1 709 753 0561. Peter Gardner, gen mgr; Marc David, principal cond.

Niagara Symphony (55). 73 Ontario St, Unit 104, St Catharines, Ont L2R 5J5, Canada *tel:* +1 905 687 4993 *fax:* +1 905 687 1149. Michael Reason, mus dir and principal cond; Laura Tilley, dir of development.

Orchestra London Canada Inc (44). Centennial Hall, 520 Wellington St, London, Ont N6A 3R1, Canada *tel:* +1 519 679 8558 *fax:* +1 519 679 8914. John David Sterne, exec dir; Mark Laycock, mus dir.

Ottawa Symphony Orchestra (90). 309-1390 Prince of Wales Dr, Ottawa, Ont K2C 3N6, Canada *tel:* 613 224 4982 *also fax.* Marian Pickering, mgr dir; David Currie, mus dir.

Québec Symphony Orchestra. 130 W Grand Allée, Québec PQ G1R 2G7, Canada *tel:* +1 418 643 5598 *fax:* +1 418 646 9665. Louis L'Atlante, orch mgr.

Toronto Symphony Orchestra (99). Suite 550, 212 King St West, Toronto, Ont M5H 1K5, Canada *tel:* +1 416 593 7769 *fax:* +1 416 593 6788 *email:* http://www.tso.on.ca. Jukka-Pekka Saraste, mus dir; Loie Fallis, artistic admin.

Vancouver Symphony (73). 601 Smithe St, Vancouver BC V6B 5G1, Canada *tel:* +1 604 684 9100 *fax:* +1 604 684 9264. Larry Blackman, personnel mgr; Sergin Comissiona, mus dir; Michael Aze, production dir.

Victoria Symphony (50). 846 Broughton St, Victoria, BC V8W 1E4, Canada *tel:* +1 604 385 9771 *fax:* +1 604 385 7767. C Stephen Smith, gen mgr; Lynn Mesher, admin asst; Peter McCoppin, mus dir; Brian Jackson, principal Pops cond; Kees Bakels, principal guest cond.

Winnipeg Symphony Orchestra (67). 101 555 Main St, Winnipeg, MB R3B 1C3, Canada *tel:* +1 204 949 3950 *fax:* +1 204 956 4271. Bramwell Tovey, artistic dir; Howard Jang, exec dir; Charles D'Amours, snr development and mkt dir; Annemarie Petrov, mus admin and operations dir; Sandra Tym, mkt and PR.

Chile

Orquesta Sinfónica de Concepción. Juan Felix Burotto, Corporation Cultural del Biobío, Casilla 1711, Concepción, Chile *tel:* +41 242525. Wilfried Junge, mus dir.

Santiago Philharmonic Orchestra (95). PO Box 18, San Antonio 149, Santiago, Chile *tel:* +56 2 638 1515 *fax:* +56 2 633 7214 *email:* http://www.municipal.cl. Andrés Pinto, admin dir.

China

Beijing Central Ensemble of National Radio. 11 Dongmeichang Xicheng, Beijing 100009, China *tel:* +86 662784/666264. Liu Wen-Jin, dir; Yang Da-Cheng, mgr.

Shanghai Symphony Orchestra (90). 105 Hunan Lu, Shanghai 200031, China *tel:* +86 21 6433 3752 *also fax.* Chen Xieyang, mus dir and principal cond; Cao Yiji, gen mgr; Cai Zhong, personnel mgr.

Colombia

Bogotá Philharmonic Orchestra (100). Calle 39 A No 14-57, Aptdo Aéreo 16034, Santa Fé de Bogotá DC, Colombia *tel:* +57 1 288 3466/4453 *fax:* +57 1 288 3162/245 6150. María Cristina Sánchez, exec mgr; Franciso Rettig, chief cond; Eduardo Carrizosa, asst cond; Marco Tulio Chacin, admin mgr.

Orquesta Sinfónica de Colombia. Calle 11, No 5-51, Santa Fé de Bogotá DC, Colombia *tel:* +57 243 5316 *fax:* +57 820854.

Croatia

Dubrovnik Symphony Orchestra (60). Put Ante Starcevica 29, 20000 Dubrovnik, Croatia *tel:* +38 52 041 7101/7110 *fax:* +38 52 041 7060. Pero Glavinic, dir; Ivan Drazinic, chief cond; Frana Krasovac, first cond; Delo Jusic, second cond.

Zagreb Philharmonic (100). Trg S Radica 4, Zagreb, Croatia *tel:* +385 1 539699/539399 *fax:* +385 1 539933. Milan Horvat, hon chief cond; Andelko Ramuscak, dir; Davorka Bajic, Ruzica Durovic, programme producers.

Czech Republic

Bohemia Symphony Orchestra. Za Nadrazim 56, CZ-290 01 Podebrady, Czech Republic *tel:* 034 35 37.

Brno Philharmonic Orchestra (115). Komenského nám 8, CZ-602 00 Brno, Czech Republic *tel:* +420 5 4221 2300/8284 *also fax.* Julius Kessner, dir; Boris Pác, concert mgr; Aldo Ceccato, principal cond; Caspar Richter, permanent guest cond; Enoch Zu Guttenberg, guest cond.

Czech Philharmonic Orchestra (120). Alsovo Nábrezi 12, CZ-110 00 Praha 1, Czech Republic *tel:* +420 2 248 93201 *fax:* +420 2 231 9051. Ing Jiri Kovár, gen dir; Vladimir Askhkenazy, cond.

Czech Symphony Orchestra FISYO (73). Trachtova 2/1130, CZ-158 00 Praha 5, Czech Republic *tel:* +420 2 684 6256 *fax:* +420 2 684 9379. Jiri Kauders, dir.

Janácek Philharmonic Orchestra (98). Michálkovická 181, CZ-710 08 Slezská Ostrava 2, Czech Republic *tel:* +420 69 622 6144/5505 *fax:* +420 69 222 886. Jan Haliska, dir; Christian Arming, chief cond.

Moravian Philharmonic Orchestra. Horní Nám 23, CZ-772 00 Olomouc, Czech Republic *tel:* +420 68 5228 971/5225 302 *fax:* +420 68 5228 511. Jiri Mikula, cond; Václav Stos, dir.

North Bohemian Philharmonic. U Zámku 1, CZ-415 28 Teplice, Czech Republic *tel:* +420 417 29463/26471 *fax:* +420 417 26471. Tomás Koutník.

North Bohemian Philharmonic Orchestra in Teplice (65). U Zámku 1, CZ-415 28 Teplice, Czech Republic *tel:* +420 417 26471 *fax:* +420 417 29463 *email:* http://www.teplice.city/kultura/scf. Jirí Malina, gen mgr; Charles Olivieri-Munroe, principal cond.

Prague Symphony Orchestra (c 100). Námestí Republiky 5, Obecní Dum, CZ-110 00 Praha 1, Czech Republic *tel:* +420 2 231 5981/200 2425 *fax:* +420 2 231 0784 *email:* fok@login.cz. Roman Belor, mgr dir; Peter Polívka, orch mgr; Gaetano Delogu, principal cond.

Radio Symphony Orchestra Pilsen (52). Nam Miru 10, 320 70 Plzen, Czech Republic *tel:* +420 19 27 22 54 *also fax.* Jan Motlík, mgr; Jan Chalupecky, cond; Frantisek Sinkule, production.

West Bohemian Symphonic Orchestra. Hlavni 51, CZ-353 21 Mariánské Lázne, Czech Republic *tel:* +420 165 2141/2567 *fax:* +420 68 5228 511. Radomil Eliska, cond; Nada Domanjová, mgr.

Denmark

Aalborg Symphony Orchestra (63). Kjellerupsgade 14, DK-9000 Aalborg, Denmark *tel:* +45 98 131955 *fax:* +45 98 130378. Owain Arwel Hughes, chief cond.

Aarhus Symfoniorkester (72). Musikhuset, Thomas Jensens Alle, DK-Aarhus C, Denmark *tel:* +45 89 318280 *fax:* +45 86 127466 *email:* aso@post3.tele.dk. Jens Nielsen, gen and artistic dir; James Loughran, chief cond.

Copenhagen Philharmonic Orchestra (74). Ny Kongensgade 13, DK-1472 Kobenhavn K, Denmark *tel:* +45 33 911199 *fax:* +45 33 149034. Tomas Vitek, mgr.

Danish National Radio Symphony Orchestra (99). Radiohuset, Rosenørns Allé 22, DK-1999 Frederiksberg C, Denmark *tel:* +45 35 203040 *fax:* +45 35 206121 *email:* ron@dr.dk. Per Erik Veng, gen mgr and artistic dir; Ulf Schirmer, chief cond; Yuri Temirkanov, Michael Schoenwandt, principal guest conds.

De Unges Symfoniorkester Dusika. Tybjergvej 30, DK-2720 Vanlose, Denmark *tel:* +45 38 791705 *fax:* +45 43 543025. Karsten Johanning.

Det Kongelige Kapel (104). Postboks 2185, DK-1017 Kobenhavn K, Denmark *tel:* +45 33 696702 *fax:* +45 33 696767. Konges Nytorv; Klas Sjöblom, asst opera dir; Paavo Berglund, chief cond; Dietfried Bernet, chief guest cond.

Foroya Synfoniorkester. Fossagata, DK-700 Klaksvik, Denmark *tel:* +45 298 55 010.

Odense Symfoniorkester (73). Odense Koncerthus, Claus Bergs Gade 9, DK-5000 Odense, Denmark *tel:* +45 66 129357 *fax:* +45 65 910047. Jan Wagner, principal cond; Per Holst, gen mgr; Marianne Granvig, chief of public relations; Asger Bondo, librarian.

Randers Byorkester (10-30). Vaerket, Mariagervej 6, DK-8900 Randers, Denmark *tel:* +45 86 412833 *fax:* +45 86 412414 *email:* rbo@post3. tele.dk; http://home3.inet.tele.dk/rbo/. Bjarne Mørchjensen, concert admin; David Riddell, principal cond and mgr dir.

Royal Danish Orchestra (99). The Royal Theatre, Tordenskjoldsgade 8, Postboks 2185, DK-1017 Copenhagen, Denmark *tel:* +45 33 696701 *fax:* +45 33 696767 *email:* kgl-teat@inet.uni-c.dk. Elaine Padmore, artistic dir; Klas Sjöblom, orch mgr; Paavo Berglund, principal cond.

Sønderjyllands Symfoniorkester. Skovvej 16, DK-6400 Sonderborg, Denmark *tel:* +45 74 426161 *fax:* +45 74 426106.

Vestjysk Symfoniorkester. Islandsgade 50, DK-6700 Esbjerg, Denmark *tel:* +45 75 139399 *fax:* +45 75 133242. Leif Pedersen.

Egypt

Cairo Symphony Orchestra (96). c/o Egyptian Opera House, Geziro, Cairo, Egypt *tel:* +202 342 0601/02/03; +202 339 8157 *fax:* +202 342 0599; +202 339 8186 *email:* opera@frcu.eun.eg. Ahmed Elsaedi, mus dir and acting gen mgr; Khaled Abd El Halim, publicity offr; Sally Mahmoud Mostafa, fundraising and PR asst; Fawzy Abd Allah, financial admin; Laila Sayed Hassan, personnel admin.

Estonia

Estonian National Opera Symphony Orchestra (97). Estonia Pst 4, EE-0105 Tallinn, Estonia *tel:* +372 6 260201 *fax:* +372 6 313080 *email:* estonia@opera.teleport.ee. Paul Himma, gen mgr; Neeme Kuningas, artistic dir; Paul Mägi, mus dir and chief cond.

Estonian National Symphony Orchestra (98). Estonia Pst 4, EE-0001 Tallinn, Estonia *tel:* +372 2 446597 *fax:* +372 6 314055 *email:* erso@ estpak.ee. Ville-Markus Kell, mgr dir; Arvo Volmer, chief cond.

Faroe Islands

Faroe Symphony Orchestra (50). Undir Brúnni 5, 700 Klaksvik, Faroe Islands *tel:* +298 56502. Bogi Lützen, mgr; Martin Mouritsen, cond.

Finland

Finnish Radio Symphony Orchestra (98). PO Box 14, FIN-00024 YLE, Finland *tel:* +358 9 1480 4366 *fax:* +358 9 1480 3551. Jukka-Pekka Saraste, cond; Helena Hiilivirta, mgr.

Helsinki Philharmonic Orchestra (98). Finlandia Hall, Karamzinikatu 4, FIN-00100 Helsinki, Finland *tel:* +358 9 40241 *fax:* +358 9 406484 *email:* helsinki.philharmonic@fin.hel.fi. Leif Segerstam, chief cond; Helena Ahonen, gen mgr.

Orchestra of Finnish National Opera (112). Helsinginkatu 58, POB 176, FIN-00251 Helsinki, Finland *tel:* +358 403021 *fax:* +358 4030 2402. Okko Kamu, chief cond; Kari Tikka, cond; Ollitapio Lehtinen, leader; Heikki Riikonen, orch mgr.

Symphony Orchestra Vivo (90). Länsitie 7B, FIN-11120 Riihimäki, Finland *tel:* +358 14 722 722 *fax:* +358 14 722 711. Riitta Nisonen, mgr dir; Kari Tikka, cond.

Tampere Philharmonic Orchestra (82). Yliopistonkatu 55, FIN-33100 Tampere, Finland *tel:* +358 3 243 4411 *fax:* +358 3 243 4400. Tuomas Ollila, artistic dir; Janos Fürst, principal visiting cond; Maritta Hirvonen, gen mgr.

Turku Philharmonic Orchestra (73). Sibeliuksenkatu 2a, FIN-20110 Turku, Finland *tel:* +358 21 2314 577 *fax:* +358 21 2328 231. Jacques Mercier, mus dir; Kalevi Kuosa, mgr.

Vaasa City Orchestra. Vaasanp 12, FN-65100 Vaasa, Finland *tel:* +358 6 325 3761.

France

La Chapelle Royale/Orchestre des Champs Elysées (50). 10 Rue Coquilliere, F-75001 Paris, France *tel:* +33 1 40 26 58 00 *fax:* +33 1 40 26 38 37 *email:* royale@micronet.fr. Philippe Herreweghe, mus dir; Stephan Maciejewski, artistic adviser; Nicolas Droin, admin; David Reveillault, stage mgr.

Orchestre de Paris (114). Salle Pleyel, 252 Rue du Faubourg St Honoré, F-75008 Paris, France *tel:* +33 1 45 61 65 60 *fax:* +33 1 42 89 24 49. Semyon Bychkov, mus dir; Michel Prada, president; Georges-François Hirsch, gen dir; Virpi Nurni, gen sec.

Orchestre des Concerts Lamoureux (96). 252 Rue du Faubourg Saint Honoré, F-75008 Paris, France *tel:* +33 1 45 63 44 34/60 62 *fax:* +33 1 45 62 05 41. Annie Foultier, admin; Michel Gauci, president.

Orchestre National Bordeaux-Aquitaine (126). BP 95, F-33025 Bordeaux Cédex, France *tel:* +33 56 44 70 71; +33 56 48 58 54 (box office) *fax:* +33 56 44 64 85. Alain Lombard, artistic dir and resident cond; Daniel Dourneau Gabory, admin dir.

Orchestre National de France (118). 116 Av du Président Kennedy, F-75786 Paris, Cédex 16, France *tel:* +33 1 42 30 26 03 *fax:* +33 1 42 30 43 33. Charles Dutoit, mus dir; Hélène Montussac, press and PR.

Orchestre National de Lille (100). 30 Place Mendès France, BP 119, F-59027 Lille Cédex, France *tel:* +33 3 20 12 82 40 *fax:* +33 3 20 78 29 10. Jacqueline Brochen, admin dir; Jean-Claude Casadesus, dir and cond.

Orchestre National de Lyon (102). 82 Rue de Bonnel, F-69431 Lyon Cédex 03, France *tel:* +33 4 78 95 95 00 *fax:* +33 4 78 60 13 08. Patrice Armengau, gen dir; Emmanuel Krivine, mus dir.

Orchestre National du Capitole de Toulouse. Halle aux Grains, Place Dupuy, F-31000 Toulouse, France *tel:* +33 61 23 21 35 *fax:* +33 61 62 10 48. Michel Plasson, artistic dir; Dominique Baudis, president; Régine Jonquière, admin.

Orchestre Philharmonique de Montpelier (91). Le Corum, BP 9056, F-34041 Montpelier, France *tel:* +33 67 61 67 21 *fax:* +33 67 61 67 20 *email:* http://www.intel-media.fr/opm. Friedemann Layer, mus dir; Dominique Stobinsky, admin dir; René Koering, gen dir.

Orchestre Philharmonique de Nice (120). 9 Rue de la Terrasse, F-06300 Nice, France *tel:* +33 93 80 59 83 *fax:* +33 93 80 34 83. Klaus Weis, mus dir; Pierre Médecin, artistic dir.

Orchestre Philharmonique de Radio-France (138). 116 Av du Président Kennedy, F-75220 Paris Cédex 16, France *tel:* +33 1 42 30 36 30 *fax:* +33 1 42 30 47 48. Marek Janowski, mus dir; Eric Montalbetti, artistic delegate.

Orchestre Philharmonique de Strasbourg (112). Place de Bordeaux, F-67070 Strasbourg Cédex, France *tel:* +33 03 88 15 09 00 *fax:* +33 03 88 15 09 01. Albert Moritz, admin dir; Theodor Guschlbauer, artistic dir; Philippe Olivier, mkt dir.

Orchestre Philharmonique des Pays de Loire (102). Maison des Arts, 25 Av Montaigne, F-49000 Angers, France *tel:* +33 41 24 11 24 *fax:* +33 41 87 80 52. Hubert Soudant, mus dir; Pierre Cueill, president.

Orchestre Symphonique et Lyrique de Nancy. 1 Rue Sainte Catherine, F-54000 Nancy, France *tel:* +33 83 85 33 20 *fax:* +33 83 85 30 66. Jean-Marie Blanchard, gen admin; Christopher Bezzone, admin.

Philharmonie de Lorraine (70). 25 Av Robert Schuman, F-57000 Metz, France *tel:* +33 87 55 12 02 *fax:* +33 87 65 69 36. Jacques Houtmann, mus dir; Christine Raffin, president.

Germany

Bamberger Symphoniker (112). Mußstr 1, D-96047 Bamberg, Germany *tel:* +49 951 964 7100 *fax:* +49 951 964 7123. Francis Hunter, mgr and mus dir; Horst Stein, cond laureate; Ingo Metzmacher, principal guest cond.

Bayerische Staatsorchester. Nationaltheater, Max-Joseph-Platz 2, D-80539 München, Germany *tel:* +49 89 2185 01 *fax:* +49 89 2185 1003. Zubin Mehta, mus dir (from Sep 98).

Berlin Philharmonic Orchestra (120). Matthäikirchstr 1, D-10785 Berlin, Germany *tel:* +49 30 254 880 *fax:* +49 30 261 4887. Claudio Abbado, mus dir; Elmar Weingarten, gen mgr; Helge Grünewald, press and PR.

Berlin Symphonic Orchestra (71). Charlottenstr 56, D-14057 Berlin, Germany *tel:* +49 30 209 02002 *fax:* +49 30 229 1818. Alun Francis, principal cond; Jochen Thärichen, mgr.

Dresden Philharmonic (119). Postfach 120368, Kulturplast Am Altmarkt, D-01005 Dresden, Germany *tel:* +49 351 486 6282 *fax:* +49 351 486 6283 *email:* philharm@.imedia.de. Olivier von Winterstein, mgr; Michel Plasson, mus dir; Juri Temirkanow, principal guest cond; Kurt Masur, cond laureate.

Düsseldorf Symphonic Orchestra (130). Ehrenhof 1, Tonhalle, D-40479 Düsseldorf, Germany *tel:* +49 211 899 3606 *fax:* +49 211 892 9143. Salvador Mas Conde, mus dir; Elisabeth von Leliwa, press; Thomas Stührk, orch mgr.

Essen Philharmonic Orchestra (101). Rolandstrasse 10, D-45128 Essen, Germany *tel:* +49 201 812 2290 *fax:* +49 210 812 292. Wolf-Dieter Hauschild, principal cond.

Hamburg Symphony Orchestra (67). Dammtorwall 46, D-20355 Hamburg, Germany *tel:* +49 40 344851 *fax:* +49 40 353788. Miguel Gómez-Martínez, principal cond; Peter Dannenberg, gen mgr.

Handelfestspielorchester (104). Opernhaus Halle, Universitätsring 24, D-06108 Halle (Saale), Germany *tel:* +49 345 511 0300 *fax:* +49 345 511 0303. Klaus Froboese, gen mgr; Reinhard Popp, dir; Roger Epple, gen mus dir.

Kölner Rundfunk-Sinfonie-Orchester (118). Westdeutscher Rundfunk, D-50600 Köln, Germany *tel:* +49 221 220 3140 *fax:* +49 221 220 2492. Hans Vonk, principal cond.

Leipziger Gewandhausorchester (193). Gewandhaus zu Leipzig, Augustusplatz 8, D-04109 Leipzig, Germany *tel:* +49 341 12 700 *fax:* +49 341 12 70200. Kurt Masur, principal cond.

MDR Sinfonieorchester (168). Springerstr 22-24, D-04105 Leipzig, Germany *tel:* +49 341 300 5505 *fax:* +49 341 300 5532 *email:* http:// www.mdr.de/klangkoerper. Hubertus Franzen, admin; Manfred Honeck, Fabio Luisi, Marcello Viotti, principal conds.

Munich Philharmonic (130). Gasteig-Kulturzentrum, Kellerstr 4/III, D-81667 München, Germany *tel:* +49 89 4809 8509 *fax:* +49 89 4809 8513. Bernd Gellermann, mgr.

Kanagawa Philharmonic Orchestra. Hanami-dai 4-2, Hodogaya-ku, Yokohama 240, Japan *tel:* +81 45 331 4001 *fax:* +81 45 331 4022. Yuzo Toyama, mus dir; Yutaka Ueno, exec dir.

Kyoto City Symphony Orchestra. 103 Izumoji Tatehoncho, Kita-ku, Kyoto-shi 603, Japan *tel:* +81 75 222 0331.

Kyushu Symphony Orchestra. 1-11-50 Shichi Kuma, Jonan-ku, Fukuoka-shi 814, Japan *tel:* +81 92 823 0101.

Nagoya Philharmonic Orchestra. c/o Shimin Hall, 1-5-1 Kanayama, Naka-ku, Nagoya 460, Japan *tel:* +81 52 322 2775 *fax:* +81 52 322 3066. Taijiro Iimori, cond; Susumu Nonoyama, mgr.

New Japan Philharmonic (100). Sumida Triphony Hall, 1-2-3 Kinshi, Sumida-ku, Tokyo 130, Japan *tel:* +81 3 5610 3820 *fax:* +81 3 5610 3825. Seiji Ozawa, hon artistic dir; Chiyoshige Matsubara.

NHK Symphony Orchestra (112). 2-16 49 Takanawa, Minato-ku, Tokyo 108, Japan *tel:* +81 3 3443 0271 *fax:* +81 3 3443 0278. Ken Soga, chmn; Takeshi Hara, dep chmn.

Osaka Philharmonic Orchestra (96). 1-1-44 Kishinosato, Nishinari-ku, Osaka 557, Japan *tel:* +81 6 656 7711 *fax:* +81 6 656 7714. Takashi Asahina, gen mus dir; Shoji Onodera, sec gen.

Sendai Philharmonic Orchestra (65). 1-3-9 Nishikicho, Aoba-ku, Sendai 980, Japan *tel:* +81 22 225 3934 *fax:* +81 22 225 4238. Yuzo Toyama, mus dir; Saneyuki Yoshi, mgr dir.

Tokyo Metropolitan Symphony Orchestra. c/o Bunka Kaikan, 5-45 Ueno Koen Taito-ku, Tokyo 110, Japan *tel:* +81 3 3822 0727.

Tokyo Philharmonic Orchestra. Eiritsu Building, 3-3 Kanda Kajicho, Chiyoda-ku, Tokyo 101, Japan *tel:* +81 3 3256 9696 *fax:* +81 3 3256 9698. Kazushi Ohno, cond; Shogo Matsuki, dir.

Korea

Korean Symphony Orchestra. c/o National Theatre, 67-San 1a, 2Ga Chang Chung-Dong, Chung-gu, Seoul, Korea *tel:* +82 2 269 2857 *fax:* +82 2 277 7222. Yun-Talk Hong, cond.

Pusan Philharmonic Orchestra. 213-4 Kaiyon 4 Dong, Nam-gu, Pusan, Korea *tel:* +82 51 625 8130 *fax:* +82 51 625 8138. Vanco Cavadarski, principal cond; Kim Jong Hae, dir gen.

Seoul Philharmonic Orchestra. Sejong Cultural Centre, 81-3 Sejong-Ro, Chong Ro-Gu, Seoul 110-050, Korea *tel:* +82 2 736 2721 *fax:* +82 2 738 0948. Kyung-Soo Won, mus dir; Pyeong-Kwon Oh, mgr; Sang-Chul Woo, PR mgr.

Latvia

Latvian National Symphony Orchestra (102). 6 Amatu St, LV-1664 Riga, Latvia *tel:* +371 7 224850/229537 *fax:* +371 7 224850. Terje Mikkelsen, mus dir; Reinis Galenieks, mgr dir; Janis Gauja, artist representative.

Latvian Philharmonic Chamber Orchestra (21). Vagnera St 4, LV-1050 Riga, Latvia *tel:* +371 2 324649/223618 *fax:* +371 2 213497. Dzintars Josts, artistic dir and principal cond; Valery Avramenko, mgr.

Liepaja Symphony Orchestra (65). Graudu 50, LV-3401 Liepaja, Latvia *tel:* +371 34 25538; +371 34 25588 *also fax.* Imants Resnis, artistic dir and chief cond; Vija Feldmane, mgr.

Lithuania

Lithuanian National Symphony Orchestra (101). Ausros Vartu 5, 2001 Vilnius, Lithuania *tel:* +370 2 627 047 *fax:* +370 2 622 859. Juozas Domarkas, artistic dir and chief cond; Gintautas Kevisas, gen dir; Eugenijus Janutenas, mgr.

Lithuanian State Symphony Orchestra (96). Zygimantu 6, 2600 Vilnius, Lithuania *tel:* +370 2 628127 *fax:* +370 2 220966. Gintaras Rinkevicius, chief cond and artistic dir; Eugenijus Butvydas, mgr dir; Alfredas Pacevicius, concert mgr; Jonas Vilimas, publicity and information mgr.

Luxembourg

Orchestre Philharmonique du Luxembourg (80). Villa Louvigny, BP 2243, L 1022, Luxembourg *tel:* +352 22 99 01205 *fax:* +352 22 99 98. Jacques Mauroy, Olivier Frank, mgr; David Shallon, chief cond.

Malaysia

Malaysian Philharmonic Orchestra. c/o IMG Artists Asia, 11th Floor Menara Dayabumi, Jalan Sultan Hishamuddin, Peti Surat 12444, 50778 Kuala Lumpur, Malaysia *tel:* +603 275 3274 *fax:* +603 275 3271. Kees Bakels, mus dir; Chean See Ooi, resident cond.

Mexico

Filarmónica de la Ciudad de México. Periférico Sur 5141, Col Isidro Fabela, 14030 México DF, Mexico *tel:* +52 905 606 8933 *fax:* +52 905 606 8401. Luis Herrera de la Fuente, cond; Namiko Jhombeck, gen mgr.

Filarmonica del Queretaro (80). Auditoria Josefa Ortiz de Dominguez, Puerta 5, Av Constituentes S/N Esquina Zimapan, 76040 Queretaro, Qro, Mexico *tel:* +91 42 231682 *fax:* +91 42 130707. Sergio Cardenas, mus dir and principal cond; Mariano Medina Gómez, gen mgr.

National Symphony Orchestra of Mexico (120). Regina 52, Centro, 06080 Mexico DF, México *tel:* +52 5 709 8118 *fax:* +52 5 709 3533. Enrique Arturo Diemecke, mus dir; Javier Cuétara-Priede, gen mgr; Eduardo Neri-Chaires, artistic mgr.

Orquesta Filarmónica de Jalisco (85). Teatro Degollado, 44100 Guadalajara, Jalisco, Mexico *tel:* +52 658 3812/3819 *fax:* +52 614 9366/658 3820. José Guadalupe Flores, principal cond and mus dir; Silvia Susana Hernandez Huerta, mgr.

State of Mexico Symphony Orchestra (85). Plaza Fray Andrés de Castro, Edif C Primer Piso, 50000 Toluca, Edo de Mexico *tel:* +52 72 44 5219 *fax:* +52 72 45 6216. Enrique Batiz, gen dir; Alfredo Higuera Hernandez, admin dir.

Moldova

National Orchestra for Radio and Television. Miorita Str 1, 277012 Chisinau, Moldova *tel:* +373 0422 721028. Gheorghe Ion Mustea, artistic dir.

Symphony Orchestra of the National Philharmonic of Moldova (93). 78 Mitropolitul Vaarlam Str, 277012 Chisinau, Moldova *tel:* +37 32 224016 *fax:* +37 32 233509. Seicanu Vladimir, dir gen; Luther Robert, chief cond and artistic dir; Valentin Doni, cond.

Monaco

Orchestre Philharmonique de Monte-Carlo (86). BP 139, 98007 Monte-Carlo, Monaco *tel:* +33 93 92 16 21 21 *fax:* +33 93 93 15 08 71. James DePreist, mus dir; René Croési, admin.

Netherlands

Arnhem Philharmonic Orchestra (94). Jansbuitensingel 29 111, NL-6811 AD Arnhem, Netherlands *tel:* +31 26 442 2632 *fax:* +31 26 443 9966. Roberto Benzi, mus dir.

Barokorkest van De Nederlandse Bachvereniging (20). Postbus 12017, NL-3501 AA Utrecht, Netherlands *tel:* +31 30 251 3522/3413 *fax:* +31 30 251 1639. Maria Hansen, mgr dir; Jos van Veldhoven, artistic dir.

Brabant Philharmonic Orchestra (80). J Van Lieshoutstraat 5, NL-5611 EE Eindhoven, Netherlands *tel:* +31 40 265 5699 *fax:* +31 40 246 3459. Marc Soustrot, chief cond; Jaap Van Zweden, principal guest cond; Detlev Weeks, mgr dir.

The Gelders Orchestra (94). Jansbuitensingel 29-III, PO Box 1180, NL-6801 BD Arnhem, Netherlands *tel:* +31 26 442 2632 *fax:* +31 26 443 9966. Roberto Benzi, principal cond; Jan Taat, mgr; Benno Brugmans, PR; Dolf Hofs, deputy mgr.

Limburgs Symphony Orchestra/Symphony Orchestra of Maastricht (66). Statenstraat 5, NL-6211 TB Maastricht, Netherlands *tel:* +31 43 350 7000 *fax:* +31 43 350 7025 *email:* lsomaafn@worldxs.worldaccess. nl. Detlev Weers, mgr dir; Shlomo Mintz, principal guest cond.

Netherlands Ballet Orchestra (90). Muziektheater, Waterlooplein 22, NL-1011 PG Amsterdam, Netherlands *tel:* +31 20 551 8823 *fax:* +31 20 620 8019 *email:* info@balletorkest.nl; http://www.balletorkest.nl. Rob Tijsen, mgr; Maurits Haenen, deputy mgr; Julia Bastiaanse, planning; Thierry Fischer, chief cond.

Netherlands Philharmonic Orchestra (140). Beurs van Berlage, Damrak 213, NL-1012 ZH Amsterdam, Netherlands *tel:* +31 20 627 1161 *fax:* +31 20 622 9939. Jan Willem Loot, mgr dir; Herbert Slegers, artistic mgr; Hartmut Haenchen, chief cond; Philippe Entremont, principal guest cond.

Netherlands Radio Philharmonic (108). Heuvellaan 33, PO Box 125, NL-1200 AC Hilversum, Netherlands *tel:* +31 35 6714 130 *fax:* +31 35 6714 171. Edo de Waart, mus dir; Rob Overman, mgr.

Noord-Nederlands Orchestra (87). Emmaplein 2, PO Box 818, NL-9700 AV Groningen, Netherlands *tel:* +31 50 126200 *fax:* +31 50 138164 *email:* nno@tref.nl. Ton Verberne, gen mgr; Viktor Liberman, chief cond.

Noordhollands Philharmonisch Orkest (NPO) (70). Klokhuisplein 2A, NL-2011 HK Haarlem, Netherlands *tel:* +31 235 31 92 48 *fax:* +31 235 32 85 33. Stan Paardekooper, gen mgr; David Porceljn, chief cond.

Radio Symphony Orchestra (93). Heuvellaan 33, PO Box 125, NL-1200 AC Hilversum, Netherlands *tel:* +31 35 6714 140 *fax:* +31 35 6714 171. Eri Klas, chief cond; Siebe Riedstra, mgr.

Residentie Orkest The Hague (109). Spuiplein 150, NL-2511 DG Den Haag, Netherlands *tel:* +31 70 360 7925 *also fax.* H van den Akker, gen mgr; Evgenii Svetlanov, chief cond; Leo Samama, artistic mgr.

Rotterdam Philharmonic Orchestra (114). De Doelen, Kruisstraat 2, NL-3012 CT Rotterdam, Netherlands *tel:* +31 10 217 1760 *fax:* +31 10 404 8023. Paul Zeegers, gen mgr; Kees Hillen, artistic leader; Valery Gergiev, principal cond.

Royal Concertgebouw Orchestra (115). Jacob Obrechtstraat 51, NL-1071 KJ Amsterdam, Netherlands *tel:* +31 20 679 2211 *fax:* +31 20 676 3331 *email:* http://www.concertgebouworkest.com. Willem Wynbergen, mgr dir; Riccardo Chailly, chief cond.

A World of Music from RTÉ

Radio Telefís Éireann, Ireland's national television and radio service, has a commitment to music which goes far beyond it's extensive broadcasting output.

It is the proud custodian of :

National Symphony Orchestra of Ireland

The National Symphony Orchestra of Ireland is among the most vibrant international orchestras playing and recording today. Since its inception as a small ensemble in 1926, it has developed, not only as an integral part of the Irish national broadcasting service, but also as the backbone of classical music throughout Ireland.

In addition to its concert season in Dublin, the NSOI also undertakes twice-yearly national tours, ensuring that in addition to fulfiling its broadcasting commitments, RTÉ brings top-class music making to thousands of people in regional centres.

Around the world too, the NSOI is creating a widespread reputation through its multi-disc contract with Naxos, one of the world's largest classical music labels and it is one of the most extensively recorded orchestras in the world. The NSOI was the resident orchestra at the Hong Kong Midsummer Classics Festival in 1996, where it was greeted with standing ovations, capacity crowds and rave reviews.

The NSOI travelled to Innsbruck and London, Glasgow and Edinburgh in 1997 and returns to Germany in 1998 and as a result of huge international interest, there are also plans to travel to the USA.

RTÉ Concert Orchestra

The RTÉ Concert Orchestra, Ireland's national radio orchestra, works right across the musical spectrum, being equally at home with the classics and pop, opera and musicals. Their versatility has earned them an enviable reputation. They have performed to acclaim at Expo'92 in Seville and have graced stages in America, Europe and at every musical venue in Ireland.

Over 300 million television viewers watched their seventh Eurovision Song Contest this year.

RTÉ's other performing groups offer further evidence of the breadth of musical talent being nurtured:

The RTÉ Vanbrugh String Quartet,
The RTÉ Philharmonic Choir,
Cór na nÓg (Young Peoples Choir)

RTÉ FM3 Classical Radio provides the world's finest music to listeners throughout Ireland every day.

For Enquiries Contact: Simon Taylor, Head of Orchestra/Performing Groups, RTE, Dublin 4, Ireland. Tel: Dublin 208 3111, Fax: 208 2511

New Zealand

Auckland Philharmonia Orchestra (55). PO Box 56-024, Auckland 3, New Zealand *tel:* +64 9 638 7073 *fax:* +64 9 630 9687. Lloyd Williams, gen mgr.

Christchurch Symphony Orchestra (110). PO Box 3260, Christchurch 8000, New Zealand *tel:* +64 3 379 3886 *fax:* +64 3 379 3861 *email:* tk@cso.co.nz; http://www.cso.co.nz. Iola Shelley, artistic dir; Jan van den Berg, concert master; A H Kunowski, gen mgr; Sir William Southgate, cond laureate.

New Zealand Symphony Orchestra (89). PO Box 6640, Wellington 6035, New Zealand *tel:* +64 4 3851 735 *fax:* +64 4 3842 824 *email:* nzso@actrix.gen.nz. Mark Keyworth, chief exec; Franz-Paul Decker, cond laureate.

Norway

Bergen Philharmonic Orchestra (97). Grieghallen, Lars Hilles Gate 3a, N-5015 Bergen, Norway *tel:* +47 5521 6100 *fax:* +47 5531 8534. Jostein Osnes, gen mgr; Dmitri Kitayenko, artistic dir; Tarjei Flotve, orch mgr.

Kristiansand Symfoniorkester (38). PO Box 777, N-4601 Kristiansand, Norway *tel:* +47 3802 2440 *fax:* +47 3802 2991. Nina Badendyck, mgr dir; Jan Stigmer, leader; Terje Mikkelsen, principal cond.

Norwegian Baroque Orchestra. c/o Tore Aasen Aune, Paul Fjermastadsv 18, N-7017 Trondheim, Norway *tel:* +47 73 51 72 10 *fax:* +47 73 51 72 24.

Norwegian Chamber Orchestra (15-40). Stockholmsgata 12, N-0566 Oslo, Norway *tel:* +47 2204 6270 *fax:* +47 2204 6290. Bernt Lauritz Larsen, mgr dir; Iona Brown, art dir.

Oslo Philharmonic Orchestra (107). PO Box 1607 Vika, Haakon VIIs gt 2, Munkedamsveien 14, N-0119 Oslo, Norway *tel:* +47 22 014900 *fax:* +47 22 014901. Trond Okkelmo, mgr dir; Mariss Jansons, mus dir.

Stavanger Symfoniorkester (65). Bjergsted, N-4007 Stavanger, Norway *tel:* +47 5150 8830 *fax:* +47 5150 8839. Alexander Dmitriev, artistic leader and chief cond; Frans Brüggen, artistic dir; Stein Slyngstad, dir; Erik Landmark, gen mgr.

Trondheim Symfoniorkester (71). Post Box 774 Sentrum, N-7001 Trondheim, Norway *tel:* +47 7353 0760 *fax:* +47 7351 4888. Siri Fristad Mathisen, gen mgr and publicity mgr; Berndt Sandotad, orch dir; Daniel Harding, chief cond.

Peru

Orquesta Sinfónica Nacional. Avda Javier Prado Este 2465, Lima 41, Peru *tel:* +51 37 7633 *also fax.* José Carlos Santos, cond and artistic dir.

Phillippines

Manila Symphony Orchestra. Manila Metropolitan Theater, Liwasang Bonifacio, PO Box 664, Manila, Phillippines. Alfredo Buenaventura, mus dir.

National Philharmonic Orchestra (80). MC PO Box 2650, Makati, Metro Manila, Phillippines *tel:* +64 817 2601/815 2651/810 7988 *fax:* +64 815 3483. Redentor L Romero, cond and mus dir; Marilou Veloso, mgr.

Philippine Philharmonic Orchestra. Cultural Center of the Philippines, Roxas Blvd, Manila, Phillippines *tel:* +63 2 832 1125 *fax:* +63 2 832 3683. Oscar Yatco, mus dir; Amelita D Guevara, exec dir.

Poland

Kielce Philharmonic (85). Plac Moniuszki 2B, PL-25334 Kielce, Poland *tel:* +48 41 368 1140/0501/0502 *fax:* +48 41 368 1191. Szymon Kawalla, gen dir, artistic dir and cond; Leonard Skrobacz, deputy dir; Zbigniew Goncerzewicz, asst cond; Sylwester Furmanczyk, admin section mgr.

Krakow Philharmonic (110). ul Zwierzyniecka 1, PL-31103 Kraków, Poland *tel:* +48 12 224312 *also fax.* Joanna Wnuk-Nazarowa, artistic and mgr dir; Jerzy Maksymiuk, principal guest cond.

Lublin Philharmonic (70). ul Kosciuski 39, PL-10503 Olsztyn, Poland *tel:* +48 81 24421. Agnieszka Kreiner, artistic and mgr dir.

Orchestra of the National Theatre. Plac Teatralny 1, PL-00-950 Warszawa, Poland *tel:* +48 22 826 3001 ext 305 *fax:* +48 22 826 0423/5012. Grzegorz Nowak, dir.

Philharmonic Orchestra. ul Narutowicza 20, PL-90135 Lodz, Poland.

Polish Chamber Orchestra. Palac Kultury i Nauki, PL-00110 Warszawa, Poland.

Polish Radio National Symphony Orchestra (118). Pl Sejmu Slaskiego 2, PL-40032 Katowice, Poland *tel:* +48 32 518903; +48 32 255 3261 *fax:* +48 32 571384. Antoni Wit, artistic dir and chief cond; Irena Siodmok, mgr dir.

Poznan Philharmonic (90). ul Sw Marcina 81, PL-61808 Poznan, Poland *tel:* +48 61 524708/9; +48 61 523451 *also fax.* Andrey Boreyko, artistic dir and cond.

Silesian State Philharmonic in Katowice (100). ul Sokolska 2, PL-40084 Katowice, Poland *tel:* +48 32 597571/598679/586261 *fax:* +48 32 589885. Jerzy Swoboda, gen dir, artistic dir and symphonic cond; Jan Wincenty Hawel, chmbr orch cond.

State Philharmonic Orchestra (100). ul Pilsudskiego 19, PL-50044 Wroclaw, Poland *tel:* +48 71 342 2001 *fax:* +48 71 342 8980. Marek Pijarowski, cond and mgr; Tadeusz Nesterowicz, asst mgr.

Szymanowski Philharmonic Orchestra (110). ul Zwierzyniecka 1, PL-310103 Kraków, Poland *tel:* +48 12 220958; +48 12 224312 *also fax.* Joanna Wnuk-Nazarowa, mgr dir; Jerzy Maksymiuk, artistic adviser; Vladimir Ponkin, cond.

Warsaw Philharmonic (112). ul Jasna 5, PL-00950 Warszawa, Poland *tel:* +48 22 826 8311/5617 *also fax; email:* phil@pol.pl. Kazimierz Kord, artistic mgr and chief cond; Borys Frydrychowicz, deputy dir.

Portugal

Gulbenkian Orchestra (70). Fundaçao Calouuste Gulbenkian, Av de Berna 45, P-1093 Lisboa, Portugal *tel:* +351 1 793 5131 *fax:* +351 1 793 5139 *email:* http://www.telepac.pt/earte/gulbenkianz. Muhai Tang, principal cond; Claudio Scimone, hon cond; Michael Zilm, principal guest cond; Max Rabinovitsz, asst cond and concertmaster.

Lisbon Metropolitan Orchestra (40). Travessa da Galé 36, P-1300 Lisboa, Portugal *tel:* +351 1 362 3830 *fax:* +351 1 362 3833. Miguel Graça Moura, artistic dir; Cristina Ribeiro, exec dir; Manuela Magallães, mkt dir.

Oporto Classical Orchestra (52). Mosteiro de S Bento da Vitória, Rua de S Bento da Vitória, P-4000 Porto, Portugal *tel:* +351 2 200 6547/8/9 *fax:* +351 2 312 111. Manuel Ivo Cruz, artistic dir and cond; António Florencio, mgr.

Portuguese Symphony Orchestra (110). Fundação São Carlos, Rua Serpa Pinto 9, P-1200 Lisboa, Portugal *tel:* +1 351 343 1734 *fax:* +1 351 343 1735. Paulo Ferreira de Castro, artistic dir of the foundation; Alvaro Cassuto, artistic dir and principal cond.

Republic of Georgia

Chamber Orchestra (21). 21/48 Chavchavadze St, Tbilisi, Republic of Georgia *tel:* +995 32 966624 *fax:* +995 32 953829. Vadim Shubladze, dir and cond; Manana Ivardava, mgr.

Republic of Ireland

National Symphony Orchestra of Ireland (88). RTE, Donnybrook, Dublin 4, Republic of Ireland *tel:* +353 1 208 2799 *fax:* +353 1 208 2522. Kasper de Roo, principal cond; Cathal MacCabe, head of mus; Simon Taylor, head of orch; Paddy McElwee, orch mgr; Claire Meehan, concerts mgr.

RTE Concert Orchestra (44). RTE, Donnybrook, Dublin 4, Republic of Ireland *tel:* +353 1 208 2779 *fax:* +353 1 208 2511. Proinnsias O Duinn, principal cond; Cathal MacCabe, head of mus; Simon Taylor, head of orch and perf groups; Sam Ellis, orch mgr; Clarie Meehan, concerts mgr.

Romania

Arad State Philharmonic (60). Piata George Enescu 1, 2900 Arad, Romania *tel:* +40 57 216284 *fax:* +40 57 217867. Dorin Frandes, gen mus dir and cond; Cristian George Neagu, cond; Codruta Blagaila, mus sec.

Brasov State Philharmonic. Str H Hirscher 10, 2200 Brasov, Romania *tel:* +40 68 143113 *fax:* +40 68 150950.

Iasi Philharmonic (105). Str Cuza Voda 29, 6600 Iasi, Romania *tel:* +40 32 114601/112100/212620 *fax:* +40 32 214160. Viorel Liviu Braica, artistic dir; Gheorghe Costin, Camil Marinescu, orch conds.

Sibiu State Philharmonic. St Filarmonicii 2, 2400 Sibiu, Romania *tel:* +40 69 433 506.

Transylvania State Philharmonic, Cluj-Napoca (110). St Emanuel de Martonne 1, 3400 Cluj-Napoca, Romania *tel:* +40 64 430060/3 *fax:* +40 64 197812. George Dudea, gen dir; Adrian Pop, programme mgr; Emil Simon, cond.

Russia

Bolshoi Symphony Orchestra (130). Bolshoi Theatre, Petrovka St 1, Moscow, Russia *tel:* +7 095 292 6570 *fax:* +7 095 292 9032. Aleksandr Lazarev, mus dir and cond; Vladimir Kokonin, dir; Sergei Selivanov, orch mgr.

Russian National Symphony Orchestra. Studio Moscow, Alexeya Tolstovo St 26-33, 103001 Moscow, Russia *tel:* +7 0 95 290 6262 *fax:* +7 0 95 292 6511. Mikhail Pletnev, founder and cond; Tatyana Sukhacheva, mgr.

Russian State Philharmonic Orchestra. 18 Murmansky Proezd, App 77, 129075 Moscow, Russia *tel:* +7 095 233 8996. Valery Poljansky, chief cond.

St Petersburg Philharmoni (105). Mikhailovskaya St 2, 191011 St Petersburg, Russia *tel:* +7 812 311 7331 *fax:* +7 812 311 2126. Yuri Temirkanov, mus dir and principal cond; Sergei Cherniadiev, orch mgr; Boris Skvortzov, orch dir.

Singapore

Singapore Symphony Orchestra (90). 2nd Floor, Victoria Memorial Hall, 11 Empress Pl, Singapore 179558, Singapore *tel:* +65 336 4417 *fax:* +65 336 6382 *email:* singsymp@temasek.teleview.com.sp. Choo Hoey, mus dir; Tisa Ng, gen mgr.

Slovak Republic

Kosice State Philharmonic (85). Dom Umenia, Moyesova, 041 23 Kosice, Slovak Republic *tel:* +421 95 622 4514/4509 *also fax.* Julius Klein, exec dir; Bystrík Rezucha, chief cond.

Slovak Radio Symphonic Orchestra (99). Mytná 1, 812 90 Bratislava, Slovak Republic *tel:* +421 17 11162 *fax:* +421 17 393947. R Stankovsky, chief cond.

Slovenia

Slovenian Philharmonic (100). Kongresni Trg 10, PO Box 156, 61000 Ljubljana, Slovenia *tel:* +386 61 213554 *fax:* +386 61 213640. Boris Sinigoj, dir; Marko Letonja, artistic dir and cond.

Slovenian Radio and Television Symphony Orchestra. Tavcarjeva 17, 61000 Ljubljana, Slovenia *tel:* +386 61 131 1333.

South Africa

Cape Town Philharmonic Orchestra (85). PO Box 4040, Cape Town 8000, South Africa *tel:* +27 21 418 9190 *fax:* +27 21 418 9187. Bernhard Gueller, principal cond; Anthony Kuhnert, artistic mgr.

Natal Philharmonic Orchestra (70). PO Box 5353, Durban 4000, Natal, South Africa *tel:* +27 31 9555/9437/9438 *fax:* +27 31 306 2166 *email:* 100075.2027@compuserve.com. Stephen Wikner, dir.

New Arts Philharmonic Orchestra Pretoria (NAPOP) (68). PO Box 566, Pretoria 0001, South Africa *tel:* +27 12 322 1665 *fax:* +27 12 322 3913. Ivan Christian, snr mgr; Isobel van der Poll, admin mgr; Gérard Korsten, principal cond.

Spain

Bilbao Symphony Orchestra (94). Ledesma 4, 7, E-48001 Bilbao, Spain *tel:* +4 423 5487 *fax:* +4 423 3889. Luis Mariá Mardaras, gen sec; Theo Alcántara, artistic dir.

City of Palma Symphony Orchestra, Baleares (67). C/Vicente Juan Rosselló 22, E-07013 Palma de Mallorca, Spain *tel:* +34 71 287 565 *fax:* +34 71 287 758. Sebastian Roig, mgr; Mariano Isasi, admin; Salvador Brotons, principal cond.

Gran Teatre del Liceu Symphony Orchestra (100). Sant Pau 1 Bis, E-08001 Barcelona, Spain *tel:* +3 485 9900 *fax:* +3 485 9919. Oriol Ponsa, mgr.

La Capella Reial de Catalunya. Traversera de Gracia, 18-20 2, E-08021 Barcelona, Spain *tel:* +34 3 580 6069. Jordi Savall, mus dir; Irene Bloc, admin.

Le Concert des Nations (30-45). Travesera de Gracia 18-20 2, E-08021 Barcelona, Spain *tel:* +34 3 580 6069 *email:* 101617.3236@compuserve.com. Jordi Savall, mus dir; Irene Bloc, admin.

National Orchestra and Chorus of Spain (124). Auditorio Nacional de Música, Principe de Vergara 146, E-28002 Madrid, Spain *tel:* +34 1 337 0213 *fax:* +34 1 563 2907. Tomás Marco, technical dir.

Orquesta de Cadaqués (60). Arcs 8, 1er 2a, E-08002 Barcelona, Spain *tel:* +34 3301 9555 *fax:* +34 3302 2670 *email:* trito@bcn:servicom.es. Llorenç Caballero, president and artistic dir; Maria Pav Roca, gen mgr.

Orquesta de Valencia (97). Palau de la Música, Paseo de la Alameda 30, E-46023 Valencia, Spain *tel:* +34 6 337 5020 *fax:* +34 6 337 0988. Javier Casal, cond; Manuel Galouf, dir.

Orquesta Filarmónica de Gran Canaria (80). Bravo Murillo 21-23, E-35003 Las Palmas de Gran Canaria, Spain *tel:* +34 28 320513 *fax:* +34 28 314747. Juan Márquez Rodríguez, mgr; Manuel Benítez González, artistic co-ord; Adrian Leaper, mus dir.

Orquesta Sinfónica de Barcelona i Nacional de Catalunya (OBC) (100). Via Laietana 41, E-08003 Barcelona, Spain *tel:* +34 3 317 1096 *fax:* +34 3 317 5439. Andreu Puig, admin dir; Abili Fort, technical dir; Lawrence Foster, artistic dir; Franz-Paul Decker, principal guest cond; Miquel Lumbierres, mgr.

Orquesta Sinfonica de Euskadi (88). Paseo de Miramón 124, E-20014 San Sebastian, Spain *tel:* +34 43 451022 *fax:* +34 43 470999 *email:* http:// www.euskadi.net. Jesus McAguirre, gen mgr; Germán Ormazabal Artolazabal, gen dir.

Orquesta Sinfonica de Galicia (85). Auditorio y Palacio de Congresos, E-15004 La Coruna, Spain *tel:* +34 81 252021 *fax:* +34 81 277499. Victor Pablo Perez, artistic dir; Enrique Rojas, mgr.

Real Orquesta Sinfónica de Sevilla (103). Imagen, 9-2 Derecha, E-41003 Sevilla, Spain *tel:* +34 5 456 1536 *fax:* +34 5 456 1888. Vjekoslav Sutej, artistic dir and principal cond; Francisco José Senra Lazo, mgr dir; José Manuel Delgado Rodriquez, technical dir.

Symphony Orchestra of Castille and Leon (75). c/o Santiago 19, 2a, E-47001 Valladolid, Spain *tel:* +34 83 370 076 *fax:* +34 83 373 275. Carlos Rubio, mgr; Max Bragado Darman, cond.

Tenerife Symphony Orchestra (83). Plaza de Espana 1, E-38001 Santa Cruz de Tenerife, Spain *tel:* +34 22 605 801 *fax:* +34 22 605 617. Victor Pablo Perez, principal dir; Dulce Xerach Perez Lopez, president; Carmen Kemper, cond.

Sweden

Göteborgs Operans Orkester. Christina Nilssons Gata, S-41104 Göteborg, Sweden *tel:* +46 31 108000 *fax:* +46 31 108026 *email:* http:// www.opera.se. Urban Ward, orch mgr.

Royal Stockholm Philharmonic Orchestra (160). Stockholm Concert Hall Foundation, PO Box 7083, S-103 87 Stockholm, Sweden *tel:* +46 8 221 800 *fax:* +46 8 791 7330. Gennady Rozdestvensky, chief cond; Niklas Willén, principal guest cond; Jan-Olav Wedin, orch mgr.

Royal Swedish Opera Orchestra (112). Box 16094, S-103 22 Stockholm, Sweden *tel:* +46 8 791 4300 *fax:* +46 8 411 0242. Bengt Hall, gen mgr; Leif Segerstam, mus dir; Staffan Carlweitz, press offr.

Swedish National Orchestra (108). Stenhammarsgatam 1, S-412 56 Gothenburg, Sweden *tel:* +46 31 778 7800 *fax:* +46 31 203 502. Neeme Järvi, principal cond; Sture Carlsson, gen mgr.

Swedish Radio Symphony Orchestra (101). Swedish Broadcasting Corporation, S-105 10 Stockholm, Sweden *tel:* +46 8 784 1801 *fax:* +46 8 667 3283. Esa-Pekka Salonen, artistic adviser; Lennart Stenkvist, gen mgr.

Switzerland

Basel Sinfonietta (80). Postfach, CH-4002 Basel, Switzerland *tel:* +41 61 335 5415 *fax:* +41 61 335 5535 *email:* 101447.3243@compuserve.com. Thomas Nidecker, mgr; Monique Fornallez, sec.

Berner Symphonie-Orchester (105). Münzgraben 2, CH-3000 Berne 7, Switzerland *tel:* +41 31 328 2424 *fax:* +41 31 328 2425. Dmitrij Kitajenko, principal cond; Margrit Lenz, mgr.

Orchester der Oper Zürich (101). Falkenstrasse 1, CH-8008 Zürich, Switzerland *tel:* +41 1 251 6920 *fax:* +41 1 251 5896. Manfred Honeck, mus master; Alexander Pereira.

Orchestre de la Suisse Romande (112). 3 Promenade du Pin, CH-1204 Genève, Switzerland *tel:* +41 22 311 2511 *fax:* +41 22 310 1789. Armin Jordan, artistic dir; Jean Cordey, gen mgr; René Wyss, admin dir.

Sinfonieorchester Basel (110). Freie Strasse 52, CH-4001 Basel, Switzerland *tel:* +41 61 269 9595 *fax:* +41 61 269 9599. Jürgen Fabritius, dir.

Tonhalle-Orchester Zürich (98). Gotthardstrasse 5, CH-8002 Zürich, Switzerland *tel:* +41 1 206 3440 *fax:* +41 1 206 3436. Trygve Nordwall, exec dir; David Zinman, mus dir and principal cond; Jürg Keller, dir of finance and admin; Chandler Cudlipp, artistic admin.

Taiwan

Taipei Symphony Orchestra. 7F, 25 Pa Teh Rd, Sect 3, Taipei 10560, Taiwan *tel:* +886 2 752 3731 *fax:* +886 2 751 8244.

Thailand

Bangkok Symphony Orchestra. Tejapaibul Building, 5th Floor, 16 Plubplaichi Rd, Bangkok, Thailand *tel:* +66 2 252 1772 *fax:* +66 2 255 3947.

Turkey

Istanbul State Symphony Orchestra (106). Atatürk Kültür Merkezi, Taksim, 80090 Istanbul, Turkey *tel:* +90 212 243 1068 *fax:* +90 212 251 0507. Türkmen Güner, dir; Ertugrul Köse, vice dir; Erol Erdinç, cond; Tadeusz Strugala, principal guest cond; Murat Gürol, programme mgr.

Izmir State Symphony Orchestra (105). Büro SSK Ishani C Blok 4, Kat Konak, 35260 Izmir, Turkey *tel:* +90 232 484 8343 *fax:* +90 232 484 5172. Tuncer Olcay, dir.

Presidential Symphony Orchestra (110). Talatpasa Bulvari 38, Ankara, Turkey *tel:* +90 312 309 1348 *fax:* +90 312 311 7548. H Hüseyin Akbulut, dir; Hüseyin Ertug, artistic dir.

Ukraine

Crimea State Symphony Orchestra (80). Yekaterynynska St 13, 334202 Yalta, Ukraine *tel:* +7 0652 325070 *fax:* +7 0652 321034. Aleksey Goulianitsky, chief cond; Vladimir Nozhov, mgr; Elgudja Kepuladze, festival mgr.

Kharkiv Philharmonic Orchestra. Rymarskaya St 21, 310057 Kharkiv, Ukraine *tel:* +7 572 470527 *also fax.* Vakhtang Jordania, mus dir; Alexander Vlasyenko, resident cond; Nicolai A Saltovsky, exec dir.

National Symphony Orchestra of Ukraine. Volodymyrsky Uzviz 2, 252001 Kiev, Ukraine *tel:* +380 44 229 6842 *also fax.* Theodore Kuchar, artistic dir and principal cond.

Odessa Philharmonic Orchestra. 15 R Lousembourg St, 270026 Odessa, Ukraine *tel:* +7 048 222 6349 *also fax.* Hobart Earle, principal cond; Victor Mitnik, mgr dir.

Ukrainian Chamber Orchestra. PO Box 64, 252150 Kiev, Ukraine *tel:* +380 44 269 8752 *also fax.* Teodore Kuchar, artistic dir and principal cond; Alexander Hornostai, gen mgr.

Ukrainian TV and Radio Symphony Orchestra. Khrestchatyk 26, 252001 Kiev, Ukraine *tel:* +7 044 229 3322 *also fax.* V Ph Syrenko, chief cond; Y N Semchenko, mgr.

USA

Arkansas Symphony Orchestra (65). PO 7328, 2417 N Tyler, Little Rock, AR 72217, USA *tel:* +1 501 666 1761 *fax:* +1 501 666 3193 *email:* asoinfo@aristotle.net. William Vickery, exec dir.

Atlanta Symphony Orchestra (96). 1293 Peachtree St NE, Suite 300, Atlanta, GA 30309, USA *tel:* +1 404 733 4900 *fax:* +1 404 733 4901 *email:* http://www.atlantasymphony.org. Yoel Levi, mus dir; J Frank Dans, artistic admin.

Baltimore Symphony Orchestra (97). 1212 Cathedral St, Baltimore, MD 21201, USA *tel:* +1 410 783 8100 *fax:* +1 410 783 8077. John Gidivitz, exec dir; David Zinman, mus dir.

Boston Symphony Orchestra (101). 301 Massachusetts Av, Boston, MA 02115, USA *tel:* +1 617 266 1492 *fax:* +1 617 638 9367. Seiji Ozawa, mus dir; Kenneth Haas, mgr dir; Anthony Fogg, artistic admin; Ray F Wellbaum, orch mgr.

Boulder Philharmonic Orchestra. The Dairy Centre for the Arts, 2590 Walnut St, Suite 6, Boulder, CO 80302-5700, USA *tel:* +1 303 449 1976 *fax:* +1 303 443 9203. Theodore Kuchar, mus dir; William Lightfoot, exec dir.

Buffalo Philharmonic Orchestra (80). PO Box 905, Buffalo, NY 14213, USA *tel:* +1 716 885 0331 *fax:* +1 716 885 9372. Maximiamo Valdes, mus dir; Constance A Miller, art admin.

Charlotte Symphony Orchestra (76). 211 N College St, Suite 202, Charlotte, NC 28202, USA *tel:* +1 704 332 0468 *fax:* +1 704 332 1963 *email:* http://www.charlottesymphony.org. Peter McCoppin, mus dir; Janna Hymes-Bianchi, resident cond; Richard L Early, president and exec dir; David Tang, asst cond; Anita Strauss-LaRowe, dir of development.

Chattanooga Symphony and Opera (up to 40). 630 Chestnut St, Chattanooga, TN 37402, USA *tel:* +1 423 267 8583 *fax:* +1 423 265 6520 *email:* cso2@chattanooga.net. Robert Bernhardt, mus dir; Elizabeth Hare, exec dir; Cynthia Loden-Dowdle, mkt and PR dir.

Chicago Symphony Orchestra (112). 220 S Michigan Av, Chicago, IL 60604, USA *tel:* +1 312 435 8122 *fax:* +1 213 786 1207. Daniel Barenboim, mus dir; Martha Gilmer, art admin.

Cincinnati Symphony Orchestra (97). 1241 Elm St, Cincinnati, OH 45210, USA *tel:* +1 513 621 1919 *fax:* +1 513 621 2132. Steven Monder, exec dir; Jesús López-Cobos, mus dir.

The Cleveland Orchestra (105). Severance Hall, Cleveland, OH 44106, USA *tel:* +1 216 231 7300 *fax:* +1 216 231 0202. Christoph von Dohnányi, mus dir; Thomas W Morris, exec dir.

Colorado Symphony Orchestra (80). 821 17th St, Suite 700, Denver, CO 80202, USA *tel:* +1 303 292 5566 *fax:* +1 303 293 2649 *email:* http://www.coloradosymphony.com. Marin Alsop, mus dir; Gene Bircher, artistic dir.

Columbus Symphony Orchestra (80). 55 East State St, Columbus, OH 43215, USA *tel:* +1 614 224 5381 *fax:* +1 614 224 7273. Alessandro Siciliani, mus dir.

Dallas Symphony Orchestra (92). 2301 Flora St, Suite 300, Dallas, TX 75201-2497, USA *tel:* +1 214 871 4000 *fax:* +1 214 871 4049 *email:* http://www.dallassymphony.com/. Eugene Bonelli, president; Andrew Litton, mus dir.

Detroit Symphony Orchestra (95). 3711 Woodward Av, Detroit, MI 48201, USA *tel:* +1 313 833 3362 *fax:* +1 313 833 3047 *email:* http://www.detroitsymphony.com. Neeme Jarvi, mus dir; Mark Volpe, exec dir; Paul Chummers, gen mgr.

Florida Orchestra Inc (88). 5670 West Cypress St, Suite C, FL 33607, USA *tel:* +1 813 286 1170 *fax:* +1 813 286 2316. Kathryn Holm, exec dir; Jahja Ling, mus dir.

Florida Philharmonic Orchestra (84). 3401 NW Ninth Av, Fort Lauderdale, FL 33309-5903, USA *tel:* +1 305 561 2997 *fax:* +1 305 561 1390. John Graham, exec dir; James Judd, mus dir; Peter Nero, pops dir.

Florida West Coast Symphony (80). 709 North Tamiami Trail, Sarasota, FL 34236, USA *tel:* +1 941 953 4252 *fax:* +1 941 953 3059. Gayle A Williams, mkt dir; Paul Wolfe, cond laureate; Gretchen Serrie, exec dir; Trevor Cramer, gen mgr.

Fort Worth Symphony Orchestra (100). 4401 Trail Lake Dr, Fort Worth, TX 76109, USA *tel:* +1 817 921 2676 *fax:* +1 817 921 9795 *email:* ticks @fwsymphony.org. Ann Koonsman, exec dir; John Giordano, mus dir.

Grand Rapids Symphony Orchestra (101). DeVos Hall, Grand Centre, 220 Lyon NW, Suite 415, Grand Rapids, MI 49503, USA *tel:* +1 616 454 9451 *fax:* +1 616 454 7477. Catherine Comet, mus dir; Stacy Ridenour, gen mgr.

Honolulu Symphony (62). 677 Ala Moana Blvd, Suite 615, Honolulu, HI 96813, USA *tel:* +1 808 524 0815 *fax:* +1 808 524 1507. Samuel Wong, cond; Michael Tiknis, exec dir.

The Houston Symphony (98). 615 Louisiana St, Houston, TX 77002-2798, USA *tel:* +1 713 224 4240 *fax:* +1 713 222 7024. Christoph Eschenbach, mus dir; Stephen Stein, cond in residence; David M Wax, exec dir.

Indianapolis Symphony Orchestra (88). 45 Monument Circle, Indianapolis, IN 46204-2919, USA *tel:* +1 317 262 1100 *fax:* +1 317 637 1917. Raymond Leppard, mus dir and cond.

Jacksonville Symphony Orchestra (52). 33 S Hogan St, Suite 400, Jacksonville, FL 32202, USA *tel:* +1 904 354 5479 *fax:* +1 904 354 9238. David Pierson, president; Roger Nierenberg, mus dir and cond.

Kansas City Symphony (77). Lyric Theatre 1660, 1020 Central, Suite 300, Kansas City, MO 64105-1672, USA *tel:* +1 816 471 1100 *fax:* +1 816 471 0976. William McBlaughlin, mus dir and cond; Susan Granano, gen mgr.

Knoxville Symphony Orchestra (80). 623 Market St, Suite 600, Knoxville TN 37902, USA *tel:* +1 423 523 1178 *fax:* +1 423 546 3766. Rick Lester, exec dir; Kirk Trevor, mus dir and cond.

Los Angeles Philharmonic (105). 135 N Grand Av, Los Angeles, CA 90012, USA *tel:* +1 213 972 7300 *fax:* +1 213 617 3065. Ernest Fleischmann, exec vice-president and mgr dir; Esa-Pekka Salonen, mus dir.

Louisiana Philharmonic Orchestra (71). 305 Baronne St, Suite 600, New Orleans, LA 70112, USA *tel:* +1 504 523 6530 *fax:* +1 504 595 8468 *email:* lpo@gnofn.org. Robert J Stiles, exec dir.

The Louisville Orchestra (70). 611 W Main St, Louisville, KY 40202, USA *tel:* +1 502 587 8681 *fax:* +1 502 589 7870. Gregg W Gustafson, exec dir; Frank Kistler, gen mgr; Max Bragado-Darman, mus dir.

Milwaukee Symphony Orchestra (90). 330 E Kilbourn Av, Suite 900, Milwaukee, WI 53202, USA *tel:* +1 414 291 6010 *fax:* +1 414 291 7610 *email:* amadeus@execpc.co; http://www.milwaukeesymphony. org. Steven A Ovitsky, vice-president and exec dir; Andreas Delfs, mus dir; Neal Gittleman, resident cond.

Minnesota Orchestra (95). 1111 Nicollet Mall, Minneapolis, MN 55403, USA *tel:* +1 612 371 5600 *fax:* +1 612 371 0838 *email:* info@mnorch. org; http://www.mnorch.org. David J Hyslop, president; Eiji Oue, mus dir; Stanislaw Skrowaczewski, cond laureate; Jeffrey Tate, cond; Doc Severinsen, cond.

Nashville Symphony Orchestra (72). 209 10th Av South, Suite 448, Nashville, TN 37203, USA *tel:* +1 615 255 5600 *fax:* +1 615 255 5656. Kenneth Schermerhorn, mus dir and cond; Stephen R Vann, exec dir.

National Symphony Orchestra (100). John F Kennedy Center for Performing Arts, Washington, DC 20566, USA *tel:* +1 202 416 8100 *fax:* +1 202 416 8105. Richard Hancock, exec dir; Leonard Slatkin, mus dir.

New Jersey Symphony Orchestra (76). 2 Central Av, Newark, NJ 07102, USA *tel:* +1 201 624 3713 *fax:* +1 201 624 2115. Zdenek Macal, artistic dir and cond; Lawrence Tamburri, exec dir; Karen Swanson, gen mgr.

New World Symphony (95). 541 Lincoln Rd, Miami Beach, FL 33139, USA *tel:* +1 305 673 3330 *fax:* +1 305 673 6749. Christopher Dunworth, president; Michael Tilson Thomas, artistic dir; Douglas Merilatt, vice-president artistic operations.

New York Philharmonic (107). 10 Lincoln Centre Plaza, New York, NY 10023-6973, USA *tel:* +1 212 875 5000 *fax:* +1 212 875 5717 *email:* http://www.newyorkphilharmonic.org. Kurt Masur, mus dir; Welz Kauffman, artistic admin.

North Carolina Symphony Orchestra (65). 2 E South St, Raleigh, NC 27601, USA *tel:* +1 919 733 2750 *fax:* +1 919 733 9920. Gerhardt Zimmermann, mus dir and cond; Hiram Black, artistic admin.

Oregon Symphony Orchestra (86). 711 SW Alder, Suite 200, Portland, OR 97205, USA *tel:* +1 503 228 4294 *fax:* +1 503 228 4150. James DePreist, cond; Peggie Schwarz, orch mgr.

Pacific Symphony Orchestra (90). 1231 E Dyer Rd, Suite 200, Santa Ana, CA 92705-5606, USA *tel:* +1 714 755 5788 *fax:* +1 714 755 5789 *email:* http://www.pso.org. Louis G Spisto, vice-president and exec dir; Carl St Clair, mus dir; James T Medvitz, dir of operations.

Philadelphia Orchestra (102). 1420 Locust St Suite 400, Philadelphia, PA 19102, USA *tel:* +1 215 893 1900 *fax:* +1 215 893 1948. Joseph H Kluger, exec dir; Wolfgang Sawallisch, mus dir.

Phoenix Symphony Orchestra. 3707 N Seventh St, Phoenix AZ 85014, USA *tel:* +1 602 277 7291 *fax:* +1 602 277 7517. James Sedares, mus dir and principal cond; Russell Allen, gen mgr.

Pittsburgh Symphony Orchestra (102). 600 Penn Av, Pittsburgh, PA 15222, USA *tel:* +1 412 392 4800 *fax:* +1 412 392 4909. Lorin Maazel, mus dir; Robert Moir, artistic admin.

Rochester Philharmonic Orchestra (59). 108 East Av, Rochester, NY 14604, USA *tel:* +1 716 454 2620 *fax:* +1 716 423 2256. Peter Bay, mus adviser.

St Louis Symphony Orchestra (101). Powell Symphony Hall, 718 N Grand Blvd, St Louis, MO 63103, USA *tel:* +1 314 533 2500 *fax:* +1 314 286 4142 *email:* http://www.stlsym.org. Bruce Coppock, exec dir; Hans Vonk, mus dir and cond.

St Paul Chamber Orchestra (32). 408 St Peter St, Suite 500, St Paul, MN 55102, USA *tel:* +1 612 292 3248 *fax:* +1 612 292 3281. Brent Assink, president and mgr dir; Hugh Wolff, mus dir.

San Antonio Symphony (76). 220 E Houston St, Suite 200, San Antonio, TX 78205, USA *tel:* +1 210 554 1000 *fax:* +1 210 554 1008. David Schillhammer, exec dir.

San Diego Symphony (81). 1245 Seventh Av, CA 92101, USA *tel:* +1 619 699 4200 *fax:* +1 619 699 4237. Yoav Talmi, mus dir and cond; Robert Shaw, principal guest cond; Jung-Ho Pak, associate cond; Elsie Weston, president.

San Francisco Symphony (106). Davies Symphony Hall, San Francisco, CA 94102, USA *tel:* +1 415 552 8000 *fax:* +1 415 431 6857. Herbert Blomstedt, cond laureate.

San Jose Symphony (89). 495 Almaden Blvd, San Jose, CA 95110, USA *tel:* +1 408 287 7383 *fax:* +1 408 286 6391. Leonid Grin, cond; Tim Beswick, artistic admin.

Seattle Symphony Orchestra (89). 305 Harrison St, 4th Floor, Seattle, WA 98109-4645, USA *tel:* +1 206 215 4700 *fax:* +1 206 215 4701 *email:* http://www.seattlesymphony.org. Gerard Schwarz, mus dir; Abraham Kaplan, associate cond (choral); Adam Stern, asst cond; Deborah R Card, exec dir.

Shreveport Symphony Orchestra. 619 Louisana Av, Shreveport, LA 71101, USA *tel:* +1 318 222 7496.

Syracuse Symphony Orchestra (67). 411 Montgomery St, Syracuse, NY 13202, USA *tel:* +1 315 424 8222 *fax:* +1 315 424 1131. Faio Mechetti, mus dir; Richard Decker, orch mgr.

Toledo Symphony Orchestra (85). 2 Maritime Plaza, Toledo, OH 43604-1803, USA *tel:* +1 419 241 1272 *fax:* +1 419 321 6890 *email:* tolsymorch@aol.com; http://www.3d-interact.com/tso. Robert Bell, president; Andrew Massey, mus dir and cond; Andrew Sewell, associate cond; Kathleen Carroll, exec vice-president development.

Utah Symphony (83). 123 W South Temple, Salt Lake City, UT 84101, USA *tel:* +1 801 533 5626 *fax:* +1 801 521 6634. Donald L Andrews, president; Joseph Silverstein, mus dir.

Virginia Symphony (49). PO Box 26, Norfolk, VA 23501, USA *tel:* +1 804 623 8590 *fax:* +1 804 623 7068. Daniel J Hart, exec dir.

Wichita Symphony Orchestra (85). 225 W Douglas, Suite 207, Wichita, KS 67202, USA *tel:* +1 316 267 5259 *fax:* +1 316 267 1937 *email:* symphony@louverture.com; http://www.wso.org. Mitchell A Berman, gen mgr; Zuohuang Chen, mus dir.

Venezuela

Orquesta Sinfónica de Aragua. Av 19 de Abril, Complejo Cultural Santos, Michelena, Edif 3 and 4, Maracay, Estado Aragua, Venezuela *tel:* +58 43 331078 *also fax.*

Orquesta Sinfónica de Maracalbo. Centro de Ballas Artes, Av 3F, No 67-217, Maracaibo 4001, Venezuela *tel:* +58 61 91 19 85 *fax:* +58 61 91 20 95. Eduardo Rahn, cond; Havid Sanchez, mgr.

Orquesta Sinfónica de Mirand. Calle Paez Sur 39, Los Teques, Estado Miranda, Venezuela *tel:* +58 32 323745 *fax:* +58 32 323747. Maria Octavia Issa, cond and president; Maria Emilia de Charme, mgr.

Orquesta Sinfónica del Estado Nueva Esparta (70). Paseo Romulo Gallegos, Sector Guaraguao, Final Calle Diaz, Porlamar Estado Nueva Esparta, Venezuela *tel:* +58 95 641282 *also fax.* Ecberth Lucena, mus dir and cond; Enmanuel Alfonzo, president.

Orquesta Sinfónica el Estado Sucre. Calle Sucre 39, Frente a la Ilesia Santa Ines, Cumana, Estado Sucre, Venezuela *tel:* +58 93 311736 *also fax.* Alcides Maestre, cond; Jesus Guevara, president.

Opera Companies

This list includes the major international opera companies. Some are touring companies, but many perform substantially at a principal venue. Details of performances are listed in *Opera Now* magazine, also available from Rhinegold Publishing.

Argentina
Teatro Colon. Cerrito 618, 1010 Buenos Aires, Argentina *tel:* +54 1 382 8924/2389 *fax:* +54 1 111232. Kive Staiff, gen and artistic dir; Carlos M Elia, admin dir.

Australia
National Chamber Opera of Australia. The Great Hall, Sydney University, Paramatta Rd, Sydney, Australia *tel:* +61 2 9266 4800.

Opera Australia. PO Box 291, Strawberry Hills, NSW 2012, Australia *tel:* +61 2 9699 1099 *fax:* +61 2 9699 3184 *email:* http://www.ausopera. org.au/. Donald McDonald, gen mgr; Moffatt Oxenbould, artistic dir; Sharolyn Kimmorley, artistic admin; Noel Stanton, technical dir.

Opera Queensland. PO Box 3677, South Brisbane, Queensland 4101, Australia *tel:* +61 7 3875 3030 *fax:* +61 7 3844 5352. Suzannah Conway, gen mgr; Jillianne Bartsch, head of mus; Tom Cullen, artistic admin.

The State Opera of South Australia. PO Box 211, Marleston BC, SA 5033, Australia *tel:* +61 8 226 4790 *fax:* +61 8 226 4791 *email:* saopera@ stateart.com.au; http://www.stateart.com.au/saopera. Stephen Phillips, gen dir; Bill Gillespie, artistic dir; Mandy MacGillivray, mkt and business affairs mgr; Nigel Bray, finance dir; Florin Radulescu, head of mus.

West Australian Opera. 3rd Floor, His Majesty's Theatre, 825 Hay St, Perth WA, Australia *tel:* +61 8 9321 5869 *fax:* +61 8 9324 1134. Pamela Foulkes, gen mgr; Richard Mills, artistic dir; Marilyn Phillips, head of mus; Michael Herrmann, acting mkt and development mgr; Judy Reid, exec asst; Lisa Johnson, mkt and development co-ord.

Austria
Haydn Festival. Schloss Esterházy, A-7000 Eisenstadt, Austria *tel:* +43 26 82 618660 *fax:* +43 26 82 61805. Walter Reicher, artistic dir.

Landestheater Linz. Promenade 39, A-4020 Linz, Austria *tel:* +43 732 761 1100 *fax:* +43 732 761 1105.

Opernhaus Bühnen Graz. 10 Kaiser Josef-Platz, A-8010 Graz, Austria *tel:* +43 316 8000 *fax:* +43 316 800 8565 *email:* info@buehnen-graz. com; http://www.buehnen-graz.com. Gerhard Brunner, gen mgr; Peter Nebel, technical dir; Michael Lakner, artistic admin.

Salzburger Landestheater. Schwarzstr 22, A-5020 Salzburg, Austria *tel:* +43 662 871512 *fax:* +43 662 87151213. Lutz Hochstraate, artistic dir; Diethmar Strasser, artistic mgr; Anton Schmidjell, financial dir.

Tiroler Landestheater. Rennweg 2, A-6020 Innsbruck, Austria *tel:* +43 512 520744 *fax:* +43 512 52 074333 *email:* tiroler@landestheater; http://www.landestheater.at. Dominique Mentha, dir; Harold Mayr.

Wiener Kammeroper. Fleischmarkt 24, A-1010 Wien, Austria *tel:* +43 1 512 0100 *fax:* +43 1 512 010010. Josef Hussek, gen dir.

Wiener Operntheater. Myrthengasse 5/11, A-1070 Wien, Austria *tel:* +43 1 526 2136 *also fax*. Sven Hartberger, gen mgr.

Wiener Staatsoper. Opernring 2, A-1010 Wien, Austria *tel:* +43 1 514440 *fax:* +43 1 514 442330 *email:* http://www.oebthv.gv.at. Ioan Holender, dir; Peter Hecht, admin; Elisabeth Sobotka; Irina Kubadinow, press.

Wiener Volksoper. Währinger Strasse 78, A-1090 Wien, Austria *tel:* +43 1 514 44 3318. Ioan Holender, dir; Irmgard Roeschnar, deputy dir.

Belgium
De Vlaamse Opera (Antwerpen). Van Ertbornstraat 8, B-2018 Antwerpen 1, Belgium *tel:* +323 233 6808/6685 *fax:* +323 232 2661. Marc Clémeur, gen mgr; Marc Minkowski, mus dir; Ray de Bouvre, admin and finance; Silvio Varviso, permanent guest cond; Peter Burian, chorus master.

De Vlaamse Opera (Gent). Schouwburgstraat 3, B-9000 Gent, Belgium *tel:* +329 225 2425. Marc Clémeur, gen mgr; Marc Minkowski, mus dir.

Opera National. Rue Léopold 4, B-1000 Bruxelles, Belgium *tel:* +322 217 22 11.

L'Opéra Royal de Wallonie. Rue de Dominicains 1, B-4000 Liege, Belgium *tel:* +32 4 221 4720 *fax:* +32 4 221 0201 *email:* http://www. moderne.org/orw. Jean-Louis Grinda, dir gen.

Théâtre Royal de la Monnaie. Rue Leopold 4, B-1000 Bruxelles, Belgium *tel:* +32 2 229 1200 *fax:* +32 2 229 1380. Antonio Pappano, mus dir; Bernard Foccroulle, dir; Yannick Vermeirsch, public relations dir.

Brazil
Teatro Municipal de Sao Paulo. Praça Ramos de Azevedo s/n, 01307-000 Sao Paulo, Brazil *tel:* +55 11 222 8698 *fax:* +55 11 223 5021.

Bulgaria
National Theater-Opera National de Sofia. Blvd Dondukov 58, 1000 Sofia, Bulgaria *tel:* +359 2 877 011. Rouslan Raichev, dir.

Canada
Calgary Opera. #601, 237-8 Av SE, Calgary, AB T2G 5C3, Canada *tel:* +1 403 262 7286 *fax:* +1 403 263 5428. David Speers, gen dir; Ty Paterson, resident cond; Heather Davies, financial offr; Barbara Burggraf, development dir; Sally Truss, mkt dir; Jacqueline Gillespie, subscriber relations admin.

The Canadian Opera Company. 227 Front St East, Toronto, Ont M5A 1E8, Canada *tel:* +1 416 363 6671 *fax:* +1 416 363 5584 *email:* http:// www.coc.ca. Elaine Calder, gen mgr; Richard Bradshaw, artistic dir.

Edmonton Opera. Box Office, Suite 320, 10232-112 St, Edmonton, Alberta T5K 1M4, Canada *tel:* +1 403 423 424 4040/1000 *fax:* +1 403 423 429 0600. Nejolla Korris, gen mgr; Irving Guttman, artistic dir; Kelly Robinson, associate artistic dir.

Manitoba Opera. PO Box 31027, Portage Place, 393 Portage Ave, Winnipeg, MB R3B 3K9, Canada *tel:* +1 204-92 7479 *fax:* +1 204 949 0377.

Opera Atelier. 87 Avenue Rd, Hazelton Lanes, Box 343, Toronto, Ont M5R 3R9, Canada *tel:* +1 416 925 3767 *fax:* +1 416 925 4895. Joan Bosworth, gen mgr; M Pynkoski, J Zingg, co-artistic dirs.

L'Opéra de Montréal. 260 Blvd de Maisonneuve Ouest, Montreal, QU H2X 1Y9, Canada *tel:* +1 514 985 2258. Bernard Uzan, gen and artistic dir.

Opéra de Québec. 1220 Av Taché, Québec, PQ G1R 3B4, Canada *tel:* +1 418 529 4142 *fax:* +1 418 529 3735. Bernard Labadie, artistic and mus dir; Grégoire Legendre, gen dir; Louis Robert, exec asst and press offr; Lucien Pouliot, accountant.

Opera Lyra Ottawa. 110-2 Daly Av, Ottawa, Ont K1N 6E2, Canada *tel:* +1 613 233 9200 *fax:* +1 613 233 5431. Jeannette Aster, artistic dir; Marcus Handman, exec dir; John Peltier, finance dir; Gerald Morris, communications mgr; Ron Ward, production mgr.

Opera Ontario (Opera Hamilton and Kitchener-Waterloo Opera). 100 King St West, Suite 200, Hamilton, Ont L8P 1A2, Canada *tel:* +1 905 527 7627; +1 519 578 5573 *fax:* +1 905 527 0014. Kenneth D Freeman, gen dir; Daniel Lipton, artistic dir; Mary Romeo, artistic admin; Christopher Richardson, office mgr; David Devan, mkt and development dir; Shelley Gadsden, mkt associate.

Pacific Opera Victoria. 1316b Government St, Victoria, BC V8W 1Y8, Canada *tel:* +1 250 385 0222; +1 250 382 1641 *fax:* +1 250 382 4944 *email:* opera@islandnet.com; http://www.islandnet.com/~opera/. Timothy Vernon, artistic dir; Jeffrey Ouellette, gen mgr; Susan Kerschbaumer, mkt mgr; Barbara Newton, artistic admin; Suzanne Bradbury, development offr; Kathy Allison, admin asst.

Vancouver Opera. Suite 500, 845 Cambie St, Vancouver, BC V6B 4Z9, Canada *tel:* +1 604 682 2871 *fax:* +1 604 682 3981. Robert J Hallam, gen dir; David Agler, mus dir.

Chile
Teatro Municipal. San Antonio 149, Santiago Centro, Chile *tel:* +56 2 638 1515 *fax:* +56 2 633 7214. Andrés Rodríguez, gen and artistic dir; Andrés Pinto, dir of admin; Christián Sepúlveda, finance dir; Enrique Bordolini, technical dir; Cristóbal Giesen, gen co-ord; Michelangelo Veltri, principal cond.

China
Central Opera Theatre. Dongzhimenwai, Zuojiazhuang, Beijing 100028, China *tel:* +86 465 2317. Wang Shi-guang, dir.

Shanghai Opera House. 10 Lane 100, Changshu Rd, Shanghai 200040, China *tel:* +86 216 248 5359 *fax:* +86 216 249 8127. He Zhao-hua, dir; Cao Ding, Lin You-Sheng, conds; Chen Guang-xiam, Zhao Zhi-ming, Li Jian-yei, admins.

Czech Republic
Moravian Theatre Olomouc. Tr Svobody 33, CZ-771 07 Olomouc, Czech Republic *tel:* +420 68 522 5727 *fax:* +420 68 522 5781. Václav Kozusnik, dir; Martin Dubovic, opera dir; Zvonimír Skrivan, chief cond; Michelle Philippe, cond.

New Productions:

Elektra
Richard Strauss
Peter Schneider, Herbert Wernicke;
Marjana Lipovsek, Gabriele Schnaut, Nadine
Secunde, William Cochran, Monte Pederson
27, 29, 31 Oct. / 4, 8, 12, 16 Nov. 97 /
17, 22 July 98

Die Fledermaus
Johann Strauß
Simone Young, Leander Haußmann, Bernhard
Kleber, Doris Haußmann; Cheryl Studer, Birgid
Steinberger, Thomas Allen, Ekkehard Wlaschiha,
Christopher Robson, Ignatz Kirchner
22, 26, 31 Dec. 97 / 3, 7, 11 Jan. / 14, 19,
21, 24 Febr. 98

The Midsummer Marriage
Michael Tippett
Mark Elder, Richard Jones, Giles Cadle, Nicky
Gillibrand, Amir Hosseinpour, Mimi Jordan Sherin;
Alison Hagley, Catherine Wyn-Rogers,
Nadja Michael, Philip Langridge, Esa Ruuttunen,
Christopher Ventris, Philip Ens
25, 28 Febr. / 3, 6, 11 March / 15, 18, 22 May 98

Was ihr wollt (As you like it)
Manfred Trojahn
(world premiere)
Michael Boder, Peter Mussbach, Andrea Schmidt-
Futterer; Iride Martinez, Jeanne Piland,
Julie Kaufmann, Rainer Trost, Dale Duesing,
Eberhard Lorenz, Jan Zinkler, Björn Waag
24, 27 May / 2, 5, 10 June 98

Tristan und Isolde
Richard Wagner
Zubin Mehta, Peter Konwitschny, Johannes
Leiacker; Waltraud Meier, Marjana Lipovsek,
Siegfried Jerusalem, Kurt Moll, Bernd Weikl
30. June / 4, 8, 12 July 98

Repertoire:
Carmen, Peter Grimes, Anna Bolena, Don
Pasquale, Lucia di Lammermoor, Giulio Cesare,
Hänsel und Gretel, Der junge Lord,
L'incoronazione di Poppea, Così fan tutte,
Don Giovanni, Le nozze di Figaro, Die Zauberflöte,
Die Liebe zu den drei Orangen, La Bohème,
Madama Butterfly, Tosca, Il Barbiere di Siviglia,
Die verkaufte Braut, Ariadne auf Naxos,
Der Rosenkavalier, Salome, Aida, Macbeth,
Nabucco, Simon Boccanegra, La Traviata,
Il Trovatore, Siegfried, Götterdämmerung,
Die Meistersinger von Nürnberg, Parsifal.

Bavarian State Ballet:

Giselle - Mats Ek,Concertante, Große Fuge,
Black Cake, Romeo und Julia, Die Kameliendame,
Chamber Symphony, Der Feuervogel,
La Bayadère, Unisono, Nacht, Sarkasmen,
Trois Gnossiennes, Déja vu, Max und Moritz,
Ein Traumspiel

Academy Concerts, Chamber Concerts, Recitals

Bavarian State Opera
Staatsintendant Peter Jonas
Box office:
Maximilianstraße 11
D-80539 München
Tel: 089/21 85 19 20
Fax: 089/21 85 19 03

1997/1998 | Bayerische Staatsoper

National Theatre Brno. Dvorakova 11, CZ-657 70 Brno, Czech Republic *tel:* +420 5 4232 1285 *fax:* +420 5 4221 3746.

The National Theatre Opera. Národní Divadlo, PO Box 865, CZ-112 30 Praha 1, Czech Republic *tel:* +420 2 24 910312/901227 *fax:* +420 2 24 911524. Zdenek Harvánek, admin; Josef Prudek, artistic dir.

Opera Furore. Sevastopolská 14, CZ-101 00 Praha 10, Czech Republic *tel:* +420 02 741095/742708 *fax:* +420 02 739064 *email:* via@gts.cz. Jirí Nekvasil, Daniel Dvorák, dirs.

Opera Mozart Praha. Sevastopolská 14, CZ-101 00 Praha 10, Czech Republic *tel:* +420 02 741095/742708 *fax:* +420 02 739064 *email:* via@ gts.cz. Daniel Dvorák, Jirí Nekvasil, dirs.

Orfeo Chamber Opera Company. Armenska 17/6, CZ-625 00 Brno, Czech Republic *tel:* +420 05 352110 *fax:* +420 05 529080. Josef Stanek, artistic chief; Anna Erdingerová, admin dir.

Statni Opera Praha. Legerova 75, CZ-111 21 Praha, Czech Republic *tel:* +420 2 242 276936 *fax:* +420 2 242 30410/29437. Eva Randová, gen mgr.

Denmark

Den Jyske Opera (The Danish National Opera). Musikhuset Aarhus, Thomas Jensens Allé, DK-8000, Arhus C, Denmark *tel:* +45 89 318260 *fax:* +45 86 133710. Troels Kold, mgr dir; Tonny Borup Mortensen, admin.

The Royal Danish Opera. The Royal Theatre, Postbox 2185, DK-1017 Copenhagen K, Denmark *tel:* +45 33 696701 *fax:* +45 33 696767 *email:* kgl-teat@inet.uni-c.dk. Elaine Padmore, artistic dir; Michael Christiansen, theatre dir.

Estonia

Estonian National Opera. Estonia Bul 4, EE-0105 Tallinn, Estonia *tel:* +372 6 260201 *fax:* +372 6 313080 *email:* estonia@opera.teleport. ee. Paul Himma, gen mgr; Neeme Kuningas, artistic dir; Paul Mägi, mus dir and chief cond.

Finland

Finnish National Opera. PO Box 176, Helsinginkatu 58, FIN-00251 Helsinki, Finland *tel:* +358 9 403021 *fax:* +358 9 4030 2305 *email:* http://www.kolumbus.fi/opera. Juhani Raiskinen, gen dir; Okko Kamu, mus dir; Jorma Uotinen, ballet dir; John E Westö, admin dir; Leena Nivanka, press offr (opera); Heidi Almi, press offr (ballet).

Joensuun Ooppera. Raimo Paltakari Kirkkokatu 10 B17, FIN-80110 Joensuu, Finland *tel:* +358 13 22 4563 *fax:* +358 13 25 14590 *email:* raimo.paltakari@jnor.joensuu.fi.

Jyväskylän Ooppera. Juhani Laurila Pitkäkatu 18-22, FIN-40700 Jyväskylä, Finland *tel:* +358 14 618 131 *fax:* +358 14 211 803.

Kotkan Ooppera. Veijo Räsänen Kottaraisentie 12, FIN-48220 Kotka, Finland *tel:* +358 5 610935 *fax:* +358 5 601936.

Kuopion Ooppera. Vuorikatu 15, FIN-70100 Kuopio, Finland *tel:* +358 17 261 8893 *also fax.*

Lahden Ooppera. Marja Tikka, Kuhilaankatu 6, FIN-15900 Lahti, Finland *tel:* +358 3 753 5236 *also fax.* Mirja Ollikainen, chmn; Eero Pulkkinen, vice chmn.

Mikkeli Opera. Vuorikatu 3A, FIN-50100 Mikkeli, Finland *tel:* +358 15 162063 *fax:* +358 15 191 2323. Kyösti Kostiainen, chmn; Kimmo Suortamo, producer.

Opera Alueooppera. Irma Rewell, Koulukatu 10C, FIN-65100 Vaasa, Finland *tel:* +358 6 317 3135 *fax:* +358 6 317 9971. Irma Rewell, opera chief; Martti Tiainen, cond; Outi Takkinen, sec.

Oulun Opera. Tuomo Rounioja, Pälästie 3 B, FIN-90230 Oulu, Finland *tel:* +358 8 314 3150.

Porin Opera. Heikki Jylhäsaari, Pietniement 22, FIN-28660 Pori, Finland *tel:* +358 2 637 8125 *also fax.*

Tampereen Opera. Vellamonkatu 2, FIN-33100 Tampere, Finland *tel:* +358 3 212 7726 *fax:* +358 3 222 0266. Jussi Tapola, artistic dir; Tarja Reijonen, exec dir.

Turku Opera. Seppo Ristilehto, Aninkaistenkatu 9, FIN-20110 Turku, Finland *tel:* +358 02 231 4563 *fax:* +358 02 233 7730. Hilkka Urho, exec mgr.

Vaasan Opera. Koulukatu 10, FIN-65100 Vaasa, Finland *tel:* +358 6 317 3135 *fax:* +358 6 317 9971.

France

L'Atelier Lyrique de Tourcoing. 82 Blvd Gambetta, F-59200 Tourcoing, France *tel:* +33 20 26 66 03. Jean-Claude Malgloire, gen dir; Catherine Noel, admin.

Châtelet Théâtre Musical. 2 Rue Edouard Colonne, F-75001 Paris, France *tel:* +33 1 40 28 28 28 *fax:* +33 1 42 36 89 75. Stéphane Lissner, gen dir; Jean-Marc Peraldi, admin dir.

Chorégies D'Orange. BP 205-84107, Orange Cedex, France *tel:* +33 90 51 83 83 *fax:* +33 90 34 87 67. Raymond Duffaut, dir gen.

L'Esplanade Saint-Etienne Opera. BP 237-42013, Saint-Etienne Cedex 2, France *tel:* +33 77 47 83 47 *fax:* +33 77 47 83 69. Jean Louis Pichon, gen mgr; Patrick Foukwillier, mus mgr; Michel Fabre, admin mgr.

Le Grand Théâtre de Bordeaux. BP 95, F-33025 Bordeaux Cedex, France *tel:* +33 56 00 85 20 *fax:* +33 56 81 93 66. Thierry Fouquet, artistic dir; Francois Vienne, admin and finance dir.

L'Opéra Comique. 5 Rue Favart, F-75002 Paris, France *tel:* +33 1 42 44 45 40/5 *fax:* +33 1 49 26 05 93. Pierre Medecin, dir; Gilles Demonet, admin; Francois Bou, production.

L'Opéra d'Avignon. Regie Municipale BP 111, F-84007 Avignon Cedex 1, France *tel:* +33 90 82 42 42 *fax:* +33 90 85 04 23. Raymond Duffaut, dir gen.

L'Opéra de Dijon. Service Location, 2 Rue Longpierre, F-21000 Dijon, France *tel:* +33 80 67 23 23.

L'Opéra de Lille. 2 Rue des Bons Enfants, F-59800 Lille, France *tel:* +33 3 20 14 99 20 *fax:* +33 3 20 14 99 27. Ricardo Szwarcer, artistic dir; Michel Defaut, admin dir.

Opéra de Lyon. 1 Place de la Comédie, F-69001 Lyon, France *tel:* +33 72 00 45 00 *fax:* +33 72 00 45 01. Jean-Pierre Brossmann, gen admin; Kent Nagano, mus dir; Jacques Hédouin, admin and finance dir.

L'Opéra de Marseille. 2 Rue Moliere, F-13001 Marseille, France *tel:* +33 4 91 55 21 12; +33 4 91 55 00 70. Elie Bankhalter, opera dir.

L'Opéra de Montpellier. 11 Blvd Victor Hugo, F-34000 Montpellier, France *tel:* +33 4 67 60 19 80/99 *fax:* +33 4 67 60 19 90 *email:* http://www.intel-media.fr./operasdemontpellier. Henri Maier, dir gen; Renée Panabière, admin.

L'Opéra de Nancy et de Lorraine. 1 Rue Sainte Catherine, F-54000 Nancy, France *tel:* +33 83 85 33 20 *fax:* +33 83 85 30 66. Jean-Marie Blanchard, gen dir; Christophe Bezzone, admin.

Opéra National de Paris-Bastille. Service de Location, 120 Rue de Lyon, F-75012 Paris, France *tel:* +33 1 40 01 17 89; +33 1 44 73 13 00. Pierre Bergé, president.

L'Opéra de Nantes. 1 Rue Moliere, F-44000 Nantes, France *tel:* +33 40 41 90 60 *fax:* +33 40 41 90 77. Philippe Godefroid, dir; Serge Cochelin, admin.

L'Opéra de Nice. 4 Rue Saint-Francois de Paule, F-06300 Nice, France *tel:* +33 93 80 59 83 *fax:* +33 93 80 34 83. Jean Albert Cartier, gen dir; François Vienne, admin.

L'Opéra de Rennes. Place de l'Hotel de Ville, F-35000 Rennes, France *tel:* +33 2 99 28 55 88 *fax:* +33 2 99 28 58 63. Daniel Bizeray, dir; Eric Le Bihan, admin.

L'Opéra de Toulouse. Place du Capitole, F-31000 Toulouse, France *tel:* +33 61 23 21 35. Jean-Claude Malgloire, gen dir; Catherine Noel, gen admin.

L'Opéra de Tours. Grand Théâtre de Tours, 34 Rue de la Scellerie, F-37000 Tours, France *tel:* +33 47 05 33 47; +33 47 05 37 87. Michel Jarry, dir; Luc Cavalier, admin.

L'Opéra de Vichy. Mairie de Vichy, BP 2158, F-03208 Vichy Cedex, France *tel:* +33 4 70 30 17 17. Diane Polya, gen and artistic mgr.

L'Opéra du Rhin. Service de Location, 19 Place Broglie BP 320, F-67008 Strasbourg Cedex, France *tel:* +33 3 88 75 48 23 *fax:* +33 3 88 24 09 34. Rudolf Berger, dir gen; Lucien Collinet, admin and finance dir; Daniel Dollé, asst to dir gen; Pierre Landau, communications dir.

Théâtre de Nimes. 6 Rue Fresque, F-30000 Nîmes, France *tel:* +33 4 66 36 65 20 *fax:* +33 4 66 21 92 67. Jean Lebeau, dir gen; Catherine Laugier, sec gen; Luc Favier, admin; Michèle Tellier, financial dir; Philippe Sarrat, information dir; François Noel, technical dir.

Théâtre des Champs Elysées. 15 Av Montaigne, F-75008 Paris, France *tel:* +33 1 49 52 50 00 *fax:* +33 1 49 52 07 41. Alain Durel, gen dir; Francis Lepigeon, deputy dir.

Théâtre Musical D'Angers. 7 Rue Duboys, F-49100 Angers, France *tel:* +33 41 60 40 40; +33 41 87 76 32.

Théâtre Municipal. 4-5 Place de la Concorde, F-57000 Metz, France *tel:* +33 87 55 51 87. D Ory, dir; Daniel Lucas, admin.

Germany

Bayerische Kammeroper. Wengertspfad 2, D-97523 Schwanfeld, Bayern, Germany *tel:* +49 93 848772 *fax:* +49 93 848678.

Bayerische Staatsoper. Nationaltheater, Max-Joseph-Platz 2, D-80539 München, Germany *tel:* +49 89 2185 01 *fax:* +49 89 2185 1003. Peter Jonas, dir; Zubin Mehta, mus dir (from Sep 98); Roland Felber, admin dir; Gerd Uecker, opera dir; Ulrike Hessler, dir of public relations.

Berlin Kammeroper. Koltbusser Damm 79, D-10967 Berlin, Germany *tel:* +49 30 693 1054 *fax:* +49 30 692 5201.

Bühnen der Landeshauptstadt Kiel. Rathausplatz 4, D-24103 Kiel, Germany *tel:* +49 431 901 2880 *fax:* +49 431 901 2838. Walter E Gugerbauer, gen mus dir; Kirsten Harms, Raymund Richter, artistic team.

Bühnen der Stadt Bielefeld. Brunnen Str 3-9, D-33602 Bielefeld, Germany *tel:* +49 521 512502 *fax:* +49 521 513430. Heiner Bruns, dir; Rainer Koch, principal cond; Alexander Gruber.

Deutsche Oper am Rhein. Heinridh-Heine-Allee 16a, D-40213 Düsseldorf, Germany *tel:* +49 211 89080 *fax:* +49 211 890 8289. Tobias Richter, artistic dir; Zoltan Pesko, mus dir; Werner Hellfritsch, gen mgr; Tim Coleman.

Deutsche Oper Berlin. Richard Wagner Str 10, D-10585 Berlin, Germany *tel:* +49 30 343 8401 *fax:* +49 30 343 84232. Götz Friedrich, gen dir; Christian Tuielemann, gen mus dir; Alard Rohr, opera dir; Richard Cragun, ballet dir.

Deutsches National-Theater Weimar. Postfach 3 und 5, D-99401 Weimar, Germany *tel:* +49 3643 755334 *fax:* +49 3643 755307. Günther Beelitz, artistic and financial dir; George Alexander Albrecht, gen mus dir; Ehrhard Warneke, opera dir.

Frankfurt Opera, Staedtische Bühnen. Untermainanlage 11, D-6000 Frankfurt am Main 1, Germany *tel:* +49 69 21202 *fax:* +49 69 212 37565 *email:* http://www.frankfurt.de/oper. Martin Steinhoff, gen mgr; Klauspeter Seibel, chief cond; Hans Peter Doll, artistic consultant.

Hamburgische Staatsoper. Grosse Theaterstrasse 34, D-20354 Hamburg, Germany *tel:* +49 40 35680 *fax:* +49 30 356 8456. Albin Hänseroth, Detlef Meierjohann, dirs.

Kammeroper Frankfurt. Nordenstr 60, D-60318 Frankfurt am Main, Germany *tel:* +49 69 556189 *also fax.* Rainer Pudenz, artistic dir; Martin Kraeke, cond.

Komische Oper. Behrenstrasse 55-57, D-10117 Berlin, Germany *tel:* +49 30 20 2600 *fax:* +49 30 20 260405 *email:* http://komischeoper.line.de. Albert Kost, intendant; Harry Kupfer, principal stage dir; Yakov Kreizberg, principal cond; Jan Linkens, principal choreographer.

LandesBühnen Sachsen. Meissner Str 152, D-01445 Radebeul, Germany *tel:* +49 351 7040 *fax:* +49 351 704201.

Nationaltheater. Mozartstr 9, D-68161 Mannheim, Germany *tel:* +49 62 1 16800 *fax:* +49 62 1 21540. Ulrich Schwab, gen intendant; Jun Märkl, gen mus dir.

Niedersächsische Staatstheater Hannover. Opernplatz 1, D-30159 Hannover, Germany *tel:* +49 511 168 6161 *fax:* +49 511 368 1768/363 2536. Hans-Peter Lehmann, dir; Andreas Delfs, gen mus dir; Knut Lehmann, admin dir.

Oper Der Bundesstadt Bonn. Am Boselagerhof 1, D-53111 Bonn, Germany *tel:* +49 228 7281 *fax:* +49 228 728371. Gian-Carlo del Monaco, intendant; Edgar Baitzel, opera dir and asst intendant.

Oper Der Stadt Köln. Offenbachplatz, Postfach 18 02 41, D-50505 Köln, Germany *tel:* +49 221 221 8282/8400. Michael Hampe, gen dir; James Conlon, gen mus dir.

Oper Leipzig. Augustusplatz 12, Postfach 346, D-04109 Leipzig, Germany *tel:* +49 341 12 610 *fax:* +49 341 12 61387 *email:* oper@leipzig-online. de. Udo Zimmermann, dir; Bettina Pesch, admin.

Opernhaus Chemnitz. Theaterplatz 2, D-09111 Chemnitz, Germany *tel:* +49 371 488 4662 *fax:* +49 371 488 4697.

Opernhaus Halle. Postfach 110554, D-06019 Halle (Saale), Germany *tel:* +49 345 51100 *fax:* +49 345 511 0102. Klaus Froboese, dir gen; Reinhard Popp, dir; Roger Epple, gen mus dir.

Pocket Opera Company. Gertrudstr 21, D-90429 Nürnberg, Germany *tel:* +49 911 329047 *fax:* +49 911 314606. Peter B Wyrsch, artistic dir; David Seaman, mus dir; Doris Gross, project mgr.

Saarlandisches Staatstheater. Schillenplatz 1, D-66111 Saarbrucken, Germany *tel:* +49 681 30920 *fax:* +49 681 309 2325.

Sächsische Staatsoper Dresden. Theaterplatz 2, D-01067 Dresden, Germany *tel:* +49 351 49110 *fax:* +49 351 491 1691 *email:* semperoper @wad.de; http://www.wad.de/semperoper. Christoph Albrecht, gen dir; Roland Beneke, admin dir; Rolf Wollrad, opera dir; Hans-Joachim Frey, artistic company dir; Matthias Brauer, chorus master; Giuseppe Sinopoli, chief cond.

Schillertheater NRW. Spinnstr 4, D-42283 Wuppertal, Germany *tel:* +49 202 563 4230 *fax:* +49 202 563 8078. Holk Freytag, Ludwig Baum, admin.

Staatsoper Unter den Linden. Unter den Linden S-7, D-10117 Berlin, Germany *tel:* +49 30 20 354555 *fax:* +49 30 20 354481.

Staatsoperette Dresden. Pimaer Landstr 131, D-01257 Dresden, Germany *tel:* +49 351 223 1261/1656 *fax:* +49 351 203 8673.

Staatstheater Braunschweig. Postfach 4539, D-38100 Braunschweig, Germany *tel:* +49 531 484 2700 *fax:* +49 531 484 2727. Detlef Grote, admin.

Staatstheater Darmstadt. Postfach 111432, D-64229 Darmstadt, Germany *tel:* +49 61 51 28111 *fax:* +49 61 51 281 1226. Gerd-Theo Umberg, dir; Michael Ostermeier, admin.

Staatstheater Stuttgart. Oberer Schlossgarten 6, Postfach 104345, D-70173 Stuttgart, Germany *tel:* +49 711 203 2520 *fax:* +49 711 203 2514. Klaus Zehelein, opera dir; Lothar Zagrosek, gen mus dir; Pamela Rosenberg, opera co-dir; Doris Szenczar, head of planning.

Städtische Bühnen Augsburg. Postfach 11 19 49, D-86044 Augsburg, Germany *tel:* +49 821 324 3933 *fax:* +49 821 324 4544. Peter Baumgardt, dir; Peter Leonard, gen mus dir; Gianfranco Paoluzi, ballet dir.

Städtische Bühnen Freiburg. Bertoldstrasse 46, D-7800 Freiburg, Germany *tel:* +49 761 34874/94. Hans Ammann, dir; Johannes Fritzsch, principal cond.

Städtische Bühnen Nürnberg. Theater Nürnberg, Richard-Wagner Platz 2-10, D-90443 Nürnberg, Germany *tel:* +49 911 231 3808 *fax:* +49 911 231 3534 *email:* http://oper.nuernberg.de. Wulf Konold, gen dir; Eberherd Kloke, gen mus dir (to Sep 98); Phillippe Auguin, gen mus dir (from Sep 98).

Städtische Bühnen Regensburg. Bismarckplatz 7, Postfach 110617, D-93047 Regensburg, Germany *tel:* +49 941 507 1422 *fax:* +49 941 507 4429. Marietheres List, artistic admin; Ottmar Bambl, admin.

Städttheater Bremerhaven. Postfach 120541, D-27519 Bremerhaven, Germany *tel:* +49 471 482 0645 *fax:* +49 471 482 0682.

Theater der Stadt Heidelberg. Friedrichstr 5, D-69117 Heidelberg, Germany *tel:* +49 6221 583502 *fax:* +49 6221 583599.

Theater Erfurt. Dalbergsweg 2, D-99084 Erfurt, Germany *tel:* +49 361 562 6267.

Greece

Greek National Opera. 18 Charilaou Tricoupi, GR-106 79 Athens, Greece *tel:* +30 1 36 00180 *fax:* +30 1 36 48309. G Kouroupos, president; Baltas Alkis, artistic dir; L Karytinos, chief cond.

Opera at the Megaron. The Athens Concert Hall, Vas Sofias Av, 1 Kokkali St, GR-115 21 Athens, Greece *tel:* +30 1 72 82000 *fax:* +30 1 72 90174. Christos Lambrakis, chmn; Nikos Manolopoulos, general mgr; N Tsouchlos, dir artistic programmes; H Spanopoulou, mkt dir; Y Papatheodorou, press offr.

Hungary

The Hungarian State Opera. Andrassy Utca 22, H-1061, Budapest, Hungary *tel:* +36 1 131 2550 *fax:* +36 1 332 7331. Miklos Szinetar, gen dir; Géza Oberfrank, mus dir.

Iceland

Icelandic Opera. Ingolfsstraeti, PO Box 1416, 121 Reykjavik, Iceland *tel* +354 56 21 077 *fax:* +354 55 27 384.

Israel

New Israeli Opera. Tel Aviv Performing Arts Centre, 28 Leonardo da Vinci St, POB 33321, Tel Aviv 61332, Israel *tel:* +972 3 692 7707 *fax:* +972 3 696 6606 *email:* opera@netvision.net.il. Hanna Munitz, gen dir.

Italy

L'Arena di Verona. Ente Lirico Arena di Verona, Piazza Bra 28, I-37121 Verona, Italy *tel:* +39 45 590109/590966/590726 *fax:* +39 45 590201/ 8011566. Gianfranco de Bosio, gen dir; Mauro Trombetta, artistic dir.

L'Arena Sferisterio Macerata. Piazza Mazzini 10, Casella Postale 92, I-62100 Macerata, Italy *tel:* +39 733 26 1335/1334/0714 *fax:* +39 733 26 1499. Claudio Orazi, dir; Bruno Carletti, technical dir.

Batignano Musica Nel Chiostro. Santa Croce, I-58041 Batignano, Comune di Grosseto, Italy *tel:* +39 56 438096.

Teatro Alla Scala. Via Filodrammatici 2, I-20121 Milano, Italy *tel:* +39 2 88791; +39 2 720 03744 *fax:* +39 2 887 9331. Carlo Fontana, gen mgr; Riccardo Muti, mus dir.

Teatro Bellini. Via Perrotta 12, Catania, Italy *tel:* +39 95 312020/325365/ 321830 *fax:* +39 95 311875/321830. Vincenzo Bianco, president; Francesco Busalacchi, dir.

Teatro Comunale (Florence). Maggio Musicale Fiorentino, Via Solferino 15, I-50123 Firenze, Italy *tel:* +39 55 27791 *fax:* +39 55 2396954. Francesco Emani, gen mgr; Zubin Mehta, principal cond; Semyon Bychkov, principal guest cond; Cesare Mazzonis, artistic mgr; Susanna Colombo, press offr.

Teatro Comunale (Treviso). Corso Del Popolo 31, I-31100 Treviso, Italy *tel:* +39 422 410130. Alfonso Malaguti, dir.

Teatro Comunale dell'Opera. Teatro Carlo Felice, Passo Al Teatro 4, I-16121 Genoa, Italy *tel:* +39 10 53811. Francesco Canessa, gen mgr.

Teatro Comunale di Bologna. Largo Respighi 1, I-40126 Bologna, Italy *tel:* +39 51 52 9901/9958/9999 *fax:* +39 51 52 9934/9905. Sergio Escobar, dir; Sindaco di Bologna, president.

Teatro Comunale di Modena. Via del Teatro 8, I-41100 Modena, Italy *tel;* +39 59 22 5443/5183.

Teatro Comunale G B Pergolesi. Piazza Della Reppublica 9, I-60035 Jesi, Italy *tel:* +39 731 59788.

Teatro Comunale Giuseppe Verdi. Riva 3 Novembre, I-34121 Trieste, Italy *tel:* +39 40 6722 111 *fax:* +39 40 6722 249. Lorenzo Jorio, dir; Gianni Gori, production mgr.

Il Teatro dell'Opera. Piazza B Gigli 8, I-00184 Roma, Italy *tel:* +39 6 481601 *fax:* +39 6 488 1253.

GÖTEBORGSOPERAN

The Gothenburg Opera

Christina Nilssons Gata
S-411 04 Gothenburg Sweden
Phone +46 (31) 10 80 00 Fax +46 (31) 10 80 30
Box Office Phone +46 (31) 13 13 00 Fax +46 (31) 10 80 51
E-mail info@opera.se
www.opera.se

FRIDERICVS REX APOLLINI ET MVSIS

s t a a t s o p e r

U n t e r   d e n   L i n d e n

Daniel Barenboim – Artistic Director

1997/1998 SEASON

New Productions Opera
(all performances in the original language)

ZAIDE
Wolfgang Amadeus Mozart
Schreier/Schulin/Grützke/Naujok
September 20, 21, 23, 25, 27,
October 7, 13, 1997

COSI FAN TUTTE
Wolfgang Amadeus Mozart
Jacobs/Rudolph/Angele
November 7, 9, 13, 15, 1997

L'OPERA SERIA
Florian Leopold Gassmann
Jacobs/Martinoty/
Schavernoch/Ogier
November 8, 10, 12, 14, 16, 1997

FALSTAFF
Giuseppe Verdi
Abbado/Miller/Kapplmüller/Mitchell
February 15, 18, 21, 24, 27,
March 2, 1998

DIE MEISTERSINGER VON NÜNRBERG
Richard Wagner
Barenboim,Weigle/
Kupfer/Schavernoch/Shiff
April 5, 12, 19,
June 14, 19, 28, 1998

KOMÖDIE OHNE TITEL
Jan Müller-Wieland
(World Premiere)
Müller-Wieland/
Peters-Messer/Meyer
April 25, 26, 28, 1998 – Munich
Performances in Berlin
in 1998/99 Season

PELLEAS UND MELISANDE
Claude Debussy
Gielen/Berghaus/Meyer
June 6, 12, 21, 1998

DER POSTILLON VON LONJUMEAU
Adolphe Adam
Weigle/Schulin/N.N.
July 1, 4, 6, 9, 12, 1998

New Productions Ballet

TANZSTUNDEN
Hans Werner Henze
October 4, 10, 16, 30, 1997
April 2, 4, 1998

SCHWANENSEE
Peter I. Tschaikowsky
December 16, 18, 21, 22, 26, 1997,
January 13, 16, 23, February 14,
June 30, July 10, 1998

PETER UND DER WOLF
Serge Prokofieff
MAX UND MORITZ
Gisbert Näther
May 13, 14, 15, 16, 17, 20, 1998

Repertory:

Die Zauberflöte, Der Freischütz, Aida, Der Rosenkavalier,
Der Barbier von Sevilla, Semele, Die wüste Insel, Fidelio,
Zar und Zimmermann, Lohengrin, Tosca, Salome, Madame Butterfly,
Die heimliche Ehe, Cavalleria rusticana/Der Bajazzo,
Elektra – Le Concours, Die Welt der Ballets Russes,
Apropos Scheherazade, Dix oder Eros und Tod, Don Quixote,
Dornröschen, Balanchine Ballettabend

motus Werbeagentur, Berlin

Information and
Booking:
Staatsoper
Unter den Linden
Visitor's Service
P.O. Box 354
D-10109 Berlin

Phone
++49-30-20 35 45 55
Fax
++49-30-20 35 44 83
Online: http://www.
staatsoper-berlin.org
E-mail:contact@
staatsoper-berlin.org

Romania
Cluj-Napoca Romanian Opera. Piata Stefan Cel Mare 24, 3400 Cluj-Napoca, Romania *tel:* +40 95 117175. Petre Sbârcea, dir.
Opera Romana. Gheorghe Gheorghiu-dej 70-72, Sector 5, Cod 70609, Bucuresti, Romania *tel:* +40 1 615 7939.

Russia
Mariinsky Theatre. 1 Theatre Sq, St Petersburg, Russia *tel:* +7 812 314 9083. Valery Gergyev, principal cond, artistic dir.

Slovak Republic
Slovak National Theatre. Gorkého 4, 815 86 Bratislava, Slovak Republic *tel:* +421 7 533 5085 *fax:* +421 7 533 5072. Ondrej Lenárd, artistic dir; Miroslav Fischer, gen dir.

South Africa
Opera of the Cape Performing Arts. PO Box 4107, Cape Town 8000, South Africa *tel:* +27 21 215470 *fax:* +27 21 215448. Angelo Gobbato, dir; Mike Bosch, mgr; Ronnie Theys, company mgr; Ieteke Oggel, publicity and press offr.
State Theatre Pretoria. Opera, PO Box 566, Pretoria 0001, South Africa *tel:* +27 12 322 1665 *fax:* +27 12 322 3913 *email:* truk@iafrica.com. Johan Maré, admin head.

Spain
Gran Teatre Del Liceu. Departament D'Abonaments 1, Localitats, Rambla dels Caputxins 61, E-08001 Barcelona, Spain *tel:* +34 3 318 9122/412 3532 *fax:* +34 3 412 1198. Josep Caminal, gen dir; Joan Matabosch, artistic mgr.
Teatre Principal. Carrer La Riera 2a, E-07003 Palma de Mallorca, Balearic Islands, Spain *tel:* +34 71 725548 *fax:* +34 71 725542.
Teatro Campoamor Melquiades. Alvarez 20 1, E-33203 Oviedo, Spain *tel:* +34 85 211705.
Teatro de la Maestranza. Paseo de Colon S/n, E-41001 Sevilla, Spain *tel:* +34 54 223344 *fax:* +34 54 225995. Jose Luis Castro, mgr dir; Giuseppe Cuccia, production mgr.
Teatro de la Zarzuela. Jovellanos 4, E-28014 Madrid, Spain *tel:* +34 1 524 5400 *fax:* +34 1 429 7157.

Sri Lanka
Opera Lanka. c/o Galle Face Hotel, 2 Kollupitiya Rd, Colombo 3, Sri Lanka *tel:* +94 1 502416 *fax:* +94 1 541072.

Sweden
Drottningholm Court Theatre. PO Box 270505, S-10251 Stockholm, Sweden *tel:* +46 8 665 1400 *fax:* +46 8 665 1473. Per Erik Öhrn, artistic dir; Per Forsström, gen mgr.
Göteborgs Operan. Christina Nilssons Gata, S-41104 Göteborg, Sweden *tel:* +46 31 1080 00 *fax:* +46 31 1080 30 *email:* http://www.opera.se. Dag Hallberg, gen dir; Kjell Ingebretsen, artistic dir; Ulf Gadd, ballet dir.
Norrlandsoperan. Box 360, S-90108 Umeå, Sweden *tel:* +46 90 154300 *fax:* +46 90 126845 *email:* info@norrlandsoperan.se. Jonas Forssell, artistic dir; Ingemar Sjölander, mgr dir.
Royal Swedish Opera. Box 16094, S-10322 Stockholm, Sweden *tel:* +46 8 791 4300 *fax:* +46 8 791 4444. Bengt Hall, gen mgr; Manuel Mardones, financial mgr; Walton Grönroos, opera dir; Frank Anderson, ballet dir; Staffan Carlweitz, press offr.
Swedish Folkopera. Hornsgatan 72, S-11821 Stockholm, Sweden *tel:* +46 8 616 0750/0700 *fax:* +46 8 844146 *email:* lasse@folkoperan.se. Claes Fellbom, artistic dir; Kerstin Nerbe, mus dir; Staffan Ryden, mgr dir; Lars Tallert, mkt mgr; Magnus Aspegren, exec producer.

Switzerland
Grand Théâtre de Genève. Administration 11, Blvd du Théâtre, CH-1211 Genève 11, Switzerland *tel:* +41 22 418 3000 *fax:* +41 22 418 3001 *email:* http://www.geneveopera.ch. Renée Auphan, gen dir; François Duchêne, gen sec; Jacques Ayrault, technical dir; Guillaume Tourniaire, choirmaster; Marcel Quillévéré, public relations and press dir; Guy Demole, president of the board.
Luzerner Theater. Theaterstr 2, CH-6002 Luzern, Switzerland *tel:* +41 41 210 6618/9 *fax:* +41 41 210 3367. Horst Statkus, artistic dir; Adrian Balmer, admin dir; Jonathan Nott, mus dir.
Opernhaus Zurich. Falkenstrasse 1, CH-8008 Zurich, Switzerland *tel:* +41 1 268 6400/6666 *fax:* +41 1 268 6401/6555. Alexander Pereira, gen dir; Franz Welser-Möst, mus dir; Grischa Asagaroff, artistic dir.
Stadttheater St Gallen. Museumstrasse 24, CH-9004 St Gallen, Switzerland *tel:* +41 71 242 0505 *fax:* +41 71 242 0506. Werner Signer, mgr dir; Peter Schweiger, dir of drama.

Theater Basel. Elisabethenstrasse 16, CH-4010 Basel, Switzerland *tel:* +41 61 295 1100 *fax:* +41 61 295 1200. Michael Schindhelm, gen mgr; Ivo Reichlin, admin dir.
TML Opera de Lausanne. CP 3972, CH-1002 Lausanne, Switzerland *tel:* +41 21 310 1616/1600 *fax:* +41 21 310 1690. Dominique Meyer, dir; Paul Durussel, admin; Bruno Boyer, technical dir; Laurence Authier, press and communication; Marie-Laure Chabloz, sec.

USA
Arizona Opera. 3501 North Mountain Av, Tucson, AZ 85719, USA *tel:* +1 520 293 4336 *fax:* +1 520 293 5097 *email:* nancy1@azopera.com; http://www.azopera.com. Glynn Ross, gen dir; Lloyd Yunker, admin dir; Dean Ryan, mus dir; Leilani Rothrock, business and finance dir; Laura Schairer, mkt dir; Monica Burrows, dir of PR.
The Atlanta Opera. 1800 Peachtree St NW, Suite 620, Atlanta, Georgia 30309, USA *tel:* +1 404 355 3311 *fax:* +1 404 355 3259 *email:* atlopera@mindspring.com; http://isotropic.com/atlopera/ophome.html. Alfred Kennedy, exec dir; William Fred Scott, artistic dir.
Austin Lyric Opera. PO Box 984, Austin, TX 78767, USA *tel:* +1 512 472 5927 *fax:* +1 512 472 4143 *email:* austinlyricopera@austin360.com; http://www.austin360.com. Jospeh McClain, gen dir.
Baltimore Opera Company. 1202 Maryland Av, Baltimore, MD 21201, USA *tel:* +1 410 727 6000 (box office); +1 410 625 1600 (admin) *fax:* +1 410 727 7854 *email:* bltopera@ix.netcom.com. Michael Harrison, gen dir; James Harp, artistic admin and chorus master; William Yannuzzi, mus dir; Peter Johnson, production mgr; Joel Purcell, business mgr.
Bohème Opera New Jersey. PO Box 4157, Trenton, NJ 08610, USA *tel:* +1 609 888 1444; +1 609 683 8000 *fax:* +1 609 888 1440; +1 609 497 0369. Joseph Pucciatti, artistic dir, cond; Sandra Pucciatti, mgr dir; Joan Slavin, development and mkt dir; Samuel Johnson, admin asst; Mary Kaye Metcalf, president elect.
Boston Lyric Opera. 114 State St, Boston, MA 02109-2402, USA *tel:* +1 617 248 8660 *fax:* +1 617 248 8810.
Central City Opera. 621 17th St, Suite 1601, Denver, CO 80293, USA *tel:* +1 303 292 6700 *fax:* +1 303 292 4958 *email:* artstozoo.org/ccopera. Pelham G Pearce, mgr dir; John Moriarty, artistic dir; Curt Hancock, artistic admin.
Chattanooga Symphony and Opera. 630 Chestnut St, Chattanooga, TN 37402, USA *tel:* +1 423 267 8583 *fax:* +1 423 265 6520 *email:* csoa@chattanooga.net. Robert Bernhardt, mus dir; Elizabeth Hare, exec dir; Cynthia Loden-Dowdle, mkt and PR dir; Susan Billings, box office mgr; Linda Morris, exec asst; Rose Helton, accounts mgr.
Chautauqua Opera. Chautauqua Institution, Chautauqua, New York 14722, USA *tel:* +1 716 357 6200/6250 *fax:* +1 716 357 9014. Jay Lesenger, artistic dir.
The Cincinnati Opera. 1241 Elm St, Cincinnati, OH 45210, USA *tel:* +1 513 621 1919/241 2742 *fax:* +1 513 621 4310. Paul Stuhlreyer, mgr dir; James de Blasis, artistic dir; Patricia Beggs, asst mgr dir; Thomas Bankston, dir of operations; Jane Killen, dir of development.
Cleveland Opera. 1422 Euclid Av, Suite 1052, Cleveland, OH 44115-1901, USA *tel:* +1 216 575 0903 *fax:* +1 216 575 1918. David Bamberger, gen dir; Carola Bamberger, associate dir and mkt dir; Marietta G Gullia, dir of development; Robert Cable, publicist; Judith Ryder, dir of outreach and educ dir; Jean Trowbridge, community support liaison.
Connecticut Opera. 226 Farmington Av, Hartford, CT 06105, USA *tel:* +1 203 953 3517/27 *fax:* +1 203 293 1715 *email:* connopera@aol.com.
The Dallas Opera. 3102 Oak Lawn Av, Suite 450, Dallas, TX 75219, USA *tel:* +1 214 443 1043 *fax:* +1 214 443 1060 *email:* opera@computek.net; http://www.dallasopera.org. Plato Karayanis, gen dir; Graeme Jenkins, mus dir; George Landis, mkt and communications dir; John Gage, production dir; Jonathan Pell, artistic admin dir; Rebecca Sherman, PR mgr.
Des Moines Metro Opera. 106 West Boston Av, Indianola, IA 50125, USA *tel:* +1 515 961 6221 *fax:* +1 515 961 2994. Jerilee Mace, exec dir; Robert Larsen, artistic dir; Donni Alley, dir of art and mkt; Randy Williams, production mgr; Denise Core, box office mgr; Arlys Kellar, business mgr.
Eugene Opera. PO Box 11200, Eugene, Oregon 97440, USA *tel:* +1 503 687 5000 *fax:* +1 503 465 2700.
Florentine Opera Company. 735 No Water St, Suite 1315, Milwaukee, WI 53202 4106, USA *tel:* +1 414 291 5700. Dennis W Hanthorn, gen dir; Joseph Rescigno, artistic adviser.
Florida Grand Opera. 1200 Coral Way, Miami, Fl 33145-2980, USA *tel:* +1 305 854 1643 *fax:* +1 305 856 1042 *email:* fgoinfo@aol.com. Robert M Heuer, gen mgr; Paul P Lapinski, asst gen mgr; Karl W Hesser, dir of artistic admin; Mark C Graf, resident associate cond.
Fort Worth Opera. 3505 West Lancaster, Fort Worth, TX 76107, USA *tel:* +1 817 731 0200 *fax:* +1 817 731 0835.

Glimmerglass Opera. PO Box 191, Cooperstown, NY 13326, USA *tel:* +1 607 547 2255 *fax:* +1 607 547 1257 *email:* glimmer@magnum.wpe.com. Christopher Warrell, exec dir; Paul Kellogg, artistic dir; Stewart Robertson, mus dir; Felicity Jackson, dir of artistic admin; Lin Smith Vincent, mkt and publications dir; Michael Willis, dir of public relations.

Greater Buffalo Opera Company. 255 Great Arrow Av #3, Buffalo, NY 14207, USA *tel:* +1 716 447 7000 *fax:* +1 716 447 7004.

Harrison Opera House. PO Box 2580, Norfolk, VA 23501, USA *tel:* +1 804 623 1223 *fax:* +1 804 622 0058. Peter Mark, gen and artistic dir; Russell P Allen, gen mgr; Lisa Jardanhazy, mkt dir; Jerome Shannon, asst artistic dir; Helen C Stevenson, dir of educ.

Houston Grand Opera. 510 Preston St, Houston, TX 77002, USA *tel:* +1 713 546 0240/0246/0272. David Gockley, gen dir; Dolores D Johnson, mgr dir; Jim Ireland, producing dir.

Indianapolis Opera. 250 E 38th St, Indianapolis, IN 46205, USA *tel:* +1 317 921 6444 *fax:* +1 317 923 5611.

Kentucky Opera. 101 S 8th St, Louisville, KY 40202-4016, USA *tel:* +1 502 584 4500 *fax:* +1 502 584 7484 *email:* kyopera@iglou.com. William Winkler, exec dir; H Charles Schmidt, dir of production; Robin Stamper, dir of mus and educ; Gerald Farrar, dir of special events and PR; Robert Curland, dir of sales; Susan G Martin, dir of finance.

Los Angeles Music Center Opera. 135 North Grand Av, Los Angeles, CA 90012, USA *tel:* +1 213 972 7219 *fax:* +1 213 687 3490. Peter Hemmings, gen dir; Christopher Hahn, artistic admin.

Lyric Opera of Chicago. 20 North Wacker Dr, Chicago, IL 60606, USA *tel:* +1 312 332 2244 *fax:* +1 312 419 8345. William Mason, gen dir; Bruno Bartoletti, artistic dir; Danny Newman, PR counsel; Farrell Frentress, dir of development; Susan Mathieson, dir of mkt and communications.

Lyric Opera Of Kansas City. Ticket Office, 1029 Central, Kansas City, MO 64105-1677, USA *tel:* +1 816 471 7344. Russell Patterson, gen artistic dir; Evan Luskin, mgr dir.

Madison Opera. 333 Glennway St, Madison, WI 53705-1310, USA *tel:* +1 608 238 8085 *fax:* +1 608 233 3431. Ann Stanke, gen dir; John De Main, artistic dir; Patricia R Helm, mkt dir; Stephanie Elkins, dir of development.

The Metropolitan Opera. Lincoln Center, New York, NY 10023, USA *tel:* +1 212 799 3100/362 6000 (tickets) *fax:* +1 212 874 2659 *email:* http://www.metopera.org. James Levine, artistic dir; Joseph Volpe, gen mgr; Sarah Billinghurst, asst mgr; Jonathan Friend, artistic admin; François Giulianni, press and PR.

Michigan Opera Theatre. Administrative Offices, Lothrop Landing, 104 Lothrop, Detroit, MI 48202, USA *tel:* +1 313 874 7850/7464 *fax:* +1 313 871 7213 *email:* http://www.motopera.com. David DiChiera, gen dir; Tom Tomlinson, mgr dir; Steve Haviaras, mkt dir; Laura Wyss, PR dir.

The Minnesota Opera. 620 North First St, Minneapolis, MN 55401, USA *tel:* +1 612 333 2700 *fax:* +1 612 333 0869. Kevin Smith, president and gen dir; Dale Johnson, artistic dir.

The Mississippi Opera. PO Box 1551, Jackson, MS 39215, USA *tel:* +1 601 960 1528. Barbara White Johnson, mgr dir.

Mobile Opera Inc. PO Box 66633, Mobile, AL 26660-1633, USA *tel:* +1 334 476 7377 *fax:* +1 334 476 7373 *email:* gendir@aol.com. Jerome Shannon, gen dir; Carole Jett, exec asst.

Nashville Opera. 719 Thompson La, Suite 401, Nashville, TN 37204, USA *tel:* +1 615 292 5710 *fax:* +1 615 292 0549. Carol Penterman, exec dir; John Hoomes, artistic dir; Cara Schneider, company mgr.

Nevada Opera. PO Box 3256, Reno, NV 89505, USA *tel:* +1 702 786 4046 *fax:* +1 702 786 4063.

New Orleans Opera. 305 Baronne St, Suite 500, New Orleans, LA 70112-1618, USA *tel:* +1 504 529 2278 *fax:* +1 504 529 7668 *email:* radelia@aol.com; http://neworleansopera.org. Ray Anthony Delia, exec dir; Arthur G Cosenza, artistic dir; Carol Rausch, educ dir.

New York City Opera. New York State Theater, 20 Lincoln Center, New York, NY 10023, USA *tel:* +1 212 870 5633/5600. Christopher Keene, gen dir; Mark Weinstein, exec dir.

The Ohio Light Opera. The College of Wooster, Wooster, OH 44691, USA *tel:* +1 216 263 2345. James Stuart, artistic dir; Bonnie Havholm, company mgr; Steven Daigle, asst dir.

Opera Carolina. 345 N College St #409, Charlotte, NC 28202, USA *tel:* +1 704 332 7177/372 1000 *fax:* +1 704 332 6448/333 1154 *email:* operacar@charlotte.infi.net. James W Wright, president and gen dir; Gaetano Staffa, vice president; Steve Dellinger, production mgr; Teresa Robertson, dir of educ and community programs; Angela Taylor, business mgr; Susan Delong, development offr.

Opera Colorado. #20, 695 S Colorado Blvd, Denver, CO 80222, USA *tel:* +1 303 986 8742 *fax:* +1 303 436 1286 *email:* opera@ossinc.net.

Opera Columbus. 177 Naghten St, Columbus, OH 43215, USA *tel:* +1 614 461 0022 *fax:* +1 614 461 0806.

Opera Company of Philadelphia. 510 Walnut St, Suite 1500, Philadelphia, PA 19106, USA *tel:* +1 215 928 21002110 *fax:* +1 215 928 2112 *email:* ostroff@operaphilly.com; http://www.operaphilly.com.

Robert Driver, gen dir; Susan Ashbaker, artistic co-ord; Don Smith, dir of development and planning; Kim Coskey, dir of mkt; Craig Hamilton, public affairs dir; Boyd Ostroff, dir of production.

Opera Delaware. 4 S Poplar St, Wilmington, DE 19801-5009, USA *tel:* +1 302 658 8063 *fax:* +1 302 658 4991 *email:* opinfo@operadel.org; http://www.operadel.org. Leland Kimball, gen dir.

Opera Memphis. University of Memphis, Campus Box 526331, Memphis, TN 38152-6331, USA *tel:* +1 901 678 2706 *fax:* +1 901 678 3506 *email:* http://gray.music.rhodes.edu/operahtmls/opera.htm. Michael Ching, gen and artistic dir; Karen Tiller, co-exec dir and dir of production; Adrienne Clark, mkt dir; David Barnwell, box office mgr; Virginia Gary, educ co-ord and company mgr.

Opera Music Theatre International. 1818 North Ode St, Arlington, Virginia, 22209-1410, USA *tel:* +1 703 527 2787 *fax:* +1 703 528 1163 *email:* omti@aol.com; http://www.omti.org. James K McCully, gen dir; Scott E Swanson, admin dir.

Opera Omaha. 1613 Farnam, Suite 200, Omaha, NE 68102, USA *tel:* +1 402 346 4398/0357 *fax:* +1 402 346 7323. Jane Hill, exec dir; Hal France, artistic dir and principal cond.

Opera Pacific. 9 Executive Circle, Suite 190, Irvine, CA 92714, USA *tel:* +1 714 474 4488 *fax:* +1 714 474 4442. David DiChiera, gen dir; Lori A Burrill, Richard H Owens, co-mgr dirs; Mary Bubb, development associate; Christine Do-Vuong, dir of finance; Todd Bentjen, dir of mkt; Kevin Chrysler, dir of community programmes.

Opera Roanoke. 54 Luck Av, Jefferson Centre, Suite 209, Roanoke, VA 24016, USA *tel:* +1 540 982 2742 *fax:* +1 540 982 3601 *email:* opera_roanoke@compuserve.com. Craig Fields, artistic dir; William Krause, exec dir.

Opera Theater of Saint Louis. PO Box 191910, St Louis, MO 63119, USA *tel:* +1 314 961 0171/0644 *fax:* +1 314 961 7463. Charles MacKay, gen dir; Colin Graham, artistic dir; Stephen Lord, mus dir.

Palm Beach Opera. 415 S Olive Av, West Palm Beach, FL 33401, USA *tel:* +1 407 833 7888 *fax:* +1 561 833 8294. Herbert P Benn, gen dir; Anton Gvadagno, artistic dir and principal cond.

Piedmont Opera Theatre. Suite 109, 7990 North Point Blvd, Winston-Salem, NC 27106, USA *tel:* +1 910 759 2277 *fax:* +1 910 759 7722. Victoria Auchincloss, interim mgr dir; Brenda Hubbard, admin.

Pittsburgh Opera. 711 Penn Av, 8th Floor, Pittsburgh, PA 15222-3407, USA *tel:* +1 412 281 0912/456 6666 *fax:* +1 412 281 4324 *email:* dma4+@andrew.cmu.edu. Tito Capobianco, artistic dir; Mark J Weinstein, exec dir; Maria Levy, dir of artistic operations.

Portland Opera. 1515 SW Morrison, Portland, OR 97205, USA *tel:* +1 503 241 1401/241 1802 *fax:* +1 503 241 4212. Robert Bailey, gen dir; Valeria Ramirez, admin dir; Kathy Park, dir of development; James Fullan, dir of public relations; Susan Thompson, dir of mkt; John Peter Jeffries, dir of production.

Sacramento Opera. PO Box 161027, Sacramento, CA 95816, USA *tel:* +1 916 264 5181 *fax:* +1 916 442 4254.

San Diego Opera. PO Box 988, San Diego, CA 92112-0988, USA *tel:* +1 619 232 7636 *fax:* +1 619 231 6915 *email:* staff@sdopera.com; http://wwwsdopera.com. Ian D Campbell, gen dir; Michael Murphy, dir of admin; Marianne Flettner, artistic admin.

San Francisco Opera. War Memorial Opera House, San Francisco, CA 94012-4509, USA *tel:* +1 415 565 6431/864 3300 *fax:* +1 415 621 7508. Lotfi Mansouri, gen dir; Donald C Runnicles, mus dir; Michael J Savage, mgr dir; Christina Scheppelmann, artistic admin; Clifford Cranna, mus admin.

The Santa Fe Opera. PO Box 2408, Santa Fe, NM 87504-2408, USA *tel:* +1 505 986 5955 *fax:* +1 505 986 5999 *email:* santafeopera@santafeopera.org. John Crosby, gen dir; Richard Gaddes, associate gen dir; Brad Woolbright, company mgr.

Sarasota Opera. 61 North Pineapple Dr, Sarasota, FL 34236-5716, USA *tel:* +1 941 366 8450 *fax:* +1 941 955 5571 *email:* http://www.sarasota-online.com/opera. Deane C Allyn, exec dir; Victor DeRenzi, artistic dir.

Seattle Opera. PO Box 9248, Seattle, WA 98109, USA *tel:* +1 206 389 7600/7676/7699 *fax:* +1 206 389 7651. Speight Jenkins, gen dir; Kathy Magiera, admin dir; Melanie Ross, company mgr; Cynthia Savage, production dir; Linda Prather, mkt dir; Tina Ryker, PR dir.

Shreveport Opera. Suite 101, 212 Texas St, Shreveport, LA 71101-3249, USA *tel:* +1 318 227 9503 *fax:* +1 318 227 9518. Gayle Norton, gen mgr; Joseph Illick, artistic dir.

Skylight Opera Theatre. 158 N Broadway, Milwaukee, WI 53202, USA *tel:* +1 414 291 7800 *fax:* +1 414 291 7815. Joan Lounsbery, mgr dir; Richard Carsey, artistic dir; Paula Suozzi, associate artistic dir.

Tacoma Opera. PO Box 7468, Tacoma, WA 98407, USA *tel:* +1 206 627 7789. Anne Farrell, gen mgr; Marian Scheele, fund development; David Bartholomew, resident stage dir.

Toledo Opera. The Valentine Theatre Complex, 406 Adams St, Toledo, OH 43601-1407, USA *tel:* +1 419 255 7464 *fax:* +1 419 255 6344. James Meena, gen dir and principal cond; Libbey McKnight, mkt dir; Joan

Eckermann, educ and outreach dir; Elizabeth Emmert, development dir; Paul Causman, box office mgr.

Townsend Opera Players. PO Box 4519, Modesto, CA 95352, USA *tel:* +1 209 523 6426 *fax:* +1 209 579 0532. Erik Buck Townsend, gen dir; Erika Townsend, operations mgr; Bunny Donalson, PR and mkt; Barbara Wesley, membership; Bryan Hoffman, production mgr.

Tri-Cities Opera. 315 Clinton St, Binghamton, NY 13905, USA *tel:* +1 607 772 0400 *fax:* +1 607 797 6344 *email:* http://www.tier.net/tco. Peyton Hibbitt, Carmen Savoca, artistic dirs; Susan MacLennan, exec dir; Kim Eaton, mkt dir.

Utah Opera. 50 West 200 South, Salt Lake City, UT 84101, USA *tel:* +1 801 323 6868 *fax:* +1 801 323 6815. Anne Ewers, gen dir; Leslie Peterson, dir of operations; John Wehrle, mus admin; Henry O Whiteside, dir of development; Judith Carleson, dir of PR and mkt; LeGrand Richins, finance dir.

The Virginia Opera. PO Box 2580, Norfolk, VA 23501, USA *tel:* +1 757 627 9545 *fax:* +1 757 622 0058. Peter Mark, gen and artistic dir; Russell P Allen, gen mgr; Helen Strickland, controller; John Harris, dir of production; Garold Whisler, asst artistic dir; Bob Minnick, technical dir.

The Washington Opera. Kennedy Center, Washington DC 20566, USA *tel:* +1 202 416 7890 *fax:* +1 202 298 6008 *email:* http://www.dc-opera.org. Patricia L Mossel, exec dir; Placido Domingo, artistic dir; Edward C Purrington, artistic admin; Heinz Fricke, mus dir; Noel Uzemack, technical dir.

Whitewater Opera Company. 1118 E Main St, Richmond, IN 47374, USA *tel:* +1 317 962 7106 *fax:* +1 317 962 7451. Charles Combopiano, artistic dir; Adele Hawks, admin asst; Curtis Tucker, mgr dir.

Wolf Trap Opera Company. Wolf Trap Foundation, 1624 Trap Road, Vienna, VA 22182-2063, USA *tel:* +1 703 255 1935 *fax:* +1 703 255 1924 *email:* http://www.wolf-trap.org. Peter Russell, gen dir; Lisa A Ostrich, admin dir.

The Washington Opera

PLÁCIDO DOMINGO, ARTISTIC DIRECTOR ⬥ PATRICIA L. MOSSEL, EXECUTIVE DIRECTOR

Nov 8 – 30 ⬥ *Leoncavallo*
Pagliacci
Conductor: Leonard Slatkin/Eugene Kohn. Director: Franco Zeffirelli. *New co-production with Los Angeles Music Center Opera. This production has been partially underwritten by members of the Domingo Circle.*

Nov 12 – 29 ⬥ *Gounod*
Roméo et Juliette
Conductor: Bertrand de Billy. Director: Giancarlo del Monaco. *New co-production with Oper der Bundesstadt Bonn, Giancarlo del Monaco, Intendant. This production has been underwritten by a grant from The Gramma Fisher Foundation of Marshalltown, Iowa.*

Dec 27 – Feb 9 ⬥ *Donizetti*
L'Elisir d'Amore
Conductor: John Keenan. Director: Stephen Lawless.
Production from Los Angeles Music Center Opera.

Jan 7 – Feb 14 ⬥ *Mozart*
The Magic Flute
Conductor: Heinz Fricke. Director: Sonja Frisell. *Revival of our 1990 production. Performances made possible by The Washington Opera Guild.*

Jan 15 – Feb 15 ⬥ *Vives*
Doña Francisquita
Conductor: Miguel Roa. Director: Emilio Sagi. *Production from Teatro Lírico Nacional de La Zarzuela, Madrid, and Teatro Colón, Buenos Aires.*

Feb 18 & 22
Samuel Ramey
February 18: "A Date with the Devil." Conductor: John DeMain
February 22: Samuel Ramey in Recital

Feb 28 – March 23 ⬥ *Puccini*
La Rondine
Conductor: Emmanuel Villaume. Director: Marta Domingo. *New co-production with Oper der Bundesstadt Bonn, Giancarlo del Monaco, Intendant, and Los Angeles Music Center Opera.*

March 7 – 28 ⬥ *Mozart*
Don Giovanni
Conductor: Heinz Fricke. Director: Jean-Pierre Ponnelle/Matthew Lata. *Revival of our 1985 production. Co-production with L'Orchestre de Paris. Performances made possible by The Washington Opera Women's Committee.*

March 12 – 29 ⬥ *Susa & Littell*
The Dangerous Liaisons
Conductor: Anne Manson. Director: Colin Graham.
East Coast premiere. Production from San Francisco Opera.

Mobil Foundation is the Official Sponsor of the 1997-98 Season.
Artists for the season include: Ainhoa Arteta, Antonio Barasorda, Dwayne Croft, Richard Croft, Franco De Grandis, Fernando de la Mora, Cecilia Díaz, Plácido Domingo, Dale Duesing, Marcello Giordani, Judith Forst, Elizabeth Futral, Marcus Haddock, Matthias Hölle, Hei-Kyung Hong, Manuel Lanza, Mary Mills, Isabel Monar, Alexandrina Pendatchanska, Nina Rautio, Richard Troxell, Verónica Villarroel and Gregory Yurisich.

1997-98
SEASON

Phone: 202-416-7800 ⬥ Fax: 202-416-7857 ⬥ http://www.dc-opera.org ⬥ Kennedy Center, Washington DC 20566

Choirs and Choruses

The following list includes professional choirs and major choruses who tour internationally and are reputed for their public performances and recording work. Some of the choirs are affiliated to orchestras, which are listed elsewhere in the **International Directory.**

Australia

Melbourne Chorale (200). 110 Keppel St, PO Box 1148, Carlton, Vic 3053, Australia *tel:* +61 3 9347 9885 *fax:* +61 3 9347 7973 *email:* melbchor@vicnet.net.au. Graham Abbott, mus dir; Nick Bailey, gen mgr.

Sydney Philharmonia Choirs. GPO Box 4972, Sydney, NSW 2001, Australia *tel:* +61 2 9251 2024 *fax:* +61 2 9251 2117.

Tasmanian Symphony Orchestra Chorus. GPO Box 9994, Hobart, Tas 7001, Australia *tel:* +61 03 62353646 *fax:* +61 03 62353651. *Associated with Tasmanian Symphony Orchestra.*

West Australian Symphony Orchestra Chorus. GPO Box 9994, Perth WA 6001, Australia *tel:* +61 8 9220 2604 *fax:* +61 8 9220 2551.

Austria

Arnold Schoenberg Choir (40). Prinz Eugenstr 16/3, A-1040 Wien, Austria *tel:* +43 1 504 2540 *fax:* +43 1 504 2549. Erwin Ortner, cond; Erich Schneider, mgr.

Concentus Vocalis Wien (26-48). Kienmayergasse 9, A-1140 Wien, Austria *tel:* +43 1 984 4634 *fax:* +43 1 982 3029. Herbert Böck, mus dir; Konstantin Moritsch, mgr.

Grosser Chor des Landeskonservatorium Tirol (60). Paul Hofhaimer Gasse 6, A-6020 Innsbruck, Austria *tel:* +43 555 232862. Günther Simonott, cond.

Vienna Male Choral Society (80-90). Bösendorferstr 12, A-1010 Wien, Austria *tel:* +43 1 505 7362 *fax:* +43 1 504 5450. Gerhard Track, dir; Kurt Schuh, mgr. *Vienna's oldest male voice choir, founded in 1843. Performs and tours world-wide. 2 concerts a season.*

Young Vienna Choral Society (60-70). Bösendorferstr 12, A-1010 Wien, Austria *tel:* +43 1 216 7333 *fax:* +43 1 212 2155. Gerhard Track, dir; Ulli Müller-Angerer, mgr.

Belarus

State Chamber Choir of Republic Belarus (30). Prospect Skaryny 50, 220005 Minsk, Belarus *tel:* +7 0172 317471 *also fax.* Igor Matyukhov, artistic adviser and principal cond; Andrey Laptjonock, mgr.

Belgium

BRTN - Omroepkoor. Magdalenazaal, Duquesnoystraat 14, B-1000 Bruxelles, Belgium *tel:* +32 2 548 0170 *fax:* +32 2 548 0177.

Choeur de Chambre de Namur (16-32). Avenue Jean 1er, No 2, B-5000 Namur, Belgium *tel:* +32 81 74 27 52 *fax:* +32 81 74 21 94. Pierre Cao, Denis Menier, mus dirs; Jean-Marie Marchal, mgr. *Classic CD Choice, Diapasson D'Or, Choc Du Monde de la Musique.*

Choeur Symphonique de Namur et de la Communauté Française de Belgique (80-120). Avenue Jean Ier, No 2, B-5000 Namur, Belgium *tel:* +32 81 74 27 52 *fax:* +32 81 74 21 94. Denis Menier, mus dir; Jean-Marie Marchal, mgr.

Bulgaria

Sofia Philharmonic Choir (100). 1 Benkovski Str, B-1000 Sofia, Bulgaria *tel:* +359 2 883197 *fax:* +359 2 874072. Gueorgui Robev, cond.

Canada

The Amadeus Choir of Greater Toronto. 168 Linden Av, Scarborough, ON M1K 3H8, Canada *tel:* +1 416 267 2796. Lydia Adams, mus dir.

Calgary Philharmonic Chorus (100). 205 Eighth Av SE, Calgary, Alta T2G 0K9, Canada *tel:* +1 403 571 0270 *fax:* +1 403 294 7424 *email:* http://www.#tn.com/cpo.

Kitchener Waterloo Philharmonic Choir. PO Box 22111, Westmount Post Office, Waterloo, Ont N2L 6J7, Canada *tel:* +1 519 746 7979 *fax:* +1 519 888 7666. Howard Dyck, mus dir.

St Lawrence Choir. PO Box 1435, Station B, Montreal, PQ H3B 3L2, Canada *tel:* +1 514 483 6922. Iwan Edwards, mus dir.

Toronto Mendelssohn Choir. 60 Simcoe St, Suite C501, Toronto, Ont M5J 2H5, Canada *tel:* +1 416 598 0422 *fax:* +1 416 598 2992. Noel Edison, cond; Donna White, gen mgr.

Vancouver Chamber Choir (20). 1254 W Seventh Av, Vancouver BC, V6H 1B6, Canada *tel:* +1 604 738 6822 *fax:* +1 604 738 7832 *email:* vcc @dowco.com; http://www.sitegeist.com/vcc. Jon Washburn, artistic and exec dir; Violet Goosen, gen mgr. *Nominated for a Juno award, won award for Oustanding Choral Recording from Association Canadian Choral Conductors. Regular broadcasts and releases.*

Croatia

Dubrovnik Chamber Choir. c/o Put Ante Starcevica 29, 20 000 Dubrovnik, Croatia *tel:* +38 52 04 17 101 *fax:* +38 52 04 17 060. Frano Krasovac, cond.

Libertas. c/o Put Ante Starcevica 29, 20 000 Dubrovnik, Croatia *tel:* +38 52 04 17 101 *fax:* +38 52 04 17 060. Viktor Lenert, cond.

Czech Republic

Cesky Filharmoniky Sbor Brno. Komenskeho nam 8, CZ-602 00 Brno, Czech Republic *tel:* +420 5 4221 5116 *fax:* +420 5 4221 1358.

Kühnuv Mixed Choir (98). Krakovská 10, CZ-110 00 Praha 1, Czech Republic *tel:* +420 2 267 96 13. Pavel Kühn, choirmaster; Vladimir Breza, sec. *Frequent performances in Europe and regular recording releases.*

Prague Radio Choir FISYO. Trachtova 2/1130, CZ-158 00 Praha 5, Czech Republic *tel:* +420 2 684 6256 *fax:* +420 2 684 9379.

Denmark

The Danish Radio Choir and Chamber Choir (30-40). Radiohuset, DK-1999 Frederiksberg, Denmark *tel:* +45 3520 6381 *fax:* +45 3520 6121 *email:* gal@dr.dk. Per Erik Veng, gen mgr and artistic dir; Stefan Parkman, principal cond. *Exclusive contract with Chandos recording company.*

Royal Opera Chorus (60). Det Kgl Teater, Tordenskjoldsgade 8, PO Box 2185, DK-1017 Copenhagen, Denmark *tel:* +45 3369 6701 *fax:* +45 3369 6767. Kaare Hansen, choirmaster; Birgitte Christiansen, admin.

Tivoli Concert Choir (80-100). Rudersdalsvej 74, DK-2840 Holte, Denmark *tel:* +45 4242 5400 *also fax.* Morten Schuldt-Jensen, artistic dir. *Resident choir of Tivoli Concert Hall.*

Estonia

Estonia Philharmonic Chamber Choir. Löhike Jalg 9, Tallinn, EE-0001 Tallinn, Estonia *tel:* +37 22 4448926.

Finland

The Jubilate Choir (c 35). Suonionkatu 7B15, FIN-00530 Helsinki, Finland *tel:* +358 9 712 281. Astrid Riska, cond.

The Polytech Choir (60). PO Box 69, FIN-02151 Espoo, Finland *tel:* +358 9 477 1434; +358 9 405 441 *fax:* +358 9 451 3277 *email:* pk@otax.tky.hut.fi; http://www.tky.hut.fi/~pk/. Tapani Länsiö, cond; Harri Lappalainen, choir sec. *Male voice choir.*

France

A Sei Voci (4-12). 32 rue Gambetta, F-72300 Sable, France *tel:* +33 2 43 92 76 58 *fax:* +33 2 43 92 76 59 *email:* 106611.657@compuserve.com. Bernard Fabre-Garrus, artistic dir; Thomas Vasseur, gr. *Researches and performs Renaissance polyphonic works. 1994 Best Vocal Ensemble of the Year in Victoire de la Musique Classique prize. Regular performances and releases.*

Choeur de Radio France. 116 Av du Président Kennedy, F-75220 Paris, Cédex 16, France *tel:* +33 1 42 30 36 30 *fax:* +33 1 42 30 47 48. Marek Janowski, mus dir. *Linked to Orchestre Philharmonique de Radio-France.*

Choeurs de Lyon - Bernardetu (80). 149 Rue Garibaldi, F-69003 Lyon, France *tel:* +33 78 95 29 40 *fax:* +33 78 62 29 03. Bernard Tetu, artistic dir; Pascaline Maugat, PR contact. *Prix de l'Academie des Beaux Arts, Institut de France.*

Choir of La Chapelle Royale. 10 Rue Coquiltiere, F-75001 Paris, France *tel:* +33 1 40 26 58 00 *fax:* +33 1 40 26 38 37. *Links with La Chapelle Royale/Orchestre des Champs Elysées.*

Ensemble Vocal Jean Sourisse (20-25). 3 Rue Jean Bart, F-75006 Paris, France *tel:* +33 1 42 22 98 17 *also fax; email:* rswyerad@artinternet.fr. Jean Sourisse, choirmaster; Claire Lamboley, pres.

Germany

Chor der Bamberger Symphoniker. Mußstr 1, D-96047 Bamberg, Germany *tel:* +49 951 964 7100 *fax:* +49 951 964 7123. R. Beck, dir. *Associated with Bamberger Symphoniker.*

Dresdner Kreuzchor (150). Eisenacherstrasse 21, D-01277 Dresden, Germany *tel:* +49 351 310 5650 *fax:* +49 351 311 3837 *email:* bucro@kreuzchor.de; http://www.kreuzchor.de. Leiter Roderich Kreile; Uwe Grüner, mgr.

Frankfurter Kantorei (120). Homburger Hohl 18, D-60437 Frankfurt am Main, Germany *tel:* +49 69 509 30041 *fax:* +49 69 509 30042. Wolfgang Schaefer, artistic dir; Johannes Kaballo, president.

Kammerchor Stuttgart (16-60). Stuttgarter Musik Podium, Christophstr 5, D-70178 Stuttgart, Germany *tel:* +49 711 239 1390 *fax:* +49 711 239 1399. Mattis Dänhardt, mgr; Frieder Bernius, cond.

Kölner Kammerchor (15-40). c/o Oberborsbacher Str 6, D-51519 Odenthal, Germany *tel:* +49 2202 70293 *fax:* +49 2202 70294. Peter Neumann, cond.

MDR Chor. Springerstr 22-24, D-04105 Leipzig, Germany *tel:* +49 341 300 5505 *fax:* +49 341 300 5532. *Associated with MDR Sinfonie-orchester.*

Philharmonischer Chor Dresden (95). Postfach 120368, Kulturplast Am Altmarkt, D-01005 Dresden, Germany *tel:* +49 351 486 6282 *fax:* +49 351 486 6283 *email:* philharm@imedia.de. *Founded 1967. Associated with Dresden Philharmonic Orchestra.*

Philharmonischer Chor München (150). Gasteig-Kulturzentrum, Kellerstr 4/III, D-181667 München, Germany *tel:* +49 89 4809 509 *fax:* +49 89 4809 513. *Links with Munich Philharmonic.*

Rheinische Kantorei (16-32). Ostpreussenallee 5, D-41539 Dormagen, Germany *tel:* +49 2133 477905 *also fax.* Hermann Max, cond; Matin Kahl, mgr. *Echo-Klassik 1996 prize for best choral recording of year.*

Städttischer Musikverein zu Düsseldorf. Ehrenhof 1, Tonhalle, D-40479 Düsseldorf, Germany *tel:* +49 211 899 3606 *fax:* +49 211 892 9143. Raimund Wippermann, dir. *Associated with Düsseldorf Symphonic Orchestra.*

Greece

Athens Broadcasting Choir (55). 432 Mesoghion Av, Aghia Paraskevi 153, 42 Athens, Greece *tel:* +30 1 606 6802/3 *fax:* +30 1 606 6099. Mrs Karniadaki, dir; Ant Kontogeogriou, choir dir.

Hong Kong

Hong Kong Philharmonic Chorus (80). 8/F Admin Building, Hong Kong Cultural Centre, 10 Salisbury Rd, Tsimshatshi, Kowloon, Hong Kong *tel:* +852 2721 2030 *fax:* +852 2311 6229. Wing-sie Yip, dir; Frances Cheung, sec. *Associated with Hong Kong Philharmonic Orchestra.*

Hungary

Hungarian State Choir (76). Vörösmarty tér 1, H-1051 Budapest, Hungary *tel:* +36 1 266 9097. Mátyás Antal, artistic dir.

Mixed Choir of the Hungarian Radio and TV (69). Bródy Sándor u 5-7, H-1088 Budapest, Hungary *tel:* +36 1 138 8405 *fax:* +36 1 138 8739. István Alföldy-Boruss, dir; Kalman Strausz, artistic dir.

Iceland

Hamrahlídarkórinn (60). Stórholti 41, IS-105 Reykjavik, Iceland *tel:* +354 562 6239 *also fax.* Thorgerdur Ingólfsdóttir, cond.

Kór Langholtskirkju (85). c/o Langholtsvegi 139, IS-104 Reykjavik, Iceland *tel:* +354 553 5750; +354 568 9430 *fax:* +354 581 1835. Jón Stefánsson, cond; Sigurbjörg Hjörleifsdóttir, office mgr.

Israel

Ichud Choir (47). 10 Dubnow St, Tel Aviv 64732, Israel *tel:* +972 3 692 7525 *fax:* +972 3 545 2659. Ada Yadlin, admin co-ord; Auner Ilay, cond and mus dir.

The Jerusalem Rubin Academy Chamber Choir. The Jerusalem Rubin Academy of Music and Dance, Givat Ram Campus, Jerusalem 91904, Israel *tel:* +972 2 759911 *fax:* +972 2 527713.

National Kibbutz Choir. Beit HaKibutz Ha'artzi, 13 Leonardo da Vinci St, Tel Aviv, Israel *tel:* +972 3 692 5223/4 *fax:* +972 3 696 6754.

Tel Aviv Philharmonic Choir. 17 Yehezkel St, Tel Aviv 62595, Israel *tel:* +972 3 699 0904 *fax:* +972 3 605 0243.

Italy

Coro Jubilate (40). Piazza S Magno 13, I-20025 Legnano, Italy *tel:* +39 331 594504 *also fax.* Paolo Alli, dir; Carlo Leonardi, president.

Japan

Japan Philharmonic Association Choir (200). 1-6-1 Umezato, Suginami-ku, Tokyo 166, Japan *tel:* +81 3 5378 6311 *fax:* +81 3 5378 6161 *email:* j-phil@suehiro.nakano.tokyo.jp. *Established 1975. Associated with Japan Philharmonic Orchestra.*

Osaka Philharmonic Choir. 1-1-44 Kishinosato, Nishinari-ku, Osaka 557, Japan *tel:* +81 6 656 7711 *fax:* +81 6 656 7714. *Associated with Osaka Philharmonic Orchestra.*

Latvia

Latvija State Academic Choir. 6 Amatu St, LV-1664 Riga, Latvia *tel:* +371 7 224850/229537 *fax:* +371 7 224850. Maris Sirmais, principal cond. *Associated with Latvian National Symphony Orchestra.*

Moldova

DOINA - State Academic Choir (70). 78 Mitropolitul, Vaarlam str, 277012 Chisinau, Moldova *tel:* +3732 22 40 16 *fax:* +3732 23 35 09. Garstea Veronica, chief cond and artistic dir. *Associated with the Moldova National Philharmonic Symphony Orchestra.*

Netherlands

Koninklijke Zangvereeniging Rotte's Mannenkoor (21). PO Box 406, NL-3067 VD Rotterdam, Netherlands *tel:* +31 10 450 2001. R Verhoeff, dir; W Glastro, pres.

Koor van De Nederlands Bachvereniging (20). De Nederlandse Bachvereniging, Postbus 12017, NL-3501 AA Utrecht, Netherlands *tel:* +31 30 2513 522/413 *fax:* +31 30 2511 639. Maria Hansen, mgr dir; Jos van Veldhoven, artistic dir.

Nederlands Theaterkoor (12-80). Houtvaartkade 28D, NL-2111 BD Aerdenhout, Netherlands *tel:* +31 23 5247 792 *fax:* +31 23 5248 162. Bart van Veen, mgr.

Netherlands Radio Choir (79). Groot Omroepkoor, Postbox 125, NL-1200 AC Hilversum, Netherlands *tel:* +31 35 6714 120 *fax:* +31 35 6714 171. Martin Wright, principal cond; Monica H M Damen, mgr dir.

Noord-Nederlands Concertkoor. Emmaplein 2, PO Box 818, NL-9700 Av Groningen, Netherlands *tel:* +31 50 126200 *fax:* +31 50 138164 *email:* nno@tref.nl. H Pruiksma, repetiteur; J Lamminga, choirmaster. *Associated with Noord-Nederlands Orchestra.*

Norway

Bergen Cathedral Choir. c/o Bjorgvin Kirkemusikk AS, PO Box 765, N-5001 Bergen, Norway *tel:* +47 5531 3320 *also fax.* Magnar Mangersnes, cond.

Grex Vocalis. Sorkesdalsvn 78, N-0376 Oslo, Norway *tel:* +47 2252 0299 *fax:* +47 2252 4738. Carl Hogset, cond.

Norwegian Soloists Choir. c/o Blinken 8, N-1349 Rykkin *tel:* +47 6713 7632 *fax:* +47 2243 1697. Christine Wille Jordheim, admin; Grete Holderød, cond.

Oslo Cathedral Choir (45). Karl Johans gt 11, N-0154 Oslo, Norway *tel:* +47 2242 7758 *fax:* +47 2241 1717. Terje Kvam, cond; Bente Johnsrud, dir.

Oslo Chamber Choir. Maridalsv 162 C, N-0161 Oslo, Norway. Marit Nybo; Grete Helgerød, cond.

Oslo Philharmonic Choir. PO Box 1607 Vika, Haaton VIIs gt. 2, NO119 Oslo, Norway *tel:* +47 22 014900 *fax:* +47 22 014901. *Associated with Oslo Philharmonic Orchestra.*

Skruk (50). v/Fredrik Mork Haskjold, Mork, N-6100 Volda, Norway *tel:* +47 7007 6667 *fax:* +47 7007 8567. Per Oddvar Hildre, cond; Fredrik Mork Haskoolp, mgr.

Trondheim Chamber Choir. Njardarvollen 19, N-7032 Trondheim, Norway *tel:* +47 7393 9528. Norunn Illevold Giske, cond.

Trondheim Symfoniorkesters Choir. Post Box 774 Sentrum, N-7001 Trondheim, Norway *tel:* +47 7353 0760 *fax:* +47 7351 4888. *Associated with Trondheim Symfoniorkester.*

Poland

Silesian State Philharmonic in Katowice (60). Ul Sokolska 2, 40-084 Katowice, Poland *tel:* +48 32 597571 *fax:* +48 32 589885. Jerzy Swoboda, gen and artistic dir; Jan Wojtacha, choir cond.

The State Philharmonic Choir. ul Pilsudskiego 19, PL-50044 Wroclaw, Poland *tel:* +48 71 3422001 *fax:* +48 71 3428980. *Associated with State Philharmonic Orchestra.*

Warsaw Philharmonic Choir (102). ul jasna 5, PL-00950 Warszawa, Poland *tel:* +48 826 56 17/826 83 11 *fax:* +48 826 56 17 *email:* phil@pol.pl. *Associated with Warsaw Philharmonic Orchestra.*

Portugal
Gulbenkian Choir. Fundaçao Calouuste Gulbenkian, Av de Berna 45, P-1093 Lisboa, Portugal *tel:* +351 1 793 5131 *fax:* +351 1 793 5139 *email:* http://www.telepac.pt/earte/gulbenkianz. *Associated with the Gulbenkian Orchestra.*

Republic of Ireland
Anúna. 5 Lakelands Lawn, Stillorgan, Co Dublin, Republic of Ireland *tel:* +353 1 283 5533 *also fax; email:* info@anuna.ie; http://www.anuna.ie. Michael McGlynn, dir and founder.

Galway Baroque Singers (65-70). 14 Montrose House, Whitestrand, Galway, Co Galway, Republic of Ireland *tel:* +353 91 561712 *also fax.* Audrey Corbett, mus dir; Joan Armitage, sec.

Irish Youth Choir (120). c/o Association of Irish Choirs, Drinan St, Cork, Republic of Ireland *tel:* +353 21 312296 *fax:* +353 21 962457. Barbara Heas, admin. *Mixed-voice, ages 17-29.*

Romania
Arad State Philharmonic Choir (47). Piata George Enescu 1, 2900 Arad, Romania *tel:* +40 57 216284 *fax:* +40 57 217867. Doru Serban, cond.

Iasi Philharmonic (70). Str Cuza Voda 29, 6600 Iasi, Romania *tel:* +40 32 114601/112100/212620 *fax:* +40 32 214160. Doru Morariu, cond. *Vocal-symphonic and a cappella repertoire. Recordings and broadcasts.*

Transilvania State Philharmonic Choir, Cluj-Napoca (70). St Emanuel de Martonne 1, 3400 Cluj-Napoca, Romania *tel:* +40 64 430060/3 *fax:* +40 64 197812. Cornel Groza, cond; George Dudea, gen dir.

Spain
Coral Agora Segovia (45). Pza S Esteban 11, 3 Segovia, Spain *tel:* +34 21 434423 *also fax.* José Miguel Arranz, sec; Marisa Martin, dir.

Coral del Conservatori Professional de Musica de Badalona (45). C/Pare Claret 2, E-08911 Badalona, Spain *tel:* +34 3 389 3957 *fax:* +34 3 389 3254. Montserrat Pi, dir.

Coro Fundación Principe de Asturias (100). Fundación Principe de Asturias, C/General Yagüe 2, E-33004 Oviedo, Spain *tel:* +34 8 525 8755 *fax:* +34 8 524 2104. José Esteban Garcia Miranda, dir; Luis Heres Prieto, sec.

La Capella Reial de Catalunya (6-10). Travesera de Gracia 18-20, E-08021 Barcelona, Spain *tel:* +33 1 48 049097 *fax:* +33 1 44 780719 *email:* 101617.3236@compuserve.com. Jordi Savall, dir; Irïne Bloc, admin.

Orfeó Catala (90). C/San Francisco de Paula 2, E-08003 Barcelona, Spain *tel:* +34 3 268 1000 *fax:* +34 3 268 4824. Jordi Casas Bayer, dir.

Sweden
Gothenburg Symphony Orchestra Chorus (200+). Stenhammarsgatam 1, S-412 56 Gothenburg, Sweden *tel:* +46 31 778 77800 *fax:* +46 31 203 502. *Associated with Swedish National Orchestra.*

Stockholm Bach Choir (30). Adolf Frederiks Church, PO Box 3270, 10365 Stockholm, Sweden *tel:* +46 8 411 2351 *fax:* +46 8 204912. Anders Öhrwall, cond.

Swedish Radio Choir (33). RH-5B, 10510 Stockholm, Sweden *tel:* +46 8 784 2406 *fax:* +46 8 784 1343 *email:* matts.boman@p2.sr.se; http://www.sr.se. Matts Boman, mgr; Tónu Kaljuste, principal cond.

Switzerland
Basler Madrigalisten (16-48). Gundeldingerstr 93, CH-4053 Basel, Switzerland *tel:* +41 61 272 8333 *fax:* +41 61 272 8338. Fritz Näf, cond; Rita Froesch, mgr dir.

Ensemble Vocal de Lausanne (c 60). Avenue du Grammont 11 bis, CH-1007 Lausanne, Switzerland *tel:* +41 21 617 4707 *fax:* +41 21 617 4867. Michel Corboz, mus dir; Frederik Sjollema, mgr.

Ukraine
Kiev Chamber Choir (23). vul Ulyanovykh 12, 252005 Kiev, Ukraine *tel:* +380 44 269 4291 *fax:* +380 44 264 7786. Mykola Gobdich, mus dir; Mykola Trofimov, gen mgr.

USA
Atlanta Symphony Orchestra Chamber Chorus (60). 1293 Peachtree St NE, Suite 300, Atlanta, GA 30309, USA *tel:* +1 404 733 4900 *fax:* +1 404 733 4901 *email:* http://www.atlantasymphony.org. *Associated with Atlanta Symphony Orchestra.*

Atlanta Symphony Orchestra Chorus (220). 1293 Peachtree St NE, Suite 300, Atlanta, GA 30309, USA *tel:* +1 404 733 4900 *fax:* +1 404 733 4901 *email:* http://www.atlantasymphony.org. *Associated with Atlanta Symphony Orchestra.*

Chanticleer (12). 650 Fifth St, Suite 311, San Francisco, CA 94107, USA *tel:* +1 415 896 5866 *fax:* +1 415 896 1660 *email:* chanticlee@aol.com. Joseph Jennings, mus dir; Susan G Duncan, exec dir.

Cleveland Orchestra Chorus. Severance Hall, Cleveland, OH 44106, USA *tel:* +1 216 231 7300 *fax:* +1 216 231 0202. *Associated with the Cleveland Orchestra.*

Colorado Symphony Chorus. 821 17th St, Suite 700, Denver, CO 80202, USA *tel:* +1 303 292 5566 *fax:* +1 303 293 2649 *email:* http://www.coloradosymphony.com.

The Dale Warland Singers (40). 120 N Fourth St, Minneapolis, MN 55401, USA *tel:* +1 612 339 9707 *fax:* +1 612 339 9826. Dale Warland, mus dir; Bonnie L McClain, exec dir.

Dallas Symphony Chorus (240). 2301 Flora St, Suite 300, Dallas, TX 75201-2497, USA *tel:* +1 214 871 4000 *fax:* +1 214 871 4049 *email:* http://www.dallassymphony.com/. *Official vocal ensemble of the DSO, founded in 1977. Volunteer organisation.*

Handel and Haydn Society (32). 300 Massachusetts Av, Boston, MA 02115, USA *tel:* +1 617 262 1815 *fax:* +1 617 266 4217. Mary Deissler, exec dir; Christopher Hogwood, artistic dir.

Houston Symphony Chorus. 615 Louisiana St, Houston, TX 77002-2798, USA *tel:* +1 713 224 4240 *fax:* +1 713 222 7024. *Associated with Houston Symphony.*

Milwaukee Symphony Chorus. 330 E Kilbourn Av, Suite 900, Milwaukee, WI 53202, USA *tel:* +1 414 291 6010 *fax:* +1 414 291 7610 *email:* amadeus@execpc.com; http://www.milwaukeesymphony.org. *Associated with Milwaukee Symphony Orchestra.*

Music of the Baroque Chorus and Orchestra (26). 100 N LaSalle St, Suite 1610, Chicago, IL 60602, USA *tel:* +1 312 551 1415 *fax:* +1 312 551 1444 *email:* baroque@baroque.org. Thomas Wikman, mus dir; Anna-Lise Pasch, concert mgr.

Nashville Symphony Chorus. 209 10th Av South, Suite 448, Nashville, TN 37203, USA *tel:* +1 615 255 5600 *fax:* +1 615 255 5656. *Associated with Nashville Symphony Orchestra.*

The National Chorale. 1650 Broadway, New York, NY 10025, USA *tel:* +1 212 333 5333 *fax:* +1 212 315 2420. Martin Josman, mus dir; Crail Conner, projects mgr.

Oratorio Singers of Charlotte. 211 N College St, Suite 202, Charlotte, NC 28202, USA *tel:* +1 704 332 0468 *fax:* +1 704 332 1963 *email:* http://www.charlottesymphony.org. David Tang, dir. *Associated with Charlotte Symphony Orchestra.*

Pacific Chorale (165). 1221 E Dyer Rd, Suite 230, Santa Ana, CA 92705-5606, USA *tel:* +1 714 755 5788 *fax:* +1 714 755 5789 *email:* http://www,pso.org. John Alexander. *Associated with Pacific Symphony Orchestra.*

The Philadelphia Singers. 1211 Chestnut St, Suite 200, Philadelphia, PA 19107, USA *tel:* +1 215 751 9494 *fax:* +1 215 751 9490.

Plymouth Music Series of Minnesota (24-110). 1900 Nicollet Av, Minneapolis, MN 55403, USA *tel:* +1 612 870 0943 *fax:* +1 612 870 9962. Philip Brunelle, art dir; Frank Stubbs, gen mgr. *Ensembles and Symphony Chorus.*

Saint Louis Symphony Chorus. Powell Symphony Hall, 718 N Grand Blvd, St Louis, MO 63103, USA *tel:* +1 314 533 2500 *fax:* +1 314 286 4142 *email:* http://www.stlsym.org. Amy Kaiser, dir. *Associated with Saint Louis Symphony Orchestra.*

St Olaf Choir (75). 1520 St Olaf Av, Northfield, MN 55057, USA *tel:* +1 507 646 3179 *fax:* +1 507 646 3527. B J Johnson, mgr.

San Francisco Symphony Chorus. Davies Symphony Hall, San Francisco, CA 94102, USA *tel:* +1 415 552 8000 *fax:* +1 415 431 6857. *Associated with San Francisco Symphony.*

Seattle Symphony Chorale. 305 Harrison St, Seattle, WA 98109-4645, USA *tel:* +1 206 215 4700 *fax:* +1 206 215 4701 *email:* http://www.seattlesymphony.org. Abraham Kaplan, leader. *Associated with Seattle Symphony Orchestra.*

Utah Symphony Chorus. 123 W South Temple, Salt Lake City, UT 84101, USA *tel:* +1 801 533 3626 *fax:* +1 801 521 6634. *Associated with Utah Symphony Orchestra.*

West Virginia Symphony Chorus. PO Box 2292, Charleston, WV 25328, USA *tel:* +1 304 342 0151. Thomas Bookhout, dir.

Wichita Symphony Orchestra Chorus. 225 W Douglas, Suite 207, Wichita, KS 67202, USA *tel:* +1 316 267 5259 *fax:* +1 316 267 1937 *email:* symphony@louverture.com; http://www.wso.org. *Volunteer choir associated with Wichita Symphony Orchestra.*

Trade Fairs

Listed below are the major international trade fairs and exhibitions that are wholly or mostly concerned with classical music. Some festivals may have an exhibition area within the festival grounds.

China

China Sound, Light and Music. Beijing International Exhibition Centre, Room 415, 4th Floor, 2nd Central Building, Hualong St, Nanheyan, Dongcheng District, Beijing 100006, China *tel:* +86 106 512 5185 *fax:* +86 106 512 5183. Wang Dongsheng, project mgr; Sun Peng, deputy gen mgr. *May. International exhibition of equipment and technology. Exhibits include professional audio systems, professional lighting equipment, musical insts, state equipment and machines, professional and household audio-video equipment, mus publications and books.*

Czech Republic

Muzika. Muzikus a Incheba Praha, Incheba Praha, PO Box 555, 28 Rijna 13, CZ-111 21 Praha 1, Czech Republic *tel:* +420 2 2419 5348 *fax:* +420 2 2419 5361. Marie Pragrová, project mgr. *17-20 Sep 1998 at Prague Exhibition Ground. Fair of insts, accs, sound and light, multimedia, w/shops and concerts.*

France

CODA - Rencontres Internationales de Musique Ancienne. 106 Blvd Richard Lenoir, F-75011 Paris, France *tel:* +33 1 43 55 47 09 *fax:* +33 1 43 55 35 17 *email:* 100532.653@compuserve.com. Philippe Suzanne, gen mgr. *Nov 1998. Covers early music from medieval to classical. Instrument manufacturers, publishers, ensembles, concerts.*

MIDEM. BP 572, 11 Rue de Colonel Pierre-Avia, F-75726 Paris Cedex 15, France *tel:* +33 1 41 90 44 39 *fax:* +33 1 41 90 46 31 *email:* jane.garton@ midem-paris.ccmail.compuserve.com. Jane Garton. *18-22 Jan 1998 in Cannes. International record mus publishing and video music market.*

Musicora. Porte de Versailles, OIP-62 Rue de Miromesnil, F-75008 Paris, France *tel:* +33 1 49 53 27 00 *fax:* +33 1 49 53 27 86. Jessie Westenholz, commissaire. *Mar. Classical mus fair; editions, instruments, concerts, festivals, associations, admin.*

Nice-Acropolis. 1 Esplanade Kennedy, F-06058 Nice, France. *Jul.*

Germany

Frankfurt Book Fair. c/o Ausstellungs und Messe GmbH, des Börsenvereins des Deutschen Buchhandels, Reineckstr 3, D-60313 Frankfurt am Main, Germany *tel:* +49 69 2102 0 *fax:* +49 69 2102 227 *email:* marketing@book-fair.com; http://www.frankfurter-buchmesse. de. Wolfgang von Schumann, PR. *7-12 Oct 1998; 13-18 Oct 1999; 11-16 Oct 2000.*

Intermedia Music and Record Expo. Interart Vertretung, Bismarkstr 83, D-28203 Bremen, Germany *tel:* +49 421 705772 *fax:* +49 421 74066 *email:* jvh@megatel.de. Claudia von Holten, PR and international mkt. *15-18 Oct 1998. Eastern Europe's main mus fair representing the world's leading producers of mus insts, electronic equipment, light, sound or special effects; publishers and labels.*

Klassik Komm/Pop Komm. Musik Komm GmbH, Kaiser-Wilhelm-Ring 20, D-50672 Köln, Germany *tel:* +49 221 916550 *fax:* +49 221 91655110 *email:* musikkomm@musikkomm.de; http://www.musikkomm.de. Uli Großmaas, dir; Racf Plaschke, dir. *13-16 Aug 1998 (Popkomm), Cologne Trade Fair; Sep 1998 (Klassik Komm).*

Musikmesse/Pro Light and Sound. Messe Frankfurt GmbH, Ludwig-Erhard-Anlage 1, D-60327 Frankfurt am Main, Germany *tel:* +49 69 75 756452 *fax:* +49 69 75 756613. Wilhelm-Peter Hosenseidl, project mgr. *11-15 Mar 1998. International trade fair for musical insts, sheet music, light and sound.*

Hong Kong

International Music Market. 703 Mannon House, 74-78 Nathan Rd, Hong Kong *tel:* +852 389 9895 *fax:* +852 312 2855. Alex Wa.

Music Convention. Reed Midem Organisation, 2805 Office Tower, Convention Plaza, 1 Harbour Rd, HK-Wanchai, Hong Kong *tel:* +852 2824 0330 *fax:* +852 2824 0271. Connie So. *May. International mus trade fair for wholesalers, retailers, distributors, import and export companies, lawyers, media and artists.*

Hungary

Hungaccord Budapest International Music Fair. PO Box 143, H-1300 Budapest 3, Hungary *tel:* +361 250 0194 *fax:* +361 250 2359. József Mészáros, dir; Eva Mihok, sec. *Nov. Sheet mus, publications, books, journals, classical insts, electronic insts, records, mus CD-Roms, accessories.*

Portugal

Expo '98. SA Avenida Marechal Gomes da Costa, 37 1800 Lisboa, Portugal *tel:* +351 1 831 9898 *fax:* +351 1 837 0022 *email:* info@expo98.pt; http://www.telepac.pt/expo98.

Russia

Music-Show Tech. Zao Expocentr, firm Mezhvystavka, Krasnopresnenskaya nab 14, 123100 Moscow, Russia *tel:* +7 095 255 3757 *fax:* +7 095 205 6055. Mrs Golossova. *7-11 Sep 1998. International exhibition of mus insts, show and stage equipment.*

Slovak Republic

Expo Music. Incheba Bratislava, Viedenska Cesta 7, SK-852 51 Bratislava, Slovak Republic *tel:* +421 7 801111/802230/802208 *fax:* +421 7 847101. Eva Komínková, commercial dir; Adela Danielová, project mgr. *Oct.*

United Kingdom

In the City. 2-4 Little Peter St, Knott Mill, Manchester M15 4PS, UK *tel:* +44 161 839 3930 *fax:* +44 161 839 3940. Anthony Wilson, Yvette Livesey, dirs; Kate Butler, Nick Neads, Phil Saxe, co-ords. *Sep. Annual meeting for the UK mus industry and its international partners.*

London Early Music Exhibition. Early Music Shop, 38 Manningham La, Bradford, W Yorks BD1 3EA, UK *tel:* +44 1274 393753 *fax:* +44 1274 393516 *email:* sales@earlyms.demon.co.uk; http://e-m-s.com. *Sep. Major international early mus exhibition held at the Royal College of Music, Kensington.*

Mad About Music. Arena Management, London Arena, Limeharbour, London E14 9TH, UK *tel:* +44 171 538 8880 *fax:* +44 171 538 5572. *Jun.*

USA

Boston Early Music Festival and Exhibition. PO Box 2632, Cambridge, MA 02238, USA *tel:* +1 617 661 1812 *fax:* +1 617 267 6539 *email:* bemf@bemf.org; http://www.bemf.org. Kathleen Fay, exec dir; Stephen Stubbs, Paul O'Dette, artistic dirs. *7-13 Jun 1999. Forum for early mus perf, scholarship and inst-making.*

South by Southwest. PO Box 4999, Austin, TX 78 765, USA *tel:* +1 512 467 7979 *fax:* +1 512 451 0754. Roland Swenson, mgr dir; Brent Grulke, programme mgr. *Mar. International industry convention; features 3-day conference and fortnight mus festival.*

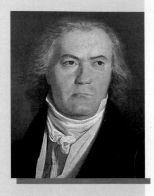

Music Publishers

The following list includes major international publishers of scores and sheet music.

Australia
Alfred Publishing (Australia) Ltd. PO Box 2355, Taren Point, NSW 2229, Australia *tel:* +61 2 9524 0033 *fax:* +61 2 9524 0023.
Allans Publishing Pty. PO Box 4072, Richmond East, Victoria 3121, Australia *tel:* +61 3 428 1600 *fax:* +61 3 428 1811. *Hire for Donemus.*
Charles Paine Pty Ltd. 8 Ferris St, North Parramatta, NSW, Australia *tel:* +61 2 9890 1388.
EMI Music Publishing Australia. PO Box C156, Cremorne Junction, NSW 2090, Australia *tel:* +61 2 9908 0788.
Holborne Australasia Pty. PO Box 282, Alexandria, NSW 2015, Australia *tel:* +61 2 519 9066 *fax:* +61 2 519 3622.
The Really Useful Company (Australia). 1st Floor, 24 Bay St, Double Bay, Sydney 2028, Australia *tel:* +61 2 9363 2499 *fax:* +61 2 9363 1589.

Austria
Bosworth & Co. Postfach 178, A-1201 Wien, Austria.
Doblinger Musikverlag. Dorotheergasse 10, A-1010 Wien, Austria *tel:* +43 1 515030 *fax:* +43 1 515 0351 *email:* music@doblinger.co.at. Helmuth Pany, gen mgr.
Josef Weinberger GmbH. Neulerchenfelderstr 3-7, A-1160 Wien, Austria *tel:* +43 1 403 59910 *fax:* +43 1 403 599113 *email:* musik@weinberger. co.at; http://www.weinberger.co.at. Hans J Granzer, mgr dir; Christian Kobee, asst mgr.
Koch Music Publishing. Gewerbegebiet/Postfach 24, A-6600 Höfen, Austria *tel:* +43 56 725500 *fax:* +43 56 725580. Franz Koch, president; Rudy Schedler, publishing mgr.
Musikwissenschaftlicher Verlag. Dorotheergasse 10, A-1010 Wien, Austria *tel:* + 43 1 515 0300 *fax:* +49 1 515 0351. Herbert Vogg, gen mgr; Mathilde Eder, confidential clerk.
Universal Edition AG. PO Box 3, A-1015 Wien, Austria *tel:* +43 1 505 8695 *fax:* +43 1 505 2720 *email:* vemusic@vemusic.co.at; http://www. vemusic.co.at/. Marion von Hortlieb, dir.
Wiener Waldhorn Verein Verlag. Postfach 134, A-1080 Wien, Austria *fax:* +43 22 393705.

Belgium
Alamire Music Publishers. PO Box 45, B-3990 Peer, Belgium *tel:* +32 11 63 21 64 *fax:* +32 11 63 49 11 *email:* musica@innet.be; http://www. innet.net/musica/alamire. Herman Baeten, mgr dir. *Facsimile editions of early musical sources; scientific publications; short studies; Musica Antiqua magazine; exclusive collection of greeting cards, posters, postcards and miniatures out of ancient musical sources.*
Hebra Music. Rue Saint-Christophe 30, B-1000 Bruxelles, Belgium. +32 2 512 7361.

Canada
Banff Music Limited. PO Box 309, Mount Albert, Ont L0G 1M0, Canada *tel:* +1 905 773 6848 *fax:* +1 905 853 2955 *email:* swain00@ibm.net. Wayne Patton, vice-president; Derek Swain, dir.
Diffusion i Média. 4580 Av de Lorimier, Montréal, QC H2H 2B5, Canada *tel:* +1 514 526 4096 *fax:* +1 514 526 4487 *email:* dim@cam.org; http://www.cam.org/~dim/.
Dominis Music. PO Box 11307, Station H, Ottawa, Ont K2H 7V1, Canada *tel:* +1 613 837 2413.
Gamelon Music Publications. PO Box 525, Station P, Toronton, Ont M5S 2T1. Michael Kleniec, mgr.
Jaymar Music Ltd. PO Box 2191, London, Ont N6A 4E3, Canada *tel:* +1 519 672 7369 *fax:* +1 519 672 0016.
Les Editions Doberman-Yppan. PO Box 2021, St-Nicholas, PQ G7A 4X5, Canada *tel:* +1 418 831 1304 *fax:* +1 418 836 3645 *email:* pgerrits@ qui.qc.cq; http://www.qui.qc/clients/doberman. Paul Gerrits, president.
Leslie Music Supply Inc. 198 Speers Rd, Oakville, Ont L6K 2E9 *tel:* +1 905 844 3109 *fax:* +1 905 844 7637.
Mayfair Music Publishing. 2600 John St, Unit 220, Markham, Ont L3R 3W3, Canada *tel:* +1 905 475 1848 *fax:* +1 905 474 9870 *email:* sales@ mayfairmusic.com. Steve Loweth, USA sales mgr; Lucie Stubbington, Canada sales mgr.
Meakin & Associates. Unit 17, 81 Auriga Dr, Nepean, Ont K2E 7TS, Canada *tel:* +1 613 226 1687.
Music Box Dancer Publications Ltd. 2600 John St, #220, Markham, Ont L3R 3W3, Canada *tel:* +1 905 475 1848 *fax:* +1 905 474 9870. Ralph Cruickshank, ed; Steve Loweth, sales mgr.

Noteworks. 60 Ottawa St, Kitchener, Ont N2G 3S7, Canada *tel:* +1 519 742 4062 *also fax.*
Patten Pending. PO Box 309, Mount Albert, Ont L0G 1M0, Canada *tel:* +1 905 841 6399 *fax:* +1 905 853 2955.
Schott Music Publishers (Canada) Ltd. 2 Bloor St West, Toronto, Ont, Canada.
Sound Ideas. 105 West Beaver Creek Rd, Suite No 4, Richmond Hill, Ont L4B 1C6, Canada *tel:* +1 905 886 5000 *fax:* +1 905 886 6800 *email:* info@sound-ideas.com; http://www.sound-ideas.com. Brian Nimens, president; Michael Bell, vice president.

Czech Republic
Divertimento Ltd. Czech Music Fund, Parizka 13, Stare Mesto, CZ-110 00 Praha 1, Czech Republic *tel:* +420 2 24 811258 *fax:* +420 2 24 810614. Vesna Padovic, Vaclav Drevikovsky, Barbara Wheeler, hire librarians.
Editio Supraphon. Chopinova 4, CZ-120 00 Praha, Czech Republic *tel:* +420 2 627 421921 *fax:* +420 2 627 4235 *email:* musicpbl@mbox. vol.cz. Dana Brozova, dir.
H Music Publishing. Mikulovice 131, CZ-533 33 Pardubice, Czech Republic *tel:* +420 40 33234. Jaroslav Horinka, mgr.
Music Cheb. Na vyhlidce 25, 350 02 Cheb, Czech Republic *tel:* +420 166 423356 *also fax.* Petr Jansky, mgr.
Muzikus. Prístavní 18, CZ-170 00 Praha 7, Czech Republic *tel:* +420 2 808780 *fax:* +420 2 876130 *email:* muzikus@mbox.vol.cz.
Nakladatelstvi Tempo. U druzstva Tempo 10, 142 00 Praha 4, Czech Republic *tel:* +420 2 472 1407 *fax:* +420 2 472 8010. Cervinkova Blanka.

Denmark
Edition Egtved A/s. PO Box 171, DK-8100 Aarhus, Denmark *tel:* +45 8620 2070 *fax:* +45 8612 0044. Ole Ugilt Jensen, mgr dir. *Organ and choral mus specialists.*
Edition Wilhelm Hansen. Bornholmsgade 1, 1, DK-1266 Copenhagen K, Denmark *tel:* +45 33 11 78 88 *fax:* +45 33 14 81 78. Tine Birger Christensen, mgr dir; Ole Hansen, promotion.
Engstrøm & Sødring AS. Borgergade 17, DK-1300 Copenhagen K, Denmark *tel:* +45 33 14 32 28 *fax:* +45 33 14 32 27. Helge Schlenkert, mgr dir.
The Society for the Publication of Danish Music. Grabrødrestraede 18, 1, DK-1156 Copenhagen K, Denmark *tel:* +45 33 13 54 45 *fax:* +45 33 93 30 44 *email:* sidmusic@inet.iui-c.dk; http://www.inet.ini-c.dk/~ sidmusic. Klaus Ib Jørgensen, chmn; Niels Prins, sec.
SteepleChase Music/Edition Kontrapunkt. PO Box 35, DK-2930 Klampenborg, Denmark *tel:* +45 39 64 42 44 *fax:* +45 39 64 50 44. Nils Winther, mgr dir. *Jazz and classical contemporary.*

Estonia
Estonian Music Foundation. Lauteri 7, EE-0001 Tallinn, Estonia *tel:* +37 22 446290. Raimo Kangro.

Finland
STM Musiikki. Hämeenpuisto 33b, FIN-33200 Tampere, Finland *tel:* +358 3 214 4416 *fax:* +358 3 222 5419. Usko Rasilainen, publishing mgr; Maija Hilden, mus sales.
Sulasol. Fredrikinkatu 51-53 B, FIN-00100 Helsinki, Finland *tel:* +358 9 4136 1100 *fax:* +358 9 4136 1122 *email:* sulasol.co@inet.fi. Matti Apajalahti, exec dir; Reijo Kekkonen, publications mgr.
Warner Music Finland Oy. PO Box 169, FIN-02101 Espoo, Finland *tel:* +358 9 435011 *fax:* +358 9 455 2162.

France
Alphonse Leduc Editions Musicales. 175 Rue Saint-Honoré, F-75040 Paris cedex 01, France *tel:* +33 1 42 96 89 11 *fax:* +33 1 42 86 02 83. Mike Warren, sales; Basile Crichton, promotion.
Breitkopf & Härtel. 20 Rue Pigalle, F-75009 Paris, France *tel:* +33 1 42 81 40 11 *fax:* +33 1 40 16 80 02.
Combre Editions. 24 Blvd Poissonnière, F-75009 Paris, France *tel:* +33 1 48 24 89 24 *fax:* +33 1 42 46 98 82. Colette Geneste, mgr; Estelle Corblin, catalogue dir.
Delrieu Edition. Palais Bellecour B, 14 Rue Trachel, F-06000 Nice, France *tel:* +33 493 82 23 69 *fax:* +33 493 82 11 00.
Editions Henry Lemoine. 24 Rue Pigalle, F-75009 Paris, France *tel:* +33 1 48 74 09 25 *fax:* +33 1 45 26 74 42. Pierre H Lemoine, president.

Editions Paul Beuscher. 27 Blvd Beaumarchais, F-75004 Paris, France *tel:* +33 1 44 54 36 00 *fax:* +33 1 44 54 36 27.

Editions Ricordi. 22 Rue Chauchat, F-75009 Paris, France *tel:* +33 1 47 70 37 28 *fax:* +33 1 42 47 17 56. Ivanka Stoianova, artistic dir.

Editions Robert Martin. 106 Grande Rue de la Coupée, F-71850 Charnay les Macon, France *tel:* +33 85 34 46 81 *fax:* +33 85 29 96 16. Paul-Louis Martin, artistic dir; Gérard Lapalus, gen dir.

Gérard Billaudot Editeur SA. 14 Rue de l'Echiquier, F-75010 Paris, France *tel:* +33 1 47 70 14 46 *fax:* +33 1 45 23 22 54. François Derveaux, chmn.

Hamelle. 175 Rue St Honore, F-75040 Paris cedex 01, France *tel:* +33 1 42 96 89 11 *fax:* +33 1 42 86 02 83.

ID Music. 29 Rue de Bitche, F-92400 Courbevoie, France *tel:* +33 1 41 88 98 98 *fax:* +33 1 47 68 74 28. Philippe C Ageon, mgr; Thierry Chevrier, mgr.

Jobert Societé des Editions. 76 Rue Quincampoix, F-75003 Paris, France *tel:* +33 1 42 72 83 43 *fax:* +33 1 42 72 27 67. Georges Denise.

Musique and Music. 19 Rue Anatole France, F-92800 Puteaux, France *tel:* +33 1 41 97 08 08 *fax:* +33 1 41 97 08 00 *email:* musetmus@calva. net. Jean-Michel Marquaille, president.

Notissimo Editeur. Informusique Ltd, 4 Rue de Brest, F-69002 Lyon, France *tel:* +33 4 72 77 07 67 *fax:* +33 4 78 42 56 53 *email:* http://www. notissimo.com.

Studio G Sarl. Chateau de Monternot, F-69220 Charentay, France *tel:* +33 4 74 66 70 53 *also fax.*

Germany

Alfred Coppenrath Musikverlag. 11 58, D-84495 Altötting, Germany *tel:* +49 8671 50652 *fax:* +49 8671 506568.

Anton Böhm & Sohn. Lange Gasse 26, D-86152 Augsburg, Germany *tel:* +49 821 502840 *fax:* +49 821 502 8433. *Sacred, secular and org mus.*

Apollo-Verlag Paul Lincke GmbH. Weihergarten 5, D-55116 Mainz, Germany *tel:* +49 6131 246300 *fax:* +49 6131 246861 *email:* schott. musik.sprang@t-online.de. Christian Sprang, company lawyer.

Bärenreiter-Verlag Karl Vötterle GmbH & Co KG. Heinrich-Schütz-Allee 35, D34131 Kassel-Wilhelmshöhe, Germany *tel:* +49 561 31050 *fax:* +49 561 3105240 *email:* http://www.baerenreiter.com. Barbara Scheuch-Vötterle; Leonhard Scheuch. *Alkor-Edition Kassel GmbH; Gustav Bosse GmbH & Co KG; Henschel Verlag für Musik GmbH; Johann-Philipp Hinnenthal Verlag; Nagels-Verlag; Süddeutscher Musikverlag GmbH & Co KG.*

Blasmusikverlag Schulz GmbH. Am Märzengraben 6, D-79112 Freiburg, Germany *tel:* +49 7664 1431/2004 *fax:* +49 7664 5123. Klaus Schulz.

Bosworth & Co. Augustinusstrasse 9b, D-50226 Frechen, Postfach 4041, D-50216 Frechen, Germany *tel:* +49 2234 61348/61397 *fax:* +49 2234 65335. Reimar Segebrecht, mgr dir.

Breitkopf & Härtel (Sales). Obere Waldstr 30, D-65232 Taunusstein, Germany *tel:* +49 612 896 6321 *fax:* +49 612 896 6350. Ulrike Lorenz, sales mgr.

Breitkopf & Härtel. Walkmühlstr 52, D-65195 Wiesbaden, Germany *tel:* +49 611 450080 *fax:* +49 611 450 0859. Lieselotte Sievers, Gottfried Möttel, gen mgrs. *Deutscher Verlag für Musik, Leipzig GmbH; Bessel.*

Carus-Verlag GmbH. Lektorat, Wannenstr 45, D-70199 Stuttgart, Germany *tel:* +49 711 960110 *fax:* +49 711 608247. Waltraud Graulich, mgr dir; Jo Kunze, sales mgr. *Sheet mus, CDs, mus books.*

Chanterelle Verlag. PO Box 103909, D-69029 Heidelberg, Germany *tel:* +49 6221 784105 *fax:* +49 6221 784106 *email:* chanterelle@t-online.de; http://www.chanterelle.com. Michael Macmeeken, owner. *Gui mus.*

Edition Schultheiss. Pasinger Str 38a, D-82182 Planegg b München, Germany *tel:* +49 89 859 9944 *fax:* +49 89 859 3323. Elisabeth Thomi-Berg.

Ewoton-International Elmar Wolf GmbH. Mittelfeldstr 4, D-66851 Queidersbach, Germany *tel:* +49 6371 92300 *fax:* +49 6371 17212 *email:* http://www.ewoton.de.

FEC Leuckart Musikverlag. Rheingoldstr 4, D-80639 München, Germany *tel:* +49 89 173928 *fax:* +49 89 176054. Marco Sander, mgr dir; Nartina Sander, asst.

Fr Kistner & CFW Siegel & Co. Adrian-Kiels-Str 2, D-51149 Köln, Germany *tel:* +49 2203 12668 *also fax.* Marianne Feder, owner.

G Henle Verlag. Forstenrieder Allee 122, D-81476 München, Germany *tel:* +49 89 759820 *fax:* +49 89 759 8240 *email:* http://www.henle.com. Martin Bente, mgr; Michael Ingendaay, sales mgr.

Gehann-Musik-Verlag. Lamperter Flur 2, D-55481 Kludenbach, Germany *tel:* +49 6763 2195 *fax:* +49 6763 2175.

Georg Löffler Publishing. Kaiser Ludwig Platz 1, D-80336 München, Germany *tel:* +49 89 5440 4534 *fax:* +49 89 5440 4535 *email:* 100605. 1067@compuserve.com. Michele Claveau, product mgr.

Gerig. Walkmühlstr 52, D-65195 Wiesbaden, Germany *tel:* +49 611 450080 *fax:* +49 611 450 0860.

Heinrichshofen's Verlag GmbH & Co KG. Liebigstrasse 16, D-26389 Wilhelmshaven, Germany *tel:* +49 4421 92670 *fax:* +49 4421 202007. Eva Noetzel, Victor Kreiner, joint presidents.

Josef Weinberger GmbH. Oeder Weg 26, D-60318 Frankfurt am Main, Germany.

Kantor Publishing. Kurfürstenallee 61, D-28329 Bremen, Germany *tel:* +49 421 499 2067 *fax:* +49 421 499 2070 *email:* 100653.2615@ compuserve.com. Karsten Arndt, mgr dir.

Karl Heinrich Möseler Verlag. Hoffmann-von-Fallersleben-Strasse 8, D-38304 Wolfenbüttel, Germany *tel:* +49 5331 95970 *fax:* +49 5331 959720. Jutta Möseler, Dietrich Möseler.

KGA Verlags Service. Postfach 10 21 80, D-3500 Kassel, Germany *tel:* +49 561 930960 *fax:* +49 561 930 9610 *email:* order@baerenreiter. com. *Distributor for Bärenreiter and other publishers.*

Koch International GmbH Music Publishing. Hermann-Schmid-Str 10, D-80336 München, Germany *tel:* +49 89 746 1350 *fax:* +49 89 725 4759. Franz Koch, president; Rudy Schedler, publishing mgr. *Foreign cats: Koch Music Publishing, Koch Records AG Music Publishing, Koch Benelux BV Music Publishing, Altantic Seven Music Library Ltd, Promo Sonor International, Shanachie Music Works, The Soundtrax Music Library.*

Kurt Maas Berklee Publications. Röntgenstr 5, D-82152 Martinsried, Germany *tel:* +49 89 856 2477 *fax:* +49 89 856 2478. Inge Maas, mgr.

Leu-Verlag Wolfgang Leupelt. Herweg 34, D-51429 Bergisch Gladbach, Germany *tel:* +49 2204 981141 *fax:* +49 2204 981143.

Lutz-Musikverlag. Schepp-Allee 17, D-64295 Darmstadt, Germany *tel:* +49 6162 84086 *also fax; email:* http://home.t-online.de/home/lutz-musikverlag. Viljem Lutz, Regina Lutz, mgrs.

Mannheimer Muisk-Verlag GmbH. Kunigundenstrasse 4, D-53179 Bonn, Germany *tel:* +49 228 347989 *fax:* +49 228 856372. Joachim von Roebel, mgr.

Melodie der Welt. Gr Friedberger Str 23-27, D-60313 Frankfurt, Germany *tel:* +49 69 29 98670 *fax:* +49 69 29 986710.

Moeck Verlag & Musikinstrumentenwerk. Inh Dr Hermann Moeck, Hans-Heinrich-Warnke Strasse 14, D-29227 Celle, Germany *tel:* +49 5141 88530 *fax:* +49 5141 885342. Hermann Moeck.

Musik-Gross-Sortiment Görz. Erletstr 14, D-85053 Ingolstadt, Germany *tel:* +49 841 61058 *fax:* +49 841 68771.

Musikverlag G Ricordi & Co. Velaskostr 6, D-85622 Feldkirchen, Germany *tel:* +49 89 903 8851 *fax:* +49 89 903 8859. Roberto Babini Cattaneo, Mimma Guastoni.

Musikverlag Zimmermann. Gaugrafenstrasse 19-23, D-60489 Frankfurt, Germany *tel:* +49 69 781022 *fax:* +49 69 789 5441 *email:* 101572. 1364@compuserve.com. Michael Henne, sales mgr; Saskia Herchenröder, hire dept.

Oertel (J). Ainmiller Str 42, D-80801 München, Germany *tel:* +49 810 54689.

Otto Wrede Regina-Verlag oHG. Schumanntrasse 35, D-65193 Wiesbaden, Germany *tel:* +49 611 523118 *fax:* +49 611 520773. Edda Wrede.

Peermusic Classical. Mühlenkamp 43, D-22303 Hamburg, Germany *tel:* +49 40 278 3790 *fax:* +49 40 2783 7940 *email:* 106332.751@ compuserve.com. Reinhard Flender, euro dir; J Glissmann; U zur Nieden, editing and promotion. *See also New York office.*

PJ Tonger Musikverlag GmbH & Co. Auf dem Brand 3, D-50996 Köln, Germany *tel:* +49 93 55640 *fax:* +49 93 556411. Peter Tonger, mgr dir.

The Really Useful Group Theater. Productions GmbH, Wilhelmstrs 62, D-65183 Wiesbaden, Germany *tel:* +49 6127 90280 *fax:* +49 6127 902 8102.

Richard Birnbach Musikverlag. Aubinger Str 9, D-82166 Lochham, Germany *tel:* +49 89 875450 *fax:* +49 89 871 4639.

Ries & Erler, Berlin Musikverlag. Charlottenbrunner Strasse 42, D-14193 Berlin, Germany *tel:* +49 30 825 1049 *fax:* +49 30 825 9721. Andreas Meurer, gen mgr.

Robert Lienau Musikverlag. Gaugrafenstr 19-23, D-60489 Frankfurt, Germany *tel:* +49 69 781022 *fax:* +49 30 789 5441 *email:* 101572. 1364@compuserve.com. Judith Picard, production mgr; Saskia Herchenröder, hire department.

Schott Musik International. Postfach 36 40, D-55026 Mainz, Germany *tel:* +49 61 31 2460 *fax:* +49 61 31 246211 *email:* http://www.schott-music.com. Peter Hanser-Strecker, Rolf Reisinger, mgr dirs; Rainer Mohrs, head of editorial dept. Also at Weihergarten 5, D-55116 Mainz.

Stockhausen-Verlag. Kettenberg 15, D-51515 Kürten, Germany *tel:* +49 2268 1813. *All scores and CDs of Karlheinz Stockhausen. Also many books about his works.*

Thomi-Berg Publisher & Sheet Music Distributor. Postfach 1736, D-82145 Planegg, Germany *tel:* +49 89 859 9944 *fax:* +49 89 859 3323. Elisabeth Thomi-Berg, mgr dir.

Tonos Musikverlags GmbH. Robert Edler Haus, Holzhofallee 15, D-64295 Darmstadt, Germany *tel:* +49 6151 39040 *fax:* +49 6151 390490 *email:* tonos@aol.com. Marian Golf, Johanna Golf, dirs.

Wolfgang Hart Musikverlag. 90 07 48, D-51117 Köln, Germany *tel:* +49 2203 988830 *fax:* +49 2203 9888350.

Hong Kong
De Wolfe Music of Hong Kong. Room 1502, 15th Floor, Fook Lee Commercial, Town Pl, 33 Lockhart Rd, Wanchai, Hong Kong *tel:* +852 527 5123.

The Really Useful Company (Asia) Ltd. Suite 9A1, Lippo Leighton Centre, 103 Leighton Rd, Causeway Bay, Hong Kong *tel:* +852 280 80860 *fax:* +852 280 80450.

Schott China Ltd. 111 Connaught Rd Central, Hong Kong.

Hungary
Editio Musica Budapest Ltd. Vörösmarty tér 1, PO Box 322, H-1370 Budapest, Hungary *tel:* +36 1 118 4228 *fax:* +36 1 138 2732. Istvan Homolya, mgr dir.

India
Routledge, Chapman & Hall. 32 Second Main Rd, CIT East, Madras 600 035, India *tel:* +91 44 434 6244 *fax:* +91 44 434 6529.

Israel
Carmel Publishers Marketing Services. PO Box 54, Gan Yavne 70800, Israel *tel:* +972 8 594552 *fax:* +972 8 596797.

Israel Music Publications Ltd. 25 Keren Hayessod St, 97188 Jerusalem, Israel *tel:* +972 2 6251370; +972 2 6241377 *fax:* +972 2 6241378. Sergey Khanukaev, dir of mus publications.

Italy
Bèrben (Edizioni Musical). Via Redipuglia 65, I-60100 Ancona, Italy *tel:* +39 71 204428 *fax:* +39 71 57414.

Boccaccini & Spada Editori. Via Francesco Duodo 10, I-00136 Roma, Italy *tel:* +39 6 3974 9858; +39 6 321 6070 *fax:* +39 6 322 1567. Pietro Spada, admin.

Casa Ricordi - BMG Ricordi. Via Berchet 2, I-20121 Milano, Italy *fax:* +39 2 88811 *email:* +39 2 8881 2212.

Fonos Edizioni Musicalli. Corso Europa 5, I-20122 Milano, Italy *tel:* +39 2 7600 2798.

Nuova Carisch SA. Via Campania 12, I-20098 San Giuliano Milanese (Milano), Italy *tel:* +39 2 982211 *fax:* +39 2 9822 1200. Adriano Solaro, president; Marco Volontè, mgr dir.

Rossini Foundation. Fondazione G Rossini, Piazza Olivieri 5, I-61100 Pesaro, Italy *tel:* +39 721 30053 *fax:* +39 721 31220.

Japan
Musicraft Co Ltd. 511 Waseda Tzurumaki-Cho, Shinjuku-Ku, Tokyo, Japan *tel:* +81 3 3202 0202.

Ongaku No Tomo Sha Corp. Kagurazaka 6-30, Shinjuku-ku, Tokyo, Japan *tel:* +81 3 3235 2111 *fax:* +81 3 3235 2110 *email:* xla06200@niftyserve. or.jp. Kazuyuki Nabeshima, head of copyright.

Schott Japan Company Ltd. Kasuga Building, 2-9-3 Iidabashi, Chiyoda-ku, Tokyo 102, Japan *tel:* +81 33 263 6530 *fax:* +81 33 263 6672.

Luxembourg
Gic-Deltaphon. Rue de Cimitiere 107, Luxembourg *tel:* +352 483289 *fax:* +352 407220. Guilliame Schu.

Letzebuerger Vollekslidderverlag ASBL. Rue Sosthene Weis 2, L-2722, Luxembourg *tel:* +352 462536 *fax:* +352 471440.

Musek Edy Noel SA. Rue Antoine Godart 21, Luxembourg *tel:* +352 488905.

Mexico
Ediciones Mexicanas de Musica AC. Avda Juarez 18, Despacho 206, 06050 D F, Mexico *tel:* +52 5 521 5855 *also fax.* Isolda Acevedo Jiménez, mgr.

Netherlands
Albersen & Co BV. 182 Groot Hertoginnelaan, NL-2517 EV Den Haag, Netherlands *tel:* +31 70 345 6000 *fax:* +31 70 361 4528. Herman Albersen, gen mgr; Michael Krens, sales dept.

Amstel Music. Middenweg 213, NL-1098 AN Amsterdam, Netherlands *tel:* +31 20 668 0232 *fax:* +31 20 692 2027. Johan de Meij, dir; Chris Abelen, chief ed.

AV Music. Soest Brote Melunweg 31, NL-3764 AZ Soest, Netherlands.

Beurskens Muziekuitgevery. 8052, NL-5993 ZG Maasbree, Netherlands *tel:* +31 77 465 1907 *fax:* +31 77 465 3883.

Donemus Publishing House. Paulus Potterstr 16, NL-1071 CZ Amsterdam, Netherlands *tel:* +31 20 676 4436 *fax:* +31 20 673 3588. L J Deuss, mgr dir.

Koch Benelux BV Music Publishing. Bredaseweg 108a, 4902 NS Oosterhout (NB), Netherlands *tel:* +31 162 470999 *fax:* +31 162 470888. Franz Koch, president; Rudy Schedler, publishing mgr.

Meta Sound BV. Postbus 22822, NL-1100 DH Amsterdam ZO, Netherlands *tel:* +31 35 235650.

XYZ International. Ambachtsweg 42, NL-1271 Am Huizen, Netherlands *tel:* +31 35 524 2104 *fax:* +31 35 524 2336 *email:* emcmusic@euronet.nl.

New Zealand
Catholic Supplies Ltd. 80 Adelaide Rd, Wellington, New Zealand *tel:* +64 4 384 3665.

Norway
Cantando Musikkforlag. Normannsgt. 24,, N-4014, Stavanger, Norway *tel:* +47 51 89 46 01 *fax:* +47 51 89 46 02.

Editio Aap. AasWangsvei 8, N-1613 Fredrikstad, Norway *tel:* +47 69 31 97 95 *also fax; email:* aap@audioattic.com; http://www.audioattic.com. Frank Nordensten, mgr; Katya Meyer, sec.

Editio Norvegica AS. Tolbugt 28, N-0157 Oslo, Norway *tel:* +47 22 42 90 90 *fax:* +47 22 42 90 91.

Fortissimo Forlag AS. PO Box 130, N-1458 Fjellstrand, Norway *tel:* +47 66 91 83 62 *fax:* +47 66 91 55 05. Trevor Ford, dir; Ann-Turi Ford, graphic dir. *Band mus and mus for wind ens.*

Frost Music A/S. PO Box 6062, Etterstad, N-0601, Oslo, Norway *tel:* +47 22 677111 *fax:* +47 22 677241 *email:* frostm@sn.no. Birger Brynjulfsen, business mgr; Fred Svendsen, mus library.

Harald Lyche & Co AS Musikkforlag. PO Box 2171 Stromso, N-3003 Drammen, Norway *tel:* +47 32 24 5000/5182 *fax:* +47 32 24 51 89.

Lunde & Co's Forlag As. Grensen 19, N-0104 Oslo, Norway *tel:* +47 22 49 91 30.

Musikk-Hussets Forlag AS. PO Box 822, Sentrum, N-0104 Oslo, Norway *tel:* +47 22 42 50 90 *fax:* +47 22 42 55 41.

Musikkverkstedet. Gutzeitsgt 4, N-1610 Frederikstad, Norway *tel:* +47 69 31 65 35 *also fax email:* forlag@online.no; http://www.forlag.no. Radnar Evensen, Christin Z Olsen, owners.

Norsk Gram AS. PO Box 4603, Valentinlyst, N-7002 Trondheim, Norway *tel:* +47 73 52 51 50 *fax:* +47 73 50 50 45.

Norsk Musikforlag A/S. Postbox 1499, Vika Postkontor, Oslo 1, Norway.

Norske Komponisters Forlag. Gjernesvn 24, N-5700 Voss, Norway *tel:* +47 56 51 33 25.

Norwegian Music Information Centre. Tollbugt 28, N-0157 Oslo, Norway *tel:* +47 22 429090 *fax:* +47 22 429091 *email:* nmic@notam. uio.no; http://www.notam.uio.no/nmi. Jostein Simble, dir; Hilde Holboek-Haussen, head of information.

Østnorsk Musikkforlag. Gullagata 15 N-3500, Hønefoss, Norway *tel:* +47 32 12 63 96 *also fax; email:* hlien@sn.no. Hans Olav Lien, mgr.

Slagerfabrikken. PO Box 2645 Solli, N-0203 Oslo, Norway *tel:* +47 22 43 60 60 *fax:* +47 22 55 16 75.

Stril Music. Edvardsensgt 19, N-5035 Bergen-Sandviken, Norway *tel:* +47 55 32 42 54.

Universitetsforlaget AS. PO Box 2959 Toyen, N-0608 Oslo, Norway *tel:* +47 22 57 53 00 *fax:* +47 22 57 53 53.

Vest-Norsk Musikforlag. PO Box 59, N-5300 Kleppesto, Norway *tel:* +47 56 14 11 02 *fax:* +47 56 14 38 00.

Warner/Chappell Music Norway AS. Nydalsvn 15 inng B, PO Box 4523, Torshov, N-0404 Oslo, Norway *tel:* +47 22 23 23 75 *fax:* +47 22 23 23 96.

Pakistan
Book Bird. Mian Chambers, 3 Temple Rd, GPO Box 518, Lahore, Pakistan *tel:* +92 42 367275/361370 *fax:* +92 42 369834.

Poland
PWM Edition Polskie Wydawnictwo Muzyczne. Al Krasinskiego 11a, PL-31111 Kraków, Poland *tel:* +48 12 227328 *also fax.* Leszek Polony, dir and chief exec; Grazyna Adamczyk, deputy dir publishing and promotion.

Portugal
Sintonia SA. Rua Profesor Mira Fernandes, Lote 1, Loja, 1900 Lisboa, Portugal.

Republic of Ireland
An Gúm. The Publications Branch, Dept of Education, 44 Sráid Uí Chonaill, Uacht, Dublin 1 *tel:* +353 1 873 4700 *fax:* +353 1 873 1140 *email:* gum@educ.irlgov.ie. Dónall ó Cuill, editor. *Trad, choral and inst mus.*

Association of Irish Choirs. Drinan St, Cork, Republic of Ireland *tel:* +353 21 312296 *fax:* +353 21 962457. Barbara Heas, admin. *Choral mus, especially Irish.*

Watermill Music. 5-6 Lombard St East, Dublin 2, Republic of Ireland *tel:* +353 16 779046.

Singapore

Alfred Publishing Co. Toa Payoh North Post Office, PO Box 841, Singapore 913135, Singapore. Larry Bong, mkt mgr.

The Really Useful Group (Singapore). 360 Orchard Rd, 10-01 International Building, Singapore 923, Singapore *tel:* +65 737 4391 *fax:* +65 737 4798.

STM Pte Ltd. Block 113, Eunos Av 3, 07-03 Gordon Industrial Building, Singapore *tel:* +65 741 8422 *fax:* +65 741 8821.

Slovak Republic

Hudobny Fond Bratislava. Medená 29, 81102 Bratislava, Slovak Republic *tel:* +421 7 533 1380 *fax:* +421 7 533 3569 *email:* his@his.sanet.sk; http://www.sarba.sk/logos/mca/mic.html. *Information sheet: Presto.*

South Africa

Peermusic (Pty) Ltd. 62 St Patrick Rd, Upper Houghton, Johannesburg, South Africa *tel:* +28 11 648 5404.

Spain

Catalana d'Edicions Musicals. CEM/SEEMSA, Layetana 23, Planta 1r-D, E-08003 Barcelona, Spain *tel:* +34 3 319 7958 *fax:* +34 3 310 1844. Josep Cruells Solvés, dir.

Clivis Publicacions. Dep de Promoció, Mila i Fontanals 14-26 3r 9a, E-08012 Barcelona, Spain *tel:* +34 3 458 8989 *also fax.* Elisenda Climent, gen mgr.

Editorial de Musica Espagnola Contempora. Alcala 70, E-28009 Madrid, Spain *tel:* +34 1 577 0751/0752 *fax:* +34 1 575 7645. Carlos Peret Caucio, president; Mauel Lopez-Quinoza, gen mgr.

Espanola de Ediciones Musicales Schott. SL Alcalá 70, E-28009 Madrid, Spain.

Monge y Boceta Asociados Musicales SL. Calle Goya, 103-2 Dcha, E-28009 Madrid, Spain *tel:* +34 431 6505/6567 *fax:* +34 577 9166.

Nueva Carsich Espana SL. Magallanes 25, E-28015 Madrid, Spain *tel:* +34 1 446 8161 *fax:* +34 1 593 3433.

Real Musical Publicaciones y Ediciones. Apartado de Correos 27, E-28670 Villaviciosa de Odón, Madrid, Spain *tel:* +34 16 16 4817 *fax:* +34 16 16 0208. J R Jiménez, mgr dir; J J Subirón, sales mgr.

Sintonia SA. Abdon Terradas 3-5, E-28015 Madrid, Spain *tel:* +341 549 2350 *fax:* +341 544 6554 *email:* sintonia@sintoniasa.es; http://www.sintoniasa.es. Bartolomé Espadalé, president, mgr dir; Clifton Williams, dir.

Tritó S L. Carrer dels Arcs 8 1/2, E-08002 Barcelona, Spain *tel:* +34 93 302 2722/+34 93 301 9555 *fax:* +34 93 302 2670.

Sweden

AB Nordiska Musikförlaget. PO Box 533, Vendevägen 85B, S-182 15 Danderyd, Sweden.

Edition Reimers. PO Box 15030, S-161 15 Bromma, Sweden *tel:* +46 8 740 0280 *fax:* +46 8 804228.

Edition Suecia. PO Box 27327, S-102 54 Stockholm, Sweden *tel:* +46 8 783 8800 *fax:* +46 8 783 9510 *email:* swedmic@stim.se. Karin Heurling, editor.

Gehrmans Musikförlag. Box 6005, S-102 31 Stockholm, Sweden *tel:* +46 8 610 0600 *fax:* +46 8 610 0625. Kettil Skarby, mgr; Staffan Carlberg, mgr, sales dept.

Scandinavian Songs AB. Box 109, S-182 12 Danderyd, Sweden *tel:* +46 8 755 9970 *fax:* +46 8 755 8870. Björn Hakanson, Kaj Lundén-Welden, dirs; Niclas Johansson, label mgr; Per Liliefeldt, mgr library division.

Switzerland

Amadeus. Postfach 473, CH-8405 Winterthur, Switzerland *tel:* +41 52 233 2866 *fax:* +41 52 233 5401.

Bärenreiter Verlag Basel AG. Neuweiler Strasse 15, CH-4015 Basel, Switzerland *tel:* +41 61 302 5899 *fax:* +41 61 302 5804. Peter G Ijler, dir; Sven Steiner, mgr.

Hug and Co Musikverlage. Limmatquai 28-30, CH-8022 Zürich, Switzerland *tel:* +41 1 251 6850 *fax:* +41 1 261 6166.

Jecklin & Co AG. Römistr 30 + 42, CH-8024 Zürich, Switzerland *tel:* +41 1 261 7733 *fax:* +41 1 251 4102 *email:* jecklin@bluewin.ch. Hannes Hinnen, gen mgr.

Koch Records AG Music Publishing. Postfach 535, Poststr 10, CH-9202 Gossau, Switzerland *tel:* +41 71 806868 *fax:* +41 71 806888. Frank Koch, president; Rudy Schedler, publishing mgr.

Kunzelmann. Grütstr 28, CH-8134, Adliswil, Switzerland *tel:* +41 1 710 3681 *fax:* +41 1 710 3817.

Really Useful Company AG. Postfach 800, CH-4021, Basel, Switzerland *tel:* +41 61 699 8810 *fax:* +41 61 699 8811.

Ruh Emil Musikverlag. Zurichstr 33, CH-8134 Adliswil, Switzerland *tel:* +41 1 710 6313 *fax:* +41 1 710 6207.

Swiss Music Edition. Postfach 7851, CH-6000 Luzern 7, Switzerland *tel:* +41 41 210 6070 *also fax; email:* sme@centralnet.ch; http://www.musicedition.ch. Ulrich Gassen, president; Peter Bitterli, sec.

Tefima. 56 Chemin des Gotettes, CH-1222 Vesenaz, Genève, Switzerland *tel:* +41 22 44 99 00.

Taiwan

De Fwo Trading Company Ltd. Nei Hu PO Box 9-59, 11411 Taipei, Taiwan *tel:* +886 2 735 3014 *fax:* +886 2 377 7735. Din-Lie Yung, chmn; Tsun-Li Chang, gen mgr. *De Wolfe Music, Rouge Music, Hudson Music and De Wolfe/Naxos Classical Music.*

Turkey

Muzikotek Ltd. 4 Gazeteciler Sitesi A 17-4, Levent 80670, Istanbul, Turkey *tel:* +90 212 282 8194 *fax:* +90 212 282 8195. D Baydur, dir; F Bezmen, T Kizilirmak, E Yenier, assts.

USA

Abingdon Press. 201 Eighth Av, Nashville, TN 37203, USA *tel:* +1 615 749 6158 *fax:* +1 615 749 6239 *email:* 72233.172@compuserve.com. Gary Alan Smith, mus resources ed.

Accura Music. PO Box 4260, Athens, OH 45701, USA *tel:* +1 614 594 3547 *fax:* +1 614 592 1609. Reginald H Fink, president.

Alfred Publishing Co Inc. PO Box 10003, Van Nuys, CA 91410-0003, USA *tel:* +1 818 891 5999 *fax:* +1 818 891 2182 *email:* 70740.475@ compuserve.com; http://www.alfredpub.com. Morton Manus, president.

Alry Publications Etc Inc. PO Box 36542, Charlotte, NC 28236, USA *tel:* +1 704 334 3413 *fax:* +1 704 334 1143 *email:* amyblu@aol.com. Amy Rice Blumenthal, president; Susan Price, Shannon Pope, assts.

American Composers Edition Inc. 170 West 74 St, New York, NY 10023, USA *tel:* +1 212 362 8900 *fax:* +1 212 874 8605. Richard Brooks, president; Catherine M Kleszczewski, operations mgr.

American International Guitar Pubs. 275 Fair St, Suite 16, Kingston, NY 12401, USA *tel:* +1 914 340 1444 *fax:* +1 914 340 1540. Jared Walker, owner.

AR Editions Inc. 801 Deming Way, Madison, WI 53717, USA *tel:* +1 608 836 9000 *fax:* +1 608 831 8200. Patrick Wall, president.

Ashgate Publishing Co. Old Post Rd, Brookfield, Vermont 05036-9704, USA *tel:* +1 802 276 3837 *fax:* +1 802 276 3651 *email:* info@ ashgate.com; http://www.ashgate.com. James Gerard, president; Barbara Church, international mkt mgr.

Augsburg Fortress Publishers. PO Box 1209, Minneapolis, MN 55440, USA *tel:* +1 612 330 3300 *fax:* +1 612 330 3455. Rev Frank Stoldt, mus and worship dir; Mark Junkert, dir of production management.

Cambridge University Press. 40 West 20th St, New York, NY 10011-4211, USA.

Carl Fischer Inc. 62 Cooper Sq, New York, NY 10003, USA *tel:* +1 212 777 0900 *fax:* +1 212 477 4129 *email:* http://www.carlfischer.com. Charles Abry, president; Lauren Keiser, exec vice-president.

Cherry Lane Music Co. 10 Midland Av, Port Chester, NY 10573, USA *tel:* +1 914 935 5200 *fax:* +1 914 937 9139. Ted Piechocinoki, snr vice president; Dan Rosenbaum, vice president.

Choristers Guild. 2834 West Kingsley Rd, Garland, TX 75041, USA *tel:* +1 972 271 1521 *fax:* +1 972 840 3113 *email:* coristers@aol.com. Patricia M Evans, exec dir; Kathy Lowrie, mus editor.

Criterion Music Corp. 6124 Selma Av, Hollywood, CA 90028, USA *tel:* +1 213 469 2296 *fax:* +1 213 962 5751. Michael H Goldsen, president.

Dantalian Inc. 11 Pembroke St, Newton, MA 02158, USA *tel:* +1 617 244 7230 *also fax.* Lora Harvey, chief admin.

De Wolfe Music Library Inc. 25 West 45th St, New York, NY 10036, USA *tel:* +1 212 382 0220.

Dover Publications Inc. 31 East 2nd St, Mineola, NY 11501, USA *tel:* +1 516 294 7000 *fax:* +1 516 742 6953. Ronald Herder, mus editor. *Reprints of classical mus.*

ECS Publishing. 138 Ipswich St, Boston, MA 02215-3534, USA *tel:* +1 617 236 1935 *fax:* +1 617 236 0261. Robert Schuneman, president.

Edwin F Kalmus & Co Inc. 6403 West Rogers Circle, Boca Raton, FL 33487, USA *tel:* +1 407 241 6340 *fax:* +1 407 241 6347. Lawrence Galison, chmn; Leon Galison, vice-president.

Elkin Music International. 16 NE 4th St, Fort Lauderdale, FL 33301, USA *tel:* +1 954 522 3611 *fax:* +1 954 522 3609 *email:* timsloan@worldnet.att.net. Timothy B Sloan, president.

European American Music Distributors Corp. PO Box 850, Valley Forge, PA 19482, USA *tel:* +1 610 648 0506 *fax:* +1 610 889 0242 *email:* eamdc@eamdc.com; http://www.eamdc.com. Ronald Freed, president.

G Schirmer Inc. 257 Park Av South, 20th Floor, New York, NY 10010, USA *tel:* +1 212 254 2100 *fax:* +1 212 254 2013 *email:* schirmer@mscgs.com. Barrie Edwards, president; Susan Feder, vice-president.

Garland Publishing Inc. 717 Fifth Av, New York, NY 10022, USA *tel:* +1 212 751 7447 *fax:* +1 212 308 9399. Leo Balk, ed; Elizabeth Borden, president.

GIA Publications. 7404 South Mason Av, Chicago, IL 60638, USA *tel:* +1 708 496 3800 *fax:* +1 708 496 3828 *email:* custserv@giamusic.com; http://www.giamusic.com. Edward Harris, chief admin.

Hal Leonard Corporation. 7777 West Bluemound Rd, PO Box 13819, Milwaukee, WI 53213, USA *tel:* +1 414 774 3630 *fax:* +1 414 774 3259 *email:* http://www.halleonard.com. Keith Mardak, president; Dan Bayer, snr vice president.

Helicon Music Corporation. c/o European American Music Corporation, Valley Forge, PA 19482, USA *tel:* +1 610 648 0506 *fax:* +1 610 889 0242 *email:* eamdc@eamdc.com; http://www.eamdc.com.

Herman and Apter. 5748 West Brooks Rd, Shepherd, MI 48883-9202, USA *tel:* +1 517 828 6987 *email:* herman.apter@sensible-net.com. Mark Herman, chief admin; Ronnie Apter. *14 dual-language piano-vocal scores.*

Hildegard Publishing Co. Box 332, Bryn Mawr, PA 19010, USA *tel:* +1 610 649 8649 *fax:* +1 610 649 8677 *email:* sglickman@hildegard.com; http://www.hildegard.com. Sylvia Glickman, president; Martha Furman Schleifer, snr ed. *Mus by women composers.*

Hinshaw Music Inc. PO Box 470, Chapel Hill, NC 27514-0470, USA *tel:* +1 919 933 1691 *fax:* +1 919 967 3399. Roberta M Van Ness, president.

Hope Publishing Co. 380 South Main Pl, Carol Stream, IL 60188, USA *tel:* +1 630 665 3200 *fax:* +1 630 665 2552 *email:* jlshope@aol.com. George H Shorney, chmn; William G Shorney, president.

Houston Publishing Inc. 222 South Lebanon St, Lebanon, IN 46052, USA *tel:* +1 317 482 4440 *also fax.* Jim Houston, president; Michelle Skow, admin asst.

Jazzmuze Inc. 80 Rumson Pl, Little Silver, NJ 07739, USA *tel:* +1 732 747 5227 *fax:* +1 732 747 7822. Joe Utterback, president; William E Todt, vice-president, sec.

Jerona Music Corp. PO Box 671, Englewood, NJ 07631-3026, USA *tel:* +1 201 568 8448 *fax:* +1 201 569 7023. Johanna I Sturm, chief admin.

Joseph Patelson MusicHouse Ltd. 160 West 56 St, New York, NY 10019, USA *tel:* +1 212 757 5587 *fax:* +1 212 246 5633. Dan Patelson.

Kendor Music Inc. PO Box 278, Delevan, NY 14042, USA *tel:* +1 716 492 1254 *fax:* +1 716 492 5124 *email:* http://www.kendormusic.com. Craig Cornwall, president; Jeff Jarvis, chief exec offr.

Lawson-Gould Music Publishers Inc. 250 West 57 St, Suite 1005, New York, NY 10107, USA *tel:* +1 212 247 3920 *fax:* +1 212 247 3991. Walter Gould, president.

Liben Music Publishers. 1191 Eversole Rd, Cincinnati, OH 45230, USA *tel:* +1 513 232 6920 *fax:* +1 513 232 1866 *email:* info@liben.com; http://www.liben.com. Madeline Bennett, chief admin.

Lorenz Corp. Box 802, 501 East 3rd St, Dayton, OH 45401-0802, USA *tel:* +1 937 228 6118 *fax:* +1 937 223 2042 *email:* order@lorenz.com. Geoffrey R Lorenz, president; Larry F Pugh, mus publishing president.

Loux Music Publishing Co. 2 Hawley La, Hannacroix, NY 12087-0034, USA *tel:* +1 518 756 2273 *also fax.* Joseph A Loux, Jr, chief admin.

Ludwig Music Publishing Co Inc. 557 East 140 St, Cleveland, OH 44110, USA *tel:* +1 216 851 1150 *fax:* +1 216 851 1958. Elizabeth Ludwig Fennell, president; Paul J Wallace, vice-president.

McGinnis & Marx Music Publishers. 236 West 26 St, No 1101, New York, NY 10001-6736, USA *tel:* +1 212 675 1630 *also fax.* Paul Sadowski.

Mark Foster Music Co. PO Box 4012, 28 East Springfield, Champaign, IL 61824-4012, USA *tel:* +1 217 398 2760 *fax:* +1 217 398 2791 *email:* markfostermus@champ.il.aads.net. Jane Menkhaus, president.

Mel Bay Publications Inc. #4 Industrial Dr, Pacific, MO 63069, USA *tel:* +1 314 257 3970 *fax:* +1 314 257 5062 *email:* email@melbay.com; http://www.melbay.com. William Bay, president; L Dean Bye, gen mgr; Doug Witherspoon, purchasing and facilities mgr.

MJQ Music Inc. 1697 Broadway, New York, NY 10019, USA *tel:* +1 212 582 6667 *fax:* +1 212 582 0627. Paul Schwartz, gen mgr.

MMB Music Inc. Contemporary Arts Building, 3526 Washington Av, St Louis, MO 63103-1019, USA *tel:* +1 314 531 9635 *fax:* +1 314 531 8384 *email:* mmbmusic@mmbmusic; http://www.mmbmusic.com. Mareia Lee Goldberg, dir, perf dept; Norman A Goldberg, president.

Music Associates of America. 224 King St, Englewood, NJ 07631, USA. George Sturm.

Neil A Kjos Music Co. 4380 Jutland Dr, San Diego, CA 92117, USA *tel:* +1 619 270 9800 *fax:* +1 619 270 3507. Neil A Kjos, president.

Oxford University Press Music Department. 198 Madison Av, New York, NY 10016-4314, USA *tel:* +1 212 726 6044 *fax:* +1 212 726 6444 *email:* mbp@oup-usa.org. Maribeth Anderson Payne, dir and exec ed; Christopher Johnson, snr editor and mgr.

Paraclete Press. PO Box 1568, Orleans, MA 02653, USA *tel:* +1 508 255 4685 *fax:* +1 508 255 5705 *email:* http://www.paraclete.press.com. Loretta Jack, sales mgr; Paul Tingley, mus ed asst. *Sacred mus.*

Paumanok Press. 974 Hardscrabble Rd, Chappaqua, NY 10514, USA *tel:* +1 914 238 9367. Theresa Vorgia, chief admin. *Exclusive publisher of the music of Michael Jeffrey Shapiro.*

Peermusic Classical. 810 Seventh Av, New York, NY 10019, USA *tel:* +1 212 265 3910 *fax:* +1 212 489 2465 *email:* classicalny@peermusic.com; http://www.peermusic.com. Todd Vunderink, vice-pres, classical; Geoffrey Hills, snr editor; Tobin W Fowler, promotions and publicity. *See also Hamburg office.*

The Really Useful Film Co Inc. 345 N Maple Dr, Suite 120, Beverley Hills, CA 09210, USA.

The Really Useful Theatre Group Inc. 1 Rockfeller Plaza, Suite 1528, New York, NY 10020, USA *tel:* +1 212 247 2123 *fax:* +1 212 247 2118.

Routledge Inc. 29 West 35th St, New York, NY 10001, USA *tel:* +1 212 244 3336 *fax:* +1 212 563 2269.

Schott Music Corporation. c/o European American Music Distributors Corporation, PO Box 850, Valley Forge, PA 19482-0850, USA *tel:* +1 610 648 0506 *fax:* +1 610 889 0242 *email:* eamdc@eamdc.com; http://www.eamdc.com.

Seesaw Music Corp. 2067 Broadway, New York, NY 10023, USA *tel:* +1 212 874 1200. Raoul R Ronson, president.

Smith Publications/Sonic Art Editions. 2617 Gwynndale Av, Baltimore, MD 21207, USA *tel:* +1 410 298 6509 *fax:* +1 410 944 5113. Sylvia Smith, ed.

Sound Adventures. PO Box 531, Wellsville, NY 14895, USA *tel:* +1 716 593 1636.

Southern Music Co. PO Box 329, 1100 Broadway, San Antonio, TX 78292, USA *tel:* +1 210 226 8167 *fax:* +1 210 223 4537 *email:* smcinfo@southernmusic.com; http://www.southernmusic.com. Arthur Gurwitz, president.

Talman Company. 131 Spring St, New York, NY 10012, USA *tel:* +1 212 431 7175 *fax:* +1 212 431 7215.

Taylor & Francis Inc. 1900 Frost Rd, Suite 101, Bristol, PA 19007, USA *tel:* +1 215 785 5800 *fax:* +1 215 785 5515.

Themes and Variations. 39 Danbury Av, Westport, CT 06880-6822, USA *tel:* +1 203 227 5709 *fax:* +1 203 227 5715 *email:* jwwaxman@aol.com; http://tnv.net. John W Waxman, chief admin.

Theodore Presser Co. Presser Pl, Bryn Mawr, PA 19010, USA *tel:* +1 215 525 3636 *fax:* +1 215 527 7841.

Transcontinental Music Publications/New Jewish Music Press. 838 Fifth Av, New York, NY 10021, USA *tel:* +1 212 650 4101 *fax:* +1 212 650 4109 *email:* tmp@mail.uahc.org; http://www.shamash.org/reform/uahc/transmp/. Judith B Tischler, dir and snr ed; Charles C Sachs, sales admin.

Viola World Publications. 2 Inlander Rd, Saratoga Springs, NY 12866, USA *tel:* +1 518 583 7177 *also fax; email:* violaworld@aol.com. Alan Arnold, dir.

Vivace Press. NW 310 Wawawai Rd, Pullman, WA 99163-2959, USA *tel:* +1 509 334 4660 *fax:* +1 509 334 3551 *email:* yordy@vivacepress.com. Jonathan Yordy.

Wayne Leupold Editions Inc. 8510 Triad Dr, Colfax, NC 27235, USA *tel:* +1 910 996 8445 *also fax.*

William Grant Still Music. 4 South San Francisco St, Suite 422, Flagstaff, AZ 86001-5737, USA *tel:* +1 520 526 9355 *fax:* +1 520 526 0321. Judith Anne Still, proprietor.

Willis Music Co. 7380 Industrial Rd, Florence, KY 41042, USA *tel:* +1 606 283 2050 *fax:* +1 606 283 1784 *email:* orderdpt@willis-music.com.

Wiscasset Music Publishing Co. PO Box 380810, Cambridge, MA 02238-0810, USA *tel:* +1 617 492 5720 *fax:* +1 617 492 4031. Betsy Warren-Davis, chief admin.

World Music Press. PO Box 2565, Danbury, CT 06813-2565, USA *tel:* +1 203 748 1131 *fax:* +1 203 748 3432.

Ybarra Music. PO Box 665, Lemon Grove, CA 91946, USA *tel:* +1 619 462 6538 *fax:* +1 619 460 4130. Dick Braun, proprietor.

Competitions

The competitions listed here are open to international entry and are usually annual. The **Fédération des Concours Internationaux de Musique** lists international competitions well in advance. Their booklet is available from 104 Rue de Carouge, CH-1205 Genève, Switzerland *tel:* +41 22 321 3620. A book detailing over 800 piano competitions worldwide is available from Drs Gustav A Alink, P O Box 85657, NL-2508 CJ Den Haag, Netherlands *tel:* +31 70 363 4760 *fax:* +31 70 365 2513.

Competitions for Performers and Conductors

Australia

The Australian Singing Competition. c/o Gridiger & Co, Solicitors, 67 Castlereagh St, Sydney N S W 2000, Australia *tel:* +61 2 9231 4888 *fax:* +61 2 9221 8201. Vivian Zeltzer, co-ord. *Sep. For opera singers and classical musicians. Must be a resident of Australia or New Zealand, aged under 26 on 23 Jun. Cash prizes of $20,000 (Aus) and $5000 (Aus).*

Melbourne International Chamber Music Competition Fellowship Program. The Australian Festival of Chamber Music, PO Box 1548, Aitkenvale Queensland 4814, Australia *tel:* +61 3 9826 3838; +61 7781 5131 *fax:* +61 3 9826 8920; +61 7781 4411. Annika Shelley, gen mgr. *Jul in Townsville. Piano trios and/or string quartets. Audition tape. Selected ensembles receive free tuition, accommodation and access to all Chamber Music Festival activities. They will then go on to participate in the National Competition in Melbourne in Oct. First prize winners in Melbourne receive the Tony Berg Award.*

Sydney International Piano Competition of Australia. PO Box 420, Double Bay, Sydney NSW 2028, Australia *tel:* +61 2 9326 2405 *fax:* +61 2 9326 2604. Claire Dan, president; Virginia Maxwell, sec. *Quadrennial. Presented by the Cladan Cultural Exchange Institute of Australia in co-operation with the Sydney Conservatorium of Music. Ages 18-32.*

Austria

Beethoven International Piano Competition. Lothringerstr 18, A-1030 Wien, Austria *tel:* +43 1 58 806190 *fax:* +43 1 58 806107. Elga Ponzer, gen sec. *Quadrennial. Age 17-32 yrs. First prize ATS 80,000, a piano and concerts.*

Das Schubertlied, International Singing Competition. Ideenagentur Austria, Opernring 1/R/3, A-1010 Wien, Austria *tel:* +43 1 587 0150 *fax:* +43 1 587 0154. Peter Weiser; Aviva Ronnefeld. *Competition inaugarated in 1997 to celebrate the 200th anniversary of Schubert. Dedicated exclusively to Schubert Lieder. 3 rounds of competition. Cash prizes ATS 50,000-100,000 plus 1 Lieder recital in the Musikverein, the Konzerthaus and Vienna's summer festival.*

Franz Schubert and the Music of the 20th Century. Hochschule für Musik und darstellende Kunst in Graz, Leonhardstrasse 15, A-8010 Graz, Austria *tel:* +43 316 389 1900/1210 *fax:* +43 316 389 1901/1710 *email:* franz.schubert@mhsg.ac.at. Petra Ernst-Kühr, head of international programmes. *Triennial. Next Feb-Mar 2000. Categories: duo for vn and pno; duo for va and pno; duo for voice and pno (Lied); str quartet. Female singers born after Jan 1968; male singers and insts born after Jan 1966; combined age of str quartet must not exceed 120 yrs by end of 2000 and no member should be over 34.*

International Belvedere Hans Gabor Competition for Opera Singers. Fleischmarkt 24, A-1010 Wien, Austria *tel:* +43 1 512 0100 *fax:* +43 1 512 010020. Isabella Gabor, mgr. *Jul, applications by Jun. Young singers of any nationality aged under 35 (male) or under 33 (female). Prize of ATS 50,000.*

International Bruckner Organ Competition. Linzer Veranstaltungs-gesellschaft, Brucknerhaus, Untere Donaulände 7, A-4010 Linz, Austria *tel:* +43 732 7612 *fax:* +43 783745. T Schlee, mus dir. *Quadrennial. Any nationality aged under 35. First prize ATS 50,000.*

International Competition for Choirs Spittal. c/o Kulturamt Burgplatz 1, A-9800 Spittal an der Drau, Austria *tel:* +43 47 623420 *fax:* +43 47 623237. *Jul, entries by Jan. Cash awards for folksong and choral works.*

International Mozart Competition. Mirabellplatz 1, A-5020 Salzburg, Austria *tel:* +43 662 88908 203 *fax:* +43 662 88908 55. Klaus Ager; Ulrike Godler, gen sec. *Quadrennial. Next 8-22 Jan 1999, applications by 30 Aug 1998. Singers, pianists, violinists, composers. Age limits: female singers born after 22 Jan 1969; male singers and instrumentalists born after 22 Jan 1967. First prize ATS 120,000 in each category.*

Belgium

International Guitar Competition. Place du Chef Lieu 9, c/o Le Printemps de la Guitare, B-6040 Charleroi-Jumet, Belgium *tel:* +32 71 350448 *fax:* +32 71 355320. André Tobie, president. *Biennial. Next 21 Sep- 3 Oct 1998. Applications by 30 Jun. Max age 32. First prize 200,000 BF and medal.*

International Singing Competition. c/o Opera Royal de Wallonie, Rue des Dominicains 1, B-4000 Liège, Belgium *tel:* +32 41 235910; +32 41 221 4720 *fax:* +32 41 210201. Raymond Rossius, dir; Cécile Duvivier, sec. *Biennial. Age 18-30 (women), 18-35 (men). First prize 200,000 BF.*

Musica Antiqua International Competitions. Festival van Vlaanderen-Brugge, Collaert Mansionstraat 30, B-8000 Bruges, Belgium *tel:* +32 50 332283 *fax:* +32 50 345204, R DeWitte MBE. *Jul-Aug, entries by Apr. Musica Antiqua competition for soloists and ens. Age limit 32 (ens), 35 (singers).*

'New Music For New Pianists' Competition. c/o Musiques et Recherches, Place de Ransbeck 3, B-1380 Ohain, Belgium *tel:* +32 2 354 4368 *fax:* +32 2 351 0094. Annette Vande Gorne, artistic dir. *Biennial. Contemporary Music for pno (post 1971), professional and amateur. No age limit.*

Queen Elisabeth International Music Competition of Belgium. 20 Rue aux Laines, B-1000 Bruxelles, Belgium *tel:* +32 2 513 0099 *fax:* +32 2 514 3297. Cécile Ferrière, sec gen. *Next Apr-May 1999, entries by 15 Jan. 1999 pno and composition; 2000 vocal; 2001 violin. Cash awards, recordings, concerts. Entry fee 2,000 BF. First prize 500,000 BF plus engagements.*

Canada

Banff International String Quartet Competition. Banff Centre for the Arts, PO Box 1020, Station 28, Banff, Alberta T0L 0C0, Canada *tel:* +1 403 762 6180 *fax:* +1 403 762 6345 *email:* arts_info@banffcentre.ab.ca; http://www.banffcentre.ab.ca/music/bisqc.html. *16-22 Aug 1998, entries by 10 Apr. String quartets of any nationality. All members under 35 yrs. Prizes: $45,000 (Can), recital tour, residency/CD and custom-made bows. Airfares paid for all competitors. First prize, $20,000 (Can) plus major concerts.*

Calgary International Organ Festival and Competition. 2nd Floor 116 8th Av SE, Calgary, Alberta T2G 0K6, Canada *tel:* +1 403 543 5115 *fax:* +1 403 543 5129 *email:* http://www.ciof.com. Timothy H Rendell, president; Cathy Nickel, mgr, communications. *Quadrennial. Next 25 Sep-3 Oct 1998. Competitive festival. Open to organists of any nationality born on or after 4 Oct 1966. Closing dates: Asia-Pacific selection round, 9 Jan; North America selection round, 12 Feb; Europe selection round, 12 Feb. Includes performances by ten selected finalists and w/shops and m/classes given by members of the jury. First prize Can $25,000 Recital Gold Medal, Can $25,000 Concerto Gold Medal.*

Eckhardt-Gramatté National Music Competition for the Performance of Canadian Music. Queen Elizabeth II Mus Building, Brandon University, Brandon, Man R7A 6A9, Canada *tel:* +1 204 728 8212 *fax:* +1 204 729 9085 *email:* eckhardt@brandonu.ca. Lorne Watson, artistic dir; Laurie Graham, admin offr. *1-3 May 1998, applications by 7 Oct 1997. Pno (1998), voice (1999), str (2000). To encourage young performers to perform contemporary and Canadian works. Open to Canadian citizens or residents in Canada since Sep 1996, born after 1 Jan 1968 and before 1 Jan 1980. First prize, $5,000 and Canadian recital tour.*

Esther Honens Calgary International Piano Competition. Third Floor, 116 Eighth Av SE, Calgary, AB T2G 0K6, Canada *tel:* +1 403 299 0130 *fax:* +1 403 299 0137 *email:* ehipc@cadvision.com. Andrew Raeburn, president; Ruth Montgomery, mgr, admin. *Quadrennial, next 2000. Cash prizes from a fund of $57,500.*

Glenn Gould Prize. Canada Council, 350 ALbert St, PO Box 1047, Ottawa, ON K1P 5V8, Canada *tel:* +1 613 566 4414 ext 5041 *fax:* +1 613 566 4390 *email:* carol.bream@canadacouncil.ca; http://www.canadacouncil. ca. Carol Bream, dir, endowments and prizes. *Triennial. Next 1999. Individuals must be nominated by three specialists in their field or in a related field. Applications by 30 Nov 1998. First prize, Can $50,000.*

Czech Republic

Concertino Praga. International Radio Competition for Young Musicians, Cêsky Rozhlas, Vinohradská 12, CZ-120 99 Praha 2, Czech Republic *tel:* +420 2409 4288 *fax:* +420 2421 8089. Josef Havel, programme dir (Czech Radio); Jana Hlinková, sec. *Nov, applications by Apr. Annual in 3 yr cycles. 1998 wind; 1999 chmbr ens. Age limit 18 yrs. First prize, concert engagements in Prague, and Southern Bohemia.*

Emmy Destinn International Singing Competition. Rudolfov 393, CZ-373 71 Ceske Budejovice, Czech Republic *tel:* +420 38 39 254 *also fax.* Antonín Kazil. *24-27 Aug 1998, applications by 30 Jun. Operatic repertoire, max age 35. First prize comprises concert opportunities and financial award.*

International Competition of Blind and Partially Sighted Musicians. SONS - Czech Blind United, Karlinské nám 12, CZ-186 03 Praha 8, Czech Republic *tel:* +420 2 2481 7393 *fax:* +420 2 2481 8398 *email:* sons_zahr@braillnet.cz. Václav Polásek, chief offr. *Triennial. Next Mar 2000, entries by 30 Oct 1999. Age range 16-35. First prize c Kc 10,000.*

International Singing Contest of Antonin Dvořák. KC Amethyst, I P Pavlova 14, CZ-360 01 Karlovy Vary, Czech Republic *tel:* +420 17 287078/28707/28708 *fax:* +420 17 23753. Marie Drlíková, contest sec. *6-13 Nov 1998, applications by 30 Jun. Category A: women under age 23 and men under age 24; category B: women under 30 and men under 32. Application fees: Category A, DM 150; Category B, DM 200 (or equivalent in US dollars). First prizes Kc 10,000 (category A) and Kc 20,000 (category B).*

Mezinárodní Sborová Soutez Bedricha Smetany. Informacní Centrum Litomysl, Smetanovo nám 72, CZ-570 01 Litomysl, Czech Republic *tel:* +420 464 4150 *fax:* +420 464 612161. Vlastislav Novák, artistic dir and cond. *May-Jun.*

Musical Competition of Beethoven's Hradec. Správa Zámku, CZ-747 41 Hradec nad Moravicí, Czech Republic *tel:* +420 653 911185/6. *Annual. Jun, entries by Feb. Two categories: aged 18 or under and aged 26 or under. 1998, vn. First prize (category I) Kc 7,000; first prize (category II) Kc 15,000.*

Prague Spring International Music Competition. Hellichova 18, CZ-118 00 Praha 1, Czech Republic *tel:* +420 2 533474 *fax:* +420 2 536040 *email:* festival@login.cz. Jarmila Nedvedová, competition sec. *Next 3-14 May 1998 for pno, str quartet; 1999 org, hpd; 2000 conducting, vc. Open to artists aged 30 and under. Application fees: $100 (pno); $200 (str quartet). First prize, Kc 120,000 (pno), Kc 200,000 (str quartet).*

Zlata Praha. Ceska Televize, Kavci Hory, CZ-140 70 Praha 1, Czech Republic *tel:* +420 6113 1111/4158/4157 *fax:* +420 6121 2891 *email:* ruzena.jeskova@czech-tv.cz. Ruzena Jeskova, head of international relations. *Early May 1998. Applications by end Jan. Entry fee DM 300. First prize DM 10,000.*

Denmark

Carl Nielsen International Music Competitions. Odense Koncerthus, Claus Bergs Gade 9, DK-5000 Odense C, Denmark *tel:* +45 66 120057 *fax:* +45 65 910047. Marianne Granvig, sec general. *1-10 Jun 1998, applications by 15 Jan 1998: flute. Max age 30. First prize DKK 125,000.*

Copenhagen Singing Competition. Det Kongelige Teater og Kapel, Postbox 2185, DK-1017 Copenhagen K, Denmark *tel:* +45 33 322020 *fax:* +45 33 143369. *May-Jun. Competition for European singers in memoriam of Lauritz Melchior. First prize DKK 100,000.*

International Organ Competition. Laessøegade 74, DK-5230 Odense M, Denmark *fax:* +45 66 136363. Henning Nielsen, admin. *Biennial. Next 13-21 Aug 1998, applications by 1 Apr. Max age 35. First prize DKK 40,000.*

Nicolai Malko International Competition for Young Conductors. Radiohuset, Rosenørns Allé 22, DK-1999 Frederiksberg C, Denmark *tel:* +45 35 206371 *fax:* +45 35 206121. Gert Herzberg, gen sec. *Triennial. Next 25-29 May 1998, applications by 1 Feb. Age 20-31. First prize, $10,000 and engagements.*

Nordic Piano Competition. The Tourist Office, Torvet 9, DK-5800 Nyborg, Denmark *tel:* +45 65 310280 *fax:* +45 65 310380. *Next 1998, applications by 1 May 1998. Age limit 29. First prize DKK 35,000 and concerts.*

Estonia

VI International Choral Festival Tallinn. Estonian Choral Society, Suur-Karja 23, EE-0001 Tallinn, Estonia *tel:* +372 2 441849 *fax:* +372 2 449147. Paul Raud, mgr dir. *Triennial.*

Finland

International Jean Sibelius Violin Competition. PO Box 31, FIN-00101, Helsinki 10, Finland *tel:* +358 9 405441 *fax:* +358 9 22002680. Minna Pitkänen, sec. *Quinquennial. Next 18 Nov-2 Dec 2000, entries by 18 Aug 2000. Open to violinists born in 1970 or later. First prize, $15,000.*

International Sibelius Conductors' Competition. Finlandia Hall, FIN-00100 Helsinki, Finland *tel:* +358 40 503 0997 *fax:* +358 40 803 0997. Elina Siltanen, sec gen. *Quinquennial. Next May 2000. Up to 35 yrs. Repertoire ranges from Mozart to contemporary Finnish works. The finalists are required to conduct a Sibelius symphony.*

Lahti International Organ Competition. Kirkkokatu 5, FIN-15110 Lahti, Finland *tel:* +358 18 782 3184 *fax:* +358 18 783 2190. *Jun-Aug.*

Mirjam Helin International Singing Competition. Finnish Cultural Foundation, PO Box 203, FIN-00121 Helsinki, Finland *tel:* +358 9 602144 *fax:* +358 9 640474 *email:* mh@skr.fi; http://www.skr.fi. Kari Vase, exec sec; Timo Arjas, exec sec. *Quinquennial. Next 8-20 Aug 1999, entries by 15 Mar. Age limits: women born in 1968 or later; men born 1966 or later. Total prize money $100,000.*

Paulo Cello Competition. PO Box 782, FIN-00101 Helsinki, Finland *tel:* +358 9 405441 *fax:* +358 9 22002680. Minna Pitkanen, sec. *Quinquennial. Next Nov 2001, entries by spring 2000. Open to cellists of all nationalities born 1968-85. First prize 70,000 FM*

Tampereen Sävel International Choir Contest and Festival. Tullikamarinaukio 2, FIN-33100 Tampere, Finland *tel:* +358 3 219 6136/6172 *fax:* +358 3 223 0121 *email:* music@tampere.fi; http://www. tampere.fi/festival/music. Aila Manninen, dir. *Biennial. Next 9-13 Jun 1999, entries by Mar. Vocal ens and choirs. No age limits. First prize 35,000 FM in both competitions.*

France

Arthur Honegger International Prize. Fondation de France, 40 Av Hoche, F-75008 Paris, France *tel:* +33 1 44 21 31 00 *fax:* +33 1 44 21 31 01. *First prize 50,000 FF and a public concert.*

Competition for Music Lovers. Concours Européen pour les Mélomanes, c/o 32 Rue Carnot, 92100 Boulogne, France *tel:* +33 1 46 04 80 02 *fax:* +33 1 47 12 09 24 *email:* hmjp@aol.com. Régine Bessis, president. *Spring 1998, entries by 1 Mar. Applicants to be aged over 25 years.*

Florilège Vocal de Tours International Choral Singing Competition. Rue des Minimes, BP 1452, 37014 Tours Cedex 1, France *tel:* +33 2 47 21 65 26 *fax:* +33 2 47 21 67 71. Christian Balandras, artistic dir. *30-31 May 1998, applications by 29 Nov 1997. Annual competition for amateur choirs. First prize 16,000 FF.*

International Competition of French Music. 28 Rue da la Paix, F-78390 Bois D'Arcy, France *tel:* +33 1 34 60 30 96 *fax:* +33 1 34 60 08 53. Désiré N'Kaoua, president. *Nov. Chmbr mus ens of two or more people; no age limit. First prize, 25,000,00 FF.*

International Maurice André Trumpet Competition. Association Acanthes, 3 rue des Couronnes, F-75020 Paris, France *tel:* +33 1 40 33 45 35 *fax:* +33 1 40 33 45 38. *Oct.*

International Musical Software Competition. Institut International de Musique Electroacoustique, BP 39 - 18001 Bourges Cedex, France *tel:* +33 48 20 41 87 *fax:* +33 48 20 45 51 *email:* agmeb10@calvacom.fr; http://www.gmeb.fr. *Jun, applications by end Apr. Musical Software Competition for the creation of musical applications from candidates of any nationality.*

International Organ Competition. Association Acanthes, 3 rue des Couronnes, F-75020 Paris, France *tel:* +33 1 40 33 45 35 *fax:* +33 1 40 33 45 38. Colette Morillon, gen sec. *Biennial. Age limit 35.*

International Rostropovich Cello Competition. Association Acanthes, 3 rue des Couronnes, F-75020 Paris, France *tel:* +33 1 40 33 45 35 *fax:* +33 1 40 33 45 38. Jacqueline Fraisse. *Quadrennial. Next 2001. All nationalities, age limit 33, entrance fee 500 FF. First prize 70,000 FF plus engagements.*

International Singing and Chamber Music Competition. Secrétariat, 10 Rue du Dôme, F-75116 Paris, France *tel:* +33 1 47 04 76 38 *fax:* +33 1 47 27 55 03. Christiane de Bayser, president. *Biennial. Chmbr mus, Oct-Nov, applications by Sep. Voice, Jul, applications by May. Women up to 32 yrs, men up to 34 yrs. First prizes 40,000 FF (chmbr mus), 50,000 FF (voice) plus performances.*

International Young Conductors Competition. 2d Rue Isenbart, F-25000 Besançon, France *tel:* +33 81 80 73 26 *fax:* +33 81 80 46 36. Yvette Cussey, admin. *Sep, applications by Mar. Age limit 35.*

Marguerite Long and Jacques Thibaud International Competition. 32 Av Matignon, F-75008 Paris, France *tel:* +33 1 42 66 66 80 *fax:* +33 1 42 66 06 43. Mrs Perin, permanent sec. *Alternates pno and vn. Nov, applications by Sep. 16-30 yrs. First prize 150,000 FF and engagements.*

Toulouse International Voice Competition. Théâtre du Capitole, F-31000 Toulouse, France *tel:* +33 61 23 21 35 *fax:* +33 61 22 24 34. George Canet, gen sec. *Biennial. Next 21-26 Sep 1998, applications by 15 Jul. Application fee 100FF. First prize: 40,000 FF.*

Germany

Brahms International Competition. Hartungstrasse 8, D-20146 Hamburg, Germany *tel:* +49 40 452 158 *fax:* +49 40 410 2888. Eckhart Besch, president. *Biennial. Next 1999.*

Carl Orff International Singing Competition. Carl Orff-Stiftung, Herzogstr 57, D-80803 München, Germany *tel:* +49 89 335033 *fax:* +49 89 335937. *10-12 Jun 1997, applications by 5 May. Soprano, tenor and baritone singers aged 34 and under. First prize DM 10,000.*

Cologne International Pianoforte Competition. Foundation Tomassoni, Dagobertstr 38, D-50668 Köln, Germany *tel:* +49 221 912 818 112 *fax:* +49 221 131 204 *email:* barbara.schmidt@uni-koeln.de; http://www.mhs-koeln.de. Isabel Pfeiffer-Poensgen, sec general; Barbara Schmidt, organisation office. *Sep-Oct 1998, applications by Jun. Pianists of all nationalities aged 30 and under. First prize DM 15,000.*

Cologne International Singing Competition. Helga and Paul Hohnen Foundation, Dagobertstr 38, D-50668 Köln, Germany *tel:* +49 221 912 818 112 *fax:* +49 221 131 204 *email:* barbara.schmidt@uni-koeln.de; http://www.mhs-koeln.de. Isabel Pfeiffer-Poensgen, sec gen; Barbara Schmidt, organisation office. *Next 21 Sep-2 Oct 1998, applications by 15 Jun. First prize: DM 15,000.*

Cologne International Violin Competition. Foundation Georg Kulenkampff, Dagobertstr 38, D-50668 Köln, Germany *tel:* +49 221 912 818 112 *fax:* +49 221 131 204 *email:* barbara.schmidt@uni-koeln.de; http://www.mhs.koeln.de. Isabel Pfeiffer-Poensgen, sec gen; Barbara Schmidt, organisation office. *Triennial. Next Sep-Oct 1998, applications by 15 Jun. Open to violinists of all nationalities aged under 30. First prize, DM 15,000.*

Ettlingen International Competition for Young Pianists. Pforzheimerstr 25a, D-76275 Ettlingen, Germany *tel:* +49 7243 101 311/2 *fax:* +49 7243 101 436. Frank Reich, dir of organisations. *Biennial. Next 15-23 Aug 1998, applications by 9 May. Two age categories: 16 and under, 21 and under. Entrance fee: DM 110. First prize DM 6500 plus concerts.*

European Chopin Competition. Chopin-Gesellschaft, Kasinostrasse 3, D-64293 Darmstadt, Germany *tel:* +49 6151 25957/55897. Prof Lukaszczyk, president. *Triennial. Next 1999. Pianists aged 30 and under. First prize DM 9,000.*

Hannover International Violin Competition. Stiftung Niedersachsen, Ferdinandstr 4, D-30175 Hannover, Germany *tel:* +49 511 990540 *fax:* +49 511 314499 *email:* stiftung.nds@t-online.de/stiftung-nieder sachsen.de/violin. Krzysztof Wegrzyn, artistic dir; Linda Anne Engelhardt, exec dir. *Triennial. Next 2000. Age 16-30. First prize, DM 50,000, CD recording and debut concerts.*

International Singers' Contest 'Alexander Girardi'. Kulturabteilung der Stadt Coburg, Steingasse 18, D-96450 Coburg, Germany *tel:* +49 956 189 1402 *fax:* +49 956 189 1029. Albrecht Tauer, culture division dir. *Next Jun-Jul 1999. Opera competition open to female singers born 1966-78 and male singers born 1964-78. First prize DM 12,000. Entrance fee DM 150.*

International Chamber-Choir Competition Marktoberdorf. c/o Bayerische Musikakademie Marktoberdorf, Kurfürstenstr 19, D-87616 Marktoberdorf, Germany *tel:* +49 8342 961825 *fax:* +49 8342 40370 *email:* 100530.317@compuserve.com. Dolf Rabus, dir. *Biennial. Mixed and female choirs of 16-36 singers. First prize DM 5,000.*

International Competition for Young Violinists. Walderseestr 57, D-22605 Hamburg, Germany *tel:* +49 880 7983 *also fax.* Prof Petru Monteanu.

International J S Bach Competition. Sekretariat Bachwettbewerbe, Thomaskirchhof 16, D-04109 Leipzig, Germany *tel:* +49 341 964410 *fax:* +49 341 964 4195 *email:* jsbach@rzaix530.rz.uni-leipzig.de. Hans-Joachim Schulze, president; Sabine Martin, gen sec. *Next 30 Jun-11 Jul 1998, applications by 15 Mar. Pno, vc, voice. Age limit 32 (voice, 34). Entrance fee DM 100. First prize DM 12,000.*

International Jazz Federation European Jazz Competition (Leverkusen). 2b Gleneagle Mews, London SW16 6AE, UK *tel:* +44 181 769 7725 *fax:* +44 181 677 7128. Charles Alexander. *15-16 Oct 1998, applications by 31 May. Jazz groups (2-7) resident in Europe. Max age 30. First prize, DM 10,000.*

International Karl-Klingler Competition 1998. c/o Hochschule für Musik "Hanns Eisler" Berlin, Charlottenstr 55, D-10117 Berlin, Germany *tel:* +49 30 20309 2487 *fax:* +49 30 20309 2402. Karl-Klingler Wettbewerb. *4-9 Apr 1998. Competition for string quartet. Total age of quintet must not exceed 130 years on 4 Apr 1998. Applications by 15 Dec 1997. First prize DM 50,000.*

International Friedrich Kuhlau Flute Competition. PO Box 2061, D-29510 Uelzen, Germany *tel:* +49 581 800240 *fax:* +49 581 800220. Hans Rudolf Mentasti, organiser. *Triennial. Next 9-13 Nov 1998. Age limit 32. First prize range, DM 2000-5000.*

International Louis Spohr Violin Competition. Burgunderstr 4, D-79104 Freiburg, Germany *tel:* +49 761 23380 *fax:* +49 761 554862. *Triennial. Max age 32.*

International Music Competition of the ARD. Bayerischer Rundfunk, D-80300 München, Germany *tel:* +49 89 5900 2471 *fax:* +49 89 5900 3091. Renate Ronnefeld, gen sec. *Annual. 1-18 Sep 1998, applications by end Apr. Age limits: inst soloists 17-30; female singers 20-30; male singers 20-32; duo and trio 17-32. Categories: voice, vc, cl, vn and pno duo, pno and str trio. First prize DM 20,000 (soloist), DM 25,000 (duo), DM 27,000 (trio).*

International Robert Schumann Choral Competition. Münzstr 12, D-08056 Zwickau, Germany *tel:* +49 375 22636 *fax:* +49 375 834130. *Next 1998, applications by 15 Jan. Open to female, male and mixed choirs. First prize, DM 6,000.*

International Robert Schumann Competition for Piano and Voice. Münzstr 12, D-08056 Zwickau, Germany *tel:* +49 375 22636 *fax:* +49 375 834130. *Quadrennial. Max age for pianists, 30 yrs and for singers 32 yrs. First prize DM 10,000 (pianists), DM 10,000 (singers).*

International Singers' Contest 'New Voices'. Carl-Bertelsmann-Str 256, PO Box 103, D-33311 Gütersloh, Germany *tel:* +49 5241 817184 *fax:* +49 5241 819513 *email:* martin.spilker@bertelsmann.de. Liz Mohn; Martin Spilker. *Biennial. Next Jun 1999, applications by autumn 1998. Male singers 32 yrs; female singers 30 yrs. First prize DM 15,000.*

International Violin Competition Leopold Mozart. Leopold-Mozart Konservatorium, Maximilianstr 59, D-86150 Augsburg, Germany *tel:* +49 821 324 4892 *fax:* +49 821 313088. Kranz Angelika, mgr dir. *Quadrennial. Next Nov 1999. Violinists of all nationalities, professional and student. Max age 30 yrs. Cash prizes, young musician awards, CD recording and concert engagements, audience prize, Mozart prize for best interpretation of contemporary compulsory set work.*

Greece

Dimitris Mitropoulos International Competition. 18 Alex Soutaou, GR-10671 Athens, Greece *tel:* +30 1 362 1477 *fax:* +30 1 362 7412. Traute Lutz, chief offr. *Annual. Nov, applications by Mar. 1998 conducting. First prize 6,000,000 Drachmas.*

International Choir Festival of Athens. Polifonia Athenaeum, 2 Spartis St, GR-153 42 Agia Paraskevi, Athens, Greece *tel:* +30 1 638 0119 *fax:* +30 1 600 9204. *Nov, entries by Feb. Entry fee US $400. First prize DR 500,000.*

Maria Callas Grand Prix for Pianists. Athenaeum International Cultural Centre, 8 Amerikis St, GR-106 71 Athens, Greece *tel:* +30 1 36 33 701/2 *fax:* +30 1 36 35 957. Riri Megas, sec. *17-26 Feb 1998, applications by 5 Jan. Max age 30. Entry fee, $100. First prize, DRS 3,000,000 and concerts.*

Maria Callas Grand Prix for Singers. Athenaeum International Cultural Centre, 8 Amerikis St, GR-106 71 Athens, Greece *tel:* +30 1 36 33 701/2 *fax:* +30 1 36 35 957. Riri Megas, sec. *Feb-Mar 1999, applications by 15 Dec 1998. Max age males 32, females 30. Entry fee, $100. First prizes, DRS 1,500,000 and engagements in three categories; male, female and oratorio-lied.*

Hungary

Budapest International Music Competition. Interart Festivalcentre, PO Box 80, Vörösmarty tér 1, H-1366 Budapest 5, Hungary *tel:* +36 1 117 9838/266 3108 *fax:* +36 1 117 9910. Maria Liszkay, mgr. *First prize $8000.*

Hungarian Television International Conductors Competition. Interart Festivalcentre, PO Box 80, Vörösmarty tér 1, H-1366 Budapest, Hungary *tel:* +36 1 266 3108/117 9838 *fax:* +36 1 117 9910. Maria Liszkay, mgr. *Triennial. Next 10-24 May 1998, applications by 1 Dec 1997. Age limit 35. First prize US$5000.*

International Choir Competition Béla Bartók. Nemzetközi Kórusverseny Irodája, Hunyadi u 1-3, H-4026 Debrecen, Hungary *tel:* +36 52 413977/419812 *fax:* +36 52 416040. Zoltàn Szabò, sec. *Jul. Member of the European Grand Prix of Choral Singing. 20th C and contemporary choral mus.*

Israel

Arthur Rubinstein International Piano Master Competition. Secretariat, 12 Huberman St, PO Box 6018, 61060 Tel Aviv, Israel *tel:* +972 3 685 6684 *fax:* +972 3 685 4924 *email:* arims@netvision.net.il. Jan J Bistritzky, founder and dir. *Triennial. Next 17 Mar-2 Apr 1998, entries by 1 Oct 1998. First prize US $25,000. Contact secretariat for further details.*

International Harp Contest. 4 Aharonowitz St, 63566 Tel Aviv, Israel *tel:* +972 3 528 0233 *fax:* +972 3 629 9524. Esther Herlitz, dir. *30 Jan-13 Feb 1998, entries by 1 Jul 1997. Max age for entry 35 in Jan 1998. First prize, Lyon and Healy concert harp.*

Leonard Bernstein Jerusalem International Music Competitions. 11 Rivka St, POB 10185, Jerusalem 91101, Israel *tel:* +972 2 673 5032 *fax:* +972 2 716 380 *email:* berncomp@netvision.net.il. Leor Segal, exec dir. *Oct. Three year cycle: conducting (1998), age limit 24-35; oratorio and song (1999), age limit 22-33; composing (2000), age limit 22-50.*

Preliminary rounds in 5 locations around world. Finals Oct in Jerusalem, entries by 1 Mar. First prize: $25,000, engagements and recording opportunities.

Italy

Alessandro Casagrande International Piano Competition. Comune di Terni-Vico S Lorenzo 1, I-05100 Terni, Italy *tel:* +39 744 549 713 *also fax.* Cesare Durante, sec. *Biennial. Next 1998. Age limit 28.*

Arturo Toscanini International Conductors' Competition. c/o Fondazione Arturo Toscanini, Office for International Competitions, Via G Tartini n 13, I-43100 Parma, Italy *tel:* +39 521 274417/27 *fax:* +39 521 272134 *email:* fondazione@toscanini.dsnet.it;˙http://www.fondazione-toscanini.it. Gianni Baratta, general mgr. *Triennial. Next Sep 2000, applications by 31 May 2000. Open to conductors of any nationality aged 32 and under. First prize (The Arturo Toscanini Award) comprises cash, contracts and diploma.*

Bellini International Voice Competition. Ibla International Foundation, 226 E Second St, Suite 5D, New York, NY 10009, USA *tel:* +1 212 387 0111 *fax:* +1 212 388 0102. Salvatore Moltisanti, chmn; Kelly Knox, exec dir. *Annual. Next Jul 1998, entries by Mar. Open to singers from all over the world. Prizes totalling $15,000, concert engagements, eventual CD recording.*

Bottega International Competition for Conducting. Corporation for the Civic Theatre of Treviso, Corso del Popolo 31, I-31100 Treviso, Italy *tel:* +39 422 410130 *fax:* +39 422 52285.

Carlo Soliva International Music Competition. Istituto Musicale Carlo Soliva, 35 Via Facino Cane, I-15033 Casale Monferrato, Italy *tel:* +39 142 55760 *also fax.* Carla Ruschena Sekawin, president. *Biennial. Next 23-28 Mar 1998, applications by 15 Feb. Any nationality. Soloists, pno duo and chmbr mus. First prize, 120,000 lire for soloists, 160,000 lire for duo, 200,000 lire for trio.*

City of Senigallia International Piano Competition. Piazza del Duca, I-60019 Senigallia, Italy *tel:* +39 71 662 9267/662 9350/65568 *fax:* +39 71 662 9349. Domenico Pergolesi, gen dir; Luigi Mostacci, artistic dir. *Aug, International Meeting of Young Pianists. Sep, pno competition. Two categories for IMYP: under 16 and under 20. Age range for pno competition 15-36. Entry fees, IMYP 100 lire; pno competition 150 lire. Entries by 30 Jun 1996. First prize for pno competition, 20,000,000 lire.*

Concorso Internazionale Cantanti Lirici "Città di Roma". Associazione Produzione Culturale Regionale, Via Aristofane, 182-00125 Roma, Italy *tel:* +39 6 523 60574 *also fax. Open to young singers aged 36 and under.*

Concorso Internazionale di Musica Viotti-Valsesia. Associazione Valsesia Musica, Sezione canto lirico, Corso Roma 38, I-13019 Varallos, Italy *tel:* +39 163 51 280. *Annual. Aug-Sep. Open to all singers, age limit 34 years (sopranos and tenors) and 35 years (mezzo-sopranos and counter-tenors, basses and baritones). Candidates must perform 6 arias chosen from the Italian and foreign lyric repertory from 1750-1950. There are three rounds to complete.*

Concorso Internazionale per 'Voci Verdiane'. Comune di Busseto, Piazza Giuseppe Verdi 10, I-43011 Busseto (Parma), Italy *tel:* +39 524 92603/91841 *fax:* +39 524 92360/92603 *email:* http://www.aspide.it/freeweb/saverio_cannara/busseto/. Sindaco di Busseto, president. *Annual. Jul 1998, applications by 27 Jun. Aged 30 and under (sop and ten), 33 and under (m-sop, bar, bs). First prize: 7,000,000 lire.*

Competition for Young Opera Singers belonging to the European Community. Istituzione Teatro Lirico Sperimentale, di Spoleto 'A Belli', Piazza G Bovio 1, I-06049 Spoleto (PG), Italy *tel:* +39 743 221645/ 220440 *fax:* +39 743 222930. Lepore Claudio, admin; Nadia Nigris, asst. *11-15 Mar 1998, applications by 24 Feb. Singers from European Community countries; sopranos and tenors aged 30 and under; mezzo-sopranos, contraltos, baritones and basses aged 32 and under. Applicants should be a citizen of an EU country. Winners will be awarded grants for a 5-month singing course culminating in a performance at the Teatro Lirico Sperimentale, Spoleto amounting to 1,300,000 lire each month.*

Dino Ciani Prize for Young Pianists. Teatro alla Scala, Via Filodrammatici 2, I-20121 Milano, Italy *tel:* +39 2 88791 *fax:* +39 2 887 9424. Riccardo Muti, jury president; Laura Colombo, sec. *Triennial. Next 1999. Age limit 30. First prize 25,000,000 lire and concerts.*

Ettore Pozzoli International Piano Competition. Via Paradiso 6, I-20038 Seregno, Italy *tel:* +39 362 222914 *also fax.* Lia Diotti, sec. *Biennial. Next 1999. First prize 20,000,000 lire.*

European Music Competition Città di Moncalieri. Via Carlo Alberto 3/b, I-10024 Moncalieri (TO), Italy *tel:* +39 11 640 8597 *fax:* +39 11 640 3060. *Oct-Nov. For pno and four hand pno. Total prizes 2,000,000 lire.*

Ferruccio Busoni International Piano Competition. Conservatorio Claudio Monteverdi, Piazza Domenicani 19, I-39100 Bolzano, Italy *tel:* +39 471 976568 *fax:* +39 471 973579 *email:* busoni@asteria.it; http://www.asteria.it/busoni.htm. Mariapia Venturi, sec. *Annual. 20 Aug-5 Sep 1998, applications by 31 May. Ages 16-32. First prize, 15,000,000 lire and about 60 concerts.*

Gian Battista Viotti International Music and Ballet Competition. Società del Quartetto, PO Box 127, I-13100 Vercelli, Italy *tel:* +39 161 252667 *fax:* +39 161 255575. *Annual. Oct. Categories of voice, pno, chmbr mus, vc. Max age: voice 35, pno 30, chmbr mus 32, vc 30. First prize 15,000,000 lire and engagements.*

Guido d'Arezzo International Choral Competition. Fondazione Guido d'Arezzo, Corso Italia 102, I-52100 Arezzo, Italy *tel:* +39 575 356203 *fax:* +39 575 324735 *email:* fondguid@krenet.it; http://www.krenet.it/unoinfo/fondguid. Remo Manganelli, commissioner. *27-30 Aug, applications by 15 Feb. Competition for amateur choirs. Max age for children 15; no age limit for other categories. First prize, 3,000,000 lire for each category; 4,000,000 lire grand prize.*

Ibla International Piano Competition. 226 E Second St, Suite 5D, NYC, NY 10009, USA *tel:* +1 212 387 0111 *fax:* +1 212 388 0102. Salvatore Moltisanti, chmn; Kelly Knox, exec dir. *Annual. Next 25 Jun-6 Jul 1998, entries by 20 Mar. Pianists worldwide. Five categories: adult, young, four hands, concerto and accompanists. Prizes are concert engagements and scholarships, totalling $20,000. Eventual CD recording.*

International Choir Competition of Riva del Garda. Associazione Concorso Chorale, Via Concordia 25, I-38066 Riva del Garda (TN), Italy *tel:* +39 4 6455 4073 *fax:* +39 4 6452 0900 *email:* http://www.garda.com. *23-26 Oct 1997.*

International Competition for Instrumental and Vocal Performance. Via Aurelia 139, I-18016 San Bartolomeo al Mare (IM), Italy *tel:* +39 183 400967/400888/400200 *fax:* +39 183 403050; +39 185 771790. Luciano Lanfranchi, artistic dir. *Annual. 10-20 Jul 1998, applications by 15 Jun. Open to insts and singers born 1962-1986. Prizes include scholarships and concerts.*

International Guitar Competition. Piazza Garibaldi 16, I-15100 Alessandria, Italy *tel:* +39 131 251207/253170 *fax:* +39 131 235507 *email:* pittalug@email.alessandria.alpcom.it. Micaela Pittaluga, president; Maria Luisa Pittaluga, vice-president. *Annual. 21-25 Sep 1998, applications by 7 Sep. For those born after Jan 1968. First prize 10,000,000 lire.*

International Verdi Requiem Vocal Competition. IUMA Worldwide Productions, Via E Filiberto 125, I-00185 Rome, Italy *tel:* +39 670 452328; +39 677 201524 *fax:* +39 677 205607 *email:* cfcatena@pelagus. it; http://www.operage.com. *Nov. Open to singers from Europe, USA, Canada, Japan and Korea. For age 39 and under. Prizes include concert opportunities in New York.*

Nicolo Paganini International Violin Competition. Corune di Genova, Via Garibaldi 9, I-16124 Genoa, Italy *tel:* +39 10 20981 *fax:* +39 10 206235. Sgnra Sanfilippo, competition sec. *Annual. 25 Sep-4 Oct 1998, applications by 31 May. Ages 33 and under. Entry fee, 170,000 lire. First prize 20,000,000 lire and exhibition concert.*

Rina Sala Gallo Piano Competition. Comune di Monza, I-20052 Monza (MI), Italy *fax:* +39 388 608. Gianna Garbagnati, president. *Biennial. 28 Sep-4 Oct 1998, entries by 15 May. Pianists aged 15-30. First prize 25,000,000 lire.*

Rodolfo Lipizer International Violin Competition. Via Don Giovanni Bosco 91, I-34170 Gorizia GO, Italy *tel:* +39 481 34775 *fax:* +39 481 536710 *email:* lipizer@mbox.vol.it; http://www.seta.it/lipizer/. Lorenzo Qualli, president; Elena Lipizer, artistic dir. *Annual. Next 5-13 Sep 1998 (4-12 Sep 1999), entries by 15 May. Violinists of any nationality born after 13 Sep 1963. First prize, 11,000,000 lire and a vn.*

Syrinx International Competition for Flute. c/o Accademia Italiana del Flauto, 43 Via Innocenza X, I-00152 Roma, Italy *tel:* +39 6 581 6225 *fax:* +39 6 588 0429. Gian Luca Morseletto, chief offr. *Biennial. Next Nov 1999, applications by Jul. Flautists of all nationalities. First prize 6,000,000 lire and a flute.*

Toti dal Monte International Singing Competition. Ente Teatro Comunale, Corso del Popolo 31, Via Diaz 7, I-31100 Treviso, Italy *tel:* +39 422 410130 *fax:* +39 422 52285. Lucio De Piccoli, press offr. *Annual. Jun. Prizes, 2,500,000-3,500,000 lire.*

Umberto Micheli International Piano Competion. c/o Resia SrL, Via Manzoni 31, I-20121 Milano, Italy *tel:* +39 2 654 161/2/3/4 *fax:* +39 2 659 7851 *email:* resiasrl@mbox.vol.it; http://www.vol.it/concorso micheli/. Patrizia Garrasi, dir; Lauro Colombo, sec. *Triennial. Next 2000. Concentrates specifically on contemporary mus, with works specially composed by Corghi, Kagel and Stockhausen. Pianists of all nationalities aged under 30. First prize 15,000,000 lire, concert engagements and a CD.*

Valentino Bucchi di Roma Capitale International Prize. Via Ubaldino Peruzzi 20, I-00139 Roma, Italy *tel:* +39 6 8720 0121 *fax:* +39 6 8713 1527. Liliana Pannella, president. *Annual. Next 9-20 Nov 1998, applications by 15 Sep (performance). Categories rotate: 1998 pno and 2 pnos in 20th C (performance and composition); 1999 cl, fl and picc; 2000 db (performance and composition); 2001 va, vc, quartet and strings (performance and composition). Ages 32-35 yrs. First prize 10,000,000 lire (pno), 13,000,000 lire (2 pnos).*

Publishers to the performing arts

RHINEGOLD PUBLISHING

YEARBOOKS

British & International Music Yearbook
Britain's most comprehensive and accurate directory of the classical music industry
Published each November £23.95

British Performing Arts Yearbook
The guide to performing companies, venues, suppliers, services, festivals, education and support organisations
Published each January £23.95

Music Education Yearbook
A guide for parents, teachers, students and musicians
Published each June £14.00

OTHER PUBLICATONS

The Musician's Handbook
A compendium of advice for the music profession
£14.95 (hardback)

Healthy Practice for Musicians
An expertly written self-help guide covering the whole spectrum of a musician's physical and mental well-being
£16.95 (hardback)

Arts Marketing
The definitive guide to audience-building through effective marketing
£18.95 (hardback)

Analysis Matters
A students' revision guide to the Group 1 London Examinations' Advanced Level Musical History and Analysis Papers for 1998 and 1999
£10.00

Kein Angst Baby
A singer's guide to German operatic auditions in the 1990s
£9.95

The Art of Conducting
A guide to essential skills
£12.95

MAGAZINES

Classical Music
The magazine of the classical music profession
Fortnightly £2.95
Annual UK Subscription £56.00

Music Teacher
Respected and enjoyed by music teachers for more than 85 years
Monthly £2.95
Annual UK Subscription £34.00

The Singer
For amateur and professional singers of every persuasion – from cabaret to grand opera
Bi-monthly £2.40
Annual UK Subscription £14.40

Piano
The magazine for performers and enthusiasts of classical, jazz and blues piano
Bi-monthly £2.40
Annual UK Subscription £14.40

Early Music Today
Britain's brightest early music news magazine
Bi-monthly £2.40
Annual UK Subscription £14.40

Opera Now
The international magazine for opera professionals
Bi-monthly £4.95
Annual UK Subscription £29.70

Music Scholar
A guide to scholarships for young musicians
Published November '97 £3.00

Rhinegold Publishing Limited
241 Shaftesbury Avenue
London WC2H 8EH
Tel 0171 333 1721 Fax 0171 333 1769
E-mail 100546.1126@compuserve.com

Vittorio Gui International Chamber Music Competition. Associazione Concorsi e Rassegne Musicali, Borgo degli Albizi n 15, I-50122 Firenze, Italy *tel:* +39 55 240672 *also fax; email:* acerm@firenze.net; http://www.firenze.net/premioqui. Massimo Bogianckino, president; Colella Ornella, organising sec. *Annual. 12-18 Oct 1998, entries by 5 Sep. Age limit 32 (for trio, quartet and quintet the average age must not exceed 32 yrs). Entry fee, 250,000 lire. First prize 15,000,000 lire and concert tour.*

Japan

Hamamatsu International Piano Competition. c/o ACT City Hammatsu Management Foundation, 111-1 Itaya-machi, Hamamatsu-shi, Shizuoka-ken 430, Japan *tel:* +81 53 4561106 *fax:* +81 53 4572237. Saichirto Sakaguchi, sec gen. *Open to pianists born between 1969 and 1981. Competition is in four stages. Cash prizes.*

International Music Competition of Japan. Japan Federation of Musicians, Kaga Bldg 2F, Toranomon 5-2-8, Minato-Ku, Tokyo 105, Japan *tel:* +81 3 3434 1781 *fax:* +81 3 3434 1784. Yumiko Ofuji. *Triennial. Next Nov/Dec 1999, applications by Jun. Age limit 17-32. First prize 2,000,000 Yen, gold medal, recital in Tokyo, concert performance in Tokyo.*

Osaka International Chamber Music Competition. C/-Yomiuri Telecasting Corporation, 2-33 Shiromi 2-chome, Chuo-ku, Osaka 540-10, Japan *tel:* +81 6 947 2184 *fax:* +81 6 947 2198. Kunihiko Tamakoshi. *Next May 1999.*

Tokyo International Music Competition for Conducting. Min-On Concert Association, 1-32-13 Kita-Shinjuku, Shinjuku-ku, Tokyo 169, Japan *tel:* +81 3 5386 2887; +81 3 3371 5103 *fax:* +81 3 3369 5206. *Jul-Nov.*

Luxembourg

ICSC International Coloratura Singing Competition - Sylvia Geszty. PO Box 1163, D-75390 Gechingen, Germany *tel:* +49 7056 8024 *fax:* +49 7056 4256. Sylvia Geszty. *Biennial. Next 4-8 May 1998, entries by 1 Mar. Age 32 and under. First round stages held in London, Berlin, Budapest and Madrid, final takes place in Luxembourg. First prize, 15,000 DM.*

Monaco

The Reding-Piette International Competition for Duo Piano. Chateau Perigord II, Monte Carlo, MC-98000, Monaco *tel:* +377 93 30 07 21 *also fax.* Janine Reding, competition president. *Triennial. Next Jun 1998, applications by 1 Apr. To select young professional piano duos preparing for an international concert career. Ages 30 and under. First prize $25,000.*

Netherlands

César Franck Organ Competition. Leeghwaterstraat 14, NL-2012 GD Haarlem, Netherlands *tel:* +31 23 532 7070. Bernard Bartelink, admin. *Triennial. Next 6-10 Oct 1998, entries by 1 Jun. Open to professional organists. First prize DFL 3000.*

IKF International Choir Festival. Plompetorengracht 3, NL-3512 CA Utrecht, Netherlands *tel:* +31 30 2313 174 *fax:* +31 30 2318 137 *email:* snlc@euronet.nl. Jos Vranken, mus mgr; Andries Ponsteen, mgr dir. *Jun-Jul 2001. Arnhem.*

International Competition for Early Music Ensembles. Singel 308, NL-1016 AE Amsterdam, Netherlands *tel:* +31 20 639 1390 *fax:* +31 20 622 7118. Martijn Jacobus, dir. *Biennial. Inst and vocal ens (max 8 persons), repertoire 1600-1800.*

International Competition for Organ Improvisation. Postbus 3333, Stadhuis, NL-2001 DH Haarlem, Netherlands *tel:* +31 23 160574 *fax:* +31 23 160576. E L S Hendrikse, sec. *Biennial. Next 7-10 Jul 1998, applications by Jan. No age limit. First prize DFL 10,000*

International Franz Liszt Piano Competition. Muziekcentrum Vredenburg PO Box 550, NL-3500 AN Utrecht, Netherlands *tel:* +31 30 233 0233 *fax:* +31 30 231 6522. *Quadrennial. Next May 2000. Age limit 16-30. First prize DFL 25,000.*

International Gaudeamus Interpreters Competition 1996. Gaudeamus Foundation, Swammerdamstraat 38, NL-1091 RV Amsterdam, Netherlands *tel:* +31 20 694 7349 *fax:* +31 20 694 7258. *All insts and vocal soloists and ens (max 12 performers). Special ens prize. Age limit 35.*

International Kirill Kondrashin Competition. c/o NOS (Netherlands Broadcasting Corp), PO Box 26444, NL-1202 JJ Hilversum, Netherlands *tel:* +31 35 775453 *fax:* +31 35 774311. Anneke Hogenstyn, project mgr. *Quadrennial. Aug-Sep 1998, entries by 1 Mar. Conducting. Max age 36.*

International Vocal Competition. PO Box 1225, NL-5200 BG's-Hertogenbosch, Netherlands *tel:* +31 73 690 0999 *fax:* +31 73 690 1166. Arthur Oostvogel, mgr dir; Bert van Mourik, artistic dir. *28 Aug-6 Sep 1998, entries for live auditions by 31 Dec 1997. Max age 35. First prizes*

of television exposure and US $10,000 for Lied, opera and oratorio categories.

Scheveningen International Music Competition. Gevers Deynootweg 970z, NL-2586 BW Den Haag, Netherlands *tel:* +31 70 352 5100 *fax:* +31 70 352 2197. Anton de Beer, competition mgr. *Annual. Mar, entries by Dec. Different inst each year. 1997: pno. Age limit 30. First prize DFL 25,000 and engagements.*

Norway

The Queen Sonja International Music Competition. PO Box 5190, Majorstua, N-0302 Oslo, Norway *tel:* +47 22 46 4055 *fax:* +47 22 46 3630. Lars Fleten, exec dir. *Triennial. Next 1999.*

Poland

Grzegorz Fitelberg International Competition for Conductors. Ul Sokolska 2, PL-40-084 Katowice, Poland, Poland *tel:* +48 32 596074 *also fax.* Karol Stryja, artistic dir; Roza Miliczek, sec gen. *Quadrennial. Next Dec 1999, applications by Apr. Age limit 35.*

Henryk Wieniawski International Violin Competition. Swietoslawska St 7, PL-61840 Poznan, Poland *tel:* +48 61 522642/528992 *fax:* +48 61 528991. Z Dworzecki, dir. *Quinquennial. Age limit 30. First prize $20,000.*

International Chopin Piano Competition. Frederick Chopin Society, Okolnik 1, PL-00368 Warszawa, Poland *tel:* +48 22 827 9589/5471 *fax:* +48 22 279599. *Quinquennial. Next Sep-Oct 2000. First prize US $25,500.*

International Festival of Choral Song. Concert Agency 'Rondo', PO Box 77, PL-70 334 Szczecin 4, Poland *tel:* +48 91 845242 *fax:* +48 91 846193 *email:* rondo@ubique.com.pl. Jan Szyrocki, mus dir; Stanislaw Zaborowski, dir. *Jun, applications by Feb. First prize PZL 5000.*

Stanislaw Moniusko Vocal Competition. Plac Teatralnyl, PL-00-950, Warszawa, Poland *tel:* +48 2226 4050 *fax:* +48 2226 1849. Maria Foltyn, artistic dir. *1-11 Oct 1998.*

Twentieth Century Music Competition for Young Performers. Polish Society for Contemporary Music, ISCM Polish Section, Ul Mazowiecka 11, PL-00 052 Warszawa, Poland *tel:* +48 22 8276981 *fax:* +48 22 8277804. Grazyna Dziura, exec sec. *Next 1998. Prize divided between prize-winner and teacher.*

Portugal

Porto International Music Competition. Rua Azevedo Coutinho 195, 4100 Porto, Portugal *tel:* +351 2 609 5099 *fax:* +351 2 600 4307. Fernanda Wandschneider, president; Elzira Calem, gen sec. *Annual. 1-12 Oct 1998, only the first 90 entries will be accepted. Contestants to have been born between 1 Jan 1965 and 30 Sep 1981. First prize 1,500,000 ptas.*

Republic of Ireland

Cork International Choral Festival. PO Box 68, Cork, Republic of Ireland *tel:* +353 21 308308 *fax:* +353 21 308309 *email:* chorfest@iol.ie. John Fitzpatrick, festival dir; Sheila Kelleher, festival admin. *30 Apr-3 May 1998, entries by 31 Jan. Amateur choirs (not children's choirs, minimum 20 voices). First prize £2000.*

Guardian Dublin International Piano Competition. City Hall, Dublin 2, Republic of Ireland *tel:* +353 1 677 3066 *fax:* +353 1 671 1385. Ann Fuller, admin. *Triennial. Next 2000, entries by 30 Nov 1999. Age limit 17-30. First prize £10,000 and international engagements.*

Limerick Church Music International Choral Festival. City Hall, Limerick, Republic of Ireland *tel:* +353 61 415799/229914 *fax:* +353 61 415266/418601 *email:* limcorp@iol.ie. Fergus Quinlivan, dir. *20-22 Mar 1998, entries by 16 Feb. Choirs and choral groups. First prize: cheque and trophy.*

Limerick International Band Festival. Shannon Development, The Granary, Limerick, Republic of Ireland *tel:* +353 61 410 777 *fax:* +353 61 315 634. Baz Millar, regional development exec. *Mar, applications by Dec. All categories marching and concert bands. First prize Shannon Development Trophy.*

Romania

Constantin Silvestri International Concerto Competition. Constantin Silvestri State Philharmonic Orchestra, Tirgu Mures, c/o LSP, 72 Warwick Gardens, London W14 8PP, UK *tel:* +44 171 603 1396 *also fax. Annual. Next end Aug 1998. All insts. Age 16-25. Prizes: concert tours with professional orchestras and recitals.*

George Enescu International Piano, Violin and Singing Competition. Calea Victoriei nr 155, bl D1 sc 8 et 2, 71012 Bucharest, Romania *tel:* +40 1 650 18 06/12 *fax:* +40 1 311 02 00 *email:* artexim@com.pcnet.ro. Mihai Constantinescu. *Next 1999.*

Nicolae Bretan International Competition for Vocal Interpretation for Vocal Interpretation. Gheorghe Dima Music Academy, Str j C Bratianu

25, Cluj-Napoca, Romania *tel:* +40 64 193879 *also fax. Biennial. 18-25 Mar 1998, entries by 1 Jan. Singers of all nationalities. Age limit: female 30, male 35.*

South Africa

Ninth International Eisteddfod of South Africa. PO Box 738, 1725 Roodepoort, South Africa *tel:* +27 11 472 2820 *fax:* +27 11 472 1014 *email:* iesa@infodoor.co.za; http://www.infodoor.co.za/exhibitions/ eisteddfod. Joe le Roux, exec dir. *Biennial. International competitive festival.*

UNISA Transnet International Music Competition. University of S Africa, PO Box 392, RSA 0001 Pretoria, South Africa *tel:* +27 12 429 3344/3353 *fax:* +27 12 429 3644. John Roos, artistic dir. *Biennial. Max age 32 yrs. First prize R60,000 for vn, vc and pno.*

Spain

Alhambra International Guitar Competition. Manufacturas Alhambra SL, Duquesa de Almodóvar, 11, 03830 Muro del Alcoy, Alicante, Spain *tel:* +34 6 553 0011 *fax:* +34 6 651 6302. D Jaime Julia Abad, mgr dir; D Yukiharu Inoue, chief officer. *13-18 Apr 1998, applications by 28 Mar. First prize 1,700,000 ptas.*

Cadaqués International Conducting Competition. Arcs 8, 1er 2, E-08002 Barcelona, Spain *tel:* +34 3301 9555 *fax:* +34 3302 2670 *email:* trito@ bcn.servicom.es. Llorenc Caballero, sec. *22-26 Jul 1998, applications by 30 Apr. First prize 500,000 ptas and orch engagements in Spain.*

Dos Hermanas International Clarinet Competition. Secretaria del Concurso Internacional de Clarinete, Ayuntamiento, E-41700 Dos Hermanas, Sevilla, Spain *tel:* +34 95 472 70 01/566 66 45/472 90 11 *fax:* +34 95 566 66 45. *Sep-Oct. Open to clarinettists of all nationalities aged 30 and under on opening date of competition. First prize 1,000,000 ptas.*

Francisco Vinas International Singing Contest. Calle Bruc 125, E-08037 Barcelona, Spain *tel:* +34 3 215 4227; 00 34 3 457 8646. Maria Vilardell Vinas, president. *Annual. 14-25 Jan 1998, entries by 4 Dec 1997. Max age: 35 male, 32 female. Application fee, 14,000 ptas. Two categories: opera and oratorio-Lieder. First grand prize for male and female singers, 1,200,000 ptas each.*

José Iturbi International Piano Competition. Diputación Provincial, Plaza de Manises 4, Servicio de Cultura, E-46003 Valencia, Spain *tel:* +34 6 388 2500 *fax:* +34 6 388 2775. *Biennial. Max age 31.*

Julian Gayarre International Singing Competition. Calle Santo Domingo 6, E-31001 Pamplona, Spain *tel:* +34 48 106072/106500 *fax:* +34 48 223906. Ignacio Aranaz, co-ord; Piero Rattalino, artistic dir. *Biennial. Sep, applications by Jul. Max age: 35 male, 32 female. First prizes (for male and female), 1,000,000 ptas and engagement.*

Maria Canals International Competition for Musical Performance. Gran Via de les Corts Catalanes 654, E-08010 Barcelona, Spain *tel:* +34 3 318 7731 *also fax.* Elisabeth Martinez, gen sec. *Annual. Apr-May, applications by Feb. Age 18-32. First prize 600,000 ptas and gold medal.*

Pablo Sarasate International Violin Competition. Calle Santo Domingo 6, E-31001 Pamplona, Spain *tel:* +34 48 106072/106500 *fax:* +34 48 223906. Ignacio Aranaz, co-ord; Vladimir Spirakov, president. *Biennial. Age limit 27. First prize 1,500,000 ptas plus engagements.*

Paloma O'Shea International Santander Piano Competition. Calle Hernán Cortés 3, E-39003 Santander, Spain *tel:* +34 42 311451/311266 *fax:* +34 42 314816. Annelies Kaufmann, gen sec. *Triennial. Next 7 Jul-7 Aug 1998. For pianists born after 1 Jan 1969. Santander Grand Prize, first prize $US46,000, total prize money $US100,000, world-wide recital tours, recordings.*

Premio Internacional de Canto Acisclo Fernández. Fundación Jacinto e Innocencio Guerrero de Música, Gran Vía 78, E-28013 Madrid, Spain *tel:* +34 1 547 66 18 *fax:* +34 1 548 34 93 *email:* jeig@adenle.es. *Biennial. 20 Apr 1998, entries by 12 Mar. Open to singers of all types of voice and all nationalities born after 1 Jan 1965. First prize: 2,500,000 ptas.*

Premio Internacional de Guitarra. Gran Via 78, c/o Fundación Jacinto e Inocencio Guerrero, E-28013 Madrid, Spain *tel:* +34 1 547 66 18 *fax:* +34 1 548 34 93. *Biennial. 26 Oct 1998, entries by 18 Sep. Open to gui players of any nationality born on or after 1 Jan 1965. First prize 2,500,000 ptas.*

Premio Internacional de Piano Fundación Guerrero. Gran Via 78, c/o Fundación Jacinto e Inocencio Guerrero, E-28013 Madrid, Spain *tel:* +34 1 547 66 18 *fax:* +34 1 548 34 93. *Biennial. Next 1999. Open to pianists of any nationality aged under 35. First prize 2,500,000 ptas.*

Sweden

Jussi Börling Tenor Competition. Borlänge Kommun 781, 81 Borläge, Högbergsgatan 76B, S-11856 Stockholm, Sweden *tel:* +46 8 243 7400 *fax:* +46 8 243 66208. Jan Hercules, dir; Charlotte Blückert, admin. *Triennial. Open to tenors aged 35 and under. Cash awards.*

Switzerland

Clara Haskil Piano Competition. PO Box 234, CH-1800 Vevey 1, Switzerland *tel:* +41 21 922 6704 *fax:* +41 21 922 6734. Patrick Peikert, dir; Christiane Susset, sec. *Biennial. Next 25 Aug-7 Sep 1999, applications by 1 Jul. Age limit 30. First prize SFR 20,000.*

Géza Anda International Piano Competition. Bleicherweg 18, CH-8002 Zürich, Switzerland *tel:* +41 1 205 1423 *fax:* +41 1 205 1429. Ruth Bossart, sec gen. *Triennial. Next Jun 2000, entries by 1 Mar 2000. Ages 32 and under. Entry fee, SFR 300. First prize, SFR 30,000, concert engagements, CD recording and management service.*

Gina Bachauer International Piano Competition. PO Box 11664, Salt Lake City, UT 84147, USA *tel:* +1 801 521 9200 *fax:* +1 801 521 9202. Paul C Pollei, founder and artistic dir; William E Gaylord, gen mgr. *Quadrennial. Next 1998 in Switzerland. Age 18-32. Artists selected at live international auditions during 1997. Also junior competition (age 11-18).*

International Tibor Varga Violin Competition. Association du Festival Tibor Varga, Case Postale 954, CH-1951 Sion, Switzerland *tel:* +41 27 23 43 17 *fax:* +41 27 23 46 62. *Annual. Aug, applications by May. Application fee SFR 100. Age limit 15-32. First prize SFR 10,000.*

Swiss Organ Competition. Place du Prieur, CH-1323 Romainmôtier, Switzerland *tel:* +41 24 531718 *fax:* +41 24 531150. Marisa Aubert. *Sep-Oct, applications by mid-May. No age limit. Repertoire changes every year. First prize SFR 4000.*

USA

Barlow International Competition. Harris Fine Arts Center, Brigham Young University, Provo, UT 84602, USA *tel:* +1 801 378 3323 *fax:* +1 801 378 5278. M Bradshaw, admin. *Entries by 1 Jul annually. No age limit. Different inst each year.*

Carmel Chamber Music Competition. PO Box 6283, Carmel, CA 93921, USA *tel:* +1 408 624 9541 *fax:* +1 408 625 6927. Amy Anderson, president; Melvin Kline, chmn. *2-3 May 1998, entries by 19 Mar. Open to non-professional chmbr ens of 3-6 players, average age under 26. Cash prizes $1250-2500.*

Center for Contemporary Opera International Opera Singers Competition. PO Box 1350, Gracie Sta, New York, NY 10028-0010, USA *tel:* +1 212 308 6728 *fax:* +1 212 308 6744 *email:* conopera @mindspring.com. Richard Marshall, dir. *Sep-Oct 1998, entries postmarked no later than 15 May. To encourage singers to explore contemporary repertory. Open to all singers who have not attained international careers. Entry fee $35. First prize $2000 and a New York recital.*

Chamber Music America Awards for Excellence in Chamber Music Teaching. 305 Seventh Av 5th Floor, New York, NY 10001-6008, USA *tel:* +1 212 242 2022 *fax:* +1 212 242 7955. Dean Stein, exec dir. *$1000 cash award granted to an individual teacher in charge of a chmbr mus programme for students aged 6-18. Applications by 1 Dec 1997.*

Chamber Music America Commissioning Program. 305 Seventh Av, 5th Floor, New York, NY 10001-6008, USA *tel:* +1 212 242 2022 *fax:* +1 212 242 7955. Dean Stein, exec dir. *Late spring 1998. Awards to enrich the chmbr mus repertoire and encourage partnerships among ens, composers and insts, made on basis of artistic excellence and demonstrated commitment to the performance of contemporary mus. Open to members of Chamber Music America. Composers must be American citizens or permanent residents of the USA.*

Chopin Foundation of the United States. 1440 79 St, Causeway, Suite 117, Miami, FL 33141, USA *tel:* +1 305 868 0624 *fax:* +1 305 865 5150. Blanka A Rosenstiel, president. *Quinquennial. Next 2000. Held in advance of the International Chopin Competition in Warsaw. Open to American pianists born between 1 Oct 1970 and 1 Oct 1982. Automatic acceptance at International Chopin Piano Competition in Warsaw, $75,000 in cash prizes and concert engagements.*

Cleveland International Piano Competition. c/o The Cleveland Institute of Music, 11021 E Boulevard, Cleveland, OH 44106, USA *tel:* +1 216 791 5000 *fax:* +1 216 791 3063. *Biennial. Age limit 17-35. First prize $12,000.*

Coleman Chamber Ensemble Competition. 202 S Lake Av, No 201, Pasadena, CA 91101, USA *tel:* +1 626 793 4191 *fax:* +1 626 787 1294 *email:* krfccma@aol.com. Kathy Freedland, exec dir. *25 Apr 1998, applications by 26 Feb. Open to non-professional chmbr ens (str, wind and br) under the direction of a coach. Average age of players in each ens must be under 26. Total of $11,200 awarded.*

Concert Artists Guild Competition. 850 7th Av, Suite 1205, New York, NY 10019, USA *tel:* +1 212 333 5200 *fax:* +1 212 977 7149 *email:* caguild@aol.com; http://www.concertartists.org. Robert Besen, associate dir. *9-17 Feb 1998, applications by 31 Oct 1997. Suggested age limit 35. Open to all solo insts, chmbr groups and singers. First prize includes management by CAG, New York recital, other prizes include recording contracts and engagements.*

East and West Artists International Auditions for New York Debut. 310 Riverside Dr, Suite 313, New York, NY 10025-4101, USA *tel:* +1 212 222 2433 *also fax.* Adolovni Acosta, exec dir; Bo Lawergren, artistic dir. *23-25 Oct 1998, entries by 1 Jun. Insts, singers, ens (up to 5 members) who have not given a New York debut recital, 18 yrs and over. Prize, fully sponsored solo debut in Weill Recital Hall at Carnegie Hall.*

Elizabeth Harper Vaughn Concerto Competition. 1200 E Center St, Kingsport, TN 37660, USA *tel:* +1 423 392 8423 *fax:* +1 423 392 8426. Debbie Robinson, mgr. *Mar, entries by Dec. To promote the performance of classical mus by young artists. Open to those aged 26 and under. Entry fee $20. First prize $1000 and concert with the Kingsport Symphony Orchestra.*

Florida Grand Opera Young Artist and Technical Apprentice Programs. 1200 Coral Way, Miami, FL 33145-2980, USA *tel:* +1 305 854 1643 *fax:* +1 305 856 1042 *email:* http://www.fgo.org. Mark Graf, dir. *Eight month programme in an environment of continuous performing and intensive training. 10 selected vocalists and an accompanist/coach given chance to perform in Florida Grand Opera Season; production and technical assistants will be assigned as assistants to the Opera's technical staff. Entry fee $10. Entries by Aug (technical and design), Oct (singers and accompanists/coaches). Auditions Dec for following season.*

Fort Smith Symphony Association Young Artist Competition. PO Box 3151, Fort Smith, AR 72913, USA *tel:* +1 501 452 7575 *fax:* +1 501 452 8985. Carol Sue Wooten, exec dir. *Feb, entries by Dec. For performers of str, br and w/wind aged 18 yrs or under on 1 Apr of the contest yr. First prize $1000 and concert.*

Friedrich Schorr Memorial Performance Prize in Voice. 110 S Madison St, Adrian, MI 49221-2575, USA *tel:* +1 517 264 3121 *fax:* +1 517 265 3607. David Katz, artistic dir. *Nov 1998, applications by 15 Sep. To choose professional singing artists to take lead roles in productions of opera and oratorio performances. Open to all professional singers. $15,000 of prizes in form of stipends and performances.*

George London Foundation for Singers Awards. 515 East 79th St, Suite 7B, New York, NY 10021, USA *tel:* +1 212 772 2768 *also fax.* Nora London, president. *Annual. 16-19 Mar 1998, entries by 15 Jan. To identify especially talented singers, aged 35 and under, in the early stage of their careers. Open to American and Canadian opera singers who have performed at least one role with a professional company and are contracted for at least one more professional engagement. Contestants are required to perform four arias in contrasting styles and languages. Five prizes of $5000 and five of $1000.*

Heida Hermanns International Young Artists Competition. 17 Morningside Drive South, Westport, CT 06880, USA *tel:* +1 203 227 8998 *also fax.* Jeanne Kimball; Eve Dillingham. *Dec, entries by Oct. Open to solo singers and solo string players not under professional management. Age limit: 19-33 for singers, 18-30 for string players. First prize in each category $2000.*

Irving M Klein International String Competition. 1600 Holloway Av, Mus Dept, San Francisco State Univ, San Francisco, CA 94132, USA *tel:* +1 415 338 7618 *fax:* +1 415 338 6159 *email:* srhall@sfsu.edu. M Klein, dir; S Hall, competition liaison. *13-14 Jun 1998, entries by 15 Feb. Age range 15-23. First prize $8000 and performances.*

Irving S Gilmore International Keyboard Festival. Kalamazoo Center, 100 West Michigan Av, Kalamazoo MI 49007, USA *tel:* +1 616 342 1166 *fax:* +1 616 342 0968. Irma Vallecillo, artistic dir. *Competition renowned for its non-competitive, anonymous selection process. The jury is able to make a careful and detailed appraisal of performance skills without candidates knowing of their participation. The focus of evaluation is changed from the artificial pressure of a competition to varied performances in natural concert settings.*

Ivo Pogorelich International Solo Piano Competition (USA). c/o Kantor Concert Management, 67 Teignmouth Rd, London NW2 4EA, UK *tel:* +44 181 208 2480 *fax:* +44 181 208 2490. Ivo Pogorelich, artistic dir. *Dec (not 1998). Open to prize winners and finalists in at least one previous international competition, with letters of recommendation. Pianists must be over 21 yrs old and submit tape or CD. First prize $100,000.*

Joanna Hodges International Piano Competition. College of the Desert, 43-500 Monterey Av, Palm Desert, California 92260, USA *tel:* +1 760 773 2575 *fax:* +1 760 776 7310. Terri Fleck, admin dir. *Next spring 1999, entry forms available winter 1998. Various categories for pianists aged 35 and under. Major prizes include debuts in New York, London, Rome and Vienna.*

Kingsville International Young Performers' Competition. PO Box 2873, Kingsville, TX 78363, USA *tel:* +1 512 5922374. J D Tryer, dir. *2-4 Apr 1998, entries by 15 Jan. Max age 25 yrs. Pno, str, wind, perc. First prize $6000 and a performance with Corpus Christi Symphony Orchestra; chmbr performance with Winter Festival de San Miguel de Allende.*

Kosciuszko Foundation Chopin Piano Competition. 15 E 65 St, New York, NY 10021-6595, USA *tel:* +1 212 734 2130 *fax:* +1 212 628 4552

email: thekf@aol.com. Thomas Pniewski, dir of cultural affairs. *2-4 Apr 1998, applications by 9 Mar. To encourage highly talented musicians to study and play the works of Chopin and other Polish composers. Open to US citizens, permanent residents or full-time foreign students with valid visa, aged 16-22. First prize $2500.*

Kurt Weill Prize. The Kurt Weill Foundation for Music, 7 East 20th St, New York, NY 10003-1106, USA *tel:* +1 212 505 5240 *fax:* +1 212 353 9663 *email:* kwf@panix.com; http://www.kwf.org. *Awarded for distinguished scholarship in 20th C music theatre, including opera. Prize $2500.*

Loren L Zachary Society National Vocal Competition for Young Opera Singers. 2250 Gloaming Way, Beverly Hills, CA 90210, USA *tel:* +1 310 276 2731 *fax:* +1 310 275 8245. Nedra Zachary, dir. *2-6 Mar (New York) and Apr-Jun (Los Angeles), applications by Jan and Apr respectively. To obtain contracts for leading roles in European opera houses. Open to female singers aged 21-33, male singers aged 21-35 ready to pursue a professional operatic career. First prize $10,000 and a round-trip flight to Europe for auditioning purposes.*

Luciano Pavarotti International Voice Competition. 1616 Walnut St, Suite 2115, Philadelphia, PA 19103, USA *tel:* +1 215 545 1121 *fax:* +1 215 545 1881. Jane Grey Nemeth, dir. *Triennial. Age limit 35 (male), 33 (female). Prizes include a performance with Luciano Pavarotti.*

MacAllister Award for Opera Singers. Indiana Opera Theatre, 7515 E 30, PO Box 1941, Indianapolis, IN 46206, USA *tel:* +1 317 253 1001 *fax:* +1 317 253 2008 *email:* http://www.iquest.net/~opera/. Elaine Morgan Bookwater, gen dir. *Annual. Aug. US citizens only. Age limit: 25 for college competition, 36 for professionals. First prize $2500 for college competition, $10,000 for professionals. To provide non-restricted funds for opera artists to pursue their careers.*

Marguerite McCammon Voice Competition. Opera Guild of Fort Worth, PO Box 100381, Fort Worth TX 76185-0381, USA *tel:* +1 817 924 1536 *fax:* +1 817 924 1886. Pat Crowley, chmn. *Biennial, next 13 Mar 1999. Open to any singer aged 21-32 working towards a professional opera career. First prize min $3,000.*

Marian Anderson Award. Marian Anderson Foundation Inc, 1 Lakeside Rd, Danbury, CT 06811, USA *tel:* +1 203 744 4454 *fax:* +1 203 748 3029. June Goodman, admin. *To recognise and advance careers of talented singers of concert and opera. US citizens by recommendation only. First prize $20,000.*

Missouri Southern International Piano Competition. Missouri Southern State College, 3950 E Newman Rd, Joplin, MO 64801-1595, USA *tel:* +1 417 625 9755 *fax:* +1 417 625 9798 *email:* burns01@vm.mssc.edu. Vivian León, dir; Fran Burns, sec. *Biennial. Next 21-25 Apr 1998, entries by 12 Jan. Age limit: 17 jnr division, 18-30 snr division. Overseas students may apply for travel assistance. First prize snr division, $8000 and Carnegie Hall recital debut. First prize jnr division, $2000.*

Murray Dranoff International Two Piano Competition. Murray Dranoff Foundation, 999 NE 72nd Street, Miami, Florida 33138, USA *tel:* +1 305 758 8700 *fax:* +1 305 757 0686. Loretta Dranoff, admin dir. *Biennial. Next 16-22 Dec 1997, entries by 30 Jul. Age 18-35. First prize $10,000.*

Naftzger Young Artists Auditions and Music Awards. Wichita Symphony Society, 225 W Douglas, Suite 207, Wichita, KS 67202, USA *tel:* +1 316 267 5259 *fax:* +1 316 267 1937 *email:* symphony@louverture.com; http://www.wso.org. Anne Marie Brown, operations mgr. *1-2 May 1998, applications by 6 Mar. For pno, inst and voice. Open to student residents of Kansas, Oklahoma, Missouri and non-residents enrolled in a college, university or conservatory in Kansas, Oklahoma or Missouri and working towards a music degree. Age Limit: 20-28 for voice, 18-26 for other insts. First prize $5000. Each division prize $2000.*

Opera at Florham Guild Vocal Competition. PO Box 343, Convent Station, NJ 07961, USA *tel:* +1 201 443 8620. Theresa Di Paulo, chmn. *18 Apr 1998, entries by 28 Feb. Aims to support the growth of young operatic singers by offering prizes and an opportunity to appear in recital or in one of the company's productions. First prize $3000.*

Oratorio Society of New York Solo Competition. Carnegie Hall Suite 504, 881 Seventh Av, New York, NY 10019, USA *tel:* +1 212 247 4199. Janet Plucknett, chmn. *Apr, applications by Feb. To seek out new talent in oratorio solo singing and give a debut platform for competition winners. Open to all singers under 40 yrs; must not have made formal New York Oratorio debut in reviewed New York concert. Cash prizes and performance contracts.*

Palm Beach Invitational International Piano Competition. PO Box 3094, Palm Beach, FL 33480-1294, USA *tel:* +1 407 8338817 *fax:* +1 407 8336735. John W Bryan, dir and press offr. *Age limit 39. By invitation only. No repertory requirements; 60 min free choice recital.*

Palm Beach Opera Vocal Competition. 415 S Olive Av, West Palm Beach, FL 33401, USA *tel:* +1 407 833 8277 *fax:* +1 407 883 8294. Herbert Benn, gen dir; Anton Guadagno, artistic dir. *Apr, entries by Feb. Open to singers aged 18-23 (jnr division), 24-30 (advance division). First prize $3000 (jnr), $6000 (snr). Total cash prizes of over $41,000.*

Pro Musicis International Award. 140 W 79 St, No 9F, New York, NY 10024, USA *tel:* +1 212 787 0993 *fax:* +1 212 362 0352. John E Haag, exec dir. *Spring 1998, entries by 1 Mar. Career development through major recitals in the US, France, Italy and Hong Kong for concert soloists prepared to perform for the aged, handicapped, infirm and imprisoned. Open to concert soloists of exceptional talent willing to repeat each of their sponsored recitals in Community Service Concerts for individuals in institutions. Eligible insts rotate. Hp, hpd, w/wind, voice (1998); gui, pno, str (1999). Prizes are major recitals in New York, Los Angeles, Boston, Paris, Rome and Hong Kong.*

Queens Opera Vocal Competition. 14 Major Dr, Sayreville, NJ 08872, USA *tel:* +1 908 390 9472 *fax:* +1 908 390 9473. Joe Messina, gen dir. *First prize $4000 in value.*

Raissa Tselentis Memorial Johann Sebastian Bach International Competitions. 1211 Pontomac St NW, Washington DC 20007, USA *tel:* +1 202 338 1111. Paul A Chadwell, dir. *To stimulate interest in the study and performance of works by J S Bach. Open to ages 20-40. Cash awards and concert appearances. Three first prizes of $3000 each.*

San Antonio International Piano Competition. PO Box 39636, San Antonio, TX 78218, USA *tel:* +1 210 655 0766 *fax:* +1 210 822 6056. Virginia Lawrence. *Pno. Triennial. Next autumn 2000, entries by spring. $50 registration fee. Age 20-32 at date of competition. First prize $10,000.*

Sorantin Young Artists Award. PO Box 5922, San Angelo, TX 76902, USA *tel:* +1 915 658 5877. Gene Smith, mgr dir. *Nov, entries by Oct. For insts aged under 28 and vocalists aged under 31. First prize $3000.*

Stefan and Wanda Wilk Prizes for Research in Polish Music. c/o Polish Music Reference Center, University of Southern California, Los Angeles, CA 90089-0851, USA *tel:* +1 213 740 9369 *fax:* +1 213 740 3217 *email:* polmusic@usc.edu; http://www.usc.edu/go/polish_music/. Maria Anna Harley, dir, PMRC. *Entries by 30 Sep annually for decision by 30 Dec. For the best unpublished papers reflecting original research in the mus of Poland; to stimulate research on Polish mus in academic circles outside Poland. No previously published essay may be submitted. First prize $1000 and publication online. Student prize $500 and publication.*

University of Maryland International William Kapell Piano Competition. University of Maryland, The Rossborough Festival, 4321 Hartwick Rd, Suite 220, College Park, MD 20740, USA *tel:* +1 301 403 8370 *fax:* +1 301 403 8375 *email:* gmoquin@umdacc.umd.edu. George Moquin, exec dir. *Biennial. 16-25 Jul 1998, applications by 15 Mar. Age limit 18-33. Finals with Baltimore Symphony Orchestra. First prize $20,000 and engagements including recital in Alice Tully Hall, Lincoln Center, New York.*

University of Maryland Leonard Rose Cello Competition. University of Maryland, The Rossborough Festival, 4321 Hartwick Rd, Suite 220, College Park, MD 20740, USA *tel:* +1 301 403 8370 *fax:* +1 301 403 8375 *email:* gmoquin@umdacc.umd.edu. George Moquin, exec dir. *Quadrennial. Next in 2001, entries by 15 Mar. Age limit 18-30. $50,000 in cash awards. Finals with Baltimore Symphony Orchestra. First prize $20,000 and engagements.*

University of Maryland Marian Anderson International Vocal Arts Competition. University of Maryland, The Rossborough Festival, 4321 Hartwick Rd, Suite 220, College Park, MD 20740, USA *tel:* +1 301 403 8370 *fax:* +1 301 403 8375 *email:* gmoquin@umdacc.umd.edu. George Moquin, exec dir. *Quadrennial. Next 15-24 Jul 1999, applications by 15 Mar. Age limit 21-39. Open to all singers regardless of race, color, gender or national origin. First prize $20,000 and engagements including recital in Alice Tully Hall, Lincoln Center, New York.*

USA International Harp Competition. PO Box 2718, Bloomington, IN 47402, USA *tel:* +1 812 336 7941 *also fax; email:* lzachry@indiana.edu. Lauren Zachry, executive dir. *Triennial. Next 5-14 Jul 1998, applications by 1 Mar. Max age 32. First prize, Lyon and Healey concert grand harp, $5000 and New York debut recital at Alice Tully Hall.*

Van Cliburn International Piano Competition. 2525 Ridgmar Blvd, Suite 307, Fort Worth, Texas 76116, USA *tel:* +1 817 738 6536 *fax:* +1 817 738 6534 *email:* cliburn@startext.net. Richard Rodzinski, exec dir. *Quadrennial. Age 18-30. First prize $20,000.*

Walter W Naumburg Foundation International Competition. 60 Lincoln Center Plaza, New York, NY 10023-6588, USA *tel:* +1 212 8741150 *fax:* +1 212 7240263. Lucy Rowan Mann. *May 1998, applications by 3 Jan. Violin. Auditions Mar-May. Age limit 17-33. First prize $5000 and concerts. Application forms on application with SAE.*

Washington International Competition. 7800 Mistic View Court, Derwood, MD 20855, USA *tel:* +1 301 869 5240. Rosemarie Houghton, chmn. *Mar, applications by Dec. Pianists age 18-32. First prize $7000.*

Young Concert Artists International Auditions. 250 W 57 St, New York, NY 10019, USA *tel:* +1 212 307 6655 *fax:* +1 212 581 8894 *email:* yca@yca.org; http://www.yca.org. Susan Wadsworth, dir. *18 Jan 1998. Preliminaries: Leipzig 8-13 Sep 1997 (applications by 20 Jun); New York 7 Nov-5 Dec 1997 (applications by 15 Oct). Semi-finals, 13-15 Jan in New York. To discover and launch the US careers of exceptional young solo musicians, string quartets and singers. Winners are presented in recital in New York and Washington, and given all management services, including concert engagements across the US and all publicity materials.*

Competitions for Composers

Argentina

Alberto Ginastera Musical Composers Competition. Marcelo T de Alvear 2371-5D, 1122 Buenos Aires, Argentina *tel:* +54 1 822 3551 *fax:* +54 1 821 2255. *Oct, entries by Aug. Composition for solo gui and orch of 17-22 mins duration. Max age 45. $15,000 prize and first performance in Argentina.*

Austria

International Mozart Competition. Mirabellplatz 1, A-5020 Salzburg, Austria *tel:* +43 662 88908 203 *fax:* +43 662 88908 55. Klaus Ager; Ulrike Godler, gen sec. *Quadrennial. Next 8-22 Jan 1999, applications by 30 Sep 1997. Composers born after 30 Sep 1962. Four prizes of ATS 50,000.*

Prix Ars Electronica. ORF/Landesstudio Oberösterreich, Europlatz 3, A-4010 Linz, Austria *tel:* +43 732 6900 227 *fax:* +43 732 6900 270 *email:* info@prixars.orf.at; http://prixars.orf.at. Wolfgang Winkler. *Annual. Festival Sep 1998, applications by 30 Apr. Competition for composition of electronic music. First prize, Golden Nica Award, ATS 150,000, two distinctions, ATS 50,000.*

Third Competition for Contemporary Music. Wiener Sommer-Seminar Für neue Musik, Postfach 345, 1061 Wien, Austria *tel:* +44 222 597 1292. Konrad Muselak. *31 Mar 1998. In association with the Vienna Summer-Seminar, works in contemporary style for accordion, cembalo, flute, guitar, mandolin, oboe (also oboe d'amore, English horn), piano, solo or ensemble (in free combination) for a duration of max 10 mins. For composers of any age and nationality. Entry fee: ATS 500 per work.*

Vienna International Composition Competition. c/o Casinos Austria, Dr-Karl-Lueger-Ring 14, A-1015 Wien, Austria *tel:* +43 1 534 4068 *fax:* +43 1 534 4034. Gerhard Skoff, dir. *Next deadline 15 Apr 1998 for 1999 competition. Different theme for competition each yr. 1999 orch work with vocal solo or soli and/or choir (applications by 15 Apr 1998); 2000 children's chmbr opera (excerpts by 15 Apr 1998, completed works*

by 30 Sep 1999). *Applicants must be aged 40 or under, and works must have been written no earlier than four years before the competition deadline. Prize: ATS 300,000-400,000.*

Vienna Modern Masters Orchestral Recording Award. Margaretenstr 125/15, A-1050 Wien, Austria *tel:* +43 545 1778 *fax:* +43 544 0785 *email:* vmmsmith@ping.at. Clyde A Smith, president. *Biennial. Next 1998, entries by 15 Dec 1998. Winning work recorded and issued internationally on a Vienna Modern Masters CD, plus 100 free CDs to composer.*

Belgium

Queen Elisabeth International Music Competition - Composition. 20 Rue aux Laines, B-1000 Bruxelles, Belgium *tel:* +32 2 513 0099 *fax:* +32 2 514 3297. *May 1997, entries by 6 Jan. No age limit. First prize 200,000 BF.*

Canada

du Maurier New Music Festival Canadian Composers Competition. 555 Main St, Ste 101, Winnipeg, MB R3B 1C3, Canada *tel:* +1 204 949 3950 *fax:* +1 204 956 4271. Bramwell Tovey, artistic dir; Annemarie Petrov, admin. *For Canadian citizens, no age restrictions, works must be unpublished and not performed professionally. First prize $8000 and a $6000 commission.*

The Nouvel Ensemble Moderne Forum 98. 200 avenue Vincent-d'Indy, CP 6128, Succursale Centre-ville, Montréal, Quèbec H3C 3J7, Canada *tel:* +1 514 3435962 *fax:* +1 514 3432443 *email:* carrieann@magellan. umontreal.ca. Lorraine Vaillancourt, artistic dir. *Nov 1998, applications by 31 Oct 1997. Composers under 30 may submit 2 scores: the first, a work of their choice, the second a work for chmbr orch or large ens. Seven chosen composers will be invited to a w/shop with the NEM in Montreal and will submit a piece of 15-20 minutes duration for 15 musicians in Nov. Prizes include concert and recording engagements.*

Republic of China

International Competition of Piano Works in the Chinese Style. Music Department, China Radio International, 2 Fuxingmenwai Av, Beijing 100866, PR China *tel:* +86 10 6851 3365/6809 2509 *fax:* +86 10 6851 3174. An Xiaoyu; Chang Haikuan. *Dec 1997, entries by Oct. Chinese-style piano solo.*

Czech Republic

International Composers' Competition - Jihlava 1998. Ipos-Artama, Kresomyslova 7, 140 16 Praha 4, Nusle, Czech Republic. *Compositions for womens' and mixed chamber choirs, a capella or maximum 3 instrument accompaniment. Applications by 30 Nov 1997. Duration 3-4 minutes. Compositions will be presented at Festival of Choral Art 1998. Total prize money: Kc 15,000.*

International Competition for Blind and Partially Sighted Composers. SONS - Czech Blind United, Karlinské nám 12, CZ-186 03 Praha 8, Czech Republic *tel:* +420 2 2481 7393 *fax:* +420 2 2481 8398 *email:* sons_zahrbraillnet.cz. Václav Polásek, chief offr. *Triennial. Next 1999, entries by 15 Oct 1999. First prize approximately Kc 10,000.*

Prague Spring International Composers' Competition. Prague Spring, Hellichova 18, CZ-11800 Praha 1, Czech Republic *tel:* +42 2 533474 *fax:* +42 2 536040. *Irregular competition. Works for chmbr orch.*

Denmark

Musical of the Year. Danmarks Radio, TV-Provins, Olof Palmes Allé 10-12, DK-8200 Aarhus N, Denmark *tel:* +45 87 39 71 11 *fax:* +45 87 39 71 04. Preben Moerkbak, exec producer. *Finals Sep. Competition for a musical drama, 2 complete scenes, min 8 songs, all texts in English. First prize DEM 100,000.*

Thad Jones Competition. Danmarks, Radio P2 Musik, DK-1999 Frederiksberg C., Denmark *tel:* +45 35 20 64 08 *fax:* +45 35 20 61 28. *International competition for jazz composers and arrangers born after 1 Jun 1965.*

France

Concours de Création Radiophonique Communiqué. La Muse en Circuit, 16-18 Rue Marcelin-Berthelot, 94140 Alfortville, France *tel:* +33 43 78 80 80 *fax:* +33 43 68 25 52.

Florilège Vocal de Tours Composition Competition. Rue des Minimes, BP 1452, F-37014 Tours Cedex, France *tel:* +33 2 47 21 65 26 *fax:* +33 2 47 21 67 71. Pierre-Marie Dizier. *29 May 1998, entries by Mar. Compositions for choir a cappella. First prize 10,000 FF.*

International Celtic Harp Festival of Dinan. La Galerie, F-22490 Plouër, France *tel:* +33 96 86 84 94 *fax:* +33 96 86 89 40. *Jul, entries by Apr. Minimum age 17. Prizes for improvisation and composition.*

International Composition Competition of the Atelier Musique. Atelier Musique de Ville d'Avray, 10 Rue de Marnes, F-92410 Ville d'Avray, France *tel:* +33 1 47 50 44 28 *fax:* +33 1 47 50 53 90. J Louis Petit. *For choirs and brass quintet. No age limit. Application fee 300 FF. First prize 10,000 FF*

International Composition Competition of the City of Le Havre. BP 5045, F-76071 Le Havre Cedex, France *tel:* +33 35 24 10 04 *fax:* +33 35 24 10 13. Philippe Langlet, chief offr. *Jul. For symphonic and jazz big band. 200,000 FF given in prizes.*

International Electroacoustic Music Competition. Institut International du Musique Electroacoustique, Place André Malraux, BP 39, F-18000 Bourges Cedex, France *tel:* +33 248 20 41 87 *fax:* +33 248 20 45 51 *email:* agmeblo@calsacom.fr. Françoise Barriere. *Jun, entries by 5 May.*

International Rostrum of Composers. International Music Council, UNESCO, 1 Rue Miollis, F-75732 Paris Cedex 15, France *tel:* +33 1 45 68 25 50 *fax:* +33 1 43 06 87 98 *email:* imc_cim@compuserve.com. Guy Huot, sec. *Annual. May-Jun. Organised by the International Music Council with the support of UNESCO. Radio music producers worldwide select contemporary works for broadcasting. The aim is to foster the exchange of performance of contemporary music between broadcasting organisations. Entries to be submitted by national broadcasting organisations only.*

Musical Composition Competition. Secrétariat, 2d Rue Isenbart, F-25000 Besancon, France *tel:* +33 381 80 73 26 *fax:* +33 381 80 46 36. Yvette Cussey, admin mgr. *Sep 1998, applications by 30 Jun 1998. Professional composers aged under 40. Symphonic works. Entry fee: 600 FF. First prize: 25,000 FF.*

Germany

Blaue Brücke. Dresdner Zentrum für zeitgenössische Muzik, Schevenstrasse 17, D-01326 Dresden, Germany. U. Zimmermann. *Competition for composers and interpreters. Selected projects should have their premieres during the Dresden Days of Contemporary Music Festival in 1999. Prize of max DM 30,000.*

International Competition for Women Composers. GEDOK, Siegstrasse 20, D-68167 Mannheim, Germany *tel:* +49 6213 4201 *also fax.* Gisela Krauss.

Greece

Dimitris Mitropoulos International Competition. 18 Alex Soutsou, GR-10671 Athens, Greece *tel:* +30 1 362 7412 *fax:* +30 1 362 1477. Traute Lutz, chief offr. *Annual. Nov 1998, applictions by 30 Apr. 1998 conducting (conductors should have been born after 30 Apr 1963). 1999 composition. First prize 5,000,000 Drachmas and concert engagements.*

Israel

Leonard Bernstein Jerusalem International Music Competitions. 11 Rivka St, POB 10185, Jerusalem, Israel *tel:* +972 2 6735032 *fax:* +972 2 6716380 *email:* berncomp@netvision.net.il. Leor Segal, exec dir. *Next 2000. Three year cycle: conductors, singers and composers. Open to any composers aged 22-50. Preliminary rounds in 5 locations around the world. Finals Oct in Jerusalem, entries by 1 Mar. First prize $20,000, engagements and recording opportunities.*

Italy

Alfred Casella International Composition Contest. Accademia Musicale Chigiana, Via di Città 89, I-53100 Siena, Italy *tel:* +39 577 46152 *fax:* +39 577 288124. *Entries by Oct. No age limit. First prize 5,000,000 lire.*

The Ennio Porrino International Piano and Composition Competition. Associazione Amici della Musica di Cagliari, Casella Postale 118, 09100 Cagliari, Italy *tel:* +39 70 42280. *Entries by October for announcement in December.*

European International Competition for Composers (Italy). 226 E Second St, Suite 5D, NYC, NY 10009, USA *tel:* +1 212 387 0111 *fax:* +1 212 388 0102. Salvatore Moltisanti, chmn; Lois Ash, asst dir. *Annual. Jun-Jul, entries by end Mar. No age limit, all nationalities. Prizes totalling $15,000.*

Gino Continelli International Competition for Composition. Segreteria dell'Accademia Filarmonica, via Giacinto 4, 98122 Messina, Italy *tel:* +39 90 343420 *fax:* +39 90 46432. *Composition competition for those aged 40 and under. Composition for symphony orchestra with or without soloist for duration of not more than 15 mins. Applications by September. First prize: 5,000,000 lire.*

Guido d'Arezzo International Composition Competition. Fondazione Guido d'Arezzo, Corso Italia 102, I-52100 Arezzo, Italy *tel:* +39 575 356203 *fax:* +39 575 324735 *email:* fondguid@krenet.it; http://www.kre net.it/unoinfo/fondguid. Remo Manganelli, commissioner. *Jun 1998, entries by 15 Mar. Open to composers of all nationalities and ages. Composition for choir (mixed, male, female or vocal ens, up to a max of 16 voices) and for choir with insts (1 or more insts up to a max of a model chmbr orch). First prize 10,000,000 lire.*

International Competition for Original Composition for Band. Segretaria Organizzativa, Via Laudati 4, I-06073 Corciano PG, Italy *tel:* +39 75 6979109 *also fax.* Antonio Pagana, president; Antonietta Trombetta, sec. *Entries by Jul. Compositions may be based on any theme and musical form, with or without inst or vocal soloists. First prize 5,000,000 lire.*

International Competition for Symphonic Composition. Palazzo Municipale, Piazza dell'Unità d'Italia 4, I-34121 Trieste, Italy *tel:* +39 40 368312/366030 *fax:* +39 40 675 4303. *Biennial. No age limit. First prize 10,000,000 lire.*

International Goffredo Petrassi Competition for Composers. c/o Fondazione Arturo Toscanini, Via G Tartini n 13, I-43100 Parma, Italy *tel:* +39 521 274417/27 *fax:* +39 521 272134 *email:* fondazione@ toscanini.dsnet.it; http://www.fondazione.toscanini.it. Gianni Baratta, mgr. *Biennial. Next Sep 2000, entries by 31 May. No age limit. For unpublished symphonic composition. First prize 10,000,000 lire.*

International Competition of Classical Guitar Composition. Piazza Garibaldi, 16-15100 Alessandria, Italy *tel:* +39 131 25 12 07 *fax:* +39 131 23 55 07 *email:* pittalug@email.alessandria.alpcom.it. Marcello Pittaluga, sec; Micaela Pittaluga, president. *25 Sep 1998, applications by 15 Jul. First prize 3,000,000 lire.*

International Mario Bernardo Angelo-Comneno Composition Competition. Accademia Angelica, Constantiniana di lettre, arti e scienze, Via delle Balduina 75, 00136 Roma, Italy *tel:* +39 6 35343557; +39 774 615465 *also fax.* Manuele Ferrari. *Nov 1998, applications by 15 Sep 1998. Composition for str quartet. First prize 3,500,000 lire.*

International New Chamber Opera Competition. Teatro Lirico Sperimentale di Spoleto, Piazza G Bovio 1, I-06049 Spoleto, Italy *tel:* +39 743 221645/220440 *fax:* +39 743 222930 *email:* teatrolirico@ mail.caribusiness.it; http://www.caribusiness.it/lirico. Claudio Lepore, mgr; Nadia Nigris, asst. *Next Mar 2000, entries by 31 Dec 1999. Open to composers of all nationalities, max age 35. For unpublished and unperformed chmbr operas with librettos in Italian, German, English,*

French or Spanish. Duration 45-60 mins. Prizes of performances in Spoleto and Ricordi publication.

Luigi Russolo International Competition for Young Composers of Analogic or Digital Electroacoustic Music. Fondazione Russolo-Pratella, Via G Bagaini 6, I-21100 Varese, Italy *tel:* +39 332 237245 *fax:* +39 332 280331. G Franco Maffina, president; Rossana Maggia, PR. *Annual. Sep. For analogic or digital electro-acoustic mus, electro-acoustic mus with insts or voice and electro-acoustic mus for the radio. Italian and foreign composers up to 35 yrs.*

Nuove Sincronie International Competition for Music Composition. The Secretary's Office, Associazione Nuove Sincronie, Via Cappuccini 8, I-20122 Milano, Italy *tel:* +39 2 7601 5954 *fax:* +39 2 7601 5970. *Entries by 31 Jul annually. Aged 45 and under. First prize 2,000,000 lire and publication of the work by Ricordi.*

Citta di Pescara International Competition of Composition. Kamerton Citta di Pescara 13, I-65131 Pescara Fontanelle, Italy. *Open to composers born after 31 Dec 1961. Aims to promote New Consonant Music and pedagogic music.*

Traiettorie Sonore International Composers Competition. v.le Varese 71/a, 22100 Como, Italy *tel:* +39 31 241365 *also fax. Established in 1995 for compositions for sop, cl and pno in various combinations. Winners pieces to be performed at Festival of 20th C Mus from Oct-Dec. Entries by September.*

Valentino Bucchi di Roma Capitale International Prize. Valentino Bucchi Foundation, Via Ubaldino Peruzzi 20, I-00139 Roma, Italy *tel:* +39 6 8720 0121/8713 1151 *fax:* +39 6 8713 1527. *Annual. 9-20 Nov 1998, applications by 30 Sep. Age 40 and under. Categories rotate: 1998 pno and 2 pnos in 20th C; 2000 db (performance and composition). First prize: 25,000,000 lire and publication.*

Japan

Irino Prize (International Composers' Competition). Irino Prize Foundation, 5-22-2 Matsubara, Setagaya-ku, Tokyo 156, Japan *tel:* +81 3 3323 0646 *fax:* +81 3 3325 5468. Reiko Takahashi Irino, president. *Jul 1998, entries by 30 Apr. Open to composers of any nationality under the age of 40. 1998 competition for orch composition. Prize 650,000 Yen. 1999 competition for chmbr mus. Prize 200,000 Yen.*

The Next Millennium Composition Award. Office of the Next Millenium Composition Award, Tokyo Opera City Cultural Foundation, PO Box 2502, 3-20-2 Nishi-Shinjuku-ku, Tokyo 163-14, Japan *tel:* +81 3 53530770 *fax:* +81 3 53530771. *30 May 1998 and Apr-May 1999, applications by Sep 1997 and 31 Mar 1998 respectively. Composers under age of 35 to submit orchestral works of 10-20 mins. First prize 3,000,000 yen and performance in the new Tokyo Opera City Concert Hall due to open in Sep 1997.*

Mexico

Competition in Music Composition through Algorithmic Models El Calleón del Ruido. Festival Callejon del Ruido, Escuela de Music, Universidad de Guanajuato, Paseo de la Presa 152, Guanajuato, Mexico *fax:* +52 473 25749. *Works must be composed with an algorithmic model. No age limit.*

Monaco

Prince Peter of Monaco Prize for Musical Composition. Centre Administratif, Rue Louis Notari 8, MC-98000, Monaco *tel:* +33 93 158 303 *fax:* +33 93 506 694. Rainier Rocchi, gen sec. *May 1998. Prize awarded to best musical composition of the year. First prize 100,000 FF.*

Netherlands

The International Gaudeamus Music Week. Gaudeamus Foundation, Swammerdamstraat 38, NL-1091 RV Amsterdam, Netherlands *tel:* +31 20 694 7349 *fax:* +31 20 694 7258 *email:* gaud@xs4all.nl. *Sep, entries by Jan. Works may already have been performed, but they must have been composed not more than three years ago. Compositions can be entered in the following categories: orchestra, choir and chamber music. First prize DFL 10,000.*

Nigeria

Nowoola International Composition/Interpreters Competition and Workshop. 32/34 Awoyokun Street, Via Ikorodu Road, Mushin, Lagos, Nigeria *tel:* +234 1 820206/825196. Nowoola Gbolahan Adbulrhapheev. *Nov, entries by Jun. Focuses on inter-relationship of composition between Africa and Europe. Open to composers and insts of all nationalities. First prize US$5000.*

Norway

Edward Grieg Memorial Competition for Young Composers. The Oslo Grieg Society, Gaustadveien 4b, N-0372 Oslo, Norway *tel:* +47 22 493630 *fax:* +47 22 492311 *email:* http://www.notam.uio.no/nmi/griegs.

Applications by Dec 1997. Write for information. First prize: 100,000 NKR.

Poland

International Witold Lutoslawski Composers' Competition. Warsaw Philharmonic, 5 Jasna Str, PL-00 950 Warsaw, Poland *tel:* +48 22 8265713 *fax:* +48 22 8265617 *email:* phil@pol.pl; http://phil.pol.pl/ rules.html. Katarzyna Andrzejowska, sec. *Next 1998, entries by 31 Dec 1997. Composition for symphony orch. No age limits. First prize PZL 3000.*

Kazimierz Serocki International Composers Competition. Polish Society for Contemporary Music, ISCM Polish Section, Ul Mazowiecka 11, PL-00 052 Warsaw, Poland *tel:* +48 22 8276981 *fax:* +48 22 8277804. Grazyna Dziura, exec sec. *Triennial. Applications by 5 Feb 1998. Composition for symphonic orch with solo instrument or voice of duration up to 30 minutes. Enrolment fee: US$20 per score.*

Spain

International Contest of Music Composition "Luis de Narváez". Fundación Caja de Granada, c/Reyes Católicos 51, 18001 Granada, Spain. *Open to composers of all nationalities to enter unlimited numbers of unpublished scores which have not been publicly performed.*

Premio International de Composició Musical Ciutat de Tarragona. Plaça de la Font 1, c/o Ajuntament de Tarragona, E-43003 Tarragona, Spain *tel:* +34 77 296121/294795 *fax:* +34 77 296118 *email:* ajtargna @tinet.fut.es; http://www.fut.es/~ajtargna. *Composition must be unpublished, unperformed, and not previously have been awarded a prize. First prize 1,000,000 ptas.*

Sweden

Stockholm Electronic Arts Award. EMS, Söder Mälarstrand 61, S-11825 Stockholm, Sweden *email:* pignon@oden.se; http://www.alognet.se/~ icem/seaa.html. Paul Pignon, competition producer. *Entries by Jun for jury decision in Sep. Competitors of any age/nationality to enter not more than 1 work. Tapes to be sent as 1/4 inch analogue tape or DAT cassette.*

Switzerland

Fribourg International Competition in Composition of Sacred Music. Fribourg Festival of Sacred Music, Case Postale 292, CH-1701 Fribourg, Switzerland *tel:* +41 26 322 4800 *fax:* +41 26 322 8331. *Biennial. Next 1999, entries by Aug. Any age and nationality.*

International Competition for Composers of Chamber Music. Kulturstiftung Winterthur, Kompositionswettbewerb, St Georgenplatz 2, Postfach, CH-8401 Winterhur, Switzerland. *Open to all composers. Unpublished pieces only.*

International Musical Composition Contest 'Queen Marie José'. Box 19 CH-1252, Meinier, Genève, Switzerland. *Biennial. Next Nov 1998, applications by 31 May. For concerted work for at least 2 solo insts (not voice), with chmbr or symph orch. First prize SFR 10,000.*

USA

ABA Ostwald Composition Contest. Harding Band Bldg, 1103 S, Sixth St, Champaign, IL 61820, USA *tel:* +1 217 333 3025. James Keene, chmn. *Biennial. 15 Nov 1998. To stimulate writing of important new compositions for band. Entry open to all except members of ABA. Works must be original, unpublished and composed within the last 2 yrs. First prize $5000 and $5000 commission.*

Biennial Competition for the AGO/ECS Publishing Award in Choral Composition. American Guild of Organists, 475 Riverside Dr, Suite 1260, NY 10115, USA *tel:* +1 212 870 2310 *fax:* +1 212 870 2163 *email:* info@agohg.org; http://www.agohg.org. *For unpublished work for SATB and org, duration 3-7 mins. $2000 of prizes, publication and performance.*

ALEA III International Composition Prize. Boston University School of Music, 855 Commonwealth Av, Boston, MA 02215, USA *tel:* +1 617 353 3340 *also fax.* Theodore Antoniou, mus dir. *Sep, entries by Mar. Max age 40. Only 1 score per composer. Works must be unpublished and must not have been publicly performed or broadcast before announcement of the prize. First prize $2500.*

The ALEA International Composition Prize. Boston University School for the Arts, Music Division, 855 Commonwealth Ave, Boston MA 02215, USA *tel:* +1 617 3533340. *A prize to promote and encourage the composition of new music. Several finalists to be chosen each year.*

ASCAP Foundation Grants to Young Composers. 1 Lincoln Plaza, New York, NY 10023, USA *tel:* +1 212 621 6327 *fax:* +1 212 595 3342. Frances Richard, dir of symphony and concert dept. *Entries by Mar. Citizens or permanent residents of the US aged under 30 on closing date. $20,000 given in prizes.*

Barlow International Competition. Barlow Endowment for Music Composition, Brigham Young University, Provo, Utah 84602, USA *tel:* +1 801 378 3323 *fax:* +1 801 378 5973. Merrill Bradshaw, exec dir. *1997 choral mus; 1998 large chmbr mus; 1999 orch mus; 2000 small chmbr mus. First prize $10,000 commission.*

Boston Chamber Ensemble Composition Contest. 65 Summer St, Hyde Park MA 02136, USA *tel:* +1 617 361 5975 *fax:* +1 617 364 1944 *email:* ebirdseye@earthlink.net. Elisa Birdseye. *Entries by 31 Jul. Compositions for chmbr ens or orch. Entry fee $15.*

Composers' Guild Annual Composition Contest. 40 North 100 W, Box 586, Farmington, UT 84025, USA *tel:* +1 801 451 2275. Ruth Gatrell, president. *Annual, entries by 31 Aug. No age limit except in young composers' category (aged under 18 on 31 Aug).*

Delius Composition Contest. c/o Jacksonville University, College of Fine Arts, Jacksonville, FL 32211, USA *tel:* +1 904 745 7371. William McNeiland. *First week in Mar, entries by 1 Oct. For vocal, keyboard and inst composition. First prize $500.*

Harvey Gaul Composition Contest. Duquesne University School of Music, Pittsburgh, PA 15282, USA *tel:* +1 412 261 0554 *fax:* +1 412 396 5479 *email:* tumielkozak@duq3.cc.duq.edu. David Stock, mus dir. *Biennial. Apr 1998, entries by 1 Apr. To encourage composition of new mus. Open to US composers. Entrance fee $15. First prize $3,000, commission and premiere.*

National Association of Composers USA Young Composers' Competition. 84 Cresta Verde Dr, Rolling Estates, CA 90274, USA *tel:* +1 310 541 8213 *fax:* + 310 373 3244. Marshall Bialosky, president. *Annual. Entries by 30 Oct. Open to ages 18-30. Cash prizes and performances in Los Angeles and New York. First prize $200 and performances.*

Pulitzer Prize in Music. Columbia University, 702 Journalism, New York, NY 10027, USA *tel:* +1 212 854 3841. Seymour Topping, admin. *Awarded for 'distinguished musical composition of significant dimension by an American that has had its first performance in the United States this year.' Works must premiere between 2 Mar 1997 and 1 Mar 1998. Entries by 1 Mar 1998.*

Rome Prize Fellowships of the American Academy in Rome. 7 E 60 St, New York, NY 10022-1001, USA *tel:* +1 212 751 7200 *fax:* +1 212 751 7220. *Entries by 15 Nov. For musical composition. Open to US citizens with a BA or equivalent. Prize is one year residency at the American Academy in Rome.*

University of Louisville Grawemeyer Award for Music Composition. School of Music, University of Louisville, Louisville, Kentucky 40292, USA *tel:* +1 502 852 6907 *fax:* +1 502 852 0520. *1998, entries by 26 Jan 1998. Compositions incorporating large musical genre: choral, orch, chmbr, electronic, opera etc. First prize $150,000 spread over 5 years. Entries must be sponsored by a professional musical organisation or individual; a composer may not therefore submit his/her own work. recent winners include Krzysztof Penderecki, Joan Tower, Witold Lutoslawski, Karel Husa, John Adams.*

Washington International Composition Competition. 6134 Tompkins Dr, McLean, VA 22101, USA *tel:* +1 703 356 1 958. E Lee Fairley, chmn. *Triennial. Age range 20-35. First prize $3,000.*

Young Composers Awards, National Guild of Community Schools of the Arts. PO Box 8018, Englewood, NJ 07631, USA *tel:* +1 201 871 3337 *fax:* +1 201 871 7639 *email:* almayadas@worldnet.att.net; http://www. natguild.org. Lolita Mayadas, exec dir. *Entries by 1 May 1998. To recognise young composers of talent and to encourage young people to write serious mus. Open to students 13-18 yrs, resident in the USA or Canada. First prize: $1000.*

Music Festivals

An asterisk denotes membership of the **European Festivals Association** (120b Rue de Lausanne, CH-1202 Genève, Switzerland *tel:* +41 22 73 22 803 *fax:* +41 22 73 84 012). Additional information on new music festivals may be obtained from the **International Society for Contemporary Music**, British Section, c/o SPNM, Francis House, Francis St, London SW1P 1DE, UK *tel:* +44 171 828 9696 *fax:* +44 171 931 9928, and from the **European Conference of Promoters of New Music**, c/o Gaudeamus Foundation, Swammerdamstraat 38, NL-1091 RV Amsterdam, Netherlands *tel:* +31 20 694 7349 *fax:* +31 20 694 7258.

Argentina

Encuentros. Fundacíon EIMC/SIMC, C Correos 1008, Correo Central, 1000 Buenos Aires, Argentina *fax:* +54 1 8221383. *Jul-Sep. Contemporary music.*

Australia

Adelaide Festival. GPO Box 1269, Adelaide 5001, Australia *tel:* +61 8 8226 8111 *fax:* +61 8 8226 8100. Nicholas Heyward, gen mgr; Robyn Archer, artistic dir. *Biennial. 27 Feb-15 Mar 1998, 3-19 Mar 2000. Opera, dance, mus, theatre, visual arts, literary.*

Australian Festival of Chamber Music. James Cook University of North Queensland, Townsville, Qld 4811, Australia *tel:* +61 77 815131 *fax:* +61 77 814411. Theodore Kuchar, artistic dir; Annika Shelley, gen mgr. *6-18 Jul 1998. Concert season of chmbr mus and chmbr mus seminar.*

Ballarat Opera Festival. Her Majesty's Theatre, PO Box 249, Ballarat, Victoria 3353, Australia *tel:* +61 53 335800/335888 *fax:* +61 53 335757.

Festival of Perth. The University of Western Australia, Nedlands, WA 6907, Australia *tel:* +61 9 386 7977 *fax:* +61 9 386 2763 *email:* festival@cyllene.uwa.edu.au. David Blenkinsop, dir; Henry Boston, gen mgr. *13 Feb-8 Mar 1998. Largest multi-arts festival in the southern hemisphere covers theatre, mus, dance, film, literature, street theatre and visual arts.*

International Music Festival Sydney. GPO 4992, Sydney 2001, Australia *tel:* +61 2 9929 5447 *fax:* +61 2 9929 5494. Odette Droulers, gen mgr. *Annual. 2-9 Jul 1998. Features school, university, community choirs, orchs and bands, with performances at Sydney Opera House, Sydney Town Hall and other venues. Cultural exchange workshops, masterclasses for up to 30 groups selected following application with audition tape or video.*

Melbourne International Festival of Organ and Harpsichord. PO Box 92, Parkville, Vic 3052, Australia *tel:* +61 3 9347 0447 *also fax; email:* mifoh@ariel.its.unimelb.edu.au; http://www.music.unimelb.edu.au/ems/mifoh.html. David Agg, dir. *14-21 Apr 1998. Early music festival featuring soloists, ens, vocal and instrumental. Over 20 separate events in various venues around Melbourne.*

Sydney Festival. Level 11, 31 Market St, Sydney, NSW, Australia *tel:* +61 2 9265 0444 *fax:* +61 2 9264 9495 *email:* sydfest@ozemail.com.au. Anthony Steel, festival dir. *4-26 Jan 1997.*

Austria

Allegro Vivo: International Chamber Music Festival Austria (Waldviertel). Festivalbüro, Wiener Str 2, A-3580 Horn, Austria *tel:* +43 2982 4319 *also fax;* +43 2252 89320 *also fax; email:* office@allegro-vivo.or.at; http://www.allegro-vivo.or.at/festival/. Mag Robert Berger; Margaret Ley, admin. *16 Aug-20 Sep 1998. Early baroque, classic Viennese, romantic, contemporary music. Concerts, summer academy.*

Austro-Hungarian Music Festival. 10 Barley Mow Passage, London W4 4PH, UK *tel:* +44 181 742 3355 *fax:* +44 181 742 1066. Martin Randall, mgr dir; Sheila Taylor, Emma Duffield. *Annual. Aug. 10 concerts in abbeys, palaces and country homes beside or within easy reach of the Danube. Max 140 participants, all concerts are exclusive to participants.*

* **Bregenz Festival.** PO Box 311, Festspiel und Kongreßhaus, Platz der Wiener Symphoniker, A-6901 Bregenz, Austria *tel:* +43 5574 40716 *fax:* +43 5574 4071400 *email:* bregenzer@festspiele.vol.at; http://www.vol.at/bregenzerfestspiele. Alfred Wopmann, artistic dir; Franz Salzmann, commercial dir. *Jul-Aug 1998. Opera, orch, chmbr mus, sacred mus, dance, drama.*

* **Carinthian Summer Festival.** Carinthischer Sommer, Gumpendorfer Strasse 76, A-1060 Wien, Austria *tel:* +43 1 596 8198; +43 1 597 9492 *fax:* +43 1 597 1236 *email:* office@carinthischersommer.at; http://www.carinthischersommer.at. *Annual. Jul-Aug. Concerts, opera.*

Chopin Festival. Biberstr 4, A-1010 Wien, Austria *tel:* +43 1 512 2374 *fax:* +43 1 512 6463. Theodor Kanitzer, dir. *XIV Chopin Festival, 20-23 Aug 1998 at Charterhouse Gaming, Lower Austria. Orch, choral mus, chamber mus, symphony mus, recitals.*

Festival Klangbogen Wien. Laudongasse 29, A-1080 Wien, Austria *tel:* +43 1 4000 8410 *fax:* +43 1 403 7540 *email:* http://www.magwien.gv.at/ma53/klangbog. Roland Geyer, mus dir. *26 Jun-6 Aug 1998. Opera and operetta, symphony concerts, chamber music, church concerts, recitals, Viennese music.*

Festival Wiener Klassik. Bossigasse 76, A-1130 Wien, Austria *tel:* +43 1 877 5208 *fax:* +43 1 876 462317. Manfred Huss, artistic dir; Manfred Seipt, mgr. *Jun-Sep 1998. Baroque, classic, early romantic music played on period instruments in historic venues.*

Franz Liszt Festival. Festivalbüro, Schloß Esterházy, A-7000 Eisenstadt, Austria *tel:* +43 2682 618660 *fax:* +43 2682 61805. Walter Reicher, artistic dir. *21-24 May 1998.*

Haydn Festival - Eisenstadt. Festivalbüro, Schloß Esterházy, A-7000 Eisenstadt, Austria *tel:* +43 2682 618660 *fax:* +43 2682 61805. Walter Reicher, artistic dir. *Annual. 1998 Festival: 11-20 Sep; concert season: 2 May-10 Oct. Orch festival focusing on Haydn's Paris Symphonies.*

* **Innsbruch Festival of Early Music.** Haspingerstr 1, A-6020 Innsbruck, Austria *tel:* +43 512 571032 *fax:* +43 512 563142 *email:* altemusik@magnet.at; http://www.tis.co.at/fest-alte-musik. René Jacobs, artistic dir; Eva Schintlmeister, mgr dir. *16-29 Aug 1998. Annual event featuring baroque music (2 operas, 16 concerts) played on period instruments at historic sites.*

International Academy for New Composition. Avantgarde Art Society, Wopfnerstrasse 16, A-6130 Schwaz/Tirol, Austria *tel:* +43 5242 65737 *fax:* +43 5242 61199. Marianne Penz-van Stappershoef, academy dir. *Annual. 24 Aug-5 Sep 1998. New mus and audio art.*

* **International Bruckner Festival.** Linzer Veranstaltungsgesellschaft mbH, Brucknerhaus Linz, Untere Donaulände 7, A-4010 Linz, Austria *tel:* +43 732 775230 *fax:* +43 732 7612201. Thomas Daniel Schlee, mus dir. *Sep. Extensive presentation of works by Anton Bruckner, plus music relating to an annual theme.*

Internationales Kammermusikfest Lockenhaus. Hauptplatz 5, A-7442 Lockenhaus, Austria *tel:* +43 2616 2072 *fax:* +43 2616 2023. Josef Herowitsch, mgr dir; Gidon Kremer, artistic dir. *27 Jun-5 Jul 1998. International chamber music festival with particular emphasis on contemporary composers. Works by composers of the year, Schubert, Mendelssohn and Brahms, along with compositions by Shostakovich, Piazolla, Tüür, Vasks and others.*

Musikprotokoll. ORF-Steiemark, Marburger Strasse 20, Graz, Austria *tel:* +43 316 470227 *fax:* +43 316 470253. Christian Scheib, dir; Rosalinde Vidic, admin. *30 Sep-3 Oct 1998. Contemporary mus.*

Salzburg Easter Festival. Herbert-von-Karajan-Pl 9, A-5020 Salzburg, Austria *tel:* +43 662 804 5328 *fax:* +43 662 840124. Robert Minder, gen mgr. *4-13 Apr 1998. Orch, choral, opera.*

* **Salzburg Festival.** Postfach 140, A-5010 Salzburg, Austria *tel:* +43 662 804501/80450 *fax:* +43 662 846682/848424. Eva Maria Wieser, artistic admin. *Annual. 21 Jul-31 Aug 1998. Drama, opera, concerts.*

Schubertiade. Gesellschaft mbH, Schweizer Strasse 1, Postfach 100, A-6845 Hohenems, Austria *tel:* +43 5576 72091 *fax:* +43 5576 75450. G Nachbauer, mgr. *Annual. 7-13 May 1998, Schloß Achberg; 14-17 May 1998, Lindau; 17-28 Jun 1998; 27 Aug-6 Sep 1998, Schwarzenberg. Classical mus, mainly Schubert.*

Styriarte Summer Music Festival in Styria. Palais Attems, Sackstr 17, A-8010 Graz, Austria *tel:* +43 316 812941 *fax:* +43 316 877 3836 *email:* styriarte@mail.styria.co.at; http://www.styria.co.at/styriarte. Mathis Huber; Irmgard Heschl, admin. *20 Jun-19 Jul 1998. Classical and baroque music, chamber and orch mus, operas, children's orch.*

* **Wiener Festwochen.** Lehárgasse 11, A-1060 Wien, Austria *tel:* +43 1 589 220 *fax:* +43 1 589 2249 *email:* festwoch@ping.at. Wolfgang Wais, sec gen. *9 May-20 Jun 1997. Drama, music and exhibitions from all periods, including contemporary.*

Wien Modern. Wiener Konzerthausgesellschaft, Lothringerstrasse 20, A-1037 Vienna, Austria *tel:* +43 1 7124686 0 *fax:* +43 1 7131709 *email:* mail@konzerthaus.at. Christoph Lieben-Seutter, sec gen; Christoph Becher, asst. *26 Oct-28 Nov 1998. 20th C mus. Interdisciplinary festival. Retrospective of mus composed after WWII.*

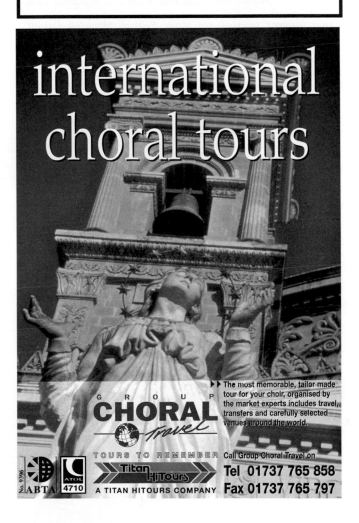

Belgium

Bruges Early Music Festival. Collaert Mansionstraat 30, B-8000 Brugge, Belgium *tel:* +32 5033 22 83 *fax:* +32 5034 62 04. Dewitte Robrecht, dir; Dens Alice, press. *24 Jul-8 Aug 1998. Hpd and f-pno international competitions, recitals, exhibitions. J S Bach and Contemporaries.*

Festival Ars Musica. 25 Rue Marche aux Herbes, B-1000 Bruxelles, Belgium *tel:* +32 2 514 2170 *fax:* +32 2 512 6649. France de Kinder, gen co-ord. *13 Mar-4 Apr 1998. Annual festival of contemporary music. Concerts, conferences, masterclasses, films.*

* **Festival de Wallonie.** Rue de L'Armee, Grouchy 20, B-5000 Namur, Belgium *tel:* +32 81 733781 *fax:* +32 81 742503. Baudouin Muylle, gen sec. *Jun-Oct 1998. 80 classical music concerts.*

Festival des Midis-Minimes. c/o F E de Wasseige, 2 Av Albert, Bte E15, B-1190 Bruxelles, Belgium *tel:* +32 2 346 1445 *fax:* +32 2 346 4647. François-Emmanuel de Wasseige, artistic dir. *Jul-Aug. One concert a day except on Sundays. Chamber and baroque music on original insts.*

* **Flanders Festival.** Kasteel Borluut, Kleine Gentstraat 46, B-905 I Gent, Belgium *tel:* +32 9 243 94 94 *fax:* +32 9 243 94 90 *email:* festival@ skynet.be; festival-gent@skynet.be. Jan Briers, co-ord. *Apr-Oct 1998. Concerts and dance.*

International Electro-acoustic Festival. Musiques et Recherches, Place de Ransbeck 3, B-1380 Ohain, Belgium *tel:* +32 2 354 4368 *fax:* +32 2 351 0094. Vande Gorne Annette, artistic dir. *Four day festival in Mar. Presents an opportunity to meet electro-acoustic composers.*

* **Les Nuits de Septembre.** Rue des Mineurs 17, B-4000 Liège, Belgium *tel:* +32 42 23 02 14 *fax:* +32 42 22 15 40 *email:* jmlg@arcadis.be. Philippe Vendrix, dir; Claire Ringlet, mgr. *Sep 1998. Early and baroque mus.*

Bulgaria

International Festival of Contemporary Music 'Musica Nova-Sofia'. ISCM Bulgarian Section, 149 Evlogy Georgiev Blvd, BG-1504 Sofia, Bulgaria *tel:* +359 2 442780 *fax:* +359 2 432675. Simeon Pironkoff, president; Gheorghi Arnaoudov, sec gen. *11-18 Jun 1998 in Sofia. Promotion of new mus. Symphonic, stage, dance, chamber, electro-acoustic music. Celebration of Messiaen.*

Plovdiv International Festival of Chamber Music. PO Box 545, BG-4000 Plovdiv, Bulgaria *tel:* +359 32 556493 *fax:* +359 32 262626. Jivko Jekov, chmn. *Sep. Chamber music. Classical, vocal, inst, ensembles, orch, opera, choral.*

* **Varna Summer International Music Festival.** Municipal Council, BG-9000 Varna, Bulgaria *tel:* +359 52 222425 *fax:* +359 52 220101. Plamena Tsoneva, musicologist. *Jun-Aug.*

Canada

Banff Arts Festival. The Banff Centre Centre for the Arts, Box 1020, Station 28, Banff, Alberta, T0L 0C0, Canada *tel:* +1 403 762 6180 *fax:* +1 403 762 6345 *email:* arts_info@banffcentre.ab.ca; http://www.banff centre.ab.ca/registrar/. *Jun-Aug. Masterclasses, chamber mus, jazz, etc.*

Boris Brott Summer Music Festival. 301 Bay St South, Hamilton, Ont L8P 3J7, Canada *tel:* +1 905 525 7664 *fax:* +1 905 526 9934. Gordon Webster, president. *21 Jul-18 Aug 1997. Jazz, classical, chamber.*

Concourse de Musique du Canada. 1030 Rue St-Alexandra, Bureau 705, Montréal, PQ H2Z 1P3, Canada *tel:* +1 514 879 1959 *fax:* +1 514 879 1835. Daniele Côté, gen dir.

duMaurier New Music Festival. 555 Main St, Room 101, Winnipeg, MB R3B 1C3, Canada *tel:* +1 204 949 3950 *fax:* +1 204 956 4271. Sandra Cherepack, mkt dir. *Jan.*

Elora Festival - A Celebration in Song. PO Box 990, Elora, Ont N0B 1S0, Canada *tel:* +1 519 846 0331 *fax:* +1 519 846 5947 *email:* elora@sentex. net. Michael Grit, gen mgr. *10 Jul-2 Aug 1998. Choral, classical and contemporary mus festival.*

Festival International de Musique Actuelle de Vitoriaville. CP 460, Victoriaville, PQ G6P 6T3, Canada *tel:* +1 819 752 7912 *fax:* +1 819 758 4370 *email:* fimav@cdcff.gc.ca. Michel Levasseur, artistic dir. *14-18 May 1998. New mus festival, jazz, rock improvised, contemporary and electro-acoustic musics.*

Festival International de Musique Baroque de Lamèque. CP 644, Lamèque, NB E0B 1V0, Canada *tel:* +1 506 344 5846 *fax:* +1 506 344 0366. Mathieu Duguay, artistic dir. *Jul. Early and baroque mus on period insts.*

Festival of the Sound. PO Box 750, Parry Sound, Ont P2A 2Z1, Canada *tel:* +1 705 746 2410 *fax:* +1 705 746 5639 *email:* festival@cancom.net; http://www.zeuter.com/parrysd. Margaret Boyd, admin. *Jul-Aug.*

Festival Orford. 3165 Chemin du Parc, Canton d'Orford, Québec J1X 3W3, Canada *tel:* +1 819 843 3981 *fax:* +1 819 843 7274 *email:* arts. orford@sympatico.ca; http://www3.sympatico.ca/arts.orford. Isabelle Langlois, communications and promotion. *3 Jul-15 Aug 1998. Chamber mus with musicians of international repute such as Janos Starker, Musici de Montreal and Menaham Pressler. Tickets: CAN $12-25.*

Guelph Spring Festival. PO Box 1718, Guelph, Ont N1H 6Z9, Canada *tel:* +1 519 821 3210 *fax:* +1 519 766 9212. Simon Wynberg, artistic dir; Lynn McGuigan, gen mgr. *22-31 May 1998. Classical, jazz, world mus and opera.*

Montréal International Jazz Festival. 822 Sherbrooke E, Montréal, PQ H2L 1K4, Canada *tel:* +1 514 523 3378 *fax:* +1 514 525 5775. Alain Simard, president; Caroline Jamet, vice-president. *Jun-Jul. Jazz, rhythm and blues, cajun.*

Northern Encounters. PO Box 257, Toronto Dominion Centre, Toronto, Ontario M5K 1J5, Canada *tel:* +1 416 214 1451 *fax:* +1 416 214 1985 *email:* info@northernc.com; http://www.northenc.com. Lawrence Cherney, artistic dir; John A Miller, exec producer. *Jun. Multicultural, wide range of music.*

Peterborough New Music. PO Box 823, Peterborough, Ont K9J 7A2, Canada *tel:* +1 705 859 2153 *fax:* +1 705 859 3851. John Lang, gen mgr.

Scotia Festival of Music. 317-1541 Barrington St, Halifax, NS B3J 1Z5, Canada *tel:* +1 902 429 9267 *fax:* +1 902 425 6785. Christopher Wilcox, mgr and artistic dir. *May-Jun.*

Summer Music from the Comox Valley. PO Box 3056, 536-6th St, Courtenay, BC V9N 5N3, Canada *tel:* +1 604 338 7463 *fax:* +1 604 334 2934 *email:* cmyc@island.net. Stacey Wright, gen mgr. *Jul-Aug. Jazz, chamber mus, orch, mus theatre.*

Vancouver Early Music Festival. 1254 West 7th Av, Vancouver, BC V6H 1B6, Canada *tel:* +1 604 732 1610 *fax:* +1 604 732 1602 *email:* earlymusic@mindlink.bc.ca; http://mindlink.net/earlymusic. José Verstappen, dir. *Jul-Aug.*

Winnipeg New Music Festival. 555 Main St, Room 101, Winnipeg, MB R3B 1C3, Canada *tel:* +1 204 949 3950 *fax:* +1 204 956 4271. Glen Buhr, co-ord. *Jan.*

Croatia

* **Dubrovnik Festival.** PO Box 132, HR-50000 Dubrovnik, Croatia *tel:* +385 59 412288/26351 *fax:* +385 59 27944. Frano Matusic, gen mgr; Valter Despalj, artistic dir. *Theatre ballet, concerts and folklore.*

Europhonia. c/o Hrvatsko Drustvo Skladatelja, Berislaviceva 9, HR-41000 Zagreb, Croatia *tel:* +385 1 423463 *fax:* +385 1 422850. Fred Dosek, mgr. *Contemporary chamber music, music for solo instruments. Electronic and multimedia presentations. Number of world and Croatian premieres.*

Zagreb Music Biennale International Festival of Contemporary Music. c/o Hrvatsko Drustvo Skladatelja, Berislaviceva, HR-10000 Zagreb, Croatia *tel:* +385 1 423463 *fax:* +385 1 422850 *email:* hdsl@zg.tel.hr. Ivo Josipovic, dir; Sanda Vojkovic, deputy dir. *Next Apr 1999. Contemporary mus.*

Czech Republic

Art Days of the Blind in Moravia. SONS, Czech Association of the Blind and Partially Sighted, Karlinské nám 12, CZ 186 03 Praha 8, Czech Republic *tel:* +420 2 2481 7393 *fax:* +420 2 2481 8398 *email:* sons_ zahr@braillnet.cz. Václav Polásek, chief offr. *Annual. Spring 1998. Six to nine towns in central Moravia. Seminars, mus, recitation, graphic art, handicrafts and theatre performances and w/shops.*

* **Brno International Music Festival.** Úvoz 39, CZ-602 00 Brno, Czech Republic *tel:* +420 5 4323 3116 *fax:* +420 5 4323 3358. Jitka Runsuková, mgr. *5-19 Apr 1998, Easter Festival of Sacred Music. 24 Sep-10 Oct, Moravian Autumn: symphony, chamber mus, opera. 30 Sep-4 Oct, Exposition of New Music: contemporary arts, mus, theatre and dance.*

Cesky Krumlov International Music Festival. Auviex, SRO, Obrovského 10, CZ-141 00 Praha 4, Czech Republic *tel:* +420 2 76 72 75 *fax:* +420 2 76 88 81. Marta Hospodková, admin dir; Oldrich Cenek, dramaturgist. *Annual. Aug. Symphony orch, inst soloists, chmbr ens, medieval, renaissance, baroque, opera.*

Emmy Destinn Music Festival. Rudolfov 393, CZ-373 71 Ceské Budejovice, Czech Republic *tel:* +420 38 39254 *also fax.* Antonín Kazil. *21 Aug-5 Sep 1998. Operatic, oratorio and chmbr mus repertoire.*

* **Forfest.** Artistic Initiative of Kromeriz, Kojetinska 1425, CZ-767 01 Kromeriz, Czech Republic *tel:* +420 634 24316 *also fax.* Zdenka Vaculovicová, mgr dir. *21-28 Jun 1998. International festival of contemporary arts with spiritual orientation; chamber music, contemporary classical, sacred, choral, electronic music, exhibitions. Member of European Conference of Promoters of New Music.*

International Jazz Festival Prague. Pragokoncert Arts Agency, Celetná 17, CZ-118 13 Praha 1, Czech Republic *tel:* +420 24 510452 *fax:* +420 24 510968. Ivo Letov, artistic dir. *Oct 1998. Jazz from traditional to modern.*

International Music Festival Janacek May. Msná 10, CZ-702 00 Ostrava 1, Czech Republic *tel:* +420 69 612 2300 *fax:* +420 69 611 4016. Jaromír Javurek, mgr and dir. *25 May-8 Jun 1998. Symphonic, chamber, opera concerts, recitals. Classical music from 17th C to contemporary. Features top international artists.*

* **Prague Spring International Music Festival.** Hellichova 18, CZ-118 00 Praha 1, Czech Republic *tel:* +420 2 532489/3474/0293 *fax:* +420 2 536040 *email:* festival@login.cz; http://www.festival.cz; http://www. festival_prague_spring.cz. Oleg Podgorny, dir. *12 May-2 Jun 1998. Classical music festival.*

Denmark

Aarhus Festival. Officersbygningen, Vester Allé 3, DK-8000 Aarhus C, Denmark *tel:* +45 89 318270 *fax:* +45 86 191336. Lars Seeberg, gen sec; Annita Hornslet, head of programme section. *Annual. 28 Aug-6 Sep 1998. Largest single concentration of cultural events in Scandinavia, including theatre, cabaret, opera, ballet and dance, classical and new music, rock, jazz and folk mus. Exhibitions, film and media, sports. Symposia, seminars and events for children.*

Albertslund Festival Week. Albertslundhuset, Bibliotekstorvet 1-3, DK-2620 Albertslund, Denmark *tel:* +45 4264 0198 *fax:* +45 4264 5798. Torben Holm Larsen, mgr. *Annual. Sep. Classical, theatre, dance.*

Composers' Biennale. c/o Dansk Komponist Forening, Gråbrødretorv 16, 1, DK-1154 Copenhagen K, Denmark *tel:* +45 33 135405 *fax:* +45 33 143219. Mogens Winkel Holm, chmn. *Biennial. Next 1998. Presentation of contemporary Danish music, organised by Danish Composers' Society.*

Contemporary Music in Suså. Tyvelsevej 26, DK-4171 Glumsø, Denmark *tel:* +45 53 648102. Anne Kristine Smith, dir. *Annual. 22-23 Aug 1998. At Suså School between Sorø and Naestved. Works by contemporary Danish composers will be performed, including world premières.*

Copenhagen Choir Festival. Wonderful Copenhagen, Gammel Kongevej 1, DK-1610 Copenhagen V, Denmark *tel:* +45 33 257400 *fax:* +45 33 257410 *email:* wolo@inet.uni-c.dk. Johannes Bo Nielsen, project co-ord. *Annual. Oct. Concerts, workshops to promote interest in choral music.*

Copenhagen Early Music Festival. Larslejsstraede 7, 3-33, DK-1451 Copenhagen, Denmark *tel:* +45 33 339320 *fax:* +45 33 339420 *email:* http://www.coco.dk. Palle Jensen, co-ord. *Biennial. 23-27 Sep 1998. Exploring musical connections between Scandinavia and the rest of Europe, little known early mus and new mus written for early mus insts.*

Copenhagen International Experimental Music Festival. Skraep, Den Anden Opera, Kronprinsensgade 7, DK-1114 Copenhagen, Denmark *tel:* +45 33 327222 *fax:* +45 33 327234; +45 32 962764 *email:* winther@ internet.dk. Niels Winther, sec. *15-21 Jun. Experimental composition and improvisation.*

Copenhagen Jazz Festival. Kjeld Langes Gade 4A, DK-1367 Copenhagen K, Denmark *tel:* +45 33 932013 *fax:* +45 33 934413 *email:* cjf@dkb.dk; http://www.cjf.dk. *3-12 Jul 1998. 10 days of jazz in jazz clubs, concert halls and on the streets and squares of Copenhagen.*

European Youth Music Festival. Ishoej Musikskole, Jaegerbuen 6, DK-2635 Ishoej, Denmark *tel:* +45 43 543025; +45 43 735664 *fax:* +45 43 542761. *Jun-Jul.*

Fanø Musikfestival. Toftestien 21, Sønderho, DK-6720 Fanø, Denmark *tel:* +45 75 164429 *fax:* +45 75 164529. Vibeke Schøtt, dir. *Classical, jazz.*

Frederiksvaerk Music Festival. Gjethuset, Gjethusgade 5, DK-3300 Frederiksvaerk, Denmark *tel:* +45 47 770607. Charlotte Lund Christiansen. *Annual. Jul. Chamber music concerts, mainly with Danish artists and ensembles, Saturdays at 8pm, Sundays at 4pm. Combined with art exhibition.*

Music Harvest Festival. Det Fynske Musikkonservatorium, Islandsgade 2, DK-5000 Odense, Denmark *tel:* +45 66 110663 *fax:* +45 66 177763. Bertel Krarup, Per Erland Rasmussen, artistic leaders. *Annual. 4-8 Nov 1998. Held in Odense, concerts and seminars on contemporary music.*

Numus Festival. c/o Musikhuset Aarhus, Thomas Jensens Allé, DK-8000 Aarhus C, Denmark *tel:* +45 89 318200 *also fax.* Karl Aage Rasmussen, artistic dir. *Annual. Apr-May. Contemporary and experimental music.*

Selsø Summer Concerts. Langs Hegnet 39, DK-2800 Lyngby, Denmark *tel:* +45 45 930778 *also fax.* Mogens Friis, dir. *Annual. Jun-Aug.*

Sorø International Music Festival. Sasserbrovej 10, DK-4173 Fjenneslev, Denmark *tel:* +45 53 60 96 39 *also fax.* Knud Vad, artistic dir; Jørgen Birkedal, sec. *24 Jun-6 Sep 1998. Classical mus, including contemporary.*

Estonia

International Festival of New Music NYYD. Eesti Kontsert, Estonia pst 4 EE0001 Tallinn, Estonia *tel:* +372 2446255/442901 *fax:* +372 631 4171 *email:* concert@netexpress.ee; http://www.bcs.ee/concert. Madis Kolk, mgr. *Biennial. 23-28 Nov 1999. Contemporary mus concerts, opera performances, workshops, multidisciplinary events, exhibitions.*

Faroe Islands

Summartónar. Reynagøta 12, FR-100 Tórshavn, Faroe Islands *tel:* +298 14815 *fax:* +298 14825 *email:* summar@olivant.fo. Kristian Blak, mgr dir. *Annual. 27 Jun-5 Jul 1998. Festival of classical and contemporary music. Indoor and outdoor locations all over Tórshavn and the Faroe Islands.*

Finland

April Jazz Espoo. Ahertajantie 6 B, FIN-02100 Espoo, Finland *tel:* +358 9 455 0003 *fax:* +358 9 465172 *email:* espoo.big.band@pp.kolumbus.fi. Martti Lappalainen, gen dir. *23-26 Apr 1998. International jazz festival.*

Avanti! Summer Sounds. Tallberginkatu 1 B 80, FIN-00180 Helsinki, Finland *tel:* +358 9 694 0091 *fax:* +358 9 694 2208 *email:* avanti@ co.inet.fi. Anssi Karttunen, artistic dir; Hanna Pursiainen, asst mgr. *25-28 Jun 1998. Orchestral and chamber music concerts, baroque and contemporary music.*

Crusell Week. Uudenkaupungin Kultuuritoimisto, Rauhankatu 10, FIN-23500 Uusikaupunki, Finland *tel:* +358 2 84515300/84515302 *fax:* +358 2 84515442.

Espoo International Piano Festival. Espoo Cultural Centre, Kulttuuriaukio, FIN-02100 Espoo, Finland *tel:* +358 09 8165051 *fax:* +358 09 81657220. Osmo Pylvänäinen, dir. *Biennial. Next Oct 1999. Classical and contemporary pno mus, recitals and orchestral concerts.*

Finland Festivals. Uudenmaankatu 36 D 21, FIN-00120 Helsinki, Finland *tel:* +358 9 621 4224 *fax:* +358 9 612 1007. Tuomo Tirkkonen, gen dir. *Various music festivals, including opera, chmbr, jazz, rock, film, dance/theatre and general mus. Apply for specific dates.*

Helsinki Biennale. c/o The Helsinki Festival, Rauhankatu 7 E, FIN-00170 Helsinki, Finland *tel:* +358 9 135 4522 *fax:* +358 9 278 1578 *email:* info@helsinkifestival.fi; http://www.helsinkifestival.fi. Risto Nieminen, dir. *11-15 Mar 1998. Part of Helsinki Festival. Contemporary mus festival which will become annual after 1998.*

* **Helsinki Festival.** Rauhankatu 7E, FIN-00100 Helsinki, Finland *tel:* +358 9 135 4522 *fax:* +358 9 278 1578 *email:* info@helsinkifestival.fi; http://www.helsinki.festival.fi. Risto Nieminen, dir. *Annual. 21 Aug-6 Sep 1998. Arts festival featuring classical, jazz, rock and pop open-air concerts, dance, theatre, opera, cinema, exhibitions, etc.*

Hetta Music Event. Virastotalo, FIN-99400 Enontekiö, Finland *tel:* +358 16 556275 *fax:* +358 16 556229 *email:* kirjasto@enontekio.inet.fi. Anneli Aro, sec of culture. *5-13 Apr 1998. Sacred and baroque music.*

Ilmajoki Music Festival. Kauppatie 26, FIN-60800 Ilmajoki, Finland *tel:* +358 6 424 7049 *fax:* +358 6 424 7171. Lasse Lintala, artistic dir; Marjatta Evasoja, gen dir. *Annual. Jun. Opera, concerts.*

Imatra Big Band Festival. Virastokatu 2, FIN-55100 Imatra, Finland *tel:* +358 5 681 6637 *fax:* +358 5 681 2001. Hannu Sopanen, artistic dir. *Jun-Jul.*

International Kalottjazz and Blues Festival. Tornion Kulttuuritoimisto, Lukiokatu 10, FIN-95400 Tornio, Finland *tel:* +358 16 432423/4 *fax:* +358 16 432612. Helena Junes, festival dir.

Joensuu Festival. Koskikatu 1, FIN-80100 Joensuu, Finland *tel:* +358 13 267 5330 *fax:* +358 13 267 5320 *email:* joensuun.laulujuhlat@co.inet.fi. Juha Iso-Aho, exec dir. *Annual. 13-20 Jun 1998. Classical to rock and pop, ethno and jazz. Dance, theatre, films, exhibitions and seminars.*

Jyväskylä Arts Festival. Kauppakatu 14 A 4, FIN-40100 Jyväskylä, Finland *tel:* +358 14 615624 *fax:* +358 14 214808. Atso Almila, artistic dir; Iiris Lehtonen, gen dir. *Annual. Jun. Chamber mus.*

Kainuu Jazz Spring. Kalliokatu 7, FIN-87100 Kajaani, Finland *tel:* +358 8 615 5514 *fax:* +358 8 615 5563. Unto Torniainen, gen dir.

Kangasniemi Music Festival. The Cultural Secretary, Kangasniemi Municipality, Otto Mannisen tie 2, FIN-51200 Kangasniemi, Finland *tel:* +358 15 780 1265 *fax:* +358 15 780 1292. *Jul. Classical and vocal music; concerts, courses and competitions for singers and liedpianists.*

Kaustinen Folk Music Festival. PO Box 24, FIN-69601 Kaustinen, Finland *tel:* +358 6 860 4111 *fax:* +358 6 860 4222 *email:* folk. fest@kaustinen.inet.fi. Jyrki Heiskanen, programme dir. *18-26 Jul 1998. Largest annual folk music and dance festival in the Nordic countries. Folk, world, traditional, ethnic, folk-dance.*

Korsholm Music Festival. FIN-65610 Mustasaari, Finland *tel:* +358 6 322 2390 *fax:* +358 6 322 2393. Frans Helmerson, artistic dir; Ros-Mari Djupsund, exec dir. *Late 21-28 Jun 1998. Chamber music with Nordic features.*

Kuhmo Chamber Music Festival. Torikatu 39, FIN-88900 Kuhmo, Finland *tel:* +358 8 520936 *fax:* +358 8 521961. Ritva Eerola, office mgr. *Annual. Jul.*

Lahti Organ Festival. Kirkkokatu 5, FIN-15110 Lahti, Finland *tel:* +358 3 782 3184 *fax:* +358 3 783 2190. Auni Myöhänen, mgr. *Annual. 2-9 Aug 1998. Organ, chamber music, ensembles and choirs. Also international organ competition during festival.*

Lakeside Blues Festival. Järvenpään Blues-Jazz Diggarit ry, PO Box 143, FIN-04401 Järvenpää, Finland *tel:* +358 9 271 1305 *fax:* +358 9 279 2550 *email:* blues@sci.fi; http://www.sjoki.uta.fi/~latvis/festivals/puisto blues/. Jussi 'Auvo' Laaksonen, festival promoter. *Annual. Last week in Jun. Rhythm and blues.*

Lieska Brass Week. Koski-Jaakonkatu 4, FIN-81700 Lieksa, Finland *tel:* +358 13 523134 *fax:* +358 13 523133 *email:* brass.week@lieksa.inet. fi; http://site.inet.fi/lieksa/matkailu. Jouni Auramo, mgr dir; Tarja Tammia, mkt mgr. *24 Jul-2 Aug 1998. Classical concerts, mus courses.*

Mikkeli Music Festival. Vuorikatu 3 A, FIN-50100 Mikkeli, Finland *tel:* +358 15 162076 *fax:* +358 15 1912323 *email:* mikkeli.music festival@iwn.fi; http://www.mediamikkeli.com/musicfestival/. Valeri Gergiev, artistic dir; Kari Moring, exec dir. *28 Jun-6 Jul 1998. Opera in stage and concert productions, symphony concerts, recitals. Main performers: Orchestra and Choir of Mariinsky (Kirov) Theatre.*

Naantali Music Festival. Henrikinkatu 1, PO Box 46, FIN-21101 Naantali, Finland *tel:* +358 2 434 5363 *fax:* +358 2 434 5425 *email:* http://www. festivals.fi/naantali. Asta Kallio, exec dir; Arto Noras, artistic dir. *Annual. 6-17 Jun 1998. Chamber music and recitals. 18-22 concerts. Main venue medieval abbey of Naantali.*

Oulainen Music Week. Oulaistenkatu 8, FIN-86300 Oulainen, Finland *tel:* +358 8 479 3272 *fax:* +358 8 473915. *Oct-Nov.*

Oulu Music Festival. Lintulammentie 1, FIN-90150 Oulu, Finland *tel:* +358 8 336830 *fax:* +358 8 336822. Ismo Sirén, artistic dir; Heli Heikkilä-Murto, concert sec. *15-21 Mar 1998. Full symphonic, chamber orchestra, chamber music, contemporary classical, recitals, children's concerts.*

Pori Jazz Festival. Etelaranta 6, FIN-28100 Pori, Finland *tel:* +358 2 550 5550 *fax:* +358 2 550 5525 *email:* http://www.porijazz.fi. Jyrki Kangas, artistic dir; Harri Kainulainen, gen mgr. *Annual. 11-19 Jul 1998. International jazz festival.*

Riihimäki Summer Concerts. Kalevankatal, FIN-11101 Riihimäki, Finland *tel:* +358 14 741615 *fax:* +358 14 741775. Juha Pesonen, artistic dir. *Jun. Recitals and chamber music.*

Sata Häme Accordion Festival. PO Box 37, FIN-39501 Ikaalinen, Finland *tel:* +358 3 458 6991 *fax:* +358 3 450 1365. Kimmo Mattila, artistic dir; Terhi Palonen, gen dir. *Annual. Jun.*

* **Savonlinna Opera Festival.** Olavinkatu 27, FIN-57130 Savonlinna, Finland *tel:* +358 15 476750 *fax:* +358 15 4767540 *email:* http://www. operafestival.fi. Paavo Suokko, gen dir. *Annual. 4 Jul-2 Aug 1998. Opera, recitals, concerts.*

Sysmä Summer Sounds. PO Box 26, FIN-19701 Sysmä, Finland *tel:* +358 18 172811 *fax:* +358 18 172831. *Jun-Jul.*

Tampere Biennale. Tullikamarinaukio 2, FIN-33100 Tampere, Finland *tel:* +358 3 84310 *fax:* +358 3 717 2831 *email:* music@tampere.fi; http://www.tampere.fi/festival/music. Aila Manninen. *Biennial. Next 1-5 Apr 1998. Contemporary Finnish music.*

Tampere Jazz Happening. Tullikamarinaukio 2, FIN-33100 Tampere, Finland *tel:* +358 3 219 6136/6172 *fax:* +358 3 223 0121 *email:* music@ tampere.fi; http://www.tampere.fi/festival/music. Aila Manninen, dir. *Annual. 30 Oct-1 Nov 1998. International contemporary jazz festival.*

Tampereen Sävel - Tampere International Choir Festival. Tullikamarinaukio 2, FIN-33100 Tampere, Finland *tel:* +358 3 219 6136 *fax:* +358 3 223 0121 *email:* music@tampere.fi; http://www.tampere.fi/ festival/music. Aila Manninen, dir. *Biennial. Next 9-13 Jun 1999. Chorus review, contest for vocal ensemble, course for choir leaders, concert series. Boy choir theme in 1999.*

Tango Festival in Seinäjoki. Kauppakatu 15 C, FIN-60100 Seinäjoki, Finland *tel:* +358 6 420 1111 *fax:* +358 6 414 2350. *8-12 Jul 1998. 100,000 people attend this festival of tango vocal and dance mus. Song and dance contest.*

Time of Music. Musiikin Aika, FIN-44500 Viitasaari, Finland *tel:* +358 14 573195 *fax:* +358 14 579 3515 *email:* time.music@festivals.fi; http:// www.festivals.fi/tom/. Harri Natunen, mgr. *8-15 Jul 1998. Contemporary music, jazz club, courses, player's band for children.*

Turku Music Festival. Uudenmaankatu 1, FIN-20500 Turku, Finland *tel:* +358 2 251 1162 *fax:* +358 2 231 3316 *email:* turku.music@tmf.pp. fi; http://turkumusic.weppi.fi. Martti Rousi, artistic dir; Alarik Repo, exec dir. *Annual. 7-16 Aug 1998. Orchestra, early, contemporary and chamber music.*

Vantaa Baroque Week. PO Box 10, FIN-01301 Vantaa, Finland *tel:* +358 9 830 6265 *fax:* +358 9 830 6261. Håkan Wikman, artistic dir. *Annual. 1-7 Aug 1998. Western European baroque mus.*

France

Auch Contemporary Dance and Music Festival. Limca, Château de Saint Cricq, Route de Toulouse, F-32000 Auch, France *tel:* +33 62 60 10 11 *fax:* +33 62 60 10 12. Philippe Prevot, dir. *Annual. Sep-Oct.*

Besançon Festival of Music. 2d Rue Isenbart, F-25000 Besançon, France *tel:* +33 81 80 73 26 *fax:* +33 81 80 46 36. Yvette Cussey, admin dir. *Sep. Classical and symphonic concerts and recitals.*

Bordeaux Festival d'Eté. Grand Théâtre, Service de Location, BP 95-33025 Bordeaux Cedex, France *tel:* +33 05 56 00 85 20 *fax:* +33 05 51 81 93 66. Catherine Lillet. *Jul.*

Chaise-Dieu Festival. PO Box 150, F-43004 Le Puy-en-Velay, France *tel:* +33 4 71 09 48 28 *fax:* +33 4 71 09 55 58 *email:* http://clrwww.in2p3. fr/chaise-dieu.html. Guy Ramona, dir; Cécile Laurent de Stredel, communications. *21-31 Aug 1998. Sacred mus, baroque, classic, contemporary. From small baroque ens to double philharmonic orch and choirs.*

Colmar International Festival. Office de Tourisme de Colmar, 4 Rue des Unterlinden, F-68000 Colmar, France *tel:* +33 89 20 68 94 *fax:* +33 89 41 34 13. Vladimir Spivakov, artistic dir; Hubert Niess, dir. *Jul. Symphonic mus, chmbr mus, recitals.*

Festival d'Aix. Palais de l'Ancien Archevêché, F-13100 Aix-en-Provence, France *tel:* +33 4 42 17 34 34 *fax:* +33 4 42 17 34 21. Valérie Samuel, dir. *Annual. Jul. Opera, concerts and vocal recitals.*

Festival Aspects des Musiques d'Aujourdhui. Conservatoire National du Region, 1 Rue de Carel, F-13027 Caen, France *tel:* +33 3186 4200 *fax:* +33 3186 1892. Jean Marc Loureau, artistic dir; Stephanie Viet, PR. *Mar. Contemporary music.*

Festival d'Auvers-sur-Oise. Manoir des Colombières, Rue de la Sansonne, F-95430 Auvers-sur-Oise, France *tel:* +33 30 36 70 82 *fax:* +33 30 36 71 55. Pascal Escande, dir. *May-Jun. Vocal, piano, chamber music, opera.*

Festival International d'art Lyrique et de Musique. Palais de l'Ancien Archevêché, 13100 Aix-en-Provence, France *tel:* +33 4 42 17 34 34 *fax:* +33 4 42 17 34 21. Jean-François Picheral, president; Bernard de Saint-Rapt, admin. *Jul. Music and dance.*

Festival International de Musique de Menton. 11 Av Delcassé, F-75008 Paris, France *tel:* +33 1 45 63 25 87 *fax:* +33 1 42 89 44 66. André Borocz, dir. *1-31 Aug 1998. Classical, chamber mus and recitals.*

Festival Musique en Scene. 9 rue du Garet, BP 1185, F-69202 Lyon Cedex 01, France *tel:* +33 4 72 07 37 00 *fax:* +33 4 72 07 37 01 *email:* grame@ rd.grame.fr; http://www.grame.fr. James Giroudon, artistic dir. *4-22 Mar 1998. Contemporary music, music theatre, films.*

Festival Synthese. Institut International de Musique Electroacoustique de Bourges, BP 39, F-18001 Bourges, France *tel:* +33 2 48 20 41 87 *fax:* +33 2 48 20 45 51 *email:* agmeb10@calvacom.fr; http://www.gmeb.fr. Françoise Barrière, dir. *Annual. 29 May-7 Jun 1998. Electro-acoustic music.*

Latour De France International Festival of Music and the Arts. c/o Mananan Festival Office, Erin Arts Centre, Port Erin, Isle of Man IM9 6LD, UK *tel:* +44 1624 835858 *also fax; fax:* +44 1624 836658. John Bethell, dir. *26-30 Jul 1998. Opportunity to appear in opera performances. Oratorio, chamber music, recitals.*

Les Estivales. La Charité, 77 Rue Cottier, PO Box 113, F-84204 Carpentras Cédex, France *tel:* +33 90 60 46 00 *fax:* +33 90 60 52 85. Joelle Pérault, admin. *Jul. Theatre, music, dance and variety show.*

Lille Festival. 64 Av du Président J F Kennedy, F-59000 Lille, France *tel:* +33 3 20 52 74 23 *fax:* +33 3 25 97 74 *email:* http://www.irgb.fr/lille festival/. Olivier Célarié, press offr. *Oct. Classical, contemporary, baroque and rock music.*

Musica International Festival of Contemporary Music. 2 Rue d'Ingwiller, F-67000 Strasbourg, France *tel:* +33 3 88 21 02 21 *fax:* +33 3 88 21 02 88 *email:* musica67@cybercable.fr. J Cloquet, admin; Jean-Dominique Marco, dir. *Annual. 18 Sep-3 Oct 1998. Contemporary music.*

Musique Action. CCAM, BP 126, F-54504 Vandoeuvre-les-Nanacy, France *tel:* +33 83 56 15 00 *fax:* +33 83 53 21 85. Dominique Répécond, artistic dir. *May. New music.*

* **Orange Festival.** Chorégies d'Orange, PO Box 205, 18 Place Silvain, F-84107 Orange Cedex, France *tel:* +33 490 51 83 83 *fax:* +33 490 34 87 67. Thierry Mariani, president; Raymond Duffaut, dir. *Annual. Jul-Aug. Opera and symphonic concerts.*

Pablo Casals Festival. Bureau du Festival (BP24), Rue Victor Hugo, F-66502 Prades Cedex, France *tel:* +33 68 96 33 07 *fax:* +33 68 96 50 95. Michel Lethiec, artistic dir. *Annual. 26 Jul-13 Aug 1998. Chamber music concerts, international music academy, instrumental and chamber music m/classes, choral session.*

Piano aux Jacobins. 61 Rue de la Pomme, F-31000 Toulouse, France *tel:* +33 61 22 40 05 *fax:* +33 61 21 74 20 *email:* pianojacobins@hol.fr. Catherine d'Argoubet, artistic dir. *Annual. 8-25 Sep 1998. Classical and contemporary music. Piano festival.*

Rencontres Musicales D'Evian. 15 Rue de Teheran, F-75008 Paris, France *tel:* +33 1 44 35 26 91 *fax:* +33 1 42 89 26 50. Mireille Vernez. *Annual. May. Symphony, chmbr mus, choral.*

Rendez-vous Musique Nouvelle. Centre Culturel, av St Rémy, F-57600 Forbach, France *tel:* +33 3 87 85 12 31 *also fax; email:* rdvmusique nouvelle@bplorraine.fr. *13-15 Nov 1998.*

Strasbourg International Music Festival. Wolf Musique, 24 Rue de la Mésange, F-67000 Strasbourg, France *tel:* +33 388 32 43 10 *fax:* +33 388 32 42 38. Harry Lapp, gen mgr; Lord Menuhin, hon chmn. *5 Jun-6 Jul 1998. Concerts, operas, recitals, jazz.*

Germany

Art Projekt. International Musikfestival GmbH, Widenmayerstr 41, D-80538 München, Germany *tel:* +49 89 290 7490 *fax:* +49 89 290 74999. Andrea Berg, project asst mgr. *Sep. Held in the Falkoner Centre Copenhagen. Classical music, jazz and various other musical genres.*

Bad Hersfeld Festival. Nachtigallenstr 7, D-36251 Bad Hersfeld, Germany *tel:* +49 662 150670 *fax:* +49 662 164355. *Bach Festival. Easter, organ and choir. Mid Jun-Aug, opera and classical music.*

* **Bayreuth Festival.** PO Box 100262, D-95402 Bayreuth, Germany *tel:* +49 921 78780. Wolfgang Wagner, dir. *Annual. Jul-Aug. Richard Wagner opera festival.*

* **Berlin Festival.** PO Box 301648, Budapester Str 50, D-10787 Berlin, Germany *tel:* +49 30 254890 *fax:* +49 30 254 89111. Dirk Nabering, mus dir. *Annual. Sep. Orch, chamber, choral, vocal.*

Donaueschingen Festival of Contemporary Music. Südwestfunk Baden-Baden, D-76522 Baden-Baden, Germany *tel:* +49 7221 922247 *fax:* +49 7221 924362. Armin Köhler, editor. *6-18 Oct 1998. Contemporary music.*

* **Dresdner Musikfestspiele.** Postfach 202723, D-01193 Dresden, Germany *tel:* +49 351 4866 317 *fax:* +49 351 4866 307 *email:* dmf@musik festspiele.com; http://www.dresdner-musikfestspiele.com. Michael Hampe, dir. *Annual. 16 May-1 Jun 1998. Theme: 'The Power of Music'. Opera, symphonic music, dance, open-air performances, solo concerts and chamber music*

Europa Cantat - European Federation of Young Choirs (EFYC). c/o Bayerische Musikakademie Marktoberdorf, Kurfürstenstrasse 19, D-87616 Marktoberdorf, Germany *tel:* +49 834 296 1826 *fax:* +49 834 240370 *email:* 100530.317@compuserve.com; http://www.introch/ecl. Dolf Rabus, sec gen. *Triennial singing festival. Next Jul 2000. Festival of choral music. International singing weeks in summer 1998 and 1999, enquire for further details.*

Gegenwelten International Festival für Neue Musik. Kulturinstitut Komponistinnen Gestern-heute, Theatrestrasse 11, D-69117 Heidelberg, Germany *tel:* +49 44 6221 166861 *fax:* +49 44 6221 182072. Roswitha Sperber, artistic dir; Rainer Koehl, exec. *17-19 Apr 1998. Contemporary music and symposium.*

Göttingen Handel Festival. Hainholzweg 3-5, D-37085 Göttingen, Germany *tel:* +49 551 56700 *fax:* +49 551 45395 *email:* http://www. haendel.org/. Susanne Litfin. *Annual. 28 May-2 Jun 1998. Baroque music and Handel operas.*

Halle Handel Festival. Grosse Nikolaistrasse 5, D-06108 Halle, Germany *tel:* +49 345 5009 0222 *fax:* +49 345 5009 0416. Hanna John, dir. *4-9 Jun 1998. Opera, concerts, oratorio, open-air performances, scientific conference.*

Heidelberg Castle Festival. Friedrichstr 5, D-69117 Heidelberg, Germany *tel:* +49 6221 583521 *fax:* +49 6221 583599. Helmut Hein, dir. *1-31 Aug 1998. Opera, musical, concerts.*

International May Festival. c/o Hessisches Staatstheater, PO Box 3247, D-65022 Wiesbaden, Germany *tel:* +49 611 1321 *fax:* +49 611 132337. Achim Thorwald, sec. *1-31 May 1998. Opera, drama, ballet, musical.*

Inventionen - Berliner Festival Neuer Musik. c/o DAAD, Berliner Künstlerprogramm, Jägerstr 23, D-10117 Berlin, Germany *tel:* +49 30 202 2080 *fax:* +49 30 204 1267 *email:* beirer@daad.b.shuttle.de; hein@gigant.kgw.tu-berlin.de. Ingrid Beirer, DAAD; Folkmaar Hein, TU Berlin. *Jun 1998. Concerts, exhibition and symposium, acousmatic music and internet.*

* **Kissinger Sommer Festival.** Postfach 2260, Marktplatz 12, D-97672 Bad Kissingen, Germany *tel:* +49 971 807110 *fax:* +49 971 807191. Kari Kahl-Wolfsjäger. *Annual. Jun-Jul. Symphony concerts, chamber music, opera, liederabende, jazz.*

Kronberg Cello Festival. International Academy of Chamber Music Kronberg, Königsteinerstr 5, D-61476 Kronberg, Germany *tel:* +49 6173 950085 *fax:* +49 6173 950086 *email:* ikacello@aol.com; http://members. aol.com/ikacello. Raimund Trenkler, artistic dir; Gabriela Denicke, Almut Latscha, admin. *Cello masterclasses.*

* **Ludwigsburg International Festival.** Festspiele Baden-Württemberg, PO Box 1022, D/W-71610 Ludwigsburg, Germany *tel:* +49 714 193960 *fax:* +49 714 193 9677. Wolfgang Gönnenwein, artistic dir; Susanne Dieterich, admin dir. *Annual. 5 Jun-25 Sep 1998. Opera, ballet, classical music, jazz.*

Markgräfler Gitarrentage - Müllheim. Stadt Müllheim, Kulturamt, Bismarckstr 3, 79379 Müllheim, Germany *tel:* +49 7631 801132 *fax:* +49 7631 801126. F D Koch, dir; Hucky Eichelmann, artistic dir. *Oct. Guitar festival.*

Metapher Festival for New Vocal Music. Musik der Jahrhunderte, Hasenbergstrasse 31/2, D-70178 Stuttgart, Germany *tel:* +49 711 6290510 *fax:* +49 711 6290515 *email:* 106673.1024@compuserve.com. Christine Fischer, mgr dir; Hans-Peter Jöhn, Manfred Schreier, artistic dirs. *Contemporary vocal music.*

Münchener Biennale - Internationales Festival für neues Musiktheater. Kulturreferat der Landeshauptstadt, Rindermarkt 3-4, D-80313 München, Germany *tel:* +49 89 280 5607 *fax:* +49 89 280 5679 *email:* 100635.2504@compuserve.com. Hans Werner Henze, Peter Ruzicka, artistic dirs. *19-30 Apr 1998. New music theatre including world premieres.*

* **Munich Opera Festival.** Bayerische Staatsoper Nationaltheater, Max-Joseph Platz 2, D-80539 München, Germany *tel:* +49 89 218501 *fax:* +49 89 218 51003. Peter Jonas, staatsintendant; Ulrike Hessler, PR dir. *Annual international opera festival, 1-31 Jul 1998. 16 opera productions, 5 ballet, liederabende and concerts.*

Musica Bayreuth. Ludwigstr 26, D-95444 Bayreuth, Germany *tel:* +49 921 67367 *also fax.* Viktor Lukas, conductor and organist. *2-17 May 1998. Classical music and opera.*

Musica Sacra International. c/o Bayerische Musikakademie Marktoberdorf, Kurfürstenstrasse 19, D-87616 Marktoberdorf, Germany *tel:* +49 8342 961825 *fax:* +49 8342 40370 *email:* 100530.317@ compuserve.com. Dolf Rabus, dir. *Biennial. Next 29 May-3 Jun 1998. Mus ens and choirs representing the main world religions.*

* **Musik-Biennale Berlin, International Festival of Contemporary Music.** Berliner Festspiele GmbH, Budapester Str 50, D-10787 Berlin, Germany *tel:* +49 30 254890 *fax:* +49 30 254 89111 *email:* http://www.berliner. festspiele.de. Heike Hoffmann. *Biennial. Next 12-21 Mar 1999.*

Musikfestspiele Saarland eV. Rotenbühlerweg 28a, D-66123 Saarbrücken, Germany *tel:* +49 681 397359 *fax:* +49 681 372310 *email:* http://www.saarbruecken.de/musikfst/start.htm. Prof Robert Leonardy, artistic dir. *Jun-Jul 1998. Theme of Hungarian music. Classical concerts, oratorios, gypsy music.*

Ruesselsheimer Floetentage. Berlinerstrasse 65, D-64589 Stockstadt-am-Rhein, Germany *tel:* +49 6158-84818. *May. Festival mainly celebrating early music performed on period insts.*

* **Schleswig-Holstein Festival.** Postfach 2655, D-23514 Lübeck, Germany *tel:* +49 451 389570 *fax:* +49 451 3895757. Franz Willnauer, dir.

* **Schwetzinger Festival.** Postfach 106040, D-70049 Stuttgart, Germany *tel:* +49 711 929 3038/+49 6202 4733 *fax:* +49 711 929 2600/+49 6202 4933. Friedmar Lueke, dir; Klaus-Peter Kehr, artistic dir. *Annual. Apr-Jun. Opera, drama, ballet, concerts.*

Summer Academy Johann Sebastian Bach, European Music Festival. Johann-Sebastian-Bach-Pl, D-70178 Stuttgart, Germany *tel:* +49 711 619210 *fax:* +49 711 619 2123. Christian Eisert, programme planning. *Annual. 31 Aug-13 Sep 1998. Music of J S Bach, Mozart and M Reger. Courses, lectures and concerts.*

Tage Alter Musik Regensburg. Postfach 100903, D-93009 Regensburg, Germany *tel:* +49 941 52687 *fax:* +49 941 53094 *email:* 100721.2242@ compuserve.com. Ludwig Hartmann, Stephan Schmid. *29-31 May 1998. Early music from middle ages to early romantic on period insts.*

Tage für Neue Musik Stuttgart. Musik de Jahrhunderte, Hasenbergstrasse 31/2, D-70178 Stuttgart, Germany *tel:* +49 711 629 0510 *fax:* +49 711 629 0515 *email:* 106673.1024@compuserve.com. Christine Fischer, mgr dir; Hans-Peter Jahn, artistic dir. *Annual. 6-14 Feb 1998. Contemporary music corresponding with visual arts, video and performances.*

Wittener Tage fur Neue Kammermusik. Kulturforum Witten, Bergerstr 25, D-58452 Witten, Germany *tel:* +49 2302 581 2427/2424 *fax:* +49 2302 581 2499. *24-26 Apr 1998. New chamber music.*

Greece

* **Athens Festival.** c/o Greek National Tourism Organisation, 1 Voukourestiou Str, GR-10564 Athens, Greece *tel:* +30 1 323 0049 *fax:* +30 1 323 5172. Nikiforos Gegos, dir. *Annual. Jun-Sep. Orchestral, opera, contemporary music, ballet and theatre.*

Patras International Festival. PO Box 1184, GR-26110 Patras, Greece *tel:* +30 61 278730 *fax:* +30 61 225948. Vassilios Philippatos, admin; Tonia Kokovika, asst artistic dir. *Jun-Aug. Classic, jazz, contemporary music, theatre, cinema, exhibitions, workshops.*

Hong Kong

Hong Kong Arts Festival. International Programme Office, 35 Little Russell St, London WC1A 2HH, UK *tel:* +44 171 637 5661 *fax:* +44 171 323 1151. Joseph Seelig, international programme consultant. *10 Feb-8 Mar 1998. Features opera, orchestral, dance, drama.*

Hungary

Bartók International Festival. Interart Festivalcenter, H-1366 Budapest PO Box 80, Hungary *tel:* +36 1 117 9838 *fax:* +36 1 117 9910. Beàta Schanda, dir. *Annual. 14-28 Jul 1998. 20th C and contemporary mus.*

* **Budapest Autumn Festival.** POB 95, Rákóczi út 65 Vl 66, H-1081 Budapest, Hungary *tel:* +36 1 133 2337/210 2792 *fax:* +36 1 133 2075. Gabor Koltay, director. *Two week multidisciplinary festival of contemporary art including concert series 'Music of our Age'.*

Budapest Farewell Party. Budapest Festival Center, Rákóczi út 65 Vl 66, H-1081 Budapest, Hungary *tel:* +36 1 133 2337/210 2792 *fax:* +36 1 133 2075. Zsófia Zimányi. *Weekend fiesta at end of June.*

* **Budapest Music Weeks.** Nemzeti Filharmónia, Vörösmarty ter 1, H-1051 Budapest, Hungary. Dr József Tóthpál, dir.

* **Budapest Spring Festival.** Budapest Festivalcenter, Ràkóczi ut 65 VI/66, H-1081 Budapest, Hungary *tel:* +36 1 133 2337/210 2792 *fax:* +36 1 133 2075 *email:* budfest@elender.hu. Zsófia Zimányi, dir. *13-29 May 1998. Opera, ballet, orchestral concerts, jazz.*

Esztergom International Guitar Festival and Seminar. Szendrey-Karper László International, Guitar Festival Foundation, PO Box 8, H-2501 Esztergom, Hungary *fax:* +36 33 313808. Istvàn Bàrdos, dir. *Next 1999. Festival, concerts, master courses, guitar orch and competition.*

* **International Kodály Festival.** POB 188, H-6001 Kecskemét, Hungary *fax:* +36 76 320160. Peter Erdei, dir. *Biennial. Next 1999. Chamber concerts and recitals, introduction of prizewinning young artists. Work of Kodály and contemporary Hungarian music.*

Kecskemét International Kodály Festival. Interart Festivalcenter, PO Box 80, Vörösmarty tér 1, H-1366 Budapest, Hungary *tel:* +36 1 266 3108/117 9910/9838 *fax:* +36 1 117 9910. Maria Liszkay, mgr. *Next Jul 1999.*

Mini Festival. c/o Hungarian Music Society, H-1025 Budapest, Pusztaszeri út 30, Hungary *tel:* +36 1 325 7313 *also fax.* Devich Sára Veszelszky, admin; Janos Devich, dir. *Annual. End of Jan for 3 days. Contemporary music, Hungarian and other.*

Music of our Age. Nemzeti Filharmónia, PO Box 49, H-1364 Budapest, Budapest, Hungary *tel:* +36 1 118 0441 *fax:* +36 1 118 0374. József Tóthpál, dir. *Annual. Early Oct for 9 days.*

Pécs Symphony Orchestra International Music Festival. Király utca 19, H-7621 Pécs, Hungary *tel:* +36 72 324350 *fax:* +36 72 242793. Péter Szkladanyi, dir. *26 Jun-3 Jul 1998. Symphonic music, oratorios, organ, chamber music.*

Sopron Early Music Days. Interart Festivalcenter, Vörösmarty tér 1, PO Box 80, H-1366 Budapest, Hungary *tel:* +36 1 117 9838; +36 1 266 3108 *fax:* +36 1 117 9910. Maria Liszkay, mgr. *20-27 Jun 1998. Early mus festival.*

Week of Hungarian Contemporary Music. Deák Ferenc u 2, H-6720 Szeged, Hungary *tel:* +36 62 310029 *fax:* +36 62 311065. Richard Weninger, admin. *Irregular. Annual or biennial for 5 days.*

Zemplén Arts Festival. Kiskorona u 7, Óbudai Társaskör, H-1036 Budapest *tel:* +36 1 2500288 *also fax.* János Rolla, dir. *21-29 Aug 1998. Chamber and symphonic music, operetta, jazz.*

Iceland

Reykjavik Arts Festival. Laekjargata 3b, PO Box 88, IS-121 Reykjavik, Iceland *tel:* +354 5 612444 *fax:* +354 5 622350 *email:* artsfest@ishoff.is; http://www.saga.is/artfest. Signy Palsdottir, exec dir. *Biennial. Next 16 May-7 Jun 1998. Mostly classical, but also features modern, pop, jazz and world music. Exhibitions, concerts, opera, dance, theatre.*

Summer Music Festival at Skálholt. Strönd, IS-225 Bessastadahreppi, Iceland. Helga Ingólfsdóttir, dir. *Annual. Jul-Aug. Baroque and sacred modern music.*

Israel

Ein Gev Music Festival. 14940 Kibbutz Ein Gev, Israel *tel:* +972 6 6658039 *fax:* +972 6 6658888. David Israel, mgr. *13-17 Apr 1998. Popular music and jazz.*

* **Israel Festival, Jerusalem.** Jerusalem Theatre, PO Box 4409, Jerusalem 91044, Israel *tel:* +972 2 5611438 *fax:* +972 2 5669850 *email:* http://www.festival.co.il/ (during festival only). Yossi Tal-Gan, gen dir; Micah Lewensohn, artistic dir. *Annual. 23 May-13 Jun 1998. Opera, symphonic and chamber music, contemporary and early music, recitals, traditional and experimental theatre, classical and contemporary dance, ethnic music, jazz, rock, performance art.*

Red Sea Jazz Festival. 6 Malkei Israel Sq, 64951 Tel Aviv, Israel *tel:* +972 3 695 9355 *fax:* +972 3 696 3528. Dan Gottfried, artistic dir. *Annual. Last week in Aug 1998. 40 concerts featuring top jazz ensembles, masterclasses and evening sessions.*

Zimriya-World Assembly of Choirs. 4 Aharonowitz St, Tel Aviv 63566, Israel *tel:* +972 3 528 0233 *fax:* +972 3 629 9524. Esther Herlitz, dir. *Triennial. Next 10-20 Aug 1998. Choral music w/shops and concerts.*

Italy

Animato. Viale Gorizia 24/a, I-00198 Roma, Italy *tel:* +39 6 854 6191 *also fax.* Lucia Ronchetti. *Sep-Dec 1998. Contemporary music.*

Batignano Musica nel Chiostro. Santa Croce, Comune di Grosseto, I-58041 Batignano, Italy *tel:* +39 564 338096 *also fax;* +44 171 607 2832. Adam Pollock, artistic dir. *Jul-Aug.*

* **Brescia and Bergamo International Piano Festival.** Direzione Artistica, c/o Teatro Grande, Via Paganora 19/A, I-25121 Brescia, Italy *tel:* +39 30 293022 *fax:* +39 30 240 0771 *email:* festival.pianistico@spm.it; http:// www.spm.it/bergamo/festival_p/. Agostino Orizio, artistic dir. *Annual. End Apr to beginning Jun 1998. Classical piano.*

Corsi Festival. Fondazione Accademia Musicale Chigiana, 89 Via di Città, I-53100 Siena, Italy *tel:* +39 577 46152 *fax:* +39 577 288124.

Corso Internazionale di Musica Antica. Festival di Musica Antica Urbino, Fondazione Italiana por la Musica Antica della SIFD, Via Monte Zebio 33, I-00195 Roma, Italy *tel:* +39 6 372 9667 *also fax.* Renato Meucci, president. *Annual. Jul. Concerts of baroque music. Instrumental courses, renaissance, baroque and folk dance.*

E' Vento Suono. Via Ciro Menotti 147, I-61100 Pesaro, Italy *tel:* +39 721 414341 *also fax; email:* musicalibera@eventsuono.it; http://www.event suono.it. Paolo Giaro, artistic dir; Antonio Cioffi, gen mgr. *Apr 1998. Annual festival held at Teatro Rossini, Pesaro. Contemporary, jazz, ethnic, world music and computer music.*

* **Festival della Valle d'Itria.** Centro Artistico Musicale, Palazzo Ducale, I-74015 Martina Franca, Italy *tel:* +39 80 4805100/4805702 *fax:* +39 80 4805120. Franco Punzi, president; Sergio Segalini, artistic dir. *Annual. Jul-Aug. Opera and concerts.*

Festival di Nuova Consonanza. Associazione Nuova Consonanza, Via Simone de Saint Bon 61, I-00195 Roma, Italy *tel:* +39 6 370 0323 *fax:* +39 6 372 0026. *Oct-Dec. Contemporary and electronic music, workshops and concerts.*

Festival Lirico Internazionale di Barga. Comune di Barga, Via di Mezzo 45, I-55051 Barga (Lucca), Italy *tel:* +39 583 723352/042 *fax:* +39 583 723745. Antonio Da Prato, president. *Jul-Aug. Open-air opera, concerts.*

Festival of Two Worlds/Spoleto Festival. Associazione Festival dei due Mondi, Via Cesare Beccaria 18, I-00196 Roma, Italy *tel:* +39 6 3210288 *fax:* +39 6 3200747. Gian Carlo Menotti, artistic dir; Francis Menotti, chmn. *Jun-Jul. Opera, symphonic concerts, choral concerts, chamber music, modern and classical dance.*

Festival Organistico Internazionale Città di Treviso. c/o Comune di Treviso, I-31100 Treviso, Italy *tel:* +39 422 658394 *fax:* +39 422 430334. Riccardo Moscatelli, sec; Andrea Marcon, artistic dir. *Sep-Oct. International Organ Academy with seminars, lectures, masterclasses. Mainly early music on ten historical organs inside the city walls.*

Festival Pontino. Viale Le Corbusier 379, I-04100 Latina, Italy *tel:* +39 773 605551 *fax:* +39 773 605548. Riccardo Cerocchi, mgr; Goffredo Petrassi, president; Raffaele Pozzi, artistic dir. *Jun-Jul. Classical and contemporary, including premieres.*

Festival Pucciniano. Biglietteria del Teatro all'Aperto, Belvedere Puccini n 4, I-55048 Torre del Lago Puccini, Italy *tel:* +39 584 359322 *fax:* +39 584 350277. Cavallaro Angelo, artistic mgr; Agostini Grazia, ticket office. *Jul-Aug. Opera, concerts, lyrical music.*

Festival Spaziomusica. Spaziomusica, Laboratorio di Studi e Ricerche, Via Liguria 60, I-09127 Cagliari, Italy *tel:* +39 70 400844 *fax:* +39 70 485439 *email:* smusica@mbox.vol.it. Franco Oppo, artistic dir. *Oct-Dec. Contemporary music.*

Gubbio Festival. Pza Oderisi 6, I-06024 Gubbio (PG), Italy *tel:* +39 75 922 0230/0693 *fax:* +39 75 927 3409. Pavel Vermikov, artistic dir; Giovanni Sammipou, admin. *Annual. 25 Jul-9 Aug 1998. Str, woodwind, piano, vocal technique, choral and chamber music concerts and masterclasses.*

Incontri Europei con la Musica. Associazione Musica Aperta, Via Borgo Palazzo 31, I-24125 Bergamo, Italy *tel:* +39 35 242287 *also fax; email:* mabg@ibguniv.unibg.it; http://www.unibg.it/~mabg. Piezalberto Cattaneo. *Feb-Apr 1998. Clasical, modern and contemporary chamber music. Member of the European Conference of Promoters of New Music.*

La Biennale di Venezia - Festival Internazionale di Musica Contemporanea. S Marco, Ca Giustinian, I-30124 Venezia, Italy *tel:* +39 41 521 8861/8711 *fax:* +39 41 520 0569/5669. Dario Ventimiglia, dir. *Sep-Oct. Contemporary music.*

* **Maggio Musicale Fiorentino.** Teatro Comunale, Via Solferino 15, I-50123 Firenze, Italy *tel:* +39 55 27791/211158 *fax:* +39 55 239 6954/277 9410 *email:* teatro.communale@infogroup.it; http://www.mega.it/maggio fiorentino/. Francesco Ernani, gen mgr. *Annual. 21 May-20 Jun 1998. Opera, concerts, ballet, exhibitions, films and meetings.*

Musica Attuale. Octandre Musica Attuale, PO Box 259, I-40100 Bologna, Italy *tel:* +39 51 676 8076. *Lectures, concerts and seminars on contemporary music. Apr-Jun.*

Musica2000 Festival. 8 Via Alpi, I-60131 Ancona, Italy *tel:* +39 71 891717 *also fax.* Corrado Canonici, artistic dir. *Sep 1998. Contemporary music.*

* **Ravenna Festival.** Via Dante Alighieri 1, I-48100 Ravenna, Italy *tel:* +39 544 213895 *fax:* +39 544 36303 *email:* ra.festival@netgate.it; http:// www.netgate.it/ra.festival. Cristina Mazzavillani Muti, president.

* **Rossini Opera Festival.** Via Rossini 37, I-61100 Pesaro, Italy *tel:* +39 721 34473 *fax:* +39 721 30979 *email:* rof@rossinioperafestival.it; http:// www.rossinioperafestival.it. Gianfranco Mariotti, gen mgr; Luigi Ferrari, artistic dir. *Annual. 8-24 Aug 1998. Rossini's operas and concerts.*

* **Settembre Musica.** Città di Torino, Assessorato per le Risorse Culturali e la Comunicazione, Piazza San Carlo 161, I-10123 Torino, Italy *tel:* +39 11 442 4715/4703 *fax:* +39 11 4424738 *email:* settembre.musica@ commune.turino.it; http://www.commune.turino.it. Laura Tori, press offr. *Annual. 1-21 Sep 1998. Classical, contemporary and ethnic music.*

* **Settimane Musicali di Stresa - Festival Internazionale.** Palazzo dei Congressi, Via R Bonghi 4, I-28049 Stresa, Italy *tel:* +39 323 31095/30459 *fax:* +39 323 33006. Italo Trentinaglia de Daverio, artistic dir. *Aug-Sep. Symphony concerts, chamber concerts (quartets, violin, cello, piano and organ recitals).*

Settimane Musicali Senese. Fondazione Accademia Musicale Chigiana, Via di Città 89, I-53100 Siena, Italy *tel:* +39 577 46152 *fax:* +39 577 288124. *Annual. Aug.*

* **Verona Festival.** Ente Lirico Arena di Verona, Piazza Brà 28, I-37121 Verona, Italy *tel:* +39 45 590109/966 *fax:* +39 45 590201. *Jan-May, Jul-Sep.*

Japan

Japan International Youth Musicale in Shizuoka. Tokoha Gakuen Educational Institute, 1 22 1 Sena Shizuoka City, Shizuoka Prefecture 420, Japan *tel:* +81 54 261 1356 *fax:* +81 54 261 5601. *Triennial.*

Kitakyushu International Music Festival. 1-1 Jonai, Kokurakita-ku, Kitakyushu 803, Japan *tel:* +81 93 582 2391 *fax:* +81 93 581 5755. Hisaki Minamimoto, sec gen. *1 week in Oct-Nov. Chamber mus.*

Kyoto International Music Festival. Saishoji-cho Okazaki, Sakyo-ku, Kyoto, Japan *tel:* +81 75 752 0202.

* **Osaka International Festival Society.** New Asahi Building, 3-18 Nakanoshima 2-chome, Kita-ku, Osaka 530, Japan *tel:* +81 6 231 6985 *fax:* +81 6 227 1262. Michi Murayama, exec dir. *Apr. Classical music, concertos, piano recitals and Noh play.*

Pacific Music Festival. Pacific Music Festival Organizing Committee, c/o Sapporo Concert Hall, 1-15, Nakajima-Koen, Chuo-Ku, Sapporo, 064 Japan *tel:* +81 11 520 2222 *fax:* +81 11 520 1687 *email:* pmf@mb. infosnow.or.jp. Toshiko Shoji, admin. *11 Jul-2 Aug 1998. International educational music festival with orchestral and chamber music course and course for voice and piano accompaniment.*

Tokyo International Chamber Music Festival. c/o Japan International League of Artists, Hidaka Bldg 1-34-8 Shinjuku, Shinjuku-ku, Tokyo, Japan *tel:* +81 3 3356 4033 *fax:* +81 3 3356 5780. Kazuhiko Hattori, chmn. *Spring. Classical and contemporary mus.*

Lithuania

Baltic Music Festival 'Gaida'. Lithuanian Composers Union, Mickeviciaus 29, 2600 Vilnius, Lithuania *tel:* +370 2 223611 *fax:* +370 2 220939 *email:* center@mipc.vno.osf.lt. Gintaras Sodeika, chmn. *Annual. Early Oct. Contemporary music from countries surrounding the Baltic Sea.*

Jauna Muzika - New Music Festival. PO Box 2489, 2051 Vilnius, Lithuania *tel:* +370 2 263291/225003 *fax:* +370 2 220939. Remigijus Merkelys, chmn. *Late Apr 1998. Lithuanian and foreign composers and musicians. Contemporary music with emphasis on music of young composers.*

Mariu Klavyrai - New Music Festival. Lithuanian Composers' Union (Klaipeda Dept), Kretingos 45-20, 5808 Klaipeda, Lithuania *tel:* +370 6 298008 *also fax.* Remigijus Silcika. *Annual. Oct. Contemporary music with an emphasis on music of the Baltic region.*

Luxembourg

Festival Européen de Wiltz-Luxembourg. Château de Wiltz, L-9516 Wiltz, Luxembourg *tel:* +352 958145 *fax:* +352 958190; +352 959310. Fernand Koenig, artistic dir. *Jul. Classical, opera, drama, ballet, jazz.*

* **Festival International Echternach.** BP 30, L-6401 Echternach, Luxembourg *tel:* +352 728347 *fax:* +352 727112. Mariette Scholtes, admin dir. *Annual. 6 May-27 Jun 1998. Mainly classical (symphonic, chamber, choral).*

Macedonia

Balkanski Festival Na Narodni Pesni i Igri. Makedonski Prosvetiteli 4, PO Box 94, 96000 Ohrid, Macedonia *tel:* +389 96 2263; +389 96 21 433 *fax:* +389 96 22 063. Dragia Sillanoska, mgr. *5-10 Jul 1998. Folk music and dance.*

* **Ohrid Summer Festival.** PO Box 23, 96000 Ohrid, Macedonia *tel:* +389 96 21304/22304 *fax:* +389 96 21133. Vasko Zorovski, programme dir. *12 Jul- 20 Aug 1998. Classical music, early music and renaissance. Orchestras, opera, ballet, chamber mus, recitals, theatre.*

Mexico

Festival Internacional Cervantino. Av Alvaro Obregon 273, Col Roma Norte, 06700 Mexico City, Mexico *tel:* +52 5 207 47 64 *fax:* +52 5 533 41 22. Sergio Vela, gen dir. *8-5 Oct 1998. Multi-art autumn festival including dance, opera, mus and theatre, academic activities, film cycles and art exhibitions.*

Festival de Música de Cámara de San Miguel de Allende. Bellas Artes, Calle Hernández Macias 75, San Miguel de Allende, Mexico *tel:* +52 41 520289 *also fax.* Carmen Masip de Hawkins, Tom Sawyer, co-dirs. *Aug. Classical, chamber music. Masterclasses and ensemble coaching for scholarship students.*

International Festival of Contemporary Music. Sones Contemporaneas Association, Seminario 179, Lomas de la Herradura, 52760 Huixquilucan Edo de Mexico, Mexico *tel:* +525 29 1 5666 *fax:* +525 56 4 4002. Cecilia Medinav. *Oct in Mexico City and Guanajuato.*

Monaco

* **Printemps des Arts de Monte-Carlo.** Direction des Affaires Culturelles, 8 Rue Louis Notari, MC-98000 (Principauté), Monaco *tel:* +33 93 158303 *fax:* +33 93 506694. Rainier Rocchi. *Annual. 11 Apr-18 May 1998. Ballet, vocal recitals, choral music, orchestral, chamber and opera.*

Netherlands

Delft Festival of Chamber Music. PO Box 404, 2260 AK Leidschendam, Netherlands *tel:* +31 70 320 25 00 *fax:* +31 70 320 26 11. Isabelle van Keulen, artistic dir. *Annual. Aug. Chamber music.*

Donemus Foundation - Dutch Music Days. Paulus Potterstraat 16, NL-1017 CZ Amsterdam, Netherlands *tel:* +31 20 676 4436 *fax:* +31 20 673 3588 *email:* donemus@pi.net; http://www.netcetera.nl/donemus. L J Deuss, mgr. *Early Dec. Dutch, mainly contemporary music.*

Festival on Spiritualism in Contemporary Music. Gaudeamus Foundation Contemporary Music Centre, Swammerdamstraat 38, NL-1091 RV, Amsterdam, Netherlands *tel:* +31 20 694 73 49 *fax:* +31 20 694 72 58 *email:* gaud@xs4all.nl. Arthur van der Drift; Michael van Eekeren. *Next 25 Sep-3 Oct 1999.*

Haarlem International Organ Festival. PO Box 3333, NL-2011 DH Haarlem, Netherlands *tel:* +31 23 160574 *fax:* +31 23 160576. Mrs E L S Hendrikse, sec. *7-31 Jul 1998. Various recitals (organ, choir, instrumental).*

* **Holland Festival.** Kleine-Gartmanplantsoen 21, NL-1017 RP Amsterdam, Netherlands *tel:* +31 70 320 25 00 *fax:* +31 70 320 26 11. Jan van Vlijmen, mus dir. *Annual. May-Jun. Opera, music theatre and dance.*

* **Holland Festival Early Music Utrecht.** Organisatie Oude Muziek, PO Box 734, NL-3500 AS Utrecht, Netherlands *tel:* +31 30 236 2236 *fax:* +31 30 232 2798. Casper Vogel, exec mgr; Tineke de Ruiter, exec mgr. *Annual. 28 Aug-6 Sep 1998. 250 events on music composed before 1900 performed on authentic period insts or copies.*

International Choir Festival - Arnhem. Stichting SNK, Plompetoren-gracht 3, NL-3512 CA Utrecht, Netherlands *tel:* +31 30231 3174 *fax:* +31 30231 8137 *email:* snt@euronet.nl. Joseph Vranken Jr, mus dir. *Quadrennial. Next Jun-Jul 2001. All types of choral music.*

International Gaudeaumus Music Week, Amsterdam. Gaudeamus Foundation, Swammersamstraat 38, NL-1091 RV Amsterdam, Netherlands *tel:* +31 20 694 7349 *fax:* +31 20 694 7258 *email:* gaud@ xs4all.nl; http://www.xs4all.nl/~gaud. H Heuvelmans, dir. *Annual. 7-13 Sep 1998. Amsterdam. Contemporary music. Performances of works by winners of the International Gaudeaumus Composers' Competition Prize (see* **Competitions***). An international selection of c 40 works in very different musical styles by composers aged 30 and under.*

International Society for Contemporary Music. c/o Gaudeamus, Swammerdamstraat 38, 1091 RV Amsterdam, Netherlands *tel:* +31 20 6947349 *fax:* +31 20 6947258 *email:* iscm@xs4all.nl; http://www. xs4all.nl/~iscm. H Heuvelmans, sec gen. *World Music Days 17-26 Apr 1998 in Manchester, UK. Contemporary music concerts.*

North Sea Jazz Festival. PO Box 87919, NL-2508 DH The Hague, Netherlands *tel:* +31 70 354 2958 *fax:* +31 70 352 4107. Paul Dankmeyer, artistic dir; Theo Van Den Hoek, mkt dir. *Jul. Soul, blues, funk, fusion, Latin.*

Orlando Chamber Music Festival. Orlando Festival Foundation, Keizersgracht 261, NL-1016 EC Amsterdam, Netherlands *tel:* +31 20 623 0469 *fax:* +31 20 622 9081. Isabelle Bensa, dir. *26 Jul-9 Aug 1998. Chamber music concerts, masterclasses, students academy.*

Norway

* **Bergen International Festival.** Strandgt 18, PO Box 183, N-5001 Bergen, Norway *tel:* +47 55 312170 *fax:* +47 55 315531 *email:* info@fib.no; http://www.fib.no/. Bergljót Jónsdóttir, festival dir. *Annual. 20-31 May 1998. Music, ballet, dance theatre, classical concerts at the homes of Edvard Grieg, Ole Bull and Harald Saeverud.*

Elverum International Festival. Elverum Tourism and Events Office, Storgate, N-2400 Elverum, Norway *tel:* +47 62 416060 *fax:* +47 62 410020. Robert Ryall, dir; Ørnulf Ring, chief exec offr. *Aug. Symphonic orch concerts and w/shops for young adults.*

Førde Folk Music Festival. PO Box 395, N-6801 Førde, Norway *tel:* +47 57 82 03 00 *fax:* +47 57 82 03 04 *email:* hildeb@telepost.no. Hilde Bjørkum, dir. *9-12 Jul 1998. Folk music from all over the world. Concerts, w/shops, exhibitions, children's events.*

Ilios Festival for Contemporary Music. NY Musik, Nord-Norge, St Olavsgt 47, N-9400 Harstad, Norway *tel:* +47 77 06 24 11 *also fax.* Kirsten Monique Jenssen, festival dir. *Feb.*

International Biennale of Contemporary Arts. Stavanger Speculum, Sandvigå 27, N-4007 Stavanger, Norway *tel:* +47 51 846676 *fax:* +47 51 846673. *1-7 Nov 1998. Thematic multimedia festival of contemporary arts containing mus, dance, theatre, exhibitions, film and conferences. 1998 theme: 'Circle'.*

* **International Chamber Music Festival, Stavanger.** Sandvigå 27, N-4007 Stavanger, Norway *tel:* +47 51 846670 *fax:* +47 51 846673 *email:* icmt@online.no. Siri Skaar, mgr. *Annual. 7-16 Aug 1998. Chamber music.*

International Church Music Festival. Kristiansand Domkirke, PO Box 321, N-4601 Kristiansand, Norway *tel:* +47 38 021311 *fax:* +47 38 027522 *email:* awilder@online.no. Andrew Wilder, cathedral organist. *Annual. 10-17 May 1998. Church music, organ music, chamber music, vocal and instrumental soloists, folk music, art exhibitions, seminars.*

Lillehammer Winter Festival. PO Box 696, N-2601 Lillehammer, Norway *tel:* +47 61 24 65 30 *fax:* +47 61 24 63 88. Olemìc Thomessen, dir; Jørgen Damskau, project leader, technics and mus. *4-8 Feb 1998. International arts festival with music of all genres, theatre, children's olympics, snow sculpture, outdoor winter activities and exhibitions of arts and handicrafts.*

Music Factory. Georgernes Verft 3, N-5011 Bergen, Norway *tel:* +47 55 231330 *fax:* +47 55 231333. Geir Johnson, artistic dir. *20 May-1 Jun 1998. Approx 12 contemporary music concerts in Bergen. Also dance and opera. Masterclass in composition. Approx 20 concerts with contemporary music presented as pedagogical programmes in schools.*

Nesbyen Music Festival. PO Box 124, N-3540 Nesbyen, Norway *tel:* +47 32 06 81 92. Per Nordal, dir. *May.*

Nordland Music Festival. PO Box 319, N-8001 Bodo, Norway *tel:* +47 75 52 2398 *fax:* +47 75 52 2387. Roar Leinan, dir; Trond Mathisen, producer. *Jul-Aug. Classical, jazz, rock.*

Nordlyd - Trondheim Contemporary Music Festival. Trond Einar Garmo, Mauritz Hansensgt 8, N-7030 Trondheim, Norway *tel:* +47 73 51 2216 *fax:* +47 73 59 6588 *email:* trondeg@notam.uio.no. *20-27 Nov 1997. Contemporary mus.*

North Norway Festival. PO Box 901, N-9401 Harstad, Norway *tel:* +47 77 066599 *fax:* +47 77 067363. *Jun. Concerts, theatre, dance, art exhibitions, literary and film, seminars and children's festival.*

Peer Gynt Festival. Turist-og Messekontoret, Nedregt 5A, N-2640 Vinstra, Norway *tel:* +47 61 29 4770 *fax:* +47 61 29 4771 *email:* peergynt@online.no. Stig R Nyhus, admin. *31 Jul-9 Aug 1998. Theatre and music festival.*

St Olav Festival of Trondheim. PO Box 2045, N-7001 Trondheim, Norway *tel:* +47 73 929470 *fax:* +47 73 503866. Eirik Kvan, dir. *25 Jul-3 Aug 1998. Church services, concerts, lectures, guided tours, exhibitions, activities for children, chamber music courses and projects in early music.*

Sandefjord Internasjonale Operafestival. PO Box 243, N-3201 Sandefjord, Norway *tel:* +47 33 46 14 88 *fax:* +47 33 46 06 20. Ronald Rörvik, dir; Trine Holthe, admin. *Biennial. Jul. International opera festival.*

Stord International Choir Festival. PO Box 433, N-5401 Stord, Norway *tel:* +47 53 496930/1 *fax:* +47 53 413077. Reidun Hagenes, festival dir. *Jun. Featuring concert choirs of high international standard. Workshops and concerts. Also soloists and chamber musicians or jazz groups; professionals only.*

Ultima Oslo Contemporary Music Festival. Tollbugt 28, N-0157 Oslo, Norway *tel:* +47 22 42 9999 *fax:* +47 22 42 4218 *email:* ultima@notam. uio.no; http://www.notam.uio.no/nmi/ultima. Åse Hedstrøm, festival dir; Beate Styri, PR officer; Howard Gamble, exec dir. *Annual. 2-11 Oct 1998. Contemporary music, including concerts and performances, sound-installations, multimedia concerts, films, educ arrangements and seminars.*

Poland

Baroque Opera Festival in Warsaw. Warsaw Chamber Opera, Ul Nowogrodzka 49, PL-00695 Warszawa, Poland *tel:* +48 82 628 3096; +48 2 229 3233 *fax:* +48 2 229 3233; +48 2 231 4764. Stefan Sutkowski, artistic dir. *Annual. 15-30 Oct 1998.*

Days of Organ Music Kraków. c/o State Philharmonic Orchestra Karol Szymanowski, Zwierzyniecka 1, PL-31103 Kraków, Poland *tel:* +48 12 220958 *fax:* +48 12 224312. Jacek Berwaldt, programme dept head. *17-25 Apr 1998. Organ recitals, oratorio concerts.*

* **International Festival Wratislavia Cantans, Music of Fine Arts.** Rynek-Ratusz 24, PL-50101 Wroclaw, Poland *tel:* +48 71 30833 *fax:* +48 71 442865. Tadeusz Strugala, artistic dir. *Annual. Sep. Oratorios, choral, instrumental, chamber, vocal recitals, lieder.*

Laboratory of Contemporary Music. Ul Klaudyny 6/83, PL-01684 Warszawa, Poland *tel:* +48 22 336859 *fax:* +48 22 619 0111. Marian Borkowski, president and artistic dir. *Annual. Oct. Symphonic, chmbr, choral and computer mus. Concerts, seminars, round tables, debates.*

Miedzyzdroje International Choral Song Festival. c/o Rondo Concert Agency, PO Box 77, 70334 Szczecin 4, Poland *tel:* +48 91 845 242 *fax:* +48 91 846 193 *email:* rondo@ubique.com.pl. Stanislaw Zaborowski.

Monteverdi's Opera Festival. Warsaw Chamber Opera, Ul Nowogrodzka 49, Pl 00695 Warszawa, Poland *tel:* +48 82 628 3096/629 3233 *fax:* +48 82 629 3233. Stefan Sutkowski, artistic dir. *Annual. 1-15 Oct 1998. All Monteverdi's stage works.*

The Mozart Festival in Warsaw. Warsaw Chamber Opera, ul Nowogrodzka 49, PL-00695 Warszawa, Poland *tel:* +48 826 28 30 96; +48 22 29 32 33 *also fax; fax:* +48 22 31 47 64. Stefan Sutkowski, artistic dir. *15 Jun-26 Jul annually. Features all Mozart's stage works (24 productions) and a selection of his concert music.*

Warsaw Autumn (International Festival of Contemporary Music). c/o Polish Composers' Union, Rynek Starego Miasta 27, PL-00272 Warszawa, Poland *tel:* +48 22 311634; +48 22 8310607 *also fax.* Olgierd Pisarenko, chmn; Krzysztof Knittel, dir. *Annual. Sep. Contemporary music; symphony orch, chmbr ens, solo recitals, electronic and computer mus, sound installations.*

Portugal

Algarve International Music Festival. Região de Turismo do Algarve, Av 5 de Outubro 18, P-8000 Faro, Portugal *tel:* +351 89 800400 *fax:* +351 89 800489. Luis Pereira Leal, dir. *May-Jun.*

* **Associaçao Internacional de Música da Costa do Estoril.** Casa dos Arcos, Estrada Marginal, P-2775 Parede, Portugal *tel:* +351 1 468 5199 *fax:* +351 1 468 5607. Piñeiro Nagy, artistic dir. *Jul-Aug. Symphonic, chamber, recitals, ballet, traditional music from Far East.*

Sintra Music Festival. Praça da República 23, 2710 Sintra, Portugal *tel:* +351 923 4895/924 3518 *fax:* +351 923 4845. Luís Pereira Leal, dir; Ana Alcântara, coordinator. *Jun-Jul 1998. Classical music in the Sintra Palaces or 'Quintas'.*

Festival Internacional de Música da Póvoa de Varzim. Rua D. Maria I 56, 4490 Póvoa de Varzim, P-4490 Póvoa de Varzim, Portugal *tel:* +351 52 61 4145 *fax:* +351 52 61 2548. J Marques, dir. *Jun-Jul. Baroque, classical, contemporary music.*

Gulbenkian Contemporary Music Encounter. Fundacao Calouste Gulbenkian, Avenida de Berna 45-A, P-1067 Lisboa, Portugal *tel:* +35 11 7935131 *fax:* +35 11 7937296 *email:* musica@gulbenkian.pt; http://www.estado-arte.pt/gulbenkian. Luís Pereira Leal, dir. *5-18 May 1998.*

Puerto Rico

Festival Casals de Puerto Rico. PO Box 41277, Minillas Sta, San Juan, Puerto Rico *tel:* +787 728 5744 *fax:* 787 723 5843. Krzysztof Penderecki, mus dir. *1-21 Jun 1998. Symphonic and chamber music.*

Republic of Ireland

Cork International Choral Festival. PO Box 68, Cork, Republic of Ireland *tel:* +353 21 308308 *fax:* +353 21 308309 *email:* chorfest@iol.ie. Sheila Kelleher, festival admin. *Annual. 30 Apr-3 May 1998; 29 Apr-2 May 1999; 27-30 Apr 2000. For amateur choirs. Featuring nightly gala concerts, fringe programme, public performances, church visits and the prestigious Fleischmann International Trophy Competition.*

Dublin International Organ and Choral Festival. Liffey House, Tara St, Dublin 2, Republic of Ireland *tel:* +353 1 677 3066 ext 416 *fax:* +353 1 679 8991. Gerard Gillen, artistic dir. *Triennial. Next 20-27 Jun 1999. Organ and choral music including international organ competition. Recitals, workshops, seminars.*

Kilkenny Arts Week. Rothe House, Parliament St, Kilkenny, Republic of Ireland *tel:* +353 56 63663 *fax:* +353 56 51704 *email:* kaw@iol.ie. Audrey Phelan, admin dir. *Aug 1998. Classical music, visual art, literature, film and theatre.*

Waterford International Festival of Light Opera. 60 Morrissons Av, Waterford, Republic of Ireland *tel:* +353 51 75437. Sean Dower, gen sec. *Annual. 19 Sep-4 Oct 1998. Competitive 16-day festival of light opera and musicals by amateur operatic and musical societies from Ireland, UK and Europe.*

West Cork Chamber Music Festival. Bantry House, Bantry, Co Cork, Republic of Ireland *tel:* +353 27 61105 *also fax; fax:* +353 27 61485 *email:* http://www.rte.ie/ music/vanbrugh/festival.html. Francis Humphrys, festival dir. *28 Jun-5 Jul 1998. Chamber music festival, poetry.*

Wexford Festival Opera. Theatre Royal, Wexford, Republic of Ireland *tel:* +353 53 22400/22144 (box office) *fax:* +353 53 24289/47438 (box office) *email:* info@wexopera.iol.ie; http://www.iol.ie/~wexopera. Luigi Ferrari, artistic dir; Jerome Hynes, chief exec; Philomena Keeling, admin. *Annual. Oct-Nov. Three productions of rare or neglected operas plus forty recitals and concerts over eighteen nights.*

Romania

Cluj Modern. Academia de Muzica 'Georghe Dima', Str IC Bratianu nr 25, 3400 Cluj-Napoca, Romania *tel:* +40 64 193879 *also fax. Biennial. Next 4-9 Apr 1999. Contemporary music.*

George Enescu International Festival. Artexim, Calea Victoriei nr 155, bl D1 sc 8 et 2, 71012 Bucharest, Romania *tel:* +40 1 650 18 06/12 *fax:* +40 1 311 02 00 *email:* artexim@com.pcnet.ro. Lord Yehudi Menuhin, hon president; Lawrence Foster, artistic dir; Mihai Constantinescu, organiser. *6-20 Sep 1998. Classical music, concert recitals, opera, ballet.*

Russia

Amber Necklace. Rokossovskogo 4, 236040 Kaliningrad, Russia *tel:* +7 095 112 443451/448830 *fax:* +7 095 112 443451.

Autumn Constellation Festival of Organ Music. Rokossovskogo 4, 236040 Kaliningrad, Russia *tel:* +7 112 443451/448830 *fax:* +7 112 443451. Grigori Nazarovski, dir. *Oct. Org mus.*

Bayan and Bayan-Players Festival. Arbat 35, 121835 Moscow, Russia *tel:* +7 095 248 3494/2939 *fax:* +7 095 230 2427. Nicolai Butov, dir. *Dec. Chmbr and folk mus.*

December Nights. Volkonkha 12, 121019 Moscow, Russia *tel:* +7 095 202 2464/203 6974 *fax:* +7 095 203 4674. Inna Pruss, co-ord, exec dir. *1-30 Dec 1998. Chamber music of Schubert, Brahms and Mendelssohn, also includes oratorios, masses and chamber operas.*

Moscow Conservatory International Summer Music Festival. c/o 41 Ashen Grove, London SW19 8BL, UK *tel:* +44 181 947 7201 *also fax.* Niel Immelman. *3-22 Aug 1998. For piano, voice and all orchestral instruments. Daily recitals by Moscow Conservatory professors and winners of international competitions.*

Moscow International Music Festival. RosInterFest, 12 Sadovaya Triumfalnaya Str, 103006 Moscow, Russia *tel:* +7 095 200 6585/209 2261 *fax:* +7 095 209 9709 *email:* rosinterfest@glas.apc.org. Igor S Gurevich, chmn of organising committee. *Jul. Summer programme of masterclasses, lessons, recitals and concerts.*

Polar Musical Autumn. Philharmonic Society, Knippovicha 20, 183049 Murmansk, Russia *tel:* +7 815 2 556268/554843 *also fax.* Alexander Kondratyev, dir. *Oct. Chamber and folk mus.*

Rakhmaninov Festival. Sovetskaya 182, 392000 Tambov, Russia *tel:* +7 7522 21664; +7 7522 21661. Aleksey Trunin. *Jun. Symphonic, chamber mus.*

Turgenev Musical Autumn. Komsomolsskaya 63, 302030 Oryol, Russia *tel:* +7 8600 66012 *also fax;* +7 8600 26681. Valeri Shapiro. *Oct. Orch, chamber mus.*

Winter Festival. Lomonosova 60, 163061 Arkhangelsk, Russia *tel:* +7 8182 441307/441863 *fax:* +7 8182 466477. Vladimir Slesaryov, dir. *Feb. Choral, chamber, folk mus.*

Serbia

Belgrade Music Festival (BEMUS). Jugokoncert, Terazije 41/I, 11000 Belgrade, Serbia *tel:* +381 11 339917 *fax:* +381 11 340478. Eduard Ile, gen dir. *Annual. Oct.*

Belgrade Summer Festival (BELEF). Jugokoncert Terazije 41/1, 11000 Belgrade, Serbia *tel:* +381 11 339917 *fax:* +381 11 340478. Eduard Ile, gen dir. *Mid Jul-end Aug.*

Singapore

Singapore Festival of Arts. Festival Secretariat, National Arts Council, 35th Storey, PSA Building, 460 Alexandra Rd, 119963, Singapore *tel:* +65 270 0722 *fax:* +65 273 6880. Liew Chin Choy, dir (artistic programmes). *Biennial. Next Jun 1998. Festival of Asian Performing Arts Jun. Traditional, classical and ethnic jazz music.*

Slovak Republic

Melos-Ethos International Festival of Contemporary Music. Michalskná 10, 815 36 Bratislava, Slovak Republic *tel:* +421 17 5331373 *also fax; email:* slovkonc@mbox.bts.sk. Slávka Ferencová, sec. *Next 1999. Contemporary music concerts and seminars.*

Slovenia

Festival Brezice. c/o Ars Ramovs Institute of Arts, Marketing, Promotion and Investment, Slovenska cesta 1, 1000 Ljubljana, Slovenia *tel:* +386 61 125 3366 *fax:* +386 61 131 3067 *email:* http://www.k-ramovs.si/. Klemen Ramovs. *18 Jul-1 Aug 1998. Medieval and baroque mus.*

* **International Summer Festival Ljubljana.** Trg Francoske Revolucije 1-2, 1000 Ljubljana, Slovenia *tel:* +386 61 126 4340/2011 *fax:* +386 61 221288 *email:* festival.ljubljana@eunet.si; http://www.festival-lj.si/. Darko Brlek, dir. *Annual. 11 Jun-31 Aug 1998. Music, dance, opera and theatre.*

Spain

Associació Côchlea. Sardenya 516 6e 2a, E-08024 Barcelona, Spain *tel:* +34 3 284 2917 *also fax; email:* cochlea@conestar.es. José Manuel Berenguer, artistic dir. *Jul-Sep. Contemporary mus, multimedia shows, free jazz and improvisation.*

* **Barcelona Summer Festival Grec.** Institut de Cultura de Barcelona, La Rambla 99, E-08002 Barcelona, Spain *tel:* +34 3 3017775 *fax:* +34 3 3016100 *email:* http://www.bcn.es. Ferran Mascarell, gen mgr; Xavier Alberti, artistic dir. *Annual. Classical, flamenco and rock music.*

* **Contemporary Music Festival of Valencia - ENSEMS.** Asociación Valenciana de Música Contemporána, c/Conde de Trenor, 1-pta 7, E-46003 Valencia, Spain *tel:* +34-63910783 *fax:* +34-63921820. Joan Cerveró, artistic dir. *20-26 Apr 1998. Contemporary music. Premieres, repertory soloists, music theatre, orch, ensembles.*

* **Cuenca Religious Music Festival.** Semenas de Música Religiosa, Apartado 97, E-16080 Cuenca, Switzerland *tel:* +34 69 178857 *also fax; email:* aef@vtx.ch.

Festival de Cadaqués. Arcs 8 1er 2a, E-08002 Barcelona, Spain *tel:* +34 33 01 95 55 *fax:* +34 33 02 26 70 *email:* trito@bcn.servicom.es. Llorenç Caballero, dir. *25 Jul-20 Aug 1998. Symphonic and chamber music.*

Festival de Música de Canarias. SOCAEM, S A, León y Castillo, 427-3, E-35007 Las Palmas de Gran Canaria, Spain *tel:* +34 28 24 7442/3 *fax:* +34 28 27 6042. Rafael Nebot, dir; Nora Krozewski, festival sec. *Annual. 7 Jan-7 Feb 1998. Classical and contemporary chamber music concerts and recitals including premieres of works commissioned by the festival. On Gran Canaria, Tenerife and throughout the Canary Islands.*

Festival de Otono de la Comunidad de Madrid. Plaza de Espand 8, E-28008 Madrid, Spain *tel:* +34 1 580 2575/7 *fax:* +34 1 580 2565. Agustín Tend, dir. *Sep-Nov. Performing arts, contemporary and traditional music.*

* **Festival Internacional de Música.** Apartat 70, E-17257 Torroella de Montgrí, Spain *tel:* +34 72 760605 *fax:* +34 72 760648 *email:* jjmmtdm@ddgi.es; http://www.udg.cs/udg/fimtdm.html. *Annual. Jul-Aug. Orchestral, chamber, vocal, choral and instrumental.*

* **Granada International Festival of Music and Dance.** Auditorio Manuel de Falla, Paseo de los Mártires s/n, E-18009 Granada, Spain *tel:* +34 958 221844 *fax:* +34 958 220691 *email:* granadafestival@tsai.es. Maricarmen Palma, admin dir. *Annual. Jun-Jul. Classical music, recitals, opera, ballet.*

International Festival of Contemporary Music. Centro para la Difusión de la Musica Contemporánea, Santa Isabel 52, E-28012 Madrid, Spain *tel:* +34 1 4682310 *fax:* +34 1 5308321 *email:* consuelo.diez@cdmc. inaem.es. Consuelo Diez, CDMC dir; José Chacón, CDMC co-ord. *Alicante. Last week of Sep. Contemporary music.*

International Guitar Festival. Ayuntamiento de Benicasim, 12560 Benicasim (Castellon), Spain *tel:* +34 64 300962 *fax:* +34 64 303432. *Aug-Sep. Classical guitar.*

Jornadas de Informatica y Electronica Musical. CDMC, Centro de Arte Reina Sofia, Santa Isabel 52, 28012 Madrid, Spain *tel:* +34 1 468 2310/2931 *fax:* +34 1 530 8321 *email:* adolfo.nunez@cdmc.es. Consuelo Diéz, CMDC dir; Adolfo Nunez, LIEM CDMC dir. *1st week of Jul. Contemporary electronic and computer mus.*

Jornadas Internacionales de Piano. Especialidad de Musicologia, Facultad de Geografia e Historia, Campus de la Vega, University de Oviedo, E-33011 Oviedo, Spain *tel:* +34 8 510 4464 *also fax.* Luis G Iberni, dir. *Jan-Feb. Piano and orchestra.*

* **Quincena Musical/Musika Hamabostaldia.** Teatro Victoria Eugenia, Reina Regente s/n, E-20003 San Sebastian, Spain *tel:* +34 943 481238/9 *fax:* +34 943 430702 *email:* http://wwwdonsnsn.com. José Antonio Echenique, dir. *Annual. 6-31 Aug 1998. Opera, ballet, ancient music, chamber music, contmeporary music, symphonic, organ, recitals.*

* **Santander International Festival.** Palacio De Festivales de Cantabria, C/Gamazo s/n, E-39004 Santander, Cantabria, Spain *tel:* +34 42 210508 *fax:* +34 42 314767. José Luis Ocejo, dir. *Annual. 1-31 Aug 1998. Classical, contemporary, chamber, opera, concert and recital. Classical and contemporary ballet and theatre.*

* **Torroella de Montgri International Music Festival.** Apartat de correus 70, E-17257 Torroella de Montgri, Spain *tel:* +972 76 10 98 *fax:* +972 76 06 48 *email:* jjmmtdm@ddgi.es; http://www.ddgi.es/tdm/fimtdm. html. *Jun-Aug. Orch, chamber music, ethnic and jazz.*

Sweden

* **Drottningholm Court Theatre Festival.** PO Box 27050, S-10251 Stockholm, Sweden *tel:* +46 8 665 1400 *fax:* +46 8 665 1473. Per Forsstrom, artistic dir; Per-Erik Óhrn, artistic dir. *Annual. Late May to early Sep. Opera.*

Festival of Electronic Music. EMS Swedish Broadcasting, Svenska Rikskonserter, Soder Malarstrand 61, S-11825 Stockholm, Sweden *tel:* +46 8 658 1990 *fax:* +46 8 658 6909 *email:* ems@ems.srk.se; http://www.srk.se/ems. Ulf Stenberg, dir. *2-7 Nov 1998. Electro-acoustic music.*

Music Festival of Piteå. The Academy of Framnäs, S-943 33 Öjebyn, Sweden *tel:* +46 911 968 16 *fax:* +46 911 968 28 *email:* sven-erik. sandlund@mh.luth.se. Ulla-Britt Sandlund. *28 Jun-5 Jul 1998. Masterclasses.*

Örebro Chamber Music Festival. Solbergavägen 6A, S-71930 Vintrosa, Sweden *tel:* +46 19 294927 *fax:* +46 19 294997 *email:* orefestspel@ swipnet.se; http://www.srk.se/orebro/festspel/index.htm. Paul Morgan, chmn. *Annual. 27-31 May 1998. Instrumental and vocal chamber music with international artists.*

Stockholm International Composer Festival. Stockholm Concert Hall, PO Box 7083, SE-10387 Stockholm, Sweden *tel:* +46 8 7860200 *fax:* +46 8 200548 *email:* lotta.bjelkeborn@konserthuset.se; http://www.konsert huset.se. *Nov.*

Stockholm Jazz. c/o The Swedish Concert Institute, PO Box 1225, SE-111 82 Stockholm, Sweden *tel:* +46 8 7914600 *fax:* +46 8 213468.

Stockholm New Music. c/o The Swedish Concert Institute, PO Box 1225, S-111 82 Stockholm, Sweden *tel:* +46 8 791 4600 *fax:* +46 8 676 0018. Martin Martinsson, dir; Christina Falk, festival co-ord. *Triennial. Next 16-20 Mar 1999. Festival of contemporary music.*

Vadstena Opera Festival. Bergsgatan 57, S-11231 Stockholm, Sweden *tel:* +46 8 652 6180. Anders Wiklund, artistic leader; Astrid Lande, mgr dir. *Jul-Aug. Rare early operas, newly commissioned works and concerts in historic setting of Vadstena's medieval town.*

Switzerland

Easter Festival Lucerne. PO Box 3842, CH-6002 Luzern, Switzerland *tel:* +41 41 210 3562/3080 *fax:* +41 41 210 7784/9464 *email:* http://www. lucernemusic.ch/. Martin Elbel, PR; Rosmarie Hohler, sponsorship; Toni J Krein, artistic mgr. *1-5 Apr 1998. Classical, sacred and choral music.*

Festival Archipel. CP67, CH-1211 Genève 25, Switzerland *tel:* +41 22 839 2114 *fax:* +41 22 839 2117. Jean Prévost, artistic dir. *8-21 Mar 1998.*

Fribourg Festival of Sacred Music. CP 292, CH-1701 Fribourg, Switzerland *tel:* +41 26 322 4800 *fax:* +41 26 322 8331. Nicole Renevey, admin. *Biennial. Next 3-12 Jul 1998. 12 concerts of early music, medieval, renaissance, baroque, romantic, contemporary. Gregorian chant w/shop. Lectures.*

* **International Festival of Music Lucerne.** Hirschmattstrasse 13, PO Box, CH-6002 Luzern, Switzerland *tel:* +41 41 210 3562/3080 *fax:* +41 41 210 7784/9464 *email:* http://www.lucernemusic.ch/. Martin Elbel, PR; Rosmarie Hohler, sponsorship; Toni J Krein, art mgr. *19 Aug-16 Sep 1998. Classical music festival with symphony concerts, chamber music, recitals, choral concerts, serenades, musica nova, 'composer in residence'. 1998 sees the opening of the new concert hall.*

Montreux International Choral Festival. PO Box 1109, 95 Grand Rue, CH-1820 Montreux, Switzerland *tel:* +41 21 962 2141 *fax:* +41 21 962 2121 *email:* rcim@choralfestival.ch; http://www.choralfestival.ch. Marcel Baudet, president; Sonia Groppi, co-ord. *14-18 Apr 1998. Includes choral work competition and concerts.*

* **Montreux-Vevey Music Festival.** Rue du Théâtre 5, CP 162, CH-1820 Montreux 2, Switzerland *tel:* +41 21 963 5450 *fax:* +41 21 963 2506. Bernard de Bonnerive, admin; Yves Petit de Voize, artistic dir. *Aug-Sep. Recitals, chamber music, orchestral music.*

* **Musiksommer Gstaad-Saanenland.** Postfach 382, CH-3780 Gstaad, Switzerland *tel:* +41 33 7488338 *fax:* +41 33 7488339. Gidon Kremer, artistic dir; Hans-Ueli Tschanz, dir. *Annual. Jul-Sep. Chamber music, orchestral music and recitals.*

Sion Summer Music Academy. Académie de Musique de Sion, CP 954, CH-1951 Sion, Switzerland *tel:* +41 27 322 6652 *fax:* +41 27 323 4662 *email:* festivargasion@vtx.ch; http://www.nouvelliste.ch/varga/trarga. htm. Liliane Martin, admin. *Jul-Aug 1998.*

Tibor Varga Festival. PO Box 954, CH-1951 Sion, Switzerland *tel:* +41 27 323 4317 *fax:* +41 27 323 4662 *email:* festivargasion@vtx.ch; http://www.nouvelliste.ch/varga/tvarga.htm. Gillioz Pierre, admin. *Annual. 25 Jul-10 Sep 1998. 30 open-air concerts and operas.*

Verbier Festival And Academy. 4 Rue Jean-Jacques Rousseau, CH-1800 Vevey, Switzerland *tel:* +41 21 922 4010 *fax:* +41 21 922 4012 *email:* verbierfestival@music.ch; http://www.music.ch/verbierfestival/. Martin T:son Engstroem, exec dir; Miguel Esteban, admin; Avi Shoshani, artistic dir. *Annual. 17 Jul-9 Aug 1998. A summer performing arts community includes symphony, chamber music, recitals, conferences, contemporary theatre and dance.*

Thailand

Thailand Festival of the Arts by Volvo. 301-3 Sukhumuit 31, Bangkok 10110, Thailand *tel:* +66 2 662 1836 *fax:* +66 2 258 8156 *email:* huckye@mozart.inet.co.th. Hucky Eichelmann, dir; Nanokthorn Viengpetchthong, asst. *Annual. Jan. Classical, jazz, ethnic and cross-cultural music and dance.*

Turkey

* **International Ankara Music Festival.** SCA Music Foundation, Tunali Hilmi Cad 114/43, TR-06700 Ankara, Turkey *tel:* +90 312 427 0855 *fax:* +90 312 467 3159 *email:* scavakfi@ada.com.tr. Mehmet A Basman, president; Elif Mülayim Basman, co-ord. *Mar-Apr. Classical music, jazz.*

* **International Istanbul Music Festival.** Istanbul Foundation for Culture and Arts, Istiklal Caddesi 146 Luvr Apt, Beyoglu, TR-80070 Istanbul, Turkey *tel:* +90 212 293 3133 *fax:* +90 212 249 5667 *email:* http:// www.istfest.org. Cevza Aktüze, dir; Ahmet Erenli, asst dir. *Annual. 15 Jun-8 Jul 1998. Orchestra, chamber, recitals, vocal, opera, dance, traditional music, young soloists.*

USA

American Landmark Festivals. Federal Hall National Memorial, 26 Wall St, New York, NY 10005, USA *tel:* +1 212 866 2086 *fax:* +1 212 825 6874. Francis Heilbut, artistic dir. *Regular recitals and concerts presented through the year at historic sites in New York.*

Amherst Early Music Festival. 65 West 95th St, #1a, New York, NY 10025, USA *tel:* +1 212 222 3351 *fax:* +1 212 222 1898 *email:* amherst@ compuserve.com. Valerie Horst.

Artpark. Box 371, Lewiston, NY 14092, USA *tel:* +1 716 754 9000 *fax:* +1 716 754 2741. David Grapes, exec dir. *1 Jul-7 Sep 1998. Summer festival featuring a wide range of music from classical to popular, dance, opera, jazz, ethnic and music theatre.*

Aspen Music Festival. 2 Music School Rd, Aspen, CO 81611, USA *tel:* +1 970 925 3254 *fax:* +1 970 925 3802 *email:* festival@aspenmusic.org. Robert Harth, president; Edward Sweeney, gen mgr. *Annual. 18 Jun-16 Aug 1998. Orchestral, chamber music, opera.*

BONK Festival of New Music 1997. 5700 N Tamiami Trail, Sarasota, Florida 34243-2197, USA *tel:* +1 941 753 1257 *fax:* +1 941 359 4479 *email:* bonk@virtu.sar.usf.edu; http://www.sar.usf.edu/~bonk. Robert Constable. *1-7 Mar 1998. Annual forum for avant-garde and experimental music held in venues all over the Tampa Bay area.*

The Boston Early Music Festival. PO Box 2632, Cambridge, MA 02238, USA *tel:* +1 617 661 1812 *fax:* +1 617 267 6539 *email:* bemf@tiac.org; http://www.bemf.org. Kathleen Fay, exec dir; Stephen Stubbs, Paul O'Dette, artistic dirs. *Biennial. Jun. Promotes early mus through festivals, annual activities, educ programmes, tours.*

Bowdoin Summer Music Festival. Bowdoin College, 6300 College Station, Brunswick, ME 04011-8463, USA *tel:* +1 207 725 3322 *fax:* +1 207 725 3047 *email:* bsmf@henry.bowdoin.edu; http://www.bowdoin. edu. Lewis Kaplan, artistic dir. *20 Jun-1 Aug 1998. Piano, strings, woodwind, composition and voice programme designed for conservatory track students aged 12-30.*

Britt Festivals, Music and Performing Arts Festival. PO Box 1124, Medford, OR 97501, USA *tel:* +1 503 779 0847 *fax:* +1 503 776 3712. Ron McUne, gen mgr. *Jun-Aug. Classical, dance, musical theatre, jazz, folk, country, popular and world music. Concerts take place in Jacksonville.*

Central City Opera Festival. 621 17th St, Ste 1601, Denver, CO 80293, USA *tel:* +1 303 292 6700/6500. Pelham Pearce, mgr dir. *Annual. Jun-Aug.*

Chautauqua Opera Festival. Chautauqua Institution, Chautauqua, NY 14722, USA *tel:* +1 716 357 6200 *fax:* +1 716 357 9014. Marty Merkley, program dir; Uri Segal, mus dir. *Jul-Aug.*

Des Moines Metro Opera Festival. 106 West Boston Av, Indianola, IA 50125, USA *tel:* +1 515 961 6221 *fax:* +1 515 961 2994. Robert Larsen, artistic dir. *Jun-Jul. Apprentice Artists programme featuring concerts, cover performances and chamber music concerts.*

Festival Miami. University of Miami, PO Box 248165, Coral Gables, FL 33124, USA *tel:* +1 305 284 3941 *fax:* +1 305 284 3901. William Hipp, dir. *Annual. Sep-Oct. Choral, jazz, symphonic, chamber, vocal, piano and violin recitals.*

Florida International Festival. PO Box 1310, Daytona Beach, FL 32115-1310, USA *tel:* +1 904 252 1511 ext 410 *fax:* +1 904 238 1663. Dewey Anderson, gen mgr. *Biennial. Principal residency of London Symphony Orchestra. Jazz, dance, country music, chamber, masterclasses. 40 performances, plus free public events.*

Gina Bachauer Piano Festival. PO Box 11664, Salt Lake City, UT 84147, USA *tel:* +1 801 521 9200 *fax:* +1 801 521 9202 *email:* gina@bachauer. com; http://www.bachauer.com. Paul C Pollei, founder and artistic dir; William E Gaylord, gen mgr. *14-27 Jun 1998. Masterclasses, concerts, seminars and junior competition for ages 11-18 organised by the Gina Bachauer International Piano Foundation.*

Grand Teton Music Festival. Walk Festival Hall, Teton Village, WY 83025, USA *tel:* +1 307 733 1128 *fax:* +1 307 739 9043 *email:* gtmf@ gtmf.org. Joanna Giesek, exec dir. *Annual. 30 Jun-22 Aug 1998. Symphony orch and chamber music. Winter recital series (Jan, Feb, Mar).*

Grant Park Music Festival. c/o Chicago Park District Admin Building, 425 East McFetridge Dr, Chicago, IL 60605, USA *tel:* +1 312 742 7638 *fax:* +1 312 742 7662. James Palermo, gen dir; Hugh Wolff, principal cond. *Jun-Aug. Classical, jazz and popular.*

Hollywood Bowl Summer Festival. PO Box 1951, 2301 N Highland Av, Hollywood, CA 90078, USA *tel:* +1 213 850 2000 *fax:* +1 213 617 3065. Anne Parsons, gen mgr. *Jul-Sep. Orchestral, pop and jazz.*

International Trumpet Guild Conference. 410 Second Av NE, Carmel, IN 46032, USA *tel:* +1 317 844 4341 *fax:* +1 317 844 2126 *email:* cpconrad@indy.net. Charles Conrad, PR dir. *Jun. Annual conference held by the International Trumpet Guild, includes performances, lectures, exhibitions and exchange of ideas on topics relevant to the trumpet.*

Irving S Gilmore International Keyboard Festival. Kalamazoo Centre, 100 W Michigan, Kalamazoo, MI 49007, USA *tel:* +1 616 342 1166 *fax:* +1 616 342 0968. Irma Vallecillo, artistic dir. *25 Apr-3 May 1998. Piano recitals, chamber music, concertos. Mainly classical, plus jazz and contemporary.*

Lake George Opera Festival. PO Box 2172, Glen Falls, NY 12801, USA *tel:* +1 518 793 3858/3859 *fax:* +1 518 793 6719. Susan Danis, exec dir. *Annual. Jul-Aug. Traditional and neglected opera masterpieces, chmbr mus and special events.*

Mostly Mozart Festival. 70 Lincoln Center Plaza, New York, NY 10023, USA *tel:* +1 212 875 5135 *fax:* +1 212 875 5145. Jane Moss, vice-president for programming. *Aug.*

National Festival of Music at Breckenridge. c/o PO Box 1254, Breckenridge, CO 80424, USA *tel:* +1 303 453 2120. Pamela Miller.

Newport Music Festival. PO Box 3300, Newport, RI 02840, USA *tel:* +1 401 846 1133 *fax:* +1 401 849 1857 *email:* staff@newportmusic.org; http://newportmusic.org. Mark P Malkovich III, gen dir; Mark Malkovich, mkt dir. *11-27 Jul 1998. Chamber music of the Romantic era with debut recitals of international artists. Rare or unusual music.*

Ninth Annual International Music Festival. Andrews University, Berrien Springs, MI 49104, USA *tel:* +1 616 471 3128/3600. Ray Landers; Jim Hanson.

Norfolk Chamber Music Festival. 135 Colleg St, New Haven, CT 06520, USA *tel:* +1 203 432 1966 *fax:* +1 203 432 2136 *email:* http://www. yale.edu/norfolk. Elaine C Carroll, festivals mgr. *Jun-Aug. Chamber music concerts, student recitals, family activities, string quartets, wind quintets, piano trios, mixed ensembles.*

Opera Theatre of St Louis. PO Box 191910 St Louis, MO 63119-7910, USA *tel:* +1 314 961 0171 *fax:* +1 314 961 7463. *May-Jun.*

Other Minds Festival. 1005 Sansome St, Suite 242, San Francisco, CA 94111, USA *tel:* +1 415 834 1946 *email:* otherminds@mainsystem. rsphere.com. Mitchell Clark, gen mgr. *Nov 1998. Contemporary music festival, featuring compositions of participating composers.*

Princeton Invitational Choir Festival. c/o AD International Inc, 136 Lawrenceville-Pennington Rd, Lawrenceville, NJ 08648-1413, USA *tel:* +1 609 896 9330 *fax:* +1 609 896 3450 *email:* adadi@aol.com. George Plasko. *18-22 Jun 1998. International festival for children and high-school age choirs. Applications for participation by 15 Jan 1998.*

Riverbend Festival. 537 Market St, Suite 16, PO Box 886, Chattanooga, TN 37401, USA *tel:* +1 615 756 2212 *fax:* +1 615 756 2719. Richard D Brewer Jr, exec dir. *Jun. Jazz, blues and light music.*

Round Top International Festival. PO Drawer 89, Round Top, TX 78954-0089, USA *tel:* +1 409 249 3129 *fax:* +1 409 249 3100 *email:* festinst@fais.net; http://www.fais.net/~festinst. James Dick, founder and artistic dir; Richard Royall, mgr dir; Alain G Declert, information dir. *6 Jun-11 Jul 1998. Classical, orchestral, chamber, solo, coaching in orch, chmbr and string quartet repertoires. Also presents an early music festival 22-25 May and 'August-to-April' series.*

The Santa Fe Opera. PO Box 2408, Santa Fe, NM 87504-2408, USA *tel:* +1 505 986 5900 *fax:* +1 505 986 5999 *email:* http://www.santefe opera.org. Tom Morris, dir of operations. *3 Jul-29 Aug 1998. Outdoor summer opera festival: classics, neglected masterpieces, world premieres.*

Sarasota Music Festival. 709 North Tamiami Trail, Sarasota, FL 34236, USA *tel:* +1 941 952 9634 *fax:* +1 941 953 3059. Paul Wolfe, artistic dir; Trevor Cramer, admin dir. *1-20 Jun 1998. Masterclasses and concerts of a wide range of chmbr mus.*

Saratoga Performing Arts Center. Saratoga Springs, NY 12866, USA *tel:* +1 518 584 9330 *fax:* +1 518 584 0809 *email:* http://www.spac.org. Donna Eichmeyer, PR. *Annual. Jun-Sep. Summer home of New York City Ballet in Jul and the Philadelphia Orchestra and Saratoga Chamber Music Festival in Aug.*

Sevenars Concerts. The Academy, South Ireland St and Rte 112, S Worthington, MA 01098, USA *tel:* +1 413 238 5854. *Aug.*

Spoleto Festival USA. PO Box 157, Charleston, SC 29402, USA *tel:* +1 803 722 2764 *fax:* +1 803 723 6383 *email:* http://www.charleston.net/ spoleto. Nigel Redden, gen dir; Nunally Kersh, dir of operations. *22 May-7 Jun 1998. Opera, dance, theatre, symph mus, chmbr and jazz.*

Summer Festival. Seattle Opera, PO Box 9248, Seattle, WA 98109, USA *tel:* +1 206 389 7676 *fax:* +1 206 389 7651 *email:* http://www.seattle opera.org. Speight Jenkins, gen dir; Linda Prather, dir mkt and communications; Tina Ryker, PR dir. *Next Aug 1998. Richard Wagner's Tristan and Isolde. Seminars, lectures and previews.*

Summer Schools and Short Courses

The music courses listed below are held at various times of the year and the course content may vary from year to year. The addresses given here are those of the organising bodies, and are not necessarily the same as the address of the course itself. Financial grants may be offered on scholarship terms. For foreign government grants, enquiries should be made to the appropriate embassy.

Jeunesses Musicales sponsors over 150 music camps for music students and experienced amateurs of all nationalities. A brochure and full details are available from the **Fédération Internationale des Jeunesses Musicales,** 10 Rue Royale, B-1000 Bruxelles, Belgium, or from **Youth and Music,** 28 Charing Cross Road, London WC2H 0DB, UK *tel:* +44 171 379 6722.

Argentina
Orchestral Conducting. Teatro Colon of Buenos Aires, Cerrito 618, 1010 Buenos Aires, Argentina *tel:* +541 352389 *fax:* +541 111232. *May.*

Australia
National Music Camp Australia. c/o Youth Music Australia, PO Box 160, Rozelle NSW 2039, Australia *tel:* +61 2 9555 7400 *fax:* +61 2 9555 7541. David Ward, operations mgr. *Annual.*

Ronald Dowd National Summer School for Singers. 171 Albion St, Surry Hills, NSW 2010, Australia *tel:* +61 2 9360 4049 *fax:* +61 2 9332 1585. Maggie Niven, exec dir; Victor Morris, artistic dir. *11-18 Jan 1998, applications by Nov 1997. Opera mastercourse in Sydney for singers and repetiteurs.*

Summer Academy. c/o Youth Music Australia, PO Box 160, Rozelle NSW 1039, Australia *tel:* +61 2 9555 7400 *fax:* +61 2 9555 7541. David Ward, operations mgr. *Annual. Jan.*

Austria
International Academy for New Composition. Wopfnerstr 16, A-6130 Schwaz/Tirol, Austria *tel:* +43 5242 65737 *fax:* +43 5242 61199. Marianne Penz-van Stappershoef. *Annual. 24 Aug-5 Sep 1998, applications by 30 Jun. Composers' seminar and inst w/shops. International Academy for New Composition. Fees: ATS 3500.*

Berwang Holiday Music Course (Austria). Willowdown, Megg La, Chipperfield, Herts WD4 9JN, UK *tel:* +44 1923 263715 *fax:* +44 1923 268412. *Aug-Sep. All ages. Strs, w/wind, singers.*

Eichendorff's Ruh Walter Hermann Sallagar. A-2564 Furth, Austria *tel:* +43 2674 88265 *also fax. 12-19 Jul 1998, applications by 12 Jun. Courses in inst making, medieval, renaissance and baroque mus, wind ens, reed-making, 'Fagottissimo'. Age 16+. Fees: ATS 7000 (including board and accommodation).*

Music Camps for Strings in Röthelstein and Steiermark. c/o Musikalische Jugend Osterreichs, Taubstummengasse 15/10, A-1040 Wien, Austria *tel:* +43 1 505 3838/12 *fax:* +43 1 504 6361. Barbara Faltl. *1-8 Aug 1998, applications by 10 Apr. For ages 8-13. Strings and recorder course. Fees: ATS 4300.*

Salzburg International Summer Academy Mozarteum. Mirabellplatz 1, A-5020 Salzburg, Austria *tel:* +43 662 88908 400/401 *fax:* +43 662 872659 *email:* michaela.bartsch@moz.ac.at. Michaela Bartsch, students' offr. *Annual. 13 Jul-22 Aug, applications by 1 Jun. No age limit, although most participants aged 20-30. M/classes for voice and insts. Fees: ATS 6700-8000.*

Salzburg Orff-Schulwerk Course. Orff Institute, Frohnburgweg 55, A-5020 Salzburg, Austria *tel:* +43 662 88 908613/908310 *fax:* +43 662 88 624867. *Annual. Jul.*

Salzburg Youth-Orchestra Camp. c/o Musikalische Jugend Osterreichs, Taubstummengasse 15/10, A-1040 Wien, Austria *tel:* +43 1 505 3838/3812 *fax:* +43 1 504 6361. Barbara Faltl. *13-23 Aug, applications by 10 Apr. Ages 12-18. All insts except pno and gui. Fees: ATS 5000.*

Vienna Summer-Seminar for Contemporary Music (Composition and Interpretation). Postfach 345, A-1060 Wien, Austria *tel:* +43 222 594 1292. Konrad Musalek. *19-30 Aug 1998, applications by 31 May. Yearly meeting of composers, performers, students and other interested people. Information, research and discussions on new mus styles and development. Daily concerts, lectures, w/shops. ATS 1000.*

Wiener Meisterkurse. Reisnerstrasse 3, A-1030 Wien, Austria *tel:* +43 1 714 88 22 *fax:* +43 1 714 88 21. Elisabeth Keschmann; Veronika Starha. *30 Jun-14 Aug 1998, applications by 1 Jun. 2-wk master courses with leading professional musicians in fl, gui, pno, vc; also choral, chmbr, opera, conducting and singing. Final concert, diploma. Fees: ATS 5200 (participants), ATS 2700 (listeners).*

Zwettl Summer Music Camp for Children. c/o Musikalische Jugend Osterreichs, Taubstummengasse 15/10, A-1040 Wien, Austria *tel:* +43 1 505 3838/12 *fax:* +43 1 504 6361. Barbara Faltl. *30 Jul-8 Aug, applications by 10 Apr. Ages 12-17. All insts except pno. Fees: ATS 4500.*

Belgium
Antwerp Summer Academy Courses. Ruckers Genootschap, c/o Museum Vleeshuis, Vleeshouwersstraat 38-40, B-2000 Antwerp, Belgium *tel:* +32 3 233 6404/383 1690 *fax:* +32 3 383 1690. Mrs J Lambrechts-Douillez. *1st week in Aug, applications by 15 May. Academy for interpretation of mus on historic insts. Course for p/grads. Fees: 7000 BF.*

Choir Conducting Masterclass - Frieder Bernns. CIMC, Av Jean 1er, B-5000 Namur, Belgium *fax:* +32 81 737872. *10-19 Jul 1998, applications by 1 Jun. W/shop for choral conductors on Bach 6 motets with professional choir in residence. Fees: c 18,500 BF.*

Europa Cantat Belgium *see* **Germany** Europa Cantat.

Harmonium Projekt. Koninklijk Vlaams Muziekconservatorium, Desguinlei 25, B-2018 Antwerp, Belgium *tel:* +32 3 244 1800 *fax:* +32 3 238 9017. J Verdin, prof of mus. *26-29 Apr Mar 1998. Four days consisting of lectures, w/shops and concerts. Course title: The French Repertoire. Fees: 2500 BF.*

Muziekactief. PO Box 45, B-3990 Peer, Belgium *tel:* +32 11 63 21 64 *fax:* +32 11 63 49 11 *email:* musica@innet.be; http://www.innet.net/musica/alamire. Bart Demuyt, co-ord. *Training programmes for adult amateur and semi-pro musicians. Weekly and evening courses.*

Bulgaria
Spring Workshop for Conductors. c/o Symphonic Workshops, 281 Pacific Av, Toronto, Ont M6P 2P8, Canada *tel:* +1 416 762 9319 *fax:* +1 416 762 6258 *email:* symphwk@interlog.com; http://www.interlog.com/~symphwk/. Harry M B Hurwitz, dir. *Mar 1998. Daily podium time with the Vratza Philharmonic Orchestra, Vratza Bulgaria for 15 participants; two concerts and prize awards. No age limit. Fees: US$1500 (including accommodation).*

Varna International Summer Academy. Varna Municipal Council, Culture Department, BG-9000 Varna, Bulgaria *tel:* +35 9 52 222425 *fax:* +35 9 52 220101. *Jun-Jul, applications by May. Pno, vn, hn and singing for ages 14-30. Fees: US$170.*

Canada
Acadia University Summer Music Institute. School of Music, Acadia University, Wolfville, NS B0P 1X0, Canada *tel:* +1 902 542 2201 ext 1171 *fax:* +1 902 542 3715 *email:* kellock@acadiau.ca; http://dragon.acadiau.ca/~conted/conted.html. *Jun-Aug, applications by May (after which a late fee is required). Summer mus camps supported by the Division of Continuing Education and the Acadia University School of Music for students and teachers, including summer bandstand, pno and vocal camps and str camps.*

Adventures in Summer Music. PO Box 5005, Red Deer, AB T4N 5H5, Canada *tel:* +1 403 342 3526 *fax:* +1 403 347 0399. Joyce Howdle, performing arts co-ord. *10-14 Aug 1998, applications by 15 Jul. Intro, jnr, intermediate band w/shop, including full band rehearsals, sectionals, options and theory for ages 9-15. For jnr and intermediate must have 2-4 yrs playing experience. Fees: $118 (not including inst rental).*

Banff Centre for the Arts. Box 1020, Station 28, Banff, Alberta T0L 0C0, Canada *tel:* +1 403 762 6180 *fax:* +1 403 762 6345. Karen Harper, asst registrar. *Long and short-term residential courses at various times May-Aug, including a series of short, intensive m/classes (str, wind, pno), jazz and chmbr mus. Self-directed programme for professional musicians (partial financial assistance available). Summer courses, 2-4 weeks (May-Aug), Autumn (Sep-Dec), Winter (Jan-Apr), applications by early Feb.*

Cammac Cedar Glen Summer Music Centre. 50 Thorncrest Rd, Toronto, Ont M9A 1S7, Canada *tel:* +1 416 236 0339. *Choir, chmbr mus, string orch, strings, opera, ens, jazz courses for all age-groups. Fees: $70-325.*

Camp Musical de Lanaudiere. PO Box 44, Joliette, PQ J6E 3Z3, Canada *tel:* +1 514 755 2496. Nicole Bourassa, exec sec. *Four sessions Jun-Aug 1998, applications by 15 Jun. Chmbr mus, choral, orch programmes for ages 9-17 who have studied for a minimum of 2 yrs. Fees: $495.*

Courtenay Youth Music Centre (CYMC). PO Box 3056, Courtenay, BC V9N 5N3, Canada *tel:* +1 604 338 7463 *fax:* +1 604 3388 7480. Stacey Wright, general mgr. *Jul-Aug. Programmes of jazz, pno, strings, harp, musical theatre, classical guitar, concert band and orchestra for beginners to advanced performers.*

Lake MacDonald Music Centre. Cammac National Office, #2509-1751 Richardson, Montreal, PQ H3K 1G6, Canada *tel:* +1 514 932 8755 *fax:* +1 514 932 9811 *email:* cammac@odyssee.net. Danièle Rhéaume, exec dir. *Wind orch, early mus, jazz, opera, choral mus for all age-groups. Fees: $15-250.*

Le Domaine Forget Academy for Music and Dance. 398 Chemin les Bains, St-Irenee, PQ G0T 1V0, Canada *tel:* +1 418 452 8111 *fax:* +1 418 452 3503. *Courses from brass and medieval mus to oriental perc and jazz. Fees: $370 (1 wk)-990 (3 wks).*

Shawnigan Lake Music Holiday. 943 Clements Av, North Vancouver, BC V7R 2K8, Canada *tel:* +1 604 980 5341 *fax:* +1 604 984 3162. *Programmes from choral singing to jazz and computer mus for age 6 and upwards. Fees: $212-425 plus membership fee.*

Summer Strings Academy. 4825 Richard Rd SW, Calgary, AB T3C 6K6, Canada *tel:* +1 403 240 6832 *fax:* +1 403 240 6594. *String w/shop for ages 6-20. Teacher recommendation and audition tape required. Fees: $380 (jnr), $510 (snr).*

Workshop in Orchestral Conducting for Choral Directors. Symphonic Workshops Ltd, 281 Pacific Av, Toronto, Ontario, Canada *tel:* +1 416 762 9319 *fax:* +1 416 762 6258 *email:* sympwk@interlog.com; http://www.interlog.com/~symphwk. Harry M B Hurwitz, dir. *Aug 1998. No age limit. Conductors get podium time and study sessions with Toronto Symfonietta. 20 places. Fees: US $1500 (including accommodation).*

Czech Republic

Brno Music Master Interpretation Courses. Janacék Academy of Music, Komenskeho nam 6, CZ-662 15 Brno, Czech Republic *tel:* +42 5 42 321307 *fax:* +42 5 42 413286. Marie Kánová, information. *14-28 Jul 1998, applications by 31 May. Courses for mus students and professional musicians; pno, vn, str quartet, vc, fl, hn, trb, elec keyboards, cl, va, singing. Age 18 and over. Application fee: US$20, tuition US$220.*

European Summer Seminar for Talented Young Musicians. Agentura Esprit, Sady Petatricátníku 1, CZ-305 29 Pilsen, Czech Republic *tel:* +42 19 222390 *fax:* +42 19 226372. *Aug-Sep, applications by May. For wind and str players aged 16-26 (gr 8 min).*

International Workshop for Composers of Orchestral Works. c/o Symphonic Workshops, 281 Pacific Av, Toronto, Ont M6P 2P8, Canada *tel:* +1 416 760 9319 *fax:* +1 416 762 6258 *email:* symphwk@interlog. com; http://www.interlog.com/~symphwk/. Harry M B Hurwitz, dir. *Mar 1998 for 10 days. Composers' new works played by Moravia Philharmonic Orchestra under established conductor. Prospects of commercial recording. Fees: US$1200 for 1 slot (2 hrs performance), US$400 accommodation.*

International Workshop for Conductors. Symphonic Workshops Ltd, 281 Pacific Av, Toronto, Ont M6P 2P8, Canada *tel:* +1 416 762 9319 *fax:* +1 416 762 6258 *email:* symphwk@interlog.com; http://www. interlog.com/~symphwk/. Harry M B Hurwitz, dir. *Three weeks Jul-Aug 1998. Large faculty of internationally known conductors, with the Bohuslav Martinu Philharmonic. Podium time for participants on alternate days as well as daily seminars, practice sessions, plus prize awards. No age limit. Fees: US$2150 (including accommodation).*

Mostly Czech Music Workshop. c/o Symphonic Workshops, 281 Pacific Av, Toronto, Ont M6P 2P8, Canada *tel:* +1 416 762 9319 *fax:* +1 416 762 6258 *email:* symphwk@interlog.com; http://www.interlog.com/ ~symphwk/. Harry M B Hurwitz, dir. *Jun 1998. Daily podium time with the Hradec Kralove Philharmonic Orchestra for 15 participants; two concerts and prize awards. No age limit. Fees: US$1750 (including accommodation).*

Opera Workshop for Conductors and Singers. c/o Symphonic Workshops, 281 Pacific Av, Toronto, Ont M6G 2Z1, Canada *tel:* +1 416 762 9319 *fax:* +1 416 762 6258 *email:* symphwk@interlog.com; http://www.interlog.com/~symphwk/. Harry M B Hurwitz. *3 wks in Opava, Jun-Jul 1998. W/shop conducted with the Silesian Opera Orchestra, soloists and chorus. Singers sing daily, conductors have podium time on alternate days, plus finalist concerts, opera productions and prize awards. No age limit. Fees: US$1995 for conductors, US$1750 for singers.*

Practical Course in Conducting. c/o Symphonic Workshops, 281 Pacific Av, Toronto, Ont M6P 2P8, Canada *tel:* +1 416 762 9319 *fax:* +1 416 762 6258 *email:* symphwk@interlog.com; http://www.interlog.com/ ~symphwk/. Harry M B Hurwitz. *Jul-Aug 1998. Podium time with the Kromeriz Orchestra for 30 participants on alternate days in addition to daily seminars, practice sessions, prize awards. No age limit. Beginners also welcome. Fees: US$1950 (including accommodation).*

Prague Rychnov NKN Summer Camp for Strings. Hudební Mlàdez CR, Krizikova 64, CZ-186 00 Praha 8, Czech Republic *tel:* +420 2 232 2470 *also fax.* Jana Klimtova, gen sec. *18-28 Aug 1998, applications by 1 Jun. Str orch and chmbr mus. Teachers from Czech conservatoires. Ages 15-25. Fees: DM 300.*

Denmark

Danish Summer School for Strings. DK-7850 Stockholm J, Denmark *tel:* +86 646002 *fax:* +86 646502. Anker Buch, dir. *Jun-Jul, applications by 10 Jun. Individual lessons, chmbr mus, orch (100 players) for all ages. Fees: £400.*

Finland

Kuhmo Chamber Music Festival Music Camp. Fredrikinkatu 77 a 2-4, FIN-00100 Helsinki, Finland *tel:* +358 9 493867 *fax:* +358 9 493956 *email:* kuhmo.festival@pp.netppl.fi. Seija Kahkonen, sec. *21-31 Jul 1998, applications by 18 Apr. Tuition for individuals and pre-formed ens, pno, str, wind insts. Ages 12-25. Fees: 2700 FM.*

France

Académie International d'Eté de Nice. 24 Blvd de Cimiez, F-06000 Nice, France *tel:* +33 04 93 81 01 23 *fax:* +33 04 93 53 33 91 *email:* http:// www.hexagone.net/art/musique. *14 Jul-10 Aug 1998. Inst, vocal, chmbr, composition m/classes. Fees: from 1950 FF for 1 week to 6850 FF for 4 weeks.*

ATEM Music and Drama Course. ATEM, Théâtre des Amandiers, 7 Av Pablo Picasso, F-92022 Nanterre Cedex, France *tel:* +33 1 46 14 70 19 *fax:* +33 1 47 25 17 75 *email:* atem@imaginet.fr; http://www.imaginet. fr/atem. Isabelle Gaudefroy, asst. *24 Aug-4 Sep 1998, applications by 30 Apr. Mus theatre, opera and orch w/shops. Ages 18 and over. Fees: 1600 FF.*

Centre Acanthes. 146 Rue de Rennes, F-75006 Paris, France *tel:* +33 1 45 44 56 50 *fax:* +33 1 45 44 26 85. Jacqueline Fraisse, public relations. *Jul, applications by end May, in Chartreuse de Villeneuve-Lez-Avignon. For composers, insts, teachers and students interested in contemporary mus. Lecture series and interpretation w/shops. Scholarships available. Fees: 1500 FF.*

Chant Sans Frontieres. 141 Inverness Av, Westcliff on Sea, Essex SS0 9DU, UK *tel:* +44 1702 349009. Isobel Tedstill. *Aug 1998, applications by end May. 1 wk intensive tuition, all aspects of singing; technique, interpretation, presentation by experienced tutors, performance opportunity. Age 18 and over. Fees: £275-325 (including tuition and board). Spectators welcome if room available.*

Deller Academy of Early Music. 2 Rural Terr, Wye, Ashford, Kent TN25 5AP, UK *tel:* +44 1233 812267. Mark Deller. *4-13 Aug 1998. Course for professional and amateur musicians, held in Lacoste-en-Provence; concerts, m/classes, solo song, vocal ens, lute solo.*

Ferrandou Summer Singing School. 'Ferrandou', 2 Lyngham Ct, Holly Park, Crouch Hill, London N4 4AB *tel:* +44 171 272 4032 *fax:* +44 171 254 0941. Helen Smith, admin; David Wilson-Johnson. *Summer singing course in Dordogne Valley for singers and actors.*

Flute 'n' French. 2 Le Bos, 33890 Juillac, France *tel:* +33 5 57 47 44 28 *fax:* +33 5 57 47 40 03. *Mar. Courses with Atarah Ben-Tovim MBE for young British and French flautists aged 12-19, held at Chateau Carbonneau Dordogne. Intensive children's course with morning and evening flute classes and orch.*

International Chamber Music Festival of Entrecasteaux and Masterclasses. AFIME, Adrech de Sainte Anne, F-83570 Entrecasteaux, France *tel:* +33 4 94 04 44 83 *fax:* +33 4 94 04 47 36. Josée Echallier. *Aug, applications by Jun. Chmbr mus with vn, va, vc and pno. Age 15-40. Fees: 5000 FF.*

International String Workshop. 187 Aqua View Rd, Cedarburg, WI 53012, USA *tel:* +1 414 377 7062 *fax:* +1 414 377 7096 *email:* thintz@ execpc.com; http://www.internationalworkshops.org. Tori Hintz. *2-15 Jul 1998, applications by 15 Jun. Biarritz. Str pedagogy and performance; orch conducting; pno pedagogy and performance; general mus; choral conducting. Ages 16-90. Fees US$1495.*

Latour De France International Festival of Music and the Arts. c/o Mananan Festival Office, Erin Arts Centre, Victoria Sq, Port Erin, Isle of Man IM9 6LD, UK *tel:* +44 1624 835858 *fax:* +44 1624 836058. Martin Norbury, admin. *26-30 Jul 1998 in France, applications by 1 May. Choral and operatic study course for young professional singers.*

Michael Procter Courses. 9 Hall Close, Godalming, Surrey GU7 3PW *tel:* +44 1483 417927 *also fax.* Michael Procter, dir; Pippa Dice, admin. *Aug 1998. Abbey of Mondaye, Calvados. Musique en Vacances. Course covering the repertoire of Anne de Bretagne.*

Music at Ladevie. Coopers Farm, Stonegate, Wadhurst, E Sussex TN5 7EH, UK *tel:* +44 1580 200386 *fax:* +44 1580 200866. Paul Roberts, dir.

Jul-Aug, pno summer school in SW France. Age 17 and over. For professionals and amateurs. Fees: £380-690.

Roujan Singing Weeks. Cantax House, Lacock, Chippenham, Wiltshire SN15 2JZ, UK *tel:* +44 1249 730468 *also fax.* Andrew van der Beek. *Aug. Two separate weeks for amateur choral singers in village near Pezenas in the south of France. All ages. Fees: 2250FF.*

Germany

Anglo-German Youth Music Week. National Association of Youth Orchestras, 2 Gilberyn Dr, Worle, Weston-super-Mare, N Somerset *tel:* +44 1934 512380 *also fax email:* malcolm.goodman@nayo.org.uk; http://www.nayo.org.uk. Malcolm Goodman, course admin. *2-9 Aug 1998, Oberwesel-am-Rhein. Annual residential mus week, alternately in Germany and the UK. Wide range of orch and chmbr mus with students from other European countries. Full symph orch forming 2 chmbr orchs. Applications age 15-25, with minimum of gr 7 on primary orch inst. Fee: £240.*

Cello Festival and Masterclasses. International Academy of Chamber Music, Koenigsteinerstr 5, D-61476 Kronberg, Germany *tel:* +49 6173 950085 *fax:* +49 6173 950086 *email:* ikacello@aol.com; http://members.aol.com/ikacello. Raimund Trenkler, artist dir; Almut Latscha; Gabriela Denicke, organisation office. *26 Sep-2 Oct 1998, applications by 15 Aug. Cello m/class. All age-groups. Cello festival in honour of Mstislav Rostropovich. Fees: DM 200 (passive), DM 400 (active).*

Europa Cantat - European Federation of Young Choirs (EFYC). c/o Bayerische Musikakademie Marktoberdorf, Kurfürstenstrasse 19, D-87616 Marktoberdorf, Germany *tel:* +49 8342 961826 *fax:* +49 8342 40370 *email:* 100530.317@compuserve.com; http://www.intro.ch/ecl. Dolf Rabus, sec gen. *Apr and Jul 1998. International singing weeks and w/shops with well-known conductors throughout Europe. Including European Youth Choir 10-25 Jul 1998, in Vitoria, Spain (ages 25 and under); European Academy for Young Choral Conductors, 10-21 Jul 1998 (ages 30 and under); International Study Tour to Belgium, end Apr in Vitoria, Spain (no age limit).*

Fortbildungszentrum für Neue Musik. An der Munze 7, D-21335 Luneburg, Germany *tel:* +49 4131 309390 *fax:* +49 4131 309390 *email:* erdmann@uni-lueneberg.de. Helmut W Erdmann. *W/end chmbr mus course for all insts, studying classical and contemporary compositions.*

IGMF (International Society for Music in Education and Therapy). PO Box 2020, D-57312 Bad Berleburg, Germany *tel:* +49 2759 7921 *fax:* +49 2759 7925. *Jul, applications by May, in Vienna. Courses in various parts of Germany and abroad from Feb-Dec, instruction on Orff insts and methods, including mus therapy. For applications conctact, MES, Ray Mason, 85b Stradella Rd, Herne Hill, London SE24 9HL, UK tel: +44 171 738 5244.*

International Masterclass for Violin and Cello. Walderseestr 57, D-22605 Hamburg, Germany *tel:* +49 40 880 7983 *also fax.* Petru Munteanu. *Jul-Aug.*

International New Music Holiday Courses. Internationales Musikinstitut, Nieder-Ramstädter Strasse 190, D-64285 Darmstadt, Germany *tel:* +49 6151 132416/17 *fax:* +49 6151 132405. Wilhelm Schlüter. *Biennial. Next Jul-Aug 1998 in Darmstadt. International vacation courses for composition and interpretation of contemporary mus. Fees: DM 1250.*

Internationale Bachakademie. Johann-Sebastian-Bach-Platz, D-70178 Stuttgart, Germany *tel:* +49 711 619210 *fax:* +49 711 619 2123. Christa Richter, course offr; Christian Eisert, programme planning. *30 Aug-13 Sep, 1998, applications by 30 Jun, in Stuttgart for any age. Conducting and vocal m/classes and seminars in musicology. Fees: DM 650-750.*

Internationaler Arbeitskreis für Musik. Heinrich-Schütz-Allee 33, D-34064 Kassel, Germany *tel:* +49 561 935170 *fax:* +49 561 313772. Adolf Lang, sec gen.

Internationales Jugend-Festspieltreffen. Aussere Badstr 7a, D-95448 Bayreuth, Germany *tel:* +49 921 9505 *fax:* +49 921 98486. Sissy Thammer, gen dir. *Aug, applications by Jun, in Bayreuth. International Youth Festival; choral, orch, perc, chmbr mus course, opera w/shop, song interpretation. Ages 18-25.*

Jeunesses Musicales Germany. Marktplatz 12, D-97990 Weikersheim/Tauber, Germany *tel:* +49 793 4280 *fax:* +49 793 48526. Thomas Rietschel, gen sec. *Aug-Sep, applications by Jul. Many courses throughout yr in one of the most beautiful castles of Germany, including international chmbr mus course for w/wind, str and pno, with internationally acclaimed teachers. Age range 22-28. Fees: DM 300 700. Grants available.*

Musicosophia International. Finkenherd 6, D-79271 Sankt Peter, Germany *tel:* +49 7760 581 *fax:* +49 7660 1536 *email:* http://www.schwarzwald.org/musicosophia. Uwe Fricke, dir; George Balan, founder. *Four courses each month for both beginners and advanced listeners in UK, France, Germany, Italy, Spain and South America. Applications by 1 week before course. Ages 6-80. No musical knowledge required. Fees: DM 220 (w/end course), DM 380 (5-day).*

String Chamber Music Course. Landesmusikrat Hessen EV, Eschersheimer Landstr 325, D-60320 Frankfurt Am Main, Germany *tel:* +49 69 567155; +49 69 637111 *fax:* +49 69 561789. Juan von Haselberg, co-ord and organiser. *3-8 Apr and 14-18 Oct 1998, applications by 6 Mar and 11 Sep respectively. Intensive str chmbr mus course for serious-minded amateurs and mus teachers aged 21-65. Fees: DM 450 (tuition and board).*

Greece

International Computer Music Conference 1997. PO Box 308, Aristotle University of Thessaloniki, 54006 Thessaloniki, Greece *tel:* +30 31 994760 *fax:* +30 31 994769 *email:* icmc97@alexandros.csd.auth.gr; http://alexandros.csd.auth.gr/icmc97/. *24-30 Sep 1997. Workshops and concerts in computer music.*

Hungary

Early Music Days. c/o Interart Festivalcenter, PO Box 80, Vörösmarty tér 1, H-1366 Budapest, Hungary *tel:* +36 1 117 9838/266 3108 *fax:* +36 1 117 9910. Mária Liszkay, mgr. *20-27 Jun 1998 in Sopron, applications by 1 May. Basso continuo; dance; choir training; history of insts and restoration. Fees: DEM 250-400.*

Europa Cantat Hungary *see* **Germany** Europa Cantat.

International Bartok Seminar and Festival. c/o Interart Festivalcenter, PO Box 80, Vörösmarty tér 1, H-1366 Budapest, Hungary *tel:* +36 1 117 9838 *fax:* +36 1 117 9910. Magdolna Szávai, sec. *14-28 Jul 1998, applications by 20 May, in Szombathely. Course for pno, chmbr mus and conducting, vn, str quartet, singing, musicology, composition.*

International Jeunesses Musicales Camp (Pécs). c/o Jeunesses Musicales, PO Box 80, Vörösmarty tér 1, H-1366 Budapest, Hungary *tel:* +36 1 117 5291 *fax:* +36 1 117 9910 *email:* jeuhun@mail.c3.hu. Beata Schanda, camp leader. *Second half of Jul 1998. Courses in symphony orch for age 16-26. Fees: SFR 550.*

International Kodály Seminar. Kodály Institute, H-6001 Kecskemét, Hungary *tel:* +36 76 481 518 *fax:* +36 76 320 160. Laura Kéri, registrar. *Next course 1999. Theoretical and practical aspects of the Kodály concept, m/classes for choral conductors, pno course, interpretation course for singers.*

International Music Camp Nyírbátor. Szaboski Miklos, Sebespyen Tinodi, Nyírbátor, H-4300 Szentver 1, Hungary *tel:* +36 42 381027 *also fax.* *Jul, applications by May. Ages 16-30. Fees: $50 (application), $200 (participation).*

International String, Keyboard and Chamber Music Masterclasses. Young European Strings, The Close, Cypress Downs, Templeogue, Dublin 6W, Republic of Ireland *tel:* +353 1 490 5263 *fax:* +353 1 492 0355 *email:* yes@iol.ie. Diana Kelemen. *Jul-Aug.*

'Pro Musica' International Summer Academy. Gyula Csetenyi, Nagymezö utca 1, H-1065 Budapest, Hungary *tel:* +36 1 3217 514 *fax:* +36 1 3228 207 *email:* http://www.6mc.hu. Gyula Csetenyi, artistic dir. *1-10 Aug 1998, applications by 15 Jun. Fl, ob, cl, bsn, vn, vc, pno and chmbr mus. Ages 14-30. Fees, US$400 (inclusive of tuition and board).*

Israel

The Israel Jeunesses Musicales International Summer Camp. c/o Jeunesses Musicales, 19 Achad-Ha'am St, Tel Aviv 65151, Israel *tel:* +972 3 560 6069 *fax:* +972 3 560 8345. Meir Wiesel, Neomi Lev, artistic dirs. *Jul-Aug, entries by 15 May. Str, w/wind, pno. Ages 13-18 (camp) and 16-26 (advanced seminar). Fees $700 and $10 registration.*

Keshet Eilon Violin Mastercourse. Keshet Eilon Violin Mastercourse, Kibbutz Eilon, Western Galilee 22845, Israel *tel:* +972 4 985 8191/4 9806 767 *fax:* +972 4 980 7323/4 9806 766. Itzhak Rashkovsky, mus dir; Gilad Sheba, mgr dir. *24 Jul-10 Aug 1998, applications by 15 Apr 1998. Age 25 and under. Course for gifted young violinists of all nationalities. Special project: Archery and the Violin. Private lessons, m/classes and solo concert experience. Fees: $1300.*

Italy

Accademia Musicale Chigiana. 89 Via di Città, 53100 Siena, Italy *tel:* +39 577 46152 *fax:* +39 577 288124. *Annual summer schools for young musicians, including masterclasses, seminars, concerts and a festival.*

Assisi Easter Academy. Institut für Kunst, Music & Sprachen, Im Speitel 3, D-76229 Karlsruhe, Germany *tel:* +49 721 482852 *also fax. Mar. 10-day course for painters and singers. Sacred and secular mus of Venetian and Roman composers, Italian language courses, excursions, Easter mass and holiday celebrations. Fees: c £450.*

Bottega International Workshop for Young Singers and Musicians. Teatro Comunale, via A Diaz no 7, 31100 Treviso, Italy *tel:* +39 422 410130 *fax:* +39 422 52285. Peter Maag.

Chamber Music for Singers (Corso per Coro da Camera). Ente Teatro Communale di Treviso, Via A Diaz 7, I-31100 Treviso, Italy *tel:* +39 422 410130 *fax:* +39 422 52285. *Sep-Feb.*

Corso Internazionale di Musica Antica. Società Italiana del Flauto Dolce, via Monte Zebio 33, I-00195 Roma, Italy *tel:* +39 6 372 9667 *also fax.* Renato Meucci, dir. *Jul, applications by Jun. Ages 6-70. Fees: 390,000 lire. Held in Urbino.*

Corso di Canto Corale di Castiglione del Lago. Cantax House, Lacock, Chippenham, Wiltshire SN15 2JZ, UK *tel:* +44 1249 730468 *also fax.* Andrew van der Beek, admin. *Aug. Two separate weeks for amateur choral singers in small lakeside town in Umbria. All ages. Fees: 650,000 lire.*

Fondazione Giorgi Cini. Seminari di Musica Antica e Concerti, Isola di S Giorgio Maggiore, I-30124 Venezia, Italy *tel:* +39 41 528 9900 *fax:* +39 41 523 8540. *Annual. Jul-Aug in Venice, entries by Jun. Fees: 100,000 lire (entry), 300,000 lire (participation).*

Incontri Musicali. Segretaria Corsi, c/o Asolo Musica, Via Robert Browning 141, I-31011 Asolo (TV), Italy *tel:* +39 423 950 150 *fax:* +39 423 529 890. *Jul-Dec. A series of courses and m/classes given by professional musicians. Held in Northern Italy Castelfranco, Veneto. Include chmbr mus, str, br, hp, gui, opera, conducting, pno, org, w/wind. Candidates must pass entrance exam to qualify for courses. Fees: c 500,000 lire.*

The Inner Voice in Italy. The White House, Aston Hill, Aston Rowant, Watlington, Oxon OX9 5SG, UK *tel:* +44 1844 351 561 *fax:* +44 1844 354 891 *email:* elisabeth@innervoice.demon.co.uk. Elisabeth Wingfield; Aliya Gordon-Creed. *Residential courses designed to help performers free themselves from problems associated with nerves, lack of self-confidence and the inner critic. Also, courses on the psychology of musical performance, held in England and Italy. Designed for teachers, students and professional singers and musicians.*

International Academy of Sacred Music. c/o IAM, Heinrich Schütz Allee 33, D-34131 Kassel, Germany *tel:* +49 561 935170. Michael Procter, dir. *May-Jun. Annual course for experienced singers. Housed at the Palazzo Giustinian, on the Grand Canal. Performances in great Venetian churches including St Mark's, with music mainly from Venice. Fees: £600.*

Michael Procter Courses. 9 Hall Close, Godalming, Surrey GU7 3PW, UK *tel:* +44 1483 417927 *also fax.* Michael Procter, dir; Pippa Dice, admin. *Many courses, mainly for singers in Renaissance sacred mus. 1998: 4-12 Apr, Assisi - Easter Academy for singers and painters with Italian classes, mus prog includes Roman and Venetian repertoires; 30 May-7 Jun, Venice - International Academy of Sacred Music, intensive course for experienced singers on sacred mus of Venice; Jul-Aug - Schola Polyphonica, international summer school.*

Music, Dance and Didactics Symposium. Coop Co Gi Tur, via Pisacane 6, I-09047 Selargius, Cagliari, Italy *tel:* +39 70 841297 *fax:* +39 70 841297. *Residential courses for renaissance and baroque mus, singing, organ, renaissance and baroque dance, international and Sardinian folk dance, mus teaching methods (Orff, Kodály). Held in Selargius, Sardinia.*

Professional Training Course for Orchestral Players. c/o Teatro Lirico Sperimentale di Spoleto, Piazza Giovanni Bovio, 1-06049 Spoleto, Italy *tel:* +39 743 221645/220440 *fax:* +39 743 222930 *email:* teatrolirico@ mail.caribusiness.it; http://www.caribusiness.it/lirico. Claudio Lepore, mgr. *Jul-Sep 1998, applications by 10 Jul. Br and str (age limits 25 and 27 respectively). No charges for these courses.*

Spazio Musica Stages Internazionali. Associazione Spazio Musica, Via Parini 10, I-16145 Genova, Italy *tel:* +39 10 317192 *also fax; email:* spimusica@tu.village.it. *Jul-Aug, applications by Jun. Various courses in pno accompaniment, opera singing, jazz, stage design, ob, hn and vc. Application fee: 250,000 lire.*

Latvia

Solvita Sejane of the Riga Early Music Centre. Brivibas 85, LV-1001, Riga, Latvia *tel:* +37 1227 5575 *fax:* +37 1227 8060 *email:* musbalt@ com.latnet.lv. *20-27 Jul 1998, applications by 1 Jun. Renaissance mus course for singers, instrumentalists and dancers in Edole Castle. Fees: GBP 200.*

Lithuania

Youth Chamber Music Days. Lithuanian Composers' Union, Mickeviciaus 29, 2600 Vilnius, Lithuania *tel:* +370 2 223611 *fax:* +370 2 220939 *email:* center@mipc.vno.osf.lt. Kestutis Bieliukas, artistic dir. *May 1998. Weekend in Druskininkai (south Lithuania). Concerts, lectures, w/shops with Lithuanian young composers and musicologists.*

Malta

Summer Music in the Mediterranean. c/o 314 Upper Richmond Rd, London SW15 6TU, UK *tel:* +44 181 785 3222 *fax:* +44 181 780 0833. *Jul. A summer school at the University of Malta for w/wind, br, strs and pno.*

University of Malta Course for String Players, Chamber Groups and Improvisati. International Office, Foundation for International Studies, University of Malta, Valletta, Malta *tel:* +356 234121/2 *fax:* +356 230538. Jean Killick. *Jul.*

Mexico

Elena Durán Flute Course. Santisimo 27, Colonia San Angel, 01000 Mexico D F, Mexico *tel:* +525 550 9449 *also fax.* Michael Emmerson, admin. *Annual. Jan, applications by Dec. M/classes and tutorials for all ages with Elena Durán, Colin Fleming, Angela Koregelds, Zoe Smith. Fees: $100.*

International Franco Donatoni Course for Composers. Medellin 251, Col Roma Sur, México DF, 06760 Mexico *tel:* +52 5 5843094 *fax:* +52 5 5644002 *email:* rasgado@mail.internet.com.mx. *Oct-Nov, applications by Jun. Daily discussions with composers and opportunity for composers of any age and nationality to compose a work for a small ensemble. Fees: US$800 (active participants); US$200 (auditors). Some scholarships available.*

International Composers Course in Mexico City. Sones Contemporaneas Association, Medellín 251 Colonia Roma Sur, 06760 Mexico DF, Mexico *tel:* +525 584 9241; +5273 123 831 *fax:* +525 564 4002 *email:* rasgado@mail.internet.com.mx. Franco Donatoni, Theo Loevendie, Victor Rasgado, teachers. *9 Feb-6 Mar 1998. Applications by Dec. Course open to composers of any age and nationality. Diploma awarded to participants. Apply with 2 recent scores and current CV. Scholarships available.*

Mexico City Flute Festival. Santísimo 27, Colonia San Angel, 01000 Mexico D F, Mexico *tel:* +525 550 9449 *also fax.* Michael Emmerson, admin. *Apr. Annual fl festival and m/classes. Open to all ages and levels. Fees: $100.*

Monaco

Reding-Piette Seminar For Duo Piano Teams. Reding-Piette School, Chateau Perigord, Monte Carlo MC-98000, Monaco *tel:* +377 93 300721 *also fax. Two-week m/classes for pno duo, given by Professor Janine Reding. No age limits. Repertory of original works written for 2 pianos. Possibility of scholarships. Accommodation provided.*

Netherlands

6th International Flute Summer Course 1997. Studio E, Vrolikstraat 195 D, 1091 TX Amsterdam, Netherlands *tel:* +31 20 6682478 *fax:* +31 20 6651425 *email:* wof@xs4all.nl; http://www.xs4all.nl/~wof. *17-22 Aug 1998. Flute course on comtemporary techniques given by Wil Offermans. Open to flute students, flautists and teachers. Technical information as well as cultural and historical references. Group sessions and private lessons. Dfl 575, with Dfl 272 advance payment.*

International Kirill Kondrashin Conductors Masterclass. Netherlands Broadcasting Corporation, PO Box 26444, NL-1202 JJ Hilversum, Netherlands *tel:* +31 35 775453 *fax:* +31 35 774311. Anneke Hogenstyn, project mgr. *Quadrennial. Age under 36. Fees: DFL 700 (participants), DFL 300 (observers).*

International Masterclass for Violin. Utrechts Conservatorium, Mariaplaats 28, NL-3511 LL Utrecht, Netherlands *tel:* +31 302 31 4044 *fax:* +31 302 31 4004. *Jun-Jul 1998, applications by 1 Jun. M/classes by Viktor Liberman and Boris Belkin. Fees: Dfl 650.*

International Summer Academy for Organists. Townhall, PO Box 3333, NL-2001 DH Haarlem, Netherlands *tel:* +31 23 160574 *fax:* +31 23 160576. Miss E L S Hendrikse, sec. *13-31 Jul 1998, applications by 15 Jun. Summer courses for qualified organists; a variety of 9 courses are offered. Held in Haarlem. Fees: from Dfl 350.*

Kurt Thomas Summer Course. SNK, Plompetorengracht 3, NL-3512 CA Utrecht, Netherlands *tel:* +31 30 231 31 74 *fax:* +31 30 231 81 37 *email:* snk@euronet.nl. *Jul, applications by May. Various group sessions for choral conductors. Course concludes with public concert. Fees: Dfl 575 (active), Dfl 300 (auditors).*

Summer School around Mozart and Dvorak. La Pellegrina, Draaiweg 103-5, NL-3515 Utrecht, Netherlands *tel:* +31 30 720339/720341 *fax:* +31 30 721961 *email:* d.horringa@inter.nl.net. Dirkjam Horringa, dir. *Aug, applications by 1 Jun. Approx £300. Orch and chmbr mus coaching for strs, wind and pno. All ages.*

Norway

Chamber Music Seminar. Nordland Akademi, PB 10, N-8490 Melbu, Norway *tel:* +47 761 58233 *fax:* +47 761 58210. Tim Challman, co-ord, musical events. *15-21 Jul 1998, applications by 30 Jun, in Melbu. For advanced students to work with professional instructors Course combined with Clarinet Seminar. All strs, individual and ens insts aged 15 and over. Fees: 1500 NKR.*

Clarinet Seminar. Nordland Akademi, PB 10, N-8490 Melbu, Norway *tel:* +47 761 58233 *fax:* +47 761 58210. Tim Challman, co-ord, musical events. *15-21 Jul 1998 in Melbu, applications by 30 Jun. For advanced students to work with professional instructors. Course combined with Chamber Music Seminar for professional or advanced level insts. Fees: 1500 NKR.*

International Festival for Youth and Children's Choirs. Norges Barne og Ungdomskorforbund, Tollbugata 28, N-0157 Oslo, Norway *tel:* +47 22 425480 *fax:* +47 22 425499 *email:* nobu@online.no. Kjetil Aamann, artistic dir. *Biennial. Next Jun 1999. Aged 25 and under. Festival organised in collaboration with the Norwegian Children's and Youth Choir Association.*

Ringve Academy. PO Box 2045, N-7001 Trondheim, Norway *tel:* +47 73 929470 *fax:* +47 73 503866. *Jul in Trondheim, applications by 1 May. early mus performance practice. Ages 20-60. Fees: 1000-1200 NKR.*

Poland

Michael Procter Courses. 9 Hall Close, Godalming, Surrey GU7 3PW, UK *tel:* +44 1483 417927 *also fax.* Michael Procter, dir; Pippa Dice, admin. *17-22 Mar 1998. Kreisau. Dresdner Akademie für Alte Musik. Vocal and instrumental mus of 17thC.*

Summer Courses for Young Composers. ISCM Polish Section, Mazowiecka 11, PL-00 052 Warsaw, Poland *tel:* +48 22 8276981 *fax:* +48 22 8277804. Grazyna Dziura, exec sec. *1-15 Sep 1998, applications by 30 Jun. US$500. Aged 30 and under. W/shops, individual lessons and lectures for young composers.*

Portugal

Fundacao Da Casa De Mateus. 5000 Vilareal, 1200 Lisboa, Portugal *tel:* +351 59 323121 *fax:* +351 59 74553. Maria Amelia Albuquerque.

International Courses for Early Music. Academia de Musica Antiga de Lisboa, Rua Ricardo Espirito Santo, 3-1 Esq, 1200 Lisboa, Portugal *tel:* +351 1 60 77 24 *also fax. Sofia de Mendia Mar-Apr, Aug, applications by Mar and Jun. M/classes and chmbr mus, singing, rcdr and traverso, vn and va, vc and gamba, hpd. Fees: 25,000 Escudos; 40,000 Escudos.*

Republic of Ireland

Association of Irish Choirs. 4 Drinan St, Cork, Republic of Ireland *tel:* +353 21 312296 *fax:* +353 21 962457. Barbara Heas, admin. *30 Jun-4 Jul 1998. Basic, intermediate and advanced choral conducting, vocal training, m/classes and lectures during an annual summer school for choral conductors and teachers. Other regional courses and choral days. Age 17 and over. Fees: IR£45-80.*

Blas. The Irish World Music Centre, University of Limerick, Republic of Ireland *tel:* +353 61 202565 *fax:* +353 61 202589 *email:* niall.keegan@ ul.ie; sandra.joyce@ul.ie. Sandra Joyce; Niall Keegan. *Jul 1998. 10-day summer school of Irish traditional mus and dance with intensive academic and practical content. For age 16 and above. Accreditation available. Fees: IR£650.*

Ennis IMRO Composition Summer School. AIC, Copyright House, Pembroke Row, Dublin 2, Republic of Ireland *tel:* +353 1 494 2880 *also fax.* Maura Eaton, exec dir. *13-25 Jul 1998, applications by early May. For 3rd level and graduate students. Lectures and tuition by course directors and international guest composer. Fees: £120-200.*

Romania

Academia de Muzica 'Gheorghe Dima'. Str I C Bratianu 25, 3400 Cluj-Napoca, Romania *tel:* +40 64 193870 *also fax. Bach Academy, Nov. Chamber Music, May. Canto and Opera, Jul.*

Russia

International Masterclass for Violin and Viola. Kulturamt Sondershausen, PO Box 30, D-99706 Sondershausen, Germany *tel:* +49 3632 622160 *fax:* +49 3632 622120. *Apr.*

International Masterclass for Violin and Viola. Raddatz Concerts, Burgunderstr 4, D-79104 Freiburg, Germany *tel:* +49 761 23380 *fax:* +49 761 554862. *Jun, Jul and Oct.*

Moscow Conservatoire International Summer School and Summer Music Festival. 41 Ashen Grove, London SW19 8BL, UK *tel:* +44 181 947 7201. *Aug. Lectures, m/classes, individual lessons, concerts and excursions.*

South Africa

International Composers Workshop. Foundation for the Creative Arts, PO Box 91122, Auckland Park, Johannesburg 2006, South Africa *tel:* +27 11 838 1383 *fax:* +27 11 838 6363. *Organised by UNESCO, alternates with Netherlands and Bulgaria.*

Spain

Casares Early Music Week. Cantax House, Lacock, Chippenham, Wiltshire SN15 2JZ, UK *tel:* +44 1249 730468 *also fax.* Andrew van der

Beek, admin. *Apr (Holy Week). For choral singers. Held in small town near Estepona in southern Spain. All ages. Fees: 50,000 ptas.*

Early Music Course in Catalonia and Andorra. Curs de Música Antiga, Departament de Cultura, Portal de Santa Madrona 6-8, E-08001 Barcelona, Spain *tel:* +34 3 412 5640 *fax:* +34 3 412 1958. Consol Vendrell, co-ord. *Annual. Aug, applications by Jul, in La Seu d'Urgell. Early mus courses in vocal technique, interpretation, cornetto, recorder, sackbut, baroque bsn, lute, baroque vn, va da gamba and hpd. Enrolment fee 14,000 ptas, plus registration fee of 6,000 ptas.*

Escuela de Musica Segovia. Tejedores 26 - El Carmen, 40004 Segovia, Spain *tel:* +34 21 43 44 23 *also fax;* email: kent@futurnet.es. Jose Miguel Arranz, mgr. *Piano, guitar and singing summer courses in Jul and Aug for national and international students. Applications by 1 Jul. Ages 16-30. Fees: £80 (tuition only).*

Francisco Viñas International Interpretation Course. Bruch 125, E-08037 Barcelona, Spain *tel:* +34 3 215 4227/457 8646. Maria Vilardell, president. *1 Dec 1997-4 Feb 1998, in Barcelona. Applications by early Nov. Various aspects of vocal interpretation, including operatic performance and acting skills, Lieder, Zarzuela, etc. Open to all voices and nationalities. Fees: 16-23,000 ptas; listeners 5000 ptas.*

Sweden

International Choral and Instrumental Week. Geijerskolan, Munkfors 1, S-68493 Ransater, Sweden *tel:* +46 552 30250 *fax:* +46 552 30448. Curt Pettersson. *Jul, applications by Jun, in Ransater. Church mus, chmbr mus, fl.*

Jeunesses Musicales 'Musik för Ungdom'. Schönfelds Gränd 1, PO Box 1225, Stockholm, Sweden *tel:* +46 8 791 4600 *fax:* +46 8 21 3468. Dag Franzén, admin. *Jul, applications by May. Week of song for ages 15-25. Fees: $100.*

Masterclasses in the Music Festival of Pitea. The Academy of Framnas, S-943 33 Ojebyn, Sweden *tel:* +46 911 96816 *fax:* +46 911 96828 *email:* sven-erik.sandlund@m.h.luth.se. Ulla-Britt Sandlund, dir; Sven-Erik Sandlund, dir. *28 Jun-5 Jul 1998.*

Orebro Chamber Music Festival Masterclasses. Kavesta Folkhogskola, S-690 72 Skollersta, Sweden *tel:* +46 19 58 7800 *fax:* +46 19 23 0802. *Aug. Summer course for advanced str players.*

Switzerland

Camp for Wind Instruments. c/o Jeunesses Musicales, Maison de la Radio, Bd Carl Vogt 66, CP 233, CH-1211 Genève 8, Switzerland *tel:* +41 22 328 7064 *fax:* +41 22 781 5218. Jean Claude Beuchat, artistic dir; Nicole Aubert, gen sec. *Jul, applications by May, in Couvet. Chmbr and wind orch. Age 15 and over. Fees: SFR 300.*

Chamber Music Course. c/o Jeunesses Musicales, Maison de la Radio, CP233, CH-1211 Genève, Switzerland *tel:* +41 22 328 7064. *Jul, applications by Jun. For age 10-16. Fees: FF 680 (all inclusive).*

International Improvisation Week. c/o Jeunesses Musicales, Maison de la Radio, Bd Carl Vogt 66, CP 233, CH-1211 Genève 8, Switzerland *tel:* +41 22 328 7064 *fax:* +41 22 781 5218. Nicole Aubert, gen sec. *Jul, applications by May. Age 14 and over. Fees: SFR 520.*

International Orchestral Course. c/o Jeunesses Musicales, Maison de la Radio, Bd Carl Vogt 66, CP 233, CH-1211 Genève 8, Switzerland *tel:* +41 22 328 7064 *fax:* +41 22 781 5218. Nicole Aubert, gen sec. *Jul, applications by Apr, in Sornetan. Symph orch and chmbr mus. Ages 15-25. Fees: SFR 580.*

International Summer Academy of Music Lenk. Stiftung Kulturforderung Lenk, Secretariat, PO Box 342, CH-3775 Lenk, Switzerland *tel:* +41 33 733 40 30 *fax:* +41 33 733 20 27. Nicole Schneider, sec. *23 Aug-5 Sep 1998, applications by 20 Jun. Inst, vocal and chmbr mus m/classes. Fees: SFR 725-1600.*

Internationale Meisterkurse. Konservatorium für Musik, Kramgasse 36, CH-3011 Berne, Switzerland *tel:* +41 31 311 6221 *fax:* +41 31 312 2053. Heinrich Forster, artistic dir; Agnes Schneiter. *Fifth International Autumn Academy 18 Sep-10 Oct 1998, in Berne, applications by 30 Jun. Master courses at the Berne Conservatoire. Str quartet, vn, hn. For advanced students and young professionals. Fees: SFR 500.*

Margess International of Switzerland. Steinmuristrasse 6B, CH-8123 Ebmatingen, Switzerland *tel:* +41 1 980 0778 *also fax; email:* rosamar@ promovis.ch; http://www.promovis.ch/rosamar. Nancy Chumachenco, dir. *12 Jul-1 Aug 1998, applications by 1 Apr. Intensive str and pno. Ages 10-22. Fees: SFR 1600.*

Music for Strings. c/o Jeunesses Musicales, Maison de la Radio, CP 233, CH-1211 Genève, Switzerland *tel:* +41 22 328 7064. Philippe Domont. *Aug. Fees: FF 770 (all inclusive).*

Music and Dance Week. c/o Jeunesses Musicales, Maison de la Radio, CP 233, CH-1211 Genève, Switzerland *tel:* +41 22 328 7064. Luc Fuchs, Manon Hotte. *Apr.*

Music Holiday Weeks. c/o Jeunesses Musicales, Maison de la Radio, CP 233, CH-1211 Genève 8, Switzerland *tel:* +41 22 328 7064. *Jul-Aug, applications by Apr. For age 10-20. Fees: FF 940 (all inclusive).*

Neuchatel Music Week of Jeunesses Musicales. c/o Jeunesses Musicales, Maison de la Radio, Bd Carl Vogt 66, CP 233, CH-1211 Genève 8, Switzerland *tel:* +41 22 328 7064. Thomas Mercado, artistic dir; Nicole Aubert. *Oct, applications by 1 Oct. Orch and chmbr mus for children and young people. Age 8-16. Fees: SFR 380.*

Orchestral and Piano Camp for Children. c/o Jeunesses Musicales, Maison de la Radio, Bd Carl Vogt 66, CP 233, CH-1211 Genève 8, Switzerland *tel:* +41 22 287064 *fax:* +41 22 781 5218. Christiane Buntschu, vice gen sec. *Jul, applications by Apr, in Geneva. Orch and pno course for children. Ages 8-15. Fees: SFR 460.*

Sion Summer Music Academy. Case postale 954, CH-1951 Sion, Switzerland *tel:* +41 27 322 66 52 *fax:* +41 27 323 46 62 *email:* festivargasion@vtx.ch; http://www.nouvelliste.ch/varga/tvarga.htm. Liliane Martin, admin. *Jul and Aug. M/classes.*

Verbier Festival and Academy. 4 JJ Rousseau, CH-1800 Vevey, Switzerland *tel:* +41 21 922 4010 *fax:* +41 21 922 4012 *email:* verbier festival@music.ch. Miguel Esteban, academy dir. *17 Jul-9 Aug 1998, applications by 15 Mar. W/shops for all ages of vn, va, vc, pno, theatre and dance. Fees: SFR 800.*

Workshop for Gregorian Chant. c/o Jeunesses Musicales, Maison de la Radio, Bd Carl Vogt 66, CP 233, CH-1211 Genève 8, Switzerland *tel:* +41 22 287064 *fax:* +41 22 781 5218. Christiane Buntschu, gen sec. *Biennial. Next 1998, applications by 31 May, in Fribourg. In collaboration with the Festival for Sacred Music. Age 15+. Fees: SFR 180 (without board and lodging).*

Youth Choir of Switzerland. c/o Jeunesses Musicales, Maison de la Radio, CP233, CH-1211 Genève 8, Switzerland *tel:* +41 22 328 7064. Pascal Mayer. *Apr-May, Jul.*

USA

American Suzuki Institute Courses. University of WI-SP, Stevens Point, WI 54481-3897, USA *tel:* +1 715 346 3033 *fax:* +1 715 346 3858 *email:* dmartz@uwsp.edu. Dee Martz, dir. *2-8 Aug 1998, applications by 8 Jun. For age 3 and over. Individual and group lessons, and teacher training using the Suzuki method. Fees: £483 (adult), $461 (student).*

Aspen Music School. Office of Student Services, 2 Music School Rd, Aspen, CO 81611, USA *tel:* +1 970 925 3254 *email:* school@aspen music.org. Dean W Harold Laster, student services. *10 Jun-16 Aug 1998, applications by 27 Feb. Full range of courses and private lessons. Ages 15 and above (average is 20). Fees include tuition, room and board.*

Baroque Music and Dance Workshop. Department of Music, Braun Music Center, Stanford University, Stanford, CA 94305-3076, USA *tel:* +1 415 723 0038 *fax:* +1 415 725 2686 *email:* melmcqee@leland. stanford.edu. Melinda McGee. *Jul-Aug. Annual summer w/shop for scholars, dancers, choreographers, musicians and theatre specialists.*

Chamber Music Institute Course. PO Box 45776, Seattle, Washington 98145, USA *tel:* +1 206 527 8839 *fax:* +1 206 526 8621. Alan Iglitzin, exec dir; Vicki Brennan, co-ord. *3 wks in Jul 1997. Intense chmbr mus instruction for ages 14-17 in a pastoral setting. Many performance opportunities and individualised coaching.*

Choral Music Workshop. School of Music, University of North Colorado, Greeley, CO 80639. Galen Darrough.

Conducting the Film Score Workshop. 281 Pacific Av, Toronto, Ontario M6P 2P8, Canada *tel:* +1 416 760 9319 *fax:* +1 416 762 6258 *email:* symphwk@interlog.com; http://www.interlog.com/~symphwk. Harry M B Hurwitz, dir. *Sep 1998. Two week w/shop held in Los Angeles.*

Education through Music Summer Institute. c/o 641 Excelsior Avenue, San Francisco CA 94112, USA *tel:* +1 415 586 2217. Trudi Richards. *Pepperdine University, Malibu, California.*

The Festival-Institute at Round Top. PO Box Drawer 89, Round Top, TX-78954-0089, USA *tel:* +1 409 249 3129 *fax:* +1 409 249 3100 *email:* festinst@fais.net; http://www.fais.net/festinst. James Dick, founder and artistic dir; Alain G Declert, artistic co-ordinator. *1-28 Jun 1998, orch and chmbr mus session; 29 Jun-12 Jul 1998, str quartet session; applications by 2 Mar 1998. Ages 17-30. A professional summer institute for advanced study and performance. Maintenance fee: $85 per week.*

Indiana University School of Music String Academy. Music Special Sessions, Merrill Hall, 121 Indiana University, School of Music, Bloomington, Indiana 47405, USA *tel:* +1 812 855 1814 *fax:* +1 812 855 4936 *email:* phillipl@indiana.edu. Leonard Phillips, dir. *Jun-Jul, applications by Mar. Age 12-18. Fees: $2000.*

International Choral Workshop. School of Music, Georgia State University, Atlanta GA 30303, USA *tel:* +1 404 651 3676. Marva Carter.

Ithaca College Chamber Music Institute. Ithaca Talent Education, PO Box 669, Ithaca, NY 14851, USA *tel:* +1 607 272 6006 *fax:* +1 607 275 0239. Sanford Reuning, dir. *5-24 Jul 1998, applications by 11 Apr. Ages 12-18. Fees: $1600.*

Ithaca Violoncello Institute. 125 Ridgecrest Rd, Ithaca, NY 14850, USA *tel:* +1 607 273 8896. Einar Holm, dir. *Late Jun-Aug for 7 weeks. Serious or professionally-minded cellists, age 16 and over. Fees: about $3000 including tuition, room and board.*

The Kodály Institute at Capital University. Conservatory of Music, Capital University, Columbus, OH 2394, USA *tel:* +1 614 236 6267 *also fax.* Sandra Mathias, dir. *13-31 Jul 1998, applications by 1 Jun. Teacher training course utilising the Kodály philosophy of mus educ, levels 1, 2 and 3. Ages 20 and above. OAKE endorsed certification course. Fees: $600 (course fee excluding accommodation).*

Magic Mountain Music Farm. 817 West End Av, New York, NY 10025, USA *tel:* +1 212 662 6634; +1 607 263 2304. Burton Kaplan, dir. *May-Sep.*

Margaret Rowell String Seminar. San Francisco Conservatory of Music, 1201 Ortega St, San Francisco, CA 94122, USA *tel:* +1 415 759 3462 *fax:* +1 415 759 3499. Irene Sharp. *Jun, applications by May. For students, performers, teachers. Morning technique sessions followed by afternoon m/classes. Fees: $425.*

New Music Miami Music Festival. School of Music, Florida International University, University Park Campus, Miami, FL 33199, USA *tel:* +1 305 348 2896 *fax:* +1 305 348 4073. Orlando Jacinto Garcia, co-dir. *15 composers invited to attend a m/class and hear a performance of one of their works. Forums, m/classes, concerts. $400 plus lodging and travel.*

Phil Mattson Vocal Jazz/Choral Workshops. Southwestern Community College, Creston, IA 50801, USA *tel:* +1 515 782 7081 ext 319. *W/shops for university students and teachers. Fees: $375.45*

Sewanee Summer Music Centre. 735 University Av, Sewanee, TN 37383, USA *tel:* +1 615 598 1225 *fax:* +1 615 598 1706. Martha McCrory, exec dir. *27 Jun-2 Aug 1998, applications by 1 Apr. Instrumental only: orch, chmbr mus, private study, theory, composition, conducting, concerts and performance. Ages 12 and over. Fees: $2100*

Summer Church Music Workshop. 3400 North IH 35, Austin, TX 78705, USA *tel:* +1 512 452 7661. Harold Rutz.

Western Wind Summer Workshops in Ensemble Singing. Western Wind Vocal Ensemble, 263 West 86th St, New York, NY 10024, USA *tel:* +1 800 788 2187 *fax:* +1 212 873 2849 *email:* info@westernwind. org; http://www.westernwind.org. Zach Nelson, workshop coordinator. *W/shops for ens singing from Renaissance to modern jazz for all ages. Fees: $149-399 (tuition), $130-450 (room and board).*

Indexes

Alphabetical Index of Advertisers

A

Abbotsholme School	326
Abingdon School	322
Academy of London	34
Ackworth School	322
Acuta Music	500
The Adderbury Ensemble	96
Aircraft Chartering Services Ltd	34, 514
Albion Brass Consort	96
Alexandre, Eva-Maria	130
Alibas	96
All Flutes Plus	459
Allegro Music	480
Alleyn's School	323
Almira String Quartet	98
Alston Hall College	381
The Amadeus Centre	270, 506
Amadeus Performance Equipment Ltd	490
Ambache Chamber Orchestra and Ensemble	34
Amos, Lisa-Maree	122
Amos-Perrett Flute and Harp Duo	118
Amoyal, Pierre	196
Anastasescu, Anda	130
Ancestral Instruments	248
Apollo Leisure Theatres	206
Ardakov, Alexander	80
The Armed Forces Music Bursary Scheme	370
The Art of Auditioning	488
Arts Marketing	372, 402, 418
Ashgate Publishing Ltd	442
Aspen Music Festival and School	597
Associated Board of the Royal Schools of Music (Publishing)	423
Association of British Choral Directors	6
Association of British Orchestras	32
Astounding Sounds	288
Athole Still International Management Ltd	78
Attwood, Merion David	248
AV Music	424
AWL Compact Disc Company Ltd	292

B

B&B Concert Services	85
The Bach Choir	58
Bach in Bath	61
The Baker Collection	256
Baker, Julian	150
Baldry, Elizabeth Jane	151
Banjo and Piano Duo	101
Barenreiter	425
Bate, Jennifer	128
Bath Festivals Trust	238
Bath Spa University College	350
Bayerische Staatsoper	560
BBC Young Musicians Events	298
Beauchamp House International Music Courses 1998	382
Beaven, Peter	122
Bedales School	322
Bedford School	323
Belfast Waterfront Hall	210
Bell Percussion Ltd Studios	507
Bennett, Elinor	152
Benslow Music Trust	382
Beyer, Isabel and Dagul, Harvey	130
Bishop's Stortford College	324
Black Box Music Limited	288
Black Cat Music	474
Blackburn Stringed Instruments	458

Blackwell's Music Shop	476
The Blue Coat School	316
Boosey & Hawkes Music Shop	460
Boulder Early Music Shop	249
The Bournemouth and Poole College of Further Education	343
Bournemouth Entertains	198
Bournemouth Orchestras	192
Bournemouth Symphony Chorus	60
Bradfield College	327
The Brandenburg Sinfonia	32, 52, 58
Brass Band Insurance Servces	498
Breitkopf Hartl	574
Brezice Festival	522
Bridge String Quartet	98
The Bridgewater Hall	204
Bridgewood and Neitzert	461
Brighton Festival Chorus	59
The Brighton Violin Shop Ltd	470
British Association of Symphonic Bands and Wind Ensembles	6
The British Federation of Young Choirs	8
The British Flute Society	10
The British Kodály Academy	10
British Music Information Centre	4
British Performing Arts Yearbook	xviii, 104, 194, 266, 418
British Reserve Insurance Co Ltd	498
British Suzuki Institute	368
British Trombone Society	10
British Youth Opera	54
Britten Sinfonia	42
Britten-Pears School for Advanced Musical Studies	372, 382
Broadway, Michael	156
Brodsky Quartet	98
Brunel University	356
Buckley, Geoffrey	141
The Burning Bush	100
Burns, Laurence	412
Byrne, John	155

C

Cadenza Concerts Ltd	95
Caithness Summer Music School	381
Caligraving Limited	500
Cambridge Early Music Summer Schools 1998	382
Cambridge Pianola Company	455
Cambridge Reed Organs	492
Cambridge University Press	426
Camden Music	424
Camden Music Typesetting	500
Canford School	324
Canterbury Cathedral Choir	316
Canterbury Festival	228
Cantiones Press	426
Canzonetta	60
Carnegie Hall	210
Caroline Ireland Management	85
Casey, Graham	146
Cecil Sharp House	507
The Centre for the Inner Voice	392
Centrepiece Music	474
Chadwick, Carolyn	160
Chameleon Arts Management	79
Chapelle du Roi	262
Chapman, Linda	414
Charivari Agreable	36
Charterhouse	324
Chelmsford Cathedral Festival	238

Chetham's School of Music 321
Chichester College of Arts, Science and Technology 344
Chlala, Hanya 412
The City of Glasgow Chorus 60
The City of London Chamber Players 36, 101
City of London School for Girls 325
City of London Sinfonia 37
City of Oxford Orchestra 37
The City Waites 256
Claremont Fan Court School 329
Classical Music 20, 42, 106, 236, 367, 417, 464, 550, 582
The Classical Recording Company 290
Claudio Records Ltd 283
Clifton College 324
Clive Morley Harps Ltd 248
Club Europe Concert Tours 310, 406, 514
Coach House Pianos 142
Colchester Institute 348
Coltman, Matthew 249
The Contemporary Music Centre Ireland 4
Contemporary Music Making for Amateurs 8
Cox, Nicholas 148
Craxton Studios 504
Cremona House Violin Shop 467
Cricklade College 343
Crofton, Robin 496
Cross, Fiona 146
Crossland, Jill 140
The Croydon Philharmonic Choir 61
Curiad 508

D
The Dalcroze Society (Inc) 12
The Dancehouse 196
Danish National Radio Symphony Orchestra 550
Dartington College of Arts 349
Dartington International Summer School 384
David Smith & Co 488
Day, Elizabeth 408
Deakin Piano Trio 102
Dean Close School 326
Derngate 202
Design and Print 410
Dewan Filharmonik Petronas 518
The Dimitris Mitropoulos International Competiti 586
Dittmer, Petronella 142
Dou Dunamis 98
The Dufay Collective viii, 258
Dulwich College 326
Dunedin Consort 62
Dyfel Management 80

E
Early Music Today 116, 250, 255, 265, 453, 574
East Sussex Academy of Music 317
East West Arts 94
Eastbourne College 326
Edmund Handy LCG 250
Edwards-Lowe, John 168
The Elizabethan Singers of London 256
English Camerata 38
English Camerata Soloists 104
English Chamber Choir 63
English Chamber Orchestra 38
The English Cornett and Sackbut Ensemble 257
The English Guitar Quartet 104
English String Orchestra 38
English Symphony Orchestra 38
Equity 8
Euphonia 278
European Discoveries Festival of Music 242
European Piano Teachers' Association 12

European Youth Summer Music 384
Ex Cathedra 62
Exmoor Singers 63

F
Fand Music Press 428
Fernandez, Wilhelmenia 196
Ferrandou 387
The Fibonnaci Sequence 106
Finchley Children's Music Group vi
The Finzi Singers 62
Fiori Musicali 260
Flutewise 10
Foster, Chris 158
Four, Jim 412
Francoise, Catherine 160
Fretwork 261
The Fusion Guitar Duo 154

G
G Henle Publishers 576
Garrett, Lesley 196
GBZ Management 83
Gemeinhardt 463
Giacalone, Nicolino 39, 168
The Godolphin School 328
Goldsmiths 358
Goldsmiths College University of London 192
Goldstone and Clemmow 132
Goodacre, Julian 249
Gordon and Breach Publishers 445
Goteborg Operan 517, 566
Graham Cole Percussion School 420
Grant Rogers Musical Artists' Management 81
Great Elm Music Festival 238
Greenhalgh, Malcolm 250
Guildford High School 328
Guildhall School of Music and Drama 352
Guildhall Summer School London 386

H
H Baron 485
Halstead, Anthony 150
Hamilton Caswell of Bristol 468
Hand/Dupre Duo 108
The Hanover Band 45
Harlequin 108
Harold Holt Limited 77
The Harpsichord Workshop 494
Harwood Academic Publishers 445
Hatstand Opera 52
Haverhill Sinfonia Soloist Competition 300
Haydn Rawstron (UK) Ltd 82
Hazard Chase Limited 83
Healthy Practice for Musicians 306, 444
Hebrides Ensemble 108
Hereford International Summer School 386
The Hidersine Co 480
Highgate School 328
Hollick, Douglas 128
Holywell Music Ltd 460
Honma Kapustka 135
Howells, David 132
Howorth Wrightson Ltd 470

I
IMG Artists 86, 87
Ibstock Place School 328
Icebreaker 110
Iceland Symphony Orchestra 517, 550
Ifeka, Althea 148
Impulse 406

The Incorporated Association of Organists 15
Incorporated Society of Musicians 14
Independent Contemporary Music Award 364
Instant Sunshine 109
International Artist Managers' Association 95, 406
International Choral Tours 60, 514, 597
International Church Music Festival in Kristiansand 597
Internationale Bachakademie Stuttgart 597
Invisible Pilots Ltd 84, 196
Isle of Wight International Oboe Competition 302
Islenska Operan 562

J
Jackdaws 1998 Residential Music Courses 386
Jane's Minstrels 110
Jaques Samuel Pianos 492
Jazz Academy 388
Jennings, Robin 249
John Boddy Agency 190
John Boyden Associates 288
John Myatt 470
JP Guivier & Co 456
Just Flutes 480
JV Pianos 455

K
Kantor Concert Management 406
Karen Durant Management 75
The Kathleen Ferrier Awards 302
Katin, Peter 135
Ken Smith Music Services Ltd 492
Kenneth van Barthold Piano Workshop Course 386
Kenny, John 151
Kensington Music Shop 462
Khan, Wajahat 156
King William's College 330
King's College, Cambridge 317
The King's Consort 44
The King's School Ely 330
Kingston University 359
Kipling, Timothy 146
Klavar 16
Kodály Institute of Britain 15
Kotzia, Eleftheria 154
Kramer, Miriam 132

L
La Brigata 262
LACCS 84
The Ladies Association of Barbershop Singers 16
Lake District Summer Music 388
Laser Music 502
Lea-Cox, Graham 122
Leeds Festival Chorus 65
Lichfield International Arts Festival 240
Lies Askonas Limited 76
Lisa Cox 485
Lisney, James 134
Litmus 118
London Choral Society 65
London College of Music 364
London College of Music and Media 353
London College of Music and Media Junior Department 342
London Festival of Chamber Music 238
London Harpsichord Ensemble 112
London International String Quartet Competition 302
London Jupiter Orchestra 46
London Musicians Limited 84
London Opera Players 54
The London Oratory School 327
London Orchestrations 508
London Sinfonietta 44

London String Ensemble 114
London Symphony Chorus 64
Longship Music 179, 430
Lucas, Claire-Louise 164

M
Machynlleth Festival 240
Maecenas Europe 430
Maeder, Suzie 414
Magenta Music International 88
Magnificat Choir and Players 67
Magnum Opus Management 89
Malaysian Philharmonic Orchestra inside front cover, 518
Malcolm Sargent Festival Choir 66
Malvern Girls' College 332
Mananan International Festival of Music and the Arts 242
Manchester Camerata 46
Markson Pianos 464
Marlborough College 332
Marshall, Anthony 248
Martens Music 470
Martin, Leon 416
May, Katharine 140
Mayfield Festival 240
McCormick, Phyllida 171
Merchant Taylors' School 330
Merchiston Castle School 333
Meriden Music 430, 578
Merrett, Louise 160
Merton College 368
Metalworks 112
Michael Harrold Artist Management 92
Minet 489
Mitchell, Madeleine 144
Montgomery, Kenneth 196
Morganstern's 488
Morley College 344
Morris, Victor 122, 179
MSM Music Publishers 433
Music Education Yearbook 28, 36, 318, 351, 408
Music Expressions 506
Music for Brass Ltd 484
Music in Print 465
Music Notables 506
The Music Sales Group 432
Music Scholar 314
Music Teacher 254, 307, 350, 438, 509, 608
Musica Europa 512
Musicfest 242
Musicians Against Nuclear Arms 19
Musicians Answering Service 490
Musicians Benevolent Fund 18
The Musician's Handbook 300, 346, 410, 552, 578, 586
Musicians' Union 26
Musicland 433
Musiclink 456
Musisca Ltd 468
Muza Rubackyte 136

N
Napier University, Edinburgh 360
The National Association of Youth Orchestras 20
National Children's Orchestra 372
National Early Music Association 246
National Federation of Music Societies 20
National Opera Studio 352
National Symphony Orchestra of Ireland 554
NB Management 89
The New Grove Dictionary of Music and Musicians 442
New London Children's Choir iv, 70
New London Orchestra 40
New Notations 173

Newcastle College 344
Newingtons 474
Ninth Wave Audio 292
The Nordoff-Robbins Music Therapy Centre 28
Norsk Musikkinformasion 530
Northern Sinfonia 48, 64
Nossek Quartet 114
NW Brown Music Division 496
Nyman Libson Paul 486

O
Oare String Orchestra 48
Olsfanger, Norman 134
The Open University 350
Opera 54, 442
Opera and Music Theatre Forum 19
Opera de Monte-Carlo 560
Opera Exclusive! 54
Opera Now 52, 436, 562
Opernhaus Zurich outside back cover, 516, 520
Orchestra of the Age of Enlightenment 48
Orchestra of the Renaissance 264
Oriole Music 261
Orion Computer Consultants Ltd 498
Oundle School 332
Oxford Bach Choir 67
Oxford 'Cello School 390
Oxford Concert Party! 114
Oxford University Press 436

P
The Palm Court Theatre Orchestra and Company 41
The Pasadena Roof Orchestra 193
Paxman Musical Instruments Limited 465
Payne, Rachel 164
Performance Ticket Printers 418
Performing Arts Library 414
Perrett, Danielle x, 151
Peter Smith & Sons 476
Peter Symonds' College 345
Phil Parker Ltd 463
The Philharmonia Chorus 68
Phillips International Auctioneers and Valuers 494
Piano 46, 110, 310, 426, 455, 508, 578
Pianoforte Tuners' Association 20
Pilgrim Harps 456
Place, Gerald 417
Poole, Sarah 160
Postern Park Digital 292
Power Music 434
PR Pictures Direct 416
Prague Classical Music Easter Festival 608
Presteigne Festival of Music and the Arts 242
Preston, Gary 134
PRIAM 488
The Princess Helena College 333
Prior's Field 334
Pro Corda 387
The Pros Kairos Players 114
Purcell School 319
PV Productions 196

Q
The Queen Elisabeth Music Competition of Belgium 582
Quintessential Sackbut and Cornett Ensemble 264

R
Radio Telefis Eirann 554
Radley College 331
Rags to Riches 130
Rathbone, Jonathan 171

RAT (Music Stands) Limited 490
Rayburn Tours Ltd 512
Read, Martin 424
Redbridge Classical 290
Regent Records 291
The Revolutionary Drawing Room 116
Reyes-Cortez, Marcel 415
Rhinegold Publishing Ltd 588
Rhinosaurus Records Ltd 290
Richard Tauber Prize for Singers 1998 x, 302
Riley, Andrew 248
RM Music 502
Robbings, Stephen 291
Robert Deegan Harpsichords 252
Robert Morley & Co Ltd 250
Roberts, Bernard 141
Robinson, Peter 196
Roland 452
Romero, Patricia 136
Rondel Ensemble 116
Rose Consort of Viols 264
Rose, Malcolm 252
The Royal Choral Society 66
Royal College of Music 352
Royal Liverpool Philharmonic Orchestra 50
Royal Marines Band Service 366
Royal Northern College of Music 202, 355
Royal Over-Seas League 304
Royal Philharmonic Orchestra 50
The Royal Society of Musicians of Great Britain 22
RTE Concert Orchestra 554
Rudolf Steiner House 196
Rugby School 334
Rushton, Virginia 164
The Ruskin Trio 116
Ryan, Gary 154
The Ryedale Festival 240

S
S & EM Turner Violins (Nottingham) 476
St Dunstan's College 335
St Edward's School Oxford 334
St John's College Choir 316
St Leonards School 336
St Margaret's School, Bushey 335
St Margaret's School Exeter 334
St Mary's School 336
St Mary's School Ascot 336
St Mary's Music School 319
St Paul's School 341
Salisbury Cathedral School 316
Salo, Satu 152
The Sarasota Opera 566
Sardos Artist Management Corporation 544
Sargent, Evelyn 135
Saunders Recorders 468
Savenko, Vassily 168
Schiller, Alan 141
Schott & Co Ltd 434
The Scottish Music Information Centre 4
Scottish Early Music Consort 266
Seldis, Dominic 144
Seraphim Piano Quartet 118
Sewanee Summer Music Centre and Festival 608
Sewell, Brian 148
Shaw, Richard 140
Shell LSO Music Scholarship 304
Sherborne School for Girls 338
Shrewsbury School 337
Shrivastav, Baluji 156
Sibelius Software iii

Sidcot School 331
Sieling, Gary 128
Signum Records 278
Silverfen 502
Sing for Pleasure 392
The Singer 24, 70, 228, 264, 300, 378, 431, 586
Singers Direct 81
Sirinu 266
Skornikova, Lenka 162
Slater, Carol 142
Slater, Carol and Jewel, Ian 109
Smart, Alison 162
Smietana, Krzysztof 144
Smith, Neil 155
Soames, Victoria 146
Society for the Promotion of New Music 22
Software Partners 504
Solid State Logic 458
Solihull School 338
Sonic Arts Network 24
Sound Moves 290
The Sound Post xii
Sound Sense 25
Sounds Classical 164
South East Music Schemes 310
Southern Concert Brass 118
Staatsoper Unter den Linden 566
The Stables Jazz Courses 392
Stafford Law Associates 93
Stagg, John W 468
Stainer & Bell Ltd 439
Stanley Thornes (Publishers) Ltd 437
Stirling, Stephen 150
Stolz, The Friends of Robert 24
Stowe School 339
Sulian Music 504
The Summer Music Summer School 390
Surrey Youth Music and Performing Arts 345
Svensk Musik 530
Swales Music Centre Ltd 484
Symphony Films 278
Symphony Hall, Birmingham 200

T
Tallis Chamber Choir 64
Teacher Stern Selby 510
Teatr Narodowy 564
Thames Chamber Orchestra 50
Thomastik-Infeld inside back cover
Tom Petzal and Associates 404
Tomes, Frank 252
Tonbridge School 340
Top Wind 466
Trinity College of Music 354
Trinity College of Music Junior Department 342
Trinity School, Croydon 338

Tunbridge Wells International Young
  Concert Artist Competition 304

U
UK Chinese Ensemble xviii, 155
Underwood, Mark 148
Universal Edition (London) Ltd 438
University College of St Martin 350
University of Huddersfield 358
University of Leeds 361
The University of Salford 360
University of Surrey 362
University of Sussex 362
University of Wales, Aberystwyth 356
University of Wales, Bangor 357
The University of Warwick Music Cente 363
University of Wolvershampton 362
University of Leicester 356
Upbeat Management 90, 91

V
Vanderbeek and Imrie 438
Vandermeer, Zoe 140, 256
Vargas Organisation 410
Vasari Singers 69
Victoria College Examinations 364
Vincent Bach 454

W
Walsh, Kate 150
The Warehouse 509
The Warehouse Waterloo 283
The Washington Opera 569
Watkins, David 434
Webb, Hugh 152
Welsh Amateur Music Federation 27
Welsh College of Music and Drama 355
West Kent College 346
Westminster Abbey Choir 318
Westminster Cathedral Choir 318
Westminster Central Hall 200
Westminster School 340
Whelpdale Maxwell and Codd Ltd 460
Wilde, Barry 144
Williams, Sioned 152
Wolff, Marguerite 138
Women in Music 27
Wooderson, Andrew 252, 496
Wu, Mary Mei-Loc x, 138
Wycliffe College 340

Y
The Yehudi Menuhin School 320

Z
Zebaida, Robin 138

Alphabetical Index of Subjects

A

abbreviations:
agents' 75
general xi
music degree and diploma 347
music publishers' 173
accessory distributors 487
accompanists and coaches 139
accountancy services 487
advertising agencies 411
agents:
international 531
jazz and light music 191
UK 75
Air Force bands, Royal 71
Alexander Technique training 369
Anglican Church music 230
annual review:
British xiii
international 519
answering services 489
antiquarian booksellers 485
Army bands 71
artists' agents:
international 531
jazz and light music 191
UK 75
Arts Council of England 2
Arts Council, Isle of Man 3
Arts Council of Northern Ireland 3
Arts Council, Scottish 3
Arts Council of Wales 3
arts:
administration courses 369
boards, regional 5
centres (concert halls) 197
associations:
for Anglican church music 230
for people with disabilities 29
musical and general 7
auctioneers, instrument 491
awards:
for study abroad 312
honorary music 348
UK 308

B

bagpipe colleges 371
ballet companies 57
bands:
brass 72
brass (youth) 376
brass band championships 307
military 71
wind (youth) 375
baritones 169
bass-baritones 169
basses 169
bassoonists 147
book publishers 443
box office services 417
brass:
band championships 307
bands 72
bands (youth) 376
instrumentalists 153
instrumentalists (early music) 268
quintets 97

British Council 2
British Legion bands, Royal 72
broadcasting:
BBC local radio stations 272
BBC radio music executives 272
BBC radio production centres 272
BBC television music executives 277
independent local radio stations 273
independent production
companies 279
independent television 277
national independent radio 273
bursaries:
for study abroad 312
UK 308

C

cassette duplication 293
cathedrals:
Anglican 230
Roman Catholic 232
CD mastering 293
cellists 147
chamber:
groups 97
groups (early music) 257
orchestras 35
championships for brass bands 307
Chapels Royal 2
choir schools 317
choirs:
cathedral and church 229
international 570
Jewish 234
UK 59
youth 377
choral directors 123
chorus-masters 123
choruses:
international 570
UK 59
church music 229
clarinettists 147
clubs, music 223
coaches (repetiteurs) 139
colleges of:
bagpipe music 371
further education 343
higher education 349
music (conservatoires) 353
competitions for:
brass band 307
composers, international 592
composers, UK 305
conductors, international 583
conductors, UK 301
performers, international 583
performers, UK 301
composers 173
competitions, international 592
competitions, UK 305
computer systems consultants 487
concert halls:
Channel Islands 208
England 199
Inner London 197
Isle of Man 208
Northern Ireland 209

Outer London 197
Scotland 208
Wales 209
concert management 407
concert promoters 221
for youth 222
conductors 123
competitions, international 583
competitions, UK 301
conservatoires 353
junior departments 342
consultants:
computer systems 487
fundraising 419
management 405
marketing 405
sponsorship 419
contraltos 165
copyists, music 501
copyright libraries 394
copyright organisations 447
cornettists 153
counter-tenors 166
courses:
Alexander Technique 369
arts administration 369
bagpipe 371
conservatoire 353
degree 357
further education 343
higher education 349
instrument repair 369
international 609
overseas 609
practical music teacher 369
psychology for musical
performance 369
recording and technology 371
recreational (international) 609
recreational (UK) 381
technology and recording 371
university 371
critics, music 448
Culture, Media and Sport,
Department of 2

D

dance companies 53
degrees and diplomas, music 347
Department of National Heritage 2
design and print 411
diary services 489
diplomas (music) 347
disabled people:
activities and courses for 30
manufacturers and retailers for 31
organisations for 29
double bassists 147
duos 97
early music 257

E

early music:
ensembles 257
fora 246
early music instrument manufacturers:
keyboard 251

early music instrument manufacturers:
    materials   253
    percussion   253
    strings   247
    wind   251
early music instrumentalists:
    keyboard   269
    strings (bowed and plucked)   268
    wind   268
editors and journalists   448
education:
    choir schools   317
    colleges of further education   343
    colleges of higher education   349
    conservatoires   353
    independent schools   323
    junior departments at
      conservatoires   342
    services schools of music   371
    specialist music schools   321
    universities   357
email services   499
engravers, music   501
ensembles   97
    early music   257
    words and music   121
equipment:
    hire   489
    manufacturers   491
examinations, external institutions   365
exhibitions, international trade   573

F

fairs, international trade   573
falsettists   166
festivals:
    England   237
    international   596
    Isle of Man   243
    London   237
    Northern Ireland   244
    Scotland   243
    Wales   244
financial services   499
Fire Service bands   72
fixers   422
flautists   147
Foundation for Sports and the Arts   3
Free Church music   234
freight forwarding   491
french horn players   153
fundraising consultants   419
further education colleges   343

G

Government offices: 2
    Arts Councils   2, 3
    Department for Culture, Media
      and Sport   2
grants:
    for study abroad   312
    UK   308
groups (ensembles)   97
    early music   257
    words and music   121
guitarists   153

H

halls, concert   197
harpists   153

harpsichordists   139
    early music   269
higher education colleges   343
hire:
    equipment   489
    instruments   493
    orchestral sets   446
honorary awards   348
horn players   153

I

independent schools   323
information centres for music:
    international   525
    UK   5
information services   491
instrumentalists   129
    early music   268
instrument:
    auctioneers   491
    hire   493
    loans for the purchase of   308
    making courses   369
    manufacturers   453
    manufacturers (early music)   247
    museums   400
    repair courses   369
    repairers   495
    retailers   459
    technicians   495
insurance services   499
international:
    agents   531
    choirs   570
    choruses   570
    competitions   583
    festivals   596
    managers   531
    music information centres   525
    music publishers   575
    opera companies   559
    organisations   525
    promoters   531
    summer schools   609
    symphony orchestras   547
    trade fairs   573
International Arts Bureau   3
internet services   499
Isle of Man Arts Council   3

J

jazz:
    agents   191
    regional organisations   191
Jeunesses Musicales courses   609
Jewish religion, music in   234
journalists   448
journals   448

K

keyboard manufacturers,
    early music   251
keyboard players, early music   269

L

leaflet distributors   417
libraries:
    church and cathedral   396
    copyright   394
    major regional public   394
    orchestral hire   446

    recorded sound   399
    regional public   394
    society and institution   398
    university and college   396
librettists   189
light music agents   191
loans for instrument purchase   308
local authority promoters:
    England   211
    Inner London   211
    Northern Ireland   220
    Outer London   211
    Scotland   219
    Wales   219
local:
    BBC radio stations   272
    independent radio stations   273
location recording services   289
London Boroughs Grants
    Committee   3
lunchtime concerts   229
lutenists   153
    early music   268

M

magazines   448
management consultants   405
manufacturers:
    disabled aids   31
    early music instruments   247
    equipment   491
    instruments   453
Marines' bands, Royal   72
marketing management   405
Master of the Queen's Music   2
media:
    buying   411
    relations   409
    sales   411
medical support organisations   499
mezzo-sopranos   165
military bands   71
miscellaneous instrumentalists   157
museums   400
music:
    and disability   29
    associations   7
    clubs   223
    colleges   353
    copyists   501
    critics   448
    degrees and diplomas   347
    engravers   501
    festivals, international   596
    festivals, UK   237
    giftware   505
    in places of worship   229
    information centres, international 525
    information centres, UK   5
    journalists   448
    novelties   505
    printers   501
    publishers, international   575
    publishers, subsidiary   440
    publishers, UK   423
    schools, specialist   321
    setters   501
    societies (associations)   7
    societies (local concert promoters) 223
    theatre   53
    therapy courses   30
Musicians' Union   28

N

National Music Council	6
newspapers	448
Non-Conformist church music	233

O

oboists	147
opera:	
companies, international	559
companies, UK	53
companies, youth	56, 379
librettists	189
producers	172
translators	189
orchestral contractors	422
orchestral hire libraries	446
orchestras:	
chamber	35
international	547
symphony	35
youth	373
organisational management	405
organisations:	
for people with disabilities	29
international	525
musical and general	7
organists	129
church and cathedral	230
overseas:	
agents	531
choirs	570
choruses	570
competitions	583
festivals	596
managers	531
music information centres	525
music publishers	575
opera companies	559
organisations	525
promoters	531
summer schools	609
symphony orchestras	547
trade fairs	573

P

percussionists	157
performers (soloists):	
accompanists and coaches	139
brass	153
cello	147
competitions, international	583
competitions, UK	301
conductors	123
double bass	147
guitar	153
harp	153
harpsichord	139, 251
keyboard (early music)	251
lute	153, 268
miscellaneous instruments	157
organ	129
percussion	157
piano	131
strings (early music)	268
viola/viola d'amore	145
violin	143
wind (early music)	268
woodwind	147
periodicals	448
personal management	407

photographers	413
pianists	131
piano trios	97
Police Force bands	72
PR consultants	409
practical music teacher courses	369
practice studios	505
printers, music	501
printing (design)	411
producers, opera	172
programme note writers	507
promoters:	
concert	221
for youth	222
local authority	211
psychology for musical	
performance courses	369
public relations consultants	409
publicity designers	411
publishers, book	443
publishers, music:	
abbreviations	173
international	575
subsidiary	440
UK	423

Q

quartets	97
early music	257
Queen's Household, The	2
quintets	97
early music	257

R

radio:	
BBC local	272
BBC national	272
independent local	273
independent national	273
record:	
companies	280
pressing	293
specialist dealers	294
recorder players	147
early music	268
recording and technology courses	371
recording studios	284
location	289
recreational courses:	
international	609
UK	381
regional arts boards	5
regional jazz organisations	191
rehearsal rooms	505
repairers, instrument	495
repetiteurs	139
retailers:	
disabled aids	31
England	469
Greater London	459
Northern Ireland	484
Scotland	482
Wales	483
Roman Catholic:	
choir schools	319
church music	232
Royal Air Force bands	71
Royal British Legion bands	72
Royal Marines' bands	72

S

saxophonists	147
scholarships:	
for study abroad	312
UK	308
schools:	
choir	317
independent	323
services	371
specialist music	321
Scottish Arts Council	3
secretarial services	513
service bands	71
services, email, internet, website	499
services' schools of music	371
setters, music	501
sheet music:	
publishers, international	575
publishers, UK	423
retailers	459
singers:	
baritones	169
basses	169
bass-baritones	169
contraltos	165
counter-tenors	166
falsettists	166
mezzo-sopranos	165
sopranos	159
tenors	166
with their own accompaniment	159
sleeve note writers	507
societies:	
music (promoting)	223
music (special interest)	7
solicitors	511
soloists *see also* performers	
early music	268
instrument	129
singers	159
sopranos	159
sound duplication	289
sound recovery and restoration	293
specialist:	
instrument insurers	499
music booksellers	485
music schools	321
record dealers	294
sponsorship consultants	419
string instrumentalists	143
early music	268
subsidiary publishers	440
summer schools:	
international	609
UK	381
symphony orchestras:	
international	547
UK	35
synagogues	234

T

taxation services	487
technicians, instrument	495
technology and recording courses	371
television:	
BBC music executives	277
independent production	
companies	279
national independent companies	277
regional independent companies	279
tenors	166

theatres (concert halls):
    Channel Islands   208
    England   199
    Inner London   197
    Isle of Man   208
    Northern Ireland   209
    Outer London   197
    Scotland   208
    Wales   209
ticket services   417
tour operators   511
trade fairs, international   573
translators   189
travel companies   511
trios   97
    early music   257
trombonists   153
trumpeters   153
tuba players   153

U
universities   357

V
venues (concert halls):
    Channel Islands   208
    England   199
    Inner London   197
    Isle of Man   208
    lunchtime concert (in churches)   229
    Northern Ireland   209
    Outer London   197
    Scotland   208
    Wales   209
video companies   513
viol players   268
viola players   145
violinists   143
Visiting Arts Office   2

W
Wales, Arts Council of   3
website services   499
wind bands, youth   375
wind quintets   97
woodwind instrumentalists   147
    early music   268
word processing services   513
words and music ensembles   121
worship, music in places of   229

Y
youth:
    brass bands   376
    choirs   377
    opera companies   56, 379
    orchestras   373
    promotion for   222
    wind bands   375

For your *free editorial entry* in the

British Music Yearbook 1999

Complete this form or a photocopy, and return to:
The Editor, British Music Yearbook, Rhinegold Publishing Ltd,
241 Shaftesbury Avenue, London WC2H 8EH, UK

ORGANISATION/INSTITUTION ....

SECTION OF BOOK ....

ADDRESS ....

....

....

....

....POSTCODE ....

TEL ....FAX ....

EMAIL...................................... WEBSITE ....

CONTACT ....POSITION ....

OTHER PERSONNEL...

....

....

COMPREHENSIVE DETAILS (PLEASE INCLUDE FOR ALL ENTRIES) ....

....

....

....

....

....

....

....

....

....

Performers and **Composers** please use the form on the next page.
Please attach any additional details to support your entry.
Editorial entries are *free*, but are included at the discretion of the editor.

Performers and Composers

For your *free editorial entry* in the

British Music Yearbook 1999

Complete this form or a photocopy, and return to:
The Editor, British Music Yearbook, Rhinegold Publishing Ltd,
241 Shaftesbury Avenue, London WC2H 8EH, UK

NAME ....

VOICE/INSTRUMENT/COMPOSER...

CONTACT ADDRESS ....

....

....

....

....POSTCODE ....

TEL..FAX ....

EMAIL... WEBSITE ....

AGENT(S)..

COMPREHENSIVE DETAILS: Performers, please list your last six performances (including date, venue, works performed etc) and include a short CV. Composers, please list your publishers and details of your last six works performed or broadcast. Ensembles, also include personnel details and a description of ensemble. **Please note that no entries can be accepted without these details.**

....

....

....

....

....

....

....

....

....

Please attach any additional details to support your entry.
Editorial entries are *free*, but are included at the discretion of the editor.